W9-AEB-458

A
CENSUS OF PENSIONERS
FOR REVOLUTIONARY
OR MILITARY SERVICES;
WITH THEIR
NAMES, AGES, AND PLACES OF RESIDENCE . . .
UNDER
THE ACT FOR TAKING THE SIXTH CENSUS

BOUND WITH
A GENERAL INDEX

Prepared by
THE GENEALOGICAL SOCIETY
of the
Church of Jesus Christ of Latter-Day Saints

A Census of Pensioners &ct.
Originally Published
Washington, D. C., 1841

Reprinted
Southern Book Company
Baltimore, 1954

Genealogical Publishing Co., Inc.
Baltimore, 1967

A General Index
Originally Published
Genealogical Publishing Co., Inc.
Baltimore, 1974, 1989, 1996

First Published in This Format
Two Volumes Bound in One
Genealogical Publishing Co., Inc.
Baltimore, 1974, 1989

Library of Congress Catalogue Card Number 74-14050
International Standard Book Number 0-8063-0631-9

Copyright © 1965
Genealogical Publishing Co., Inc.
Baltimore, Maryland
All rights reserved

Made in the United States of America

A

CENSUS OF PENSIONERS

FOR

REVOLUTIONARY OR MILITARY SERVICES;

WITH THEIR

NAMES, AGES, AND PLACES OF RESIDENCE,

AS

RETURNED BY THE MARSHALS OF THE SEVERAL JUDICIAL DISTRICTS,

UNDER

THE ACT FOR TAKING THE SIXTH CENSUS.

PUBLISHED BY AUTHORITY OF AN ACT OF CONGRESS, UNDER THE DIRECTION OF THE SECRETARY OF STATE.

WASHINGTON:
PRINTED BY BLAIR AND RIVES.
1841.

INDEX TO STATES

CENSUS

OF

PENSIONERS FOR REVOLUTIONARY AND MILITARY SERVICES,

AS

RETURNED UNDER THE ACT FOR TAKING THE SIXTH CENSUS,

IN 1840.

STATE OF MAINE.

Names of pensioners for revolutionary or military services.	Ages.	Names of heads of families with whom pensioners resided June 1, 1840.	Names of pensioners for revolutionary or military services.	Ages.	Names of heads of families with whom pensioners resided June 1, 1840.
YORK COUNTY.			**YORK COUNTY**—Continued.		
WATERBOROUGH.			*SHAPLEIGH.*		
Noah Ricker	78	Noah Ricker.	Keziah Warren	81	John Pitts.
Jonathan Knight	77	Simeon C. Knight.	Jonathan Horn	85	Simon Ross.
Moses Deshon	76	Moses Deshon.	Jonathan Ross	91	Gideon Ross.
Abigail Hutchens	87	Abigail Hutchens.			
Elizabeth Smith	85	Abner Thing.	*SACO.*		
Thomas Carpenter	76	Thomas Carpenter.	Stephen Googins	86	Alexander Googins.
Sarah McKenney	74	Rufus McKenney.	John Grace	79	Moses Grace.
John Hamilton	75	John Hamilton.	Abraham Tyler	77	Abraham Tyler.
Caleb Lassell	79	Ivory Parcher.			
Moses Rhodes	74	Moses Rhodes.	*PARSONSFIELD.*		
			Noah Wedgwood	81	Allen Henry.
SOUTH BERWICK.			Levi Chadbourn	82	Levi Chadbourn.
Mary Chambertin	80	Josiah W. Seaver.	James Brown	83	Edmund Chase.
Lydia Jay	92	Ivory Jay.	Jacob Eastman	77	Jacob Eastman.
Henry Beedle	80	Henry Beedle.	Josiah Davis	90	Enoch Hale.
Timothy Berdens	76	John Brooks.	Wentworth Lord	84	Wentworth Lord.
Peliliah Stevens	83	John Welch.	William Campnell	80	Nathan Moulton, jr.
Barsham Allen	76	Barsham Allen.	George Newbegin	76	George Newbegin.
Charles Sargent	86	Charles Sargent.	Thomas Pendexter	68	Thomas Pendexter.
Lydia Marr	72	Reuben Bennett.	John Stone	82	John Stone.
John Hearl	85	John Hearl.	Thomas Towle	98	Thomas Towle.
Peace Peirce	69	Samuel Peirce.	Nathan Wiggin	80	Nathan Wiggin.
Hannah Peirce	81	Hannah Peirce.	Jonathan Wingate	82	Lot Wedgwood.
Betsey Nasan	81	Betsey Nasan.			
Seammon Chadbourn	85	Seammon Chadbourn.	*NORTH BERWICK.*		
Benjamin Nealey	58	Benjamin Nealey.	Ichabod Wentworth	52	Ichabod Wentworth.
			Absalom Stacpole	88	Absalom Stacpole.
WELLS.			Jacob Allen	82	Jacob Allen.
Aaron Warren	83	Walter Warren.	Simeon Applebee	88	Benjamin Applebee.
Samuel M. Jefferd	77	Samuel Jefferd.	Jonathan Hamilton	85	Abraham Henderson.
Mary Gawen	73	James Goodwin.			
Joseph Hilton	85	Joseph Hilton.	*NEWFIELD.*		
Miriam Littlefield	85	Joseph Littlefield, 3d.	Simeon Tibbets	88	Silvester Tibbets.
Daniel Stuart	87	Joseph Stuart.	Ebenezer Colby	81	Ebenezer Colby.
William Eaton	85	William Eaton.	Paul Roberts	78	Nathaniel Roberts.
Abigail Hobbs	72	James Hobbs.			
David Hatch	79	David Hatch.	*LYMAN.*		
Joseph Williams	90	Moses Williams.	Nathan Raymond	86	Francis Eldreg.
Benjamin Penny	79	Benjamin Penny.	Thomas Murphey	85	Joseph Murphey.
Joseph Wheelwright	88	Joseph Wheelwright.	Joshua Gilpatrick	82	Benjamin Goodwin.
			Silas Grant	86	Peter Grant.
SANFORD.			Jeremiah Roberts	86	Jeremiah Roberts.
John Hurton	77	John Hurton.	Rebecca Ricker	83	George W. Ricker.
Hepribeth Jacobs	85	Theodore Jacobs.	Simeon Chadbourn	91	Simeon Chadbourn.
Betsey Leavitt	72	Daniel L. Littlefield.	Elizabeth Lord	78	Elizabeth Lord.
Eunice Goodwin	72	John Lard.	John Burbank	88	Reuben Goodwin.
John Quint	79	John Quint.	Uriah Hanscomb	59	Felard Davis.
Samuel Shaw	83	Samuel M. Shaw.	William Clark	88	William Clark.
Samuel Shackford	79	Christopher Shackford.	Amaziah Goodwin	77	James Goodwin.
Robert Tripp	76	Robert Tripp.	Isaac Coffin	84	Issac Coffin.
William Worster	86	Samuel Worster.			

CENSUS OF PENSIONERS.

MAINE—Continued.

Names of pensioners for revolutionary or military services.	Ages.	Names of heads of families with whom pensioners resided June 1, 1840.	Names of pensioners for revolutionary or military services.	Ages.	Names of heads of families with whom pensioners resided June 1, 1840.
YORK COUNTY—Continued.			**YORK COUNTY—Continued.**		
LYMAN—Continued.			**YORK—Continued.**		
Jacob Rhodes	76	Jacob Rhodes.	Elizabeth Witham	83	Luther Grow.
Joanna Littlefield	72	Joanna Littlefield.	Abigail Grant	94	Joshua Grant, jr.
LIMINGTON.			Anna Mendum	81	William Mendum.
Josiah Black	89		Susannah McDaniel	74	Robert Norton.
Ephraim Clark	84		Pelatiah Perkins	86	Pelatiah Perkins.
Joshua Brackett	78		Mary Phillips	84	George Phillips.
Isaac Dyer	82		Susannah Littlefield	81	Samuel Plaisted, jr.
Elias Foss	74		Abraham Shaw	77	Abraham Shaw.
Richard Edgerly	79		Eliakim Sevey	77	John Sevey.
Susannah Foss	85		Aaron Bocker	88	William Voudy.
Mary Kendall	76		Dinah Prince	105	George Woodward.
Lois Gove	70		Jeremiah Weare	83	Jeremiah Weare.
Walter Higgins	75		Hannah Young	83	Hannah Young.
Libby Harvey	76	Libby Harvey.	**ELLIOT.**		
Lois Sutton	76	Rufus Meserve.	Lucy Simpson	82	Lucy Simpson.
Deborah Robinson	77	Eliakim Robinson.	Eunice Stacey	80	Eunice Stacey.
Joseph Rose	78	Ambrose P. Rose.	Elliot Frost	79	Elliot Frost.
Elizabeth Small	81	Elizabeth Small.	Dorcas Knowlton	69	Dorcas Knowlton.
Daniel Small	80	Daniel Small.	Sarah Frost	76	Joshua Frost.
Ebenezer Sawyer	82	Ebenezer Sawyer.	Alexander Goold	88	Alexander Goold.
Spencer Thomas	76	Spencer Thomas.	John Goold	85	Hiram Goold.
Caleb Hopkinson	94	Joshua Spencer.	Rebecca Hill	76	William Fogg.
LIMERICK.			Thomas Scriggins	76	John Staples.
Mary Leavitt	79	Mary Leavitt.	Hannah Spinney	86	Jedediah Witham.
Nathaniel Libby	77	Nathaniel Libby, Esq.	Peggy Wherren	79	John Lydston.
Daniel Warren	75	Daniel Warren.	Elizabeth Knight	79	Elizabeth Knight.
Hannah Lord	77	Hannah Lord.	Parker Foster	79	Parker Foster.
Elizabeth Boothby	80	Elizabeth Boothby.	Elizabeth Fernald	79	Hiram Fernald.
Josiah Berry	78	Joseph Berry.	**KITTERY.**		
LEBANON.			Betsey Wilson	82	Betsey Wilson.
Mary Goodwin	76	Mary Goodwin.	John Stevens	82	Theodore Parker.
Love Robberts	88	Love Robberts.	Charity Sargent	76	Henry Sargent.
Samuel Hersom	77	Nathaniel Hersom.	**CORNISH.**		
Reuben Goodwin	79	Reuben Goodwin.	John O'Brion	78	William L. O'Brion.
Susan Gowell	–	Wentworth Goodwin.	Chase Sargent	83	William Sargent.
Patience Clark	88	Jonathan Clark.	Timothy Berry	87	Timothy Berry.
Ruth Goodwin	74	Ruth Goodwin.	Moody Brown	75	Moody Brown.
Sarah Cook	87	Samuel Wentworth.	James Wormwood	87	James Wormwood.
KENNEBUNK PORT.			Daniel Eastman	83	Daniel Eastman.
Abraham Currier	81	Nathaniel Currier.	Joseph M. Thompson	88	Dr. Benjamin Thompson.
Daniel Huff	86	Daniel Huff.	**HOLLIS.**		
Robert Hanscom	77	Sally Hanscom.	Noah Hill	50 to 60	Noah Hill.
Thomas Boston	77	Elijah Littlefield.	Edmund Bradesh	49	Edmund Bradesh.
Lemuel Miller	89	Lemuel Miller.	James R. Bean	67	James R. Bean.
John Millet	77	John Millet.	John Gilford	76	John Gilford.
Jacob Merrill	81	Jacob Merrill.	Ebenezer Carll	82	Robert Carll.
Edward Nason	85	James Nason.	Joshua Warren	83	Joshua Warren.
Samuel Smith	91	Andrew Smith.	Carll Tarbox	70 to 80	Gilbert Tarbox.
Jonathan Stone	77	Jonathan Stone.	**BUXTON.**		
James Thompson	79	James Thompson.	John Chamberlain	90 to 100	Orin Dennett.
Nathan Thompson	85	Nathan Thompson.	James Woodman	87	James Woodman.
Benjamin Wildes	78	Thomas Wildes.	Jabez Sawyer	72	Jabez Sawyer.
KENNEBUNK.			Richard Dresser	81	Paul Dresser.
Daniel Wise	78	Daniel Wise.	Roger Plasted	86	Roger Plasted.
Patty Young	74	Patty Young.	Joshua Woodman	83	Joshua Woodman.
Daminicus Lord	79	Daminicus Lord.	**BIDDEFORD.**		
John Bragden	86	Enoch Bragden.	Elizabeth Moore	77	John Moore.
Mehitable Day	87	John Walker, jr.	Louisa Staples	77	Louisa Staples.
Hannah Wakefield	77	Joshua Wakefield.	Solomon Hopkins	85	Hannah Cole.
Jonathan Boster	86	Harriet Stone.	Elizabeth Zouldthwait	62	Jacob R. Cole.
Joseph Gillpatrick	77	Joseph Gillpatrick.	**ACTON.**		
Susan Treadwell	83	Joshua E. Treadwell.	Joshua Brackett	82	Joshua Brackett.
Oliver Perkins	42	Oliver Perkins.	Ralph Farnham	84	Ralph Farnham.
Hannah Watterhouse	84	Joseph Watterhouse.	Daniel Horn	88	Frederick Horn.
Samuel Emerson	76	Samuel Emerson.	Jonathan Hubbard	78	John Lord.
Dorothy Littlefield	92	Jesse Taylor.	Stephen Marsh	79	Thomas D. Marsh.
Joseph Towne	78	Elias Stephen.	**BERWICK.**		
Jowel Stephens	94	Luther Stephens.	Aaron Downs	79	Aaron Downs.
Jacob Fisher	78	Jacob Fisher.	Samuel Lord	80	Samuel Lord.
YORK.			Charles G. Clark	75	Charles G. Clark.
Abigail Berry	73	Abigail Berry.	Timothy Wentworth	93	Timothy Wentworth.
Sarah Banks	88	Sarah Banks.	Ephraim Tebbets	78	James Tebbets, 2d.
Daniel Bridges	79	John Beedle.	Moses Foye	79	Moses Foye, jr.
Isaac Chick	81	Adrial Chick.	Jonathan Horsaw	83	Jonathan Horsaw.
Abigail Donnell	79	Deborah Donnell.			
Mary Baker	88	Mark Fernald.			

MAINE—Continued.

Names of pensioners for revolutionary or military services.	Ages.	Names of heads of families with whom pensioners resided June 1, 1840.	Names of pensioners for revolutionary or military services.	Ages.	Names of heads of families with whom pensioners resided June 1, 1840.
CUMBERLAND COUNTY.			**CUMBERLAND—Continued.**		
BALDWIN.			*FALMOUTH—Continued.*		
Charles Hall	85	Jonathan Burnell.	Benjamin Hodsdon	83	Andrew Hodsdon.
Joseph Bryant	83	Joseph Bryant.	Daniel Lunt	78	Daniel Lunt.
Eleanor Spencer	75	Daniel Cram.	*FREEPORT.*		
Molly Richardson	87	Joseph Richardson.	Joseph Talbot	76	
Webber Rowe	77	Webber Rowe.	Josiah Reid	79	
SEBAGO.			Jonathan Soule	84	
Rebecca Moody	83	John Moody.	Elizabeth Winslow	75	
Tyler Porter	82	Tyler Porter.	David Dennison	79	
Robert Libby	79	John Pugsley.	Elizabeth T. Beal	78	
Phebe Robinson	72	Phebe Robinson.	James Soule	85	
BRIDGTON.			Rachael Hooper	89	
Robert Andrews	87	Robert Andrews.	Robert Townsend	79	
Phineas Ingalls	82	Phineas Ingalls.	John Addison	89	
Joseph Kimball	81	Joseph Kimball.	Samnet Seales	81	
David Martin	71	David Martin.	Mary Aldrich	79	
John Kilborn	85	John Kilborn.	Joseph Mum	79	
Ebenezer Choate	75	Ebenezer Choate.	Mary Morr	97	
Jacob Hazen	78	Edmund Hanson.	*GORHAM.*		
BRUNSWICK.			Deborah Blake	70 to 80	William Bartlett.
Philip Owen	84	Nathaniel Badger.	Timothy Bacon	70 to 80	Timothy Bacon.
John Bennet	58	John Bennet.	Esther Files	70 to 80	Esther Files.
John Cornish	84	John Cornish.	Hannah Fogg	60 to 70	Hannah Fogg.
Ichabod Doughty	86	Ichabod Doughty.	Edward Libby	70 to 80	Edward Libby, jr.
William Gatchell	84	William Gatchell.	John Lombard	80 to 90	John Lombard.
Sarah Graffam	81	Joseph Graffam.	William McLellan	80 to 90	William McLellan.
Elizabeth Hall	79	Elizabeth Hall.	Thomas Morton	70 to 80	Thomas Morton.
Martha McGill	85	Martha McGill.	Matthias March	80 to 90	Matthias March.
Daniel McMannus	74	Daniel McMannus.	John Phinney	70 to 80	John Phinney.
John McMannus	80	Henry Meryman.	Joshua Swett	70 to 80	Joshua Swett.
Sarah Ross	82	Jonathan Snow.	Eben Storer	80 to 90	Eben Storer.
Charles Thomas	82	Charles Thomas.	Edward Webb	80 to 90	William Peter.
Seth Toothaker	82	Seth Toothaker.	*GRAY.*		
Thomas House	65	John Woodside, 2d.	Amasa Dilano	82	Amasa Dilano.
John McDonald	74	John Woodside, 2d.	James Welch	76	Abel Welch.
Nathaniel Ham	85	John Woodside, 2d.	Samuel Swett	76	Samuel Swett.
CAPE ELIZABETH.			John Merrill	81	Edward Harmon.
Lucy Fickett	88	John Fickett.	Joseph Allen	81	Emery Allen.
John Stanford	77	John Stanford.	*HARPSWELL.*		
Hannah Dyer	77	Catharine Dyer.	James Doughty	76	David Doughty.
Joshua Gammon	78	George Webster.	William Coombs	86	Joseph Coombs.
Samuel Crockett	79	Samuel Crocket.	Levi Dingley	84	Levi Dingley.
CUMBERLAND.			Mary Dyer	76	Leonard Dyer.
Samuel Gurney	76	Samuel Gurney.	John Coombs	77	Jesse Easters.
William Cleaves	80	William Cleaves.	*HARRISON.*		
Cotton Murray	-	Cotton Murray.	John Brackett	79	Walker Brackett.
Richard Colley	86	Thomas Leighton.	Simeon Caswell	77	Philip Caswell.
Joseph Shaw	78	William Shaw.	Nicholas Bray	89	Edward Brag.
DANVILLE.			Charles Walker	80	Charles Walker, jr.
Joseph Penly	83	Joseph Penly.	Daniel Jumper	76	Daniel Jumper, jr.
George Leach	83	George Leach.	*MINOT.*		
Jacob Larrabe	76	Jacob Larrabe.	Samuel Hatch	84	Samuel Ray.
Theophilus Libby	47	Theophilus Libby.	John Bridgham	86	Garish Bridgham.
Robert Maxwell	74	Robert Maxwell.	Lucy Hilborn	89	Ira Hilborn.
Samuel Tarbox	82	Samuel Tarbox.	Hannah Sanborn	77	Samuel Versall, 2d.
Joanna Jordan	76	Joanna Jordan.	Nathan Warren	77	Thomas Warren.
Aaron Dresser	81	Mickel Holland..	John Downing	74	John Downing, jr.
William Maxwell	83	William Maxwell.	Peabody Bradford	82	Lewis Bradford.
DURHAM.			Nehemiah Packard	74	Nehemiah Packard.
Daniel Robinson	86	James Jordan, jr.	Lucy Moody	76	David Moody.
James Wagg	86	Joshua Miller, 2d.	Lucy Bridgham	74	Hersey Freeman.
Isaac Davis	82	Isaac Davis.	Gersham Holmes	75	Gershom D. Holmes.
Jarvis Beal	41	Jarvis Beal.	Amasa Pribou	81	Amasa Pribou, jr.
Joseph Lancaster	83	Joseph Lancaster.	Nathaniel Chandler	80	George Dean.
Elisha Stetson	81	Charles Stetson, 2d.	James Murdock	83	James Murdock.
FALMOUTH.			James Goff	80	William Goff.
Josiah Hobbs	77	Josiah Hobbs.	Lucy Bailey	73	Edmund Penny.
Benjamin Creesey	83	Benjamin Creesey.	Azael Kinsley	79	Austin Kinsley.
William Colley	89	Joseph Colley.	William Campbell	42	William Campbell.
Jacob Elliott	77	Jacob Elliott.	Ruth Crooker	80	William Crooker.
James Dobbin	88	James Dobbin.	John Dillingham	77	John Dillingham.
Benjamin Prince	83	Benjamin Prince.	Daniel Kinsley	82	Daniel Kinsley.
Job Pool	76	Job Pool.	Mary King	70	Paul Bowker.
Jacob Knight	83	Jacob Knight.	Sarah Willis	79	Sarah Willis.
William R. York	83	William R. York.	Isaac Allen	83	Isaac Allen.
			Jacob Bates	80	Jacob Bates.
			Jonathan Nash	87	John Narsh.

Names of pensioners for revolutionary or military services.	Ages.	Names of heads of families with whom pensioners resided June 1, 1840.	Names of pensioners for revolutionary or military services.	Ages.	Names of heads of families with whom pensioners resided June 1, 1840.
CUMBERLAND—Continued.			**CUMBERLAND—Continued.**		
MINOT—Continued.			STANDISH.		
John Chandler - - -	82	John Chandler.	Isaac York - - -	81	Isaac York.
Joseph Haws - - -	87	Joseph Hodge.	Margaret Menow - - -	86	Samuel F. Boultie.
Samuel Downing - - -	75	Samuel Downing.	Isaac Chase - - -	82	Isaac Chase.
RAYMOND.			Samuel Davis - - -	78	Samuel Davis.
			William Harmon - - -	78	William Harmon.
Daniel Small - - -	76	Daniel Small.	Abigail Hunnewell - - -	78	Ebenezer Howe.
William Mayberry - -	82	William Mayberry.	Jedediah Lombard - - -	81	Jedediah Lombard.
Joseph Wight - - -	82	Joseph Wight.	Peltiah McDonald - - -	86	Peltiah McDonald.
NAPLES.			Benjamin Morton - - -	55	Benjamin Morton.
Sally Senter - - -	76	Isaac Senter.	Lydia Plaisted - - -	72	Ebenezer Moulton.
			Aaron Parker - - -	81	Benjamin Parker.
NORTH YARMOUTH.					
Isaac Ross - - -	84	Isaac Ross.	SCARBOROUGH.		
Elizabeth Jones - - -	79	Elizabeth Jones.	Lydia Milliken - - -	79	Sewall Milliken.
James Bibber - - -	84	James Bibber.	Margaret Milliken - - -	83	Stephen Sewall.
Amos M. Hayes - - -	85	Amos M. Hayes.	Abigail Libby - - -	77	Abigail Libby.
Nehemiah Porter - - -	83	Rufus Porter.	Dorothy Libby - - -	78	Hiram Libby.
William Hamilton - -	78	William Hamilton.	James Small - - -	83	James Small.
Robert Maxfield - - -	78	Reuben Maxfield.	Mark Libby - - -	90	Mark Libby.
Samuel Doten - - -	83	Samuel Doten.	Edmund Higgins - - -	83	Edmund Higgins.
Seth Blanchard - - -	81	Seth Blanchard.	Abigail Libby - - -	76	Sherley Libby.
Mary Baker - - -	71	Samuel Baker.	Abigail Libby - - -	78	Daniel Libby, jr.
OTISFIELD.			Hannah McLaughlin - -	78	Hannah McLaughlin.
Aaron Fuller - - -	83	Aaron Fuller.	Jacob Allen - - -	76	Jacob Allen.
Relief Moors - - -	83	Johnathan Moors.	James Snow - - -	87	James Snow.
James Sampson - - -	76	Reuben Sampson.	Zebulon Berry - - -	80	Zebulon Berry.
John Winship - - -	80	John Winship.	Jonathan McKenney - -	80	Jonathan McKenney.
Eunice Ray - - -	94	Henry Holden.	Joseph Moulton - - -	83	Joseph Moulton.
Robert Anderson - - -	79	Samuel P. Anderson.	Zechariah Eastman - -	95	Zechariah Eastman.
John Lombard - - -	76	Asa Andrews.	Joseph Pilsbury - - -	84	Joseph Pilsbury.
Enoch Spurr - - -	79	Enoch Spurr.			
John Knight - - -	83	John Knight.	WESTBROOK.		
Thomas Edes - - -	78	Emery Edes.	John Sawyer - - -	75	John Sawyer.
			Catharine Porterfield - -	84	Sarah Johnson.
POLAND.					
John Bragdon - - -	80	Nathaniel Bragdon.	WINDHAM.		
Mehitable Dacy - - -	94	Jacob Scillenger.	Herd Brackett - - -	47	Herd Brackett.
Paul Stanton - - :	82	William Stanton.	John Swett - - -	82	John Swett.
Abraham Knight - - -	74	Abraham Knight.	John Mugford - - -	79	John Mugford.
Samuel Godding - - -	80	Allen Bangs.	Jedediah Elliott - - -	79	John Elliot.
Jeremiah Elwell - - -	50	Jeremiah Elwell.			
Mary Partridge - - -	90	George Hanscom.	NEW GLOUCESTER.		
Joseph Johnson - - -	77	James Johnson.	Zebulon Rowe - - -	91	Zebulon Rowe.
William Allen - - -	83	Reuben Allen.	John Lunt - - -	54	John Lunt.
Hepzibah May - - -	89	David Madcaff.	William Pickett - - -	76	William Pickett.
PORTLAND.					
1st Ward.			**OXFORD COUNTY.**		
Elizabeth Mountfort - -	72	Elizabeth Mountfort.	ALBANY.		
Sarah Henick - - -	76	Joseph Hay.	Isaac Turner - - -	87	Hezekiah Pingue.
			David Jordon - - -	79	David Jordon.
2d Ward.					
Samuel Colby - - -	78	Samuel Colby.	WATERFORD.		
			Benjamin Hale - - -	77	Benjamin Hale.
3d Ward.			Israel Hale - - -	80	Israel Hale.
John McLellan - - -	71	John McLellan.	Thaddeus Brown - - -	79	Thaddeus Brown
			Josiah Procter - - -	79	Josiah Procter.
4th Ward.			Louis Gage - - -	81	Amos Gage.
None.			Oliver Hale - - -	79	Oliver Hale.
			Lydia Chaplin - - -	78	John S. Chaplin.
5th Ward.			Joel Atherton - - -	77	Joel Atherton.
Daniel Cobb - - -	79	Daniel Cobb.	Mary Stevens - - -	92	Jonathan Stevens.
Polly Shaw - - -	77	Polly Shaw.	Eliphalet Alvin - - -	80	Chandler Perry.
Mary Preble - - -	65	Edward D. Preble.	Abijah Carter - - -	78	Abijah Carter.
Rebecca Bailey - - -	91	Sally N. Waite.			
John K. Smith - - -	86	William Smith	ANDOVER.		
Elijah Kellogg - - -	79	Joseph Kellogg.	Ebenezer Bodwell - -	55	Ebenezer Bodwell.
6th Ward.			NEWRY.		
Thomas B. Parsons - -	51	Thomas B. Parsons	John Kilgore - - -	~	John Kilgore.
			Benjamin Barker - - -	77	Moses Coburn, jr.
7th Ward.			Jesse Barker - - -	75	Jesse Barker.
Thomas Runnells - -	79	Thomas Runnells.	Benjamin Russell - - -	76	Benjamin Russell.
Elizabeth Martin - -	66	Elizabeth Martin.	James Eames - - -	78	James Eames.
POWNAL.			ANDOVER NORTH SURPLUS		
Job Allen - - -	77	Job Allen.	Joshua Dun - - -	81	Joshua Dun.
Josiah Walker - - -	84	Josiah Walker.			
Nehemiah Allen - - -	87	David Allen.	GILEAD.		
Thomas Paine - - -	84	Thomas Paine.	Stephen Hodgdon - - -	82	Stephen Hodgdon.
Jacob Bemis - - -	83	Jacob Bemis, jr.	Jonathan Blodget - - -	83	Jonathan Blodget.

MAINE—Continued.

Names of pensioners for revolutionary or military services.	Ages.	Names of heads of families with whom pensioners resided June 1, 1840.	Names of pensioners for revolutionary or military services.	Ages.	Names of heads of families with whom pensioners resided June 1, 1840.
OXFORD—Continued.			**OXFORD—Continued.**		
BETHEL.			*GREENWOOD.*		
Nathaniel Seger	85	William Barker.	James Barker	80	James Barker.
Lydia Holt	76	Hiram Holt.	Frederick Ballard	77	Joshua W. Ballard.
Phinehas Frost	46	Phinehas Frost.	Rachel Field	88	Paul Winth orth.
Thaddeus Bartlett	81	James C. Bean.	Joshua Pool	78	Nathaniel Cobb.
James Swan	77	John Williamson.	Daniel Haney	86	Amos Young.
Eunice Mason	80	Aaron Mason.			
Eli Twitchell	81	Curatia T. Bartlett.	*HARTFORD.*		
Peter Twitchell	80	Eli Twitchell, 3d.	William Hayford	78	William Hayford.
Margaret Bean	82	George W. Grover.	William Cushman	75	William Cushman.
Daniel Gage	79	Daniel Gage.	Jabez Churchill	86	Joab Churchill.
			Mercy Holmes	70	Mercy Holmes.
DENMARK.			Olive Bicknell	89	Nathaniel Bicknell.
Obadiah True	82	Robert True.	Abijah Bryant	79	Abijah Bryant.
John Douglass	80	John Douglass.	Moses Dunham	84	Otis Alley.
Sampson Whiting	75	Sampson Whiting.	Ebenezer Washburn	78	Ebenezer Washburn.
Jotham Bragdon	42	Jotham Bragdon.			
			HEBRON.		
BROWNFIELD.			Hannah Bumpus	76	
Joseph Howard	81	Richard Paine.	William Cobb	75	
John Greenlaw	74	John Greenlaw.	Mary Fuller	89	
Ebenezer Seavy	53	Ebenezer Seavy.	Jennet Washburn	79	
			Gideon Cushmon	89	
BUCKFIELD.			Elias Monk	86 or 87	
Jacob Whitman	86	Jabez Taylor.	Ebenezer Perkins	83	
Job Packard	77	Job Packard.	Gideon Bearse	82	
Gashum Davis	81	Gashum Davis.	Jacob Gurney	76	
Abigail Record	82	Thomas Irish, jr.	Samuel Crafts	77	
Simon Record	87	Lewis Record.	John Goodin	77	
Thomas Berry	78	Peter Berry.			
Nathaniel Chase	78	David W. Swett.	*HIRAM.*		
Samuel Gilbert	78	Samuel Gilbert.	John Goodmon	89	Alpheus Spring.
Jonathan Record	90	Samuel Furnald.	Thomas Spring	85	Marshal Spring.
Jerusha Drew	83	Mercy Drew.			
Eleazer Parsons	79	Eleazer Parsons.	*RUMFORD.*		
Tobias Ricker	80	Obadiah Berry.	Philip Abbot	83	Henry Abbot.
Josiah Smith	77	Jonathan Buck, jr.	Samuel Akley	76	Samuel Akley.
Josiah Parris	75	Jeremiah Bean.	Richard Dolloff	85	John Dolloff.
Jane Record	82	Rodney Chaffin.	Joseph Wardwell	80	Aaron Graham.
Sarah Gardner	73	Hiram Coburn.	Daniel Gould	86	Daniel Gould.
Larnard Swallow, jr.	32	Larnard Swallow, jr.			
Benjamin Woodbury	78	Benjamin Woodbury.	*LOVELL.*		
Jabez Churchill	80	Amos Winslow.	Nathaniel Day	77	Nathaniel Day.
Thaddeus Pratt	85	Samuel Chesley.	Levi Dresser	79	Job A. Dresser.
			James Kilgore	82	James Kilgore.
MEXICO.					
Benjamin R. York	79	Benjamin R. York.	*LIVERMORE.*		
Ammi Mitchell	47	Ammi Mitchell.	Elijah Fisher	82	Elijah Fisher, jr.
			Jabez Delano	79	Jabez Delano.
ROXBURY.			Pelatiah Gibbs	83	Isaac Noyes.
Nathaniel Philbric	47	Nathaniel Philbric.	William Churchill	75	William Churchill.
Benjamin Lufkin	78	Rufus K. Bunker.	Thomas Chase	84	Thomas Chase.
			William Swett	62	William Swett.
CANTON.			Robert Low	80	C. L. Lyford.
William French	78	William French.	Ithamas Farrington	84	Ithamas Farrington.
Joel Ireland	49	Joel Ireland.			
Joseph Coolidge	79	Joseph Coolidge.	*OXFORD.*		
Joshua Davis	81	Joshua Davis.	Nathan Nelson	80	Nathan Nelson.
			Polly Soule	71	Lathrop L. Soule.
DIXFIELD AND PERU.			Sarah Perkins	77	Luther Perkins.
Joseph Peterson	57	Joseph Peterson.	Samuel Brown	72	Samuel Brown.
Joseph Foss	81	Samuel Foss.	Sarah Cushman	73	Bartlett H. Cushman.
Spencer Thomas	53	Spencer Thomas.	William Chipman	77	William Chipman.
William Brakett	88	William Brakett.	John Gardner	79	John Gardner.
FRYEBURG.			*PARIS.*		
Sarah Eastman	78		Ruby Field	81	Galen Field.
Thaddeus Bemis	81		John Rowe	82	Mary Sturtevant.
John Fifield	78		Seth Morse	76	Elisha Morse.
Isaac Abbot	78		Amzi Breth	79	Martin Breth.
Uriah Ballard	80		Edmund Dean	81	Edmund Dean.
William Eveans	75		Mary Hubbard	75	Mary Hubbard.
Ann Hatch	84		Naomi Briggs	78	Naomi Briggs.
			Sarah Sturtevant	72	Leonard Sturtevant.
NORWAY.			Joseph Besse	–	Alden Besse.
Timothy Jordan	74	John P. Jordan.	Mehitable Perkins	70	Simeon Perkins.
Joseph Gammond	76	Seba Gammond.	Huldah Bumpus	78	Nathaniel Bumpus.
Joel Stevens	88	Andrew Mills.	Abigail Lord	79	John L. Thorn.
Darius Holt	76	Pleamon Holt.	Joseph Swift	80	Joseph Swift.
Samuel Ames	81	Baker Ames.	Jorius Shaw	85	Jorius Shaw.
Isaac Turner	87	Hoyet Pingrey.			
Margaret Cushman	79	Joseph Cushman.	*PORTER.*		
Mary Needham	75	Jefferson Needham.	John Thompson	71	John Thompson.
Daniel Knight	81	Daniel Knight.			

Names of pensioners for revolutionary or military services.	Ages.	Names of heads of families with whom pensioners resided June 1, 1840.
OXFORD—Continued.		
PORTER—Continued.		
Josiah Wood	92	Josiah Wood.
John Pearl	41	John Pearl.
Widow Samuel Brooks	75	Asahael Brooks.
SUMNER.		
James Hursey	82	James Hursey.
Meshack Keen	83	Tulob Keen.
Abijah Warren	78	Abijah Warren.
Isiah Cushman	84	Isiah Cushman.
Elizabeth Fletcher	68	Cyrus Fletcher.
Charles Ford	82	Charles Ford.
Oliver Turner	79	Oliver Turner.
Seth Sturtavant	80	Seth Sturtavant.
Isaac Bonney	85	Isaac Bonney.
Anna Tucker	84	Anna Tucker.
John Bartlett	89	Evan Robinson.
SWEDEN.		
Daniel Holden	76	Luther Holden.
David Stone	78	Hinam Stone.
TURNER.		
Sylvia Conant	84	Silvanus Conant.
Hannah Lumbard	68	Emery Lumbard.
Elizabeth Pumpilly	67	Allen Pumpilly.
Silence Phillips	74	Jarius Phillips.
Sarah French	93	Charles French.
Dan Pratt	79	Dan Pratt.
Elijah Dresser	89	Trius Dresser.
Luther Cary	79	Luther Cary.
John Keen	79	John Keen.
James Laria	85	Isaiah Laria.
Cornelius Jones	77	Cornelius Jones.
Abigail Phillips	84	Deborah Phillips.
Nathaniel Shaw	76	Nathaniel Shaw.
LINCOLN COUNTY.		
BATH.		
Huldah Grace	78	Joshua Purrington.
John Fanin	80	John Fanin.
Sarah Stockbridge	79	Sarah Stockbridge.
William Brown	80	William Brown, jr.
John Sanford	80	John Sanford.
Mary Low	80	Benjamin Paten.
James M. Mitchell	80	Benjamin Mitchell.
Peleg Pallman	77	Peleg Pallman.
Abigail Hodgkins	80	Samuel Crowell.
Thomas Lement	81	Thomas Lement.
Joseph Pulcifer	75	Joseph Pulcifer. .
Pammey Mitchell	80	Pammey Mitchell.
BOOTHBAY.		
Dorcas Farnham	85	John Farnham.
Ephraim Alley	80	John Alley.
Asa G. Baker	50	Asa G. Baker.
Daniel Landerkin	90	Daniel Landerkin.
David Keniston	82	William Keniston.
Benjamin Babcock	82	William Keniston.
Abijah Kinney	85	Abijah Kinney.
Thomas Decker	86	Thomas Decker.
David Reed	74	Jacob Reed.
Henry Abbot	85	Henry Abbott.
Ezekiel Webber	80 to 87	Ezekiel Webber.
BOWDOIN.		
Daniel Allen	86	Rufus Allen.
Joseph Tarr	82	Joseph Tarr.
John Harris	75	John Harris.
Isaac Chase	80	James Chase.
Samuel Walker	80	Joseph Whiten.
Thomas Briniyion	85	Thomas Briniyion.
Stephen Rideout	80	Stephen Rideout.
James Potter	88	Jesse Potter.
Samuel Adams	83	Hannah P. Adams.
John Temple	84	John Temple.
Ephraim Small	81	Amos Small.
BOWDOINHAM.		
Jonathan Brown	68	Jonathan Brown.
Eunice Watson	84	Benjamin Foster.
Susannah Allen	69	Stephen Elliot.
Rebecca Adams	77	Stephen Cromwell.

Names of pensioners for revolutionary or military services.	Ages.	Names of heads of families with whom pensioners resided June 1, 1840.
LINCOLN—Continued.		
BOWDOINHAM—Continued.		
John Sedgley	80	Emery Center.
Rachel Coombs	79	Samuel Coombs.
Michael Crips	58	Michael Crips.
BREMEN.		
Mary Wellman	78	Fanny Wellman.
Mary M'rit	78	Ensign Merit.
Sarah Palmer	80	Benjamin Palmer.
BRISTOL.		
John Little	84	John Little.
Jean Sproul	78	Hiram Murphy.
John Nichels	81	John Nichels.
Philip Hatch	86	Philip Hatch.
Stephen Tibbets	88	Stephen Tibbets.
WARREN.		
Peggy Delano	88	James Copeland.
Rowland Cobb	82	Charles Copeland.
Aaron Davis	79	Aaron Davis.
James Stevens	44	James Stevens.
Willing Blake	78	Willing Blake.
Amos Lawrence	86	Joshua Lawrence.
Abner Farrington	86	Thomas Mallet.
Rufus Crane	83	Moses Crane.
James W. Head	74	James W. Head.
Josiah Merb	85	Josiah Merb.
CUSHING.		
William Burton	83	William Burton.
Samuel Paysons	79	Samuel Paysons.
Mary Norton	73	Darius Norton.
Hannah Fuller	85	James Chaples.
EDGECOMB.		
Ebenezer Chase	74	Ebenezer Chase.
Isaac Moore	88	Osborn Moore.
Nathaniel Moore	84	Nathaniel Moore.
Josiah Gorham	80	Josiah Gorham.
Daniel Huff	80	Daniel Huff.
Moses Huff	76	Moses Huff.
DRESDEN.		
Solomon Blanchard	77	Charles Blanchard.
UNION.		
Jerson Ware	84	Vinal Ware.
Jemima Adams	83	Cornelius Irish.
Sarah Barnard	80	Sarah Barnard.
Levi Morse	78	Levi Morse.
WALDOBORO'.		
Margaret Hoffses	88	James Hoffses.
Catharine Vanner	77	Andrew Vanner.
Jacob Burnheimer	75	Joseph Burnheimer.
Cornelius Heyer	88	Cornelius Heyer.
Frank Miller	75	James Miller.
Hannah Russell	82	Thomas Russell.
Charles Heavner	81	Charles Heavner.
George Deab	89	George Miller, 2d.
Mary C. Cole	81	James Cole.
John Crammer	76	John Crammer.
John C. Mink	77	John C. Mink.
Abigail Farnsworth	90	James Trobridge.
Andrew Gentner	81	Andrew Genter.
GEORGETOWN.		
John Sadler	70	John Sadler.
Robert Chase	79	William Chase.
Isaac Hall	94	William Huntt.
Mary Oliver	70	Joseph Berry.
Margaret McKinney	70	John S. McKinney.
Estor Nichols	78	Michael Fogg, jr.
Thomas Linnen	79	Thomas Linnen.
Nancy Weber	73	Noah Weber.
Jeremiah Spinney	77	Jeremiah Spinney.
JEFFERSON.		
Ammi Dunham	75	Daniel Curtis.
Mary Shepherd	79	James Shepherd.
Mary Tobey	78	George Tobey.

MAINE—Continued.

Names of pensioners for revolutionary or military services.	Ages.	Names of heads of families with whom pensioners resided June 1, 1840.	Names of pensioners for revolutionary or military services.	Ages.	Names of heads of families with whom pensioners resided June 1, 1840.
LINCOLN—Continued.			**LINCOLN—Continued.**		
LEWISTON.			WESTPORT.		
David Paul - - -	79	David Paul.	Caleb Hodgdon - - -	87	Thomas Hodgdon.
John P. Read - - -	46	John P. Read.	James Shattuck - - -	83	James Heal.
Samuel Cole - - -	83	Jeremiah Cole.	Samuel Colby - - -	79	Samuel Colby.
Robert Anderson - -	84	Barton Anderson.			
Joel Thompson - - -	86	Isaac C. Thompson.	WHITEFIELD.		
John Merrill - - -	80	Nathan L. Merrill.	Isaac Heath - - -	83	
William Bickford - -	84	William Bickford.	Abram Tarr - - -	78	
William Atkinson - -	75	William Atkinson.			
Mercy Carvill - - -	82	Benjamin Carvill.	WISCASSET.		
Bradbury T. Jepson -	54	Bradbury T. Jepson.	John Williams - - -	79	Daniel Carr.
Oliver Herrick - -	57	Oliver Herrick.	Benjamin Greenleaf - -	80	Benjamin Greenleaf.
John Skinner - - -	87	Andrew Skinner.	Joseph Clark - - -	74	Joseph Clark.
Loved Lincoln - - -	82	Loved Lincoln.	Nathaniel Norton - -	79	Nathaniel Norton.
William True - - -	80	William True.	Ezekiel Averill - - -	85	Ezekiel Averill.
NEW CASTLE.			WOOLWICH—SMITH—FAIRFIELD.		
Ephraim Taylor - -	81	John Taylor.	John Shaw - - -	88	Reuben Wright.
			James Walch - - -	50	James Walch.
LISBON.			Thurston Card - - -	48	Thurston Card.
Calvin Cowing - - -	88	Calvin Cowing.	John Wright - - -	82	John Wright.
Isaac Whitney - - -	83	Isaac Whitney.	Joseph Wright - - -	78	Joseph Wright.
WEBSTER.			PATRICKTOWN PLANTATION.		
Foster Wentworth - -	75	Foster Wentworth.	Simeon Fish - - -	68	Simeon Fish.
James Colby - - -	76	James Colby.			
Benjamin Henderson -	86	Thomas Smith.	**KENNEBEC COUNTY.**		
James Weeks - - -	81	James Weeks.	ALBION.		
			Samuel Baker - - -	85	Ralph Baker.
NOBLEBOROUGH.			Stephen Rider - - -	79	Stephen Rider.
Levi Heall - - -	83		Nehemiah Stratton - -	81	Nehemiah Stratton.
Elijah Dunbar - - -	85		Edward Plummer - -	86	Edward Plummer.
Andrew Knowlton - -	89		Obadiah Wetherel - -	95	George Shaw.
Benjamin Chapman - -	80		AUGUSTA.		
Samuel A. Flagg - -	78	John Flagg.	John Kincaid - - -	78	John Kincaid.
PHIPSBURG.			Daniel Cony - - -	87	Daniel Cony.
Samuel Small - - -	83		Shubael Pitts - - -	74	James C. Pitts.
William Sprague - -	73		John Chandler - - -	78	John Chandler.
Abraham Day - - -	77		William Dorr - - -	84	John Dorr.
Daniel Morse - - -	94		Benjamin Gilbreth - -	56	Benjamin Gilbreth.
William Maine - - -	82		Charles Clark - - -	78	Elan Lyon.
Moses Morrison - -	84		Elijah D. Savage - -	52	Josiah Rollins.
			Henry Servall - - -	87	Henry Servall.
RICHMOND.			Amos Church - - -	84	Amos Church.
Sarah Blanchard - -	86		John Lancaster - - -	78	John Lancaster, jr.
Rebecca Blackstone - -	79		George Read - - -	80	George Read.
Anna Booker - - -	75		Seth Pitts - - -	82	Seth Pitts.
Abigail Webber - - -	79		William Stone - - -	75	William Stone.
William Welch - - -	85		Timothy Goldthwait - -	78	Timothy Goldthwait.
David Perry - - -	77		Ephraim Leighton - -	72	Ephraim Leighton, jr.
			Asa Wilbur - - -	80	David Wilbur.
ST. GEORGE.			John Rollins - - -	74	John Rollins.
Samuel Hinds - - -	80	Samel Hinds.	Henry Doe - - -	73	Hannah Gaild.
Benjamin Marshall - -	49	Benjamin Marshall.			
David Keller - - -	82	Alexander Keller.	ROME.		
Joseph Barter - - -	57	Joseph Barter.	Stephen Morrill - - -	65	
Mark Barter - - -	54	Mark Barter.			
			DEARBORN.		
THOMASTON.			Eleanor Whitney - -	57	
Nathan Sherman - -	78	Asa Sherman.			
Elizabeth Snowdeul - -	75	Edward Snowdeul.	CHINA.		
Robert Thorndike - -	79	Robert Thorndike.	Samuel Andress - -	85	Samuel Andress, jr.
Joseph Perry - - -	79	Joseph Perry.	Patience Breck - - -	75	Samuel Breck.
Darius Brewster - -	76	Darius Brewster.	Michael Crowell - -	83	Michael Crowell.
Aaron Massman - -	82	Memik Massman.	William Farris - - -	81	William Farris.
Beulah Ott - - -	82	Memik Massman.	Jotham Calvin - - -	80	Jotham Calvin.
William Tillson - -	87	William F. Tillson.	Sherman Lincoln - -	83	Sherman Lincoln.
Margaret George - -	78	John Ruggles.	Hannah Hall - - -	77	Nathaniel F. Norton.
Phineas Butler - -	82	George Butler.	Abram Talbot* - -	87	Abram Talbot.
Josiah Haskell - - -	80	Josiah Haskell.			
Mary Thomas - - -	80	George Thomas.	CLINTON.		
Job Perry - - -	75	Eben Swett.	Nathan Brackett - -	55	Nathan Brackett.
			James Lamb - - -	69	James Lamb.
TOPSHAM.			Levi Flint - - -	86	David Pratt.
Caleb Curtis - - -	82	Caleb Curtis.	Michael McNally - -	88	Arthur McNally.
Dorcas Dunlap - - -	76	Dorcas Dunlap.	Mordecai Moor - - -	102	John Moor.
William Hunter - -	76	Obadiah E. Frost.	Benjamin Roundey - -	48	Benjamin Roundey.
William Mallett - -	83	Isaac Mallett.	Isaac Keen - - -	86	Josiah Keen.
Jane Whitten - - -	78	Libbey Smith.	Lemuel Jenkins - -	76	Lemuel Jenkins.
			Ebenezer Whitney - -	79	Ebenezer Whitney.
WASHINGTON.					
Levi Hall - - -	–	James Hall.			
John Yarrow - - -	–	Worster Yarrow.	* Died since June 1st.		

MAINE—Continued.

Names of pensioners for revolutionary or military services.	Ages.	Names of heads of families with whom pensioners resided June 1, 1840.	Names of pensioners for revolutionary or military services.	Ages.	Names of heads of families with whom pensioners resided June 1, 1840.
KENNEBEC—Continued.			KENNEBEC—Continued.		
CLINTON GORE.			MONMOUTH—Continued.		
Thomas Hunter - - -	69	Thomas Hunter.	Pelatiah Warren - - -	86	Charles Warren.
			John Freeman - - -	80	John Freeman.
GREENE.					
Susannah Adams - - -	73	Moses Adams.	WALES.		
Samuel Mower - - -	79	Samuel Mower.	James Campbell - - -	81	James Campbell.
Simon Dearborn - - -	77	Aaron Daggett.	Hugh Owen - - -	71	Joseph Foss.
Joan Turner - - -	78	Edwin Turner	George Fogg - - -	73	George Fogg.
Lydia Beals - - -	74	Cyrus Beals.	Mary Larbree - - -	78	Daniel Larbree.
Cynthia Allen - - -	81	Benjamin Allen.			
John Mower - - -	81	Calvin Mower.	LITCHFIELD.		
William Sawyer - - -	77	John E. Sawyer.	Richard Fennin - - -	79	Elenor Dow.
Joseph McKenny - - -	86	Solomon McKenney.	Lydia Knowles - - -	84	Caleb C. Knowles.
			Abner Danforth - - -	75	Samuel Danforth.
WAYNE.			Andrew Brown - - -	79	Andrew Brown.
Keziah Burgese - - -	80	John True.	Roger Merril - - -	78	Roger Merril.
Bethiah Weeks - - -	78	Noah Chandler.	Abiah Stinson - - -	70	James B. Sawyer.
Lydia Fairbanks - - -	74	George W. Fairbanks.	James Dunlap - - -	88	James Dunlap.
John Smith - - -	83	John Smith.	Mary Hutchinson - - -	81	Robert Patten, jr.
Jabez Besse - - -	75	Jabez Besse.	Saul Cook - - -	82	Saul Cook.
			Abigail Fitts - - -	89	John Smith.
LEEDS.			Noah Towns - - -	85	Noah Towns.
Mary Bates - - -	77	William Bates.			
Lydia Turner - - -	88	Stephen Wellcome.	MOUNT VERNON.		
Jabez R. Bates - - -	79	Cyrus Bates.	John Jacobs - - -	85	John Jacobs.
John Ham - - -	81	Joshua Rayban.	Laban Smith - - -	79	Eldridge Wiggins.
William Pettengill - - -	80	William Pettengill, jr.			
Zadoc Bishop - - -	91	Joseph Bishop.	PITTSTON.		
James Lindsay - - -	84	James Lindsay.	David Rollins - - -	65	David Rollins.
Obadiah Pettengill - - -	78	Obadiah Pettengill.	Nathaniel Berry - - -	84	Leonard Blanchard.
Increase Leadbetter - - -	90	Ezra Leadbetter.	William Batchelder - - -	79	William Batchelder.
Francis George - - -	77	Francis George.	Levi Shepherd - - -	76	Levi Shepherd.
Andrew Cashman - - -	79	Isaac Cashman.	David Moores - - -	84	David Moores.
Anne Stowe - - -	76	Ithamar F. Stowe.			
James Lamb - - -	79	Ira Lamb.	READFIELD.		
Stephen Foster - - -	74	Stephen Foster.	Luther Sampson - - -	80	Luther Sampson.
			Joseph Woodford - - -	78	W. H. Woodford.
FAYETTE.			William Vance - - -	80	William Vance.
James Young - - -	80	James Young.	Oliver Bean - - -	42	Oliver Bean.
Joseph P. Mauton - - -	78	Josiah Elkins.	David Smith - - -	42	David Smith.
Philip Morse - - -	85	Philip Morse.	Job Sherburn - - -	82	Job Sherburn.
Sylvester Jones - - -	79	Sylvester Jones.	Moses Nickerson - - -	76	Moses Nickerson.
Philip Davis - - -	82	Joseph French.	Isaac Case - - -	79	Isaac Case.
Robert Blake - - -	87	Robert Blake.	Andrew Mace - - -	83	Andrew Mace.
William Raymond - - -	92	Nathan Raymond.			
Andrew Sturdevant - - -	79	Andrew Sturdevant, jr.	SIDNEY.		
Asa Hutchinson - - -	89	Asa Hutchinson.	Jabez Rollins - - -	73	Jabez Rollins.
Richard Jackman - - -	84	Richard Judkins.	Robert Ellis - - -	74	Carey Ellis.
			Thomas Stevens - - -	82	Samuel Shorey.
GARDENER.			Samuel Shorey - - -	47	Samuel Shorey.
Mary McCausland - - -	75	Thomas McCausland.	David Reynolds - - -	82	Charles Reynolds.
John Jakes - - -	80	John L. Foy.	Susanna Hayward - - -	65	Ambrose Hayward.
Mehitable Jones - - -	75	Henry Leeman.	Edward Mulikin - - -	71	Edmund Hayward.
Jedediah Robinson - - -	87	William Hopkinson.	Ebenezer Trask - - -	77	Asa Trask.
William Crawford - - -	82	William Crawford.	Elizabeth Cowan - - -	77	Isaac Cowan.
Joseph Collins - - -	80	Joseph Collins.	Jacob Morse - - -	75	James Daugherty.
John Lowell - - -	83	Benjamin B. Lowell.			
James P. Evans - - -	68	James P. Evans.	VASSALBOROUGH.		
Hugh Potter - - -	78	Hugh Potter.	Reliance Baxter - - -	84	Daniel Baxter.
Joseph Rollins - - -	85	Anelm. Bucke.	Lydia Bragg - - -	71	Lydia Bragg.
Hannah Hazen - - -	65	Hannah Hazen.	Amos Childs - - -	75	Amos Childs.
Rebecca Sweatland - - -	82	James Sherburn.	Sylvenus Hows - - -	77	Sylvenus Hows.
William Fuller - - -	79	William Fuller.	Squire Bishop - - -	85	John Tabor.
			Jonathan Burgess - - -	81	Jonathan Burgess.
HALLOWELL.			Desire Mathews - - -	78	James Mathews.
Benjamin Stickney - - -	84	Benjamin Stickney.	Jonathan Carleton - - -	79	Jonathan Carleton.
Abraham Pray - - -	79	Abraham Pray.	Jane Cowan - - -	75	Jane Cowan.
Samuel Prescott - - -	83	Samuel Prescott.	Samuel Bassett - - -	94	Jabez Bassett.
John Couch - - -	54	John Couch.	Caleb Randal - - -	87	Samuel Cross.
			Richard Warren - - -	85	Jared Warren.
MONMOUTH.					
Sarah Kelley - - -	78	Jason King.	VIENNA.		
Ruth Norris - - -	74	Greenlief K. Norris.	Joseph Holland - - -	79	Joseph Holland.
Mary Brown - - -	73	William G. Brown.	Robert Cofren - - -	75	Robert Cofren.
James F. Norris - - -	67	James F. Norris.	Mary Wells - - -	76	John Wells.
John Moody - - -	59	John Moody.	John Allen - - -	81	John Allen.
John Wilcox - - -	80	Washington Wilcox.	Ebenezer Mason - - -	77	Ebenezer Mason.
Benjamin Ayer - - -	76	William Richardson.			
Hannah Blue - - -	78	Nathaniel Blue.	WATERVILLE.		
Benjamin Clough - - -	75	Asa Clough.	Richard Sweetser - - -	90	David Parker.
David Marston - - -	89	David Marston.	Manoah Crowell - - -	78	Manoah Crowell.
John Witherell - - -	87	Rufus Witherell.	Sampson Freeman - - -	75	Sampson Freeman.
			Timothy Littlefield - - -	81	Timothy Littlefield.

MAINE—Continued.

Names of pensioners for revolutionary or military services.	Ages.	Names of heads of families with whom pensioners resided June 1, 1840.	Names of pensioners for revolutionary or military services.	Ages.	Names of heads of families with whom pensioners resided June 1, 1840.
KENNEBEC—Continued.					
WATERVILLE—Continued.			PENOBSCOT—Continued.		
Sarah Gilman	82	Nathaniel Gilman, jr.	CORINTH.		
John Cool	83	John Cool.	Aaron Bragdon	83	Aaron Bragdon.
Salathiel Penney	83	Arba Penney.	Susannah Rollins	87	Anthony Rollins.
Seth Getchell	86	Susan Stackpole.			
Elisha Hallet	82	Jonathan Hallet.	HOWLAND.		
Solomon Hallet	86	Solomon Hallet.	Arnold Glidden	87	Samuel Cram.
Lot Sturtevant	81	Reward Sturtevant.			
Thomas Bates	83	Thomas Bates, jr.	MATTAMASCONTIS.		
Asa Redington	78	Asa Redington.	Leah Tourtlotle	84	Levi Lancaster.
WINDSOR.			CHESTER.		
Abraham Cleaves	76	Abraham Cleaves.	Benjamin Walton	78	Benjamin Walton.
Mary Hallowell	85	John Hallowell.			
Mary Ridlow	74	Robert Hutchason.	DIXMONT.		
Joseph Linn	55	Joseph Linn.	Jacob Sawyer	92	Bryant Morton.
Caleb Leonard	80	Enoch Merrill.	Moses Littlefield	85	David Simpson.
Simon Palmer	79	Simon Palmer.	Charles Peabody	41	Charles Peabody.
Nehemiah Ward	55	Nehemiah Ward	William W. Reed	85	William W. Reed.
			Joseph Spaulding	79	Joseph Spaulding, jr.
WINTHROP.			Thomas Lowell	78	Thomas Lowell.
Nathaniel Levering	77	Nathaniel Levering.			
Judith Smith	79	Greenleaf Smith.	EXETER.		
Daniel Allen	86	Daniel Allen.	Stephen Bachelder	85	Stephen Bachelder.
Asa Robbins	81	Samuel True.	Leighton Colbath	45	Leighton Colbath.
Jonathan Russell	87	William Russell.	John Oakes	84	John Oakes, jr.
Jeremiah Brown	79	Cephas Thomas.	John S. Peavy	44	John S. Peavy.
Samuel Wood	81	Samuel Wood.	George Shaw	86	Andrew Shaw.
David McDuffin	66	David McDuffin.			
Elizabeth Heselton	85	Joseph Heselton.	GARLAND.		
Thomas Fillebrown	76	Thomas Fillebrown.	Phineas Batchelder	80	John H. Batchelder.
Rial Stanley	80	Jonathan L. Stanley.			
Hannah Chandler	75	Hannah Chandler.	HAMPDEN.		
Nathaniel Kimbal	83	Nathaniel Kimbal.	Amos Doane	82	Edward Doane.
Adin Stanley	78	Adin Stanley.	Samuel Cone	89	Samuel Cone.
Abigail Renson	85	Ezekiel Holmes.	Harding Snow	84	Harding Snow.
			William March	81	Newhall P. March.
WINSLOW.					
Simeon Simson	76		MILFORD.		
Enoch Fuller	85		Ruth Johnstone	88	Benjamine Johnstone.
PENOBSCOT COUNTY.			DEXTER.		
EDENBURG.			Joshua Elder	76	
Nathaniel Hoit	45	Nathaniel Hoit.	John Tucker	80	
BANGOR.			CORINNA.		
Peter Perham	89	David Perham.	Susan Adams	99	
Mary H. Downe	68	Mary H. Downe.	Mehitable Hubbard	85	
James Mayhew	81	James Mayhew, jr.	Eunice Sawtelle	82	
William A. B. Phillips	32	William A. B. Phillips.	Josiah Hammon	77	
Abigail Dix	90	Elijah Dix.			
Robert Mann	52	Robert Mann.	LEVANT.		
Joseph Mansell	89	Joseph Mansell.	Joseph Pomroy	67	Joseph Pomroy.
Oliver Randall	79	William Randall.			
William Forbes	78	William Forbes.	NEWBURG.		
			Simeon Farnum	85	
GLENBURN.			David Gilman	75	
John McLellen	79	Solomon Hutchinson.			
			NEWPORT.		
KIRKLAND.			Lydia Richardson	82	Jonathan Richardson.
Amos Munn	79	Amos Munn.	Isaac Lawrence	81	Isaac Lawrence, jr.
			Hannah Stuart.		
BRADFORD.			Sally Steward	77	
Daniel Maxfield	55	Daniel Maxfield.	James Clark	77	James Clark, jr.
James Harvey	78	James Harvey.			
George D. Marshal	-	George D. Marshal.	STETSON.		
			Oliver Hartwell	80	
EDDINGTON.					
Park Holland	87	Park Holland.	PLYMOUTH.		
Celia Eddy	78	William Cook.	Sylvanus Harlow	79	
Tamar Putnam	74	Benjamin Putnam.			
William Davis	78	William Davis.	ORONO.		
			William Colburn	79	Edward Colburn.
BREWER.					
Daniel Shed	77	Daniel Shed.	ORRINGTON.		
John Fannington	83	John Fannington.	Matilda Dole	75	William H. Dole.
Samuel Gilmore	77	Samuel Gilmore.	Oliver Doane	85	James Smith.
John Blake	86	Charles Blake.	Solomon Bolton	82	James Bolton.
			Nathaniel Severance	92	Nathaniel Peirce.
CARMEL.			Elizabeth Severance	69	Joseph S. Severance.
James Mayhew	81				
			OLD TOWN.		
CHARLESTON.			Joshua Sinclair	-	Joshua Sinclair.
Levi Gould	54	Otis Smith, jr.			

MAINE—Continued.

Names of pensioners for revolutionary or military services.	Ages.	Names of heads of families with whom pensioners resided June 1, 1840.	Names of pensioners for revolutionary or military services.	Ages.	Names of heads of families with whom pensioners resided June 1, 1840.
PENOBSCOT—Continued.			WALDO—Continued.		
WEST HALF TOWNSHIP NO. 6.			HOPE.		
Allen Dwelley - - -	78	Allen Dwelley.	George Ulmer - - -	80	James P. Brown.
			Richard Cummings - -	45	Richard Cummings.
WALDO COUNTY.			John Nayson - - -	84	Abner Dunton.
SEARSMONT.			Lemuel Wentworth - -	86	Daniel Hilt.
Cyril Brown - - -	84	Thomas S. Brown.	Stephen Sweatland - -	79	James Sweatland.
Andrew L. Robinson - -	84	John L. Robinson.	Benjamin Smith - -	83	Benjamin Smith.
Martha Willman - - -	77	Jacob Willman.			
			JACKSON.		
APPLETON.			Joseph Crary - - -	83	Joseph Crary.
Titus Metcalf - - -	86	Titus Metcalf.			
			KNOX.		
BELFAST.			Isaac Hall - - -	86	Isaac Hall.
Rhoda Hall - - -	70		Widow of Paul Wentworth	76	Stephen Wentworth.
Lemuel Dillingham - -	82		Ruth Sufferance - -	76	
Mary Patterson - - -	90		Henry Colburn - -	79	Moses Blake.
Hannah Smith - - -	73		Benjamin Johnson - -	75	
Charles Smith - - -	85		Mary Haskill - - -	83	Nathaniel Haskill.
Daniel Johnson - - -	76		Sarah Smith - - -	73	Levi Smith.
Eunice Edmuns - - -	83				
Joseph Gordon - - -	81		LINCOLNVILLE.		
Walter Hatch - - -	82		Abigail Rankins - -	68	Abigail Rankins
			John Wade - - -	85	John Wade.
BELMONT.			George W. Warren - -	39	George W. Warren.
James Weymouth - -	81	James Weymouth.	Noah Miller - - -	66	Noah Miller.
Charles White - - -	90	William White.	John Calderwood - -	88	James Calderwood.
James Greer - - -	81	James Greer.			
Isaac Neal - - -	58	Isaac Neal.	MONTVILLE.		
			Ebenezer Allen - -	80	Nelson Allen.
BROOKS.			John Milliken - - -	78	John Milliken.
Samuel Bowen - - -	76	Barzillar Bowen.	Susannah Terry - -	71	William Terry.
Benjamin Silley - -	79	Benjamin Silley.	Joseph Emery - - -	63	Alexander Emery.
James Means - - -	86	James Means.	Lucy Ripley - - -	75	Nahum Ripley.
Joseph Roberts - - -	87	Alford J. Roberts.	Thomas Carter - - -	63	Thomas Carter.
			Richard McAlister - -	78	Richard McAlister.
TROY.			Noah Norton - - -	92	David Norton.
Richard Whitten - -	77	Richard Whitten.	Betsey Abbot - - -	73	Joel Abbot.
			Luther Gregory - -	60	Luther Gregory.
UNITY.					
Phebe Harden - - -	83	Seth Hardin.	PALERMO.		
Amos Jones - - -	78	Amos Jones, jr.	John Dean - - -	81	John Dean.
Daniel Whitmore - -	81	Jesse Whitmore.	Thaddeus Bailey - -	80	Thaddeus Bailey.
Nancy Aspenwall - -	77	Hezekiah Chase, 2d.	Asenath Brown - -	76	Isaac Brown.
James Packard - - -	82	Moses Boynton.	William Davis - - -	83	Lewis Sabin, jr.
Henry Stuart - - -	78	James Fowler.	Daniel Plummer - -	85	Eli Carr.
Matthew Fowler - -	77	Matthew Fowler.	Oliver Pullen - - -	78	Franklin Newel.
			Mary Longfellow - -	81	Mary Longfellow.
BURNHAM.			Isaac Worthing - -	78	Nathan Worthing.
Olive Doe - - -	87	Raymond S. Doe.			
Elisha Douglass - -	71	Elisha Douglass.	LIBERTY.		
Betsey Dodge - - -	75	Nathan P. Dodge.	Joseph Knowlton - -	90	Joseph F. Knowlton.
Asa Lassell - - -	78	Asa Lassell.	Ichabod Tibbets - -	90	Benjamin Tibbets.
			Martha Lanson - -	80	William Lanson.
CAMDEN.					
Elizabeth Harkness - -	76	Robert Harkness.	MONROE.		
Beulah Ott - - -	82	Robert Thorndike.	Samuel Smith - - -	82	Samuel Smith.
Deborah Ames - - -	79	Alexander Thomas.	Eleazer B. Dickey - -	80	Eleazer B. Dickey.
Martha Hopkins - -	69	Richard Hopkins.	John Sanborn - - -	50	John Sanburn.
Ephraim Sheldon - -	75	Ephraim Sheldon.	Benjamin Curtis - -	83	Benjamin Curtis.
John Santell - - -	81	Asa Santell.	Hannah Jourdan - -	83	John Ward.
Peter Barrows - - -	85	Peter Barrows.			
Lucy Brewster - - -	89	William Brewster.	NORTHPORT.		
Simeon Tyler - - -	87	Benjamin F. Tyler.	Nathaniel Gitchel - -	79	Nathaniel Gitchel.
Benjamin J. Porter - -	77	Benjamin J. Porter.			
			PROSPECT.		
FRANKPORT.			Joseph Martin - - -	79	Joseph P. Martin.
Samuel Spaulding - -	76		David Halbrook - -	75	David Halbrook.
Andrew Tyler - - -	80		Moses Smith - - -	81	Moses Smith.
John Dwelly - - -	74				
William Carr - - -	84		SWANVILLE.		
—— Nickerson - - -	82		Simeon Haynes - -	82	Simeon Haynes.
Joseph Stubbs - - -	47				
Abner Bicknell - - -	76		THORNDIKE.		
Solomon Collins - -	77		William Philbrick - -	80	William Philbrick.
John Carlton, 2d - -	59		Shubal Bumps - - -	81	Benjamin Bumps.
Edward Cole - - -	59				
James Clark - - -	51		VINALHAVEN.		
			Sarah Bowen - - -	77	Silvanus Banks.
FREEDOM.					
John Plummer - - -	69	Brentnal Searl.	WALDO PLANTATION.		
Timothy Walker - -	82	Luther Small.	Susan Sayward - -	87	Abiel Gay.
Philip Flanders - - -	82	Phineas Warren.	John Maddin - - -	63	Samuel Bassett.

MAINE—Continued.

Names of pensioners for revolutionary or military services.	Ages.	Names of heads of families with whom pensioners resided June 1, 1840.	Names of pensioners for revolutionary or military services.	Ages.	Names of heads of families with whom pensioners resided June 1, 1840.
HANCOCK COUNTY.			**SOMERSET—Continued.**		
BLUEHILL.			STARKS—Continued.		
Edith Hinckley - - -	74	Robert W. Hinckley.	Jabes Bowing - - -	82	Jabes Bowing.
			Bethsheba Waugh - -	89	John Waugh.
ELLSWORTH.					
Samuel Maddocks - - -	78	Samuel Maddocks.	*ST. ALBANS.*		
			Benjamin Collins - -	73	Benjamin Collins.
BROOKSVILLE.			Edward Hartwell - -	93	Samuel Hartwell.
Jeptha Benson - - -	81	Jeptha Benson.	Mary Jewett - - -	76	Samuel S. Jewett.
Jacob Ames - - -	83	Robert Redman.	Amasa Steward - -	78	Amasa Steward.
Thomas Stevens - -	74	Thomas Stevens.			
Thomas Watson - -	77	Thaddeus Shepardson.	*HARTLAND.*		
John Warson - - -	86	John Warson.	Uzizeel Withee - -	75	David Hayden.
			John Whiting - - -	82	Leonard Whiting.
DEER ISLE.					
Judah Covill - - -	87	William Morey.	*FAIRFIELD.*		
Samuel Stinson - -	81	Samuel Stinson.	Simon Doe - - -	81	Simon Doe.
Joseph Whitmore - -	84	Joseph Whitmore.	Susannah Bates - -	82	Susannah Bates.
			Heman Nye - - -	37	Heman Nye.
BUCKSPORT.			Jonathan Nye - - -	83	Jonathan Nye.
Benjamin Gross - -	85	Benjamin Gross, jr.	Nathaniel Barrett - -	74	Nathaniel Barrett.
Nathan Atwood - -	82	Zabeth Atwood.	Abigail Emery - -	80	Caleb Emery.
Free G. Parker - -	85	Harriet Goodnow.	Abigail Kendall - -	74	David Hudson.
			Reuben Wyman - -	77	Reuben Wyman.
CASTINE.					
Edmund Bridges - -	77	Edmund Bridges.	*PALMYRA.*		
Richard Jaques - -	85	Richard Jaques.	Elizabeth Lancey - -	74	Daniel T. Robinson.
Henry Keler - - -	48	Henry Keler.	Asa Longley - - -	78	Asa Longley.
Ebenezer Richardson -	38	Ebenezer Richardson.	Joseph Pratt - - -	82	James Pratt.
PENOBSCOT.			*PITTSFIELD.*		
Alexander McCaslin -	77	Alexander McCaslin.	Robert M. Causland -	82	Robert M. Causland.
Nathaniel Patten - -	79	Mark S. Patten.	Jotham Buzzell - -	48	Jotham Buzzell.
David Dunbar - -	83	David Dunbar.			
William Hutchings -	75	William Hutchings.	*CHANDLERVILLE.*		
Theodore Bowden -	76	Theodore Bowden.	Sarah Pray - - -	74	Thomas Pray.
John Condon - - -	65	John Condon.			
			EMBDEN.		
MOUNT DESERT.			John Wilson - - -	78	John Wilson.
William Heath - -	76	William Heath.	Benjamin Colbey - -	89	Benjamin Colbey.
Rebecca Branscomb -	95	Charles Branscomb.	Joseph Felker - -	80	Joseph Felker.
Davis Hasgatt - -	89	Davis Hasgatt.			
Sarah Savage - - -	77	John Savage.	*CORNVILLE.*		
			Samuel Fogg - - -	83	Samuel Fogg.
EDEN.			William H. Hilton -	80	William Fox.
Phebe Remick - - -	73	Seth D. Remick.	Moses Cass - - -	82	Moses Cass.
SULLIVAN.			*S. ROWHEGAN.*		
Abigail Pettee - - -	60	Barry Pettee.	John Wyman - - -	64	William Wyman.
			Solomon Whitten - -	86	Benjamin Emery.
SOMERSET COUNTY.					
MADISON.			*NORRIDGEWOCK.*		
Andrew Russel - -	81	Nathan Haughton.	Lucy Gould - - -	79	William W. Dinsmore.
Joseph Maynard - -	81	Joseph Maynard.	Sybil Wood - - -	81	Samuel Smith.
Jonathan Hayden - -	77	Isaac McKenny.	Josiah Spaulding - -	79	Josiah Spaulding.
Amos Adams - - -	94	Ephraim Washburn.	William Spaulding - -	82	William Spaulding.
John Piper - - -	79	Wentworth Viles.			
Samuel C. Walker -	50		*SMITHFIELD.*		
William Walker - -	73		Susannah Whitehouse -	84	Susannah Whitehouse.
Ebenezer Dean - -	80		George Sawyer - -	82	George Sawyer, jr.
SOLON.			*BLOOMFIELD.*		
William Hilton - -	81		Tilley Mason - - -	80	George Pratt.
Benjamin Patten - -	80		Lydia Pratt - - -	78	Thomas Pratt.
Matthew P. Sanborn -	81		John Emery - - -	87	Samuel Pollard.
Solomon Russel - -	82				
			CAMBRIDGE.		
MERCER.			Philip Judkins - -	82	Leonard Judkins.
Ezra Willard - - -	72	Amasa Willard.			
Peltiah Boyington - -	82	Waterman Boyington.	*BINGHAM.*		
Phebe Ingalls - - -		Hermance Ingalls.	Calvin Russell - -	78	Calvin Russell.
Susannah Church - -	84	Andrew Croswell.			
Benjamin Young - -	90	Benjamin Young.	*HARMONY.*		
Rufus Sanderson - -	82	Rufus Sanderson.	Samuel Marble - -	-	William Roberts.
Nahum Baldwin - -	78	Nahum Baldwin.			
Nathaniel Farnham -	83	Nathaniel Farnham.	*ANSON.*		
			William Paine - -	79	William Paine.
STARKS.			Anna Williams - -	79	Anna Williams.
John Greenleaf - -	84	John Greenleaf.	Robert Leathhead - -	81	Joseph S. Houghton.
Ruth Dalino - - -	85	Daniel Greenleaf.	Joseph Bray - - -	76	
Amreah Meso - - -	83	Charles Meso.			
Luke Lawyer - - -	80	Luke Lawyer.	*NEW PORTLAND.*		
David Lerry - - -	86	Edward L. Lerry.	Josiah Parker - -	76	Josiah Parker.
William Young - -	87	William Young.	Thomas Wilber - -	74	Thomas Wilber.

Names of pensioners for revolutionary or military services.	Ages.	Names of heads of families with whom pensioners resided June 1, 1840.
SOMERSET—Continued.		
NEW PORTLAND—Continued.		
Josiah Everett	80	Josiah Everett.
LEXINGTON.		
David Morse	79	David Morse.
Jonathan Allbee	97	
WASHINGTON COUNTY.		
HARRINGTON.		
Joseph Libby	92	Ephraim Libby.
Zebulon Fickett	81	Zebulon Fickett.
CHERRYFIELD.		
Benjamin Sanborn	78	Nathaniel Sanborn.
Elisha Small	82	William Small.
CALAIS.		
John Noble	78	James Noble.
ROBBINSTON.		
Jonas Bond	80	William Jenkins.
Gideon Dean	80	Gideon Dean, jr.
CHARLOTTE.		
Robert Ramsey	76	Robert Ramsey.
ADDISON.		
Josiah Moore	80	Richmond D. Norton.
Eliphalet Reynolds	80	Benjamin Reynolds.
William Merit	81	William Merit, jr.
JONESBOROUGH.		
Samuel Watts	85	Samuel Watts.
COLUMBIA.		
Isaac Bussel	84	Robert Bussel.
DENNYSVILLE.		
Daniel Bosworth	79	Daniel Bosworth.
Christopher Benner	84	James Farley.
PEMBROKE.		
Jacob Dunbar	98	Moses Gardiner.
Thomas Jones	62	Thomas Jones.
Zadok Hersey	88	Zadok Hersey, jr.
PERRY.		
John Johnston	97	Samuel Trott.
EASTPORT.		
Daniel Granger	78	Daniel Granger.
Patrick Mulligan	52	Patrick Mulligan.
LUBEC.		
Joshua Oaks	81	Ebenezer Oaks.
Ebenezer Ramsdall	78	Ebenezer Ramsdall.
Martha Gove	69	Martha Gove.
MACHIAS.		
Levi Bowker	77	Levi Bowker.
Lunun Atus	–	Lunun Atus.
Sarah Getchell	84	Stillman Getchell.
Ebenezer Inglee	76	Ebenezer Inglee.
PISCATAQUIS COUNTY.		
BROWNVILLE.		
Ichabod Thomas	82	
Polly Stickney	68	
PARKMAN.		
Abner Merrill	49	Abner Merrill.
ABBOT.		
Jeremiah Ralf	82	Jeremiah Ralf.
SANGERVILLE.		
John Burrill	83	John Burrill.
John Leach	83	Jeremiah Leach.
Enoch Leathers	79	Jonathan Roberts.
GUILFORD.		
Ephraim Andrews	83	Robert Herring.

Names of pensioners for revolutionary or military services.	Ages.	Names of heads of families with whom pensioners resided June 1, 1840.
PISCATAQUIS—Continued.		
GUILFORD—Continued.		
Consider Glass	81	Consider Glass
Isaac Plumer	56	Isaac Plumer.
FOXCROFT.		
Aaron Tucker	56	Aaron Tucker.
SEBEC.		
Enoch Brown	89	Samuel Brown.
Ezekiel Chase	77	Ezekiel Chase.
ATKINSON.		
John Hart	78	John Hart, jr.
FRANKLIN COUNTY.		
WELD.		
Elizabeth Grover	85	Edsel Grover.
BERLIN.		
Lucy Handy	77	Charles Heath.
James Brackett	76	James Brackett.
Peter Adley	79	Peter Adley.
MADRID.		
Joel Pelton	83	Joel Pelton.
LETTER E.		
Ezra Carlton	76	Ezra Carlton.
FARMINGTON.		
Jesse Butterfield	88	
Thomas Riant	80	
Eliphalet Ginings	75	
Abraham Smith	78	
Samuel Stowers.		
Elihu Norton	53	
Ebenezer Childs	52	
INDUSTRY.		
Zoe Withee	78	
Lemuel Collings	83	
Josiah Gordin	83	
Trustum Daggtt	90	
Daniel Collings	84	
SALEM.		
George Pratt	76	George Pratt.
William Carle	77	William Carle.
PHILLIPS.		
Charles Church	78	Charles Church.
Josiah Blake	80	J. L. Blake.
Uriah Howard	77	Darius Howard.
John Clough	80	Luther Russell.
Jacob Whitney	77	Jacob Whitney.
AVON.		
Nathan Hanscom	93	Seth Carson.
George Goodwin	77	A. D. Goodwin
FREEMAN.		
Elezer Parlin	83	
Jonathan True	83	
Anna Winch	80	
NEW SHARON.		
Jephthah Coburn	81	Manly Coburn.
Samuel Bradley	74	Samuel Bradley.
Nathaniel Tibbetts	85	John Tibbetts.
Thomas Fields	90	Thomas Fields.
James Dyer	86	Henry Dyer.
STRONG.		
Silas Baker	82	James P. Baker.
Eliab Eaton	77	Joshua T. Eaton.
TEMPLE.		
Mitchell Richards	81	Moses A. Richards.
Mary Howe	81	James Richards.
Betsy Ballard	83	Jonathan A. Ballard.
Joel Varnum	78	Joel Varnum.
Polly True	80	Gideon Staples.

MAINE—Continued.

Names of pensioners for revolutionary or military services.	Ages	Names of heads of families with whom pensioners resided June 1, 1840.	Names of pensioners for revolutionary or military services.	Ages	Names of heads of families with whom pensioners resided June 1, 1840.
FRANKLIN—Continued.			**FRANKLIN—Continued.**		
WILTON.			JAY.		
Thomas Wutting - - -	72	Thomas Wutting.	Joseph Adams - - -	74	Abrazus Adams.
Jesse Woods - - -	75	James L. Woods.	Mary French - - -	82	Nancy French.
Thomas Colborn - - -	82	William Webster.	Jemima Keyes - - -	75	Lorenzo Keyes.
John Wheler - - -	90	Jesse Hiscock.	Silas Alven - - -	74	Louis Packard.
Samuel Whiten - - -	83	Thomas B. Whiten.			
Abigail Roach - - -	73	Samuel Jones.	**AROOSTOOK COUNTY.**		
Moses Averrill - - -	85	Moses Averrill.	HOULTON.		
Silas Gould - - -	83	Perham Gould.	Ephraim M. Condra - -	48	

STATE OF NEW HAMPSHIRE.

Names of pensioners for revolutionary or military services.	Ages.	Names of heads of families with whom pensioners resided June 1, 1840.	Names of pensioners for revolutionary or military services.	Ages.	Names of heads of families with whom pensioners resided June 1, 1840.
ROCKINGHAM COUNTY.			**ROCKINGHAM—Continued.**		
PORTSMOUTH.			DEERFIELD.		
Caroline N. Berry - - -	43		Sally Mathers - - -	75	
Martha Holbrook.			Moses Chase - - -	78	
Ann Huntress - - -	91		Francis Rollins - - -	79	
Polly Lord - - -	75		Joshua Veasey - - -	80	
George Libbey.			John Stearns - - -	80	
The heirs of Robert and Charlotte			Ezekiel Knowles - - -	85	
N. R. Thorne—			Jenett Blue - - -	75	
One aged - - -	17		Asa Folsom - - -	86	
Do. - - -	19		Abijah Ring - - -	65	
Sarah Willard - - -	34		Joseph Robinson - - -	84	
Anna Welch - - -	84				
George Boyles - - -	55	George Boyles.	NEW MARKET		
George Colbath - - -	84	George Colbath.	Betsey Tuttle - - -	76	
George Fishley - - -	80	George Fishley.	Thomas Brown - - -	80	
John Grant - - -	56	John Grant.	Josiah Clark - - -	80	
John Hodgkins - - -	50	John Hodgkins.	David Watson - - -	80	
Sarah Randall - - -	79	Sarah Randall.			
Alexander Smith - - -	42	Alexander Smith.	HAMPTON FALLS.		
			Robert Marshall - - -	87	
RYE.			Abigail Marshall - -	91	
John Y. Randall - - -	55	John Y. Randall.			
Mary Green - - -	80	William Caswell.	EPPING.		
James Robinson - - -	58	James Robinson.	Gordon Fruse - - -	78	
Betsey Smith - - -	79	Ephraim Philbrick.	Ebenezer Keniston - -	80	
Michael Dalton - - -	87	Michael Dalton.	Zebulon Dow - - -	84	
			Martha Hayley - - -	82	
NORTH HAMPTON.			Philip Blaisdell - - -	78	
Jeremiah Brown - - -	76	Jeremiah Brown, jr.	Sarah Rollins - - -	77	
Abigail Marston - - -	79	Dearborn Marston.	Aaron Huntoon - - -	83	
Heprebath Marston - - -	96	Daniel Marston.			
William Moulton - - -	82	John Haven.	NOTTINGHAM.		
Ebenezer Lovering - - -	84	Ebenezer Lovering.	Betsey Langley - - -	88	
Simon Leavitt - - -	87	Thomas C. Leavitt.	Sally Witham - - -	85	
			Abigail Wescott - - -	75	
EXETER.			Sarah Chapman - - -	78	
Martha Speed - - -	77	Martha Speed.	Lovey Pickering - - -	88	
Temperance Walker - - -	81	Temperance Walker.	Abner Davis - - -	86	
Relief Taft - - -	78	Nathaniel Rundletts.	Jonathan Davis - - -	84	
Sally Durant - - -	83	Susan Durant.	Joseph Cilley - - -	49	
John Tilton - - -	–	Timothy Tilton.	John Crawford - - -	55	
Jacob Carter - - -	–	Henry Carter.			
Enoch Rowe - - -	82	Enoch Rowe.	NORTHWOOD.		
			Abigail Right - - -	86	
STRATHAM.			Lydia Weeks - - -	68	
John Adams - - -	81	John Adams.	John Chesley - - -	89	
Joseph Green - - -	79	Nicholas Rollins.	Joseph Shaw - - -	90	
			Simon Bachelder - - -	82	
GREENLAND.			John Johnson - - -	83	
Joseph Dearborn - - -	78	Joseph Dearborn.	John Bickford - - -	80	
			Betsey Furber - - -	95	
NEWINGTON.			Sarah Fogg - - -	82	
Mary Huntress - - -	81	Mary Huntress.	Ebenezer Bennett - - -	78	
HAMPTON.			SEABROOK.		
Jonathan Seavey - - -	81	Jonathan Seavey.	John R. Beckman - - -	86	
Anna Moulton - - -	82	Anna Moulton.	Nicholas Felch - - -	85	
Daniel Lamprey - - -	81	Daniel Lamprey.	Sarah Eaton - - -	70	
Mary Godfrey - - -	74	Josiah Nudd.	Jeremiah Brown - - -	80	
Mary Stickney - - -	77	Comfort Leach.	Mariam Brown - - -	80	

NEW HAMPSHIRE—Continued.

Names of pensioners for revolutionary or military services.	Ages.	Names of heads of families with whom pensioners resided June 1, 1840.	Names of pensioners for revolutionary or military services.	Ages.	Names of heads of families with whom pensioners resided June 1, 1840.
ROCKINGHAM—Continued.			**ROCKINGHAM—Continued.**		
SEABROOK—Continued.			CHESTER.		
Sylvanus Eaton - - -	84		Thomas Anderson - -	78	Thomas Anderson.
David Eaton - - -	83		Lydia Shannon - -	84	Josiah Morse.
Mary Lock - - -	70		Thomas Shannon - -	79	Thomas Shannon.
Samuel George - - -	84		Jacob Eliot - -	84	Jacob Eliot.
KINGSTON.			Michael Worthen - -	81	Michael Worthen.
Sarah Proctor - - -	78		Mary Sanborn - -	76	Simon M. Sanborn.
Elizabeth Chellis - -	80		Benjamin True - -	76	Osgood True.
John Davis - - -	85		John Shannon - -	83	Meny Lane.
KENSINGTON.			Joshua Brown - -	84	Joshua Brown.
Winthrop Wiggin - -	96		Phebe Abbott - -	80	Jeremiah Rann.
Lydia Fogg - - -	72		Sarah Clark - -	84	Sarah Clark.
Ruth Dow - - -	82		John Heath - -	80	John Heath.
Hanson Hodgdon - -	82		Martha Aiken - -	76	Martha Aiken.
EAST KINGSTON.			John Downing - -	76	James Calep.
Christopher Challis - -	82		John Wason - -	86	John Wason.
Dolly Blaisdell - -	75		Richard Heath - -	78	Richard Heath.
HAMPSTEAD.			CANDIA.		
James Brickett - - -	77	James Brickett.	Hannah Taylor - -	81	John Moore, jr.
Isaac Noyes - - -	79	Isaac Noyes.	Phineas Swain - -	77	Phineas Swain.
Daniel Little - - -	90	Tristram Little.	Moses Turner - -	86	Moses Turner, jr.
ATKINSON.			Dorothy Knowles - -	82	Eleazer Knowles.
Judith Cogswell - -	74	Joseph B. Cogswell.	Ann Marden - -	85	Ann Marden.
PLAISTOW.			Mehitable McClure - -	91	John Buswell.
Hannah Clement - -	83	Amos C. Clement.	William Patten - -	76	Willis Patten
Nathaniel Clark - -	74	Nathaniel Clark, jr.	RAYMOND.		
Moses Bly - - -	82	Moses Bly.	Mary Prescot - -	78	John Bachelder, jr.
NEWTOWN.			Jacob Smith - -	83	Jacob Smith.
Sarah Hanson - - -	76	John Hasty.	Mary Richardson - -	78	Mary Richardson.
SANDOWN.			Theophilus Lorring - -	81	Moses Brown.
Dolly Fitts - - -	72	Nathaniel Fitts.	**STRAFFORD COUNTY.**		
Elizabeth Clough - -	89	Josiah Clough.	DOVER.		
DANVILLE.			Mary Watson - -	86	Samuel Watson, 2d.
Moses Hoyt - - -	86	William Huntington.	Reuben Ricker - -	82	Reuben Ricker.
Lydia Bean - - -	84	Lydia Bean.	Daniel Cushing - -	88	Daniel Cushing.
Judith Showell - -	81	Nathaniel George.	Margaret Tibbets - -	76	Nathaniel Tibbets.
Abigail Diamond - -	83	Obadiah Diamond.	Sarah Nute - -	88	Sarah Nute.
SALEM.			Ezra Green - -	94	Ezra Green.
Martha Harriss - -	96	Dudley W. Jones.	SOMERSWORTH.		
Sarah Hastings - -	76	Sarah Hastings.	Elizabeth Furber - -	82	Joshua Furber.
Lydia Webster - -	63	Thomas Webster.	James Burnham - -	86	James Burnham.
Moses Austin - -	85	Moses Austin.	Rachel Randall - -	75	Benjamin Andrews.
Maria Stevens - -	88	Tristram Kimball.	Moses Yeaton - -	86	Leavitt H. Yeaton.
Elisha Woodbury - -	78	Elisha Woodbury, jr.	Martha Roberts - -	79	Lydia Twombly.
Israel Woodbury - -	80	Israel Woodbury.	John Roberts - -	84	John Garvin.
Elizabeth Woodbury -	77	Elizabeth Woodbury.	John Philpot - -	83	Eliza Philpot.
WINDHAM.			Ann Hodgdon - -	78	Olive Abbott.
Hannah Center - -	84	Syntha Claggett.	GILMANTON.		
Elizabeth Emerson - -	78	John Hill.	Abigail Smith - -	79	Abigail Smith.
Mehitable Huges - -	93	John Huges.	Moses Currier - -	80	Moses Currier.
LONDONDERRY.			Jemima Burtet - -	77	Russell Phillips.
Allen Anderson - -	84	Eliza Holmes.	Elizabeth Perkins - -	87	Elizabeth Perkins.
Olive Eastman - -	76	John Follinsbee.	Anna Hunt - -	81	Jacob Hunt.
Benjamin Griffin - -	74	Benjamin Griffin.	Abigail Burley - -	69	Abigail Burley.
William Hogg - -	79	Nathan Conner.	Jonathan Taylor - -	75	Joseph Rowe.
David Crowell - -	82	Peter Crowell.	John Dow - -	76	John Dow.
DERRY.			Eleazer Young - -	83	Eleazer Young.
Deborah Waters - -	82	Margaret Adams.	Mary Folsom - -	85	Mary Folsom.
John Burnham - -	90	George Burnham.	Thomas Adams - -	82	John Adams.
James Choat - -	79	Humphrey Choat.	Jonathan Hilliard - -	80	Jonathan B. Hilliard.
Thomas Carlton - -	77	Thomas Carlton.	Mehitable Hutchinson -	87	James Hutchinson.
Ruth Carlton - -	85	Daniel Carlton.	Abraham Parsons - -	85	Abraham Parsons.
Hannah Cheney - -	86	William Cheney.	Paul Otiss - -	85	Eliphalet F. Gilman.
William Rowell - -	91		Dinah Sands - -	74	Samuel G. Kelley.
Moses Hoyt - -	67	Moses Hoyt.	Micajah Kelley - -	80	Ithiel Smith.
Sarah Remicks - -	76	Sarah Remicks.	Ithiel Smith - -	69	John Lougee.
Benjamin Shute - -	81	Benjamin Shute.	John Lougee - -	63	Rhoda Gutterson.
Benjamin Warner - -	83	Benjamin Warner.	Mary Gutterson - -	79	
Robert Willson - -	81	Robert Willson.	GILFORD.		
			Susan Nichols - -	81	Martha Nichols.
			J. V. Barron - -	53	J. V. Barron.
			David Thompson - -	83	David Thompson.
			Martha Sawyer - -	79	Israel Sawyer.
			Benjamin Jewett - -	75	Benjamin Jewett.
			Anna Whitcher - -	78	Timothy Whitcher.
			Jabez James - -	80	Jabez James.

NEW HAMPSHIRE—Continued.

Names of pensioners for revolutionary or military services.	Ages.	Names of heads of families with whom pensioners resided June 1, 1840.	Names of pensioners for revolutionary or military services.	Ages.	Names of heads of families with whom pensioners resided June 1, 1840.
STRAFFORD—Continued.			**STRAFFORD—Continued.**		
BARNSTEAD.			SANDBORNTON—Continued.		
Robert Tebbetts - - -	81	Robert Tebbetts -	Nathaniel Morrill - - -	77	Nathaniel Morrill.
James Marden - - -	85	David Marden.	Sarah Brimhall - - -	90	Joseph Vaughen.
Molly Jacobs - - -	84	Joseph Tuttle.			
Valentine Chapman - -	82	Valentine Chapman.	ALTON.		
John Aikens - - -	88	John Aikens.	Jonathan Richards - -	49	Jonathan Richards.
Ephraim Tebbetts - -	86	Robert Tebbetts.	Jeremiah Woodman - -	79	Jeremiah Woodman.
Ebenezer Nutter - -	83	Ebenezer Nutter.	Benjamin Sluper - -	81	Joseph Stuper.
Mary Avery - - -	84	Samuel Rollins.	John Rollins - - -	84	John Rollins.
Pelatiah Penney - -	83	Noah Holmes.	Thomas Baker - - -	84	Daniel Baker.
Lucy Hill - - -	83	John Hill..	Benjamin Morrison - -	84	Susannah Morrison.
Anthony Nutter - -	78	Anthony Nutter.	Elizabeth Bennet - -	86	Benjamin Bennet.
John Nutter - - -	83	Ira Parsley.	Hannah Webster - -	74	Hannah Webster.
			Mary Peavy - - -	73	Enoch Peavy.
STRAFFORD.			Anna Dudley - - -	84	Abel Dudley.
Nancy Kemuston - -	80		Polly Dudley - - -	78	Samuel Dudley, jr.
Mary Lougee - - -	80	Nathaniel E. Hanson.			
George Foss - - -	83	George Foss, jr.	MIDDLETON.		
John Peavey - - -	86	John Peavey, jr.	Elizabeth Roberts - -	77	John Roberts.
George Foss - - -	86	George Foss.	Dorothy Pike - - -	77	Robert Pike.
Abigail McNeal - -	87	Mary Wingate.	Martha Buzzell - -	73	Jacob P. Buzzell.
Samuel Parsley - -	91	Enoch Libbey.	Eleanor Stevens - -	76	George W. Stevens.
Mary Leighton - -	82	Sally Clark.	Hannah Garland - -	81	Ham Garland.
Joseph Caswell - -	84	Joseph Caswell.			
			FARMINGTON.		
BARRINGTON.			Sarah Tilcomb - - -	78	Jeremiah Wingate.
Mary Buzzell - - -	88	Jonathan Buzzell.	Alice Watson - - -	77	Alice Watson.
Patience Watson - -	75	Joseph Hall..	Joseph Roberts - -	78	Joseph Roberts.
Mary Rermick - - -	73	Solomon Waldson.	Hannah Walker - -	87	John Walker.
			Isaac Hanson - - -	82	Isaac Hanson.
LEE.			Benjamin Ham - - -	85	Benjamin Ham.
Deborah Williams - -	82	James Langley.			
Hannah Dearborn - -	77	Hannah Durgin.	MILTON.		
Josiah Bartlett - -	57	Josiah Bartlett.	Sarah Nute - - -	77	David Nute.
Charles Willey - -	83	Charles Willey.	Amos Bragdon - - -	78	Amos Bragdon.
			Elizabeth Roberts - -	80	James C. Roberts.
MADBURY.			Jonathan Dore - - -	83	Jonathan Dore.
John Twombly - -	80	Paul Brock.	David Corsen - - -	79	David M. Corsen.
Dorothy Jackson - -	78	Ephraim Jackson.	Thomas Applebee - -	84	James Applebee.
Ruth Huckins - - -	78	John Huckins.	Bennaiah Dore - - -	75	Bennaiah Dore.
DURHAM.			NEW DENHAM.		
Hannah Emerson - -	91	Joshua F. Emerson.	Elizabeth Sumner - -	78	William S. Sumner.
John Starbird - - -	85	John Starbird.	Abigail Mitchel - -	87	Samuel Mitchel.
William Applebee - -	79	William Applebee.	Charles Powers - -	78	Samuel Gilman.
Hannah Crumnet - -	84	Winthrop Smith.	Jacob Leighton - -	82	Jacob Leighton.
Eleazer Bennett - -	92	John Bennett.	Winthrop Davis - -	73	Winthrop Davis.
Sarah Stillson - -	89	William Stillson.			
Joseph Dame - - -	82	Asa Dame.	BROOKFIELD.		
Andrew Drew - - -	82	Andrew Drew.	Judith Chamberlain -	77	William T. Cate.
			Phineas Johnson - -	93	Phineas Johnson.
ROCHESTER.			Edmund Tibbets. - -	78	Edmund Tibbets.
Samuel Runnels - -	86	John Hanson.	Mary Watson - - -	89	Nathan Watson.
Henry Buzzell - -	80	Henry Buzzell.			
Sarah Hoyt - - -	92	Sarah Hoyt.	EFFINGHAM.		
John McDaffee - -	87	John Richards.	John Drake - - -	87	John Drake.
Sarah Sargeant - -	83	Joseph Dame.	Abraham Marston - -	81	John L. Marston.
John Gray - - -	75	John Gray, jr.	James Garland - - -	87	William Mason.
			Samuel Lear - - -	75	Samuel Lear.
SANDBORNTON.					
Caleb Aldrich - - -	75	Caleb Aldrich.	TUFTONBOROUGH.		
Sarah Burhigh - -	87	Peter Burhigh.	Elisha Smith - - -	63	Elisha Smith.
Elisha Chapman - -	70	Elisha Chapman.	James Renolds - - -	88	James Renolds
Ebenezer Colby - -	79	Ebenezer Colby.	Eliphalet Drake - -	92	John Drake.
Amos Blodgett - -	83	Ebenezer Colby, jr.	Miles Renolds - - -	78	Miles Renolds.
Asa Currier - - -	79	Asa Currier.	James Wiggin - - -	80	James Wiggin.
Samuel Davis - - -	48	Samuel Davis.	Mehitable Severence -	74	Benjamin Severance.
John Dungin - - -	83	John Dungin.	Ichabod Horn - - -	81	Ichabod Horn.
Elizabeth Morrill - .	76	Willoughby Dungin.	Lydia Veazey - - -	83	Lydia Veazey.
Moses Gilman - - -	47	Moses Gilman, jr.	James Whitehouse - -	89	Nathaniel Whitehouse.
Eunice Jaques - -	80	Eunice Jaques.	Benjamin Bean - -	83	Benjamin Bean.
Jonathan Morrison -	80	Simon R. Morrison.	Joshua Neal - - -	85	John Neal.
Olive Putnam - - -	75	William B. Putnam.	Jonathan Morrison -	81	Ebenezer Morris.
John Sanders - - -	83	John Sanders.	Benjamin Wiggin - -	84	Benjamin Wiggin.
Jonathan Smart - -	82	Asa R. Smith.			
Henry Smith - - -	79	Josiah C. Smith.	WAKEFIELD.		
Dolly Sanborn - -	76	Dolly Sanborn.	Betsey Cook - - -	70	Peter Cook.
Dudley Swain - -	81	Dudley Swain.	Solomon Hutchins - -	80	Solomon Hutchins
Louchance Smith - -	89	Mark Smith.	Mehitable Cook - -	80	John Fellows.
Jeremiah Swain - -	81	Jeremiah Swain.	Ebenezer Hill - - -	82	Ebenezer Hill.
John Taylor - - -	83	William Taylor.			
Elias Buswell - - -	85	Dearborn Taylor.	WOLFSBOROUGH,		
Josiah Sanborn, 2d -	80		Sally Lucas - -	84	John Lucas

3

NEW HAMPSHIRE—Continued.

Names of pensioners for revolutionary or military services.	Ages.	Names of heads of families with whom pensioners resided June 1, 1840.	Names of pensioners for revolutionary or military services.	Ages.	Names of heads of families with whom pensioners resided June 1, 1840.
STRAFFORD—Continued.			**STRAFFORD**—Continued.		
WOLFSBOROUGH—Continued.			CENTRE HARBOR—Continued.		
Nathan Lee - - -	78	Nathan Lee.	James Tibbets - - -	76	
Ichabod Colby - - -	79	John T. G. Colby.	Sargeant Kimball - -	83	
John Shory - - -	85	Lyford Shory.	Hosea Sturdavant - -	77	
David Piper - - -	84	David Piper.	Jonathan Kelley - -	79	
Martha Moody - - -	79	Joseph W. Moody.			
Hannah Nudd - - -	75	Samuel Nudd.	FREEDOM.		
John Clough - - -	78	John Clough.	Richard Taylor - - -	89	Richard Taylor.
Polly Leavett - - -	68	Barron T. Leavett.	Moses Harmon - - -	81	Moses Harmon.
George Yeaton - - -	80	Hannah Furber.	Thomas Lord - - -	83	Thomas Lord.
			Pelatiah Harmon - -	84	Pelatiah Harmon.
TAMWORTH.			Sarah Mills - - -	82	James R. Mills.
Benjamin Sullivan - -	77	Benjamin Sullivan.	John Andrews - - -	77	John Andrews.
Sally Gilman - - -	78	Polly Gilman.			
Nathaniel Hayford - -	84	Warren Hayford.	EATON.		
Sarah Washburn - -	77	Sarah Washburn.	Judith Fall - - -	81	Samuel H. Allard.
Drusilla Head - - -	76	Andrew Nealy.	Eli Glenis - - -	76	Thomas Glenis.
Martha Jackson - - -	93	Noah J. Sanborn.	Moses Ferrin - - -	80	Samuel Ferrin.
Andrew Nealley - -	94	Timothy Tewksbury.	Jonathan Towle - -	85	Jonathan Towle.
OSSIPEE.			CONWAY.		
Hannah Docken - -	69	Moses Harrison.	William Burbank - -	47	William Burbank.
Joseph White - - -	73	Joseph White.	James Howard - - -	71	James Howard.
Silas White - - -	81	Silas White.	William Thorns - -	79	William Thorns.
Charity Cauney - -	80	John C. Thompson.	Ebenezer Bean - - -	84	Ebenezer Bean.
Stephen Nason - - -	82	John Weeks.	Samuel Willey - - -	87	Samuel Willey.
Rhoda Marston - - -	75	Simon Philbrook.	Elijah Dinsmoor - -	77	Fox Dinsmoor.
John Thompson - -	52	John Thompson.	Amos Barnes - - -	84	Amos Barnes.
			Miles Dolloff - - -	67	Miles Dolloff.
MOULTONBOROUGH.			Jonathan Leavitt - -	81	Jonathan Leavitt.
Ebenezer Horn - - -	85	Ebenezer Horn.	Moses Patten - - -	90	David Carr.
John Knowles - - -	80	Joseph Knowles.			
William Morrill - -	77	Jacob Graves.	SANDWICH.		
Samuel B. Mason - -	82	Benjamin M. Mason.	Theodore Atkinson - -	75	
Stephen Strong - -	77	Stephen Strong.	Jonathan Gilman - -	52	
Martha Adams - - -	77	Martha Adams.	Jonathan Vittum - -	59	
Nancy Morse - - -	74	Benjamin E. Morse.	David Kenistan - -	84	
Abigail Richardson -	90	Samuel Richardson.	Eliphalet Smith - -	76	
Hannah Horn - - -	75	Jonathan Copp, 2d.	Anna Webster - - -	85	
Charles Brown - - -	78	Charles Brown.	Betty Furguson - -	76	
Jemima Brown - - -	71	John Brown.	David Collins - - -	82	
Charlotte Cook - -	77	Samuel S. Cook.	Jane Etherage - - -	76	
			Abigail Mason - - -	75	
NEW HAMPTON.			John Church - - -	80	
Naomi Farmer - - -	87		John Watson - - -	83	
Levi Robinson - - -	86		John Marston - - -	82	
Eunice Harris - - -	79		Dorcas Thompson - -	69	
Richard Durgin - -	89		Ebenezer Cook - - -	80	
Sarah Wells - - -	82		Waymouth Wallace -	83	
Judith Tilton - - -	69		Samuel Ladd - - -	62	
Josiah Magoon - - -	82				
Benjamin Smith - -	82		CHATHAM.		
John Smith - - -	80		Louda Smith - - -	78	
Thomas Woodman - -	88		William Eaton - - -	74	
Rachel Sincler - - -	81		Elizabeth Heard - -	84	
Joseph Smith - - -	80		Lydia Wyman - - -	75	
MEREDITH.			**MERRIMACK COUNTY.**		
Benjamin Perkins - -	79		CONCORD.		
John Robinson - - -	80		Daniel Arlin - - -	71	Daniel Arlin.
Eunice Merrill - - -	80		John Carter - - -	81	Moses Davis.
Amos Leavitt - - -	81		Samuel Davis - - -	81	Moses Davis.
Jonathan Russell - -	87		Jonathan Wheelock -	81	Lewis Dowaing.
Thomas Dalloff - -	81		John Elliot - - -	84	John Elliot.
Joseph Danforth - -	77		Huldah Evans - - -	76	Huldah Evans.
Daniel Tilton - - -	82		Mary Boardman - -	85	Samuel Fletcher.
Reuben Morgan - -	92		Asa French - - -	98	Asa French.
Mariam Swain - - -	78		Thomas Haines - -	79	Thomas Haines.
Oliver Clough - - -	77		Elizabeth Stickney -	82	Gersham Hanson.
Stephen Fogg - - -	30		Miriam Hoit - - -	72	Jonathan H. Hoit.
Abel Cass - - -	83		Levi Hutchins - - -	78	Levi Hutchins.
Betsey Cram - - -	30		John Virgin - - -	57	Samuel Hutchins.
Hannah Gorden - -	75		Samuel Jackman - -	91	Samuel Jackman.
Josiah Moulton - -	61	Moses Buzell.	Anna Griffin - - -	84	Nancy Morrill.
John Wadleigh - -	37		Tabatha Gilman - -	82	Thomas Potter.
Simeon Wadleigh - -	78		Joseph Runnels - -	81	Joseph Runnels.
Abigail Gorden - -	83		Jonathan Uran - - -	85	Jonathan Uran.
John Bryant - - -	72		Stephen Webster - -	82	Atkinson Webster.
Phebe Pike - - -	78		Andrew Willey - - -	85	Andrew Willey.
CENTRE HARBOR.			HOPKINTON.		
Bening Wilkinson - -	74		Ephraim Fisk - - -	81	Ephraim Fisk, jr.
Jacob Davis - - -	81		Esther Putney - - -	79	Esther Putney.

Names of pensioners for revolutionary or military services.	Ages.	Names of heads of families with whom pensioners resided June 1, 1840.	Names of pensioners for revolutionary or military services.	Ages.	Names of heads of families with whom pensioners resided June 1, 1810.
MERRIMACK—Continued.			**MERRIMACK—Continued.**		
HOPKINTON—Continued.			BRADFORD—Continued.		
Joseph Putney	87	Joseph Putney.	Abel Severance	85	John Severance.
Samuel Eastman	79	Samuel Eastman.	Daniel Lord	88	Peter A. Cook.
William Weeks	85	William Weeks.	Abel Blood	82	Robert Fulton.
Moody Smith	82	Moody Smith.	Jonathan Knight	86	Jonathan Knight.
Abigail Chadwick	76	Abigail Chadwick.	Abraham Smith	85	Abraham Smith.
Moses Long	79	Moses Long.	Daniel Hale	84	Daniel Hale.
Moses Cross	79	Moses Cross.	NORTHFIELD.		
Ruth Tabor	77	Ruth Tabor.	Elias Abbott	82	Elias Abbott.
HENNIKER.			Jesse Carr	83	Jesse Carr.
Oliver Noyes	82	Oliver Noyes.	John Dinsmore	85	Edmund Dearborn.
James Brown	86	James Brown.	Samuel Dinsmore	87	Samuel Dinsmore.
Polly How	79	Oliver Whitcomb.	Samuel Goodwin	93	James Goodwin.
Mary Greenleaf	77	Mary Greenleaf.	Abner Flanders	85	Nancy Haniford.
Ruth Goss	77	Cyrus Goss.	Joseph Cofran	50	John Rogers.
PEMBROKE.			WILMOT.		
Timothy Hall	81	Timothy Hall.	Edward Courrier	77	Edward Courrier.
Hannah Connor	88	John Brown.	Jethro Barber	79	Jethro Barber.
Joanna Parker	84	Bailey Parker.	Daniel Emery	79	Eben. White.
ALLENSTOWN.			Daniel Poor	79	Charles Poor.
Samuel Libby	84	Samuel Libby.	Joseph Pedrick	75	Joseph Pedrick.
			Eliphalet Rollins	84	Eliphalet Rollins.
DUNBARTON.			Jeremiah Bean	74	Jeremiah Bean.
Elizabeth Leach	93	Samuel Leach.	SALISBURY.		
Esther Hammond	84	Esther D. Hammond.	Samuel McGuin	104	William Clay, jr.
Janette Stinson	89	John Stinson, 3d.	Benjamin Thompson	79	Benjamin Thompson.
Walter Harris	79	Walter Harris.	Abraham Fifield	85	Daniel Fifield.
Sarah Whipple	84	Benjamin Whipple.	Jabez True	82	Jabez True.
Esther Adams	85	John Adams.	Nathan Bullard	76	Reuben Greeley.
Isabel McCauly	85	James McCauly.	Enoch Adams	86	Samuel Scribner.
HOOKSETT.			Moses Fellows	85	Moses Fellows.
Ebenezer Currier	77	Ebenezer Currier.	FRANKLIN.		
James Otterson	83	James Otterson.	Thaddeus Gage	86	David Gage.
Alice Mitchell	71	Joseph Mitchell.	David Flanders	83	Amos Hoid.
Samuel Poor	82	Samuel Poor.	Caleb Brown	81	Caleb Brown.
Anna Abbot	73	Ann Abbot.	William Ash	72	William Ash.
BOW.			Edward Sawyer	79	Edmund Sawyer.
Nancy Currier	84	Nancy Currier.	Samuel Morse	87	Samuel Morse, jr.
David Hammond	84	David Hammond.	Daniel Bean	84	Daniel Bean.
Thomas Colley	85	Thomas Colley.	ANDOVER.		
Stephen McCoy	81	Asa Morgan.	Samuel Cilley	87	Samuel Cilley.
Jonathan McCoy	83	Asa Morgan.	Mark Batchelder	82	Mark Batchelder.
WARNER.			William Glines	80	Lewis Davis.
Stephen Badger	82	Stephen Badger.	NEW LONDON.		
Dudley Bailey	85	Albridge D. Bailey.	Levi Everett	79	Levi Everett.
Richard Straw	85	Richard Straw.	Josiah Davis	83	Josiah Davis.
Joseph Sargent	89	Caleb Sargent.	Moses Trussell	86	Moses Trussell.
Samuel Cheney	77	Chilis F. Colby.	NEWBURY.		
Joseph Evans	85	John Withington.	William Leach	84	William Leach.
Joseph B. Hoyt	78	Joseph B. Hoyt.	Charles Colburn	77	Charles Colburn.
Anthony Clark	88	Anthony Clark.	William Sargent	78	William Sargent.
BOSCAWEN.			John Eaton	77	John Eaton.
Samuel Morse	81	Samuel Morse.	CANTERBURY.		
Eliphalet Kilburn	87	Eliphalet Kilburn, jr.	Sampson Battis	89	Sampson Battis.
Joseph Little	79	Joseph Little.	John Lovis	80	John H. Bennett.
Nathaniel Burpey	84	Joseph Burpey.	Morrill Shepherd	75	Morrill Shepherd.
Jonathan Burpey	74	Jonathan Downing.	Joseph Cleasby	76	Joseph Cleasby.
Nathaniel Atkinson	86	Nathaniel Atkinson.	Sarah Clough	80	Joseph Clough.
Eliakim Walker	87	Benjamin Walker.	Benjamin Bradley	79	Benjamin Bradley.
Nathan Carter	78	Nathan Carter.	Elizabeth Moore	76	Elizabeth Moore.
SUTTON.			LOUDON.		
Theodore Richards	76	George W. Richards.	Abner Clough	83	Abner Clough.
Benjamin Colby	84	David Farmer.	Sarah Wiggins	83	Samuel Haines.
Philip Nelson	84	Philip Nelson.	Joseph Clough	83	Joseph Clough.
Isaac Littlefield	46	Isaac Littlefield.	Isaac Clifford	87	William Jackson.
James Buswell	57	James Buswell.	Jeremiah Bennett	85	Jeremiah Bennett.
Wells Davis	87	Edward Ordway.	Amos Currier	85	George B. Johnston.
Simon Stevens	76	John Stevens.	Joanna Hayes	96	Joseph E. Clifford.
Jonathan Stevens	96	John Hubburt.	Benjamin Page	81	Benjamin Page.
Abner Ward	85	Abner Ward.	Jonathan Davis	80	Jonathan Davis.
BRADFORD.			Eleanor Gleeson	80	Jeremiah Gleeson.
Micah How	81	Micah How.	Daniel Seavey	77	Daniel Seavey.
Rufus Fuller	79	Parley Martin.	Eleanor Berry	80	Walter Berry.
Abraham P. Sweat	80	Abraham P. Sweat.	William Wheeler	80	William Wheeler

NEW HAMPSHIRE—Continued.

Names of pensioners for revolutionary or military services.	Ages.	Names of heads of families with whom pensioners resided June 1, 1840.	Names of pensioners for revolutionary or military services.	Ages.	Names of heads of families with whom pensioners resided June 1, 1840.
MERRIMACK—Continued.			**HILLSBOROUGH—Continued.**		
PITTSFIELD.			*PETERBOROUGH.*		
Thomas R. Swett	79	Thomas R. Swett.	John Todd	83	John Todd.
Anna Sanborn	82	Simon Mason.	Samuel Morrison	79	Samuel Morrison.
John Shaw	88	John Shaw.	Sarah Matthews	79	Thomas Matthews.
Anna Sanborn	89	Anna Sanborn.	Rebecca Diamond	78	John Diamond.
Hannah Drake	76	James Drake.	David Smiley	80	David Smiley.
David Bennett	24	David Bennett.	James Porter	85	Samuel Maynard.
John True	78	John True.	Abner Hagget	81	Peter Twiss.
CHICHESTER.			Elizebeth Blair	84	James Swan.
Gardner Edmunds	46	Gardner Edmunds.	Phebe Hadley	85	Thomas Hadley.
Molly Knox	90	Molly Knox.	*LYNDEBOROUGH.*		
Susannah Benson	61	Susannah Benson.	Jonathan Butler	87	Jonathan Butler.
Leavitt Hook	43	Leavitt Hook.	Jedediah Russell	88	Ebenezer Russell.
Dudley Smart	82	Dudley Smart.	Joshua Sargent	82	Joshua Sargent.
Moses Towns	86	Moses Towns.	Oliver Perham	78	Oliver Perham.
Richard Maxfield	77	Richard Maxfield.	Abraham Rose	80	Abraham Rose.
Joseph Dow	90	Joseph Dow.	Edmund Perkins	80	Burnham Russel.
Rhoda Maxfield	85	Daniel P. Maxfield.	Phineas Kidder	84	Phineas Kidder.
EPSOM.			*GREENFIELD.*		
Ruth Philbrick	83	Ruth Philbrick.	Joseph Eaton	81	Lewis Martin.
Sarah McClary	84	Jonathan Steele.	William Holley	75	William Holley.
Dorothy Grant	86	John Grant.	Abigail Johnson	89	Frederick A. Mitchell.
Eunice Sargent	84	John Marshall.	Ebenezer Farrington	83	Ebenezer Farrington.
Mark Emerson	78	Simeon P. Locke.	Jacob McIntire	84	Jacob McIntire.
John Bachelder	79	Levi Locke.	Lucy Perey	73	Lucy Perey.
Phebe Prescott	82	Samuel Cate.	William Brooks	79	William Brooks.
Samuel Lear	78	Samuel L. Lear.	Simeon Fletcher	80	Simeon Fletcher.
David How	75	David How.	Ruhama Burnham	76	Ruhama Burnham.
Abigail Bickford	84	Samuel B. Bickford.	Simon Low	85	Simon Low.
HILLSBOROUGH COUNTY.			*FRANCESTOWN.*		
HILLSBOROUGH.			Eleanor Brewster	77	Isaac Brewster.
William Dickey	85	William Dickey.	William Hopkins	77	William Hopkins.
David Livermore	78	David Livermore.	Sarah Dustin	77	Emerson Favor.
Mary Gould	79	George Gould.	Mehitable Fisher	78	Winslow Lakin.
Martha Mann	77	Martha Mann.	Winslow Lakin	81	Winslow Lakin.
Thomas Killom	80	Thomas Killom.	Abigail Morse	75	Mark Morse.
Daniel Killom	84	Daniel Killom.	William Campbell	89	Richard Fisher.
Nathaniel Parmenter	85	Nathaniel Parmenter.	William McAlvin	86	William McAlvin.
Isaac Farrar	79	Isaac Farrar.	Robert Butterfield	83	Oliver Butterfield.
Thaddeus Goodwin	87	Thaddeus Goodwin.	Thomas Fisher	79	Phineas Butterfield.
Isaac Andrews	84	Isaac Andrews.	Amos Batchelder	78	Amos Batchelder.
William Parker	84	William Parker.	Eleanor Follansbee	80	John Follansbee.
Daniel Russell	85	Denizen Gould.	Daniel Fuller	79	Daniel Fuller.
Abigail Robbins	75	Charles D. Robbins.	*NEW BOSTON.*		
Lucy McNeil	82	Solomon McNeil.	Jacob Curtice	80	Josiah Kendall.
WINDSOR.			Abner Hogg	81	Abner Hogg.
Mrs. William Jones	89	Mrs. John Averile.	Jennett Dickey	83	Elias Dickey.
Mrs. John Priest	73	Richard S. Smart.	Elizabeth Howe	71	Jacob Davis.
DEERING.			Hannah Griffin	82	Daniel Griffin.
John Morrill	78	John Morrill.	Joseph Haradon	81	Josiah Warren.
ANTRIM.			Sarah Jones	82	George Jones.
Josiah Herrick	76	Josiah Herrick.	Joseph Lamson	80	Joseph Lamson.
Mary Dinsmore	71	Samuel Dinsmore.	Elizabeth Mullet	86	Elizabeth Mullet.
Martha McClure	79	Manly McClure.	William Morgan	79	Ezra Morgan.
Samuel Chandler	76	Samuel Chandler.	*AMHERST.*		
Abijah Barker	80	Abijah Barker.	Hannah Bills	73	Hannah Bills.
James Neswith	82	James Neswith.	Joseph Crosby	87	Joseph Crosby.
Sarah Barker	84	Moody Barker.	Benjamin Damon	79	Benjamin Damon.
George Gates	86	Mary Hutchinson.	David Fisk	83	David Fisk, 3d.
Daniel Bazzell	76	William Bazzell.	Ephraim Goss	74	Ephraim Goss.
John Thompson	79	Thomas Thompson.	Mary Howard	72	Levi Howard.
Sarah Hardy	75	Benjamin M. Buckminster.	Nathan Kendall	85	Nathan Kendall.
Thomas Brown	77	Thomas Brown.	Mary Leavitt	75	Mary Leavitt.
HANCOCK.			Thomas Melendy	91	Luther Melendy.
Mary Priest	74	Daniel Priest.	John Purple	97	John Warren.
Samuel Eaton	82	Samuel Eaton.	*BEDFORD.*		
Ebenezer Pratt	86	Ebenezer Pratt.	John Ferguson	83	Daniel Ferguson.
Mary Barker	79	Mary Barker.	John Gault	77	Daniel Gault.
Jeremiah Fogg	81	Charles Fogg.	Sarah Holbrook	75	Thomas G. Holbrook.
Moses Dennis	88	Moses Dennis.	William Moore	80	William Moore.
Daniel Kimball	84	Daniel Kimball.	Lydia Rundlet	90	Thomas Rundlet.
Abraham Moors	79	Isaac A. Moors.	Eunice Shepard	77	Charles Shepard.
Oliver Lawrence	84	Nathaniel Dow.	*GOFFSTOWN.*		
John Brooks	80	John Brooks.	Jonathan Bell	85	Jonathan Bell.
Timothy Moors	85	Timothy Moors.	Michael Carter	76	Michael Carter.
Peter Fletcher	77	Peter Fletcher.	Mary Poor	76	Mary Poor.

NEW HAMPSHIRE—Continued.

Names of pensioners for revolutionary or military services.	Ages.	Names of heads of families with whom pensioners resided June 1, 1840.	Names of pensioners for revolutionary or military services.	Ages.	Names of heads of families with whom pensioners resided June 1, 1840.
HILLSBOROUGH—Continued.			**HILLSBOROUGH—Continued.**		
LITCHFIELD.			MILFORD.		
Reuben Barns - - -	81	Reuben Barns.	Samuel Lovejoy - - -	84	William Lovejoy.
			Isaac Burpee - - -	84	Francis Wright.
MOUNT VERNON.					
Daniel Averill - - -	74	Daniel Averill.	WILTON.		
Ella Heywood - - -	73	John Heywood.	Sally Marble - - -	80	Susannah Burton.
Zephaniah Kittredge -	83	Zephaniah Kittredge.	Joseph Gray - - -	79	James B. Gray.
Solomon Kittredge -	85	Solomon Kittredge.	William Pettingill -	80	William Pettingill.
Andrew Leavitt - -	87	William Leavitt.	Mary Herrick - -	85	Elijah Stockwell.
Jonathan Lamson - -	84	Betsey Lamson.			
Israel Farnum - -	81	Mark D. Perkins.	NEW IPSWICH.		
Hannah Perkins - -	75	Hiram Perkins.	John Emery - - -	93	John Emery.
			Sarah Walker - - -	77	Sarah Walker.
MERRIMACK.					
Rebecca Carlton - -	68	Rebecca Carlton.	MASON.		
John Fields - - -	84	John H. Colburn.	Molly Adams - - -	82	Jonas Adams.
John Gilson - - -	79	John Gilson.	James Gilman - - -	86	James Gilman.
Rachel French - - -	82	Daniel Lanabee.	Micah Gates - - -	77	Betsey Green.
John Odall - - -	78	John Odall.	Daniel Hill - - -	77	Daniel Hill.
			Tryphena Kemp - -	80	Jonas Prichard.
MANCHESTER.					
Peter Emerson - - -	82	James Emerson.	**CHESHIRE COUNTY.**		
Archibald Gamble - -	78	Samuel Gamble.	ALSTEAD.		
Aphia Wyman - - -	68	David Gibson.	Mary Allen - - -	92	Mary Allen.
Abigail Stearns - -	74	Moulton Mace.	Samuel Garfield - -	83	John Colburn.
Ephraim Stevens - -	82	Ephraim Stevens.	Sarah Howard - -	83	Samuel Howard.
Olive Pollard - - -	79	John Stark.	Levi Pratt - - -	84	Hannah Hutchinson.
Sarah Manning - -	76	Samuel Worthley.	Sarah Murphy - -	78	David Murphy.
			Samuel Slade - - -	78	Samuel Slade, jr.
PELHAM.			William Slade - -	83	Allen Slade.
Seth Cutter - - -	82	Seth Cutter.	Elisha Towne - - -	77	Matthew W. Towne.
Sarah Richardson - -	91	James Griffin.	Nathan Twining - -	86	Nathan Twining.
Elizabeth Gage - -	85	Nathan Gage.	Eliphalet Taylor - -	82	Eliphalet Taylor.
Abel Gage - - -	80	Abel Gage.	James Wood - - -	79	James Wood.
Nathaniel Ingalls - -	83	Nathaniel Ingalls.	John Watts - - -	81	John Watts.
Jacob Marsh - - -	79	Prescott Jones.			
Isaac Marshall - -	82	Isaac Marshall.	GILSUM.		
Thomas Thissell - -	80	Thomas Thissell, jr.	William Barron - -	74	William Barron.
Edmund Tenney - -	84	Edmund Tenney.	Samuel Corey - - -	86	Benjamin Corey.
			Luna Foster - - -	76	Luna Foster.
HUDSON.			Levina Richardson -	77	Jesse Hemmingway.
Betsey Cutter - - -	87	Betsey Cutter.	David Adams - - -	83	Calvin May.
Betsey Marsh - - -	72	Hiram Marsh.	Samuel Smith - -	82	David Ware.
Andrew Stimpson - -	81	Andrew Stimpson.			
			MARLOW.		
WEARE.			Samuel Comstock - -	84	Samuel Comstock, jr.
Edmund Barnard - -	84	Edmund Barnard.	Prudence Whittemore -	77	Prentiss Whittemore.
William Hogg - -	85	Benjamin Colby.			
Thomas Cilley - -	89	Thomas Cilley.	SULLIVAN.		
John Day - - -	88	John Day.	Berthier Boynton - -	72	David Boynton.
Mary Lull - - -	76	Moses Lull.	Mary Sawyer - - -	82	Lyman Gates.
Hannah Cilley - -	—	Abraham Morrill.	Benjamin Hastings -	72	Benjamin Hastings.
Samuel Blaisdell - -	75	Osgood Paige.	Benjamin Kemp - -	78	David Kemp.
Rachel Whittle - -	73	John Whitle, 2d.	Eliakim Kemp - -	88	Edmund Nims.
HOLLIS.			STODDARD.		
Abigail Youngman - -	78	Jonas Blood, jr.	George Coffin - - -	79	George Coffin.
Stephen Conrey - -	81	Stephen Conrey.	Nathaniel Evans - -	81	Nathaniel Evans.
Abigail Colburn - -	85	Nathan Colburn.	Sarah Bardin - - -	88	Nathaniel Gilson.
Mary Colburn - - -	84	Peter U. Colburn.	Rebecca Joslin - -	72	Luke Joslin.
William Hale - - -	79	William P. Hale.	Nathaniel Joslin - -	79	Nathaniel Joslin.
Nathaniel Hubbard - -	75	Stephen Lovejoy.	David Jenkins - -	82	David Jenkins.
Solomon Pierce - -	90	William Newton.	Edward Phelps - -	77	Edward Phelps.
Enoch Jewett - - -	83	Andrew Willoby.	Peter Wright - - -	88	John Procter.
Daniel Bailey - - -	84	Daniel Bailey.	Rebecca Stacey - -	77	William Stacey.
			Zubah Gerould - -	77	Roxana Thurston.
NASHUA.			George Holems - -	78	Jesse Wilder.
Lydia Lovejoy - - -	80	Sarah Chase.	Samuel Wilson - -	85	William Wilson.
Israel Hunt - - -	82	Israel Hunt.	Eunice Dow - - -	84	Eunice Dow.
Joshua Palmer - -	75	Joshua Palmer.			
Eleazer Fish - - -	75	Joseph Waugh.	SURRY.		
			Sarah Joslyn - - -	75	John Joslyn.
BROOKLINE.			Asa Wilcox - - -	84	Hollis Wilcox.
Abel Hodgman - -	82	Abel Hodgman.	Enoch Whitcomb - -	80	David Whitcomb.
Hannah Hoit - - -	80	Elisha Hoit.			
Eleazer Gilson - -	83	Joseph F. Jefts.	WESTMORELAND.		
			Ichabod Albee - -	81	Ichabod Albee.
SHARON.			Lydia Carlisle - -	83	Lydia Carlisle.
Daniel Davis - - -	79	Daniel Davis.	John Curtis - - -	78	John Curtis.
Reuben Law - - -	89	James Law.	Darius Dagget - -	79	Darius Dagget.
Margaret Moor - -	80	Margaret Moor.	Benjamin Howe - -	53	Caleb C. Daggett.
			Betsey Goodrich - -	77	Draco Goodrich.
TEMPLE.			John Wheeler - - -	80	Ambrose Gravis,
Elias Boynton - - -	85	Elias Boynton,			

NEW HAMPSHIRE—Continued.

Names of pensioners for revolutionary or military services.	Ages.	Names of heads of families with whom pensioners resided June 1, 1840.	Names of pensioners for revolutionary or military services.	Ages.	Names of heads of families with whom pensioners resided June 1, 1840.
CHESHIRE—Continued:			**CHESHIRE**—Continued.		
WESTMORELAND—Continued.			WINCHESTER—Continued.		
Joseph Sawyer - - -	87	Wilson Gleason.	Francis Cook - - -	81	Abel H. Cook.
Amasa Highland - -	80	Ira Highland.	Eunice Dodge - - -	79	Clark Dodge.
Abiather Shaw - - -	81	Abiather Shaw.	Oliver Wright - - -	81	Edwin Jewell.
Timothy Skinner - -	79	Barton Skinner.	John Jones - - -	85	John Jones.
Rebecca Wier - - -	77	John Wier.	Mary Kendall - - -	81	George Kendall.
Chary White - - -	81	Charles White.	Submit Lawrence - -	82	Luther Lawrence.
			William Rixford - -	85	William Rixford, jr.
WALPOLE.			Lydia Combs - - -	87	Phebe Turtelot.
Thomas C. Drew - -	78	Thomas C. Drew.	Daniel Wise - - -	85	Leonard Wise.
Cynthia Eldrige - -	74	Cynthia Eldrige.			
Sarah Fay - - -	77	Sarah Fay.	**DUBLIN.**		
James Holland - - -	79	James Holland.	Amos Alexander - -	79	Amos Alexander.
Eliza Mead - - -	84	Eliza Mead.	Phineas Gleason - -	83	Phineas Gleason.
Daniel Marsh - - -	75	Daniel Marsh.	Lucy Hardy - - -	79	Elias Hardy.
William Rust - - -	84	Aaron Priest.	Olive Phillips - - -	85	Richard Phillips.
Ephraim Stearns - -	85	Stephen Stearns.	Abijah Richardson -	79	Abijah Richardson.
Ebenezer Wellington -	77	William Wellington.	John Snow - - -	80	John Snow.
			David Townsend - -	84	David Townsend.
CHESTERFIELD.					
Oliver Brown - - -	83	Alexander Willard.	**FITZWILLIAM.**		
Asa Britton - - -	77	Asa Britton.	Leonard Colburn - -	44	Leonard Colburn.
Ebenezer Cheeny - -	77	Ebenezer Cheeny.	Mathias Felton - -	84	Mathias Felton.
William Clark - - -	83	William Clark.	Joel Whitney - - -	80	Benjamin B. Morse.
Francis Henry - - -	86	Francis Henry, 2d.	Joel Miles - - -	84	Noah Miles.
William Black - - -	78	William Black.	Ebenezer Potter - -	91	Ebenezer Potter, jr.
Betsey Mead - - -	77	Bradley Mead.	John Shirley - - -	85	Harry Shirley.
Constant Merrick - -	81	Constant Merrick.	Nathan Smith - - -	76	Nathan Smith.
John Phillips - - -	83	John Phillips.	Artemas Wilson - -	83	Benjamin Wilson.
John Putnam - - -	80	John Putnam.	Stephen White - - -	78	Silas White.
Hannah Rice - - -	86	Stephen Rice.	Sarah Whitney - - -	92	David Whitney.
Eunice Witt - - -	85	Eunice Witt.			
Jacob Wetherbee - -	81	Jacob Wetherbee.	**JAFFREY.**		
			Ithamar Wheelock -	79	Nathan Blodgett.
HINSDALE.			Rebecca Bacon - -	84	Rebecca Bacon.
Eunice Dickinson - -	80	Erastus Dickinson.	Jacob Baldwin - - -	80	William Baldwin.
Ivory Soule - - -	80	Ivory Soule.	Joseph Cutter - - -	88	Joseph Cutter.
David Wooley - - -	80	David Wooley.	Abel Winship - - -	84	David Cosey.
			Lydia Buss - - -	91	James Gillmore.
KEENE.			Nathan Hunt - - -	80	Nathan Hunt.
Martha Bassett - -	83	Nathan Bassett.	Rachel Cutter - - -	73	Sarah Law.
Isaac Miller - - -	86	Dorcas Balch.	Rebecca Pierce - -	88	Josiah Pierce.
David Carpenter - -	81	David Carpenter.	Joseph Robbin - -	82	Joseph Robbin.
Sarah Devinell - -	77	Sarah Devinell.	Polly Stratton - - -	74	John Town.
Susanna Davis - - -	84	Aaron Davis.			
Phineas Hamblett - -	85	Benjamin Hamblett.	**MARLBOROUGH.**		
Olive Seward - - -	82	Oliver Heaton.	Jonas Gary - - -	79	Joseph Butler.
Elijah Knight - - -	83	Elijah Knight.	Abigail Worsley - -	93	William Greenwood.
Silas Perry - - -	77	Silas Perry.	Ebenezer Herrick - -	81	Ebenezer Herrick.
William Vose - - -	52	William Vose.	Sarah Joslin - - -	79	David Joslin.
Philemon Wright - -	58	Philemon Wright.	Martha Lewis - - -	78	Martha Lewis.
			Lawson Moore - - -	84	Lydia Mason.
RICHMOND.			Asa Porter - - -	83	Asa Porter.
Jeremiah Barrus - -	83	Alvin Barrus.	Benjamin Thatcher -	79	Levi Thatcher.
Naomi Bacon - - -	77	Uriah Brown.	Jacob Woodward - -	78	Jacob Woodward.
Waitstill Starkey - -	80	William Woodward.	Aaron Willard - - -	82	Aaron Willard.
Oliver Whipple - -	89	Rufus Whipple.	Mary Tayntor - - -	89	John Wiswell.
ROXBURY.			**NELSON.**		
Gideon Phillips - -	82	Benjamin Foster.	Philip Atwood - - -	84	Philip Atwood.
Mary Hemingway - -	86	Aaron B. Kidder.	Thomas Baker - - -	83	Thomas Baker.'
William Parker - -	84	William Parker.	Timothy Bancroft - -	82	Timothy Bancroft.
Mary Toser - - -	83	Elias Toser.	Joseph Felt - - -	82	Joseph Felt.
			Naomi Felt - - -	81	Naomi Felt.
SWANZEY.			David Kimball - - -	80	David Kimball.
Russell Ballou - - -	76	Russell Ballou.	Samuel Scripture - -	79	Samuel Scripture.
Molly Cummings - -	76	Charles Cummings.	Benjamin Sawyer - -	83	Benjamin Sawyer.
Elisha Chamberlain -	77	Elisha Chamberlain.	Nehemiah Wright - -	83	Nehemiah Wright.
Mary Scott - - -	88	Abel Dickinson.	John White - - -	82	Jane White.
Jonathan Eames - -	84	Jonathan Eames.			
Benjamin Howard - -	70	Elizabeth Green.	**RINDGE.**		
Rosilla Hill - - -	80	Benjamin Howard.	Sarah Bowen - - -	84	Sarah Bowen.
Asaph Lane - - -	83	David Hill.	Eleazer Blake - - -	84	Eleazer Blake.
Samuel Lane - - -	81	Asaph Lane.	Joshua Chadwick - -	85	Joshua Chadwick.
Phebe Long - - -	81	Elisha Lane.	Abner Foster - - -	79	Abner Foster.
Mary Ockington - -	80	Joseph Long.	Eunice Faulkner - -	69	Eunice Faulkner.
Jemima Stone - - -	85	Josiah Leach.	Francis Green - - -	85	Harry Green.
Ivory Snow - - -	86	David Stone.	Asa Jones - - -	82	Asa Jones.
Abijah Whitcomb - -	78	Joseph Snow.	Enos Lake - - -	81	John E. Lake.
	88	Rosewell Whitcomb.	Hepsabeth Lake - -	77	John E. Lake.
WINCHESTER.			Joseph Moors - - -	82	Hubbard Moors.
Ama Bartlett - - -	84	Ama Bartlett.	Francis Smith - - -	87	Silas Smith.

NEW HAMPSHIRE—Continued.

Names of pensioners for revolutionary or military services.	Ages.	Names of heads of families with whom pensioners resided June 1, 1840.	Names of pensioners for revolutionary or military services.	Ages.	Names of heads of families with whom pensioners resided June 1, 1840.
CHESHIRE—Continued.			SULLIVAN—Continued.		
TROY.			ACWORTH—Continued.		
Joseph Forestall - - -	82	Joseph Forestall.	Anna Merrill - - -	76	David Merrill.
Benjamin Tolman -	84	Benjamin Tolman.	Johnson Prouty - - -	88	Robert Morrison.
			CHARLESTOWN.		
SULLIVAN COUNTY.			William Bend - - -	80	Silas Bond.
CLAREMONT.			Nathaniel Challis - - -	78	Benjamin Challis.
Jabez Downs - - -	78		Clement Corbin - -	75	Ezborn Corbin.
Roswell Clapp - -	85		Eleanor Watts - - -	78	Gardner Cutler.
Ebenezer Sperry - -	84		Sally Carryl - - -	76	Parmelia Carryl.
Peter Niles - - -	87		John Hodskins - - -	76	Frederick S. Hodskins.
Joseph Fuller - -	86		Betsey Hawkley - -	73	Adams Millikin.
Abigail Handerson -	81		Daniel Adams - - -	89	Alpheus Nevers.
Anna Draper - -	76		Sybil Palmer - - -	71	Asahel Porter.
Margaret Moore - -	86		Rachel Powers - - -	83	Walter Powers.
Lorrin Munger - -	84				
Sarah Jackson -	73		GOSHEN.		
Thankful Bowman -	76		Mary Chase - - -	76	Bartlett Wise.
Abigail Sperry - -	89		Lydia McLaughlin - -	78	Ebenezer Stevens.
Mary Goodwin -	82		Edward Dame - - -	85	Samuel Smart.
Samuel Abbott - -	75		Samuel Sischo - -	84	Samuel Sischo.
			James Libbey - - -	89	Samuel White.
NEWPORT.					
Joel Kelsey - - -	78		LEMPSTER.		
P. W. Kibbey - -	76		Lydia Littlehale - -	82	Penuel Allen.
Solomon Dunham -	82		Jabez Alexander - -	84	Jabez Alexander.
Joel McGregor - -	78		Jemima Beckwith -	80	Byron Beckwith.
			Lassell Silsby - -	85	Joel Fletcher.
CORNISH.			Noah Fuller - - -	82	Noah Fuller.
David Davis - - -	82		Joseph Hull - - -	80	Anthony Guild.
Philip Tabor - -	79		John Lewis - - -	87	William Lewis.
Daniel Robertson -	79		Rachel Miner - - -	75	Rachel Miner.
William York - -	82		Torrey Maxon - -	79	Torrey Maxon.
			Mary Tuck - - -	83	John Tuck.
PLAINFIELD.					
Simeon Hildreth - -	82		LANGDON.		
Daniel Cole - -	82		Anna Bidwell - - -	81	Anna Bidwell.
George Every - -	81		Stephen Whipple - -	64	Samuel Garfield.
Thomas Watsan - -	78		Anna Warker - - -	83	Elisha Garfield, jr.
Samuel Clark - -	83		Asa Holden - - -	82	Aaron G. Holden.
Philip Spalding - -	85		Levi Jennison - - -	58	Levi Jennison.
Elizabeth Hall - -	82		Nathaniel Lamb - -	80	Nathaniel Lamb.
Haden Cutter - -	83		Lemuel Royel - -	84	Lemuel Royel.
GRANTHAM.					
Lydia Sanders - -	74		WASHINGTON.		
John Eaton - - -	80		John Barney - - -	88	John Barney.
Edna Smith - -	73		Jonathan Clark - -	84	Jonathan Clark.
Henry Eastman - -	77		James Faxon - - -	75	James Faxon.
William Molton - -	77		William Graves - -	83	William Graves.
Jonathan Bachelder -	83		Olive Lowell - - -	76	Olive Lowell.
Eleanor Newton - -	85		Eunice May - - -	81	John May.
Morrell Coburn - -	87		Asa Stevens - - -	79	Sarah Mead.
Permela Stowell - -	83		John Putney - - -	82	John Putney.
Salisbury Wheeler -	76		Keziah Reed - - -	76	Keziah Reed.
Elijah Rekord - -	84		Emma Spaulding - -	81	Gardner Spaulding.
			Abraham Shattuck -	84	Abraham Shattuck.
SPRINGFIELD.			Ebenezer Wood - -	86	Ebenezer Wood.
Anna Huggins - -	80		Jacob Wright - - -	81	Jacob Wright.
Abigail Gilman - -	85				
Eunice Heath - -	85		GRAFTON COUNTY.		
			HILLS.		
UNITY.			Timothy Kelley - -	77	Timothy Kelley.
Nathan Carr - - -	81	Nathan Carr.	Mary Straw - - -	80	Moses Straw.
Moses Wright - -	78	Moses Wright, jr.	Anna Daniels - - -	86	Hiram Daniels.
Jeremiah Gilman -	79		Phineas Sargent - -	94	George W. Sargent.
Susanna Huntoon -	77				
			BRISTOL.		
CROYDON.			John Ross - - -	83	Luke Sumner.
Sherman Cooper - -	82		David Fowler - - -	60	David Fowler.
			Josiah Fellows - -	87	David C. Willey.
WENDELL.			Stephen Bohonon -	50	Stephen Bohonon.
Samuel George - -	78		Benjamin Sanbone -	81	Benjamin Sanbone.
Christopher Gardner -	77				
			ALEXANDRIA.		
ACWORTH.			Molly Tenney - - -	80	Eliphalet Blake.
Joseph Blanchard - -	84	David Blanchard.	Moses Atwood - - -	79	Elizabeth Sleeper.
Solomon Blodget - -	74	Samuel Blodget.	Betsey Sleeper - -	81	Colby Sleeper.
Supply Reed - -	85	David Currier.	Alexander McMurphy -	80	Daniel McMurphy.
Richard Chapman - -	82	Horace Chapman.	George Bayley - -	49	George Bayley.
Martha McClure - -	79	Samuel McClure.			
Charles Matthewson -	83	Horace Matthewson.	HEBRON.		
John McKeen - -	80	John McKeen.	Lemuel Fuller - - -	83	Lemuel Fuller.
John Brigham - -	81	Samuel McKeen.	Jerahmeel Bowers -	95	Samuel Hartshorn.

NEW HAMPSHIRE—Continued.

Names of pensioners for revolutionary or military services.	Ages.	Names of heads of families with whom pensioners resided June 1, 1840.	Names of pensioners for revolutionary or military services.	Ages.	Names of heads of families with whom pensioners resided June 1, 1840.
GRAFTON—Continued.			**GRAFTON—Continued.**		
HEBRON—Continued.			LEBANON—Continued.		
Mary Hazelton	84	Sarah Neal.	Enoch Freeman	86	Enoch Freeman.
James Putney	84	John Smith.	David Wright	83	Zelia Durkee.
David Pratt	74	David Pratt.	Silas Hall	84	Nathaniel Hall.
Bruce Walker	80	Nathaniel Walker.	Diarca Allen	79	Abner Allen.
Levi Day	87	Lemuel Kendall.	Chloe Fay	77	Joseph Fay.
			Anna Buswell	70	Hammond Buswell.
BRIDGEWATER.			John Gilbert	76	John Gilbert.
Nathan Hoyt	77	Enoch Brainard.	Meriam Colburn	83	Benjamin Colburn.
Reuben Rundlett	77	Reuben Rundlett.			
Sarah Jewett	76	William B. Nichols.	**HANOVER.**		
Benjamin Boardman	83	Benjamin Boardman.	Hezekiah Goodrich	83	Pearl K. Hutchings.
Ezekiel Fellows	86	Joseph Fellows.	Eli Washburn	81	Cyrus Breck.
Frederick McCutcheon	90	William Fogg.	Elias Buckman	77	Elias Buckman.
Seth Spencer	80	Seth Spencer.	Ruth Houston	68	Charles Houston.
			Thomas Ross	79	David M. Pelton.
DANBURY.			Samuel Simmons	83	Caleb Ward.
Jonathan Clark	83	Jonathan Clark, jr.	Stockman Sweatt	80	Aden Sweatt.
Isaac Palmer Curtis	82	Philbrick Curtis.	Tabitha Woodward	90	David Woodward.
Mary Flanders	79	Reuben S. Long.	Luther Ingalls	82	Sylvester Ingalls.
			David Tenney	81	David Tenney.
GRAFTON.			Daniel Kendrick	81	Nathaniel Kendrick.
Jonathan Barbank	74	Samuel Davis.	John Durkee	79	John Durkee.
Betty Whitney	85	Silas Whitney.	Asa Risley	86	Asa Risley.
Sarah Barber	79	John Kimball.	Rebecca Newell	82	Mary Dewey.
Mercy Williams	92	Alexander Williams.	Barney Tisdale	84	Barney Tisdale.
Hannah Peck	77	Hannah Peck.	Benjamin Preston	79	Benjamin Preston.
Alexander Pixley	88	Alexander Pixley.	Joseph Pineo	80	Oramel Pineo.
Nancy Potter	80	George W. Potter.	Ezra Lowell	83	William Hills.
Charles Stickney	42	Charles Stickney.	Joseph Wilmarth	89	Nathan Stark.
William Bowen	85	Peter Bullock.			
			DORCHESTER.		
ORANGE.			Gideon Bridgman	86	Thomas Bridgman.
Nathaniel Briggs	93	Nathaniel Briggs.	William Elliott	88	John Hobart.
Thomas Whittier	80	Peter Adams.	Lavinia Wheeler	78	Amos Stetson.
Jesse Dow	86	Thomas Cole.	Elizabeth Burley	74	Benjamin Burley.
			Benjamin Abbott	82	Samuel S. Abbott.
CANAAN.					
Bridgett Wheat	83	Joseph Wheat.	**GROTON**		
Warren Wilson	77	Warren Wilson.	Theophilus Cass	84	Jonathan Hall.
Elizabeth Currier	74	Theophilus Currier.			
Josiah Clark	82	Josiah Clark.	**LYME.**		
Nathaniel Bartlett	83	John Presey.	Temperance Sloan	75	Asahel Sloan.
Dan. Parker	83	Dan. Parker.	Caleb Conant	78	Samuel W. Baker.
Joshua Richardson	82	Joshua W. Richardson.	Sarah Chapman	76	Sarah Chapman.
Daniel Colley	87	Andrew Elliott.	Mary Scott	72	Charles T. Scott.
Sarah Poland	79	Elijah Gove.	John Bishop	80	Samuel Hervey.
Sarah Longfellow	88	Stephen Williams.	David Pushee	80	Harvey Pushee.
Lydia Whitney	88	Isaac Whitney.	Samuel Bixby	86	William Bixby.
Daniel Kimball	77	David Townsend.	Jonathan Franklin	87	Jonathan Franklin.
			John Porter	80	Nathaniel Lancaster.
ENFIELD.			Daniel Hervey	76	Philander Allen.
Jonathan French	80	Jonathan French.	James Downer	78	Isaac Farnsworth.
Nathan Follansbee	78	Nathan Follansbee.	Arthur Latham	82	Berer Latham.
Matthew Greeley	80	Matthew Greeley.	John Culver	79	John Culver.
Benjamin Powell	76	Enoch Nickols.	Mary Wise	85	Robert Latham.
David Choate	77	David Choate.	Deborah Mason	78	Moses Edgell.
James Stevens	83	James Stevens.	William Porter	79	William Porter.
John Bowley	88	Ezra Tucker.	David Whitman	78	David Whitman.
Lydia Colley	78	Thomas J. Colley.			
Joseph Johnson	79	Joseph Johnson.	**OXFORD.**		
Lucy Howe	75 ⎱	Thomas Goodhue.	Hannah Griggs	87	Philip E. Bundy.
Hannah Johnson	81 ⎰		Abel Sawyer	88	Jonathan P. Sawyer.
Sarah Colby	80	Milton Aldrich.	Israel Morey	75	Israel Morey.
Mary Green	81	Bradbury Green.	John Hale	84	Aaron Hale.
Elisha Fox	82	Franklin Fox.	Henry Sloper	81	Priscilla Maxwell.
Moses Flanders	78	Daniel Smith.	William Brown	84	William Brown.
Jonathan Howe	79	Jonathan Howe.	Eunice Rogers	83	Eunice Sergent.
Daniel Stickney	79	Hiram Stickney.	Ichabod Palmer	81	David Blood.
			Martha Dame	87	Henry S. Perren.
LEBANON.			Elihu Corliss	82	Elihu Corliss.
Joseph Wood	80	Samuel Wood, 2d.			
Wills Kimball	80	Elisha Kimball.	**WARREN.**		
Rebecca Demary	75	John Ela.	Mary Currier	89	Tristram Brown.
Jason Downer	84	Jason Downer.	William Alexander	76	William Alexander.
William Hadley	93	George French.	Stephen Lund	89	Hosea Lund.
Lois Lathrop	75	Thomas Freeman.	Hannah Abbott	86	True Merrill.
Lydia Hough	79	Clark Hough.	Lydia Bayse	86	Jabez Kimball.
Catharine Lathrop	78	George H. Lathrop.	Phebe Abbott	71	George Libbey.
Amy Hurlburt	77	Amasa Hurlburt.			
Bridget Simonds	82	Hiram A. Simonds.	**WENTWORTH.**		
Parthena Allen	81	Howard Benton.	Caleb Keith	85	Caleb Keith.
Thomas Barrows	89	Samuel S. Barrows.	Samuel Smart	77	Samuel Smart.

NEW HAMPSHIRE—Continued.

Names of pensioners for revolutionary or military services.	Ages.	Names of heads of families with whom pensioners resided June 1, 1840.	Names of pensioners for revolutionary or military services.	Ages.	Names of heads of families with whom pensioners resided June 1, 1840.
GRAFTON—Continued.			**GRAFTON**—Continued.		
WENTWORTH—Continued.			LYMAN—Continued.		
Sarah Rowen	78	Jacob Rowen.	Lemuel Barrett	77	Ezra Barrett.
Molly Stevens	87	Rufus Stevens.	Yanaca Young	79	John Young.
Rebecca Smith	77	Oliver Ellsworth.	Lydia Sanborn	84	Herod Stevens.
Samuel Johnson	84	Henry Johnson.	Solomon Parker	87	Samuel Parker.
Ebenezer Gove	85	William Gove.	Rhoda Burkley	80 to 90	Russell Underwood.
			Anna Moulton	75	David Moulton.
ROMNEY.			Jonathan Moulton	84	Jonathan Moulton.
Reuben French	80	Reuben French.	Noah Moulton	82	Rinaldo Moulton.
William Preston	84	William Preston.	Susan Olmstead	88	Henry Olmstead.
Moses Smart	85	Moses Smart.	Moses Moore	75	Moses Moore.
Elizabeth Craig	88	Tappan W. Craig.	Abigail Moore	84	Archibald Moore.
Abigail Kimball	74	David Ramsay.	Martin Barny	80	Daniel White.
Josiah Barton	75	Josiah Barton.			
James Herbert	81	Samuel Herbert.	PIERMONT.		
			Amos Gould	79	Aaron P. Gould.
BATH.			Andrew Crook	80	John Crook.
Aby Harris	76	Absalom Harris.	Ware McConnel	49	Ware McConnel.
Edward Pollard	84	Edward Pollard.			
Samuel Chase	83	Moses Chase.	PLYMOUTH.		
Sarah Knight	75	Moses Knight.	Samuel Kimball	–	John Emery.
Josiah Martin	78	Jirah Martin.	Samuel Morse	–	Stephen Morse.
Jesse Hardy	79	Jesse Hardy.	Ezekiel Keyes	–	Ezekiel Keyes.
Robert Rollins	84	Beri Bartlett.	Elizabeth Heath	–	Samuel C. Heath.
John Clement	78	John Clement.	Sarah Homan	–	Leonard George.
			Moor Russell	–	Moor Russell.
COVENTRY.					
Jonathan Tylor	89	James Haniman.	BETHLEHEM.		
			Jonas Brooks	85	Jonas Brooks.
HAVERHILL.			Lot Woodbury	80	Lot Woodbury.
Nathaniel Rix	74	Nathaniel Rix.	Thomas Hatch	82	Thomas Hatch.
Andrew Martin	84	Andrew Martin.	Jonathan Blanden	87	Jonathan Blanden.
Michael Johnson	76	Michael Johnson.			
William Cross	98	William Cross.	CAMPTOWN.		
Ebenezer Whitteker	86	Peter Whitteker.	Tamer Taylor	74	Gilman R. Taylor.
Stephen Morse	83	Hiram Morse.	Anna Phillips	76	Henry C. Phillips.
Daniel Dotey	76	Daniel Dotey.	Edmund Mash	82	Newton Mash.
Abiah Knight	72	Kinsley H. Batchelder.			
Asa Hinkley	80	Asa Hinkley.	FRANCONIA.		
Hannah Wills	79	Riley Wills.	John Wallace	77	John Wallace.
James King	75	James King.	Lemuel Barret	75	Lemuel Barret.
Human Penock	78	Jefferson Penock.	Caleb Young	82	Samuel Bolls.
Simon Ward	78	Simon Ward.			
Ezra Gates	82	Isaac F. Allen.	THORNTON.		
James Eastman	86	Moses Eastman.	Winthrop Bagley	78	Winthrop Bagley.
Lucy Sanborn	88	Elisha Hibbard.	Ruth Smart	82	Elijah Smart.
Sarah Glynn	74	Sarah Glynn.	John Foss	85	John Foss, jr.
Elias Stearns	86	Elias Stearns.	Silas Whitney	73	Silas Whitney.
			Hannah Ferrin	79	Jonathan Ferrin.
HOLDERNESS.			Phebe Patee	84	Richard Patee.
Daniel Page	–	Daniel Page.	James P. Patee	84	Silas W. Patee.
			Isaac Blake	75	Isaac Blake.
LANDAFF.					
Benjamin York	79	Benjamin York.	WOODSTOCK.		
Hannah Clark	72	Moses Clark.	Thomas Vincent	79	Stephen Vincent.
James Simonds	79	James Simonds.	Abigail Barron	80	Benjamin M. Barron.
Jeremiah Bowen	86	John A. Bowen.	Jacob Selingham	79	Jacob Selingham.
Benjamin Moody	78	Benjamin Moody.	Royal Jackman	49	Royal Jackman.
David Garnsey	76	Abner Garnsey.	Betsey Boies	95	Jonathan Darling.
LISBON.			**COOS COUNTY.**		
Joseph Young	73	Joseph Young.	CLARKSVILLE.		
Obadiah Morse	76	Obadiah Morse.	Norman Clark	97	Joseph Wiswell.
Moses Barron	85	Fletcher Barron.			
Bela Young	51	Bela Young.	STEWARTSTOWN.		
Hannah Smith	76	Ebenezer Wetherby.	Abial Chandler	75	Abial Chandler.
Lydia Howard	87	Elijah Howard.	Elijah Benton	80	Elijah Benton.
Sally Walker	74	Leonard Morse.	Thomas Chase	75	George Chase.
LITTLETON.			COLEBROOK.		
Judith Huntoon	86	Daniel Carter.	Lemuel Stoddard	81	Asa Stoddard.
Sarah Williams	96	Timothy A. Edson.	Joseph Loomis	74	Joseph Loomis.
Ezra Foster	78	Ezra Foster.			
Phebe Lewis	78	Titus Hutchinson.	COLOMBIA.		
Susannah Bemes	91	Alvin Stow.	Job Pierce	81	Ora Pierce.
Samuel Hudson	78	Samuel Hudson.	Jared Cone	79	Jared Cone.
			Benjamin Jorden	79	Benjamin Jorden.
LYMAN.			Joseph Hackett	48	Joseph Hackett.
Annis Merrill	89	Annis Merrill.	Abel Marshall	75	Abel Marshall.
Eli Hoskins	81	Eli Hoskins.			
Joshua Thornton	75	Joshua Thornton.	STRATFORD.		
William Martin	91	William Martin.	William Curtis	81	William Curtis, jr.
John Barber	78	Libbeus Hastings.	Isaac Stevens	88	Isaac Stevens.
			Elizabeth Rider	84	Lydia Schoff.

4

CENSUS OF PENSIONERS.

NEW HAMPSHIRE—Continued.

Names of pensioners for revolutionary or military services.	Ages.	Names of heads of families with whom pensioners resided June 1, 1840.	Names of pensioners for revolutionary or military services.	Ages.	Names of heads of families with whom pensioners resided June 1, 1840.
COOS—Continued.			COOS—Continued.		
NOTHCMBERLAND.			DATTON.		
Antipas Marshall - -	83	Antipas Marshall.	Jacob Barrows - -	92	Jacob Barrows.
Alpheas Hutchins - -	47	Alpheas Hutchins.	William Fisk - -	52	William Fisk.
STARK.			BARTLETT.		
Abijah Potter - -	80	Daniel Rowell, jr.	Enoch Abbot - -	48	Enoch Abbot.
			Rebecca Carlton - -	85	Woodman Carlton.
LANCASTER.			Richard Garland - -	77	Richard Garland.
Samuel S. Wentworth - -	83	Joseph Wentworth.	Lydia Hall - -	71	Lydia Hall.
Phineas Hodgden - -	81	John Hodgden.	Noah Sinclare - -	49	Noah Sinclare.
John McIntire - -	75	John McIntire.			
Sally Stanley - -	77	Sally Stanley.	JACKSON.		
Ebenezer Twambly -	81	Ebenezer Twambly.	Peter Coffin - -	81	Peter Coffin.
Rebecca White - -	78	Samuel White.	Pike G. Burnham - -	88	Pike G. Burnham.
George W. Lucas - -	47	George W. Lucas.	William Gates, alias William Nute	49	William Gates.
Benjamin Stephenson - -	52	Benjamin Stephenson.			
			RANDOLPH.		
JEFFERSON.			Joseph Morse - -	77	Joseph Morse.
Benjamin Hicks - -	85	Benjamin Hicks, jr.			
Lazarus Holmes - -	86	Lazarus Holmes.	SHELBURNE.		
			Nathaniel Porter - -	76	Nathaniel Porter.
WHITEFIELD.			Moses Ingalls - -	85	Moses Ingalls.
John Burns - -	84	John Burns.			
Moses Huntoon - -	81	George Huntoon.	HENKOAR.		
George Huntoon - -	49	George Huntoon.	Isaac Ilsley York -	87	Isaac Ilsley York.
Susanna Eastman - -	77	William Eastman.			
Isaac Minor - -	76	Isaac Minor.			

STATE OF MASSACHUSETTS.

Names of pensioners for revolutionary or military services.	Ages.	Names of heads of families with whom pensioners resided June 1, 1840.	Names of pensioners for revolutionary or military services.	Ages.	Names of heads of families with whom pensioners resided June 1, 1840.
NANTUCKET COUNTY.			BARNSTABLE—Continued.		
NANTUCKET.			HARWICH.		
John Wilber - -	78	John Wilber.	Abigail Smith - -	85	Ebenezer Smith.
			Eleanor Hall - -	81	Eleanor Hall.
DUKES COUNTY.			Zuba Cahoon - -	76	Zuba Cahoon.
EDGARTOWN.			Nathan Underwood -	86	Nathan Underwood.
James Brecher - -	63		Samuel Cash - -	78	Samuel Cash.
Lucy Norris - -	78		Naomi Phillips - -	77	Naomi Phillips.
Joseph Linton - -	77		Mary Doane - -	89	James Long.
Peggy Crosman - -	81		Ebenezer Eldredge -	–	Jacob Eldredge.
Love Norton - -	85		Stephen Nickerson -	86	Stephen Nickerson.
Caroline Smith - -	80				
Mary Holley - -	74		CHATHAM.		
Huldah Coffin - -	81		Salathel Nickerson -	80	Salathel Nickerson.
			Joseph Young - -	78	Joseph Young.
VISBURY.			Reliance Hopkins -	80	Reliance Hopkins.
Thankful Smith - -	85	George Smith.			
Rhoda Baxter - -	80	Dwight Boyce.	ORLEANS.		
Anna Luce - -	85	Shubael Luce.	Hezekiah Rogers - -	89	Yates Rogers.
Mehitable Luce - -	84	Mehitable Luce.	Richard Rogers - -	82	Alvah Rogers.
Obed Norton - -	90	Susan Worth.	Eunice Taylor - -	82	Asa Rogers.
Thomas Luce - -	83	Thomas Luce.	Jabez Sparrow - -	86	Jabez Sparrow.
Nathan Clifford - -	82	Nathan Clifford.	David Taylor - -	77	David Taylor.
Ann Waldron - -	75	Warren Waldron.	Hannah Rogers - -	82	Hannah Rogers.
			Isaac Snow - -	82	Isaac Snow.
CHILMARK.					
John Hayden - -	55	John Hayden.	BARNSTABLE.		
			Deborah Freeman - -	74	Benjamin Hinckley.
BARNSTABLE COUNTY.			Thankful Hedge - -	72	Thankful Hedge.
DENNIS.			Violet Coffin - -	78	Violet Coffin.
James Taylor - -	78	James Taylor.	Alvan Jenkins - -	–	Alvan Jenkins.
Henry Hall - -	78	Hiram Hall.	Ansel Adams - -	78	Ansel Adams.
Samuel Baker, 3d - -	40	Samuel Baker, 3d.	Chloe Hinckley - -	78	Chloe Hinckley.
Abner Robbins - -	82	Emanuel Spindle.	Benjamin Hallett - -	80	Benjamin Hallett.
Samuel Chase - -	79	Samuel Chase.	Prince Hinckley - -	81	Prince Hinckley.
			Leonard Chase - -	38	Leonard Chase.
EASTHAM.			Ebenezer Case - -	83	Ebenezer Case.
John Hopkins - -	83	John Hopkins.	Sylvanus Hinckley - -	83	Moses H. Bearse.
			Zenas Gage - -	81	Zenas Gage.
BREWSTER.			Jabez Bacon - -	83	Jabez Bacon.
Daniel Rogers - -	81	Eunice Mayo.	George Lewis - -	80	Washington Crowell.
Anguish McCloud - -	97	Aaron Crowel.	Richard Lewis - -	89	Richard Lewis.
Susanna Paine - -	73	Susan Paine.	Rebecca Bearse - -	84	Melinda Eldridge.

MASSACHUSETTS—Continued.

Names of pensioners for revolutionary or military services.	Ages.	Names of heads of families with whom pensioners resided June 1, 1840.	Names of pensioners for revolutionary or military services.	Ages.	Names of heads of families with whom pensioners resided June 1, 1840.
BARNSTABLE—Continued.			**BRISTOL—Continued.**		
FALMOUTH.			WESTPORT—Continued.		
Joseph Hatch	82	David Bowman.	Job Sowle	84	Job Sowle.
Isaac Parker	82	Isaac Parker.	Lydia Shaw	87	Lydia Shaw.
Thomas Fish	77	Thomas Fish.	Francis Tripp	80	Francis Tripp.
Silas Lawrence	92	Silas Lawrence.			
Braddock Dimmock	79	Braddock Dimmock.	FALL RIVER.		
Sylvanus Fish	85	Sylvanus Fish.	Thomas Butts	81	Thomas Butts.
Nathaniel Bourne	86	Nathaniel Bourne.	Peleg Brightman	77	Peleg Brightman.
Jonathan Green	80	Jonathan Green.	Austus Bushee	76	Daniel Brightman.
Rebecca Swift	74	Melatiah Lawrence.	Ephraim Boomer	77	Ephraim Boomer.
Zuriel Bourne	84	Zuriel Bourne.	James Talman	78	William Cudworth.
			Ezekiel Chace	80	Ezekiel Chace.
MARSHPEE.			Ephraim Larkin	78	John Eddy.
Isaac Wickhams	78	Isaac Wickhams.	John Reynolds	77	Uriah Holmes.
			George Crocker	84	Nathan Harding.
SANDWICH.			Hannah Hart	85	Almeda Raymond.
Joseph Fuller	82	Joseph Fuller.	Gardner Thomas	80	Gardner Thomas.
Joshua Avery	76	Joshua Avery.	Elijah Reed	80	Pardon Wordell.
Thankful Packard	81	Benjamin Packard.			
Edward McGowns	80	James P. Nye.	BERKLEY.		
John Perry	81	John Perry.	Mary Lindal	80	
John Gardner	77	Bela White.	Joanna Crane	94	Abiatha Crane.
Mary Nye	80	Ebenezer Nye.	Thomas Andros	81	Thomas Andros.
Lemuel Fisher	80	Allen Fish.	Josiah Macomber	83	Venus Macomber.
			Hannah Paull	86	Hannah Pawll.
TRURO.			Isaac Babbit	77	Adoniram Babbit.
Joseph Rich	78	Joseph Rich.	Simeon Chace	84	Simeon Chace.
WELLFLEET.			RAYNHAM.		
Jeremiah Newcomb	81	Jeremiah Newcomb.	Abigail Robinson	79	Abigail Robinson.
Stephen Young	79	Stephen Young.	Seth Dean	83	Seth Dean.
Nathan Harding	88	Henry Harding.	Israel Washburn	85	Israel Washburn.
James Newcomb	87	Elisha Rich.	Olive Andrews	87	Carmi Andrews.
Hannah Morris	73	Hannah Morris.	Philip Knapp	85	Philip Knapp.
John Taylor	-	John Taylor.	Phebe Richmond	81	Lydia Richmond.
Mary Harding	76	Mary Harding.	Stephen Williams	87	Stephen Williams.
			Joseph Shaw	88	Joseph Shaw.
YARMOUTH.			Benjamin Keen	84	Benjamin Keen.
Betsey Berry	79	Betsey Berry.	John Gilmore	81	John Gilmore.
George Baker	64	George Baker.			
Reuben Chase	78	Reuben Chase.	FREETOWN.		
Abigail Hall	85	David Hall.	Joseph Durfee	90	Joseph Durfee.
Samuel Taylor	84	Samuel Taylor.	James Richmond	80	James Richmond.
Polly Thacker	82	Polly Thacker.	Elizabeth Burr	76	Ebenezer Pierce.
Bethiah Miller	79	Bethiah Miller.	Asenath Leonard	80	Susan Allen.
			Benjamin Haskell	44	
BRISTOL COUNTY.			John Laurence	78	William N. Laurence.
NEW BEDFORD.			Lucy French	85	Apollos Dean.
Daniel Brett	78	Daniel S. Brett.	Mercy Pitsley	78	
Thomas Taber	75	James B. Watkins.	Priscilla Richmond	75	
William Bliss	82	William Bliss.	William Pratt	80	
William Grinnell	77	James M. Cranston.			
John Elliot	85	Thomas Allen.	EASTON.		
John Hathaway	86	John Hathaway.	Sarah Ward	78	Benjamin Ward.
Jaber Hathaway	83	Jabez Hathaway.	Stimpson Williams	76	Stimpson Williams.
Brownell Armsby	82	Lemuel M. Armsby.	Freelove Packard	80	Almshouse.
Barzaliel Washburn	78	Barzaliel Washburn.	Polly French	80	Polly French.
			Marcy Snow	78	Marcy Snow.
FAIRHAVEN.			Lyman Wheelock	78	Lyman Wheelock.
Thomas Westgate	79	Thomas Westgate.	Susanna Phillips	86	Susanna Phillips.
Lettice Washburn	82	Lettice Washburn.	Adam Drake	81	Cynthia K. Drake.
Simeon Demoranville	76	Simeon Demoranville.			
Elnathan Pope	80	Elnathan Pope.	NORTON.		
Jared Chase	79	Jared Chase.	Nathan Andrews	78	Nathan A. Andrews.
Noah Stoddard	85	Noah Stoddard.	Abisha Smith	79	Seth Smith.
Patience Tupper	92	Patience Tupper.	John Carver	91	Clifford Carver.
			Jason Blake	84	Benjamin Sweet.
DARTMOUTH.			Francis Guillo	77	Francis Guillo.
Joseph Whalon	83	Joseph Whalon.	Anna Lincoln	78	Thompson Tripp.
Benjamin Woodcock	88	Benjamin Woodcock.	John L. Monroe	85	John L. Monroe.
Elijah Macomber	85	Elijah Macomber.	Isaac Rodgers	82	Isaac Rodgers.
Joseph Weaver	83	Joseph Weaver.	Rufus Hodges	81	Leonard Hodges.
Lewis Gifford	85	Lewis Gifford.	Sylvanus Braman	87	Sylvanus B. Braman.
Samuel Sabins	84	Samuel Sabins.	Josiah King	78	Josiah King.
John Reed	79	John Reed.	Thomas Danforth	79	Thomas Danforth.
Thomas Wilbur	84	Thomas Wilbur.	Solomon Lothrop	79	Solomon Lothrop.
Lemuel Reed	76	Lemuel Reed.			
			SWANSEY.		
WESTPORT.			Thomas Lewin	81	Thomas Lewin.
Barzilla Manchester	78	Thomas Allen.	Stephen Luther	79	Stephen Luther.
Ann Cory	83	Ann Cory.	Ebenezer Holmes	77	Richard Walker.
Robert Cottle	83	Robert Cottle.	Aaron Luther	77	Mason G. Brown.
Joshua Petty	85	Moses Petty.			

MASSACHUSETTS—Continued.

Names of pensioners for revolutionary or military services.	Ages.	Names of heads of families with whom pensioners resided June 1, 1840.	Names of pensioners for revolutionary or military services.	Ages.	Names of heads of families with whom pensioners resided June 1, 1840.
BRISTOL—Continued.			**BRISTOL—Continued.**		
SOMERSET.			SEEKONK—Continued.		
Noble Cummings - -	80	Noble Cummings.	John Coomer - - -	93 }	Calvin Wood.
			Charles Cushing - -	76 }	
DIGHTON.			Alexander Mason - -	82	Alexander Mason.
James Briggs - -	81	James Briggs.	Nathaniel Vial - -	78	Nathaniel Vial.
Sarah Briggs - -	84	Sarah Briggs.	Peter Whitaker - -	86	Joel Whitaker.
Littis Wood - -	89	Gilford Waldron.	Abel Whitaker - -	83	Abel Whitaker.
George Walker - -	79	George Walker.	Moses Walker - -	79	Moses Walker.
Thomas Rose - -	82	Thomas Rose.			
Joshua T. Williams	80	Joshua S. Williams.	PAWTUCKET.		
Hodizah Baylies -	83	Hodizah Baylies.	Molly Bowers - -	99	Caroline M. Read.
Ebenezer Stetson -	79	Ebenezer Stetson.	Abba Eldridge - -	43	Abba Eldridge.
Nathan Ide - -	81	Nathan Ide, jr.			
Rebecca Fish - -	79	Rebecca Fish.	ATTLEBOROUGH.		
Abizer Briggs - -	87	Abizer Briggs.	Elizabeth Briggs - -	74	Elizabeth Briggs.
Ann Pearce - -	77	Anna Pearce.	Caleb Parmenter - -	82	Draper Parmenter.
			Charles Freeman - -	76	William A. Freeman.
TAUNTON.			Nathan Richards - -	80	Nathan Richards.
Sally Lincoln - -	74	Joseph Wilbar.	Joel Ellis - - -	83	Joel Ellis.
Edmund Davis - -	78	Perry Davis.	David Brown - -	83	David Brown.
Jonathan Ingell -	85	Jonathan Ingell.	Jeremiah Peck - -	76	Jeremiah Peck.
Dier Pratt - -	86	Dier Pratt.	Samuel Tingley - -	88	Samuel Tingley.
Marcy Blake - -	78	Caleb Blake.	Mary Bowers - -	93	Milton Bowers.
James Walker - -	80	James Walker.	John Chase - -	84	Barton Chase.
Preserved Haskins -	77	Preserved Haskins.	Joseph Cushman - -	85	Bartholomew Cushman.
Cato Fillebrown -	78	John Brown.	Obed Robinson - -	78	Obed Robinson.
Jane Fisher - -	88	Joseph Potter.	Caroline Woodcock -	79	Joseph Field, jr.
Wiltha Godfrey -	75	George G. Godfrey.			
Thomas Hewitt -	83	Thomas Hewitt.	MANSFIELD.		
Roby Wheeler -	79	William Wheeler.	Benjamin Billings - -	79	Benjamin Billings.
Robert Holmes -	74	Robert Holmes.	Matilda White - -	80	Matilda White.
Amos Rounds - -	76	Amos Rounds.	Ruth Lincoln - -	99	Schuyler Shepard.
Nathaniel Lincoln -	75 }		Joseph Titus - -	80	A. F. Lunt.
Levi Woodward -	79 }	Almshouse.	John White - -	81	John White.
Elisha Eddy - -	78 }		Experience Dunham -	74	Experience Dunham.
Sarah Drown - -	80	Sarah Drown.	Caleb Atherton - -	79	David Holmes.
Sarah Morey - -	75	Daniel Morey.	David Grover - -	84	Robert B. Grover.
Susanna Knapp -	73	Edward N. Knapp.	Ruth Drake - -	77	Ruth Drake.
Amos Kelton - -	80	Amos Kelton.	Rhoda Paine - -	88	Simeon Grover.
John Wilde - -	86	John Wilde.			
Daniel Woodward -	81	Daniel Woodward.	**PLYMOUTH COUNTY.**		
Timothy White -	79	Timothy White.	PLYMOUTH.		
Deborah Philips -	79	Deborah Philips.	Bethiah Bagnele - -	84	Samuel W. Bagnele.
Elijah Haskins -	83	Samuel Haskins.	Amasiah Preston - -	83	Joseph White.
Henry Haskins -	79	Edward Haskins.	Isabella Thomas - -	76	Isabella Thomas.
Ezra Clark - -	79	Ezra Clark.	Samuel N. Holmes - -	85	Samuel N. Holmes.
Richard Clark -	78	William Seekell.	John Adlington - -	76	John Adlington.
George Reed - -	82	George Reed.	James Thatcher - -	83	James Thatcher.
Jemima Cain - -	87	Samuel Cain, jr.	Lucy Hardy - -	81	Betsey Peterson.
Lemuel Dean - -	85	Lemuel Dean.	William Robbins - -	82	Edmund Robbins.
Enos Dean - -	78	Enos Dean.	Moses Nichols - -	77	Moses Nichols.
Jerusha Godfrey -	79	Jerusha Godfrey.	Bathsheba Barnes - -	73	Bathsheba Barnes.
Abigail Paddleford	78	James Paddleford.	Mary Ripley - -	76	William Ripley.
Ebenezer Robinson	82	Ebenezer Robinson.	Reubah Lucas - -	82	Ephraim Washburn.
Eunice Richmond -	86	Asa Richmond.	Betsey Lucas - -	81	Sylvanus Rogers, jr.
Peter Adams - -	98	Peter Adams.	Susan Wright - -	84	Joseph Wright.
John Presbrey -	80	John Presbrey.	Lucy Briggs - -	77	Lucy Burgess.
Temperance Dean -	85	Leander B. Dean.	Phebe Warren - -	86	Phebe Warren.
John Marston - -	84	John Marston.	John Burgess - -	74	John Burgess.
Lydia Bassett -	80	Anselm Bassett.	James Harlow - -	77	James Harlow.
Mary Dean - -	78	Mary Dean.	Patience Nickerson -	82	Patience Nickerson.
Anna Robinson -	86	Ann Robinson.	Deborah Raymond -	73	Deborah Raymond.
			William Stevens - -	88	Lemuel Stevens.
REHOBOTH.					
Mary Peck - -	90	Benjamin Peck.	KINGSTON.		
Israel Goff - -	80	Israel Goff.	Hezekiah Ripley - -	83	Hezekiah Ripley.
Thomas Handy -	86	Isaac Pearce.	Ezra D. Morton - -	72	Ezra D. Morton.
Thomas Pearce -	76	Jarvis Wheeler.	Ebenezer Covel - -	82	Ebenezer Covel.
Elnathan Lake -	87	William Covel.	James Sever - -	78	James Sever.
Asa Bliss - -	79	Asa Bliss.	Noah Bradford - -	77	Ezekiel Bryant.
Martha Blanding -	79	Martha Blanding.	Thankful D. Drew - -	90	Elisha Ford.
Joseph Wheaton -	87	Joseph Wheaton.	Lucy Washburn - -	74	Francis Washburn.
Jonathan Nash -	86	Jonathan Nash.	Saba Cushman - -	77	Mary Perkins.
Priscilla Bowen -	69	Priscilla Bowen.			
Amos Martin - -	85	Amos Martin.	CARVER.		
Nathan Hicks -	78	Nathan Hicks.	Daniel Bumpus - -	79	Edmund P. Bumpus.
			Edward Bumpus - -	86	Edward Bumpus.
SEEKONK.			Gideon Shurtliff - -	78	Nathaniel Shaw.
William Daggett - -	83	Zebina Horr.	Jerima Lucas - -	83	Consider Robbins.
Richard Walker - -	82	Lewis Walker.	Lydia Crocker - -	87	Haman Crocker.
Sarah Radloff - -	82	James Radloff.	Job Aplin - -	83	Isaac Vaughn.
Joel Bowen - -	79	Joel Bowen.	Nehemiah Cobb - -	88	Nathan Cobb.
Lydia Perry - -	79	Lydia Perry.			

MASSACHUSETTS—Continued.

Names of pensioners for revolutionary or military services.	Ages.	Names of heads of families with whom pensioners resided June 1, 1840.	Names of pensioners for revolutionary or military services.	Ages.	Names of heads of families with whom pensioners resided June 1, 1840.
PLYMOUTH—Continued.			**PLYMOUTH—Continued.**		
WAREHAM.			*SCITUATE—Continued.*		
Mesey Bumpus	87	Mesey Bumpus.	Lydia Curtis	83	Job Curtis.
Silas Bessey	79	Constant Bessey.	Luther Damon	84	Luther Damon.
Thomas Washburn	79	Thomas Washburn.	William Hyland	87	Hannah Litchfield.
Josiah Smith	83	Josiah Smith.	Martha Clapp	85	Thomas Clapp.
Joseph Gibbs	78	Joseph Gibbs.	Charles Cole	80	Alfred Litchfield.
Silvia Bates	86	Silvia Bates.	Simeon Pierson	87	Simeon Pierson.
Jesse Briggs	83	Jesse Briggs.	John Studley	80	John Studley.
Axy Bumpus	71	Axy Bumpus.	Cornelius Bates	78	Cornelius Bates.
Betsey Lucas	75	Charles Lucas.	Rhoda Morris	85	Robert Williams.
PLYMPTON.			Francis Litchfield	79	S. O. Ruggles.
Noah Thomas	80	Henry L. Thomas.	Lemuel Jacobs	–	Lemuel Jacobs.
Jacob Cushman	92	Jacob Cushman.	Anna Webb	82	Paul Webb.
Jerusha Ripley	85	Simeon Churchill.	Judith Cook	80	William Cook.
Ebenezer Wright	77	Ebenezer Wright.	Gideon Young	79	Moses F. Rich.
Deborah Pliney	90	Barnabas Pliney.	Rachel Clapp	80	N. B. Sylvester.
John Bisbee	84	John Bisbee.	Calvin Jenkins	82	Calvin Jenkins.
Zebedee Chandler	76	Zebedee Chandler.	Lydia Turner	77	Samuel A. Turner.
Benjamin Cushman	78	Amos Fuller.	*HINGHAM.*		
Joseph Wright	83	Willard Ellis, jr.	Peter Kersey	82	J. B. Mayhew.
Simeon Loving	77	Simeon Loving.	Philippi Dunbar	82	Peter Kersey, jr.
Polly Sherman	78	George Sherman.	Bethsheba Tower	82	Moses Tower.
Samuel Briggs	76	Samuel Briggs.	Nabby Dunbar	77	S. L. Fearing.
Levi Wright	83	Levi Wright.	David Gardner	86	E. D. Blossom.
Sarah Shurtliff	73	Zenas Washburn.	Mary Stoddard	74	W. A. Hessey.
Patience Wright	73	George E. Wright.	Jedediah Jay	86	Lydia Stoddard.
DUXBURY.			Israel Stowell	84	Israel Stowell.
			Rachel Lincoln	82	Rachel Lincoln.
Joseph Kinney	85	Alethea Soul.	Susanna Lincoln	80	Alexander Anderson.
Priscilla Peterson	75	Ruth Peterson.	Lot Marsh	82	Lot Marsh.
Howland Sampson	85	Howland Sampson.	Mileah Dill	84	Mileah Dill.
Andrew Sampson	91	Andrew Sampson.	Susan Stoddard	78	Susan Stoddard.
Thomas Chandler	87	Samuel Chandler.	Perez Gardner	78	Perez Gardner.
Samuel Gardner	76	Samuel Gardner.	Elizabeth Corthell	75	Elizabeth Corthell.
Howard Chandler	81	Howard Chandler.	Ezekiel Hersey	79	Ezekiel Hersey.
Jerusha Waterman	75	Jerusha Waterman.	Israel Whiton	81	Lyman Barnes.
Marcia Taylor	72	Marcia Taylor.	Edmund Hobart	85	Edmund Hobart.
James Weston	79	James Weston.	John Kersey	79	S. S. Kersey.
Oliver Delano	81	Oliver Delano.	Jonathan Cushing	81	Jonathan Cushing.
Lucy Glass	80	Nancy Glass.	*HULL.*		
Reuben Daws	95	Peleg Simmons.	Olive Lovell	83	Pyam Cushing.
Nathaniel Hodges	78	Joseph F. Wadsworth.	Winefred Hunt	86	Winefred Hunt.
Isaiah Alden	81	Isaiah Alden.	Mary Dill	73	William Pope.
Abner Sampson	88	Abner Sampson.	*ABINGTON.*		
Levi Weston	83	Levi Weston.	Nancy Curtis	67	Nancy Curtis.
Judah Alden	89	Judah Alden.	Oliver Stetson	82	Alvin Studley.
Sarah Burgess	83	Sarah Burgess.	Ruth Lovell	74	Jacob Lovell.
Wealthy Drew	83	Wealthy Drew.	Sarah Reed	94	Jesse Reed.
Rebecca Peterson	86	Joseph Wadsworth.	Huldah Penniman	84	Harris G. Prouty.
Drusbury Wadsworth	79	Drusbury Wadsworth.	Sarah Cook	80	Thomas J. Cook.
Uriah Sprague	92	Uriah Sprague.	Ruth Dyer	80	Ruth Dyer.
Seth Sprague	80	Seth Sprague.	Joseph P. Gurney	79	Joseph P. Gurney.
Margaret Delano	79	Jesse Delano.	Lydia Cotherell	82	John Cotherell.
Abigail Kent	75	Abigail Kent.	Asa Gurney	81	Asa Gurney.
Joshua Brewster	77	Joshua Brewster.	Luther Lazell	86	Luther Lazell.
Jeptha Delano	81	Jeptha Delano.	Patience Chamberlin	83	Patience Chamberlin.
Abigail Kent	94	Amos Ames.	Matthew Noyes	82 }	Almshouse.
Lucy Stoddard	75	Sally Walker.	Caleb Lane	77 }	
Abigail Weston	77	Abigail Weston.	Anna Hill	88	Anna Hill.
Edward Arnold	92	Galen Arnold.	Susanna Tarrey	65	Barker C. Young.
MARSHFIELD.			Gridley Thaxter	84	Gridley Thaxter.
Susanna Delano	82	Susanna Delano.	David Noyse	79	Albert Reed, 2d.
John Bourn	81	John Bourn.	*EAST BRIDGEWATER.*		
Abigail Baker	76	Dwelly Baker.	Molly French	73	Nathaniel French.
Luther Little	84	Luther Little.	Eunice Thayer	83	Parmo Stetson.
Wales Tilden	84	Wales Tilden.	Philip Torrey	80	Philip Torrey.
Asa Lapham	95	Asa Lapham.	Lydia Ramsdell	72	Lydia Ramsdell.
Anthony Hatch	87	Anthony Hatch.	Susanna Whitmarsh	71	Susanna Whitmarsh.
Bethial Rogers	93	Bethial Rogers, jr.	Benjamin Pincin	80	Dexter Pratt.
Thomas Rogers	88	Hatel Oakman.	Luther Hatch	78	Luther Hatch.
Rachel Rogers	75	Constant Oakman.	Margaret Wesley	91	William Pratt.
SCITUATE.			Nathan Alden	89	Nathan Alden.
John Turner	79	John Turner.	Molly Chamberlin	75	Calvin Chamberlin.
Martha Stetson	82	Samuel Stetson.	*WEST BRIDGEWATER.*		
Elisha Briggs	79	Elisha Briggs.	Asa White	78	Asa White.
Laban Souther	77	Laban Souther.	Richard Thayer	81	Richard Thayer.
Robert Pierce	79	Paul Litchfield.	Daniel Hartwell	85	Daniel Hartwell.
Jerusha Tower	84	E. T. Fogg.	Seth Burr	82	Almshouse.
Deborah Gross	87	Lewis Gross.			
Alice Cushing	83	Nathaniel Cushing.			

CENSUS OF PENSIONERS.

MASSACHUSETTS—Continued.

Names of pensioners for revolutionary or military services.	Ages.	Names of heads of families with whom pensioners resided June 1, 1840.	Names of pensioners for revolutionary or military services.	Ages.	Names of heads of families with whom pensioners resided June 1, 1840.
PLYMOUTH—Continued.			PLYMOUTH—Continued.		
WEST BRIDGEWATER—Continued.			MIDDLEBOROUGH—Continued.		
Elijah Alden	77	Almshouse.	Lydia Wood	74	Lydia Wood.
Samuel Wood	75	Samuel Wood.	Elisha Freeman	89	John Freeman.
			Hannah Ellis	85	Ebenezer Ellis.
NORTH BRIDGEWARH.			Moses Thompson	78	Moses Thompson.
Joseph Sylvester	76	Joseph Sylvester.	Jedediah Caswell	87	Jedediah Caswell.
Mary Crafts	77	Mary Crafts.	Joseph Clark	84	Joseph Clark.
Sarah Faxon	80	William Faxon.	Benjamin Thompson	77	Benjamin Thompson.
Thomas Wales	89	Lewis Bunker.	Mary Hoar	78	William Bourne.
Abigail Sturdifant	73	Willard Howard.			
Oliver Howard	82	Daniel Howard.	ROCHESTER.		
Jonas Howard	79	Naham Battles.	Lois Handy	82	Henry P. Young.
Zachariah Gurney	78	Zachariah Gurney.	Elizabeth Tinkham	90	Levi Handy.
Relief Packard	79	Jesse Packard.	Thomas Barrows	81	Thomas Barrows.
Hannah Jackson	86	Almshouse.	Gideon Hammon	86	Gideon Hammon.
Nathaniel Hobart	76	Nathaniel Hobart.	Eben Ellis	78	Eben Ellis.
Jonathan Carey	83	Jonathan Carey.	Sarah Church	81	Jonathan Church.
Andrew Freeman	75	Andrew Freeman.	Earl Church	81	Joseph M. Church.
Abiel Hartwell	83	Alfred Snell.	Mary Lumbnot	83	Phebe Peirce.
			Joshua Chandler	84	Joshua Chandler.
HANSON.			Mehitable Kenny	–	Lucy Tripp.
Lydia Keen	78	Lydia Keen.	Mehitable Clark	79	James H. Clark.
J. Bowen Barker	87	J. Bowen Barker.	Susanna Doty	86	Amos Combs.
Mary Josselyn	78	Mary Josselyn.	Deborah Briggs	79	Deborah Briggs.
Betsey Joel	77	Betsey Joel.	Stephen Rider	80	Joseph E. Smith.
Seth Perry	85	Seth Perry.	William Clark	82	John Pitcher.
Ezekiel Bonney	78	Ezekiel Bonney.	Timothy Hiller	80	Timothy Hiller.
			Jane Look	83	Alden Look.
HANOVER.			Levi Gunney	93	Levi Gunney.
Benjamin Bates	80	Jared Whiting.	Thankful Gunney	–	Samuel Gunney.
Patience Mann	80	John Brooks.	Isaiah Cobb	80	Isaiah Cobb.
Rufus Farnum	70	Rufus Farnum.			
Leavitt Lane	79	Lebbeus Stockbridge.	HALIFAX.		
Mary Mann	83	Mary Mann.	Judah Wood	79	Samuel Wood, 3d.
Elizabeth Perry	84	Elizabeth Perry.	Ebenezer Thompson	86	Jabez P. Thompson.
Lydia Tilden	79	Lydia Tilden.	Zebedee Thompson	81	Zebedee Thompson.
			Lydia Holmes	89	Oliver Holmes.
PEMBROKE.			Mercy Sears	77	William Sears.
Lemuel Lapham	78	Lemuel Lapham.	Nathaniel Holmes	79	Nathaniel Holmes.
Ruth Garnett	77	Ruth Garnett.	Abigail Sturtevant	92	John Sturtevant.
John Osburn	72	John U. Osburn.	Samuel Churchill	80	Samuel Churchill.
Billy Ford	83	Billy Ford.	Zenas Sturtevant	79	Zenas Sturtevant.
Betsey Nash	80	Zebulon Nash.	Thomas Pope	82	Dexter C. Thompson.
Christopher Pierce	80	Christopher Pierce.	Lydia Loring	79	Levi Morse.
Joshua Magoun	79	Joshua Magoun.			
Averick Thomas	74	Ebenezer S. Thomas.	BRIDGEWATER.		
John Hix	83	Almshouse.	Jonah Benson	81	Jonah Benson, jr.
Benjamin Bearce	82	Philip M. Tew.	Samuel Leonard	77	Samuel Leonard, jr.
Sally Stetson	78	Abel Stetson.	Simeon Pratt	81	Simeon Pratt.
Ursula Fish	77	Job Fish.	Azor Howe	75	Azor Howe.
Isaiah Sampson	82	Isaiah Sampson.	Jacob Leonard	82	Jacob Leonard.
			Cornelius Holmes	85	Cornelius Holmes.
MIDDLEBOROUGH.			Lydia Ashport	86	Lydia Ashport.
Lydia Lyon	80	Isaac Lyon.	Bethiah Bottom	82	Martin Leonard.
Abiel Washburn	79	George Shaw.	Mary Perkins	78	Simeon Perkins.
Daniel Tucker	80	Woodward Tucker.	Mary Forbes	83	Ezra Forbes.
Samuel Sampson	76	Samuel Sampson.	Joanna Wilbar	79	Isaac Wilbar.
Bethiah White	83	Bethiah White.	Abiah Forbes	87	Abiah Forbes.
Edward Thomas	81	James G. Cushman.	James Alger	85	James Alger.
William Drake	79	William Drake.			
Jane Gurney	83	Daniel Gurney.	NORFOLK COUNTY.		
George Hackett	81	George Hackett.			
Stephen Bennett	74	Stephen Bennett.	DOVER.		
Seth Thomas	86	Mary Carver.	Bethshebee Larabee	87	
Leonard Briggs	90	Silvanus Lovell.	Esther Chickering	79	
William Porter	77	William Porter.	Levi Sawin	79	
Earl Sears	78	Earl Sears.	Mary Battell	78	
Samuel Robbins	78	Samuel Robbins, jr.	Sarah Kerring	71	
Caleb Bassett	83	Caleb Bassett.			
Humphrey Alden	77	Joseph Shockley.	SHARON.		
Henry Andress	77	Henry Andress.	Philip Curtis	85	
Joshua Haskins	85	Apollos Haskins,	Joseph Cummings	83	
Joseph Cole	96	Joseph Cole.	Josiah Talbot	84	
Andrew Cole	85	Andrew Cole.	Edward French	79	
Deborah Thompson	91	Abner Wood.	Nehemiah Leonard	80	
Hope Wood	74	Hope Wood.			
Eliphus Weston	76	Ira Haskins.	MEDFIELD.		
Samuel Smith	89	Samuel Smith.	Nathaniel Kingsbury	91	
Hope Faunce	83 }	Seneca Thomas.	Nathan Allen	87	
Deliverance Cobb	76 }		Oliver Cutler	78	
Silvanus Wood	81	Benjamin O. Wood.	Oliver Fisher	85	
Isaac Benson	80	Isaac Benson.	John Bullard	82	
Arispa Thomas	77	Eleazer Thomas.	Nathaniel Stearns	76	

MASSACHUSETTS—Continued.

Names of pensioners for revolutionary or military services.	Ages.	Names of heads of families with whom pensioners resided June 1, 1840.	Names of pensioners for revolutionary or military services.	Ages.	Names of heads of families with whom pensioners resided June 1, 1840.
NORFOLK—Continued			**NORFOLK—Continued**		
FOXBOROUGH.			ROXBURY—Continued.		
Ezra Carpenter	88		Ebenezer Fox	78	
Jesse Hartshorn	78		Thomas Runnell	72	
Daniel Sallvy	73				
Cornelius Morse	83		DEDHAM.		
Oliver Comee	83		Lewis Colburn	88	
Benjamin Wilbur	82		Hezekiah Turner	88	
			William Fairbanks	87	
WALPOLE.			Joshua Whiting	82	
Timothy Monn	93		Seth Edson	79	
Josiah Hall	90		Jesse Wheaton	77	
Jesse Barden	80		Joseph Stone	78	
Jeremiah Smith	85				
William Hodges	85		DORCHESTER.		
			David Clap	81	Theophilus C. Clap.
WRENTHAM.			Chandler Russell	76	Susan Whitcomb.
James Holbrook	85		James Humphreys	87	James Humphreys.
Enoch Wilson	81		Edward Kilton	84	Edward Kilton.
Jared Wilson	78		Nancy Glover	74	Nancy Glover.
David Hawes	81		Edward Howard	53	Edward Howard.
Elkanah Whiting	83		Thomas Leeds	77	Thomas Leeds.
Cyrus Fisher	79		Ann Wheeler	87	John Preston, 2d.
Jeremiah Hartshorn	89		Thomas Withington	76	Thomas Withington
Jabez Pond	79		Hannah Lewis	78	Hannah Lewis.
Samuel Sales	77		Samuel Capen	80	Samuel Capen.
Daniel Gillmore	82		Lemuel Withington	83	Jacob Bacon.
Cornelius Kollock	84		Anna Allen	80	Thomas Reed.
George Hawes	78		Jeremiah McIntosh	80	Jeremiah McIntosh.
Moses Craige	85		Abigail Bailey	73	Abigail Bailey.
Elias Ware	86		John Bussey	89	John Bussey.
Hannah George	94		Susanna Pierce	82	Susanna Pierce.
Elizabeth Allen	78		Thomas Lyon	82	Thomas Lyon.
Patience White	86				
Nancy Colman	77		RANDOLPH.		
			Lydia Thayer	86	Ezra Thayer.
BILLINGHAM.			Rachel Whitcomb	75	Rachel Whitcomb.
Ruth Wadeworth	82	Bethiel Slorum.	Sylvanus French	77	Rhodolphus Porter.
Aaron Fanrington	85	Aaron Fanrington.	Relief Kingman	84	Relief Kingman.
Samuel Darling	80	Samuel Darling.	Samuel Ludden	79	Samuel Ludden.
Deborah Scott	76	Amos A. Wales	Elizabeth Thayer	82	Aminadab Thayer.
Eliab Wight	79	Eliab Wight.	Aaron Littlefield	81	Aaron Littlefield.
Lavina Laret	79	Daniel Larel.	Seth Turner	84	Seth Turner.
Elizabeth Spear	75	Perry Dawley.	Elizabeth Martin	84	Charles Allen.
Molly Holbrook	81	John Wales.	Simeon Alden	76	Simeon Alden.
			Bethiah Clark	90	Luther Thayer.
MEDWAY.			Micah White	86	Micah White.
Quinda Everton	80	Artem Brown.	Rachel Thayer	78	John Niles.
Beulah Farebank	79	Leonard Farebank.	Nathaniel Holbrook	84	Nathaniel Holbrook.
Jedediah Philops	85	Jedediah Philops.	Hepsibah Howard	97	Thomas Howard
Samuel Patrige	87	Samuel Patrige.			
Mercy Richardson	84	Jeremiah D. Richardson	BRAINTREE.		
Jonathan Adams	87	William Adams.	Bryant Newcomb	78	Bryant Newcomb.
Elijah Dewing	78	Elijah Dewing.	Thomas Hancock	76	Thomas Hancock.
Ameriah Force	82	Ameriah Force.	Hannah Clark	93	Hannah Clark.
			David Loud	79	David Loud.
FRANKLIN.			Rachel Faxon	79	Minott Newton.
Thomas Gay	86		Asa Copland	84	Asa Copland.
Leonard Fisher	74		Eliphaz Thayer	78	Eliphaz Thayer.
William Makepiece	76		Lydia Thayer	88	Lydia Thayer.
Abijah Clarke	85		Jonathan Wild	80	Jonathan Wild.
Timothy Fisher	78		Abigail White	78	Moses Holbrook.
Samuel Guild	77		Ruth Pratt	67	Ruth Pratt.
Elaher Pond	77		Lydia Thayer, 2d.	82	Gardner Penniman.
David Hartshorn	77		Susanna Fogg	76	Charles M. Fogg.
William Metcalf	85		Elizabeth Thayer	86	Jechonias Thayer.
Asa Fisher	83		Mary Wales	82	Nathaniel Wales.
Nathan Daniels	91		Levi Wild	82	Levi Wild.
Timothy Fisher	73				
James Metcalf	82		STOUGHTON		
Daniel Sayles	82		Rebecca Littlefield	75	Rebecca Littlefield.
Lydia Richardson	72		Anna Kieth	88	William Curtis, jr.
Mary Daniels	77		Thomas Curtis	83	Thomas Curtis.
Rhoda Thayer	81		Elizabeth Williams	92	Elizabeth Williams.
Adena Dean	75		Amos Guild	87	Amos Guild.
Margaret Knap	82		Silence Holmes	82	Silence Holmes.
Juleka Tarebant	78		Benjamin Bisbee	80	Benjamin Bisbee.
Anna Rockwood	84		Relief Harris	74	Relief Harris.
Mary Pierce	77		Lemuel Smith	81	Jesse Pierce.
Betsey Hartshorn	68		Asa Waters	80	Asa Waters.
Susan Fisher	77		Chloe Drake	77	Benjamin Drake.
			Samuel Wales	80	Samuel Wales.
BOXBURY.					
Samuel Trash	83				

MASSACHUSETTS—Continued.

Names of pensioners for revolutionary or military services.	Ages.	Names of heads of families with whom pensioners resided June 1, 1840.	Names of pensioners for revolutionary or military services.	Ages.	Names of heads of families with whom pensioners resided June 1, 1840.
NORFOLK—Continued.			**BERKSHIRE—Continued.**		
MILTON.			SHEFFIELD—Continued.		
Amos Holbrook	87		Ichabod West	75	Ichabod West.
Polly Horton	87		Stephen Stevens	83	Stephen Stevens.
			Joseph Hewing	76	Joseph Hewing.
CANTON.			Mary Andrews	84	Hannah Austin.
Elizabeth Crane	85		Amos Holden	76	Rodney Sage.
Charles Echard	47		Hannah Whitney	81	Henry Sanders.
Samuel Bisby	76		Reuben Buckman	81	Heman McIntyre.
Martha Howard	80		David Allen	88	David Allen.
Nathaniel French	77		Joseph Brown	80	Joseph Bower.
Sarah Billings	80		Bartholomew Parsons	84	Bartholomew Parsons.
Nathaniel Wentworth	80				
Ephraim Hunt	78		WEST STOCKBRIDGE.		
Rachel Wentworth	86		Joseph Wilber	87	Joseph Wilber.
Ruth Blockman	73		Amos Woodruff	77	Chester L. Woodruff.
Mary Burr	89		John Easland	82	John Easland.
Israel Bailey	93		William Payns	80	Philo Olds.
			Christopher French	88	C. French.
QUINCY.			Shubal Snow	80	Shubal Snow.
John Pray	86	Benjamin Curtis.	David Bradly	82	E. S. Bradly.
Gideon F. French	80	Elisha Turner.	Silas Barns	76	Theodore Avery.
COHASSET.			EGREMONT.		
Aaron Pratt	78		Jacob Cline	79	Jacob Cline.
Priscilla Bates	81		David Sandford	81	Stephen Sandford.
Lydia Nichols	80		James Baldwin	81	Albert Lewis.
Deborah Briggs	80		Darius Lewis	82	Albert Lewis.
Elizabeth Lincoln	81		Stephen Barnum	80	M. Millard.
Joseph Neal	88				
Susanna Wilcutt	77		RICHMOND.		
Joseph Beal	88		Noah Rossiter	81	Noah Rossiter.
Ruth Orcutt	84		Levi Crittenden	82	Asa Cone.
Nathan Buck	58				
Celia Beals	78		NEW MARLBOROUGH.		
Abigail Nichols	80		William Jaquins	88	William Jaquins.
			Jeremiah Corvet	76	Jeremiah Corvet.
WEYMOUTH.			John Stannard	84	John Stannard.
Thaddeus Bates	84		Thomas Clark	76	Thomas Clark.
Azariah Beals	84		Mary Hall	81	Amy Griswold.
Job Nash	85		Elizabeth Foot	88	Salmon Foot.
William Loud	78		Isaac Brewer	78	Isaac Brewer.
Sylvanus Loud	79		Louisa Stebbins	77	Rawson Harmon.
Benjamin Tirrell	81		Zenas Wheeler	84	Zenas Wheeler.
Isaac Pratt	80		Elizabeth Warner	77	Gad Warner.
Thomas Vinson	85		Michael Goodrich	91	Walter Goodrich.
Samuel Whitmarsh	80				
Lucy Holbrook	82		STOCKBRIDGE.		
Jonathan Lewis	81		Lillis Churchill	86	Seymour Churchill.
Rebecca Ripley	82		James Davidson	88	James Davidson.
Deborah Humphrey	80		Agrippa Hull	79	Agrippa Hull.
Mary Ricknell	81		Caleb Bennett	81	Caleb Bennett.
Patience Pratt	76				
Betty Pratt	84		LEE.		
Mary Blanchard	90		Joseph Willis	81	Joseph Willis.
Anna Loud	80		Reuben Marsh	78	Reuben Marsh.
Elizabeth Bates	74		Nathaniel Bassett	89	Nathaniel Bassett.
Hannah Pratt	75		Joel Hayden	78	Arthur Perry.
Rebecca Vinson	87		Cornelius Bassett	79	Cornelius Bassett, jr.
Timothy Nash	81		Levi Robinson	78	Levi Robinson.
John Webb	83				
Sarah Shaw	84		BECKET.		
Elizabeth Laulor	40		Anthony Church	79	Cyrus Church.
			John Messenger	99	John Messenger.
BERKSHIRE COUNTY.			Levi Snow	80	Edward C. Snow.
GREAT BARRINGTON.			Jonah Cushman	81	Alden Cushman.
Martin Hart	82	Martin Hart.	James Harris	86	James Harris.
Abram Seely	79	Gilbert Ford	Andrew Broga	82	Andrew Broga.
Asa Coles	82	Benjamin Coles.	Nathaniel Rudd	87	John W. Rudd.
Hugh Humphrey	90	Daniel Humphrey.	John Haskins	80	John Haskins.
Wethy A. Patterson	77	B. Patterson.	Elizabeth Snow	81	Stephen Snow.
Hezekiel Grant	75	H. Grant.			
Mary Pyncheon	74	George Pyncheon.	SANDISFIELD.		
Esther Lewis	86	George Stanley.	Leonard Bettes	69	Leonard Bettes.
			Elizabeth Markham	72	Aaron F. Couch.
ALFORD.			Jedediah White	89	Allen Bennett.
Enoch Sperry	79	Enoch Sperry.	Stephen Sage	91	Silas Sage.
Samuel Willoby	84	Samuel Willoby.	Chester Couch	78	Chester Couch.
Abiatha Fowler	85	A. Fowler.	Aaron Heth	85	Alvah Heth.
Jerusha Flint	70	Jerusha Flint.			
			OTIS.		
SHEFFIELD.			Oliver Judd	79	Oliver Judd.
Benjamin Spaulding	85	Benjamin Spaulding.	Daniel Webb	77	Daniel Webb.
Joel Root	85	Joel Root.	John Davidson	77	John Davidson.

MASSACHUSETTS—Continued.

Names of pensioners for revolutionary or military services.	Ages.	Names of heads of families with whom pensioners resided June 1, 1840.	Names of pensioners for revolutionary or military services.	Ages.	Names of heads of families with whom pensioners resided June 1, 1840.
BERKSHIRE—Continued.			**BERKSHIRE—Continued.**		
Otis—Continued.			Williamstown—Continued.		
William Crittenden	86	William S. Crittenden.	William B. Sherman	81	William B. Sherman.
John Fry	83	John Blair.	Henry Green	82	Henry Green.
Richard Chase	80	Richard Chase.			
James Haskell	51	James Haskill.	LANESBOROUGH.		
			David Jewet	81	Oliver Jewet.
LENOX.			Elijah Phelps	79	George R. Rockwell.
Asahel Lunduz	75	Asahel Lunduz.	Asa Lane	74	David Barnes
Elijah Thomas	79	Elijah Thomas.	Amos Pettibone	79	Amos Pettibone.
John Eells	87	Richard Parker.	Elnathan Gregory	83	Eli Bradley.
Daniel Canfield	80	Daniel Canfield.			
			N. ASHFORD.		
WASHINGTON.			John Stills	82	John Stills.
Daniel Sanger	79	Daniel Sanger.	Huldah Cole	79	Otis Cole.
Samuel Brooker	79	Samuel Brooker.	Jonathan Ingraham	80	Jonathan Ingraham.
John Kent	76	John Kent.			
William Millikan	78	William Millikan.	CHESHIRE.		
			Sarah Viner	69	Isaac Viner.
HINSDALE.			Susan Bliss	78	John M. Bliss.
James Winy	83	James Winy.	Nathan Wood	80	Arvin Wood.
John Adams	73	John Adams.	Reuben Albe	77	Reuben Albe.
Nathaniel Mourey	89	Nathaniel Mourey.	Zilpha Childs	78	Dexter Cole.
Abraham Washburn	86	Abraham Washburn.	Amos Carr	42	Amos Carr.
			Stephen Temple	76	Stephen Temple.
PERU.					
Daniel Cone	81	Daniel Cone.	SAVOY.		
Joseph Bacon	78	Joseph Bacon.	Elijah Turner	79	Elijah Turner.
John Geer	–	John Geer.	Ruth Davis	81	Abiger Davis.
Roger Haskell	87	Roger Haskell.	Benjamin Burlingame	57	Benjamin Burlingame.
			Snellern Babbit	79	Edward Babbit.
PITTSFIELD.			Simeon Goff	86	Simeon Goff, jr.
Joseph Howland	78	Joseph Howland.			
Hosea Merrills	79	Hosea Merrills.	TYRINGHAM.		
Josiah Lawrence	85	Thomas Lawrence.	Ziba Bush	74	Ziba Bush.
John Daniels	77	John Daniels.	Ellen Hill	81	Ellen Hill.
Reuben Brooks	78	Reuben Brooks.	Mary Patton	81	Freeman Stanley.
Zenas Root	76	Zenas Root.	Olive Cannon	78	John Cannon.
Robert Francis	78	Robert Francis, jr.	Lucy Buel	78	Samuel Fargo, jr.
Nathaniel Freeman	83	Edward P. Goodrich.	William Heath	77	William Heath.
Simeon Guilford	87	Willard Gay.			
John Peory	88	John Peory.	**FRANKLIN COUNTY.**		
Richard Barnard	81	Richard Barnard.	COLERAIN.		
			Mary Handy	75	Charles Handy.
DALTON.			Reuben White	90	Reuben White.
Henry Cleaveland	97	Cyrus Cleaveland.	James McCullock	84	James McCullock.
			George Walkup	77	George Walkup.
WINDSOR.			Gideon Lake	84	Gideon Lake.
Jacob Snow	82	Jacob Snow.	James White	84	James White.
Jacob Dawes	77	John Dawes.	Stoddard Totman	84	Stoddard Totman.
Stephen Hume	86	Richard Hume.	Jonathan Peterson	86	Sylvanus Peterson.
Jacob Fisk	77	Jacob Fisk.	Samuel Eddy	77	Samuel Eddy.
Sebeus Bates	80	William H. Bates.	Walter Bell	78	William Bell.
			George Shaw	77	George Shaw.
ADAMS.					
James Potter	80	Mercy Harkness.	HEATH.		
John Sheldon	91	Amasa Harrington.	Prudence Warfield	85	Job Warfield.
Zeniah Paul	85	Trueman Paul.			
Mary Temple	81	John Temple.	ROWE.		
Lyman Hall	85	Jabez Hall.	Jemima Stanford	93	Ebenezer Stanford.
Lydia Colgrove	75	Jeremiah Colgrove.	Asa Burton	87	Thomas White.
Edmund Badger	60	Edmund Badger.	Anna Ide	85	Anna Ide.
Tryphina Starks	76	Willard Starks.	Benjamin Shumway	88	Daniel Nelson.
Eli Gould	74	Eli Gould.	Meribath Wheeler	69	John W. Wheeler.
FLORIDA.			LEYDEN.		
Zebulon Benton	80	Loring Benton.	Matthew Clark	80	Calvin Davenport.
John Manning	44	John Manning.	Henry Thorn	81	Crandall Thorn.
Edmund Jordan	77	Edmund Jordan.			
Aaron Hayes	78	Aaron Hayes.	DEERFIELD.		
			Jesse Billings	75	Jesse Billings.
CLARKSBURG.			Abner Goodnow	77	Abner Goodnow.
Isaac Carter	76	Isaac Carter.	Abijah Harding	80	Abijah Harding.
Jacob Brown	77	Jacob Brown.	Roswell Lanfair	78	Robert Lanfair.
			Jeremiah Newton	84	Jeremiah Newton.
WILLIAMSTOWN.			Joel Smith (since deceased)	82	Lester Sammis.
Elijah Hawley	96	Cooe Danforth.	Charles Warren	80	Phineas Warren.
Mindwell Waters	77	Mindwell Waters.			
Nathaniel Chamberlin	83	Nathaniel Chamberlin.	GREENFIELD.		
Thomas Reed	101	Thomas Reed.	Job Graves	83	Job Graves.
Obadiah Bardwell	82	Obadiah Bardwell.	Uriah Martindale	82	Theodore Martindale.
Benjamin Briggs	80	Benjamin Briggs.	Elizabeth Clapp	82	Susan Ripley.
Azabia Dunsett	80	John Leney.	Samuel Pickett	80	Aaron Spalding.
Asa Russel	87	Nabby Mills.			

5

MASSACHUSETTS—Continued.

Names of pensioners for revolutionary or military services.	Ages.	Names of heads of families with whom pensioners resided June 1, 1840.
FRANKLIN—Continued.		
LEVERETT.		
William Winchester -	80	Daniel Gardner.
Andrew Gardner (since deceased)	91	Elihu Hemenway.
Josiah Rice -	76	Josiah Rice.
MONTAGUE.		
Moses Andrews -	85	Moses Andrews.
Samuel Bardwell -	83	Ezra Bardwell.
David Clary -	80	David Clary.
Moses Gunn -	86	Moses Gunn.
Salmon Gunn -	80	Henry A. Gunn.
Enos Marsh -	80	Lucius Marsh.
Joel Shepherd -	75	Joel Shepherd.
Obed Taylor -	78	Obed Taylor.
Ebenezer Whitney -	78	Ebenezer Whitney.
SUNDERLAND.		
Sylvanus Clark -	80	Sylvanus Clark.
Caleb Hubbard -	86	Caleb Hubbard.
Justus Clark -	83	Moses Montague.
WHATELY.		
Isaiah Brown -	88	Isaiah Brown.
Graves Crafts -	80	Graves Crafts.
Josiah Gilbert -	78	Josiah Gilbert.
Oliver Graves -	79	Oliver Graves.
Reuben Graves -	80	Reuben Graves.
Isaac Sanderson -	82	Isaac Sanderson.
Asa Sanderson -	84	Asa Sanderson.
CONWAY.		
John Avery -	82	John Avery.
Josiah Boyden -	77	Josiah Boyden.
John Boyden -	76	John Boyden.
Reuben Childs -	85	Reuben Childs.
Seth Hopkins -	87	Reuben Hopkins.
Daniel Newhall -	80	Daniel Newhall.
Bezaleel Smith -	78	Bezaleel Smith.
Caleb Sherman -	78	Caleb Sherman.
ASHFIELD.		
David Vincent -	77	David Vincent.
Ziba Leonard -	84	Paul Leonard.
Caleb Packard -	79	Willard Packard.
Timothy Warren -	79	R. Taylor.
Solomon Hill -	80	Solomon Hill.
Ezekiel Taylor -	83	J. Taylor.
Joseph Gurney -	82	Josiah Gurney.
Stephen Warren -	85	Stephen Warren.
Abigail Sears -	85	Asarelah Sears.
Asa Selden -	80	Jesse Selden.
Bethiah Howes -	88	David Howes.
Robert Gray -	82	Foster King.
Caleb Ward -	87	Luther Ward.
Timothy Catlin -	87	Timothy Catlin.
BERNARDSTOWN.		
Samuel Green -	80	Samuel Green.
Lucy Root -	73	Ralph Cushman.
BUCKLAND.		
Susanna Brackett -	77	Martin Brackett.
Asa Nichols -	78	Asa Nichols.
Eunice Forbes -	79	William Forbes.
Joseph Shepard -	86	Amos Shepard.
Jesse Pratt -	79	Jesse Pratt.
William Hubbard -	86	Joseph Hubbard.
Lucy Chapin -	73	John Porter.
Amos Wood -	83	Amos Wood.
Hannah Smith -	75	Emory Smith.
Dan. Townsley	76	Dan. Townsley.
Stephen Allis -	82	Stephen Allis.
CHARLEMONT.		
Ruth Bullard -	79	Calvin Walker.
Jonathan Avery -	84	Elihu Avery.
Jonathan Howard -	78	Jonathan Howard.
Susanna Willis -	75	Joab Willis.
Martin Rice -	91	Samuel Upton.
Joshua Vincent -	85	Orain Vincent.
Josiah Pierce -	89	Richard Pierce.
Hannah Mayhew -	82	Holmes Hayhew.
FRANKLIN—Continued.		
ERVING.		
Asa Albu -	87	Asa H. Albu.
GILL.		
Elisha Munn -	84	Elisha Munn.
Gideon Tenney -	80	Gideon Tenney.
George Goodrich -	88	Alfred Goodrich.
Augustus Davis -	80	Horatio Roberts.
HAWLEY.		
Isaac Toby -	90	John Toby.
Hannah Howard -	87	Chester Smith.
Paul Marcy -	84	David Pratt.
Phineas Scott -	84	Phineas Scott.
Edmund Longley -	93	Thomas Longley.
NORTHFIELD.		
Charles Blake -	69	Marshall S. Mead.
Elisha Alexander -	86	Josiah Alexander.
Eba Church -	77	William J. Church.
Eldad Wright -	–	Xenophon Turner.
Simeon Alexander -	83	Samuel Alexander.
Eunice Scott -	77	Medad Field.
John Darling -	80	Daniel G. Darling.
John Caldwell -	84	Rufus Caldwell.
Isaac Reed -	87	Moses Reed.
Hannah Foster -	77	Harvey Stratton.
Silas Bruce -	76	Warren Stratton.
NEW SALEM.		
Abijah Thayer -	85	Abijah Thayer.
R. Ellis -	77	R. Ellis.
Abigail Holden -	76	J. B. Holden.
Betsey Walker -	81	Calvin Hunt.
Shipman Shaw -	78	Samuel Shaw.
Jesse Trask -	74	Isaac Gibbs.
Electa Bangs -	75	Electa Bangs.
J. Vaughan -	78	Joseph King.
ORANGE.		
Jacob Tyrell -	80	Jacob Tyrell.
SHELBURNE.		
Nancy Long -	82	Stephen Long.
Elethe Coleman -	77 }	Elisha Barnard.
Elisha Barnard -	77 }	
David Anderson -	79	James Anderson.
Reuben Bardwell -	86	Moses Dole.
SHUTESBURG.		
Josiah Beaman -	86	P. Hemenway.
Stephen Jones -	79	Stephen Jones.
Mary Dorathy -	77	Rachel Sanderson.
Luther Spear -	80	Luther Spear.
Thomas Kibby -	81	Thomas Kibby.
Samuel Wheeler -	87	Samuel Wheeler.
Jacob Harwood -	79	Jacob Harwood.
WARWICK.		
Bulah Cook -	84	Daniel Evans.
Philip Atwood -	81	Philip Atwood.
Israel Fisher -	80	J. Fisher.
WENDAN.		
Samuel Reed -	78	Samuel Reed.
Zedekiah Fisk -	76	Zedekiah Fisk.
Nathaniel Wilder -	89	Daniel Wilder.
Samuel Oreutt -	74	Samuel Orcutt.
Timothy Armstrong -	79	Timothy Armstrong.
Joseph Merchants -	80	Joseph Merchants.
Julia Clark -	72 }	James Clark.
Aaron Tyler -	82 }	
Stephen Felton -	83	Ebenezer Felton.
HAMPSHIRE COUNTY.		
NORTHAMPTON.		
Elijah Bartlett -	82	
Lydia Marble -	77	
Simeon Clapp -	80	
Sarah Gardner -	71	
Elisha Babcock -	79	
Elizabeth Phelps -	77	

MASSACHUSETTS—Continued.

Names of pensioners for revolutionary or military services.	Ages.	Names of heads of families with whom pensioners resided June 1, 1840.	Names of pensioners for revolutionary or military services.	Ages.	Names of heads of families with whom pensioners resided June 1, 1840.
HAMPSHIRE—Continued.			**HAMPSHIRE—Continued.**		
NORTHAMPTON—Continued.			WARE—Continued.		
Reuben Taylor	78		Lemuel Andrews	79	
Gersham Randall	90		Stephen Andrews	81	
Samuel Hinckley	83		John Wheeler	79	
Asa French	83		Alice Stearns	70	
Nathan Brooks	82		Mille Gould	79	
Shubal Wilder	81		John Osborne	84	
Chloe Wright	73				
Esther Clark	80		WILLIAMSBURG.		
Thomas Lyman	83		Abner Hunt	75	
J. C. Flanders	47		Solomon Snow	85	
Elihu King	81		Anthony Hunt	84	
Levi Strong	60		Timothy Kingsley	81	
John Hoxie	65		Elias Root -	78	
			Cornelius Tileston	83	
EAST HAMPTON.			Judith Wait	86	
Payson Williston	76		Phebe Thayer	84	
Stephen Wright	81		Ann Hayden	82	
Luke Packard	80		Miriam Wires	90	
			Lucy Skiff	77	
BELCHERTOWN.					
Josiah Dunbar	76		GOSHEN.		
Robert Brown	76		Ambrose Stone	83	
Erastus Kentfield	75		Zebulon Wilcott	80	
Thomas Squires	75		Abigail Manning	77	
Ebenezer Hawkes	81		Rachel Gloyd	83	
Andrew Howard	78				
Eleazer Owen	79		PLAINFIELD.		
James Walker	82		Ebenezer Dickinson	87	
William Clark	88		Josiah Shaw	77	
			James Richards	83	
AMHERST.			Joseph Gloyd	76	
Ebenezer Mattoon	85		Vinson Curtiss	78	
Silas Johnson	75		John Hamlen	78	
Barnabas Seares	75		Samuel Streeter	86	
Mary Cushman	83		Philip Packard	77	
Rhoda Graves	86		Jacob Nash	79	
John Dickinson	82		Susanna Clark	74	
Judah Clark	83		Deborah Gardner	75	
Jonathan Thayer	76				
Willis Coy	76		WORTHINGTON.		
Nathan Sprout	77		Gersham Brown	79	
Samuel Thompson	80		Samuel Fallett	86	
Simeon Dickinson	83		John Stone	77	
Peter King	84		Joseph Holcomb	81	
			Luther Pomeroy	82	
HADLEY.			Lot Drake -	80	
John Smith	87		Marsh Zepporah	78	
Levi Dickinson	85		Lear Tower	93	
Joseph Smith	90		Mary Parsons	73	
Thomas Smith	78				
Ebenezer Pomeroy	81		MIDDLEFIELD.		
Daniel Bartlett	86		John Newton	82	
Olive Emes	84		Jemima Taylor	87	
Patience Washburn	95				
Sybel Montigue	88		CHESTERFIELD.		
Experience Corbin	84		Asa Todd -	84	
			Patrick Bryant	75	
SOUTH HADLEY.			Joseph Torry	86	
Sarah Bellows	77	Stephen Pepper.	Abel Cushing	76	
			Joseph Burnell	83	
PELHAM.			Asa Shaw -	92	
Solomon Whipple	88		Isaac Damon	78	
Ichabod Woods	80		Deborah Whiting	80	
Aseneth Grout	79		Theodoma Phelps	84	
Oliver Smith	78		Sally Utley	77	
Silas Cook	88		Margaret Davis	73	
			Catharine Wilcutt	84	
PRESCOTT.			Mercy Damon	75	
Nathan Fish	77		Hannah King	79	
John Atkinson	75		Deborah Hatch	76	
Roland Sears	77				
Sarah Stacy	76		NORWICH.		
Stephen Powers	75		Sandford Holsey	74	
Silas Williams	76		Samuel Wicks	75	
Alexander Conkey	87		Stephen Angell	75	
			Giles Lyman	82	
GREENWICH.			Nathan S. Colkins	86	
David Whipple	81		Soloman Thomas	79	
			Isaac Coit -	86	
WARE.			Sally Wetherby	85	
James Lumberton	78				

CENSUS OF PENSIONERS.

MASSACHUSETTS—Continued.

Names of pensioners for revolutionary or military services.	Ages.	Names of heads of families with whom pensioners resided June 1, 1840.	Names of pensioners for revolutionary or military services.	Ages.	Names of heads of families with whom pensioners resided June 1, 1840.
HAMPSHIRE—Continued.			**WORCESTER—Continued.**		
WEST HAMPTON.			*MILLBURY—Continued.*		
Oliver Atwell	85		Jonathan Gould	84	Jonathan Gould.
Joel Burt	81		Benjamin Bancroft	87	Isaac Lincoln.
Seberry Fisk	79		Joseph Wadsworth	82	Benjamin Wadsworth.
Samuel Edwards	87		Mary Lovell	85	
Sybel Bridgman	78				
Submit Clark	78		*SHREWSBURY.*		
Dorothy Alvard	82		Relief Harrington	73	Halloway Harrington.
Rachel Bartlett	82		Phebe Lathrop	75	Orville Lathrop.
			Lydia Bellows	81	Stephen Bellows.
HATFIELD.			Jonas Stone	82	Jonas Stone.
Seth Frary	81		Nathan Pratt	80	Nathan Pratt.
Silas Porter	80		Samuel Smith	83	Samuel Smith.
Joseph Guild	80		Jonathan Harrington	81	Jonathan Harrington.
Sarah Smith	85		John Park	81	Solomon Bothwick.
Martha Geary	80		Jonas Hastings	84	Jonas Hastings.
Orpha Swift	77				
			BROOKFIELD.		
SOUTHAMPTON.			Simeon Draper	75	Simeon Draper.
Jacob Pomeroy	88		Lucretia Hastings	79	Jainos Abbott.
Mansford Avery	85		Jason Walker	80	Jason Walker.
Aaron Bates	82		Amos Rice	80	Amos Rice.
Abraham Losee	82		Lydia Richardson	72	Ch. Richardson.
Timothy Clapp	87		Reuben Olds	79	Reuben Olds.
Lemuel Bates	85		William Rice	80	William Rice.
Thomas Rowley	87		Miriam Adams	76	Miriam Adams.
Anna Hannum	82		E. Richardson	80	E. Richardson.
			Ezra Richmond	88	Ezra Richmond.
WORCESTER COUNTY.			Thankful Ross	79	Esther Gilbert.
WEBSTER.			Israel Smith	85	Israel Smith.
Jonathan Cady	85	Jonathan Cady.	Elisha Converse	82	Elisha Converse.
			Benjamin Barrett	82	H. P. Barrett.
SOUTHBRIDGE.			Seth Field	79	Seth Field.
Lydia Plimpton	78	Lydia Plimpton.	Ruth Gilbert	85	Dexter Bruce.
Simeon Mason	89	Alvin Streeter.	Mercy Blair	80	Benjamin Blair.
Dennison Wheelock	87	Davis Wheelock.	Andrew Barrister	78	Linus Barrister.
Lemuel Clark	89	Lemuel Clark.	Sarah Henshaw	83	Josiah Henshaw.
Charles West	81	Charles West.	Susan Blair	76	Reuben Blair.
Nathan Brown	82	Nathan Brown, jr.			
			WARREN.		
DUDLEY.			Isaac Moore	87	John Moore.
Mary Brown	79	Artemas C. Pickering.	Robert Hathaway	77	Robert Hathaway.
Asa Keith	83	Asa Keith.	John Combs	83	Levi Combs.
Josiah Barns	88	Moses Barns.	Rebecca Barnes	76	Rufus Barnes.
Thomas Larned	78	Thomas Larned.	Elizabeth Burbank	81	John Burbank.
Dolly Healy	73	Harvey Conant.	Hannah Parker	75	Orison Hill.
Joshua Corbin	89	Carlton Combs.	Olive Holbrook	86	Ebenezer Holbrook.
John Edmonds	81	Asa E. Edmonds.			
			CHARLTON.		
OXFORD.			Nathaniel Burden	85	Nathaniel Burden.
David Lamb	82	Alfred Mower.	Nahum Lamb	–	Calvin Lamb.
John Larned	81	John Larned.	Jonathan Fuller	87	Charles Curtis.
Chloe D. Robinson	74	Jonas Larnard.	Sylvia Willard	70	Aaron Willard.
Jason Collier	96	Jason Collier.	Hannah Hooker	90	Jonathan Winslow.
Elisha Livermore	90	Calvin Stockwell.	Mary Williams	–	Mary Williams.
			Susanna Child	83	Samuel May.
GRAFTON.			James Dickey	95	James Dickey.
Caleb Segar	89	} Ithamar Stow.	Lucretia Barton	70	Lucretia Barton.
Henry Rixford	85		Nathan Dexter	82	Isaac Tower.
Tabitha Roberts	86	Isaac Southwick.	Humphrey Bigelow	78	Isaac Tower, 2d.
Polly Sawyer	71	Samuel Houghton.	Nehemiah B. Stone	80	N. B. Stone.
Thankful Nichols	80	Thankful Nichols.	Sally Smith	77	Sally Smith.
Assenath Walker	77	John V. Leland.	Amos Merritt	79	Amos Merritt.
Lois Walker	83	John C. Knap.			
Thomas Richmond	76	Thomas Richmond.	*AUBURN.*		
			Nathan Knowlton	80	Ezra Rice.
NORTHBRIDGE.			David Hosmer	82	David Hosmer.
William Rawson	89	Caleb Rawson.	Susan Craig	86	A. and W. Craig.
Nathan Streeter	89	Aldrich Streeter.			
Israel Taft	79	Israel Taft.	*STURBRIDGE.*		
Patty Flagg	79	William Trask.	Asa Bullard	85	John Albee.
			Elijah Alden	78	Martha Taft.
MILLBURY.			Stephen Newell	80	Moses Newell.
Susanna Holman	80	Asa Waters.	Mary Plimpton	76	George W. Holmes.
Ammi Faulkner	84	Cyrus Faulkner.	Anna Plimpton	81	Anna Plimpton.
Samuel Bixby	84	Samuel Bixby.	Silas Dunton	79	Silas Dunton.
Hannah Dwinnell	87	Solomon Dwinnell.	Deliverence Marsh	82	S. M. Freeman.
Joshua Carter	81	Joshua Carter.	Mary Plimpton	94	Mary Plimpton.
Amariah Brigham	85	Amariah Brigham.	George Thomson	84	George Thomas.
Amos Pierce	78	Amos Pierce.	Samuel Shumway	91	L. Shumway.
Mrs. Pierce	75	Abraham Pierce.	Lucy Shumway	79	Samuel Shumway, 2d.
Ithran Harris	49	Ithran Harris.			

MASSACHUSETTS—Continued.

Names of pensioners for revolutionary or military services.	Ages.	Names of heads of families with whom pensioners resided June 1, 1840.	Names of pensioners for revolutionary or military services.	Ages.	Names of heads of families with whom pensioners resided June 1, 1840.
WORCESTER—Continued.			**WORCESTER—Continued.**		
HARDWICK.			*RUTLAND—Continued.*		
John Gorham	81	John Gorham.	Hezekiah Newton	87	C. L. Newton.
Samuel Hinckley	83	Samuel Hinckley.	Tilly Flint	82	Tilly Flint.
Theophilus Hastings	78	Theophilus Hastings.	Barsella Miles	89	B. Miles.
Jeremiah Campbell	88	Jeremiah Campbell.	Jonas Stone	85	Jonas Stone.
Adonijah Dennis	80	Adonijah Dennis.	M. Parmeter	81	R. L. King.
Timothy Hathaway	84	Timothy Hathaway.	Abraham Hager	85	Joel Temple.
Zenas Phinney	88	Zenas Phinney.	Betsey Bryant	74	William Bryant.
Sarah Hudson	87	Apollos Fay.	James Cowden	84	James Cowden.
Olive Ruggles	80	Martin Ruggles.			
Lucy Ruggles	83	Gardner Ruggles.	*BARRE.*		
Elizabeth Washburn	84	Hannah Washburn.	Noah Harrington	76	Timothy Adams.
Elizabeth Howland	78	Elizabeth Howland.	Tilby Mead	84	Tilby Mead.
Abigail Mandell	82	Martin Mandell.	Mary Smith	84	Samuel French.
Eleanor Harrington	83	Eleanor Harrington.	Hannah Sears	84	Hannah Sears.
			Daniel Nourse	83	Daniel Nourse.
PAXTON.			Isaac Bassett	84	J. P. Bassett.
Braddyll Livermore	76	Braddyll Livermore.	Jason Hause	82	Jason Hause.
Abigail Willson	81	Abigail Willson.	Abraham Stevens	83	Nathan Stevens.
Micah Harrington	81	Micah Harrington.	Anna Brigham	83	Anna Brigham.
Ruth Pike	78	Ruth Pike.	Peter Fessenden	78	Peter Fessenden.
NORTH BROOKFIELD.			*WORCESTER.*		
Jonathan Parks	87	Jonathan Parks.	John Bigelow	85	S. D. Barker.
Levi Hathaway	78	Levi Hathaway.	Zenith Walker	85	B. P. Rice.
Nathan Moore	78	Nathan Moore.	Martha Whitney	–	Martha Whitney.
Sarah Waite	79	Sarah Waite.	William Tanner	–	Henry Tanner.
Jonas Bigelow	83	Jonas Bigelow.	Simon Gates	–	Simon Gates.
Mary Bartlett	86	Eli Bartlett.	Frost Rockwood	–	Frost Rockwood.
Jeduihan Stevens	74	Jeduthan Stevens.	Lydia Johnson	73	Lydia Johnson.
Rhoda Potter	87	Lovey Potter.	William Drury	82	William Drury.
			Rachel Wheaton	81	Ephraim Drury.
LEICESTER.					
Austin Flint	80	Austin Flint.	*LUNENBURG.*		
Huldah Yainter	84	Huldah Yainter.	Daniel Wetherbee	83	Daniel Wetherbee.
Elizabeth Burton	69	Charles Burton.	David Wood	83	David Wood.
Samuel Frink	75	Samuel Frink.	Reuben Adams	80	Enoch Adams.
Joseph Wilson	78	} Town farm.	Jonathan Adams	81	Jonathan Adams.
Asahel Matthews	75		John Peabody	77	John Peabody.
David Bryant	78	David Bryant.			
Elijah Warren	81	Henry E. Warren.	*FITCHBURG.*		
Rebecca Waite	77	Elizabeth Jackson.	Abijah Goodrich	86	Joshua Goodrich.
			Elizabeth Fullum	74	Elizabeth Fullum.
NEW BRAINTREE.			Azariah Fuller	76	Dixon L. Gill.
Phineas Warner	76	Phineas Warner.	Ephraim Osborn	75	Ephraim Osborn.
Eleazer May	83	Eleazer May.	Polly Burnap	74	Polly Burnap.
Robert Hoyt	87	Town farm.	John Meriam	78	John Meriam.
Pelatiah Hawes	84	Mary Bartlett.	Rebecca Pratt	74	John D. Pratt.
Silas Knight	83	Prince Knight.	Rebecca Flint	84	Rebecca Flint.
Stephen Parker	78	Stephen Parker.			
Ruth Newell	81	Welcome Newell.	*WESTMINSTER.*		
			Hannah Williams	88	Hannah Williams.
HOLDEN.			Abijah Wood	86	Abijah Wood.
Martha Stratton	76	Samuel Stratton.	Abel Wood	84	Abel Wood.
James Potter	82	James Potter.	Eleazer Drewry	85	Eleazer Drewry.
Samuel Nash	85	Samuel Nash.	Joanna Dike	76	Joanna Dike.
Molly Cheny	80	Molly Cheny.	Ann Knower	82	Thomas Knower.
Jonathan Mower	83	J. Mower.	Abner Sawin	77	Abner Sawin.
Artemas Dryden	83	Artemas Dryden.	Rebecca Nichols	80	Rebecca Nichols.
Jonathan Rodgers	85	J. Rodgers.	Jeduthan Warren	84	Jeduthan Warren, jr.
Timothy Marshall	83	T. Marshall.	Ebenezer Mann	89	Ebenezer Mann.
Andrew Brown	85	E. Brooks.			
Jonathan Flagg	83	Jonathan Flagg.	*ASHBURNHAM.*		
			Joseph Meriam	77	Joseph Meriam.
BOYLSTON.			Margaret Townsend	77	Reuben Townsend.
Molly Howe	77	Jotham Howe.	John Bowman	81	John Bowman.
John Howe, 1st	77	John Howe, 1st.	Cyrus Fairbanks	88	Jacob Fairbanks.
			Jonathan Sampson	81	Jonathan Sampson.
WEST BOYLSTON.			Joshua Fletcher	78	Joshua Fletcher.
Eunice Holt	95	Asa Holt.	David Clark	82	Lewis L. Willard.
John Winn	81	John Winn.	Thomas Gibson	87	John Gibson.
Prudence Prouty	81	Prudence Prouty.	Isaac Whitmore	85	Enoch Whitmore.
Oliver Glazier	77	Oliver Glazier.	Jabez Marble	85	Joel Marble.
Mary Stearns	81	P. Stearns.	Charlotte Lowe	73	William H. Cutler.
Thomas White	82	Joseph White.	Joseph Jewett	79	Joseph Jewett.
Silas Walker	96	S. Walker.	Leonard Stimpson	82	Lemuel Stimpson.
			Zilpher Rice	84	Samuel Brooks, 2d.
RUTLAND.			Charles Hastings	79	Joseph P. Hastings.
Sarah Skinner	89	Joseph Skinner.	William Ward	80	Benjamin Ward.
Samuel Heywood	81	Samuel Heywood.			
John Powers	86	John Powers.	*LANCASTER.*		
Benjamin Mead	81	William Mead.	Thomas Davis	86	
Joseph Hubbard	81	Joseph Hubbard.	Phebe Emerson	67	

CENSUS OF PENSIONERS.

MASSACHUSETTS—Continued.

Names of pensioners for revolutionary or military services.	Ages.	Names of heads of families with whom pensioners resided June 1, 1840.	Names of pensioners for revolutionary or military services.	Ages.	Names of heads of families with whom pensioners resided June 1, 1840.
WORCESTER—Continued.			WORCESTER—Continued.		
LANCASTER—Continued.			TEMPLETON—Continued.		
Jacob Lincoln	79		Hannah Turner	96	Asa Turner.
Nancy Goodarel	69		Mary Dolbear	75	Joel Dolbear.
Mary Wilden	93		Oliver Brown	85	Abel Davis.
LEOMINSTER.			GARDNER.		
Betsey Cobbern	87		Rebecca Nichols	80	Martin Dunster.
Calvin Hale	78		Jude Sawyer	89	Jude Sawyer.
John Bass	81		Sarah Hill	81	Sarah Hill.
John Cooledge	75		Reuben Haynes	86	Reuben Haynes.
Benjamin Hows	86		Ebenezer Brooks	77	Asa Reed.
Samuel Jones	79		Levi Fairbanks	85	Levi Fairbanks.
Thomas Robins	79		Ephraim Temple	80	Levi Holden.
HUBBARDSTON.			SPENCER.		
Samuel Morse	81		Phineas Jones	78	Phineas Jones.
Moses Hanting	82		Nathan Craige	86	Nathan Craige.
Rachel Church	88		Paul Wheelock	84	Ephraim Wheelock.
Ephraim Holt	78		Ellen Bacon	75	James Sprague.
Sybel Morcon	93		Jonas Bemis	79	Jonas Bemis.
Catharine Smith	93		Elias Adams	76	Elias Adams.
Hannah Hapgood	83		Hannah Bemis	76	Reuben Bemis.
STERLING.			Lucy Watson	86	William Watson.
Mary Darling	86		Andrew Morgan	79	Andrew Morgan.
Sylvester Roper	77		Joseph Wheat	85	Joseph Wheat.
Elizabeth Roper	79		Amasa Bemis	82	Amasa Bemis.
Jonas Bailey	89		Joel Howe	79	Joel Howe.
Deborah May	74		Rebecca Prouty	79	Eli Prouty.
James Wilder	77		OAKHAM.		
Isaac Bock	83		James Conant	84	James Conant.
Joseph Pearson (since dead)	82		Mary Rice	78	Nathan Rice.
Abigail Baker	74		Lucy Packard	77	Parley Packard.
Calvin Moore	85		Keziah Fales	86	William Ware.
Joel Pratt	88		Elizabeth Leonard	85	Caleb Packard.
PRINCETON.			Susanna Robinson	75	Susanna Robinson.
Nehemiah Parker	79		Susanna Conant	73	Luther Spear.
Israel Keyes	81		Grindal Chase	83	Josiah R. Deane.
Luther Parmeter	84		BOLTON.		
Calvin Kilbern	83		Jonas Houghton	80	Jonas Houghton.
Aaron Hagner	81		Israel Woodbury	84	Israel Woodbury.
ATHOL.			Job Howard	82	Job Howard.
David Young	84	Moses Fisk.	Benjamin Sawyer	82	Benjamin Sawyer.
Aaron Hager	82	Jesse Hager.	Jonas Welch	87	Jonas Welch.
Royal Humphreys	79	Henry Humphreys.	Nathaniel Longley	84	Nathaniel Longley.
ROYALSTON.			BERLIN.		
David Cook	87	David Cook, jr.	Benjamin Brown	96	William Eager.
Nathan Bliss	77	Nathan Bliss.	John Larkin	79	John Larkin.
Squire Davis	78	Joseph Davis.	SOUTHBOROUGH.		
Enoch Whitmore	80	Enoch Whitmore.	Persis Moore	87	Elijah Crouch.
WINCHENDON.			Martha Fay	79	Martha Fay.
John Day	87	Joseph Day.	Elizabeth Angier	79	Anna Fay.
John Kilburn	84	John Kilburn.	James Dunton	80	Elijah Bemis.
Stephen Emory	92	Isaac Cummings.	Ebenezer Newton	82	
PETERSHAM.			Patty Fay	79	Ephraim Ward.
Josiah Taft	84	Josiah Taft.	Daniel Warner	81	Daniel Warner.
Sophia Sanderson	78	Jonathan Sanderson.	NORTHBOROUGH.		
Samuel Hoskins	78	Samuel Hoskins.	Alice Brigham	84	Alice Brigham.
Stephen Thayer	86	George Walker.	Elizabeth Newton	73	Elizabeth Newton.
Widow Dunn	85	John Dunn.	Jonathan Barrett	79	Samuel Nurse.
Sarah Filmore	95	William Mann, 2d.	Silas Bailey	84	Silas Bailey.
PHILLIPSTON.			Seraphina Eager	72	Nahum Eager.
John Hagar	82	Washington Hagar.	HARVARD.		
James Stone	83	James Stone.	Elias Warner	76	Elias Warner.
David Pike	81	David Pike.	Jonathan Baird	85	Jonathan Baird.
Prudence Shepherd	82	John Shepherd.	Polly Smith	74	Henry Smith.
Susan Lamb	82	Ezra L. Bates.	Lemuel Stone	87	Reuben Whitney.
Earl Cutting	82	Earl Cutting.	Samuel Dickinson	88	Willard Dickinson.
TEMPLETON.			Lewis Hayden	78	Lewis Hayden.
James Crocker	—	James Crocker.	John Stacy	81	Nathaniel Stacy.
Stephen Knowlton	78	Stephen Knowlton.	Moses Tyler	82	Moses Tyler.
Josiah Haskell	84	Josiah Haskell.	WESTBOROUGH.		
Mehitable Mann	83	Josiah Cutting.	Reuben Babcock	88	Jesse Wood.
Silas Church	89	Joshua Church.	Fortunatus Nickols	80	Fortunatus Nickols.
Noah Kendall	87	Noah Kendall.	Benjamin Smith	76	Benjamin Smith.
Lucy Simonds	89	Joshua Sawyer.	Henry Marble	85	Henry Marble.
			Levi Smith	83	Levi Smith.

MASSACHUSETTS—Continued.

Names of pensioners for revolutionary or military services.	Ages.	Names of heads of families with whom pensioners resided June 1, 1840.	Names of pensioners for revolutionary or military services.	Ages.	Names of heads of families with whom pensioners resided June 1, 1840.
WORCESTER—Continued.			**MIDDLESEX—Continued.**		
UPTON.			*WOBURN.*		
Samuel Morse	89	Samuel Morse.	Jonathan Tidd	84	William Tidd.
Enoch Batchelder	84	Levi Batchelder.	Joshua Reed	77	Joshua Reed.
Silas Warren	86	Elijah Warren.	Aaron Smith	31	Aaron Smith.
			Ebenezer Lawrence	85	Ebenezer Lawrence.
MENDON.			Sylvanus Wood	90	Sylvanus Wood.
Rhoda Streeter	88	George Been.	Isaac Reed	84	Isaac Reed.
George Taft	80	Arnold Aldritch, jr.	Nathan Pierce	80	Nathan Pierce,
Henry Mowry	80	Henry Mowry.	Mary Thompson	78	
David Pickering	78	David Pickering.			
Benjamin Pickering	82	Benjamin Pickering.	*BILLERICA.*		
Bilota Burden	78	Aaron Burden.	James Bennett	82	James Bennett.
Lovina Engly	80	Joseph Engly.	Joseph Dows	81	Joseph Dows.
David Legg	84	Daniel Legg.	Bill Russell	77	Bill Russell.
John Remington	80	John Remington.	Samuel Whiting	81	Samuel Whiting.
Jemima Wood	82	George Wood.			
Enos Taft	84	Enos Taft.	*WEST CAMBRIDGE.*		
Thomas Burbeck	81	Joseph Wheelock.	Thomas Hill	79	Pauper.
MILFORD.			*MALDEN.*		
Darius Sumner	84	Darius Sumner.	Jane Mills	66	William S. Mills.
Abigail Morse	87	Clarke Ellis.	Sarah Cheever	86	Jacob Cheever.
Hackaliah Whitney	78	Hackaliah Whitney.	William Emerson	80	William Emerson.
Ezekiel Jones	82	Ezekiel Jones.	John Edmonds	83	John Edmonds.
Caleb Alber	75	Caleb Alber.			
Anna Lawrance	80	Anna Lawrance.	*SOUTH READING.*		
Samuel Warfield	84	Samuel Warfield.	Cornelius Sweetser	91	Stephen Sweetser.
Nathan Wood	80	Nathan Wood.	Elias Boardman	82	Benjamin L. Boardman.
Edmond Bowker	83	Edmond Bowker.	Nathaniel Cowdry	81	Nathaniel Cowdry.
			John Sweetser	80	John Sweetser.
DOUGLASS.			Oliver Walton	82	Oliver Walton.
David White	82	David White.	Barseliel Sturtevant	77	Barseliel Sturtevant.
David Bolcom	86	David Bolcom.			
Eli Stockwell	80	Eli Stockwell.	*MEDFORD.*		
Jedediah Jepherson	78	Jedediah Jepherson.	Patty Stetson	82	Jotham Stetson.
Noah Hill	80	Noah Hill.	John King	67	John King.
			Rebecca Cutter	75	Rebecca Cutter.
UXBRIDGE.			Elizabeth Symmes	83	Edward Symmes.
John Jepherson	80	John Jepherson.	Mary Johnson	81	Mary Johnson.
Benjamin Tucker	78	Benjamin Tucker.			
Moses Taft	80	Newell Taft.	*STONEHAM.*		
James Tilley	93	Nathan Aldritch.	Nathaniel Upton	85	A. P. Smith.
Elisha Murdock	85	Edward F. Seagraves.	Thomas Williams	77	Thomas Williams.
			Mary Bryant	80	Mary Bryant.
SUTTON.					
Simeon Morse	80	Simeon Morse	*LEXINGTON.*		
Zelek Darling	79	Zelek Darling.	Levi Harrington	79	Levi Harrington.
Francis Putnam	84	Silas Putnam.	Sulivan Burbank	63	Sulivan Burbank.
Daniel Sibley	83	Daniel Sibley, jr.	Isaac Smith	76	Isaac Smith.
Thomas Smith	82	Thomas Smith.	Eunice Thorning	84	Mary Wood.
Stephen Marsh	79	Stephen Marsh.			
Jonathan Pike	48	Jonathan Pike.	*WATERTOWN.*		
			Eunice Brigham	72	Luke Robinson.
MIDDLESEX COUNTY.					
CHARLESTOWN.			*CAMBRIDGE.*		
			John Stone	83	John Stone.
Hannah Wiley	85	Peter B. Wiley.	Joseph Rumrill	85	Joseph Rumrill.
Mary Flint	80	Mary Flint.	Parsons Smith	66	Elijah F. Valentine.
Amos Samson	78	Amos Samson.			
Mary Crowningshield	–	James Armstrong.	*READING.*		
Abigail Gibbs	83	Laban Turner.	Joseph Damon	81	Joseph Damon.
Jane Richardson	80	Asa Caldwell.	Joseph Bontwell	83	Joseph Bontwell.
Mary Blestill	77	Lydia Staples.	William Parker	80	William Parker.
Hannah Kidder	88	Mary Rand.	Aaron Parker	83	Aaron Parker.
Mary Thompson	84	Mary Thompson.	Daniel Damon	83	Daniel Damon.
Abigail Locke	81	Elias Crafts.	Timothy Wakefield	85	Timothy Wakefield.
Eleanor Fuller	76	Charles C. Fuller.	David Parker	85	Thomas Rainer, jr.
Ebenezer Evans	43	Convict in prison.			
Betsey Hay	74	Betsey Hay.	*WILMINGTON.*		
Mary Rea	81	Nathaniel R. Mansir.	Jonathan Eames	83	Jonathan Eames.
Mary Babbitt	76	Edward B. Babbitt.	Jonathan Nichols	83	Charles Nichols.
Naomi Downes	80	John Downes.	Jerusha Upton	82	Paul Upton.
William B. Brown	58	William B. Brown.	Lois H. Persons	75	
Caroline Lord	15	J. R. Covington.	Joseph Bond	79	Joseph Bond.
Hannah Bubibeer	78	John Bubibeer.			
William Watley	79	} Paupers.	*BEDFORD.*		
Robert Barry	68		John Webber	80	John Webber.
John Skinner	82		David Lane	81	David Lane.
Thomas Walcott	83				
John Leland	86	John Leland.	*ASHBY.*		
William Cutter	82	Paschal Sprague.	William Foster	51	William Foster.
Rachel Dickson	73	Rachel Dickson.	Asa Kendall	77	Asa Kendall.
			William Johnson	79	William Johnson.

MASSACHUSETTS—Continued.

Names of pensioners for revolutionary or military services.	Ages.	Names of heads of families with whom pensioners resided June 1, 1840.	Names of pensioners for revolutionary or military services.	Ages.	Names of heads of families with whom pensioners resided June 1, 1840.
MIDDLESEX—Continued.			**MIDDLESEX—Continued.**		
ASHBY—Continued.			CARLISLE—Continued.		
William Green - - -	85	William Green.	John Jacobs - - -	81	John Jacobs.
Abel Richardson - -	86	Abel Richardson.	Joan Adams - - -	83	Benjamin Adams.
TOWNSEND.			LITTLETON.		
Deborah Green - -	92	George Green.	Peter Wright - - -	80	Elizabeth Wright.
Hannah Searles - -	92	Samuel Searles.	Thomas Burbuk - -	80	Samuel Connant.
Caleb Sylvester - -	87	Caleb Sylvester.			
Daniel Prentice - -	83	Daniel Prentice.	DRACUT.		
William Manning - -	83	William Manning.	Rachel Coburn - -	78	Nathaniel B. Coburn.
Nahum Gassett - -	–	Nahum Gassett.	Mary Coburn - - -	76	Julia Carter.
Jonathan Bailey - -	92	Benjamin Robinson.	Abiah Bowers - -	92	Peter Bowers.
Josiah Reed - - -	92	Josiah Reed.	Joel Fox - - -	83	Joel Fox.
			William Richardson	82	William Richardson.
PEPPERELL.			William Clough - -	99	William Clough.
Thomas Yarbell - -	92	Abijah Whitney.	Amos Wood - - -	85	Micajah Wood.
Jonathan Bancroft -	80	Jonathan Bancroft.	Jonathan Bancroft -	79	Jonathan Bancroft.
Jonathan Messer - -	81	Jonathan Messer.			
Nathaniel Sowtell -	80	Nathaniel Sowtell.	SUDBURY.		
Noah Wright - -	79	Noah Wright.	John Goodnow - -	78	John Goodnow.
Dudley B. Kemp -	86	Dudley B. Kemp.	Sarah Cutler - -	82	Christopher Cutler.
			Isaac Pratt - - -	78	Solomon C. Pratt.
DUNSTABLE.			Ebenezer Parmenter	78	Ebenezer Parmenter.
Jonathan Woodward -	101	Jonathan Woodward, Jr.	Elizabeth Brigham -	83	Reuben Moore.
Jonas French - -	83	Jonas French.			
William French - -	88	William French.	WAYLAND.		
			John T. Roberts -	80	Susan Lawrence.
GROTON.			Susanna Grout - -	79	William C. Grout.
Abel Prescott - -	80	Abel Prescott.	Richard Heard - -	86	Richard Heard, jr.
William Prescott - -	72	Merrick Lewis.	Edmund Rice - -	85	Edmund Rice.
Joshua Parker - -	76	Joshua Parker.			
William Yarbell - -	76	William Yarbell.	WESTON.		
Jacob Nutting - -	93	Jacob Nutting.	Rebecca Brackett -	83	Isaac Brackett.
Isaac Patch - - -	78	Isaac Patch.	Alpheus Bigelow -	83	Alpheus Bigelow.
Joseph Sowtell, 2d. -	76	Joseph Sowtell, 2d.	Lydia Traverse -	82	John Williams.
David Lakin - -	89	David Lakin.	Abel Pierce - -	85	Charles Weston.
Amos Farnsworth -	86	Amos Farnsworth.			
Stephen Pingrey -	92	John Pingrey.	LINCOLN.		
			Isaac Monroe - -	83	Isaac Stearns.
SHIRLEY.			Mary Hartwell - -	92	George Hartwell.
James Carter - -	80	Jonas K. Putney.	Leonard Hoar - -	83	Leonard Hoar, jr.
Benjamin Hartwell -	81	Benjamin Hartwell.	Joseph Colburn - -	82	William Colburn.
Moses Jennison - -	85	Moses Jennison.	Azuba Jones - -	80	Ephraim Brown.
			Josiah Parks - -	80	Josiah Parks.
WESTFORD.			Amos Baker - -	84	James Baker.
Joan Chandler - -	85	William Chandler.	Eunice Parks - -	77	Jonas Parks.
Abigail Wight - -	79	Caleb Wight.			
Mary Perry - -	86	} Gilbert Farmer.	ACTON.		
Elihu Reed - -	75		Daniel White - -	80	Daniel White.
Abijah Reed - -	86	Samuel Farwell.	Abel Proctor - -	86	Lucy Hendley.
Isaac Durant - -	83	Ebenezer Blood.	Thomas Thorp - -	84	Thomas Thorp.
Huldah Robbins - -	75	Jedediah Robbins.	John Oliver - -	92	John Oliver.
			Charles Hendley -	77	Charles Hendley.
CHELMSFORD.			Nathaniel Johnson -	78	Rufus Tenney.
Josiah Fletcher - -	81	Josiah Fletcher.	Hannah Leighton -	94	Harriet Davis.
Samuel Davis - -	75	Samuel Davis.	Samuel Hosmer - -	79	Samuel Hosmer.
Samuel Brown - -	75	Samuel Brown.	Peter Wright - -	80	Nathan Wright.
Samuel Parkhurst -	81	Samuel Parkhurst.			
Levi Proctor - -	73	Levi Proctor.	CONCORD.		
John Crosby - -	80	John Crosby.	Isaac Hurd - - -	84	Isaac Hurd.
Hezekiah Thorndike -	86	Hezekiah Thorndike.	Abel Davis - - -	83	Abel Davis.
William Adams - -	78	William Adams.	Daniel Wood - -	79	James Wood.
Martha Merrill - -	68	Charles A. Frost.			
Amy Wibber - -	89	Hugh Pettingill.	NEWTON.		
Polly Pierce - -	83		Nicholas Thwing -	92	William Park.
Rachel Dunn - -	80		George Stearns - -	80	Samuel Hyde.
			Samuel Trowbridge -	83	Samuel Trowbridge.
TEWKSBURY.			Ebenezer Brown -	92	Ebenezer Brown.
Noah Hunt - -	77	Noah Hunt.	Catharine Hyde -	76	Catharine Hyde.
Joel Shed - - -	81	Joel Shed.	Mehitable Seger -	92	William Hall.
Joseph Foster - -	80	Moses Foster.	Solomon Richards -	89	Solomon Richards.
Russell Mears - -	74	Joseph Parkhurst.	Zibeon Hooker -	89	Ezra Nichols.
Esther Baldwin - -	82	William Baldwin.			
John Danforth - -	83	Jonathan B. Averell.	BOXBOROUGH.		
			Peter Wheeler - -	76	Peter Wheeler.
TYNGSBOROUGH.					
Elizabeth Flint - -	80	Charles Flint.	BRIGHTON.		
Hannah Jaques - -	–	Daniel Jaques.	Patience Wood - -	81	William Fletcher.
William Blodgett -	–	William Blodgett.			
Eleazer Farwell -	81	Eleazer Farwell.	WALTHAM.		
			Rebecca Dole - -	77	Almira Wyman.
CARLISLE.			Nathaniel Hagg -	78	Samuel Ryan.
Amos Russell - -	93	Thomas Heald, jr.			

MASSACHUSETTS—Continued.

Names of pensioners for revolutionary or military services.	Ages.	Names of heads of families with whom pensioners resided June 1, 1840.	Names of pensioners for revolutionary or military services.	Ages.	Names of heads of families with whom pensioners resided June 1, 1840.
MIDDLESEX—Continued.			**ESSEX—Continued.**		
FRAMINGHAM.			*ANDOVER—Continued.*		
Thomas Nixon - - -	78	Thomas Nixon.	Joseph Shattuck - - -	82	Joseph Shattuck.
Ezekiel Howe - - -	84	Ezekiel Howe.	Lucy Bailey - - -	73	James Bailey.
Mary Trowbridge - -	85	Charles Trowbridge.	Dorcas Ames - - -	91	Simeon Ames.
Jacob Belcher - - -	79	Jacob Belcher.	Rachel Furbush - -	75	Rachel Furbush.
Nathan Kendall - - -	83	Nathan Kendall.	Abigail Stickney - -	82	William Stickney.
Luther Eaton - - -	78	Luther Eaton.	*METHUEN.*		
Uriah Rice - - -	83	Uriah Rice.	Hannah Barker - - -	84	Mrs. Buck.
Phineas Rice - - -	78	Phineas Rice.	Isaac Austin - - -	84	Frye Austin.
Hannah Belcher - -	83	Hannah Belcher.	John Richardson - -	88	Ben. Richardson.
Ebenezer Eaton - -	90	Ebenezer Eaton.	Amos Morse - - -	77	Amos Morse, 3d.
Joel Coolidge - - -	81	Joel Coolidge.	John Gage - - -	83	John Gage.
Betsey Davis - - ?	81	Timothy Davis.	Joshua Swan - - -	85	Joshua Swan.
Betsey Fisk - - -	81	Joseph Ballard.	Jonathan Howe - -	85	Jonathan Howe.
Sally Greenwood - -	78	Abel Greenwood.	Abial Heath - - -	75	Enoch Marshall.
Nathan Knowlton - -	80	Nathan Knowlton.	Abijah Cross - - -	82	Abijah Cross, jr.
Abel Benson - - -	74	Abel Benson.	Benjamin Kimball - -	79	Benjamin Kimball.
MARLBOROUGH.			*HAVERHILL.*		
William Gates - - -	78	William Gates.	James Walker - - -	90	James Walker.
Micah Balcom - - -	82	Joseph Balcom.	David How - - -	84	David How.
Betty Brigham - - -	69	Betty Brigham.	Daniel Bradbury - -	77	Daniel Bradbury.
James Dalrymple - -	83	James Dalrymple.	James Simpson - - -	83	James Simpson.
Sarah Whitcomb - -	80	Lucien B. Drury.	Daniel Silver - - -	77	Daniel Silver.
Sarah Thompson - -	78	Curtis Searles.	Daniel Clough - - -	77	Daniel Clough.
William Goodell - -	83	David Goodell.	*BRADFORD.*		
Isaac Brown - - -	80	Charles Miles.	Silas Noyes - - -	76	Almshouse.
Mary Williams - - -	76	Mary Williams.	Day Mitchel - - -	80	Day Mitchel.
STOW.			Lydia Chase - - -	85	Uriah Hopkinson.
Patty Rogers - - -	75	Samuel Rogers.	Mehitable Burbank -	95	J. W. Reed.
Ruth Stow - - -	78	Ruth Stow.	Timothy Phillips - -	81	Timothy Phillips.
Abraham Whitcomb -	82	Abraham Whitcomb.	*WEST NEWBURY.*		
Ezra Mosman - - -	78	Ezra Mosman.	Nehemiah Follansbee -	81	Nehemiah Follansbee.
Elizabeth Conant - -	82	Artemas Conant.	Ebenezer Hossum - -	76	Ebenezer Hossum.
Mary Tower - - -	72	Charles Tower.	Sarah Follansbee - -	76	Enoch Follansbee.
Zaccheus Robinson -	75	Zaccheus Robinson.	*GLOUCESTER.*		
Sarah Brown - - -	77	Calvin Taylor.	Sally Ellery - - -	75	William Ellery.
SHERBURN.			John Lowe - - -	80	John Lowe.
William Clark - - -	87		Zachariah Stevens - -	75	Zachariah Stevens.
Daniel Coolidge - -	87		William Haskell - -	79	Charles Haskell, jr.
Asa Clark - - -	76		William Dolliver - -	81	William Dolliver.
Sally Holbrook - - -	84		James Millet - - -	85	James Millet.
HOPKINTON.			Nathaniel Warner - -	79	James Millet.
Abial Watkins - - -	86		Miriam Akins - - -	86	William Blackford.
John Bowker - - -	78		Nathaniel Tucker - -	79	Nathaniel Tucker.
Lois Walker - - -	83		Lucy Davis - - -	76	Lucy Somes.
Sarah McFarland - -	91		Andrew Mattison - -	56	Andrew Mattison.
Samuel Goddard - -	81		Patience Fears - - -	91	Patience Fears.
Benjamin Pond - -	82		Moses Lufkin - - -	83	Moses Lufkin.
Abigail Greenwood -	78		Molly Parsons - - -	79	Molly Parsons.
Hannah Phipps - -	77		Elizabeth Elwell - -	86	Joseph W. Hillier.
Joseph Walker - - -	79		Dolly Adams - - -	85	Nehemiah Adams.
Elizabeth Pratt - - -	74		Solomon Rowe - - -	86	Richard Edgar.
HOLLISTON.			Susan Davis - - -	84	Experience Tucker.
Timothy Leland - -	88		Isaac Dennison - - -	78	Isaac Dennison.
John Fairbanks - -	81		Caleb Lane - - -	81	Caleb Lane.
Isaac How - - -	82		Fanny Dade - - -	74	William Dade.
Rebecca Hill - - -	86		Jonathan Robinson -	80	Jonathan Robinson.
Anna New - - -	79		Ruth Burnham - - -	73	Andrew Burnham.
NATICK.			Eunice Hodgkins - -	81	Eunice Hodgkins.
Abigail Sawin - - -	79		Anna Poland - - -	86	Enoch Bray.
Phebe Goodnow - -	79		Jerusha Rust - - -	83	Jerusha Rust.
Benoni Muzzy - - -	78		Joanna Andrews - -	96	Joanna Andrews.
Abel Perry - - -	83		Benjamin Webber - -	86	Benjamin Webber,
Lucy Rice - - -	79		*NEWBURY.*		
Ebenezer Bacon - -	57		Nehemiah Follansbee -	81	
ESSEX COUNTY.			Aaron Rogers - - -	78	
ANDOVER.			Moses Cheeney - - -	80	
Benjamin Carlton - -	84	Sarah Carlton.	Moses Short - - -	80	
Eleanor Johnson - -	92	John Johnson.	Moses Davis - - -	88	
Tabitha Gray - - -	75	William Styles.	Parker Jaques - - -	86	
Joshua Johnson - -	84	Joshua Johnson.	William Custis - -	79	
Isaac Giddings - -	85	Isaac Giddings.	Farnham Howe - -	77	
Hannah Berry - - -	71	Hannah Berry.	Daniel Flanders - -	80	
Samuel Gunnison - -	53	Samuel Gunnison.	Silas Pearson - - -	83	
Dudley Woodbridge -	80	Dudley Woodbridge.	Daniel Adams, jr. - -	80	
Lucy Frye - - -	84	Job T. Cole.	Molly Dole - - -	78	
			Sarah Follansbee - -	78	

6

MASSACHUSETTS—Continued.

Names of pensioners for revolutionary or military services.	Ages.	Names of heads of families with whom pensioners resided June 1, 1840.	Names of pensioners for revolutionary or military services.	Ages.	Names of heads of families with whom pensioners resided June 1, 1840.
ESSEX—Continued.			ESSEX—Continued.		
NEWBURY—Continued.			AMESBURY.		
Lydia Woodwell	80		Betty Hoyt	83	William Hoyt.
Lydia Chase	87		Jerusha Clark	81	Lucius W. Clark.
Ann Harris	80		John Pressy	83	John Pressy.
Sarah Hanson	77		Elizabeth Morrill	77	Thomas J. Pratt.
Elizabeth Woodman	86				
Hannah Lunt	82		SALISBURY.		
			Elizabeth Knight	76	Elizabeth Knight.
NEWBURYPORT.			William Morrill	80	William Morrill.
James Bradbury	79		Rhoda Greely	81	Rhoda Greely.
Jeremiah Blanchard	78		Robert Fowler	80	Robert Fowler.
Samuel Pilsbury	78		Abigail Nye	86	Abigail Clark.
William Tappan	80		Edward Dorr	81	Edward Dorr.
Jonathan Gage	80		Polly Crocker	79	James Crocker.
Jonathan Kettell	79		Moses Collins	83	Moses Collins.
John Rutherford	79		Joseph Stevens	83	Joseph Stevens.
Abraham Wheelwright	83		Mary Carr	81	John Hinkson.
Benjamin Gould	89		Moses Pike	89	Moses Pike.
Moses Somerby	80		Jonathan Stockman	78	Jonathan Stockman.
Samuel Emerson	82				
Philip Bagley	84		HAMILTON.		
Moses Davenport	84		Stephen Brown	82	Stephen Brown
Abraham Dodge	75		James Brown	87	James Brown.
Ann Levering	81		Joseph Patch	75	Joseph Patch.
Olive Folsom	77				
Mary Beck	82		IPSWICH.		
Martha Bragdon	71		Thomas Kimball	79	Thomas Kimball.
Sarah Murray	87		Susan S. Farley	70	Susan S. Farley.
Sarah Pearson	87		Samuel Lancaster	83	Samuel Lancaster.
Mercy Richards	82		James Fuller	81	James Fuller.
Ellen Clark	90		Nathaniel Herd	76	James Peatfield.
Hannah Davis	85		William F. Andrews	78	William F. Andrews.
Hannah Dowell	84		Daniel Ross	83	Daniel Ross.
Catharine Coffin	83		William Kinsman	86	William Kinsman.
Lydia Brag	86		John Burnham	85	John Burnham.
Sarah Hills	76		Jeremiah Ross	85	Thomas Foster.
Sarah Tucker	76		John H. Boardman	87	Aaron Cogswell, jr.
Mehitable Cutter	78		Susanna Treadwell	93	Susanna Treadwell.
Ednah Haskell	80		Henry Russell	82	Henry Russell.
Rebecca Rogers	77		Thomas Spiller	83	Thomas Spiller.
Patience Silloway	77		Abraham Perkins	93	Abraham Perkins.
			Thomas Ross	85	Thomas Ross.
BOXFORD.			Daniel Smith	85	Daniel Smith.
Eleanor Hall	77	Samuel Hall.	Nathaniel Fuller	80	Nathaniel Fuller.
Enos Runnels	83	Enos Runnels.	John Clement	51	Ira Worcester.
Sarah Peabody	86	Benjamin Peabody.	Mary Staniford	82	Mary Staniford.
Simeon Cole	78	Simeon Cole.			
Samuel Carleton	89	Samuel Carleton.	BEVERLY.		
Rebecca Russell	77	Peabody Russell.	Thomas Barrett	81	Thomas Barrett.
Olivia Bixby	85	Solomon Perley.	Samuel Cole	88	Samuel Cole.
Josiah Woodbury	86	Josiah Woodbury.	Rebecca Butman	69	Rebecca Butman.
			Isaac Smith	80	Isaac Smith.
GEORGETOWN.			Ebenezer Ray	81	Ebenezer Ray.
John Fitts	76	David Mighill.	Mark Morse	82	Mark Morse.
Abigail Poor	88	Daniel Palmer.	Rachel Lakeman	85	Rachel Lakeman.
Nathaniel Burpee	79	Almshouse.	Mary Porter	85	Mary Porter.
			Nathaniel Friend	76	Nathaniel Friend.
ROWLEY.			Benjamin Woodberry	82	Benjamin Woodberry.
Sarah Hobson	85	Sarah Lambert.	Judith Pickett	84	Judith Pickett.
Susanna Dresser	88	Benjamin Dresser.	Anna Nash	85	Anna Nash.
Mehitable Scott	77	James T. Scott.	Mary Brown	76	Mary Brown.
Elizabeth Clark	73	Elizabeth Clark.	Hale Hilton	80	Hale Hilton.
Annes Spiller	76	Annes Spiller.	John Annable	80	John A. Bartel.
Caleb Jackson	86	Caleb Jackson.	Thomas Dodge	77	Almshouse.
TOPSFIELD.			LYNNFIELD.		
Elijah Cummings	77	Elijah Cummings.	Ebenezer Parsons	79	Ebenezer Parsons.
Abigail Perkins	80	David Perkins.	Daniel Needham	79	Daniel Needham.
Lydia Dennen	75	Joel R. Peabody.			
Joshua Town	85	Ebenezer Town.	SAUGUS.		
Benjamin Pike	86	Benjamin Pike.	Abijah Cheever	81	Abijah Cheever.
Timothy Ross	89	Hezekiah B. Perkins.	Sarah Carleton	91	Isaac Carleton.
Samuel Flood	78	John G. Flood.	Lydia Danforth	77	Lydia Danforth.
ESSEX.			MIDDLETON.		
Miriam Choate	68	David Choate.	Sarah Wilkins	90	Sarah Thomas.
William Andrews	81	William Andrews.			
Abigail Butler	79	Abigail Butler.	DANVERS.		
Aaron Low	85	Warren Low.	Benjamin Fuller	65	John Edmonds.
Susan Foster	74	Eli Shelden.	Lemuel Horton	80	John Edmonds.
Benjamin Burnham	85	Benjamin Burnham.	Edward Shehane		
Sarah Burnham	79	Sarah Burnham.	Nancy Harwood	74	Nancy Harwood.
			Anna Larrabee	85	Sarah Larrabee.

MASSACHUSETTS—Continued.

Names of pensioners for revolutionary or military services.	Ages.	Names of heads of families with whom pensioners resided June 1, 1840.	Names of pensioners for revolutionary or military services.	Ages.	Names of heads of families with whom pensioners resided June 1, 1840.
ESSEX—Continued.			**ESSEX—Continued.**		
DANVERS—Continued.			CITY OF SALEM—Continued.		
Gideon Foster - - -	91	Gideon Foster.	Joseph Thompson - - -	84	J. Thompson.
Aaron Porter - - -	83	Aaron Porter.	William Mugford - - -	77	W. Mugford.
William Flint - - -	80	William Flint.	Jesse Smith - - -	83	Jesse Smith.
John Josselynn - - -	79	James Goodale.	Edward Brown - - -	84	George F. Brown.
Elizabeth Waitt - - -	78	Samuel Wait.	Stephen Wood - - -	93	E. Low.
Richard Elliot - - -	78	Richard Elliot.	Jonathan Edwards - -	55	J. Edwards.
Elizabeth Ross - - -	82	Elizabeth Rust.	John Henfield - - -	84	J. Towne.
Francis Peabody - - -	80	E. B. Wilkins.			
			LYNN.		
ROCKPORT.			Polly Berry - - -	69	Rachel Tapley.
Joshua Gott - - -	86	Joshua Gott, jr.	Sarah Ireson - - -	82	Samuel J. Ireson.
Annis Tarr - - -	78	Annis Tarr.	Ann Lye - - -	73	Ann Lye.
Jabez Tarr - - -	81	Jabez Tarr.	Mary Ann Holmes - -	49	Mary Ann Holmes.
Isaac Rowe - - -	86	David Brewer.	James Newhall - - -	83	James Newhall.
Martha Abbot - - -	77	Martha Abbot.	Abigail Tarbox - - -	87	John Coates.
Joshua Clark - - -	84	Peter Clark.	Hannah Bruce - - -	77	Hannah Bruce.
Betsey Rowe - - -	78	Samuel Parker.	Eliza Simonds - - -	49	Eliza Simonds.
James Story - - -	77	James Story.	Eliza Organ - - -	75	Edmund Waite.
			Mary Mansfield - - -	76	Mary Mansfield.
MANCHESTER.			Rebecca Batts - - -	84	William Newhall.
Isaac Allen - - -	82	Isaac Allen.	James Mullen - - -	79	Henry B. Mullen.
Isaac Lee - - -	79	Isaac Lee.	Sarah Newhall - - -	74	Sarah Newhall.
John West - - -	92	Nehemiah Goldsmith.	Amos Blanchard - -	74	Amos Blanchard.
Nathaniel Allen - -	81	Luther Allen.	Israel Wing - - -	88	Henry Benton.
Elizabeth Norwood -	86	Elizabeth Norwood.	William Laskey - - -	78	Peter Parks.
Jane Burges - - -	80	Jane Burges.	Dinah Haymore - -	84	Rebecca Moulton.
William Catham - -	84	William Catham.	Rebecca Higgins - -	33	Rebecca Higgins.
Anna Lendall - - -	79	Thomas S. Blanchard.	Betty Low - - -	54	George Jillson.
			Daniel Watts - - -	74	Daniel Watts.
MARBLEHEAD.			William Wiggins - -	77	William Wiggins.
William Thompson -	83	William Thompson.			
Mary Cash - - -	92	George Ramsdell.	**HAMPDEN COUNTY.**		
Peter Rix - - -	60	Peter Rix.	WESTFIELD.		
Mary Curtiss - - -	84	Mary Curtiss.	Abel Griswold - - -	80	Abel Griswold.
Mary Brown - - -	75	Mary Brown.	Ephraim Slaughter - -	85	Sylvanus Slaughter.
Stephen Twist - - -	75	Stephen Twist.	Hannah Noble - - -	98	Electar Norton.
Ambrose Allen - - -	79	Ambrose Allen.	Timothy Stebbins - -	78	Timothy Stebbins.
Mary Trefry - - -	78	Mary Trefry.	Samuel Reed - - -	82	Samuel F. Reed.
Jane Nutting - - -	85	Jane Caswell.	Simon Smith - - -	81	Daniel Smith.
Hannah Bridges - -	82	Richard Caswell.	Patience Gaylord - -	73	Patience Gaylord.
Richard Frost - - -	71	Richard Frost.	Luther Atkins - - -	82	Luther Atkins.
John Union - - -	56	Peter Union.			
Nancy Stacey - - -	86	Asa Hooper.	RUSSEL.		
Margaret Savage - -	84	Margaret Savage.	Newman Bishop - - -	82	Newman Bishop.
Sarah Furniss - - -	89	John Felton.	Jacob Loomis - - -	83	Jacob Loomis.
Hannah Hooker - -	82	Hannah Hooker.			
Mrs. Cheever - - -	75	Mrs. Cheever.	MONTGOMERY.		
Sarah Russell - - -	78	Samuel Porter.	George Gorham - - -	84	Russel Gorham.
Elizabeth Colley - -	84	Edward Dixley.			
David Quill - - -	63	David Quill.	SOUTHWICK.		
Lydia Grant - - -	75	Thomas Nichelson.	Elisha Parker - - -	74	Elisha Parker.
Sarah Homan - - -	92	Sarah Homan.	Jonathan Hutchinson -	87	Jonathan Hutchinson.
Mary Wells - - -	75	Mary Wells.	James Taylor - - -	82	James B. Taylor.
Elizabeth Devereux -	83	Joshua Goss.			
Mrs. Homan - - -	80	John Homan.	CHESTER.		
Mary C. Harriss - -	68	Hannah Harriss.	Elijah Churchill - - -	84	
Abigail Cowell - - -	47	Abigail Cowell.			
Deborah Lindsey - -	71	Deborah Lindsey.	BLANDFORD.		
Sarah Roundey - - -	88	Sarah Roundey.	Anthony Sizer - - -	87	Anthony Sizer.
Mary Kelly - - -	83	Samuel Cloutman.			
Mary Stephens - - -	87	Polly Proctor.	WEST SPRINGFIELD—*Feeding Hills parish.*		
Samuel Green - - -	67	Samuel Green.	Benjamin Copley - -	78	Benjamin Copley.
Hannah Caswell - -	73	Sarah Knapp.	Stephen Bumphrey - -	87	Stephen Bumphrey.
Samuel Bowden - -	89	Samuel Bowden.	Phineas Leonard - -	89	Dwight Leonard.
Thomas Tindley - -	48	Thomas Tindley.	Jeremiah Liswell - -	42	Thomas Liswell.
Tabitha Darby - - -	75	} Almshouse.			
Hannah Gilbert - - -	78		*Agawam parish.*		
John D. Hammond -	56		Amy Clark - - -	80	A. S. Starkweather.
Hannah Hamson - -	81	Nancy Butman.	Mary Porter - - -	87	Harvey Porter.
Mary James - - -	82	Samuel P. Bassett.	Mabel Bowe - - -	82	Asa Austin.
Sally Williams - - -	83	Stephen Hathaway.	Gad Warriner - - -	82	Gad Warriner.
Jane Roundey - - -	73	Jane Roundey.	John Egleston - - -	84	John Egleston, jr.
			First parish.		
CITY OF SALEM.			Simeon Smith - - -	86	Simeon Smith.
Jane Peabody - - -	78	J. Peabody.	Abigail Allen - - -	83	Michael Marsh.
Moses Townsend - -	82	M. Townsend.	Abigail Colton - - -	78	Jesse McIntire.
Noah Hobart - - -	83	N. Hobart.	Joseph Telt - - -	81	Louisa Rogers.
John Howard - - -	85	J. Howard.	Roger Cooley - - -	79	Roger Cooley.
Aaron Purbeck - - -	84	A. Purbeck.			
W. Prossy - - -	91	M. Saunders.			
Joseph Eveleth - - -	84	J. Eveleth.			

Names of pensioners for revolutionary or military services.	Ages.	Names of heads of families with whom pensioners resided June 1, 1840.	Names of pensioners for revolutionary or military services.	Ages.	Names of heads of families with whom pensioners resided June 1, 1840.
HAMPDEN—Continued.			**HAMPDEN—Continued,**		
WEST SPRINGFIELD—Ireland parish.			MONSON.		
David Wood - - -	77	David Wood.	Paul Chapin - - -	85	Patty Pease.
Naomi Ludington - -	85	Jason Ludington.	John Shaw - - -	85	John Shaw.
Judith Perkins - -	72	Edwin Perkins.	Ruth Thayer - - -	80	Alexander Maxfield.
Jabez Edwards - -	77	Joseph Edwards.	Isaac Jones - - -	87	Charles B. Jones.
Jube Ely - - -	78	Jube Ely.	Fanny Gates - - -	77	Henry Gates.
Enoch Ely - - -	85	Enoch Ely.	Stephen W. Warner - -	80	Stephen Warner.
Caleb Tuttle - -	79	Caleb Tuttle.	Joseph Peck - - -	83	Solomon L. Peck.
Lydia Jones - - -	78	Pliny Jones.	Anna Harvey - - -	86	Stephen Nichols.
Erastus Morgan - -	76	Erastus Morgan.	Sarah Munn - - -	80	Calvin Munn.
Joseph Ely - - -	83	Joseph Ely.	Ezra Tucker - - -	90	Joel Tucker.
			Ezra Tupper - - -	78	E. Tupper.
LONG MEADOW— West parish.			Daniel Mixter - - -	85	Azariah Butler.
Freelove Chandler -	84	Dimond Chandler.			
Stephen Keep - -	75	Stephen Keep.	PALMER.		
Gaius Bliss - - -	79	Gaius Bliss.	Jonathan Hunt - - -	80	Jonathan Hunt.
Mary Parker - -	79	Ira Parker.	Naomi Strickland - -	78	Warner C. Lemon.
Levi Crandall - -	80	Levi Crandall.	Alice Perry - - -	70	John Perry.
Naomi Robinson - -	76	Naomi Robinson.	Huldah Ball - - -	79	Huldah Ball.
East parish.			Samuel Taylor - - -	79	Samuel Taylor.
Anna Lathrop - -	79	Nathaniel Billings.	Eleanor McClintock - -	85	Tryphena McClintock.
Jacob Hills - - -	76	Jacob Hills.			
James Stebbins - -	79	Samuel Markham.	SPRINGFIELD.		
Philip Butterfield -	82	F. M. Hamblet.	Elsea Loomis - - -	73	Elsea Loomis.
Lewis White - -	80	Susan Ashley.	Buller Thayer - - -	70	Carlton Thayer.
			Jonathan Smith - -	79	Benjamin Walcot.
WILBRAHAM—North parish.			Francis Bliss - - -	47	Francis Bliss.
Charles Cooley - -	84	Luther B. Bliss.	Thaddeus Ferry - -	80	Roswell Clements.
David Shields - -	84	David Shields.	Catharine Allen - -	80	Calvin Hunter.
Joshua Wallbridge -	81	Joshua Wallbridge.	Desire Bangs - - -	79	Oliver Shattuck.
Isaac Lewis - -	80	Isaac Lewis.	Caleb Stacey - - -	79	Caleb Stacey.
Titus Amidon - -	77	Titus Amidon.	Simson Pomeroy - -	86	Simson Pomeroy.
Esther Calkins - -	77	Mary Calkins.	Hannah Taylor - -	79	Wid. Julius Dart.
Wealthy Hancock -	77	Wealthy Hancock.	Susanna Richmond - -	79	Zimri Richmond.
South parish.			John Stevenson - -	82	John Stevenson.
Stephen Newell - -	82	John Newell.	Levi Dart - - -	76	Levi Dart.
Ephraim Chaffee - -	79	David Burt.	John S. Edwards - -	76	John S. Edwards.
Elijah Button - -	85	Justus Bedortha.	Dorcas Whitley - -	77	Dorcas Whitley.
Olive Chaffee - -	78	Daniel Chaffee.	Peneller Cooley - -	82	Abner Cooley.
David Stebbins - -	80	David Stebbins.	George Blake - - -	82	George Blake.
			Hannah Stevens - -	90	Jonathan Blake.
TOLLAND.			Reuben Burt - - -	92	Reuben Burt, jr.
Jesse Hall - - -	83	Jesse Hall.	Amos Skeele - - -	92	Amos Skeele.
Titus Hubbard - -	76	Titus Hubbard.	Mehitable Griswold - -	84	Mehitable Griswold.
William Moore - -	80	William Moore.			
Dolly Marshall - -	74	Dolly Marshall.	**SUFFOLK COUNTY.**		
Isaac Miller - -	82	Jesse Miller.	CITY OF BOSTON—1st ward.		
Cephas Mills - -	80	Cephas Mills.	John Fillebrown - -	84	Lewis Smith.
			Nathaniel Emmes - -	80	Nathaniel Emmes.
GRANVILLE—East parish.			Martin Loyd - - -	78	Hezekiel Putnam.
Olive Buttles - -	79	R. & L. Buttles.	Joseph F. Ferdand - -	87	John F. Conant.
George Hubbard - -	85	George Hubbard.	Michael Orcutt - -	84	Thomas Loring.
Thomas Pexton - -	80	Stephen Spelman, 2d.	Judith Clark - - -	79	Judith Clark.
Timothy Gibbons -	78	Lucius Gibbons.	John Sholes - - -	78	Edward Carnes.
West parish.			Elizabeth McMillion -	81	Jonathan Cushing.
Seth Parsons - -	82	Seth Parsons.	Elizabeth Cunill - -	69	Daniel Conant.
			Mary Bradford - -	86	Samuel Jones.
BRIMFIELD.			*2d ward.*		
Sevia Sivzer - -	98	Sevia Sivzer.	Sarah Gray - - -	80	Michael Anderson.
C. Ward - - -	83	Christopher Ward.	Elizabeth Stockwell -	77	Robert Hodge.
Joseph Griggs - -	90	Orlando Griggs.	John Stevens - - -	82	John Jewell.
Thomas Charles - -	82	Thomas Charles.	*3d ward.*		
David Nichols - -	85	David Nichols.	Hannah Lilly - - -	83	John Lilly.
Lucy Lambert - -	82	Elijah Lambert.	Sarah Baldwin - -	70	William French.
Baly Bond - - -	80	Harvey Russell.	James Cussell - -	84	Edmund D. Cussell.
William Jones - -	82	William J. Sherman.	Lydia Beals - - -	78	Lydia Beals.
			Sally Annis - - -	72	William Annis.
HOLLAND.			Rachel Peabody - -	72	Rachel Peabody.
Maly Pike - - -	83	David B. Dean.	*4th ward.*		
Eunice Sherman - -	87	Zebina Fletcher.	Ruth Arnold - - -	82	Ruth Arnold.
			Oliver Johonnet - -	80	Oliver Johonnet.
LUDLOW.			Abigail Selman - -	87	Eleazer Johnson.
Timothy Jones - -	78	Henry Graves.	*5th ward.*		
Jonathan Rice - -	80	Alpheus Rice.	Jonas Welch - - -	86	James Ridgway.
Peninah Goodell - -	83	Sarah Goodell.	Richard Caswell - -	83	Lewis Hinchman.
Patience Pratt - -	79	Patience Pratt.	Sarah Ramsden - -	99	Reuben Ramsden.
			Elizabeth Smaledge -	84	Stephen D. Salmon.
WALES.			William Jemeson - -	81	William Jemeson.
Sevia Thayer - -	81	Alfred Nelson.	Lucy Stodder - - -	82	Susan Fisk.
Josiah Eaton - -	84	Josiah Eaton.	Priscilla Darling - -	76	
Caleb Edson - -	85	Nancy Munger.	Mary Lemuir - - -	76	
James Walker - -	87	James Walker.			

MASSACHUSETTS—Continued.

Names of pensioners for revolutionary or military services.	Ages.	Names of heads of families with whom pensioners resided June 1, 1840.	Names of pensioners for revolutionary or military services.	Ages.	Names of heads of families with whom pensioners resided June 1, 1840.
SUFFOLK—Continued.			**SUFFOLK—Continued.**		
Boston—Continued.			*Boston—Continued.*		
6th ward.			*12th ward—Continued.*		
Elizabeth Adams - - -	73	Ralph Smith.	Nathaniel Hayden - - -	78	Nathaniel Hayden.
Elias Cotton - - -	84	Elias Cotton.	Hannah Kent - - -	65	
Catharine Gibbs - -	73	James C. Wild.	Hannah Allen - - -	69	Samuel Allen.
Sarah H. Haywood - -	70	Sarah H. Haywood.	James McFarlen - - -	40	James McFarlen.
7th ward.			Susanna Parker - - -	77	Susanna Parker.
Sarah Neagles - - -	71	George Gibson.	Elizabeth Hayden - - -	75	Jonathan Dunbar.
Sarah Homans - - -	68	John Homans.	Catharine Johnson - - -	50	Cartharine Johnson.
8th ward.			George Bender - - -	89	
David Hill.			Samuel Dow - - -	87	William B. Harding.
9th and 10th wards.			William Mills - - -	76	William Mills.
None.			Lucy Wells - - -	74	Eleazer M. P. Wells.
11th ward.			*CHELSEA.*		
Mary Johnson - - -	74	James B. Johnson.	Susanna Green - - -	81	Susanna Green.
Margaret Kilton - -	79	John Kilton.	Persis Thayer - - -	63	Zachariah Hall, jr.
Ann Hancock - - -	79	Henry K. Hancock.	Mary Pratt - - -	83	Mary Pratt.
Elizabeth Spear - -	80	Elizabeth Spear.	Caleb Pratt - - -	77	Caleb Pratt.
Zachariah Rhodes - -	85	Zachariah Rhodes.			
Rebecca Copeland - -	83	Joseph Copeland.	**NANTUCKET COUNTY.**		
12th ward.			*NANTUCKET.*		
James Bradford - - -	63		John Wilber - - -	78	John Wilber.
Jemima Burnham - - -	84				

STATE OF RHODE ISLAND.

Names of pensioners for revolutionary or military services.	Ages.	Names of heads of families with whom pensioners resided June 1, 1840.	Names of pensioners for revolutionary or military services.	Ages.	Names of heads of families with whom pensioners resided June 1, 1840.
PROVIDENCE COUNTY.			**PROVIDENCE—Continued.**		
CITY OF PROVIDENCE—1st ward.			*CITY OF PROVIDENCE—Continued.*		
Mary Daggett - - -	84	Mary Daggett.	*4th ward—Continued.*		
Sarah Olney - - -	84	Mary J. Carr.	Sarah Dyer - - -	95	Sarah Dyer.
Elisha Dillingham - -	87	Elisha Dillingham.	Benjamin Eddy - - -	26	Benjamin Eddy.
Thomas Luther - -	87	Josias L. Luther.	Elizabeth Slocum - - -	85	Ruth Spink.
Susanna Bradford -	80	Susanna Bradford.	Pardon Mason - - -	81	Pardon Mason.
Lewis Hill - - -	49	Lewis Hill.	Thomas Coles - - -	87	Thomas Coles.
Jabez Allen - - -	78	Mary Montgomery.	Benjamin Peck - - -	70	Benjamin Peck.
2d ward.			Sarah Larned - - -	72	Sarah Larned.
William Harding - -	80	William Harding.	*5th ward.*		
Mary Vaughan - -	84	Ably Vaughan.	Charles Lippitt - - -	86	Charles Lippitt.
Rhoda Barton - -	88	Rhoda Barton.	Martha Fales - - -	77	Betsey Paine.
William Wilkinson - -	79	William Wilkinson.	Barnard Eddy - - -	77	Barnard Eddy.
Mary Spelman - -	85	Robert Perkegs.	Elizabeth Rauson - - -	75	Joseph Rauson.
James Calder - - -	85	John Calder.	Rosamond Brown - - -	79	John Humphrey.
Hannah Wilbour - -	82	Hannah Wilbour.	Samuel Currie - - -	79	Samuel Currie.
Samuel McClanan - -	80	Samuel McClanan.	Sarah Westcott - - -	87	Sarah Westcott.
Daniel Dexter - -	82	Stanton Thurber.	Elizabeth Hull - - -	80	Jacob C. Gould.
Hannah Robinson - -	78	Mary Lovell.	Phebe Gladding - - -	77	John Gladding.
Rhoda Newcomb - -	49	Rhoda Newcomb.	Zipporah Field - - -	77	Zipporah Field.
Grace Man - - -	66	Grace Man.	Nathan B. Leonard - - -	78	Luther Buffington.
Fenna Angell - -	83	Fenna Angell.	Elizabeth Dawley - - -	83	Welthon Dawley.
Andrew Burnett - -	69	Andrew Burnett.	Thankful Clarke - - -	83	Pardon Clarke.
3d ward.			Ruth Oswell - - -	73	Hezekiah Willard.
Benjamin Hodges - -	73	Peter Langley.	Aaron Turner - - -	82	Patience T. Battey.
Elias D. Trafton - -	84	Elias D. Trafton.	*6th ward.*		
Elizabeth Page - -	84	William Aplin.	Sabia Walcott - - -	73	Isaac Field, 2d.
Simeon Ingraham - -	91	Simeon Ingraham.	Tabitha Smith - - -	84	Tabitha Smith.
Samuel Ezhforth - -	85	Samuel Ezhforth.	Daniel Pettey - - -	83	Enos H. Weeden.
John Howland - -	82	John Howland.	Lydia Fenner - - -	73	Cornelius G. Fenner.
Elizabeth Rogers - -	80	Frances R. Arnold.	Sarah Smith - - -	85	Sarah Smith.
4th ward.			Peleg Hull - - -	85	Peleg Hull.
Mary Cranston - -	85	William B. Cranston.	Mary Low - - -	85	Mary Low.
Mary Hoppin - -	88	Royal Farnum.	Penelope Williams - - -	75	Sheldon Battey.
Ephraim Bowen - -	87	Ephraim Bowen.	Henry Whitman - - -	76	Benjamin R. Whitman.
John Perrin - -	87	John Perrin.	Mary Sweet - - -	84	Mary Sweet.
Thomas Philburk - -	80	Henry Cushing.	Betsey Williams - - -	76	Benajah Williams.
Susanna Weld - -	79	Susanna Weld.			
Sarah Collins - -	68	Welcome Collins.	*NORTH PROVIDENCE.*		
Esther Stone - -	78	Ethan Stone.	Benjamin Burrell - - -	81	Benjamin Burrell.
Reuben Wright (naval service)	53	Reuben Wright.	Huldah Swetland - - -	84	Huldah Swetland.
Susanna Anthony - -	85	Burrington Anthony.	Lois Marsh - - -	89	Jefferson Inmorn.
Huldat Mahony - -	84	Horace Capson.	Lucy Field - - -	75	Lucy Field.
Calvin Tower - -	42	Calvin Tower.	Calvin Ripley - - -	93	Charles Ripley.

Names of pensioners for revolutionary or military services.	Ages.	Names of heads of families with whom pensioners resided June 1, 1840.
PROVIDENCE—Continued.		
NORTH PROVIDENCE—Continued.		
John Montgomery	81	John Montgomery.
Elizabeth Gregory	91	Joseph Smith.
Dorcas Sherman	77	Dorcas Sherman.
Sarah Hawkins	80	Sarah Hawkins.
Stephen Randall	79	Stephen Randall.
Leonard Williams	81	Leonard Williams.
Waite Brown	87	Jason Young.
SMITHFIELD.		
Jane Vose	79	Mary Eddy.
Jemima Tucker	93	Nancy Tucker.
Abial Tripp	77	Abial Tripp.
Jesse Carrol	77	Jesse Carrol.
Mary Morse	80	Ellis Tompson.
David Calwell	85	Willard Calwell.
Noah Crossman	86	Alpheus Crossman.
Joel Aldrich	82	Joel Aldrich.
Abigail Sayles	82	Olney Mowry.
Zelotes Tyler	80	David S. Standley.
Delia Sprague	84	Daniel P. Sprague.
Ebenezer Balcome	48	Ebenezer Balcome.
Tampson Tripp	73	Tampson Tripp.
Israel Arnold	85	Israel Arnold.
Mary McIntire	84	Mary Jencks.
Lois Baker	79	Benjamin F. Holley.
Smith Sayles	81	Smith Sayles.
Rose Sayles	78	Rose Sayles.
Jeremiah Mowry	79	Jeremiah Mowry.
Daniel Wilbour	79	Daniel Wilbour.
Jonathan Mowry	78	Benjamin Cushing.
Susanna Mowry	76	Susanna Mowry.
Oliver Smith	83	Oliver Smith.
Salsbury Freeman	80	Salsbury Freeman.
Betty Matthewson	86	Lewis Follett.
Elijah Smith	80	Simon Smith.
Benjamin Evans	77	Benjamin Evans.
Phebe Mann	93	Anna Mann.
Olive Aldrich	88	Welcome Aldrich.
Hannah Gross	83	Stephen Gross.
Stephen Hawkins	86	Hannah Taylor.
Lucretia Whitman	84	Lucinda Butler.
Nathaniel Arnold	77	John Waiscott.
Simon Paine	78	Amey Burlingame.
SCITUATE.		
Joseph Carpenter	84	Joseph Carpenter.
Waity Luther	81	Zadoc Luther.
Abigail Jencks	84	Abigail Jencks.
Thomas Smith	79	Joshua Smith.
Hannah Hill	89	Thomas Hill.
Priscilla Davis	77	Stephen R. Davis.
Sarah Walker	83	Jarvis Eddy.
Sarah Randall	69	Sarah Randall.
Job Taylor	78	Richard Olny.
Marcy Pakham	87	Josiah Westcott.
Ezekiel Bishop	78	Ezekiel Bishop.
Lydia Westcott	82	Thomas R. Westcott.
Jonathan Smith	94	Jonathan Smith.
Nicholas Thomas	84	Richard R. Thomas.
Amey Salesbury	–	Abel Salsbury.
Benjamin Boss	83	Benjamin Boss.
Stephen Harris	81	Russell Harris.
Samuel Kemball	78	Robert S. W. Hopkins.
Ruth Staples	79	Simon Staples.
Lydia Cole	80	Lydia Cole.
Reuben Stern	85	Reuben Stern.
Roby Atwood	84	Job W. Fiske.
David Burlingame	83	David Burlingame.
Huldah Aldrich	90	Huldah Aldrich.
Welthan Hughes	83	Welthan Hughes.
Martha Colwell	77	Uriah Colwell.
Abel Mowry	82	Abel Mowry.
John W. Cook	78	John W. Cook.
Stephen Westcott	77	Joshua Angell.
Christopher Edwards	83	Otis Mathewson.
Mary Randall	78	Oliver Randall.
Israel Knight	79	Israel Knight.
Samuel Henrys	83	Samuel Henrys.
Elizabeth Colvin	84	Moses Colvin.
Roby Collins	83	Richard Matteson.
Rebecca Eldred	78	Rebecca Eldred.
Sarah Ralph	77	Sarah Ralph.

Names of pensioners for revolutionary or military services.	Ages.	Names of heads of families with whom pensioners resided June 1, 1840.
PROVIDENCE—Continued.		
SCITUATE—Continued.		
William Battey	80	William Battey.
Nabby Manchester	74	Nehemiah Manchester.
Stephen Young	82	Stephen Young.
Comfort Knight	80	John Graves.
Sarah Baker	81	Sarah Baker.
John Vaughan	86	Eharer Phillips.
CUMBERLAND.		
Hannah Tower	93	Elijah Brown.
Noah Ballow	89	Noah Ballow.
Noah Butterworth	79	Susan Bullock.
Nathaniel Cook	92	Nathaniel Cook.
Stephen Chace	81	Stephen Chace.
Joseph Capron	89	Elisha Capron.
John S. Dexter	86	John S. Dexter.
Jerusha Darling	83	Jerusha Darling.
William Follett	82	William Follett.
Amey Fisk	79	Amey Fisk.
Lepha Haskill	72	Lepha Haskill.
Darius Hawkins	81	Rufus Hawkins.
Oliver Harris	81	Oliver Harris.
Abigail Havens	75	Lovett Havens.
Levi Lee	81	Levi Lee.
Jonathan Peck	80	Jonathan Peck.
William Rude	88	William Rude.
Amey Scott	84	Olney Scott.
Mary Sawyer	81	Mary Sawyer.
Ann Wilkinson	91	James Thompson.
Jeremiah Vose	74	Jeremiah Vose.
Leah Weatherhead	81	Daniel Weatherhead.
Samuel Haskill	85	Whipple Weatherhead.
Sylvia Whipple	81	Sylvia Whipple.
Elizabeth Grant	74	Eliab Whipple.
Lavina Whipple	84	Nathan Whipple.
Amaziah Weatherhead	82	Joseph Whipple.
Jedediah Jencks	79	Welcome Whipple.
Priscilla Faxon	75	Horatio Stockbridge.
Mary Howard	84	Ichabod Howard.
CRANSTON.		
Esek Dyer	82	Esek Dyer.
Richard Fenner	87	Welcome Fenner.
Elisha Arnold	76	Elisha Arnold.
John Arnold	76	John Arnold.
Simeon Smith	95	Remington Smith.
Reuben Smith	80	Reuben Smith.
Esther Waterman	79	Henry Waterman.
Sarah Greene	83	Caleb Williams.
Mary Ramsey	89	Anstress Waterman.
Abigail Mathewson	89	Mary G. Potter.
Mary Calvin	89	Caleb Calvin.
Mary Westcott	80	Niles Westcott.
Jonathan Knight	80	Sheldon Knight.
James Hill	87	James A. Hill.
Pardon Burlingame	84	Pardon Burlingame.
Mary Brayton	86	Mary Brayton.
JOHNSTON.		
James Olney	77	James Olney.
Jeremiah Manton	77	Jeremiah Manton.
Catharine Manton	79	Catharine Manton.
Esther Waterman	85	Resolved Waterman, 2d.
John Alverson	83	John Alverson.
Edward Waterman	82	Edward Waterman.
Russell Hall	84	Russell Hall.
GLOCESTER.		
Rachel Keech	89	Stephen Keech.
Samuel Winsor	82	Hannah Winsor.
Squire Williams	88	Joshua Williams.
Molly Wade	90	Oliver Wade.
Willard Wade	83	Willard Wade.
Jeremy Sweet	83	Jeremy Sweet.
Roby Wood	84	Luther Wood.
Sarah Mann	93	Charles Wade.
Aaron Bardine	77	Horace Bardine.
Nathaniel Sheldon	51	Nathaniel Sheldon.
John Trask	81	John Trask.
James Bowen	80	James Bowen.
Jesse Armstrong	80	Job Armstrong.
Obed Seaver	80	John Hawkins.
Esek Brown	85	Esek Brown.

RHODE ISLAND—Continued.

Names of pensioners for revolutionary or military services.	Ages.	Names of heads of families with whom pensioners resided June 1, 1840.	Names of pensioners for revolutionary or military services.	Ages.	Names of heads of families with whom pensioners resided June 1, 1840.
PROVIDENCE—Continued.			NEWPORT—Continued.		
GLOCESTER—Continued.			PORTSMOUTH.		
Reuben Place	78	Reuben Place.	Peleg Almy	79	Peleg Almy.
Thankful Wilbour	84	Thankful Wilbour.	Sophia Sisson	93	Sophia Sisson.
Elizabeth Mitchell	75	Joseph Mitchell.	William Lawton	85	William Lawton.
Sarah Andrews	81	Sarah Andrews.	Elizabeth Allen	84	Job Gray.
Temperance Edwards	75	Temperance Edwards.	George Sisson	89	George Sisson.
Simeon Bowen	82	Lyman Bowen.	Giles Lake	88	Christopher Lake.
Jemima Warner	78	Jemima Warner.	Samuel Cory	83	Samuel Cory.
David Kelley	88	Abel Whitaker.			
Martha Medbury	79	Samuel Steere.	MIDDLETOWN.		
Mary Steere	77	Mary Steere.	Elizabeth Taggart	73	Elizabeth Taggart.
Sarah Daggett	76	Seril M. Daggett.			
Thankful Smith	79	Pardon Hunt.	TIVERTON.		
			Richard Durfee	81	Richard Durfee.
FOSTER.			Susanna Dring	72	Thomas Dring.
Oliver Arnold	80	Oliver Arnold.	Elizabeth Dively	78	Elizabeth Dively.
Patience Brayton	77	John Brayton.	Isaac Negus	84	Isaac Negus.
Mary Bennett	82	Mary Bennett.	Daniel Sherman	82	Daniel Sherman.
Mary Bennett	83	Asher Bennett.	Elihu Gifford	81	Elihu Gifford.
Francis Brayton	76	Francis Brayton.	Mary Durfee	86	Mary Durfee.
Dorothy Cole	71	Dorothy Cole.	Margaret Manchester	78	Abraham Manchester.
Betsey Drown	81	Betsey Drown.	Giles Manchester	36	Giles Manchester.
Obadiah Easton	90	Obadiah Easton.	William Sherman	87	William Sherman.
Dorothy Howard	82	Dorothy Howard.	Thomas Remington	79	Thomas Remington.
Elizabeth Wilkinson	90	Benjamin Hopkins.	Knight Springer	83	Knight Springer.
Josiah Harrington	80	Josiah Harrington.	William Albert	78	William Albert.
Peleg Hopkins	85	Peleg Hopkins.	Borden Brayton	80	Borden Brayton.
Freelove Harrington	72	Freelove Harrington.	Lydia Humphrey	78	Lydia Humphrey.
James Howard	81	James Howard.	Thomas Wilcox	81	Thomas Wilcox.
Pernilepa Harrington	85	Peleg Harrington.	David Lake	78	David Lake.
Ezekiel Hopkins	82	Ezekiel Hopkins.	Nancy Taber	79	Peleg Wilcox.
Peter Hopkins	85	Peter Hopkins.	Abraham Manchester	78	Abraham Manchester.
Bethiah Morse	84	Bethiah Morse.	William Cook	84	William Cook.
Marcy Stone	77	Barton Randall.	Mary Wilcox	70	Samuel Lake.
Solomon Shipper	92	Solomon Shipper, jr.	Pardon Wilcox	78	Pardon Wilcox.
Mercy Taylor	77	Mercy Taylor.	Phebe Manchester	96	John Grinnell.
Drusilla Tucker	83	Drusilla Tucker.	John Carr	79	John Carr.
Ephraim Williams	84	Ephraim Williams.	Ichabod Simmons	78	William Simmons.
Martha Cornell	87	Daniel Walker.	Abner Simmons	77	Abner Simmons.
BURRILLVILLE.			LITTLE COMPTON.		
Asa Shelldin	83	Asa Shelldin.	John Almy	82	John Almy.
Elisha Sayles	83	Angell Sayles.	Sandford Almy	80	Sandford Almy, jr.
John Williams	80	John Williams.	George Brown	82	Humphrey Brown.
Lydia Mathewson	87	John Mathewson.	Ruth Clapp	86	Abner Brownell.
Rachel Logee	83	Joseph Emerson.	John Brown	78	John Brown.
Othenial Young	82	Alpheus Young.	Phebe Brownell	83	Phebe Brownell.
Olive Phillips	71	Silas Mowry.	Francis Wilbor	85	Alfred Brownell.
Rose Bowen	69	Rose Bowen.	Stephen Brownell	78	Stephen Brownell.
George Whipple	81	George Whipple.	Deborah Brownell	91	James Brownell.
John Esteen	78	John Esteen.	Thomas Briggs	80	Thomas Briggs.
Joanna Inmon	87	Jeremiah Mowry.	Sarah Briggs	77	Job Briggs.
Martha Cook	94	John Arnold.	Gideon Church	78	Lydia Church.
			Betsey Hunt	84	Betsey Hunt.
NEWPORT COUNTY.			Susanna Sisson	66	William Jordan.
NEWPORT.			Esther Manchester	78	Ephraim Manchester.
Martha Taber	96	Caleb S. Knights.	Ichabod Pearce	77	Ichabod Pearce.
Thankful Briggs	78	Gilbert Stanton.	Ruth Brownell	82	Israel Palmer.
Sarah Boss	82	Sarah Boss.	Emblem Palmer	91	Jonathan D. Palmer.
Rebecca Heath	60	Rebecca Heath.	Brownell Stoddard	84	Perry Simmons.
Abigail Weaver	77	Abigail Weaver.	Noah Shaw	82	Noah Shaw.
Elizabeth Mays	67	Elizabeth Mays.	Benjamin Tompkins	81	Thomas G. Tompkins.
Samuel Buffam	85	Gardiner Smith.	Mary Tompkins	74	Mary Tompkins.
Hannah Clarke	75	Sally Clarke.	Mary Tompkins	85	Mary Tompkins.
Samuel Young	89	Samuel Young.	Samuel Wilbor	81	Samuel Wilbor.
Martha Yeomans	89	Martha Yeomans.	John Springer	80	Hezekiah Woodworth.
Edith Holt	87	Nathaniel Holt.	Isaac Simmons	75	Charles Wood.
Asa Gates	84	Asa Gates.	James Walden	79	James Walden.
Nicholson Ward	80	Nicholson Ward.	Thomas White	79	Thomas White.
James Barker	60	James Barker.			
Elizabeth C. Perry	49	Elizabeth C. Perry.	NEW SHOREHAM.		
Elizabeth M. Perry	20	Arthur Ross.	Hannah Steadman	75	John E. H. Champlin.
Rebecca Alger	81	Mary Richmond.	Margaret Paine	75	Nathaniel B. Paine.
Daniel Peckham	82	Daniel Peckham.			
Sarah Smith	56	Sarah Smith.	JAMESTOWN.		
William Card	87	William Card.	John Remington	79	George Weeden.
Nathaniel Smith	76	Nathaniel Smith.			
Mary Dayton	83	Mary Dayton.	WASHINGTON COUNTY.		
Henri'tta Scott	70	George E. Nason.	SOUTH KINGSTON.		
Sally 'i ifft	85	Augustus Tifft.	Samuel R. Potter	83	Samuel R. Potter.
Francis Anderson	92	William Vars.	Ebenezer Smith	84	John A. Smith.
Sarah Clarke	66	Russell J. Clarke.	Mary Gardner	84	Mary Gardner.
			William Willson	79	William Willson.

RHODE ISLAND—Continued.

Names of pensioners for revolutionary or military services.	Ages.	Names of heads of families with whom pensioners resided June 1, 1840.
WASHINGTON—Continued.		
South Kingston—Continued.		
Thomas Billington	83	William Hill.
Sweet Briggs	85	Job Briggs.
Stephen Greene	84	Stephen Greene.
William C. Clarke	83	William C. Clarke.
Abigail Gardner	78	James A. Gardner.
Joseph Champlin	81	Frederick Chappell.
Gideon Greenman	88	Gideon Greenman.
Enoch Lewis	87	Enoch Lewis.
Sylvester Willcox	84	William P. Willcox.
Mary Oatley	75	Isaac J. Hopkins.
David Knight	84	Nathan Knight.
Silas Gardner	85	Cranston Gardner.
Margaret Barber	94	Moses Barber.
Abigail Gardner	94	William Sims.
Mary Smith	86	Mary Smith.
John Aldrich	81	Luke Aldrich.
William Lunt	95	William Lunt.
Timothy Peckham	85	Timothy Peckham.
William Tourjee	89	William Tourjee.
James Reynolds	83	James Reynolds.
Gideon Lillibridge	86	Gideon Lillibridge.
WESTERLY.		
John Cranston	87	John Cranston.
Rebecca Sims	85	Maxson Chase.
Desire Govit	86	Benajah Govit.
Smith Murphy	88	Smith Murphy.
Paul Babcock	80	Paul Babcock, jr.
Arnold Crumb	87	Coddington Bliven.
Sarah Ray	83	Gideon Ray.
Catharine Edwards	83	Clarke Edwards.
Thomas Sisson	81	Lebeas Sisson.
Esther Greene	78	Charles K. Greene.
Jude Taylor	86	Jude Taylor.
Perry Brumbley	81	Perry Brumbley.
Lois Chapman	80	Lois Chapman.
James Crandal	77	James Crandal.
Mary Peckham	88	William York.
Nathan Blivin	79	Nathan Blivin.
Clarke Hiscox	79	Clarke Hiscox.
Peleg Pukham	78	Peleg Pukham.
NORTH KINGSTON.		
William Reynolds	87	William Reynolds.
Oliver Spink	85	Oliver Spink.
Robert Eldred	79	Robert Eldred.
Elizabeth Reynolds	70	Emily Reynolds.
Ruth Whitehorne	73	Annos Baker.
Hannah Sherman	86	Joshua C. Baker.
Mary Nichols	77	George M. Shaw.
David Bissel	79	David Bissel.
James Updike	78	James Updike.
Elsey Babcock	77	Elsey Babcock.
George Congdon	80	George Congdon.
Sarah Clarke	86	Sarah Clarke.
Sylvester Johnson	84	Sylvester Johnson.
Joseph Corey	83	Joseph Corey.
Elizabeth Reynolds	79	Ezra D. Davis.
Samuel Browning	86	Stephen Smith.
Isaac Hall	79	Isaac Hall, jr.
Sarah Brown	85	Sarah Brown.
Zebulon Northup	98	William Corey.
Elizabeth Sweet	67	Elizabeth Sweet.
Peleg Card	85	Peleg Card.
Stukely Hill	85	Stukely Hill.
Sylvester Northup	79	Sylvester Northup.
EXETER.		
Anne Kinsley	73	Caleb Lawton.
Sarah Ann Gardner	75	Varnum Gardner.
Joshua Brown	83	Joshua Brown.
John Place	75	John Place.
Sarah Bales	86	Sarah Bales.
William Greene	85	Christopher C. Greene.
Landerick Sherman	78	Clarke Sherman.
Job Sherman	83	Job Sherman.
Daniel Sunderlin	85	Daniel Sunderlin.
Rufus Sherman	82	Othanial Sherman.
Deborah Whitman	70	Deborah Whitman.
Ezekiel Austin	83	Ezekiel Austin, jr.
Roger Sheldin	83	Roger Sheldin.
Daniel Barber	92	Daniel Barber.

Names of pensioners for revolutionary or military services.	Ages.	Names of heads of families with whom pensioners resided June 1, 1840.
WASHINGTON—Continued.		
CHARLESTOWN.		
Isaiah Burdich	79	Augustus Burdich.
Sarah Stanton	92	Lodowick Hoxsie.
Ethan Crandall	82	Ethan Crandall.
Augustus J. Lewis	81	Joseph H. Lewis.
Margaret Anthony	69	Margaret Anthony.
Thomas Chappell	84	Scranton Chappell.
Martha Kenyon	78	Martha Kenyon.
HOPKINTON.		
Joseph Braman	77	George W. Braman.
James Stanbry	81	James Stanbry.
Christopher Brown	84	Christopher Brown.
Thomas Brightman	89	Thomas Brightman.
Adam B. Champlin	77	Adam B. Champlin.
Nathaniel Hall	76	Nathaniel Hall.
RICHMOND.		
Moses Clark	92	Moses Clark.
Silas Moore	80	Silas Moore.
John Vallet	85	John Vallet.
William Kenyon	84	William Kenyon.
KENT COUNTY.		
WARWICK.		
Nathan Miller	88	
Joseph Arnold	84	
Anna Budlong	80	
Susanna Browning	81	
Caleb Arnold	86	
Phebe Levally	78	
Anna Clapp	94	
Betsey Baker	88	
Mary Bennett	87	
Phebe Gorton	87	
Catharine Rhodes	86	
Mary Rhodes	85	
Mary A. Budlong	86	
James Greene	83	
Phebe Phillips	83	
Mary Potter	82	
Hannah Arnold	81	
Martha Pearce	81	
Elizabeth Arnold	81	
Matthew Price	80	
Martha Potter	80	
Remington Arnold	79	
Remington Sherman	78	
James Rhodes	76	
Stephen Budlong	78	
Dorcas Clanning	76	
Waity Gardner	76	
Festus L. Thompson	52	
Ruth Whipple	64	
COVENTRY.		
Benjamin Greene	80	Benjamin Greene.
Mary Gorton	79	Mary Gorton.
Orpah Stafford	87	Jared Stafford.
Lucy Matteson	79	Henry A. Matteson.
Olive Peck	82	Olive Peck.
Caleb Whitman	86	Caleb Whitman.
James Capevill	84	James Capevill.
Betty Blanchard	85	Oliver Greene.
Abigail Briggs	83	Joseph Hart.
Reuben Porter	81	Charles Griffiths.
Mary Healy	–	Asahel Matteson.
David Reynolds	–	David Reynolds.
George Andrews	86	George Andrews.
Abel Wickes	85	Abel Wickes.
Rhoda Matteson	87	Benjamin A. Matteson.
Ezekiel Johnson	80	Ezekiel Johnson.
Jerusha Whaley	89	Raymond P. Goff.
William Waterman	77	Jonathan Whaley.
Robert Harnes	84	William Harris.
Mary Nichols	78	Mary Nichols.
John Hammond	84	John Hammond.
Susanna Matteson	89	Peleg Brown.
Stephen Matteson	81	Stephen Matteson.
Phebe Matteson	91	Rufus Matteson.
James Stafford	90	Daniel Tiffany.
Richard Arnold	78	Richard Arnold.
Dorcas Matteson	93	Cory Matteson.

RHODE ISLAND—Continued.

Names of pensioners for revolutionary or military services	Ages.	Names of heads of families with whom pensioners resided June 1, 1840.	Names of pensioners for revolutionary or military services.	Ages.	Names of heads of families with whom pensioners resided June 1, 1840.
KENT—Continued.			BRISTOL—Continued.		
COVENTRY—Continued.			BRISTOL—Continued.		
Thomas Cruff	86	Thomas Cruff.	Rachel Bourn	72	John Chadwick.
Elias Young	77	Hazard Champlin.	Aaron Easterbrooks	89	Aaron Easterbrooks.
Sarah Spencer	83	Orrin Spencer.	William Diman	81	Calvin Simmons.
Sarah Mitchell	87	John Wilcox.	Elizabeth Dimond	80	Fanny M. Jones.
Elizabeth Knight	90	Lawton Johnson.	Catharine Lindsey	88	Catharine Lindsey.
Sarah Potter	82	Loury C. Potter.	Susanna Smith	84	Mary Paine.
			Jonathan Fales	89	Jona. Fales.
EAST GREENWICH.			Lydia Attwood	78	Husey Bradford.
Jonathan Andros	78	Jonathan Andros.	Tabitha Bosworth	81	Ann Storrs.
Oliver Wickes	82	Oliver Wickes.	Palmela Lindsey	65	Palmela Lindsey.
Daniel Updike	79	Daniel Updike.	Betsey Smith	89	Palmela Lindsey.
Eunice Miller	91	Waity Sweet.	Phebe Smith	92	Phebe Smith.
Anna Whitmash	82	Mary Spencer.	Mary Brown	86	William Hoar.
Dute Weaver	82	Thomas A. Howland.	Benjamin Luther	79	Sylvester Luther.
Peleg Weden	83	Peleg Weden.	John D. Wolf	80	John D. Wolf.
Benedict Remington	80	Benedict Remington.	Elizabeth Slocum	86	Samuel Reed.
Benjamin Gardner	84	Betsey Tanner.	Jonathan Reynolds	77	Jonathan Reynolds.
Wanton Casey	81	Wanton Casey.	Bernard Haile	81	Stillman Welsh.
James Miller	86	James Miller.	Joseph Munro	79	Joseph Munro.
Anthony Spencer	78	Ezra Spencer.	Lydia Bunn	74	Bosworth Munro.
James Sweet	87	James Sweet.	Anthony Snell	78	Anthony Snell, jr.
John Carpenter	90	Colonel A. Carpenter.	Anna Cole	83	Benjamin Greene.
John Spencer	80	Richard Spencer.	Thomas Church	79	Thomas Church.
Peleg Whitman	78	Peleg Whitman.			
Greene Capron	82	Greene Capron.	WARREN.		
Andrew Fry	77	Andrew Fry.	Anna Cole	85	Samuel Luther, 2d.
Jeremiah Place	83	Jeremiah Place.	Anna Short	84	James Short.
Joseph Briggs	83	Joseph Briggs.	Seth Cole	84	Andrew Cole.
			Seabury Sisson	75	Betsey Kelley.
WEST GREENWICH.			Elizabeth Cole	87	Elizabeth Cole.
Job Whitford	84	Job Whitford.	Ichabod Cole	91	Philip Short.
Phebe James	72	Phebe James.	Jesse Brown	80	Fracil W. Brown.
Mary Bennet	84	Mary Bennet.	Lydia Kinnecutt	86	Oliver Johonnett.
Mary Allen	95	Mary Allen.	Frederick Luther	78	Allen Luther.
Nathan Straight	85	Nathan Straight.	Martin Luther	75	Martin Luther.
Joseph Bailey	84	Joseph Bailey.			
Olive Weaver	90	Robert Hall.	BARRINGTON.		
Desiah Ellis	86	Desiah Ellis.	Elizabeth Humphrey	78	Elizabeth Humphrey.
Job Harrington	80	Job Harrington.	Amy Bicknal	77	Amy Bicknal.
Abiah Watson	84	Abiah Watson.	Grindal Chase	83	Grindal Chase.
			Elizabeth Martin	85	Ambrose Martin.
BRISTOL COUNTY.			Anne Heath	95	Anne Heath.
BRISTOL.			Jonathan J. Drown	79	Jonathan J. Drown.
Stephen Talbee	85	Stephen Talbee, jr.	Lucy Peck	67	Lucy Peck.

STATE OF CONNECTICUT.

Names of pensioners for revolutionary or military services.	Ages.	Names of heads of families with whom pensioners resided June 1, 1840.	Names of pensioners for revolutionary or military services.	Ages.	Names of heads of families with whom pensioners resided June 1, 1840.
HARTFORD COUNTY.			HARTFORD—Continued.		
CITY OF HARTFORD.			HARTFORD CITY—Limits excepted—		
Isaac Bliss	80	Isaac Bliss.	Continued.		
Amos Ransom	80	Amos Ransom.	Lucy Sedgewick	67	William Sedgewick.
Elizabeth Seymour	74	Elizabeth Seymour.	Abigail Whitman	77	Abigail Whitman.
Susanna Dodd	84	Susanna Dodd.	Abijah Flagg	85	Abijah Flagg.
Elizabeth Kilborn	86	Elihu Denslow.	Mahetible Hurlbut	74	Roswall Hurlbut.
Martha Sedgewick	90	Charles Burr.	Ruth Elmer	78	Oliver S. Elmer.
Isaac Spencer	80	Isaac Spencer.	John W. Smith	56	John W. Smith.
Hepsebah Knowles	70	Heppy Knowles.	Frederick Lord	80	Frederick Lord.
Catharine Putnam	84	George Sumner.	Abigail Anderson	81	Jesse B. Bull.
Abner Squires	78	Abner Squires, jr.	Theodore Spencer	81	Theodore Spencer.
Rebecca Wilcox	77	Rebecca Roberts.			
Joel Carter	75	Joel Carter.	WEATHERSFIELD.		
Jonathan Olcott	82	Jonathan Olcott.	Jemima Filley	84	Hiram E. Stoddard.
Nathaniel Hooker	79	Nathaniel Hooker.	Mary Belden	76	Mary Belden.
Oliver Clapp	82	Betsey Clapp.	Richard Belden	78	Richard Belden.
Jacob Sargent	70	Jacob Sargent.	Marian Ackley	76	John Flint.
Mary Kingsbury	78	Mary Kingsbury.	Deborah Goodrich	72	Allen Robins.
Silas Fuller	65	Silas Fuller.	John Kilby	79	James Hurlbut, 2d.
Sarah Wickham	79	James S. Wickham.	William Wolcott	86	William Wolcott.
			Bezaleel Thrasher	82	Bezaleel Thrasher.
HARTFORD CITY—Limits excepted.			Mary Dickinson	88	Joseph Wright.
Simon Wells	86	Simon Wells.	Abigail Wright	84	Abigail Wright.
Amny Mix	82	Amny Mix.	George Aboy	78	Elisha R. Wells.
			Joseph Stillman	79	Harriet Stillman.

CONNECTICUT—Continued.

Names of pensioners for revolutionary or military services.	Ages.	Names of heads of families with whom pensioners resided June 1, 1840.	Names of pensioners for revolutionary or military services.	Ages.	Names of heads of families with whom pensioners resided June 1, 1840.
HARTFORD—Continued.			**HARTFORD—Continued.**		
WEATHERSFIELD—Continued.			EAST WINDSOR—Continued.		
Abigail Woodhouse	80	Abigail Woodhouse.	Catherine Bowers	79	Cyrus Bowers.
Mary Belden	82	Erastus F. Cook.	Roger Burnham	79	Roger Burnham.
Lucy Wilcox	80	Lucy Wilcox.	Nathaniel Chatman	58	Nathaniel Chatman.
Elisha Williams	81	Stephen Francis.	Stephen Elmer	86	Stephen Elmer.
Thede Hale	86	Simeon Hale.	Eleanor Felley	82	Horace Felley.
Rebecca May	83	Sylvester May.	Gustavus Grant	81	Lucius Grant.
Anice Cook	82	Talcott A. Arnold.	Rhoda Eldridge	82	John S. Goodale.
Ichabod Goodrich	81	Jasper Goodrich.	Grace Green	83	Asahel Green.
Gideon Goff	79	Gideon Goff.	Lucy Grant	79	Harvey Grant.
Calvin Chapin	76	Calvin Chapin.	Samuel Hunn	77	Samuel Hunn.
Hezekiah Whitmore	84	Hezekiah Whitmore.	Zerviah Haden	94	Edward Haden.
Thomas Holmes	84	Thomas Holmes.	Ruth Morton	78	Ruth Morton.
			Hezekiah Munsell	87	Hezekiah Munsell.
BERLIN.			Jonathan Pasco	82	Jonathan Pasco.
Lucy Dickenson	69	Lucy Dickinson.	Elizabeth Strong	74	Hiram Strong.
Abijah Porter	83	Abijah Porter.	Mehitable Sloughton	79	Mehitable Sloughton.
Levi North	80	Levi North.	Flora Sloughton	78	Horace Sloughton.
Seth Savage	84	Amasa Savage.	Jerusha Woolcott	84	Ursula Skinner.
Selah Savage	81	Selah Savage.	Elizabeth Skinner	82	Elizabeth Skinner.
Phebe Norton	71	Henry Norton.	Eleanor Sloughton	85	William Sloughton.
Hezekiah Hart	82	Mary Meriman.	Ephraim Warfield	70	Chester Wolcott.
—— Bunnel	83	Luther Stocking.			
Ruth Hart	98	Lucy Hartford.	**EAST HARTFORD.**		
Jabez Cowles	84	Jabez Cowles.	Esther House	81	Elisha Smith.
Grace Elton	83	James Elton.	Daniel Roberts	79	Daniel Roberts.
Giles Curtiss	85	Giles Curtiss.	Timothy Hall	82	Timothy Hall.
Sarah Riley	87	D. Buckley.	Lucy Derning	75	Abigail Derning.
Daniel Galpin	83	Daniel Galpin.	Russell Treat	82	Russel Treat.
Hannah Palmer	78	Peter Jacocks.	Ashbel Warren	78	Ashbel Warren.
Esther Judd	82	Henry Judd.	Lucretia Roberts	84	Lucretia Roberts.
Elijah Francis	80	Elijah Francis.	Hannah Reynolds	77	Hannah Reynolds.
John Bunnel	81	Alfred Baley.	Timothy Anderson	78	Norman Anderson.
Lois Carter	82	Benjamin Hart.	John Bennett	78	J. Hubbard Wellis.
Hooker Gilbert	88	Hooker Gilbert.	Mary Porter	74	Mary Porter.
Hannah Hooker	79	Seth Hooker.	Abigail Roberts	89	Isaac Roberts.
Hannah Hooker	78	George Cornwall.	Anna Norton	83	Emily Pitkin.
Sarah Hart	71	Horace Hart.			
Fidelia Bronson	77	Theodore Bronson.	**MANCHESTER.**		
Rhoda Andrews	83	Selah Andrews.	Mabel Marsh	77	Marcus Marsh.
Elizabeth Mugs	84	Thomas Lee.	Ashna Symonds	82	Ashna Symonds.
Sarah Morse	83	William Morse.	Moses Evans	81	Moses Evans.
			George Buckland	82	George Buckland.
SOUTHINGTON.			David Squire	81	Daniel Squire.
Samuel Hitchcock	83	Samuel Hitchcock.	Hannah Jacklin	80	Henry C. Woodbridge.
Josiah Boot	87	Betsey Buck.	Richard Keeney	75	Richard Keeney.
Elthir Carter	78	Elihu Carter.	Elizabeth McKee	85	Elizabeth McKee.
Julia Tyler	80	Julia Tyler.	Eleanor Geer	83	Joseph Thompson.
Ichabod C. Frisby	79	Ichabod C. Frisby.			
Channey Lewis	79	Channey Lewis.	**GLASTONBURY.**		
Caleb Ray	82	Jared Stephens.	Richard Smith	82	Jennett Gillett.
Daniel Pardu	77	Daniel Pardu.	Joseph Tryon	78	Joseph Tryon.
			Azariah Taylor	82	Azariah Taylor.
SUFFIELD.			Edward Potter	81	Horace Roberts.
Phebe Allen	79	Ambrose Bemont.	Abel Lewis	79	Abel Lewis.
Jacob Cooper	77	Judah Cooper.	Daniel Miles	89	Daniel Miles.
Silas Dewey	79	Silas Dewey, jr.	Louis House	77	Giles House.
Ebenezer Chaplain	90	Ebenezer Chaplain.	Mabel Wright	73	Mabel Wright.
Jehiel Harmon	79	Jehiel Harmon.	James McLean	85	Ogden McLean.
Ezra Hanchell	81	Ezra Hanchell.	Elizabeth Bidwell	83	Elizabeth Bidwell.
John K. Kent	81	John K. Kent.	Mary Fer	81	Elijah Sparks.
Rosanna Miller	77	John Miller.			
Elizabeth Phelps	77	Elizabeth Phelps.	**MARLBOROUGH.**		
Moses Bliss	87	Henry A. Pikes.	John Uxford	85	Gibson W. Uxford.
Gideon Sikes	87	Gideon Sikes.	Ezra Blish	72	Ezra Blish.
John Warner	84	Rowland Taylor.			
Richard Warner	79	Richard Warner.	**GRANBY.**		
			Thomas Stevens	82	Thomas Stevens.
ENFIELD.			Ahinoam Holcomb	80	Elihu E. Holcomb.
Lydia Abbey	75	Lydia Abbey.	Rebecca Sands	75	Rebecca Sands.
Mary Chaffee	81	Samuel Chaffee.	Joseph Dyer	72	Joseph Dyer.
Calvin Squires	76	John S. Davis.	James Bartholomew	80	James C. Bartholomew.
Roxannah Gowdy	68	Henry Gowdy.	Prudence Smith	80	Joseph Smith.
Windsor Buker	82	Austin King.	Chloe Holcomb	76	Ebenezer S. Holcomb.
Ebenezer Prior	95	Ebenezer Prior.	Samuel Benjamin	83	Samuel Benjamin.
John Pease	87	John Pease.	Zabina Burr	88	Zabina Burr.
Abigail Pease	86	Heber Pease.	Benoni Gillett	78	Benoni Gillett.
Simeon Pease	82	Simeon Pease.	William Pratt	89	William H. Pratt.
Betsey Thompson	69	Betsey Thompson.	Abraham Osborne	84	Abraham Osborne.
			Ebenezer Godard	88	Arsepheus Godard.
EAST WINDSOR.			Mary Holcomb	69	Mary Holcomb.
Arnold Allen	71	Arnold Allen.	Samuel Warner	84	Samuel Warner.
Thomas Bissell	82	Thomas Bissell.			

CONNECTICUT—Continued.

Names of pensioners for revolutionary or military services.	Ages.	Names of heads of families with whom pensioners resided June 1, 1840.	Names of pensioners for revolutionary or military services.	Ages.	Names of heads of families with whom pensioners resided June 1, 1840.
HARTFORD—Continued.			**HARTFORD—Continued.**		
GRANBY—Continued.			BRISTOL—Continued.		
John O'Brien	84	Harry Alky.	Elizabeth Gladden	70	Elizabeth Gladden.
John Godard	81	Grove Godard.	Anna Bishop	74	Anna Bishop.
Ephraim Gillett	79	James Gillett.			
Chrispus Fox	84	Chrispus Fox.	FARMINGTON.		
Dudley Hayes	80	Dudley Hayes.	Chauncey Royce	83	John Royce.
			Eunice Eaton	86	Gideon Watkins.
WINDSOR.			Daniel Tilotson	81	Edward Tilotson.
Samuel Woodruff	80	Samuel Woodruff.	Timothy Olmstead	82	Clarissa Tryon.
Phineas Picket	83	Phineas Picket.	Moses Morse	89	Chauncey Morse.
Eunice Munsell	86	Rodney Munsell.	Dorcas Woodruff	76	Henry Mygatte.
Roswell Miller	80	Roswell Miller.	Christiana Woodruff	76	Ephraim Woodness.
Frederick Chapman	79	Delia Wilson.	Phebe Janes	73	Phebe Janes.
Elisha N. Sill	79	Elisha N. Sill.	Elias Brown	81	Elias Brown.
Elijah Denslow	76	Elijah Denslow.	Rhoda Warna	94	Sylvester Tubs.
Elizabeth Stanard	93	Eli Wilson.	Lydia Sherman	84	Johiah Wilcox.
Abel Barnes	86	Lyman Barnes.			
Submit Wilson	74	Horace Thrall.	**NEW HAVEN COUNTY.**		
Jemima Graham	85	Ruth Bartholomew.	CITY OF NEW HAVEN.		
Philip Halsey	80	Henry Halsey.	James Nicolson	52	James Nicolson.
Loomis Warner	83	Thomas Warner.	Mary Wakelee	80	Charles H. Wakelee.
			Jacob Wilcox	82	Norris Wilcox.
SIMSBURY.			Anna Cornwall	86	Alvan Wilcox.
Loisa Eno	76	Chester Eno.	John Trumbell	84	Benjamin Sillaman.
Elijah Griswold	78	Elijah Griswold.	Benjamin Lines	78	Benjamin Lines.
John Tyler	74	John Tyler.	Nathan Beers	87	Nathan Beers, sr.
Joab Wilson	78	Chester Roberts.	Eneas Monson	76	A. E. Monson.
Obed Higley	83	Obed Higley, jr.	William Storer	75	William Storer.
Levi Humphrey	75	Levi Humphrey.	Mary A. Dwight	86	Timothy Dwight.
Salathel Chapman	80	Salathel Chapman.	Marcus Meraman	78	Marcus Meraman.
Abel Case	84	Abel Case.	Catharine Ramsdell	83	Mary L. Ramsdell.
Roswell Noble	82	Roswell F. Noble.	Isaac Bussett	82	Isaac Bussett.
Ambrose Hoskins	78	Ambrose Hoskins.	Sarah Burney	80	Julia Gorham.
Catharine Andrus	87	Abigail Andrus.	Samuel Hicks	82	George Sandford.
Esther Slater	77	Chauncey Goodrich.	Henry Daggett	82	Henry Daggett.
George Cornish	79	George Cornish.	Lois Peck	82	Lois Peck.
			Lydia Bradley	87	Nathan Thomas.
HARTLAND.			Mary Woolcott	75	John Williams.
Asa Cowdrey	82	James Cowdrey.	Charles Larrabee	58	Park Brown.
Hulda Daniels	86	Sterling G. Daniels.	Huldah Barker	80	Huldah Barker.
Daniel Bills	82	Daniel Bills.	William Wise	80	Timothy Alling.
Cleopatra Skinner	74	Cleopatra Skinner.	Lois Willard	80	Stephen Willard.
Ebenezer Hoadley	83	Ebenezer Hoadly.	Garritt De Witt	77	Garritt De Witt.
Achsah Giddings	77	Achsah Giddings.	Abiah Smith	72	John Fitch.
Affiah Giddings	69	Henry Fuller.	Elizabeth Tuttle	75	Isaac Tuttle.
Stephen Goodyear	78	Stephen Goodyear.	Mabel Hull	82	Thaddeus Austin.
Timothy Coe	79	Timothy Coe.	Sylvanus Bills	74	Sylvanus Bills.
John M. Case	77	Charles Case.	Jarius Sandford	77	Jarius Sandford.
Thomas Fox	77	Thomas Fox.	Benoni Gillett	80	Benoni Gillett.
Timothy Tiffany	86	Timothy Tiffany.			
			COUNTY OF NEW HAVEN.		
BLOOMFIELD.			Elijah Hatchkiss	78	Elijah Hatchkiss.
Louis Colton	79	Samuel Colton.			
William Seymour	79	Ruel Gridley.	HAMDEN.		
Silas Rowley	79	Silas Rowley.	Samuel Warner	80	Stephen Warner.
Joseph Millard	77	Joseph Millard.	Joel Huff	83	Silas Andrews.
Daniel Hooker	79	Daniel Hooker.	Lois Merriman	76	Lois Merriman.
AVON.			NORTH HAVEN.		
Isaac Osborne	79	Isaac Osborne.	John Smith	85	John Smith.
Thomas F. Bishop	76	Thomas F. Bishop.	Sibenu Barnes	80	Merit Barnes.
Rosanna Wilcox	83	Josiah A. Wilcox.	John Pierpont	87	John Pierpont.
Elijah Barnes	77	Elijah Barnes.	Rebecca Chace	72	Horace Chace.
			James Donnow	–	James Donnow.
CANTON.			Martin Jethro	–	Martin Jethro.
Sophia Andrus	76	Henry Andrus.	Joel Brockett	80	Joel Brockett.
Margaret Wright	69	Henry J. Wright.			
Solomon Ackart	90	David Ackart.	MILFORD.		
Aber Alford	79	Aber Alford.	Eunice Ford	75	Stephen B. Ford.
Francis Bacon	81	Alvin Bacon.	Ephraim Strong	85	William Strong.
Elizabeth Barber	86	Alson Barber.	Samuel Higby	81	Samuel Higby.
Abi Barber	73	Miles Foot.	Rhosmantu Rhodus	53	Samuel C. Mervin.
			Eunice Wise	69	Eunice Wise.
BURLINGTON.			Benjamin Gillet	82	Benjamin Gillet.
Oliver Barnes	92	Caleb Barnes.	Mary Glenney	–	William Glenney.
Lois Benham	85	Lois Benham.	Martha Sacket	80	Martha Sackett.
Ebenezer Benham	84	Ebenezer Benham.	Abigail Baldwin	77	Abigail Baldwin.
Samuel Hotchkiss	84	Samuel Hotchkiss.	Molly Ston	87	Isaac J. Gum.
Lucy Culva	69	Nathan Culva.	William Durand	80	William Durand.
			Nathan Oviatt	75	Nathan Oviatt.
BRISTOL.			Anna Northrop	78	Thomas Lawrence.
Martha Manross	75	Elisha Manross.	Anna Ball	82	Abel Baldwin.
			Samuel Gurn	78	Joseph Fowler.

CONNECTICUT—Continued.

Names of pensioners for revolutionary or military services.	Ages.	Names of heads of families with whom pensioners resided June 1, 1840.	Names of pensioners for revolutionary or military services.	Ages.	Names of heads of families with whom pensioners resided June 1, 1840.
NEW HAVEN—Continued.			**NEW HAVEN—Continued.**		
MILFORD—Continued.			EAST HAVEN—Continued.		
Mary Dickinson	81	Samuel W. Dickinson.	John A. Thomas	70	John A. Thomas.
Mary Bryan	79	Addison Beard.	John Rowe	86	John Rowe.
David Bristol	76	David Bristol.	Enos Herringway	85	Enos Herringway.
Samuel Peck	75	Samuel Peck.	Lucinda Miles	77	Stephen Smith, 2d.
Joseph C. Clark	89	Joseph C. Clark.	Sarah Smith	81	Degrasse Mallby.
Susan Beard	81	Joseph Beard.	Jared Grannis	85	Frederic Grannis.
David Smith	84	David Smith.	Jesse Luddington	84	Joseph Grannis.
Samuel B. Smith	84	Samuel B. Smith.			
Elisha Clark	85	Amos Clark.	BRANFORD.		
Samuel Durand	79	Samuel Durand.	Martha Rogers	86	John Jowner.
Nathan Nettleton	76	Nathan Nettleton.	Mason Hobart	88	Mason Hobart.
Isaac Clark	77	Isaac Clark.	Desire Baldwin	83	Desire Baldwin.
Jedediah Ston	83	Jedediah Ston.	Iriphena Palmer	86	Timothy Bradley, jr.
Elisha Sandford	89	Elisha Sandford.	Edmund Morris	82	Edmund Morris.
			Phebe Beach	82	John Beach.
ORANGE.			John Monro	87	Woodward Page.
Daniel Allen	82	Enoch Summers.	James Goodrich	82	Joseph Goodrich.
Lelia Trowbridge	70	Leman Brockett.	Mary Barker	78	James Barker.
Abigail Allen	85	Octural Catlin.	Josiah Irisbie	89	Josiah Irisbie.
John Bryan	86	Thomas Painter.	Heman Rogers	84	Heman Rogers.
Samuel Parsons	79	Samuel Parsons.			
Miles Mallet	77	Miles Mallet.	GUILFORD.		
			John Stone	80	John Stone.
WALLINGFORD.			Jerry Scranton	84	Jerry Scranton.
Anna Tyler	78	Cyral Tyler.	Mabel Meigs	83	Isaac Meigs.
Ichabod Ires	81	Ichabod Ires.	Nathan Chittenden	82	Nathan Chittenden.
Ruth Hall	74	Ruth Hall.	Abraham Chittenden	89	H. W. Chittenden.
Andrews Hall	81	Andrews Hall.	Mary Hart	73	George London.
Jeremiah Hull	77	Jeremiah Hull.	Timothy Seward	86	Timothy Seward.
Fanny Henry	73	Fanny Henry.	James Davis	75	James Davis.
Hannah Davidson	74	Hannah Davidson.	Sarah Talmage	82	Sarah Talmage.
Jonathan Batholomew	85	Jonathan Batholomew.	Medad Potter	84	Russell Potter.
David Barnes	76	David Barnes.	John Coan	77	John Coan, jr.
Meriman Catherine	82		Jared Dudley	83	Jared Dudley.
Marlin Buel	81	Marlin Buel.			
Mabel Allen	75	Mabel Allen.	MADISON.		
			Gilead Bradley	83	Gilead Bradley.
NORTH BRANFORD.			Timothy Grave	81	Timothy Grave.
Abram Wheldon	78	Abram Wheldon.	Jeffrey Smith	78	Jeffrey Smith.
John Robinson	79	John Robinson.	Jonathan Lee	78	Jonathan Lee.
Ruth Rogers	83	Ebenezer Rogers.	Saul Foster	85	Frederick Foster.
Othiel Stent	88	Othiel Stent.	Abraham Hill	77	Abraham Hill.
Stephen Smith	89	Stephen Smith.	Vial Richmond	76	Vial Richmond.
John Potter	80	David Page.	Morris Jones	85	Morris Jones.
Hannah Rose	78	Hannah Rose.	Noah Benton	77	Noah Benton.
Eunice Russell	71	David A. Russell.	Timothy Scranton	88	Timothy Scranton.
Desire Baldwin	84	Bessie Levi.			
Jonathan Munson	84	Chauncy Munson.	DERBY.		
Sarah Lindsley	76	John Lindsley, 2d.	Samuel Hawkins	78	Samuel Hawkins.
Elihu Foot	83	Edwin Foot.	John Beers	81	John Beers.
Pure Bunnel	85	Luther Bunnel.	Mary Morris	74	Mary Morris.
Kesiah Baldwin	76	Anson Baldwin.	Bradford Steele	84	Bradford Steele.
			Nathaniel Johnson	82	Nathaniel Johnson.
MERIDEN.			William Kenney	83	Isaac Kenney.
Robert Smith	83	Thomas T. Baldwin.	Abel Holbrook	77	Thomas C. Holbrook.
Elizabeth Benham	81	Elizabeth Benham.	James Bassett	83	Josiah Bassett.
Martha Ives	85	Phineas T. Ives.	Lucy Tomlinson	69	Philo Bassett.
Huldah Johnson	86	Huldah Johnson.	Wilson Hurd	77	Wilson Hurd.
Amasa Merriam	82	Amasa Merriam.	Abigail Pool	75	Betsey Hawkins.
Joseph Juiss	79	Benjamin Juiss.	Ruth Hallock	71	Garrett Smith.
Abner Way	86	Abner Way.	Anna Hawkins	84	Isaac Hawkins.
Jerusha Brown	76	Jerusha Brown.			
			OXFORD.		
CHESHIRE.			Edward Bassett	84	Edward Bassett.
Samuel Talmage	80	Samuel Talmage.	Prudence Lounsbury	76	Edward E. Mallory.
Susanna Durand	77	Susanna Durand.	Samuel Candee	87	Samuel Candee.
John Field	81	John Field.	Phineas Johnson	79	Chester Matfield.
Stephen Parker	81	Stephen Ives.	Timothy Johnson	82	Timothy Johnson.
Lydia Clark	87	Aaron A. Hitchcock.	Job Candee	80	Daniel Tuckee.
			Uri Scott	81	Uri Scott.
EAST HAVEN.					
Elijah Bradley	80	Elijah Bradley.	WOODBRIDGE.		
Sylvia Brown	76	Sylvia Brown.	Isaac Northrop	80	William Hargee.
Hannah Chidsey	83	Hannah Chidsey.			
Abigail Goodsel	94	Trueman Colt.	WATERBURY.		
Phebe Davenport	81	Phebe Davenport.	Edward Field (Mary)	62	Edward Field.
Temperance Hotchkiss	79	Lyman Hotchkiss.	Ransom Mix	48	Ransom Mix.
Rosanna Pardee	78	Ceba Munson.	Selah Bronson	77	Selah Bronson.
Mabel Tyler	74	William Tyler.	Sarah Judd	81	Sarah Judd.
Abraham W. Johnson	89	Wylly Thompson.	Giles Brockett	79	Giles Brockett.
Eli Forbes	80	Eli Forbes.	Thomas Judd	63	Thomas Judd.
Anna Smith	88	Daniel Smith.	Sarah Merrell	85	Elijah F. Merrell.

CONNECTICUT—Continued.

Names of pensioners for revolutionary or military services.	Ages.	Names of heads of families with whom pensioners resided June 1, 1840.	Names of pensioners for revolutionary or military services.	Ages.	Names of heads of families with whom pensioners resided June 1, 1840.
NEW HAVEN—Continued.			**NEW LONDON—Continued.**		
WATERBURY—Continued.			EAST LYME—Continued.		
Ebenezer Brown	82	Samuel Bunnell.	Joseph Latham	81	Lebsey Latham.
Ward Peck	77	Ward Peck.	James Denison	47	James Denison.
Mercy Miles	76	Samuel Stocking.	Horace Smith	32	Horace Smith.
Sarah Welton	81	Isaac B. Castle.	William Tinker	78	William Tinker.
Elihu Spencer	78	Elihu Spencer.	Jonathan Rathbun	75	Jonathan Rathbun.
Francis P. Gardner	26	Frances Fowler.	Joseph Gillet	85	B. F. Gillet.
Culpepper Hoadley	75	Culpepper Hoadley.			
Abigail Poole	75	William H. Tomlinson.	LYME.		
Ursula Wooster	79	Ursula Wooster.	Nathan H. Jewit	79	Benjamin Beckwith.
Jared Merrill	49	Jared Merrill.	Benajah Bill	70	Lodowick Bill.
Jared Terrell	82	Horace Terrell.	Robert Bramble	78	Robert Bramble.
Sarah Pitts	85	Sarah Pitts.	James Greenfield	88	James Greenfield.
Ansel Spencer	76	Ansel Spencer.	John Lay	76	John Lay.
			Silas Champlin	–	Silas Champlin.
WOLCOTT.			Usual Johnson	80	Usual Johnson.
Lucius Tuttle	91	Betsey H. Hall.	Reuben Champion	–	Reuben Champion.
Isaac Bronson	78	Isaac Bronson.	Waitstill Cone	79	Oliver Cone.
Joseph Miner	84	Joseph Miner.	Phebe Champion	75	Phebe Champion.
Lydia Alcox	74	Lydia Alcox.	Sarah Peck	78	Sarah Peck.
Nathaniel Lane	76	Anson G. Lane.	Seth Miner	82	Seth Miner.
Benjamin Bement	85	Benjamin Bement.	Mehitable Burnham	–	William S. Ely.
Ruth Wooden	83	Ruth Finch.	Naomi Huntley	85	Naomi Huntley.
Phebe Peck	74	Moses Pond.	John Brockway	84	John Brockway.
			Thomas Pilgrim	87	Thomas Pilgrim.
PROSPECT.			John Wood	83	John Wood.
Elizabeth Lewis	85	Chester Scovill.	Rhoda Miner	75	Erastus Bramble.
Eben. Hatchkiss	82	Eben. Hatchkiss.	Joseph Plumb	81	Clement Fosdeck.
Archibald Sanford	81	Archibald Sanford.	Gideon Rogers	79	Gideon Rogers.
Mabel Munson	80	Mabel Munson.	Lucy Way	84	Jonathan Chapel.
			Hannah Spencer	85	Oliver Spencer.
MIDDLEBURY.			Elizabeth Sisson	86	Amos ———.
Benjamin Fenn	84	Benjamin Fenn.	Hoell Huntley	–	Howell Huntley.
Hannah Bronson	85	Hannah Bronson.			
Asahel Bronson	80	Asahel Bronson.	GROTON.		
Ebenezer Richardson	56	Aaron Freeman.	Catharine Crandall	77	John Merrit.
Daniel Clark	77	Daniel Clark.	Soloman Tift	82	John Beneham.
Aaron Benedict	95	Aaron Benedict.	Simeon Comstock	86	Thomas Comstock.
			Christopher Latham	84	Christopher Latham.
SOUTHBURY.			Nicholas Morgan	78	Nicholas Morgan.
Aaron Tuttle	84	Aaron Tuttle.	Silas Lamb	77	Silas Lamb.
Sarah Henman	78	Sarah Henman.	Rufus Avery	81	Rufus Avery.
Sarah Lines	78	John E. Smith.	Mary White	78	Mary White.
Abijah Peck	83	Abijah Peck.	Jonathan Langford	88	Jonathan Langford.
Mary Bassett	81	Bronson Wheeler.	Mary Chester	76	Willys Clark.
William Burr	78	William Burr.	Mary Avery	71	Mary Avery.
Samuel Smith	78	Samuel Smith.	Benjamin Daball	83	Benjamin Daball.
Ebenezer Hyde	81	Laurens Hyde.	Hannah Holdredge	70	Hannah Holdrege.
Samuel Botsford	79	Samuel Botsford.	Jabez Edgecomb	77	Jabez Edgecomb.
Nathan Gregory	79	Nathan Gregory.	Samuel Edgecomb	80	Samuel Edgecomb.
			Mary Heath	81	Mary Heath.
NEW LONDON COUNTY.			Thomas Wells	86	Thomas Wells.
NEW LONDON.			Mary Brightman	74	William P. Brightman.
Lebues Maynard	76	A. F. Maynard.	Peter Every	76	Peter Every.
Anthony Jerome	59	Anthony Jerome.	Hannah Packer	82	Hannah Packer.
James Edgerton	82	James Edgerton.	Sabina Packer	77	Sabina Packer.
Ezekiel Fox	84	Ezekiel Fox.	Cathine Burrows	82	Caleb Latham.
Henry Burbeck	85	Henry Burbeck.	Elisha Lyman	75	Thankful Clift.
John Carrol	79	John Carrol.			
Christopher Culver	87	John Culver.	LEDYARD.		
Richard Law	78	Richard Law.	Ichabod Badcock	82	Ichabod Badcock.
Charles Bukely	87	Charles Bukely.	Oliver Morgan	79	Stephen Stoddard.
James Chapman	89	James Chapman.	Daniel Stoddard	79	Daniel Stoddard.
Ephraim Dayton	79	Jonathan Lane.	Robert Stoddard	83	William Green.
John G. Muson	32	John G. Muson.	William Forsyth	78	William Forsyth.
William Ashcraft	86	Joshua Getchel.	Joshua Bill	79	Gurdon Bill.
			Mary Rose	87	Mary Rose.
WATERFORD.			Mary Williams	80	William M. Williams.
Job Daniels	81	Job Daniels.	John Packer	83	John Packer, 2d.
Christopher Brown	81	Christopher Brown.	Andrew Gallup	79	Andrew Gallup.
Stedman Newbury	89	Stedman Newbury.	Thomas Smith	86	Thomas Smith.
John Murtins	55	John Murtins.	Jebanah Williams	82	Nathan Barns.
Ebenezer Darrow	86	Ebenezer Darrow.	William Noyes	76	William Noyes.
Ebenezer Maynard	82		Adam Larabee	53	Adam Larribee.
Lydia Bukwith	79		William Lathum	75	William Adams.
Jason Chapman	78		Nehemiah Gallup	88	Nehemiah Gallup.
			Deborah Davis	87	Ichabod Davis.
EAST LYME.			Thomas Roach	73	Thomas Roach.
Benjamin Jinker	80	Benjamin Jinker.			
Elisha Way	83	Elisha Way.	STONINGTON.		
Asa Woodward	79	Asa Woodworth.	Asa Driscoll	90	Henry Spencer.
John Tubs	80	John Tubs.	Isaac Williams	82	Isaac Williams.
Mary Dosset	86	Abby Harding.	Lydia Smith	73	Elisha Bennet.

CONNECTICUT—Continued.

Names of pensioners for revolutionary or military services.	Ages.	Names of heads of families with whom pensioners resided June 1, 1840.	Names of pensioners for revolutionary or military services.	Ages.	Names of heads of families with whom pensioners resided June 1, 1840.
NEW LONDON—Continued.			**NEW LONDON—Continued.**		
STONINGTON—Continued.			PRESTON—Continued.		
Cato Cuff	83	Cato Cuff.	Prudence Denison	83	Prudence Denison.
Amos Gallup	84	Amos Gallup.	Jacob Meach	82	Jacob Meach.
Jonathan Wheeler	78	Jonathan Wheeler.	Phebe Rude	77	Rix Rude.
Asa Baldwin	84	Asa Baldwin.	Hannah Tracy	88	Elisha Clark.
Ichabod Dickerson	81	Ichabod Dickerson.	Alas Bromley	75	Alas Bromley.
William Robinson	75	William Robinson.	Hezekiah Ingraham	80	Hezekiah Ingraham.
Jedediah Austin	78	Jedediah Austin.			
Hannah Stanton	72	Charles P. Stanton.	GRISWOLD.		
Mary Tinker	76	Asa Willcox.	Dixwell Lathrop	87	Dixwell Lathrop.
Jane Birtch	81	George Howe.	Mary Mulkins	86	Job Lawton.
			Bishop Tyler	72	Bishop Tyler.
CITY OF NORWICH.			Nathan Belcher	82	Nathan Belcher.
Sarah Trumbull	80	Peter Sanman.	Elisha Prentice	74	Elisha Prentice.
Elizabeth Backus	74	Gurdon Pendleton.	Gideon Ray	84	Joseph Wilber.
Christopher Vail	82	Christopher Vail.	Lucy Hutchinson	77	Hazard Hawkins.
Benjamin Coit	81	Benjamin Coit.	Enoch Baker	86	Enoch Baker.
Clark Case	55	Francis B. Lee.			
Anna Coit	81	Erastus Coit.	NORTH STONINGTON.		
Anna Griswold	70	Joseph A. Griswold.	Hannah Grant	82	Elisha Kinney.
Abby Holt	75	Elizabeth Cox.	Elizabeth Ecclestone	95	Caleb Ecclestone.
Sarah Comstock	81	Otis Hilton.	Lucretia Billings	91	Sanford Main.
Mary Clark	75	Mary Clark.	Elisha Palmer	90	Elisha Palmer.
Reuben Godfrey	83	Benjamin Godfrey.	James Thompson	88	James Thompson.
Ichabod Ward	80	Ichabod Ward.	Philemon Baldwin	–	Philemon Baldwin.
			Jeremiah York	76	Jeremiah York.
NORWICH, (without the city limits.)			Gershom Ecclestone	78	Gershom Ecclestone.
Elizabeth Yeomany	80	David Yeomany.	Martha S. Phillips	80	Bradford Phillips.
Hannah Caswell	71	Gilbert Huntington.	Bridget Leray	74	Bridget Leray.
John Foster	78	John Foster.	Jeptha Brown	82	Jeptha Brown
Hannah Ames	80	Erasmus Ames.	David Main	88	David Main.
Desire Morgan	74	Charles Morgan.	Oliver Avery	83	Stanton Hewitt, jr.
Susan Fanning	81	Sidney Gardner.	Anna Bently	83	George W. Bentley.
Joseph Pettes	81		Wareham Williams	81	Wareham Williams.
			Lucy Davis	75	David Caswell.
MONTVILLE.					
Joseph Church	80	Joseph Church.	SALEM.		
Eleazer Tracy	75	Anson Gleason.	Jesse Beckwith	88	Israel Beckwith.
James Comstock	90	James Comstock.	Ebenezer Rogers	96	Ebenezer Rogers.
Thomas Rogers	83	Thomas Rogers.	William C. Beebe	68	William C. Beebe.
John Smith	80	John Smith.	Samuel C. Smith	46	Samuel C. Smith.
John Uncas	90	Mary Church.	Elijah Treadway	86	Elijah Treadway.
Samuel Atwell	80	Samuel Atwell.	Lucretia Dodge	80	Lucretia Dart.
Guy Chapel	81	Betsey Chapel.	James Ransom	78	James Ransom.
Anna Bishop	82	Robert Bishop.			
David Dart	79	David Dart.	BOZRAH.		
Elisha Holms	81	Jonathan Forseth.	Alpheus Kingsley	77	Alpheus Kingsley.
Anna Chapel	82	Isaac Whipple.	Perez Chesbrongh	78	Perez Chesbrough.
Daniel Ames	84	Daniel Ames.	Molly Vergason	76	Oliver Landpher.
Lucy Chapel	87	Willard Wickwise.	Abigail ——	82	Asa Smith.
LISBON.			COLCHESTER.		
Mary Perrigo	79	Betsey Abel.	Lucretia Ramond	80	Jonathan Morgan.
Wealthy Fuller	83	Wealthy Fuller.	Gideon Unash	86	Gideon Unash.
Ebenezer Fuller	80	John Rathbone.	David Shattuck	82	Giles Shattuck.
Ruth Rathbone	81	Ruel Cook.	Solomon Dowd	82	Solomon Dowd.
James Storey	80	Roswell Adams.	Gamaliel R. Tracy	81	James R. Tracy.
William Adams	87	Joseph Baldwin.	Elijah Taylor	81	John Bogue.
Joseph Baldwin	89	Joel Hyde.	Sally Lewis	80	Clark Lewis.
Joel Hyde	76	Daniel Downing.	Frederick Smith	78	Thomas Smith.
Daniel Downing	78		Eunice Clark	73	George Clark.
			John B. Wartrons	86	John B. Wartrons.
FRANKLIN.			John T. Otis	81	John T. Otis.
Isaac Butts	80	Almira Bellows.			
Nabby Armstrong	75	Cheney Armstrong.	LEBANON.		
Frederick Brewster	77	Frederick Brewster.	Asa Jones	86	Andrew Lathrop.
			William A. Morgan	85	Griswold A. Morgan.
PRESTON.			Ebenezer Metcalf	83	Ebenezer Metcalf.
Absalom Pride	84	Absalom Pride.	Solomon Loring	78	Solomon Loring.
Mary Giddings	76	Charles Brewster.	Amasa Dutton	86	Amasa Dutton.
Joshua Bill	78	Robert M. Palmer.	Abigail Fitch	85	Jabez Fitch.
George Harvey	77	George Harvey.	Elijah Smith	76	Elijah Smith.
Frederick Stoddard	79	Frederick Stoddard.	Asel Gay	84	Asel Gay.
Simeon Hewitt	–	Charles E. Hewitt.	John Willes	89	Charles Gardner.
Philip Prince	80	Bristow Swan.	Eleazer Bill	81	
Uriah Corning	–	Jedediah Corning.	Elizabeth Bliss	75	
Eunice Guile	81	Alfred Guile.	Jacob Clark	81	
Abel Shoals	47	Abel Shoals.	Isaiah Loomies	82	
Jonah Witter	82	Jonah Witter.	Rebecca Fowler	81	
Isaac Williams	80	Jonah Witter, jr.	Stephen Champlin	77	
Sally Runnolds	76	Luke Runnolds.	Simon Loomies	79	
Ebenezer Avery	78	Ebenezer Avery.	David Avery	75	
James Treat	77	James Treat.	John Loomies	88	

CONNECTICUT—Continued.

Names of pensioners for revolutionary or military services.	Ages.	Names of heads of families with whom pensioners resided June 1, 1840.	Names of pensioners for revolutionary or military services.	Ages.	Names of heads of families with whom pensioners resided June 1, 1840.
FAIRFIELD COUNTY.			**FAIRFIELD**—Continued.		
CITY OF BRIDGEPORT.			FAIRFIELD—Continued.		
Stiles Nichols	79	Stiles Nichols.	Nathaniel Perry	84	Nathaniel Perry.
Dorcas Wordin	76		Lebius Brown	83	Charlotte Buckley.
Abigail Hyde	75		Mary Perry	86	David B. Perry.
Molly Smith	83				
Anna Lord	73		STRATFORD.		
Lucy Hawley	75	Lucy Hawley.	Nathan Burrett	77	Nathan Burrett.
Griswold Odell	79		Sally Burrett	79	Josiah Hubbed.
Archibald Baldwin	87		Patience Lewis	89	Patience Lewis.
Hannah Hilliard	79		Sally Curtis	73	Sally Curtis.
Hannah Merritt	82		Sarah Blakeman	83	Beard Blakeman.
Joseph Polly	82	Joseph Polly.	Joemna Blakeman	79	Gould Blakeman.
Sally Beardslee	73		Jabez H. Tomlinson	79	Jabez H. Tomlinson.
Hannah Crawford	72		Samuel Wells	79	Samuel Wells.
			Elnathan Willcox	91	Elnathan Willcox.
BRIDGEPORT.			Ellen Birdsey	79	Hepsibah Wooster.
John Brooks, sr.	76	John Brooks, sr.	Naomi Judson	81	Naomi Judson.
Abiah Lewis	76	Federal Ward.	Samuel Ufford	79	Samuel H. Ufford.
Eunice Saully	74	Russel Morgan.	Mary Hubbell	82	Mary Hubbell.
Thomas Stratton	82	Samuel Stratton.	Charity Lewis	78	Charity Lewis.
Elijah Pect	79	Elijah Pect.	Dorothy Benjamin	72	Dorothy Benjamin.
			Daniel Jackson	77	Whitney Jackson.
WESTPORT.			John McEwen	96	Aaron Beard.
Thomas Saunders	79	Thomas Saunders.	Massa Louthworth	78	Lewis Chatfield.
Gillen Platt	75	Gillen Platt.	Phebe Tomlinson	75	David Plant.
Joseph Platt	75	Joseph Platt.	Alice Thompson	76	Alice Thompson.
Anna Nash	68	Keeler Nash.	Jerusha Dayton	84	Denra Dayton.
Josiah Gregory	79	Josiah Gregory.	Ellen Peck	90	Job Peck.
Edmund Tuttle	76	Edmund Tuttle.	Mary Peck	83	Levi Peck.
Joseph Downs	75	Joseph Downs.			
Nancy Taylor	73	Paul L. Taylor.	HUNTINGTON.		
Elizabeth Bennett	73	Marvin O. Bennett.	David Blackman	82	
Joshua Couch	82	Joshua Couch.	Nathan Fairchild	78	
William Allen	75	William Allen.	Thomas Gilbert	85	
Joseph Meeker	80	Silas Meeker.	Dan. Chatfield	79	
Betsey Hanford	82	Samuel Disbro.	Agur Tomlinson	84	
Samuel Wood	82	Samuel Wood.	Nathan Lewis	85	
Daniel Dikeman	83	John Stephenson.			
			MONROE.		
FAIRFIELD.			Eli Mitchel	72	
Thomas Brothwill	74	Thomas Brothwill.			
Samuel Wilson	79	Samuel Wilson.	TRUMBULL.		
Joseph Hayes	84	Joseph Hayes.	Hezekiah Edwards	79	
Caroline M. Wheeler	79	Nichols C. Wheeler.	Everard Curtiss	81	
Abraham Morehouse	82	Abraham Morehouse.	Lewis Burton	78	
David Potter	79	David Potter.	James Beardslee	83	
Aaron Hubbell	79	Aaron Hubbell.	David Booth	79	
Margaret Beardslee	78	John W. Beardslee.			
Thaddeus Hubbell	74	Thaddeus Hubbell.	DANBURY.		
Benjamin Brothwell	81	Benjamin Brothwell.	Hannah Ambler	77	Thomas Ambler.
John Wilson	76	John Wilson.	Enos Nichols	80	Enos Nichols.
James Penfield	82	James Penfield.	Stephen Allen	74	Stephen Allen.
Ann Morehouse	83	Ann Morehouse.	Josiah Bennett	74	Josiah Bennett.
Anna Mallett	82	Anna Mallett.	Hezekiah Bailey	85	Hezekiah Bailey.
Abel Turney	75	Abel Turney.	David Weed	92	David Weed.
Benjamin Bennett	86	Henry C. Graves.	Anna Weed	78	Anna Weed.
William Jennings	74	William Jennings.	Sarah Crofut	81	Mos. Crofut.
Sarah A. Burr	78	Sarah A. Burr.	William Patch	79	William Patch.
Catharine M. Burt	40	Catharine Mills.	Mary Peters	85	Uriel Gunn.
Thomas Turner	55	Thomas Turner.	John Gregory	79	John Gregory.
Abigail Sherwood	80	Samuel Perry.	Russell Hamlin	85	Russell Hamlin.
George Wakeman	76	Gershon Wakeman.	Eli Taylor	80	Eli Taylor.
Ephraim Nichols	81	Ephraim Nichols.	Samuel Taylor	78	Samuel Taylor.
Joseph Gray	82	Joseph Gray.	Thaddeus Starr	80	Thaddeus Starr.
Nathan Banks	80	Nathan Banks.	Anna Platt	67	Nehemiah Gillett.
Ruth Banks	86	Abraham Banks.	Eliud Taylor	82	Eliud Taylor.
Hyat Banks	76	Hyat Banks.	Betsey Gunn	71	Betsey Gunn.
Mabel Banks	64	Benjamin Wilson.			
Benjamin Smith	93	Benjamin Smith.	NEWTOWN.		
Joseph Buckley	81	William Bradley.	Mary Botsford	82	Jabez B. Botsford.
Abigail Sherwood	80	Abigail Sherwood.	Abigail Davis	78	Zar Winton.
Amelia Buckley	86	Timothy Buckley.	Jerusha Crittenden	80	Eleazer Dancomb.
Sally Ogden	76	Sally Ogden.	Sarah Colburn	77	James Boyer.
Mary Sherwood	79	Burr Sherwood.	Kellogg Berry	77	Kellogg Berry.
Reuben Sherwood	87	Reuben Sherwood.	Eunice Taylor	82	Daniel Summers.
John Osborn	84	John Osborn.			
Peter Jennings	77	Peter Jennings.	BROOKFIELD.		
Jeremiah Osborn	77	Jeremiah Osborn.	Lucy Ruggles	76	Lucy Ruggles.
Grace Darrow	77	Grace Darrow.	Clarina Northrop	78	Clarina Northrop.
Eleazer Buckley	77	Eleazer Buckley.	Anna Hawley	81	Benjamin Hawley.
John Alvord	90	Nehemiah B. Alvord.	David Reeler	87	David Reeler.
Mary Smith	69	Mary Smith.	Abel Smith	83	Abel Smith.
Sarah Robertson	78	Sarah Robertson.	Anna Bostwick	84	Asa Reeler.

CONNECTICUT—Continued.

Names of pensioners for revolutionary or military services.	Ages.	Names of heads of families with whom pensioners resided June 1, 1840.	Names of pensioners for revolutionary or military services.	Ages.	Names of heads of families with whom pensioners resided June 1, 1840.
FAIRFIELD—Continued.			**FAIRFIELD—Continued.**		
Brookfield—Continued.			Darien.		
Hannah Quintard -	70	Cyrus Beers.	Mary Weed -	76	Samuel Bates.
Huldah Reeler -	82	Albert Judson.	John Little -	79	John Little.
			Samuel Matha -	75	Samuel Matha.
New Fairfield.			Jonathan Bell -	85	Jonathan Bell.
Gideon Chase -	79	Daniel Chase.	William Waterbury	78	William Waterbury.
James Wheeler -	81	James Wheeler.	John Weed -	83	Joseph H. Leeds.
Uriah Mead -	80	Uriah Mead.	Thadeus Bell -	84	Thadeus Bell.
Benjamin Treadwell -	77	Benjamin Treadwell.	Henry Weed -	75	Henry Weed.
Benjamin Peck -	78	Benjamin Peck.	John Dibble -	81	Frederic Waterbury.
			Benjamin Weed -	81	Benjamin Weed.
Sherman.			Abigail Darkam -	80	William Howe.
Rumas Renedict -	74	Hanley Hungerford.	Ebenezer Hoyt -	76	Ebenezer Hoyt.
Hannah Hungerford -	81	Uriel Hungerford.			
Mary Wakeman -	75	Mrs. Pepper.	Norwalk.		
Mercy Hinman -	73	Thomas Bennett.	Esther Ayatt -	77	
Joanna Squires -	83	Isaac Squires.	Esther Fitch -	77	
			Esther Banks -	79	
Bridgefield.			Jacob Bishop -	85	
Elisha Hawley -	83	Elisha Hawley.	Stephen Hyatt -	79	
Ezra Mead -	82	Ezra Mead.	James Jelliff -	81	
Thomas Mead -	76	Thomas Mead.	Thomas Trowbridge -	77	
Jeremiah Mead -	85	Seth Mead.	Thomas Aiken -	81	
Matthew Olmsted -	80	Jeremiah Olmsted.	Abigail Edwards -	79	
Thomas Hawley -	84	Thomas Hawley.	David Mawin -	81	
Wakeman Barrett -	87	Wakeman Barrett.	Henry Chichester -	77	
			Nathaniel Raymond	87	
Reading.			Nathan Odell -	79	
Abiah Sanford -	95	Zalmon Sanford.	David St. John -	78	
Joel Merchant -	78	Joel Merchant.	Rebecca Seymond -	88	
Ebenezer Sanford -	78	Ebenezer Sanford.	Darius Benedict -	83	
Sarah Gould -	83	Aaron Gould.	Seth Seymond -	76	
Zalmon Read -	81	Zalmon Read.	Samuel Beers -	81	
Isaac H. Bartram -	88	Isaac H. Bartram.	Sarah Gregory -	73	
Abraham Couch -	73	Abraham Couch.	Hannah Murray -	87	
Stephen Baterson -	79	Stephen Baterson.	Hannah Macvin -	79	
Asell Solomons -	82	Asell Solomons.	Elijah Dinge -	82	
Jacob Packen -	76	Jacob Pachen.	Sarah Bonton -	88	
James Sanford -	81	James Sanford, jr.	Moses Webb -	84	
			John Woolsey -	79	
Weston.			Nathan Knapp -	77	
Samuel Fairwether -	79	Samuel Fairwether.	Daniel Hoyt -	82	
John Knapp -	87	Nathaniel W. Knapp.	Ann Knight -	78	
Betsey Lacey -	80	Jesse Lacey.			
Nehemiah W. Lyon -	81	Nehemiah Lyon.	Wilton.		
Ebenezer Seeley -	79	Ebenezer Seeley.	Rebecca Dikeman -	90	
Joseph Seeley -	84	Joseph Seeley.	Phebe Whitlock -	75	
Justus Whitlook -	85	Justus Whitlook.	Deodate Gaylord -	80	
Wildman Hall -	75	Wildman Hall.	Seth Bonton -	86	
Eleanor Wilson -	80	Walter Wilson.	Eber Dudley -	87	
Hannah Whaley -	81	Jonathan Whaley.	Clapp Rockwell -	77	
Ezekiel Obanks -	81	Ezekiel Obanks.	Mary Cole -	77	
Isaac Hubbell -	82	Hannah Fanton.	Daniel Birchard -	80	
Hannah Robertson -	84	Alanson Robertson.	Samuel Stewart -	95	
Elias Bennett -	88	Elias Bennett.	Jesse St. John -	81	
Jonathan Godfrey -	87	Samuel Smith.	Job Hodges -	82	
Thomas Squairs -	79	Thomas Squairs.	Zadok Raymond -	76	
Fanton Beers -	85	Fanton Beers.	Cato Treadwell -	74	
			Thad. Mead -	76	
Stamford.			Daniel Wescott -	86	
Joseph Selleck -	81	Joseph Selleck.	Isaiah Betts -	75	
Hezekiah Knapp -	90	Hezekiah Knapp.	Daniel Betts -	84	
Ezra Scofield -	84	Ezra Scofield.			
Josiah W. Scofield -	77	Edward Scofield.	New Canaan.		
Samuel Provost -	75	Samuel Provost.	Mary Waterbury -	75	
William Knapp -	84	William Knapp.	Warren Hoyt -	78	
Enos Waterbury -	79	Enos Waterbury.	John Conly -	41	
Jonathan Weed -	82	Jonathan Weed.	Elizabeth Wrid -	84	
Jared Scofield -	84	Jared Scofield.	Lavis Stebbens -	83	
Ebenezer Dean -	74	Ebenezer Dean.	Isaac Smith -	78	
Samuel Dean -	77	Samuel Dean.	Isaac Benedict -	89	
David Raymond -	80	Gould Raymond.	Ann Comstock -	85	
Hait Scofield -	84	Hait Scofield.	Enoch St. John -	75	
			Aaron Abbott -	82	
Greenwich.			Elias Gregory -	89	
Noah Lockwood -	73	Noah Lockwood.	Allen Clinton -	77	
Messenger Lockwood -	75	Messenger Lockwood.	Daniel Weed -	74	
Ebenezer Jessup -	77	Ebenezer Jessup.			
Joshua Lyon -	87	Joshua Lyon.	**WINDHAM COUNTY.**		
Smith Mead -	80	Seely Mead.	Canterbury.		
Phineas Rundle -	81	Gilbert Close.	Samuel C. Adam -	76	Samuel C. Adam.
Charles Smith -	73	Charles Smith.	Susanna Monroe -	79	Susanna Monroe.
Solomon Mills -	84	Soloman Mills.	Benjamin Smith -	77	Benjamin Smith.

CONNECTICUT—Continued.

Names of pensioners for revolutionary or military services.	Ages.	Names of heads of families with whom pensioners resided June 1, 1840.
WINDHAM—Continued.		
CANTERBURY—Continued.		
Sarah Manning	78	Mansur Manning.
Philena Bradford	70	Archibald Bradford.
Richard Cady	78	Richard Cady.
Gideon Popple	94	Gideon Popple.
Hezekiah Kingsley	81	Hezekiah Kingsley.
Ebenezer Packes	81	Ebenezer Packes.
Lucy Smith	89	Asher Smith.
Nathaniel Luce	82	Nathaniel Luce.
Samuel Shepard	79	Samuel Shepard.
Abigail Brown	70	Abigail Brown.
Candes Lilly Bristee	83	Theodore Bristee.
Martha Hough	77	Samuel L. Hough.
Susanna Adams	98	Peleg Lewis.
Phebe Leach	87	Harvey Leach.
PLAINFIELD.		
Judith Watson	87	Moses Packes.
Marvil Laurence	75	Marvil Laurence.
Reuben Briant	77	Reuben Briant.
Stephen Bennet	83	Stephen Bennet.
Squire Cady	88	Squire Cady.
STERLING.		
Reuben Camp	85	Reuben Camp.
Simon Titus	87	Joseph Titus.
VOLUNTOWN.		
Thomas Robins	75	Thomas Robins.
Zeruviah Robins	85	Zeruviah Robins.
William Stewart	89	William Stewart.
Gershom Ray	80	Gershom Ray.
Benjamin Palmer	83	Benjamin Palmer.
Freelove Kinney	89	Avery Kinney.
Agnes Laurence	82	Charles Kennada.
Moses Thompson	76	Charles W. Thompson.
Income Potter	94	Income Potter.
WINDHAM.		
Mercy Bingham	97	——— Lincoln.
Loisa Raymond	81	Edward Raymond.
Eliphalet Ripley	55	Eliphalet Ripley.
Jonathan Robinson	80	Jonathan Robinson
Andrew Robinson	77	Andrew Robinson.
John S. Billings	77	Gilbert Billings.
Peter Sanders	88	Peter Sanders.
Benjamin Willard	85	Benjamin Willard.
Nehemiah Ripley	78	Nehemiah Ripley.
Asa Bates	82	Asa Bates.
Lucy Snow	87	Edward Chappel.
Pompey McCuffe	80	Pompey McCuffe.
Abner Weble	81	Abner Weble.
Dudley Hovey	78	Dudley Hovey.
Seabry Manning	76	Gamaliel Manning.
Mary Manning	93	Walter Kingsley.
Lydia Losell	95	John Losell.
Eunice Rudd	87	William R. Dorrance.
Nathan Fuller	76	Nathan Fuller.
Prudence Welch	72	
CHAPLIN.		
Eunice Fisk	85	Eunice Fisk.
Lucy Kenneda	76	Thomas Baldwin.
David Dean	81	David Dean.
Matthew Smith	80	Matthew Smith.
——— Foster	78	Joseph Foster, jr.
Lucy Simons	76	Otis Whiton.
Abigail Utley	82	James Utley.
Amos Clark	78	Amos Clark.
Elizabeth Lamphere	81	Solomon Lamphere.
HAMPTON.		
David Spencer	78	David Spencer.
Amasa Clark	76	Amasa Clark.
Amos Ford	78	Amos Ford.
Amasa Martin	76	Amasa Martin.
William Durkee	81	William Durkee, 1st.
Nathaniel F. Martin	80	Nathaniel F. Martin.
Chloe Farnham	79	Philip Pearl.
Joseph Ashley	84	Joseph Ashley.
Silas Cleaveland	84	Mason Cleaveland.
Lucy Dennison	77	William Clark.
Daniel Ashley	82	Daniel Ashley.
WINDHAM—Continued.		
HAMPTON—Continued.		
Anna Holt	79	Ezra D. Beers.
Tamma Barnham	74	Tamma Barnham.
BROOKLYN.		
Jaben Kingsley	82	Jaben Kingsley.
Ezra Franklyn	87	Ezra Franklyn.
Anna Wheeler	72	Timothy Herrick.
Joseph Davison	82	Joseph Davison.
KILLINGLY.		
Oliver Chase	79	Oliver Chase.
Simon Place	88	Calvin Place.
Reuben Robinson	84	Reuben Robinson.
Elihu Warner	77	Elihu Warner.
Seth Babbit	80	Silas Tucker.
Mary Eddy	79	James Bussey.
Daniel Farman	80	Daniel Farman.
Seth Short	82	William Button.
Samuel White	82	Samuel White.
Shubal Hutchins	81	Shubal Hutchins.
Nathaniel Thurber	80	Nathaniel Thurber.
Hannah Adams	80	Joseph Adams.
Aaron Buck	86	Aaron Buck.
John Fisher	84	Laben Fisher.
Oliver Torry	84	Oliver Torry.
Edward Babbit	77	Edward Babbit.
Margaret Raynolds	82	Matilda Raynolds.
Moses Lippet	89	Nathaniel Lippet.
James Simmons	77	James Simmons.
Annis Day	79	Annis Day.
POMFRET.		
Olive Hyde	79	William Sherman.
Jeremiah Wheaton	84	Jeremiah S. Wheaton.
Amasa Copeland	82	Amasa Copeland.
Deliverance Caswell	86	Jedida Griggs.
Elisha Cady	91	Rachel Richmond.
Reuben Sharp	77	Reuben Sharp.
Lucinda White	76	Lucinda White.
Sarah Bugbee	88	Aaron Tucker.
Albey Stone	78	Albey Stone.
ASHFORD.		
Amasa Robinson	77	Amasa Robinson.
Hannah Bedlow	86	Hannah Bedlow.
George Dunworth	81	Horace Whiton.
Ambrose Brown	73	Ambrose Brown.
Samuel Whitney	82	Warren Whitney.
Ebenezer Robbins	83	Ebenezer Robbins.
Josiah Eaton	83	Josiah Eaton.
Willard Watkins	75	William Orcutt.
Sarah Lawson	74	Ariel Keys.
Jacob Bosworth	79	David Fuller.
Prudence Scarborough	71	Uriah B. Carpenter.
Eliphal Carpenter	72	Lucius Carpenter.
Esther Chapman	71	Timothy Backus.
Ephraim Squire	92	Ephraim Squire.
Philip Squire	83	Philip Squire.
Martha Bugbee	82	Martha Bugbee.
David Seares	87	David Seares.
James B. Felch	47	James B. Felch.
Aaron Flint	81	Aaron Flint.
Frederick Knowlton	79	Frederick Knowlton.
Nathaniel Round	81	Nathaniel Round.
John Davis	85	John Davis.
THOMPSON.		
Sarah Allton	77	Daniel Allton.
Phebe Stone	87	Joseph Wheaton.
Thomas Elliott	81	Ira Elliott.
Jonathan Converse	80	Jonathan Converse.
Susanna Day	77	George Day.
Robert Tucker	80	Robert Tucker.
Susanna Goodell	68	Amos Goodell.
Ebenezer Covill	81	Ebenezer Covill.
Arculaus Sibley	79	Arculaus Sibley.
Eleazer Bowen	86	Eli R. Gleason.
Joseph Matthews	88	Nathan Matthews.
Stephen Robbins	79	Amos Robbins.
William Town	83	Harmon Shumway.
Rebecca Davis	76	Thomas Davis.
William Walker	82	Richard Carpenter.

8

CENSUS OF PENSIONERS.

CONNECTICUT—Continued.

Names of pensioners for revolutionary or military services.	Ages.	Names of heads of families with whom pensioners resided June 1, 1840.	Names of pensioners for revolutionary or military services.	Ages.	Names of heads of families with whom pensioners resided June 1, 1840.
WINDHAM—Continued.			LITCHFIELD—Continued.		
THOMPSON—Continued.			HARRINGTON—Continued.		
Ebenezer Greene	81	Samuel Greene.	Lyman Clark	89	Lyman Clark.
Jacob Blackmar	80	Jacob Blackmar.			
Joseph Richardson	78	Joseph Richardson.	BARKHAMSTEAD.		
Asa Jacobs	80	Asa Jacobs.	Abner Slade	82	Abner Slade.
Molly Woodlin	88	Christopher Corlis.	Tahpoenes Wilder	79	Thomas Wilder.
Sarah Benson	88	Ebenezer Thompson.	Medad Munson	83	Medad Munson.
Alpheus Bowers	85	Deluno White.	Esther Moses	76	Evelin Kibom.
Aaron Bixby	79	Aaron Bixby.	Mercy Wilson	82	Martin Rust.
Molly Bixby	72	Halsey Bixby.	David Lee	76	Daniel Lee.
Chester Chaffee	85	Chester Chaffee.	David Hoskins	81	Lyman Hoskins.
Joseph Tourtelott	82	Joseph Tourtelott.	Strong Sanford	79	Strong Sanford.
Nancy White	93	Martin White.	Martin Moses	79	Martin Moses.
			Mary Gilbert	74	Franklin Gilbert.
WOODSTOCK.			John Mash	82	John Mash.
Anna Fowler	86	John F. Williams.			
Andrew Parsons	79	Nelson L. Elmer.	NEW HARTFORD.		
John Fox	83	Nehemiah Fox.	Roswell Marsh	79	Roswell Marsh.
David Clark	85	Mary Clark.	Levi Watson	79	Levi Watson.
Hezekiah Herrendeen	–	Hezekiah Herrendeen.	Reuben Messenger	87	Reuben Messenger.
Oliver Dorsett	68	Phebe Austin.	Lydia Thorp	78	Lydia Thorp.
Elijah Mason	83	Jacob Lyon.	Salome Marsh	77	Miles Marsh.
John Clark	85	Thaddeus Clark.	Nathan Barns	–	Nathan Barns.
Calvin Holbrook	82	Calvin Holbrook.	Susan Seymour	77	Martin S. Goodwin.
Lucy Underwood	82	Rufus Child.	Mitchel Spencer	74	Mitchel Spencer.
Mary Curtis	86	Ebenezer Hibbard.	Israel Barns	82	Israel Barns.
Jemima Harding	80	Hezekiah Bugbee.	Huldah Crow	74	William Butter.
Willard Child	82	Willard Child.			
William Carter	88	Abigail Child.	COLEBROOK.		
Abiel Chaffee	79	Abiel Chaffee.	John Thomas	80	Miles H. Bidwell.
			Ephraim White	86	Asa White.
LITCHFIELD COUNTY.			Jesse Taylor	87	Hiram Smith.
LITCHFIELD.			John Phelps	84	John Phelps.
Amos Galpin	86	Amos Galpin.	Mehitable Simons	78	Abel Bunnell.
Martha Moss	90	Lery Catlin.	—— Simons	82	Abial Cose.
Eunice Sanford	84	Stephen Moss.	Titus Hart	83	Titus Hart.
Athnel Gileot	81	Athnel Gileot.	Mary Tinker	82	James Marvin.
Elisha Mason	81	Elisha Mason.	David Orris	93	Chandler Wutten.
James Baldwin	82	James Baldwin.	Eleazer Bidwell	88	Phineas Bidwell.
William Gibbs	86	William Gibbs.			
Solomon Gibbs	80	Solomon Gibbs.	WINCHESTER.		
Eliada Orsborne	79	Eliada Orsborne.	Seth Bishop	82	Alonzo Bishop.
Samuel Blakesly	80	Samuel Blakesly.	Hooma Rogers	80	Samuel Rogers.
Levy ——	74	Levy ——.	Zebina Smith	80	Zebina Smith.
Thomas Stone	86	Thomas Stone.	Jamima Jose	70	Lavina Hawly.
Rhoda Chase	82	Charles Buel.	Daniel H. Cone	87	Ira Loomis.
James Birge	82	James Birge.	Abigail Hatch	–	Washington Hatch.
Oliver Pickinson	83	Samuel Wright.	Sillimon Hubbel	75	Silliman Hubbel.
Thankful Potter	76	Oliver Pickinson.			
John Hall	85	John Hall.	ROXBURY.		
Gershom Gibbs	90	Willis Gibbs.	Deliverance S. Painter	75	Henry Painter.
Patience Gibbs	75	Jarvis Grisnold.	Thomas Beardsley	85	Nathan Beardsley.
John Welch	82	John Welch.	Roswell Wheaton	80	Roswell Wheaton.
Ruth Waugh	79	Ruth Waugh.	Philo Hodge	83	Philo Hodge.
Lydia Parmer	85	Alanson Hall.	David Buel	83	David Buel.
Olive Barwes	89	Rufus Ames.			
Rachel Porter	79	John Porter.	MILFORD.		
Grant Wicknire	80	Grant Wicknire.	John Waoner	76	John Waoner.
Rebecca Seymour	78	Rebecca Seymour.	Nathaniel Wilson	76	Nathaniel Wilson.
Elisha Taylor	79	Elisha Taylor.	—— Beardsley	57	Sylvester R. Lane.
Joseph Mason	85	Chester Emmons.	Henry Nearing	82	Henry Nearing.
—— Smith	81	George Smith.	Daniel Copley	84	Daniel Copley.
			David ——	79	David ——.
TORRINGTON.			John Cavenan	82	John Cavenan.
Thomas White	76	Thomas White.	John Camp	78	John Camp.
Mary Brown	80	Sylvester Coe.	Timothy Randall	82	Timothy Randall.
Rhoda Birrell	78	Henry Bristol.	Phineas Gorham	83	Phineas Gorham.
Justice Reed	79	Justice Reed.	Benjamin Hamblin	76	Benjamin Hamblin.
Ebenezer Miller	76	Ebenezer Miller.	David Lockwood	80	David Lockwood.
Noah Drake	82	Noah Drake.	Jonathan ——	78	Jonathan ——.
Polly Filer	82	Julia Filer.	Samuel Oviatt	77	Samuel Oviatt.
Prudence Taylor	86	Fanny Taylcr.	Levi Smith	76	Levi Smith.
Thomas Watson	79	George Watson.	Charles Randall	76	Charles Randall.
HARRINGTON.			WOODBURY.		
Darius Foot	78	Darius Foot.	John Strong	87	John Strong.
Martha Bull	76	John Bull.	Enoch Hayes	75	Enoch Hayes.
Benoni Johnson	73	Sherman Cloveland.	Jesse Hayes	77	Jesse Hayes.
George Jones	85	George Jones.	Abram Smith	80	Abram Smith.
John Winchel	77	John Winchel.	Benjamin Andrews	84	Benjamin H. Andrews.
Simeon Barhour	87	Simeon Barhour.	Josiah Bacon	84	William H. Bacon.
Widow Barnes	78	Barson Barnes.	Nehemiah Judson	82	Nehemiah Judson.
Erastus Baldwin	80	Erastus Baldwin.			

CONNECTICUT—Continued.

Names of pensioners for revolutionary or military services.	Ages.	Names of heads of families with whom pensioners resided June 1, 1840.	Names of pensioners for revolutionary or military services.	Ages.	Names of heads of families with whom pensioners resided June 1, 1840.
LITCHFIELD—Continued.			**LITCHFIELD—Continued.**		
PLYMOUTH.			SHARON—Continued.		
Electa Allen	79	Roger Allen.	John Hatch	80	Daniel Hatch.
David Adkins	80	David Adkins.			
Thaddeus Brack	76	Janus Brack.	GOSHEN.		
Theophilus M. Smith	82	Theophilus M. Smith.	William Browne	83	William Brown.
Henry Stevens	75	Horace Stevens.	Ruth Hart	79	Warren Brown.
Lydia Jones	79	Horace Tolles.	Samuel Miles	84	Charles H. Dear.
			Elizabeth Osborn	85	William F. Osborn.
WATERTOWN.			Jeremiah M. Kelly	81	Augustus Miles.
Anne Bradley	82	Anne Bradley.	Mary Howe	85	Mary Howe.
Obed Doolittle	76	Obed Doolittle.	Parmelia Thompson	76	Charles M. Thompson.
Thomas Frun	77	Thomas Frun.	Francis Beach	85	Francis Beach.
Chauncey Garnsey	80	Chauncey Garnsey.	Julius Beach	75	Julius Beach.
Benjamin Huil	76	John P. Hungerford.			
Anne Merriman	76	George F. Merriman.	CORNWELL.		
Samuel Woodruff	81	Samuel Woodruff.	Jane Baldwin	81	Henry Baldwin.
			George Clark	88	George Clark.
BETHLEHEM.			Abel Avery	79	Abel Avery.
Ebenezer Hall	82	Brack Zophar.	Burret Jennings	81	John Jennings.
Champion Clark	79	Edwin Clark.	David Mallery	86	David Mallery.
Abner Everett	77	Abner Everett.	Chloe Prout	68	Chloe Prout.
Samuel Jackson	82	Samuel Jackson.	Oliver Burnham	79	Oliver Burnham.
Sarah Brown	78	Leman Thomas.	Abigail Pratt	89	Abigail Pratt.
			Jacob Scoville	88	Jacob Scoville, 2d.
WASHINGTON.			Martha Dean	78	Ethel Dean.
Meriam Armstrong	84	Meriam Armstrong.	Adonijah Pangman	82	Gideon P. Pangman.
John Day	74	John Noble.			
Susanna Osborn	77	Daniel Prentiss.	NORFOLK.		
Joseph Titus	82	Joseph Titus, jr.	Richard Beckley	80	Richard Beckley.
Olive Whitney	86	Elisha Whitney.	John Strong	79	John Strong.
			Reuben Palmer	79	Reuben Palmer.
WARREN.			Joseph Rockwell	82	Joseph Rockwell.
Daniel Beeman	84	Daniel Beeman.	Ichabod Atwater	80	Ichabod Atwater.
Mary Batterson	77	Mary Batterson.	Hessibah Warner	79	Russell Allen.
Lysander Curtis	77	Dilly Curtis.	Ephraim Brown	68	Ephraim Brown.
Lovisa James	82	Lovisa James.	Mary Heady	79	John Heady.
Benjamin Sackett	78	Benjamin Sackett.	Esther White	77	Daniel White.
Lydia Tanner	85	Ebenezer Tanner.	Elin Tilbals	79	Orrin Tilbals.
John Welch	77	John Welch.			
Sarah Wickwire	80	Alvan Wickwire.	CANAAN.		
			Thomas Judd	86	Chauncey Morriss.
KENT.			Esther Post	76	Esther Post.
Michael Bailey	96	Philo Bailey.	Esther Hunt	77	John Hunt.
Naomi Burton	92	Joseph Benson.	Abraham Holcomb	78	Timothy Morton.
Lucy Roots	76	Hiram H. Roots.	Joshua Bolden	77	Jeremiah Bolden.
Silas Leonard	83	Amasa Leonard.	Nathaniel Merrils	80	Nathaniel Merrills.
Joseph Segar	82	Joseph Segar.	Jonathan Gillett	78	Jonathan Gillett.
Mary Stone	81	Levi W. Stone.	Nela Wadsworth	77	Benjamin Wadsworth.
Elias Taylor	87	Agur Beardsley.	Olive Jaqrua	77	Daniel Jaqrua.
Elizabeth Hubbell	77	Chester Hubbell.	Amy Stevens	79	Seth Stevens.
David Whitehead	75	David Whitehead.	Edmina Demming	75	Edmund Demming.
Tracy Beeman	78	Tracy Beeman.			
Daniel Stone	81	Daniel Stone.	**MIDDLESEX COUNTY.**		
—— Judd	92	Joseph J. Cass.	MIDDLETOWN (without the city.)		
			Rachel Crowell	79	Henry Crowell.
SALISBURY.			Allen Evans	79	William Butler.
Rufus Landon	81	Henry Landon.	Zarnah Phelps	79	Zarnah Phelps.
John Russell	78	John Russell.	Jesse Caples	92	Jesse Caples.
Sylvia Sardam	63	Solomon Sardom.	Sylvanus Nichols	77	Sylvanus Nichols, jr.
Archibald Campbell	75	Archibald Campbell.	Joshua Stow	78	Joshua Stow.
Elijah H. Bundy	72	Elijah H. Bundy.	Elijah Roberts	78	Elijah Roberts.
Joseph Hollista	88	Horace Hollista.	William Bacon	82	Oliver Atkins.
Catharine Wilsey	74	Lewis German.	Samuel Golpin	81	Samuel Golpin.
Simeon Sage	87	Simeon Sage.	Ebenezer Roberts	82	Harley Bowes.
Mary Evaets	91	Mary Evaets.	Elizabeth Treat	82	Seth Cornwell.
			Benjamin Gilbert	79	Benjamin Gilbert.
SHARON.			John Cornwell	80	John Cornwell.
Daniel Clark	78	Daniel Clark.	Samuel Butler	74	Samuel Cutler.
Asahel Hotchkiss	80	Asahel Hotchkiss.	Christina Belden	85	Christina Belden.
James Lloyd	76	William Loyd.	Elizabeth W. Sage	83	Elizabeth W. Sage.
Thomas Heth	85	Thomas Heth.	Hannah Taylor	79	Samuel Miner.
Adonijah Maxam	86	Clark Maxan.			
David ——	76	Henry Van Densen.	CITY OF MIDDLETOWN,		
Lois Lambert	79	Lois Lambert.	Jack Randall	84	Jack Randall.
Johanna Lyman	85	Abram Weed.	Hamet Achmet	81	Hamet Achmet.
Tabitha Merchant	82	Samuel Merchant.	Samuel Frothingham	81	Samuel Frothingham.
Alpheus Jewitt	85	Alpheus Jewitt.	Thaddeus Nichols	78	Thaddeus Nichols.
John Fuller	76	Cyrus Fuller.	Rachel Carter	91	Rachel Carter.
Samuel Ames	47	Samuel Ames.	William Plumb	91	William Plumb.
John Fullerton	81	Rufus Chamberlin.	Louis Crofoot	82	Ephraim Crofoot.
Nathaniel Hunter	82	Nathaniel Hunter.	William Sumner	83	William Sumner.
Joel Chaffee	81	Joel Chaffee.	Rebecca Burr	78	William Warner.
John Wilson	78	John Wilson.			

CONNECTICUT—Continued.

Names of pensioners for revolutionary or military services.	Ages.	Names of heads of families with whom pensioners resided June 1, 1840.	Names of pensioners for revolutionary or military services.	Ages.	Names of heads of families with whom pensioners resided June 1, 1840.
MIDDLESEX—Continued.			**MIDDLESEX—Continued.**		
CHATHAM.			SAYBROOK.		
Rachel Strong	79	Rachel Strong.	Rufus Clark	75	Rufus Clark.
Esther Warner	93	Esther Warner.	Ambrose Waterhouse	83	Ambrose Waterhouse.
Rebecca Bowers	82	Rebecca Bowers.	Joel Drane	78	Joel Drane.
Jacob Hurd	79	Jacob Hurd.	Oliver Chalker	80	Oliver Chalker.
Benjamin Hurd	77	Benjamin Hurd.	Moses Chalker	81	Moses Chalker.
Richard Flood	78	Richard Flood.	John Jones	79	John Jones.
Jesse Graham	79	Jesse Graham.	Elias Tully	88	Samuel M. Tully.
John Markham	83	John Markham.	George Clark	78	George Clark.
Abel Abel	77	Abel Abel.	John Salter	83	John Salter.
Elijah Abel	79	Elijah Abel.			
Elisha Niles	79	Elisha Niles.	CHESTER.		
Daniel Morgan	78	Daniel Morgan.	Harmon Dudley	82	Harmon Dudley.
Anna Usher	91	Sophron Usher.	Joseph Clark	78	Joseph Clark.
Philip White	92	Philip White.			
John Johnson	81	John Johnson.	WESTBROOK.		
Sparro Smith	78	S. Smith.	Richard Stokes	76	Richard Stokes.
Benjamin Cobb	79	Benjamin Cobb.	Elijah Stannard	87	Elijah Stannard.
Amos Clark	83	Amos Clark.	Jedediah Chapman	81	Jedediah Chapman.
Rebecca Johnson	85	Rebecca Johnson.	Cornelius Chittenden	74	Cornelius Chittenden.
Benjamin Pettis	84	Benjamin Pettis.	John Chittenden	83	John Chittenden.
David Sears	85	David Sears.	Nathan Kirtland	77	Nathan Kirtland.
Stephen Clark	83	Stephen Clark.	Job Stannard	78	Job Stannard.
Seymour Hurlbut	83	Seymour Hurlbut.	John Stannard	80	John Stannard.
Simeon Penfield	85	Simeon Penfield.			
David Shepard	82	David Shepard.	**TOLLAND COUNTY.**		
George Bush	83	George Bush.	HEBRON.		
Ezra Potter	85	Asa Dickerson.	Sarah Flint	78	Joshua C. Flint.
			John Taylor	83	John Taylor.
DURHAM.			Andrew Mann	85	Caleb Hubbard.
Jabez Chalker	83	Jabez Chalker.	Daniel Phelps	81	Daniel Phelps.
Eber Lee	79	Elah Camp, 2d.	Amos Phelps	83	Amos Phelps.
John Barkhardt	–	Daniel Thompson.	Joseph Mann	78	Joseph Mann.
James Parmalee	79	James Parmalee.	Roger Phelps	77	R. L. Phelps.
Rejoice Camp	81	Lemuel Camp.	Hannah White	80 to 90	Hannah White.
Manoah Camp	79	Manoah Camp.	Deborah Brown	81	Harvey Brown.
Elizabeth Bishop	71	Henry Canfield.	Robert Holdridge	77	Robert Holdridge.
			Hannah Peter	78	Hiram Goodale.
HADDAM.			Mary Mack	78	P. R. Gilbert.
Abisha Smith	86	Abisha Smith.			
Nehemiah Tyler	80	Nehemiah Tyler.	VERNON.		
Sarah Lewis	86	Sarah Lewis.	Roswell Smith	82	Roswell Smith.
Phebe Cow	71	Ephraim Parsons.	Justus Talcott	80	Justus Talcott.
Jonathan Sabin	83	Jonathan Sabin.	Jane King	72	Elisha Pember.
Noadiah Cone	80	Noadiah Cone.	Leonard Rogers	85	Leonard Rogers.
Huldah Cook	86	Huldah Cook.	Leavitt Millard	80	Leavitt Millard.
Concurrence Bonfoy	78	Concurrence Bonfoy.			
James Thomas	87	James Thomas.	BOLTON.		
			John Coleman	87	John Coleman.
EAST HADDAM.			Abigail Fitch	88	Elijah Fitch.
William Gelston	84	William Gelston.	Tabitha Carver	83	Tabitha Carver.
John Foster	92	John Foster.	Abner Backus	78	Abner Backus.
Olive Hungerford	82	Olive Hungerford.	Cary Clark	84	Cary C. Clark.
Gurdon Ely	80	Gurdon Ely.			
William Babcock	54	William Babcock.	COLUMBIA.		
Samuel Fargo	79	Samuel Fargo.	Simon Babcock	82	Simon Babcock.
Samuel Palms	85	Samuel Palms.	Jemima Dewey	83	Jemima Clark.
Samuel Lord	85	Samuel Lord.	Samuel Barstow	80	Samuel Barstow.
Lydia Brainerd	82	Lydia Brainerd.	David Skinner	88	David Skinner.
Temperance Smith	76	Temperance Smith.	David Strong	78	David Strong.
Jabez Maynerd	83	Jabez Maynerd.			
John Watson	76	John Watson.	MANSFIELD.		
George Plum	74	George Plum.	Temperance Bennett	95	Temperance Bennett.
Joel Spencer	77	Joel Spencer.	Esther Bennett	79	Ann Bills.
Nathan Burnham	81	Nathan Burnham.	Samuel Dunham	85	Samuel Dunham.
Samuel Emmons	79	Samuel Emmons.	Nathaniel Brown	83	Nathaniel Brown.
Daniel S. Emmons	83	Daniel S. Emmons.	Selah Turner	74	Selah Turner.
Isaac C. Ackeley	80	Isaac C. Ackeley.	Marilla Bronson	71	Greene Capron.
Joshua Cone	82	Joshua Cone.	Ruth Janes	77	Josiah Janes.
Crippen Hurd	77	Crippen Hurd.	Sylvanus Conant	89	Sylvanus Conant.
			Jonathan Atwood	79	Jonathan Atwood.
KILLINGWORTH.			Lydia Dewey	72	Alathea Jones.
Jonathan Wellman	78	H. Griffin.	Isaac Arnold	76	Isaac Arnold.
			Mary Davis	76	Joseph Solace.
CLINTON.			Josiah Fuller	87	Josiah Fuller.
Elnathan Hurd	83	Elnathan Hurd.	Gardiner Spencer	81	Gardiner Spencer.
Constant Parmelee	79	Constant Parmalee.	Martha Martin	79	Martha Martin.
John Wright	78	John Wright.			
Jimmy Post	79	Jimmy Post.	COVENTRY.		
Elias Stevens	76	Elias Stevens.	John Clark	88	John Clark.
David Griffin	77	David Griffin.	Mary Lyman	88	Martin Lyman.
			Ebenezer L. Sweetland	87	E. L. Sweetland.
			Bela Boynton	87	Bela Boynton.

CONNECTICUT—Continued.

Names of pensioners for revolutionary or military services.	Ages.	Names of heads of families with whom pensioners resided June 1, 1840.	Names of pensioners for revolutionary or military services.	Ages.	Names of heads of families with whom pensioners resided June 1, 1840.
TOLLAND—Continued.			**TOLLAND—Continued.**		
COVENTRY—Continued.			UNION.		
Celia Crossman	82	David Robertson.	Orthanial Brown	81	Orthanial Brown.
Asa Parker	83	Asa Parker.	Joseph Snell	85	Joseph Snell.
Solomon Judd	82	Solomon Judd.	Samuel Stone	86	Samuel Stone.
Asher Wright	86	Asher Wright.	Hannah Sessions	86	Joanna D. Sessions.
Stephen Dunham	79	Stephen Dunham.	Ebenezer Lawson	81	Isaac B. Booth.
James Dunham	76	James Dunham.			
Mary Philips	80	Samuel Cooper.	TOLLAND.		
Elijah Morley	72	Elijah Morley.	Hannah Bugbee	77	Alanson Bugbee.
Lucy Slocumb	74	David Man.	Jacob Benton	80	Jacob Benton.
Daniel Avery	78	Daniel Avery.	Lydia Chapman	81	Ashbel Chapman.
Nathaniel Root	84	Nathaniel Root.	Elnathan Grant	78	Elnathan Grant.
Rebecca Talcott	81	Chester Talcott.	Ebenezer Grover	86	Ebenezer Grover.
Daniel Loomis	82	Daniel Loomis.	Lemuel Pinney	88	Daniel Griggs.
Benjamin House	82	Benjamin House.	Samuel Johnson	83	Ira Johnson.
Mary Ensworth	80	Jedediah Ensworth.	Jabez Kingsberry	84	Jabez Kingsberry.
Dow C. Brigham	77	D. C. Brigham.	Medad Kellogg	91	Medad Kellogg.
			Ellis Lillibridge	79	Daniel Lillibridge.
SOMERS.			Ammi Paulk	84	Joshua Luce.
Eleanor Jones	87	Jonathan Clark.	Ruth Scott	67	Leverett Luce.
Abigail Morgan	78	Charles Morgan.	Samuel Reed	79	Samuel Reed.
James Spencer	80	James Spencer.	Simeon Webster	80	Milton Webster.
George Risley	77	George Risley.			
Oliver Chapin	82	Oliver Chapin.	ELLINGTON.		
Huldah Bourn	77	John Bourn.	Jonathan Buckland	76	Jonathan Buckland.
Asa Wood	78	Martin Wood.	Timothy Carpenter	74	Timothy Carpenter.
Jonathan Clark	78	Jonathan Clark.	Charlotte Foster	74	Ephraim Ely.
Lorica Russell	84	Lorica Russell.	Solomon Eaton	82	Solomon Eaton.
Frederick Kibber	78	Frederick Kibber.	Sarah Wallis	84	James M. Gardener.
Sarah Pease	81	Sarah Pease.	John Dimmick	86	Ezekiel Newell.
Martin Enoe	76	Martin Enoe.	Jemima Steele	77	Oliver W. Steele.
Daniel Brace	83	Daniel Brace.			
Anna Pease	92	Oliver Pease.	WILLINGTON.		
			Mary Brigham	87	Elisha Atwood.
STAFFORD.			Ellis Anderson	72	Thomas Anderson.
Abigail Blodgett	87	Abijah Blodget.	Mrs. Walker	92	Jacob Clarke.
William Rice	78	William Rice.	Solomon Fenton	81	Solomon Fenton.
Amy Ellethorp	86	Samuel E. Fairfield.	Eunice Fuller	77	Chester Fuller.
Abigail Rogers	84	Samuel Colburn, jr.	John Fuller	87	John Fuller.
Hannah Thresher	77	Thomas H. Thresher.	Joseph Scott	77	Hazzard Hull.
Sarah Converse	79	Parley Converse.	Sarah Crocker	82	Joseph Hull.
Sarah Converse	84	Roswell Converse.	Nathan Jennings	86	Elisha Jennings.
Molly Cady	78	Absalom Cady.	Thomas Knowlton	74	Thomas Knowlton.
Israel How	81	Israel How.	Andrew Manning	86	Lathrop Manning.
Stephen Orcutt	83	Stephen Orcutt.	Lois Pearl	76	Austin Pearl.
Silas Dean	85	Silas Dean.	Frederick Pearl	78	Frederick Pearl.
William Patten	88	William Patten.	Eleanor Sparks	78	Roxana Sparks.
Stephen Whitaker	81	Stephen Whitaker.	Seth Vinton	84	Seth Vinton.
Rebecca Huntington	79	Rebecca Huntington.			
Noah Saunders	84	Noah Saunders.			

STATE OF VERMONT.

Names of pensioners for revolutionary or military services.	Ages.	Names of heads of families with whom pensioners resided June 1, 1840.	Names of pensioners for revolutionary or military services.	Ages.	Names of heads of families with whom pensioners resided June 1, 1840.
CHITTENDEN COUNTY.			**CHITTENDEN—Continued.**		
BURLINGTON.			CHARLOTTE—Continued.		
David Russell	82	David Russell.	Skiff Morgan	79	Skiff Morgan.
Nathan Seymour	84	William Seymour.	Samuel Andrews	77	Samuel Cunningham.
William Kilburne	77	William Kilburne.	Asa Narramore	78	Samuel L. Narramore.
Lydia Sawyer	65	Lydia Sawyer.	Ephraim Page	45	Ephraim Page.
John Stacy	79	John Stacy.			
Stephen Russell	75	Stephen Russell.	MILTON.		
Alanson Adams	48	Alanson Adams.	Benjamin Adams	74	Benjamin Adams.
Reuben Bostwick	81	Reuben Bostwick.	Elisha Owen	80	Elisha Owen.
			Alpheus Hall	83	Alpheus Hall.
SHELBURN.			Oliver Howard	77	Oliver Howard.
Samuel Mills	77	Samuel Mills.	John Blake	81	Jonathan Blake.
Dorcas Pierson	73	Hiram Pierson.	William Hewes	79	Benjamin Hewes.
Elizabeth Collamer	74	Ira A. Collamer.			
			ST. GEORGE.		
CHARLOTTE.			Jehiel Isham	78	Jehiel Isham.
Stephen Turrill	94	Lucy Simons.			

VERMONT—Continued.

Names of pensioners for revolutionary or military services.	Ages.	Names of heads of families with whom pensioners resided June 1, 1840.	Names of pensioners for revolutionary or military services.	Ages.	Names of heads of families with whom pensioners resided June 1, 1840.
CHITTENDEN—Continued.			**FRANKLIN**—Continued.		
HINESBURG.			BERKSHIRE—Continued.		
George Palmer	79	Robert Palmer.	Arthur Danow	81	Arthur Danow.
Nanny Wilcox	88	John Wilcox.	Elisha Shaw	78	Elisha Shaw.
Moses Dow	80	Moses Dow.	Lucy Chaffee	82	John Chaffee.
Rhoda Beach	79	Thaddeus L. Beach.	Benj. B. Searle	74	Benjamin B. Searle.
			Elizabeth Bowen	84	Otis Clapp.
COLCHESTER.			Levi Darling	78	Hiram Darling.
Jeremiah Fisher	77	Jeremiah Fisher.			
Lemuel Tubbs	91	Amos C. Richardson.	FAIRFIELD.		
Amos Preston	85	Amos Preston.	Dolly Beardsley	80	Lewis Beardsley.
Elizabeth Alford	75	Joshua Barnes.	Abel Fairbanks	86	Benj. Fairbanks.
David Webster	81	John S. Webster.	John B. Mitchell	81	John B. Mitchell.
Claud Monty	88	John Monty.	Sarah Runnels	70	Ebenezer Runnels.
Amos Mansfield, jr.	47	Amos Mansfield.	Josiah Osgood	82	Lucy Page.
WILLISTON.			MONTGOMERY.		
Daniel Isham	88	Daniel Isham.	Joshua Wade	75	Joshua Wade.
Thaddeus Graves	84	Thaddeus Graves.			
Ebenezer Bradley	79	Timothy M. Bradley.	RICHFORD.		
Zachariah Hart	81	Zachariah Hart.	Hezekiah Goff	86	Hezekiah Goff.
Solomon S. Miller	79	Harry Miller.	Gideon Wood	79	Gideon Wood.
John Brown	82	John Brown.			
Paul Clark	83	Wright Clark.	SHELDON.		
Leonard Hodges	81	Leonard Hodges.	Ebenezer Chamberlain	86	John Fish.
			Francis Duclous	85	Philip W. Duclous.
RICHMOND.			Elim Gilbert	76	Amira Tracy.
John Deveraux	84	Alanson Deveraux.	Joseph Lamb	76	Nathan Lamb.
William Humphrey	57	William Humphrey.	Uriah Higgins	68	Stephen Marvin.
Daniel Robbins	76	Daniel Robbins.	Josiah Peckham	85	Josiah Peckham.
HUNTINGTON.			ST. ALBANS.		
Benjamin Hawley	79	Nathan Hawley.	Jehiel Holdridge	88	Jehiel Holdridge, jr.
John Fitch	85	John Fitch.	John Delaway	82	Chauncey Smith.
John Moses	81	Jonathan Moses.	Eleazer Brooks	73	Eleazer Brooks.
Sophia Buel	77	Ebenezer Buel.	Jeremiah Virginia	83	Jeremiah Virginia.
			William Isham	81	Asahel Isham.
ESSEX.			Noel Potter	79	Levi Beals.
Stephen Butler	81	Stephen Butler.	Daniel B. Meigs	77	Daniel B. Meigs.
David Day	82	Horatio Day.	Hezekiah Keeler	81	Lewis Keeler.
Abigail Bradley	81	Horace Halbert.	Bates Turner	80	Bates Turner.
Gideon Curtis	71	Gideon Curtis.			
			FAIRFAX.		
WESTFORD.			J. Danforth	79	Jonathan Danforth.
James Taylor	75	Bartholomew F. Taylor.	E. Faxan	81	Francis Faxan.
Simeon Hooker	100	Hart Woodruff.	George Magars	85	George Magars.
Jesse Ide	80	Jesse Ide.	Thomas Keyes	85	Thomas Keyes.
Sylvester Crandal	87	John Coon.	Archibald Cook	77	Hiram Cook.
Huldah Wilmouth	84	Henry Woodruff.	Joseph Cross	80	
John Macomber	80	John Macomber.	Eunice Starks	93	
Solomon Hobert	80	Solomon Hobert.	Hannah Blaisdell	85	
Thomas Atwood	85	Thomas Atwood.			
			GEORGIA.		
BOLTON.			Abel Parker	74	Abel Parker.
James Bennett	83	James Bennett.	Elisha Bartlett	82	Orson Bartlett.
Edmund Town	77	Ira Town.	Frederick Cushman	82	Roswell Cushman.
			Ethiel Scott	78	Ethiel Scott.
UNDERHILL.					
Josiah Sheldon	85	Josiah Sheldon.	HIGHGATE.		
Rebecca Wells	85	Rebecca Wells.	Israel Jones	80	Israel Jones.
Barnard Ward	76	Barnard Ward.	John Johnson	82	Nathaniel Johnson.
George Olds	90	Peter Martin.	Philip Shelters	78	Philip Shelters.
Caleb Sheldon	84	Caleb Sheldon.			
Samuel Calhoun	79	Alonzo Calhoun.	SWANTON.		
Chauncey Graves	79	Chauncey Graves.	John Otis	81	Joseph Otis.
Esther Rider	73	Esther Rider.	John B. Joyall	96	John B. Joyall.
			James Fiske	77	James Fiske.
JERICHO.			Peter Barsha	83	Peter Barsha.
Isaac Benham	79	Isaac Benham.	Erastus Hathaway	80	Harry Hathaway.
J. I. Warner	79	J. I. Warner.	John Austin	82	John Austin.
Esther Chapin	81	Esther Chapin.			
Benoni Chapin	82	Benoni Chapin.	**CALEDONIA COUNTY.**		
Roger Stevens	79	Roger Stevens.	BARNET.		
Ichabod Chapin	79	Ezra Church.	William Strobridge	84	William Strobridge.
Peter L. Allen	52	Peter L. Allen.	Levi Hall	79	Nathaniel Hall.
Tryphena Hathaway	86	Arthur Bostwick.			
Ellen Lee	89	Ellen Lee.	ST. JOHNSBURY.		
Simeon Davis	82	Simeon Davis.	Lemuel Jenkins	82	Lemuel Jenkins.
			Simeon Cobb	82	Elkanah Cobb.
FRANKLIN COUNTY.			Samuel Clark	77	Nathan W. Clark.
BERKSHIRE.			Oliver Phelps	77	Oliver Phelps.
Ezekiel Pond	79	John Busbee.	Isaac Stowell	82	Lewis Pierce.
Job Barber	78	Job Barber.	Daniel Fuller	80	Daniel Fuller.
Edward Whitmore	77	Edward Whitmore.	Lydia Farnam	83	Aaron Farnam.

VERMONT—Continued.

Names of pensioners for revolutionary or military services.	Ages.	Names of heads of families with whom pensioners resided June 1, 1840.	Names of pensioners for revolutionary or military services.	Ages.	Names of heads of families with whom pensioners resided June 1, 1840.
CALEDONIA—Continued.			CALEDONIA—Continued.		
St. Johnsbury—Continued.			PEACHAM.		
Comfort Healey - - -	75	Comfort Healey.	Simeon Walker - - -	84	Abel Walker.
Barnabas Barker - -	78	Barnabas Barker.	Judson Farrar - - -	58	Judson Farrar.
Jedediah Coe - - -	78	Nathaniel Kelly.	Ebenezer Spencer - -	76	Ebenezer Spencer.
Joel Roberts - - -	78	Joel Roberts.	James Miner - - -	82	James Miner.
			Lemuel Northrop - -	92	Joseph Northrop.
LYNDON.			Rebecca Bartlett - -	86	Alfred Bartlett.
Abel Carpenter - -	86	Abigail Willard.	Hastings Blanchford - -	50	Isaac Sturtevant.
Ephraim Niles - -	86	Oliver Niles.			
John Bly - - -	83	Reuben Pike.	RYEGATE.		
			Wells Goodwin - - -	47	Wells Goodwin.
WATERFORD.			Sylvanus Larnard - -	77	Sylvanus Larnard.
Samuel Hill - - -	79	Cyrus Hill.	Samuel Johnson - - -	78	Hugh Johnson.
Thaddeus Potter - -	76	Thaddeus Potter.	Allen Stuart - - -	86	Cyrus Heath.
John Melendy - -	83	John Melendy.	Sarah Gray - - -	80	William Nelson, 2d.
John Chaplin - -	73	John Chaplin.			
Samuel Spalding - -	76	Carlton Spalding.	GRAND ISLE COUNTY.		
Moses Huntly - -	90	Dennis Huntly.	ISLE LA MOTT.		
			Gardner Wait - - -	91	Gardner Wait.
BRADLEYSVALE.			Elisha Reynolds - -	77	Elisha Reynolds.
Asa Parker - - -	81	Asa Parker, jr.			
			NORTH HERO.		
SUTTON.			Samuel Doty - - -	84	Samuel Doty.
Jesse Anger - - -	79	Jesse Anger.	Abram Woodard - -	51	Abram Woodard.
Jonathan Sprague - -	82	Jonathan Sprague.			
Samuel Winslow - -	85	James Ruggles.	GRAND ISLE.		
			William Hodgkins - -	82	William Hodgkins.
BURKE.					
Benjamin Farmer - -	90	Uriah Farmer.	ORLEANS COUNTY.		
Abner Coe - - -	77	Oliver Coe.	CRAFTSBURY.		
Seth Clark - - -	80	Seth Clark, jr.	Joseph Scott - - -	79	Joseph Scott.
			Daniel Davison - -	75	Daniel Davison.
KIRBY.			Robert Trumbull - -	86	Robert Trumbull.
Stephen Watkins - -	75	Stephen Watkins.	John Hadley - - -	50	John Hadley.
Jonathan Lewis - -	82	Jonathan Lewis.			
Zebulon Boroughs -	82	Zebulon Boroughs.	ALBANY.		
			Merrill Pillsbury - -	44	Merrill Pillsbury.
DANVILLE.			Samuel Russell - -	43	Samuel Russell.
Benjamin Deming - -	85	Benjamin Deming.	Joshua Johnson - -	76	Joshua Johnson.
Uri Babbit - - -	80	Uri Babbit.	Ebenezer Watson - -	52	Ebenezer Watson.
Thomas Colby - -	82	Page Colby.			
Ebenezer Sawyer - -	84	Jeremiah Kittredge.	LOWELL.		
Sarah Rollins - - -	92	Benjamin Rollins.	Hosea Sprague - - -	89	Hosea Sprague.
Jethro Bachelder - -	93	John Bachelder.	Jonathan Powers - -	82	Jonathan Powers.
Clarissa Trescott - -	72	Matilda Bussell.			
Elizabeth Sanbern - -	68	Jonathan Clifford.	TROY.		
Eli Bickford - - -	85	Eli Bickford.	Cyrus Allen - - -	69	Cyrus Allen.
Eleazer Nutting - -	79	Moses B. Nutting.	Moses Hunt - - -	79	Moses Hunt.
Thomas Hoyt - - -	78	Abner H. Hoyt.			
Stephen Dexter - -	85	William H. Stone.	NEWPORT.		
			John Jenness - - -	79	John Jenness.
WHEELOCK.			Stephen Barnard - -	64	Stephen Barnard.
Ebenezer Chandler - -	85	Theophilus Chandler.			
Nehemiah Phillips - -	78	Nehemiah Phillips.	IRASBURG.		
Judith Darling - -	78	David Darling.	Benjamin Burton - -	85	Benjamin Burton.
Edward Magoon - -	83	Edward M. Magoon.	Benjamin Hardy - -	79	Asa Hardy.
HARDWICK.			COVENTRY.		
Jonathan Stevens - -	79	Jonathan Stevens.	Frederick Herman - -	87	Frederick W. Herman.
John Fox - - -	83	John Fox.	Joseph Priest - - -	78	Joseph Priest.
Abel Conant - - -	84	Joseph Conant.	Edward Welch - - -	72	Edward Welch.
Jonathan Curtis - -	87	Benjamin Thomas.	David Lathe - - -	42	David Lathe.
Reuben Wheatley - -	79	Ward Wheatley.			
			DERBY.		
WALDEN.			Timothy Hinman - -	78	Timothy Hinman.
Nathan Barker - -	76	Nathan Barker.	Isaac Hinman - - -	85	Isaac Hinman.
Benjamin Dow - -	81	Benjamin Dow.	Simeon Pope - - -	78	Simeon Pope.
Timothy Shurtliff - -	82	George Miller.	John Healey - - -	79	John Healey.
Nathaniel Dow - -	82	James B. Dow.	Abram Alexander - -	76	Abram Alexander.
Elisha Cate - - -	83	Elisha Cate, jr.			
Nathaniel Perkins, 1st	84	Nathaniel Perkins, 1st.	GLOVER.		
			Jesse Thomas - - -	77	Samuel Hoyt.
CABOT.			Paul Cook - - -	82	Amos Cook.
Mehitable Webster - -	80	Alpha Webster.			
Deborah Warner - -	78	Oliver A. Warner.	GREENSBOROUGH.		
Fifield Lyford - -	78	Fifield Lyford.	John Cross - - -	86	John S. Ayres.
Thomas Osgood - -	79	Thomas Osgood.	Thomas Tolman - -	84	John C. Ellsworth.
			Amos Smith - - -	83	Amos Smith, jr.
GROTON.			Samuel Badger - -	87	Samuel Badger.
Hepzebah Johnstone -	85	Barnard Brickett.			
John Clark - - -	85	Elijah S. Clark.	CHARLESTON.		
Ebenezer Fisk - -	53	Ebenezer Fisk.	John Palmer - - -	84	D. W. Palmer.
Samuel Randal - -	74	Samuel Randal.	William Sawyer - -	84	William Sawyer, jr.

VERMONT—Continued.

Names of pensioners for revolutionary or military services.	Ages.	Names of heads of families with whom pensioners resided June 1, 1840.
ORLEANS—Continued.		
BROWNINGTON.		
Joel Priest	92	Joel Priest.
HOLLAND.		
John Bishop	46	John Bishop.
Isaac Clement	81	Isaac Clement.
MORGAN.		
James Taylor	72	James Taylor.
Christopher Bartlett	73	Christopher Bartlett.
Samuel Elliot	76	Samuel Elliot.
Nathan Wilcox	81	John M. Wilcox.
Nathaniel S. Clark	84	Nathaniel S. Clark.
Joshua Bailey	77	Joshua Bailey.
BARTON.		
Jonathan Robinson	75	Jonathan Robinson.
John Moncam	73	John Moncam.
Joseph Hyde	74	Jarid Hyde.
John Adams	77	Ammon Jourdon.
WASHINGTON COUNTY.		
CALAIS.		
Richard Ringe	84	Davis Flint.
Welcome Ainsworth	60	Welcome Ainsworth.
John Martin	80	John Martin.
Nathaniel Jacobs	78	Nathaniel Jacobs.
Stephen Hall	82	Stephen Hall.
MARSHFIELD.		
Jonas Cummings	78	True Eaton.
John Pike	78	Sylvester Pike.
Joseph T. Eaton	82	Joseph T. Eaton.
Jonathan Willis	82	Jonathan Willis.
Nathaniel Corbin	87	Rufus Flood.
Henry Dwinnell	89	Henry Dwinnell.
Stephen Rich	78	Stephen Rich.
Daniel Bemus	85	Daniel Bemus.
MONROE.		
Comfort Wheeler	82	Comfort Wheeler.
MONTPELIER.		
Timothy Hatch	87	Timothy Hatch.
Micah Hatch	81	Bulah Wentworth.
Mrs. Davis	82	Samuel Davis.
Edward West	85	Edward West.
Hezekiah Tinkham	81	Hezekiah Tinkham.
Samuel Patterson	87	Samuel Patterson.
Elias Metcalf	80	Elias Metcalf.
John Putnam	76	John Putnam.
Richard Paine	83	Richard Paine.
PLAINFIELD.		
Phebe Shattuck	74	James M. Shattuck.
WATERBURY.		
Roswell Hunt	63	Roswell Hunt.
Levi Gleason	62	Hiram Gale.
Cephas Sheldon	86	Cephas Sheldon.
Asaph Allen	88	Asaph Allen.
Nancy Wright	69	Tilman Wright.
Paul Dillingham	80	Paul Dillingham.
John Hutson	83	John Hutson.
WORCESTER.		
Stephen Spear	76	Stephen Spear.
NORTHFIELD.		
Ebenezer Fox	87	Ebenezer Fox.
Betsey Nickols	67	William Nickols.
John Loyd	51	David R. Tilden.
Susanna Latham	88	James Latham.
Silas Roise	80	Silas Roise.
BARRE.		
Malin Stacy	76	Malin Stacy.
Ansel Paterson	77	Ansel Paterson.
Rebecca Parker	75	John Parker.
Zebedee Beckley	76	Zebedee Beckley.
Francis Davis	82	Samuel Davis.
Nathaniel Holden	87	Elijah Holden.
James Briton	73	James Briton.

Names of pensioners for revolutionary or military services.	Ages.	Names of heads of families with whom pensioners resided June 1, 1840.
WASHINGTON—Continued.		
BARRE—Continued.		
Elizabeth Harrington	74	Joseph D. Harrington.
Jonas Nickols	95	Peter Nickols.
Abijah Holden	87	Eli Holden.
BERLIN.		
James Braman	75	James Braman.
Thomas Spears	80	Thomas Spears.
Molly Townsend	81	Abraham Townsend.
James Perley	75	James Perley.
Nabby Sawyer	74	Moses H. Sawyer.
Stephen Persons	81	Jeremiah Persons.
Solomon Nye	76	Solomon Nye.
Nathaniel Bosworth	87	Nathaniel Bosworth.
ROXBURY.		
Jedediah Smith	78	Jedediah Smith.
Benjamin Sampson	84	Benjamin Sampson.
Hannah Haines	74	Hannah Haines.
Stephen Rumney	49	Stephen Rumney.
MORETOWN.		
Reuben Hawks	85	John Patrial.
Bissel Phelps	86	Bissel Phelps.
DUXBURY.		
Mehitable Lyman	73	Richard Lyman.
Samuel Ridley	87	Samuel Ridley.
David Phelps	85	David Dow.
Thankful Wallice	87	Frederick Wallice.
John Colt	86	Elias Wells.
WAITSFIELD.		
Gaas Hitchcock	71	Lewis Dumas.
Mary Smith	75	Ithamer Smith.
Doud Bushnel	77	Doud Bushnel.
FAYSTON.		
Jesse Mix	76	Jesse Mix.
William Waite	84	Nathaniel Waite.
Elizabeth Hutcherson	77	Benjamin Adams.
Ebenezer Cutler	81	Ebenezer Cutler.
WARREN.		
Ruel Sherman	77	Elias D. Sherman.
William Portler	91	Oliver Portler.
ESSEX COUNTY.		
BLOOMFIELD.		
Adin Bartlett	46	Adin Bartlett.
BRUNSWICK.		
Samson Wait	69	James B. Davis.
CANAAN.		
Mary Luther	74	Moses Luther.
Oliver Goss	79	Oliver Goss.
John Hugh	77	John Hugh.
Gilman Clough	79	Gilman Clough.
Lucy Beecher	79	Marcus Beecher.
CONCORD.		
Hinds Reed	82	J. M. Darling.
Patty Adams	80	Samuel Adams.
Hannah Woodbury	76	Hannah Woodbury.
Martha Woodbury	80	Benjamin Woodbury, 2d.
David Hibbard	85	Josiah Gregory.
Josiah Goodale	86	William Nichols.
GUILDHALL.		
Samuel Howe	83	E. H. Webb.
LUNENBURG.		
Moses Quimby	84	Z. Snow.
Zuriah Marshall	87	Levi Bowker.
Samuel Gates	79	Samuel Gates.
Polly Belknap	83	Stephen Adams.
Azariah Webb	93	J. R. Webb.
Louis Cook	77	William Cook.
Susanna Daniels	77	Leonard Hatch.
Samuel Martin	80	Samuel C. Martin.
Dorcas Bastin	70	Isaac Bastin.

VERMONT—Continued.

Names of pensioners for revolutionary or military services.	Ages.	Names of heads of families with whom pensioners resided June 1, 1840.	Names of pensioners for revolutionary or military services.	Ages.	Names of heads of families with whom pensioners resided June 1, 1840.
ESSEX—Continued.			**ORANGE—Continued.**		
LEMINGTON.			BROOKFIELD—Continued.		
Mills De Forest	77	Abdil Blodget.	Lucy Bigelow	74	W. L. Bigelow.
Anna Abbot	77	Stephen Harris, jr.	Ruth Fisk	87	Artemas Fisk.
			Elizabeth Williams	83 }	Hezekiah Williams.
MAIDSTONE.			Amaziah Grove	86 }	
Jacob Schoff	83	Jacob Schoff.	Amasa Edson	76	Amasa Edson.
			Abigail Adams	76	Elijah Howes.
ORANGE COUNTY.			Philomela Lyman	80	Elijah Howes.
TOPSHAM.			Solomon Smith	77	Jos. G. Smith.
Jacob Wilds	78	Jacob Wilds.	Samuel Bayley	87	Benjamin Bayley.
Adam Dickey	89	Adam Dickey.	Elisha Wilcox	77	Elisha Wilcox.
Anna Banfill	82	Ephraim Bagley.			
Dorothy Weed	88	Isaac Weed.	NEWBURY.		
			William Tice	80	Joshua Bayley, jr.
ORANGE.			Asa Coburn	83	Asa Coburn, jr.
Alden Freeman	80	Bradford Freeman.	Sarah Ladd	72	Sarah Ladd.
Samuel Judkins	78	Samuel Judkins.	Daniel Heath	76	Daniel Heath.
			Joseph Herriman	85	Arad Kent.
WASHINGTON.			John Smith	82	John Smith.
Hannah Clements	94	John Hoyt.	Samuel Johnson	77	Joseph Whitcher.
Joseph Kinneson	76	Joseph Kinneson, jr.	Sarah Ladd	79	Ward Buell.
Enoch Cheney	83	David Cheney.	Mary Smith	79	Jonathan Smith.
Shubal Smith	78	Shubal Smith.	Thomas Mellen	83	Thomas Mellen.
Thaddeus White	81	Thaddeus White.	Peter Bagley	87	Peter Bagley.
			Nathan Avery	81	Geo. W. Avery.
WILLIAMSTOWN.					
Elijah Whitney	85	Elijah Whitney, jr.	TUNBRIDGE.		
James Kilburn	76	L. A. Simons.	William Ballou	81	Sanford Ballou.
Submit Cowdry	82	Orpha Cowdry.	Cyrus Tracy	82	Moses Lunt.
Asa Hatch	80	Asa Hatch.	Hannah Allen	89	Eli Austin.
Joshua Gilman	85	Richard Martyn.	Jonathan Foster	81	Jonathan Foster.
			Enoch Hoytt	80	Enoch Hoytt.
BRADFORD.			Lydia Morsell	78	Lydia Morsell.
Israel Putnam	79	Israel Putnam.	William White	77	William White.
Lucy Blood	74	Elijah Blood.	Timothy Dewey	85	Asahel Dewey.
Emerson Corliss	82	Emerson Corliss.	Daniel Hackett	87	Ephraim Hackett.
Elizabeth Pratt	80	Elizabeth Pratt.			
Dorothy Eastman	70	Samuel F. Eastman.	BRAINTREE.		
Theodore Barker	79	Theodore Barker.	Daniel Flint	79	Nathaniel Flint.
James McFarlin	81	Francis De Cato.	Jonah Flint	85	Augustus Flint.
Samuel Aspenwall	73	Samuel Aspenwall.	Mary Battles	99	Caroline Battles.
Susan Bean	78	Thomas Morey.	Susanna French	89	Gilman Vose.
Reuben Martin	85	William Martin.	Dorcas Nichols	103	Isaac Nichols.
			Bathsheba Bass	89	Samuel Patridge.
CORINTH.			John Gooch	83	Micah Ford.
Daniel Stevens	75	Daniel Stevens.	Lydia Cleavland	81	Abel Thayer.
Reuben Page	86	Reuben Page, jr.	David Smith	82	Jabez Smith.
Nella Towle	85	Ira Towle.			
Jeremiah Bowen	86	Jeremiah Bowen.	RANDOLPH.		
Ebenezer Berry	80	Ebenezer Berry.	David Grow	78	David Grow.
Peter V. Mahew	89	Paul Bickford.	Olive Carpenter	83	George Carpenter.
Amos Boardman	76	Amos Boardman.	Deborah Carlisle	84	Michael Carlisle.
Dorothy Raymond	69	Simon Raymond.	Henry Blodget	80	Henry Blodget.
			Chancy L. Temple	38	Chancy L. Temple.
VERSHIRE.			Nathan Nye	78	Perley Orcott.
Lyman Child	79	Spencer Town.	Ruth Kibbee	80	Ruth Kibbee.
Enoch Cotton	78	Solomon Cotton.	William Corley	74	Alpheus Corley.
Martha Frizzle	83	Eliakim Frizzle.	Lydia Wales	81	Anson Wales.
Samuel Southworth	83	Sewel Godfrey.	Huldah Weston	73	Edman Weston.
Jesse Paine	81	Jesse Paine.	Benj. Blodgett	81	James Blodgett.
Nathan Pierce	82	Lemuel Church.	Levi Wilder	81	Levi Wilder.
			Benj. Woodworth	84	Wm. Woodworth.
CHELSEA.			Dyer Hebard	83	Simeon Boothe.
Anna Dearborn	76	Wilder Dearborn.	Stephen Herrick	80	L. D. Herrick.
Enos Smith	78	Enos Smith.	Isaac Thayr	76	J. C. Thayr.
Ananiah Bohonon	75	Ananiah Bohonon.	Elizabeth Martin	74	Joshua Martin.
Thomas Moore	84	Salmon J. Moore.	Joseph Hobart	84	Jonathan Hobart.
Annis Calkins	85	Ebenezer Merrill.	Elisha Lilley	76	Elisha Lilley.
Laban Brown	69	Jonathan Scribner.	John McIntire	79	Reuben McIntire.
Emma Brigham	84	Samuel Brigham.	Abner Washburn	82 }	John Smith.
Elkanah Stevens	79	Elkanah Stevens.	Sarah Smith	82 }	
Jonah Gates	76	Jonah Gates.	Alvin Edson	43	Luther Edson.
Mary Snow	84	Joseph Thompson.	Jacob Cobb	82	Jacob Cobb.
Hannah Allen	75	Hannah Allen.			
Samuel Lincoln	87	Samuel Lincoln.	STRAFFORD.		
Ebenezer Allen	86	Obed Allen.	Nathan Cobb	76	Daniel Cobb.
			Robert Hayes	76	David Hayes.
BROOKFIELD.			Mary Lillie	89	John Hilliard.
John Slade	88	John Slade.	Benj. Tucker	78	Benj. Tucker.
Timothy Kendall	79	Samuel Kendall.	Edward Felch	53	Edward Felch.
Gashum York	88	W. York.	Elias Carpenter	78	Elias Carpenter.
Asahel Durkee	74	A. Durkee.	Lydia Bourrows	78	Ashley Bourrows.
Edmund Pease	76	Edward Pease.]	Phebe Miller	76	Moses Miller.
			John Reynolds	81	John Reynolds, jr.

9

CENSUS OF PENSIONERS.

VERMONT—Continued.

Names of pensioners for revolutionary or military services.	Ages.	Names of heads of families with whom pensioners resided June 1, 1840.	Names of pensioners for revolutionary or military services.	Ages.	Names of heads of families with whom pensioners resided June 1, 1840.
ORANGE—Continued.			WINDHAM—Continued.		
THETFORD.			WARDBORO'—Continued.		
Mary Hubbard - - -	84	Orange Hubbard.	Daniel Read - - -	79	Daniel Read, jr.
Betheal Briant - - -	75	James Campbell.	Ephraim Rice - - -	82	Ephraim Rice.
Eunice Parker - - -	74	Justus Newcomb.	Lucy Smith - - -	82	Gardner Smith.
Edward S. Meeder - -	47	Edward S. Meeder.	Thomas Simpson - -	85	Thomas Simpson.
Richmond Crandall - -	86	Richmond Crandall.	Edward Walker - -	84	Bliss Walker.
Robert Farris - - -	81	Robert Farris.	Asa Wheelock - -	82	Asa Wheelock.
Simon Gillett - - -	83	Joseph Gillett.			
Mary Emerson - - -	79	Joseph Fletcher.	MARLBOROUGH.		
Samuel Shepard - -	79	Samuel Shepard.	Huldah Mather - -	81	Rufus Mather.
James Tyler - - -	80	James Tyler.	Amos Prouty - - -	76	Fosdick Prouty.
Joseph Bruce - - -	82	David Bruce.	Justus Angurs - -	99	Sally Allen.
Jeremiah Tyler - -	74	Wm. M. Tyler.	John Philips - - -	78	John Philips.
			Mary Chamberlain -	86	Mary Chamberlain.
FAIRLEE.			Boomer Jenks - -	79	Andrew N. Jenks.
Asa Woodward - -	83	Asa Woodward, jr.			
Benj. Follett - - -	85	Benj. Follett.	SOMERSET.		
Sarah Houghton - -	75	A. L. Houghton.	Elijah Morse - - -	82	Joseph Morse.
Francis Churchill - -	86	John E. Churchill.	Hannah Putnam - -	73	P. B. Putnam.
WEST FAIRLEE.			DOVER.		
Jonathan Lougee - -	83	Jonathan Lougee.	Ebenezer Sears - -	83	Ebenezer Sears, jr.
Stephen May - - -	85	Elisha May.	Luther Ward - - -	80	Wm. M. Wood.
Hannah Colton - -	75	Ebenezer P. Colton.	David Dexter - - -	80	David Dexter, jr.
Joseph Foster - - -	93	John L. Wilson.	Balah Kendall - -	82	Ebenezer Sparks.
Calvin Morse - - -	47	Calvin Morse.	Joseph Briggs - -	83	Joseph Briggs.
John Guild - - -	79	John Guild.	Gardner Howe - -	80	Gardner Howe.
Solomon Dickinson -	83	Jefferson Dickinson.	Anna Perry - - -	77	A. P. Perry.
Francis Whitcomb -	79	Daniel West.	Elijah Baldwin - -	84	Ezra Baldwin.
			Gamaliel Ellis - -	83	Joseph Ellis.
WINDHAM COUNTY.					
BROOKLINE.			TOWN OF HALIFAX.		
Samuel Bennett - -	82	Samuel Bennett, jr.	Lydia Allen - - -	84	Daniel Allen.
Ebenezer Harwood -	87	Joel Harwood.	Francis Phelps - -	83	Francis Phelps, jr.
Rebecca Rist - - -	82	Samuel Rist.	Chloe Bullock - -	74	Stephen Niles.
Jotham Stebbins - -	79	Jotham Stebbins.	Jesse Guild - - -	75	Jesse Guild.
Jonathan Woolley -	82	Jonathan Woolley.	Anna Collins - - -	85	Robert Collins.
Timothy Wellman -	83	Deluis Wellman.	Elijah Pike - - -	77	Elijah Pike.
			John Farnham - -	77	John Farnham.
JAMAICA.			Eleazer Whitney - -	85	Jonathan Whitney.
Timothy Fisher - -	78	Abi Ames.	Moses Larned - -	78	Nathan Larned.
Nathaniel Cheney - -	82	Nathaniel Cheney.	Hezekiah Smith - -	88	Elisha Harris.
Ichabod Higgins - -	81	Elisha Higgins.	Artemas Woodard -	80	Benjamin Woodward.
Joel Hill - - -	83	Joel Hill.	Israel Jones - - -	79	Israel Jones.
Hannah Jenison - -	68	Elias Jenison.	John Harris - - -	74	John Harris.
Jerusha Kellogg - -	77	Alpheus Kellogg.	Samuel Stafford - -	84	Samuel Stafford, jr.
Esther Puffer - - -	78	Sally Puffer.			
Bailey Rawson - -	79	Bailey Rawson.	WILMINGTON.		
John Bradley - - -	79	Harvey Stone.	Judah Moore - - -	85	Zephaniah S. Moore.
Elizabeth Chase - -	72	Russel Underwood.	Jesse Mosman - -	88	Levi Cushman.
			Calvin P. Perry - -	61	Calvin P. Perry.
NEWFANE.			Sarah Winchester -	71	Franklin Winchester.
William Hills - - -	82	Nathaniel Hills.	Israel Lawton - -	82	Israel Lawton.
William King - - -	78	Wm. King.	Margaret Blodget -	79	Randolph Blodget.
Elizabeth Lincoln - -	74	Amasa Lincoln.	Simeon Chandler -	86	Ezra B. Chandler.
Ephraim Hall - - -	78	William H. Morse.			
Pain Phillips - - -	76	George Phillips.	WHITTINGHAM.		
Esther Allen - - -	84	William Stedman.	Deborah Tothingham -	78	Burden Lake.
			Jonathan Carley - -	80	Joseph Carley.
STRATTON.			Amy Dix - - -	81	Jonathan Dix.
Jonathan M. Bissell -	77	Jonathan M. Bissell.	David Jillson - -	79	David Jillson, jr.
Abel Grout - - -	82	Abel Grout, jr.	Stephen Putnam - -	79	Stephen Putnam.
Amos Parsons - -	81	Amos Parsons.	Samuel Parker - -	76	L. A. Warner.
Bille Mann - - -	83	Richard Scott.			
			WESTMINSTER.		
TOWNSHEND.			Seth Arnold - - -	82	Seth S. Arnold.
Mary Austin - - -	76	Asa Austin.	Mary Hall - - -	72	Mary Hall.
George Austin - -	77	George Austin.	Aaron Bixby - - -	76	Aaron Bixby.
Ruth Burt - - -	95	Warner Burt.	Josiah Eaton - - -	81	Josiah Eaton.
Martha Mansfield - -	86	Harry Cary.	Mark Richards - -	79	Mark Richards.
Amos Gray - - -	79	Amos Gray.	Hezekiah Abby - -	85	Hezekiah Abby.
Meriam Holbrook - -	90	Meriam Holbrook.	Jabez Paine - - -	84	Jabez Paine.
Mary Seargeant - -	81	Ruth Dunkle.	Seth Gould - - -	80	Seth Gould.
Thomas Low - - -	53	Thomas Low.	Elisha Johnson - -	104	Elisha Johnson.
			John Priest - - -	95	John Priest.
WARDBORO'.			Amaziah Richmond -	78	Amaziah Richmond.
Hannah Bartlett - -	84 }	Joel Bartlett.	Benjamin Stone - -	81	Benjamin Stone.
Elizabeth Phillips - -	81 }		Reuben Lippenwill -	80	Reuben Lippenwill.
Nathaniel Chamberlin -	79	Moses Chamberlin.	Maverick Eaton - -	85	Jere. Eaton.
Samuel Kenney - -	84	Almond B. Freeman.			
Pearly Fairbanks - -	79	Pearly Fairbanks.	ATHENS.		
Daniel Harris - - -	79	Daniel Harris.	George Porter - -	81	George Porter.
Abner Lewis - - -	84	Abner Lewis.	Charles Colton - -	78	Charles Colton.

VERMONT—Continued.

Names of pensioners for revolutionary or military services.	Ages.	Names of heads of families with whom pensioners resided June 1, 1840.	Names of pensioners for revolutionary or military services.	Ages.	Names of heads of families with whom pensioners resided June 1, 1840.
WINDHAM—Continued.			**WINDHAM—Continued.**		
WINDHAM.			**BRATTLEBORO'—Continued.**		
John Gould - - -	80	John Gould.	Ben. Chamberlain - - -	82	S. Chamberlain.
Archibald Mack - - -	87	Archibald Mack.	Benajah Dudley - - -	77	Ben. Dudley.
Abial Whitman - - -	82	Abial Whitman.	Salathiel Harris - - -	81	Alfred Harris.
James Smith - - -	90	James Smith.	Income Jones - - -	83	Benson Jones.
			Lucy Kelsey - - -	77	Aaron Kelsey.
LONDONDERRY.			Reuben King - - -	94	Isaac King.
Jemima Geryl - - -	87	Waldo Barton.	George Loveland - - -	80	R. Loveland.
Edmond Ingalls - - -	83	Edward Ingalls.	Reuben Stearns - - -	81	Reuben Stearns.
Thomas Read - - -	74	Thomas Read.	Sylvanus Sartwell - - -	82	M. Sartwell.
Samuel Davis - - -	87	Amos Davis.	John Carpenter - - -	84	Jotham Warren.
Mary Shalluck - - -	81	Silas Davis.			
Bethiah Howard - - -	76	Allen Howard.	**GUILFORD.**		
Benjamin Pierce - - -	78	Benjamin Pierce.	Betsey Andrews - - -	86	Solomon Andrews.
Nathan Whiting - - -	75	Jabez Temple.	Thomas Harris - - -	86	Reuben Colgrove.
Berreck Bolster - - -	78	Berreck Bolster.	Ebenezer Chamberlain -	89	W. Chamberlain.
Jeremiah Wheeler - - -	82	Jeremiah Wheeler.	Eliel Washburn - - -	87	Joel Eddy.
Abraham Abbott - - -	87	Reuben Harrington.	Samuel Larabee - - -	82	Samuel Larabee.
			William Marsk - - -	76	William Marsk.
GRAFTON.			Eunice Rose - - -	83	George Rose.
Asa M. Wyman - - -	82	Asa Wyman.	Tabitha Smith - - -	83	Tabitha Smith.
Margaret Palmer - - -	78	Hiram Palmer.	Aaron Wilder - - -	86	John Wilder.
Henry Davis - - -	82	Henry Davis.	Eunice Wild - - -	75	Isaac Wild.
Jonathan Warner - - -	80	Elisha Warner.			
Mima Goodnough - - -	75	Henry Goodnough	**VERNON.**		
Ruth Hill - - -	73	Thomas Hill.	Jabez Clark - - -	82	Jabez Clark.
John Kider - - -	79	John Kider.	Sarah You - - -	88	G. W. Lee.
Nathaniel Cutler - - -	80	George W. Beard.			
Solomon Gilson - - -	79	Solomon Gilson.	**ELMORE.**		
David Blood - - -	78	David Blood.	Ebenezer Capin - - -	81	Hiram S. Putnam.
Samuel Spaulding - - -	79	Samuel Spaulding.			
Betsey Conant - - -	73	Betsey Conant.	**LAMOILLE COUNTY.**		
			WOLCOTT.		
ACTON.			Esther Peirce - - -	97	Samuel Stiles.
Susanna Huzzy - - -	88	Susanna Huzzy.	Jabez Newland - - -	76	Jabez Newland.
Judith Jennerson - - -	74	Joseph Jennerson.			
Eleazer Cobley - - -	87	Eleazer Cobley.	**HYDEPARK.**		
			Amos McKinstry - - -	81	George McKinstry.
ROCKINGHAM.			John Collins - - -	54	John Collins.
Lydia Wyman - - -	75	John Wyman.	John McCloud - - -	63	John McCloud.
Jonathan Stearns - - -	77	Jonathan Stearns.			
John Fish - - -	84	Joseph Davis.	**EDEN.**		
Lona Holt - - -	79	Levi Hoit.	Samuel Plumley - - -	80	William Plumley.
Philip Adams - - -	89	Philip Adams.	Isaac Lackey - - -	86	Samuel Plumley, jr.
John Dudley - - -	79	John Dudley.	Peter Wylie - - -	84	Peter Wylie.
William Stearns - - -	84	William Stearns.	Jonas Harrington - - -	54	Jonas Harrington.
John Stearns - - -	77	William B. Stearns.	Eli Hinds, Jr. - - -	48	Eli Hinds, jr.
Abraham Tuttle - - -	85	Sylvester Tuttle.			
Joshua Reed - - -	79	Joshua Reed, jr.	**CAMBRIDGE.**		
Nathan Woolley - - -	83	Nathan Woolley.	Parker Page - - -	79	Amos Page.
Joseph Muzzy - - -	77	Joseph Muzzy.	Joel F. Perham - - -	79	Joel F. Perham.
			Jane Fullington - - -	76	John Fullington.
PUTNEY.			Lucretia Parker - - -	78	D. C. Hatch.
Abigail Haynes - - -	84	H. H. Barton.	Elizabeth Prior - - -	82	Alva Prior.
Huldah Reed - - -	80	F. T. Glynn.	Trueman Powell - - -	81	Egbert Powell.
Zenas Hyde - - -	81	Zenas Hyde.	Elias Green - - -	84	Giles A. Barber.
Elijah Houghton - - -	77	Elijah Houghton.	Elihu Grant - - -	80	Bridgeman Grant.
Isaac Palmer - - -	89	R. W. Palmer.	Sarah Stearnes - - -	75	Benjamin W. Harvey.
Ezekiel Pierce - - -	86	Ezekiel Pierce.			
John Smith, 1st - - -	81	John Smith, 1st.	**WATERVILLE.**		
			Daniel Morse - - -	79	Ezekiel P. Morse.
DUMMERSTON.			Sally Keith - - -	77	Scot Keith.
David Bennett - - -	79	D. Bennett.			
Jemima Bernis - - -	87	Joseph Bernis.	**BELVIDERE.**		
Elijah Brown - - -	81	Elijah Brown.	Moses Brown - - -	79	Asahel Brown.
Nathaniel Bixby - - -	81	Nathaniel Bixby.	John Rosier - - -	85	Lewis Carpenter.
James Chase - - -	88	A. T. Chase.			
Isaac Taylor - - -	79	John Foster.	**JOHNSON.**		
Elijah Gibbs - - -	75	Elijah Gibbs.	Daniel Perkins - - -	77	Joseph Fletcher.
Arad Holton - - -	87	W. Holton.	Solomon Briggs - - -	87	William Brown.
Ellis Griffith - - -	79	C. Haladay			
Joel Knight - - -	79	Joel Knight.	**STOWE.**		
Rachel Moore - - -	72	Martin Moore.	Asa Poland - - -	75	Asa Poland.
Calvin Munn - - -	79	Calvin Munn.	Susanna Bennett - - -	69	Zebina W. Bennett.
Benjamin Peirce - - -	74	Benjamin Peirce.	Lucy Town - - -	84	Nehemiah Town.
Prudence Fairbank - -	82	David Reed.	Noah Robinson - - -	83	John R. Robinson.
William Robertson - -	89	William Robertson.	Abraham Moses - - -	84	Abraham Moses.
Martha Lester - - -	87	A. Stockwell.	Aaron Clough - - -	76	Thomas Bigford.
			Polly Alden - - -	81	Adam Alden.
BRATTLEBORO.					
Thomas Akeley - - -	85	R. Akeley.	**MORRISTOWN.**		
Joel Bolster - - -	78	Joel Bolster.	Joseph E. Westgate - -	79	William Westgate.
Mary Chapin - - -	74	Mary Chapin.	Adam Sumner - - -	65	Daniel F. Gates.

CENSUS OF PENSIONERS.

VERMONT—Continued.

Names of pensioners for revolutionary or military services.	Ages.	Names of heads of families with whom pensioners resided June 1, 1840.	Names of pensioners for revolutionary or military services.	Ages.	Names of heads of families with whom pensioners resided June 1, 1840.
LAMOILLE—Continued.			**BENNINGTON—Continued.**		
MORRISTOWN—Continued.			RUPERT.		
Joseph Burk	77	Sampson Burk.	Joel Taylor	76	Stephen Taylor.
Thomas Youngman	80	Simeon Whitcomb.	Israel Hayes	88	Isaac Hays.
John Cole	87	Harvey Cole.	Ashbel Sykes	85	
Phebe Wilkins	86	Aaron Wilkins.	John Parker	83	
Crispas Shaw	76	Crispas Shaw.	Enoch Shirman	77	
James Little	82	Roswell Clark.	Isaac Clapp	77	
Joshua Morrill	80	Aaron B. Morrill.	Daniel Warner	87	Daniel Warner.
			Moses Sheldon	89	Aaron Sheldon.
STERLING.			Harry Sykes	47	Harry Sykes.
Elisha Town	81	Amos Paine.	John Blanchard	76	John Blanchard.
BENNINGTON COUNTY.			DORSET.		
STAMFORD.			Noah Fuller	77	Noah Fuller.
Elisha Raymond	79	J. Harris.	Stephen Martindale	80	Stephen Martindale.
Ira Hill	76	Ira Hill.	Elizabeth Manly	72	William Manly.
			Nathaniel Vial	78	
BENNINGTON.			Jonathan Crandall	75	Jonathan Crandall.
Martin Norton	75	Martin Norton.	James Wrin	79	James Wrin.
Esther Robinson	89	Stafford Robinson.	Asahel L. Finton	78	Isaac Finton.
Samuel Rockwood	83	Samuel Rockwood.	Benedict Eggleston	77	
Simeon Thayer	75	S. Thayer.	Hannah Brock	89	
Aaron Hubbell	82	Aaron Hubbell.	Mary Dunton	78	William B. Dunton.
Cornelius Bracy	74	C. Bracy.	John Sergeant	79	John Sergeant.
Sarah Rudd	95	Enos Rudd.			
			WINHALL.		
WOODFORD.			Daniel Benson	79	Daniel Benson.
Ebenezer Temple	83	E. Temple.			
Hannah Knapp	86	Cyrus Knapp.	MANCHESTER.		
			Caroline Goodwin	75	Matthew Goodwin.
READSBORO'.			Samuel Walker	87	Hiram Walker.
Archelaus Dean	78	A. Dean.	Eunice Tucker	74	
Ezra Keyes	77	Ezra Keyes.	Gideon Moody	76	Gideon Moody.
			Samuel Vial	81	
POWNAL.			Elijah Burton	79	
Moses Hastings	85	A. Hastings.	Eli Pettibone	84	Eli Pettibone.
Zacheus Hovey	76	Z. Hovey.	Elisha Cook	80	
Lucy Angel	82	Lucy Angel.	Nathan Eaton	84	
John Sherman	84	J. Sherman.	Abigail Wakefield	76	
Benjamin Grover	73	B. Grover.	Frederick Smith	69	
Jerusha Lilly	86	Caleb Lilly.	Martha Purdy	78	
John Magoon	75	John Magoon.	Lucy Hollister	80	
Louis Dunham	75	Eber Dunham.			
Joseph Thorp	79	Joseph Thorp.	**RUTLAND COUNTY.**		
David Jipson	77	D. Jipson, jr.	CASTLETON.		
			Elias Hall	86	Elias Hall.
SHAFTSBURY.			Daniel Eaton	78	Daniel Eaton.
Cynthia Hewlett	70	A. Johnson.	William Bromley	77	William Bromley.
Prosper Wheeler	83	B. Wheeler.	Daniel Lowden	80	Daniel Lowden.
John Fuller	80	J. Fuller.			
James Sweet	79	James Sweet.	BENSON.		
Aaron Denio	85	Aaron Denio.	Solomon Martin	87	Ebenezer Martin.
Hezekiah Carey	77	Henry Carey.	William Manning	82	Joel Manning.
Thankful Elwell	88	L. Elwell.	Simeon Goodrich	81	Eleazer Goodrich.
			Ozias Johnson	82	Ozias Johnson.
SANDGATE.			James Noble	79	James Noble.
Lewis Hurd	81	—— Hurd.	Allen Goodrich	79	Allen Goodrich.
Adam Hurd	83	—— Hurd.	Rufus Ewen	80	John D. Hunt.
Deborah Wakely	69	Deborah Wakely.			
Abel Buck	85	Abel Buck.	ORWELL.		
John Wyman	81	John Wyman.	Samuel Griswold	81	M. Griswold.
Mercy Parsons	93	David Hill.	Ephraim Blood	78	Ephraim Blood.
			Jonathan Belden	79	Joseph Simons.
PERU.					
Luther Barnard	89	E. Messenger.	SUDBURY.		
Peter Gould	77	Peter Gould.	Adams Stevens	89	Adams Stevens.
			Azel Williams	80	Azel Williams.
LANDGROVE.			Noah Merritt	85	Noah Merritt.
Mary Shattuck	80	Maria Walker.	Abner Hull	79	Abner Hull.
Judy Clark	83	Robert Clark.	Peter Reynolds	79	John Hull.
			Stephen Murray	82	Stephen Murray.
SUNDERLAND.					
Simeon Hicks	85	Simeon Hicks.	HUBBARDTON.		
John Rowen	90	David Little.	Jonathan Slason	80	Jonathan Slason.
			John Rumsey	82	John Rumsey.
ARLINGTON.			Azel Wright	89	Azel Wright.
Simeon Littlefield	74	Simeon Littlefield.	Frederick Dikeman	80	Frederick Dikeman.
John Calkins	77	David Rounds.			
Benoni Hawkins	79	Benoni Hawkins.	CHITTENDEN.		
Mary Wright	86	Wm. C. Campbell.	Asa Durkee	45	Asa Durkee.
Ephraim Blowers	77	Ephraim Hastings.			
Mary Leonard	82	Edward Brownson.	CLARENDON.		
Hepsebeth Pollord	79	Hepsebeth Pollard.	John Smith	78	John C. Smith

VERMONT—Continued.

Names of pensioners for revolutionary or military services.	Ages.	Names of heads of families with whom pensioners resided June 1, 1840.	Names of pensioners for revolutionary or military services.	Ages.	Names of heads of families with whom pensioners resided June 1, 1840.
RUTLAND—Continued.			**RUTLAND—Continued.**		
CLARENDON—Continued.			WALLINGFORD.		
Samuel Parker	85	Joseph Parker.	Nathaniel Keyes	80	Nathaniel Keyes.
Ephraim Parker	80	Ephraim Parker.	Eli Calkin	79	Eli Calkin.
Zebulon Crane	79	Orin Hewitt.	Asa Anderson	77	Philo D. Hart.
Abel Titus	79	Abel Titus.	Andrew Hewitt	79	Andrew Hewitt.
Isaac Southworth	81	Isaac Southworth.	Mary Ives	75	John Ives.
Sarah Smith	84	John Learnard.	Nathan Dennison	82	Trueman L. Reed.
James Eddy	76	James Eddy.	Eunice Soverence	75	Wm. Johnson.
David Dean	81	Eli Baxter.	Philbrook Barrows	85	Philbrook Barrows.
Abel Horton	83	Hopkins Horton.	Jerchamell Doty	76	J. Doty.
			Sarah Holden	83	Luther Holden.
DANBY.			Mary Hubbard	84	Ebenezer Miles.
Ruama Lincoln	74	Wm. Johnson.			
Miner Hilyard	76	Miner Hilyard.	WELLS.		
Elijah Lilly	84	Hiram Lilly.	Samuel S. Merriam	78	S. S. Merriam.
			Peter Blossom	83	Seth Blossom.
IRA.			John Davis	79	J. S. Davis.
Jason Newton	78	Jason Newton.			
Savia Tower	86	Amos Tower.	RUTLAND.		
			Artemus Taft	90	
MENDON.			Asa Hall	80	
Isaac Sanderson	85	Parley Wilkins.	Simeon Post	88	
Hilkiah Grout	78	Hilkiah Grout.	Nathan M. Loundsberry	84	
			Nathan Osgood	79	
MIDDLETOWN.			Moses Head	74	
David Enos	79	David Enos.	Benj. Cheney	77	
David Griswold	90	David Griswold.	Roswell Staples	80	
Jedediah Edgerton	80	Jedediah Edgerton.	Ephraim Jackson	80	
Peter Crocker	82	David Stafford, jr.	Eleazer Wheelock	83	
Richard Haskins	78	Ezra Haskins.			
Philo Stoddard	81	Philo Stoddard.	PITTSFORD.		
Francis Perkins	81	Francis Perkins.	Amos Lawrence	82	
David Parker	77	David Parker.	Margaret Ingersol	80	
			Sarah Gilbert	75	
MOUNT HOLLY.			Dennis Miller	83	
Silas Proctor	89	Silas Proctor.	Lucy B. Bauge	79	
Royal Crowley	74	Royal Crowley.	Thomas Hammond	80	
Ichabod G. Clark	85	John White.	Rufus Wheeden	79	
Ebenezer Andrews	86	Jurial Andrews.	Luvitia Kellogg	76	
Mary Foster	77	Mary Foster.	Hannah Jackson	86	
			Oliver Wolcott	79	
MOUNT TABOR.			Prudence Molton	76	
Joseph Daggett	82	Abel Kelly.	James Walker	80	
			Sabia Bowen	75	
PAWLET.			Peter Powers	75	
Isaac Reed	85	Solomon T. Reed.	Jeremiah Rann	78	
Sibal Leach	84	Sibal Leach.	Zebulon Pond	75	
Jacob Sacks	82	Jacob Sacks.	Joel Will	80	
Mary Evings	96	Mary Evings.			
Nathaniel Robinson	88	Nathaniel Robinson.	BRANDON.		
Ephraim Robinson	80	Ephraim Robinson, jr.	Ebenezer Squires	82	
Josiah Munroe	76	Josiah Munroe.	Sophia Burnell	80	
Judah Moffit	79	Judah Moffit.	Roger Smith	78	
James Pratt	78	Ervin Pratt.	David Meriam	80	
Jennett Halister	79	Hartley Halister.	Phebe Tracy	73	
PITTSFIELD.			**WINDSOR COUNTY.**		
Penuel Childs	83	Penuel Childs, jr.	HARTFORD.		
Elijah Segar	83	Elijah Segar.	David Colburn	78	David Colburn.
			Roger Huntington	82	Roger Huntington.
POULTNEY.			William Champlin	84	Wm. Champlin.
Oliver Wright	70	Oliver Wright.	Jacob Hall	92	Jacob Hall.
James Hooker	80	James Hooker.	Hannah Kilbee	81	Samuel Nutt.
Abel Hubbard	72	Thomas Davis.	Samuel Harrington	79	Samuel Harrington.
Samuel Prindle	93	Samuel Prindle.	Philip Sprague	75	Philip Sprague.
Seth Ruggles	83	Seth Ruggles.	Burpy Prouty	78	Burpy Prouty.
Joseph Manning	78	Hiram H. Swallow.	Solomon Hazen	81	Solomon Hazen.
William Lewis	83	William Lewis.	Josiah Tilden	80	Josiah Tilden.
Jeremiah Armstrong	79	Jeremiah Armstrong.			
Jesse Soper	78	Jesse Soper.	HARTLAND.		
			Peter Gibson	76	
SHERBURNE.			Mehitable Bugbee	81	Wm. Lemmex.
Joseph Adams	91	Roswell Adams.	Solomon Brown	79	Solomon Brown.
Amasa Fuller	82	Amasa Fuller.	Moses Webster	85	John Webster.
			Elizabeth Lamphear	73	David Lamphear.
SHREWSBURY.			Elizabeth Lamphear	75	Reuben Lamphear.
Abram Eaton	85		Eliphalet Rogers	83	Eliphalet Rogers.
			Daniel Brick	92	Daniel Brick.
TINMOUTH.			Hannah Perkins	78	John Short.
Nathaniel Chipman	87	Nathaniel Chipman.	Mary Alexander	82	H. S. Alexander.
Thomas Rogers	81	Thomas Rogers.	Quartus Alexander	81	Consider Alexander, 2d.
Abigail Ambler	73	Abigail Ambler.	Lucy Cushman	76	Lucy Cushman.
			Noah Aldrich	75	Noah Aldrich.

VERMONT—Continued.

Names of pensioners for revolutionary or military services.	Ages.	Names of heads of families with whom pensioners resided June 1, 1840.	Names of pensioners for revolutionary or military services.	Ages.	Names of heads of families with whom pensioners resided June 1, 1840.
WINDSOR—Continued.			**WINDSOR—Continued.**		
HARTLAND—Continued.			*ROYALTON—Continued.*		
Elizabeth Raymond	82	David Rogers.	Tryphena Davis	79	Calvin Davis.
Patuma Billings	83	Willard Billings.	Permilla Cleveland	78	Bradford Cleveland.
Elizabeth Marcy	77	Elizabeth Marcy.	Gideon Crandall	78	Tracy Crandall.
Phebe Dinsmoor	79	J. R. Dismoor.	Samuel Metcalf	77	Samuel Metcalf.
Hannah Richardson	83	Hannah Richardson.	Abraham Waterman	85	Abraham Waterman.
			Ebenezer Dewey	78	Ebenezer Dewey.
WOODSTOCK.			Benjamin Cole	79	Alsop Latham.
Seenee Hatch	83	John D. Powers.	William Waterman	82	William Waterman.
Henry Roby	81	Henry Roby.	Polly Root	71	Stephen E. Root.
Esther Sterns	78	Jacob Eaton.	Lyman Back	79	Lyman Back.
Rhoda Marsh	74	Henry Marsh.	Daniel Lovejoy	79	Daniel Lovejoy.
Mary Wales	77	Mary Wales.	Matthew Aritherton	81	Matthew Aritherton.
Jacob Wilder	83	Jacob Wilder.	Elias Stevens	85	Elias Stevens.
Eleazer Wood	78	Orrin Wood.	Darius Dewey	83	Darius Dewey.
George Sampson	81	George Sampson.			
Acenath Darling	74	Acenath Darling.	*BETHEL.*		
Hannah Shaw	75	Barnabas Thompson.	B. L. Cotton	77	B. L. Cotton.
Philemon Sampson	78	Philemon Sampson.	Amos Crain	75	Amos Crain.
Barnabas Caswell	84	Earl Cox.	Joseph Wood	79	Joseph Wood.
Prudence Emmons	77	Harry Emmons.	Steph. Fisk	82	Stephen Fisk
Asahel Dubledee	88	S. C. Dunham.	Hannah Cleveland	72	Charles E. Cleveland.
Seth Starling	77	Seth Starling.	Ezra Putnam	88	Daniel Putnam.
Sylvanus Shaw	88	Sylvanus Shaw.	Reuben Brooks	76	Reuben Brooks.
Elizabeth Waldron	76	L. Ransom.	Jason Bannister	77	Jason Banister.
Abram Snow	78	Abram Snow.	Moses Bragg	76	Moses Bragg.
Zebedee Hackett	77	L. Benjamin.			
Catharine Fletcher	80	Catharine Fletcher.	*BARNARD.*		
Noah Crocker	79	Noah Crocker.	William Buckman	89	William Buckman.
Elijah Royce	80	Chester Royce.	John Ellis	81	John Ellis.
			Charles French	74	Charles French.
BRIDGEWATER.			Gideon Newton	79	Gideon Newton.
James Topliff	80	Josiah Joslin, jr.	William Harlow	74	Daniel Sharp.
Phineas Sanderson	80	Artimas Sanderson.	Daniel Sharp	86	Daniel Sharp, jr.
Isaac Bisbee	80	Isaac Bisbee.	Nathaniel Richmond	75	Nathaniel Richmond.
Mary Robinson	78	Nathaniel Robinson.	Samuel Bennett	80	Lemuel Gibbs.
Nathan Pratt	88	Hiram Pratt.	William Chamberlin	87	C. Chamberlin.
Joseph French	76	Jacob French.	George Cox	78	George Cox, jr.
Josiah Gibbs	77	Jesse Gibbs.	John Foster	83	John Foster.
			Roger French	82	Roger French.
NORWICH.			Ezra Spalding	88	Bela Spalding.
Joseph Cushman	82	Joseph Cushman.	Charles Spooner	76	Charles Spooner.
Jos. Tucker	87	Asa Whitcomb.	Benjamin Clapp	78	Benjamin Clapp.
John Gould	81	Elisha Culver.	John Gambel	78	John Gambel.
Solomon White	81	Solomon White.	Thomas Freeman	78	Thomas Freeman.
Mendwell Strong	82	Samuel H. Clark.	Hannah Kinney	88	L. S. Kinney.
Jonathan Spear	74	Jonathan Spear.			
Henry Burton	81	Henry Burton.	*STOCKBRIDGE.*		
Elizabeth Boardman	81	Eleazer J. Boardman.	Jonathan Norris	67	Jonathan Norris.
Mabel Goodrich	76	William Wilson.	Walter Pollard	78	Walter Pollard.
Hezekiah Goodrich	83	H. G. Knapp.	Stukely Angel	77	Asa Chamberlin.
Ruth Waterman	83	Joel Morris.	Lydia Taggart	73	Lydia Taggart.
Sarah Waterman	78	Aaron Keyes.			
Sarah Hatch	75	Sarah Hatch.	*ROCHESTER.*		
Daniel Nye	84	Daniel Nye.	Seth Tinkham	79	Seth Tinkham.
Calvin Seaver	82	Otis Seaver.	David Clough	83	David Clough.
Ruth Poor	82	Thomas W. Poor.	Kiles Paul	84	Kiles Paul.
Betsey Hews	81	Daniel Menard.	Clark Young	87	Clark Young.
Calvin Johnson	84	Calvin Johnson.			
Jerome Hutchinson	77	Jerome Hutchinson.	*CHESTER.*		
			Reuben Ray	72	Reuben Ray.
SHARON.			John Kibling	83	Joshua Church, jr.
Susanna Foster	82	Isaac Parkhurst.	Jemima Holden	91	Joseph S. Holden.
Nathan Hitchcock	84	Henry Hitchcock.	Benjamin Whitmore	89	Benjamin Whitney, jr.
Seth Hart	83	Seth Hart.	David Earl	93	Roswell Earl.
Reuben Spalding	82	Reuben Spalding.	Jason Rice	79	Jason Rice.
Benjamin Metcalf	84	John Mamsel.	Lydia Leland	76	Phineas Leland.
Mary Benjamin	79	Ira Benjamin.	Simeon Keth	75	Aaron Harrington.
Joel Barrett	77	Joel Barrett.	Ebenezer Farrington	75	Abraham Farrington.
Asahel Holt	75	Asahel Holt.	Daniel Fletcher	85	Daniel Fletcher.
Ebenezer Currier	83	Samuel Gilman.	Jeremiah Dean	85	Jeremiah Dean.
Nicholas C. Wells	70	L. Harrington.	Amos Weatherby	82	Newel Weatherby.
Oliver Sexton	75	H. Fuller.	Amasa Turner	51	Amasa Turner.
			Joshua Church	75	Joshua Church.
ROYALTON.			Solomon Wilson	79	George Wilson.
Benjamin Bosworth	84	Benjamin Bosworth.	William Stoodley	75	Amos G. Gould.
Temperance Skinner	79	Jonathan Kinney.	John Thurston	83	John Thurston.
Isaac Pinney	82	Isaac Pinney, jr.	Joshua Jordan	79	Joshua Jordan.
Isaac Skinner	81	Isaac Skinner.			
Benjamin Parkhurst	95	Simon Parkhurst.	*ANDOVER.*		
John Hutchinson	85	Jonathan Dyer.	Solomon Howard	83	Solomon Howard.
Stephen Baccus	82	Andrew Baccus.	Ebenezer Farnsworth	82	Ebenezer Farnsworth.
Sarah Waldo	67	Warren Waldo.	Lucy Abbott	80	Luther Abbott.

VERMONT—Continued.

Names of pensioners for revolutionary or military services.	Ages.	Names of heads of families with whom pensioners resided June 1, 1840.	Names of pensioners for revolutionary or military services.	Ages.	Names of heads of families with whom pensioners resided June 1, 1840.
WINDSOR—Continued.			**WINDSOR—Continued.**		
ANDOVER—Continued.			PLYMOUTH.		
Thankful Walker	88	Thankful Walker.	Daniel Clark	87	Caleb Weaver.
Hart Balch	89	Obadiah Parker.	Esther Knight	73	Elbridge Knight.
Vashti Gassett	91	David Gassett.	Francis Ackley	89	Francis Ackley, jr.
			Benjamin Green	78	Joseph Green.
BALTIMORE.			Caleb Snow	75	Eliphalet Wood.
Leah Harris	79	Luke Harris.	Robert Bishop	79	Daniel Bishop.
			Samuel G. Allen	81	Samuel G. Allen.
WESTON.			Elizabeth Holt	78	Elizabeth Holt.
Samuel Proctor	75	Samuel Proctor.	Asa Pratt	81	Asa Pratt.
Nicholas Lawrence	76	Nicholas Lawrence.	Asa Green	79	Asa Green.
Ezra Ritter	79	Ezra Ritter.			
Henry Hall	82	Elijah Fuller.	LUDLOW.		
			Jonathan Whitcomb	78	Hiram Whitcomb.
SPRINGFIELD.			Ephraim Dutton	87	Zelotus Dutton.
Joseph Hodgman	87	W. L. Hodgman.	Thomas Weatherby	82	Thomas Weatherby.
Joseph Hulet	88	John Jenkins.			
Eunice Woodward	85	N. Woodward.	CAVENDISH.		
Silas Parker	81	William F. Parker.	John Spaulding	79	John Spaulding.
Jed. Ward	80	Simeon Randall.	Elnathan Reed	85	Elnathan Reed.
William Bragg	77	Joshua Spencer.	Sally Proctor	78	Stilman Proctor.
Asahel Powers	81	Asahel Powers.	Timothy Adams	78	Timothy Adams.
Josiah Belknap	81	Josiah Belknap.	John McLane	83	John McLane.
Mary Chase	71	Joel Griswold.	Joel Davis	85	Timothy Davis.
Samuel Dyke	76	Samuel Dyke.	Nabby Giddings	89	Hiram Giddings.
Hannah Lynds	85	Aaron P. Lynds.	Nathaniel Farr	94	Nathaniel Farr.
David Stimson	78	David Stimson.	Lincoln Stiles	76	Lincoln Stiles.
William Brown	75	Josiah Wells.	Eunice Morse	90	Abel Burbank.
Jonathan Luke	78	Daniel Luke.			
Prudence Kirk	75	William Kirk.	**ADDISON COUNTY.**		
Stephen Dyer	85	Stephen Dyer.	ADDISON.		
Lucy Bradford	79	Richard Bradford.	Oliver Smith	75	Ephraim C. Goodale.
Damaris Williams	81	Jasper Williams.	Benjamin Everett	88	Benjamin Everett.
Benjamin Spooner	93	Benjamin Spooner.	Lorain Everts	76	George Everts.
			Sylvanus Chapin	83	Sylvanus Chapin.
WEATHERSFIELD.			Sally Eaton	73	Zadoc Everest.
Priscilla Cheney	87	Benjamin Page.	Jacob Post	78	Jacob Post.
Jewitt Boynton	78	J. Boynton, jr.			
William Nichols	84	William Nichols.	BRIDPORT.		
Lucretia Stone	65	Lucretia Stone.	Solomon Howe	87	Solomon Howe, jr.
John Mallard	77	Samuel Mace.	Jonathan Eldridge	88	Joseph Eldridge.
John Chase	79	John Chase.	Ephraim Holdridge	84	Ephraim Holdridge.
Stephen Reed	86	Stephen Reed.	Windsor Johnson	78	Lewis Johnson.
Lydia Chapin	77	Wolcot Chapin.	David Whitney	83	David Whitney.
Thomas Prentiss	81	Thomas Prentiss.			
Sarah Bennett	80	John Bennett.	CORNWALL.		
John Haskill	77	John C. Haskill.	Daniel Foot	80	Daniel Foot.
Isaac Brown	48	Isaac Brown.	William Pratt	73	Trueman Dewey.
Molly Hatch	74	Nathaniel Hatch.	Reuben Peck	80	Reuben Peck.
Caleb Litchfield	80	Caleb Litchfield.	Felix Benton	78	Felix Benton.
			Samuel Richards	81	Samuel Richards, jr.
WINDSOR.			Jeremiah Bingham	92	Jeremiah Bingham.
Thomas Craig	86	Thomas Craig.			
William Gilkey	82	William Gilkey.	FERRISBURGH.		
Simeon Pomeroy	86	Thomas M. Pomeroy.	Mary Ingham	77	Abner Wing.
Henry Stevens	79	Henry Stevens.	Rebecca Powers	72	Hartwell Powers.
Mary Hunter	82	Asa Aiken.	Daniel Champion	77	Daniel Champion.
Jonathan Hall	83	Jonathan Hall.	Sarah House	81	Hiram Curler.
Nathaniel Cobb	81	Nathaniel Cobb.			
Elizabeth Cady	81	Lyman Cady.	LEICESTER.		
Jonas Adams	77	Jonas Adams.	Joseph Swinington	78	Adin A. Swinington.
John Blood	81	John Blood.	Isaac Atwood	80	Isaac Atwood.
Oliver Osgood	78	Oliver Osgood.	Benjamin Whitman	83	Benjamin Whitman.
Abel Fling	76	Abel Fling, jr.			
Susanna Aiken	74	Israel Aiken.	MIDDLEBURY.		
Sibel Houghton	82	Peter Houghton.	Lydia Judd	73	Daniel Judd.
Huldah Chapin	86	James Bailey.	Justus Cobb	75	Justus Cobb.
Reuben McAlister	81	Reuben McAlister.	Benoni Shurtleff	83	Benoni Shurtleff.
Rufus Root	77	Rufus Root.	Ethan Andrews	84	Ethan Andrews.
Asahel Smith	84	Asahel Smith.	Samuel Cook	87	Samuel Cook, jr.
Jerome Sawins	78	Jerome Sawins.	Eleazer Barrows	75	Lucius Barrows.
Samuel Hutchinson	90	Samuel Hutchinson.	Alpheus Brooks	82	Alpheus Brooks.
			James Crane	78	James Crane.
READING.			Nathan Case	77	Nathan Case.
Molly Chubb	85	Molly Chubb.	Mary Hooker	88	Charles Hooker.
Sally Orcutt	79	Roland Fletcher.	Israel Wadsworth	80	William Dewey.
Bathsheba Nichols	78	Amos Williams.	Calvin Goodno	78	Asa Goodno.
Abiah Rice	81	Abiah Rice.	Freeman Foot	80	Allen Foot.
Lucy Rust	88	Oliver Rust.	Ebenezer Sumner	82	Ebenezer Sumner.
Daniel Weatherby	82	Daniel Weatherby.			
Ebenezer Robinson	75	Ebenezer Robinson.	PANTON.		
—— Robinson	72	Ezra Robinson.	Rupee Bacheller	90	Jesse Grandy.
Elijah Williams	82	Elijah Williams.	Lucy Haven	84	Lucy Haven.

VERMONT—Continued.

Names of pensioners for revolutionary or military services.	Ages.	Names of heads of families with whom pensioners resided June 1, 1840.	Names of pensioners for revolutionary or military services.	Ages.	Names of heads of families with whom pensioners resided June 1, 1840.
ADDISON—Continued.			**ADDISON—Continued.**		
SHOREHAM.			MONKTON.		
Elizabeth Hunsden	76	Robert R. Hunsden.	Lemuel Tracy	79	Lemuel Tracy.
William Jones	81	William Jones.	William Niles	84	William Niles.
Samuel Sunderland	87	Charles Turner.			
Noah Jones	81	Noah Jones.	NEWHAVEN.		
Stephen King	84	Stephen King.	William Seymour	76	William Seymour.
Ruth North	81	Ruth North.	Lois Andrews	73	Oliver D. Cole.
Martha Pratt	85	Benjamin Hunt.			
Eliakim Culver	85	Eliakim Culver, jr.	STARKSBOROUGH.		
			Hebbord Morrill	82	Hebbord Morrill.
WEYBRIDGE.					
Sarah Porter	81	Timothy O. Flanagan.	GRANVILLE.		
Pliny Stannard	83	James Kelly.	Eli Lewis	77	Eli Lewis.
Thomas Dickenson	84	Silas Herendeen.	James Shaw	77	Amos Rice.
John Halsey	84	John Halsey.	Jeremiah Snow	72	Jeremiah Snow.
			Isaac Cady	75	Isaac Cady.
WHITING.			Abiathar Austin	85	James H. Jinney.
Gershom Justin	89	Azim M. Goodrich.			
Elijah White	77	Lyman P. White.	HANCOCK.		
			Patience Bidwell	89	Patience Bidwell.
BRISTOL.					
John Curry	82	Peter Danforth.	SALISBURY.		
Amaziah Hawkins	81	Elisha Briggs.	Thomas Savery	82	William Savery.
Abraham Vreedenburgh	53	A. Vreedenburgh.	Hannah Pierce	79	William Pierce.
Samuel Hall	81	Samuel Hall.			
Jiriah Chamberlin	78	Jiriah Chamberlin.	WALTHAM.		
Rufus Barnard	78	Rufus Barnard.	Mary McKenzie	78	William McKenzie.
Jeremiah Hatch	73	Jeremiah Hatch.			
Joseph Bird	79	Frederick A. Bird.	LINCOLN.		
John D. Holly	49	John D. Holly.	Dorothy Palmer	76	Simeon Palmer.
Paul P. Holly	44	Paul P. Holley.	Joshua Rugg	78	Eli Vasney.
Walcott Burnham	76	Walcott Burnham.	Owen Briggs	82	Thomas Briggs.

STATE OF NEW YORK—NORTHERN DISTRICT

Names of pensioners for revolutionary or military services.	Ages.	Names of heads of families with whom pensioners resided June 1, 1840.	Names of pensioners for revolutionary or military services.	Ages.	Names of heads of families with whom pensioners resided June 1, 1840.
ALBANY COUNTY.			**ALBANY—Continued.**		
CITY OF ALBANY—First ward.			NEW SCOTLAND.		
Jonathan Kidney	75	Jonathan Kidney.	John Ramsay	81	John Ramsay.
Mathias Rimhart	77	Henry Chandler.	Ganet J. Sager	87	G. J. Sager.
Second ward.			Rachel Van Hosen	80	John Taylor.
Richard Hilton	81	Edwin James.	Christopher Winne	80	
Jonathan Hoard	85	Jonathan Hoard.			
Walter Whitney	87	Walter Whitney.	KNOX.		
Nathaniel Smith	77	John Davison.	Mary Dennison	81	Amos Crary.
Joshua Weldon	83	J. Weldon.	Jacob Shoultes	80	Jacob Shoultes.
Mathew Gregory	82	Mathew Gregory.	Johan Jost Deitz	79	Jacob Deitz.
Third ward.					
Gideon Deming	84	Sylvester Hale.	BERN.		
Fourth ward.			Andrew Secor	87	Andrew Secor.
Wilhelmus Ryckman	81	Albert Ryckman.	John Salsburg	89	Harmon Salsburg.
Fifth ward.			Evan Philips	63	Evan Philips.
Abraham Vosburgh	84	Abraham Vosburgh.	Thomas Frisbee	79	Thomas Frisbee.
Frederick Dumph	94	Eli Van Volkenburgh.	Francis Garvy	77	Isaac J. Garvy.
Anthony Van Sanford	81	A. Van Sanford.	Joseph Owen	81	Joseph Owen.
			Levit Head	84	Paul White.
BETHLEHEM.			William Ball	76	John Ball.
Conrad Goss	90	Conrad Goss.	Simeon Church	89	Simeon C. Church.
Jacob Laraway	82	Jacob Laraway.	Esau King	77	Jackson King.
Joshua Bailey	76		Paul J. Hogstrasser	78	Jacob Hoghstrasser.
Minardt P. Vandenburg	83		Elizabeth Skinner	82	Chester Skinner.
WATERVLIET.			RENNSELAERVILLE.		
Samuel Gallatin	91		Nathan Dayton	82	Nathan Dayton.
Mary Hills	83		Doctor Smith	76	Jared Smith.
Isaac Grote	82		Mathew Mulford	83	Charles L. Mulford.
			John Rogers	84	Sands Jervis.
GUILDERLAND.			Mary Bliven	77	Augustus L. Cross.
Abraham Lowe	82	James L. Lowe.	Sylvanus Purrington	85	Sylvanus Purrington.
Henry Sever	82	Peter Sever.	Eliphaz Kilbourn	83	Eliphaz Kilbourn.
John Vanderpool	86	Abraham Vanderpool.	John J. H. Burnett	83	John J. H. Burnett.

NEW YORK—NORTHERN DISTRICT—Continued.

Names of pensioners for revolutionary or military services.	Ages.	Names of heads of families with whom pensioners resided June 1, 1840.	Names of pensioners for revolutionary or military services.	Ages.	Names of heads of families with whom pensioners resided June 1, 1840.
ALBANY—Continued.			**ALLEGANY**—Continued.		
RENSSELAERVILLE—Continued.			HUME—Continued.		
Reuben King - - -	75	Asa Woodford.	Joel Elmer - - -	78	Joel Elmer.
Henry Cline - - -	86	George Benn.	Billing Starkweather - -	77	B. Starkweather.
Apollos Moore - - -	75	Apollos Moore.	David Smith - - -	81	
			John Bostwick - - -	78	J. Bostwick.
WESTERLOO.					
Simeon Whitcomb - -	84	Simeon Whitcomb.	NEW HUDSON.		
John Preston - -	84	Ezra Preston.	Hugh McKeen - - -	85	S. McKeen.
Jacob Ingalls - -	76	Jacob Ingalls.			
Stephen V. Tompkins -	82	Abraham Tompkins.	PIKE.		
William Wheaton - -	83	Darius Lockwood.	Seymour Talmadge - -	86	J. Talmadge.
Stephen Allen - - :	79	Stephen H. Allen.	William Vanslyke - -	81	William Vanslyke.
Sarah Hurlbert - -	83	Simeon Lobbdell.	Henry Bennet - -	78	H. Bennet.
Johiel Lamb - -	84	Johiel Lamb.	Robert L. Hurd - -	76	Robert L. Hurd.
Margaret Wilsey - -	83	John Arnold.	Joshua Whitney - -	80	Joshua Whitney.
Joseph Hinkley - -	80	Josiah Hinkley.			
David Sullivan - -	88	David Sullivan.	RUSHFORD.		
Levi Tracy - -	80	Daniel Spalding.	Billa Root - - -	84	Billa Root.
			Ephraim Morrison - -	77	E. Morrison.
COEYMANS.			Zachariah Dodds - -	89	Z. Dodds.
Sarah Mead - -	74	David Mead.	Elisha Coy - - -	77	Elisha Coy.
Daniel Wickham - -	78	Daniel Green.	Enos Gary - - -	83	
Jacob Spaunberg - -	74	George Spaunberg.			
Gertrude Vanderpool -	83	John Vanderpool.	SCIO.		
			Benjamin Jones - -	83	Benjamin Jones.
ALLEGANY COUNTY.			John Gowdy - -	81	E. Gowdy.
ANGELICA.			Stephen Taylor - -	72	
Charles Stewart - -	80	Solomon S. Childs.			
Simon Grant - -	83	County poor-house.	WIRT.		
			Aaron Swarthout - -	79	J. Swarthout.
AMITY.			Carey Crandall - -	79	Carey Crandall.
Hezekiah Wadsworth -	84	Trueman C. Wadsworth.	William Sherman - -	77	J. Sherman.
			Elisha Dakin - -	91	E. Dakin.
ALMOND.					
Isaiah Crandall - -	81	John How.	**BROOME COUNTY.**		
			CHENANGO.		
WEST ALMOND.			Jesse Hinds - - -	81	Jesse Hinds, jr.
Richardson Dunham -	80	Richardson Dunham.	John P. Smith - -	86	M. Smith.
			Peter Mills - - • -	62	Peter Mills.
BURNS.			Abel De Forest - -	79	Abel De Forrest.
Jesse Tuttle - -	83	Jesse Tuttle.	Mary McNelly - -	40	Mary McNelly.
			William Rose - -	76	Elanson Rose.
PORTAGE.			Jedediah Seward - -	82	Jedediah Seward.
Joseph Hasford - -	78	Franklin Hasford.			
Samuel Fuller - -	74	Samuel Fuller.	UNION.		
Erastus Booth - -	80	David Booth.	Elias Bayless - -	88	John Bayless
Wm. G. Deake - -	79	Wm. G. Deake.	Stephen Rust - -	67	S. Rust.
Allen Sears - -	80	Nathaniel Rathburn.	John Wilson - -	80	John Wilson.
Oliver Cary - -	80	Oliver Cary.	John Wilkinson - •	79	J. Wilkinson.
David Mosher - -	–	Jabez Mosher.	Daniel Chamberlain -	86	D. Chamberlain.
Ebenezer Patteson - -	–	Wm. B. Patteson.	Samuel Ingham - -	80	S. Ingham.
NUNDA.			VESTAL.		
William Gould • -	84	William Gould.	William Weston - -	78	**William Weston.**
BELFAST.			CONKLIN.		
Borden Potter - -	76		John Conklin - -	84	James Conklin.
John Vreeland - -	89				
Josiah Haywood - -	76		WINDSOR.		
John Phelps - - ✓	82		Samuel Scoville - -	80	S. M. Scoville.
			Paul Atwell - -	75	Paul Atwell.
CUBA.			Patience Heath - -	79	John Heath.
Joseph Gilbert - -	85		John Heath - -	84	J. Heath, jr.
Ezra Stanard - -	76		Joel Gamsey - -	75	Joel Gamsey.
John Burt - - •	78				
			COLESVILLE.		
CANEADIA.			Luther Mason - -	83	L. Mason.
Benjamin Webster - -	80		Joel Curtiss - -	76	Joel Curtiss.
			Seth Edson - - -	79	S. Edson.
CENTREVILLE.			James Wiley - -	88	James Wiley.
Edward Dewolf - -	75	Edward Dewolf.	Joseph Pike - -	82	J. Hurlbert.
Samuel Leach - -	84	S. Leach.	Joshua Baker - -	77	J. Baker.
Heman Hatch - -	74				
			SANDFORD.		
FRIENDSHIP.			Nathan Burlingame - -	78	Nathan Burlingame.
John Baxter - -	79		Jonas Underwood - -	77	J. Underwood, jr.
			Silas Seward - -	80	S. Seward.
GENESEE.					
Daniel Edwards - -	83		BARKER.		
Zacheus Maxson - -	84		John Rogers - -	78	J. Rogers.
			Solomon Armstrong - -	89	H. Ferguson.
HUME.			NANTICOKE.		
Remember Pratt - -	84	S. H. Pratt.	Asaph Morse - -	80	J. French.

10

Names of pensioners for revolutionary or military services.	Ages.	Names of heads of families with whom pensioners resided June 1, 1840.	Names of pensioners for revolutionary or military services.	Ages.	Names of heads of families with whom pensioners resided June 1, 1840.
BROOME—Continued.			**CATTARAUGUS**—Continued.		
NANTICOKE—Continued.			NEW ALBION.		
Samuel Phipps	80	Samuel Phipps.	Joseph Davis	80	Eben. Davis.
John Durfee	77	H. Durfee.	DAYTON.		
			James Gordon	87	James Gordon.
LISLE.			Jesse Worden	86	Abram Eastward.
Keen Robinson	87	M. Livermore.			
			ELLICOTTVILLE.		
TRIANGLE.			Alexander Phelps	83	Ralph R. Phelps.
Joseph Sanders	77	J. Sanders.	Justin Rust	76	Huldah Rust.
Joseph Sandford	84	J. Sandford.	Abiathar Vinton	81	Abiathar Vinton.
Elijah Gaylord	77	E. Gaylord.			
Ashbel Olmsted	76	J. Standish.	ASHFORD.		
Nathaniel Rogers	79	J. Sparrow.	Henry Hill	79	Henry Hill.
Ephraim Hodges	83	B. Hodges.			
			PERRYSBURG.		
CATTARAUGUS COUNTY.			James Mallory	78	M. Mallory.
FREEDOM.			Isaac Rugg	75	Isaac Rugg.
Betsey Fuller	83	Chase Fuller.	Ezekiel Perkins	76	Ezekiel Perkins.
John Nichols	80	Samuel Nichols.	Lemuel Mynard	91	Lemuel Mynard.
Zera Norton	76	John C. Moore.	Edmund Farnsworth	79	Edmund Farnsworth.
Susanna Champlin	78	Samuel Champlin.			
			OTTO.		
YORKSHIRE.			John Boutell	78	John Boutell.
Elisha Randall	79	Elisha Randall.	Sylvanus Parkinson	78	John T. Ferris.
Jacob Winters	54	Jacob Winters.			
Bishop Coston	81	James Coston.	RANDOLPH.		
William Gould	88	William Gould, jr.	Seth Berry	75	Seth Berry.
Abner Reckard	76	William Langmade.	Jehial Niles	86	Jehial Niles.
Elisha Plumb	53	Elisha Plumb.			
			FRANKLINVILLE.		
FARMERSVILLE.			John Doty	88	Palmer Doty.
Jeremiah Parish	75	Jeremiah Parish.	Samuel Sullivan	83	Samuel Sullivan.
Susanna Champlin	76	Elizabeth Champlin.	Pyram Ripley	77	Walter Blount.
Matthias Lane	81	Matthias Lane.			
Stephen Volentine	48	Stephen Volentine.	BURTON.		
Robert Burdick	52	Robert Burdick.	Hannah Clark	81	James R. Clark.
John Lafferty	85	Daniel Phillips.			
Oliver Holt	84	Elnathan Toby.	**CAYUGA COUNTY.**		
Zachariah Blackman	79	Gain R. Blackman.	AUBURN.		
			Joseph Marshall	82	F. Richardson.
MACHIAS.			Richard Connell	81	Hiram Bostwick.
Gad Taylor	81	Gad Taylor.	Abel Williams	83	Nathaniel Williams.
John Farrar	81	John Farrar.	Lois Sexton	81	Charles Sexton.
Richard Odell	80	Richard Odell.	E. B. Cobb	42	E. B. Cobb.
Edward Burt	68	Edward Burt.	James Pease	87	James Pease.
HINSDALE.			BRUTUS.		
Moses Fay	78	Moses Fay.	Nathaniel Bristol	85	J. St. John.
Enos Luddon	79	Enos Luddon.			
Jonathan Gowing	78	Eliab Gowing.	MENTZ.		
			Ashbel Treat	76	A. Treat.
PORTVILLE.			Benjamin F. Wellington	36	S. P. Trimper.
Daniel Carpenter	80	Daniel Carpenter.	Marietta Avery	75	E. Avery.
			Philip King	78	E. A. King.
OLEAN.			Josiah Baldwin	83	J. Baldwin.
Ebenezer Reed	79	Ebenezer Reed.	Russell Willis	77	R. Willis.
			Aaron Fredenburgh	87	A. Fredenburgh.
LITTLE VALLEY.			Richard Daimwood	81	Richard Daimwood.
Zebulon Stratton	88	James Stratton.			
			AURELIUS.		
CONEWANGO.			Benjamin Barrett	80	B. Barrett.
John Ash	77		Nathaniel Scofield	77	J. Scofield.
Abner Lovejoy	79	Almond Lovejoy.	Joseph Barron	77	J. Barron.
John Cowen	86	John Cowen.			
Joseph Woodsworth	82	Joseph Woodsworth.	SENNETT.		
			Thomas Willson	81	T. Willson.
NAPOLI.			Ira Pomeroy	81	I. Pomeroy, jr.
Caleb Adye	86		Frances Ganett	72	William Sprague.
Jacob Rice	79	Zyenas Rice.	William Mitchell	83	William Sprague.
COLD SPRING.			SPRINGPORT.		
Charles Crooks	89	Charles Crooks, 2d.	Barnet Crisse	80	Barnet Crisse.
			Samuel Wesner	77	Samuel Wesner.
LEON.			Gideon Allen	93	Zimri Allen.
Anthony Day	77	Anthony Day.	Reuben Weed	77	Reuben Weed.
Nicholas Blur	94	Abraham Low.			
Samuel Whitcomb	87	Samuel Whitcomb.	OWASCO.		
Ambrose Squires	74	Ambrose Squires.	Samuel Hanbeck	86	Samuel Hanbeck.
Dudley Noyes	76	Frederick Noyes.	Powell P. Ammerman	78	Richard Ammerman.
			Martin Cuykendal	76	Martin Cuykendal.
GREAT VALLEY.			Garret Van Fleet	84	Daniel Bevier.
Jonathan Fuller	87	Jonathan Fuller.			
Benjamin Chambers	83	Benjamin Chambers.			

Names of pensioners for revolutionary or military services.	Ages.	Names of heads of families with whom pensioners resided June 1, 1840.	Names of pensioners for revolutionary or military services.	Ages.	Names of heads of families with whom pensioners resided June 1, 1840.
CAYUGA—Continued.			**CAYUGA—Continued.**		
LEDYARD.			SUMNER HILL.		
Daniel A. Ward	80	Joseph Esters.	Ebenezer Hathaway	84	Ebenezer Hathaway.
Sarah York	76	Stephen Gifford.	Harman Peters	78	Cornelius Peters.
Asa Burnham	87	Sherman Smith.	Jesse Woodward	76	Horace Woodward.
Daniel McDowel	83	Daniel McDowel.	John Vermilye	76	John Vermilye.
GENOA.			CATO.		
David Price	87	David Price.	David Bartlett	47	David Bartlett.
Sarah Palmer	78	Edward Palmer, 2d.	John Bennett	75	John Bennett.
Henry Studwell	84	Aaron Lyon.			
James Mead	86	James Mead.	IRA.		
Margaret Henderson	74	Charles Denison.	Benjamin Bartlett	77	Harry Ferris.
Samuel Branch	73	Samuel Branch.	Reuben Peck	80	Jonathan Smith.
Hannah Tilly	75	Hannah Tilly.			
Rosina Napp	74	Gilbert Lockwood.	CONQUEST.		
			Joshua Fuller	77	Francis R. Petty.
VENICE.			Thomas Frost	77	Charles J. Frost.
Benjamin Clark	84	Benjamin Clark.	Valentine Wheeler	84	Valentine Wheeler.
William Huffman	78	Caleb Nye.			
Zadiack Bateman	78	Zadiack Bateman.	VICTORY.		
Ebenezer Parks	94	Ebenezer Parks.	Elijah Starkweather	84	Reuben Blanchard.
William Mane	82	William Mane.	Levi Wilkinson	84	Levi Wilkinson.
Henry Hewitt	77	Henry Hewitt.	Jacob Stanley	85	Thomas Chapman.
James Thompson	75	James Thompson.	Christian Finck	81	Phebe Finck.
Hannah Neely	77	Dennis Robinson.			
Asa Way	80	Asa Way.	STERLING.		
Gilbert Tracy	80	Gilbert Tracy.	William McCoy	84	William McCoy.
Sarah Weeks	66	Sarah Weeks.	James Wasson	79	James Wasson.
			Abijah Hunt	78	Abijah Hunt.
SCIPIO.			Cornelius Ackerson	85	William Ackerson.
Joseph Culver	79	Ansel Culver.	William Deusenbury	82	William Deusenbury.
Samuel Gray	46	Samuel Gray.			
Lucenia Johnson	77	Lucenia Johnson.	**CHATAUQUE COUNTY.**		
Elias Manchester	82	Elias Manchester.	HARMONY.		
William Graham	89	James Easterly.	Phineas Chamberlain	74	Phineas Chamberlain.
Nathan Sheffield	76	Nathan Sheffield.	John Willman	78	William Blanchard.
Eleanor Elliott	82	William Elliott.	Thomas Shepherd	47	Thomas Shepherd.
			Nathaniel Mather	81	Nathaniel Mather.
LOCKE.			David Holister	86	Anson Phelps.
Jacob Barret	76	Jacob Barret, jr.	Samuel Benedict	87	William Dean.
John Croft	78	John Croft.			
Amy Bowker	70	Abraham Dates.	POLAND.		
Daniel Harris	82	Joseph Harris.	Seth Baker	78	Seth Baker.
Benjamin Heath	75	Benjamin Heath.	Elias Tracy	78	Elias Tracy.
Ebenezer King	79	Benjamin King.	Joshua Woodard	84	Peer Woodard.
Aaron Murphy	47	Aaron Murphy.	Phineas Allen	81	Sumner Allen.
Esther Martin	77	Erastus Southworth.	Nathaniel Fenton	77	Nathaniel Fenton.
John White	84	J. Thompson.	Joel J. Reynolds	79	Joel J. Reynolds.
William Wattles	84	William Wattles.	Jonathan Bill	85	Joseph Bill.
MORAVIA.			ELERY.		
Eliphaz Alexander	76	Eliphaz Alexander.	Lemuel Bacon	77	William Bacon.
Zadock Cady	76	Zadock Cady.	Luther Barney	83	Luther Barney.
Daniel Wood	88	Thomas Ferguson.	Jonah Maples	78	Charles G. Maples.
Nancy McGuigan	73	Zebulon Hall.	Jeremiah Griffith	82	A. Griffith.
Susanna Terry	77	Anselm Terry.	Selah Scofield	82	Haran Scofield.
Henry Thomas	85	Henry Thomas.	Jonathan Babcock	78	Benjamin Parker.
Esther White	83	John White.	Jacob Annies	77	Jacob Annies.
			Joseph Boyd	81	Alvin Boyd.
NILES.					
Cornelius D. Dewitt	80	Cornelius D. Dewitt.	ELLINGTON.		
Egbert Dewitt	79	Egbert Dewitt.	Abijah Hitchcock	81	Abijah Hitchcok.
John Ellis	69	John Ellis.			
Roswell Fairman	77	Roswell Fairman.	SHERMAN.		
William Hall	78	William Hall.	David Waldo	76	David Waldo.
Samuel Jones	83	John D. Hakes.	William Turner	85	Richard Platt.
David Johnson	82	David Johnson.	Reuben Thompson	77	Jos. A. Hubbard.
Sarah Lazell	69	Joseph Lazell.	Isaac Osborn	79	Isaac Osborn.
Ebenezer Plumby	86	Allen J. Plumby.			
Joseph Newland	89	Lemuel A. Newland.	CLYMER.		
Job Shirley	83	Simpkins Snow.	Gardner Cleavland	77	Gardner Cleavland.
Henry Van Etten	80	Levi W. Van Etten.	John Campbell	78	John Campbell.
Othniel Williams	75	Othniel Williams.			
			BUSTI.		
SEMPRONIUS.			John Smiley	79	Samuel Smiley.
Samuel Gurnee	43	Samuel Gurnee.	Barnabas Willman	83	Homer Willman.
Elisha Hewitt	82	Elisha Hewitt.	Martin L. Comstock	83	Martin L. Comstock.
Joseph B. Miller	58	Joseph B. Miller.	Phineas Parmenter	78	John Parmenter.
Nicholas Potter	80	Nicholas Potter.	Stephen Wilcox	78	Ephraim Wilcox.
Puryer Reeves	90	Manassah Reeves.			
Hannah Lake	73	George Sawyer.	FRENCH CREEK.		
Reuben Woodworth	79	Reuben Woodworth.	William Adams	85	William Adams.

Names of pensioners for revolutionary or military services.	Ages.	Names of heads of families with whom pensioners resided June 1, 1840.	Names of pensioners for revolutionary or military services.	Ages.	Names of heads of families with whom pensioners resided June 1, 1840.
CHATAUQUE—Continued.			**CHATAUQUE—Continued.**		
MINA.			SHERIDAN—Continued.		
Juvenile Winters	82	Juvenile Winters.	Jesse Clothier	81	A. R. Clothier.
David Madden	77	Ichabod Thayer.	Susanna Swift	70	Lyman Swift.
CARROLL.			Stephen Bush	81	Stephen Bush, jr.
Asa More	75	Joseph R. More.	Otis Ensign, 1st.	78	Otis Ensign, 1st.
Jasper Marsh	80	Jasper Marsh.	ARKWRIGHT.		
John Owens	100	Reuben Owens.	Stephen Pratt	76	Stephen Pratt.
ELLICOTT.			Hannah Evans	78	Stephen Hill.
Thomas Matthews	93	Jabez Blackmar.	James Olmstead	86	Chauncy Webster.
Daniel Deming	77	Daniel Deming.	Nathan Hatch	84	Edmund Hatch
William Washburn	72	William Washburn.	Eliakim Thatcher	78	Eliakim Thatcher.
Charles Wood	80	Edward F. Wood.	William Wood	76	Arna Wood.
			CHARLOTTE.		
GERRY.			Anna Seaver	74	R. W. Seaver.
Benjamin Matthews	85	Caleb Matthews.	CHERRY CREEK.		
John Coe	83	John Coe.	Darius Wiard	83	Darius Wiard.
RIPLEY.			Daniel Osborne	89	Daniel Osborne.
Benjamin Bennet	84	A. F. Bennet.	Isaac Stone	75	Isaac Stone.
Moses Dustin	75	Moses Dustin.	VILLANOVIA.		
David Jenkins	49	David Jenkins.	Thomas Phillips	78	Thomas Phillips.
Levi Adams, sen.	86	Levi Adams, sen.	Elias Clark	87	Jesse Jay.
WESTFIELD.			Mehitable Spencer	78	John Spencer.
Daniel Barnham	78	Daniel Barnham.	Nathaniel Warner	71	Nathaniel Warner.
Samuel Wheeler	76	Samuel Wheeler.	Solomon Norton	90	G. B. Aldritch.
Samuel Penfield	76	Samuel Penfield.	Joseph Mather	85	John Mather.
Sarah Hall	77	Sylvester Hall.	HANOVER.		
Fisk Durand	74	Fisk Durand.	Christopher McManus	82	Christ. McManus.
Jonathan Dyer	75	B. Parrish.	Isaac Van Camp	80	Joseph Van Camp.
Reuben Wright	91	Reuben Wright.	Reuben Barns	84	Dennis Barns.
David Rumsey	82	David Rumsey.	Silas Nash	78	Silas Nash.
Lent Bradley	84	Lent Bradley.	Thomas Frink	77	Harvey Frink.
Nathaniel Bird	77	Nathaniel Bird.	Robert Love	86	Levi Love.
William Chase	78	William Chase.	Zilpha Cranston	60	William Cranston.
CHATAUQUE.			Solomon Rothbone	76	Solomon Rothbone.
Bethuel Bond	77	Bethuel Bond.	Comfort Herrington	86	Andrew Irish.
Jonathan Brigham	86	Jonathan Brigham.	Cornelius Phelps	77	Cornelius Phelps.
Adonijah Fenton	86	Henry Whitney.	Phebe Howard	81	Abram Osborne.
Nancy Hawkins	74	W. W. Hawkins.			
Richard Whitney	81	Richard Whitney.	**CHEMUNG COUNTY.**		
Abigail Thayer	82	Abigail Thayer.	BIG FLATS.		
PORTLAND.			William Mapes	79	Elijah Mapes.
Anne Taylor	77	Anne Taylor.	Frederick Vaughn	72	Wm. F. Reeder.
William Couch	81	William Couch.	CATHERINES.		
Joseph P. Peters	79	J. P. Peters.	George Brink	80	George Brink.
Calvin Barns	74	Calvin Barns.	Noah Agard	85	Levi Beardsley.
Daniel Barns	76	Daniel Barns.	John Cooper	87	Aaron Cooper.
Simon Burton	71	Simon Burton.	Joseph Frost	85	Eli C. Frost.
Erastus Taylor	52	Erastus Taylor.	Jonathan Hitchcock	79	Jonathan Hitchcock.
Mary Eaton	87 }	David Eaton.	Israel Lee	81	John S. Lee.
David Eaton	58 }		Levi Sylvester	85	Levi Sylvester.
Samuel Munson	78	Samuel Munson.	John Mitchell	82	John Mitchell, jr.
Amos Standish	90	John Robins.	CHEMUNG.		
POMPRET.			Daniel Van Campen	79	Daniel Van Campen.
William Seymour	85	John Seymour.	James Green	90	James Green.
Roswell W. Fitch	77	R. W. Fitch.	Jacob Decker	84	Jacob Decker.
Elizabeth Crane	86	Elizabeth Howes.	CAYUTA.		
William Lamont	84	William Lamont.	Abraham Losey	73	Abraham Losey.
Vaniah Fox	78	Vaniah Fox.			
Nicholas M. Bovee	81	Ebenezer Baldwin.	CATLIN.		
Silas Marsh	78	Silas Marsh.	Samuel Shoemaker	79	J. M. Shoemaker.
Sarah Barker	75	Sarah Barker.			
Jonathan Phelps	76	Jonathan Phelps.	DIX.		
Sarah Matteson	85	D. J. Matteson.	Mary Rosengrant	76	Tunis Voorhees.
Lucy Ingham	83	Isaac Ingham.	Ebenezer Smith	79	Ebenezer Smith.
Zimri Hills	77	Heman Hills.			
Reuben Thompson	78	Reuben Thompson.	ERIN.		
			Richard Andrews	76	Richard Andrews.
STOCKTON.					
Elijah Look	82	Elijah Look.	ELMIRA.		
Thankful Cleland	82	Nathan Cleland.	James B. Decker	102	Pamelia Decker.
Asa Turner	75	Reuben Jones.	Silas Hall	84	Joshua Hall.
Thomas Curtice	79	Jeremiah Curtice.	Theodore Norton	76	Theodore Norton.
			James Swartwood	93	Benj. Smith.
SHERIDAN.			Jonathan Sturdevant	79	Jonathan Sturdevant.
James White	82	James White, jr.	Benjamin Woodward	76	Benj. Woodward.
Ephraim Herrick	85	Ephraim Herrick.			

NEW YORK—NORTHERN DISTRICT—Continued.

Names of pensioners for revolutionary or military services.	Ages.	Names of heads of families with whom pensioners resided June 1, 1840.	Names of pensioners for revolutionary or military services.	Ages.	Names of heads of families with whom pensioners resided June 1, 1840.
CHEMUNG—Continued.			**CHENANGO—Continued.**		
SOUTHPORT.			SHERBURNE—Continued.		
John Carr	83	Nathan Carr.	Jeremiah Purdy	77	Jeremiah Purdy.
Edward Comfort	78	Edward Comfort.	Amos Cole	80	Amos Cole.
John Fitz Simmons	79	John Fitz Simmons.	Josiah Lathrop	83	Josiah Lathrop.
David Griswold	79	David Griswold.	Timothy Hatch	82	Timothy Hatch.
Eleanor Hass	77	Wm. Jenkins.			
Sarah McCormick	72	Abraham Miller.	SMYRNA.		
Samuel Nichols	76	Samuel Nichols.	Timothy Dunn	84	Timothy Dunn.
Ezekiel Rhodes	86	Ezekiel Rhodes.	William Jones	81	William Jones.
Nathan Sayre	92	Nathan Sayre.	Joseph Simonds	83	Joseph Simonds.
			Jesse Wheeler	83	Merritt Wheeler.
VETERAN.			Conrod Mowers	79	Henry Mowers.
Joshua Kendall	79	Joshua Kendall.			
Ichabod Meeker	90	Elijah Meeker.	COVENTRY.		
			Abigail Goodnough	89	David Goodnough.
CHENANGO COUNTY.			Catharine Smith	69	Matthew B. Smith.
LINCKLEAN.			Mercy Packard	77	O. H. Packard.
Joseph Breed	85	Joseph Breed.	Sarah Parker	83	Lucia Parker.
Anna Corey	79	Amasa Corey.	Heth Helsey	83	Clark Smith.
Jacob Allen	85	Jacob Allen.	Roger Edgarton	79	Roger Edgarton.
George Champlin	83	Joshua Sanders.	Joseph Fairchild	82	Joseph Fairchild.
Jonathan Babcock	76	Harvey Babcock.			
Elizabeth Cook	83	Loren Cook.	GREENE.		
			Zemis Jones	79	Betsey Wheeler.
OTSELIC.			Nathan Bennett	87	Nathan Bennett.
Joseph Carey	80	Joseph Carey.	William Root	80	R. Lyon.
William Coley	82	William Coley.	Robert Gallup	79	Erastus Foote.
NEW BERLIN.			SMITHVILLE.		
Thomas Loomis	84	Charles Knapp.	Thankful Matteson	83	Jesse Matteson.
Richard Goff	76	Elisha Herrington.			
Daniel Sage	83	William Shaw.	PITCHER.		
Matthew Calkins	76	Matthew Calkins.	John Blanchard	76	John Blanchard.
Joseph Sheffield	80	Joseph Sheffield.			
Reuben Huntly	89	Ezra Huntly.	PHARSALIA.		
Elisha Babcock	78	Elisha Babcock.	Jonathan Champlin	84	Michael Champlin.
Comfort Meeker	76	Fanny Brown.			
			NORWICH.		
GUILFORD.			Jedediah Randall	83	Jedediah Randall.
Nancy Richmond	90	Seth Richmond.	Thomas Hadlock	81	Thomas Hadlock.
Rachael Twilager	80	Josiah Twilager.	George H. King	77	George H. King.
John Secor	78	John Secor.	John King	87	John King.
Elisha Sage	86	Gilbert Jewel.	Nathaniel Church	92	Nathaniel Church.
Theophilus White	86	Jeremiah White.	Peter Keith	85	Peter Keith.
Daniel Johnson	80	Seth Johnson.	Nathan Daniels	80	Leonard Daniels.
John Dickerman	74	William Dickerman.	John McNitt	79	John McNitt.
Anna Denning	80	Nicholas Slater.	Joshua Aldrich	80	Joshua Aldrich.
Elisha Smith	84	Elisha Smith.	John Hicks	79	John Hicks.
Sarah Clark	88	William Clark.			
Polly Aylesworth	80	Polly Aylesworth.	PLYMOUTH.		
Abram Terry	86	Abram Terry.	Eliphalet Cutting	73	E. Cutting.
			John Brewer	78	John Brewer.
COLUMBUS.					
Esick Olney	84	Esick Olney.	PRESTON.		
Jacob Tillotson	80	Jacob Tillotson.	William Clark	86	William Clark.
Hope Howard	76	Richard Dutton.	Roswell Dudley	79	Roswell Dudley.
Henry Williams	77	Henry Williams.	Daniel Eccleston	85	Daniel Eccleston.
James C. Church	79	Eli Church.	John H. Avery	79	John H. Avery.
John Willis	54	John Willis.			
James P. Denison	78	Nathaniel Denison.	OXFORD.		
John Fletcher	78	John Fletcher.	Mary Throop	69	Nancy Packer.
Caleb Church	86	Varnum Church.	Phebe Hancox	76	Charles Hancox.
			Josiah Hacket	82	Daniel Hacket.
BAINBRIDGE.			Thomas Welch	84	Benjamin Welch.
James Whitmore	79	James Whitmore.	Zophar Betts	80	Warren Betts.
John Elsworth	84	John Elsworth.	Polly Vickery	84	Silas Blowers.
Charity Banks	79	William Banks.	Catharine Bennett	76	Samuel Wheeler.
Solomon Hallet	81	Solomon Hallet.	Hezekiah Brackets	78	Hezekiah Brackets.
William Johnston	89	James Johnston.	Mary Cooley	80	David Polly.
William King	81	Jacob King.	John Harrington	83	John Harrington.
Edward Walker	83	Edward Walker.	Asa Wells	71	Daniel Hall.
Ebenezer Landers	82	Solomon Landers.	Matilda Brown	73	David Brown.
James Basford	80	James Basford.			
			CLINTON COUNTY.		
SHERBURNE.			PLATTSBURG.		
Abram Crego	82	Daniel S. Crego.	Levi M. Roberts	45	Levi M. Roberts.
Newcomb Raymond	76	Newcomb Raymond.	Charles Cortwite	53	Charles Cortwite.
Garrett Reed	86	Garrett Reed.	Joshua Buzzel	49	Joshua Buzzel.
Samuel Blackman	78	Horace Morse.	Placid Monty	74	Placid Monty.
Andrew Stafford	84	Andrew Stafford.	John A. Ferris	82	John A. Ferris.
Thomas Higgins	85	Thomas Higgins.	John Lee	80	John Lee.
Isaac Sheldon	84	S. Harrington.	Mary Wilson	83	John Rugar.
Joseph Guthrie	80	Joseph Guthrie.	Polly Reed	75	Zanthy Reed.

NEW YORK—NORTHERN DISTRICT—Continued.

Names of pensioners for revolutionary or military services.	Ages.	Names of heads of families with whom pensioners resided June 1, 1840.
CLINTON—Continued.		
PLATTSBURG—Continued.		
Francis Rogers - - -	47	Francis Rogers.
John Roberts - - -	80	John Roberts.
Isaac Kennon - - -	84	David Kennon.
Allen Smith - - -	81	Allen Smith.
Mary Young - - -	72	John T. Addoms.
Joshua Hilyard - - -	83	Joshua Hilyard.
Lucy Bradford - - -	79	Elisha Bradford.
Rebecca Hilyard - - -	74	Rebecca Hilyard.
S. Francis Huttinack -	79	Stephen F. Huttinack.
Adoniram Parrot - -	83	A. Parrot.
Esther Scribner - - -	83	Jeremiah Scribner.
BEEKMANTOWN.		
Lorin Larkin - - -	85	Elam Larkin.
Reuben Stiles - - -	80	Reuben Stiles.
Israel Rand - - -	79	Ephraim Rand.
John Monty - - -	66	John Monty.
Luther Drury - - -	78	Luther Drury.
Phebe Howe - - -	93	Almshouse.
Nicholas Constantine - -	84	
Thomas Eddy - - -	50	Thomas Eddy.
Jonathan Scribner - -	81	Jonathan Scribner.
Thomas Reynolds - - -	45	Thomas Reynolds.
CHAMPLAIN.		
Samuel Ashmun - -	76	Samuel Ashmun.
Arcosh Martin - - -	73	Nelson Martin.
Amable Bilow - - -	72	Joseph K. Bilow.
Mary Currier - - -	86	Michael Currier.
Bozziel Nadeau - - -	84	Francis Nadeau.
Reuben Huntoon - -	78	Reuben Huntoon.
Ezra Loomis - - -	84	Alva Loomis.
Dan. Beaumont - - -	77	Dan. Beaumont.
John Wilson - - -	79	Chester Wilson.
CHAZY.		
Joseph C. Marsh - -	77	Joseph C. Marsh.
Gardner Goodspeed - -	59	Gardner Goodspeed.
Benjamin Graves - -	80	Benjamin Graves.
George Merriman - -	84	Francis Kinsley.
Mary Amlaw - - -	80	Mary Amlaw.
Alexander Feriole - -	76	Alexander Feriole.
Mary Lezotte - - -	80	Joseph Lezotte.
Peter Robarge - - -	82	Peter Robarge, 3d.
Agal Amlaw - - -	72	John Breette.
Walter Durfee - - -	89	Walter Durfee.
Joseph Monty - - -	67	Joseph Monty.
Francis Delong - - -	80	Francis Delong.
Margaret Belonga - -	74	Isaac Abare.
Daniel Bixby - - -	78	Joel Hickok.
John Wilson - - -	57	John Wilson.
Asa Stearns - - -	83	Asa Stearns.
Stephen Howard - - -	82	Stephen Howard.
MOOERS.		
David Southwick - -	78	David Southwick.
Margaret Smith - - -	76	Chauncey Sperry.
Levi Stockwell - - -	86	Levi Stockwell.
PERU.		
Martha Blanchard - -	69	A. Blanchard.
Josiah Terry - - -	82	Josiah Terry.
Joseph Westcott - - -	75	Joseph Westcott.
Jephtha Hewit - -	60	Jephtha Hewit.
Clarissa Marvin - - -	75	Hiram Marvin.
Isaac Webb - - -	73	Sally Fish.
ANSABLE.		
Avery Sanders - - -	78	Avery Sanders.
Lydia Woodward - - -	77	Hiram Safford.
Ezra Pond - - -	84	Cephas Clark.
ELLENBURG.		
Frederick Perrigo - -	75	James D. Perrigo.
J. Knight - - -	79	Elijah Knight.
CORTLAND COUNTY.		
TRUXTON.		
Allen Webster - - -	75	Hiram Webster.
Ezekiel Kent - - -	78	Jerome Kent.
Paul James - - -	84	Sheffield James.
Stephen Pendleton - -	84	Esther Maxham.

Names of pensioners for revolutionary or military services.	Ages.	Names of heads of families with whom pensioners resided June 1, 1840.
CORTLAND—Continued.		
TRUXTON—Continued.		
Betty Andrews - - -	80	Asa W. Andrews.
Timothy Crosby - - -	84	Timothy Crosby.
John Maxson - - -	85	Roxana Perry.
Walcott Justice - - -	76	Joseph Justice.
Darius Benjamin - -	82	Varnum M. Burdick.
David Morse - - -	79	David Morse.
Reuben Cadwell - -	77	Reuben Cadwell.
Elias Benjamin - - -	57	Elias Benjamin.
EAST HALF CORTLANDVILLE.		
Aaron Day - - -	73	Aaron Day.
Nathan Blodget - - -	83	Enoch Mosely.
Timothy Andrews - -	88	Timothy Andrews.
HOMER.		
Samuel Goff. - - -	89	Benj. Goff.
John Albright - - -	79	
Daniel Durkee - - -	85	Nathaniel Durkee.
Hannah Price - - -	74	Aaron L. Price.
Geradus Clute - - -	85	James Clute.
Nancy Alvord - - -	72	Jacob B. Alvord.
Margaret Houton - -	69	Margaret Houton.
Helen Devou - - -	65	Helen Devou.
Daniel Broom - - -	78	L. B. Canfield.
Isaac Bellows - - -	78	Zebulon Bellows.
Abram Rosa - - -	79	Rufus Rosa.
SCOTT.		
James Brown - - -	82	Samuel Ames.
Alexander Kinyon - -	81	Alexander Kinyon.
PREBLE.		
Asa Blood - - -	76	Asa Blood.
Richard Severson - -	85	Nicholas Severson.
Juliana White - - -	82	Henry W. Anderson.
Amos Skeel - - -	73	Amos Skeel.
Lucretia Trowbridge -	74	Job J. Johnson.
William White - - -	77	William White.
William Collins - - -	67	William Collins.
Eli Pierce - - -	79	George D. Pierce.
VIRGIL.		
Jeremiah Chase - - -	84	Jeremiah Chase.
Elizabeth Ryan - - -	75	Jonathan Ryan.
Elizabeth Robinson - -	71	L. Robinson.
Joel Hancock - - -	49	Joel Hancock.
Thos. Kingsbury - -	88	Marvin Baulch.
Stephen Kelly - - -	84	Stephen Kelly.
Simeon Leroy - - -	85	Simeon Leroy.
George Totman - - -	78	Lorenzo Totman.
Joel Morton - - -	87	E. Jones.
John Gee - - -	77	A. Gee.
Elisha Brewer - - -	75	Elisha Brewer.
Cornelius Lament - -	85	Hiram Lament.
John Stanbro - - -	82	J. Stanbro.
Enoch Smith - - -	70	Enoch Smith.
SOLON.		
Ebenezer Blake - - -	82	Ebenezer Blake.
Edward Goddard - - -	89	Edward Goddard.
CINCINNATUS.		
Peter Fosburgh - - -	85	
Enoch Blackman - - -	77	Enoch Blackman.
James Walker - - -	87	James Walker.
Samuel Roberts - - -	79	Eliza Roberts.
Laurence White - - -	81	Laurence White.
M. Robins - - -	79	J. L. Robins.
MARATHON.		
Asahel Bently - - -	80	Caleb Sherwood.
Lucy Barnes - - -	82	James Burgess.
FREETOWN.		
John Tinker - - -	82	Isaac Hawley.
Nancy Richardson - -	83	Alvah Harman.
Elisha Wood - - -	79	E. Wood, jr.
WILLETT.		
Archibald Campbell - -	87	Archibald Campbell.
Joseph Gordon - - -	80	Joseph Gordon.

NEW YORK—NORTHERN DISTRICT—Continued.

Names of pensioners for revolutionary or military services.	Ages.	Names of heads of families with whom pensioners resided June 1, 1840.	Names of pensioners for revolutionary or military services.	Ages.	Names of heads of families with whom pensioners resided June 1, 1840.
CORTLAND—Continued.			DELAWARE—Continued.		
WILLETT—Continued.			BOVINA.		
Edward Nickerson - - -	80	E. Nickerson.	James Vanderburgh - -	81	Clarion F. Vanderburgh.
Hezekiah Allen - - -	77	Horace Allen.			
			ANDES.		
WEST HALF CORTLAND.			Abigail Newton - - -	79	Robert Jones.
Alexander Milliner - - -	74	A. Milliner.	Trueman White - - -	48	Trueman White.
Hezekiah Herrick - - -	83	W. B. Sturtevant.	Jotham Hanks - - -	75	Jotham Hanks.
Sibbel Craim - - -	75	Wm. Goodell.	John Shaver - - -	77	John Shaver.
Anstis Daboll - - -	76	Elias Daboll.			
Gilbert Edgecomb - - -	78	G. Edgecomb.	COLCHESTER.		
Hope till Haskins - - -	85	G. Lamphier.	Lydia Allen - - -	80	Lydia Allen.
Mead Merrill - - -	77	S. R. Hunter.	Abigail Elwood - - -	73	Hezekiah Elwood.
Martha White - - -	86	J. R. White.			
Darius Waterman - - -	79	Tercius Eels.	HAMDEN.		
Lydia Bassett - - -	76	Lydia Bassett.	Abigail Hitt - - -	84	Isaac Hitt.
Benajah Story - - -	93	Stephen Story.	Sarah Barber - - -	93	Sarah Barber.
Anna Kinney - - -	76	M. L. Hopkins.			
			HARPERSFIELD.		
			Roswell Hotchkiss - -	78	Roswell Hotchkiss.
DELAWARE COUNTY.			Susanna Mark - - -	76	Susanna Mark.
TOMPKINS.			Jedediah Gaylord - -	82	Jedediah Gaylord.
Silas Underwood - - -	78	Samuel R. Underwood.	James Smith - - -	78	James Smith.
Joseph Webb - - -	80	Joseph Webb.	Abijah Baird - - -	83	David Baird.
Aaron Stiles - - -	78	Samuel Stiles.	Robert Inglis - - -	91	Wm. Inglis.
Rachel Butterfield - -	78	Samuel Butterfield.	Roswell Mallison - -	78	Roswell Mallison.
			Submit Rickey - - -	72	Thomas Rickey.
SIDNEY.					
David Hall - - -	75	David Hall.	MIDDLETOWN.		
Josiah Thatcher - - -	76	Josiah Thatcher.	Elizabeth Delamater - -	82	Abram J. Delamater.
Benonah Paige - - -	88	Benonah Paige.	John Nicholas Taple - -	78	John Nicholas Taple.
Levi Bartlett - - -	80	Luman Cohoon.	Thomas Sweet - - -	91	Valentine Sweet.
Ichabod Case - - -	85	Ichabod Case.	Issachar Robinson - -	78	Samuel Termilgar.
			Samuel Todd - - -	83	Darling Todd.
MASONVILLE.					
Benjamin Wheaton - -	80	George A. Northrup.	WALTON.		
Mehitable Clarke - - -	84	Jeremy Thurbur.	Matthew Hawin - - -	86	Thomas Hawin.
Nicholas Groat - - -	79	Nicholas Groat.	Levi Hanford - - -	80	Wm. B. Hanford.
Moses Lyon - - -	78	Richard Lyon.	Wm. Andrews - - -	82	Wm. Andrews.
			Susanna Weed - - -	77	Daniel Weed.
DELHI.			Hannah Webb - - -	78	Daniel White.
John Moore - - -	78	Greene Moore.	Patty Butler - - -	77	Jabez Wakeman.
Jonathan Finney - - -	86	Jonathan Finney.			
Sarah Bishop - - -	71	John Bishop.	STAMFORD.		
Joseph Howland - - -	77	Gideon Frisbee.	Wm. Johnson - - -	83	Elisha Wetmore.
March Farrington - - -	80	Henry More.	Noah Davenport - - -	82	Nicholas P. Champlin.
Rufus Perkins - - -	79	Rufus Perkins.	Aaron Rollins - - -	82	Bern Rollins.
Josiah Shaw - - -	84	Josiah Shaw.	Shubal Randall - - -	86	Hiram Skinners.
Seth Whitney - - -	78	Seth Whitney.			
			Nelly Pattison - - -	76	Abm. Lockwood.
DAVENPORT.			Samuel Cranston - -	83	Samuel Cranston.
Jesse Utter - - -	91	Stephen Utter.	Edmund Kelley - - -	72	Martin Kelley.
Hugh McGuire - - -	95	Sarah Teneick.	Avery Benton - - -	61	Avery Benton.
Daniel Herrick - - -	81	James Harlow.	Nathan Osborn - - -	76	Moses Sherwood.
Daniel R. Campbell - -	78	Daniel R. Campbell.	Ephraim Decker - - -	82	Martin Decker.
Uriah White - - -	80	Daniel White.	Cornelius Cator - - -	78	Abm. J. Cator.
Gershom Van Wager - -	85	Hontice H. Coux.	Solomon Jenkins - -	48	Solomon Jenkins.
			John C. Cator - - -	83	John C. Cator.
HANCOCK.			Richard Conkey - - -	78	Richard Conkey.
Christopher Roff - - -	78	Christopher Roff.	Bridget Benham - - -	70	Matthew Benham.
Elijah Thomas - - -	87	Elijah Thomas.	Zophar Wicks - - -	85	Zophar Wicks.
			Lovina Gleason - - -	76	Fisher Gleason.
FRANKLIN.			Philip B. Travis - - -	77	Philip B. Travis.
Levi Miles - - -	77	Levi Miles.	Nathaniel Jenkins - -	84	Nathaniel Jenkins, jr.
David Ogden - - -	75	David Ogden, jr.	Daniel Wood - - -	83	Daniel Wood.
Ebenezer Bennet - - -	88	Ebenezer Bennet.			
Edward Gay - - -	77	William Gay, 1st.	ERIE COUNTY.		
Anthony Judd - - -	88	Jesse Judd.	CITY OF BUFFALO—1st ward.		
Mary Parker - - -	82	Epaphras Bowles.	Manuel Grace - - -	90	Andrew Murray.
Ada Phelps - - -	74	Horace Phelps.	2d ward.		
			Daniel Hicks - - -	80	John Hicks.
CORRICT.			Stephen Champlin - -	50	Stephen Champlin.
Hannah Hunt - - -	79	Hiram Hunt.			
Solomon Raney - - -	84	Harvey Davis.	TONAWANDA.		
Samuel Andrus - - -	83	Joseph Mud.	Hezekiah Mosby - -	86	Hezekiah Mosby.
John Armstrong - - -	78	John Cease.			
Jesse Stewart - - -	81	Foreman Denison.	EDEN.		
			David Corbin - - -	82¼	John Baker.
MEREDITH.			Amos Conant - - -	78	Benjamin Grover.
Chloe Fox - - -	78	Amasa Fox.			
Eleazer Wright - - -	85	Eleazer Wright, jr.	CLARENCE.		
Ruth Dutton - - -	81	Street Dutton.	Benjamin Nesmith - -	84	David Nesmith.
Silas Brooks - - -	78	Silas Brooks.	Jacob Cummings - -	77	Simeon R. Cummings.
			Abraham Carmer - -	79	Abraham Carmer.

Names of pensioners for revolutionary or military services.	Ages.	Names of heads of families with whom pensioners resided June 1, 1840.	Names of pensioners for revolutionary or military services.	Ages.	Names of heads of families with whom pensioners resided June 1, 1840.
ERIE—Continued.			**ESSEX—Continued.**		
NEWSTEAD.			ELIZABETTOWN.		
George Bugbee	77	George Bugbee.	Levi Brown	59	Levi Brown.
Martin Lewis	73	Martin Lewis.	Josiah Fisher	80	Josiah Fisher.
Robert Pennell	78	Robert Pennell.	Thomas Mitchel	77	Thomas Mitchel.
William Anderson	90	Samuel Anderson.	Joseph Durand	76	Alyron Durand.
Andrew Bell	84	Ebenezer J. Brown.			
Olive Pixley	81	Abigail Gilman.	ESSEX.		
Gad Sutlief	85	Asa Greenman.	Sarah Derby	85	Asa Derby.
Thomas C. Love	50	Thomas C. Love.	Oliver Barker	78	Oliver Barker.
			Betsey Gardner	81	Richard C. Gardner.
LANCASTER.			Eldad Sabin	75	Erastus W. Sabin.
Benjamin Clark	81	James Clark.	Nathaniel Rogers	79	Nathaniel Rogers.
Betsey Johnson	70	Isaac S. Johnson.	John Greely	81	John Greely.
Pardon Peckham	77	Pardon Peckham.	Thomas Warden	75	Thomas Warden.
Joseph Williams	43	Joseph Williams.			
Asa Severence	78	Corbin W. Powers.	JAY.		
			Shubal Sumner	81	Shubal Sumner.
WALES.			David Nichols	83	Thaddeus Bowman.
Enoch Kellogg	78	James Kellogg.	Sarah Clark	84	Sylvanus Minor.
Ithamar Arkley	77	Ithamar Arkley.	Isaac Finch	56	Isaac Finch.
Omer Warner	78	Omer Warner.	Aaron Fenne	79	Joel Bull.
HAMBURG.			KEENE.		
Johnson Guin	81	Obed Guin.	Sally Hull	70	William H. H. Hull.
Moses Smith	84	Joseph D. Wethwell.	Caleb Ingalls	84	Caleb Ingalls.
Reuben Cobleigh	79	Reuben Cobleigh.			
Jonathan Skinner	78	Stephen Cetchell.	LEWIS.		
Selathial Alen	76	Samuel Okes, jr.	Ephraim Pratt	79	Ephraim Pratt.
Caleb West	75	Caleb West.	Oliver Edwards	83	Stephen Perry.
Abner Amsdill	79	Benj. J. Clapp.	Jacob Sargeants	49	Jacob Sargeants.
Dennis Canfield	78	Dennis Canfield.	Elizabeth Smith	74	John Smith.
Peter Ferro	86	Peter Ferro.			
			MINERVA.		
COLDEN.			Martha West	70	Anson West.
Asa Gould	88	Asa Gould.			
Asa Partrige	80	Asa Partrige.	MORIAH.		
			John Titus	76	John Titus.
HOLLAND			Ebenezer Bailey	79	Ebenezer Bailey.
Joseph Cooper	84	Joseph Cooper.	Rufus Mason	81	Rufus Mason.
David Hunt	80	Zaccheus Hunt.	Oliver Parmenter	78	Ira Dutton.
Joseph Brant	76	Joseph Conner.	Thomas Dudley	83	Joel Dudley.
			Abel Allen	84	Abel Allen.
BOSTON.			Rhoda Spear	80	Hiram Spear.
Richard Carey	83	Richard Carey.	Timothy Moore	70	Benjamin Whitney.
CONCORD.			SCHROON.		
Consider Bement	79	Consider Bement.	Russell Pitkin	47	Russell Pitkin.
			Charles Abraham	50	Charles Abraham.
EVANS.			Daniel Cushman	85	Allen Baker.
Joseph Ross	79	Chauncey Ross.	Joseph Gray	86	Joseph Gray.
John Frost	81	Richard Hurd.	John Wyckum	55	John Wyckum.
			Anna Rawzon	81	Josiah H. Rawzon.
SARDINIA.			David Stowell	83	David Stowell.
Reuben Nichols	77	Clark Nichols.	Freeman Perry	86	Phineas Hodgkins.
Caleb Hamet	93	Erastus Graves.			
Roswell Goodrich	84	Josiah Goodrich.	TICONDEROGA.		
Ephraim Briggs	87	Allen Briggs.	Ezra Snow	85	Ezra Snow, jr.
David Shedd	83	David Shedd.	Jason Eager	67	Jason Eager.
Elisha Pomeroy	77	Elisha Pomeroy.	Robert Hammond	76	Robert Hammond.
			Moses Finney	76	Moses Finney.
COLLINS.			Abraham Holden	79	Aaron Holden.
Wm. Morgan	84	Elias Morgan.	Constant Whitford	79	Constant Whitford.
Margaret Gilbert	74	Wm. Potter.	Joel Allen	64	Joel Allen.
John Stanclift	85	John Stanclift.	Michael Spicer	74	Michael Spicer.
			Aaron Haskins	53	Aaron Haskins.
ESSEX COUNTY.			Paul Harvey	78	Paul Harvey.
CHESTERFIELD.			William Graves	81	Oliver Graves.
David Watter	78	Harry Watter.	Elijah Gould	83	Elijah Gould.
Joseph B. Covel	79	Joseph B. Covel.	Jacob Winter	53	Jacob Winter.
Elnathan Stephens	82	Enos Stephens.	Jonathan Treadway	82	Thomas J. Treadway.
Clotilda Harford	72	Louis Grinean.	Nathaniel Miller	80	Nathaniel Miller.
CROWN POINT.			WESTPORT.		
Sarah Nichols	79	Aaron Nichols.	Samuel Pangburn	82	Samuel Pangburn.
Israel Gillet	48	Israel Gillet.	Ziba Howard	80	Ziba Howard.
Stephen Spaulding	63	Stephen Spaulding.	Jonathan Cady	80	Jonathan Cady.
William Shearer	88	Thomas Shearer.	Asa Grandy	83	Asa Grandy.
Benjamin Warner	83	Samuel Warner.	Brazilla Myrick	81	Brazilla Myrick.
Abijah Winch	82	Elisha Rhoades.	Abner Fisk	81	Asahel Havens.
William Perkins	88	Obadiah Baldwin.	Ebenezer Durfee	78	Ebenezer Durfee.
Asa Stowell	79	Asa Stowell.	Levi Frisbee	67	Levi Frisbee.
Edmund Farnsworth	78	Thomas Farnsworth.	Levi Cole	88	Levi Cole.
			Sarah Hardy	83	Jason Dunstead.

NEW YORK—NORTHERN DISTRICT—Continued.

Names of pensioners for revolutionary or military services.	Ages.	Names of heads of families with whom pensioners resided June 1, 1840.	Names of pensioners for revolutionary or military services.	Ages.	Names of heads of families with whom pensioners resided June 1, 1840.
ESSEX—Continued.			**FULTON**—Continued.		
WILLSBOROUGH.			JOHNSTOWN—Continued.		
Abraham Allen	57	Abraham Allen.	George Newton	60	George Newton.
Ephraim Hayward	80	Ephraim Hayward.	Catharine Van Voast	80	John Van Voast.
Joseph Stafford	81	Joseph Stafford.	Louis Bennett	79	Elisha Bennett.
Elisha Collins	77	Elisha Collins.	Stephen Gillet	87	Chester Gillet.
Job Stafford	58	Job Stafford.	Samuel Giles	83	Amos Beach.
			Elijah Cheadle	78	Elijah Cheadle.
WILMINGTON.			Jesse Foote	82	Jesse Foote.
David Fuller	80	David Fuller.	Charles Belden	79	Norman Belden.
			William Van Ostead	73	William Van Ostead.
FRANKLIN COUNTY.			Lemuel Lewis	79	William Lewis.
MALONE.			John J. Wilson	71	John G. Wilson.
Simeon Graves	87	Simeon Graves.	George Walter	84	George Walter.
Enos Wood	79	Enos Wood.	Jonathan Smith	40	Charles Peck.
Aaron Parks	75	Harry C. Parks.	Deborah Graff	67	James A. Stewart.
Samuel Smith	81	Samuel Smith.	Alexander Hay	85	Alexander Hay.
Jesse Chipman	85	Elon S. Chipman.	Samuel Kennedy	79	Samuel Kennedy.
Samuel Forbs	74	Samuel Forbs.	James Van Atten	84	James Van Atten.
Nathan Beman	86	Aaron Beman.	James Wilson	63	Matthew Potter.
Chester Morris	71	Chester Morris.			
			PERTH.		
FORT COVINGTON.			Abel Dunning	77	Abel Dunning.
Francis Clark	86	Joseph Briggs.	David Blood	75	David Blood.
DICKINSON.			STRATFORD.		
Betsey Lathrop	78	Matthew Davidson.	Mary Bleekman	87	Thomas Bleekman.
BOMBAY.			MAYFIELD.		
Asa Jackson	79	Eliphalet Jackson.	Peter McArthur	90	Peter McArthur.
			Mary Van Sickler	73	Mary Van Sickler.
WESTVILLE.			Samuel Woodworth	76	Samuel Woodworth.
Barnabas Berry	82	Philemon Berry.	Samuel Petit	78	Samuel Petit.
			John Schoonmaker	77	John Schoonmaker.
BANGOR.			Frances Gurner	84	Frances Gurner.
Gabriel Cornish	82	Gabriel Cornish.	Sarah McKinlay	76	Alexander McKinlay.
			Samuel Bigford	78	Samuel Bigford.
FRANKLIN.			Samuel Blowees	78	Alanson Warner.
Sally Merrill	83	John Merrill.	Eldert Fonda	89	John Holenbeck.
			Abiel Kinsley	50	Abiel Kinsley.
BRANDON.					
Henry Stevens	83	Andrew Stevens.	BROADALBIN.		
			Jonathan Pinckney	79	James Smith.
MOIRA.			Angelica Banta	72	John Hartley.
Jonathan Lawrence	78	Sidney Lawrence.	Deborah Kennedy	94	Deborah Kennedy.
Thomas Spencer	84	Eleazer Austin.	Joseph Degolyea	77	James Degolyea.
John Kimball	76	Samuel Philips.	Zenas Hathaway	84	Levi Ingraham.
Elkanah Philips	84	Lucinda Philips.	David Atkins	80	David Atkins.
Uriah Kingsley	80	George Kingsley.	Jacob Groves	49	Jacob Groves.
			Lydia Thorp	76	Lydia Thorp.
BELLMONT.			John Green	81	John T. Green.
Ebenezer Webb	82	Samuel Webb.	Isaiah Betts	82	Isaiah Betts.
			Isaac Newman	74	Henry Winney.
FULTON COUNTY.			Asa Markham	79	Asa Markham.
NORTHAMPTON.			Gideon Potter	80	Varnum Potter.
Jacob Shew	77	Jacob Shew.	Timothy Green	77	Timothy Green.
John Chambers	79	John Chambers.	Noah Wells	85	William J. Monteith.
Abigail Bennett	65	Giles C. Van Dyke.	Dennis McCormick	78	Peter Robertson.
Joseph Collins	86	David Collins.	John Loder	77	Henry Loder.
John Gifford	79	John Gifford.	Samuel Thatcher	87	Samuel Thatcher.
Joseph Brown	80	Joseph Brown.	Henry Perry	77	John Perry.
			Anna Clark	79	Alexander Clark.
BLEEKER.			Richard Van Vranken	77	Richard Van Vranken.
Nicholas Stoner	73	Nicholas Stoner.	Samuel Putney	83	Samuel Putney.
			Stephen Sherman	78	Stephen Sherman.
OPENHEIM.			James Benedict	78	James Benedict.
Jacob Yonker	83	Jacob Yonker.			
Jonathan Bacon	81	Jonathan Bacon.	EPHRATAH.		
Hannah Yonker	77	Hannah Yonker.	Giles Miller	80	Peter Miller.
Jacob Failing	79	Nicholas Failing.	Abraham Philips	92	E. B. Gilbert.
Joseph Stark	89	Phebe Failing.	Ichabod Peck	79	Ichabod Peck.
Marcus Dusler	78	Isaac Dusler.	William Smith	77	William Smith.
Frederick Baum	78	Jacob F. Baum.	Samuel Hills	78	Sylvester Hills.
Augustus Flanders	83	Augustus Flanders.	Elizabeth Spontmable	88	J. I. Spontnable.
John J. Failing	74	John J. Failing.	Elizabeth Kretcher	79	Henry Kretcher.
			Elizabeth Getman	76	Peter C. Getman.
JOHNSTOWN.			Rachael Kumble	78	Isaac Padrick.
Joseph Balch	80	Joseph Balch.	Elizabeth Coppernoll	88	George E. Coppernoll.
Benjamin Sammons	82	Jacob Sammons.	Peter Getman	76	Peter Getman.
Rachael Van Antwerp	77	Peter Conghuet.	William Powell	80	William Powell.
Nelly Putman	98	Peter Putman.	John Shaver	51	John Shaver.
Jacob Davis	78	Jacob Davis.	Philip Johnson	76	Philip Johnson.
Elias Crum	75	Elias Crum.			
David Morse	88	Eldad Nutting.			

11

Names of pensioners for revolutionary or military services.	Ages.	Names of heads of families with whom pensioners resided June 1, 1840.	Names of pensioners for revolutionary or military services.	Ages.	Names of heads of families with whom pensioners resided June 1, 1840.
GENESEE COUNTY.			**GENESEE—Continued.**		
ALEXANDER.			*CASTILE.*		
Humphrey Willard	82	Humphrey Willard.	Daniel Foster	86	Hepzee Brady.
William Hoyt	74	William Hoyt.	Sailor Weels	79	Sailor Weels.
Benjamin Porter	80	Philo Porter.	Green Hungerford	76	H. Martin.
Philo Porter	53	Philo Porter.	Hannah Gilbert	84	Jonathan Gilbert.
Richard Covill	74	Richard Covill.	Elkney Fuller	76	Elkney Fuller.
Leverett Seward	48	Leverett Seward.			
Eliphalet Peck	82	Eliphalet Peck.	*COVINGTON.*		
Rodolphus Hawkins	82	Rodolphus Hawkins.	Isaac Storme	87	Isaac Storme.
Lot Burge	78	Lot Burge.			
Abel Baker	64	T. C. Ashton.	*PERRY.*		
			Silas Ranson	75	Silas Ranson.
BATAVIA VILLAGE.			Abraham Vookers	86	Abraham Vookers.
Huldah Brunson	71	John D. Gillet.	Jacob Sent	84	Jacob Sent, jr.
Anne Wells	74	Elizabeth Williams.	John Willard	78	Mary Walson.
			Mark Andrews	80	Mark Andrews.
BATAVIA.			Ebir Higgins	83	William Tebbets.
Samuel S. Foster	79	Samuel S. Foster.	Bela Armstrong	86	John Brown.
John Vaughan	80	John W. Vaughan.	Stephen Barthwick	83	Stephen Barthwick.
John Hubbard	78	John Hubbard.			
Daniel Barker	84	Aram Beardsley.	*BERGEN.*		
Thomas Beckwith	80	Richard Beckwith.	Ebenezer Green	77	Ebenezer Green.
Samuel Huntington	84	John W. Martin.	Jacob Spafford	80	Jacob Spafford.
Baxter Sherman	53	Balden Potter.	Amos Allen	80	Horace Sandon.
Joseph Osborn	85	Joseph Osborn.			
			ATTICA.		
BETHANY.			Benjamin Nelson	82	
John Willard	85	Thaddeus Rowe.	Rowland Cotton	82	
Seth Allen	79	Seth Allen.	Eliphalet Hodges	80	Eliphalet Hodges.
Lydia Churchill	82	Nathaniel Churchill.	Temperance Tinney	85	Festus Tinney.
Isaac Davis	89	Samuel Bartlet.	Ebenezer Bullock	84	Ebenezer Bullock.
Theophilus Crocker	78	Theophilus Crocker.	John Fisk	79	John Fisk.
William E. Persons	82	William E. Persons.	Peleg Peck	78	Peleg Peck.
Nathaniel Brown	75	Lysander Brown.	Reynolds Whaley	76	Alanson Whaley.
Sibbilla Taylor	91	Nathaniel Huggins.	Josiah Gardner	84	Josiah Gardner.
Edmund Hoar	86	Edmund Hoar.	Isaac Smith	77	Isaac Smith.
DARIEN.			*BENNINGTON.*		
Samuel Mattison	77	Samuel Mattison.	Thomas Gratton	83	David M. Gratton.
Vine T. Hibbard	74	Vine T. Hibbard.	Moses Holmes	93	William Holmes.
Benjamin Willis	76	Benjamin Willis.			
Joshua Clark	82	Joshua Burdich.	*CHINA.*		
William Williams	53	William Williams.	Thomas Root	86	
Annah Roberts	81	Urania Farnham.			
Sally Humphrey	73	Alva Jefferson.	*GAINESVILLE.*		
Crary Gratton	79	Crary Gratton.	Jabez Ely	85	Jabez Ely, jr.
David Long	79	David Long.	Conrad Ten Eyck	83	
John Bordwell	83	Samuel Edson.	Lucy Warrener	75	Lucy Warrener.
			Isaac Amsdem	86	Elihu Amsdem.
ELBA.			Nathan Fuller	81	William Fuller.
Gideon Dunham	78	Gideon Dunham.	Oliver Butrick	92	
Nathan Waldo	78	Nathan Waldo.			
Borden Wilcox	79	Borden Wilcox.	*JAVA.*		
Sunderland Patterson	83	Sunderland Patterson.	Timothy Torry	74	Timothy Torry.
Sherman Patterson	87	Josiah Patterson.	Enoch Jenkins	76	Enoch Jenkins.
John Fuller	80	John Fuller.	Joanna Bartlett	84	
John C. Wilford	53	John C. Wilford.	Nathan Mann	80	
Stephen Sellech	78	Stephen Sellech.	Aaron Francis	75	Aaron Francis.
Solomon Hill	86	Jesse Lord.			
Abraham Benedict	94	John T. Benedict.	*MIDDLEBURY.*		
			Peter Kendall	77	Peter Kendall.
PEMBROKE.			Alexander Tackles	85	
Daniel Church	87	Arson Church.	Elkanah Brown	82	
Abigail Safford	77	Abigail Safford.	Abram Bishop	78	Abram Bishop.
Ebenezer Martindale	82	Ebenezer Martindale.			
Daniel Delong	80	Daniel Delong.	*ORANGEVILLE.*		
John Webb	80	John Webb, jr.	Jotham Mead	84	Jotham Mead.
Thomas Cathcart	81	Enos Cathcart.	Samuel Pethey	75	
Zaccheus Darrow	80	Zaccheus Darrow.	Mary Babbett	78	Harry Babbett.
Asa Wright	80	Asa Wright.	Michael Morse	80	
Wait Lewis	85	Curtis Childs.	John Laman	80	John Laman.
Samuel Luscombe	89	William Brown.			
Nathan Durkee	80	Nathan Durkee.	*SHELDEN.*		
			Royatt Palmer	75	Elijah W. Palmer.
STAFFORD.			Ivory Luce	82	Ivory Luce.
Isaac Bishop	82	Isaac Bishop.	Joseph Potter	85	Zebina Potter.
Mercy Hall	81	Hiram Hall.	Paul McKinstry	80	Porter McKinstry.
Philena Disbrow	68	Philena Disbrow.	Lodowick Thomas	85	Lodowick Thomas.
Peter Davidson	84	Martha Annis.	James Bentley	88	
			Martin Terry	98	John Howe.
BYRON.					
Samuel Parker	82	Samuel Parker.	*WETHERSFIELD.*		
Leonard Perkins	78	Harlow Perkins.	Weltham Davis	79	
John Quimby	86	John Whimley.			

NEW YORK—NORTHERN DISTRICT—Continued.

Names of pensioners for revolutionary or military services.	Ages.	Names of heads of families with whom pensioners resided June 1, 1840.	Names of pensioners for revolutionary or military services.	Ages.	Names of heads of families with whom pensioners resided June 1, 1840.
GENESEE—Continued.			HERKIMER—Continued.		
WETHERSFIELD—Continued.			WARREN.		
Joseph Warren	80	Joseph Warren.	Simeon Ely	78	Horace Ely.
Mary Langdon	77		Abigail Ward	79	Joel Northrup.
			Arnold Bennett	42	Arnold Bennett.
WARSAW.			FRANKFORT.		
Lyman Noble	82	Jabez B. Noble.	Andrew Piper	80	Andrew Piper.
William Whiting	81	William Whiting.	Eli Brown	82	Edmond Adams.
Benjamin Seeley	81	Benjamin Seeley.	Anne Dygert	78	John B. Dygert.
Samuel Conable	78	Samuel Conable, jr.	Joseph French	79	Joseph French.
Jared Knapp	88	Jared Knapp.	Anne Francisco	81	Samuel C. Frances.
Lucy Kinman	77		Conrad Eddee	78	Conrad Eddee.
Oliver Holt	85		Benjamin Harvey	105	Benjamin Harvey.
Niles Giddings	75	Niles Giddings.	Jacob Lints	90	Phillips Lints.
			Roswell Stevens	66	Roswell Stevens.
HERKIMER COUNTY.			FAIRFIELD.		
COLUMBIA.			Robert Nolton	81	Robert Nolton.
Marks Grants	78	Marks Grants.	Joseph Lobdell	79	Emelias Pickert.
Thomas Smith	80	Thomas Smith.	Eliab Peirce	78	Eliab Peirce.
Mary Getman	74	Mary Getman.	Samuel Evans	89	Silas S. Evans.
Katharial Ackler	77	Adam Ackler.	Cyrus Potter	75	Robert Potter.
Mary Wormworth	75	William Wormworth.	Nathan Rix	80	Nathan Rix.
Nicholas Chrisman	86	Henry Chrisman.	John Wood	81	John Wood, 4th.
Henry Crim	78	John H. Crim.	Reuben Mather	92	David Raynor.
Asahel Alford	79	Cyrus Alford.	Isaac Churchill	85	Isaac Churchill.
			David Bensley	85	David Bensley.
GERMAN FLATS.			Hannah Nelson	86	Zachariah Reed.
Joseph Hess	83	Dennis Clapsaddle.			
Eli Brown	80	John W. D. Heald.	HERKIMER.		
George R. T. Hawes	106	William Morrison.	Margaret Weatherstone	70	David Weatherstone.
James Haight	76	James F. Haight.	Reuben Hildreth	85	Thaddeus Hildreth.
Barnabas Youngs	81	Barnabas Youngs.	Ansteen Sterling	80	Henry Jellyers.
Flavel Clark	79	Flavel Clark.	John Rowland	78	Samuel Rowland.
Henry Seeber	99	Sylvanus Seeber.	John Dockstader	80	Frederick Dockstader.
Richard Casler	73	Richard Casler.	Elizabeth Shoemaker	81	Michael Hartman.
Lodowick Moyer	79	Lodowick Moyer.	William Hagadom	83	William Hagadom.
Peter Flagg	89	Peter Flagg.			
Robert Babock	82	Stanton Denison.	LITTLE FALLS.		
George Lighthall	93	Giles R. Brown.	Edward Arnold	80	Edward Arnold.
Absalom Giffords	75	William Giffords.	Catharine Rankin	68	Catharine Rankin.
			Nicholas Spluk	74	Robert Beasley.
WINFIELD.			Catharine Moseley	72	Elizabeth Blood.
Jacob C. Edick	77	Josiah Ackler.	Stephen Hammond	73	Stephen Hammond.
Adam Burdock	80	Adam Burdock.	Elijah Stanton	85	John Eaton.
Joseph Moors	79	Joseph Moors.	Jonas Churchill	79	Jonas Churchill.
John Goff	85	Orange Goff.	John Buell	91	Erastus Hall.
Nathan Brown	75	Nathan Brown.	Henry Wallradt	80	Richard J. Casler.
Anthony Rhodes	79	Rodley Randall.	Martha Wheeler	82	Charles S. Daniels.
Judah Eldred	86	Zenas Eldred.	Dan. Chapman	85	Dan. Chapman.
LITCHFIELD.			MANHEIM.		
William Bacon	82	William Bacon.	Stephen Every	77	Stephen Every.
Mary White	64	Milton White.	William Fecter	84	William Fecter, jr.
			Barbara Casselman	77	John Casselman.
DANUBE.			Henry Ritter	80	Joseph Ritter.
Nathaniel Waldron	82	George D. Rightmyer.	Peter Wolever	75	Nicholas Wolever.
Anna Eve Shall	75	John Shall.	Jacob Pettibone	80	Jacob Pettibone, jr.
Neal McNeal	83	Joseph Sholl.			
Solomon Waggoner	77	Abraham S. Waggoner.	NEWPORT.		
Adam Armstrong	75	John H. Starring.	Charlotte Waterman	76	Henry Waterman.
			Darius Hawkins	68	Darius Hawkins.
SCHUYLER.			Eleazer Daniels	79	Eleazer Daniels.
Chloe Cady	93	Amos Smith.	Lois Munn	85	Cady Howe.
Jacob Widrig	79	Jacob Widrig.			
Israel Ward	89	Nathan Ward.	NORWAY.		
Jonathan Gilbert	78	Jonathan Gilbert.	Aaron Buck	78	Stephen M. Tompkins.
Cheney Luke	91	Samuel Luke.	John Parsons	85	Addison Manley.
Sarah Sweet	78	Vaughn Sweet.	John Vanderburgh	80	John Vanderburgh.
Thomas Wood	85	Thomas Wood.	Jabez Green	86	Jabez Green.
Joseph Willis	77	Joseph Willis.			
			OHIO.		
STARK.			William McIntosh	80	William McIntosh.
John Shall	80	David J. Shall.	Gilbert Ferguson	77	Gilbert Ferguson.
Chris. John House	85	John Siver.	Simeon Dutcher	78	Simeon Dutcher.
Hannah Wendell	86	Jacob Wendell.			
Richard Kenter	74	Richard Kenter.	RUSSIA.		
Lucy Baccus	88	William Baccus.	Phineas Briggs	91	Daniel Carpenter.
Richard Skimmel	74	Richard Skimmel.	Elisha Hall	79	Elisha Hall.
John Mount	90	John Mount.	Abel Rust	83	Hiram Rust.
Christopher Norton	78	Felix Bronner.	Sarah Enos	87	Alva Enos.
Henry Shaver	80	Henry Shaver.	Isaiah Johnson	84	Isaiah Johnson.
Margaret Snyder	81	Daniel Snyder.	Thomas Kellogg	82	Ebenezer Kellogg

Names of pensioners for revolutionary or military services.	Ages.	Names of heads of families with whom pensioners resided June 1, 1840.	Names of pensioners for revolutionary or military services.	Ages.	Names of heads of families with whom pensioners resided June 1, 1840.
HERKIMER—Continued.			**JEFFERSON—Continued.**		
SALISBURY.			*ELLISBURG—Continued.*		
Amos Ives	91	Philo Stiles.	James Gault	83	Noah Lamon.
Jemima Seamans	76	Jemima Seamans.	Simeon Russell	84	Jesse Littlefield.
			Samuel Mixer	82	Grant Mixer.
HAMILTON COUNTY.			Simeon Russell	89	Simeon Russell.
HOPE.			Levi Smith	85	Hiram J. Babbit.
Olive Wooster	89	J. P. Groff.	Abiezar Phillips	81	M. Phillips.
Ezekiel Sloan	76	Ezekiel Sloan.	Thomas Worden	82	Benjamin Randall.
Joseph Courier	80	Joseph Courier.	Ebenezer Wallace	79	Charles Wallace.
Tryphenia Crain	79	Tryphenia Crain.	Stephen Hicks	85	Barney Hicks.
			Henry H. Fall	90	Henry H. Fall.
WELLS.					
Charles Turner	77	Charles Turner.	*HENDERSON.*		
Ebenezer Dunham	81	Ebenezer Dunham.	John Pettingell	73	John Pettingell.
			Ebenezer Sawyer	86	Ebenezer Sawyer.
JEFFERSON COUNTY.			Abijah Stickney	82	Alexander Carte.
ANTWERP.			John Carter	78	John Denison.
Lydia Turner	76	Allen Thompson.	John Morris	81	John Morris.
Noah Russell	86	Noah French.	Stephen Hawkins	82	Stephen Hawkins.
Martha Clark	76	Asa Southworth.			
Josiah Drake	78	Josiah Drake.	*HOUNDSFIELD.*		
			Jared Olcott	81	Jared Olcott.
ORLEANS.			Charles Ripley	76	Charles Ripley.
Joseph Rhodes	78	Joseph Rhodes.	Sumner Adams	65	John Gill.
Adolphus Picket	79	Adolphus Picket.	Solomon Livermore	78	Solomon Livermore.
William Collins	80	Hannah Horr.	Anna Dorchester	79	Alfred Dorchester.
John Monk	89	John Monk.	Elias Taylor	72	George W. Taylor.
Moses Limon	78	Walter Chandler.	Thomas Cole	72	John Cole.
Elizabeth Rixford	75	Anson Squares.	Julius Terry	64	Julius Terry.
Nicholas Smith	85	Robert Smith.	Ebenezer Phillips	80	Ebenezer Phillips.
Elizabeth Barret	80	Chesterfield Persons.			
Caleb Willis	78	Caleb Willis.	*RUTLAND.*		
M. Contreman	70	M. Contreman.	Mary Barney	74	John Barney.
			Stephen Durham	88	Stephen Durham.
LYME.					
Samuel J. Mills	81	Samuel J. Mills.	*ADAMS.*		
Jacob H. Ores	83	Jacob H. Ores.	Peter Doxtater	88	Peter Doxtater, jr.
Nicholas Smith	85		Lucy Thompson	73	Lucy Thompson.
Prudence Hodges	73	Timothy Soper.	Cynthia White	77	Joseph Green.
Lucretia Marsh	84	Luther Steadman.	John Merriam	84	David H. Parham.
Felix Powell	77	Olive Butterfield.	Abel Bassett	80	Abel Bassett.
			Danforth Doty	85	Danforth Doty, jr.
ALEXANDRIA.					
George Rappole	89	Henry Rappole.	*LORRAINE.*		
William Carter	83	James Carter.	Jacob Weaver	83	
Daniel Whorry	75	Daniel Whorry.	Benjamin Fletcher	80	
Edith Patten	80	Ira J. Patten.	Caleb Tift	81	Caleb Tift.
Ephraim Hogert	84	Daniel S. Hoyt.			
Peter Lutz	76	John Sharon.	*RODMAN.*		
Abram Newman	81	Abram Newman.	Ephraim Wright	73	Ephraim Wright.
			John Russell	–	John Russell.
CLAYTON.			Elijah Walsworth	78	Elijah Walsworth.
Solomon Ingalls	90	Henry Ingalls.			
Hosey Randolph	79	Allen Randall.	*LE RAY.*		
Lydia Dixon	85	Samuel Perry.	Timothy Tomblin	83	John W. Tomblin.
Amos Richards	82	Polly Richards.	Joel Dodge	79	Clark Dodge.
James Bothell	82	David Bothell.	Hiel Truesden	78	
Mary Davis	73	John Rummell.	Ezekiel Lyman	80	
Abraham Joy	78	David Joy.	William Rogers	83	William Rogers.
James Rankin	82	Daniel Casler.	Hannah Harwick	81	Jacob B. Harwick.
Thomas Fetterly	76	Thomas Fetterly.	Elizabeth Ainstead	74	
			Elisha Scofield	76	Elisha Scofield.
PAMELIA.					
J. Gloyd	85	Nathaniel White.	*PHILADELPHIA.*		
			Editha Tailor	84	
BROWNVILLE.			James Hewitt	77	
John Baxter	88		Jonathan Carr	83	
Walter Wilson	85		Isaac Hurd	79	Isaac Hurd.
Selah Burton	79				
David Rimiston	93		*WILNA.*		
John P. Beecher	78		Peter Brown	88	
			Stephen Shew	79	Stephen Shew.
ELLISBURG.			Josiah Hurlbert	79	Josiah Hurlbert.
Solomon Tracey	81	Solomon Tracey.	Solomon Cleavland	86	Fassett Cleavland.
Jonathan Fish	83	Jonathan Fish.			
Stephen Lindsey	81	R. Waaliver.	**LEWIS COUNTY.**		
Mrs. Deuse	80	Mrs. Deuse.	*DENMARK.*		
Bryant Eddy	79	C. Boomer.	Elizabeth Graves	77	Lewis Bond.
Lyman Ellis	80	Lyman Ellis.	John S. Clark	78	Owen Clark.
Jonathan Matteson	78	Samuel Matteson.	Louisa Munger	79	Abner Munger.
Rufus Richardson	79	Rufus Richardson.	Hannah Mores	88	Levi Mores.
Abel Potter	80	Abel Potter.	Elias Sage	83	Elias Sage.
Samuel Hubbard	79	Moses Burret.	Joseph Van Ingen	–	Joseph Van Ingen.
			Peter Ryall	80	Peter Ryall.

NEW YORK—NORTHERN DISTRICT—Continued.

Names of pensioners for revolutionary or military services.	Ages.	Names of heads of families with whom pensioners resided June 1, 1840.	Names of pensioners for revolutionary or military services.	Ages.	Names of heads of families with whom pensioners resided June 1, 1840.
LEWIS—Continued.			**LIVINGSTON—Continued.**		
GREIG.			SPRINGWATER—Continued.		
John Slaughter - - -	86	Stephen Murphy.	Reuben Gilbert - - -	83	Reuben Gilbert.
			Elisha Capron - - -	74	Sylvester Capron.
HARRISBURG.					
Elias Jones - - -	81	Elias Jones.	SPARTA.		
William Risner - - -	81	William Risner.	William Sprague - - -	77	William Sprague.
Garrett Marcellus - - -	80	Garrett Marcellus.	Shem Truman - - -	87	Ebenezer Porter.
			Benjamin Sweeter -	78	Ezekiel Reed.
LOWVILLE.			James Palmer - -	85	James Palmer.
John Buck - - -	76	Samuel Buck.	James Scott - - -	80	James Scott.
Elisha Back - - -	75	Henry Back.	William Perine - - -	85	William Perine.
William Chadwick - -	79	Joseph Chadwick.	James Roles - - -	80	James Roles.
Altha Gordon - - -	80	J. V. Gordon.	Susanna Jencks - - -	80	L. Jencks.
			Moses Van Campen -	84	Moses Van Campen.
LEYDEN.			John Sample - - -	79	John Sample.
Lydia Dewey - - -	79	Abram Dewey.	William Howell - - -	82	William Howell.
Elizabeth Cone - - -	76	Curtis Higby.			
Ada Miller - - -	86	Ada Miller.	LIMA.		
Lewis Smith - - -	87	Lewis Smith.	Benjamin Knapp - - -	78	
William Topping - -	75	William Topping.	Pehial Bunnel - - -	76	Dennis Bunnel.
Hezekiah Johnson - -	79	Nathan Bassett.	Moses S. George - - -	45	Moses S. George.
MARTINSBURG.			LEICESTER.		
Ruth Adams - - -	—	Melas Adams.	Abijah Crabbe - - -	86	Abijah Crabbe.
Jesse Benjamin - - -	81	Jesse Benjamin.	Samuel Horton - - -	75	Samuel Horton.
Anna Easton - - -	69	Henry Easton.	Alexander Murray - -	78	Alexander Murray.
Lydia Green - - -	80	Willard Green.	Noah Bigelow - - -	75	Noah Bigelow.
Edward Johnson - -	81	Edward Johnson, jr.			
Salmon Root - - -	77	Salmon Root.	AVON.		
Peter Vandriesen - -	75	Richard Vandriesen.	Ephraim Trickey - - -	86	
Bartholomew Williams -	76	Bartholomew Williams.	Thomas Torrance - -	85	Richard Torrance.
			William Rich - - -	77	William Rich.
PINCKNEY.			John Whetmore - - -	84	John Whetmore.
Catharine Forbes - -	84	William Ralston.			
			MOUNT MORRIS.		
TURIN.			Christopher Bergen - -	81	Jacob Bergen.
Benjamin Doud - - -	79	Eli Doud.	Eli Mead - - -	70	
Giles Foster - - -	83	Giles Foster.			
			YORK.		
WEST TURIN.			Giles Lyman - - -	75	Giles Lyman.
Jonathan Collins - -	84	Jonathan C. Collins.	Robert McKnight - -	86	Robert McKnigh .
Simeon Strickland - -	54	Simeon Strickland.			
			CALADONIA.		
WATSON.			David Fuller - - -	80	David Fuller.
Sarah Puffer - - -	75	Ebenezer Puffer.			
Jacob Shults - - -	78	C. J. Shults.	**MONROE COUNTY.**		
Elizabeth Webb - -	81	Elizabeth Webb.	CITY OF ROCHESTER.		
Lewis Day - - -	73	Lewis Day.	*First ward.*		
Sarah Farr - - -	73	Alvin Farr.	Joy Babbett - - -	73	Joy Babbett.
			Barney McGuire - -	76	Barney McGuire.
LIVINGSTON COUNTY.			Loisa Ann Mathews -	73	C. M. Bartlett.
CONESUS.			John D. Concklin - -	83	E. S. Treat.
Abram Holden - - -	78	George Robbins.	*Second ward.*		
Paul Sanburn - - -	79	Paul Sanburn.	Sarah Root - - -	78	Silas Pierce.
Thaddeus Gage - - -	81	Thaddeus Gage.	*Third ward.*		
Lemuel Richardson - -	74	Lemuel Richardson.	None.		
David Soper - - -	97	Richard Blasdell.	*Fourth ward.*		
			Carine Hills - - -	76	Marcus Holmes.
GENESEO.			Levi H. Parish - - -	47	Levi H. Parish.
Abijah Hutchinson - -	83	James Hutchinson.	John Chamberlin - -	76	O. P. Chamberlin.
Aaron Adams - - -	78	Aaron Adams.	Jehial Felt - - -	71	Jehial Felt.
Theoda Bissell - - -	75	D. H. Bissell.	Philip Allen - - -	83	Philip Allen.
Lucy Justin - - -	75	Ralzamon Beckwith.	*Fifth ward.*		
Margaret Wickham - -	83	James Wood.	Moses Hall - - -	74	Moses Hall.
			John Gifford - - -	49	John Gifford.
GROVELAND.			Mary Reynolds - - -	83	Levi Brown.
William Parker - - -	79	William Parker.			
			GATES.		
LIVONIA.			Alexander McGregor -	88	
Robert Baker - - -	78	Robert Baker.	David Gage - - -	82	Moses Gage.
Joseph M. Pine - - -	77	Samuel Benham.			
Selah Stedman - - -	77	B. L. Stedman.	RIGA.		
Noah Amsden - - -	82	Noah Amsden.	Oliver Church - - -	76	J. B. Avery.
Philo Gibbs - - -	75	Philo Gibbs.	Thomas Hill - - -	78	Joseph Emmons.
Rhoda Pierpont - - -	74	William McCoy.	James Gay - - -	96	James Gay.
Nehemiah Olmsted - -	87	Nehemiah Olmsted.	Thomas Adams - - -	78	Thomas Adams.
Timothy Baker - - -	80	Timothy Baker.	Rufus Hibbard - - -	82	Hezekiah Hibbard.
Oliver Woodruff - -	86	Oliver Woodruff.			
			SWEDEN.		
SPRINGWATER.			Charles Treat - - -	84	Charles Treat.
Gilbert Weed - - -	72	Gilbert Weed.	Jonathan Fanning - -	86	Anson Sparlin.
Lewis Carpenter - -	70	Lewis Carpenter.	Thomas Cooley - - -	76	Thomas Cooley.
Joel Tiffany - - -	80	Trueman Tiffany.	Anson Comstock - - -	77	A. Comstock.

NEW YORK—NORTHERN DISTRICT—Continued.

Names of pensioners for revolutionary or military services.	Ages.	Names of heads of families with whom pensioners resided June 1, 1840.	Names of pensioners for revolutionary or military services.	Ages.	Names of heads of families with whom pensioners resided June 1, 1840.
MONROE—Continued.			**MONROE**—Continued.		
SWEDEN—Continued.			MENDON.		
Elisha Locke - - -	79	Elisha Locke.	John Dixon - - -	79	John B. Dixon.
Ebenezer Martin - -	78	Ebenezer Martin.	Jonathan Ogden - -	74	Jonathan Ogden.
			Josiah Crossman - -	78	Josiah A. Crossman.
BROOKPORT VILLAGE.			Cornelius Treat - -	74	Cornelius Treat.
Sarah Smith - - -	75	Rebecca Hinman.			
			MADISON COUNTY.		
OGDEN.			LEBANON.		
Hannah Stone - -	73	Hannah Stone.	Abigail Willis - -	71	Hezekiah Willis.
Nathan Walden - -	75	N. Walden.	Joseph Bachellor - -	77	Joseph Bachellor.
Elizabeth Paterson -	91	Samuel Kilborn.	Hannah Watson - -	80	Hannah Hartshorn.
			John Younglove - -	83	Daniel Younglove.
CLARKSON.			Rhoda Eddy - -	89	Adolphus Eddy.
David Smith - - -	73	David Smith.	Archibald Campbell -	81	Archibald Campbell.
William Pennett - -	–	Henry Seabott.			
			DE RUYTER.		
WHEATLAND.			Betsey Jones - -	76	Charles Jones.
Ira Merrill - - -	81	Israel Merriman.	Stephen Maxson - -	86	Stephen Maxson.
			Rowland Swift - -	84	Jonathan Coon.
CHILI.			Betsey Clark - -	83	Eliakim Clark.
Abijah Britton - -	84	Robert Thompson.	Elias Wells - -	78	Matthew Wells.
PARMA.					
Noah Downs - -	80	Nathan Wright.	BROOKFIELD.		
Jeremiah Perry - -	86	Jeremiah Perry.	Lucy Davis - -	75	Erastus S. Fitch.
			Pain Wait - -	85	Stephen Whitford.
GREECE.			Thomas Griffin - -	73	Thomas Griffin.
Bethia Reed - -	81	Samuel Reed.	Samuel Reed - -	83	Samuel Reed.
Kitchel Reed - -	80	Silas Walker.	Joseph Congdon - -	82	John Miller.
Philip Caldwell - -	84	Philip Caldwell.	Jason Miller - -	77	
Samuel Parder - -	88	S. F. Hunting.	Mary Murphy - -	82	Randall Whitman.
Jacob Hayden - -	78	Jacob Hayden.	Thomas Giles - -	86	Thomas Giles, jr.
J. C. Doss - -	48	M. Warner.			
			CAZENOVIA.		
PENFIELD.			Nicholas Welch - -	77	Nicholas Welch.
Samuel L. Brooks - -	83	Garry Brooks.	Simeon Dodge - -	76	Isaac Dodge.
Joseph Burrows - -	77	Amos Chappell.	Matthew Chandler -	76	Lury Chandler.
Lucy Owen - -	72	Calvin W. Owen.	Cirad Cook - -	77	Cirad Cook.
Levi Francisco - -	83	Levi Francisco.	Jotham Hall - -	80	Jotham Hall.
Othniel Preston - -	84	Othniel Preston.	Edward Parker - -	80	Edward Parker.
Elizabeth Shoecraft -	84	William Harris.	Abigail Tilloson - -	81	Ephraim Tilloson.
			Kesiah Pollard - -	73	Fletcher Billings.
WEBSTER.			Sally May - -	85	Luke May.
Samuel Millard - -	79	Samuel Millard.	James Williams - -	74	James Williams.
Mary Robbe - -	66	Henry Robbe.	William Shankland -	79	William Shankland.
Josiah Barce - -	84	William Roe.	Mary Taber - -	88	David Taber.
David Parkhurst - -	72	David Parkhurst.	Gideon Anthony - -	87	Gideon Anthony.
Chester Cleaveland -	78	Chester Cleaveland.	Rinaldo Webber - -	78	Rinaldo Webber.
			Hannah Hamblin - -	77	Abner J. Hamblin.
HENRIETTA.			Elizabeth Davenport -	81	Adson Davenport.
Edward Dunham - -	93	Seneca Dunham.			
Melinda Burr - -	79	W. Burr.	HAMILTON.		
William Huston - -	83	Samuel Titus.	Samuel White - -	77	Samuel White.
Joel Clark - -	72	Joel Clark.	Louis Blanchard - -	78	Walter Blanchard.
Aaron Webster - -	87	Samuel Webster.	Elizabeth Cranston -	75	Phineas Cranston.
			David Craw - -	83	Justus Craw.
BRIGHTON.			Abram Avery - -	86	Abram Avery.
Ichabod Worden - -	79	Ichabod Worden.	Versalla Newton - -	76	Anson Newton.
Eliphalet Edmonds -	76	Eliphalet Edmonds.	Jonathan French - -	75	Jonathan French.
John Smith - -	25	Horatio Adams.	Abigail Torrey - -	86	Hosea Thayer.
Ezra Sibley - -	78	Chauncey Sibley.	Sarah Collister - -	74	William Cobson.
			David Brown - -	78	Daniel Brown.
PERINTON.			Edward Wilcox - -	80	Sandford Wilcox.
Catharine Butler - -	77	Elisha Fulham.	White Osborn - -	82	Sally Carder.
David Cady - -	75	George Cady.	Huldah Warner - -	83	Thomas A. Warner.
William Tyler - -	75	William Tyler.	Oliver Teal - -	81	Oliver Teal.
Robert Jackson - -	79	Robert Jackson.			
Lydia Scovil - -	80	Henry Scovil.	GEORGETOWN.		
			Josiah Purdy - -	78	Isaac Purdy.
PITTSFORD.					
Ebenezer Graves - -	78	Samuel Hughes.	MADISON.		
Peter Rose - -	76	Peter Rose.	Abner Burnham - -	84	Abner Burnham.
Jeronimus Vannest -	74	Mumford Clark.	Ezra Holmes - -	82	Ezra Holmes.
Andrew Huntington -	79	Andrew Huntington.	John Brown - -	73	Asher Brown.
			John Wheeler - -	79	Alexander White.
RUSH.			Peggy M. Carpenter -	72	J. E. Burton.
Isaac Campbell - -	78	Isaac Campbell.	Rhoda Blatch - -	71	J. Urgeburger.
Noah Pratt - -	77	Philip B. Keeler.	Mary Tompkins - -	70	Philip Tompkins.
Amos Jones - -	94	Amos Jones.	Benj. Simmons - -	82	Benj. Simmons.
Eliphalet Gordon - -	82	Emery Bowen.	Seth Blair - -	80	Seth Blair.
Abigail Green - -	80	John Green.	Elizabeth Barker - -	80	Elizabeth Barker.
Wells Clark - -	80	Wells Clark.	Israel Rice - - -	79	Francis Rice.
Elnathan Perry - -	80	Elnathan Perry.			
John Pratt - - -	77	Jacob Thomas.			

NEW YORK—NORTHERN DISTRICT—Continued.

Names of pensioners for revolutionary or military services.	Ages.	Names of heads of families with whom pensioners resided June 1, 1840.	Names of pensioners for revolutionary or military services.	Ages.	Names of heads of families with whom pensioners resided June 1, 1840.
MADISON—Continued.			MONTGOMERY COUNTY.		
STOCKBRIDGE.			CHARLESTON.		
			Thomas Thompson	77	Thomas Thompson.
Thomas Powell	75	Thomas Powell.	George Young	81	George Young.
Ebenezer Hills	100	Thomas Stanton.	Samuel Hubbs	75	Samuel Hubbs.
Sarah Sloan	87	Lyman G. Sloan.	Martin Becker	91	Martin Becker.
Asel Powel	81	Asel Powel.	Elijah Herrick	79	Elijah Herrick.
George Buck	80	Austin Carver.	Hendrick Kunck	83	Hendrick Kunck.
Philip Peterson	82	Philip Peterson.			
Job Francis	75	Job Francis.	ROOT.		
Oliver Stewart	79	Oliver Stewart.	Daniel Dey	83	James Dey.
Lemuel Smith	88	Lemuel Smith.	James Lettis	86	Jacob Lettis.
John Nelson	79	John Nelson.	Philip Hamestreet	95	Benjamin Hamestreet.
			William Allen	52	William Allen.
LENOX.			Albert Vedder	80	Albert Vedder.
George Ratnom	75	George Ratnom.	David Parks	75	David Parks.
John Roberts	53	John Roberts.	Coonrad Friday	77	Coonrad Friday.
Nathan Stewart	82	Nathan Stewart.			
Reuben Perkins	76	Caleb Perkins.	CANAJOHARIE.		
Peter Hendrickson	75	P. Hendrickson.	Peter Lambert	84	Peter Lambert.
Adam Phillips	80	A. A. Phillips.	Nicholas Dunckle	81	Nicholas Dunckle.
Asa Cranson	79	Asa Cranson.	George Dunckle	84	George G. Dunckle.
Jacob Laughton	74	John Laughton.	John Roof	78	John Roof.
			Elizabeth Cochran	74	Phenix Lone.
NELSON.			John Wood	77	Isaac Wood.
Phebe Truesdell	79	George Rich.	Hiram Chappell	76	Benj. Sixbury.
Abraham Humphrey	78	Willis Humphrey.	Daniel Spencer	77	Daniel Spencer.
Chloe Lyon	76	Eliphaz Lyon.	Benj. Button	81	Jacob Hodges.
Paul Griffith	87	Otis Griffith.	Adam Brown	92	Daniel Brown.
Jesse Carpenter	91	Elijah Carpenter.	Christian Rapp	69	Christian Rapp.
Dyer Mattison	77	Dyer Mattison.	Margaret Stillwell	77	John Wemple.
Joanna Grummond	90	John Simons.	Margaret Van Netter	72	C. Frolick.
			Maria Gates	87	Andolph Seeber.
FENNER.			Henry Lake	73	Henry Lake.
Eunice May	81	A. C. Ehle.	John H. Waffle	78	Peter Hevener.
Elijah Farnham	80	Daniel Farnham.	Christian Hufnoglo	77	Henry Stam.
Samuel Nichols	82	Samuel Nichols.	Gideon Elliot	77	Gideon Elliot.
Roswell Welch	75	H. Cushing.	Hannah Ritter	76	John K. Ritter.
Siblius Stannard	82	Alvan Stannard.	Percy Elliot	79	Percy Elliot.
Mary Harris	71	Elisha Bradley.	Jonathan Silsbury	78	Jonathan Silsbury.
Wm. Loundsberry	92	James Loundsberry.	Abijah White	77	Abijah White.
Benj. Woodworth	80	Benj. Woodworth.			
Alice Hill	72	O Howes.	MINDEN.		
Asa Dana	86	Wm. Johnson.	Nicholas Casler	76	Nicholas Casler.
Nathaniel Kaler	81	Nathaniel Kaler.	Peter Sitts	81	Peter Sitts.
			Frederick Weller	82	Frederick Weller.
SULLIVAN.			Adam Casler	75	Peter A. Casler.
			Elizabeth Wilson	82	John Wilson.
Phineas Cadwell	83	E. S. Cadwell.	Jacob A. Diefendorf	72	Jacob A. Diefendorf.
Stephen Northrup	82	Stephen Northrup, jr.	Peter Young	80	Peter Young.
Abner Sherman	78	Abner Sherman.	William Hackney	75	Adam Hackney.
Lucas Salsbury	80	Lucas Salsbury.	Peter Eggabroat	82	George Phillips.
Adonijah Bond	87	Adonijah Bond.	Margaret Charlesworth	74	James Burns.
Daniel Shippey	64	Daniel Shippey.			
Elizabeth Tuttle	77	P. Tuttle.	FLORIDA.		
Timothy Page	80	Timothy Page.	Amos Daws	79	Palmer Oblin.
Catharine Ehle	88	John C. Young.	Nicholas Hill	74	Nicholas Daws.
Henry Rightmyer	87	H. Rightmyer.	Joseph Earl	83	Joseph Earl.
Peter H. Ehle	86	Peter H. Ehle.	John Lott	80	
			Derrick Van Vechten	87	Derrick Van Vechten.
SMITHFIELD.					
Benj. Wilber	83	Andrew Crout.	AMSTERDAM.		
Rhoda Woods	88	Eli Wood.	Catharine Craw	75	Abraham Craw.
John Bush	80	John Bush.	Amos Schenehorn	76	
Abraham Bartlett	81	John G. Curtis.	Banajah Mills	99	
Francis Dodge	82	Francis Dodge.	Gerrit Smith	88	Gerrit Smith.
			Abraham Hoagland	82	Jacob Hoagland.
EATON.			Abraham Siesco	92	Abraham Siesco.
			Samuel French	82	William French.
Daniel Rider	75	Daniel Rider.	Lucinda Shepard	86	Horace Shepard.
Ichabod Woodworth	74	Enos Merill.	Mary Lepper	88	Jacob F. Lepper.
Benj. Hatch	86	Benj. Hatch.	Israel Stearns	76	Israel Stearns.
Ezekiel Merritt	73	Ezekiel Merritt.			
Simeon Chubbuck	84	Simeon Chubbuck.	MOHAWK.		
Thomas Omans	80	Thomas Omans.	Ann Schenk	82	Edward J. Schenk.
Mary Phelps	85	Stephen Coman.	John Degraff	86	Haronymus Degraff.
Lois Burdwin	79	J. R. Burdwin.	Abraham Vosburgh	82	John Vosburgh.
Constant Avery	81	D. Avery.	Nancy Van Dusen	75	Abraham Van Dusen.
Benj. Blanchard	80	Daniel Green.	Jacob Van Alstine	91	Jacob Van Alstine.
Moses Bump	79	Moses Bump.			
Deborah Morse	77	Sylvester Macomber.	GLEN.		
Gideon Simmons	95	Judson Boothe.	John Mount	80	John Mount.
Ashbel Mason	83	A. Mason.	John Serviss	85	Samuel Serviss.
			Abigail Vanslyke	80	Richard Hudson.

NEW YORK—NORTHERN DISTRICT—Continued.

Names of pensioners for revolutionary or military services.	Ages.	Names of heads of families with whom pensioners resided June 1, 1840.	Names of pensioners for revolutionary or military services.	Ages.	Names of heads of families with whom pensioners resided June 1, 1840.
MONTGOMERY—Continued.			**ONEIDA—Continued.**		
GLEN—Continued.			*DEERFIELD—Continued.*		
James Williamson - - -	81	James Williamson.	Justin Cooley - - -	80	Justin Cooley.
Ruth Cady - - - -	82	Heny Cady.	Thomas Cummings - -	86	Hosea Cummings.
Susan Wooliver - - -	86	Susan Wooliver.	Calvin Preston - - -	78	Philip Preston.
Caty Quackenbuss - -	78	John Quackenbuss.			
Magdalem Quackenbuss -	79	Isaac Quackenbuss.	*FLOYD.*		
Caty Newkirk - - -	79	Catharine Newkirk.	Joseph Merchant - -	80	Joseph Merchant.
Isaac Conhover - - -	80	Isaac Conhover.	Salmon Moulton - -	82	Salmon Moulton.
Catharine Frank - - -	85	Widow Frank.	Obadiah Wheelock - -	78	Obadiah Wheelock.
			Stephen Moulton - -	78	Stephen Moulton.
ST. JOHNSVILLE.			Lot Fuller - - -	80	Lot Fuller.
Elizabeth Tumierman - -	88	Jacob H. Tumierman.	Mary Ward - - -	76	Josiah Ward.
William M. Sanderson - -	75	William M. Sanderson.	George Hopkins - -	82	George Hopkins.
George R. Turca - - -	85	Betsey Wright.	Sarah Jacobs - - -	73	Sarah Jacobs.
Catharine Nestle - - -	86				
			KIRKLAND.		
FALATINE.			Dinah Root - - -	81	Dinah Root.
Henry Flanders - - -	80	John Flanders.	Elisha Lee - - -	76	Enoch Lee.
Hannah Walker - - -	86	Jacob Shill.	Eli Bristol - - -	84	Eli Bristol.
John Nellis - - -	78	John J. Nellis, jr.	Eleazar Warner - -	76	Eleazar Warner.
Peter Fox - - -	81	Peter Fox.	Thomas Goodsell - -	99	Obadiah M. Benedict.
George Ecker - - -	79	George Ecker, jr.	Samuel Bingham - -	87	Thomas Goodsell.
Elizabeth Kelly - - -	80	John Kelly.	Charles Bartholomew -	81	Charles Bartholomew.
Gloudy Vandusen - -	86	Gloudy Vandusen.	Solomon Wood - -	79	Solomon Wood.
Delilah Casler - - -	84	John Casler.	John Fitch - - -	90	John Fitch.
			Frederick Gibbs - -	79	John Currie, 2d.
NIAGARA COUNTY.			David Comstock - -	79	David Comstock.
NEWFANE.			Thankful Foot - -	83	Noel Foot.
David Wisner - - -	83	David Wisner.	James Look - - -	86	Harrison Earl.
Christopher Lewis - -	84	Oliver Lewis.	Barnabas Pond - -	84	Barnabas Pond.
George Fults - - -	88	Conrad Fults.	Archibald C. Crary -	45	Daniel Parkhurst.
			Samuel Royce - -	83	Samuel Royce.
SOMERSET.			Molly Merritt - -	81	Molly Merritt.
John Cassway - - -	48	Charles Pratt.	Asa H. Morse - -	53	Asa H. Morse.
George Thrasher - -	77	Jared C. Aldrich.	Henry McNiel - -	76	Henry McNiel.
			Ruth Hibbard - -	78	Burnham Hibbard.
HARTLAND.			Ozias Marvin - -	77	Ozias Marvin.
Noel Potter - - -	82	Noel Potter, jr.	Sarah Marsh - - -	65	William N. Marsh.
David Waterman - -	80	David Waterman.			
Asa Ripley - - -	80	Asa Ripley.	*MARCY.*		
James Edmonds - -	79	James Edmonds.	Edward Burlison - -	75	Edward Burlison.
			Jabez Carey - - -	79	Jabez Carey.
ROYALTON.			Nancy Howe - - -	74	Ezra Clark.
John Coakley - - -	84	Roswell Kelsey.	Cynthia Risley - -	70	Cynthia Risley.
Reuben Clane - - -	81	Samuel S. Foot.	Eleazar Russell - -	78	Eleazar Russell.
Roger Avery - - -	79	Alanzo Smedley.	Loomis Kellogg - -	82	Loomis Kellogg.
			Nathaniel Thompson -	88	Ethan Thompson.
WHEATFIELD.			Martin Porter - -	81	Martin Porter.
John Swency - - -	52	John Sweney.	Ephraim Buss - -	95	Ephraim Buss.
			Thomas Wadworth -	76	Thomas Wadworth.
CAMBRIA.			Stukely Sayles - -	79	Artemas Sayles.
Daniel Smith - - -	87	Josiah Crane.	Clemence Hurlburt -	82	Benjamin F. Hurlburt.
Amos Benedict - -	84	Ira Benedict.			
			ROME.		
LEWISTON.			Henry F. A. Kirkland -	90	Henry F. A. Kirkland.
Jeremiah Allen - - -	76	Jeremiah Allen.	Jeremiah Steves - -	78	Joshua S. Steves.
Dependance Colbreath -	77	Dependance Colbreath.	Silas Wells - - -	91	Russell Tennant.
Luther Smith - - -	76	Luther Smith.	Mary House - - -	88	Phineas Abbe.
Nathan Baxter - -	79	Nathan Baxter.	Erastus Root - - -	–	Erastus Root.
			Hannah Hamlin - -	73	Josiah Hills.
LOCKPORT.			Daniel Green - - -	84	Daniel Green.
Thadeus Wright - -	79	Solomon C. Wright.	Adin Swan - - -	76	Adin Swan.
Alexander Roman - -	60	William A. Townsend.	Martha Hubbard - -	94	John Elden.
Ezra Doty - - -	81	Z. S. Doty.	Martin Van Buren -	81	John Van Buren.
Noah Levings - - -	76	John Downing.	William Horton - -	77	Joseph Sheles.
Jonathan Rumery - -	81	Jonathan Rumery.	Rhoda Adams - -	85	Horace Adams.
Stephen Wakeman - -	78	Stephen Wakeman.	Jason Bushnell - -	76	Jason Bushnell.
Alexander Freeman - -	79	Alexander Freeman.	Solomon Williams - -	86	Solomon Williams.
			John Williams - -	81	John Williams.
LOCKPORT VILLAGE.			Lucy Williams - -	80	Jesse Williams.
Benajah Malory - -	76	Benajah Malory.	Molly Fellows - -	89	Molly Fellows.
			John Griswold - -	79	John Griswold.
ONEIDA COUNTY.			Betsey Bloomfield -	77	John W. Bloomfield.
CITY OF UTICA—2d ward.			Abigail Fuller - -	86	Orrin Fuller.
James Battles - - -	81	Samuel Cruckshank.	Roxana Graves - -	77	Asa Graves.
3d ward.			Lucy Dickinson - -	86	Lucy Dickinson.
Levi Kellogg - - -	82	Spencer Kellogg.	Winslow Clark - -	53	Winslow Clark.
Daniel Buckly - - -	82	Ely Platt.			
			WESTMORELAND.		
DEERFIELD.			Peleg Havens - -	78	Peleg Havens.
Gate Root Weaver - -	73	Amasa Weaver.	Abigail Goodwin - -	81	Israel T. Goodwin.
Richard Harter - -	78	Richard Harter.	Phineas Bell - - -	79	Phineas Bell.
Andrew Mann - -	81	Andrew Mann.	Ebenezer Benjamin -	76	Ebenezer Benjamin.

NEW YORK—NORTHERN DISTRICT—Continued.

Names of pensioners for revolutionary or military services.	Ages.	Names of heads of families with whom pensioners resided June 1, 1840.	Names of pensioners for revolutionary or military services.	Ages.	Names of heads of families with whom pensioners resided June 1, 1840.
ONEIDA—Continued.			**ONEIDA—Continued.**		
WESTMORELAND—Continued.			STEUBEN.		
Samuel P. Goodsell	48	Samuel P. Goodsell.	Catharine Suits	77	Catharine Suits.
Asa Ellis	97	Daniel Ellis.	William Tripp	78	Stephen Tripp.
Sarah Yale	74	Moses Yale.	Lydia Myers	82	William E. Myers.
Roderick Morrison	76	Orville P. Loomis.	Nathaniel Ames	79	Nathaniel Ames.
William Hatch	77	William Hatch.			
Nathaniel Sweeting	81	Philip B. Sweeting.	TRENTON.		
Selah Woodruff	78	Selah Woodruff.	Lydia Wilkinson	77	William Wilkinson.
			Elisha Davis	80	Elisha Davis.
WHIT‧‧‧N.			Phebe Clark	87	Porter Davis.
James Green	76	William O. Pennfield.	Sarah Catlin	74	John Warren.
Rosanna Olmsted	78	Oliver Olmsted.	Pelatiah Razey	82	Pelatiah Razey.
Savil Moors	51	Savil Moors.	Elizabeth Wilber	83	Elizabeth Wilber.
Enoch Storey	84	Stephen Storey.	Roderick Hopkins	84	Roderick Hopkins.
Jeremiah Powell	89	Liberty Powell.	David Chapin	78	David Chapin.
Reuben Wilcox	77	Reuben Wilcox.	Elisha Wells	82	Ira Wells.
Fortune C. White	52	Fortune C. White.	Joseph Pelton	78	Joseph Pelton.
William Gallup	81	Micajah Morrell.	William Platt	81	Cyrus Cook.
Simeon Rogers	78	Simeon Rogers.	John Williams	76	Linnial Williams.
			Joseph Prince	88	Harvey Hitchcock.
WESTERN.			Samuel Rockwell	87	Samuel Rockwell.
Ahasuerus Teller	83	Ahasuerus Teller.	Joseph Halsted	80	Joseph Halsted.
			David Demming	79	David Demming.
VIENNA.			Samuel Church	80	Samuel Church.
Calvin Dunham	86	Ezekiel Dunham.			
Jonathan Harvey	80	Jonathan Harvey.	AUGUSTA.		
Caleb Robinson	77	David Bristoll.	Thomas Thomson	83	Thomas Thomson.
Thomas Harrison	80	Thomas Harrison.	Amos Parker	78	Amos Parker.
Lucretia Murray	81	Benjamin B. Murray.	Eli Risley	76	Eli Risley.
Richard J. Wilson	80	Richard J. Wilson.	David Powers	79	David Powers.
David Newland	88	Josiah Newland.	Abel Guthrie	75	Abel Guthrie.
William Gates	82	Asa Fitch.	Elijah Shepard	77	Riley Shepard.
Isaac Seeley	88	Lucinda Seeley.	Noah Leonard	75	Noah Leonard.
Jeremiah Gifford	78	Jeremiah Gifford.	Matthew Scovill	78	Isaac Richmond.
Samuel Bloss	88	Samuel Bloss.	Daniel Warren	76	Daniel Warren.
CAMDEN.			BRIDGEWATER.		
Zephaniah Smith	89	Erastus Devereux.	Abraham Monroe	75	Abraham Monroe.
Bartholomew Pond	85	Merritt Pond.	Eli Andrews	82	Thomas Convers.
Daniel Tuthill	82	Hubbard Tuthill.	Lorin Robbins	78	Clark Robbins.
Luther Washburn	83	Freeman Washburn.	Luke Woodbury	82	Cooning Morgan.
Sela Sanford	55	Sela Sanford.	Samuel Guild	78	Samuel Guild.
Joseph Lathers	83	Joseph Lathers.	Hawley Guile	43	Hawley Guile.
			William Ray	50	William Ray.
FLORENCE.			Susan De Wolf	79	Jabez De Wolf.
Jonathan Barnes	80	David S. Grilley.	Sarah Sholes	74	Sarah Sholes.
Mary Robinson	92	Alpheus Robinson.			
Daniel Letts	78	Chester Letts.	MARSHALL.		
Samuel Loomis	78	Anson Loomis.	Nathaniel Ford	74	Nathaniel Ford.
			Moses Swartwout	83	Daniel Swartwout.
AMESVILLE.			Joseph Eastman	81	Joseph S. Eastman.
Peter Mowers	75	Peter Mowers.			
Eliakim Miller	77	Alva Miller.	PARIS.		
Levi Hitchcock	85	Levi Hitchcock, jr.	Frederick Gibbs	79	Augustus Butler.
Mary Fowler	79	James Chapman.	Elon Norton	82	Elon Norton.
Nathan Frink	75	Nathan Frink.	Sarah Norton	74	Ezekiel Pierce.
			Peter Selleck	83	Peter Selleck.
LEE.			Hannah Burrite	82	George Steward.
Mary Potter	74	Almon Potter.	Uriah Doolittle	77	Ralph Head.
Isaac Buell	84	Isaac Buell.	Ruth Laraby	75	David Laraby.
Elisha Niles	75	John B. Hall.	Caleb Simmons	86	Isaac Simmons.
James Eames	77	James Eames.	Asahel Curtiss	74	Asahel Curtiss.
Reuben Marsh	88	James Eames.	Josiah Mosier	84	S. Emerson Mosier.
Abner Fisk	86	Alvin Walker.	Rufus Chapman	96	Daniel Willard.
Stephen Cornish	80	Samuel P. Cornish.	James Parker	76	Alva Parker.
Samuel Wyman	81	Simeon Thrall.	Asa Priest	83	Asa Priest.
Stephen Cleveland	83	Harry Cleveland.	Robert Dixson	86	Robert Dixson.
Medad Comstock	76	Medad Comstock.	Elijah Davis	75	Channey Davis.
Jerradus Dingman	75	Harmonious Dingman.	Abel Porter	83	Lenthel Eells.
			Hobert Graves	75	Hobert Graves.
REMSEN.					
Stephen Manchester	78	Nathaniel Manchester.	SANGERFIELD.		
Anne Green	80	Eleazar Green.	Mary Forest	75	George Green.
John Stebbins	80	John Stebbins, jr.	Lodowick Green	80	Hall Green.
Enoch Hall	75	Enoch Hall.	Oliver Robbins	66	James Young.
			Tabitha Terry	83	Horace A. Terry.
BOONVILLE.			Mary Rugg	78	Abner Eaton.
Martha Harrington	92	Timothy Jackson.	Mary Stetson	85	Ezra Stetson.
Bernard Carpenter	84	Benjamin Carpenter.	Philip Harris	82	Thomas Weaver.
Cromwell Traffarn	77	Cromwell Traffarn.	Stephen Pierce	87	Mrs. Reuben Tower.
Daniel Buck	77	Jonathan Buck.	Aaron Stafford	53	Aaron Stafford.
Peter Sippell	82	Peter Sipple, jr.			

12

Names of pensioners for revolutionary or military services.	Ages.	Names of heads of families with whom pensioners resided June 1, 1840.	Names of pensioners for revolutionary or military services.	Ages.	Names of heads of families with whom pensioners resided June 1, 1840.
ONEIDA—Continued.			ONONDAGA—Continued.		
VERNON.			SPAFFORD—Continued.		
Jacob Ellis	82	Jacob Ellis.	John Green	79	John Green.
Stephen Brigham	86	Stephen Brigham.	Samuel Prindle	81	Samuel Prindle.
Daniel Pettibone	87	Daniel Pettibone.	Allen Breed	81	Rufus Breed.
Chloe Gridley	75	Leander Gridley.			
Thomas Tryon	82	Thomas Tryon.	SALINA.		
Samuel Cody	80	Rodolphus Cody.	Calvin Tripp	82	Elijah Tripp.
Seth Holmes	78	Seth Holmes.	Vine Coy	74	William Ranger.
Isaiah Carpenter	75	George Murray.	Lewis Sweeting	88	Lewis Sweeting.
Lawrence Schoolcraft	80	Joseph Pixley.	Dennison Avery	90	Dennison Avery.
David Murray	82	David Murray.	Joseph Wilson	81	Jonas Mann.
Tobias Weygint	85	Tobias Weygint.	Solomon Huntley	86	Solomon Huntley.
Gilbert Hart	82	Joel Pomroy.			
Adino Goodenough	85	John B. Goodenough.	CICERO.		
			Elijah Loomis	79	Elijah Loomis.
VERONA.					
Ephraim Covill	80	Lorenzo R. Covill.	CLAY.		
Daniel Vanderhyden	81	Abram Vanderhyden.	John Lynn	88	John Lynn.
Rhoda Ensign	85	Thomas Ford.	James Smith	80	Leonard Smith.
Benjamin Wilcox	76	Joseph Wilcox.	Samuel Bragden	78	Thomas Bragden.
Benjamin Alexander	75	McIntosh Alexander.			
Ezekiel Jones	79	Ezekiel Jones.	ONONDAGA.		
David Douglass	82	David Douglass.	Daniel Peck	82	Daniel Peck.
Solomon Bishop	82	Calvin Bishop.	Richard Caton	77	Leonard Caton.
			James Herrington	70	Henry B. Herrington.
ONONDAGA COUNTY.			George Clarke	82	David D. Fellows.
SKANEATELES.			Ephraim Hall	79	Ephraim Hall.
William Webber	77	William Webber.	Jonathan Belding	80	Jonathan Belding.
Nehemiah Cleaveland	87	Lewis W. Cleaveland.	Justus Johnson	84	Justus Johnson.
Isaac Staples	75	Isaac Staples.	Ebenezer Moore	81	Almira Wilson.
John Beach	76	Samuel P. Rhoades.	William Evans	80	Noah Evans.
			Jabez Cole	80	Sterling Cole.
JORDONVILLE.			Caleb Potter	78	Caleb Potter.
James Betts	80	James Betts.	Jonathan Conklin	80	Jonathan Conklin.
ELBRIDGE.			MANLIUS.		
Gill Mallory	85	Joel Mallory.	Benjamin Darling	78	Benjamin Darling.
Stephen Pratt	79	Mary Lilly.	George Edick	84	George Edick.
			Jacob Shaver	78	Jacob Shaver.
MARCELLUS.			Lewis Bishop	79	Levi Bishop.
Job Barber	86	Erastus Whiting.	Martin Walter	90	Isaac Walter.
John Balch	80	John Balch.	Absalom Denny	73	Abijah Miller.
Lemuel Barrows	78	Ezekiel Baker, jr.	Roswell Cleveland	81	Roswell Cleveland.
Lois Baker	73	William Baker.	Elijah Gridley	80	Elijah Gridley.
Benoni Reynolds	86	Benoni Reynolds.	George Ransin	84	George Ransin, jr.
Jonathan Baker	78	Jonathan Baker.	John Cole	75	John Cole.
Ezekiel Baker	75	Anson Baker.	Levi Carr	78	Levi Carr.
Sarah Van Meter	76	Garret Sharp.	Zebedee Potter	86	Zebedee Potter.
Chancy Gaylord	83	Asaph Gaylord.	Asa Merrill	80	Asa Merrill.
Joseph Bishop	81	Ira Bishop.			
Reuben Dorchester	92	Eliakim Dorchester.	POMPEY.		
John Daliba	75	Sanford Daliba.	Thomas Dixan	80	Thomas Dixan.
Robert McCullock	79	Robert McCullock.	Moses Knapp	86	Moses Knapp.
			Richard Hiscock	81	Luther Hiscock.
LYSANDER.			Conrad Bush	84	Conrad Bush.
William Johnson	88	William Johnson.	David Beard	85	David Beard.
Abigail Northrop	88	Jacob Northrop.	Benjamin Hayes	82	Benjamin Hayes.
John Slawson	76	John Slawson.	William Cook	79	Albert Cook.
William Foster	88	Ira Foster.	Jeremiah Crandal	84	Elanson Watkins.
Lucy Clark	74	Theodore E. Clark.	James Bookhunt	79	James Bookhunt.
Nathaniel Root	73	Nathaniel Root.	Jehiel Foote	80	Jehiel Foote.
Stiles Freeman	52	Stiles Freeman.	Ralph Wheelock	81	Gershom B. Wheelock.
Shubal Preston	82	Shubal Preston, jr.	Samuel Jones	80	Samuel Jones.
Israel Hooker	82	Israel Hooker.	Zadock Seymour	83	Eliza Seymour.
			Adonijah Cole	83	Chauncey Cooper.
VAN BUREN.			Moses Moultrup	76	Moses Moultrup.
John C. Britton	84	John Conets.			
Daniel Bennet	51	Daniel Bennet.	FABIUS.		
Dow Smith	105	Augustus Smith.	Ambrose Gron	83	Ambrose Gron.
Calvin Waterman	85	Calvin Waterman.	Rufus Carter	75	Rufus Carter.
			Ebenezer Foot	87	Thomas T. Beden.
CAMILLUS.			Manuel Truair	81	John Truair.
Dorcas Case	80	John Case.	James Steward	70	James Steward.
John Clark	88	Joel Chapman.	Daniel Hills	78	Daniel Hills.
John Dill	82	Samuel Dill.			
Miles Bennet	74	Miles Bennet.	TULLY.		
Enoch Wood	76	Enoch Wood.	Enoch Baily	81	Enoch Baily.
Helen Clute	77	Helen Clute.			
			LAFAYETTE.		
SPAFFORD.			Benjamin June	87	Benjamin June.
Stephen Albro	81	Maria Hinman.	Jacob Goodrich	86	Elijah Goodrich.
Lydia Owen	81	Thomas Babcock.	Samuel Humphrey	84	Samuel Humphrey.
Phebe Pressey	86	Moses Pressey.	Benjamin Webb	84	Hiram Leonard.

NEW YORK—NORTHERN DISTRICT--Continued.

Names of pensioners for revolutionary or military services.	Ages.	Names of heads of families with whom pensioners resided June 1, 1840.	Names of pensioners for revolutionary or military services.	Ages.	Names of heads of families with whom pensioners resided June 1, 1840.
ONONDAGA—Continued.			**ONTARIO—Continued.**		
LAFAYETTE—Continued.			HOPEWELL.		
Jedediah Winchell - -	88	Jacob Winchell.	Samuel Andrews - - -	86	Samuel Andrews.
Zenas Northway - -	75	Zenas Northway	Joseph Stoddard - -	49	Joseph Stoddard.
Nathaniel Gage - -	77	Amos Gage.	Hannah Thompson -	80	George Thompson.
DE WITT.			FARMINGTON.		
Jacob G. Low - -	84	Jacob G. Low.	Sylvester Worden - -	87	Henry S. Worden.
Andrew Balsley - -	85	James Balsley.			
Pelham W. Ripley - -	76	Pelham W. Ripley.	VICTOR.		
Silas Burke - -	75	Silas Burke.	Wynant C. Vanderburgh -	79	Heman Van Veghten.
William Vermilyea -	74	William Vermilyea.	Samuel Tubbs - -	58	Samuel Tubbs.
Major Watson - -	93	Daniel Downs.	Esther Rawson - -	84	Joseph Rawson.
Henry Bogardus - -	77	Henry P. Bogardus.	Amos Wooddin - -	87	Henry Wooddin.
			Israel M. Blood - -	78	Nathaniel Blood.
OTISCO.			Abigail Pardee - -	84	Henry Pardee.
Chauncy Atkins - -	77	Hiram Perkins.	Asa Eddy - -	74	Asa Eddy.
Christopher Monk - -	82	Anna Monk.	Job Hart - -	81	Asa Hart.
Apollos King - -	76	Apollos King.	John Fiddler - -	78	Henry Task.
			Eleazer Boughton -	75	Asahel Boughton.
ONTARIO COUNTY.			Abijah Williams - -	83	Abijah Williams.
CANANDAIGUA.					
Polly Gildersleeve -	84	James Williams.	EAST BLOOMFIELD.		
William Cox - -	89	William Cox.	Edmund Richards - -	84	Edmund Richards.
Abner Barlow - -	89	J. G. Haskins.	Timothy Buell - -	83	Timothy Buell, jr.
Mary Gould - -	89	Phineas P. Bates.	Gershom Salmon - -	86	Stephen Salmon.
John Debow - -	78	Harvy Debow.	Benjamin Gauss - -	75	Benjamin Gauss.
James Blair - -	85	William Blair.	Ebenezer French - -	79	Ebenezer French.
Isaac Morse - -	84	Orlando Morse.			
Celia Wheeler - -	77	Andrew Sleght.	WEST BLOOMFIELD.		
Isaac Booth - -	84	Isaac Booth.	John Adams - -	80	John Adams.
Cyrel Eaton - -	73	Cyrel Eaton.	John Martin - -	79	John Martin.
Daniel Ensign - -	79	Daniel Ensign.	Anna Hogan - -	65	Anna Hogan.
Ephras Nott - -	84	Ephras Nott.	John Shepard - -	75	John Shepard.
PHELPS.			BRISTOL.		
Ezra Post - -	76	William Post.	Israel Conant - -	77	Jonas Pickarel.
Joseph Vandermark -	78	Benjamin F. Salisbury.	Elihu Morse - -	81	Elihu Morse, jr.
James Davis - -	75	James Davis, jr.	John Worden - -	86	Barzilla Worden.
James McMillan -	76	Charles S. Jenkins.	Seth Gerry - -	76	Seth Gerry.
Susanna Cozart - -	75	William Henry.			
Daniel Tibbits - -	51	Daniel Tibbits.	SOUTH BRISTOL.		
Mercy Humphrey -	77	Cornelius Vanalstine.	Roxana Tuttle - -	77	Jeffrey A. Blackman.
Oliver Humphrey - -	81	Oliver Humphrey.	Thomas Brown - -	86	Jacob Shaw.
Susan Benton - -	81	Moses Cortright.	James Parmely - -	82	James Parmely, jr.
William Palmiter -	77	Asenath Palmiter.	Israel Butler - -	80	Israel Butler.
Timothy Ray - -	78	Timothy Ray.	William Pierce - -	73	William Pierce.
George Willson - -	84	George Willson.	Joseph Snow - -	92	Sherman Snow.
Darius Seager - -	89	Darius Seager.	Thomas Covel - -	49	Thomas Covel.
Thomas Wood - -	85	Thomas Wood.	Asa Brown - -	92	John Brown.
Elisha Crain - -	86	Chester Crain.	Hannah Crocker - -	70	Chauncey Pease.
Enoch Crosby - -	76	Enoch Crosby.			
Jonathan Melvin - -	89	Jonathan Melvin.	RICHMOND.		
			Andrew Palmer - -	85	William F. Reed.
MANCHESTER.			James Voorhees - -	95	James Voorhees.
Oliver Fletcher - -	84	Oliver Fletcher.	Joseph Cleveland - -	92	Joseph Cleveland.
Thomas Hill - -	86	Thomas Hill, jr.	Aaron Briggs - -	85	Aaron Briggs.
Philip Lemangon -	85	Pardon Butts.	Jesse Stevens - -	77	Jesse Stevens, jr.
Robert Robinson -	77	Randal Robinson.	Abijah Wright - -	77	Abijah Wright.
			Elijah Laton - -	66	Elijah Laton.
SENECA.					
Jonathan Presler - -	89	Northrup Green.	CANADICE.		
Samuel Smith - -	83	Samuel Smith.	Nathan Morse - -	90	John Adams.
Cornelius Roberds -	84	Cornelius Roberds.			
Mary Ryder - -	78	Sylvester Brown.	NAPLES.		
Isaac Amsden - -	85	William Amsden.	Mary Kibbe - -	90	Betsey Pottle.
Hugh W. Dobbin -	73	Hugh W. Dobbin.	Otis Pierce - -	49	Otis Pierce.
Sarah Wells - -	77	Mary Jane Black.	Rebecca Pierce - -	86	Rebecca Pierce.
Charlotte Thurston -	77	Joseph Clement.	John Hinckley - -	77	John Hinckley.
Catharine Tellinghart	76	Ezekiel Lewis.	Margaret Cassady - -	93	Tunis Moshier.
Jane Hay - -	90	Philip C. Hay.	Eleazer Wales - -	84	Solomon Wales.
Wheeler Lanphire -	56	Wheeler Lanphire.	Amasa S. Tifft - -	52	Amasa S. Tifft.
			John Cronk - -	52	John Cronk.
GORHAM.			Benjamin Garlinghouse -	78	Benjamin Garlinghouse.
Salmon Child - -	75	William Child.			
Lydia Dunham - -	73	Joseph Smith.	**ORLEANS COUNTY.**		
Stephen Marcy - -	84	Stephen Marcy.	BARRE.		
Ebenezer Crittenden -	83	Orrin Crittenden.	Lot Swift - -	82	Henry Swift.
William Morrison -	96	William Morrison.	Stephen Angevine - -	39	Stephen Angevine.
Solomon Blodgett -	84	Solomon Blodgett.	William Butts - -	84	Lockwood Butts.
Henry Green - -	77	Henry Green.	Artemas Thair - -	77	Washington Thair.
Joseph Chase - -	87	Benjamin Blodgett.	Elisha Wright - -	87	Elisha Wright, jr.
Ludim Blodgett - -	76	Joseph Blodgett.	Israel Root - -	80	Amos Root.
John Walter - -	94	Luman Walter.	Elisha Shelden - -	78	Elisha Shelden.

NEW YORK—NORTHERN DISTRICT—Continued.

Names of pensioners for revolutionary or military services.	Ages.	Names of heads of families with whom pensioners resided June 1, 1840.	Names of pensioners for revolutionary or military services.	Ages.	Names of heads of families with whom pensioners resided June 1, 1840.
ORLEANS—Continued.			**OSWEGO—Continued.**		
BARRE—Continued.			READFIELD.		
Silas Phelps	80	Calvin C. Phelps.	Experience Warren	102	Samuel Warren.
Daniel Bennett	84	Levi Bennett.	Joshua Wood	74	Joshua Wood.
Abial Harding	79	Abial Harding.	Amos Johnson	76	Samuel N. Johnson.
Stephen Brown	80	Stephen Brown.	William Lord	81	William Lord.
Samuel Lazendry	80	Elisha Lazendry.			
Joseph Root	77	Joseph Root.	RICHLAND.		
			Sally Weed	82	Elihu Phillips.
RIDGEWAY.			Ezra Lampher	83	Ezra Lampher.
Hannah Hubbard	83		Abigail McChesany	76	J. A. McChesany.
			Ruth Price	80	Isaac Price.
SHELBY.			Isaac Fellows	82	Augustus Fellows.
Benjamin Porter	80		Levi Cary	81	Zenas Cary.
John Letts	80	John Letts.	Mary Mason	82	E. Mason.
Oliver Cone	80		John Earskin	88	John Earskin.
			Edward Wade	87	Edward Wade.
GAINES.			Ebenezer Roberts	84	Ebenezer Roberts.
Moses Bacon	52		John Breed	85	Joseph Breed.
			Abijah Hubbel	79	Abijah Hubbel.
CLARENDON.			Dennis Wright	79	N. Wright.
Lemuel Cook	75	Lemuel Cook.			
Nathan Chadwick	75	Nathan Chadwick.	SANDY CREEK.		
Benj. Petingal	79	Benj. Petingal.	Nathaniel Jacobs	80	Nathaniel Jacobs.
Samuel Millikin	87		Peter Barga	84	L. Widick.
			Ephraim Kimdle	84	E. Kimdle.
MURRAY.			Nicholas Winters	83	N. Winters.
Amos Frink	80				
Aaron Warren	78	Aaron Warren.	WILLIAMSTON.		
Thomas Kelicott	87		Peter Bergen	91	Peter Bergen.
John Rutherford	42	John Rutherford.			
			HANNIBAL.		
YATES.			Daniel Dunham	77	David Dunham.
Joshua Brigs	87	Austin Brigs.	Epaphious Loomis	84	Joseph Langden.
KENDALL.			GRANBY.		
Chaffe Green	80	Chaffe Green.	Austin Smith	87	Sidney Tracy.
William Ogle	78		James Wheeler	79	L. A. Wheeler.
Eve Bird	80	Edmund Bird.	Joseph H. Perigo	77	Robert Perigo.
OSWEGO COUNTY.			VOLNEY.		
			Elihu Bradley	84	Elihu Bradley.
ALBION.			Aaron Fish	81	H. Norton.
Sarah Powers	87	Benj. Cross.			
Ebenezer Carr	85	Stillman Preston.	PALERMO.		
			Samuel Murray	84	T. Seely.
AMBOY.					
Billings Worden	87	Billings Worden.	SCHROEPPEL.		
Lydia Coop	67	James Riddle.	Isaac Packard	78	Isaac Packard.
Jesse Kinney	78	Jesse Kinney.			
Esther Brown	79	Asa Brown.	SCRIBA.		
			Aaron Wheeler	80	Aaron Wheeler.
BOYLSTON.					
Almon Ormsby	92	Alanson Ormsby.	NEW HAVEN.		
			Richard Risley	86	Richard Risley.
CONSTANTIA.					
Anna Ford	75	William Ford.	OSWEGO.		
Joel Legg	82	Stephen Taft.	Samuel Starks	79	Samuel Starks.
Moses Nelson	75	Moses Nelson.	Jason Thomas	78	Jason Thomas.
			William Colby	80	William Colby.
HASTINGS.			Sylvanus Bishop	74	Lewis Bishop.
William Heiner	84	William Heiner.	Simon J. Vrooman	81	Simon J. Vrooman.
Joseph Farrer	67	Joseph Farrer.			
Gilbert Parkhurst	70	Gilbert Parkhurst.	**OTSEGO COUNTY.**		
			HARTWICK.		
MEXICO.			Edward Bowe	83	Edward Bowe.
Jesse Smith	83	Jesse Smith.	Benjamin Camp	77	Benjamin Camp.
Caleb C. Whipple	78	Caleb C. Whipple.	Samuel Holman	78	Samuel Holman.
Experience Ormsby	71	Philander Ormsby.	Nicholas Camp	85	Nicholas Camp.
John Kinyon	80	John Kinyon.	Joseph Crofts	78	Joseph Crofts.
Amos Reed	87	Amos Reed.	Joseph C. Hawley	83	M. Blackford.
Alexander Beebe	81	Asa Beebe.	Noah Eddy	80	William Eddy.
Bathsheba Alexander	87	Gardener Hagan.	T. Whaley	80	T. Whaley.
			James Newton	81	J. S. Newton.
ORWELL.			John Wells	81	John Wells.
Samuel Stowell	77	Samuel Stowell.	John Tucker	77	Ira Tucker.
John Brooks	81	Michael Calb.	John Wells	46	Stephen Holden.
Allen Gilbert	84	Jabez H. Gilbert.	Elisha Bills	91	Elisha Bills.
PARISH.			WESTFORD.		
Philip Chesley	78	Philip Chesley.	Jonas Babcock	76	Jonas Babcock.
Nathan Franklin	78	Nathan Franklin.	David Smith	80	Samuel Shellan.
Timothy Rider	76	Putnam Rider.	David Hull	81	David Hull.
			Swain Seward	63	Swain Seward.

NEW YORK—NORTHERN DISTRICT—Continued.

Names of pensioners for revolutionary or military services.	Ages.	Names of heads of families with whom pensioners resided June 1, 1840.	Names of pensioners for revolutionary or military services.	Ages.	Names of heads of families with whom pensioners resided June 1, 1840.
OTSEGO—Continued.			**OTSEGO—Continued.**		
WESTFORD—Continued.			BUTTERNUTS.		
Aaron Baldwin	78	Aaron Baldwin.	Nehemiah Daniels	77	Nehemiah Daniels.
Timothy Canfield	81	Timothy Canfield.	Ebenezer M. Holden	76	Ebenezer M. Holden.
Henry Stever	91	Alexander Loyd.	Norris Collar	93	Norris Collar.
MARYLAND.			Alexander Bryant	78	Alexander Bryant.
Samuel Ketchum	78	Jonathan Ketchum.	Daniel Nash	77	Daniel Nash.
Simeon Durham	73	C. Chamberlin.	Timothy Donaldson	89	Eli Donaldson.
Cyrus Brown	76	Amos Brown.	John Marsh	78	John Marsh.
DECATUR.			Mordecai Bedient	76	Mordecai Bedient.
Isaac Lane	76	Isaac Lane.	Jared Parmer	80	Jared Parmer.
John Magee	82	John Magee.	Reuben Chitenden	81	Reuben Chitenden.
Henry Cooper	67	Henry Cooper.	Calvin Donaldson	85	
Justice Lewis	78	Justice Lewis.	Josiah Beardslee	—	
MIDDLEFIELD.			Jeremiah Townsend	83	
Mary Gilbert	74	Mary Gilbert.	Isaac Bedient	76	
Oliver Cory	76	Oliver Cory.	Mary Weston	89	
Peter Slingerland	73	Geo. W. Stillman.	UNADILLA.		
Wm. Straight	82	Wm. Straight.	Sarah Collins	76	
John Loudon	75	John Loudon.	Seth Rowley	80	
Caleb Babcock	86	I. Pierce.	Abner Griffis	88	
Jehiel Todd	86	M. Hamilton.	Josiah Reed	72	
Nicholas Righton	87	N. Righton.	Thomas Card	78	
George Boyd	78	George Boyd.	Thomas Wild	77	
WORCESTER.			Asahel Packard	77	
Francis Dickson	77	Francis Dickson.	Ezra Allen	83	
Sarah Childs	80	Amasa Childs.	Elisha Luther	85	
John Brooks	87	Ira Lane.	Susan Hough	82	
Joseph Powers	85	Chester Powers.	EDMESTON.		
Samuel Hartwell	80	D. Refinburgh.	Polly Bennett	76	Lewis Hammond.
David Jones	88	Enoch Jones.	Amos Sherman	62	Leonard Powers.
CHERRY VALLEY.			Stephen Colegrove	77	Stephen Colegrove.
Andrew Pette	81	Anna Gillet.	Daniel Green	82	Horace Green.
Benj. Allen	76	Isaac Allen.	Thomas Terry	81	Thomas Terry.
James Bradley	85	James Bradley.	Jacob Campbell	78	Squire Campbell.
John Thompson	82	John Thompson.	Gideon De Forest	75	Gideon De Forest.
Zebe Granger	78	Zebe Granger.	Peter Parker	72	Peter Parker.
Benj. Denslow	80	Benj. Denslow.	Lemuel Anderson	76	Lemuel Anderson.
Asa Glazier	55	Asa Glazier.	BURLINGTON.		
Jerome Clark	83	Jerome Clark.	John Jackson	85	John Jackson.
Stephen McGown	78	Stephen McGown.	John Hood	86	David Hood.
Archibald McKillip	85	A. McKillip.	Levi Miller	85	Henry Newton.
Jesse Wilson	40	David Cary.	Samuel Blanden	80	Zeno Blanden.
ONEONTO.			Lydia Story	78	Rufus Lines.
James Young	79	James Young.	Susanna Herrington	73	Susanna Herrington.
Henry Larue	84	Henry Larue.	Chloe Meacham	82	Chloe Meacham.
Walter Fitch	77	Walter Fitch.	Tabitha Peck	74	Nathaniel Bolton.
Michael Hilsinger	81		Elizabeth Cushman	74	Almon Cushman.
Jacob Van Wort	86		Daniel Rolo	78	Daniel Rolo.
Lawrence Swart	86	David Swart.	Lemuel Hubbell	85	Lemuel Hubbell.
MILFORD.			EXETER.		
James Westcott	77		Hannah Palmer	75	Christopher Palmer.
Joseph Vars	79	Augustus Vars.	Humphrey Palmer	82	Humphrey Palmer.
Olive Waters	75	Amos Waters.	Elizabeth Wilber	—	Elizabeth Wilber.
Barnabas Bates	79	Dewitt Bates.	William McKoun	45	William McKoun.
Ezekiel Seger	87	Edward Seger.	Asahel Williams	86	Sherman Williams
William Russel	84		Smith Hollister	78	Smith Hollister.
William Barnard	75	Moses Barnard.	David Janes	77	David Janes.
William Pettingill	82	Samuel Pettingill.	NEW LISBON.		
Benoni Wellman	75	William Welman.	Patience Briggs	82	Patience Briggs.
LAURENS.			Abiel Cooke	77	Abiel Cooke.
John Hubbard	82		Joseph Nearing	77	Joseph Nearing.
Ezekiel Bennett	78	Ezekiel Bennett.	Asaph Buck	78	Asaph Buck.
John Potter	85	John Potter.	William Russell	55	William Russell.
John Cooke	84	John Cooke.	Uriah Warren	54	Uriah Warren.
PITTSFIELD.			Mary Mars	85	Robert Barton.
Elisha Wood	79	Elisha Wood.	Zachariah Downer	84	Zachariah Downer.
John White	85	John White.	Caroline Mather	74	Caroline Mather.
OTEGO.			OTSEGO.		
Moses Stephens	70	Simeon Stevens.	Mary Spencer	89	Mary Wood.
Judy Hyatt	79	Charles Hyatt.	Uriah Luce	77	Harry Knowlton.
Polly Emerson	77	Charles L. Emerson.	Abijah Farchild	85	Stephen Gregory.
Benjamin Edson	81	Freeman Edson.	Elizabeth Hand	75	Hannah Ray.
Joseph Northrup	86	Joseph Northrup, jr.	John Reed	63	John Reed.
David Smith	85	John Smith.	Samuel Short	74	Samuel Short.
			Amos Rexford	71	Amos Rexford.
			Mercy Smith	70	Eleazar Joslyn.
			John Dunbar	74	John Dunbar.

CENSUS OF PENSIONERS.

NEW YORK—NORTHERN DISTRICT—Continued.

Names of pensioners for revolutionary or military services.	Ages.	Names of heads of families with whom pensioners resided June 1, 1840.	Names of pensioners for revolutionary or military services.	Ages.	Names of heads of families with whom pensioners resided June 1, 1840.
OTSEGO—Continued.			**RENSSELAER—Continued.**		
otsego—Continued.			nassau—Continued.		
James Baily	86	John S. Baily.	Amaziah Baily	90	Asa Upham.
Samuel McKeen	75	Samuel McKeen.	Rufus Tifft	85	Green Tifft.
Joel Squire	80	Joel Squire.	Joseph Carr	82	Joseph Carr.
Abigail Bover	84	Eleazer Brown.			
Allen Geer	86	Elias Geer.	**SANDLAKE.**		
Daniel Preston	77	Joan Preston.	Elizabeth Frothingham	82	Elizabeth Frothingham.
			Stephen Gregory	83	Stephen Gregory.
PLAINFIELD.			William Sliter	–	William Sliter.
Ezekiel Sheldon	80	Elisha Bently.	Reuben Babcock	82	Reuben Babcock.
David Treadway	97	David McLaughlin.	Joseph Huntington	82	Joseph Huntington.
RICHFIELD.			**STEPHENTOWN.**		
Parley Herrington	85	S. P. Herrington.	Moses Bishop	83	Moses Bishop.
Daniel Patchem	81	Daniel Patchem.	Amos James	80	Amos James.
John Stewart	77	John Stewart.	John Horton	78	John Horton.
John Bloodgood	77	John Bloodgood.	Nathan Williams	84	Nathan Williams.
Daniel Hannahs	73	Amos Beardsley.	Eli Young	84	Eli Young.
Wardwell Green	82	Wardwell Green.	Jesse Bennett	93	H. Bennett.
William Eddey	80	Willard Eddey.	Jacob Wright	80	William Boughton.
Sisson Cole	94	Leroy Cole.	Benjamin Andrews	83	Reuben Andrews.
Nancy Young	84	Salathiel Young.	Job Taylor	83	Job Taylor.
			BERLIN.		
SPRINGFIELD.			William Bell	77	William Bell.
Robert Wood	89	Robert Wood.	Moses Hendrick	85	Moses Hendrick.
Anthony Davoe	77	Anthony Davoe.	Joseph Crandall	84	Joseph Crandall.
Polly Fargo	79	Nathaniel P. Ransom.	Caleb Bentley	74	Caleb Bentley.
William Thayer	46	William Thayer, jr.	Asa Beebe	79	Asa Beebe.
Merrit Hoke	93	Jacob Hoke.			
Thomas Van Horne	96	Philip Van Horne.	**PETERSBURG.**		
Nancy House	73	Hamilton Coleman.	William Scriver	84	William Scriver.
H. Vedder	81	Richard Vedder.	John Armsbry	89	John Armsbry.
Polly Hicks	69	Polly Hicks.	Stephen Potter	81	Stephen Potter.
Christer Walter	81	C. Walter.	Christopher Colegrove	79	C. Colegrove.
William Brown	82	William Brown.	Augustus Lewis	87	Augustus Lewis.
Anson Hall	83	Anson Hall.	Sterry Hewitt	84	Sterry Hewitt.
George Dunbar	81	John Shaw.	Jason Babcock	85	Benjamin Babcock.
Moses Franklin	76	Moses Franklin.			
Jedediah Beech	85	Jedediah Beech.	**SCHODACK.**		
Henry Sitts	86		Sarah Potter	84	Henry Potter.
Joseph Farnham	76	Joseph Farnham.	John Ostrander	87	Sarah Ostrander.
			Abraham Van Buren	89	Abraham Van Buren.
RENSSELAER COUNTY.			Phebe Birch	81	Isaiah Birch.
hoosick.					
Freeborn Sweet	83	Freeborn Sweet.	**GREENBUSH.**		
Nathaniel Barnett	86	Nathaniel Barnett.	Albert Claflin	84	William Claflin.
John Palmer	82	John Palmer.	Nicholas Van Rensselaer	89	Nicholas Van Rensselaer.
Frederick Outerkirk	85	Frederick Outerkirk.	William Van Benthuysen	86	William Van Benthuysen.
Timothy Graves	88	Timothy Graves.	Peter Best	81	Peter Best.
Abner Crandall	78	Abner Crandall.			
Jacob Boovie	77	Jacob Boovie.	**BRUNSWICK.**		
Darling Shaw	81	Darling Shaw.	Christopher Gray	92	Martin Springer.
Morriss Tucker	83	Morriss Tucker.	Charles Hall	82	Charles Hall.
			Henry Smith	84	Henry Smith.
PITTSTOWN.					
Asahel Eastman	76	Isaiah F. Eastman.	**GRAFTON.**		
Isaac Van Wart (since dead)	89	A. Van Wart.	David Barnhart	–	David Barnhart.
Richard Anthony	76	Richard Anthony.	Rufus Parks	80	Rufus Parks.
Gilbert Eddy	79	Gilbert Eddy.	James Scrivner	89	Caleb W. Scrivner.
			Rufus Gallop	84	Rufus Gallop.
LANSINGBURG.			Amos Martin	82	Nathaniel Martin.
Margaret Louk	80	Margaret Louk.			
Mary Biggs	–	Peter Morriss.	**TROY—1st ward.**		
Stephen Pelton	79	Chauncey Ives.	Elijah Reed	76	Elijah Reed.
Prudence Barton	77	Prudence Barton.	Ephraim Whittaker	85	Ephraim Whittaker.
Lucy Morgan	79	Lucy Morgan.	John Folliard	88	John Folliard.
Catharine Oakly	80	Andrew Follett.	Elizabeth Grace	76	Elizabeth Grace.
Timothy Cone	77	Timothy Cone.	Love Perady	–	Henry Hart.
Mary Leonard	79	F. B. Leonard.	Sarah Wilbur	–	Curtis Wilbur.
			2d ward.		
SCAGHTICOKE.			None.		
John Welch	77	John Welch.	**3d ward.**		
Elisha Phelps	82	Freeman Baker.	Martha Bootle	87	Benjamin F. Randall.
Peter Akart	84	Peter Akart, jr.	Benjamin Pierce	77	Benjamin Pierce.
John L. Van Antwerp	80	P. Y. Van Antwerp.	Phebe Prescot	79	E. Prescot.
Nathaniel Robinson	82	Nathaniel Robinson.	Amasa Tiffney	73	Amasa Tiffney.
			Esther Hendryx	82	I. J. Hendryx.
NASSAU.			**4th ward.**		
Charles Dickinson	83	Jane B. Gale.	Elizabeth Crowley	77	G. Buckingham.
Abijah Bush	85	Abijah Bush.	**5th ward.**		
Simeon Griswold	87	Simeon Griswold.	Sally Knight	71	Sally Knight.
William Hunt	84	Alva Hunt.			
Quain Tanner	78	Quain Tanner.			

NEW YORK—NORTHERN DISTRICT—Continued.

Names of pensioners for revolutionary or military services.	Ages.	Names of heads of families with whom pensioners resided June 1, 1840.	Names of pensioners for revolutionary or military services.	Ages.	Names of heads of families with whom pensioners resided June 1, 1840.
RENSSELAER—Continued.			**SARATOGA—Continued.**		
TROY—Continued.			*BALLSTON—Continued.*		
6th ward.			Aurt Hanson	79	Aurt Hanson.
Henry S. Myers	49	P. C. Marble.	Thaddeus Scribner	78	Thaddeus Scribner.
7th ward.			Elijah Armstrong	55	Elijah Armstrong.
Jacob Miller	82	Charles Moray.	Justus Jennings	84	Justus Jennings.
Olive Woodward	74	Lewis Woodward.	James A. McDonald	63	James A. McDonald.
SARATOGA COUNTY.			*CHARLTON.*		
GREENFIELD.			Esther Lefferts	86	Esther Lefferts.
Jared Hood	78	Norton Hood.	Jacob Layport	–	Jacob Layport.
Abraham Weed	81	Abraham Weed.	Lydia Chambers	–	Ann Chambers.
Giles Fitch	78	Giles Fitch.	Alexander Van Eppes	78	Teunis Nisbeth.
Nathaniel Seymour	83	Thomas Seymour.	Ahasuerus Wardwell	84	A. Wardwell.
Elijah Smith	82	Elijah Smith.	Benjamin Marvin	77	Timothy Marvin.
Hiel Savage	80	Samuel Wood.	Elijah Spencer	85	Elijah Spencer.
Catharine Bishop	88	William Woodcock.	John P. K. Taylor	77	John P. K. Taylor.
Daniel Scott	87	Daniel Scott.			
Joseph Bemiss	84	Daniel Davis.	*CLIFTON PARK.*		
			James Knights	83	James Knights.
SARATOGA.			Mayhew Daggett	83	Mayhew Daggett.
Charles Cluky	97	Charles Cluky.	Elnathan Finch	79	Elnathan Finch.
Anthony Glean	89	Anthony Glean.	Abijah Peck	82	Abijah Peck.
			Evert E. Van Vranken	83	Evert E. Van Vranken.
SARATOGA SPRINGS.			Benjamin Chadsey	72	Benjamin Chadsey.
Isaac Weatherbee	78	John Weatherbee.	Marybee Jones	70	Robert D. Graff.
James Ide	83	James Ide.	Samuel Brewster	85	Samuel Brewster.
Caleb Fish	84	Othniel Corbel.	Reuben Stokeham	98	Reuben Stokeham.
Ezra Ketchum	91	Job Reynolds.			
James Barhyte	78	James Barhyte.	*GALWAY.*		
			Elijah Curtiss	79	Elijah W. Curtiss.
CORINTH.			Joel Burr	81	Joel Burr.
John Rhodes	80	Stephen F. Rhodes.	John Carter	88	John Carter.
			George Hart	82	Jonathan Weeden.
HADLEY.			Desire Tourgie	–	Joseph Berniss.
N. Scofield	86	A. Scofield.	Martha Murray	86	Catharine Murray.
Squire Wood	79	Comfort Wood.	Aaron Berniss	80	Aaron Berniss.
Thomas Reed	74	Thomas Reed.	Israel Phelps	82	Israel Phelps.
Joseph Gilbert	85	Joseph Gilbert.	Joseph Brewster	80	Joseph Brewster.
			Andrew Sprague	86	Joseph Van Every.
DAY.			Arthur Colwell	78	Arthur Colwell.
S. Holcomb	76	W. K. Holcomb.			
Mary Demming	81	Mary Demming.	*MALTA.*		
			Vincent Foster	85	Deborah Foster.
EDINBURGH.			Dean Chase	78	Dean Chase.
Maria Simpson	80	Isaac Rhodes.			
Andrew Albro	77	Andrew Albro.	*MILTON.*		
Samuel Downing	76	Samuel Downing.	Samuel Barnum	81	Anna H. King.
Joseph Olmsted	82	Joseph Olmsted.	Isaac Lent	88	Daniel A. Collamer.
Sampson Hosley	86	Sampson Hosley.	George T. Waiger	50	Daniel A. Collamer.
Robert Sumner	78	Henry Noyes.	Sarah Wandle	81	Sarah Wandle.
Ormel King	77	Anthony De Golier.	Sarah Danforth	83	John Dunning.
Elkanah Sprague	80	Benjamin Axley.	James Merrill	82	James Merrill.
Benjamin Axley	81		Sarah Radford	86	Sylvester Alexander.
			John Ellsworth	89	John Ellsworth.
MOREAU.			Asa Beach	78	Asa Beach.
Joseph Carr	83	William Carr.	Jonathan Nash	80	Isaac Nash.
Nehemiah Stevens	78	J. B. Stevens.	Lucy Herrick	78	Miles Herrick.
Zachariah Ray	81	Zachariah Ray.	John Whitid	80	John Whitid.
Peter Stephenson	87	Peter Stephenson.	David Ames	77	Jacob Goodrich.
Nathaniel Calkins	87	John Roberts.	Catharine Crumb	101	J. S. Waiger.
John Bitely	84	J. L. Bitely.			
Caleb Burrows	75	Amos Burrows.	*PROVIDENCE.*		
			Lucy Hall	76	Ruth Hall.
WILTON.			Elizabeth Bundy	67	Elijah Bundy.
Amos Goldin	84	Amos Goldin.	Elijah Walworth	49	Elijah Walworth.
Jonathan Woodward	81	Jonathan Woodward.	Isaac Colony	77	Isaac Colony.
Benjamin Dimmick	84	Giles Dimmick.	Rachel Smith	78	H. V. Smith.
Roswell Ray	74	Roswell Ray.	Mehitable Landers	79	Moses Landers.
			William Bearsly	77	William Bearsly.
NORTHUMBERLAND.					
John Crage	84	John Crage.	**SCHENECTADA COUNTY.**		
Grace Wood	83	A. Wood.	*DUANESBURG.*		
Gideon Whitmore	80	David Coffinger.	Jonathan Herrick	79	
			Isaiah Tower	80	Isaiah Tower.
BALLSTON.			David Hillard	80	
Sanborn Ford	84	Sanborn Ford.	Enos Howard	80	Enos Howard.
David Howe	78	David Howe.	Henry Head	82	Henry G. Head.
Sarah Fitzgerald	87	James Fitzgerald.	Samuel Rogers	76	Samuel Rogers.
Uriah Gregory	86	Uriah Gregory.			
Mary De Forest	81	William C. De Forest.	*GLENVILLE.*		
Paul Wilson	85	Paul Wilson.	Sally Gondenough	78	
William Kingsley	75	William Kingsley.	Rebecca Shelly	80	
Catharine English	92	Ephraim Miller.	Job Hedden	86	G. Hedden.

NEW YORK—NORTHERN DISTRICT—Continued

Names of pensioners for revolutionary or military services.	Ages.	Names of heads of families with whom pensioners resided June 1, 1840.	Names of pensioners for revolutionary or military services.	Ages.	Names of heads of families with whom pensioners resided June 1, 1840.
SCHENECTADA—Continued.			**SCHOHARIE**—Continued.		
GLENVILLE—Continued.			JEFFERSON—Continued.		
Benjamin Crandall - -	77	Benjamin Crandall.	Eli S. Rolly - - -	76	Eli S. Rolly.
Abraham Seppius - -	81		Rachel Epner - -	82	Betsey Towls.
Garret Van Eps - -	79	Garret Van Eps.	MIDDLEBURGH.		
Nicholas G. Veeder -	78	William Veeder.	Charity Acherson - -	77	Charity Acherson.
Angelica Kane - -	99		Joseph Efner - -	79	Joseph Efner, jr.
Andrew Seaman - -	76	Andrew Seaman.	Henry Yanson - -	80	Henry Ward.
Philip Carner - -	79	Jacob Carner.	Margaret Yanson - -	76	John Yanson.
Jacob Wallace - -	80		Isaac Laraway - -	78	Isaac Laraway.
Frederick Van Patten -	79		Samuel Palmer - -	87	Moses Palmer.
James Van Vorst - -	77	James Van Vorst.	Anna Gridley - -	78	John Gridley.
Joseph Carley • -	80		Benjamin Esterbrooks -	78	Benjamin Esterbrooks.
Reuben Wheaton - -	82	William Wheaton.	Oldren Gates - -	80	Oldren Gates.
PRINCETOWN.			David Lynes - -	76	Samuel Lynes.
Margaret Brougham - -	88	John J. Brougham.	Robert B. White - -	49	Robert B. White.
			Martinus Borst - -	76	Benjamin Borst.
ROTTERDAM.			SHARON.		
William Coyt - -	80	William Coyt.	Sylvanus Cooper - -	89 }	
Bartholomew Schermerhorn -	83	Bartholomew Schermerhorn.	Christopher Moyer -	89 }	Andrew C. Moyer.
John Myers - - -	78		Adolphus Dingman - -	88	Killian Dingman.
Lewis D. Peck - -	75		John Anthony - -	79	Christopher Anthony.
NISKAYUNA.			SEWARD.		
Dinah C. Groat - -	81	Beruch C. Groat.	John A. Strobeck - -	77	Paul Strobeck.
			John Martin - -	80	John Martin.
SCHENECTADA CITY—1st ward.			Conrad Van Wagenen -	87	R. Van Wagenen.
Joseph Peck - -	84	Joseph Peck.	James Vandewaker -	82	James Vandewaker.
Catharine Mercellis -	76	Catharine Mercellis.	SUMMIT.		
C. L. Van Santford -	83	C. L. Van Santford.	Levi Ives - - -	79	Isaac Ives.
2d ward.			Daniel Williams - -	79	Peter Revenburg.
Sarah Vedder - -	75	Sarah Vedder.	Aaron Wheeler - -	77	Benjamin Wheeler.
John Carl - -	83	John Carl.	John Kling - - •	77	John Kling.
Mary Perry - -	82		SCHOHARIE.		
John Van Voast - -	90		Joel Messenger - -	85	Joel Messenger.
John J. Schermerhorn -	76	John Schermerhorn.	John Larkin - -	80	John Larkin.
Rebecca Groat - -	72		Eleanor Burgh - -	67	David Burgh.
Joseph Brittian - -	84		Ebenezer Williams -	90	Ebenezer Williams.
Jacob Leport - -	90	Jacob Leport.	Abram Caton - -	88	Abram Caton.
3d ward.			Francis Becraft - -	87	Jacob Becraft.
Rachel Van Desbogart -	86	Joseph Van Desbogart.	Lydia Smith - -	78	Lorenzo Haugh.
Jerome Barhydt - -	75	Jerome Barhydt.	Henry Plough - -	76	John H. Kyser.
Jacob D. Clute - -	84	Jacob D. Clute.	Jacob Becker - -	87	Peter Becker.
4th ward.			Jabez Holmes - -	86	Henry Rosefelt.
Charles Geer - -	79	Charles Geer.	John Schoolcraft - -	75	Jacob Schoolcraft.
Bartholomew Clute -	75	Bartholomew Clute.	Angelica Shafer - -	78	Christian H. Shafer.
Isaac Imax - -	83	Isaac Imax.	Andrew Slater - -	80	Andrew Slater.
Reuben Finch - -	82		Elizabeth Bivin - -	83	Benjamin Bivin.
Henry Kellar - -	67	Henry Kellar.	BLENHEIM.		
Henry H. Peck - -	77	Henry H. Peck.	Molly Patchen - -	79	Charles Patchen.
			Henry Hager - -	75	Henry Hager.
SCHOHARIE COUNTY.			BROOME.		
CONESVILLE.			James Johnson - -	84	Charles Duncan.
Thaizer Sage - -	74	Thaizer Sage.	John Winans - -	78	Adam Mattice.
CARLISLE.			**SENECA COUNTY.**		
Elizabeth Hutton -	79	George Hutton.	OVID.		
Frederick Utman - -	85	Frederick Utman.	Samuel Ferris - -	86	L. Ferris.
Margaret Hannis - -	82	Maria Johnson.	Thomas Covert - -	86	T. Covert.
COBLESKILL.			Abraham Low - -	85	A. Low.
Philip Becker - -	80	Philip Becker.	Nicholas Huff - -	84	N. Huff.
Abram Coon - -	94	John Coon.	Richard Huff } twins	84	P. J. Huff.
David Zeah - -	84	David Zeah, jr.	ROMULU'S.		
George Patrick - -	85	George Patrick.	Peter Depew - -	84	Peter Depew.
Henry Shafer - -	76	Henry Shafer.	SENECA.		
Elijah Hatchel - -	77	Elijah Hatchel.	Randall Hewitt - -	79	Henry Robinson.
Jacob France - -	80	Jacob France, jr.	Silas M. Wood - -	48	Henry Shoemaker.
Peter L. Myers - -	84	Stephen Myers.	William Sackett - -	86	Cornelius Boylon.
Benjamin Rulin - -	82	Reuben Rulin.	Needham Maynard -	85	Lyman Dodge.
FULTON.			Ezekiel Beebel - -	86	Margaret Jerolomon.
Everett Tripp - -	85	Everett Tripp.	VARICK.		
Isaac Willsey - -	86	Isaac Willsey.	John Pronty - -	77	Thomas Blain.
Jacob Vandyke - -	70	Jacob Vandyke.	Samuel Corwin - -	86	Isaac Atchley.
Powls Moor - -	88	Powls Moor.	COVERT.		
JEFFERSON.			Noah Jennings - - -	80	
Sally Patchen - -	68	Wadwood Patchen.			
Frederick Smith - -	80	Frederick Smith.			
David Gainsey - -	82	Benjamin Heesick.			
Demas Judd - -	87	Demas Judd.			

NEW YORK—NORTHERN DISTRICT—Continued.

Names of pensioners for revolutionary or military services.	Ages.	Names of heads of families with whom pensioners resided June 1, 1840.	Names of pensioners for revolutionary or military services.	Ages.	Names of heads of families with whom pensioners resided June 1, 1840.
SENECA—Continued.			ST. LAWRENCE—Continued.		
LODI.			DE PEYSTER.		
Sylvanus Travers - - -	85	Joseph Benedict.	Joseph Shaw - - -	79	Lebus Curtis.
John Emmons - - -	83	Amos Peterson.	Jonathan Fellows - - -	78	Jari Fellows.
Peter Van Zandt - -	82	John Myers.			
John Garrison - - -	85	Christopher Quick.	OSWEGATCHIE.		
William Stacy - - -	77	Peter Covert.	Sarah June - - -	81	James Beaty.
			Benjamin Salts - - -	78	Benjamin Salts.
TYRE.			Esther Dollestun - - -	78	Benjamin Edsell.
Asa Smith - - -	82	Stephen B. Crane.	Richard Van Ornum - -	82	R. Van Ornum.
Nathaniel Burchard - -	78	Lucas Ekerson.	Noah Spencer - - -	87	Noah Spencer.
Henry Brink - - -	89	Calvin Pinson.	Daniel Chapman - - -	81	Daniel Chapman.
ST. LAWRENCE COUNTY.			MORRISTOWN.		
PARISHVILLE.			Phinehas Maxon - - -	85	Uriah Mead.
Joseph Armsby - - -	76	Joseph Armsby.	M. Demming - - -	80	N. Worden.
Hepsebah Mitchell - -	78	Horatio Mitchell.	Stephen Smith - - -	84	Stephen Smith.
Simeon Howard - - -	79	Jabez Healey.	Sarah K. Thurber - -	91	John Thurber.
Elijah Allen - - -	82	Samuel Hoit.	William Lee - - -	74	William Lee.
HOPKINTON.			HAMMOND.		
Solomon Chittenden - -	78	Asel H. Chittenden.	Emanuel Dake - - -	79	David Fell.
STOCKHOLM.			ROSSIE.		
Ephraim Knapp - - -	83	Moses Knapp.	Henry Apple - - -	86	Thiciam Apple.
Mercy Dunham - - -	78	Reuben Dunham.			
Luke Fletcher - - -	81	Luke Fletcher.	GOUVERNEUR.		
Martin Brockway - -	79	Martin Brockway.	John Garrett - - -	85	Willard Smith.
Rhoda Skinner - - -	83	Ashbel Skinner.	Polly Hulbert - - -	72	Augustus Hulbert.
William Burrows - -	81	William Burrows.	Solomon Cross - - -	82	Solomon Cross.
Thomas Scott - - -	80	James Scott.	Eli Skinner - - -	81	O. S. Skinner.
Elizabeth Whiston - -	83	Joseph W. Glidden.	Stephen Porter - - -	79	Stephen Porter.
LAWRENCE.			HERMON.		
Elizabeth Sanders - -	78	Daniel C. Bastin.	David Page - - -	57	David Page.
Sarah Barnes - - -	74	Joseph Eggleston.	Asher Williams - - -	79	Asher Williams.
NORFOLK.			DE KALB.		
Daniel Bradish - - -	79	Daniel Bradish.	John C. Cook - - -	27	John C. Cook.
Tryphena Collamer - -	79	Dolly H. Collamer.			
Theodorus Woodard - -	79	Theodorus Woodard.	LISBON.		
Elizabeth Lawrence - -	81	Hiram Lawrence.	Isaac Mitchell - - -	80	Isaac Mitchell.
Elijah Brown - - -	84	Ira Brown.	Samuel Wallace - - -	80	Samuel Wallace.
Jemima Sawyer - - -	75	Benjamin Sawyer.	Hughey Willson - - -	84	Hughey Willson.
Griffin Place - - -	78	Nathaniel Flagg.	Amon Lawrence - - -	49	Amon Lawrence.
Guy Carpenter - - -	56	Guy Carpenter.	Jane Turner - - -	89	Jane Turner.
Russel Atwater - - -	79	Phineas Atwater.			
			CANTON.		
MASSENA.			Asa Briggs - - -	88	George Simmon.
Daniel Kenney - - -	80	Hiram Anderson.	Eber. Goodnow - - -	75	Eber. Goodnow.
Elijah Flagg - - -	80	Elijah Flagg.	Joshua Conkey - - -	80	Joshua Conkey.
Daniel Kinney - - -	80	Peabody Kinney.	Lucy Tuttle - - -	95	Azariah Place.
John Polley - - -	79	Foster Polley.	Isaac Robinson - - -	79	Isaac Robinson.
Eben. Polley - - -	53	Eben. Polley, jr.	Lydia Low - - -	72	Alvin C. Low.
John Polley - - -	55	John Polley.	Olive Tuttle - - -	67	James Lemon.
			John Daniels - - -	80	Theodore Trisba.
LOUISVILLE.					
Asa Day - - -	80	Asa Day.	POTSDAM.		
Oliver Barrett - - -	79	Salsbury Barrett.	William Carpenter - -	87	Samuel Carpenter.
Asher Blunt - - -	81	Palmer Blunt.	Eunice Perigo - - -	93	Nathan Giffin.
Elias Kingsley - - -	79	Elias Kingsley.	Elijah Ames - - -	79	Elijah Ames.
			Ebenezer Atwood - -	74	Henry Robinson.
PIERPONT.			Mary Aikins - - -	74	John Aikins.
Frederick Squire - -	45	Frederick Squire.	John Bowker - - -	85	John Bowker.
Reuben Butler - - -	45	Reuben Butler.	Jane Dailey - - -	88	Simeon Hall.
Joseph Dirnick - - -	73	Joseph Dirnick.	Stephen Chandler - -	86	John Chandler.
Nathan Crary - - -	78	Nathan Crary, jr.	Lucy Chandler - - -	76	Charles C. Chandler.
David Bradley - - -	81	David Bradley.	Daniel Shaw - - -	86	Daniel Shaw.
			Nathan Estabrook - -	80	Joel Higley.
RUSSELL.			Nathaniel Parmeter - -	54	Nathaniel Parmeter.
Miles Cook - - -	75	Miles Cook.	Nathan Parmeter - -	81	Nathan Parmeter.
John Knox - - -	81	Henry Knox.	Ruth Brush - - -	77	Ebenezer Brush.
Samuel Barrows - -	73	John Kelsey.	Dyer Williams - - -	81	Dyer Williams.
Abraham Wells - - -	83	Charles Ellis.	Giles Parmele - - -	76	Benjamin Lane.
Gilbert Ray - - -	76	G. B. Clark.	John Fobes - - -	78	John Fobes.
John Gillmore - - -	87		John Moore - - -	82	Trueman Moore.
			Ammi Courier - - -	75	Ammi Courier.
FOWLER.			Sylvanus Willes - - -	84	Wilder Willes.
Ebenezer Parker - -	84	Charles Ryon.			
Jacob Beland - - -	78	Benjamin Ross.	VILLAGE OF POTSDAM.		
			Thomas Palmer - - -	80	Thomas Palmer.
EDWARDS.					
Abel Pratt - - -	83	Abel Pratt.	MADRID.		
Comfort Johnson - - -	87	Hugh McGill.	John Erwin - - -	59	John Erwin.

13

NEW YORK—NORTHERN DISTRICT—Continued.

Names of pensioners for revolutionary or military services.	Ages.	Names of heads of families with whom pensioners resided June 1, 1840.	Names of pensioners for revolutionary or military services.	Ages.	Names of heads of families with whom pensioners resided June 1, 1840.
ST. LAWRENCE—Continued.			**STEUBEN—Continued.**		
MADRID—Continued.			PRATTSBURG.		
Samuel Daniels	78	Samuel Daniels.	Enoch Niles	82	A. D. Voorhees.
Abiram Hurlbut	76	Abiram Hurlbut.	Nathan S. Strong	85	Nathan Strong.
Peter Eaton	58	Peter Eaton.	Erastus Foster	79	E. Foster.
Rebecca Packard	66	Samuel Bailow.	Moor Wilson	90	Moor Wilson.
Lucy Byington	80	Henry Hilliard.	Jonathan Sweet	90	David Herrick.
James Covey	78	James Covey.	John Riker	75	Arthur Odell.
Isaac Buck	77	Leonard Doran.	Isaac Polmentier	80	Isaac Polmentier.
Manasseh Sawyer	81	John Lockwood.	John Spore	80	John Spore.
Isaac Bartholomew	78	Charles D. Bartholomew.	Samuel Orris	80	Saml. Orris.
Margaret Allen	86	Samuel Allen.	Samuel Hotchkiss	86	Saml. Hotchkiss.
Jacob Ridington	81	Nathaniel A. Ridington.	James Sturdevant	84	James Sturdevant.
STEUBEN COUNTY.			POULTNEY.		
READING.			Peter Tyler	80	Luther Parker.
Elijah Bacon	79	Peter Hanmer.	Benjamin Watrous	78	John Watrous.
David Barrett	47	David Barrett.	Phineas Parker	83	Asel Parker.
James Hawkins	81	James Hawkins.	Thomas Horton	76	Thos. Horton.
TYRONE.			BATH.		
John Rapellee	66	John Rapellee.	Lucy Kanna	84	John Handy.
Samuel Bigelow	77	Benjamin Carpenter.	Stephen Smith	79	Stephen Smith.
David Silsbe	47	David Silsbe.	Samuel Thompson	72	Saml. Thompson.
Silas Daily	84	Silas Daily.	John McCoy	90	E. McCoy.
Joseph Paulding	76	Joseph Paulding.	Allen Butler	86	Allen Butler.
John Hight	85		Alexander Arnold	85	Alexander Arnold.
			Nehemiah Sherwood	76	Nehemiah Sherwood.
WAYNE.					
Timothy Hastings	78	Timothy Hastings.	JASPER.		
Anthony Swarthout	81	Asa Swarthout.	Philip Hailing	76	Philip Hailing.
			Andrew Simpson	79	Andrew Simpson.
URBANNA.			Levi Holcomb	74	Levi Holcomb.
David Hawkins	82	David Hawkins.	John Heliker	81	John Heliker.
Amos Stone	81	Amos Stone.	Nathaniel Kellogg	82	James Ingersoll.
Robert Harrison	80	Robert Harrison.			
Nathaniel Kellog	78	Nathaniel Kellog.	HORNELLSVILLE.		
William Foster	76	William Rowley.	Chloe Harding	78	Chloe Harding.
Benjamin Eaton	78	Jonathan Eaton.	Elizabeth Hurlbut	81	Christopher Hurlbut.
Isaac Train	81	William Bird.	John M. Dake	74	Bartlett Dake.
			Stephen Allen	78	John Hood.
BRADFORD.					
Daniel Bartholomew	85	Daniel Bartholomew.	GREENWOOD.		
Abraham Vangorder	75	James Barclay.	Nathaniel Shelden	100	Ithamar Farrell.
Luke Covert	82	Luke Covert.			
			ERWIN.		
ORANGE.			Peter Tice	45	Peter Tice.
Charles Jones	66	Charles James.	Daniel Mulholon	45	Daniel Mulholon.
Abraham Dewitt	72	Abraham Dewitt.			
			CAMERON.		
			Jonas Yournans	83	Abijah Yournans.
HORNBY.			Elias Vananken	79	William A. Loghery.
Christopher Shelts	77	Christopher Shelts.			
Peter Fero	77	Abraham Fero.	CANISTEO.		
			Uriah Stevens	80	George H. Stevens.
CAMPBELL.			John Moore	62	James W. Moore.
David Minor	83	Jedediah Minor.			
Stephen Corbin	80	Alson Pierce.	WOODHULL.		
Reuben Eddy	86	Jesse J. Madison.	John Boldman	74	John Boldman.
William Woodworth	76	William Woodworth.	David Cook	88	David Cook.
Sampson Bixby	81	Samuel Bixby.			
Hinsdell Hammond	80	Simeon Hammond.	TROUPSBURGH.		
			Eli Moffitt	76	Eli Moffitt.
WHEELER.					
Peter Robins	87	Peter Robbins.	PAINTED POST.		
Sylvanus Dygart	80	Sylvanus Dygart.	Joseph Gillet	68	Joseph Gillet.
			Lambert Burget	78	Lambert Burget.
CONHOCTON.					
Ebenezer Pettis	78	Ebenezer Pettis.	ADDISON.		
Walter Patchen	76	Walter Patchin.	Samuel Haskins	100	James F. Haskins.
Mathew Halsey	87	Andrew W. More.	James Miles	77	Isaac Miles.
Isaac Blood	80	Constant Cook.			
Selah B. Benjamin	75	E. Bentley.	DANSVILLE.		
Nicholas Rouse	86	Nicholas Rouse.	Joseph Ogden	77	Joseph Ogden.
Henry Southard	87	Wm. McCaslin.	Amos Holiday	89	Amos Holiday.
Daniel Spike	84	Daniel Spike.	Elnathan Phelps	45	Elnathan Phelps.
Gabriel Dasenbury	90	Seth Dasenbury.	Thos. Buck	79	Joshua Woodard.
			William S. Lemen	79	William S. Lemen.
HOWARD.			James Moore	81	James Moore.
Timothy Chapin	80	Timothy Chapin.	Samuel Gillet	81	Samuel Gillet.
Pardon Dolbie	–	Pardon Dolbie.			
Nathan Delano	75	Nathan Delano.	**TIOGA COUNTY.**		
Ephraim Chambers	68	Ephraim Chambers.	BERKSHIRE.		
Samuel Chriswell	88	J. M. Armstrong.	Elizabeth Prentice	74	Joseph Prentice.
Daniel Everett	76	Daniel Everett.	Sarah Akins	76	Lyman P. Akins.

Names of pensioners for revolutionary or military services.	Ages.	Names of heads of families with whom pensioners resided June 1, 1840.	Names of pensioners for revolutionary or military services.	Ages.	Names of heads of families with whom pensioners resided June 1, 1840.
TIOGA—Continued.			**TOMPKINS—Continued.**		
BERKSHIRE—Continued.			ULYSSES—Continued.		
Bilb Torney	79	Bilb Torney.	Jabez Hanson	79	Jabez Hanson.
Waterman Baker	77	Waterman Baker.	Lemuel Beckwith	79	Lemuel Beckwith.
William Dony	77	John Dony.	John Robinson	84	John Robinson.
Samuel Collings	76	Abbent Collings.			
Olive Leonard	76	Isaac Hitchcock.	ENFIELD.		
			John Flitcher	81	Joseph Flitcher.
BARTON.			Judah Baker	77	Judah Baker.
Luke Saunders	82	Christopher Saunders.	Benjamin Bennett	89	Aham Bennett.
John Hannah	93	William Hannah.			
William Knapp	76	William Knapp, jr.	HECTOR.		
Stephen Mills	89	Stephen Mills.	William Curry	92	Robert Curry.
Ralecha Moor	79	Joseph L. Moor.	Jesse Youngs	48	Jesse Youngs.
Joshua Monroe	77	Joshua Monroe.	Jacob Doty	78	Jeremiah Doty.
			James Smith	85	James Smith.
CANDOR.					
Jasper Taylor	76	Jasper Taylor.	CAROLINE.		
Joel Strong	77	Joel Strong.	Laurence Johnson	83	Laurence Johnson.
Abel Galpin	84	Simeon Galpin.	Solomon Midaugh	84	Solomon Midaugh.
Moses Brink	76	Wilman R. Brink.	Francis Norwood	85	Jonathan Norwood.
Rhoba Tallmadge	79	John Elwell.	Salathiel Dunham	82	Salathiel Dunham.
Samuel Hull	85	Libeus Hull.	James Geeman	78	James Geeman.
Thomas Gridley	79	Adney Gridley.			
Joel Smith	83	George W. Smith.	NEWFIELD.		
Penley Rodgers	82	Penley Rodgers.	John Abbott	77	John Abbott.
Richard Hewitt	78	Richard Hewitt, jr.	Peter Puff	82	John Puff.
			Job Beckwith	80	Job Beckwith.
NICHOLS.					
Griffin Kinyon	87	Daniel Burch.	LANSING.		
Anna Miens	81	William Osborn.	William Hunt	76	William Hunt.
Mercy Lyans	74	Sidney Baldwin.	Mary Bishop	75	Lambert Bishop.
Francis Conyell	82	Francis Conyell.	Ebenezer Brown	87	Ebenezer Brown.
			Zenas Conger	84	Zenas Conger.
NEWARK.					
Abraham Wright	83	Sanford Comstock.	DRYDEN.		
Samuel Johnson	83	Samuel Johnson.	Catharine Townley	71	Henry Townley.
Phineas Spaulden	80	John Henman.	Lydia Williams	82	Louis Clark.
Joseph Jones	88	Joseph Jones.	Samuel Knapp	82	Samuel Knapp.
			Joseph Mosley	79	Joseph J. Mosley.
OWEGO.			Samuel Fox	81	Samuel Fox.
Richard Walen	80	Hiram Dennison.	Henry Steward	74	Henry Steward.
Amos Mead	84	Amos Mead.	George McCutcheon	80	George McCutcheon
Jeremiah French	81	Jeremiah French.	Isaac Carmer	80	Isaac Carmer.
John Jewitt	83	John Jewitt.	Jonathan Sperry	82	Rexford Sperry.
Asa Camp	81	Asa Camp.	Edward Griswold	82	Timothy Stone.
Joseph Smith	83	Paddock Smith.	Elias Laraby	74	Elias Laraby.
Bethiah Tuesdell	80	Jonathan Tuesdell.	Moses Stephens	84	Moses Stephens.
Mary Pratt	80	Abijah Pratt.			
Marcus Williamson	81	Marcus Williamson.	GROTON.		
G. Cortrite	86	Oso Hall.	Abel Cobb	77	Abel Cobb.
Richard Sarles	87	Richard Sarles.	Simon Loomis	82	Simon Loomis.
James Holmes	85	James Holmes.	Ede Hatch	79	Ede Hatch.
			Admatha Blodget	81	Admatha Blodget.
OWEGO VILLAGE.			Hulah Eldrege	74	Elisha Eldrege.
Catharine Frank	77	John Frank.	Ama Austin	82	Francis F. Hasting.
Elijah Dewey	78	Alanson Dean.	Lodowick Weaver	77	Denison Weaver.
Nathaniel Dearborn	81	Asa Dearborn.	Ziporah Virgil	72	Philip Luther.
			Isaac Seamans	82	Isaac Seamans.
RICHFORD.			Alexander Miller	84	John Hopkins.
Eli Osborn	81	Eli Osborn.	John Brown	81	John R. Brown.
Eliakim Hamilton	84	Eliakim Hamilton.	Philemon Tiffany	78	Noah Tiffany.
Mathias Park	79	Whiting Russell.	George McKenzie	85	George McKenzie.
			Gedor Woodruff	79	Gedor Woodruff.
SPENCER.			Eunice Brabrook	82	William Brabrook.
Clatira Cumings	64	Daniel McQuigg.	Thomas Benedict	87	Thomas Benedict.
Hannah Martin	73	Ward Martin.			
John Jones	79	John Jones.	DANBY.		
Tunis Riker	70	Tunis Riker.	John S. Huntington		John S. Huntington.
Richard Ferris	78	Richard Ferris.	Mathias Mount	84	Mathias Mount.
			Jemima Babb	83	Benjamin Elliott.
TIOGA.			Isaac Wright	82	Isaac Wright.
Josiah Cleveland	85	Elijah Cleveland.	Ezekiel Montgomery	78	Ezekiel Montgomery.
Stephen Emerson	88	Stephen Emerson.	Job Lockwood	84	Titus Dawson.
			Peter Demoriest	83	Gradis Vaninwagen.
TOMPKINS COUNTY.			William Swartwout	87	James Swartwout.
ITHACA.			Lament Duplex	85	George Duplex.
Britton Head	77	Britton Head.	John Bruce	82	John Bruce.
ULYSSES.			**WASHINGTON COUNTY.**		
Jacob Levingston	53	Jacob Levingston.	SALEM.		
Jeptha Lee	77	Jeptha Lee.	George Field	80	Perry Wilkinson.
Isaac Markhams	86	Isaac Markhams.	James Harvey	46	James Harvey.
Conrad Teetu	84	Conrad Teetu.			

NEW YORK—NORTHERN DISTRICT—Continued.

Names of pensioners for revolutionary or military services.	Ages.	Names of heads of families with whom pensioners resided June 1, 1840.	Names of pensioners for revolutionary or military services.	Ages.	Names of heads of families with whom pensioners resided June 1, 1840.
WASHINGTON—Continued.			**WASHINGTON—Continued.**		
SALEM—Continued.			KINGSBURY—Continued.		
Robert Stewart	73	Robert Stewart.	Elijah Butterfield	77	Elijah Butterfield.
Sarah Willson	70	N. W. Willson.	Uriah Yates	87	Augustus Underhill.
Robert McCarter	87	Robert Hanna, jr.	Philip Loraway	82	Phipps Loraway.
Sarah Sanderson	80	Lyman Sanderson.	John King	75	John King.
Sarah McNish	82	William McNish.	ARGYLE.		
George Fowler	79	George Fowler.	John Smith	76	John Smith.
Asa Fitch	74	Asa Fitch.	HARTFORD.		
Margaret Gray	75	Margaret Gray.	Asher Ford	79	Asher Ford.
HEBRON.			Samuel Taylor	78	Samuel Taylor.
Eunice Tyrrell	78	Eunice Tyrrell.	JACKSON.		
John Willson	85	John Willson.	Benjamin Scott	83	Anderson Simpson.
James Rogers	77	James Rogers.	CAMBRIDGE.		
Ebenezer Chapman	77	Ebenezer Chapman.	Azor Bonton	75	John Donehugh.
HAMPTON.			FORT EDWARD.		
Thomas Todd	79	Thomas Todd.	Zachariah Reynolds	82	William Bugber.
Eleazer Lyman	74	Eleazer Lyman, jr.	Nathan Hatch	82	Nathan Hatch.
Samuel Beeman	84	Samuel Beeman.	Thomas Galusha	87	John Galusha.
Caleb Warren	76	Caleb Warren.	DRESDEN.		
Benjamin C. Owen	77	Benjamin C. Owen.	Thomas Huntington	83	Erastus Huntington.
Joseph C. O'Brien	44	Mary O'Brien.			
GRANVILLE.			**WAYNE COUNTY.**		
Reuben Van Gilder	80	Reuben Van Gilder.	ARCADIA.		
Nehemiah Hewlet	75	Nehemiah Hewlet.	Wessel Cornue	76	Wessel Cornue.
Noah Day	83	Noah Day.	Shevah Houghton	85	
Benijah Hill	85	Benijah Hill.	Thomas Treet	77	
Jonathan Brown	80	Jonathan Brown.	George Babcock	77	George Babcock.
William Town	81	Benjamin Brown.	MARION.		
Simeon Howard	87	Lyman Howard.	Obediah Archer	79	John W. Archer.
Samuel Standish	86	Samuel Standish.	Solomon Leonard	81	Solomon Leonard.
Jacob Allen	79	Jacob Allen.	ONTARIO.		
John Kirkland	82	Edwin S. Kirkland.	John Mack	82	Abraham Mack.
Jesse Averill	86	Jesse Averill, jr.	John Speller	74	
Lewis Hatch	80	Lewis Hatch.	Willard Church	82	Willard Church.
Samuel Weeks	82	Harry Weeks.	PALMYRA.		
Mason Law	75	Mason Law.	William Jackways	81	William Jackways.
Isaac Doty	81	Levi Doty.	Daniel Wood	83	Daniel Wood.
FORT ANN.			Durfee Hicks	83	Gardner Hicks.
Moses Harvey	75	Moses Harvey.	James G. Smith	56	
Sally Root	78	Lucy Root.	WALWORTH.		
David Butler	50	David Butler.	Joseph Carey	83	Joseph Carey.
George Clark	81	George Clark.	WILLIAMSON.		
Lucinda Weller	78	Lucinda Weller.	James Calhoun	77	James Calhoun.
Israel Lamb	78	Israel Lamb.	Isaac Curtiss	86	Isaac Curtiss.
John Parish	89	John Parish.	Marshal Barmore	84	
Samuel Fenton	83	Samuel Fenton.	Valentine Hahn	80	Valentine Hahn.
Benjamin Cutter	78	Benjamin Cutter.	BUTLER.		
John Granger	79	John Granger.	Simeon Merrill	80	Simeon Merrill.
Jenkins White	79	John White.	Roger Olmstead	76	Philo Olmstead.
Michael Mason	80	Ebenezer Mason.	Reuben Barnes	84	Reuben Barnes.
Jonathan Kingsley	80	Jonathan Kingsly.	Ezekiel Scott	81	Ezekiel Scott.
John Simmons	79	John Simmons.	Josiah Munson	75	Hiram Munson.
Dorcas Goss	87	Benjamin Bacon.	Ebenezer Pierce	78	Ebenezer Pierce.
William Patison	80	William Patison.	GALEN.		
Amos Allen	88	Amos Allen.	Beeri Foot	78	Albert Foot.
John Baker	84	John Baker.	Benjamin McClary	59	Benjamin McClary.
WHITE HALL.			John Selfridge	82	Sarah Smith.
Peleg Dewey	79	George Johnson.	Timothy McIntosh	80	Timothy McIntosh.
Jonathan Reynolds	99	Nicholas Reynolds.	Gilbert Hooker	82	Zina Hooker.
Judith Burbank	71	John S. Burbank.	LYONS.		
Levi Falcounbury	79	Levi W. Falcounbury.	Josiah Dunning	86	John Dunning.
Reuben Smalley	78	Reuben Smalley.	Jacob Patrick	76	Jacob Patrick.
Simeon Hotchkiss	85	John Meriam.	Nathan Smith	79	Nathan Smith.
Abigail Russell	74	Mary Ann Prindle.	Elijah Whiting	82	Elijah Whiting.
Hannah Jones	77	Dennis Jones.	David Plidden	81	David Plidden.
Israel Warner	72	Israel Warner.	Benjamin Avery	82	Cyrus Avery.
John Porter	77	John N. Porter.	ROSE.		
Sarah Parrons	89	Arel Parrons.	John Featherly	80	John Featherly.
Annah Barrett	76	L. Bartholomew.	Emanuel Winfield	79	Reuben S. Parshal.
KINGSBURY.					
Joshua Harris	80	Joshua Harris.			
John Gray	84	William Gray.			
Simeon Moss	83	Simeon Moss.			
Asa Barney	83	Throop Barney.			
Solomon Day	78	Eliza Day.			
William Moore	79	William Moore.			
Roger Haladay	75	Roger Haladay.			

NEW YORK—NORTHERN DISTRICT—Continued.

Names of pensioners for revolutionary or military services.	Ages.	Names of heads of families with whom pensioners resided June 1, 1840.	Names of pensioners for revolutionary or military services.	Ages.	Names of heads of families with whom pensioners resided June 1, 1840.
WAYNE—Continued.			**WARREN—Continued.**		
SODUS.			HORICON.		
James Green	82	Isaac R. Green.	David Culver	82	David Culver.
Elizabeth Fitzhue	74	Elizabeth Fitzhue.	Hamsah Dickerson	84	Samuel C. Dickerson.
Jonathan Clemmons	85	Jonathan Clemmons.			
John Norris	86	John Norris.	CHESTER.		
Philip Demarest	79	Philip Demarest.	Ezekiel Ellis	76	Ezekiel Ellis.
			Seba Higbey	77	Seba Higbey.
SAVANNAH.			Isaac Cara	82	Alpha Cara.
Moses Lent	78	Moses Lent.	Benjamin Rathburn	75	Jonathan Mead.
Jabez Carter	80	Benjamin S. Carter.	William Lake	80	William Lake.
Francis Needham	73	Francis Needham.	Augustus Angle	80	Augustus Angle.
Benjamin Derrell	75	Miles Hodges.	Benjamin Knap	75	Benjamin Knap.
			Samuel Grisel	80	Thomas Grissel.
HURON.					
Charles Kent	78	Charles Kent.	JOHNSBURG.		
Darius Howard	75	Darius Howard.	Abigail Pasco	74	Leonard Pasco.
Abm. Vas Sise	77	Morgan Wilde.	Barney Hewit	84	Barney Hewit.
Paul Sherman	81	Paul Sherman.	John Ward	86	John Ward.
Gad Hall	81	Gad Hall.	Abiram Galutia	77	Reuben Galutia.
Bulkley Johnson	83	Daniel Chase.	Nehemiah Grovier	86	Nehemiah Grovier.
WOLCOTT.			WARRENSBURG.		
Jacob Ward	84	Alven Ward.	Harvey Nuton	83	Dick Nuton.
Jerusha Pease	80	David H. Pease.	Stephen Millard	81	Stephen Millard.
			Joshua Combs	76	Joshua Combs.
WARREN COUNTY.			**YATES COUNTY.**		
LUZERNE.			BENTON.		
Abner Reehordron	81	Abner Reehordron.	Titus Harman	73	Titus Harman.
Jacob Randal	81	Moses Randal.	Asa Olcott	80	Benjamin Havens.
			Isaac Whitney	91	Jacob Whitney.
CALDWELL.			John McLewin	93	W. F. McLewin.
Sarah Pike	65	Sarah Pike.	William Bates	79	William Bates.
			Daniel Brown	82	Daniel Brown.
HAGUE.					
Samuel Patchin	82	John Patchin.	BARRINGTON.		
John Holman	69	John Holman.	Joseph Finton	79	Joseph Finton.
QUEENSBURY.			ITALY.		
Ebenezer Demask	82	Ebenezer Demask.	William Smith	75	Daniel Smith.
John Kay	83	John Kay.	Thomas Treat	78	Waster Berk.
David Barber	73	Hiram Barber.			
Anson Comstock	76	Daniel Comstock.	JERUSALEM.		
Joseph Reed	77	Joseph Reed.	Elisha Benedict	80	N. G. Benedict.
			Castle Daines	91	Castle Daines.
ATHOL.			Jacob Fradenburgh	81	James Fradenburgh.
William C. Allen	87	William C. Allen.	John Beal	84	John Beal.
Asa Smith	88	Asa Smith.			
Samuel Ross	76	Samuel Ross.	MILO.		
Stephen Griffing	86	Nathaniel Griffing,	Samuel Abby	80	Samuel Abby.
BOLTON.			MIDDLESEX.		
Reuben Smith	81	Reuben Smith.	Michael Pearce	84	Michael Pearce.
Daniel Nims	78	Daniel Nims.	Robert McNair	85	Jacob Van.
Jonathan Fish	78	John K. Fish.	John Cole	81	John Walford.
John Bates	86	Joseph Putney.			
Zaith Tucker	81	Zaith Tucker.	POTTER.		
Timothy S. Barton	81	Perley Barton.	Isaac Hoard	83	Isaac Hoard.
John Dickson	81	John Dickson.	Isaac Page	82	David Page.
Nehemiah Brown	73	Nehemiah Brown.	Philip Dinturff	88	Philip Dinturff.

NEW YORK—SOUTHERN DISTRICT.

CITY OF NEW YORK.			CITY OF NEW YORK—Continued.		
1st ward.			3d ward—Continued.		
None.			Edward Van Wyck	24	John K. Liston.
2d ward.			Mary Dunscomb	79	Mary Dunscomb.
Bartholomew Delapier	60	Bartholomew Delapier.	Abner Osborn	78	Ithamar Osborn.
3d ward.			Daniel Palmer	44	Daniel Palmer.
William Dodge	81	William Dodge.	Ann G. McCullough	57	Boyden, Coleman, & Stetson.
Jarret Stilwell	82	Jarret Stilwell.	4th ward.		
Abigail Woodruff	81	William Woodruff.	None.		
Maria Varick	78	Maria Varick.	5th ward.		
Abraham B. Martling	79	Abraham B. Martling.	Jacob Van Tassel	96	Jacob Van Tassel.
Sarah Cunningham	73	Harriet N. Mann.	Ebenezer Belknap	76	Ebenezer Belknap.
Alexander Moran	15	Jane Haight.	Joseph Whitley	81	Joseph Whitley.
Lucretia Stevens	84	Samuel Stevens.			
Dinah Benson	79	Dinah Benson.			

NEW YORK—SOUTHERN DISTRICT—Continued.

Names of pensioners for revolutionary or military services.	Ages.	Names of heads of families with whom pensioners resided June 1, 1840.	Names of pensioners for revolutionary or military services.	Ages.	Names of heads of families with whom pensioners resided June 1, 1840.
CITY OF NEW YORK—Continued.			GREEN—Continued.		
6th ward.			WINDHAM—Continued.		
None.			Reuben White - - -	89	Giles White.
7th ward.			William Henson - -	79	William Henson.
William Gayler - - -	88	Mary Wardaline.	James Tompkins - - -	85	Nicholas Nicholas.
William Rowdon - -	76	William Rowdon.	PRATTSVILLE.		
Samuel Cornwell - -	90	Samuel Cornwell.	Elias Bates - - -	80	Elias Bates.
Roger Sherman - -	92	Roger Worden.	Asel Hull - - - -	81	Isaac P. Hull.
8th ward.			LEXINGTON.		
Henry Willis - -	80	Henry Willis.	David Foster - - -	84	Ruth Foster.
Enoch Hoyt - - -	79	Enoch Hoyt.	Peter T. Smith - -	80	James Smith.
Uriah Travis - -	95	Robert Travis.	Elijah Towner - -	82	Elijah Towner.
9th ward.			Chester Hull - - -	74	Nathaniel Hull.
Alletta Storms - - -	82	Alletta Storms.	Ebenezer Johnson - -	77	Ebenezer Johnson.
Charles Gilmore - -	81	Charles Gilmore.	Adnah Beach - - -	81	Adnah Beach.
Samuel McGee - -	77	Samuel McGee.	Daniel Angle - - -	109	Jacob Angle.
Asa Holden - -	79	Asa Holden.	HUNTER.		
John De Camp - -	79	John De Camp.	Wilhelmus France - -	86	Wilhelmus France.
Charles Beakley - -	82	Christian Beakley.	CAIRO.		
Hulda Taylor - -	78	Maria A. Hoag.	William Burton - - -	77	William Burton.
Morris Thorp - -	35	Ezra Thorp.	Seth Warner - - -	77	Seth Warner.
10th ward.			Williams Avery - -	76	Williams Avery.
Richard Nixon - -	82	Richard Nixon.	Jeremiah Mandigo - -	85	Archibald Mandigo.
Aaron Dupee - - -	88		Nathan Lockwood - -	81	Nathan Lockwood.
Josiah W. Wentworth -	86		Ethan Rogers - - -	82	Ethan Rogers.
11th ward.			Eliab Alden - - -	78	Eliab Alden.
Daniel Banks - -	83	Daniel Banks.	Amos Finch - - -	85	Amos Finch.
Charles Gilman - -	82	Charles Gilman.	ATHENS.		
12th ward.			Lemuel Raymond - -	77	Lemuel Raymond.
None.			Andrew Stover - - -	84	William G. Edwards.
13th ward.			CATTSKILL.		
Thomas Kearns - -	69	Richard Newman.	David Porter - - -	79	David Porter.
James Miner - - -	74	Thomas Miner.	Abijah Dewey - - -	75	Lafayette Delamater.
Robert Leonard - -	73	Robert Leonard.	Ezekiel Whitney - -	90	David Whitney.
14th ward.			Peter P. Egner - - -	83	Henry Egner.
Thomas Ayres - -	86	James McFallen.	ULSTER COUNTY.		
Daniel Smith - -	86	Daniel Smith.	ESOPUS.		
15th ward.			William Smith - - -	80	William Smith.
Jonathan Owens - -	79	Ruth Owens.	Catharine Ostrander - -	70	Catharine Ostrander.
Dennis Striker - -	80	Dennis Striker.	William Teerpening - -	87	William Teerpening.
Seba Brinkerhoff - -	82	Seba Brinkerhoff.	NEW PALTZ.		
Charles Anderson - -	82	Charles Anderson.	John Dunn - - - -	79	John Dunn.
William Popham - -	87	William S. Popham.	Bridget Deyo - - -	81	Benjamin A. Deyo.
John A. Harring - -	90	John A. Harring.	Jemima Wilklow - -	73	Jemima Wilklow.
James Ervin - -	87	John B. Ervin.	John Ruger - - -	78	John Ruger.
17th ward.			John York - - -	81	John York.
Peter Tappan - -	76	Peter Tappan.	MARLBOROUGH.		
Elias Varbenscoter - -	96	C. Varbenscoter.	Jacob Lawson - - -	87	Jacob Lawson, sen.
Abraham Legget - -	87	J. L. Smith.	Andrew Ely - - -	84	Andrew Ely.
GREEN COUNTY.			PLATTEKILL.		
COXSACKIE.			Joseph Rhodes - -	83	Joseph Rhodes.
Peter Curtis - - -	28	Oliver Van Valin.	Jonathan Tompkins - -	87	Jane Berrian.
Nicholas Hoose - -	81	Nicholas Hoose.	Samuel Brodhead - -	82	Ann Cab.
NEW BALTIMORE.			SHAWANGUNK.		
Henry Bogardus - -	88	Jacob Slater.	John Irvin - - -	81	John Irvin.
James Yale - -	75	James Yale.	Simon Lambertson - -	83	Simon Lambertson.
GREENVILLE.			Eleanor Johnson - -	84	Christian Roosa.
Reuben Rundell - -	83	Reuben Rundell, jr.	HURLEY.		
Benjamin Reynolds - -	79	Benjamin Reynolds.	Frederick Bush - - -	90	Thomas Hallock.
Aelel Wakeley - -	79	Russel Wakeley.	WOODSTOCK.		
Caleb Foster - -	78	Richard Foster.	Henry Plinley - - -	96	Henry Plinley.
Daniel Lake - -	73	Daniel Lake.	SHANDAKEN.		
Peter Simpson - -	82	Peter Simpson.	James Rosakrans - -	87	James Rosakrans.
Joshua Baker - -	81	Joshua Baker.	Frederick Myers - -	85	Frederick Myers.
Reuben Stevens - -	79	John N. Bogardus.	KINGSTON.		
Richard Tripp - -	87	Richard Tripp.	Cornelius Winne - -	76	Cornelius Winne.
DURHAM.			Elizabeth Winne - -	84	Gilbert Cooper.
John Wright - -	81	Silvester Hanson.	Abm. Whitaker - -	80	James S. Whitaker.
Moses Earle - -	79	Moses Earle.	Herman Munkier - -	84	Peter Van Aken.
Augustus Pratt - -	89	Augustus Pratt.			
WINDHAM.					
Orange Munson - -	76	John Munson.			
Michael G. Kuran -	82	Peter Kuran.			
David Travis - -	83	Charles Frayer.			
Eli P. Robinson - -	58	Eli P. Robinson.			
Leisure Miller - -	81	Jeremiah Miller.			
Oliver Lommis - -	80	Willis Lommis.			

Names of pensioners for revolutionary or military services.	Ages.	Names of heads of families with whom pensioners resided June 1, 1840.	Names of pensioners for revolutionary or military services.	Ages.	Names of heads of families with whom pensioners resided June 1, 1840.
ULSTER—Continued.			**SULLIVAN—Continued.**		
KINGSTON—Continued.			THOMPSON.		
Jacob Brink	96	William J. Brink.	Jonathan Brown	78	Jonathan Brown.
John E. Roosa	79	Stephen Ousterhoudt.	Asahael Frisbee	84	Asahael Frisbee.
Adam Traver	80	Philip Folandt.	Mrs. Avis Coger	78	Charles P. Coger.
			Catharine Munroe	80	John Munroe.
SAUGERTIES.			John Garrett	87	Trueman Strong.
Margaret Brink	87	James Brink.	Stephen Stratton	87	Benjamin Beardsley.
Adam Brink	78	Martin Snyder.	Nathaniel Travis	80	Elias Champlin.
Wilhelmus Emerick	82	William H. Emerick.	Ezekiel Maston	80	Ezekiel Mastin.
Ephraim Myers	81	John S. Myers.	Zepheniah Bowers	81	Zepheniah Bowers.
John Crawford	78	John Crawford.	Samuel Jones	78	Samuel Jones.
Adam France	82	Adam France.	Ebenezer Lounsbury	85	Ebenezer Lounsbury.
OLIVE.			COCHECTON.		
Joseph Fish	80	Joseph Fish.	Jacob Mariquot	76	Jacob Mariquot.
Jon. Elmendorf	82	Jon. Elmendorf.			
Abraham Winfield	78	Abraham Winfield.	LUMBERLAND.		
Andrew Davis	82	Andrew Davis.	Daniel Skinner	93	Daniel Skinner.
Benjamin Buley	80		Elizabeth Peck	88	Adam White.
Uriah Hill	84				
			LIBERTY.		
MARLBOROUGH.			William Fitch	75	William Fitch.
Abraham Masten	78	Michael Enderly.	Ann Partridge	80	Merrit Hurd.
Mary Lyons	82	Isaac Lyons.	Reuben Lewis	86	Reuben Lewis.
Christopher Snyder	84	Christopher Snyder.	Ede Shaw	80	Amos Shaw.
John Morris	81	Dewalt Morris.	John Gray	102	William Gray.
Blandinah Janson	83	Hulbert Elmondorf.	James Douglass	83	James Douglass.
Benjamin A. Krun	81	Peter Snyder.			
Cornelius Krun	85	James C. Krun.	ROCKLAND.		
Jacob J. Roosa	79	Jacob J. Roosa.	Jonathan French	76	Gabriel Beech.
Catharine Oliver	75	Jacobus Hardenbergh.	David Joscelyn	79	David Joscelyn.
Jacob P. Markle	77	Jacob P. Markle.	Mary Mott	92	Thomas Mott.
Garret Dubois	77	Conrad Dubois.	John Cornelius Van Sice	80	Hiram Rose.
ROCHESTER.					
Penelope Keldar	84	Henry Keldar.	**COLUMBIA COUNTY.**		
Benjamin Rider	80	John J. Davis.	CHATHAM.		
Cornelius Quick	83	Cornelius Quick.	Isaac Beeman	85	Joseph Ashley.
William Turner	81	William Turner.	Hannah Gillet	82	Abram Palmer.
John Depuy	81	James Hardenbergh.	Anna Beebe	82	Andrew Lovejoy.
George P. Frost	83	George P. Frost.	Harvey Gaylor	56	Harvey Gaylor.
			Hosea Birge	80	Hosea Birge.
WAWARSING.			Edward Lay	78	Edward Lay.
Thomas Crosman	82	Thomas Crosman.	James Simpson	87	James Simpson.
Cornelius Baldwin	85	Ezekiel Baldwin.	Guy Lester	79	Guy Lester.
Maria Wilson	71	Peter Bull.			
Henry T. Oosterhoudt	75	Henry T. Oosterhoudt.	NEW LEBANON.		
Abraham Hornbeck	77	Abraham Hornbeck.	Asa Evans	87	William H. Baley.
			Jane Wright	72	Jane Wright.
SULLIVAN COUNTY.			Cornelius Earle	81	Cornelius Earle.
FALLSBURG.			Ezra Gates	93	Elias Gates.
John Simpson	77	John Simpson.	Seba Moses	78	Seba Moses.
John Tappan	67	James Tappan.	Ezekiel Merrill	84	Zenas Goodrich.
John Eller	77	John Eller.	Zenas Goodrich	78	Zenas Goodrich.
Mary Tarket	76	Francis Tarket.	Nathan Young	52	Nathan Young.
Jabez Wakeman	70	Elijah Beardsley.	Eliab Perkins	84	Orson Hayward.
			Peleg Spencer	81	Peleg Spencer.
NEVERSINK.			Lucretia Murdock	79	John Murdock.
Joab Bowers	75	Joab Bowers.			
Hannah Townsend	83	Joshua Townsend.	CANAAN.		
James Davenport	80	James Davenport.	Daniel Christie	69	Daniel Christie.
Jeremiah Smith	78	Jeremiah Smith.	Ælizabeth Freeman	63	John Dana.
Sands Raymond	79	Sands Raymond.	Joseph Wilbur	89	Alexander Wilson.
Mrs. Amy Childs	75	Richard D. Childs.	Abigail Marks	74	Abigail Marks.
Philip Mullin	78	Philip Mullin.	Dulana Law	84	Hezekiah Marks.
Peter Hornbeck	81	Peter Hornbeck.	Sarah Frisbee	88	Lewis Frisbee.
John Barns	80	Ebner Townsend.	Stephen Churchifl	78	Stephen Churchill.
Peter Coon	87	Peter Coon.	Anna Parks	78	Anna Parks.
Hannah Low	70	Hannah Low.	James Aikin	86	James Aikin.
Philip Quick	80	Peter Lercy.			
			AUSTERLITZ.		
MAMAKATING.			Sarah Gott	75	Sarah Gott.
John Woodward	85	John Woodward.	Seth Jennings	76	Seth Jennings.
Ebenezer Price	82	Ebenezer Price.	Jacob Bice	81	Jacob Bice.
Jemima Lockwood	80	Alfred Lockwood.	Nathan Lester	85	Elisha Curtis.
David Dickerson	84	David Dickerson.	John Harmon	79	Ruth Crouter.
Elizabeth Dalloway	107	Jacob Dalloway.	Jonathan Benton	82	Calvin Killogg.
Sarah Berry	79	John F. Brown.	Abigail Doty	78	Ebenezer P. Doty.
Wilhelmus Kerkendall	78	Henry Kerkendall.	James Platt	80	James Platt.
Sarah Cremer	71	Mrs. S. Cremer.	Milla Evans	76	Tunis Moore.
Sarah Clearwater	83	Hiram Clearwater.	Joseph Foot	79	Joseph Foot.
Jacob Mastin	77	Jacob Mastin.	Story Gott	74	Story Gott.
			Hussy Stratten	86	John P. Harde.

NEW YORK—SOUTHERN DISTRICT—Continued.

Names of pensioners for revolutionary or military services.	Ages.	Names of heads of families with whom pensioners resided June 1, 1840.	Names of pensioners for revolutionary or military services.	Ages.	Names of heads of families with whom pensioners resided June 1, 1840.
COLUMBIA—Continued.			**PUTNAM**—Continued.		
GHENT.			*PUTNAM VALLEY*—Continued.		
Jacob Maul - - -	82	Jacob Maul.	Amos Odell - - -	85	Aaron Odell.
John Luffman - -	90	Thomas Luffman.	Rufus Gillet - - -	80	Rufus Gillet.
John Halsapple -	84	William Halsapple.	*KENT.*		
John Maul - - -	86	Jacob J. Maul.	Josiah Smawley - -	79	Josiah Smawley.
KINDERHOOK.			Gilbert Carragan - -	82	Gilbert Carragan.
John Clapper - - -	81	John Clapper.	Stephen Hults - -	83	Isaac Hults.
Ann M. Stufflebun -	70	David Mickle.	William Barrit - -	92	William Barrit.
STUYVESANT.			Peter Robertson - -	82	Peter Roberison.
Elizabeth Vosburgh -	77	John P. Vosburgh.	*SOUTHEAST.*		
Christopher Hutton -	83	Isaac Hutton.	Samuel Purdy - -	79	Samuel Purdy.
Wm. Van Valkenburgh -	77	Wm. Van Valkenburgh.	Amos Niffin - -	83	Charles Niffin.
STOCKPORT.			Hannah Townsend - -	85	William Townsend.
Barrust Van Valkenburgh	84	Jas. Van Valkenburgh.	William Reneval - -	86	Nathaniel Heverland.
Lydia Butler - -	71	Lydia Butler.	*PATERSON.*		
CLAVERACK.			Benjamin Cowl - -	77	Benjamin Cowl.
Mary Kilmer - -	83	Peter Brasee.	Hannah Haight - -	76	David D. Haight.
Jacob Eeletyne - -	78	Jacob Eeletyne.	**WESTCHESTER COUNTY.**		
Henry W. Phillips -	84	Wm. Phillips.	*MOUNT PLEASANT.*		
HILLSDALE.			Elizabeth Trobridge -	80	B. W. Trumbull.
Henry Speed - -	74	Henry Speed.	Abraham Hitchcock -	75	William Stanton.
Eli Rood - - -	81	Eli Rood.	William Davids - -	75	Moses Stanton.
Comfort Bullock - -	77	Major Bullock.	Peter Paulding - -	91	John Paulding.
Dorothy Hawley - -	92	Amos Hawley.	Benjamin Acker - -	80	Peter Davids.
James Shepherd - -	77	Albert Shepherd.	Phele Ansen - -	80	Jemima Miller.
Hannah Tyle - -	81	Archibald Olmsted.	Samuel Miller - -	84	Samuel Miller.
John Jones - - -	76	Moses Jones.	Elizabeth Van Tassel -	84	John Van Tassel.
Parley Foster - -	81	Parley Foster.	Letty Yerks - -	84	Thomas Lyon.
Wm. Scutt - - -	83	Wm. Scutt.	Joseph Benedict - -	90	John Newman.
COPAKE.			Jesse Fisher - -	85	Smith Clason.
Catharine Pulver - -	83	John Silvernail.	John Yerks - -	82	John Yerks.
GALLATIN.			Stephen Mills - -	87	Almshouse.
Winneson Brasee - -	79	Winneson Brasee.	*GREENBURGH.*		
Joseph Bush - -	75	John T. Bush.	Mary Dean - -	85	Mary Hammond.
TAGHKANIC.			Lane Storms - -	80	Jonathan Bayles.
Saml. Myres - - -	73	Abraham Myres.	Abraham Martling -	79	Abraham Martling.
LIVINGSTON.			Catharine Bancker -	82	Garrett Storms.
Philip Race - - -	75	Henry Best.	Joel Cock - - -	81	Jane Vicar.
John Root - - -	78	John Root.	Dennis Crouk - -	78	Dennis Crouk.
Saml. Ten Broeck -	95	Leonard W. Ten Broeck.	*NORTH CASTLE.*		
GERMANTOWN.			Alice Weycoff - -	80	Samuel Palmer.
William Snyder - -	84	William Snyder.	Michael Foster - -	79	Samuel Foster.
Catharine Salpaugh -	78	Philip Salpaugh.	Joseph Waring - -	89	David D. Hemted.
Nicholas Halsapple -	86	Nicholas Halsapple.	Samuel Miller - -	83	Joseph Teeks.
Henry Dick - -	79	Henry Dick.	John Smith - - -	83	Silas Southerland.
1ST WARD HUDSON.			*HARRISON.*		
Deborah Reynolds -	74	Thos. W. Smith.	Simeon Tyler - -	80	William Tyler.
Polly Younglowe -	77	Jacob Whitbeck.	*RYE.*		
Hannah Parkman -	73	Wm. E. Parkman.	Charles McDonald -	82	Charles McDonald.
Abigail Allen - -	81	Oliver Allen.	*CORTLANDT.*		
2D WARD HUDSON.			Isaac Conklin - -	90	Isaac Conklin.
Maria Ten Broeck -	84	Maria Ville.	Samuel Wheeler - -	80	Samuel Wheeler.
Prosper Hosmer - -	83	Secon Gantley.	Henry C. Vought - -	80	Henry Christian.
John Hardie - -	88	Abrom T. Hardie.	John Peterson - -	90	John Peterson.
John Kempor - -	84	John Kempor.	*NEW CASTLE.*		
John Jaquins - -	77	Candy Jaquins.	Oliver Stewart - -	77	Oliver Stewart.
GREENPORT.			William Cooney - -	83	Stephen Archer.
John Elindorf - -	88	William Van Dusen.	*YORKTOWN.*		
Nicholas Stickles -	85	Peter Stickles.	Abraham Regna - -	81	Abraham Regna.
PUTNAM COUNTY.			*LEWISBORO.*		
PHILLIPSTOWN.			Stephen Van Tassel -	93	Joshua Culver.
James Darrow - -	75	James Darrow.	Samuel Laurence - -	80	George W. Laurence.
Bertheany Baily - -	85	John Baily.	Rachel Grummond -	87	Rachel Brown.
Timothy Wood - -	81	Timothy Wood.	Jeremiah Keeler - -	80	Jeremiah Keeler.
John Bishop - -	83	Harry Garrison.	Joseph Monroe - -	77	Joseph Monroe.
Elizabeth Jenkins -	80	Isaac Jenkins.	Amon Marshall - -	87	A. Marshall.
PUTNAM VALLEY.			Keziah Webster - -	74	Keziah Webster.
Elizabeth Silick - -	83	Nathaniel Silick.	Stephen Gillert - -	78	Stephen Gillert.
			Jonathan Taylor - -	86	Jonathan Taylor.
			Nathaniel Reynolds -	86	Nathaniel Reynolds.
			Moses Boughton - -	83	Edwin Bouton.

Names of pensioners for revolutionary or military services.	Ages.	Names of heads of families with whom pensioners resided June 1, 1840.	Names of pensioners for revolutionary or military services.	Ages.	Names of heads of families with whom pensioners resided June 1, 1840.
WEST CHESTER—Continued.			**DUTCHESS—Continued.**		
NORTH SALEM.			BEEKMAN.		
Susanna Smith	75	George P. Smith.	Thomas Martin	86	Thomas Martin.
Abraham Van Scoy	81	Abraham Van Scoy.	Morris Baxter	75	Morris Baxter.
Timothy Van Scoy	90	Timothy Van Scoy.	Daniel Worden	84	Daniel Worden.
BEDFORD.			PAWLINGS.		
Samuel Barrett	90	Joseph Barrett.	John Haviland	84	John Haviland.
Elizabeth Higgins	91	David Higgins.	Catel Holmes	87	John Holmes.
Jeremiah Reynolds	77	Jeremiah Reynolds.	Martha Watts	80	Stephen Worden.
Elizabeth Miller	82	John Miller.	Stephen Turner	78	Stephen Turner.
Abraham Barrett	90	Abraham Barrett.	Elisha Turner	84	Elisha Turner.
James Raymond	87	James Raymond.	Abel Van Scoy	85	Abel Van Scoy.
Nathan Clark	88	Nathan Clark.	Nathan Bennett	75	Nathan Bennett.
Abijah Harris	85	Abijah Harris.			
Abijah Holmes	83	Abijah Holmes.	NORTHEAST.		
James Williams	85	James Williams.	Bezaleel Rudd	89	Bezaleel Rudd.
Jonathan Mills	75	Joseph S. Platt.			
Ebenezer Whelpley	81	Ebenezer Whelpley.	PINE PLAINS.		
David Holmes	83	David Holmes.	Hannah Dennis	72	John Simmons.
Zadock Seeley	61	Zadock Seeley.	Simeon Taylor	74	E. Taylor.
POUNDRIDGE.			MILAN.		
Amy Scofield	79	Sutton Sarles.	Jacob Conse	89	Henry J. Conse.
Amos Dixon	75	Amos Dixon.			
Nathaniel Hoyt	76	Nathaniel Hoyt.	RED HOOK.		
Thomas Pott	76	Thomas Pott.	Ebenezer Adams	88	Ebenezer Adams.
Mary Scofield	86	Job Hoyt.	Helen Mosher	82	John Snook.
James Dan	80	James Dan.	Adam Ryphenburgh	89	Jeremiah Ryphenburgh.
Samuel Dan	87	Samuel Dan.			
Elnathan Weed	82	Elnathan Weed.	RHINEBECK.		
Thomas Peck	79	Thomas Peck.	Daniel McCarty	87	Stephen McCarty.
Stephen Green	85	Thaddeus K. Green.			
Eleazar Slawson	81	Nathan Slawson.	CLINTON.		
Nathan Slawson	88	Nathan Slawson.	Jane Smith	77	Jane Smith.
Lydia Platt	87	Mehitable Brown.	Abigail Webb	84	John Webb.
RICHMOND COUNTY.			HYDE PARK.		
SOUTHFIELD.			Joseph Teal	95	Cyrus Braman.
Amos Rooke	–	Amos Rooke.	Frederick Banker	82	Thomas Banker.
			Hannah Russell	81	James Russell.
CASTLETON.			Morgan Lewis	85	Morgan Lewis.
John McDonald	65	Sailors' Snug Harbor.	Matthias D. Spencer	88	Schuyler Crapser.
Robert Thompson	81	James Thompson.	Jacob Lent	74	John Marshall.
DUTCHESS COUNTY.			POUGHKEEPSIE.		
PLEASANT VALLEY.			John C. Brower	80	George Remer.
John C. Lake	85	Samuel C. Lake.	Mary Bogardus	73	Mary Bogardus.
Peter Lake	77	Jeremiah Johnson.	Oliver Drew	79	Oliver Drew.
Gitty Stansbury	84	Crapo Lake.	Jane Schoonmaker	77	Cornelia Schoonmaker.
Henry Vanderburgh	85	Henry Vanderburgh.	Abel Gunn	85	Abel Gunn.
Mary Mott	82	Mary Mott.	John Dubois	85	John M. Cable.
			Abner Miller	76	Abner Miller.
FISHKILL.			Stephen Trobridge	89	Stephen B. Trobridge.
John Finch	–	John Finch.	John Sherwood	88	Rachel Lapham.
Sarah Bush	79	Elizabeth Smith.			
Aleta Schenck	74	Barnet Smith.	**SUFFOLK COUNTY.**		
Ann Bartlett	–	Henry Bartlett.	EASTHAMPTON.		
Daniel Annin	87	Samuel Annin.	Elizabeth Bennet	–	Miller Bennet.
Nicholas Berry	83	Nicholas Berry.	Abraham Sherril	86	Abraham Sherril.
David Mead	82	Robert P. Howe.	Hannah Hedges	76	Robert Hedges.
Abraham Sleight	85	Abraham Sleight.			
			SOUTHAMPTON.		
WASHINGTON.			James Sayre	86	James Sayre.
Margaret Arnnusmun	78	Margaret Redell.	Hamutual Halsey	78	Hugh Halsey.
			Sylvanus Halsey	84	Sylvanus Halsey.
DOVER.			Stephen Talmage	80	Stephen Talmage.
David Thayer	81	Daniel Thayer.	Henry White	90	Henry White.
Silas Curtis	81	Silas Curtis.	Elizabeth Smith	74	Horace Smith.
Anna Jones	76	Anna Jones.			
John Johnson	81	John Johnson.	HUNTINGTON.		
Jacob Parks	83	Thruston Wing, jr.	Ephraim Oaks	87	Jesse Oaks.
Christopher Fry	78	William Fry.	Martha Bennett	81	John Bennett.
			Solomon Ketcham	83	Isaac Conklin.
AMENIA.					
Prudence Stevens	78	Elijah Stevens.	ISLIP.		
Anne Winchester	87	David Winchester.	Daniel Rogers	81	Timothy Rogers.
David Rundal	83	David Rundal.	Henry Crum	79	Henry Crum.
Jabez Flint	84	Jabez Flint.			
			SOUTHOLD.		
STANFORD.			Daniel Hallock	87	Micah W. Hallock.
Aman Canfield	80	Aman Canfield.	John Clark	78	John Clark.
Joel Thompson	85	Isaac Thompson.	Wells Ely	86	Irad Reeve.
			Peter Vail	78	Peter Vail.

14

NEW YORK—SOUTHERN DISTRICT—Continued.

Names of pensioners for revolutionary or military services.	Ages.	Names of heads of families with whom pensioners resided June 1, 1840.	Names of pensioners for revolutionary or military services.	Ages.	Names of heads of families with whom pensioners resided June 1, 1840.
SUFFOLK—Continued.			**ROCKLAND—Continued.**		
RIVERHEAD.			*CLARKSTOWN—Continued.*		
Henry Ross - - -	–	Henry Ross, sen.	Matthew Conklin - -	74	
Christopher Youngs -	84	Neuter Youngs.	Mary O'Blennis - - -	84	Mary O'Blennis.
			John House - - -	81	John House, jr.
SMITHTOWN.			Mary Eckerson - -	84	Abram Eckerson.
Amy Rose - - -	80	Phineas Rose.	Mary Snider - - -	81	Henry Snider.
			Rebecca Brower - -	79	Abram Brower.
BROOKHAVEN.			Cornelius Depew - -	81	Cornelius Depew.
Alexander Wicks - -	85	Alexander Wicks.	Peter Stevens - - -	79	Henry R. Stevens.
Nathan Davis - -	87	Nathan Davis.	Harriet Blanch - -	75	
Moses Clark - -	81	William Clark.	John Vanhouten - -	84	John Vanhouten.
Temperance Davis -	76	Richard Davis.	Elizabeth Williamson -	74	
Justus Overton -	82	Justus Overton.	Tunis Tallman - -	91	
Zachariah Green -	80	Zachariah Green.	Rachel Tallman - -	69	
Joseph Tooker -	83	Joseph Tooker.	Jane Vanhouten - -	71	John T. Vanhouten.
Zopher Hawkins -	83	Zopher Hawkins.	John Hutton - - -	79	John Hutton.
John Williamson -	88	John Williamson.			
			ORANGETOWN.		
KINGS COUNTY.			Cornelius T. Blauvelt -	91	Daniel G. Blauvelt.
CITY OF BROOKLYN.			John Hudson - - -	88	James Hudson.
First ward.			Cornelius Mabie - -	86	
John Langdon - -	86	John Langdon.	Ralph Verbryck - -	75	
Second ward.			Elizabeth Hendrick -	93	
John Simons - -	79	Allen E. Simons.	Samuel G. Verbryck -	79	Samuel G. Verbryck.
Third ward.			John G. Bogart - -	85	
None.			Hannah Vanorden - -	80	
Fourth ward.			Clarissa Blauvelt - -	78	
None.			Mary Carson - -	72	
Fifth ward.			John G. Blauvelt - -	81	
David Davis - -	82	David Davis.			
James Thompson - -	63	James Thompson.	**ORANGE COUNTY.**		
Edmond Brett - -	68	Edmond Brett.	*MONROE.*		
John Legrange - -	39	John Legrange.	John James - - -	81	John James.
Michael Fitzpatrick -	41	Michael Fitzpatrick.	Peter C. Bloom - -	73	Peter C. Bloom.
Francis H. Ellison -	78	Francis H. Ellison.	Henry Wood - -	86	Henry Wood.
Robert W. Blair - -	31	Daniel P. Blair.	Henry Gibson - -	98	Henry Gibson.
John Clough - -	74	John Clough.	Abigail Letz - -	78	Isaac Chase.
Sixth ward.			Henry Davenport - -	98	Ezekiel Davenport.
None.					
Seventh ward.			*BLOOMING GROVE.*		
John McCoy - -	42	John McCoy.	William Buchanan - -	86	William Buchanan.
Richard Tice - -	78	Richard Tice.	Jeremiah Horton - -	88	Benjamin Horton.
GRAVESEND.			Job Sayre - - -	83	Job Sayre.
Henry Ward - - -	49	John H. Brower.	*MONTGOMERY.*		
			Abraham Wood - -	88	Abraham Wood.
NEW UTRECHT.			Andrew Wilson - -	79	Andrew Wilson.
Jacob Smith - -	33	Jacob S. Smith.	Jane Van Orsdoll - -	93	Jane Van Orsdoll.
William S. Red - -	35	James C. Church.	Elizabeth Taylor - -	78	Elizabeth Taylor.
			Samuel Sly - - -	84	Samuel Sly.
FLATBUSH.			Eve Miller - - -	88	J. M. Hunter.
John Scroder - -	55	Thomas Baisley.	House Skelp - - -	83	House Skelp.
Thomas Murdock - -	28	Jerome Suydam.	John Sears - - -	89	Jacob Sears.
			Samuel Sears - -	82	Samuel Sears.
QUEENS COUNTY.			John Hamilton - -	81	John Hamilton.
NORTH HEMPSTEAD.					
Noah Mason - - -	82	Noah Mason.	*NEW WINDSOR.*		
			Samuel Liscum - -	78	Samuel Liscum.
JAMAICA.			Robert Humphrey - -	84	George C. Humphrey.
Samuel D. Mills - -	83	Samuel D. Mills.	Samuel S. Crawford -	76	James McKinny.
			Isual Knapp - -	79	Isual Knapp.
NEWTOWN.			Robert Burnet - -	78	Robert Burnet.
Leonard Bleeker - -	84	Leonard Bleeker.	Elizabeth Kelso - -	83	James Kelso.
			Joseph Beaty - -	83	Maria Beaty.
ROCKLAND COUNTY.					
HAVERSTRAW.			*NEWBURG.*		
Jacob Lent - - -	85	Jacob Lent.	Keziah Ann Kidd - -	87	James R. Kidd.
Nathaniel Yeoumans -	79	Nathaniel Yeoumans.	John Newkirk - -	81	John Newkirk.
Mary Conklin - -	97	Mary Montanya.	Robert Blair - -	79	Robert Blair.
Matthew Benson - -	77		Rachel Johnson - -	76	Rachel Johnson.
			John McMikle - -	79	John McMikle.
RAMAPO.			Jamaico J. Collins - -	85	James Collins.
John Stormes - -	78	John Stormes.	Benjamin H. Eaton - -	77	Mary Brundage.
Daniel Martine - -	85				
Rachel Talman - -	83	Daniel Talman.	*CORNWALL.*		
Peter S. Vanorden - -	77	Peter S. Vanorden.	Michael Smith - -	85	Michael Smith.
			George Brown - -	83	George Brown.
CLARKSTOWN.			Henry Van Duzen - -	82	Henry Van Duzen.
John J. Blanvette - -	89	John J. Blanvette.	James Edmondson - -	80	James Edmondson.
Elizabeth Garrison -	83		William House - -	86	William House.
Sarah Coe - - -	71	Richard Coe.	Henry Beal - - -	87	Joseph Brown.
Ann Rampson - -	94		Polly Whetmore - -	84	Polly Whetmore.
Abram Vanhouten - -	81	Abram J. Vanhouten.	John Daniels - - -	79	John Daniels.

NEW YORK—SOUTHERN DISTRICT—Continued.

Names of pensioners for revolutionary or military services.	Ages.	Names of heads of families with whom pensioners resided June 1, 1840.	Names of pensioners for revolutionary or military services.	Ages.	Names of heads of families with whom pensioners resided June 1, 1840.
ORANGE—Continued.			**ORANGE—Continued.**		
MINISINK.			GOSHEN—Continued.		
Mary Smith - - -	77	William Smith.	Hannah Coleman - -	78	
Effa Reed - - -	84		Elizabeth Hall - -	74	
Bethia Bailey - -	88		James W. Wilkins - -	75	James W. Wilkins.
Mehitable Boyd - -	83				
Samuel Brown - -	87	Samuel Brown.	WALKILL.		
Jacob Otis - - -	82	Jacob Otis.	John Warden - -	101	John Warden.
Amelia Reed - - -	73		Thomas Knight - -	80	Thomas Knight.
Samuel Parsons - -	84	Samuel Parsons.	Keziah Oliver - -	70	
Mary Green - - -	76	Jesse Green.	Margaret Denniston - -	92	John Denniston.
Elizabeth Kimber - -	80		John L. Fink - -	54	John L. Fink.
Winans Harris - -	79	Winans Harris.	Sarah Brown - -	86	
Phebe Aber - - -	75		Joel Coleman - -	75	Joel Coleman.
George Wood - -	87	George Wood.	Daniel Bailey - -	82	
Joseph Schoonover - -	78	Joseph Schoonover.	Lawrence Cortwright - -	81	Lawrence Cortwright.
			John Jordan - -	93	
CRAWFORD.					
Mary Cox - - -	76	John Cox.	WARWICK.		
Margaret Elder - -	76	Robert Elder.	Noah Morford - -	89	Noah Morford.
Sarah Gillespie - -	89	Sarah Gillespie.	John Hall - -	84	John Hall.
			James Burt - -	77	James Burt.
DEERPARK.			Samuel Benjamin - -	79	Samuel Benjamin.
Margaret Samons - -	72		Benjamin Davis - -	80	Benjamin Davis.
Jane Rosacrontz - -	72	Jacob Rosacrontz.	Ogis B. Stinard - -	82	
Margaret Carpenter - -	71	Benjamin Carpenter.	William Winfield - -	96	William Winfield.
			David Stephens - -	85	David Stephens.
GOSHEN.			Samuel Ketcham - -	82	Samuel Ketcham.
Daniel Popinoe - -	81	Daniel Popinoe.			

STATE OF NEW JERSEY.

Names of pensioners for revolutionary or military services.	Ages.	Names of heads of families with whom pensioners resided June 1, 1840.	Names of pensioners for revolutionary or military services.	Ages.	Names of heads of families with whom pensioners resided June 1, 1840.
ATLANTIC COUNTY.			**BERGEN—Continued.**		
EGG HARBOR.			HACKENSACK.		
John Tilton - - -	85	James Tilton.	Benjamin P. Westervelt - -	76	Benjamin P. Westervelt.
John Jeffrys - - -	82	Nicholas Jeffrys.	Sarah Demarest - -	74	Sarah P. Demarest.
			Peter D. Demarest - -	78	Peter D. Demarest.
GALLOWAY.			Cornelius C. Teshune - -	79	Cornelius Teshune.
Parker Clark - - -	74	James H. Clark.			
Reuben Clark - - -	86	Reuben Clark, sen.	NEW BARBADOES.		
			John C. Post - -	79	John J. Post.
HAMILTON.			Henry Berdan - -	88	Henry Berdan.
Edward Downs - -	82	Edward Downs.	Abel Studder - -	86	Rynear Vanderbick.
			Ichabod Vreeland - -	75	Ichabod Vreeland.
MULLICA.			Simon Simonson - -	93	Hannah Simonson.
Samuel Denike - -	79	Samuel Denike.			
Peter Johnson - -	80	Peter Johnson.	LODI.		
			Daniel Van Sciven - -	90	Benjamin Van Sciven.
BERGEN COUNTY.			James Brinkerhoff - -	82	Jacob J. Brinkerhoff.
FRANKLIN.					
Lewis Keeler - - -	82	Mary Burk.	WASHINGTON.		
James J. Blauvelt - -	77	James J. Blauvelt.	Garret F. Haring - -	78	Garret F. Haring.
Henry Roome - -	77	Henry Roome.	Sarah Blauvelt - -	80	John R. Blauvelt.
William Courter - -	89	Henry Starr.	Daniel Van Horn - -	79	Daniel Van Horn.
John Packer, jr. - -	79	John Packer, jr.			
Abraham H. Garrison - -	82	Abraham H. Garrison.	**BURLINGTON COUNTY.**		
John P. Post - -	79	John J. Post.	MANSFIELD.		
Samuel Romaine - -	84	Albert Romaine.	James Tower - -	87	Daniel Ivins.
William Van Voorhis - -	84	John P. Smith.			
John S. Bertholf - -	79 }	John Bertholf, jr.	CHESTERFIELD.		
John Storms - -	77 }		William Everingham - -	93	William Everingham.
Aaron Garrison - -	85	Peter A. Garrison.			
Lewis Keeler - - -	81	Stephen Lawrence.	**CUMBERLAND COUNTY.**		
John A. Van Houten - -	78	John A. Van Houten.	HOPEWELL.		
Ann Bamper - -	86	Garret A. Bamper.	David Gandy - -	8)	Almshouse.
Charity Perry - -	81	Catharine Wiggins.			
John A. Hopper - -	78	John A. Hopper.	DEERFIELD.		
			Mary Dare - -	80	Philip Dare.
HARRINGTON.			Philip Shimp - -	83	Philip Shimp.
Cornelius Ackerman - -	85	Cornelius Ackerman.	Ebenezer Elmer - -	88	Ebenezer Elmer.
John Walling - -	76	John Walling.	Samuel Tomlinson - -	78	William Brookfield.
John A. Blauvelt - -	79	Abraham J. Blauvelt.	Frederick Fauver - -	77	Frederick Fauver.

NEW JERSEY—Continued.

Names of pensioners for revolutionary or military services.	Ages.	Names of heads of families with whom pensioners resided June 1, 1840.	Names of pensioners for revolutionary or military services.	Ages.	Names of heads of families with whom pensioners resided June 1, 1840.
CUMBERLAND—Continued.			**ESSEX—Continued.**		
FAIRFIELD.			LIVINGSTON.		
Robert Levick - - -	78	Robert Levick.	Sally Ward - - -	79	James L. Ward.
Daniel Bateman - -	83	Daniel Bateman.	Abner Ball - - -	80	Abner Ball.
Moses Bateman - -	80	Moses Bateman.	Mary King - - -	84	Mary King.
MILLVILLE.			Jacob Edwards - -	77	Jacob Edwards.
Peter Kempton - - -	80	William Blake.	Phebe Steel - - -	69	Geo. C. Steel.
			Joseph Green - - -	81	Joseph Green.
MAURICE RIVER.			CITY OF NEWARK—East ward.		
Henry Feaster - - -	80	Henry Feaster.	Catharine Parker - -	80	Catharine Parker.
Jeremiah Towser - -	84	Jeremiah Clark.	Mary Gardner - -	81	Samuel J. Gardner.
DOWNES.			Aaron Thompson - -	82	Aaron Thompson.
Jonathan Hand - -	78	Jonathan Hand.	Mary Speer - - -	75	Samuel Davis.
Sarah Daniels - - -	83	Sarah Daniels.	Thomas Belton - -	108	Thomas Belton.
Samuel Lard - - -	80	Samuel Lard.	Johanna Lyon - -	74	Johanna Lyon.
Dayton Irelan - - -	84	Dayton Irelan.	Daniel Fitch - - -	79	Daniel Fitch.
Benjamin Crozier - -	96	Benjamin Crozier.	South ward.		
George Taylor - - -	93	George Taylor.	David Tichenor - -	82	David Tichenor.
			Ann Plum - - -	77	Ann Plum.
ESSEX COUNTY.			Aury King - - -	86	Moses R. King.
BELLEVILLE.			Turner Hull - - -	67	Hugh Heath.
Catharine Campbell -	84	Mary G. Francisco.	North ward.		
			Sarah Cummings - -	78	Sarah Cummings.
RAHWAY.			Mary Harriss - -	84	Samuel D. Harriss.
Char. Mooney - - -	73	Char. Mooney.	Harriet Leayre - -	76	Harriet Leayre.
Josiah Gray - - -	84	Josiah Gray.	West ward.		
			U. Baldwin - - -	80	William W. Baldwin.
NEW PROVIDENCE.			Henry Willis - - -	83	
John Tilue - - -	85	John Tilue.	UNION.		
Nathan Elmer - - -	78	Nathan Elmer.	David Williams - -	81	William S. Williams.
Jacob Potter - - -	85	Jacob Potter.	Michael Meeker - -	85	Michael Meeker.
James Doty - - -	83	James Doty.	James Wilcox - -	77	James Wilcox.
			Thomas Woodruff -	71	David M. Woodruff.
WESTFIELD.			Stephen Headley - -	79	Stephen Headley.
Benjamine Crane - -	79	Benjamin Crane.	ORANGE.		
John Dunham - -	78	John Dunham.	Thomas Harrison - -	81	Henry Harrison.
Aaron Ball - - -	85	Aaron Ball, jr.	Japhia Condit - -	89	Japhia Condit.
Margaret Ludlow - -	74	John Ludlow.	Abijah Harrison - -	89	Abijah Harrison, jr.
Mary Pierson - - -	79	Jonathan Cory.	Isaac T. Tichenor -	79	
Clark Miller - - -	83	Clark Miller.	CLINTON.		
William Clark - - -	85	William Clark.	Joseph Lyon - - -	76	Joseph Lyon.
Enoch Miller - - -	80	Enoch Miller.	Nancy Stockman - -	81	Moses Stockman.
Robert Woodruff - -	83	James Enders.	Sayres Roberts, sen. -	85	Sayres Roberts, sen.
James Lambert - -	85	James Lambert.	Sarah Meeker - -	89	Zadock Meeker.
Moses Dickerson - -	87	Moses Dickerson.	Timothy Bigelow - -	76	Timothy Bigelow.
J. B. Osborn - - -	86	J. B. Osborn.			
J. H. Osborn - - -	80	J. H. Osborn.	**GLOUCESTER COUNTY.**		
Daniel Hatfield - -	84	Daniel Hatfield.	NEWTON.		
Sarah T. Phillips - -	37	Sarah T. Phillips.	James B. Cooper - -	80	James B. Cooper.
Mary Dolbeer - - -	85	Mary Dolbeer.	WASHINGTON.		
Nancy Terrill - - -	76	Nancy Terrill.	Daniel Park - - -	84	Almshouse.
Sarah Murry - - -	85	Elijah Shotwell.	GLOUCESTER.		
Rachel De Camp - -	81	Rachel De Camp.	Benjamin Bates - -	81	Benoni Bates.
Ichabod Clark - - -	78	Ichabod Clark.	John Mapes - - -	92	John Mapes.
Isaac Manning - -	82	Isaac Manning.	DEPTFORD.		
ELIZABETHTOWN.			Jonas Cattell - - -	82	Jonas Cattell.
David Williams - -	83	David Williams.	GREENWICH.		
Jerusha Crittendon -	81	Sophia Crittendon.	Hugh Aggings - -	86	Hugh Aggings.
Charlotte Townly - -	83	Charlotte Townley.	Abraham Jones - -	80	Nehemiah Cowgill.
BLOOMFIELD.			WOOLWICH.		
Moses Harrison - -	79	Moses Harrison.	Lewis Bender - - -	108	John E. Bender.
Timothy Gould - -	88	Timothy Gould.	FRANKLIN.		
Aury King - - -	86	Edmund H. Davey.	James Ferrell - - -	91	James Ferrell.
John E. Smith - -	86	John E. Smith.			
Isaac Dodd - - -	78	Isaac Dodd.	**HUNTERDON COUNTY.**		
SPRINGFIELD.			BETHLEHEM.		
Aaron Hand - - -	76	Isaac M. Hand.	Jacob Johnston - -	87	Jacob S. Johnston.
David Dean - - -	76	David Dean.	John Head - - -	83	James Smith.
Stephen Lyon - - -	84	Stephen Lyon.	John Bigler . - -	84	John Bigler.
Thomas F. Randolph -	77	Margaret Hutchings.	Leonard Martin - -	84	Leonard Martin.
Matthias Denman - -	89	Matthias Denman.	John Clifford - - -	92	John Clifford.
Samuel Tubs - - -	66	Samuel Tubs.	AMWELL.		
CALDWELL.			Jacob Williamson, sen. -	86	Jacob Williamson.
Henry Lane - - -	78	Henry Lane.			
Isaac Pear - - -	81	Isaac Pear.			
Josiah Gould - - -	79	Josiah Gould.			
Jacob Kent - - -	87	Simon Kent.			
William Gould - -	82	William Gould.			

NEW JERSEY—Continued.

Names of pensioners for revolutionary or military services.	Ages.	Names of heads of families with whom pensioners resided June 1, 1840.	Names of pensioners for revolutionary or military services.	Ages.	Names of heads of families with whom pensioners resided June 1, 1840.
HUNTERDON—Continued.			**MERCER—Continued.**		
AMWELL—Continued.			PRINCETON.		
Peter Williamson	77	Peter Williamson.	Mary H. Stockton	32	Mary Hunter.
John Abbott, sen.	82	John Abbott, sen.	Mary S. Hunter	79	
Amos Peters	81	John Peters.	Jacob Gray	93	Jacob Gray.
Jacob Williamson	80	Jacob Williamson.	Mary G. Fergeson	80	Mary G. Fergeson.
RARITAN.			Oliver Hunt	84	David Bartine.
Martin Smith	84	Peter Smith.	EAST WINDSOR.		
Joseph Gray, sen.	81	Joseph Gray, sen.	Jacob Hall	89	John Shepard.
John Besson	90	Andrew Bearder.	William Morris	87	Mary Barbour.
John Howe	86	John Dilts.	William Fisher	81	Samuel Chamberlain.
READINGTON.			WEST WINDSOR.		
Cornelius Latourette	85	James Williams.	John Stevens	82	John Stevens.
Adrian Johnson	85	Adrian Johnson.	William Updike	81	Levi Updike.
Cornelius Messler	81	Isaac Messler.	John Rue, sen.	86	Joseph J. Rue.
Edward Mitchell	85	Jacob Mitchell.	John Hulfish	81	John Hulfish.
Peter Shirts, sen.	92	Peter Shirts, sen.	Robert Ayres	86	Robert Ayres.
DELAWARE.			John Wiley	78	Eli Rogers.
William Dilts	86	William Dilts.	**MIDDLESEX COUNTY.**		
Elijah Hummell	84	Elijah Hummell.	MONROE.		
Tunis Case	79	Tunis Case.	Isaac Snedaker	85	Peter Snedaker.
Andrew Butterfoss	81	Andrew Butterfoss.	James Clinton	87	James Clinton.
James Underwood	77	Henry Seaght.	PISCATAWAY.		
William Geary	85	E. Butterfoss.	James T. Dunn	80	James T. Dunn.
Daniel Ent	83	Daniel Ent.	Benjamin Sullard	75	Benjamin Sullard.
Samuel Barber	84	Samuel Barber.	Sarah Martin	81	Benajah Martin.
ALEXANDRIA.			Gabriel Munday	81	Gabriel Munday.
Catharine Hogland	85	James Larreson.	James Longstaff	86	Henry Longstaff.
Edwin Dalrymple	88	Elizabeth Dalrymple.	Sarah Kent	78	Samuel Stelle.
John Witing (since dead)	77	Nathaniel Witing.	Benjamin Field	77	Michael Field.
LEBANON.			Dennis Field	79	Dennis Field.
Jacob Nitzer	97	Jacob Nitzer.	WOODBRIDGE.		
John Blane	82	John Blane.	Thomas Lee	76	Adam Lee.
KINGWOOD.			Isaac Sayre	79	Isaac Sayre.
John Mires	81	Francis Mires.	Thomas Bloomfield	70	Thomas Bloomfield.
John Bray	85	John Bray.	Archibald Augar	75	Archibald Augar.
Richard Heath	84	Richard Heath.	NORTH BRUNSWICK.		
Christy Little	77	Christy Little.	Anthony Collins	78	Anthony Collins.
TEWKSBURY.			Enoch Dunham	79	Enoch Dunham.
Christopher Philhower	86	Adam J. Apgar.	Hannah Norman	79	Edgar Hardenbrook.
			Runyon Barcalew	84	Runyon Barcalew.
MERCER COUNTY.			Abm. Merserell	82	Stephen Wines.
			Francis Letis	81	James Townsend.
TRENTON.			Lewis Johnson	80	Lewis Johnson.
Josiah Jones	79	Clemens Jones.	Abm. Vantine	93	John Strong.
John Burroughs	86	Charles Burroughs.	Darby Oram	88	Darby Oram.
Joseph Reed	92	Jane Hart.	Daniel Kemper	91	Daniel Kemper.
William Robinson	62	William Robinson.	John Vanderventer	85	Jacob Wyckoff.
EWING.			David Voorhees	83	David Voorhees.
Mary Laning	72	Ralph Laning.	David Vliet	93	David Vliet.
Elizabeth Green	83	James B. Green.	John Nevius	77	John Nevius.
LAWRENCE.			Margaret Hulse	78	Margaret Hulse.
Sarah Reeder	78	Charles Reeder.	SOUTH AMBOY.		
Ralph Laning	81	Ralph Laning.	Cornelius Suydam	79	Cornelius Suydam.
John Lott	83	John Lott.	Mary McGee	80	William McGee.
HOPEWELL.			David Lamberson	80	David Lamberson.
Israel Hunt	83	Israel Hunt.	David Hall	82	David Hall.
John Fidler	82	John Fidler.	David Owens	80	David Owens.
John R. Hart	87	Dean Hart.	John Booraem	80	John Booraem.
Deborah Golden	76	Anna Lewis.	Daniel Petty	77	John Burlew.
Sarah Swaim	80	Sarah Swaim.	Ruth Burlew	73	
Rachel Stout	74	Westly Burroughs.	Mary Hillyer	81	Ruth Martin.
NOTTINGHAM (INCLUDING SOUTH TRENTON.)			Thomas Lamberson	87	Thomas Lamberson.
Joseph Parker, sen.	81	Joseph Parker.	James Campbell	80	Rice Campbell.
Robert Carson	77	Washington Carson.	SOUTH BRUNSWICK.		
Robert Phares	78	Elizabeth Nelson.	Henry Cortleyou	79	Hendrick Cortleyou.
Gershom Loveless	84	Gershom Loveless.	Elizabeth Groves	79	John Slover.
Jabez Ashmore	79	Jabez Ashmore.	Garret Breese	80	Garret Breese.
Mary Davis	77	Joseph Ashmore.	John Groves	92	John R. Applegate.
Martha Cannon	93	Hannah Thompson.	John Gulick	80	John Gulick.
Sarah Lipes	68	William H. Dye.	Peter Wyckoff	83	Johnson Stout.
			Richard Sutphen	85	Richard Sutphen.
			Benjamin Griggs	85	Reuben Griggs.
			David Chambers	91	Mary Lewis.

CENSUS OF PENSIONERS.

NEW JERSEY—Continued.

Names of pensioners for revolutionary or military services.	Ages.	Names of heads of families with whom pensioners resided June 1, 1840.	Names of pensioners for revolutionary or military services.	Ages.	Names of heads of families with whom pensioners resided June 1, 1840.
MONMOUTH COUNTY.			**MORRIS COUNTY.**		
MIDDLETOWN.			*PEQUANNOCK.*		
John Eldridge	81	John Eldridge.	John Estler	92	James Doremus.
Henry Johnson	85	Lambert Johnson.	Jonathan Morgan	78	Jonathan Morgan.
Leah Maxen	75	William Maxen.	David Provost	90	David Provost.
Job Compton	76	Job Compton.	Evont Vangelder	88	Evont Vangelder.
Euphemia Willet	75	Euphemia Willet.	John Sanford	82	John Sanford.
Daniel Wallen	81	Daniel Wallen.			
William Ribbet	84	William Ribbet.	*MORRIS.*		
John Chacy	85	John Chacy.	Hannah Wager	78	Hannah Wager.
John Rulshart	81	John Rulshart.	Nehemiah Osborn	79	Nehemiah Osborn.
Nicholas World	84	Nicholas World.	Peter Hendrixon	79	Peter Hendrixon.
John Brewer	80	Aaron Brewer.	David Lindsly	79	David Lindsly.
John P. Leister	76	John P. Leister.	Catharine Parrot	78	Catharine Parrot.
James Bowne	86	James Bowne	James Rodgers	79	James Rodgers.
John Carhart	84	Jacob Von Brockle.	Ebenezer Little	82	Ebenezer Little.
William Ommuck	79	William Ommuck, sen.	Peter Mesler	79	Peter Mesler.
			Martha Emmet	81	Martha Emmet.
SHREWSBURY.			Israel Canfield	79	Israel Canfield.
Zebel Maps	84	Elias West.			
John Springsteen	82	Enos Patterson.	*CHATHAM.*		
Amelia Lippincott	89	Amelia Lippincott.	Isaac Genung	63	Isaac Genung.
Mary Wall	88	James Schureman.	Daniel Wilcox	78	Daniel Wilcox.
John Matthews	78	John Matthews.	David Bennet	78	David Bennet.
William Paviton	89	William Paviton.	Luke Miller	82	Luke Miller.
Anthony Holmes	81	Anthony Holmes.	Benjamin Sturges	83	Benjamin Sturges.
			Brown Brookfield	80	Brown Brookfield.
FREEHOLD.			John Campfield	83	John Campfield.
William McIntire	77	Thomas McIntire.			
Thomas Errickson	78	Thomas Errickson.	*MENDHAM.*		
Ann Conover	77	Ann Conover.	Henry Clark	82	Henry Clark.
Daniel Applegate	82	Mathias Applegate.	Isaac Bedell	78	Isaac Bedell.
James Chambers	76	James Chambers.	J. Martin Mundy	90	Isaac M. Mundy.
Elizabeth Burk	86	Joseph T. Parker.	Peter Kise	82	Peter Kise.
Peter M. Johnson	89	Peter M. Johnson.	Ephraim Carns	88	Ephraim Carns.
Catharine Mount	84	John H. Mount.	Job Loree	79	Job Loree.
Aaron F. Walker	81	William Crawford.			
John Clayton	76	John Clayton.	*HANOVER.*		
Samuel Herbert	85	Samuel Herbert.	Jeremiah Howell	92	Jeremiah Howell.
David Sutphen	80	William R. S. Betts.	Stephen Cook	87	Stephen Cook.
James Yetman	80	William McDormat.	William Ball	86	William Ball.
Michael Neighmaster	77	John Leonard.	Abraham Fairchild	86	Abraham Fairchild.
Stephen Seabrook	82	William H. Herbert.	Mary Tuttle	80	Mary Tuttle.
John Read	86	John Read.	Charles P. Christian	56	Charles P. Christian.
Elizabeth Hays	78	Charles Hays.	John Garrigus	80	John Garrigus.
Matthew M. Hulshart	84	Matthew M. Hulshart.	Eunice Casterline	78	Daniel Casterline.
Joseph Van Cleaf	80	William J. Van Cleaf.	David Gordon	84	David Gordon.
John Anderson	88	John Anderson.			
John Conk	78	William Conk.	*RANDOLPH.*		
William Applegate	81	William Applegate.	David Horton	89	David Horton.
Lewis Conover	88	Lewis Conover.	Aaron Voorhees	80	Aaron Voorhees.
Garret Wickoff	81	Garret Wickoff.	Robert Pierson	81	Robert Pierson.
John Aumock	81	John Aumock.			
Levah Williamson	86	Garret W. Wickoff.	*ROXBURY.*		
Sarah Striker	78	Philip Striker.	John Ross	83	John Ross.
Aaron Sutphen	79	John A. Sutphen.	John Muir	77	Walter S. Dickerson.
Thomas Gearon	80	Thomas Gearon, jr.	Daniel Jones	83	Daniel Jones.
Mathias Smith	87	Thomas M. Smith.	John Wiley	86	John Wiley.
Richard Thorn	86	Richard Thorn.	Samuel Maize	80	Ann Merritt.
Elizabeth Craig	71	Elizabeth Craig.			
			CHESTER.		
UPPER FREEHOLD.			Ada King	77	Ada King.
Walter Karr	81	Walter Karr.	Margaret Dorland	74	Margaret Dorland.
George Haley	80	George Haley.	John Locke	86	John Locke.
William Parent	83	William Parent.	Hugh Runyan	84	Hugh Runyan.
Jesse Mount	82	Ezekiel Mount.	Richard Runyan	82	Richard Runyan.
HOWELL.			*WASHINGTON.*		
Aaron Chamberlin	85	Aaron Chamberlin.	Cornelius Vansyche	84	Cornelius Varsyche.
John Chamberlin	91	John Chamberlin.	Daniel Swezey	84	Daniel Swezey.
James Hendrickson	88	James Hendrickson.			
Samuel Johnson	79	Samuel Johnson.	**PASSAIC COUNTY.**		
Joseph Miller, sen.	89	Joseph Miller, sen.	*MANCHESTER.*		
James Smith	91	James Smith.	William Shippy	84	James Shippy.
			Naomi Lyon	74	John Lyon.
DOVER.			Henry Cooper	79	Francis Hendrick.
William Williams	85	William Crawford.	Thomas Blane	90	Thomas B'ane.
Bartholomew Applegate	83	Bartholomew Applegate.	Benjamin Romine	94	Peter Demirest.
STAFFORD.			*WEST MILFORD.*		
Samuel Bennett	79	Samuel Bennett.	Joseph D. Tichenor	78	James Tichenor.
			Nathaniel Sisco	78	Nathaniel Sisco.
			Peter J. Sisco	84	Peter J. Sisco.
			Giles Sisco	94	Giles Sisco.

NEW JERSEY—Continued.

Names of pensioners for revolutionary or military services.	Ages.	Names of heads of families with whom pensioners resided June 1, 1840.	Names of pensioners for revolutionary or military services.	Ages.	Names of heads of families with whom pensioners resided June 1, 1840.
PASSAIC—Continued.			**SOMERSET—Continued.**		
POMPTON.			BRIDGEWATER.		
Tunis Felter - - -	78	Tunis Felter.	John A. Autin - - -	78	John A. Autin.
Anthony Beam - - -	88	Josiah Beam.	Henry Vroom - - -	83	Henry Vroom.
Robert Gould - - -	78	Robert Gould.	Richard Brokaw - - -	83	Richard Brokaw.
Abraham Vreeland - -	82	Abraham Vreeland.	Jacob Degroot - - -	90	Jacob Degroot.
Thomas Carman - - -	76	Thomas Carman.	Robert Little - - -	86	Robert Little.
			Lucius Vosseller -	83	Lucius Vosseller.
PATERSON.			Paul Voorhees - - -	82	Philip A. Tunison.
Abraham Rutan - -	77	Abraham Rutan.	John Steele, sen. - -	85	John Steele, sen.
Mary Pope - - -	78	Mary Pope.	Rulif Van Pelt - -	82	Rulif Van Pelt.
Richard Galway - -	32	Richard Galway.			
Mary Brower - - -	79	Mary Brower.	HILLSBOROUGH.		
Sarah Colt - - -	82	Sarah Colt.	Peter J. Quick - -	81	Peter J. Quick.
			Willet Taylor - - -	81	Gilbert B. Taylor.
AQUACKAWONK.			Dinah Van Cleaf -	86	Jacob S. Van Cleaf.
John H. Post - - -	81	John H. Post.	Peter Voorhees - -	84	Binear Staat.
Mary Tures - - -	65	John Tures.	George N. Scamp -	89	George N. Scamp.
Garret G. Vreeland -	80	Garret G. Vreeland.	Adam Bellis - - -	91	John Hall.
SALEM COUNTY.					
UPPER PENN'S NECK.			**SUSSEX COUNTY.**		
John Jourden - - -	80	John Jourden.	MONTAGUE.		
			Margaret Quick - -	69	
UPPER ALLOWAY'S CREEK.			Abraham Kittle - -	82	
William Brown - -	84	William Brown.	Henry Holdron - -	84	
Charles Wintzell - -	90	Benjamin Fogg.			
Abraham Harris - -	94	Samuel Harris.	FRANKFORD.		
James Reed - - -	76	James Reed.	David Silsbee - - -	79	David Silsbee.
William Smick - - -	86	Andrew Shidener.	Lemuel Tingley - -	79	Lemuel Tingley.
SALEM.			HARDYSTON.		
Thomas Ware - - -	87	Lewis Mairs.	George Anthony - -	77	George Anthony.
MANNINGTON.			NEWTON.		
Joshua Allen - - -	51	Josiah Allen.	Jacob Drake - - -	84	Jacob Drake.
PILES' GROVE.			WANTAGE.		
Reuben Peterson - -	88	Joseph Titus.	Caspar Rorick - - -	89	Caspar Rorick.
			Lewis Mead - - -	75	Lewis Mead.
PITTSGROVE.			Samuel Lambert - -	82	Samuel Lambert.
Jacob Briant - - -	84	Richard Burt.			
			VERNON.		
SOMERSET COUNTY.			Luke Degraw - - -	81	Luke Degraw.
BEDMINSTER.			Ichabod Tompkins -	79	Evi S. Tompkins.
William Todd - - -	79	William Todd.	John Cooper - - -	77	John Cooper.
Joseph Annin - - -	89	Joseph Annin.	George Parker - - -	76	George Parker.
Hendrick Field - -	88	Hendrick Field.			
			WARREN COUNTY.		
BERNARD.			HOPE.		
Hannah Van Sickel -	84	Hannah Van Sickel.	Jesse Parr - - -	80	Jonathan A. Parks.
John Toulin - - -	69	Samuel Stanbury.			
Joseph Kennan - -	58	Jonathan Hand.	HARDWICK.		
Mary Kennan - - -	76	Alva Lewis.	Isaac Dickerson - -	89	Henry M. Sherrer.
Henry Southard - -	92	Samuel S. Doty.			
Nathaniel Whitaker -	80	Nathaniel Whitaker.	GREENWICH.		
Ziba Norris - - -	78	Ziba Norris.	Philip Weller - - -	84	Philip Weller.
FRANKLIN.			FRANKLIN.		
Isaac Brokaw - - -	–	Isaac Brokaw.	John Wilson - - -	89	John Wilson.
James D. Perrien - -	–	Henry Hagaman.	Elijah Warne - - -	80	Abraham Warne.
Ellen Van Tyne - -	78	Ellen Van Tyne.			
John C. Wyckoff - -	83	John C. Wyckoff.	OXFORD.		
			John Daylay - - -	80	Philip Daylay.
WARREN.					
John Coddington - -	78	John Coddington.			
John Pennington - -	78	John Pennington.			

CENSUS OF PENSIONERS.

PENNSYLVANIA—EASTERN DISTRICT.

Names of pensioners for revolutionary or military services.	Ages.	Names of heads of families with whom pensioners resided June 1, 1840.	Names of pensioners for revolutionary or military services.	Ages.	Names of heads of families with whom pensioners resided June 1, 1840.
ADAMS COUNTY.			RUSCOMBMANE.		
HAMILTON BAN.			John Everhart - - -	81	
Captain David Wilson -	89	Captain David Wilson.	Simon Link - - -	82	
Joshua Heidler. sen. -	77				
			ROCKLAND.		
MOUNT PLEASANT.			Jacob Walter - - -	84	
Michael Clapsadale -	91		Conrad Fry - - -	85	
FRANKLIN.			OYEY.		
Joseph Chamberlin.			John Yeager.		
READING.			WASHINGTON.		
William Johnston - -	83		Frederick Glass - -	87	
BUCKS COUNTY.			**CHESTER COUNTY.**		
SOUTHAMPTON.			WEST CALU.		
John Scott - - -	60		James Brown - -	79	John Calwell.
BENSALEM.			BRANDYWINE.		
Andrew Ott - - -	103		William Moore, sen. -	84	William Moore, sen.
			John Byres - -	86	John Wilson.
DOYLESTON.					
Eleanor Lacy - -	75		WEST NANTMEAL.		
Nathan James - -	85	John D. James.	Thomas Rankin - -	58	Thomas Rankin.
Andrew Denison - -	84	Andrew Denison.			
Jacob Conrad - -	78		EAST NANTMEAL.		
			Borick Beagle - -	88	Jacob Starrett.
BUCKINGHAM.			Alexander Neisbit -	85	Mary Robinson.
Martin Herlinger - -	78				
			WEST FALLOWFIELD.		
NEWTON.			Charles Wallace - -	79	Edmund Taylor.
William Willard - -	76				
Nathaniel Burrows -	85		WEST BRADFORD.		
			William Walker - -	48	William Walker.
NOCHAMIXION.					
Thomas Custerd - -	84	Thomas Custerd.	EAST VINCENT.		
Benjamin Hawldren -	89	Benjamin Hawldren.	Anthony W. Hayman -	55	John Miller.
Andrew Stull - -	85	Andrew Stull.			
			WEST VINCENT.		
PLUMSTEAD.			Lewis Harple - -	82	Lewis Harple.
Robert Beaty - -	78		James Thomas - -	83	James Thomas.
			Evan Evans - -	82	Evan Evans.
DURHAM.					
Michael Fackenthall -	84	Michael Fackenthall.	COVENTRY.		
			Jacob Zombro - -	80	John Byer.
MILFORD.			Colonel Caleb North -	87	Colonel Caleb North.
Christian Huber - -	84	Christian Huber.	Philip Nimon - -	80	Jacob Nimon.
WEST ROCKHILL.			SCHUYLKILL.		
Adam Richert - -	88	Adam Richert.	William Jones - -	49	William Jones.
RICHLAND.			CHARLESTOWN.		
Henry Heft - - -	82	Henry Heft.	Thomas Bodly - -	81	Matilda Carter.
BERKS COUNTY.			Jacob Wisner - -	78	Jacob Wisner.
READING.					
Michael Spats - -	78		TREDYFRIN.		
Sebastian Algiar - -	83		Elizabeth Howell - -	82	Elizabeth Howell.
Peter Stickles - -	78		Sarah Woodman - -	81	William S. Woodman.
Aaron Wright - -	78				
Henry Styles - -	84		LONDONDERRY.		
Christian Miller - -	85		Carswell Gardner - -	84	George Thomas.
William James - -	79				
Joseph Snabble - -	84		EAST NOTTINGHAM.		
John P. Nagle - -	83		James All - - -	82	Levi K. Brown.
			James A. Dremren -	88	William Collingsworth.
MAXATAWNY.			James Ewing - -	88	John Allen.
Henry Grim - -	75				
Frederick Bower -	83		LOWER OXFORD.		
Jacob Wink - -	82		George Rudolph - -	60	William W. Lyle.
Philip Noyes - -	84				
Christian Smick -	76		UPPER OXFORD.		
			Peter Fry - - -	85	James Ross.
GREENWICH.			**CUMBERLAND COUNTY.**		
Andrew Camp - -	84		NORTH MIDDLETON.		
George Hincley - -	82		Jacob Hefflebower - -	85	Michael Frisburn.
Peter Stiger - -	80		Philip Lehnhart - -	79	Benjamin Thompson.
WINDSOR.			EAST PENNSBORO'.		
Nicholas Grate - -	81		Peter Beaty - -	78	Peter Beaty.
RICHMOND.			CARLISLE.		
Henry Stine - -	71		James Hutton - -	83	
John Hains - - -	—		Archibald London - -	86	
			Michael Tanno - -	65	

PENNSYLVANIA—EASTERN DISTRICT—Continued.

Names of pensioners for revolutionary or military services.	Ages.	Names of heads of families with whom pensioners resided June 1, 1840.	Names of pensioners for revolutionary or military services.	Ages.	Names of heads of families with whom pensioners resided June 1, 1840.
CUMBERLAND—Continued.			FRANKLIN—Continued.		
WEST PENNSBORO'.			SURGAN.		
Elizabeth Ferguson	75		Peter Pinkey	70	
			George Gunter	83	
FRANKFORD.					
George S. Rinehart	94		METAL.		
			John Goyer	80	
DELAWARE COUNTY.			Thomas Forsythe	35	
NETHER PROVIDENCE.			John Jones	110	
George Hizer	93	Thomas Deram.			
			WARREN.		
MIDDLETOWN.			Frederick Keefer	78	
John Lindsay	88	William Saunders.			
			LANCASTER COUNTY.		
MARPLE.			RAPHO.		
Samuel Carr	54		Jacob Brown	85	
DAUPHIN COUNTY.			MONHEIM.		
HARRISBURG—South ward.			Peter Maurer	83	
Ann Maria Keefer	70	John J. Black.			
Justina Weiser	82	John Lingle.	WEST DONEGAL.		
			Peter Sheaffer	89	
UPPER SWATARA.					
John Rickerd, sen.	79	John Rickerd, sen.	EAST HEMPFIELD.		
George Yeager	76	Peter Landes.	John Patterson	81	
Robert Gray	83	John Levingstone.			
			WEST HEMPFIELD.		
LONDONDERRY.			Isaac O'Donnel	67	
Jacob Scheller	80				
			LANCASTER CITY.		
DERRY.			John Roberson	–	Mrs. Roberson.
Philip Fishburn	86		Joseph Peterman	–	Mrs. Peterman.
Ludwig Fishburn	84		Polly Merrit	–	George Merrit.
			Mary Carpenter	–	Ann Green.
LOWER PAXTON.			Jacob Keller	78	Mrs. Keller.
Jacob Schope	78		Eliza Trisler	–	Mrs. C. Trisler.
			Molly Longnecker	–	John Longnecker.
SUSQUEHANNA.			Samuel Ludwig	–	David Roger.
Simon Fulk	97		Susan Roth	–	Mrs. Moyer.
John Lehman	84		Catharine Gonech	–	Peter Gonech.
			Caspar Hubbert	78	Caspar Hubbert.
FRANKLIN COUNTY.			George Leonard	82	George Leonard.
CHAMBERSBURG.			John Gontz	–	Elizabeth McGrann.
John Henebarger	85		Michael Gumph	76	Michael Gumph.
			Frederick Seip	–	Rudolph Suter
ANTRIM.			Catharine Gemshorn	–	James Roger.
Jacob Skully	84		Legal Dutrich	–	James Corey
Frederick Byers	85		Jacob Long	82	Jacob Long.
Joseph Davidson	86		John Gonter	79	John Gonter.
			Peter Shindle	80	Peter Shindle.
GREEN.			Christopher Gumph	80	C. Gumph.
John Dine	96		Peter Bruner	77	Peter Bruner.
Nicholas Fritz	82		Catharine Eichholty	–	Susan Eichholty.
George Kehl	82		Thomas Shay	–	Thomas Shay.
Peter Stambaugh	89		Catharine Fry	–	Catharine Luty
John Renfrew	87		William Low	83	Jacob Eshleman.
MERCERSBURG.			EAST COCALICO.		
William Dick	53		Andrew Ream	84	
James Irwin	84		Harry Ream	84	
WASHINGTON.			WEST COCALICO.		
Adam Hartman	77		David Landis	84	
			Henry Rinchold	82	
QUINCY.					
John Barnsheeser	94		ELIZABETH.		
			Abraham Eshleman	82	
FANNET.					
John Krouse	83		EARL.		
Peter Foreman	87	Peter Foreman.	David Diffenderfer	91	
			Jacob Diffenderfer	83	
HAMILTON.					
Christian Weest	95		CAERNARVON.		
Fred. Stucky	100		Adam Northamer	81	
PETERS.			BRECKNOCK.		
Leonard Croborga	90		Barbara Sweigan	–	
			Jesse Stover	–	
ST. THOMAS.			LITTLE BRITAIN.		
Jacob Line	87		Robert Dugless	76	
George Harmony	52				
			MARTICK.		
LETTERKENNY.			John Bain	103	
Michael Fitz Strasburg	84		William Henzell	90	

15

PENNSYLVANIA—EASTERN DISTRICT—Continued.

Names of pensioners for revolutionary or military services.	Ages.	Names of heads of families with whom pensioners resided June 1, 1840.	Names of pensioners for revolutionary or military services.	Ages.	Names of heads of families with whom pensioners resided June 1, 1840.
LEBANON COUNTY.			**LEHIGH**—Continued.		
LEBANON BOROUGH.			NORTH WHITEHALL—Continued.		
George Hess - - -	79	George Hess.	Christian Acker - - -	85	Elias Semel.
			George Fisher - - -	84	John Esh.
SWATARA.					
Peter Witmoyer - - -	80	F. Witmoyer.	**MONROE COUNTY.**		
Anna Barbara Yeagley -	78	Anna Barbara Yeagley.	HAMILTON.		
Peter Sailor - - -	77	Peter Sailor.	Moses Swartwood - -	75	John Actman.
John Shalley - - -	79	John Shalley.	John Staples - - -	87	
Jacob Heim - - -	75	Jacob Heim.	Aaron Depuy - - -	80	
John Bickel, jun. - -	88	John Bickel, sen.			
Valentine Shoufler - -	88	Valentine Shoufler.	SOUTH SMITHFIELD.		
Martin Meily - - -	78	Martin Meily.	Daniel Labar - - -	76	
George Heilman - -	81	George Heilman.			
			STROUDSBURG.		
EAST HANOVER.			John Fenner - - -	78	
Thomas Kopenhaver -	80	William Kopenhaver.	John Coolbaugh - -	80	
John Hetrich - - -	77	John Hetrich.	John Cooper - - -	–	
Jacob Decker - - -	84	Jacob Decker.			
Philip Witmoyer - -	80	Philip Wittmoyer.	MIDDLE SMITHFIELD.		
John Garberich - -	81	John Garberich.	Margaret Vananaken -	75	
James Steward - -	83	John Winter.			
			TOBYHANNA.		
LONDONDERRY.			Philip Trausu - - -	82	
Jacob Lentz - - -	81	Jacob Lentz.			
Adam Frist - - -	80	David Flory.	ROSS.		
Jacob Keaner - - -	86	Jacob Keaner.	Mary Smith - - -	75	
Andrew Robeson - -	81	Joshua Robeson.			
			CHESNUT HILL.		
HEIDELBERG.			Benjamin Vanhorn - -	81	
George Wolf - - -	79	Christian Smith.			
Margaretta Leob - -	79	Henry Leob.	**MONTGOMERY COUNTY.**		
Elizabeth Derr - -	81	Elizabeth Derr.	ABINGTON.		
			Baker Barns - - -	80	
LEBANON—*South ward.*					
Andrew Hoover - -	75	Andrew Hoover.	MOORLAND.		
North ward.			William Prikhe - -	86	
Dilman Doup - - -	81	Dilman Doup.	Marlain Freas - - -	77	
Mary Weaver - - -	75	Jacob Weaver.			
			WHITEMARSH.		
BETHEL.			Christopher Carr - -	98	Elizabeth Lentz.
Catharine Walborn -	85	John Walborn.			
			MONTGOMERY.		
JACKSON.			Daniel Harrar - - -	84	
Mary Bainny - - -	75	Mary Bainny.			
Rebecca Bowers - -	74	Rebecca Bowers.	GWYNEDD.		
John Smith - - -	86	John Smith.	Henry Neavel - - -	87	
			Henry Yelles - - -	87	
LEHIGH COUNTY.					
ALLENTOWN.			HATFIELD.		
Charles Deshlu - -	82	Charles Deshlu.	Edward Hoxworth - -	78	
John Miller - - -	71	John Miller.			
Frederick Kemerer -	84	Timothy Geidner.	WORCESTER.		
Peter Houk - - -	88	Peter Houk.	Adam Homsher - - -	86	
Andrew Gangwer - -	92	Andrew Gangwer.			
Philip Lehr - - -	57	Philip Lehr.	POTTSTOWN.		
			George Leader - - -	87	George Leader.
SALISBURY.			Catharine Drace - -	91	Major M. Kinney.
Jacob Wilt - - -	79	Andrew Wilt.			
			POTTSGROVE.		
UPPER SAUCON.			Frederick Miller - -	79	Jonas Freed.
George Deily - - -	87	Joseph Morey.	Mathias Laughman - -	83	Jos. Laughman.
George Rumfeldt - -	86	Elizabeth Rumfeldt.			
			LIMERICK.		
LOWER MACUNGY.			Christian Mattis - -	84	Christian Mattis.
Michael Kehm - -	87	Michael Kehm.			
			UPPER PROVIDENCE.		
UPPER MILFORD.			Widow Harple - - -	84	Mary Harple.
John Titlow - - -	81	John Titlow.			
David Alshouse - -	86	David Eberhad, jr.	NEW HANOVER.		
			Widow Deeker - - -	77	Jacob Deeker.
LOWHILL.			Sophia Barnhart - -	86	John Barnhart.
Andrew Knerr - -	83	Andrew Knerr, sen.	Jacob Erb - - -	80	Jacob Erb.
			MARLBORO'.		
SOUTH WHITEHALL.			Catharine Rushon - -	80	John Shaid.
George Gangewer - -	82	George Gangewer.	Christopher Brey - -	62	Christopher Brey.
			Catharine Shively - -	79	John Haring.
WEISENBERG.			John Salada - - -	76	John Salada.
Christian Boyer - -	82	Christian Boyer.			
Andrew Rupp - - -	82	Jeremiah Snyder.	LOWER MERION.		
Lorenz Holben - -	91	Solomon Holben.	Jacob Latch, sen. - -	81	Jacob Latch.
			John Wilfong, sen. - -	80	John Wilfong, sen.
NORTH WHITEHALL.			Griffith Smith - - -	79	Griffith Smith.
Peter Gross - - -	79	Peter Gross.	William Holdgate - -	79	Jacob Rodenboh.
			John C. Ferl - - -	50	John C. Ferl.

PENNSYLVANIA—EASTERN DISTRICT—Continued.

Names of pensioners for revolutionary or military services.	Ages.	Names of heads of families with whom pensioners resided June 1, 1840.	Names of pensioners for revolutionary or military services.	Ages.	Names of heads of families with whom pensioners resided June 1, 1840.
NORTHAMPTON COUNTY.			**PIKE—Continued.**		
LEHIGH WARD.			*MILFORD.*		
Daniel Yansen	86	Daniel Yansen.	Elizabeth Bunnel	82	Elizabeth Bunnel.
			Isaac Blackmore	89	Isaac Blackmore.
LOWER MOUNT BETHEL.			Samuel Hellems	79	Hyram Hellems.
Thomas Silaman	84	Thomas Silaman.			
William Stinson	81	William Stinson.	**SCHUYLKILL COUNTY.**		
Ludwick Shoup	76	Ludwick Shoup.	*ORWIGSBURG.*		
			Frederick Hesser	78	
PLAINFIELD.					
Philip Diley	86	Philip Diley.	*WAYNE.*		
			Adam Snyder	82	
WILLIAMS.			George Zegman	83	
John Eckert	87	John Eckert.			
			PINEGROVE.		
ALLEN.			John Dollinger	91	
One female	83				
One female	85		*UPPER MAHANTANGO.*		
			Philip Bechtel	82	
BUSHKILL.			Abraham Zimerman	83	
William Seifert	78		Jacob Reinert	81	
M. Miller	69				
P. Steinmetz	69		*BARRY.*		
			Valentine Kuter	81	
LEHIGH.					
—— Heckman	80	Charles Heckman.	*SCHUYLKILL.*		
			Godfreid Duher	84	
MOORE.					
C. Schlegel	85	C. Schlegel.	*RUSH.*		
P Deemer	80	Phil. Deemer.	Adam Kline	78	
J. Frey	80	Jacob Frey.			
			WEST PENN.		
LOWER SAWCON.			Peter Steighwalt	78	
John Mann	83	John Mann.	James Nunimacher	80	
Henry Brown	85	Henry Brown.			
Ad. Frey	79	Ad. Frey.	*WEST BRUNSWICK.*		
John Ohl	82	John Ohl.	Adam Mengle	87	
PERRY COUNTY.			*EAST BRUNSWICK.*		
CENTRE.			Philip Swartz	86	
Miniran Dickson	84	William H. McClain.	Barnard Kepner	76	
			Frederick Bensinger	80	
GREENWOOD.			Henry Hoffman	80	
Benjamin Bonsell	79		Abraham Knittle	80	
Andrew Burd	78		Christopher Boyer	77	
			Andrew Bolich	83	
LIVERPOOL.			John Miller	76	
Jacob Essick	81				
Michael Lepkichler	81		**CITY OF PHILADELPHIA.**		
			NORTH MULBERRY WARD.		
NEWPORT.			Ann Fletcher	75	Benjamin Rodgers.
Ephraim Williams	85		Susan Kollock	84	John McDowell.
			Sarah Sianert	81	Edward Dickinson.
WHEATFIELD.					
Andrew Lash	79		*SOUTH MULBERRY WARD.*		
			Patrick Dougherty	45	John McDowell.
RYE.					
Paul Musser	84		*NORTH WARD.*		
			Frederick Burkart	79	Frederick Burkart.
BOROUGH OF LIVERPOOL.					
Richard Baker	81		*MIDDLE WARD.*		
			Elizabeth Billingham	39	Jonas P. Falum.
MADISON.					
Melchoir Spohn	81	Melchoir Spohn.	*SOUTH WARD.*		
			Jacob Stremback	85	Jacob Stremback.
SAVILLE.			John G. Watmough	45	John G. Watmough.
Elizabeth Jacobs	72	George Jacobs.			
Nicholas Barack	81	Nicholas Barack.	*LOCUST WARD.*		
			Elizabeth Nagle	48	Elizabeth Nagle.
JUNIATA.			Mary Savel	95	Mary Savel.
Michael Robison	81	William Robison	Susan Bainbridge	62	Susan Bainbridge.
Adam Netrow	52	Adam Netrow.	Leonora Parsons	77	L. Parsons.
			Comfort Richards	80	Delia Richards.
CARROLL.			Abigail Conover	77	M. A. Lawrence.
Robert Lackey	76	Robert Lackey.	Mary Hodgson	80	Alexander Hodgson.
John Murphy	81	John Murphy.	Mary Baton	75	James Hickey.
			Ann Butler	89	Samuel Butler.
PIKE COUNTY.			Sarah Parris	73	Sarah Parris.
LEHMAN.			Sarah Inskeep	83	Sarah Inskeep.
Peter Benson	45	Chalin Chamberlain.			
Barnadus Swartwood	80		*NEWMARKET WARD.*		
			Ann Mayhew	79	Enoch Mayhew.
DELAWARE.					
Frederick Shoff	88	Frederick R. Shoff.	*CEDAR WARD.*		
			Sarah O'Neill	83	Humphrey Hunt.

PENNSYLVANIA—EASTERN DISTRICT—Continued.

Names of pensioners for revolutionary or military services.	Ages.	Names of heads of families with whom pensioners resided June 1, 1840.	Names of pensioners for revolutionary or military services.	Ages.	Names of heads of families with whom pensioners resided June 1, 1840.
CITY OF PHILADELPHIA— Continued.			**PHILADELPHIA—**Continued.		
PINE WARD.			OXFORD.		
Andrew Kee	30	John C. Righter.	Benjamin Vandergrift	81	Benjamin Vandergrift.
Margaret E. Shaw	50	Wm. H. Odenheimer.	Jacob Foulkrod	80	Jacob Foulkrod.
Barnet Rogan	21	Lewis Perot.	John McVaugh	88	John McVaugh.
			ROXBOROUGH.		
PHILADELPHIA COUNTY.			Elizabeth Matthias	90	Charles Silverthorn.
NORTHERN LIBERTIES—5th ward.			Phebe Righter	81	Phebe Righter.
John Revel	40	John Revel.	Edith Nunemaker	79 }	Joseph H. Hoffman.
7th ward.			Mary Levering	75 }	
Jacob Madlock	83		Ann Bigony	82	Joseph Lare.
			Christopher Ozies	89	Christopher Ozies.
SOUTHWARK—1st ward.			Margaret Stritzel	79	Margaret Stritzel.
Jane Culbert	78	James Culbert.			
Mary T. Philler	57	Andrew Philler.			
Robert M. Wilson	84	Robert M. Wilson.	**WAYNE COUNTY.**		
Jemima Smith	72	James S. Smith.	BERLIN.		
John Douglass, sen.	94	John Douglass, sen.	John Bunnell	83	
2d ward.					
James Ferguson	56	James Ferguson.	BETHANY.		
John Nugent	57	Prudence Taylor.	Eliphalet Kellogg	75	Eliphalet Kellogg.
John Price	35	Sarah Richardson.			
Ezekiel H. Teal	71	Ezekiel Teal.	CANAAN.		
Baltus Stone	96	George Copes.	Abraham Frisbie	78	
Ann Steel	81	Lester F. Donnell.	Abigail Seely	75	
Henry Wilmer	30	Sarah Philips.	Jesse Morgan	78	
4th ward.			John A. Schenck	80	
Hannah Turney	87				
Isaac Harding	32	Samuel H. Foster.	CLINTON.		
5th ward.			John Griswold	84	
Henry Boyer	82	Evan Boyer.	Jason Stanton	79	
Anna Maria Clunet	42	Anna Maria Clunet.			
Catharine Rinker	64	Catharine Rinker.	MOUNT PLEASANT.		
Elizabeth Buck	35	Elizabeth Buck.	Elizabeth King	71	
			Sarah Benjamin	84	
SPRING GARDEN—1st ward.					
Olive Fullinsbury	88		PALMYRA.		
Elizabeth Niles	80		Ethal Jones	75	
George Turner	93				
George Tripner	78	George Tripner.	PRESTON.		
Dragoon Recruitz	–	Samuel F. Eltz.	Gideon Woodman	82	
2d ward.			Silas Tyler	94	
Mary Bunting	84				
Nathan B. Jennings	91	Nathan B. Jennings.	SALEM.		
Philip Bevan	84		Jeremiah Osgood	78	
William Elliott	82	Evan Baily.	John Andrews	82	
3d ward.			Rachel Weston	81	
Catharine Owen	97	William Lawrence.			
Paul Russell	83	Paul Russell.	STERLING.		
4th ward.			John Benett	87	
Mary Sexton	79	Silas W. Sexton.			
Mary Brown	78	John Ellison.	**YORK COUNTY.**		
Elizabeth Ludwick	80	Elizabeth Ludwick.	YORK BOROUGH—South ward.		
			Lewis Shive	80	Lewis Shive.
KENSINGTON—1st ward.			Jacob Rudy	91	Jacob Rudy.
Christopher Deum	81	John Lunshum.	John Stroman	84	John Stroman.
			John Koch	82	John Koch.
BLOCKLEY.			North ward.		
John Elliott	80	John Elliott.	Michael Warner	78	Henry Stauffer.
John Frailey	80	John Frailey.	Jonathan Jacobs	84	Jonathan Jacobs.
WEST PHILADELPHIA.			BOROUGH OF DILLSBURG.		
Rachel Gaudy	72	Moses Hopkins.	Adam Keener	90	Adam Keener.
James O'Donnell	63 }				
Hugh Merrill	62 }		FRANKLIN.		
Samuel Floyd	56 }	Alms House.	Edward Cavenaugh	89	Edward Cavenaugh.
Richard Hallowell	69 }				
George Ernest	81 }		DOVER.		
			George Switzer	77	Jesse Barnes.
LOWER DUBLIN.					
Simon Krewson	86		HANOVER.		
Jacob Snyder	87		John Lipp	86	Joseph Deck.
			Peter Grumbine	78	Joseph Aldhoff.
GERMANTOWN.			William Fanschelt	89	William Fanschelt.
Henry Young	86	Edwin Runkle.			
			OLD CODORUS.		
MOYAMENSING.			George Krebs	86	George Krebs.
John T. Lewis	75	John T. Lewis.	Andrew Miller	86	Andrew Miller.
Nicholas Mack	93	Ann McNichols.	George Bailey	90	Henry Bailey.
UNINCORPORATED NORTHERN LIBERTIES.			MANHEIM.		
Harman Sutton	34	Henry Davis.	Melchor Riffel	90	Melchor Riffel.
John Steiner	55	Eli Kenderhine.			

PENNSYLVANIA—EASTERN DISTRICT—Continued.

Names of pensioners for revolutionary or military services.	Ages.	Names of heads of families with whom pensioners resided June 1, 1840.	Names of pensioners for revolutionary or military services.	Ages.	Names of heads of families with whom pensioners resided June 1, 1840.
YORK—Continued.			YORK—Continued.		
HOPEWELL.			PEACHBOTTOM—Continued.		
Thompson Alexander	82	Daniel Grimm.	John Bullock	87	
YORK.			Benjamin Jones	90	Matthew Clarke.
Philip Wambaugh	85	Adam Musser.			
PEACHBOTTOM.			CHANCEFORD.		
Isaac Jones	85	Isaac Jones.	George Keener	87	George Keener.

PENNSYLVANIA—WESTERN DISTRICT.

ALLEGANY COUNTY.			ALLEGANY—Continued.		
LOWER ST. CLAIR.			FRANKLIN.		
William Barr	90	William Barr.	Jacob Rosensteel	54	Jacob Rosensteel.
Daniel McDarmit	95	Daniel Hunter.	Margaret Shrum	76	Margaret Shrum.
Joseph McDarmit	90	Robert Hays.	Richard Easton	88	Richard Easton.
JEFFERSON.			PINE.		
James Wallace	89	James Wallace.	John Walter	86	John Walter.
William Wilson	86	William Wilson.	Jacob Burkhardt	74	Jacob McDonald.
James Hindman	86	James Hindman.	Robert Scott	84	Robert Scott.
			Hardy Reynolds	80	George Wallace.
MIFFLIN.			John Hillman	80	John Hillman.
Joseph Forsyth	84	Joseph Forsyth.	Samuel Arbuthnot	81	Samuel Arbuthnot.
			William Trenary	98	Henry Trenary.
FINDLEY.			George Grove	89	George Grove.
Thomas McClanen	76	Thomas McClanen.	George Greer	84	Thomas Greer.
			William Beggs	86	William Beggs.
ROBINSON.					
Alexander Walker	70		ROSS.		
William Stockdale	56	William Stockdale.	James Watson	75	David Reel.
Robert Cockran	83	Robert Cockran.			
			EAST DEER.		
ELIZABETH.			John Davis	54	John Noel.
Thomas Clark	90		Daniel Howe	75	William Plumer.
Christopher Doughty	85		William Leslie	81	Thomas Leslie.
Thomas Drennen	86	William M. Drennen.			
			CLINTON COUNTY.		
INDIANA.			DUNSTABLE.		
Mrs. Clink	65	Jacob Clink.	Jeremiah Shearer	50	Jeremiah Shearer.
Miss Grubs	38	Andrew Grubs.			
Mrs. Hicky	73	James Hicky.	GROVE.		
Miss Clows	10	William Clows.	John Ramage	-	John Ramage.
CITY OF ALLEGHANY.			LOGAN.		
Rossin Tivis	-	R. Tivis.	Ludwig Fridley	90	Ludwig Fridley.
Lewis Coaps	-	Lewis Coaps.	Christopher Colby	103	Christopher Colby.
Thomas Pardy	-	Peter Pardy.	Henry Hening	87	Henry Hening.
Elizabeth Shannon	77		John Kitchen	89	John Keller.
Sarah Brannon	77				
E. Grub	75		WARREN COUNTY.		
Samuel Crawl	81		WARREN.		
Peter Brown	83		John Andrews	68	John Andrews.
Margaret Williams	70				
Mary Conner	77		BROKENSTRAW.		
James Chambers	52		Solomon Jordan	85	Elijah Jordan.
			George Long	75	George Long.
CITY OF PITTSBURG—West ward.					
George Hinsey	74		COLUMBUS.		
			Zacheus Raymond	78	Zacheus Raymond.
5th ward.			Bashabe Beels	88	Ezra Beels.
Margaret Larance	73	Thomas McKee.			
			SUGARGROVE.		
East ward.			Josiah Chandler	85	Alva Evens.
James McCollough	86	James McCollough.			
			PINEGROVE.		
PITT TOWNSHIP.			Noah Chappel	83	Noah Chappel.
Eshi Powers	96	John Graham.	Squire Philips	82	Squire Philips.
			Gideon Northrop	86	David Northrop.
PEEBLES.					
Thomas Campbell	85	John Horshman.	SOUTHWEST.		
			Mrs. Hannah Smith	71	John R. Smith.
VERSAILLES.					
Cary Quigley	108	John McKee.	LIMESTONE.		
Catharine Orgin	90	James Coulter.	Mrs. Margaret McGee	76	Henry McGee.
OHIO.			BEDFORD COUNTY.		
Charles Brooks	79	Charles Brooks.	AIR.		
James Brown	66	Moses Blazer.	Robert Alexander	86	Robert Alexander.

CENSUS OF PENSIONERS.

PENNSYLVANIA—WESTERN DISTRICT—Continued.

Names of pensioners for revolutionary or military services.	Ages.	Names of heads of families with whom pensioners resided June 1, 1840.	Names of pensioners for revolutionary or military services.	Ages.	Names of heads of families with whom pensioners resided June 1, 1840.
BEDFORD—Continued.			COLUMBIA—Continued.		
BELFAST.			ORANGE.		
James Hollingshead - -	84	James Hollingshead.	Peter Blank - - -	84	Peter Blank.
BETHEL.			HEMLOCK.		
Mary Bishop - - -	77	Margaret Bishop.	John Hartman - -	84	John Hartman.
Sarah Truax - -	78	Hester Truax.	Abraham Shoemaker - -	81	Abraham Shoemaker.
BEDFORD.			MONTOUR.		
William Clark - - -	80	William Clark.	John Foust - - -	84	John Foust.
CUMBERLAND.			DANVILLE.		
Frederick Simons - -	78	Frederick Simons.	William Clark - - -	84	William Clark.
Valentine Miller - -	86	Valentine Miller.	WASHINGTONVILLE.		
William Drenning - -	77	William Drenning.	Rachel McCoy - -	85	Robert McCoy.
HOPEWELL.			MADISON.		
John McNey - - -	75	John McNey.	Christopher Woolheaver - -	85	Christoper Woolheaver.
Maty Gordon - - -	92	Thomac Fredrigal.	John Allen - -	83	John Allen.
COLERAIN.			Valentine Christian - -	84	Valentine Christian.
Christopher Hart - -	87	Christopher Hart.	VALLEY.		
Peter Morgan - -	82	Peter Morgan.	Phebe Gray - - -	86	John Gray.
UNION.			Frederick Calehoofer - -	84	Frederick Calehoofer.
John Artis - - -	86	John Artis.	LIBERTY.		
Leonard Curl - -	76	Leonard Curl.	Jane Bell - - -	69	Jane Bell.
BROADTOP.			Daniel Evellon - -	81	Daniel Evellon.
John Lain - - -	85	John Lain.	LIMESTONE.		
SOUTHAMPTON.			Joseph Fulton - -	87	Joseph Fulton.
William Davis - -	83	William Davis.	SUGARLOAF.		
John Brumley - -	40	John Brumley.	John Keeler - - -	76	John Keeler.
LONDONDERRY.					
William Masters - -	83	John Lafferly.	GREEN COUNTY.		
ST. CLAIR.			WAYNE.		
Samuel Elseroad - -	45	Samuel Elseroad.	Jotham Black - - -	80	Jotham Black.
William Slick - -	91	William Slick.	William Cornwell - -	86	William Cornwell.
NAPIER.			RICHHILL.		
John McCrackin - -	89	Joseph Mortimore.	Abraham Staggers - -	67	George Wright.
William Frasey - -	80	William Frasey.	WASHINGTON.		
GREENFIELD.			Jacob Johns - - -	76	Jacob Johns.
Thomas Wilt - - -	62	Jacob Wilt.	Lewis Wright - -	87	Lewis Wright.
			John Weir - - -	81	John Weir.
MIFFLIN COUNTY.			MORRIS.		
WAYNE.			Stephen Simpson - -	90	Stephen Simpson.
Thomas Holt - - -	76		William Rush - -	91	Michael Rush.
MENO.			CENTER.		
James McGriger - -	85		Lewis Martin - - -	79	William L. Martin.
Eli Williams - - -	81		Isaac Dunn - -	83	Isaac Dunn.
			Salome Longstreth - -	85	Thomas Longstreth.
DERRY.			DUNKARD.		
Joseph Woods - -	81		Jacob Stoneking - -	75	Jacob Stoneking.
James Glasgow - -	77		Jonathan Morris - -	88	Jonathan Morris.
John Ridean - -	82		Elizabeth Smith - -	72	Elizabeth Smith.
GRANVILLE.			Isaac Cowell - -	82	Isaac Cowell.
James Cupples - -	84		Hannah Long - - -	75	Benjamin Long.
ARMAGH.			Benjamin Titus - -	81	Benjamin Titus.
Jacob Brown - - -	84		WHITELY.		
			Andrew Myres - -	78	Andrew Myres.
COLUMBIA COUNTY.			Moses Moreland - -	88	Moses Moreland.
MIFFLIN.			Joseph Fox - -	84	John Fox.
Jacob Sewank - -	81	Jacob Sewank.	William Latimore - -	88	William Latimore.
Eve Mary Stahler - -	92	John P. Klingeman.	John Anderson - -	80	John Anderson.
Anna Mary Durnbauch - -	67	Anna Mary Durnbauch.	CUMBERLAND.		
Laurence Christ - -	77	Thomas Knox.	Abraham Scott - -	87	Abraham Scott.
Henry Erwine - -	88	Henry Erwine.	George Wiscarver - -	82	Meredith Ingram.
ROARING CREEK.			MONONGAHELA.		
Andrew McClure - -	85	Andrew McClure.	Caleb Crumlow - -	82	Caleb Crumlow.
BRIAR CREEK.			Henry Sycks - -	83	Henry Sycks.
Christian Marical - -	81	Christian Marical.	Stephen Maple - -	81	Stephen Maple.
Thomas Ward - -	92	Thomas Ward.	JEFFERSON.		
Jacob Johnson - -	65	George Snider.	Abraham Kelly - -	80	James Kelly.

PENNSYLVANIA—WESTERN DISTRICT—Continued.

Names of pensioners for revolutionary or military services.	Ages.	Names of heads of families with whom pensioners resided June 1, 1840.	Names of pensioners for revolutionary or military services.	Ages.	Names of heads of families with whom pensioners resided June 1, 1840.
COLUMBIA—Continued.			**SUSQUEHANNA—Continued.**		
JEFFERSON—Continued.			*RUSH—Continued.*		
Abijah McClain	85	Abijah McClain.	Isaac Rynearson	82	Cornelius Rynearson.
James Maxwell	83	Peter Sharpnack.	Lucy Tower	82	Rial Tower.
William Pugh	85	Barbary Stronnan.			
			NEW MILFORD.		
FRANKLIN.			Garret Schnedicar	85	Anna Newman.
Thomas Smith	85	Hugh Smith.	Elsa Miller	75	Joseph P. Miller.
David White	89	David White.	Nathan Buel	77	Arphaxed Buel.
William Maple	77	William Maple.			
Reuben Mickle	77	Reuben Mickle.	*RUSH.*		
			John Blasdell	74	John Blasdell.
SUSQUEHANNA COUNTY.					
FOREST LAKE.			*SPRINGVILLE.*		
Hannah Southell	75	Asahel Southell.	Joseph Button	80	Abner Burdick.
Luther Kellum	80	Luther Kellum.	Mary Wakelee	73	Arad Wakelee.
			Pardon Fish	89	Justus Knapp.
MIDDLETOWN.					
John Darrow	82	John Darrow.	**FAYETTE COUNTY.**		
Andrew Canfield	86	Andrew Canfield.	*MENALLEN.*		
			Joseph Mendenhall	94	Joseph Mendenhall.
CHOCONUT.					
Westol Scovill	85	Daniel Chamberlin.	*TYRONE.*		
			Benjamin Mackey	55	Benjamin Mackey.
AUBURN.			Samuel Wilson	76	Samuel Wilson.
Ezekiel Avery	77	Ezekiel Avery.			
			BULLSKIN.		
BRIDGEWATER.			John Washington	69	John Washington.
Moses Tyler	74	Moses Tyler.	Robert Fleming	71	Robert Fleming.
Asahel Gregory	82	Samuel Gregory.	George Ullery	62	George Ullery.
William Shufelt	79	William Shufelt.	Simon Rufleam	97 }	George Huey.
Eseck Thayre	77	Eseck Thare.	George Huey	56 }	
Henry Congdon	81	William Shipman.			
Henry Primes	74	Henry Primes.	*SALTLICK.*		
Ezekiel Maine	80	Ezekiel Maine.	William Herns.	85	Jonathan Herns.
Darius Cook	87	Nathan Moss.	Dennis Coon	61	Dennis Coon.
Lawrence Tarpinning	78	Lawrence Tarpinning.	James Rodgers	73	James Rodgers.
John Reynolds	86	John Reynolds.	Charles Warick	79	Charles Warick.
James Eldredge	86	John Stroud.	William Turner	86	William R. Turner.
Elijah Bullard	95	Elijah Bullard.	Alexander Cumings	90	Alexander Cumings.
Simeon Reynolds	78	Simeon Reynolds.			
			CONNELLSVILLE.		
BROOKLYN.			James Whaley	52	James Whaley.
Isaac Brown	88	William Squires.	Azariah Davis	72	Azariah Davis.
Joshua Jackson	78	Joshua Jackson.	Elizabeth Stellwagon	95	Elizabeth Stellwagon.
Bristol B. Sampson	84	Bristol B. Sampson.			
			DUNBAR.		
DIMOCK.			William Cox	54	William Cox.
Amy Babcock	76	Mason Tingley.	William Harden	65	William Dickerson.
Eunice Brownson	86	John Lathrop.	William Cottorn	98	Edward Davis.
Dyer Crocker	76	Dyer Lathrop.	Isaac Artist	82	William Hardey.
David Shearer	82	Samuel Shearer.	Daniel Cole	84	Tobias Johnston.
			William Kennear	64	William Kennear.
FRANKLIN.					
Jedediah Adams	78	Joel Morse.	*WHARTON.*		
Isaac Tunells	77	David Watson.	Cato Harden	62	Elizabeth Teach.
			William Williams	78	William Williams.
GREAT BEND.			Reuben Thasp	86	William Thasp.
Lydia Staples	95	Daniel Lyon.	Thomas Pearce	85	Thomas Pearce.
Putnam Catlins	74	Putnam Catlins.			
			HENRY CLAY.		
GIBSON.			Benjamin Miller	61	Benjamin Miller.
Abial Bills	81	Peleg Bills.	Job Clark	88	Andrew Flanagan.
Enos Whitney	78	Enos Whitney.	George Berker	80	James McGlaughlin.
George Gelats	82	George Gelats.			
Ruth Fuller	83	William Belcher.	*GEORGES.*		
Elias Van Winkle	81	Elias Van Winkle.	Jacob Blackford	81	Jacob Blackford.
			James Davis	79	Catharine Davis.
HARFORD.			John Combs	87	Graham Combs.
Huldah Richardson	75	Caleb C. Richardson.	Jeremiah Archey	55	Jeremiah Archey.
John Thatcher	80	Daniel Thatcher.	John Harden	77	John Harden.
Ichabod Seaver	81	Ichabod Seaver.	Jacob Price	49	Jacob Price.
Sally Hewitt	83	Thomas Tiffany.	Conrad Rager, sen.	85	Jacob Rager.
Rufus Kingsley	77	Rufus Kingsley.	Solomon Gladden	76	Solomon Gladden.
			Joseph Stillwell	85	John Stillwell.
HERRICK.					
Stephen Ellis	76	Stephen Ellis.	*GERMAN.*		
			John Hanning	89	John Hanning.
LIBERTY.			Abraham Franks	71	Abraham Gallenton.
Josiah Davis	83	Josiah Davis.	James Ritchey	80	James Ritchey.
Ichabod Buck	83	Ichabod Buck.	Jacob Lawrence	83	Jacob Lawrence.
			Gabriel Abrams	91	Gabriel Abrams.
LENOX.			Alexander McDugle	81	Alexander McDugle.
Zerah Scott	75	Zerah Scott.			

PENNSYLVANIA—WESTERN DISTRICT—Continued.

Names of pensioners for revolutionary or military services.	Ages.	Names of heads of families with whom pensioners resided June 1, 1840.	Names of pensioners for revolutionary or military services.	Ages.	Names of heads of families with whom pensioners resided June 1, 1840.
FAYETTE—Continued.			**BUTLER**—Continued.		
UNION BOROUGH.			DONEGAL.		
Andrew Gardner	65	John Vankirk.	John Moser	85	John Moser.
Thomas Olden	83	Sophia Stephens.	Elizabeth Rencill	90	Elizabeth Rencill.
			John Warner	87	John Warner.
UNION TOWNSHIP.					
Samuel Garwood	75	James Lenox.	CENTRE.		
John Lincoln	81	Patterson Lincoln.	Charles Campbell	93	Peter Grubb.
Joseph Taylor	65	Joseph Taylor.	John Corathers	96	Thomas Corathers.
Archibald Stewart	80	Edward Bell.	Samuel McCall	70	Samuel McCall.
David Buchanon	–	David Buchanon.			
Charles Williams	49	Charles Williams.	PARKER.		
			Enoch Vernum	75	Enoch Vernum.
SPRING HILL.			John Chambers	67	John Chambers.
Peter Bricker	84	Benjamin Bricker.	John Allen	85	William Allen.
Osburn Helery	78	Osburn Helery.			
			VENANGO.		
BROWNSVILLE.			Amos Dunbar	77	Amos Dunbar.
Michael Fee	81	Michael Fee.			
John Fleming	79½	John Fleming.	MERCER.		
			John Welsh	78	John Welsh.
PERRY.			BUTLER TOWNSHIP AND BOROUGH.		
James Moon	70	James Moon.	Clark McPherrin	37	Clark McPherrin.
			John McCullough	70	John McCullough.
LUZERNE.			Mary Crutchlow	74	Mary Crutchlow.
Joseph Wilson	80	Joseph Wilson.	John Buckhart	71	John Buckhart.
WASHINGTON COUNTY.					
EAST FINDLEY.			MUDDY CREEK.		
Dr. John Hair	84	James Hair.	William Harvey	70	George King.
William Adams	94	Samuel Donley.			
—— Newland	84	William Sprowls.	CONEQUENESSING.		
			Peter McKinney	75	Peter McKinney.
CANONSBURG.			Elizabeth Scott	70	Elizabeth Scott.
George Wilkey	78	George Hagerdy.			
			CRANBERRY.		
AMWELL.			Cory Meeker	88	Cory Meeker.
John Ruckman	96	John Ruckman.	James Jordan	70	James Jordan.
			Martha Reed	85	Francis Pierce.
CHARTIERS.					
James Kerr	– }	Almshouse.	**ARMSTRONG COUNTY.**		
John Fitherman	– }		ALLEGHENY.		
			Peter Yungst	80	Peter Yungst.
MORRIS.			Daniel Davis	–	Daniel Davis.
Joseph Pipes	75	Joseph Pipes.			
			RED BANK.		
WEST FINDLEY.			Addy Anderson	70	Abraham Anderson.
Isaac Lucus	81	John Lucus.	David Shields	80	Hans Ferguson.
FALLOWFIELD.			CLARION.		
Thomas S. Shaffer	84	Thomas Shaffer.	John Brown	80	John Brown.
			Thomas Meredith	–	Joshua Rea.
SOMERSET.					
Robert Campbell	87	Robert Campbell.	PLUM CREEK.		
John Hipple	84	Frederick Hipple.	Henry Davis	73	Henry Davis.
Andrew Vanemon	84	Andrew Vanemon.	Sarah Smith	67	James Robb.
			James McCaine	64	James McCaine.
PETERS.			Martha Stone	77	
James Mitchell	90	John Wright.			
Jos. Denniston	90	Jos. Denniston.	PERRY.		
			James Buccannon	85	William Logue.
WASHINGTON.			Joseph Everet	63	Joseph Everet.
Hugh Workman	81	Hugh Workman.	Gideon Gibson	76	Gideon Gibson.
Henry Arnold	100	Joseph Arnold.			
			TOBY.		
CROSS CREEK.			Hugh Callen, sen.	67	Hugh Callen.
Peter Perrine	83	Peter Perrine.	Samuel Austin	84	Samuel Austin, jun.
John Sutherland	93	Margaret Sutherland.	John Wilson, sen.	71	John Wilson.
SOUTH STRABANE.			MADISON.		
Benjamin Day	54	Benjamin Day.	Mary Soliday	72	Jacob Money.
Matthew Murdock	84	John Colmery.			
Benedict Reynolds	82	Benedict Reynolds.	SUGAR CREEK.		
John Bollen	84	John Bollen.	Isaac Steel, sen.	77	Isaac Steel.
			Daniel Gould	69	Daniel Gould.
BUTLER COUNTY.			Ezekiel Lewis	85	Ezekiel Lewis.
MIDDLESEX.					
John Davis	84	John Davis.	FRANKLIN.		
			Manassa McFadden	53	Manassa McFadden.
BUFFALO.			Joseph McDonald	77	Joseph McDonald.
Robert Riddle	72	Robert Riddle.			
William Coleman	67	William Coleman.	BUFFALO.		
Abraham Leasure	77	Abraham Leasure.	Henry Reefer	48	Henry Reefer.
Daniel Malarkey	68	Daniel Malarkey.	William Hill	69	William Hill.

PENNSYLVANIA—WESTERN DISTRICT—Continued.

Names of pensioners for revolutionary or military services.	Ages.	Names of heads of families with whom pensioners resided June 1, 1840.	Names of pensioners for revolutionary or military services.	Ages.	Names of heads of families with whom pensioners resided June 1, 1840.
ARMSTRONG—Continued.			BEAVER—Continued.		
BUFFALO—Continued.			BRIGHTON.		
Samuel Murphey -	82	Samuel Murphey.	Abraham Lockwood -	50	Abraham Lockwood.
Margaret Laughrey -	69	Margaret Laughrey.			
John Sipe -	70	John Sipe.	LITTLE BEAVER.		
Eleanor Rayburn -	72	James Rayburn.	George Swager -	70	George Swager.
KITTANING.			DARLINGTON.		
Andrew Daugherty	71	Andrew Daugherty.	Isaac Leonard -	50	Isaac Leonard.
Kilian Briney -	73	John Terfastz.			
John Davis, sen. -	77	Jacob Davis.	CHIPPEWA.		
Michael Shall, sen. -	70	Michael Shall, sen.	Thomas Stratton -	80	Samuel Stratton.
Michael Hartman -	81	Michael Hartman.			
Sarah Wiliard -	70	Jacob Wiliard.	BIG BEAVER.		
Michael Truby, sen. -	-	Michael Truby, jr.	Philip Young -	83	John Bales.
			Joseph S. Line -	81	Joseph S. Line.
PINE.					
James Walker -	68	James Walker.	NORTH BEAVER.		
Thomas Taylor -	70	Thomas Taylor.	Esther Lenard -	79	Abna Lenard.
Robert Patrick, sen. -	68	Robert Patrick, sen.	John Fulkerson -	83	Richard Fulkerson.
			Elizabeth Justice -	74	George Justice.
JUNIATA COUNTY.			James Alsworth -	79	David Meanon.
BOROUGH OF MIFFLINTOWN.			Agnes Bannon -	79	George Coalman.
Jacob Wise -	83	Jacob Wise.	John Elder -	85	John Elder.
			John Coalman -	93	John Coalman.
WALKER.			SOUTH BEAVER.		
George Rhiam -	83	Jonas Hauffman.	Jacob Grostcost -	98	Jacob Grostcost.
			Philip Mason -	77	Jacob Grostcost, jr.
GREENWOOD.			John Partredge -	88	John Partredge.
Mary Cox -	93	William Cox.			
Lawrence Koon -	82	Lawrence Koon.	RACCOON.		
Frederick Keller -	83	Frederick Keller.	Jesse Lum -	68	Jesse Lum.
FAYETTE.			FALLSTOWN.		
Thomas Burchfield	85	Absalom Jones.	Henry Woods -	79	David Woods.
John Bell -	88	John Bell.			
Emanuel Ebbs -	106	Emanuel Ebbs.	NORTHUMBERLAND COUN-		
James Deviney -	104	James Deviney.	TY.		
			TURBUT.		
TURBET.			Nicholas Long -	81	Nicholas Long.
John Middaugh -	81	Asher Middaugh.	John Sample -	85	William Sample.
William Patton -	82	William Patton.	John Loas -	84	John Loas.
			Michael Walizer -	87	John Walizer.
TUSCARORA.			George Davis -	85	Jacob Shook.
Sarah Nicholson -	87	Sarah Nicholson.	Dewalt Lynn -	85	Dewalt Lynn.
Elizabeth Conn -	81	Daniel Conn.			
David Hackendorn -	77	David Hackendorn.	MILTON.		
			Peter Egner -	76	Peter Egner.
LACK.					
John Lemmon -	72	John Lemmon.	NORTHUMBERLAND.		
			Peter Bucklew -	85	Peter Bucklew.
BEAVER COUNTY.					
NEW BRIGHTON.			BOROUGH OF SUNBURY.		
Nathaniel Coburn -	75	N. Coburn.	Elizabeth Weitzel -	75	
			Mary Gray -	77	
NEW SEWICKLY.					
James Moore -	82	John Borring.	AUGUSTA.		
Samuel Lane -	73	Samuel Lane.	Elizabeth Schmick	85	
			Deborah Grant -	77	
SHENANGO.					
Alexander Long -	83	A. G. Long.	RUSH.		
Sebastian Mershomer -	84	Henry Mershomer.	Sarah Scott -	78	
James Johnston -	70	James Johnston.			
Robert Boyd -	80	Matthew Reed.	UPPER MAHANOY.		
			George Kump -	87	
SLIPPERY ROCK.					
James Robison -	82	James Robison.	LOWER MAHANOY.		
			John Tschoop -	82	
NORTH SEWICKLY.					
Sampson Pearsal -	76	Sampson Pearsal.	SHAMOKIN.		
			Joseph Richardson -	80	
HANOVER.			George Hummel -	79	
George White -	53	George White.	Frederick Hummel -	78	
			Elizabeth Harman -	85	
HOPEWELL.			Mary Campbell -	77	
Thomas Liggett -	85	James Liggett.			
William Hall -	84	Obadiah Crider.	INDIANA COUNTY.		
			BLACKLICK.		
MOON.			Alexander Campbell -	86	
William Pittman -	56	William Pittman.			
James Read -	89	Andrew McCullock.	BRUSHVALLEY.		
			James Kelly -	71	Robert Kelly.
BOROUGH OF BRIDGEWATER.					
John Javens -	73	Thomas Javens.			
Christian Poorman -	51	C. W. Bloss.			

16

CENSUS OF PENSIONERS.

PENNSYLVANIA—WESTERN DISTRICT—Continued.

Names of pensioners for revolutionary or military services.	Ages.	Names of heads of families with whom pensioners resided June 1, 1840.	Names of pensioners for revolutionary or military services.	Ages.	Names of heads of families with whom pensioners resided June 1, 1840.
INDIANA—Continued.			**ERIE—Continued.**		
BLAIRSVILLE.			WASHINGTON.		
Zebulon Doty	85		Nathaniel B. Gordon	75	
Mott Wilkinson	75		Martin Van Worken	72	
			Joseph Walker	82	
CONEMAUGH.					
James Kane	80		UNION.		
John Montgomery	80	Martha Errington.	Michael Hare	114	
			William Miles	80	
CENTRE.			Darius Orton	84	
Joseph Moorhead	72				
James Huston	82		BOROUGH OF ERIE.		
Benjamin Williams	65	Michael Ressinger.	Simeon Smith	85	
John Ferguson	76				
			GIRARD.		
GREEN.			Peter D. Watts	84	
George Bowers	82	George Bowers.	Dennis Carroll	81	
Henry Kifer	97	Henry Kifer.			
			SPRINGFIELD.		
WHEATFIELD.			Benjamin Cheeseman	85	
Cornelius Hutcheson	84	Cornelius Hutcheson.	Samuel Currier	84	
			Ebenezer Doy	77	
YOUNG.			William Southworth	82	
John Ewing, sen.	75	Alexander Ewing.	William Hamilton	76	
ARMSTRONG.			HARBOR CREEK.		
Isaac Akeright	56	Isaac Akeright.	William Gifford	86	
			Alexander Wilson	80	
WASHINGTON.			Nathaniel Walker	77	
James R. Bill	46	James R. Bill.			
John Jamieson	67	John Jamieson.	CONNEAUT.		
William McHenry	70	William McHenry, jr.	Medad Pomroy	84	
			Rufus Thompson	78	
MAHONING.			James Morrison	83	
John Leasure	76	Andrew Shields.	Elihu Crane	82	
John Brady	63	John Brady.			
Isaiah Vanhorn	80	Isaiah Vanhorn.	NORTH EAST.		
Thomas Neil	78	Thomas Neil.	Thaddeus Histed	77	
James Ewing	73	James Ewing.	Jesse Belnap	80	
James Shields	101	Robert Shields.	James Dickson	83	
John Brady	64	John Brady.	Orange Spencer	76	
MONTGOMERY.			McKEAN.		
William White	84	William White.	Samuel Stancliff	75	
Job Pearce	88	George Pearce.	Comfort Stancliff	88	
			Stephen Oliver	75	
UNION COUNTY.			David Pollock	86	
CENTRE.					
Conrad Swartzlander	95	George Swartzlander.	**HUNTINGDON COUNTY.**		
			ALLEGHENY.		
UNION.			John Adams	78	J. Adams.
George Miller	81	George Miller.			
Jacob Bickel	85	Samuel Ulrich.	MORRIS.		
John Derr	86	Israel Yearger.	John Clark	94	John Clark.
MIFFLINBURG.			WALKER.		
Peter Lenhart	85	Jacob Lenhart.	Valentine Hefner	84	Valentine Hefner.
John Linn	84	John Linn.	Simon Fox	84	Simon Fox.
			John Geissenger	68	John Geissinger.
WEST BUFFALO.					
Robert Barbes	89	Robert Barbes.	ANTES.		
			Lemuel Root	80	L. Root.
EAST BUFFALO.			Timothy Vanskyhock	72	Timothy Vanskyhock.
Jacob Mook	86	Jacob Mook.			
Adam Schout	86	George Baker.	DUBLIN.		
			Andrew Sands	86	Andrew Sands.
WHITE DEER.			Stephen Flemming	36	Stephen Flemming.
Joseph Bedding	83	Henry Bedding.			
			HENDERSON.		
HARTLEY.			James Hight	89	John Hight.
Peter Klingaman	85	Peter Klingaman.	John Fee	80	John Fee.
ERIE COUNTY.			BARRE.		
BOROUGH OF WATERFORD.			John Gregory	90	Alexander Gregory.
Moses Warner	82		William Johnston	81	William Johnston.
CONCORD.			**LYCOMING COUNTY.**		
John Lilly	84		FAIRFIELD.		
			Philip Andas	85	Jacob Agly.
AMITY.					
Gideon Roberts	83		WOLF.		
			Daniel Morris	87	Daniel Morris.
LE BOEUF.					
Nathan Parker	80		MUNCY.		
Nathaniel Mallory	79		Andrew Flatt	83	Andrew Flatt.

PENNSYLVANIA—WESTERN DISTRICT—Continued.

Names of pensioners for revolutionary or military services.	Ages.	Names of heads of families with whom pensioners resided June 1, 1840.	Names of pensioners for revolutionary or military services.	Ages.	Names of heads of families with whom pensioners resided June 1, 1840.
LYCOMING—Continued.			**SOMERSET—Continued.**		
MUNCY CREEK.			SOUTHAMPTON.		
James Barret	77	Peter Michael.	Peter Troutman	84	Peter Troutman.
John Gardner	82	Charles Feagles.			
			TURKEYFOOT.		
MORELAND.			Peter Gary	77	Peter Gary.
Peter Sones	84	Peter Sones.	George Beal	89	George Beal.
			Benjamin Jennings	81	Benjamin Jennings.
MIFFLIN.			Jacob Rush	85	Jacob Rush.
Robert Covenhoven	85	Robert Covenhoven.			
Robert King	88	Robert King.	**McKEAN COUNTY.**		
			NORWICH.		
LYCOMING.			Edward Corwin	81	Edward Corwin.
Conrad Kress	79	Conrad Kress.			
Daniel Vergison	76	Daniel Vergison.	SERGEANT.		
Philip Grove	80	Philip Grove.	Rhoda White	82	Samuel Beckwith.
			Benjamin Lamphier	79	William Lamphier.
CUMMINGS.					
John English	87	Thomas Ramsay.	**CENTRE COUNTY.**		
			HAINES.		
BROWN.			Nicholas Bressler	86	Nicholas Bressler.
Rachel Campbell	76	Jeremiah Campbell.	William Taylor	74	William Taylor.
HEPBURN.			BOGGS.		
William Vanhorne	83	William Vanhorne.	Philip Barnhart, sen.	82	Philip Barnhart, sen.
			Lawrence Bathurst	83	Henry A. Bathurst.
LOYALSOCK.					
Sarah Palhaines	85	Abraham Palhaines.	FERGUSON.		
			Samuel McWilliams	85	Samuel McWilliams.
SUSQUEHANNA.					
James Armstrong	77	James Armstrong.	GREGG.		
			Adam Sundy	77	Adam Sundy.
CLINTON.					
William Fitzsimmons	87	Thomas Davis.	HOWARD.		
Michael Sechler	79	Michael Sechler.	John Marsden	84	John Marsden.
WASHINGTON.			POTTER.		
Cornelius Vanfleat	81	Cornelius Vanfleat.	James Watt	85	John Fye.
VENANGO COUNTY.			SPRING.		
SANDY CREEK.			John Garretson	85	John Garretson.
Andrew Alsworth	88	Alexander Strain.			
John Morrison	82	John Morrison.	WALKER.		
			John Glontz	95	John Glontz.
TIONESTA.					
Phineas Bates	76	Phineas Bates.	**TIOGA COUNTY.**		
			JACKSON.		
RICHLAND.			George Dill	87	Samuel D. Wright.
Adam Sheffer	80	Joseph Redick.	John Lefler	85	Mary Lefler.
SUGAR CREEK.			MIDDLEBURG.		
Thomas Carter	88	Thomas Carter.	Jesse Lowcy	79	Jesse Lowcy.
PLUM.			WELLSBORO'.		
Anna Maria Herring	79	Simon Sterling.	Israel Greenleaf	74	Israel Greenleaf.
James Daugherty	89	John Daugherty.	Mary Waklee	72	John Waklee.
ROCKLAND.			TIOGA.		
Eve Stroup	79	Daniel Stroup.	Harvis Hotchkiss	76	Harvis Hotchkiss.
			Mercy Wright	75	J. N. Wright.
CRANBERRY.					
William Nelles	77	William Nelles.	ELKLAND.		
			Oliver Phelps	75	Oliver Phelps.
FRANKLINBORO'.			Samuel Tubbs	85	Benjamin Tubbs.
William Brown	69	William G. Brown.			
Nimrod B. Grace	52	Nimrod B. Grace.	WESTFIELD.		
			John Hyler	76	John Hyler.
SOMERSET COUNTY.					
ALLEGHENY.			RUTHLAND.		
Jacob Burchart	82	Jacob Burchart.	Jacob Cummings	67	Levi Osgood.
George Platz	75	George Platz.	Andrew Sharp	75	Andrew Sharp.
BROTHER'S VALLEY.			SULLIVAN.		
Jacob Lowry	81	John Whetson.	Abraham Westbrook	78	Abraham Westbrook.
			Jeremiah Rumsey	77	Jeremiah Rumsey.
SHADE.					
Christopher Burket	93	Christopher Burket.	CHARLESTON.		
			Samuel Van Gorden	76	Chancy Terry.
PAINT.			Hannah Dart	82	Agnes Dart.
David Levingston	79	David Levingston.			
			DEERFIELD.		
MILFORD.			Thomas Cumings	82	Thomas Cumings.
Christian Rice	77	Christian Rice.	Christopher Schoonover	77	Christopher Schoonover.
Peter Henry	80	Peter Henry.			
William Critchfield	87	William Critchfield.			

PENNSYLVANIA—WESTERN DISTRICT—Continued.

Names of pensioners for revolutionary or military services.	Ages.	Names of heads of families with whom pensioners resided June 1, 1840.	Names of pensioners for revolutionary or military services.	Ages.	Names of heads of families with whom pensioners resided June 1, 1840.
TIOGA—Continued.			**CRAWFORD—Continued.**		
BROOKFIELD.			*NORTH SHENANGO—Continued.*		
Godfrey Bowman - - -	47	Godfrey Bowman.	Henry Williams - - -	79	Henry Williams.
			Jonathan Herrington - -	78	Jonathan Herrington.
JEFFERSON COUNTY.					
ROSE.			*BEAVER.*		
John Kirker - - -	71	John Kirker.	Abijah Learned - - -	80	Silvanus Learned.
			John Colman - - -	78	John Colman.
SNYDER.					
John Wilkins - - -	69	John Wilkins.	*OIL CREEK.*		
			Nathan Winton - - -	80	Bradley Winton.
YOUNG.					
Henry Hurn - - -	77	John Hurn.	*ROME.*		
			Christopher Connell - -	82	Isaac Connell.
POTTER COUNTY.			Robert Stanton - - -	78	Robert Stanton.
HARRISON.					
Maria Rose - - -	83	Solomon Burtis.	*FAIRFIELD.*		
			William Dean - - -	69	William Dean.
ALLEGANY.			John Wintworth - -	75	John Wintworth.
Royal Cole - - -	81	L. B. Cole.			
			VENANGO.		
HEBRON.			William Ely - - -	84	Elam Holcomb.
Lavina Sparks - - -	71	William Sparks.			
			SUMMERHILL.		
HECTOR.			Potter White - - -	72	Potter White.
Joseph Throckmorton -	75	E. Throckmorton.	Oliver Lawrence - -	84	Oliver Lawrence.
WESTMORELAND COUNTY.			*FALLOWFIELD.*		
NORTH HUNTINGDON.			Peter Mattocks - - -	81	Peter Mattocks.
Eli Brawner - - -	66	Eli Brawner.	John Ralston - - -	80	John Ralston.
Jacob Byerly, sen. - -	80	Jacob Byerly, sen.	James Randolph, sen. -	70	James Randolph, sen.
FRANKLIN.			*MEADVILLE.*		
Sarah Davis - - -	72	Sarah Davis.	John Bliss - - -	52	John Bliss.
George Richey - - -	98	George Richey.	James McNamara - -	93	James McNamara.
William Donald - -	89	James Donald.	Phineas Andrews - -	85	Phineas Andrews.
George Hamilton - -	55	George Hamilton.			
George McWilliams -	69	John McWilliams.	*WOODCOCK.*		
			James Wygant - - -	79	James Wygant.
UNITY.			Samuel Graff - - -	82	Samuel Graff.
Michael Waugh - -	67	Joseph Bush.			
Adam Weaver - - -	89	Adam Weaver.	*RANDOLPH.*		
			Joel Jones - - -	76	Joel Jones.
DONEGAL.					
Zebulon Parke - - -	87		*VERNON.*		
Robert Ewing - - -	78		Cornelius Vanhorn - -	90	Cornelius Vanhorn.
John Harbison - - -	77				
Thomas Paine - - -	105	Thomas Paine.	*MEAD.*		
			Oris Filer - - -	75	James Masters.
ALLEGHENY.			David Thurston - -	78	David Thurston.
John Johnston - - -	93		James Adams - - -	69	James Adams.
Jacob Bear - - -	84		John Ellis, sen. - -	77	John Ellis, sen.
			Zavan Sackett - - -	91	Zavan Sackett.
DERRY.			Samuel Lord - - -	73	Samuel Lord.
Sarah Patterson - -	72				
			MERCER COUNTY.		
SALEM.			*NESHANOCK.*		
Robert Barnet - - -	78		John Moore - - -	70	John Moore.
David Shaw - - -	87				
John Young - - -	86		*MAHONING.*		
Samuel Mehaffy - -	84		George Cassadey - -	59	George Cassadey.
HEMPFIELD.			*LACKAWANNOCK.*		
Jonathan Gunnell - -	84		James Young - - -	70	James Young.
Christian Isaman - -	80		James Spears - - -	71	John Spears.
			Archibald McNair - -	82	A. McNair.
MOUNT PLEASANT.					
Charles Richard - -	85		*COOLSPRING.*		
Frederick Septer - -	78		William McGaw - - -	88	William McGaw.
Christopher Ackerman -	83				
John J. Hemminger - -	84		*WEST SALEM.*		
			John Brown - - -	70	John Brown.
CRAWFORD COUNTY.			Martin Grinder - -	90	Martin Grinder.
HAYFIELD.			Hugh McGill - - -	64	Hugh McGill.
Joseph Carter - - -	78	Joseph Carter.	Samuel Howard - -	84	Samuel Howard.
Abner Jinnings - - -	82	Abner Jinnings.			
			PYMATUNING.		
SPRING.			James Duncan - - -	84	John Duncan.
Joshua Church - - -	79	Jesse Church.	Godfrey Carnes - -	79	John Carnes.
NORTH SHENANGO.			*DELAWARE.*		
Jared Crouk - - -	82	Jared Crouk.	Josiah Weslick - - -	59	Josiah Weslick.
Martin Kingsley - -	84	Martin Kingsley.			
William Reed - - -	79	William Reed.			

PENNSYLVANIA—WESTERN DISTRICT—Continued.

Names of pensioners for revolutionary or military services.	Ages.	Names of heads of families with whom pensioners resided June 1, 1840.	Names of pensioners for revolutionary or military services.	Ages.	Names of heads of families with whom pensioners resided June 1, 1840.
MERCER—Continued.			**LUZERNE—Continued.**		
WOLF CREEK.			NORTHMORELAND.		
John Sutherland - - -	84	John Sutherland.	Lydia Strong - - -	82	Josiah Rogers.
HICKORY.			John S. Jenks - - -	70	John S. Jenks.
Samuel Quimby - - -	87	Charles S. Quimby.	ABINGTON.		
Abraham Deforest - -	92	Isaac Deforest.	John Phillips - - -	88	John Phillips.
SLIPPERY ROCK.			Marcy Colvin - - -	83	Joab Colvin.
Henry Jordon - - -	79	Henry Jordon.	George Reynolds - -	79	William Rice.
CAMBRIA COUNTY.			SALEM.		
CONEMAUGH.			John Varner - - -	81	John Varner.
Ludwick Wisinger - -	84	George Wisinger.	William Moore - -	82	William Moore.
			Nathan Beach - -	78	Nathan Beach.
JOHNSTOWN.			FALLS.		
George Lucas - - -	90	David Lucas.	Azor White - - -	74	Nathan Philo.
RICHLAND.			NICHOLSON.		
Plinn Hays - - -	88	Plinn Hays.	Simeon Foot - - -	78	Simeon Foot.
SUMMERHILL.			DALLAS.		
John Plott - - -	85	Joseph Plott.	Elam Spencer - -	76	Simeon Spencer.
Godfrey Settlemyre -	88	Godfrey Settlemyre.	Daniel Spencer - -	79	John Waldon.
JEFFERSON.			Dorothy Darby - -	78	Tiffany Darby.
Samuel Cole - - -	79	Samuel Cole.	MONROE.		
			Ebenezer Parrish - -	79	Ebenezer Parrish, jr.
LUZERNE COUNTY.			BRAINTRIM.		
BUTLER.			David Lovelass - -	77	David Lovelass.
William Betterley - -	75	William Betterley.	Ambrose Gaylord - -	84	Ambrose Gaylord.
HANOVER.			David Doolittle - -	74	David Doolittle.
Elisha Blackman - -	80		PLYMOUTH.		
PROVIDENCE.			William Walton - -	77	Abram Walton.
Parley Hughs - - -	85	Parley Hughs.	George P. Ransom -	78	George P. Ransom.
PITTSTON.			Catharine Fuller - -	80	Freeman Atherton.
Samuel Carey - - -	77	Samuel Carey.	FAIRMOUNT.		
SUGARLOAF.			Sears Shay - - -	64	Sears Shay.
Jacob Rittenhouse - -	82	Jacob Rittenhouse.	Adam Shafer - -	75	Adam Shafer.
WILKESBARRE.			UNION.		
John Carey - - -	82	John Carey.	Ichabod Shaw - -	94	John Glass.
WILKESBARRE BOROUGH.			HUNTINGDON.		
Job Barton - - -	71	Job Barton.	Thomas Stevens - -	82	Thomas Stevens.
Rufus Bennett - -	81	Rufus Bennett.	Epaphras Wadsworth -	86	Epaphras Wadsworth.
Jonathan Buckley - -	62	Jonathan Buckley.	Josiah Edson - -	77	Josiah Edson.
GREENFIELD.			Joseph Potter - -	79	Joseph Potter.
Reuben Taylor - -	85	Reuben Taylor.	Christopher Boston -	86	Christopher Boston.
William O'Bryon - -	95	William O'Bryon.	Thomas Taylor - -	85	Thomas Taylor.
James Brown - -	85	James Brown.	**CLEARFIELD COUNTY.**		
Reuben Taylor - -	75	Reuben Taylor.	JORDAN.		
Josiah Pell - - -	75	Josiah Pell.	John Swan - - -	85	
BENTON.			John Scott - - -	82	
Solomon Freeland - -	75	Solomon Freeland.	Hugh Jordan - - -	84	
WINDHAM.			**BRADFORD COUNTY.**		
Chandler Robinson -	79	Chandler Robinson.	ASYLUM.		
Josiah Rogers - -	79	Josiah Rogers.	Henry W. Cornelius -	81	H. W. Cornelius.
Isaiah Adkins - -	79	Isaiah Adkins.	John Wood - - -	86	John Wood, jun.
Elisha Ames - -	80	Elisha Ames.	Anthony Vanderpool -	95	Henry Pool, jun.
KINGSTON.			BURLINGTON.		
Abiathar Jenkins - -	88	Abiathar Jenkins.	David Campbell - -	72	David Campbell.
Aaron Perkins - -	77	Aaron Perkins.	Jacob Scouten - -	85	William Nicholls, jr.
Peregrine Jones - -	83	Peregrine Jones.	Alexander Lane - -	78	Alexander Lane.
Benjamin Bedlock - -	81	Benjamin Bedlock.	Benjamin Bosworth -	85	John Haythorn.
TUNKHANNOCK.			CANTON.		
Gabriel Eley - - -	85	Horatio G. Eley.	Noah Wilson - - -	79	Noah Wilson.
EXETER.			COLUMBIA.		
Samuel Van Scoy - -	74	Daniel Van Scoy.	Asa Howe - - -	80	Asa Howe.
Elizabeth Jacobs - -	100	John Jacobs.	Joanna Corey - -	84	Ebenezer Corey.
EATON.			John Budd - - -	77	John Budd.
Lydia Harding - -	77	Stephen Harding.	Oliver Canfield - -	78	Oliver Canfield.
Thomas Hawkins - -	83	Thomas Hawkins.	Anna M. McClelland -	80	Peter McClelland.
			GRANVILLE.		
			John Putnam - - -	72	Luman Putnam.

PENNSYLVANIA—WESTERN DISTRICT—Continued.

Names of pensioners for revolutionary or military services.	Ages.	Names of heads of families with whom pensioners resided June 1, 1840.	Names of pensioners for revolutionary or military services.	Ages.	Names of heads of families with whom pensioners resided June 1, 1840.
RRADFORD—Continued. GRANVILLE—Continued.			**BRADFORD—Continued.** WINDHAM—Continued.		
Caleb White	79	David White.	Martha Dunham	77	Henry Dunham.
Simon Chesley	74	Simon Chesley.	Joseph Gibbs	77	Joseph Gibbs.
HERRICK.			Stratton Sherwood	91	Stratton Sherwood.
Mary Squires	97	Charles Squires.	WARREN.		
			Esther Heacock	81	Reuben Heacock.
LEROY.			Christopher Avery	75	George Avery.
Benjamin Reynolds	79	Benjamin Reynolds.	Preserved Buffington	80	Preserved Buffington.
			Joseph Lomoreaux	87	John Dickerson.
MONROE.			Abraham Whitaker	76	Henry Whitaker.
Samuel Seeley	98	Amos Ackler.	RIDGEBURY.		
			Job Stiles	81	Job Stiles.
BOROUGH OF TOWANDA.			Alpheus Gillott	80	Alphens Gillott.
Amos Mix	85	Hiram Mix.	ORWELL.		
James Dickey	86	James Dickey.	Ebenezer Chubbuck	78	James Cleavland.
			John Kneeland	75	Hiram Frost.
TROY.			ROME.		
Levi Preston	76	Ebenezer Preston.	Reuben Bump	84	Hiram Drake.
John Wilber	79	John Wilber.	Walter S. Minthorn	56	Walter S. Minthorn.
			Elijah Towner	81	Jos. Towner.
WYALUSING.			William Elliott	88	Samuel Elliott.
James B. Decker	102	Levi Decker.	Godfrey Vought	79	Godfrey Vought.
Isaac Custard	80	Isaac Custard.	SHESHEQUIN.		
Daniel Brewster	–	Daniel Brewster.	Sarah Gore	76	Sarah Gore.
Joseph Elliott	83	Joseph Elliott.	Wealthy Ann Spalding	73	Zebulon R. Spalding.
			Joseph Kinney	84	Joseph Kinney.
WYSOX.			Jared Norton	83	Jared Norton.
Ozias Bingham	89	Cornelius Coolbaugh.	Benjamin Brink	76	John Brink.
Daniel Gardner	62	Daniel Gardner.	WELLS.		
Samuel Cole	54	Samuel Cole.	William Carr	79	Moses J. Carr.
James Drake	84	James Drake.	SPRINGFIELD.		
Sartile Holden	89	Octavius A. Holden.	William Salisberry	82	Chauncey Guthin.
Jonathan Stevens	75	Jonathan Stevens.	George Upham	53	George Sergeant.
William Huyck	77	William Huyck.	Benjamin McAffee	77	Benjamin McAffee.
			Simeon King	82	Alvin Parmenter.
ATHENS.			John Harkness	80	John Harkness, jun.
Cynthia Satterlee	71	J. F. Satterlee.	Azuba Severence	77	Samuel Severence.
Elizabeth Mathewson	75	E. Mathewson.	Lucretia Kent	78	Isaac Cooley.
Julius Tozer	76	Julius Tozer.	SMITHFIELD.		
Zephon Flower	74	Zephon Flower.	Ebenezer Pease	80	Ebenezer Pease.
			Rowena Phelps	76	Augustus Phelps.
LITCHFIELD.			Mary Scott	88	John Scott.
Margaret Wolcott	83	Benjamin Wolcott.	James Satterlee	77	James Satterlee.
Abigail Park	79	Thomas Park.	ULSTER.		
			Christopher Simonson	79	Garret Simonson.
PIKE.					
Stephen Gregory	86	Jesse Gregory.			
Isaac Ford	76	Isaac Ford.			
WINDHAM.					
John Plum	75	John Plum.			
Isaac Bronson	81	Isaac Bronson.			

STATE OF DELAWARE.

Names of pensioners for revolutionary or military services.	Ages.	Names of heads of families with whom pensioners resided June 1, 1840.	Names of pensioners for revolutionary or military services.	Ages.	Names of heads of families with whom pensioners resided June 1, 1840.
NEW CASTLE COUNTY.			**KENT COUNTY.**		
Isaac Janvier	54	Isaac Janvier.	Duncan McCather	57	James E. Boyer.
John Robinson	78	John Robinson.			
John Gardiner	82	Abraham Eves.			

STATE OF MARYLAND.

Names of pensioners for revolutionary or military services.	Ages.	Names of heads of families with whom pensioners resided June 1, 1840.	Names of pensioners for revolutionary or military services.	Ages.	Names of heads of families with whom pensioners resided June 1, 1840.
ALLEGHANY COUNTY.			**MONTGOMERY COUNTY.**		
1ST DIVISION.			1ST DIVISION.		
Christian Smith - - -	88	Christopher Smith.	Giles Easton - - -	80	Lewis Easton.
2D DIVISION.			3D DIVISION.		
Peter McMahon - - -	86	Peter McMahon.	Francis Hutchinson - -	87	Samuel Thrift.
Thomas Clinton - - -	84	Thomas Clinton.	Heister Pennefill - -	71	Asa Claggett.
James Skinner ' - - -	85	James Skinner.			
William Groves - - -	83	William Groves.	4TH DIVISION.		
George King - - -	78	George King.	William Layman - - -	87	Thomas Worthington.
WASHINGTON COUNTY.			5TH DIVISION.		
3D DISTRICT.			Mary Tailor - - -	78	
Peter Feighly, sen. - -	86	Peter Feighly, sen.	Mary Watkins - - -	81	Thomas Watkins.
Polly Lewis - - -	82	George Schryock.	Christian Miller - -	88	Christian Miller.
			Elizabeth Warfield - -	86	N. D. Warfield.
4TH DISTRICT.					
Mark Coil - - -	85	Mark Coil.	**PRINCE GEORGE'S COUNTY.**		
Francis Krick - - -	80	Francis Krick.	4TH DIVISION.		
			Martha Wall - - -	78	Martha Wall.
5TH DISTRICT.					
Anthony Belsor - - -	88	George Hamilton.	5TH DIVISION.		
			James Evans - - -	56	Henry Martin.
FREDERICK COUNTY.			Richard Coe - - -	87	Richard Coe.
3D DISTRICT.			John Smith (colored) - -	71	Richard Taylor.
James Cochrane - - -	77	James Cochrane.	Basil Hatton - - -	80	Basil Hatton.
Laurence Everhart - -	85	Laurence Everhart.			
			ST. MARY'S COUNTY.		
8TH DISTRICT.			2D DISTRICT.		
George Ovelman - - -	81	George Ovelman.	George Dent - - -	83	William Dent.
			Thomas Haywood - -	84	John A. Haywood.
9TH DISTRICT.					
John Montgomery, sen. -	80	John Montgomery, sen.	3D DISTRICT.		
			William Matton - - -	41	William S. L. Abell.
10TH DISTRICT.					
Peter Zollinger - - -	84	Peter Zollinger.	**CHARLES COUNTY.**		
			3D DISTRICT.		
CARROLL COUNTY.			Adam Adams - - -	80	
4TH DISTRICT.					
William Lynch - - -	70	William Lynch.	**ANNE ARUNDEL COUNTY.**		
William Fanning - - -	48	William Fanning	1ST DISTRICT.		
			Susan O'Harra - - -	81	William O'Harra.
6TH DISTRICT.			James Davidson - -	79	James Davidson.
Jacob Shennick - - -	75				
Samuel Dewees - - -	91		2D DISTRICT.		
Christian Snyder - -	84		Richard Hall - - -	97	Richard Cadle.
7TH DISTRICT.			3D DISTRICT.		
David Cochrane - - -	78	David Cochrane.	Richard Kelly - - -	78	Sarah Stinchcomb.
BALTIMORE COUNTY.			4TH DISTRICT.		
1ST DISTRICT.			Samuel Baldwin - - -	82	Levi Baldwin.
Thomas Crampton - -	80	Henry Chaney.			
Arthur McLane - - -	79	John Moke.	ANNAPOLIS.		
Thomas White - - -	86	Charles White.	Deborah Randall - -	77	Alexander Randall.
			Rebecca Sewell - -	65	Rebecca Sewell.
2D DISTRICT.			Henry Maynadier - -	81	Henry Maynadier.
General John Armstrong -	83	Horatio G. Armstrong.	Sarah Windham - - -	92	Eleanor Windham.
Anthony Pitsch - - -	57	Anthony Pitsch.	Susan Brewer - - -	81	Susan Brewer.
			Solomon Frazier - -	80	James Frazier.
4TH DISTRICT.			Ann Hollydeoke - -	99	Ann Hollydeoke.
Joseph Harper - - -	94	Joseph Harper.			
			CECIL COUNTY.		
5TH DISTRICT.			1ST DISTRICT.		
Joseph West - - -	85	Joseph West.	Thomas M. Forman - -	82	Thomas M. Forman.
			Stephen Shea - - -	55	Sylvester Megee.
HARFORD COUNTY.					
2D DISTRICT.			2D DISTRICT.		
Andrew Gorrell - - -	50		John McLean - - -	84	John McLean.
3D DISTRICT.			**KENT COUNTY.**		
William Wilgis - - -	75	William Wilgis.	1ST DISTRICT.		
Andrew McAdew - -	84	Andrew McAdew.	John Humphries - -	85	L. M. Recaud.
4TH DISTRICT.			2D DISTRICT.		
Jarrett Tracy - - -	51	Jarrett Tracy.	Elijah Dailey - - -	46	Benjamin Greenwood.
Thomas Schivengton - -	56		Major James H. Gale - -	45	Major James H. Gale.
William Slone - - -	65				
Henry Long - - -	45		**CAROLINE COUNTY.**		
Nancy Long - - -	86		2D DIVISION.		
John Heaps - - -	80		Stephen Phillips, sen. -	77	Stephen Phillips, sen.
5TH DISTRICT.			**TALBOT COUNTY.**		
Archibald Heape - -	82		1ST DISTRICT.		
			Solomon Barrott - -	76	Solomon Barrott.
			John Weyman - - -	47	John Weyman.

MARYLAND—Continued.

Names of pensioners for revolutionary or military services.	Ages.	Names of heads of families with whom pensioners resided June 1, 1840.	Names of pensioners for revolutionary or military services.	Ages.	Names of heads of families with whom pensioners resided June 1, 1840.
TALBOT—Continued.			**BALTIMORE CITY.**		
3D DISTRICT.			*1st ward.*		
Elisha Draper	—	Elisha Draper.	Samuel Hutson	77	Ed. Cleary.
Anna Maria Tilghman	85	Tench Tilghman.	George Rentzall	55	Sister Mary Olympia.
QUEEN ANNE COUNTY.			*2d ward.*		
1ST DISTRICT.			None.		
Jacob Jeffers	80	William Cornelius.	*3d ward.*		
5TH DISTRICT.			Evan Griffith	83	James Parkinson.
Nathan Allan	85	Nathan Allan.	*4th ward.*		
SOMERSET COUNTY.			Henry Cook	82	Obed Pearce.
1ST DIVISION.			*5th ward.*		
Levin Willing	84	Levin Willing.	Mary Allen	75	Ann Allen.
3D DIVISION.			Elizabeth Bowen	79	Joseph Davenport.
John Purnell	85	Dryden Purnell.	*6th ward.*		
DORCHESTER COUNTY.			None.		
4TH DISTRICT.			*7th ward.*		
Nehemiah Beckwith	76	Nehemiah Beckwith.	None.		
Levin Frazier	86	Levin Frazier.	*8th ward.*		
NEWMARKET DISTRICT.			Christopher Lambert	89	Christian Cook.
William Merick	81	John Merick.	Ann Elizabeth Lorentz	65	Ann E. Lorentz.
8TH DISTRICT.			Susanna Haney	83	Catharine Williams.
Aaron Vinson	78	Aaron Vinson.	*9th ward.*		
WORCESTER COUNTY.			Laura Nicholson	35	Laura Nicholson.
SOUTHERN DISTRICT.			Catharine Kelty	64	Eliza Jones.
Nancy Handy	—	Nancy Handy.	*10th ward.*		
			Elizabeth Phillips	68	James League.
			Richard Wells	82	John G. Dorcy.
			11th ward.		
			None.		
			12th ward.		
			Elizabeth Haupt	81	Elizabeth Haupt.
			Henrietta Frazier	79	Alexander Yearly.

STATE OF VIRGINIA—EASTERN DISTRICT.

Names of pensioners for revolutionary or military services.	Ages.	Names of heads of families with whom pensioners resided June 1, 1840.	Names of pensioners for revolutionary or military services.	Ages.	Names of heads of families with whom pensioners resided June 1, 1840.
ACCOMACK COUNTY.			**AMELIA—Continued.**		
ACCOMACK PARISH.			Claiborn Wade	85	Claiborn Wade.
Elkaneh Andrews	77	Elkaneh Andrews.	Boswell Richards	53	Boswell Richards.
ST. GEORGE'S PARISH.			John Hutcherson	76	John Hutcherson.
John Charnock	81	John Charnock.	Samuel Burton	85	Chas. H. Featherston.
Peter P. Copes	76	Peter P. Copes.			
William Kinnehorn	91	William Kinnehorn.	**AMHERST COUNTY.**		
ALBEMARLE COUNTY.			Jones Gill	78	Jones Gill.
FREDERICKSVILLE PARISH.			William Lockard	110	William Lockard.
James Dunn, sen.	80	James Dunn, jr.	Thomas Coppedge	88	Abraham Martin.
James Gentry	82	James Gentry.	William Cashwell	78	William Cashwell.
William Harris, sen.	80	William Harris, jr.	Alexander Logan	79	Alexander Logan.
James Herring	90	James Herring.	James Evans	82	Nancy Blair.
George Gentry	80	James A. Johnson.	Jeremiah Brown	82	Jeremiah Brown.
William Jordan	79	William Jordan.	Thomas Miles	79	Thomas Miles.
Adam Keblinger	77	Adam Keblinger.	Dudley Calaway	90	Jesse Beck.
Walter Watson	79	F. F. Kirby.	Jesse Beck	85	Jesse Beck.
William Maupin	80	William Maupin, jr.	Giles Davidson	78	Giles Davidson.
Richard Snow	86	Richard Snow.	George Wise	83	Almshouse.
John Wood, sen.	83	John Wood, sen.	Ebenezer Hickok	81	Ebenezer Hickok.
ST. ANN'S PARISH.			**BEDFORD COUNTY.**		
Samuel Backsdale	81	Samuel Backsdale.	Jonathan Grooms	84	Reuben Atkinson.
M. Bowen	83	William Bowen.	William Oliver	85	James C. Oliver.
William Boyd	90	William Boyd.	Thomas Andrews	79	Thomas Andrews.
L. Drumheller	75	L. Drumheller.	Thomas Pullin	78	Joseph Pullin.
Richard Harrison	83	Richard Harrison.	Joseph White	100	Joseph White.
John Jones	82	John Jones.	John Arthur, sen.	82	John Arthur, sen.
Jesse Lewis	77	Jesse Lewis.	Isaac Gross, sen.	96	Isaac Gross, sen.
William Morgan	51	William Morgan.	Isaac Cundiff	79	Isaac Cundiff.
Thomas Burton	83	William Reynolds.	John McCormahay	78	John McCormahay.
David Strange	78	David Strange.	John Hudnall	78	John Hudnall.
AMELIA COUNTY.			William J. Walker, sen.	79	William J. Walker, sen.
Larkin Foster	79	Larkin Foster.	Francis Woods	79	William Green.

VIRGINIA—EASTERN DISTRICT—Continued.

Names of pensioners for revolutionary or military services.	Ages.	Names of heads of families with whom pensioners resided June 1, 1840.	Names of pensioners for revolutionary or military services.	Ages.	Names of heads of families with whom pensioners resided June 1, 1840.
BEDFORD—Continued.			**CAROLINE—Continued.**		
Jane Hancock	75	Samuel Hancock.	Edmund Gatewood	78	Edmund Gatewood.
John Buford	83	John Buford.	William Madison	75	William Madison.
John Carter	88	Thomas Stewart.	Betsy Perry	72	Betsy Perry.
William Arthur, sen.	78	William Arthur, sen.	Moses Stanly	82	Moses Stanly.
John Haynes	88	Edmund Haynes.	Robert Satterwhite	87	Robert Satterwhite.
Jonathan Dakin	79	Jonathan Dakin.	Lucy Southworth	75	Lucy Southworth.
Henry Brown, sen.	79	Henry Brown, sen.	George Saunders	79	George Saunders.
Abram Blankenship	82	Abram Blankenship.	Bartholomew Taylor	78	Bartholomew Taylor.
Gray Jones	84	Gray Jones.	Catlett Thomas	77	Catlett Thomas, sen.
T. Minor, sen.	82	T. Minor, sen.	James Thomas	75	James Thomas.
John Wigginton	80	John Wigginton.	William Tucker	75	William Tucker.
Ann Hancock	79	Mary Brown.	Agnes Yarborough	74	Agnes Yarborough.
Jacob Shepperd	80	Jacob Shepperd.			
David Saunders, sen.	80	David Saunders, sen.	**CHARLOTTE COUNTY.**		
Joseph Crews	84		Elizabeth Ashworch	69	Elizabeth Ashworch.
John Halley	79		Joanna Bouldin	88	Joanna Bouldin.
Mary Beard	85		Martha Brown	78	Martha Brown.
William Davenport	75		Clement Carrington	77	Clement Carrington.
Richard Austin	84		Susan Davis	91	Susan Davis.
John Gills	80		Solomon H. Elam	82	Solomon H. Elam.
Ann Moseley	75		David Barree	74	George Harvey.
Philip Lockhust	90		William P. Hamlett	81	William P. Hamlett.
Benjamin Robinson	86		Daniel Hendrick	78	Daniel Hendrick.
			Ambrose Hailey	82	Ambrose Hailey.
BRUNSWICK COUNTY.			James Mullins	80	James Johnson.
Jesse Vaughan	83	John M. Vaughan.	James Rudder	80	Major J. Drury.
Ruel Lewis	81	Ruel Lewis.	Nancy Mathews	80	Nancy Mathews.
Thomas Whitlock	84	Thomas Whitlock.	Isaac Robertson, sen.	86	Isaac Robertson, sen.
William Wilkinson	79	William Wilkinson.	Isaac Smith	74	Isaac Smith.
Thomas Delbridge	74	Thomas Delbridge.	Agnes St. John	75	Jacob A. St. John.
			Lucy Spencer	80	William W. Spencer.
BUCKINGHAM COUNTY.			Joseph Sammons	55	Joseph Sammons.
NORTHERN DISTRICT.			William Skelton	83	William Skelton.
William Starks	85	William Harrison.	Elizabeth Tombs	75	Charles Tombs.
Abram Jones	79	Abram Jones.	William Walker	78	William Walker.
John C. Harris	85	James Harris.			
Mary Mosely	75	Rolfe Eldridge.	**CHESTERFIELD COUNTY.**		
John Thomas	85	John C. Thomas.	UPPER DISTRICT.		
Charles Howel	80	Gideon Howel.	William Hill	80 to 90	William Hill.
John Harris	79	Joseph Riddle.	Jordan Anderson	80 to 90	Jordan Anderson.
			Nathaniel Puckett	85	Nathaniel Puckett.
SOUTHERN DISTRICT.			Moses Fergusson	79	Moses Fergusson.
Timothy Scruggs	86	Timothy Scruggs.	William Goode, sen.	79	William Goode, sen.
James Routon	79	James Routon, sen.	John Bass, sen.	79	John Bass, sen.
Olive Branch	80	Olive Branch.	John Spears	80	John Spears.
William Thornhill	82	William Thornhill, sen.	Jacob Flournoy	79	Jacob Flournoy.
John Doss	85	Rane Walker.			
William Duval	92	Major William Duval.	LOWER DISTRICT.		
James Wilkerson	85	Archibald Drinkard.	John Dyson	78	John Dyson.
William Bigbie	83	William Bigbie.	Isham Andrews	93	Isham Andrews.
			Ezekiel Perkenson	82	Ezekiel Perkenson.
CAMPBELL COUNTY.			Levi Newby	85	Levi Newby.
SOUTHERN DISTRICT.			Thomas Newby	79	Thomas Newby.
John Preble	84	John Preble.	Thomas Gregory, sen.	88	Thomas Gregory, sen.
Thomas P. Franklin	76	Thomas P. Franklin.			
John Cobbs	80	John Cobbs.	**CULPEPPER COUNTY.**		
Jesse Rice	80	Jesse Rice.	Catharine Allen	79	Catharine Allen.
Isham Hall	90	Isham Hall.	Nancy Bailey	75	Armstead Bailey.
John Willard	84	John Willard.	John Creel		John Creel.
Edward Herndon	87	Edward Herndon.	Sarah Calvin	78	Sarah Calvin.
			John Cannady	77	John Cannady.
NORTHEASTERN DISTRICT—LYNCHBURG.			Lucy Pettit	78	John L. Conner.
General Joel Leftwich	80	Rug Leftwich.	Elizabeth Edwards	90	Elizabeth Edwards.
Arthur Litchford	82	Arthur Litchford.	John Freeman	83	John Freeman.
Richard Daniel	92	Richard Daniel.	Zachariah Griffin	79	Zachariah Griffin.
David Calleham	82	David Calleham.	Gabriel Gray	77	Gabriel Gray.
Sampson Evans	89	Sampson Evans.	Humphrey Hill	77	Humphrey Hill.
James Brooks	85	James Brooks.	Julius Hunt	78	Julius Hunt.
Thomas Franklin	83	Thomas Franklin.	John Hall	79	John Hall.
Harry Walthal	79	Harry Walthal.	William Jett	77	William Jett.
Samuel Mathews	77	Samuel Mathews.	William Lewis	77	William Lewis.
James Howard	75	James Howard.	Mary Lambkin	78	Mary Lambkin.
James Whitaker	77	James Whitaker.	Hannah Clark	87	Madden Willis.
			Abner Newman	85	Abner Newman.
CAROLINE COUNTY			Richard Payne, sen.	77	Richard Payne, sen.
			Reuben Rosson	87	Reuben Rosson.
Daniel Atkinson	89	Daniel Atkinson.	Randolph Stallard	83	Randolph Stallard, jr.
James Bradley	89	James Bradley.	Philip Slaughter	82	Philip C. Slaughter.
William Coates	85	William Coates.	Peter Triplett	88	Peter Triplett.
Patrick Carnall	80	Patrick Carnall.	Almond Vaughan	84	Almond Vaughan.
William Gatewood	76	William Gatewood.	Isaiah Welsh		Isaiah Welsh,

17

CENSUS OF PENSIONERS.

VIRGINIA—EASTERN DISTRICT—Continued.

Names of pensioners for revolutionary or military services.	Ages.	Names of heads of families with whom pensioners resided June 1, 1840.	Names of pensioners for revolutionary or military services.	Ages.	Names of heads of families with whom pensioners resided June 1, 1840.
CUMBERLAND COUNTY.			**FRANKLIN COUNTY.**		
Bartlett Cox - - -	85	Bartlett Cox.	Walter Bernard - - -	82	Walter Bernard.
Richard Taylor - - -	84	Richard Taylor.	Thomas Crag - - -	90	Thomas Crag, sen.
Daniel Tolty - - -	75	Daniel Tolty.	Lewis Davis - - -	84	William Davis.
James Morton - - -	83	William S. Morton.	Richard Dale - - -	81	Richard Dale.
William Walker - - -	83	William Walker.	Martel Lashow - - -	85	Martel Lashow.
			Richard Robertson - -	79	Richard Robertson.
DINWIDDIE COUNTY.			Bednego Hodge - - -	81	William Stegall, sen.
			Martin Woody - - -	80	Martin Woody.
James Bishop, sen. - -	79	James Bishop, sen.	Elisha Walker - - -	94	Elisha Walker.
Samuel Major - - -	78	Samuel Major.	Abraham Absher - -	92	George A. Absher.
George Simmons - -	83	George Simmons.	Elisha Barton - - -	80	Elisha Barton.
Thomas Wilkinson - -	82	Thomas Wilkinson.	John Campbell - - -	79	John Campbell.
Josiah Grigg - - -	79	Theodorick H. Grigg.	Will Cuff - - -	92	Will Cuff.
Joel Sturdivant, sen. -	78	Joel Sturdivant, sen.	Isles Cooper - - -	90	Isles Cooper.
Claiborne Elder - -	82	Claiborne Elder.	Cheseham Griffeth - -	80	Cheseham Griffeth.
Bolling Wells - - -	81	Bolling Wells.	Leonard Hutts - - -	86	Leonard Hutts, sen.
Peter Epes - - -	81	Peter Epes.	Jacob McNeal - - -	81	Jacob McNeal.
William Nunnally - -	84	William Nunnally.	Richard Pew - - -	82	Richard Pew.
James Boss - - -	80	Jane Boss.	Jacob Paitsell, who was a pensioner,		
James Spicely - - -	78	James Spicely.	and lost his warrant - -	83	Jacob Paitsell.
PETERSBURG—Centre ward.			Richard Richerson - -	84	Richard Richerson.
			Abraham Sink - - -	75	John Sink.
Joseph Scott - - -	55	Joseph Scott.	William Stuard - - -	80	William Stuard.
			John Wright - - -	94	John Wright.
South ward.			Benjamin Wray - - -	84	Benjamin Wray.
William R. Cheeves - -	55	William R. Cheeves.	**GLOUCESTER COUNTY.**		
ESSEX COUNTY.			Thomas Hogg - - -	75	Thomas Hogg.
			Lucy Berry, widow of Robert		
John Armstrong - -	78	Joseph Armstrong.	Berry - - - -	88	James Berry.
Carter Croxton - -	80	Carter Croxton.	William James - - -	80	William James.
Benjamin H. Munday -	77	Benjamin H. Munday.			
Reuben Atkinson - -	90	Robert Atkinson.	**GOOCHLAND COUNTY.**		
Thomas Cognell - -	78	Thomas Cognell.			
Ann D. Butler - - -	80	Lewis Warner.	Elizabeth Clark, widow of Turner		
			Clark - - - -	78	Elizabeth Clark.
FAIRFAX COUNTY.			Elizabeth Johnson - -	83	Elizabeth Johnson.
			Jesse Wite - - -	74	Jesse Wite.
Daniel Saunders - -	90	Daniel Saunders.	Joseph D. Watkins - -	85	Joseph D. Watkins.
			William Grinstead - -	80	John P. Wite.
FAUQUIER COUNTY.			Elizabeth Alvis - - -	70	Elizabeth Alvis.
			John Sanders - - -	78	Samuel H. Sanders.
Ann Blackweel - - -	79	James Blackweel.	James Gray - - -	77	James Gray.
Susan Burke - - -	96	Susan Burke.	Jacob Woodson - -	79	Jacob Woodson.
Robert Combs - - -	87	Robert Combs.	John Mallory - - -	79	John Mallory.
Anthony Ethel - - -	88	Anthony Ethel.	Henry Isbell - - -	79	H. Isbell.
George Purcell - - -	90	William German.	John Beadshaw - -	78	John Beadshaw.
George Green - - -	80	George J. Green.	Benjamin Isbell - -	77	Z. Isbell.
Martha Howell - - -	70	Martha Howell.	Richard Toler - - -	79	Richard Toler.
Alexander Jeffries - -	77	George Jeffries.	John Banks - - -	92	N. Banks.
Hannah Lear - - -	70	James Lear.	S. Chandoin - - -	87	S. Chandoin.
Elizabeth Maffett - -	82	John A. Maffett.	B. Woodward - - -	82	B. Woodward.
William Pattie - - -	78	William Pattie.	John Salmon - - -	87	John Salmon.
Martha Roach - - -	80	James M. Roach.	Joseph Shelton - -	79	Joseph Shelton.
William Rawles - - -	80	William Rawles.	Nathaniel Smith - -	77	Nathaniel Smith.
Michael Wiser - - -	85	Michael Wiser.	Robert Pace - - -	77	Robert Pace.
Rose Merry - - -	75	Samuel Wharton.	A. Layne - - -	81	A. Layne.
John Welch - - -	68	William A. Bowen.	Thornton Lowry - -	78	Thornton Lowry.
Amie Claggett - - -	68	Ferdinand Claggett.	John Martin - - -	88	John Martin.
Elizabeth Arrowsmith -	75	Day Mildred.	John Richards - - -	86	John Richards.
Ann Vowles - - -	88	Newton Vowles.			
Frances Walker - -	80	Solomon Walker.	**GREENSVILLE COUNTY.**		
			John Goodrum - - -	84	John Goodrum.
FLUVANNA COUNTY.			Balaam Bowers, sen. -	87	Balaam Bowers, sen
Stephen Mayo - - -	82	Stephen Mayo.	**GREENE COUNTY.**		
Isaac Lucado - - -	82	Littlebury Lucado.			
Hopper Ward - - -	88	Archibald Creary.	John Davis, sen. - -	80	John Davis, sen.
Martin Faris - - -	77	Martin Faris.	William Davis - - -	82	William Davis.
Charles Clements, sen. -	81	Charles Clements, sen.	Richard Goodall - -	82	Richard Goodall.
John S. Haislip - -	80	John S. Haislip.	Nehemiah Greening - -	84	Nehemiah Greening.
Daniel Thacher - -	81	Daniel Thacher.	Robert Holbert - -	39	Robert Holbert.
Zaccheus Granger - -	79	Allen T. Watson.	James Holmes - - -	82	James Holmes.
Jesse Saunders - -	88	Jesse Saunders.	William Parrott, sen. -	86	William Parrott, sen.
Richard Cawthorn, sen. -	76	Richard Cawthorn, sen.	George Sherman - -	77	George Sherman.
Thomas Shores - - -	85	Thomas Shores.	Bland Shiflett (died 15th of July,		
Jesse Wood - - -	86	Jesse Wood.	1840) - - -	89	Bland Shiflett.
John Maddox - - -	76	John Maddox.			
Nathaniel Harlow -	97	Nathaniel Harlow.			

Names of pensioners for revolutionary or military services.	Ages.	Names of heads of families with whom pensioners resided June 1, 1840.
GREENE—Continued.		
Zachariah Taylor - - -	81	Zachariah Taylor.
Richard White - - -	84	Richard White.
HALIFAX COUNTY.		
NORTHERN DISTRICT.		
William Abbott - - -	84	William Abbott.
Charles Allen - - -	78	James Allen.
Thomas Bailey - - -	75	Thomas Bailey.
John Coats, sen. - - -	84	John Coats, sen.
Charles Hudson - - -	75	Hilary Hudson.
William Hubbard - - -	82	William Hubbard.
David Street - - -	86	David Street.
Moses Woosley - - -	86	Holeman Woosley.
John Yates - - -	87	John Yates.
SOUTHERN DISTRICT.		
Edward Tuck, sen. - - -	78	
Wallace Wilson - - -	87	
William White - - -	78	William White.
James Willis - - -	77	James Willis.
Andrew Porgan - - -	79	
John Wesby - - -	76	John Wesby.
Alva Oliver - - -	76	
Alexander Kent - - -	84	
Patrick Mason - - -	75	Patrick Mason.
Thomas Tuck - - -	77	
Lewis Harley - - -	100	Ambrose Harley.
Noah Harbour - - -	83	Hartwell Harbour.
John Phillips - - -	80	John Phillips.
William Guill - - -	77	William Guill.
HANOVER COUNTY.		
Richard Shackelford - - -	84	John P. Shackelford.
John Gilman - - -	80	John Gilman.
John Woodson - - -	77	John Woodson.
John Hope - - -	77	John Hope.
Edmund Gilman - - -	78	Edmund Gilman.
Ann Fontaine - - -	74	Edmund Fontaine.
John Hall - - -	85	John Hall.
James Seay - - -	80	James Seay.
Hensley Grubbs - - -	83	Stephen V. Stone.
HENRICO COUNTY.		
Samuel Drewin - - -	76	Samuel Drewin.
John Hudson, sen. - - -	89	John Hudson, sen.
Thomas Clopton - - -	79	R. M. Pulleam.
John Whitlock, sen. - - -	77	Charles Whitlock, sen.
John Tinsley - - -	81	John Tinsley.
William Roundtree - - -	77	William Roundtree.
Samuel Drewin - - -	76	
CITY OF RICHMOND.		
Jefferson ward, No. 1.		
Jane Dunn - - -	74	Richard Deny.
Isaiah Parker - - -	52	Jabez Parker.
Madison ward, No. 2.		
Robert Pollard - - -	84	Robert Pollard.
Monroe ward, No. 3.		
None.		
HENRY COUNTY.		
John Redd - - -	84	John Redd.
Moses Spencer - - -	88	Elizabeth Stone.
Lewis Franklin - - -	82	Lewis Franklin.
Nusom Pau - - -	86	Nusom Pau.
Elisha Arnold - - -	82	Elisha Arnold.
John Price - - -	78	John Price.
Matthew Seay - - -	75	Matthew Seay, sen.
Benjamin Stratton - - -	87	James Stratton.
William Shackleford - - -	81	William Shackleford.
James Johnson - - -	84	James Johnson.
John Thompson - - -	83	John Thompson.
James Johnston - - -	94	James Johnston.
ISLE OF WIGHT COUNTY.		
Joseph Parkinson - - -	53	Joseph Parkinson.

Names of pensioners for revolutionary or military services.	Ages.	Names of heads of families with whom pensioners resided June 1, 1840.
KING GEORGE COUNTY.		
George Strother - - -	80	James Strother.
George Strother - - -	80	Benjamin Weaver.
KING WILLIAM COUNTY.		
John Butler - - -	76	John Butler.
James Whitlock - - -	77	James Whitlock, sen.
Mason Collins - - -	82	Mason Collins.
KING AND QUEEN COUNTY.		
Wilson Lumpkin - - -	86	Susanna Watkins.
William Gatewood - - -	82	William Gatewood.
John Clarke - - -	80	John Clarke.
Leonard Shackleford - - -	81	Leonard Shackleford.
LOUDOUN COUNTY.		
James Hogland - - -	81	John Hogland.
John Russell - - -	92	John Russell.
Charles B. Atwell - - -	75	Hugh Smith.
Edward Harvin - - -	86	Edward Harvin.
Issachar Brown - - -	80	Issachar Brown.
Enoch Furr - - -	95	Enoch Furr.
Hannah West - - -	68	John Onison.
Sarah Copeland - - -	72	Sarah Copeland.
1ST CITY DISTRICT.		
Margaret M. Stousonberger	78	Margaret M. Stousonberger.
Joseph Gilbert - - -	92	Joseph Gilbert.
Mary Magdalena - - -	73	Samuel Dan.
Sarah Butler - - -	78	George Marlow.
John H. Richardson - - -	83	John Wor.
Elizabeth Quick - - -	78	Elizabeth Quick.
Mary E. McPherson - - -	40	John S. Edwards.
Benjamin Widington - - -	76	Benjamin Widington.
Jacob Long - - -	88	Jacob Long.
Jesse Dailey - - -	79	Jesse Dailey.
William Newton - - -	52	Judith Newton.
LOUISA COUNTY.		
Joseph Spicer - - -	79	Joseph Spicer, sen.
John Morrison - - -	79	John Morrison.
Thomas Poindexter - - -	79	Thomas Poindexter.
Samuel Wharton - - -	77	Samuel Wharton.
Austin Hancock, sen. - - -	78	Austin Hancock, sen.
Henry Bibb - - -	81	Henry Bibb.
Robert Tate - - -	88	Robert Tate.
Thomas Badget - - -	82	Thomas Badget.
Dudley Degges - - -	80	Seneca T. P. Degges.
Nathaniel Snelson - - -	88	Nathaniel Snelson.
John Meeks, sen. - - -	76	John Meeks, sen.
Harden Duke - - -	80	Harden Duke.
Nathaniel Scales - - -	82	Nathaniel Scales.
LUNENBURG COUNTY.		
Charles Cooksey - - -	78	Charles Cooksey.
Shadrach Clark - - -	81	S. S. Field Clark.
John Estes - - -	84	John Estes.
John Frame - - -	83	John Frame.
Peter Hudson - - -	78	Peter Hudson.
Julius Hite - - -	83	Julius Hite.
John Mohorn - - -	84	John Mohorn.
Robert Mitchell - - -	80	Robert Mitchell.
William Stokes - - -	79	William Stokes.
MADISON COUNTY.		
Churchill Gibbs - - -	84	Churchill Gibbs.
J. & B. Haneson - - -	81, 83	John Haneson.
L. Taylor - - -	90	Ann Huffman.
Tavner Jones - - -	86	Tavner Jones.
William Madison - - -	82	William Madison.
Abram Tanner - - -	78	Abram Tanner.
William Taylor - - -	86	William Taylor.
William Tuyman - - -	84	William Tuyman.
MATTHEWS COUNTY.		
Thomas Davis - - -	78	Thomas Davis, son.
Avarilla Owen - - -	74	James D. Owen.

VIRGINIA—EASTERN DISTRICT—Continued.

Names of pensioners for revolutionary or military services.	Ages.	Names of heads of families with whom pensioners resided June 1, 1840.	Names of pensioners for revolutionary or military services.	Ages.	Names of heads of families with whom pensioners resided June 1, 1840.
MATTHEWS—Continued.			**ORANGE**—Continued.		
George Callis	78 }	George Callis, sen.	James Chiles	81	James Chiles.
Johanna Watson	84 }		William Fisher	79	William Fisher.
Nancy Morgan	74	Nancy Morgan.	George Morris	75	George Morris.
William Degges	80	William Degges, sen.	Jonathan Pratt	74	Jonathan Pratt.
Bathsheba Brooks	75	Bathsheba Brooks.	Philomel Richards	84	Philomel Richards.
Mary Minter	76	Mary Minter.	Daniel Young	49	Daniel Young.
Josiah Pugh	78	Josiah Pugh, sen.			
Matthias Gayle	78	Matthias Gayle, sen.	**PATRICK COUNTY.**		
Thomas Hall	75	Thomas Hall, sen.			
Dorothy White	78	Dorothy White.	William Tinch	81	William Tinch.
William D. White	48	William D. White.	James Harris	85	William Cassel.
Elizabeth White	67	Elizabeth White.	Benjamin Beasley	82	William Blancitt.
Mary Davis	86	Mary Davis.	Martha Martin	81	Stephen Martin.
Hugh Hudgins, sen.	76	Hugh Hudgins, sen.	Elihu Ayers	80	Elihu Ayers.
Joice Gayle	79	Bartlett Gayle.	James Boyd	81	John Boyd.
			William Carter	82	William Carter, sen.
MECKLENBURG COUNTY.			James Boaz	94	James Boaz, sen.
			Joseph Varner	82	Joseph Varner.
Joseph Butler, sen.	84	Joseph Butler, sen.	John Spencer	80	John Spencer, sen.
Charles Hudson	89	Charles Hudson, sen.			
James McCarton	81	James Henareck.	**PITTSYLVANIA COUNTY.**		
Royall Lockett, sen.	88	Royall Lockett.			
			James Thomas	81	James Thomas.
EASTERN DISTRICT.			James Hopkins	75	James Hopkins.
William Coleman	79	Wesley Coleman.	John Robertson	78	John Robertson.
Daniel Hicks	78	Daniel Hicks.	Moore Lumpkin	78	Moore Lumpkin.
Abel Farrar	75	Abel Farrar.	Henry H. Norvell	82	George Dove.
Varney Andrews	86	Varney Andrews.	Joseph Hundley	95	John Parker.
Bartlett Cox	74	Bartlett Cox.	Elisha Jones	82	Alexander Jones.
			Joseph Hubbard	78	Joseph Hubbard.
MIDDLESEX COUNTY.			Anthony P. Lipford	85	Anthony P. Lipford.
			Ann Miller, (died July 28, 1840)	73	Samuel J. Miller.
Elizabeth Daniel	78	Mecklenburg Daniel.	James Roach	78	James Roach.
George Gardner	85	George Gardner.	John Neal	79	John Neal.
			William Dove, sen.	82	William Dove, sen.
NANSEMOND COUNTY.			Griffeth Dickenson	84	Griffeth Dickenson.
Henry Skinner	81		SOUTHERN DISTRICT.		
William Boytt, sen.	82	William Boytt, sen.	Robert W. Fitz	83	Tandy W. Fitz.
William Byrd	81		William M. Nance	82	William M. Nance.
Jeremiah Peale	83	Jeremiah Peale.	William Dickson	85	William Dickson.
			Peter Wall	87	Peter Wall.
NELSON COUNTY.			Jennings Thompson	78	Jennings Thompson.
			Zachariah Pruit	83	Zachariah Pruit.
Hawes Coleman	83	Hawes N. Coleman.	John D. Martin	45	John D. Martin.
Benjamin Fitzgerald	81	Benjamin Fitzgerald.	Elisha Ford	79	Elisha Ford.
Richard Hare	91	Richard Hare.	Jacob Anderson	90	Jacob Anderson, jun.
William Jordan	90	William Jordan.			
Alexander McAlexander	84	Alexander McAlexander.	**POWHATAN COUNTY.**		
Hudson Martin	79	Hudson Martin.			
Henry McLayne	90	Henry McLayne.	Henry Lipford	91	George W. Pace.
Micass Pendleton	82	Micass Pendleton.	Thomas Tucker	86	Thomas Tucker.
John Pugh	82	John Pugh.	Seth Hatcher	80	Seth Hatcher.
Clifton Tombs	46	Clifton Tombs.	Susanna Mosby	72	Edward C. Mosby.
Bransford West	85	Bransford West.	Sally Taylor	72	Sally Taylor.
Micass Wheeler	81	Micass Wheeler.	Susanna Mosby	75	Susanna Mosby.
Thomas Ware	78	Thomas Ware.	Archibald Short	79	Dutoy Bass.
			John Sledd	81	John Sledd.
NEW KENT COUNTY.			James Hall	87	James Hall.
Anselm Bailey, sen.	—	Anselm Bailey, sen.	**PRINCESS ANNE COUNTY.**		
Samuel Moss	77	Samuel Moss.			
James Williams	—	James Williams.	John Brown, sen.	82	John Brown, sen.
			Charles Anderson	85	Charles Anderson.
NORFOLK COUNTY.					
			PRINCE EDWARD COUNTY.		
John Butler	85	J. O. Butler.			
D. Wright	84	D. Wright.	Charles Brightwell	83	Charles Brightwell, sen.
William Stark	85	William Stark.	John Crute	85	John Crute.
			John Cunningham	82	John Cunningham.
NORTHAMPTON COUNTY.			Bartholomew Cyrus	82	Bartholomew Cyrus.
			Joseph Davidson	86	Joseph Davidson.
Obadiah Johnson	48	Obadiah Johnson.	Mary Dupey	73	Mary Dupey.
James Carter	85	Sarah Becket.	Nathan Grubbs	81	Nathan Grubbs.
William Dennis	87	Nathaniel Dalby.	Obadiah Hendrick	82	Obadiah Hendrick.
			William Hill	82	William Hill, sen.
ORANGE COUNTY.			William Jesse	81	William Jesse.
			James Moss	80	James Moss.
John Almond	86	John Almond.	Ann Pugh	74	John M. Pugh.
Lucy Cowherd	77	Lucy Cowherd.	William F. Scott	80	William F. Scott.
Susan Campbell	71	Susan Campbell.	Jehu Simmons	78	Jehu Simmons.
William Crittendon	80	William Crittendon.	Samuel Walker	48	Samuel Walker.

VIRGINIA—EASTERN DISTRICT—Continued.

Names of pensioners for revolutionary or military services.	Ages.	Names of heads of families with whom pensioners resided June 1, 1840.	Names of pensioners for revolutionary or military services.	Ages.	Names of heads of families with whom pensioners resided June 1, 1840.
PRINCE GEORGE COUNTY.			SPOTTSYLVANIA—Continued.		
Samuel Temple - - -	78	Samuel Temple.	BERKELEY PARISH.		
Augustine Heath - - -	78	Augustine Heath.	William Cason - - -	75	William Cason.
Daniel Hair - - -	80		Thomas R. Jones - - -	85	Thomas R. Jones.
Joel Cheives - - -	85	Joel Cheives.	William Knight - - -	80	William Knight.
PRINCE WILLIAM COUNTY.			John Pierce, sen. - - -	88	John Pierce, sen.
			P. Pendleton - - -	79	Phil. Pendleton.
John Sullivan - - -	82	John Sullivan.	Richard Stears - - -	78	Jenny Stears.
John Gill - - -	80	John Gill.	John Stewart - - -	79	John Stewart.
Hugh Davis - - -	81	Hugh Davis.	Philip Smith - - -	83	Philip Smith.
			James Smith - - -	90	James A. Smith.
PORTSMOUTH COUNTY.			George Trible - - -	85	George Trible.
			Philip Vass - - -	78	Philip Vass.
Elizabeth Porter - - -	75		H. Willoughby - - -	79	Henry Willoughby.
Ann Watts - - -	74		Abr. Wilson - - -	80	Abr. Wilson.
RAPPAHANNOCK COUNTY.			ST. GEORGE'S PARISH.		
			William Griffin - - -	86	William Griffin.
George M. Houck - - -	83	Francis Carey.	George Mansfield - - -	84	George Mansfield.
Mary Drummond - - -	75	Mary Drummond.	John Sorrill - - -	88	Frances Strutton.
William Brown - - -	85	William Brown.			
Lucy Slaughter - - -	71	Robert Slaughter.	**STAFFORD COUNTY.**		
Elizabeth Towles - - -	80	Samuel Decamp.			
Mason Colvin - - -	80	Mason Colvin.	James Nickens - - -	85	James Nickens.
John Corder - - -	80	John Corder.	Travers Fritter - - -	43	Travers Fritter.
Spencer Withers - - -	75	Spencer Withers.			
William Smith - - -	84	William Smith, sen.	**SURRY COUNTY.**		
John Roberts - - -	82	John Roberts.			
Vincent Tapp - - -	76	Vincent Tapp.	Jesse Brown - - -	83	Benjamin Brown.
David Kennaird - - -	82	David Kennaird.	Jesse King - - -	86	Jesse King.
Delpha Smith - - -	68	John W. Garner.			
George Mozingo - - -	79	George Mozingo, sen.	**SUSSEX COUNTY.**		
James Jones - - -	83	James Jones.	William Chappell - - -	78	William Chappell.
			Absalom Flowers - - -	82	Absalom Flowers.
RICHMOND COUNTY.			Joseph Prince - - -	76	Joseph Prince.
			John Wrenn - - -	78	John Wrenn.
John France, sen. - - -	78	John France, sen.	Henry Bailey - - -	84	Henry Bailey.
James Burgess, sen. - - -	77	James Burgess, sen.	William Shands, sen. - - -	82	William Shands, sen.
John Brown - - -	58	John Brown.			
			WESTMORELAND COUNTY.		
SOUTHAMPTON COUNTY.					
			William Brann - - -	93	William Brann, sen.
Jesse Croker - - -	80	Jesse Croker.	Robert Beale - - -	82	Robert Beale.
Samuel Corbit - - -	83	Johnson Corbit.	James Deatly - - -	90	James Deatly.
Joshua Joyner - - -	83	Joshua Joyner.	Charles Green - - -	81	Charles Green.
William Owney - - -	78	William Owney.	Charles Hegdon - - -	76	Charles Hegdon.
Revell Holiday, sen. - - -	83	Revell Holiday, sen.	Gerard Hutt - - -	75	Gerard Hutt, sen.
			William S. Jett - - -	76	William Starke Jett.
SPOTTSYLVANIA COUNTY.			James McKoy, sen. - - -	80	James C. McKoy, sen.
TOWN OF FREDERICKSBURG.			Samuel Templeman - - -	82	Samuel Templeman.
James Jones - - -	80	James Jones.			

VIRGINIA—WESTERN DISTRICT.

Names of pensioners for revolutionary or military services.	Ages.	Names of heads of families with whom pensioners resided June 1, 1840.	Names of pensioners for revolutionary or military services.	Ages.	Names of heads of families with whom pensioners resided June 1, 1840.
ALLEGANY COUNTY.			**BROOKE COUNTY.**		
ALLEGANY.					
Jacob Persinger - - -	96	Jacob Persinger	Joachim Wicoff - - -	90	Robert Moore.
Jacob Hoover - - -	93	Jacob Hoover	David Craig - - -	58	David Craig.
George Semmon - - -	82	Conrad Semmon.	Samuel Corey - - -	86	Elijah Corey.
			Daniel Corkle - - -	93	William McConnell.
			Samuel Ogden - - -	87	Samuel Ogden.
AUGUSTA COUNTY.			William Baxter - - -	91	William Baxter.
			Patrick Gass - - -	70	Patrick Gass.
Mary Knowles - - -	85	John Gorden.	Captain Oliver Brown - - -	88	Stephen Colwell.
John McWilliams - - -	82	Andrew Anderson.	Samuel Miller - - -	85	Joseph Miller.
William Armstrong - - -	81	Archibald Armstrong.			
John McCutchin - - -	91	James McCutchin.	**BOTTETOURT COUNTY.**		
Thomas Johnston - - -	79	Thomas Johnston.			
David Steele - - -	83	John Steele.	Francis Hunter - - -	79	Francis Hunter.
Alexander Hamilton - - -	76	William Brown.	Richard Litteral - - -	75	Richard Litteral.
Robert Porterfield - - -	88	Robert Porterfield.	Henry Cartmile - - -	86	Henry Cartmile.
John Nee - - -	80	John Nee.	John Camper - - -	92	John Camper.
Christian Gregory - - -	74	John S. Kesterson.	James Simpson - - -	83	Mary Simpson.
Claudius Buster - - -	76	Claudius Buster.	John Hacket - - -	81	James R. Trainor.
Elizabeth Eskridge - - -	73	George Walls.	Michael Gwartney - - -	80	Zachariah Gwartney.
Peter Lohr - - -	88	Peter Lohr.	Jacob Lemmon - - -	77	Jacob Lemmon.

VIRGINIA—WESTERN DISTRICT—Continued.

Names of pensioners for revolutionary or military services.	Ages.	Names of heads of families with whom pensioners resided June 1, 1840	Names of pensioners for revolutionary or military services.	Ages.	Names of heads of families with whom pensioners resided June 1, 1840.
BOTTETOURT—Continued.			**GREENBRIER COUNTY.**		
John Hewitt	77	John Hewitt.	NORTHERN DISTRICT.		
Philip Crist	82	Philip Crist, jr.	John Fryer	81	John Fryer.
BATH COUNTY.			Eli Perkins, sen.	82	Eli Perkins, jr.
Ann Payne	80	James Howell.	SOUTHERN DISTRICT.		
Robert Thompson	84	James Thomas.	Berryman Jones	78	Berryman Jones.
James Stuart	84	St. Clair Stuart.	James McLaughlin	58	James Scott.
John Stuart	79	John Stuart.	Thomas Perry	89	Thomas Perry.
William Boner, sen.	80	William Boner, sen.	**GILES COUNTY.**		
Rachel Cameron	68	Andrew W. Cameron.			
Samuel Gilmor	80	Alexander Gilmor.	William Neel	79	John M. Neel.
Timothy Holcomb	85	Roger Gum	William Brown	86	William H. Brown.
BERKELEY COUNTY.			John Kirk	86	John Kirk, jr.
			Andrew Straley	88	James Straley.
Charles Young	84	Charles Young.	**HARRISON COUNTY.**		
Catharine McKeeven	84	Elizabeth McKeeven.			
Erasmus Gant	81	Erasmus Gant.	Joshua Jones, sen.	79	Joshua Jones, sen.
Paul Taylor	90	Paul Taylor.	Job Goff, sen.	79	Job Goff, sen.
Basil Lucas	83	Basil Lucas.	Peter Knight	81	Peter Knight.
Henry Bedinger	86	Henry Bedinger.	Jacob Harrow	84	Jacob Harrow.
Susan Shober	70	Susan Shober.	Peter Johnson	88	Peter Johnson.
BRAXTON COUNTY.			William Shingleton	80	William Shingleton.
			John Waldo	79	John Waldo.
Jacob Fisher	77	William Cutlip.	Pamela Keyser	76	George Keyser.
CABELL COUNTY.			John Latham	74	John Latham.
			Susanna Roe	77	James Roe.
John Everritt, sen.	87	John Everritt, jr.	Leonard Cutzer	81	Leonard Cutzer.
Asher Crocket	81	Asher Crocket.	William Martin	78	William Martin.
Valentine Blose	82	Isaac Blose.	John Bennet	61	John Bennet, sen.
John Stephenson	79	John Stephenson.	John Nay	91	Oliver Nay.
Robert Rutherford	77	Thomas Rutherford.	Jacob Thompson	80	Jacob Thompson.
Thomas Roberts	78	Thomas Roberts.	Elisha Griffith	89	Charles McEntire.
James Gellengwaters	74	John Gellengwaters.	William Nichol	84	Kezin Fowler.
John Lesley	79	Milton Stratton.	Edward Stewart	81	Edward Stewart, sen.
William Meade	78	Theophilus Goodwin.	Christopher Nutter	80	Christopher Nutter.
Adam Crom	85	Adam Crom.	Rhodam Rogers	84	Benjamin Harvey.
John Adkins, sen.	84	John Adkins.	Mary Lindsey	76	Mary Lindsey.
Peter Sullivan	85	Aaron Sullivan.	William Davis	82	John Sutton.
Thomas Chandler	78	Thomas Chandler.	Jonathan Hughes	86	Robert Stutler.
CLARK COUNTY.			Henry McWhorter	80	Leonard S. Ward.
			HARDY COUNTY.		
Jacob Berlin	95	Philip Berlin.	John Rosebraugh	101	John Rosebraugh.
FREDERICK COUNTY.			Adam Bullinger	73	Adam Bullinger.
			Jacob Randall	81	Jacob Randall.
George Escridge	84	Stephen Prichards.	Cichman Ours	85	Cichman Ours.
Philip Booher	90	Philip Booher.	John Ebills	76	John Ebills.
Robert Finley	76	Robert Finley.	Christopher Goodnight	78	Christopher Goodnight.
Henry Bailis	80	Henry Bailis.	Daniel Ketterman	78	Daniel Ketterman
John Lewis	92	John Lewis.	John Berry	96	John Berry.
George Black	82	James Garvin.	Richard Redman	84	John Martin.
Jacob Shade	84	Jacob Shade.	**HAMPSHIRE COUNTY.**		
FAYETTE COUNTY.			George Little	84	George Little.
			John Mailick	78	John Mailick.
Abraham Vandal	80	E. D. Vandal.	John Queen	85	Stephen Queen.
John Reins	96	John Reins.	Henry Powelson	79	Henry Powelson
William Richmond	89	Shadrick Martin.	Asa Simons	81	Asa Simons.
FLOYD COUNTY.			John Peters	86	John Peters.
			Christian Hass	88	Peter Hass.
John King	80	John King.	Thomas Shores	86	William Abernathy, jr.
Benjamin Edwards	87	Benjamin Edwards.	Alexander Doran	80	Joseph Doran.
Daniel Shelor, sen.	89	George Shelor, sen.	John Hansbrough	75	John Hansbrough.
GRAYSON COUNTY.			Wilmore Male (colored)	84	Wilmore Male.
EASTERN DISTRICT.			Henry Kump	82	Henry Kump.
Mary Frost	79	Simon Frost.	Major William Heron	78	William Heron.
Lawrence Stephens	85	Lawrence Stephens.	Daniel Taylor	83	Daniel Taylor.
Susanna Dean	75	Susanna Dean.	Isaac James	78	Isaac James.
Mary Spencer	79	Mary Spencer.	**JEFFERSON COUNTY.**		
Anthony Foster	84	Anthony Foster.	CHARLESTOWN.		
William Cloud	89	William Cloud.	Peter Haines	90	John Avis.
Sarah McCraw	81	Levi Jones.	SHEPERDSTOWN.		
Joel Ashworth	78	Joel Ashworth.	Daniel Folck	86	Daniel Folck.
WESTERN DISTRICT.			**JACKSON COUNTY.**		
William Vaughn	79	William Vaughn.	Thomas Good	82	Thomas Good.
			Andrew Welch	82	Andrew Welch.

VIRGINIA—WESTERN DISTRICT—Continued.

Names of pensioners for revolutionary or military services.	Ages.	Names of heads of families with whom pensioners resided June 1, 1840.	Names of pensioners for revolutionary or military services.	Ages.	Names of heads of families with whom pensioners resided June 1, 1840.
JACKSON—Continued.			WESTERN MONONGALIA—Continued.		
John McKown - - -	83	John McKown.			
Samuel Carpenter - -	77	Samuel Carpenter.	Charles Simkins - - -	82	Charles Simkins.
Elijah Runnion - - -	78	Elijah Runnion.	Benjamin Chesney - -	80	William Cole.
David Harris - - -	71	David Harris.	James Scott - - -	75	James Scott.
Henry Raburn - - -	100	Weden Carney.	John Dent - - - -	85	John Dent.
			Elisha Clayton - - -	83	Elisha Clayton.
KANAWHA COUNTY.			Asaph M. Colegate - -	77	Asaph M. Colegate.
			Samuel Dudley - - -	77	Samuel Dudley.
Benjamin Stone - - -	80	Benjamin Stone.	Robert Derrah - - -	71	Robert Derrah.
			Amos Morris - - -	77	Amos Morris.
LEE COUNTY.			Zadoc Morris - - -	79	Zadoc Morris.
Edward Smyth - - -	75	Edward Smyth.	**MONTGOMERY COUNTY.**		
Francis Mills - - -	83	Francis Mills.			
Samuel Marion - - -	94	Samuel Marion.	Frederick Bolt - - -	90	Frederick Bolt.
Jacob Crabtree - - -	81	Jacob Crabtree.	Francis Charlton - -	82	Francis Charlton.
Enoch Bush - - -	91	Enoch Bush.	John Emmons - - -	77	John Emmons.
William Carmack - -	77	William Carmack.	Jesse Hall, sen. - -	80	John L. Hall.
William Ely - - -	91	William Ely.	Asa Hall, sen. - -	82	Asa Hall, sen.
Samuel Gilbert - - -	77	Samuel Gilbert.	Mary Lucas - - -	82	Wilson Lucas.
			Andrew Lewis - - -	82	Andrew Lewis.
LOGAN COUNTY.			Alexander McClure - -	64	Thomas Moses.
			Rice D. Montagu, sen. -	72	Rice D. Montagu, sen.
William Davis - - -	96	William Davis.	Elijah Meacham - -	80	Elijah Meacham.
John S. Barsden - -	90	Edward Barsden.	John Miles, sen. - -	89	John Miles, sen.
Samuel Mead - - -	90	Samuel Mead.	Elizabeth Elliott - -	66	Samuel Otey.
			James P. Preston - -	66	James P. Preston.
LEWIS COUNTY.			Elizabeth Crow - -	84	William S. Ronald.
			Bolen Rogers - - -	78	Bolen Rogers.
John Waggoner - - -	90	Samuel Waggoner.	Giles Thomas - - -	76	William Thomas.
John Rains - - -	83	William R. Sturcher.	Elizabeth Robinson -	82	William L. Woolwine.
Jacob Hunt - - -	85	John Hunt.			
Philip Reeger - - -	73	Nathan Reeger.	**MARSHALL COUNTY.**		
James Tenney - - -	75	James Tenney.			
Jacob Hyse - - -	83	Jacob Hyse.	David Ferrel - - -	75	David Ferrel.
John Cutright - - -	87	Christopher Cutright.	John Caldwell - - -	90	Ezekiel Caldwell.
John Davis - - -	86	Benjamin Shammon.	John Cummins - - -	85	John Cummins.
William Powers - -	75	William Powers.	John Fox - - -	85	John Fox, jr.
Joseph Wilson - - -	83	Dolpheas D. Holbert.	Henry Yoho - - -	88	Henry Yoho.
Peter Cogar - - -	85	Adam Starcher.			
Phebe Cunningham - -	80	Benjamin Hardman.	**MORGAN COUNTY.**		
			Nicholas Henry - - -	84	Peter Henry.
MASON COUNTY.					
			MERCER COUNTY.		
John Hereford - - -	83	John Hereford.			
Samuel Hayes - - -	59	Samuel Hayes.	Josiah Meadows - - -	83	Green Meadows.
James Harrison - -	85	George Chapman.			
George Lemastor - -	43	George Lemastor.	**OHIO COUNTY.**		
John Kersey - - -	78	John Kersey.			
Luman Gibbs - - -	75	Luman Gibbs, sen.	James Holliday - - -	86	James Holliday.
William Hawkins - -	76	Nancy Hawkins.	Samuel Miller - - -	85	Joseph Miller.
Robert Love - - -	78	Robert Love.	John Curtis - - -	89	James Darling.
Andrew Eckard - -	80	Andrew Eckard.			
			PENDLETON COUNTY.		
MONROE COUNTY.					
			Charles Borror - - -	83	Charles Borror.
John Wright - - -	82	David G. Givins.	John Devericks, sen. -	78	John Devericks, sen.
John Foster - - -	80	John Foster.	William Eagle - - -	79	William Eagle.
Flora Smith - - -	95	Thomas Pritt.	Michael Hoover - -	88	Michael Hoover.
James Jones - - -	79	James Jones.	Thomas Kinkead - -	76	Thomas Kinkead.
James Larkin - - -	96	Robert Young.	William Lawrence - -	73	William Lawrence.
John Hutchinson - -	86	Isaac Hutchinson.	Edward Morton - -	75	Edward Morton.
James Boyd - - -	81	James Boyd.	Zachariah Rexroad - -	79	Solomon Rexroad.
Nathaniel Garlen - -	78	Nathaniel Garlen.	George Rymer, sen. -	90	George Rymer, sen.
Henry Arnott, sen. -	80	Henry Arnott, jr.	Eli B. Wilson - - -	84	Eli B. Wilson.
Samuel Clarke - -	76	Samuel Clarke.			
William Kirby - -	81	Martin Kirby.	**POCAHONTAS COUNTY.**		
Samuel Allen - - -	95	George Allen, sen.			
Thomas Walker - -	77	Thomas Walker.	John Young, sen. - -	73	John Young, sen.
			Adam Abegart, sen. -	80	Adam Abegart, sen.
EASTERN MONONGALIA COUNTY.			John Webb - - -	89	Martin Dilley.
Evan Morgan - - -	88	Evan Morgan.	**PAGE COUNTY.**		
William Wilson - -	84	William Wilson.			
Isaac Reed - - -	82	Isaac Reed.	Daniel Anderson - -	88	Daniel Anderson.
James Devars - - -	86	James Devars.	Sarah Anderson - -	–	Moses Wood.
George Keller - - -	81	John Keller.	Thomas Tharp - - -	80	Thomas Tharp.
			John C. Aleshire - -	84	Henry Mauck.
WESTERN MONONGALIA COUNTY.			James McCullough - -	–	Joseph McCullough.
			—— Cook - - -	–	Strawther Cook.
James Collins - : -	85	James Collins.	Virginia Page Carder - :	:	Robert Carder.

VIRGINIA—WESTERN DISTRICT—Continued.

Names of pensioners for revolutionary or military services.	Ages.	Names of heads of families with whom pensioners resided June 1, 1840.	Names of pensioners for revolutionary or military services.	Ages.	Names of heads of families with whom pensioners resided June 1, 1840.
PAGE—Continued.			**SMYTH—Continued.**		
Sarah Strickler	–	David J. Strickler.	Nathaniel Harris, sen.	78	Nathaniel Harris, sen.
John Burkholder	–	William Burkholder.	John Musser	83	John Musser.
—— Burner	–	John R. Burner.	William Reagan	84	William Reagan.
Jane Roads	–	John H. Roads.	**SCOTT COUNTY.**		
Ann Stover	–	Joseph Stover.	Absalom Hamonds	86	Sarah Hamonds.
Henry Aleshire	89	Conrad Aleshire.	William Stewart	83	Nimrod Taylor.
PULASKI COUNTY.			William Fields	86	William Fields.
Jacob Anderson	83	Jacob Anderson.	John Smith	79	William B. Smith.
John Carper	80	John Carper, jr.	William Lawson, sen.	76	William Lawson, sen.
Henry Wysor, sen.	86	Henry Wysor, sen.	Alexander M. Gray	52	Alexander M. Gray.
PRESTON COUNTY.			William Sloane, sen.	82	William Sloane, sen.
Isaac Matthew	84	Isaac Matthew.	**SHENANDOAH COUNTY.**		
John Jennings	90	Jonathan Jenkins.	Daniel Gray	76	James McCan.
John Hartman	84	John Hartman.	Michael Rootz	94	Thornton A. Bowman.
Daniel Martin	89	Daniel Martin.	Thomas Hudson	83	Thomas Hudson.
Dabney Ford	89	Frederick K. Ford.	**TAZEWELL COUNTY.**		
Asa Wilson	78	Asa Wilson.	Low Brown, sen.	89	Low Brown, sen.
Nathan Ashby	75	Elijah Hardesty.	Joseph Oney	90	Isaac Oney.
Abner Messenger	81	Samuel Messenger.	Jarrett Bolling	72	Jarrett Bolling.
ROCKINGHAM COUNTY.			Thomas Witten, sen.	88	James S. Witten, jr.
Elizabeth Brown	83	Peter Brown.	Lyles Dollsberry	80	Lyles Dollsberry.
Andrew Huling	79	Joseph Weltshire.	William Brooks	88	William Brooks.
Philip Koontz	95	Philip Koontz.	John McGlotholin	75	John McGlotholin.
James Meadows	81	James Meadows.	**TYLER COUNTY.**		
Henry Hammer	84	Henry Hammer.	Charles Swan	86	Charles Swan.
Leonard Davis	79	Susanna Marshall.	Thomas Weekley, sen.	88	Thomas Weekley, sen.
Francis Yancy	70	Francis Yancy.	William Bennet	94	William Bennet.
William Bryan	78	Elisha Bryan.	Sarah Wells	85	Eli Wells.
Agnes Vanpelt	77	Jacob Vanpelt.	Jacob Lewis	85	Jacob Lewis.
David Ralston	79	David Ralston.	Philip Miller	83	Philip Miller.
Magdaline Bible	75	Christian Bible.	Samuel Wheeler	80	Samuel Wheeler.
Mary Gibbons	80	Samuel Gibbons.	Richard Dotson	88	James Dotson.
Philip Hartman	83	Elias Horn.	James S. Ferrell, sen.	78	James S. Ferrell, sen.
Matthew Tate	87	Russel Wright.	Jeremiah Williams, sen.	79	Jeremiah Williams, sen.
James Palmer	77	James Palmer.	John Burden, sen.	81	John Burden, sen.
RUSSELL COUNTY.			Temperance Cochran	79	Samuel Cochran.
Michael Sword, sen.	82	Michael Sword, jun.	**WARREN COUNTY.**		
Benjamin Ray	83	William Wallis.	Thomas Buck, sen.	84	Thomas Buck, sen.
Francis Browning, sen.	87	Francis Browning, sen	William Monroe	80	William Monroe.
Thomas Lovelady	93	George Gose.	Samuel Stokes	87	Samuel Stokes.
John Hackney	86	John Hackney.	Moses Henry	86	Moses Henry.
Daniel Price	77	Daniel Price.	Benjamin McKnight	80	} John Sansberry.
John Sykes	83	James Sykes.	John Sansberry	60	
Joel Ramsey	81	Joel Ramsey.	Daniel Edmonds	83	Jos. Brown.
James Rose	80	Jona. Skeen.	Jeffrey Collins	85	Jeffrey Collins.
Jesse Vermillion	88	Jesse Vermillion.	Robert Russell	84	Robert Russell.
RANDOLPH COUNTY.			James Cheek	77	James Cheek.
Mary Chenoweth	76	Jehu Chenoweth.	**WYTHE COUNTY.**		
John Neville, sen.	75	John Neville, sen.	Joseph Ramsey	80	Joseph Ramsey.
Henry Tansler	79	Andrew Tansler.	Hugh McGavock	79	Hugh McGavock.
Jacob Kittle	83	Jacob Kittle.	**WASHINGTON COUNTY.**		
Nancy Ann Hart	83	Nancy Ann Hart.	Edward Barker	88	Edward Barker.
ROCKBRIDGE COUNTY.			Samuel Henseley	86	Samuel Henseley.
BROWNSBURG.			James Hilland	82	David G. Hilland.
Captain William Moore	90	Nancy Harvey.	Samuel Johnson	81	Samuel Johnson.
John Green	91	Lawrence Green.	James Keyes	84	Robert Keyes.
John Strickland	91	Joseph Strickland.	Henry Low	94	Henry Low.
William Smith	76	William Smith.	Frederick Leonard	82	Henry Leonard, sen.
James Barley	80	Samuel Barley.	John McCauly	84	John McCauly.
Adam Hickman	78	Adam Hickman.	Robert Pippin, sen.	83	Robert Pippin, sen.
David Shepperson	77	David Shepperson.	Thomas McGee	99	Hannah Roe.
Absalom Ailstock	84	Absalom Ailstock.	John Shaffer	87	Samuel Shaffer.
ROANOKE COUNTY.			Jacob Woodard	80	Jacob Woodard.
Douglass Ebley	87	John Reley.	Michael Widener	82	Michael Widener.
William Henry	87	William Henry.	**WOOD COUNTY.**		
Joel Davenport	87	Joel Davenport.	Thomas Leach	78	John Cooper.
Eusom Hannon	91	Eusom Hannon.	Bailey Rice	85	Bailey Rice.
SMYTH COUNTY.			Patrick Sumett	83	George Sumett.
Moses Allen	89	Moses Allen.	William Cunningham	82	William Cunningham.
Zachariah Hurt	75	Washington Hurt.	Moses Rollins	76	Henry Rollins.

STATE OF NORTH CAROLINA.

Names of pensioners for revolutionary or military services.	Ages.	Names of heads of families with whom pensioners resided June 1, 1840.	Names of pensioners for revolutionary or military services.	Ages.	Names of heads of families with whom pensioners resided June 1, 1840.
ANSON COUNTY.			**BRUNSWICK COUNTY.**		
James Ross	79		Ebenezer Hewett	95	
Rachael High	79	Rachael High.	John Cason	100	
Jordan Woodard	81	Jordan Woodard.	**CAMDEN COUNTY.**		
Absalom Candle	73	Berry Candle.	None.		
William Ricketts	92	William Ricketts.			
John Hough	80	John Hough.	**CHATHAM COUNTY.**		
Job Williams	82	Job Williams.			
Michael Nash	87	Michael Nash.	William Marsh, sen.	81	William Marsh, sen.
William Johnson	79	William Johnson.	Richard Pope, sen.	79	Richard Pope, sen.
Josiah Abshear	87	Josiah Abshear.	James Barns	77	James Barns.
William Garman	80	William Garman.	Richard Stokes	78	Richard Stokes.
Kinchin Martin	78	Kinchin Martin.	James Carter	77	William A. Reaves.
Charles Hinson	78	Charles Hinson.	Hurbart Lewis	82	Isaiah Williams.
Richard Tomlinson	92	Richard Tomlinson.	John Foshee, sen.	82	John Foshee, sen.
William Vaughan	91	William Vaughan.	Joshua Adcock, sen.	79	Joshua Adcock, sen.
William O. Bryant	85	William O. Bryant.	Moses Merack	82	Tabitha Merack.
ASHE COUNTY.			Grace Webb	83	Grace Webb.
			James Dollar	80	James Dollar.
Francis Johnson	79	Francis Johnson.	Joseph Yarbrough	83	Joseph Yarbrough.
John Baldwin	79	John Baldwin, jr.	Thomas Dickens	82	Thomas Dickens.
John Wagg	84	John Wagg.	Andrew Peddy	83	Andrew Peddy.
			William Laseter, sen.	83	William Laseter, sen.
BUNCOMBE COUNTY			Abner Laseter	85	Abner Laseter.
SOUTHERN DIVISION.			Mary Pendergrass	77	Candace Pendergrass.
William Dever	77	Reuben Dever.	James Kinby	78	James Kinby.
William Brittain	78	William Brittain.	Hardy Lewter	100	Hardy Lewter.
Samuel Patton	79	Samuel Patton.	Bias Rogers	90	Bias Rogers.
Daniel Ball, sen.	–	Daniel Ball, sen	John Mooring, sen.	75	John Mooring, sen.
Joseph Cross	93	Joseph Cross.			
James Alexander	84	James Alexander.	**CABARRUS COUNTY.**		
Thomas Paine	74	Thomas Paine.			
Thomas Jester	78	Thomas Jester.	Henry Furr	80	Henry Furr.
James Rector	75		Thomas McClure	77	William Fisher.
			James Bradford	81	James Bradford.
BURKE COUNTY.			William Carregan	79	William Carregan.
			James Hamilton	79	James Hamilton.
Birch Allison	78	Birch Allison.	George Thomaston	91	Francis Ray.
Daniel Sullivan	80	E. D. Sullivan.	Thomas Irvine	80	Thomas Irvine.
John Arrowood, sen.	78	John Arrowood, sen.	Archibald McCurdy	88	Archibald McCurdy.
Adam Hoppis	86	Adam Hoppis.			
George Hodge	80	George Hodge.	**COLUMBUS COUNTY.**		
John Duckworth	83	John Duckworth, jr.			
Sherwood Boman, sen.	81	Sherwood Boman, sen.	John Money	84	Augustus Smith.
Lewis Powell	78	Lewis Powell.	David Ross	77	John N. Hill.
Nicholas Fry	97	John Berry.	Benjamin Sasser	84	Stephen Jernegan.
Benjamin Spencer	80	Benjamin Spencer.			
John Swink	88	John Swink.	**CHOWAN COUNTY.**		
			Jonathan Overton	86	Samuel Overton.
BLADEN COUNTY.			Henry Halsey	84	Henry Halsey.
Josiah Singletory	76	Josiah Singletory.	**CRAVEN COUNTY.**		
Richard Cheshire	97	Richard Cheshire.			
John Darrah	83	John Darrah.	Enoch Masters	83	Enoch Masters.
Francis Davis	87	Francis Davis.	Samuel Ipock, sen.	80	Samuel Ipock, sen.
Jacob B. Boit	89	Jacob B. Boit.	William Witherington	82	William Witherington.
William Prigen	112	Elizabeth Johnson.	Benjamin White	78	Benjamin White.
James Shipman	89	James Shipman.	Solomon Witherington, sen.	80	Solomon Witherington, sen.
John McElthan	83	Malcom McLeod.			
Musgroves Jones	88	Musgroves Jones.	**CASWELL COUNTY.**		
William Smith	85	William Smith.			
			Sterling Gum	76	Sterling Gum.
BEAUFORT COUNTY.			John B. Davis	83	John B. Davis.
			Jeremiah Buren	86	Willie Garner.
Anthony Kinion	77	Anthony Kinion.	James Matkins	80	John Matkins.
Isaac Buck, sen.	88	Isaac Buck, sen.	William Roberts	79	William Roberts.
			Charles Cox	78	Charles Cox.
BURKE COUNTY.			Elisha Evans	80	Elisha Evans.
			Braxton Carter	65	Braxton Carter.
Stephen Ballew	77	Stephen Ballew.	Keziah Donoho	89	Keziah Donoho.
Daniel Moore, sen.	76	Daniel Moore, sen.	Nathan Adkins	90	William Adkins.
Samuel Alexander	80	Samuel Alexander.	John Dill	77	John Dill, jr.
Benjamin Austin	81	Benjamin Austin.	Richard Morton	85	Richard Morton.
David Hayes	92	David Hayes.			
			CUMBERLAND COUNTY.		
BERTIE COUNTY.					
			Alexander Johnson	80	Alexander Johnson.
John White	82	John White.	Sherwood Fort	81	Sherwood Fort.
William Watford	88	William Watford.	Hardy Mathews	86	Hardy Mathews.
John Hoggard	82	John Hoggard.	Will. S. Walker	–	Will. S. Walker.

18

CENSUS OF PENSIONERS.

NORTH CAROLINA—Continued.

Names of pensioners for revolutionary or military services.	Ages.	Names of heads of families with whom pensioners resided June 1, 1840.	Names of pensioners for revolutionary or military services.	Ages.	Names of heads of families with whom pensioners resided June 1, 1840.
DISTRICT OF FAYETTEVILLE.			FRANKLIN—Continued.		
John Lumsden - - -	82	John Lumsden.	Robert Coggin - - -	95	Robert Coggin.
			Elizabeth Fawn - - -	78	Elizabeth Fawn.
CURRITUCK COUNTY.					
			GUILFORD COUNTY.		
Willoughby West - - -	84	Willoughby West.			
Samuel Ferubee - - -	79	Samuel Ferubee.	James Henderson - - ;	79	Jesse Henderson.
A. Williams - - -	85	James Williams.	Thomas Smith, sen. - -	75	Thomas Smith, sen.
Thomas Gregory - - -	81	Thomas Gregory.	John Scott, sen. - -	84	John Scott, sen.
			Jacob Hickman - - -	87	Robert Cor.
CHEROKEE COUNTY.			John McBride - - -	91	John McBride.
			George Nux - - -	95	Adam Nux.
Peter Leadford - - -	86	Peter Leadford.	John White - - -	85	John White, sen.
Amos Brown - - -	84	Amos Brown.	Matthew Roe - - -	78	Matthew Roe.
			William Ryan - - -	74	William Ryan.
DAVIE COUNTY.			Richard C. Taylor - - -	96	Richard C. Taylor.
			William Pailer - - -	84	John W. Pailer.
Henry Lee - - -	78	Henry Lee.	John A. Smith.		
Edmond Etchison - -	85	Edmond Etchison.			
John Myers - - -	79	John Myers, sen.	GRANVILLE COUNTY.		
Edward Stewart - - -	78	Edward Stewart.			
			John Phillips - - -	85	
DUPLIN COUNTY.			Fanny Bledsoe - - -	84	
			Peter Cash - - -	84	
Kadar Harrell - - -	94	Almshouse.	Samuel Chopell - - -	85	
William Alfin - - -	74	William Alfin.	Cyrus Davis - - -	82	
Samuel Gauff - - -	81	Samuel Gauff.	Charles Bullock - - -	80	
Nathaniel Waller - - -	76	Nathaniel Waller.	William Allen - - -	80	
Jesse Brown - - -	79	Jesse Brown.	John Lock - - -	86	
Thomas Kennaday - - -	78	Thomas Kennaday.	Petteford George - - -	89	
Bezzent Brock - - -	82	Bezzent Brock.	Samuel Andrew - - -	87	
James Holland - - -	93	James Holland.	Joseph Lumpkin - - -	81	
John Davis - - -	78	John Davis.			
John Rigby - - -	78	John Rigby.	GATES COUNTY.		
James Moore - - -	77	James Moore.			
William Carr - - -	87	William Carr.	William Pierce - - -	96	William Pierce.
David Charlton - - -	84	David Charlton.			
James Blauton - - -	79	James Blauton.	HAYWOOD COUNTY.		
Thomas Wright - - -	78	Thomas Wright.			
William Taylor - - -	83	William Taylor.	Leonard Hice - - -	77	
Daniel Withington - -	85	Daniel Withington.	Andrew Shook - - -	85	
			Absalom Hooper - - -	80	
DAVIDSON COUNTY.			William Underwood - -	80	
			Robert Love - - -	80	Robert Love.
Alexander Thomas - -	82	Alexander Thomas.	Elijah Henson - - -	77	
Joel Riggans - - -	80	Jacob Riggans.	Lewis Smithe - - -	77	
Joseph Esseck - - -	98	Jeremiah Mix.			
Jacob Lockinghour - -	89	Felix Mottsinger.	HYDE COUNTY.		
George Murrell, sen. - -	81	George Murrell, sen.			
John Graham - - -	78	John Graham.	None.		
Stephen Bailey - - -	78	Elkins Bailey.			
John Rickard - - -	85	John Rickard.	HALIFAX COUNTY.		
George Thomason, sen. -	77	George Thomason, sen.			
John Koontz - - -	85	John Koontz.	William Edmonds - - -	77	William Edmonds.
George Fritts, sen. - -	87	George Fritts, sen.	William Wood, sen. - -	79	William Wood, sen.
Stephen Osburn, sen. - -	87	Daniel Clinard, jr.	George Green, sen. - -	72	George Green, sen.
Sherwood Keneday, sen. -	79	Sherwood Keneday, sen.	John Lee, sen. - - -	79	
Joseph Northern - - -	77	David Beck.	George Powell - - -	78	George Powell.
William Thompson - -	92	John Morriss.	Robert L. Whitaker - -	75	Robert L. Whitaker.
Harwood Pope - - -	78	Harwood Pope.			
			10TH DISTRICT.		
EDGECOMBE COUNTY.			James Lock, sen. - - -	86	
Isaac Jackson, jr. - - -	86	Isaac Jackson, jr.	HENDERSON COUNTY.		
Major Glandens - - -	75	Sally Worrell.			
Lewis Todd - - -	76	Lewis Todd.	William Erwin - - -	89	William Erwin.
Micajah Petway - - -	80	Micajah Petway.	Widow of Elijah Williamson	75	Sarah Williamson.
John Webb, sen. - - -	80	John Webb, sen.	Mary Tredaway - - -	85	Arthur Tredaway.
Henry Kea - - -	87	Henry Kea.	Matthew Maybin - - -	84	Matthew Maybin.
			John Peter Corn - - -	91	John Peter Corn.
FRANKLIN COUNTY.			Joseph Henry, sen. - -	77	Joseph Henry, sen.
			James Johnson - - -	79	James Johnson, sen.
Green Walker - - -	80	Henry Walker.			
William Saunders - -	94	William Saunders.	HERTFORD COUNTY.		
Martha Davis - - -	70	Mrs. Martha Davis.			
John King - - -	102	John King.	Joseph Dilday - - -	84	Seth Dilday.
William Leonard - - -	79	William Leonard.	James Weston - - -	83	James Weston.
John Bartholomew - -	84	John Bartholomew.	Michael Britton - - -	79	Augustus Boss.
Tillman Patterson - -	79	James Dent.	Charles Powell - - -	83	Charles Powell.
Ephraim Conyers - - -	85	Ephraim Conyers.	Amos Rayner - - -	80	Amos Rayner.
Miles Hicks - - -	70	Miles Hicks.			
William Jones - - -	81	William Jones, S. C.	IREDELL COUNTY.		
Moses Carr - - -	95	Moses Carr.	David Beaty - - -	77	David Beaty.
			Matthew McPherson - -	82	James McPherson.

NORTH CAROLINA—Continued.

Names of pensioners for revolutionary or military services.	Ages.	Names of heads of families with whom pensioners resided June 1, 1840.	Names of pensioners for revolutionary or military services.	Ages.	Names of heads of families with whom pensioners resided June 1, 1840.
IREDELL—Continued.			**MECKLENBURG—Continued.**		
Andrew Ramsey	85	Andrew Ramsey.	James Orr	80	James J. Orr.
Matthew Vancliver	88	Matthew Vancliver.	William Pyrow, sen.	84	William Pyrow, sen.
William Fuinster	80	William Fuinster.	Samuel Wilson	91	Samuel Wilson.
Joseph Gibson	80	Hugh Gibson.	Andrew Walker	84	Andrew Walker.
Claborn Howard	78	John Carlton.	Jephtha Yarborough	42	Jephtha Yarborough.
John Grant, sen.	80	John Grant, sen.			
Thomas Brotherton	89	William B. Brotherton.	**MONTGOMERY COUNTY.**		
Joseph Sharpe	88	Joseph Sharpe.			
Jacob Bostian	85	Jacob Bostian.	David Green	79	David Green.
Andrew Carson	87	Andrew Carson.	Kenchen Pennington	81	Kenchen Pennington.
Laurence Maiden	89	Samuel Henderson.	Lucy Poplin	89	F. Hingon.
William Mason	90	William Mason.	Solomon Burroughs, sen.	78	Solomon Burroughs, sen.
John Scroggs	88	David Scroggs.	Philip Cell	86	Philip Cell.
John Luck	81	John Luck.	James Duke, sen.	77	James Duke, sen.
Randle Shoemaker	82	Randle Shoemaker.	Williamson Ross	75	Williamson Ross.
Hugh Andrews	82	Hugh Andrews.	B. Pemar	78	B. Pemar.
Robert Gracy	77	James B. Gracy.	Winny Allmar, sen.	75	Winny Allmar, sen.
George Lackey, sen.	87	George Lackey, sen.	Benjamin Boles	83	Benjamin Boles.
Andrew Bastian	79	Peter Frieze.	Nancy Parsons	67	James Bruton.
Abram Hill	83	Abram Hill.	Edward Wright	85	Edward Wright.
John Wallace	82	John Wallace.	Joshua Hurley	77	Joshua Hurley.
Daniel Boyed	102	Daniel Boyed.	John Barmer	86	John Barmer.
Thomas Lawson	86	Thomas Lawson.	Benjamin Bell	79	Benjamin Bell.
Thomas Lackey	92	Thomas Lackey.	Jesse Jones	87	Jesse Jones.
			Thomas Blake	96	Colwell Pool.
JOHNSTON COUNTY.					
			MACON COUNTY.		
James Holt	86	James Holt.			
William Talton	85	William Talton.	William Garrett	85	William Garrett.
Valentine Shepard	90	Valentine Shepard.	Daniel Bryson	84	Daniel Bryson.
James Odom	88	Gary Sydevant.	Thomas Plemmons	80	Jacob Plemmons.
			Aaron Thomas	81	Amos Thomas.
LENOIR COUNTY.			William McLeod	80	William McLeod.
			Thomas Williams	80	Thomas Williams.
Martin Wootus	81	Martin Wootus.	Nathan Thompson	78	Nathan Thompson.
			Samuel Manteath	85	Samuel Manteath.
LINCOLN COUNTY.					
			MOORE COUNTY.		
Martin Coulton	81	Elkanah Coulton.			
Jacob Blouk	94	Jacob Blouk.	James Monk	–	James Monk.
Nicholas Heoner	90	Nicholas Heoner.	James Gaines	75	James Gaines.
Joshua Roberts	80	Joshua Roberts.			
Robinson Goodin	76		**MARTIN COUNTY.**		
Humphrey Parker	80	Humphrey Parker.			
John Harman	77	John Harman.	John Clark	85	John Clark.
John Dickson	84	John Dickson.	William Price	79	
Joseph Willis, sen.	89	Joseph Willis, sen.			
Michael Reep	78	Michael Reep.	**NASH COUNTY.**		
Marmaduke Maples	78	Marmaduke Maples.			
George Poplin	88	George Poplin.	William Turner, sen.	88	William Turner, sen.
James T. Henry	89	James T. Henry.	Jordan Sherrod	79	Jordan Sherrod.
Philip Titman	91	Manuel Rhyne.	Abram Hedgepeth	72	Abram Hedgepeth.
John Rid	87	John Rid.	Benjamin Williams	80	Benjamin Williams.
Abraham Forney	81	Abraham Forney.	Thomas Hambleton	86	Thomas Hambleton.
Elisha Weathers	76	Elisha Weathers.			
William Ranken	79	William Ranken.	**NEW HANOVER COUNTY.**		
James Holsclau	87	James Holsclau.			
John D. Abernathy	80	John D. Abernathy.	William News	84	William News.
Richard Hanks	77	Richard Hanks.	John Kennair	91	John R. Taylor.
Samuel Pryor	83	Samuel Pryor.	Jacob Wells	89	Thomas Wells.
Simon Hager	83	Simon Hager.	John Pages	79	John Pages.
Andrew Strane	81	Andrew Strane.	Mary Powel	68	Mary Powel.
			Josiah Sikes	106	Eleanor Larns.
MECKLENBURG COUNTY.			James Lee	80	James Lee.
			George Bannerman	88	Evan Larkins.
Major Thomas Alexander	87	Major Thomas Alexander.	Elizabeth Kerr	77	Ann Taylor.
Andrew Berry	81	Andrew Berry.	James Malpas	88	F. J. Croom.
Thomas Barnet	80	Thomas Barnet.	Zack Holmes	90	Zack Holmes.
Jeremiah Clontz	85	John A. Clontz.	James Lewis	84	James Lewis.
Harry Emerson	84	Henry Emerson.	Francis Predgin	79	Francis Predgin.
Hugh Forbus	83	Hugh Forbus.			
Gabriel Ferrel	85	Gabriel Ferrel.	**NORTHAMPTON COUNTY.**		
John Gardner	81	John Gardner.			
Samuel Givens	77	Samuel Givens.	Christopher Cook	84	Lazarus Cook.
Richard Griffin	80	Richard Griffin.	James Seat	86	James Seat.
John Horfland, sen.	78	John Horfland, sen.	Samuel Williams	76	Samuel Williams.
Robert Huddleston	79	Robert Huddleston.	Nicholas Tyner	90	Nicholas Tyner.
James Knox, sen.	81	James Knox, sen.	Jesse Britton	88	Jesse Britton.
Robert Kerr	89	Robert Kerr.			
George Kiker	87	George Kiker.	**ORANGE COUNTY.**		
Michael McLeary, sen.	77	Michael McLeary, sen.	John Porterfield	77	John Porterfield.
George McWhorter	79	George McWhorter.	Samuel Allen	79	Samuel Allen.

NORTH CAROLINA—Continued.

Names of pensioners for revolutionary or military services.	Ages.	Names of heads of families with whom pensioners resided June 1, 1840.	Names of pensioners for revolutionary or military services.	Ages.	Names of heads of families with whom pensioners resided June 1, 1840.
ORANGE—Continued.			**ROCKINGHAM—Continued.**		
Henry Trollinger	77	Henry Trollinger.	Samuel Woodall	82	William Knight.
Philip Mason	88	John Danielly.	Alexander Semmons	81	Alexander Semmons.
Abner James	77	Abner James.	**ROWAN COUNTY.**		
Elizabeth Lackey	86	William Lackey.			
John Dolly	86	John Dolly.	Archibald Woodside	84	Archibald Woodside.
Thomas Bowles	78	Thomas Bowles.	Joseph Sawyers	76	George Wilhelm.
George Foster	83	George Foster.	Nathan Morgan, sen.	85	Nathan Morgan, sen.
John Strader	82	John Strader.	John Melchor Eller	88	John Melchor Eller.
Nathan Mann	82	Nathan Mann.	Martin Hoffner	78	Martin Hoffner.
			Abraham Arey	84	Abraham Arey.
SOUTHERN DIVISION.			John McLaughlin	88	Robert McLaughlin.
William Dollar	85	William Dollar.	Benjamin Knox	82	Robert Knox.
George Carrington	84	George Carrington.	Richard Smith	84	Hiram Smith.
Alexander Gattes	77	Alexander Gattes.	John McNeely	84	John McNeely.
Thomas Jacobs	73	Thomas Jacobs.	**RICHMOND COUNTY.**		
Alexander Hatch	76	Alexander Hatch.			
James Carter	81	James Carter.	Edwin Ingram	89	Elisha Bostick.
James Turner	78	James Turner.	John Currie	92	Duncan Currie.
John Efeland	77	John Efeland.	Walter Leak, sen.	79	Walter Leak, sen.
John Rawson	91	John Rawson.	Tillotson O'Brian	81	Tillotson O'Brian.
Christopher Daniel	82	Christopher Daniel.	Jn. Macalister	76	Jn. Macalister.
John Bowers	79	John Bowers.	Lot Stricklin	81	Calvin Stricklin.
Charles Rowe	90	Charles Rowe.	James Hasty	86	James Hasty.
John Bowden	85	John Bowden.	William Brown	78	William Brown.
ONSLOW COUNTY.			[Of this number, one has discontinued his pension for a year or two]		
Stephen Costen	85	Stephen Costen.			
PASQUOTANK COUNTY.			**RUTHERFORD COUNTY.**		
Will. Palmer	85	Will. Palmer.	Robert Lemons	84	Robert Lemons.
Colonel John Roen	84	John Roen	Thomas Hutchins	87	Thomas Hutchins.
PERSON COUNTY.			James Dobbins	78	James Dobbins.
			Moses Warters	—	William Doggett.
John Wilkerson	81	John Wilkerson.	William Brooks	96	William Brooks.
Isaac Lint	86	George Gray.	Edward Cook	83	Edward Cook.
Abram Gregory	79	Abram Gregory.	Sereny Monroe	27	
George Duncan	83	George Duncan.	Asey Walrop	48	
PERQUIMANS COUNTY.			Richard Ledbetter	65	
			William Dalton	74	William Dalton.
John Goodwin	90	Caleb Goodwin.	Thomas Dalton	77	Thomas Dalton, sen.
PITT COUNTY.			John Hyder, sen.	38	John Hyder, sen.
			Cornelius Clemmons	82	Cornelius Clemmons.
Charles Smith, sen.	106	Charles Smith, sen.	**RANDOLPH COUNTY.**		
Giles Nelson	86	Caleb Nelson.			
Britton Jones	81	Britton Jones.	Starling Cooper	86	John Cooper.
Thomas Bently	80	Thomas Bently.	Richard Bell	81	Richard Bell.
Robert Williams, sen.	83	Robert Williams, sen.	Elizabeth Luther	78	Charles Slack.
Henry Smith	83	James Smith.	Margaret Slack	74	Charles Slack.
John Bryant	80	Jesse Thomas.	Elizabeth Gatting	80	Edward Gatting.
Moses Hysmith	80	Moses Hysmith.			
Henry Barnhill	83	Henry Barnhill.	NORTHERN DIVISION.		
Charles Rollings	87	Charles Rollings.	Lemuel Glascow	91	Miles Glascow.
Reuben Gaganus	78	Saving Jolly.	Dan. Merrill	85	Dan. Merrill.
William Spain	78	William Spain, sen.	Edmond Hags	79	Edmond Hags.
ROBESON COUNTY.			William Wadsworth	77	William Wadsworth.
James McNatt	81	James McNatt, sen.	**STOKES COUNTY.**		
Nazra Mitchell	82	Nazra Mitchell.	Noah Baley	89	Thomas Sprinkle.
William Lewis	79	William Lewis.	George Kreeger	81	George Kreeger.
Nathan Musselwhite	86	John Jackson.	Benjamin Marshall	81	Martin Marshall.
ROCKINGHAM COUNTY.			Thomas Jones	76	Thomas Jones.
			William Beck	75	William Beck.
James Griffin	79	John Griffin.	Abner Powel	87	Abner Powel.
Robert Burton	78	Robert Burton.			
William H. Rice	79	W. H. Rice.	NORTHERN DIVISION		
Peter Crawford	80	Peter Crawford.	William Merrit	77	William Merrit.
Elijah Brown	88	H. Hulgan.	Thomas Ring, sen.	83	Thomas Ring, sen.
William Stratton	82	William Stratton.	Jacob Hilsabeek	78	Jos. Hilsabeek.
Nicholas McCubbin	81	N. McCubbin.	John Tuttle	80	John Tuttle.
Adam Sharp	77	Adam Sharp.	Jerusha Hooker	83	Elizabeth Lawson.
William Godsey	78	J. Godsey.	Edwin Hickman	78	Edwin Hickman.
John Riddle	91	Ran. Riddle.	Stephen Rierson	83	Stephen Rierson.
Thomas Carter	92	Thomas Carter.	Howel Hartgrove	77	Howel Hartgrove.
John May	84	John May.	Leonard Zeglar	77	Leonard Zeglar.
			William Young	90	William Young.

NORTH CAROLINA—Continued.

Names of pensioners for revolutionary or military services.	Ages.	Names of heads of families with whom pensioners resided June 1, 1840.	Names of pensioners for revolutionary or military services.	Ages.	Names of heads of families with whom pensioners resided June 1, 1840.
STOKES—Continued.			**WAKE—Continued.**		
NORTHERN DIVISION—Continued.			William Sledd	79	William Sledd.
William Eaton	57	William Eaton.	James Harward	80	Daniel Parham.
William Pofford	78	William Pofford.	Burwell Whitehead	95	Lazarus Whitehead.
Hartwell Borham	85	Hartwell Borham.	James Rigsbee	76	James Rigsbee.
Henry Carter	83	George W. Carter.	James Browne, sen.	91	James Browne, sen.
Francis Steel	84	Andrew Steel.	Jesse Horris	80	Jesse Horris.
John Quillin	85	John Quillin.	John Williams	86	John Williams.
Benjamin Jones	84	Elizabeth Jones.	James Hughes	79	James Hughes.
William Steel	86	John Boyles.	Robert Sneed	80	Robert Sneed.
			John Walker	85	John Walker.
SAMPSON COUNTY.			Richard Pipen	86	Willie Chamblee.
			Samuel Scarborough, sen.	80	Samuel Scarborough, sen.
Daniel Merritt	78	Daniel Merritt.	Rufus Willie	75	Rufus Willie.
Thomas Gregory	91	Thomas Gregory			
William Gainy	88	William Gainy.	**WARREN COUNTY.**		
Thomas Tart	80	Thomas Tart.			
Jeremiah Simmons	87	Jeremiah Simmons.	John Watkins	77	Thomas G. Watkins.
John Stewart	78	John Stewart.	Thomas Hilliard	78	Thomas Hilliard.
Elizabeth Hollingsworth	88	Nathan Dudley.	William Duke	90	Doctor M. Duke.
William Hays	88	William Hays.	Augustin Baltrip	80	Augustin Baltrip.
Micajah Springs	85	Micajah Springs.	Burrell Davis	83	Edward Davis.
Henry Hollingsworth	80	H. Hollingsworth.	Francis Riggan	76	Francis Riggan.
Christopher Manuel	90	Christopher Manuel.	John Dowton	79	John Dowton.
Peter O. Ryan	89	Peter O. Ryan.	James Durham	81	James Durham.
John Boykin, sen.	77	John Boykin, sen.	Frederick Shearin	77	Frederick Shearin.
Lott Ritch, sen.	82	Lott Ritch, sen.	Henry Southall	82	Henry Southall.
John Wright, sen.	81	John Wright, sen.	William Askew	103	William Askew.
			Robin Harris	82	Robin Harris.
SURRY COUNTY.			David King	78	David King.
William Going	78	William Going.	**WILKES COUNTY.**		
Morris Richards	79	Morris Richards.			
John Reaves	79	John Reaves.	Abednego Easpe	82	Abednego Easpe.
Felix Vansant	85	Felix Vansant.	John Swanson	79	John Swanson.
Edmund McKinny	53	Edmund McKinny.	David Laws, sen.	85	David Laws, sen.
Benjamin Shinalt	78	Benjamin Shinalt.	Alexander Gilreath	85	Alexander Gilreath.
Robert Davis	85	Robert Davis.	James Smoot	78	James Smoot.
David Cockram	78	David Cockram.	John Love	78	John Love.
Thomas Wright	82	Thomas Wright.	Sterling Rose	83	Sterling Rose.
Perry Chinn	77	Perry Chinn.	James Gray	77	James Gray, sen.
Widow Eliz. Apperson	77	Thomas Apperson.	William Spicer, sen.	93	William Spicer.
John Marler	82	John Marler.	William Harris	88	James Harris.
William Allgood	79	William Allgood.	Jacob Wall	92	Joseph Wall.
Daniel Cockram	78	Daniel Cockram.	Edmund McKenney	59	Edmund McKenney.
Reuben Bryant	85	Reuben Bryant.	George Combs	82	George Combs.
John Rose	91	John Rose.	Jarret Crabb	82	Jarret Crabb.
George Nix	85	George Nix.	John Sparks	97	Reuben Sparks.
John Angel	79	John Angel.	Jacob Lyon	78	Jacob Lyon.
			Jemima Yates	86	David Yates.
WAYNE COUNTY.			John Lane	85	Edward Lane.
			Samuel Castle	100	Jesse Farmer.
Ezekiel Slocumb	79	Ezekiel Slocumb.	Amos Church	89	Amos Church, sen.
John Wiggs	78	John Wiggs.	John Montgomery	84	Hugh Montgomery.
John Howell	87	John Howell.	Abel Rollen	75	Abel Rollen.
			John Bryan, Esq.	87	John Bryan, Esq.
WAKE COUNTY.			William Jenkins	80	Thomas D. Kelly.
Thomas Holland	84	Lewis Barker.	**YANCEY COUNTY.**		
Joseph Shaw	83	Drury King.			
William Wood	82	Markham Wood.	Z. Horter, sen.	79	Z. Horter, sen.
Frederick Rigsbee	85	Frederick Rigsbee.	John Green	73	James Buchanan.
Aaron Roberts	84	Aaron Roberts.	Edward Wardrup	90	Solomon Wardrop.
William Burton	80	William Burton.	Jonathan McPeeters	84	Charles McPeeters.
John Green	88	Samuel Green.	Thomas Reede	84	Thomas Reede, sen.
Jesse Bryant	84	Wyott Freeman.	John Blaylocker, sen.	78	John Blaylocker, sen.

CENSUS OF PENSIONERS.

STATE OF SOUTH CAROLINA.

Names of pensioners for revolutionary or military services.	Ages.	Names of heads of families with whom pensioners resided June 1, 1840.	Names of pensioners for revolutionary or military services.	Ages.	Names of heads of families with whom pensioners resided June 1, 1840.
CITY OF CHARLESTON.			**EDGEFIELD—Continued.**		
1st ward.			Zilpha Nobles	–	Theophilus Loudy.
Joseph Righton	78	Joseph Righton.	Abner Corley	82	J. W. Devore.
Marty G. Mathews	79	O. L. Dubson.	Phebe Randal	76	Alfred Randal.
Richard Wall	102	Richard Wall.			
Elizabeth Jeffords	86	Richard Clark.	**LEXINGTON DISTRICT.**		
Mrs. Isaac Motte	85	Mrs. Isaac Motte.	Clem. Clemmons	75	Clem. Clemmons.
2d ward.			Needham Busby	80	Needham Busby.
David Sarzedas	80	F. Spencer.			
S. Cardozo	74	S. Cardozo.	**RICHLAND DISTRICT.**		
Susanna Hall	81	Susanna Hall.	Nancy Higgins	83	Martha Howell.
Mrs. C. C. Smith	68	Mrs. C. C. Smith.			
Mrs. Rachel Lazarus	78	Mrs. Marks Lazarus.	**SUMTER DISTRICT.**		
Mrs. Mary Brown	78	Mrs. Mary Brown.	Obadiah Spears	76	Obadiah Spears.
3d ward.			Redden McCoy	82	Redden McCoy.
Margaret B. Gruber	81	Margaret B. Gruber.	John China	76	George Broadway.
Mary R. Hatch	64	Mary M. Hatch.	John James	80	John James.
4th ward.			Joseph West	80	Joseph West.
Sarah Godfrey	74	Ann Jacks.	William Vaughan	76	William Vaughan.
Catharine Lafar	78	Catharine Lafar.	Charles Spann, sen.	88	Charles Spann, sen.
Judith Abrahams	77	Judith Abrahams.	Samuel Huggins	81	Samuel Huggins.
Charlotte Head	80	Mathias Mathewson.	Peter Dubose	79	Peter Dubose.
Nap Raymond	79	C. P. Frasier.	John McDonald, sen.	83	John McDonald.
Ann Kingman	65	Ann Kingman.	Ripley Copeland, sen.	79	Ripley Copeland, sen.
Job Palmer	93	Basil Lanneau.	William McIntosh	76	William McIntosh.
CHARLESTON NECK.			Samuel Chandler, sen	77	Samuel Chandler, sen.
Charlotte Haskell	71	James Rhett.			
Catharine Edwards	80	H. L. Banks.	**WILLIAMSBURG DISTRICT.**		
William Purse	79	William Purse.	Archy Campbell	75	Archy Campbell.
ST. JAMES'S (GOOSE CREEK) PARISH.			Jesse Hicks, sen.	78	Jesse Hicks, sen.
John Stoutmay	95	John Stoutmay.			
Thomas Burbage	83	Rev. Thomas Burbage.	**ABBEVILLE DISTRICT.**		
ST. GEORGE'S, DORCHESTER.			**1ST PART.**		
Elizabeth Stroble	71	David Stroble.	Willis Scroggins	78	W. Scroggins.
			James Lockhart	84	James Lockhart.
ST. LUKE'S PARISH.			James Carlisle	78	James Carlisle.
Richard Freeman	80	Richard Freeman.	Solomon Hall	82	S. Hall.
			Pollard Brown	78	P. Brown.
BARNWELL DISTRICT.			Peter Roberts	79	P. Roberts.
Tarlton Brown	83	Tarlton Brown.	Christiana Teulon	85	William Beazly.
Jesse Griffin	81	Mathew Alexander.	**2D PART.**		
Daniel O. Dom	83	Daniel O. Dom.	James Frashier	74	James Frashier.
Henry B. Rice	26	Henry B. Rice.	Zachariah Corwill	90	Zachariah Corwill.
ORANGE PARISH.			Thomas Milford	84	Thomas Milford.
Leven Argrove	85	Leven Argrove.	Joseph Black	77	Joseph Black
Hugh Phillips	85	Hugh Phillips.			
Andrew Houser	82	Andrew Houser.	**LAURENS DISTRICT.**		
Erasmus Gibson	86	Erasmus Gibson.	Captain Ambrose Hudgens	76	Major John Hudgens.
ST. MATTHEW'S PARISH.			Andrew Burnside	78	Andrew Burnside.
Adam Garick	80	Adam Garick.	Thomas Word	88	John Walcomb.
			Robert Long, Esq.	79	Robert Long, Esq.
EDGEFIELD DISTRICT.			John Freeman	73	Henry Pope.
Smith Brooks	76	Smith Brooks.	Sally Downs	83	James Bruster.
Miles Radford	94	Richard Prescott	John Osborn	77	John Osborn.
Basil Lowe	81	Basil Lowe.	Joseph Griffin	77	Joshua Burns.
Dennis Lowe	70	Samuel Posey.	Charles Allen, Esq.	76	Charles Allen, Esq.
John B. Mitchell	83	William Riley.	Leonard Beasly	76	Leonard Beasly.
George Seigler	76	George Seigler.	John Farrow	82	John Farrow.
Richard Burton	81	Richard Burton	Henry Pitts	81	Henry Pitts.
William Nobles	80	William Nobles.	Henry Meredith	83	Henry Meredith.
U. Richardson	81	U. Richardson.	John Knight	92	William Pucket
Drewry Hearn	85	Drewry Hearn.	William Blakely, sen.	80	William Blakely, sen.
James King	82	Margaret Sharpton.	Paul Finley	78	Paul Finley.
Daniel Rodgers	82	Daniel Rodgers.			
William Howle	85	William Howle.	**NEWBERRY DISTRICT.**		
Colonel Samuel Hammond	85	Colonel Samuel Hammond.	Thomas Denson	77	Thomas Denson.
James Eidson	74	James Eidson.	John Hays	76	John Hays.
Benjamin Lindsey	87	Benjamin Lindsey.	Edmund Kelly	95	Robert Kelly.
William Smith	78	William Smith.			
Moses Harris	88	Moses Harris.	**FAIRFIELD DISTRICT.**		
Jacob Wise	82	Jacob Wise.	Robert Killpatrick	105	Thomas Killpatrick, sen.
Elizabeth Carter	74	Elizabeth Carter.	John Sloan	77	J. Sloan.
Thomas M. Chandler	29	Thomas M. Chandler.	**KERSHAW DISTRICT.**		
Thomas Williams	98	Warde Glover.	Delilah Williams	66	Delilah Williams.
Henry Timmanson	82	Wm. T. Timmanson.	Lewis Cook	84	Lewis Cook.
William Cook	86	Jeremiah Cook.			
Peter Hilliard	–	Peter Hilliard.			

SOUTH CAROLINA—Continued.

Names of pensioners for revolutionary or military services.	Ages.	Names of heads of families with whom pensioners resided June 1, 1840.	Names of pensioners for revolutionary or military services.	Ages.	Names of heads of families with whom pensioners resided June 1, 1840.
KERSHAW—Continued.			**GREENVILLE DISTRICT.**		
			1ST PART.		
Adam Teem - - -	79	Adam Teem.	William Bagwell - - -	83	Jesse Bagwell.
John Steward - - -	86	John Steward.	John Brooksher - - -	80	John Brooksher.
Nathaniel Jones - - -	86	Nathaniel Jones.	Henry Canon - - -	89	Henry Canon.
Samuel Jones - - -	78	Samuel Jones.	Greenbury Caps -	80	Greenbury Caps.
			William Crane, sen. -	76	William Crane, sen.
DARLINGTON DISTRICT.			Jonathan Davis -	82	Jonathan Davis.
			Robert Duncan - - -	78	Robert Duncan.
Martin Dewett - - -	77	Martin Dewett.	Runnels Dill - - -	76	Runnels Dill.
Albert Forte - - -	85	Albert Forte.	Philip Evans - - -	81	Philip Evans.
Ephraim Gandy - - -	98	Ephraim Gandy.	Isaac Gregory - - -	102	Isaac Gregory.
Jesse Jordan - - -	80	Jesse Jordan.	Ezekiel Henderson -	78	Ezekiel Henderson.
John Kolb - - -	83	John Kolb.	Jacob Kittle - - -	80	Jacob Kittle.
James Neill - - -	85	James Neill.	Richard Locke - - -	79	Richard Locke.
Augustin Wilson - -	85	Augustin Wilson.	Lewis Land - - -	78	Lewis Land.
			David Morton - - -	80	David Morton.
MARION DISTRICT.			Alexander Peden - -	84	Robert Peden.
			John Rogers - - -	91	John Rogers.
Ezekiel Daniel - - -	76	Mary Meggs.	Samuel Roberts, sen. -	79	Samuel Roberts, sen.
Levi Odam - - -	83	Levi Odam.	2D PART.		
L. R. Munnerling - -	88	Thomas M. Munnerling.	William Gossett - -	75	William Gossett.
Dura Pilkington, sen. -	79	Dura Pilkington, sen.			
			SPARTANBURGH DISTRICT.		
PICKENS DISTRICT.			1ST PART.		
			Newman Wilson - - -	85	Isham Wilson.
Levi Phillips - - -	94	Levi Phillips.	Joel Calaham - - -	81	Joel Calaham.
Charles Williamson - -	76	Charles Williamson.	Samuel Fowler - - -	93	Samuel Fowler.
Jacob Jones - - -	87	Major Cole.	William Wingo - - -	81	John Wingo.
John Verner - - -	77	John Verner.	George Roebuck - -	89	Willis Pierson.
William Day - - -	83	Reuben Day.	Reuben Newman - -	80	Reuben Newman.
William Hughes - - -	79	James Hughes.	Paul Castleberry - -	83	Paul Castleberry.
William Guest - - -	77	William Guest.	John Collins, sen. -	85	John Collins, sen.
Jesse Neville - - -	83	Alexander Neville.	Ellis Johnston - - -	86	Samuel Brice.
John Wilson - - -	107	John Wilson.	Thomas Farrar - - -	85	Thomas Farrar.
John Buckner Smith -	79	Buckner Smith.	William Holme - - -	85	Mordecai Taylor.
John Thrift - - -	79	John Thrift.	Solomon Crocker - -	86	Solomon Crocker.
William Dodd - - -	80	William Dodd.	Samuel Morrow - -	81	Samuel Morrow.
Benjamin Neighbour -	78	Benjamin Neighbour.	William West, sen. -	80	William West, sen.
Andrew Hughes - -	85	James Hughes.	Drury Parkham - -	85	Drury Parkham.
John Craig - - -	81	John Craig.	John O'Shields - - -	80	John O'Shields.
John Cobb - - -	82	John Cobb.	James Seay - - -	88	James Seay.
Jordan Holcomb - -	78	William Holcomb.	Mourning Smith - -	77	Mourning Smith.
Charles Smith - - -	81	Cullen Rains.	Geoffrey O'Shields -	78	Geoffrey O'Shields.
Thomas Hays - - -	89	Thomas Hays.	Howell Johnson - -	78	Howell Johnson.
Archibald McMahan -	82	Archibald McMahan.	John King - - -	82	John King.
Jesse Smith - - -	82	Jesse Smith.	Anthony Crocker - -	82	Anthony Crocker.
Thomas Henderson -	79	Thomas Henderson.	Rowland Johnson - -	80	Rowland Johnson.
			Claburn Holt - - -	87	Claburn Holt.
ANDERSON DISTRICT.			Solomon Abbott - -	83	Solomon Abbott.
1ST PART.			Robert Belcher - - -	82	Cyrus Belcher.
Joseph Caldwell - - -	78	Joseph Caldwell.	William G. Hopkins -	80	William G. Hopkins.
James Caldwell - - -	84	James Caldwell.	John McClure - - -	81	John McClure.
James Brown - - -	83	James Brown.	Edward Clement - -	81	T. J. Rollins.
William Grant - - -	80	William Grant.			
John Burns - - -	83	John Burns.	2D PART.		
John Harris - - -	87	Andrew Harris.	Henry Emerson - -	78	Henry Emerson.
Samuel Warren - -	86	Samuel Warren.	George Walker - - -	75	George Walker.
David Saddler, sen. -	78	David Saddler, sen.			
William Armstrong -	78	Thomas Runnels.	**UNION DISTRICT.**		
Harmon Cummins - -	84	Harmon Cummins.			
Joshua Betterton - -	78	John Chappel.	Richard Addis - - -	91	A—— Culbertson.
David Verner - - -	81	Mary Ledbitter.	Robin Savage - - -	82	Robert Savage.
James Young - - -	88	John Young.	Hancock Porter - -	92	Hancock Porter.
			Mordecai Chandler -	78	Mordecai Chandler.
2D PART.			Mrs. E. F. Farr - -	75	Mrs. E. F. Farr.
William Moore - - -	83	James Moore.	James Smith - - -	89	James Smith.
John Warnock - - -	84	John Warnock.	Ann Rochester - -	70	Ann Rochester.
William Entreken - -	79	William Entreken.	Thomas Word - - -	88	John D. Word.
Frederick Owen - -	83	Frederick Owen.	Major Thomas Young -	76	Major Thomas Young.
Shedrick Owen - -	79	Shedrick Owen.	Meshack Chandler -	96	Meshack Chandler.
William Hubbard - -	79	James Smith.	Major Joseph McJemkin -	85	Major Joseph McJemkin.
Stephen Huff - - -	83	Nicholas Tripp.	Perry Evans - - -	80	Perry Evans.
Aaron Guyton - - -	79	Aaron Guyton.	Tilmon Bobo - - -	78	Tilmon Bobo.
Peter McMahan - -	85	Peter McMahan.	James Hollis - - -	82	Thomas Hollis.
William Gibbs - - -	76	William Gibbs.	James Howard - - -	78	James Howard.
John Willson - - -	85	John Willson.	Daniel Palmer - - -	85	Daniel Palmer.
Reuben Brock - - -	86	Headon Brock.	Daniel Holder - - -	83	Daniel Holder.
John Bagwell - - -	79	John Bagwell.	Sherwood Nance - -	86	David Adams.
William Williamson -	77	William Williamson.	James McWherter - -	83	James McWherter.
Joshua Pruett - - -	87	William Pruett.	William Morehead - -	77	Walter Morehead.
John Parker - - -	84	Robert Parker.	William Bailey - - -	92	William Bailey.
Nicholas Bishop - -	79	Nicholas Bishop.	Nicholas Cump, sen. -	88	Nicholas Cump, sen.
Major William Millun -	87	Major William Millun.	John Bird - - -	82	Daniel Smith.

CENSUS OF PENSIONERS.

SOUTH CAROLINA—Continued.

Names of pensioners for revolutionary or military services.	Ages.	Names of heads of families with whom pensioners resided June 1, 1840.	Names of pensioners for revolutionary or military services.	Ages.	Names of heads of families with whom pensioners resided June 1, 1840.
YORK DISTRICT.			**CHESTER—Continued.**		
1ST PART.			Isabella King	88	Martin King.
Daniel Gilmore	76	Daniel Gilmore.	Francis Wylie	90	Francis Wylie.
Daniel Quinn	82	David Gaston.	John Holcomb	52	John Holcomb.
J. B. Fulton	75	A. Fulton.	Colonel George Gill	79	Colonel George Gill.
John McElwee	75	John McElwee.	Stephen McElhenny	80	Stephen McElhenny.
John Barber	80	Robert Barber.	John Con	85	John Con.
Gilly Moss	76	Samuel Moss.	John Colwell	79	John Colwell.
Samuel Turner, Esq	77	Samuel Turner, Esq.	Robert Cowley	88	Robert Cowley.
William Carson	77		**LANCASTER DISTRICT.**		
James Campbell	86	James Campbell.			
James Brian, sen.	80	James Brian, sen.	John Hinson, sen.	89	John Hinson, sen.
Robert Wilson	82	Robert Wilson.	Mrs. Bell, widow of George Bell	80	Nelson Bell.
Jacob Black	86	Jacob Black.	William Hopkins	84	William Hopkins.
Joseph Jameson	76	Joseph Jameson.	Isham Peoples	70	Isham Peoples.
Henry Rhay	81	Henry Rhay.	Thomas McKay	78	Thomas McKay.
David Stinson, sen.	84	David Stinson, sen.	Reuben Bennett	80	Reuben Bennett.
Thomas Bailey	84		P. Conner	88	Philemon Conner.
Robert Harris	83	Robert Harris.	W. Valendenham	87	William Valendenham.
William Shaw	82		James Ramsey	80	James Ramsey.
Andrew Kerr	85	Andrew Kerr.	John McMurry	92	John McMurry.
William Clark	79	William Clark.	R. James Hunter	70	James Hunter.
David Patton	78	David Patton.	**CHESTERFIELD DISTRICT.**		
Benjamin McWhorter	75				
2D PART.			Peter Arant	91	Peter Arant.
Thomas Boggs	95	J. W. Jennings.	John Blakney	82	John Blakney.
John Starr	70	Mary Boggs.	George Bone	77	George Bone.
Robert Hannah	80	Eli More.	Thomas Davis	81	Thomas Davis.
Samuel McElhenny	81	Allen Robertson.	Ahaz Rogers	84	Ahaz Rogers.
CHESTER DISTRICT.			**MARLBOROUGH DISTRICT.**		
John Brown	87	David Sexton.	John Haskew	76	John Haskew.
Jane Gaston	75	James A. H. Gaston.	William Hodges	83	William Hodges.
John McDill	78	James McDill.	Lewis Stubbs, sen.	81	Lewis Stubbs, sen.
John Culp	79	John Culp.	William Coxe	77	William Coxe.
John Bishop	79	John Bishop.	William Lister, sen.	81	William Lister.

STATE OF GEORGIA.

Names of pensioners for revolutionary or military services.	Ages.	Names of heads of families with whom pensioners resided June 1, 1840.	Names of pensioners for revolutionary or military services.	Ages.	Names of heads of families with whom pensioners resided June 1, 1840.
CAMPBELL COUNTY.			**CAMDEN COUNTY.**		
William R. Gunnell	88	William R. Gunnell.	Lewis Welford	95 to 100	Lewis Welford.
William Clinton	80	William Clinton.	**COBB COUNTY.**		
George Norwood	77	Harrison McCain.			
Benjamin Bledsoe	77	Benjamin Bledsoe.	Jeremiah Nesbit	105	Lindsey Ellsbury.
James Akins	90	James Akins.	Peter Grover	79	Daniel Grover.
CHATTOOGA COUNTY.			John Sumers	77	William Gann.
			Robert McDowell	86	R. McDowell.
Daniel Orear	83	Daniel Orear.	John Barnwell	88	John Barnwell.
CHEROKEE COUNTY.			Israel Eastwood	82	Mary Avery.
			John Collins	80	John Collins.
Charles Smith	75	Charles Smith.	Adonijah Edwards	73	Adonijah Edwards.
Nathan Willaford	82	Nathan Willaford.			
Ephraim Martin	80	G. W. Crawley.	**CRAWFORD COUNTY.**		
CASS COUNTY.			Philip Matthews	88	Philip Matthews.
			Jason Meador	81	Jason Meador.
John Lewis	83	Bayles W. Lewis.	James Bailey	80	James H. Wright.
Reuben Edwards	82	Reuben Edwards.	Joel Ethridge	77	John Anthony.
Hugh Brewster	80	William Brewster.	Thomas Turner	89	Thomas Turner.
Benjamin Haris	81	John Stokes.	Daniel Hartley	97	Daniel Hartley.
Charles Baker	79	Charles Baker.	Lewis Goodwin	74	L. Goodwin.
CLARK COUNTY.			Jacob Fudge	82	Jacob Fudge.
Francis Farrar	76	John Killgoar.	**CARROLL COUNTY.**		
John Oliver	78	John Oliver.			
John Espy	84	John Espy.	Zachariah Stedham	89	James H. Stedham.
Benjamin Parr	83	E. H. Rodgers.	Jesse Rowell	87	Jesse Rowell.
George Wilson	88	Reuben Hambleton.	John Robinson, sen.	88	John Robinson, sen.

Names of pensioners for revolutionary or military services.	Ages.	Names of heads of families with whom pensioners resided June 1, 1840.	Names of pensioners for revolutionary or military services.	Ages.	Names of heads of families with whom pensioners resided June 1, 1840.
COWETA COUNTY.			**FRANKLIN COUNTY.**		
Allen Gay - - -	75	Allen Gay.	Ann Cash - - -	75	Howard Cash.
William Smith - -	91	William Smith.	Elisha Dyer - - -	77	John Dyer.
John Neely - -	83	Rebecca Neely.	William Murdock -	81	Thomas H. Murdock.
James Akens - -	74	James Akens.	William Mitchell -	81	William Mitchell.
William Bunster - -	83	James Bunster.	John Stonecypher -	84	John Stonecypher.
BURKE COUNTY.			Stephen Fuller - -	88	Stephen Fuller.
			Thomas Clarke - -	79	Thomas Clarke.
Abraham Thomas -	86		William Aaron - -	93	William Aaron.
James Allen - -	84	James Allen.	Jesse Holbrook - -	76	Jesse Holbrook.
BALDWIN COUNTY.			William Spears - -	95	William Spears.
			Samuel McCoy - -	79	Samuel McCoy.
William Anderson -	78	William Anderson.	Robert Flemming -	77	Robert Flemming.
Benjamin Talbot -	76	Benjamin Talbot.	Abner Sherdin - -	80	Abner Sherdin.
Jeriah Robinson -	70	Luke Robinson.	**FAYETTE COUNTY.**		
James G. Russell, sen. -	78	James G. Russell.	Karen Hapuck Mills -	79	Richard Phipps.
BIBB COUNTY.			James Waldroup -	85	David Waldroup.
None.			Jared Suddeth -	76	James N. Suddeth.
BULLOCK COUNTY.			William Black - -	76	Samuel Black.
			Susan Gilleland -	80	
John Banks - -	34	Elijah Aspinwall.	**FORSYTH COUNTY.**		
BUTTS COUNTY.			Leonard Wells - -	84	Leonard Wells.
			Ambrose Brown -	83	Ambrose Brown.
E. Price - - -	79	E. Price.	James Nolen - -	90	Thomas Wiley.
DADE COUNTY.			John N. Lagran -	87	John N. Lagran.
			Philip Whitten -	95	William Arons, jr.
Moses Perkins - -	87	Isham Perkins.	James Carroll - -	75	Martin R. Paxton.
DE KALB COUNTY.			**GWINNETT COUNTY.**		
			John Davis - -	109	Joseph Rutledge.
Lewis Stowers, sen. -	76	Lewis Stowers, sen.	Benjamin Conger -	84	Benjamin Conger.
William Terrell -	84	William Terrell.	Daniel Clowers -	79	Daniel P. Clowers.
William Copeland -	75	William Copeland.	Isaac Horton - -	81	Isaac Horton.
George Brooks - -	79	Stacy Strickland.	Joseph Curbo - -	86	Joseph Curbo.
Thomas Roberts -	95	Simeon Acre.	William McRight -	21	William McRight.
John Macomeson -	84	John Macomeson.	Nathan Williams -	89	Nathan Williams.
William Reeve - -	84	William Reeve.	Nathan Dobs - -	85	Nathan Dobs.
ELBERT COUNTY.			Stephen Harris -	86	Stephen Harris.
			John McDadde -	93	Lucinda Saxton.
John Cook - -	79	John Cook.	Owen Anders - -	87	David Anders.
William Kelley -	82	William Kelley.	John Laurence -	80	John Laurence.
David Carter - -	82	David Carter.	Philip Iseley - -	91	Philip Iseley.
James Riley - -	82	James Riley.	Edward Jackson -	86	Edward Jackson.
Richard Gully - -	85	William Robertson.	Robert Patison -	78	George A. Patison.
John Davis - -	87	John Davis.	Reuben Bramlett -	75	Reuben Bramlett.
Benjamin Brown -	77	Benjamin Brown.	Littleton Hunt -	97	Sarah Chambers.
William Ward - -	82	William Ward.	Abel Gowers - -	86	Abel Gowers.
John Daniel - -	80	John Daniel.	Enoch Benson - -	84	Enoch Benson.
William Gains - -	83	William Gains.	George Thrasher -	85	George Thrasher.
Amos Richardson -	76	James V. Richardson.	Joseph Herringdon -	77	Joseph Herringdon.
William Trammel -	83	William Trammel.	**GILMER COUNTY.**		
Leonard Rice - -	81	Leonard Rice.	Richard Cox, sen. -	79	Richard Cox, sen.
William Glasgow -	78	William Glasgow.	Enoch Smith - -	81	Asahel Smith.
EMANUEL COUNTY.			James Kell - -	81	Alexander Kell.
			Ebenezer Fain -	78	Ebenezer Fain.
Benjamin Fareclauth -	83	Benjamin Fareclauth.	Mary Ellis - -	84	Elijah Ellis.
David Edenfield -	79	David Edenfield.	**GREENE COUNTY.**		
Matthew Curl - -	78	Matthew Curl.	George Sloughter -	77	George Sloughter.
Wilson Drew - -	75	Levi Drew.	Robert Pullin - -	85	Robert R. Pullin.
Henry Brown - -	70	Henry Brown.	Stephen Gatlin -	54	Stephen Gatlin.
A. Sutton - -	82	Abner Sutton.	Matthew Harris -	88	Matthew Harris.
Jacob Durdan - -	85	Jacob Durdan.	John Shurr - -	77	John Shurr.
EFFINGHAM COUNTY.			**HEARD COUNTY.**		
Jonathan Rahn - -	78		James Stewart - -	75	John Stewart.
EARLY COUNTY.			**HALL COUNTY.**		
Redman Wells - -	58	Redman Wells.	Joseph Bonds - -	84	Joseph Bonds.
Josiah Bagget - -	78		James Anderson -	72	James Anderson.
Elizabeth Jordan -	57	Charles B. Jordan.	Isaac Reed - -	84	Joseph Reed.
			John Moore - -	83	John Moore.
			James McCleskey -	86	James McCleskey.

19

GEORGIA—Continued.

Names of pensioners for revolutionary or military services.	Ages.	Names of heads of families with whom pensioners resided June 1, 1840.	Names of pensioners for revolutionary or military services.	Ages.	Names of heads of families with whom pensioners resided June 1, 1840.
HALL,—Continued.			**LIBERTY COUNTY.**		
William Flanagan	91	William Flanagan.	Mary Hart	72	Joseph Jones.
Robert Kell	89	William Kell.	**LUMPKIN COUNTY.**		
James Gilmer, sen.	80	James Gilmer, sen.			
Elias Allread	82	Elias Allread.	William Allen	101	William Allen.
Milliner Childers	77	Wiley Childers.	William Fleming	79	Isaac N. Fleming.
Jesse Hulsey	81	Jesse Hulsey.	John Hames	94	John Hames.
James Pitts	77	James Pitts.	Reuben Hill	69	Reuben Hill.
John Nicholson	77	John Nicholson.	Richard Ledbetter	101	Johnson Ledbetter.
Charles Gunter	78	Charles Gunter.	Edmond Singleton	85	Overstreet Singleton
Beal Baker	84	Beal Baker.	John Nix	75	Micajah Walker.
Robert Robertson	83	Robert Robertson.	Michael Pilgrim	86	Samuel Eires.
William Clark	84	William Clark.			
Basil Shaw	92	Roland Johnson.	**LINCOLN COUNTY.**		
Benjamin West	81	Benjamin West.			
			William Linvill	85	William Linvill.
HENRY COUNTY.			John Guyse	79	John Guyse.
Ezekiel Cloud	78	Ezekiel Cloud.	**LAURENS COUNTY.**		
Francis Adams	77	Francis Adams.			
James Gilbert	87	James Gilbert.	None.		
Thomas Cook	88	Jesse M. Cook.			
Charles Upchurch	85	Charles Upchurch.	**MACON COUNTY.**		
Shelldeake Chandler	88	Joel Chandler.			
			Daniel Whatley	87	Daniel Whatley.
HARRIS COUNTY.			Joseph Passmore	79	Joseph Passmore.
			Dempsey Baker	77	Dempsey Baker.
William Norris	84	William Norris.			
William B. Swan	82	W. B. Swan.	**MORGAN COUNTY.**		
			William Barkly	80	R. J. D. Barkly.
HABERSHAM COUNTY.			M. Cochran	83	Matthew Cochran.
Daniel McCollans	86	John Stovall.	George Campbell	86	George Campbell.
Thomas Pilgrim	74	Thomas Pilgrim.			
Garrett Vandegriff	89	Garrett Vandegriff.	**MADISON COUNTY.**		
Robert Turner	80	Robert Turner.			
			Robert L. Tate	76	Robert L. Tate.
HANCOCK COUNTY.			Charles Tugle	87	Martin Rowe.
Malone Mullins	80	Malone Mullins.	James Thompson	77	James Thompson, sen.
William Shuffield	70	William Shuffield.	Alexander Haman	80	Alexander Haman.
Timothy Rossiter	80	Timothy Rossiter.	William Cheek	89	William Cheek.
John Hill	80	John Hill.			
John Dennis	70	John Dennis.	**MURRAY COUNTY.**		
Bird Brasel	70	Bird Brasel.			
Isaac Blount	80	Isaac Blount.	William Stone	–	James Stone.
Joseph Grant	80	Levi Spights.			
Mills Howel	70	Mills Howel.	**MARION COUNTY.**		
William Faison	70	William Faison.			
			George Buchanan	81	George Buchanan.
JONES COUNTY.			John Mayo	81	Axom Mayo.
Oliver Morton, sen.	77	Oliver Morton, sen.	**McINTOSH COUNTY.**		
Reuben Roberts	85	Reuben Roberts.			
John C. Slocumb	80	John Slocumb.	George White	81	Waldegrave C. Street.
			John Calder	77	John Calder.
JASPER COUNTY.					
Sion Barnett	79	Sion Barnett.	**MONROE COUNTY.**		
David Waters	105	Wiley Henderson.			
John Davidson	79	John Davidson.	Tolover Davis	84	Tolover Davis.
William Jones, sen.	82	William Jones, sen.	William Stewart	87	William Stewart.
John Spears	89	John Spears.	William Jones	45	John M. Woolsey.
Lewis D. Yancy	78	Lewis D. Yancy, sen.			
			MERIWETHER COUNTY.		
JEFFERSON COUNTY.			Alexander Smith	81	Alexander Smith.
			Samuel Bowen	83	Samuel Bowen.
Jacob Sodown	80	Jacob W. Sodown.	Lewis Jenkins	87	Lewis Jenkins.
			John Black	77	John Black.
JACKSON COUNTY.			Giles Kelley	78	Giles Kelley.
			George Earnest	80	Elisha Earnest.
Isaac Mathews	79	Milton Mathews.			
William Mathews	77	William Mathews.	**MUSCOGEE COUNTY.**		
Solomon Saxon	73	Solomon Saxon.			
Ansell Cuningham	77	Ansell Cuningham.	Philemon Hodges	83	Samuel K. Hodges.
Levi Lowery	76	Levi Lowery.	Richard Christmas	77	Richard Christmas.
Jesse White	79	Jesse White.			
John King	85	John King.	**NEWTON COUNTY.**		
George Levay	85	George Levay.			
Henry Anglin	81	Henry Anglin.	John Webb	85	John T. Webb.
Sherrod Thompson	83	Sherrod Thompson.			
James Wheeler	85	James Wheeler.			

GEORGIA—Continued.

Names of pensioners for revolutionary or military services.	Ages.	Names of heads of families with whom pensioners resided June 1, 1840.	Names of pensioners for revolutionary or military services.	Ages.	Names of heads of families with whom pensioners resided June 1, 1840.
NEWTON CITY.			**WARREN—Continued.**		
Richmond Terrell	80	Richmond Terrell.	John Jackson	85	Lewis Jackson.
Richard Fretwell	87	Richard Fretwell.	Charles Studevent	80	Charles Studevent.
Valentine Weathers	76	Valentine Weathers.	**RABUN COUNTY.**		
Wyatt Hewell	84	Jesse W. Hewell.			
Robert Carter	84 }		Edward Williams	102	Edward Williams.
Thomas McLane	80 }	Thomas McLane.	John McLain	81	John McLain.
			John Dillard	81	John Dillard.
OGLETHORPE COUNTY.			Josias Collahan	81	Josias Collahan.
			Jonathan Dunlap	81	Jonathan Dunlap.
William Finch	76	William Finch.			
Thomas Dunn, sen.	76	Thomas Dunn, sen.	**RICHMOND COUNTY.**		
Joseph Woodall	76	Joseph Woodall.			
Miller Bledsoe	78	Whitfield Landrum.	John Marten	103	John Marten.
Samuel Ward	85	Samuel Ward.	**RANDOLPH COUNTY.**		
Jacob Eberhart	83	Jacob Eberhart.			
Charles Carter	88	Charles Carter.	Peter Bucholter	77	John S. Harrison.
William Kidd, sen.	77	William Kidd, sen.	Ezekiel Bryan	75	Ezekiel Bryan.
Charles Strong	77	Charles Strong.	John Brown	77	John P. Taff.
			Thomas Davis	85	Thomas Davis.
UNION COUNTY.			Richard Darby	102	Richard Darby.
Michael Tanney	81	Michael Tanney.	**TALIAFERRO COUNTY.**		
			Thomas McCormack	90	Thomas McCormack.
UPSON COUNTY.			Richard King	88	Richard King.
			William Evans	98	William Evans.
Hiram Chelfench	35	Hiram Chelfench.	Henry Stewart	81	Henry Stewart.
PIKE COUNTY.			**TELFAIR COUNTY.**		
John Jenkins, sen.	85	John Jenkins, sen.	Joseph Williams	80	Joseph Barrows.
John Wise	84	Nathan Vinson.			
William Harper	88	William Harper.	**TALBOT COUNTY.**		
David Grisham	83	David Grisham.			
Faddy Whittington	87	Faddy Whittington, jun.	Shadrach Ellis	80	John Ellis.
WILKINSON COUNTY.			**TWIGGS COUNTY.**		
Robert Rosier, sen.	84	Robert Rosier, sen.	John Keeth	90	John Keeth.
John Meadows	78	Joseph Meadows.	Ephraim Lile	77	Ephraim Lile.
William Jenkins	83	Jorial Bennet.	Thomas Taylor, sen.	77	Thomas Taylor, sen.
WILKES COUNTY.			**TROUP COUNTY.**		
John Combs	78	John Combs, sen.	William Thomason	92	John C. Thomason.
William Williams	78	William Williams.	Fountain Jordan	77	Fountain Jordan.
Andrew Woolf	88	Andrew Woolf, sen.	Joseph Johnson	86	Daniel Johnson.
WASHINGTON COUNTY.			**PULASKI COUNTY.**		
William Williams	86	William Williams.	Jacob Parkerson	79	J. Parkerson.
Lustatia Thompson	74	Greene H. Warthin.			
George F. Howard	27	James Collins.	**CITY OF SAVANNAH.**		
Uriah Peacock	88	Uriah Peacock.			
Thomas Love	90	Lovey Love.	Sheftall Sheftall	78	Sheftall Sheftall.
Moses Cox	86	Moses Cox, jun.	Elias Bullough	77	J. K. Bullough.
Isaac Jones	79	Isaac Jones.	John Cabos	94	John Cabos.
WALTON COUNTY.			**SUMTER COUNTY.**		
Henry Harden	89	Henry Harden.	Daniel Flanigan	83	G. H. Hayship.
Benjamin Harris	87	Benjamin Harris.			
James Swords	92	James Swords.	**SCRIVEN COUNTY.**		
WALKER COUNTY.			John Arnett	80	Levi H. Best.
Daniel Newnan	—	Daniel Newnan.	**STEWART COUNTY.**		
Robert Story	25	John Foster.			
			Zachariah Elliott	84	Zachariah Elliott.
WARREN COUNTY.			Benjamin Smith	88	Benjamin Smith.
			Robert Melton	82	William Melton.
William Cason	93	William Cason.	Prescott Bush	81	Prescott Bush.
John Doud	85	John Doud.	Thomas Glenn	81	Thomas Glenn.
James Draper	89	James Draper.	Nathaniel Statham	76	Nathaniel Statham.
John Wilson	85	Elias Wilson.			
Benjamin Rickerson	80	Benjamin Rickerson.			

CENSUS OF PENSIONERS.

STATE OF ALABAMA—NORTHERN DISTRICT.

Names of pensioners for revolutionary or military services.	Ages.	Names of heads of families with whom pensioners resided June 1, 1840.	Names of pensioners for revolutionary or military services.	Ages.	Names of heads of families with whom pensioners resided June 1, 1840.
BLOUNT COUNTY.			**LAWRENCE COUNTY.**		
WESTERN DIVISION.			Samuel McGaughy	78	Samuel McGaughy.
			Abrm. Haughton - - -	81	William Boyee.
Charles Holt - - -	78	C. Holt.	John Harvey - - -	82	John Harvey.
Jeremiah Files - - -	75	J. Files.	Jarvis Ellett - - -	75	Jon. Wilson.
			Abrm. Ellege - - -	80	Abrm. Ellege.
EASTERN DIVISION.			William Mitchell - -	86	A. Mitchell.
			William Lackey - - -	87	William Lackey.
George Husstullar - -	76	G. Husstullar.	Thomas Fulton - - -	81	Thomas Fulton.
Thomas C. Jones - -	82	Thomas C. Jones.	Andrew White - - -	78	Andrew White.
Jos. McDerment - -	83	John Cook.	James McDonell - - -	82	James McDonell.
BENTON COUNTY.			**LIMESTONE COUNTY.**		
Hezekiah Posey - - :	90	Hezekiah Posey.	Thomas Holland - -	78	Thomas Holland.
John Presnell - - -	81	John Presnell.	John Craig - - -	75	John Craig.
James Watkins - -	92	James Watkins.	William Malone - -	85	William Malone.
Samuel Tolbert - -	87	Samuel Tolbert.	James McConnell, sen. -	83	James McConnell, sen.
John Landers - -	82	Abel Brooks.	Jesse Mitchell - - -	75	Jesse Mitchell.
Tobias Honey - -	78	John Landers.			
John Chandler - -	89	John Chandler.	**MARION COUNTY.**		
Samuel Ridner - -	80	Jos. Ridner.			
John Mallory - -	75	Henry H. Mallory.	Thomas Stanford - - -	—	
William Cunningham -	93	William N. Cunningham.	William Kennedy - - -	—	J. Kennedy.
John Roper - - -	75	Stephen Roper.			
Samuel Warden - -	84	David Barnwell.	**MORGAN COUNTY.**		
CHEROKEE COUNTY.			Thomas Queen - - -	80	Thomas Queen.
			E. Thompson - - -	91	E. Thompson.
E. Moss - - -	74	E. Moss.	James Lynn - - -	76	James Lynn.
John Grewer - -	42	John Grewer.	N. Thompson - - -	81	N. Thompson.
Jos. Garner, sen. -	95	Jos. Garner.	Jos. Nelson - - -	87	Jos. Nelson.
			Cornelius Malone - -	81	Cornelius Malone.
DE KALB COUNTY.			Robert Barclay, sen. -	76	Robert Barclay, sen.
			Thomas Hubbard, sen. -	87	Thomas Hubbard, sen.
Jacob Froxil - - -	85	J. Froxil.			
William Walker - -	78	G. Walker.	**MARSHALL COUNTY.**		
George Upton - - -	80	George Upton.			
			Samuel West - - -	103	Butcher West.
FRANKLIN COUNTY.			John Bradley, sen. -	83	John Bradley, sen.
			Thomas Cargill - -	77	Thomas Cargill.
Hugh Randolph - -	85	David Fuller.	Thomas T. Doty - -	44	Thomas T. Doty.
Elijah White - - -	78	Samuel B. White.	Robert Rains - - -	56	Robert Rains.
FAYETTE COUNTY.			**MADISON COUNTY.**		
			NORTH DIVISION.		
Reuben Cook - - -	80	Reuben Cook.			
Fred. Bagwell - -	80	Fred. Bagwell.	Clement Blackbourn -	80	
Thomas Glaze - -	89	Thomas Glaze.	Richard Harris - -	82	
Isaac Lansdale - -	80	Isaac Lansdale.	Andrew Martin - -	105	Andrew Martin.
Benjamin Guess - -	83	Jesse Howard.	Peyton Powell - -	80	Peyton Powell.
Johnson Strong - -	82	Johnson Strong.	Samuel Davis - -	85	Samuel Davis.
David Black - - -	80	David Black.	Jacob Caulk - - -	85	John H. Webster.
			Edward Bevill - -	78	Edward Bevill.
JACKSON COUNTY.			Reuben Stone - - -	84	Reuben Stone.
			Richard Johnson - -	82	Richard Johnson.
John Duncan - - -	83	Robert Duncan.	Sturdy Garner - -	78	Sturdy Garner.
Jesse Sampels - -	79	Jesse Sampels.			
Jos. R. McCormack -	96	Joseph R. McCormack.	*SOUTH DIVISION.*		
Jonah McInally - -	52	Jonah McInally.			
John Wood - - -	89	Thomas Campbell.	Ezekiel Craft - - -	77	Ezekiel Craft.
Thomas Russell - -	79	Thomas Russell.	John Wright - - -	48	John Wright.
John Bryant - - -	85	John Bryant.	Richard Dean - - -	81	Richard Dean.
John Morris - - -	76	John Morris.	Jer. Gurley - - -	81	John Gurley.
John McCravy - -	87	Thomas Coleman.			
Benjamin Matthews -	73	Benjamin Matthews.	**RANDOLPH COUNTY.**		
Elizabeth Calton - -	21	John Owens.			
Elizabeth Bryant -	71	H. M. Bryant.	John Kinard - - -	82	Barnett Kinard.
Lewis Clark - - -	77	Lewis Clark.	James Simpson - -	79	William Simpson
John Smith - - -	77	Larkin Smith.	Hugh Card - - -	84	Hugh Card.
Joshua Townsel - -	80	Joshua Townsel.			
Rebecca Smith - -	39	Rebecca Smith.	**ST. CLAIR COUNTY.**		
James Smith - - -	81	James P. Smith.			
Andrew J. Kirby - -	25	John McReynolds.	Noel Battles - - -	100	William Battles.
			Robert Reed - - -	75	
LAUDERDALE COUNTY.					
			TALLADEGA COUNTY.		
Charles Littleton - -	79	Charles Littleton.			
Samuel Burney - -	60	Samuel Burney.	David Caldwell - -	87	Charles Caldwell.
Lewis Markham - -	75	L. Markham.	Spencer Pendegrass -	69	Spencer Pendegrass.

ALABAMA—SOUTHERN DISTRICT.

Names of pensioners for revolutionary or military services.	Ages.	Names of heads of families with whom pensioners resided June 1, 1840.	Names of pensioners for revolutionary or military services.	Ages.	Names of heads of families with whom pensioners resided June 1, 1840.
AUTAUGA COUNTY.			**JEFFERSON**—Continued.		
Littleton Reese	76	L. Reese.	James Tarrant, sen.	86	James Tarrant, jr.
Clement Billingsley	84	C. Billingsley.	Michael McCarty	90	Michael McCarty.
John Thomas, sen.	81	Mary Johnson.			
Walter Ross, sen.	81	Walter Ross, sen.	**LOWNDES COUNTY.**		
			Thomas Hamilton	81	Thomas Hamilton.
BARBOUR COUNTY.					
W. R. Cowan	26	W. R. Cowan.	**MACON COUNTY.**		
			Barret Brewer	77	
BIBB COUNTY.			Adam J. Files	78	A. J. Files.
Henry Haggard	94	James Fancher.			
John Wallace	80 to 90	John Wallace.	**MOBILE COUNTY.**		
Zaccheus Corley	77	Zaccheus Corley.	John Mason	72	John Mason.
George Maberry	89	George Maberry.	Mr. Alexander	98	Mr. Alexander.
			John Bailey Williams	86	John B. Williams.
BUTLER COUNTY.					
John Linton	82	Hugh Linton.	**MARENGO COUNTY.**		
Theophilus Petty, sen.	82	Theophilus Petty, sen.	Joshua Cherry	79	J. W. Cherry.
Adam Skanes	85	Adam Skanes, sen.	John Kinnard	77	John Kinnard.
			John Gilmore	81	
CONECUH COUNTY.					
None.			**MONROE COUNTY.**		
			Owen Daily	76	Owen Daily.
COOSA COUNTY.			Benjamin Cook	82	Benjamin Cook.
Reuben Blankenship	73	Reuben Blankenship.			
William Casey	80	M. B. Casey.	**MONTGOMERY COUNTY.**		
Joshua Rowe	79	Daniel Rowe.	Mary Lucas	80	Jane W. Freeney.
			Samuel Fleming	85	Samuel Fleming.
CLARK COUNTY.					
Axiom Lewis	75	William R. Hamilton.	**PERRY COUNTY.**		
Joshua Wilson	80	Joshua Wilson.	Isaac Oaks	81	Willis Osbourn.
John Bradley, sen.	83	John Bradley, sen.			
William Armistead	77	William Armistead.	**PIKE COUNTY.**		
Elias Scarbrough	94	Elias Scarbrough.	Aaron Lewis	80	Aaron Lewis.
			John Griffin	97	John Griffin.
COVINGTON COUNTY.			Stephen Living, sen.	80	Stephen Living, sen.
Samuel Williams	85	Samuel Williams.	John A. Hidecker	93	Sarah Reeks.
John Lyle	84	John B. Dixan.	James Cadenhead, sen.	98	James Cadenhead, sen.
			John Fowler, sen.	99	John Fowler.
CHAMBERS COUNTY.					
Daniel Galespie	77	David Taylor.	**PICKENS COUNTY.**		
Thomas Taylor	56	Jonathan Music.	Meredith Taylor	78	James Bonner.
James Langley	80	James Langley.	Mildra Tollifero	78	John A. Tollifero.
Reuben Stephens	77	Reuben Stephens.	James McCrory	82	Robert McCrory.
Richard Henderson	54	Richard Henderson.	Peter Williams	86	Peter Williams.
			James Rodgers	80	James Rodgers.
DALE COUNTY.			James Galaspy	78	John O. Galaspy.
Joseph Watford	92	Barnabas Watford.			
Bartholomew Fields	79	Bartholomew Fields.	**RUSSELL COUNTY.**		
John Merrick, sen.	82	John Merrick, sen.	Samuel Pool	80	Matthew Pool.
DALLAS COUNTY.			**SHELBY COUNTY.**		
James Porter	80	James Porter.	Henry Gragg	79	Henry Gragg.
John Pierce	95	Benjamin Grumblin.	James Butler	83	James Butler.
Morgan Mills	78	Morgan Mills.			
William Brown	88	William Brown.	**SUMTER COUNTY.**		
			Thomas M. Dearman	94	Thomas M. Dearman.
GREENE COUNTY.			Andrew McCosklin	78	Andrew McCosklin.
Richard Johnson, sen.	79	Richard Johnson, sen.	Samuel Hammond	88	Samuel Hammond.
Henry Hart	76	Henry Hart.	Jesse Alsobrook	77	Jesse Alsobrook.
Hambleton Brown	86	Hambleton Brown.			
James Petigrew	79	James Petigrew.	**TUSCALOOSA COUNTY.**		
William Hillhouse	81	William Hillhouse.	Charles Geasling	98	Charles Geasling.
James McCarter	76	James McCarter.			
John Tidmore	84	John Tidmore.	**WILCOX COUNTY.**		
David Campbell	80	David Campbell.	Dempsey Carroll	78	Dempsey Carroll.
			John Young	90	Samuel Young.
JEFFERSON COUNTY.			John Garner	81	William H. Wait.
R. S. Shepherd	73	Sarah Nabers.			
John McDonald	81	Launcelot Armstrong.			
William Pullin, sen.	82				

ALABAMA—SOUTHERN DISTRICT—Continued.

Names of pensioners for revolutionary or military services.	Ages.	Names of heads of families with whom pensioners resided June 1, 1840.	Names of pensioners for revolutionary or military services.	Ages.	Names of heads of families with whom pensioners resided June 1, 1840.
WASHINGTON COUNTY.			**WALKER—Continued.**		
John Washam, sen. -	78	John Washam, sen.	Mathey Payne - - -	76	Mathey Payne.
			Andrew Nelson - - -	76	Robert Howard.
WALKER COUNTY.			Varder Mabgly - - -	102	Robert Mabgly.
Jeremiah Alexander - -	76		**BENTON COUNTY.**		
David Walling - - -	76	David Walling.			
Stephen Garison - - -	83	Silas Garison.	John Robinson - - -	81	J. H. Morison.

STATE OF MISSISSIPPI—NORTHERN DISTRICT.

Names of pensioners for revolutionary or military services.	Ages.	Names of heads of families with whom pensioners resided June 1, 1840.	Names of pensioners for revolutionary or military services.	Ages.	Names of heads of families with whom pensioners resided June 1, 1840.
CHICKASAW COUNTY.			**NOXUBEE COUNTY.**		
Thomas Mullin - - -	76	James Clark.	William Robinson - -	83	Dr. Foreman.
			Christopher White - -	77	E. Desmarkes.
CHOCTAW COUNTY.			William McIntosh - -	83	John Liddell.
Charles Holland - - -	82	Charles Holland.	**PANOLA COUNTY.**		
ITAWAMBA COUNTY.			Matthew Armstrong - -	76	Matthew Armstrong.
John Mangam - - -	77	John Mangam.	George Alexander - -	77	George Alexander.
LAFAYETTE COUNTY.			**PONTOTOC COUNTY.**		
Thomas Walker - -	81	John Walker.			
William Gillespie - -	81	D. G. Willis.	Charles Cornelius - -	85	Charles Cornelius
Leonard Miller - -	87	Ben. Miller.			
David Manow - - -	82	William Sims.	**TIPPAH COUNTY.**		
MARSHALL COUNTY.			William Vance - - -	84	Peyton A. Vance.
NORTHERN DISTRICT.			John Morgan - - -	80	John Morgan.
Alexander Milton - -	83	Alexander Milton.			
SOUTHERN DISTRICT.			**TISHAMINGO COUNTY.**		
Alexander Meek - -	76	Alexander Meek.	James Morgan - - -	80	James Morgan.
Harrison Jones - -	84	Weldon Jones.	Mayfield Crane - - -	105	John Moor.
Edward Corbet - -	78	Edmund Corbet.			
MONROE COUNTY.			**WINSTON COUNTY.**		
William Johnson - -	80	John F. Fowlkes.	Airs Hudspeth - - -	83	Airs Hudspeth.
George Wigington - -	85	George Wigington.	Robert Smith - - -	75	Ben. B. Smith.
John Kitchen - -	85	Joseph Laud.	William Tabor - - -	81	William Tabor.
David Adams - -	79	David Adams.	Sherwood White - -	82	James White.
Gideon Harmon - -	59	Gideon Harmon.	Simeon Watson - - -	78	Simeon Watson.
Robert Williams - -	74	Robert Williams.			
David Wright - -	83	James W. Tyler.			
Thomas Wilks - -	81	Thomas G. Wilks.			
OCKTIBBEHA COUNTY.			**YALOBUSHA COUNTY.**		
John Brown - - -	79	John Brown.	Hilary Hendricks - - -	89	Hilary Hendricks.

MISSISSIPPI—SOUTHERN DISTRICT.

Names of pensioners for revolutionary or military services.	Ages.	Names of heads of families with whom pensioners resided June 1, 1840.	Names of pensioners for revolutionary or military services.	Ages.	Names of heads of families with whom pensioners resided June 1, 1840.
AMITE COUNTY.			**KEMPER—Continued.**		
Christopher Gartington	80	Wilson Clark.	Charles P. Coleman	77	Charles P. Coleman.
Grief Whitington	78	Grief Whitington.	Ezekiel Haws	87	Ezekiel Haws.
John Sibley, sen.	82	John Sibley, sen.	**LAWRENCE COUNTY.**		
CLARK COUNTY.			John Stewart	82	William Sassor.
John Finton	81	John Finton.	**LAUDERDALE COUNTY.**		
COPIAH COUNTY.			James Whitehead	85	James Whitehead.
Shadrach McClenden	88	Jesse McClenden.	**MARION COUNTY.**		
William Fairbanks	83	William Fairbanks.	John Bowsman	70 to 80	John Bowsman.
FRANKLIN COUNTY.			**MADISON COUNTY.**		
Daniel Hawley	78	John B. Ducker.	Caleb Johnson	85	Caleb Johnson.
GREENE COUNTY.			**NESHOBA COUNTY.**		
Alexander Morse	77	Alexander Morse.	Samuel Boydstun	77	Samuel Boydstun.
Thomas Bateman	86	John Roberts.	Joel Vaughn	104	James Barnes.
HINDS COUNTY.			**NEWTON COUNTY.**		
Charles Campbell	82	Hugh Campbell.	William Harris	87	William Harris.
JEFFERSON COUNTY.			James Boyd	77	James Boyd.
S. Johnson	80	Eldridge Scissan.	**SIMPSON COUNTY.**		
J. Burke	80	Wiley B. Burke.	James Courtney	76	James Courtney.
KEMPER COUNTY.			**SMITH COUNTY.**		
John Tatton	—		William Stroud	85	
Kenneth McCaskill	—	Kenneth McCaskill.			

STATE OF LOUISIANA—EASTERN DISTRICT.

Names of pensioners for revolutionary or military services.	Ages.	Names of heads of families with whom pensioners resided June 1, 1840.	Names of pensioners for revolutionary or military services.	Ages.	Names of heads of families with whom pensioners resided June 1, 1840.
PARISH EAST FELICIANA.			**PARISH OF EAST BATON ROUGE.**		
Thomas Jackson	83	Chesley Jackson.	Patrick McNorton	68	Patrick McNorton.
PARISH OF JEFFERSON.			FAUXBOURG.		
C. Vattier	71	J. F. Francisco.	P. B. Hardy	83	P. B. Hardy.
WASHINGTON PARISH.			**CITY OF NEW ORLEANS.**		
John Brumfield	93	Fleming Brumfield.	Etienne Silvestre	76	Etienne Silvestre.
John Pierce	98	Augustus Pierce.			

LOUISIANA—WESTERN DISTRICT.

NATCHITOCHES PARISH.			CALDWELL PARISH.		
John J. Laplace	78	J. J. Laplace.	Hampton Stroud	84	Henry Young.
UNION PARISH.			**CADDO PARISH.**		
None.			William Davis	80	
RAPIDES PARISH.			**CLAIBORNE PARISH.**		
John Spencer Umphrey	46	John S. Umphrey.	Jethro Butler	88	Jethro Butler.
			Benjamin Goodson	82	Benjamin Goodson.

STATE OF TENNESSEE—EASTERN DISTRICT.

Names of pensioners for revolutionary or military services.	Ages.	Names of heads of families with whom pensioners resided June 1, 1840.	Names of pensioners for revolutionary or military services.	Ages.	Names of heads of families with whom pensioners resided June 1, 1840.
ANDERSON COUNTY.			SCHOOL DISTRICT NO. 8.		
			John Miller	75	John Miller.
James Trowell	78	James Trowell.	George Emert	83	Elizabeth Emert.
Douglas Oliver	88	Douglas Oliver.	Richard Kelley	76	Richard Kelley.
William Cross	80	William Cross.			
William Patterson	87	William Patterson.	DISTRICT NO. 9.		
Peter Johnson	81	Peter Johnson.	Leonard Bowers	80	Leonard Bowers.
Page Portwood	83	Page Portwood.			
Thomas Brummett	87	Thomas Brummett.	**CLAIBORNE COUNTY.**		
J. J. Williams	81	J. J. Williams.			
			Harman Hopper	78	John Hopper.
BRADLEY COUNTY.			Richard Harper	76	Richard Harper.
			Andrew Presley	90	Squire J. Harper.
Charles Lain	81	Charles Lain.	Thomas Nun	90	Sarah Larcham.
Joseph Lain	83	Joseph Lain.	Jesse Webb	63	Jesse Webb.
Sarah Cry	78	Sarah Cry.	Thomas Hardy	74	Thomas Hardy.
Robert McCormack	83	Lemuel Carpenter.	John Ousley	82	John Ousley.
James Hamilton	84	James Hamilton.	Solomon Lewis	90	David Rogers.
William McAllister, sen.	80	William McAllister.	John Braden	80	John Braden.
Robert Forrester	80	William Forrester.	John Jones, sen.	77	John Jones, sen.
William Dodd	83	George Couch.	Peter Peck	78	Peter Peck.
James Sellers	85	James Sellers.	Whorton Nunn	85	Henry Nunn.
			Matthew Bussle	93	Matthew Bussle.
BLOUNT COUNTY.					
			COCKE COUNTY.		
Robert McCay	81	Robert McCay.			
Thomas Hunter	82	Thomas Hunter.	William Bragg	75	William Bragg.
James Houston	82	Robert Tedford.	Peter Wise	89	Joseph Wise.
William Tipton	79	William Tipton.	Darius O'Neal	76	Darius O'Neal.
James Taylor	82	Joshua Taylor.	Bartlett Sisk	79	Lawson Sisk.
John Davis	86	John Davis, sen.	Samuel Yeates	83	Samuel Yeates.
Robert Tedford	80	Robert A. Tedford.	Joseph Burke	75	Joseph Burke.
James McKensey	87	William McKensey.	Henry Click	59	Henry Click.
Robert Bryant	93	Thomas Bryant.	Allen Seratt	77	Allen Seratt.
George Haden	91	George Haden.			
James Symms	90	John Symms.	**CAMPBELL COUNTY.**		
George Ewing	80	Samuel McColley.			
James Carathers	80 to 90	James Carathers.	John Cabbage	83	Champlen Waters.
Robert Rhea	76	Robert Rhea.	James McDonald	79	James McDonald.
William Hamby	97	William Dunn.	Martha Rogers	75	William A. Wright.
			Dennis Trammel	--	David Trammel.
BLEDSOE COUNTY.			Richard Crabtree	76	Richard Crabtree.
DISTRICT NO. 1.					
John Narramore	79	John Narramore.	**GREENE COUNTY.**		
DISTRICT NO. 2.			Peter Kent	80	Peter Kent.
Chatten D. Pollard	79	Chatten D. Pollard.	John Sexton	79	John Sexton.
John Ford, sen.	78	John Ford, sen.	William Houston	77	William Houston.
			George House	78	Washington House.
DISTRICT NO. 3.			Thomas Morgan, sen.	88	Thomas Morgan, sen.
Charles Shurmon	86	Charles Shurmon.	Martin Waddle	80	Martin Waddle.
			Nasma Sevier	97	John Rector.
DISTRICT NO 6.			Joseph Dunlap	92	William Wykle.
Philip Shurmon	82	Philip Shurmon.	William Sharp	79	William Sharp.
John Hail	86	John Hail.			
Andrew Davis	83	Andrew Davis.	NORTHERN DIVISION.		
			Jacob Bruner	76	Ide Bruner.
DISTRICT NO. 7.			John Morrison	83	John Morrison.
Andrew McDonough	80	Anna McDonough.	John Gass, sen.	83	John Gass, sen.
			Azariah Doty	96	Ephraim Doty.
DISTRICT NO. 9.			John Carter	83	Ezekiel Carter.
Francis Hughs	80	Margaret Hughs.	Thomas Bryant	86	Austin Bryant.
			Frederick Shaffer	82	Frederick Shaffer.
CARTER COUNTY.			John Kesterson	85	John Kesterson.
DISTRICT NO. 1.					
Charles Moreland	76	Wright Moreland.	**GRAINGER COUNTY.**		
James Campbell	80	James Filyou, jr.			
			John Tanner	81	John Tanner.
DISTRICT NO. 3.			Lewis Collins	87	Lewis Collins.
Jeremiah Campbell	78	Jeremiah Campbell.	Chapman Poindexter	81	Chapman Poindexter.
			Richard Grantham	85	Richard Grantham.
CIVIL DISTRICT NO. 5.			John Bethel	84	John Bethel.
Ephraim Buck	49	Ephraim Buck.	Joseph Yadon	84	Joseph Yadon.
John Scott	87	John McInturff.	James Hines	89	James Hines.
Isaac Taylor	84	Isaac Taylor.	William Clay	80	William Clay.
			Thomas Brown	77	Thomas Brown.
DISTRICT NO. 6.			Joseph Ellis	77	Joseph Ellis.
Solomon Hendrix	86	Solomon Hendrix.	Adam Cabbage	86	Adam Cabbage.
Andrew Taylor	80	Andrew Taylor.	John Hammock	86	John Hammock.
			Israel McBee	79	Israel McBee.
DISTRICT NO. 7.			Thomas Lay	79	Thomas Lay.
Abner McLeod	44	Abner McLeod.			
Elizabeth Carter	75	Benjamin Brewer.			

TENNESSEE—EASTERN DISTRICT—Continued.

Names of pensioners for revolutionary or military services.	Ages.	Names of heads of families with whom pensioners resided June 1, 1840.
HAMILTON COUNTY.		
Moses Nelson	41	Moses Nelson.
Robert Martin	84	Alexander Martin.
William Reid	75	James Roy.
James Davis	80	James Davis.
Thomas Palmer	81	Thomas Palmer.
Joseph Campbell	86	Joseph Campbell.
HAWKINS COUNTY.		
William Thurman	79	Benjamin Thurman.
Robert Hensley	81	John Hicks.
Mary Beaty	86	Samuel Beaty.
Henry Frazier	57	Henry Frazier.
Thomas A. Fletcher	90	Anthony Smith.
Robert Campbell, sen.	80	Robert Campbell, sen.
Washington Denham	54	Washington Denham.
William Molsbey, sen.	82	William Molsbey, sen.
James Simmons, sen.	81	James Simmons, sen.
Henry Blevins	84	Henry Blevins.
John Hicks	80	John Hicks, sen.
Thomas Brooks	80	Thomas Brooks.
Wright Bond	87	Arthur Bond.
James Lovin	81	Edmund Lovin.
Richard Matlock	79	George Matlock.
Notley Thomas	93	Notley Thomas, sen.
John Sowel	80	William Ritter.
Momon Lawson	95	Peter Lawson.
Littleton Brooks	90	Littleton Brooks.
Seth Manis	78	Seth Manis.
Alexander Trent	81	Alexander Trent, sen.
Bartlet Belcher	76	Bartlet Belcher.
Francis Winstead	81	Margaret Winstead.
John Rains	81	John Rains.
Abner Gordon	82	Abner Gordon.
Pharaoh Cobb	90	Jesse Cobb.
Samuel Riggs	80	Samuel Riggs.
Elizabeth Smith	79	Joseph Mooney.
Thomas Price	79	Thomas Price.
Jonathan Long, sen.	78	Jonathan Long, sen.
Letitia Rorack	93	Letitia Rorack.
John Leonard	82	John Leonard.
Daniel Jones, sen.	86	Daniel Jones, jr.
William Bussell	77	William Bussell.
John Light, sen.	76	John Light, sen.
William Jewell	97	William Jewell.
James Morrison	86	James Morrison.
Flower Mullins	77	Flower Mullins.
William Skelton	79	William Skelton.
Joseph Britton	87	Joseph Britton.
JOHNSON COUNTY.		
William Wilson	82	William Wilson, jr.
James McDaniel	82	James McDaniel.
Jacob Hood	96	Nancy Morley.
JEFFERSON COUNTY.		
NORTHERN DIVISION.		
Stephen McLaughlon	82	Stephen McLaughlon.
John Petty	83	William T. Allerson.
Jacob Maddox	76	Jacob Maddox.
Allen Kelley	55	Allen Kelley.
William Murphy	83	Samuel Box.
Benjamin Bradshaw	82	Benjamin Bradshaw.
William Caldwell, sen.	80	William Caldwell, sen.
John McCoy	88	William McCoy.
John Hasket	90	John Hasket.
Samuel McSpadden	83	Thomas McSpadden.
Jesse Gammon	75	Jesse Gammon.
Spencer Watkins	80	Spencer Watkins.
Richard Cheek	79	Richard Cheek.
Tide Lane	78	Tide Lane.
James Anderson	80	James Anderson, sen.
Michael Treace	85	Michael Treace.
SOUTHERN DIVISION.		
George Turnley	78	George Turnley.
John Fain	51	John Fain.
Zaccheus Copeland	76	Zaccheus Copeland.
George Gregory	61	George Gregory.
James Fuller	49	James Fuller.

Names of pensioners for revolutionary or military services.	Ages.	Names of heads of families with whom pensioners resided June 1, 1840.
JEFFERSON—Continued.		
SOUTHERN DIVISION—Continued.		
John Russell	55	John Russell.
Michael Barnet	80	Michael Barnet.
John Henry	81	John Henry.
Jesse Webb	74	Jesse Webb.
Joel Davis	77	Joel Davis.
Ely Sartin	55	Ely Sartin, sen.
KNOX COUNTY.		
David Pinn	80	Lutilda Dabney.
Philip Titlow	57	Philip Titlow.
Edward Smith	80	Edward Smith.
Samuel Tarver	80	Samuel Tarver.
Thomas Dove	86	Thomas Dove.
Perrin Cardwell	76	Perrin Cardwell.
Absalom Rutherford	78	Absalom Rutherford.
Vincent Jackson	95	Alexander Blain.
Marcus Swadley	80	Ann Defriese.
Thomas Sumpter	76	Thomas Sumpter.
Joseph Brown	84	Joseph Brown.
Mitchell Childress	90	Mitchell Childress.
John Fox	83	John Fox.
David Falkner	83	David Falkner.
Joseph Large	84	Joseph Large.
Edmund Newman	77	Edmund Newman.
James Campbell	83	James Campbell.
Harris Gammon	83	Lewis Gammon.
John Childress	81	John Childress.
Garnett Smith	78	Bolin Smith.
Jesse Wells	91	Michael Davis.
Jacob Gallespie	86	Jacob Gallespie.
Card Cox, sen.	77	Card Cox, sen.
Luke Stansbury	88	Luke Stansbury.
Richard Porterfield	82	Richard Porterfield.
Jesse Perry	83	Lewis Perry.
James Crews	86	James Crews.
Robert Johnson	81	Robert Johnson.
John McLemore	85	William McLemore.
Abraham Hankins	86	Abraham Hankins.
McMINN COUNTY.		
Isaac Lane	81	Isaac Lane.
Jno. Honey	79	John Honey.
Will Peters	79	George Monroe.
William Norman	76	William Norman.
Spencer Benson	76	John Benson.
Edmond Roberts	83	Ed. Roberts.
Elizabeth McNabb	80	William McNabb.
James Cunningham	80	J. B. Cunningham.
John Raney	84	John Raney.
James Riggins	88	James Riggins.
Maximilian Rector	82	Maximilian Rector.
Henry Matlock	54	Henry Matlock.
Charles Carter	73	Charles Carter.
William Barnett	79	James M. Barnett.
Simeon Eldridge	78	Simeon Eldridge.
John Kurtus	85	John Kurtus.
Benjamin Brown	87	Benjamin Brown.
E. Cooper	45	Ebenezer Cooper.
MONROE COUNTY.		
26TH REGIMENT.		
Gideon Morgan	65	Gideon Morgan.
Henry Stephens	66	Nathaniel Watson.
Nathaniel Watson	99	John Harris.
Christopher Boston	81	Christopher Boston.
Bergiss Wit	79	Bergiss Wit.
William Duggan	49	William Duggan.
John Allgood	85	John Allgood.
27TH REGIMENT.		
Thomas Vernon	88	Thomas Vernon.
Jacob Patton	83	Jacob Patton.
Thomas Duncan	76	Thomas Duncan.
James Montgomery	49	James Montgomery.
John Pannel	49	John Pannel.
John Simms	90	John Gentry.
John Denton	81	John Denton.
James McGill	83	Harvey McGill.
Samuel Steel	81	Samuel Steel.

TENNESSEE—EASTERN DISTRICT—Continued.

Names of pensioners for revolutionary or military services.	Ages.	Names of heads of families with whom pensioners resided June 1, 1840.	Names of pensioners for revolutionary or military services.	Ages.	Names of heads of families with whom pensioners resided June 1, 1840.
MORGAN COUNTY.			**ROANE**—Continued.		
Betsey Staples - - -	76	B. Staples.	William Boyd - - -	84	William Boyd.
Rebecca Holloway -	76	Rachel Holloway.	William Moore - -	82	James Moore.
Joseph McPeters - -	83	Joseph McPeters.	Benjamin Clark - -	77	Benjamin Clark.
Marsha Green - -	87	Marsha Green.	William Hyden - -	76	William Hyden.
Abel Peak - -	79	Abel Peak.	David C. Demey - -	86	David C. Demey.
Esther Sexton - -	79	Timothy Sexton.			
Nathaniel Milton - -	80	Nathaniel Milton.	**SULLIVAN COUNTY.**		
Jonathan Deldine -	77	J. Deldine.			
John Howard - -	73	John Howard.	Thomas King - - -	86	Thomas King.
Ryal Pren - -	77	Ryal Pren.	David Hughes - -	82	David Hughes.
John Williams - -	80	John Williams.	John Almoney - -	58	John Almoney.
Joseph Patton' - -	78	Joseph Patton.	John Grier - -	79	Jacob Crumley.
Joseph Stincuphor -	85	Joseph Stincuphor.	Thomas Jones - -	78	Thomas Jones.
Thomas Kindred - -	81	Thomas Kindred.	Thomas Morrell - -	80	Thomas Morrell.
John Crinshaw - -	83	John Crinshaw.	Joshua Hamilton -	79	Joshua Hamilton.
Matthew Williams -	85	Matthew Williams.	Elijah Cross - -	84	David L. Cross.
			Abraham Cross - -	90	Abraham Cross.
MEIGS COUNTY.			Edward Cox - -	83	John Cox.
			Jacob Bealer - -	89	Jacob Bealer.
John Dyer - - -	80	Robert Phariss.	Joseph Grey - -	76	Joseph Grey.
John Sutton - - -	90	Thomas P. Davis.	Jacob Hawk - -	82	Jacob Hawk.
			George Bushong - -	48	George Bushong.
MARION COUNTY.			Jacob Slaughter -	84	Jacob Slaughter.
			William Snodgrass -	80	William Snodgrass.
Ransom Smith - -	81	Ransom Smith.	Samuel Taylor - -	85	Edward Taylor.
Ezekiel Stone - -	83	Richard W. Stone.	Thomas Cox - -	84	Stephen Miller.
Letitia Rains - -	71	Robert Rains.	Henry Maggot - -	80	Richard Shipley.
Laton Smith - -	84	Aaron Smith.	John Hudson - -	85	Hamilton Perry.
William Everett - -	78	William Everett.	Henry Maggot - -	54	Henry Maggot.
James Morgan - -	81	James Morgan.	Ankey Godsey - -	77	Jacob Millers.
			William King - -	88	Benjamin H. King.
POLK COUNTY.			William Bolen - -	83	William Bolen.
			David Childress - -	78	W. P. Nelms.
William May - -	75	William May.	Benjamin Birdwell -	74	Benjamin Birdwell.
William Longley - -	82	William Longley.	William Goad - -	86	William Goad.
Samuel Walker - -	80	William Parker.	Richard Parkers - -	55	Richard Parkers.
Thomas Towns - -	89	John Towns.	John Chester - -	86	John Chester.
Samuel Carter - -	85	Amos Carter.	John Douglass - -	76	John Douglass.
			Robert Tribbett - -	57	Robert Tribbett.
RHEA COUNTY.			Micajah Adams - -	81	Micajah Adams.
Daniel Broiles - -	80	Cornelius Broiles.			
James Furgison - -	81	Samuel Furgison.	**SEVIER COUNTY.**		
Thomas Hamilton -	80	Thomas Hamilton.			
Thomas McKeddy -	86	William McKeddy.	Penelope Porter - -	77	Ashley Winn.
Mary Reace - -	23	Mary Reace.	Lydia Atchley - -	75	Noah Atchley.
Harris Ryan - -	76	Harris Ryan.	Jacob Layman - -	78	Jacob Layman.
			William Trotter - -	77	William Trotter.
ROANE COUNTY.			Jeremiah Compton -	87	Cyrus Compton.
			George Parsons - -	79	George Parsons.
Thomas Landrim - -	86	Thomas Landrim.	Daniel Fox - -	66	Martha James.
James Acree - -	86	James Acree.	John McCroskey - -	84	John McCroskey.
John Baman - -	86	John Baman.			
Adam Miller - -	83	Adam Miller.	**WASHINGTON COUNTY.**		
David Blackwell - -	82	David Blackwell.			
Benjamin Chapman -	78	Benjamin Chapman.	John Crouch - -	84	David Mains.
Samuel Evans - -	84	L. B. Davis.	Loyd Ford - -	83	Loyd Ford.
John Hood - -	78	John Hood.	Amon Hale - -	83	Amon Hale.
John Wooddy - -	81	Samuel Wooddy.	William Ledmon - -	67	William Ledmon.
John McNatt - -	78	John McNatt.	Jeremiah Keys - -	43	Jeremiah Keys.
James Allen - -	81	James Allen.	Elizabeth Lacky - -	80	Elizabeth Hundley.
Edward Wyatt - -	81	Daniel White.	James Simmons - -	49	James Simmons.
James Akin - -	80	James Akin.	William Slaughter -	85	David Lawson.
Robert Liles - -	81	Robert D. Liles.	John Thornburg - -	61	John Thornburg.
Thomas Ives - -	82	Thomas Ives.	Jacob Brown - -	91	Jacob Brown.
Carter Barnard - -	78	Carter Barnard.	Hugh Harriss - -	84	Hugh Harriss.
Solomon Gearran - -	80	Solomon Gearran.	Adam Harman - -	75	Adam Harman.
Tandy Senter - -	82	Tandy Senter.	Andrew Hannah - -	79	Andrew Hannah.
Lard Burns - -	85	Lard Barns.	Zadoc Freeman - -	55	Zadoc Freeman.
John Cox - - -	82	Samuel Cox.	Adam Ingle - -	86	Adam Ingle.
George Fuller, sen. -	83	George Fuller, sen.	James Sevier - -	76	James Sevier.
Nathaniel Orsbourn -	89	Elizabeth Burk.	Elizabeth Jackson -	75	Alfred Jackson.
			Darling Jones - -	77	Darling Jones.

TENNESSEE—MIDDLE DISTRICT.

Names of pensioners for revolutionary or military services.	Ages.	Names of heads of families with whom pensioners resided June 1, 1840.	Names of pensioners for revolutionary or military services.	Ages.	Names of heads of families with whom pensioners resided June 1, 1840.
BEDFORD COUNTY.			**DAVIDSON—Continued.**		
			CIVIL DISTRICT NO. 9—Continued.		
Robert Majors - - -	79	Robert Majors.	Joseph Vick - - -	78	Joseph Vick.
Samuel Knox - - -	83	William Eoff.	CIVIL DISTRICT NO. 10.		
Richard Keel - - -	87	Richard Keel.	John Williamson - -	79	John Williamson.
Matt Martin, sen. - -	77	Matt Martin, sen.			
John Davidson - - -	77	John Davidson.	CIVIL DISTRICT NO. 11.		
Zadoc Wood - - -	74	E. B. Jones.	John McCutchin - -	87	John McCutchin.
John Moore, sen. - -	80	John Moore, sen.			
John Gibbs - - -	81	Ebenezer F. Gibbs.	CIVIL DISTRICT NO. 12.		
Horatio Coop - - -	84	James Coop.	William Watkins - -	85	William E. Watkins.
Jackson Lisle - - -	78	Jackson Lisle.	Caleb Mason - - -	87	John Davis.
John Morrison - - -	77	John Morrison.			
David Ostean - - -	79	David Ostean.	CIVIL DISTRICT NO. 18.		
John Tacke - - -	86	John Tacke.	John Casey - - -	77	Charles S. Casey.
Jacob Bledsoe - - -	79	Jacob Bledsoe.	Isaiah Alley - - -	91	Thomas Alley.
Ezekiel Reynolds - -	80	Michael Reynolds.			
Abram Hilton - - -	90	Abram Hilton.	CIVIL DISTRICT NO. 19.		
James Murray - - -	88	James Murray.	Peter Bashaw - - -	78	Peter Bashaw.
John Williams - - -	79	John Williams.	Benjamin Morgan - -	78	Benjamin Morgan.
CANNON COUNTY.			CIVIL DISTRICT NO. 20.		
John Bynum - - -	83	John Bynum.	William Coats - - -	80	Beverly E. Coats.
Enoch Berry - - -	77	Enoch Berry.	CIVIL DISTRICT NO. 22.		
John Stephenson - -	89	Abner Alexander.	John McCaslin - - -	90	Joshua Drake.
Isaac Eoff - - -	79	Isaac Eoff.			
Daniel Carroll - - -	77	George W. Thurston.	DISTRICT NO. 23.		
Hardy Lassetor - -	88	Luke Lassetor.	Thomas Hickman - -	78	Thomas Hickman.
David Faulkenburg - -	101	William Pace.			
Gisbin Lane - - -	89	James C. Greer.	DISTRICT NO. 24.		
COFFEE COUNTY.			Thomas Douglass - -	84	Thomas Douglass.
			George Smith - - -	80	George Smith.
Isaac Street - - -	78	Isaac Street.	**FENTRESS COUNTY.**		
Morton Jones - - -	91	Morton Jones.			
John Nelson - - -	81	John Nelson.	Lucy Chapman - - -	70	Lucy Chapman.
Lewis Taylor - - -	79	Lewis Taylor.	Andrew Shortridge - -	85	Andrew Shortridge.
Charles Pearson - -	80	William Pearson.	Anna Flowers - - -	78	Archibald Stonie.
Sterling Pearson - -	87	Ellis Pearson.	Jane Evans - - -	72	Thomas Evans.
George D. Sherrell - -	77	George D. Sherrell.	Bailey Owen - - -	82	Bailey Owen.
			George Chilton - -	88	George Chilton.
DICKSON COUNTY.			George Helm - - -	89	George Helm.
Benjamin C. Waters -	92	Benjamin C. Waters.	Smith Willis - - -	78	Smith Willis.
Abraham Hogins - -	85	Archibald D. Hogins.	William Dorse - - -	78	William Dorse.
William Willie - - -	96	Reddick Myatt.	**FRANKLIN COUNTY.**		
James Daniel - - -	54	James Daniel.			
George Clark - - -	94	Benjamin Clark.	Samuel Handley - -	89	John Handley.
Christopher Strong - -	80	Christopher Strong.	Enoch Breedon - -	82	Enoch Breedon.
John Nesbitt - - -	84	Allen Nesbitt.	Thomas Wakefield - -	76	Thomas Wakefield.
Robert Nesbitt, sen. -	80	Robert Nesbitt, sen.	Elihu Berk - - -	75	Alexander Donaldson.
Simon Deloach - -	57	Simon Deloach.	Patrick McElyea - -	91	Archer Hatchet.
William James - -	45	William James.	Richard Erwin - - -	30	Richard Erwin.
Gideon Carr - - -	90	John B. Carr.	William Calwell - -	78	William Calwell.
John Maybourn - -	97	Howell Underwood.	Larkin Ragan - - -	93	Larkin Ragan.
Isaac Walker - - -	85	Isaac Walker.	Ann Wilson - - -	40	Mrs. Ann Wilson.
Gustavus Rape - -	77	Gustavus Rape.	William Jackson - -	78	William Jackson.
William Tatorn - -	80	William Tatorn.	William Calwell - -	78	William Cowan.
Mary Thompson - -	71	Mary Thompson.	Jonas Hill - - -	76	Jonas Hill.
Benjamin Darrow - -	78	Benjamin Darrow.	Jacob Reynolds - -	47	Jacob Reynolds.
			Samuel Reynolds - -	84	Samuel Reynolds.
DE KALB COUNTY.			**GILES COUNTY.**		
John Fite - - -	81	Henry Fite.			
Leonard Fite - - -	81	Leonard Fite.	Joseph Jones - - -	82	Joseph Jones.
James Saunders - -	79	Joseph Saunders.	Nathaniel Tatum - -	79	Nathaniel Tatum.
Elijah Duncan - - -	90	Elijah Duncan.	Henry Goodnight - -	79	David Goodnight.
Elijah Hooton - - -	93	John Reeves.	John Jones - - -	90	Hizar Jones.
Joseph Rankhorn - -	81	Joseph Rankhorn.	John Everly - - -	74	George Everly.
John Pucket - - -	76	John Pucket.	John Ross - - -	89	George B. Ross.
John Bevert - - -	86	John Bevert.	Thomas Williams - -	79	Henry E. Williams.
			Benjamin Cheatham -	80	Benjamin Cheatham.
DAVIDSON COUNTY.			James Tinner - - -	81	James Tinner.
Norvell Lipscomb - -	84	James Walker.	Aaron Grigsby - -	85	Amos Grigsby.
Perkinson Jackman - -	77	Perkinson Jackman.	John Erwin - - -	85	John Erwin.
James Haley - - -	84	James Haley.	Richard Jones - - -	77	Richard Jones.
Peter Leslie - - -	80	Peter Leslie.	George Dodson - -	79	George Dodson.
Gideon Johnson - -	86	George Chadwell.	Hugh King - - -	85	Hugh King.
James Barnes - - -	79	James Barnes.	Elles Wood - - -	87	George Erwin.
Nicholas Hale - - -	78	Nicholas Hale.	John Bradberry - -	104	J. Bradberry.
			James Higgins, sen. -	89	James Higgins, jun.
CIVIL DISTRICT NO. 9.			John Watkins - - -	83	John Watkins.
Cabler Frederick - -	82	John Corbett.			

TENNESSEE—MIDDLE DISTRICT—Continued.

Names of pensioners for revolutionary or military services.	Ages.	Names of heads of families with whom pensioners resided June 1, 1840.	Names of pensioners for revolutionary or military services.	Ages.	Names of heads of families with whom pensioners resided June 1, 1840.
GILES—Continued.			LINCOLN—Continued.		
			DISTRICT NO. 3.		
Lester Morris	80	T. A. Westmoreland.	Samuel Isaacs	82	Samuel Isaacs.
Robert Patterson	83	Robert Patterson.	Josiah Brandon	80	Josiah Brandon.
Samuel Baker	86	Robert Chapman.			
Lawson Hobson	86	Lawson Hobson.	DISTRICT NO. 6.		
Thomas Hudson	78	John Sandusky.	Thomas Armstrong	85	John Armstrong.
Samuel Watson	79	Richard Suttle.	Aaron D. Gage	82	Easter Westerman.
			William Pamplin	77	Henry Pamplin.
HICKMAN COUNTY.					
			DISTRICT NO. 7.		
Elijah Mayfield	80	Elijah Mayfield.	William Shaw	82	William Shaw.
Josiah Grimett	74	Josiah Grimett.			
Jerdon Milum	90	Jerdon Milum.	DISTRICTS NOS. 10 AND 11.		
John Tucker	87	John Tucker.	William George	85	William George.
Richard Campbell	82	Richard Campbell.	David Henderson	49	David Henderson.
Richard Nalls	77	Richard Nalls.	W. C. Smith	82	Larkin Smith.
			Benjamin Rowe	82	Benjamin Rowe.
HUMPHREYS COUNTY.			Philip Koonce	75	Philip Koonce.
DISTRICT NO. 1.					
John Plant	56	John Plant.	DISTRICT NO. 14.		
			John Gibson	80	John Gibson.
DISTRICT NO. 3.					
Simon Steptoe	77	Hilary Caps.	DISTRICT NO. 17.		
			William Beard	80	Francis A. Beard.
DISTRICT NO. 5.					
Josiah Pucket	91	Josiah Pucket.	DISTRICT NO. 22.		
Alexander Anderson	85	Alexander Brown.	William Brown	70	Joshua B. Brown.
DISTRICT NO. 9.			DISTRICT NO. 23.		
Isaac Hale	78	Isaac Hale.	John R. Vickers	91	John R. Vickers.
William Gibson	98	Patrick Spicer.	Alexander Forbes, sen.	79	Alexander Forbes, sen.
			Rapel Smith, sen.	77	Rapel Smith, sen.
JACKSON COUNTY.					
DISTRICT NO. 1.			LAWRENCE COUNTY.		
James Cayson	83	Edm. Cayson.	Wilson Rogers	82	Jacob Blyche, sen.
Richard Gordon	78	Richard Gordon.	Palmore Kendred	95	William Ayers.
			Richard Robinson	104	Catharine Brown.
DISTRICT NO. 2.			Joseph Spears	80	Joseph Spears.
Thomas Wilkerson	77	Jesse Jinkins.	John Evans	77	John Evans, jun.
			Jeremiah Bentley	82	J. Bentley.
DISTRICT NO. 3.			James Waters, sen.	88	James Waters, sen.
Reuben Graves	79	Reuben Graves.	William H. Redding	81	William H. Redding.
DISTRICT NO. 4.					
William Carlisle	75	William Morse.	MARSHALL COUNTY.		
Yelvaton Neville	76	Yelvaton Neville.	Lewis Parham	55	Lewis Parham.
			Benjamin Copeland	76	Benjamin Copeland.
DISTRICT NO. 5.			William Martin	81	William Martin.
John Wood	92	Philip Condra.	John Dysart, sen.	91	John Dysart.
			Richard Long, sen.	82	Richard Long, sen.
DISTRICT NO. 9.			James Shaw	69	James Shaw.
Joseph Hawkins	74	Joseph Hawkins.	Robert Walker	86	Robert Walker.
Jeremiah Brown	86	Jeremiah Brown.	James Wilson	86	James Wilson.
			Ezekiel Billington	82	Ezekiel Billington.
DISTRICT NO. 10.			James Bass	83	James Bass.
David Phillips	86	David Phillips.	Sylvester Chunn	86	Sylvester Chunn.
Charles Harmon	83	Charles Harmon.	Robert Cowden	86	Robert Cowden, 3d.
			Frederick Fisher	78	Frederick Fisher.
DISTRICT NO. 11.			Shadrach Weaver	74	Shadrach Weaver.
David Lyles	84	Joshua Draper.	William Dickson	54	William Dickson.
Daniel Ramsey	77	Daniel Ramsey.	Emanuel McConnell	84	Emanuel McConnell.
			Jacob Lawrance	82	John Lawrance.
DISTRICT NO. 12.			Samuel Hilles	81	John Hilles.
Michael Saylers	82	Thomas Saylers.	William Bingham	84	William Bingham.
			Elijah Alexander	81	Elijah Alexander.
DISTRICT NO. 13.			Alexander Ewens	79	Alexander Ewens.
John Henley	89	John Henley.			
Peter Crumb	81	Peter Crumb.			
Joseph Jared, sen.	80	Joseph Jared, sen.	MONTGOMERY COUNTY.		
Jacob Newman	75	Catharine Murphy.	Benjamin P. Persons	58	Benjamin P. Persons.
			Lucinda Pool	75	John Pool.
DISTRICT NO. 15.			John Vick	84	John Vick.
			James Fentress	77	James Fentress.
William Ferrel	83	William Ferrel.	Alexander Frazier	81	Sol. Neville.
			Joseph Ligon	85	Joseph Ligon.
LINCOLN COUNTY.			Thomas Hackney	88	D. W. Hackney.
DISTRICT NO. 1.			James Bowers	84	James Bowers.
Thomas Davis	81	Thomas Davis.			
DISTRICT NO. 2.			MAURY COUNTY.		
John McNott	105	Charles McNott.	4TH DISTRICT.		
			Joseph Haynes	89	Joseph Kennedy.

TENNESSEE—MIDDLE DISTRICT—Continued.

Names of pensioners for revolutionary or military services.	Ages.	Names of heads of families with whom pensioners resided June 1, 1840.	Names of pensioners for revolutionary or military services.	Ages.	Names of heads of families with whom pensioners resided June 1, 1840.
MAURY—Continued.			**RUTHERFORD—Continued.**		
9TH CIVIL DISTRICT.			John Stone - - -	76	John Stone.
Zachariah Butler - -	76	Zachariah Butler.	Daniel McCoy - - -	89	Thomas Dalton.
Jacob Biffle - - -	78	Jacob Biffle.	Nathaniel Winston - -	73	Nathaniel Winston.
			Sylvania Tucker - -	84	David Tucker.
10TH CIVIL DISTRICT.			John Clark - - -	80	John Clark.
Samuel Mayers - -	81	Samuel Mayers.			
Joel Fagg - - -	88	Joel Fagg.	**ROBERTSON COUNTY.**		
			John C. Coon - - -	85	Eliza Saunders.
19TH CIVIL DISTRICT.			Charles Gent - - -	85	James W. Gent.
William Gordon - -	88	Josiah Gordon.	James Jones - - -	88	James Jones.
James Mitchell - -	74	James Mitchell.	David Jones - - -	86	David Jones, sen.
			Martin Walton - -	79	Martin Walton.
14TH CIVIL DISTRICT.			William W. Walker - -	25	William W. Walker.
Jacob Gilliam - -	79	Jacob Gilliam.	David Henry - - -	89	David Henry.
			Fendal Roland - -	80	Reuben Adams.
15TH CIVIL DISTRICT.			John Zeck - - -	81	John Zeck.
James Love - - -	78	James Love.	Charles Ellison - -	76	Charles Ellison.
			Ann White - - -	81	Ann White.
17TH CIVIL DISTRICT.					
Martin True - - -	80	Martin True.	**SMITH COUNTY.**		
David Dobbins - -	82	David D. McFalls.			
Abner Johnson - -	81	Abner Johnson.	Willis Hodges - -	93	Willis Hodges.
			Philip Pope - - -	78	Philip Pope.
20TH CIVIL DISTRICT.			William Denny - -	47	William Denny.
Abraham Parker - -	77	Abraham Parker.	Isom Beasley - -	87	Isom Beasley.
			Elizabeth Darnes - -	79	Elizabeth Darnes.
22D CIVIL DISTRICT.			Ann Ford - - -	67	Ann Ford.
Jacob W. Young - -	78	Jacob W. Young.	Robin Hayse - - -	46	Robin Hayse.
			Berry Gregory - -	79	Berry Gregory.
23D CIVIL DISTRICT.			William Gregory - -	76	William Gregory.
James Lockridge - -	84	James Lockridge.	Francis Cauly - -	100	Francis Cauly.
James Hardison - -	81	James Hardison.	Dabney Cooper - -	84	Dabney Cooper.
Elisha Williams - -	80	Elisha Williams.	Henry Wakefield - -	88	Henry Wakefield.
David Long - - -	82	David Long.	Benjamin Jones - -	81	Simeon Jones.
			Susanna Boon - -	79	Susanna Boon.
24TH CIVIL DISTRICT.					
George Barker - -	81	George Barker.	**STEWART COUNTY.**		
OVERTON COUNTY.			Thomas French - -	88	Thomas French.
			John Ross - - -	88	John Ross.
Samuel Tays - - -	79	Samuel Tays.	Benjamin Daniel - -	87	Benjamin Daniel.
Cornelius Carmack -	82	John Carmack.	Alexander Anderson -	88	John Brown.
William Phillips, sen. -	91	William Phillips.			
Jesse Ashlock - -	84	Jesse Ashlock.	**SUMNER COUNTY.**		
Abraham Sevier - -	80	Abraham R. Sevier.			
Henry Dillon - -	80	Abraham Grimsley.	Bathl. Stovall - -	80	Bathl. Stovall.
Benjamin Reader - -	80	John Walker.	Thomas Parrish - -	80	Thomas Parrish.
Henry Hoover, sen. -	86	Henry Hoover, sen.	John Carney, sen. -	105	John Carney, sen.
Joseph Taylor, sen. -	78	Joseph Taylor, sen.	Reuben Pruett - -	80	Reuben Pruett.
Smith Ferril - -	80	Smith Ferril.	William Fortune - -	94	Joseph Smith.
Andrew Swallow - -	80	Andrew Swallow.	James Gamblin - -	90	James Gamblin.
David Gentry, sen. -	97	David Gentry, sen.	Hudson Thompson -	77	H. Thompson.
George Henderson -	81	George Henderson.	William Beard - -	86	Frank Youn, sen.
			William Bruce - -	77	William Bruce.
RUTHERFORD COUNTY.			James Pond - - -	75	Mary Rice.
			John McMurtry - -	86	John McMurtry.
Cornelius Saunders -	79	Cornelius Saunders.	Joseph Jackson - -	84	Joseph Jackson.
William Burnett - -	91	William Burnett.	Henry Pitt - - -	75	Henry Pitt.
John M. Leak - -	88	John M. Leak.	John B. Miller - -	79	J. B. Miller.
George C. Booth - -	82	George C. Booth.	Richard Johnson - -	80	W. A. Sanders.
John Ealter - - -	81	John Ealter.	Elijah Bayles - -	81	Elijah Bayles.
Joseph Bennett - -	83	Thomas Bennett.	John Sloan - - -	82	John Sloan.
John Bruce - - -	45	John Bruce.	John Cleburne - -	82	George Cleburne.
Peter Jennings - -	88	Peter Jennings.	Benjamin Haynes - -	94	Thomas Haynes.
William Mitchell - -	75	William Mitchell.	William Morris - -	80	William Morris.
William Leckie - -	77	W. Leckie.	John McClung - -	80	John McClung.
A. Miles - - -	91	Patterson Miles.	Albert Hendricks - -	80	Albert Hendricks.
John Bradly - - -	84	John Bradly.	Samuel Cockram, sen. -	84	Samuel Cockram, sen.
Samuel Rillough - -	77	Samuel Rillough.	William May - - -	85	Major May.
Joshua Ford - - -	83	Joshua Ford.	John McAdams - -	79	John McAdams.
James Saunders - -	77	Mary Acuff.	Ezekiel Marshall - -	82	Ezekiel Marshall.
John Brown - - -	80	John Brown.	William Bell - -	82	William Bell.
John Stephenson - -	87	Enos McKnight.			
John Barclay - -	77	John Barclay.	**WHITE COUNTY.**		
Jordan Williford - -	85	Robert Williford.	DISTRICT NO. 2.		
Benjamin Todd - -	78	Benjamin Todd.	Patrick Hewet - -	100	Jonathan Clenny.
Daniel Bowman - -	82	Daniel Bowman.	John White, sen. - -	83	John White, sen.
John Newman, sen. -	85	John Newman, sen.	Turner Lane, sen. -	78	Turner Lane, sen.
Thomas Blanton - -	78	Thomas Blanton.	John H. Miller - -	77	John H. Miller.
Stephen White - -	77	Stephen White.			
Joseph Newman - -	81	Joseph Nesbitt.	DISTRICT NO. 3.		
Timothy Parker - -	81	Timothy Parker.	Edward Helton - -	77	Joseph B. Glenn.
George Bruce - -	81	Joseph Arthur.			

TENNESSEE—MIDDLE DISTRICT—Continued.

Names of pensioners for revolutionary or military services.	Ages.	Names of heads of families with whom pensioners resided June 1, 1840.	Names of pensioners for revolutionary or military services.	Ages.	Names of heads of families with whom pensioners resided June 1, 1840.
WHITE—Continued.			**WILLIAMSON—Continued.**		
DISTRICT NO. 3—Continued.			Joshua Pierce	82	Joshua Pierce.
Thomas Hill	84	Winkfield Hill.	Richard Vernon	82	Leonard Vernon.
Elijah Alverson	78	Elijah Alverson.	Jacob Grimmer	84	Jacob Grimmer.
DISTRICT NO. 4.			John Secrest	82	John Secrest.
Thomas Crawley	86	Thomas Crawley.	William Kennedy	85	William Kennedy.
DISTRICT NO. 5.			Zachariah Smith	81	Chas. S. McCall.
Burgess Clark	77	Burgess Clark.	Robinson Ross	78	Robinson Ross.
George Ailsworth	83	George Ailsworth.	20TH DISTRICT.		
DISTRICT NO. 8.			David Ivey	82	David Ivey.
John Ditty	84	John Ditty.	Laban Hartley	95	Lycurgus McCall
John Ellisson	78	John Ellisson.	Sherrod Smith	79	Sherrod Smith.
DISTRICT NO. 11.			John Hall	83	John Hall.
Thomas Welch	91	Thomas Welch.	**WILSON COUNTY.**		
DISTRICT NO. 12.			Samuel Shepard	78	Samuel Shepard.
Alexander Cooper	77	Alexander Cooper.	Abednego Rutland	80	Joseph Rutland.
Samuel Weaver	78	Reuben Briles.	Samuel Williams	80	Samuel Williams.
Henry Marsh	75	Henry Marsh.	John Crunk	78	John Crunk.
William Bertram	81	William Bertram.	John W. Beashamp	33	John W. Beashamp.
Isaac Graham	100	Charles Graham.	John Garrison	82	John Garrison.
John Weaver	78	John Weaver.	John Gunn, sen.	80	John Gunn, sen.
DISTRICT NO. 13.			Robert Crisswell	80	John Crisswell.
Solomon Yager, sen.	82	Solomon Yager, sen.	Nancy Williams	83	Nancy Williams.
DISTRICT NO. 15.			George Avery	70	George Avery.
Thomas Moore	78	William Shockley.	William L. Sypert	45	W. L. Sypert.
Abel Pearson	78	Joseph Cummings.	Thomas Conner	83	Thomas Conner.
Thomas Shockley	80	William Moore.	John Bonner	76	John Bonner.
Joseph Cummings	78	Joseph Cummings.	William Colly	88	William Colly.
Jesse Hopkins	78	Jesse Hopkins.	Austin Colly	84	Austin Colly.
Samuel Moore	81	Samuel Moore.	Susan Oakley	82	Susan Oakley.
WAYNE COUNTY.			Moses Allen	86	Moses Allen.
Benjamin Shaw	75	Hugh Liston.	Henry Criswell	80	Henry Criswell.
Richard Copeland, sen.	81	Richard Copeland.	Jonathan Tipton	85	James Tipton.
Zachariah Goforth	81	Humphrey Goforth.	Charles Blalock	75	Charles Blalock.
Robert Cypert	85	Robert Cypert.	William Donald	94	Thomas Pentacost.
Isaac Horton, sen.	81	Isaac Horton, sen.	Charles Smith	88	Archibald Ray.
John Broadway	80	John Broadway.	William Teag	78	John Pemberton.
WILLIAMSON COUNTY.			**WARREN COUNTY.**		
James Potts	81	James Potts.	Robert Brown	78	Robert Brown.
Benjamin Ragsdale	82	James Ragsdale.	Thomas Brown	91	Thomas Brown.
Tapley M. Lightfoot	81	Tapley M. Lightfoot.	William Bond	75	William Bond.
Isaac Ferguson	83	Isaac Ferguson.	John Cunningham	93	William Kennard.
Charles Allen, sen.	82	Charles Allen, sen.	Samuel Hand	85	James Hand.
			Reuben Roberts, sen.	80	Reuben Roberts, sen.
			Robert Carson	87	Andrew Michael.
			John Lockheart	83	Robert Tate.
			John Kersy	84	Jonah Duty.

WESTERN DISTRICT.

Names	Ages.	Heads of families	Names	Ages.	Heads of families
BENTON COUNTY.			**DYER COUNTY.**		
William Cockran	73	J. T. Florance.	John Given	76	Alexander McCullock.
Samuel Wadkins	80	Samuel Wadkins.	Joseph Scoby	66	Joseph Scoby.
Thomas Petty	76	Thomas Petty.	**FAYETTE COUNTY.**		
CARROLL COUNTY.			Samuel Martin	84	Samuel Martin.
Elias Miars	83	William Stoker.	David Blalock	93	Margaret Hurley.
Thomas Seamore	80	William Seamore.	Mark Miller	75	Jefferson Miller.
William Matheny	96	Peter Matheny.	James McKee	76	James McKee.
Pleasant Henderson	84	James M. Henderson.	Benjamin Starret	76	Benjamin Starret.
John McKenzie	84	John McKenzie.	John Birdsong	77	John Birdsong.
Frederick Miller	81	Frederick Miller.	Andrew Pickens	86	J. S. Pickens.
Matthew Sparks	79	Isaac Sparks, sen.	James Belloat	80	C. S. Belloat.
Jonathan Montgomery	78	Jonathan Montgomery.	Henry Randolph	84	Samuel Morgan.
John Chambers	88	Wilson Chambers.	Charles Turner	75	Colin Turner.
Arthur Brown	78	Arthur Brown.	Hugh Luckey	77	Hugh Luckey.
William Whitesides	77	John Whitesides.			

TENNESSEE—WESTERN DISTRICT—Continued.

Names of pensioners for revolutionary or military services.	Ages.	Names of heads of families with whom pensioners resided June 1, 1840.	Names of pensioners for revolutionary or military services.	Ages.	Names of heads of families with whom pensioners resided June 1, 1840.
GIBSON COUNTY.			**HENRY—Continued.**		
Thomas Frazier	81	Thomas Frazier.	Susanna Palmer	77	John L. Palmer.
Thomas May	78	Thomas May.	Matthew Alexander	85	Matthew Alexander.
David Hambleton	89	David Hambleton.	William Powel	74	William Powel.
Stephen Richards	75	Patrick Glason.	Joseph Weatherington	82	Joseph Weatherington.
John Crisp	85	William Crisp.	Matthew Myrick	88	William Myrick.
Beverly Williams	57	Beverly Williams.	James Haynes	79	James Haynes.
Thomas Morton	45	Thomas Morton.	Martin Neace, sen.	82	Martin Neace, sen.
James Givens	76	James Givens.	William Bunton	73	William Bunton.
Anderson Davis	30	Benjamin Wickum.	Robert Ramsey	82	Robert Ramsey.
Josiah Reed	84	Josiah Reed.	Britton George	102	Britton George.
Jacob Trout	105	Joseph Trout.			
James Bell	79	James Bell.	**LAUDERDALE COUNTY.**		
HARDIN COUNTY.			James Barefield	58	James Barefield.
1st district.			Shadrach Elkins	79	Robert Walker.
William Lingo	44	William Lingo.			
Allegany McGuire	78	Halladay McGuire.	**McNAIRY COUNTY.**		
2d district.			Pugh Cannon	80	Terrill Siveat.
Ezekiel Fortner	79	Ezekiel Fortner.	Jovan Cox	79	Jovan Cox.
			Alexander N. McColler, sen.	81	Alex. McColler, sen.
5th district.			William Barns	75	William Barns.
John Thorp	63	John Thorp.	Robert Moore	78	Janey Moore.
			James Roland	87	James Roland.
7th district.			John Stewart	83	Jane Edwards.
George Ross	79	George Ross.	Daniel Hill	83	Daniel Hill.
			Robert Rankin	83	Robert Rankin.
8th district.			Allen Sweat	81	Allen Sweat.
Stephen Austin	82	Saunders Austin.			
John Perkins	77	James Saxson.	**MADISON COUNTY.**		
9th district.			Daniel Madding	45	Francis Madding.
Shadrach Nolen	89	Shadrach Nolen.	Ann Fenner	73	Ann Fenner.
			David Eckleburger	43	Isaac Malett.
10th district.			Jonas Clark, sen.	82	Jonas Clark, sen.
Richard Strame	77	Richard Strame.	Bradley Medlin	80	Eaton Lenusford.
12th district.			**OBION COUNTY.**		
Samuel McFerren	79	Smith D. Cooper.	Thomas Parker	85	Thomas Parker.
HARDIMAN COUNTY.			**PERRY COUNTY.**		
Sames Vales	82	Samuel Vales, jr.	Philip Rushing	78	Berrill Rushing.
Richard Glasgow	87	John Glasgow.	Bartholomew Murphey	81	Bartholomew Murphey.
Jeremiah Doxey	87	Stephen H. Doxey.	John Tolly	78	John Tolly.
John Holliday	78	John Holliday.	William Higginbottom	79	William Higginbottom.
Elijah Warren	87	William Warren.	James Kelly	81	James Kelly.
			John Eply	78	John Eply.
HENDERSON COUNTY.			Edward Box	68	Edward Box.
Joseph Purviance	78	Joseph Purviance.	William Gibson	92	William Gibson.
Nathan Green	80	Nathan Green.	Richard Rushing	92	Richard Rushing
Archibald McCorcle	81	Archibald McCorcle.	John Bregins	67	John Bregins.
John Foster	86	John Foster.			
Daniel Murphy	78	Daniel H. Murphy.	**SHELBY COUNTY.**		
John Andrews	52	John Andrews.	A. B. Shannon	48	A. B. Shannon.
HAYWOOD COUNTY.			William Hope	79	William Hope.
Westword A. Jones	64	James Waddill.	**TIPTON COUNTY.**		
John Maxwell	76	John Maxwell.	Colonel Thomas Good	81	Colonel Thomas Good.
Hemdon Hamilton	82	Hemdon Hamilton.	William McFerrin	85	Cullin Curlee.
John Moore	77	John Moore.	Vincent Voss	84	E. O. Chambers.
			Henry Yarbrough, sen.	84	Henry Yarbrough.
HENRY COUNTY.			**WEAKLEY COUNTY.**		
Elias Bowden	77	Elias Bowden.	John Chester	88	John Chester.
Daniel Rogers	72	Daniel Rogers.	Presley Thonton	86	William Jones.
Alexander Craig	85	Alexander Craig.			
Polly Simmons	74	James P. Simmons.			

CENSUS OF·PENSIONERS.

STATE OF KENTUCKY.

Names of pensioners for revolutionary or military services.	Ages.	Names of heads of families with whom pensioners resided June 1, 1840.	Names of pensioners for revolutionary or military services.	Ages.	Names of heads of families with whom pensioners resided June 1, 1840.
ADAIR COUNTY.			**BATH—Continued.**		
			WEST OF SLATE CREEK—Continued.		
Thompson C. Loyd - -	52	Thompson C. Loyd.	William Boyd - - -	74	William Boyd.
Samuel Ellis - -	79	Samuel Ellis.	James McClehany - -	80	James McClehany.
John Montgomery - -	78	Robert M. Montgomery.	Richard Thomas - -	81	Richard Thomas.
James Irvin - -	85	John Irvin.	*EAST OF SLATE CREEK.*		
William Hurt - -	82	William Hurt.	Moses Botts - - -	94	Benjamin Botts.
Thomas White - -	77	Thomas White.			
Alexander Elliott - -	75	Alexander Elliott.	**BOONE COUNTY.**		
William Warnack - -	76	William Warnack.			
William James - -	82	Elijah Leech.	Elizabeth Allen - -	65	Elizabeth Allen.
Zachariah Holliday - -	78	William Holliday.	John H. Craig - -	77	John H. Craig.
John Hamilton - -	83	John Hamilton.	A. Ross - - -	77	A. Ross.
Philip Winfree - -	76	Reuben Winfree.	Isaac D. Sanders - -	51	Isaac D. Sanders.
Solomon Royce - -	76	Solomon Royce.	Hugh Steers - -	81	Hugh Steers.
William Mosby - -	85	William Mosby.	Jane Bridgis - -	74	James Bridgis.
Henry Armstrong - -	85	Elijah Green.	Peter Brumback - -	87	Peter Brumback.
Elisha Bailey - -	75	Elisha Bailey.	Jerusha Alexander -	86	John T. Alexander.
Thomas Cochran - -	77	Thomas Cochran.	Richard Hubbell - -	74	G. L. Hubbell.
			George Vest - -	80	George Vest.
ALLEN COUNTY			Joseph Barlow - -	80	Catharine Barlow.
James McIlroy - -	80	William B. McIlroy.	Daniel Goff - -	80	Alexander Marshall.
Asa Tiffany - -	60	Joseph Martin.	Joseph Cobbs - -	50	Samuel Craig.
Elizabeth Wright - -	81	Elizabeth Wright.	Cave Johnson - -	79	Cave Johnson.
John Durham - -	88	John Durham.	Jacob Brewno - -	86	Moses Brewno.
Nancy Gatewood - -	74	Fletcher Gatewood.	John Grant - -	51	John Grant.
Dorcas Alexander - -	74	John G. Alexander.	William Brady - -	81	John Brady.
George T. Hector - -	89	George T. Hector.	John Tomlinson - -	81	John Tomlinson.
Daniel Pitchford - -	79	Daniel Pitchford.			
Stephen Merritt - -	78	Stephen Merritt.	**BOURBON COUNTY.**		
Christopher Haines - -	80	Christopher Haines.	*NORTHERN DIVISION.*		
George Stovall - -	79	George Stovall.	Abner Shropshire - -	76	Abner Shropshire.
John Brooks - -	86	John Brooks.	Joseph Jackson - -	85	Joseph Jackson.
Michael Hatter - -	81	Michael Hatter.	Edward McConnell - -	68	Edward McConnell.
			Michael Smith - -	88	Peter Smith.
ANDERSON COUNTY.			Phœbe Pritchard - -	78	Phœbe Pritchard.
Roadham Petty - -	89	Roadham Petty.	Benjamin Henniss - -	80	William Sugg.
Ann Hill - -	75	James Searey.	Thomas Hays - -	80	Griffin Kelly.
Jane Hawkins - -	77	John Hackly.	John Hinkson - -	69	John Hinkson.
George Jordan - -	87	George Jordan.	Nathaniel Harriss - -	81	Jacob Jacoby.
William Cummins - -	53	William Cummins.	James Davis - -	79	James Davis.
Benjamin Warford - -	89	Samuel B. Petty.	George Bryan - -	82	William S. Bryan.
Reuben Boston - -	75	Joel Boston.	Archibald Bell - -	84	Pamela Bell.
James Robertson - -	86	James Robertson.	Henry Wiggington - -	84	Henry Boyer.
			John Debruler - -	92	Beverly B. Wright.
BARREN COUNTY.					
NORTHEASTERN DIVISION.			*SOUTHERN DIVISION.*		
Frederick Smith - -	86	Frederick Smith.	Isaac Clinkinbeard - -	81	Isaac Clinkinbeard.
John Watson - -	77	John M. Watson.	Andrew Hause - -	94	William Hause.
Thomas Goodman - -	77	Littleberry Goodman.	William B. Branham - -	77	William B. Branham.
Callam Bailey - -	92	William T. Bailey.	Henry Towles - -	54	Henry Towles.
Sarah Key - -	78	James Bennett.	Henry Willson - -	84	James Willson.
			John Brest, sen. - -	81	John Brest, sen.
SOUTHWESTERN DIVISION.			John Brest, jun. - -	52	
Ambrose Huffman - -	86	Henry Huffman.	William Scott, sen. - -	67	William Scott, sen.
Margaret Higdon - -	74	Margaret Higdon.	Joseph L. Stevens - -	76	Joseph L. Stevens.
William Bell - -	89	William W. Bell.			
Richard Bailey - -	78	Richard Bailey.	**BRACKEN COUNTY.**		
Philip Carter - -	74	Philip Carter.	*NORTHERN DIVISION.*		
Thomas Green - -	77	Thomas Green.	James Arbuckle - -	80	James Arbuckle.
Philemon Sanders - -	78	Philemon Sanders.	Philip King - -	53	Philip King.
Jonathan Hunt - -	80	Jonathan Hunt.	William Sargent - -	81	William Sargent.
John Renfro - -	80	Joseph Renfro.	John Hamilton - -	76	John Hamilton.
Liddy Harris - -	78	John R. Harris.	Bartholomew Taylor -	80	Joseph Taylor.
Absalom Hughes - -	86	Absalom Hughes.	John J. Thomas· - -	82	William Thomas, jr.
William Carson - -	80	William Carson.	*SOUTHERN DIVISION.*		
John Cosby - -	99	John Cosby.	John King - - -	78	John King.
John Duff - -	80	John Duff.	William King, sen. - -	80	William King, sen.
Rodeham Laurence - -	78	Rodeham Laurence.			
John Cole - -	88	John Cole.	**BREATHITT COUNTY.**		
			Roger Turner - -	83	Thomas Turner.
BATH COUNTY.			Drury Bush - -	82	Drury Bush.
OWINGSVILLE.			Jesse Boling - -	82	Jesse Boling.
William Kearns - -	84	William Kearns.			
WEST OF SLATE CREEK.			**BRECKENRIDGE COUNTY.**		
John Sims - -	79	John Sims.			
Michael Moors - -	84	Jacob Tregely.	James Wells - -	77	James Wells.
Josiah Collins - -	83	Silas Moors.	George Seaton - -	86	William K. Seaton.
Andrew Linam - -	81	Andrew Linam.	George Pullin - -	81	Elisha Pullin.
Holman Rice - -	82	Holman Rice.	Susanna Sharp - -	71	Isom Sharp.
Gordon Griffin - -	86	Gordon Griffin.			

Names of pensioners for revolutionary or military services.	Ages.	Names of heads of families with whom pensioners resided June 1, 1840.	Names of pensioners for revolutionary or military services.	Ages.	Names of heads of families with whom pensioners resided June 1, 1840.
BRECKENRIDGE—Continued.			**CASEY COUNTY.**		
John Goattey	88	John Goattey.	John Royalty	70	John Royalty.
James Bramblett	78	James Bramblett.	James Carson	70	James Carson.
			Jacob Coffman	84	Chloe Coffman.
BULLITT COUNTY.			Elizabeth Haifley	83	Jacob Haifley.
			William Sutherland	95	William Sutherland.
Lawrence Bishop	79	Lawrence Bishop.			
Reuben Northern	81	Reuben Northern.	**CHRISTIAN COUNTY.**		
Joseph Lloyd	79	Joseph Lloyd.			
Jacob Hubbs	78	Jacob Hubbs.	James Sullenger	77	James Sullenger.
L. Pilkenton	70	Larkin Pilkenton.	Isaac Palmer	93	Isaac Palmer.
Isaac Skinner	83	Isaac Skinner.	Charles Thomas	76	Charles Thomas.
John Buzan	84	John Buzan.	John Cain	77	John Cain.
John Humphrey	77	John Humphrey.	Thomas Woolsey	79	Thomas Woolsey.
John Stringer	85	John Stringer.	Jona. Clark	81	Jona. Clark.
			William Gray	86	William Gray.
BUTLER COUNTY.					
			CLARK COUNTY.		
John Sorel	81	John Sorel.			
John Clark	103	Braxton Clark.	James Bush	83	James Bush.
Abner Wornack	76	Abner Wornack.	Reuben Franklin	85	David Fanner.
Jesse Scowfield	83	Jesse Scowfield.	Smallwood Acton	82	Smallwood Acton.
Mark Whitaker	92	Mark Whitaker.	Richard Oliver	97	Joel Oliver.
Matthew Kirkendoll	82	Matthew Kirkendoll.	Thomas Lourey	79	Thomas Lourey.
William Beesley	78	William Beesley.	Vachael Faudre	79	Vachael Faudre.
			John Arnald	86	John Arnald.
CALDWELL COUNTY.			Robert Bush	53	Younger Histle.
			Lincefield Burbridge	80	Thomas Burbridge.
Reuben Bowers	74	Reuben Bowers.			
Joseph McConell	56	Joseph McConell.	**CLAY COUNTY.**		
Thomas Beck	75	George Beck.			
Michael Freeman	76	Michael Freeman.	John Chandler	75	Joseph Philpot.
John Blick	77	Dennis Blick.	David Burge, sen.	80	David Burge, sen.
Solomon Freer	76	Solomon Freer.	John Garland	102	John Garland.
Judith Freeman	80	Hardy F. Freeman.	William Burnes	87	Sarah Bishop.
William Ford	77	William Ford.			
William Asher	79	William Asher.	**CLINTON COUNTY.**		
William Blackburn	82	Harrison Blackburn.			
John Hart	88	John Hart.	Charles Worsham	88	James C. Sutherland.
Major Groom	75	Major Groom.	Richard Wade	88	Richard Wade.
			John Miller	78	John Miller.
CALLOWAY COUNTY.			Francis Purce	81	Francis Purce.
			Nicodemus Barnes	80	James Bell.
Kimbrough Ogilvie	78	Kimbrough Ogilvie.	John Davis	83	James Davis.
Rolling Stone	75	Rolling Stone.	James Woody	79	James Woody.
Peter Waterfield	80	Orville E. Waterfield.			
Charles Galloway	83	Charles Galloway.	**CUMBERLAND COUNTY.**		
Joseph Dunn	89	John P. Dunn.	NORTHERN DIVISION.		
Nicholas Henson	81	Nicholas Henson.	Samuel Smith	98	Samuel Smith.
William Wilkins	81	William Wilkins.	Martin Grider	88	Martin Grider.
Nathan Frizzell	82	William Frizzell.	Elijah Bledsoe	68	Elijah Bledsoe.
			John Self	78	Guy Self.
CAMPBELL COUNTY.			Abram Esters	68	Abram Esters.
			Joseph Jewell	88	Richard T. Phelps.
Jacob Mefford	77	Jacob Mefford.	Thomas Cash, sen.	65	Thomas Cash, sen.
Joseph Dickens	75	Levi Dickens.	David Bowen	56	David Bowen.
Samuel Todd	83	Samuel Todd.	Thomas Brothers	62	Thomas Brothers.
Thomas Stevens	65	Thomas Stevens.	John Hurt	71	John Hurt.
David Dukes	28	David Dukes.			
Henry Smith	90	Henry Smith.	SOUTHERN DIVISION.		
Thomas Harris, sen.	93	Thomas Harris, sen.	Solomon Prewet, sen.	96	Solomon Prewet, sen.
Edward Turner	63	Edward Turner.	James Sewel	86	James Sewel.
Benjamin Sutton	85	Benjamin Sutton.	John Gibson	95	Jesse Gibson.
Nicholas Long	85	William Coldwell.	George King	90	George King.
William De Comcy	85	William De Comcy.			
William Orcutt, sen.	81	William Orcutt, sen.	**DAVIESS COUNTY.**		
Edward Morin	96	Edward Morin.	NORTHERN DIVISION.		
			Charles Hansford	80	William Hansford.
CARROLL COUNTY.			James Jones	79	James Jones.
			SOUTHERN DIVISION.		
John Short	78	R. M. Tandy.	Benjamin Tayloe	84	John A. Tayloe.
John Deen, sen.	84	John Deen, sen.	Benjamin Field	84	Benjamin Field.
Robert Scott	77	James Scott.			
David Driskill	79	Green Driskill.	**ESTILL COUNTY.**		
James Coghill	82	James Coghill.			
Amos V. Matthews	79	Amos Matthews.	Phebe Witt	82	Silas Witt.
			Barbara Meadowes	91	Barbara Meadowes.
CARTER COUNTY.			Mary Eastes	81	Eli Steward.
			Susan Horn	77	Lewis Barnett.
No returns.			Andrew Leckey	78	Andrew Leckey.
			Susan Winkler	81	William Winkler.
21			William Johnson, sen.	81	William Johnson, sen.

Names of pensioners for revolutionary or military services.	Ages.	Names of heads of families with whom pensioners resided June 1, 1840.	Names of pensioners for revolutionary or military services.	Ages.	Names of heads of families with whom pensioners resided June 1, 1840.
ESTILL—Continued.			**FRANKLIN—Continued.**		
			SOUTHERN DIVISION.		
Dudley Fardin	49	Dudley Fardin.	Mrs. Polly Reading	78	George Williams.
Ambrose Powell	79	Ambrose Powell.	Robert Hedges	80	Robert Hedges.
Joseph Proctor	86	Joseph Proctor.	John Crutcher	78	Mrs. N. Crutcher.
Martha Elkins	74	Robert Crow.			
Elizabeth Ward	107	H. Ward.	**GALLATIN COUNTY.**		
John Stuffleban	101	David Snowden.			
William Harris	72	William Harris.	John Birks	67	John Birks.
Barbara Noland	80	Silas Noland.	Abijah North	80	Abijah North.
			James Furnish	74	James Furnish.
FAYETTE COUNTY.			John Waters	55	John Waters.
EASTERN DIVISION.			Charles Goins	71	Charles Goins.
Francis Epperson	90	Chesley Epperson.	Jeremiah Haydon, sen.	78	Jeremiah Haydon, sen.
Thomas Clark	85	Thomas Clark.	William Thompson	77	William Thompson.
Cornelius Sullivan	84	James M. Smith.	Mary Slaughter	89	
Abraham Ferguson	79	Abraham Ferguson.			
Lyttleton Geter	86	Dorothy Rogers.	**GARRARD COUNTY.**		
Joseph Mosby	84	Joseph Mosby.	Michael Salter	82	Michael Salter.
John Graves, sen.	83	John Graves, sen.	John Floyd	82	Davis Floyd.
Randall Haley	84	Randolph Haley.	Mary Sutton	68	Benjamin Sutton.
			Goolsbury Childers	85	John Orr.
WESTERN DIVISION.			John Buford	73	John Buford.
James Laffoon	78	Anderson Laffoon.	David Kennedy	70	David Kennedy.
Sarah Bowman	84	George H. Bowman.	Leanna Pollard	77	James Pollard.
Daniel Cowgill	85	George Cowgill.	Thomas Ramsey, sen.	85	Thomas Ramsey, sen.
Francis Falconer	79	Jos. Falconer.	John Walden	78	John Walden.
James McDowell	84	John L. McDowell.	Arabia Brown	86	Arabia Brown.
Elizabeth Scruggs	74	Thomas M. Scruggs.	Robert Brank	79	B. G. Brank.
			Naman Roberts	75	Fountain Rothwell.
FLEMING COUNTY.			John Slavin	83	John Slavin.
1st DIVISION.			William Haggard	84	William Haggard.
Burtis Ringo	78	Burtis Ringo.	John Crutchfield	87	Mordecai Cruchfield
Daniel Ferhune	81	Daniel Ferhune.	Jesse Robbards	80	Jesse Robbards.
Zaccheus Cord	64	Zaccheus Cord.	Jane Poore	72	Robert C. Poore.
Elizabeth Madden	87	Jeremiah Madden.	Averriler Edgington	75	B. P. Edgington.
			Timothy Logan	84	Timothy Logan.
2d DIVISION.			Jane Rasson	65	Jane Rasson.
Samuel Blackburn	80	Samuel Blackburn.	Sarah Bryant	70	Sarah Bryant.
Peter Mauzy	80	Peter Mauzy.	Thaddeus Wormoth, sen.	79	Thaddeus Wormoth, sen.
Redman Smith	80	Redman Smith.			
Hugh Drennan	80	Hugh Drennan.	**GRANT COUNTY.**		
			John Linn	79	John Linn.
3d DIVISION.			Daniel Seward	79	Lucinda Seward.
John McKee	88	John McKee.	John Jump, sen.	96	John Jump, sen.
William Proctor	82	William Proctor.	Aaron Adams	71	Aaron Adams.
Jesse Davis	76	Matthew Lee.	John Lawless	89	Uriel Tongate.
Moses Clark	76	Moses Clark.	James Theobald	81	James Theobald.
John Frazure	78	John Frazure.	Joshua Jones	79	Joshua Jones.
William Davis	83	John Swer.	Stephen Barker	81	Stephen Barker.
Aley Humphreys	86	Harrison Hupres.	William Cook	47	William Cook.
John Page	78	John Page.			
Patrick McCann	80	Patrick McCann.	**GRAVES COUNTY.**		
Joseph Goddard	79	Joseph Goddard.	John Brimage	85	Thomas Brimage.
			John Stafford	74	John Stafford.
FLOYD COUNTY.			Joshua Gamblin	75	Joshua Gamblin.
Amy Justice	80	Amy Justice.	Daniel Fox	75	Daniel Fox.
Sally More	80	John More.	Charles Gilbert	84	Catharine Gilbert.
Rebecca Henrel	90	James Herring.	Willis Odem	85	Lewis Odem.
Anthony Hall	78	Anthony Hall.	William Thompson	80	James Birch.
Reuben Thacker	65	Reuben Thacker.	Joseph Glover	80	Joseph Glover.
Patey Harris	85	Samuel Harris.			
Benedict Watkins	84	Benedict Watkins.	**GREENUP COUNTY.**		
Cudbeth Stone, sen.	80	Cudbeth Stone, sen.	James Lawson	80	Jamec Lawson.
John Porter	74	John Porter.	Godfrey Smith	76	Godfrey Smith.
Elizabeth Preston	85	Jeffrey Preston.	James Patton	89	John Patton.
Thomas C. Brown	80	Thomas C. Brown.	James Norton	73	James Norton.
Philip Williams	87	Philip Williams.	John Chadwick	75	James Chadwick.
Mexico Pits	75	Mexico Pits.	Thomas Hackwith	77	R. Hackwith.
			Thomas Dixon	75	Thomas Dixon.
FRANKLIN COUNTY.					
NORTHERN DIVISION.			**GRAYSON COUNTY.**		
George Swingle	83	John Swingle.	Henry Skaggs	80	James Skaggs.
Virgil Poe	83	Andrew Baldwin.	Isaac Goar	80	Jacob Hart.
Mrs. Etherton	90	Mrs. Hall.	Simon Pryor	80	Simon Pryor.
James Biscow	80	James Biscow.	Edward De Haven	84	John De Haven.
Silas Douthard	76	Silas Douthard.	John Decer	90	John Decer.
John McDonak	75	John McDonald.	Isaac Vanmetre	85	Isaac Vanmetre.
Charles Tyler	78	Alfred Tyler.	John Row	98	John Row.
Francis Brown	65	Isaac Morgan.			

KENTUCKY—Continued.

Names of pensioners for revolutionary or military services.	Ages.	Names of heads of families with whom pensioners resided June 1, 1840.	Names of pensioners for revolutionary or military services.	Ages.	Names of heads of families with whom pensioners resided June 1, 1840.
GREENE COUNTY.			**HENRY—Continued.**		
SOUTHERN DIVISION.			WESTERN DIVISION—Continued.		
James Sherrill	81	James H. Sherrill.	Joseph Davis	77	James Wentworth.
Thomas Parsons	92	Thomas Parsons.	Little Berry Wells	79	Little Berry Wells.
John S. Sublett	47	John S. Sublett.	William Jeffries	77	William Jeffries.
Thomas Smith	77	William Hall.			
Jeremiah Ingram	81	Harriet Ingram.	**HICKMAN COUNTY.**		
Sherrod Griffin	81	Sherrod Griffin.	NORTHERN DIVISION.		
Daniel Trabal	80	Sally Anderson.	Jacob Williams	75	Benjamin Garrison.
Thomas Gains	81	Thomas Gains.	W. B. Warden	49	W. B. Warden.
Andrew Barnett	81	Ardrew Barnett.	Henry Pickett	96	Elizabeth Kimber.
			John Depoister	86	Gabriel Davis.
NORTHERN DIVISION.					
John Thurman	73	John Thurman.	SOUTHERN DIVISION.		
James Cowherd	81	James Cowherd.	Murril Cunningham	81	Thomas J. Cunningham.
Moses Meers	80	Moses Martin.	Thomas Vincent	81	George Vincent.
William Sturman	85	William Sturman.	Lewis Huey	79	Lewis Huey.
Peter D. Spain	75	Peter D. Spain.	Jesse Meshew	79	William Meshew.
Andrew Chaudoin	78	Andrew Chaudoin.	John Bane, sen.	84	John Bane, sen.
Mary Wright	75	Elizabeth Ship.			
Joshua Lee	83	James Lewis.	**HOPKINS COUNTY.**		
Jonathan Cowherd	85	Coleby Cowherd.			
James Bibb	87	Robert Bibb.	George Timmonds	82	George Timmonds.
John Greenwell	80	Reason Sterling.	Lemuel Hulett	51	Lemuel Hulett.
Richard Piercell	99	James Newcomb.	Manley Winstead	80	Manley Winstead.
John Dickin	81	John Dickin.	William Givins	78	William Givins.
			Samuel Downey	78	Samuel Downey.
HART COUNTY.			John Herron	102	John Herron.
			James Curtis	84	James Curtis.
Lawrence Campbell	75	Benjamin Shrieve.	John Montgomery	72	John Montgomery.
John Bomar	83	John Bomar.			
Joseph Timberlake	88	M. K. Dye.	**HANCOCK COUNTY.**		
Daniel Morris	74	Daniel Morris.			
Benjamin D. Corder	77	B. D. Corder.	Edmund Newman	78	Colonel Ed. Newman.
John Potterson	77	John Potterson.			
Joshua Crump	75	Jos. Crump.	**HARDIN COUNTY.**		
Jeremiah Harber	47	Jeremiah Harber.			
			John Smoot	69	Elijah Smoot.
HARLAN COUNTY.			John Scott	99	William Scott.
			Warren Cash	80	W. P. Cash.
James Jackson, sen.	84	James Jackson, sen.	Thenas Hoskins	82	William Harrington.
Stephen L. Jones	99	Sally Holanes.	Anthony Ament	83	Anthony Ament.
Benjamin Caurod	80	George Buckhart.	Samuel Aubry	82	Craven Aubry.
			Michael Hargan	85	Joseph Hargan.
HENDERSON COUNTY.			Rebecca Van Meter	63	
			Joseph Smith, sen.	78	Joseph Smith, sen.
James M. Edwards	53	James M. Edwards.	Susan Hardin	79	
John Ramsey	84	John Ramsey.	Alexander McDugle	101	Alexander McDugle.
Edward Baldwin	78	Barret Baldwin.	Richard Winchester	86	Richard Winchester.
			Patrick Marven	82	Patrick Marven.
HENRY COUNTY.			Margaret Haycraft	80	
EASTERN DIVISION.					
Benjamin Haydon	82	Benjamin Haydon.	**HARRISON COUNTY.**		
Thomas Bell	81	Thomas Bell.	EASTERN DIVISION.		
Joshua Wallace	79	John Wallace.	Ann Whiteaker	79	Josiah Whiteaker.
Charles Hugeley	80	Charles Hugeley.	Benoni Jameson	67	Benoni Jameson.
Archibald Johnston	91	P. Johnston.	Samuel Caswell	77	Samuel Caswell.
David Criswell	77	David Criswell.	William Smith	58	William Smith.
Peter Force	96	J. P. Force.	Thomas McCalla	87	Joseph McCalla.
Samuel Hisle	78	Samuel Hisle.	James Rees	77	William Rees.
David Welch	44	David Welsh.	William H. Layton	83	James Whiteaker.
William Morgan	79	William Morgan.	Philip Roberts	77	Philip Roberts.
Darcus Antle	77		Andrew Ward	55	Andrew Ward.
Thomas Wooldridge	89	Thomas Wooldridge.	Mrs. Meares (since dead)	76	George W. Rohr.
Elisha Bishop	83	Elisha Bishop.			
Richard Minyard	91	John Minyard.	WESTERN DIVISION.		
Mary Jevidend	75	Mary Jevidend.	Lewis Wolf, sen.	89	Lewis Wolf, sen.
Thomas Pettit	76	Thomas Pettit.	Jacob Miller	75	Jacob Miller.
Jacob List	81	Jacob List.	Leonard Eddleman	79	Aaron Eddleman.
James Johnston	77	James Johnston.	William Sutton	78	William Sutton.
William Adams	92	William Adams.	John Wood	90	Benjamin Brandon.
Matthias Shuck	84	Matthias Shuck.			
Henry Kephart	78	Jacob Kephart.	**JESSAMINE COUNTY**		
			Daniel Bryan	82	Thomas Bryan.
WESTERN DIVISION.			Samuel B. Todd	47	Samuel B. Todd.
John Martin	80	Mary Browning.	Henry Overstreet	77	Joseph Baughn.
George K. Mitchell	77	George K. Mitchell.	Betsey Knight	77	Grant Knight.
John Blakemore	78	Lewis Blakemore.	Kesiah Jenkins	78	Elisha Jenkins.
James Logan	76	James R. Logan.	James Martin	82	James Martin.
Rebecca Goode	85	Lemuel Goode.	Alexander Willoughby	80	Alexander Willoughby.
Sarah Powell	83	John Powell.	Ann Hunter	75	John Portwood.
William Simmons	97	William Simmons.	Jeremiah King	81	Jeremiah King.
Barrack Bryant	99	Barrack Bryant.	John Carroll	85	John Carroll.
Thomas Robertson	58	Thomas Robertson.			

CENSUS OF PENSIONERS.

KENTUCKY—Continued.

Names of pensioners for revolutionary or military services.	Ages.	Names of heads of families with whom pensioners resided June 1, 1840.	Names of pensioners for revolutionary or military services.	Ages.	Names of heads of families with whom pensioners resided June 1, 1840.
JESSAMINE—Continued.			**LIVINGSTON—Continued.**		
James Graves	79	James Graves.	William Fires	81	John Fires.
Abraham Cassell	84	Thomas J. Cassell.	James Clinton	80	Peter Clinton.
Jacob Grindstaff	88	Benjamin Willis.			
James Ervir	85	James Ervin.	**CITY OF LEXINGTON.**		
James Walker	81	James Walker.			
Mary Hicks	80	Benjamin Goforth.	Thomas Chamberlain	59	Thomas Chamberlain.
Giles Hawkins	86	Giles Hawkins.	John Baker	40	John Baker.
Robert Campbell	79	Robert Campbell.	Fielding Jeter	81	Fielding Jeter.
Benjamin Adams	96	George W. Adams.	John Fowler	85	John Fowler.
John Megee	79	John Megee.	John Peck	70	John Peck.
			E. K. Hendley	48	E. K. Hendley.
JEFFERSON COUNTY.			Leslie Combs	47	Leslie Combs.
NORTHERN DIVISION.					
Samuel Conn	78	Michael Shroat.	**LOGAN COUNTY.**		
Benjamin Wilkenoon	95	Benjamin Wilkenoon.			
			William Addison	72	William Addison.
SOUTHERN DIVISION.			Judith Williams	75	J. C. Jones.
Levin Cooper, sen.	87	Levin Cooper, sen.	John Wited	76	John Wited.
Jane Wilson	78	Jane Wilson.	William Patillo	80	W. E. Johns.
John Murphy	76	John Murphy.	Alexander Guffey	77	Alexander Guffey.
			John P. Gillum	79	John P. Gillum.
KNOX COUNTY.			John Ham	95	Joseph Ham.
			George Blakey	91	George Blakey.
Richard Baloo	72	Richard Baloo.	James Stevenson	75	James Stevenson.
Edward Brownin	100	Paschal G. Bryant.	Lawrence Houx	80	Sarah S. Gill.
Jacob Cooper	109	Eli Blackburn.	Rodham Kenner	77	Rodham Kenner.
John B. Horton	81	William Horton.	George Herndon	78	Richard Burnett.
Joshua Mullins	82	Joshua Mullins.	Moses Hendricks	75	Moses Hendricks.
Peter Hammonds	78	Peter Hammonds.			
James Miller	93	Thomas Marsa.	**MADISON-COUNTY.**		
			EASTERN DIVISION.		
KENTON COUNTY.			John Crook	74	Kiah Crook.
			Robert Covington	77	Robert Covington.
Nancy McGlassen	72	Nancy McGlassen.	Richard Oliver	87	Isaac Oliver.
Joseph Casey	78	Joseph Casey.	Joseph Todd	81	Joseph Todd.
William Worthington	90	William Worthingt, n.	Robert Burnside	80	Robert Burnside.
Stephen Collins	85	Stephen Collins.	Samuel Walkup	82	Samuel Walkup.
Edmund Massey	95	Joseph Wayland.	Thomas Morris	80	Thomas Morris.
John Ducker	81	John Ducker.	John Hunter, sen.	78	John Hunter, sen.
John Keen	81	John Keen.	William Kindred	80	William Kindred.
			Jacob Dooly	85	Jacob Dooly.
LAUREL COUNTY.			Thomas Mason	74	Thomas Mason.
			Jesse Oglesby	76	Jesse Oglesby.
Solomon Stansberry	85	Solomon Stansberry.	Henry Duke	81	Henry Duke.
John Nicks	84	John Nicks.	Joseph Kennedy	81	Joseph Kennedy.
John Simpson	87	John Simpson.	Yelverton Peyton	86	Yelverton Peyton.
Ambrose Pitman	92	Ambrose Pitman.	Richard Gentry	77	Richard Gentry.
Titus Mersham	91	Titus Mersham.	Thomas Becknell	77	Thomas Becknell.
John Fanbush	81	John Fanbush.	John Cook	81	Hezekiah Cook.
			Joseph Watson	86	William Watson.
LAWRENCE COUNTY.			Thomas Dunbar	80	Thomas Dunbar.
			Isham Lane	82	Isham Lane.
Gilbert Bloomer	87		Loftus Pullin	80	Loftus Pullin.
Josiah Marcum	81		Nathan Gutherage	76	Nathaniel Gutherage.
George Hardwick	82				
James Ward	80		WESTERN DIVISION.		
Bilas Wooton	84		Gabriel Duncan	80	Gabriel Duncan.
Moses Henny	83		Mary Barnett	77	James B. Miller.
William Lyons	88		John Ross	78	David P. Ross.
			George Tennal	89	George Tennal.
LEWIS COUNTY.			John Wood	44	John Wood.
			James Cooly	80	William Cooly.
Richard Bane	88	Richard Bane.	John Land, sen.	86	John Land, sen.
John Dyal	77	John Dyal.	Ralph Magee, sen.	86	Ralph Magee, sen.
			Anthony Purkins	76	Anthony Purkins.
LINCOLN COUNTY.			Richard Harris	78	Richard Harris.
Caldwell Wood	83	Caldwell Wood.			
Anthony Gale	78	W. A. Gale.	**McCRACKEN COUNTY.**		
Abraham Sublett	84	Abraham Sublett.			
Micajah Frost	79	Micajah Frost.	Sarah Moore	83	Edward Stevens.
Samuel Duncan	80	Samuel Duncan.	Nancy B. Lovelace	84	Robert R. Hester.
Joseph Hall	79	Joseph Hall.	Benjamin Junes	79	Isaac Davis.
Dunn Salyers	81	Dunn Salyers.			
Mark McPherson	86	Mark McPherson.	**MARION COUNTY.**		
John S. Alverson	85	John S. Alverson.			
Robert Givins	83	Robert H. Givins.	Mrs. Hardin	80	Lewis C. Raley.
Abraham Eastas	76	Abraham Eastas.	James White Cotton	91	James White Cotton.
			Perry Tharp	83	Perry Tharp.
LIVINGSTON COUNTY.			William Hendrick	95	Archibald Brown.
			James Ramsey	79	Frances Ann Ramsey.
William Wells	80	William Wells.	Coonrod Beams	82	Coonrod Beams.
Arthur Travis	76	Arthur Travis.	James Corbet	81	Jacob Corbet.

KENTUCKY—Continued.

Names of pensioners for revolutionary or military services.	Ages.	Names of heads of families with whom pensioners resided June 1, 1840.	Names of pensioners for revolutionary or military services.	Ages.	Names of heads of families with whom pensioners resided June 1, 1840.
MARION—Continued.			**MONTGOMERY COUNTY.**		
Margaret Smock	79	Margaret Smock.	James Dunlap	99	William Dunlap.
George Spalding, sen.	84	George Spalding, sen.	James Ramsey	78	Matthew Divine.
			James Bourn	78	James Bourn.
MERCER COUNTY.			John M. Howard	45	John M. Howard.
			John B. Fisher	70	John B. Fisher.
Samuel Hackney	79	Samuel Hackney.	William Conner	74	Abraham Ingram.
Mary Pipes	81	Mary Pipes.	Benjamin Grigsby	91	James Grigsby.
Henry Sparrow	79	Henry Sparrow.	John Stephens	79	John Stephens, jun.
William Kelly	84	William Kelly.	William Gray	85	William Gray.
Timothy Corn	84	Timothy Corn.	Beverly Daniel	78	Beverly Daniel.
James Rains	82	James Rains.	Daniel McCarty	78	Daniel McCarty.
Leonard Taylor	83	Leonard Taylor.	Edward Steen	70	Sarah Vise.
Matthew Colter	81	Matthew Colter.	Robert Garrett	88	Robert Garrett.
George Gabbard, sen.	79	George Gabbard, sen.	Samuel McKee	76	Samuel McKee.
Henry Hamler	81	Henry Hamler.	Benjamin Robenson	84	Moses Groomer.
Lewis Webb	83	Lewis Webb.			
Henry Deshazer	81	Henry Deshazer.	**MORGAN COUNTY.**		
John Sneed	86	John Sneed.			
Christian Snail	89	Christian Snail.	Mary Hopkins	84	William Defer.
Rebecca Verbryck	83	Rebecca Verbryck.	Benjamin Wages	106	John Wages.
Cornelius O. Vanarsdale	80	Cornelius O. Vanarsdale.	Levi Sevanson	85	Levi Sevanson.
Edward Willis	78	Edward Willis.	Thomas Lewis	85	Thomas Lewis.
Ebenezer Cary, sen.	83	Ebenezer Cary, sen.	Gilbert Stevens	78	Gilbert Stevens.
Charles Brown	88	Charles Brown.	David Ellington	78	David Ellington.
Robert Jones	75	Robert Jones.	B. Hamilton	76	David Hamilton.
John Comingore	90	John Comingore.	Rebecca Day	74	Jesse Day.
Elias Fisher	87	Elias Fisher.	John Smothers	79	John Smothers.
Peter Huff	85	Peter Huff.	John Kulby	87	John L. Little.
John Grant	85	John Grant.	Martha Jones	80	John Jones.
Jane Shelton	82	Jane Shelton.	Isaac Kuton	79	Isaac Kuton.
Claiborne Bradshaw	83	Claiborne Bradshaw.	John Preewitt	85	John Preewitt.
John Rice	78	John Rice.			
Susanna Jourdon	79	Susanna Jourdon.	**MUHLENBURG COUNTY.**		
Mary Wilson	76	Mary Wilson.			
Elizabeth Moore	75	Elizabeth Moore.	John Bone	79	John Bone.
Martha Sandefer	83	Jackson Roberts.	Sihez Garriz	77	Sihez Garriz.
Thomas Graham	78	Thomas Graham.	Joshua Elkins	86	Joshua Elkins.
Thomas Kyle	83	Thomas Kyle.	Brit. 'n Willis	80	Britain Willis.
Edward Houchins	80	Edward Houchins.	William Hopkins	73	William Hopkins.
Philip Bourd	80	Philip Bourd.	Benjamin Neal	80	Benjamin Neal.
James Galloway	84	James Galloway.	Andrew Glenn	88	A. Glenn.
Sarah Bohon	76	Sarah Bohon.			
Isaac Follis	77	Isaac Follis.	**NELSON COUNTY.**		
Reuben Smithy	85	Reuben Smithy.	WESTERN DIVISION.		
John Potter, sen.	79	John Potter.	William Thompson	101	William Thompson.
Charles Hart	81	Charles Hart.	Barnabas Carter	84	Barnabas Garter.
			NORTHEASTERN DIVISION.		
MASON COUNTY.			Susan McCown	74	Susan McCown.
NORTHERN DIVISION.			Benjamin Smith	79	Benjamin Smith.
Mary Ann Shepherd	75	Mary Ann Shepherd.	John Bell	91	William Bell.
Leonard Bean	80	Leonard Bean.	John Lawson	83	John Lawson.
William Bickley	83	William Bickley.			
Isabella Pelham	74	John Pelham.	**NICHOLAS COUNTY.**		
Elizabeth Cole	81	Elizabeth Cole.			
John Campbell	65	Thomas Holland.	James Fitzpatrick	88	James Fitzpatrick.
John Ward	78	Benjamin Kirk.	Reuben Walls	86	Reuben Walls.
Samuel H. Stitt	49	Samuel H. Stitt.	Edward Adkins	85	Thomas Adkins.
John White	82	Caleb White.	Edward Stoker	77	Edward Stoker.
			William H. Layton	86	James Whitaker.
SOUTHERN DIVISION.			Esau Ritchey	63	Esau Ritchey.
Daniel Bell	76	James Morris.	Coleman A. Collier	61	Coleman A. Collier.
William Owens	77	Albert Owens.	Hugh McClintock	82	Hugh McClintock.
William Devin	71	William Devin.	Sarah Barnett	76	James P. Barnett.
Abram Williams	98	Abram Williams.			
John Rust	86	Mason Rust.	**OHIO COUNTY.**		
John Solomon	85	Delilah Vincamp.			
			Zebra Arnold	83	Bayliss Axton.
MONROE COUNTY.			William L. Barnard	81	William L. Barnard.
			William Campbell	87	William Campbell.
Joseph Gist	89	Joseph Gist.	William Carter, sen.	80	William Carter, sen.
Jacob Goodman	80	Jacob Goodman.	John Maddox, sen.	78	John Maddox, sen.
Pleasant Haily	84	Pleasant Haily.	Francis Petty	87	Pinkney Petty.
Matthew Kidwell	80	M. Kidwell.	Peter Parks	81	Peter Parks.
Fleming Smith	96	Dorcas Page.	Diadama Shutts	78	Joseph Shutts.
Elijah Veach	89	Samuel B. Jinkins.	Chesley Calloway	81	William Simmons.
John Rainer	85	John Painter.			
John Giles	84	John Giles.	**OLDHAM COUNTY.**		
Harden Denham	78	Harden Denham.			
Solomon Dickerson	80	Solomon Dickerson.	Benjamin Coons	66	Benjamin Coons.
Thomas Brown, sen.	84	Thomas Brown, sen.	James Hoskins	83	James Hoskins.
Thomas Bartlee	77	Thomas Bartlee, jun.	Merrett Humphrey	80	Merrett Humphrey.
John Morehead	90	Rebecca Morehead.	John Austin	102	John Austin.
			Edmund Archer	81	E. Archer.

KENTUCKY—Continued.

Names of pensioners for revolutionary or military services.	Ages.	Names of heads of families with whom pensioners resided June 1, 1840.
OWEN COUNTY.		
John Guill	82	John Guill.
William Ligon	78	John Morgan.
John Bond	78	John Bond.
Lewis Vallandingham	79	Lewis Vallandingham.
Edward D. Kenny	78	Edward D. Kenny.
John Searcy	78	James Crowder.
Rebecca McCormack	88	Margaret Stuart.
James McHatton	56	James McHatton.
Jacob Hunter	83	Jacob Hunter.
Robert Burk	78	Robert Burk.
William Lorance	77	William H. Lorance.
Nancy Ellis	77	Duncan Ellis.
John Sanders, sen.	89	John Sanders, sen.
Thomas Parsley	78	Thomas Parsley.
Henry Carter	91	Henry Carter.
Samuel Boone	88	Smallwood Moon.
PENDLETON COUNTY.		
Adam Taylor	78	Adam H. Taylor.
James Pribble	79	James Pribble.
Gabriel Mullins	87	Patrick Mullins.
Robert Taylor	82	Robert Taylor.
John Glinn	80	Martha Talbott.
Isaac Conner	85	Isaac Conner.
Phebe Clarkson	66	Isaac S. Clarkson.
James Cordy	87	W. Cordy.
Elizabeth Wyatt	78	Elizabeth Wyatt.
Leonard Highfill	52	Leonard Highfill.
Ebenezer Jane	55	Ebenezer Jane.
John H. Frigate	59	John H. Frigate.
James Hammerty	70	James Hammerty.
William Cleveland	83	W. Cleveland.
Jane Hand	75	James S. Hand.
James Yelton	94	James Yelton.
Peter Demoss	88	Peter Demoss.
PERRY COUNTY.		
James Candill	90	William Candill.
Archilous Croft	81	Archilous Croft.
Simon Justice	87	Simon Justice.
Edmund Pally	84	David Pally.
PIKE COUNTY.		
Moses Stepp	86	John Burgett.
Christian Trant	87	Christian Trant.
Jos. Ford	88	Polly Ford.
PULASKI COUNTY.		
George Decker	80	George Decker.
Robert Anderson	70	Robert Anderson.
Robert Sayers	80	Robert Sayers.
John Wilson	70	John Wilson.
Barnabas Murray	80	Barnabas Murray.
ROCKCASTLE COUNTY.		
Elijah Denny	77	Elijah Denny.
Reuben C. Pew	81	Reuben C. Pew.
William Lawrence	76	Neely Lawrence.
George Harloe	89	George Harloe.
Moses Farris	78	John Newcom.
William Sweney	80	William Sweney.
Nicholas Houke	100	Richardson Roberts.
Humphrey Bates	70	Humphrey Bates.
William Abney	86	William Abney.
Jacob Stephens	84	Jacob Stephens.
George Sigmon	83	George Sigmon.
Francis Ramsey, sen.	76	Francis Ramsey, sen.
RUSSELL COUNTY.		
Thomas Graves	77	Thomas Graves.
Isham Sharp	85	Isham Sharp.
Henry Law	82	Coleman Law.
Matthew Robertson	78	Matthew Robertson.
William Perryman	81	William Perryman.
Jordan George	76	Jordan George.
John Polly	80	John Polly.

Names of pensioners for revolutionary or military services.	Ages.	Names of heads of families with whom pensioners resided June 1, 1840.
SCOTT COUNTY.		
William Beaty	78	G. G. Gorham.
David Keer	93	John A. Gorham.
James Dooly	106	Nancy Leach.
Thomas H. Graves	46	Thomas H. Graves.
Herman Hill	87	William T. Wood.
Achilles Stapp	86	Achilles Stapp.
James Jones	74	James Jones.
Mary Chisam	86	Benjamin Chisam.
Eleanor Tarlton	78	James W. Fenwick.
John Payne	44	John Payne.
Jeremiah Miner	95	Jeremiah Miner.
Paul Leinhers	96	Margaret A. Lemon.
Robert Nimley	48	Robert Nimley.
Kindness Grisham	97	Robert Power.
Daniel Ganoe, sen.	82	Daniel Ganoe, sen.
Joseph Burch	77	Joseph Burch.
Abigail Patterson	70	William Moore.
Henrietta Downing	95	John Downing.
Samuel Sharon	48	Samuel Sharon.
John Hiles	80	John Hiles.
John Jacobs	78	John Jacobs.
Samuel Barnhill	82	James Vance.
John Gatewood	77	John Gatewood.
John Campbell	75	John Campbell.
Thomas H. Graves	46	Thomas H. Graves.
Herman Hill	87	William F. Wood.
SHELBY COUNTY.		
Benjamin Conyers	91	Bryant Davis.
Daniel McCalister, sen.	80	Daniel McCalister, sen.
Peter Carnine	88	Peter Carnine.
John Riely	79	John Riely.
Robert F. Gale	72	Robert Gale.
Charles Mitchell	83	Gideon Mitchell.
Delilah Maddox	72	James McCann.
Joseph Thompson	70	Joseph Thompson.
Samuel White	64	Samuel White.
Sutherland Mayfield	55	Sutherland Mayfield.
Francis Basket	73	Jesse Basket.
James Hickman	81	James Hickman.
Benjamin Washburn	72	Benjamin Washburn.
Joseph Reeves	73	Willis Reeves.
Mesheck Pearson	86	Mesheck Pearson.
Sarah Christy	79	Sarah Christy.
Sarah Ford	75	Oswell Herron.
SHELBYVILLE.		
William French, sen.	80	William French, jr.
B. W. Ballard	81	B. W. Ballard.
Nich. Blankenbaker	82	Luke Blankenbaker.
Elisha Gibson	95	John Painter.
Seth Strattan	78	Seth Strattan.
Nancy Davis	81	Prisly Davis.
Robert Woolfolk	85	John Carvan.
George Hawkins	92	Gilbert Hawkins.
Henry Wiley	95	Henry Wiley.
Elizabeth Collett	71	John Collett.
Samuel Burke	84	Samuel Burke.
Edward Miller	89 }	Robert Miller.
Nancy Clark	76 }	
SIMPSON COUNTY.		
Mary Roper	75	Mary Roper.
Laton Cooper	82	Joseph Wright.
George Pearce	85	George W. Pearce.
William West	87	James Millikin.
Nancy Kelley	85	Nancy Kelley.
James Moore	84	Edward L. Gaines.
SPENCER COUNTY.		
John Barr	85	John Barr.
John Davis	82	John Davis.
M. Reason	85	James Reason.
John Strange	90	John Strange.
Brant Stone	90	B. Stone.
John Ringoe	80	John Ringoe.
Philip Taylor	75	Philip Taylor.

KENTUCKY—Continued.

Names of pensioners for revolutionary or military services.	Ages.	Names of heads of families with whom pensioners resided June 1, 1840.	Names of pensioners for revolutionary or military services.	Ages.	Names of heads of families with whom pensioners resided June 1, 1840.
TODD COUNTY.			WASHINGTON—Continued.		
Jonathan Smith	83	H. B. Davidson.	Andrew Young	82	Andrew Young.
Robert Acock	86	Robert Acock.	Jacob Lea	75	Jacob Lea.
Anna Boone	67	H. G. Boone.	Martin Hughs	81	Richard Smith.
John M. Boyd	77	G. W. Boyd.	Peter Adams	79	Peter B. F. Adams.
James Flack	79	James Flack.	Samuel Booker	82	Samuel Booker.
Samuel Gordon	81	G. W. Gordon.	Amos Graham	85	Amos Graham.
George Gibson	78	George Gibson.			
Jeanette Mabon	70	Thomas Martin.	**WHITLEY COUNTY.**		
Elizabeth Qualls	75	Thomas Moss.			
Benjamin Pannel	83	Benjamin Pannel.	Darley Smithheart	81	D. Smithheart.
Peter Petree	77	Peter Petree.	Michel Stephens	54	Michel Stephens.
William Turner	85	William Turner.	Thomas Adkins	82	Thomas Adkins.
				85	
TRIGG COUNTY.			Henry Porch	75	Henry Porch.
			Daniel Twig	86	Daniel Twig.
John Mabry, sen.	76	John Mabry, sen.	James Rogers	86	James Rogers.
Balaam Ezell	84	Balaam Ezell.	Anes Witt	80	Samuel Witt.
Miles Hallowell	79	Miles Hallowell.	John Hood	80	John Hood.
James Barham	78	James Barham.	Thomas Laughlin	77	Thomas Laughlin.
TRIMBLE COUNTY.			**WAYNE COUNTY.**		
Isaac Gray	66	Isaac Gray.	Bartholomew Haden	64	Bartholomew Haden.
Thomas Hardin	81	Thomas Hardin.	Patrick Coyle	71	Patrick Coyle.
George Wright	76	George Wright.	William Doss	76	William Doss.
Joshua Prewett	77	Joshua Prewett.	George Rogers	76	George Rogers.
Samuel Vanhorn	86	John Wright.	Isaac Crabtree	82	Isaac Crabtree.
Samuel Kelly	53	Samuel Kelly.	James Jones, sen.	81	James Jones, sen.
Kennard Younger	85	Kennard Younger.	Frederick Cooper	80	Frederick Cooper.
John Logan	82	Joseph Logan.	John Parmley	79	John Parmley.
Thomas Morgan	79	John Lamastus.	Mastin Durham	85	Mastin Durham.
Thomas McIntosh	83	James Johnson.	James Piercey	80	James Piercey.
			Reuben Coffey	81	Reuben Coffey.
UNION COUNTY.			James Turner, sen.	77	James Turner, sen.
			Stephen Pratt	75	Stephen Pratt.
Armisted Anderson	83	Armisted D. Anderson.	James S. Davis	60	James S. Davis.
Lewis Richards	77	Lewis Richards.	Abram Hunt	80	Abram Hunt.
A. Davenport	81	A. Davenport.	John Adair	87	John Adair.
			Charles Washam	80	Charles Washam.
WARREN COUNTY.			Zachariah Sanders	81	Zachariah Sanders.
			Peter Catun	86	Peter Catun.
Miles Bellows	80	William W. Bowers.	Caleb Cooper	80	Caleb Cooper.
John Billingsley	87	John Billingsley.			
William Hayse	77	William Hayse.	**WOODFORD COUNTY.**		
Christopher Haven	88	Samuel Haven.	NORTHERN DIVISION.		
Jesse Kerby, sen.	83	Jesse Kerby, sen.	Bird Smith	53	Bird Smith.
Leonard Kerby	79	Leonard Kerby, jr.	Dennis Dayley	79	Dennis Dayley.
Ralph Young	87	Ralph Young.	John Gregory	84	John Gregory.
			Jane Ellis	77	George Byvis.
WASHINGTON COUNTY.			John Mitchell	75	John Mitchell.
			Peter Alexander	83	Robinson Ruddle.
Jonathan White	78	Jonathan White.			
John Combs	81	Joseph Good.	SOUTHERN DIVISION.		
Joseph Sweeney	81	Joseph Sweeney.	John Cox	78	John Cox.
Elijah Farris	80	Elijah Farris.	Stephen Chilton	80	Stephen Chilton.
Philip Burns	84	Philip Burns.	James Hamilton	77	James Hamilton.
John Lambert	81	John Lambert.	John McQuiddy	80	John McQuiddy.
Nathan Lawson	85	Chesley Lawson.	George W. New	76	Daniel Taylor.

STATE OF OHIO.

Names of pensioners for revolutionary or military services.	Ages.	Names of heads of families with whom pensioners resided June 1, 1840.	Names of pensioners for revolutionary or military services.	Ages.	Names of heads of families with whom pensioners resided June 1, 1840.
ASHTABULA COUNTY.			**ATHENS COUNTY.**		
CONNEAUT.			HOMER.		
Haunaniah Brooks	83	Daniel Chapman.	Amos Stackhouse	82	Joshua Hinds.
Shadrach Dodge	78	Ezekiel Bonney.	William Stanly	65	V. C. Stanly.
MONROE.			CANAAN.		
Joseph Rathburn	78	Joseph Rathburn.	Thomas Arnold	84	William Arnold.
PIERPONT.			AMES.		
William Gould	79	Harlow B. Seager.	Jason Rice	88	Sabinas Rice.
ANDOVER.			George Wolf	87	George Wolf.
Isaac Bartlett	81	Isaac W. Bartlett.	Jonathan Sweat	79	Jonathan Sweat.
John Pickett	86	Luther Wight.	TROY.		
Seth Hillver	81	Seth Hillyer.	Phebe Waterman	83	Jonas Smith.
Nathan Mason	83	Calvin Mason.	Eunice Griffith	81	Nica Griffin.
WILLIAMSFIELD.			ALEXANDER.		
Elnathan Pratt	83	Ranseller S. Pratt.	Thomas Huderal	80	Thomas Huderal.
WAYNE.			Uriah Tippy	82	Uriah Tippy.
Benjamin Ward	77	Benjamin Ward.	Nathan Burrell	80	Josiah Hook.
Joel Pease	79	Joel Pease.	Joel Louther	85	Asa Wade.
Joseph M. Jewett	77	Joseph M. Jewett.	MARION.		
DENMARK.			Nathan Brewster	82	Nathan Brewster.
Joseph Rogers	87	Joseph Rogers.	Aaron Fall	79	Aaron Fall.
SHEFFIELD.			BERNE.		
Nancy Schermerhorn	84	John D. Clute.	Samuel Collins	87	W. W. Collins.
John McManners	80	John McManners.	Samuel Brown	82	John Henry.
KINGSVILLE.			CARTHAGE.		
Obadiah Ward	87	Elijah Ward.	C. Vanderhoff	89	C. Vanderhoff.
Benjamin Barrett	80	Amos Barrett.	BROWN.		
COLEBROOK.			Ephraim Pratt	80	Luther Pratt.
Samuel Phillips	80	Samuel Phillips.	ELK.		
NEW LYME.			Daniel Gill	83	Joseph Gill.
Asa Doty	77	Oliver Brown.	ATHENS.		
Philip Bovee	51	Philip Bovee.	Jane Brown	86	A. G. Brown.
Luther Reeves	81	Luther Reeves.	Daniel Stewart	77	D. Stewart.
LENOX.			**ADAMS COUNTY.**		
Benjamin Waters	78	Benjamin Waters.	GREEN.		
Thomas Holman	85	Thomas Holman.	John Toland	76	John Toland.
JEFFERSON.			Nathaniel Reynolds	77	Charity Reynolds.
Allen Hackett	83	James M. Hackett.	Nathaniel Foster	80	Nathan Foster.
PLYMOUTH.			MONROE.		
Thomas Willis	81	Asahel Willis.	William Yates	90	William Yates.
ASHTABULA.			Charles Stevenson	78	Charles Stevenson.
Thomas Benham	81	Thomas Benham.	LIBERTY.		
ORWELL.			John Stivers	74	Robert Stivers.
George Smith	79	George Smith.	John McPike	90	John McPike.
ROME.			JEFFERSON.		
Henry Straight	80	Henry Straight.	James Williams	82	Newton Williams.
AUSTINBURG.			Richard Woodworth	85	Richard Woodworth.
John Crissey	83	Ebenezer A. Mills.	SPRING.		
Nathaniel Austin	87	Lewis Austin.	John Blair	78	Andrew Marton.
SAYBROOK.			Jesse Ellis	86	Jesse Ellis.
Jacob Jenks	80	John Sherman.	WEST UNION.		
Ezra Sexton	83	William C. Sexton.	John Killin	83	John Killin.
Nancy Streeton	80	Rhoda Knowles.	**ALLEN COUNTY.**		
GENEVA.			DUCHOUQUET.		
Levi Gaylard	81	Harvey R. Gaylard.	John Ridley	81	John Ridley, jr.
Enoch Barnum	52	Enoch Barnard.	GERMAN.		
HARPERSFIELD.			Simon Cochran	86	Simon Cochran.
John Lamont	82		AMANDA.		
Selina Hendry	73		Ann Place	76	Abraham Miller.
Hannah Skinner	87		**BUTLER COUNTY.**		
WINDSOR.			ST. CLAIR.		
Caleb Thomas	77	Oliver Loomis, jr.	William Davis	90	Jackson Davis.
Skene D. Sackett	76	Jonathan Wilder.	James Reiley	93	J. and F. Reiley.
			William Caldwell	76	William Caldwell.

Names of pensioners for revolutionary or military services.	Ages.	Names of heads of families with whom pensioners resided June 1, 1840.	Names of pensioners for revolutionary or military services.	Ages.	Names of heads of families with whom pensioners resided June 1, 1840.
BUTLER—Continued.			**BELMONT**—Continued.		
WAYNE.			RICHLAND.		
John Craig - -	79	James Craig.	Richard Hardesty - - -	86	Richard Hardesty.
Thomas Simmons - -	75	Thomas Simmons.	William Rennison - - -	83	Joseph Rankin.
MADISON.			William Craig - - -	85	James Parrish.
Pardon Starks - -	76	Pardon Starks.	Robert Thompson - - -	81	Poorhouse.
UNION.			SMITH.		
Ashabel Waller - - -	81	Ashabel Waller.	William Dawson - - -	47	William Dawson.
John Beckett - - -	87	James C. Beckett.	GOSHEN.		
James Irwin - - -	82	James Irwin.	Sarah Windham - - -	79	Sarah Windham.
LIBERTY.			MORRISTOWN, UNION TOWNSHIP.		
William Knox - - -	70	Robert S. Knox.	William Ramsey - - -	84	William Ramsey.
John Carnes - - -	77	John McGuire.	UNION.		
William Wright - - -	79	William Wright.	William Musgrove - - -	79	William Musgrove.
John Line - - -	76	John Line.	Eve Mitchell - - -	85	Sarah Berry.
LEMON.			FLUSHING.		
James Grimes - - -	80	James Grimes.	George Brokaw, sen. - -	86	George Brokaw, sen.
Joseph Compton - - -	80	Joseph Compton.	John N. Smith - - -	76	John N. Smith.
HAMILTON.			MEAD.		
John Reily - - -	77	John Reily.	Rosell Beach - - -	86	Rosell Beach.
Pierson Sayre - - -	77	Pierson Sayre.	David Lockwood - - -	70	David Lockwood.
FAIRFIELD.			WAYNE.		
John Walker, sen. - -	75	John Walker, sen.	Abraham Gray - - -	86	John Gray.
ROSS.			SOMERSET.		
Nathan Griffith - - -	82	Nathan Griffith.	Levi Davis - - -	76	Levi Davis.
HANOVER.			George Morgan - - -	92	George Morgan.
Ezekiel Ross - - -	84	Amos Ross.			
Joshua Leach - - -	85	Joshua Leach.	**CARROLL COUNTY.**		
Martin Rinehart - - -	82	George Rinehart.	ORANGE.		
REILEY.			John Raignsbearger - -	81	John Raignsbearger.
James Deneen - - -	84	Alexander Deneen.	Robert West - - -	86	James West.
John Smith - - -	78	John Smith.	Henry Martin - - -	83	Henry Martin.
Heman Adams - - -	79	Warren Smith.	PERRY.		
OXFORD.			Mordecai Amos - - -	94	Henry Amos.
John Freeman - - -	83	John Freeman.	AUGUSTA.		
MILFORD.			Diana Westfall - - -	80	Simeon Westfall.
Daniel Baker - - -	85	David Baker.	HARRISON.		
BROWN COUNTY.			John Gribbins - - -	89	William D. Gribbins.
STERLING.			ROSE.		
James Waits - - -	78	James Waits.	Nicholas Criss - - -	74	Nicholas Criss.
WASHINGTON.			**COSHOCTON COUNTY.**		
Michael Conley - - -	94	Michael Conley.	FRANKLIN.		
George Marshall - - -	82	George Marshall.	Israel Buker - - -	84	Israel Buker.
William Reeves - - -	76	William Reeves.	JEFFERSON.		
GREEN.			James Beatty - - -	80	Samuel Martin.
Theodore Melott - - -	89	Prater Melott.	PERRY.		
SCOTT.			William Watson - - -	84	George Beckley.
Joshua Davidson - - -	87	John Bingaman.	David Lee - - -	56	David Lee.
FRANKLIN.			Christian Musser - - -	80	Christian Musser.
Benjamin Wills - - -	87	Sarah Rice.	WEST CARLISLE.		
Benjamin Wells - - -	88	Benjamin Wells.	Richard Smith - - -	48	Richard Smith.
James Erwin - - -	77	James Erwin.	WASHINGTON.		
CLARK.			Lloyd Pyott - - -	52	Lloyd Pyott.
James Rounds - - -	82	James Rounds.	VIRGINIA.		
HUNTINGTON.			Joseph Thompson - - -	79	James L. McGregor.
Edward McDaniel - - -	95	Edward McDaniel.	ROCHESTER.		
DECATUR.			William Critchfield - -	77	William Critchfield.
Benjamin Sutton - - -	87	Benjamin Sutton.	MILL CREEK.		
BOYD.			Luke Tipton - - -	85	Adam Bible.
Samuel Pickerill - - -	77	Samuel Pickerill.			83	
BELMONT COUNTY.			KEENE.		
ST. CLAIRSVILLE.			Samuel Wiley - - -		Samuel Wiley.
Marmaduke S. Davis -	80	Marmaduke S. Davis.			

22

OHIO—Continued.

Names of pensioners for revolutionary or military services.	Ages.	Names of heads of families with whom pensioners resided June 1, 1840.	Names of pensioners for revolutionary or military services.	Ages.	Names of heads of families with whom pensioners resided June 1, 1840.
CHAMPAIGN COUNTY.			**COLUMBIANA COUNTY.**	82	
ADAMS.			KNOX.		
Thomas Tipton	108	Asahel Wilkinson.	James Beer	82	
GOSHEN.			SMITH.		
John Davis	65	John Odle.	John Allerton	77	John Allerton.
RUSH.			MIDDLETON.		
Daniel Baker	72	Daniel Baker.	James Boyd	80	James Boyd.
URBANNA.			Matthias Shirts	90	Matthias Shirts, jun.
John Dawson	92	John Dawson.	Thomas Kent	94	Thomas Kent.
Frederick Gump	99	Frederick Gump.	WAYNE.		
WAYNE.			James Figgins	80	
Elizabeth Barret	85	Elizabeth Barrett.	LIVERPOOL.		
James Witty	73	James Witty.	Samuel Lyons	78	Samuel Lyons.
William Gutridge	64	William Gutridge.	William Carnagey	86	William Carnagey.
CLARK COUNTY.			CALCUTTA.		
MOORFIELD.			Samuel Quigley, sen.	84	Samuel Quigley, sen.
William Rogers	83	William Rogers.	ST. CLAIR.		
MADISON.			John Hight	83	John Hight.
Isaac Wilson	80	Isaac Wilson.	James Smith	84	James Smith.
MAD RIVER.			UNITY.		
John Parsons	93	George Parsons.	Bernard Boatman	83	Bernard Boatman.
BETHEL.			Alfred Stewart	51	Alfred Stewart.
William G. Servace	53	William G. Servace.	ELK RUN.		
PIKE.			William Mankins	80	William Mankins.
Samuel Lippencot	81	Samuel Lippencot.	FAIRFIELD.		
CLERMONT COUNTY.			John Crozer	86	Jonathan Piggott.
BATAVIA.			NEW LISBON.		
John Henlick	88	Jane Gest.	Jacob Hawke	81	William Sanders.
Nathaniel Reeves	84	Nathaniel Reeves.	CENTRE.		
TATE.			James McClelland	80	James McClelland.
Oakey Van Osdol	83	Oakey Van Osdol.	GREEN.		
MONROE.			Philip Bowman	85	Joshua Bowman.
John Dennis	80	John Dennis.	William Snyder	55	William Snyder.
Hugh Mulloy	88	Hugh Mulloy.	**CUYAHOGA COUNTY.**		
Barton Lowe	78	Barton Lowe.	NEWBURGH.		
OHIO.			Edmund Rathban	83	Edmund Rathban.
Nehemiah Ward	84	Nehemiah Ward.	Elizabeth Cochrane	83	Aliner Cochrane.
John Wheeler	89	William Wheeler.	CLEVELAND.		
Thomas Manning	77	Thomas Manning.	Nathaniel Andrews	77	N. Andrews.
Christian Placard	88	Jeremiah Gaskins.	Rice Beckworth	85	Joseph Wyley.
NEW RICHMOND.			BROOKLYN.		
James Arthur	76	James Arthur.	Phineas Shepard	83	Phineas Shepard.
Zebulon Applegate	86	Levi Moss.	Sybil Sawtle	77	Benjamin Sawtle.
STONELICK.			ROYALTON.		
William Cowen	85	William Cowen.	Elias Keyes	77	Elias Keyes.
WAYNE.			John Miner	78	John Miner.
James Carter	85	James Carter.	STRONGSVILLE.		
JACKSON.			Joshua Hudson	80	Joshua Hudson.
Sarah Stoner	74	Ann Smith.	J. Meyreck	84	Justin Meyreck.
John Hair	86	Arthur Clark.	DOVER.		
CLINTON COUNTY.			Joseph Porter	89	John Porter.
LIBERTY.			Jared Farren	79	J. Farren.
David Shields	87		Jedediah Crocker	78	J. Crocker.
VERNON.			PARMA.		
Thomas Hardin	85		Isaac Burnam	75	Isaac Burnam.
CLARK.			Mrs. Azuba Norton	87	Asher Norton.
Aaron Ruse	78	Aaron Ruse.	WARRENSVILLE.		
John Jones	84	John Jones.	Moses Warner	80	Moses Warner.
WASHINGTON.			MAYFIELD.		
George Howard	92	Mary H. Howard.	William Elsworth	79	William Elsworth.
George Nixon	89		BRICKSVILLE.		
			Joseph Willcox	86	Doolittle Willcox.

OHIO—Continued.

Names of pensioners for revolutionary or military services.	Ages.	Names of heads of families with whom pensioners resided June 1, 1840.	Names of pensioners for revolutionary or military services.	Ages.	Names of heads of families with whom pensioners resided June 1, 1840.
CUYAHOGA—Continued.			**ERIE—Continued.**		
CLEVELAND CITY.			HURON.		
Second ward.			John McMillen	80	John McMillen.
Samuel Adams	78	Samuel Adams.	GROTON.		
			Joseph M. Remington	77	Joseph Turner.
DELAWARE COUNTY.			PORTLAND.		
SCIOTO.			David Carswell	76	Esther Hurd.
William Warrington	86	William Warrington.			
			FAIRFIELD COUNTY.		
HARLEM.			CLEAR CREEK.		
Elam Blain	80	Elam Blain, jr.	Joshua Chrishfield	87	
Mille Hills	77	Sherman Fairchild.	Peter Wotring	83	
Elizabeth Adams	73	Silas Adams.	John Runnels	89	
TRENTON.			HOCKING.		
Philemon Bidlack	76	Philemon Bidlack.	John Thompson	82	
Sarah McCoy	71	John Simpson.			
John Wort	84	Israel B. Wort.	WALNUT.		
Martha Hough	82	Owen Hough.	Walker Newman	79	
Sibel Orton	78	Polly Gall.	BLOOM.		
PORTER,			Charles Bolen	75	Charles Bolen.
Peter Vansickle	90	Ira Finch.			
William Steward	88	James White.	**FAYETTE COUNTY.**		
			UNION.		
BENNINGTON.			Felix McElhany	90	Felix McElhany.
Eunice Smith	76	William Smith.	Ralph Boon	95	George W. Ritchie.
			Charles Sexton	78	
GENOA.			JEFFERSON.		
Katharine Bennett	80	Katharine Bennett.	Adam Allen	81	Adam Allen.
Adam McKnight	76	Adam McKnight.	George Rupert	84	
BERKSHIRE.			CONCORD.		
Morgan Young	89	Andrew Young.	John Newlin	97	Nich. Newlin.
Johanna Jones	80	Johanna Jones.	Thomas Crawford	87	
Andrew Hemrod	80	Zelotus Jones.			
Jacob Fisher	81	George Fisher.	GREEN.		
Stiles Parker	75	Stiles Parker.	John Priddy	82	
Ebenezer Landon	79	Ebenezer Landon.	Jesse Roe	86	
Ezekiel Brown	80	Samuel Leonard.			
			FRANKLIN COUNTY.		
KINGSTON.			CITY OF COLUMBUS.		
Pelatiah Morgan	74	Ira Blackman.	*Third ward.*		
Katharine Coykendall	77	Katharine Coykendall.	Henry Stoving	57	Henry Stoving.
			Thomas Smith	81	Thomas Smith.
LINCOLN.			George Whiteman	80	George Whiteman.
Alexander Kingman	75	Alexander Kingman.	JEFFERSON.		
			Mathias Dague	87	
BERLIN.			NORWICH.		
Eunice Caulkins	77		Phœbe Champe	83	William Champe.
Thomas Beddo	80	Thomas Beddo.	JACKSON.		
			William Ballard	81	William Ballard.
WESTFIELD,			TRURO.		
Reuben Martin	93	Samuel Martin.	Joseph Mapes	79	Joseph Mapes.
Phebe Hopkins	81	Abraham Hopkins.	WASHINGTON.		
Elizabeth Patee	75	Henry Patee.	Rebecca Beal	73	
DELAWARE,			BROWN.		
Benjamin Newell	73	Peter Poland.	Samuel Davis	73	
Azariah Root	78	Azariah Root.			
			GEAUGA COUNTY.		
TROY.			THOMPSON.		
Perris Main	77	Perris Main.	Katharine Morey	73	Moses Stragler.
			Retire Trask	82	Cooper Blakeslee.
MARLBOROUGH,			William Thompson	95	William Thompson.
Jehiel Wilcox	81	Jehiel Wilcox.	CHESTER.		
			John More	90	John More.
NORTON,			Lavina Phelps	77	Lavina Phelps.
Abel Spaulding	75	John Spaulding.	Ezekiel Morley	81	Ezekiel Morley.
			Lucy Brass	71	Reuben Gillmore,
DARK COUNTY.			RUSSEL.		
TWIN.			Josiah Rogers	74	Josiah Rogers.
Henry Penney	86	Henry Penney.	AUBURN.		
Ezekiel Farmer	79		David Smith	77	David Smith.
GERMAN,					
John Reed	74	John Reed.			
HARRISON.					
William Graham	76	Addison Graham.			
ERIE COUNTY.					
OXFORD.					
Chauncey Cooke	82	Chauncey Cooke.			

Names of pensioners for revolutionary or military services.	Ages.	Names of heads of families with whom pensioners resided June 1, 1840.	Names of pensioners for revolutionary or military services.	Ages.	Names of heads of families with whom pensioners resided June 1, 1840.
GEAUGA—Continued.			GUERNSEY—Continued.		
NEWBURY.			LIBERTY.		
Ephraim Jewell	80	Ephraim Jewell.	John Lewis	68	John Lewis.
Frederick Loveland	76	Frederick Loveland.			
			HAMILTON COUNTY.		
HAMPDEN.			SPRINGFIELD.		
Samuel M. Starr	74	Samuel M. Starr.	James Woodruff	64	
Abel Damon	80	Abel Damon.	Henry Tucker	84	
Daniel Morgan	87	Lydia Brigham.	John Hay	53	
Nathaniel Hickock	82	Daniel Ingraham.	Robert Watson	64	
Ichabod Pomeroy	83	Noah Pomeroy.	Shubael Carpenter	52	
Squire Davenport	76	Squire Davenport.	Andrew Norris	78	
			John Wilkinson	80	
CLARIDON.					
Rebecca Elliot	75	Lewis Elliot.	COLERAIN.		
Priscilla Dimock	75	Daniel Dimock.	Henry Deatz	84	
			Henry Love	85	
BENTON.			Alexander McNutt	62	
James Goff	78	James Goff.			
Nathan Parks	81	Nathan Parks.	DELHI.		
Meriman Cook	79	E. Cook.	Charles Vathier	78	Charles Vathier.
Thaddeus Bradley	84	Thaddeus Bradley.	Reuben Gage	74	
			Elijah Sargent	82	
TROY.					
Ira Phelps	78	Richard Phelps.	CROSBY.		
			Othniel Looker	83	
MONTVILLE.					
Israel Wilson	81	Lyman Williams.	COLUMBIA.		
			William Finch	78	
GALLIA COUNTY.			Israel Ward	77	
SPRINGFIELD.			John W. Langdon	81	
Amasa Howe	74	Amasa Howe.	Daniel Davis	91	
HARRISBURG.			Abraham Parmetor	79	
Abraham Haptonstall	79				
			ANDERSON.		
RACOON.			Amos Mitchel	80	
Oliver Scott	74	Oliver Scott.	Robert Welsh	58	
			John Charlton	78	
CHESHIRE.					
James Martindale	93	James Martindale.	SYCAMORE.		
			Bethnal Norris	89	
ADDISON.			Price Thompson	84	
Gideon Viah	84	Samuel Viah.	Alexander Martin	80	
HUNTINGTON.			FULTON.		
David Keeton	83		John Hamond	87	
Moses Gee	85	Moses Gee.			
			MILL CREEK.		
GREEN.			James Lyon	85	
Daniel Wiggin	85	Daniel Wiggin.	George Gwinnup	85	
Benjamin Williams	77	Benjamin Williams.	Andrew Cox	81	
Alice Newton	82				
			CITY OF CINCINNATI.		
HARRISON.			1st ward.		
John Straighter	82	John Straighter.	Abijah Phelps	79	
			4th ward.		
GREENE COUNTY.			John Brooks	78	
BATH.			William Worthington	91	
Benjamin Bridge.					
			5th ward.		
XENIA.			Daniel Moss	91	
Thomas Adams	83	Thomas Adams.	John Nelson	77	
James Small	81	James Small.			
			6th ward.		
CÆSAR'S CREEK.			James Skaats, sen.	87	
George Deeds	75	George Deeds.	John Hudson	73	
			John R. Douglass	80	
SILVER CREEK.					
S. B. Hebb	80		WHITE WATER.		
			John Halsted	86	
GUERNSEY COUNTY.					
RICHLAND.			HANCOCK COUNTY.		
Ephraim Dilly, sen.	85	Ephraim Dilly, sen.	UNION.		
			Jacob Fox	77	Jacob Fox.
SPENCER.			John Fox	72	John Fox.
William Wallace	86	William Wallace, jr.	William Carroll	84	Elizabeth Gwin.
Robert Bay	86	Peter Whitaker.			
			PORTAGE.		
WELLS.			Nicholas Helmeck	81	Nicholas Helmeck.
George W. Morrison	47	George W. Morrison.			
MILLWOOD.			CASS.		
Michael L. Montgomery	101	Michael L. Montgomery.	Samuel Freeman	78	Job Freeman.

OHIO—Continued.

Names of pensioners for revolutionary or military services.	Ages.	Names of heads of families with whom pensioners resided June 1, 1840.	Names of pensioners for revolutionary or military services.	Ages.	Names of heads of families with whom pensioners resided June 1, 1840.
HANCOCK—Continued.			**HIGHLAND—Continued.**		
MARION.			DODSON.		
Hugh Pierce - - -	84	Hugh Pierce.	George Speckard, sen. - -	84	George Speckard, sen.
AMANDA.			LIBERTY.		
Zebulon Lee - - -	83	Richard Lee.	William Higgins - -	97	James Higgins, sen.
			John W. Harper - -	82	
RIDGE.			John Crawford - -	92	John Crawford.
John Fisher - - -	85	John Fisher.			
Ephraim Hubbard - -	86	David Graham.	**HOCKING COUNTY.**		
			STARR.		
HARDIN COUNTY.			Caleb Williams - - -	75	Caleb Williams.
BENTON.					
John Briby - - -	78		SALT CREEK.		
			Samuel Wycoff - - -	82	Jacob Alexander.
HARRISON COUNTY.					
RUMLEY.			**HOLMES COUNTY.**		
George Dickerson - -	94		MECHANIC.		
			John Palmer - - -	84	
WASHINGTON.			William Hendrickson - -	83	
John Parker - - -	81				
			WASHINGTON.		
VILLAGE OF CADIZ.			John Critchfield - - -	81	
William Boggs.					
			KILLBUCK.		
TOWN OF CADIZ.			John Guinn - - -	78	
Robert Alexander - - -	45	Robert Alexander.			
Charles D. Wells - -	82	Charles D. Wells.	**HURON COUNTY.**		
			RIPLEY.		
HANOVER.			Joseph More - - -	84	William Irvins.
Charles Conaway - -	88	Charles Conaway.			
			WAKEMAN.		
NORTH.			Lemuel Kingsbury - -	81	Lemuel Kingsbury.
Mordecai Amos - - -	90	Mordecai Amos.	Isaac Curtiss - - -	86	Isaac Curtiss.
STOCK.			GREENWICH.		
Frederick Walters - -	80	Frederick Walters.	Charles Eastman - - -	88	Charles Eastman.
NOTTINGHAM.			BRONSON.		
William Todd - - -	84	Alexander Todd.	Michael Parks - - -	82	Michael Parks.
Isaac Suddith - - -	80				
			SHERMAN.		
HIGHLAND COUNTY.			Abram Bennet - - -	75	Abram Bennet.
FAIRFIELD.					
Evan Evans - - -	87	Evan Evans.	FITCHVILLE.		
Beverly Milner - - -	85	Beverly Milner.	E. H. Cook - - -	81	E. H. Cook.
Daniel Tyler - - -	83	Daniel Tyler.	Abram Hand - - -	79	Abram Hand.
MADISON.			CLARKSFIELD.		
John Robbins - - -	82	John Robbins.	Noah W. Norton - - -	76	Z. C. Norton.
John Strange - - -	85	John Strange.			
			NEW HAVEN.		
BRUSH CREEK.			Henry Brewer - - -	85	Henry Brewer.
George Gall, sen. - -	75	George Gall, sen.			
John Middleton - -	85		RIDGEFIELD.		
Jos. West - - -	83	Benjamin West.	Benjamin Reed - - -	84	James Brakenridge.
FAINT.			PERU.		
John West - - -	84		Prince Haskell - - -	—	Admiral Haskell.
Robert Montgomery - -	81	Robert Montgomery.			
Peter Snider - - -	86	Jacob Snider.	NORWALK.		
John W. Sparger, sen. -	86	John W. Sparger, sen.	Abner Baker - - -	86	Timothy Baker.
JACKSON.			**JACKSON COUNTY.**		
Joseph Horn, sen. - -	84		FRANKLIN.		
James Anderson, sen. -	74	James Anderson, sen.	James Dawson - - -	77	
			Job Foster - - -	84	
CONCORD.					
William Smith - - -	90	Thomas Miller.	LIBERTY.		
John Richardson - -	78		John Hanna - - -	85	
Stephen Ogden - - -	84				
			WASHINGTON.		
NEWMARKET.			Enoch Russell - - -	81	
William Vanwinkle - -	84	William Vanwinkle.			
William Boatman, sen. -	84	Mitchell Boatman.	**JEFFERSON COUNTY.**		
			WARREN.		
WHITE OAK.			John McElroy - - -	85	John McElroy.
Anthony Sonner - -	79	Anthony Sonner.	John Humphrey - - -	87	David Humphrey.
Lewis Robinson - - -	86		John Fry - - -	85	Susanna Staver.
John Mahappy - - -	81	Andrew Mahappy.	Thomas McCune - - -	86	James McCune.
DANVILLE.			WELLS.		
Andrew Shaper, sen. - -	81	Andrew Shaper, sen.	James Barcus - - -	80	James Barcus.

OHIO—Continued.

Names of pensioners for revolutionary or military services.	Ages.	Names of heads of families with whom pensioners resided June 1, 1840.	Names of pensioners for revolutionary or military services.	Ages.	Names of heads of families with whom pensioners resided June 1, 1840.
JEFFERSON—Continued.			**LAKE—Continued.**		
SALINE.			*MADISON.*		
———— Willis	90	Isaac Willis.	Joseph Fuller	82	Joseph Fuller, jun.
ROSS.			Joseph Green	74	Jesse Green.
William Starr	100	William Starr.	William Branch	80	William Branch.
William Roach	100	Jeremiah Roach.	Joshua Emmes	88	Joshua Emmes.
SPRINGFIELD.			Joseph Emerson	86	Joseph Emerson, jun.
Philip Crabs	50	Philip Crabs.	Samuel Smead	93	Oliver Smead.
			Amasa Hill	77	Amasa Hill.
KNOX COUNTY.			Abel Kimball	74	Abel Kimball, 2d.
FRANKLIN.					
Abraham Blair	82	Abraham Blair.	**LAWRENCE COUNTY.**		
HOWARD.			*FAYETTE.*		
Benjamin Critchfield	79	Benjamin Critchfield.	Joseph L. Rowley	90	Thomas Rowley.
CLINTON.			*PERRY.*		
Thomas Davis	87	Thomas Davis.	Elisha B. Greene	54	Elisha B. Greene.
PLEASANT.			*ELIZABETH.*		
Carey McClelland	89		Jacob Huffman	80	Jos. Huffman.
Jos. Northrup	89		*UPPER.*		
LIBERTY.			George Sparling	62	George Sparling.
Christopher Myers	83		Peter Wakefield	75	Peter Wakefield.
MIDDLEBURG.			*LAWRENCE.*		
John Ackerman	84	John Ackerman.	Samuel Lane	81	Samuel Lane.
Samuel Dowd	77	Samuel Dowd.	*MASON.*		
David Welch	85	Peter Welch.	Cornelius Vansarsdall	81	Minedred W. Vanarsdall.
WAYNE.			Humphrey Brimfield	96	Humphrey Brimfield.
Peter Doty	84	Ephraim Doty.	*ROME.*		
MORRIS.			William Losey	89	William Losey.
Benjamin Jackson	88	Benjamin Jackson.	Nathaniel Pritchard	77	Nathaniel Pritchard.
MONROE.			**LICKING COUNTY.**		
H. H. Young	82	H. H. Young.	*GRANVILLE.*		
Levi Chadwick	88	Levi Chadwick.	Stephen Mead	81	Stephen Mead.
CHESTER.			Solomon Freeman	78	William Freeman.
John Holt	80	John Holt.	Achsa Rose	77	C. C. Rose.
John Riney	—	John Riney.	*BURLINGTON.*		
BERLIN.			Samuel Edman	84	Samuel Edman.
David Hess	97	David Hess.	*BENNINGTON.*		
			Mary Perkins	85	Wesley Perkins.
LAKE COUNTY.			*LIMA.*		
PAINESVILLE.			George Horne	76	Jesse Horne.
Mary French	78	Warren French.	*HARRISON.*		
Elkanah Jones	79	Jonathan Goldsmith.	Benjamin Dewolf	81	Benjamin Dewolf.
Roger Crane	78	Tower W. Crane.	*ST. ALBANS.*		
Cypnam Parish	74	Lewis Parish.	Sewell Gilbert	75	Sewell Gilbert.
Edward Paine	96	Sally M. Paine.	Chloe McCuller	81	W. W. Blake.
CONCORD.			Henry Trevitt	80	Henry Trevitt.
Samuel Rogers	73	Samuel Rogers.	Jesse Stockwell	81	Benjamin Bills.
Oliver Brown	79	Oliver Brown.	*JERSEY.*		
Mary Carll	81	Aaron Scribner.	Joseph Headley	83	Benjamin Parkhurst.
William R. Eddy	79	William R. Eddy.	Michael Beam	84	Michael Beam, jun.
Jacob Tyler	79	William Fox.	S. D. Ball	85	S. D. Ball.
KIRTLAND.			Henry Jolly	82	Vachel Dickerson.
Thomas Morley	82	Alfred Morley.	*ETNA.*		
Joseph Bryant	60	Joseph Bryant.	George E. Lloyd	89	J. D. Shank.
Oliver Harmon	83	Oliver Harmon, jun.	*MONROE.*		
WILLOUGHBY.			Caleb Hill	83	Thomas Lunn.
Horace Simmons	78	Horace Simmons.	Elijah Adams	87	Elisha Adams.
John Campbell	78	James Campbell.	*JOHNSTOWN.*		
John Furguson	84	John Furguson.	Jacob Martin	100	Jacob Martin.
LEROY.			Rachel Scovell	78	David Scovell.
Nathan French	80	Nathan French.	*UNION.*		
Lydia Chappell	93	Erastus Rogers.	John Colter	78	John Colter.
Joel Hokum	80	Joel Hokum.	Jonathan Benjamin	101	Mary Ford.
PERRY.			James Taylor	86	James Taylor, jr.
Mary Hanks	77	John Youngs.	*BOWLING GREEN.*		
			William Harris, sen.	85	William Harris, sen.

Names of pensioners for revolutionary or military services.	Ages.	Names of heads of families with whom pensioners resided June 1, 1840.	Names of pensioners for revolutionary or military services.	Ages.	Names of heads of families with whom pensioners resided June 1, 1840.
LICKING—Continued.			**LORAIN—Continued.**		
JACKSONTOWN.			AMHERST.		
Anthony Pitzer	70	Anthony Pitzer.	Calvin Dyke	78	Calvin Dyke.
Japhet Mentzer	87	Gershom Richerson	79	James Cossing.
PERRY.			EATON.		
John Ferrell	89	James Ferrell.	John Taylor	89	Nicholas Taylor.
NEWTON.			AVON.		
Zachariah Albaugh	82	Zachariah Albaugh.	Joseph Moor	76	J. Moor.
UTICA.			HENRIETTA.		
Elias Hughes	86	Jonathan Hughes.	Rebecca Wellman	78	Chauncey Remington.
WASHINGTON.			RUSSIA.		
Zarah Curtis	78	Zarah Curtis.	Joshumy Campbell	78	R. A. Campbell.
MADISON.			Jonathan Buck	90	J. Buck.
John Larabee, sen.	86	John Larabee, sen.	BRIGHTON.		
Ebenezer Mattox	45	Ebenezer Mattox.	Abner Looveland	76	S. H. Looveland.
NEWARK.			Josiah Ward	78	J. Ward.
George W. Parks	47	George W. Parks.	Justice Battle	86	S. T. Battle.
Anna Shenefelt	78	John Shenefelt.	Jos. Kingsbury	79	Austin Kingsbury.
Eldad Steele	76	Eldad Steele.	BROWNHELM.		
			Seth Morse	63	Seth Morse.
LOGAN COUNTY.			COLUMBIA.		
PERRY.			John Howard	83	John Howard.
Peter Howard	95	Peter Howard.	Thomas Williams	78	Abel Goodwin.
Henry Kudisilly	85	Josiah Whitecar.	Samuel Hoadly	68	Samuel Hoadly.
MONROE.			CARLISLE.		
William Carrell	73	William Carrell.	Zachariah Beers	82	Abiram Drakely.
			Eli Pember	78	Eli Pember.
UNION.			Moses Allis	86	William Allis.
Judah Chamberlin	80	Judah Chamberlin.	Jesse Morgan	79	E. H. Morgan.
James Hays	50	John W. Hays.	HUNTINGTON.		
MIAMI.			Ben. Rising	92	Oliver Rising.
Michael Cox	84	Evan J. Schooler.	**LUCAS COUNTY.**		
HARRISON.			GORHAM.		
James Sargent	85	James Sargent.	John Kendall	47	John Kendall.
RUSH CREEK.			ROYALTON.		
Christian Neighbarger	76	Jacob W. Neighbarger.	Richard Tiney	77	Richard Tiney.
James L. New	77	James L. New.	Amos Jordan	84	Amos Jordan.
JEFFERSON.			**MORGAN COUNTY.**		
Codema Knapp	76	Sarah J. Brooks.	BROOKFIELD.		
			Benjamin Severance	78	Benjamin Severance.
LORAIN COUNTY.			Jesse George	86	Jesse George.
ELYRIA.			John Bain	72	John Bain.
Abraham Wellman	60	Abraham Wellman.	BRISTOL.		
Adna S. Clark	77	A. S. Clark.	Hugh Osborn	75	Ezra Osborn.
Betsey Squires	73	Andrew Myers.	Matthew Wilson	85	Matthew Wilson.
SULLIVAN.			JACKSON.		
Jonathan Crapo	77	Jonathan Crapo.	Eddy Birch	80	Oliver Birch.
RIDGEVILLE.			MANCHESTER.		
Eunice Terrel	81	Wyllis Terrel.	Casper Mohler	81	Casper Mohler.
Elihu Terrel	81	David M. Tyler.	WINDSOR.		
David Beebe	93	Garry Root.	Timothy Blackmore	72	Timothy Blackmore.
Jonah Hanchett	83	J. Hanchett.	MORGAN.		
LAGRANGE.			John Clancy	-	Charles Clancy.
Submit Langden	90	F. Langden.	DEERFIELD.		
Charles Rounds	80	Nathaniel Rounds.	Philip Saylor	89	Philip Saylor.
SHEFFIELD.			**MEIGS COUNTY.**		
Elisha Brown	86	E. Bartlet.	COLUMBIA.		
WELLINGTON.			William Howell	92	Philip D Barnhous.
Samuel Pelton	83	Samuel Pelton.	Anthony Haly	81	Anthony Haly.
BLACK RIVER.			ORANGE.		
Eleazer Crawford	78	Eleazer Crawford.	Asa Dains	76	Leonard Dains.
GRAFTON.			Isaac Moss	91	Jeptha Dains.
E. A. Turner	49	E. A. Turner.	Daniel Stivers	77	John Cam.
Aaron Burt	82	Aaron Burt.			

OHIO—Continued.

Names of pensioners for revolutionary or military services.	Ages.	Names of heads of families with whom pensioners resided June 1, 1840.	Names of pensioners for revolutionary or military services.	Ages.	Names of heads of families with whom pensioners resided June 1, 1840.
MEIGS—Continued.			MEDINA—Continued.		
CHESTER.			YORK.		
John White - - -	82	Samuel Fair.	Ezra Brown - - -	77	E. D. Brown.
			Ebenezer Armstrong - -	80	Ebenezer Armstrong.
OLIVE.					
Miles Oakley - - -	84	Bennett Oakley.	HARRISVILLE.		
Jeriah Osborn - - -	78	John Coleler.	John Hogeboom - - -	83	Bartholomew Hogeboom.
			Elizabeth Poe - - -	87	D. W. Poe.
LETART.					
George Harrell - -	93	George Harrell.	MONTGOMERY COUNTY.		
			DAYTON.		
SCIPIO.			Benjamin Cox - - -	94	William Cox.
Robert Townsend - -	84	Daniel Dutton.	George Snider - - -	89	George Snider.
SUTTON.			CLAY.		
George Roush - - -	80	George Roush.	Conrad Witters - -	83	Conrad Witters.
Jonas Roush - - -	77	David Chemiller.			
Luther Danielson - -	84	Luther Danielson.	GERMAN.		
			Philip Negly - - -	92	John C. Negly.
SALEM.			Peter Kesler - - -	81	Peter Kesler.
Esther Russell - -	78	Moses Russell.	Charles Brooks - - -	–	Peter Frank.
			George Clency - -	96	George Clency.
RUTLAND.					
Brewster Higby - -	82	Cyrus Higby.	MIAMI.		
Abijah Hubbell - -	77	Abijah Hubbell.	Jacob Larose - - -	86	Jacob Larose.
Thomas Everton - -	79	Benjamin Dickerson.			
			MUSKINGUM COUNTY.		
SALISBURY.			ZANESVILLE.		
James Whaly - - -	90	James Whaly.	William Davis - - -	86	William Davis.
			John Campbell - - -	79	John Campbell.
MARION COUNTY.					
BIG ISLAND.			UNION.		
Joshua Vanfleet - -	76	Joshua Vanfleet.	John Kelley - - -	80	John Kelley.
			David Findley - - -	75	David Findley.
SALT ROCK.					
Frazier Gray - - -	80	Frazier Gray.	WASHINGTON.		
			Samuel Beavers - -	78	Samuel Beavers.
GILEAD.					
Campbell McDonald -	86	Campbell McDonald.	PERRY.		
			Philip Richcreek - -	77	Philip Richcreek.
MORVEN.					
Amariah Chase - -	77	Solomon Chase.	MONROE.		
Jacob Foust - - -	85	Jonas Foust.	John Baird - - -	82	John Baird.
			James Sprague - - -	84	James Sprague.
MEDINA COUNTY.					
CHATHAM.			WAYNE.		
Jehiel Green - - -	78	Jehiel Green.	John Kent - - -	92	John Kent.
Ephraim Palmer - -	79	Ephraim Palmer.			
Nebediah Cass - -	55	Nebediah Cass.	JACKSON.		
Susannah Allen - -	74	Jacob Allen.	John Johnson - - -	81	Thomas Berry.
WADSWORTH.			DRESDEN.		
Joseph Bartholomew -	82	Joseph Bartholomew.	Lucinda Henry - -	80	Henry Shutts.
SHARON.			LICKING.		
Elizabeth Stephenson -	71	G. W. Stephenson.	David Brondage - -	74	David Brondage.
GRANGER.			NASHPORT.		
Samuel McCloud - -	80	Samuel McCloud.	John Davis - - -	82	John Davis.
Seth Goodwin - - -	77	David Goodwin.			
			MUSKINGUM.		
KINKLEY.			Amos Mix - - -	82	Amos Mix.
Isbuel Jennings - -	–	Isbuel Jennings.	Enos Devose - - -	49	Enos Devose.
Josiah Brown - - -	76	Melville Brown.			
			HOPEWELL.		
GUILFORD.			John Reddick - - -	81	John Reddick.
Jane Wilson - - -	82	James Huffman.	Jacob Crigger - - -	87	Jacob Crigger.
Hannah Pelton - -	87	Corydon Culver.			
Thomas Leland - -	83	Thomas Leland.	FALLS.		
Mary Shields - - -	79	William Shields.	Captain James Taylor -	71	James Taylor.
Katharine Raduback -	75	Thomas Raduback.			
			NEWTON.		
SEVILLE.			Martin Rohrer - - -	68	Martin Rohrer.
Nathan Gray - - -	80	Nathan High.	Jeremiah Woods - -	86	Jeremiah Woods.
Anna Houghton - -	79	Oliver Houghton.			
			SPRINGFIELD.		
BRUNSWICK.			Jesse Smith - - -	81	Ezra Smith.
Solomon Denning - -	76	Carrol Denning.	Jacob Addison - -	79	Jacob Addison.
John Hulet - - -	85	Fletcher Hulet.			
Asa Hulet - - -	82	Elisha Mason.	BRUSHCREEK.		
John Stearns - - -	89	Daniel Stearns.	Robert Boyd - - -	80	Robert Boyd.
			HARRISON.		
WESTFIELD.			John Wolf - - -	80	Michael Wolf.
Deliverance Eastman -	79	J. M. Eastman.	Josiah Thomas - - -	83	William Thomas.

OHIO—Continued.

Names of pensioners for revolutionary or military services.	Ages.	Names of heads of families with whom pensioners resided June 1, 1840.	Names of pensioners for revolutionary or military services.	Ages.	Names of heads of families with whom pensioners resided June 1, 1840.
MUSKINGUM—Continued.			**PERRY COUNTY.**		
MEIGS.			READING.		
Richard Marshall - - -	79	Richard Marshall.	Samuel Parrot - - -	85	Samuel Parrot.
MADISON COUNTY.			THORN.		
SOMMERFORD.			Johnson Cook - - -	80	Johnson Cook.
Thomas Davis - -	83	Thomas Davis.			
David Colver - - -	76	David Colver.	CLAYTON.		
			Ruel Sayres - - -	87	Isaac Bennet.
FAIRFIELD.					
Stephen Morris - -	94	Stephen Morris.	MADISON.		
			Edward Ward - - -	86	Edward Ward.
PIKE.			Jer. Simms - -	79	Jer. Simms.
George Jones - -	77	Michael Rosenbery.	William Dusenberry - -	84	William Dusenberry
			Thomas Moore - -	79	Israel Moore.
CANAAN.					
Oble Beach - - -	81	Oble Beach.	**PREBLE COUNTY.**		
			ISRAEL.		
DARBY.			David Madill - -	77	Samuel Austin.
Samuel Smith - - -	83	James Smith.	Samuel Heran - - -	80	Samuel Heran.
UNION.			DIXON.		
Andrew Sifard - -	88	Andrew Sifard.	Thomas B. McCohan.		
			William Gray - - -	84	William Gray.
MERCER COUNTY.			David Truax - - -	84	
DUBLIN.					
John Sutton - - -	84	Isaac H. Sutton.	JACKSON.		
			John Campbell - -	79	
WAYNE.			William Williams - -	77	
John Latimer - - -	84	William Latimer.			
			WASHINGTON.		
WASHINGTON.			Barnabas Vandeventer -	85	Barnabas Vandeventer.
James Scoonover - - -	44	James Scoonover.			
			MONROE.		
MIAMI COUNTY.			David Heriman - - -	84	Charles Vanhorn.
CONCORD.					
John W. Meredith - -	80	John W. Meredith.	JEFFERSON.		
John R. Bold - -	50	John R. Bold.	Elijah Mitchell - -	79	
Alexander Telford - -	86	James Telford.			
Aaron Tullis - -	95	Aaron Tullis.	**PIKE COUNTY.**		
Abram Thomas - -	85	Abram Thomas.	SEAL.		
			John Violet - - -	90	John Violet.
BETHEL.			Benjamin Daniels - -	64	Benjamin Daniels.
Daniel Fielding - - -	75	Daniel Fielding.	William Price - -	96	William Price.
			John Hall - - -	92	Elijah Holt.
ELIZABETH.					
Isaac Taylor - -	83	Benjamin Goodwin.	BEAVER.		
John Barnes - -	87	Michael G. Gavon.	Zachariah Cook - -	90	Zachariah Cook.
Jacob Prillainan - -	88		Philip Wolfinberger - -	80	Philip Wolfinberger.
			John Steward - -	92	John Steward.
UNION.					
John Oblinger - - -	89	Amos Oblinger.	MIFFLIN.		
			Reuben Bristol - -	86	Reuben Bristol.
SPRING CREEK.					
Benjamin Winans - -	100	John Winans.	PREBBLE.		
Benjamin Regg - -	85	Benjamin Regg.	Charles Love - -	60	Charles Love.
Lewis Boyer - - -	73	Lewis Boyer.			
			PICKAWAY COUNTY.		
MONROE COUNTY.			JACKSON.		
GREEN.			John Fisher, sen. - - -	84	John Fisher, sen.
Thomas Jordan - -	93	Thomas Jordan.			
			PERRY.		
SUNBURY.			John Devauss - -	87	John Devauss.
Joseph Tomlinson - -	84	Joseph Tomlinson.	John Derham - -	80	John Derham.
ADAMS.			HARRISON.		
John Walters - - -	81	John Walters.	John Brown, sen. - -	76	John Brown, sen.
FRANKLIN.			WALNUT.		
John Carmichael - -	94	John Carmichael.	Charles Dea - - -	85	Charles Dea.
SENECA.			WASHINGTON.		
Lemuel Rucker, sen. -	89	Lemuel Rucker, sen.	Jos. Clark - - -	70	Jos. Clark.
ENOCH.			CIRCLEVILLE.		
Basil Morris - - -	82	Robert Morris.	John C. C. Smith - -	78	Zadoc Smith.
OHIO.			**PORTAGE COUNTY.**		
William McClain - -	81	William McClain.	FRANKLIN.		
			John Gaylord - -	79	John Gaylord.
CENTRE.			Moses Adams - - -	86	Moses Adams.
Joseph Fulherson, sen. - -	85	Joseph Fulherson, sen.	BRIMFIELD.		
Nathan Hollester - -	80	Nathan Hollester.	Constant Chatman - -	79	Henry C. Chatman.
John Pratt - - -	83	John Pratt.	John Agard - -	78	John Agard.

23

OHIO—Continued.

Names of pensioners for revolutionary or military services.	Ages.	Names of heads of families with whom pensioners resided June 1, 1840.	Names of pensioners for revolutionary or military services.	Ages.	Names of heads of families with whom pensioners resided June 1, 1840.
PORTAGE—Continued.			RICHLAND—Continued.		
STREETSBOROUGH.			William Gillaspie - - -	104	William Gillaspie.
Reuben Randall - - -	73	Reuben Randall.			
Zebulon Whipple - - -	76	Zebulon Whipple.	VERNON.		
David Crocker - - -	80	David Crocker.	James Gamble - - -	81	Silas Mavier.
AURORA.			ORANGE.		
Ebenezer Hecox - - -	83	Joshua Hecox.	John Tilton - - -	82	John Tilton.
John Seward - - -	82	John Seward.	James McKenzie - - -	71	James McKenzie.
CHARLESTOWN.			Christian Fast - - -	88	Christian Fast.
Ozias Norton - - -	80	Leverett Norton.	Jacob Heiffner - - -	83	Jacob Heiffner.
HIRAM.			MONTGOMERY, (including ASHLAND.)		
Allen Turner - - •	78	Lewis M. Turner.	James Sweney - - -	84	James Sweney.
RAVENNA.			Philip Shafer - - -	82	Philip Shafer.
Dr. Bostwick - - -	75	Dr. Bostwick.	VERMILION.		
Darius Ely - - -	79	Ashley Ely.	John Mowdy - - -	95	John Mowdy.
Obadiah Stephenson - -	82	Obadiah Stephenson.	Aaron Hoaglan - - -	75	Aaron Hoaglan.
J. Lane - - -	85	John Lane.	Charles Stewart - - -	72	Charles Stewart.
NELSON.			GREEN.		
Samuel Backus - - -	75	Roswell Manby.	Joseph McCumber - - -	72	Joseph McCumber.
FREEDOM.			Jacob Freed - - -	73	Frederick Shafer.
Paul Larkcom - - -	76	Arvillas C. Larkcom.	Clement West - - -	82	Clement West.
Ebbe Durkee - - -	72	Joel Durkee.	Joseph Jones - - -	84	Joseph Jones.
WINDHAM.			WORTHINGTON.		
David Wolcott - - -	75	David Wolcott.	Amasa Flaharty - - -	84	Nicholas Flaharty.
PALMYRA.			Moses Beeman - - -	84	Moses Beeman.
Amariah Daniels - - -	69	Amariah Daniels.	Samuel Phips - - -	104	Jephtha Carlton.
Nathan Muzzy - - -	77	Nathan Muzzy.	MONROE.		
Elijah Canfield - - -	82	Charles Canfield.	Charles Young - - -	80	Sol. Gladden.
Amos Thurber - - -	80	Amos Thurber.	MIFFLIN.		
Truman Gilbert - - -	87	Margaretta Gilbert.	Matthias Young - - -	84	Michael Young.
DEERFIELD.			MILTON.		
Lewis Day - - -	86	Solomon Day.	William Anderson - - -	79	William Anderson.
Ebenezer Williams - -	82	Ebenezer Williams.	MADISON.		
SHALERSVILLE.			Alex. McDougle - - -	86	John A. McDougle.
Ichabod Lord - - -	77	Ichabod Lord.	Samuel Taylor - - -	49	Samuel Taylor.
Noah Shirtleff - - -	75	Selah Shirtleff.			
John Turrel - - -	78		ROSS COUNTY.		
Job Thompson - - -	81	James Thompson.	SCIOTO.		
ATWATER.			John Poe - - -	91	
Jona. Baldwin - - -	82	Jona. Baldwin.	Peter Robinson - - -	84	
ROOTSTOWN.			CONCORD.		
Josiah Mix - - -	86	Samuel R. Mix.	Thomas Arrowhood • -	79	
Valentine Coosard - -	97	Valentine Coosard.	Chris. Depoy - -	79	
Solomon Payne - - -	79	Solomon Payne.	Hendrick Roseboon • -	84	
EDINBURGH.			TWIN.		
Eliza Bostwick - - -	83	Edmund Bostwick.	Caspar Pliley - - -	77	William Pliley.
Nathan Freeman - - -	78	Stephen R. Freeman.	UNION.		
PUTNAM COUNTY.			William Beard - - -	81	Jos. Beard.
OTTAWA.			EAGLE.		
James Jack - - -	60	James Jack.	John Clark - - -	86	John Clark.
RILEY.			HUNTINGTON.		
Israel Hubbard - - -	80	Bildad Hubbard.	Chris. Young - - -	81	Jacob Miller.
RICHLAND COUNTY.			Sampson Price - - -	77	Sampson Price.
SPRINGFIELD.			Benning Wentworth - -	77	Benning Wentworth.
David Post - - -	87	John Post.	BUCKSKIN.		
PLYMOUTH.			Joseph Waugh - - -	76	Lemmon Waugh.
William Bodley - - -	76	William Bodley, jun.	Adam Howard - - -	90	
SANDUSKY.			James Collier - - -	89	
Christian Riblet - - -	80	Christian Riblet.	COLERAIN.		
CONGRESS.			Philip Kerner - - -	75	
David Snell - - -	79	David Snell.	Catharine Dumm - - -	78	
PERRY.			FRANKLIN.		
Jona. Howell - - -	80	Paul Broderic.	Thomas Elsey - - -	81	Patrick Elsey.

OHIO—Continued.

Names of pensioners for revolutionary or military services.	Ages.	Names of heads of families with whom pensioners resided June 1, 1840.	Names of pensioners for revolutionary or military services.	Ages.	Names of heads of families with whom pensioners resided June 1, 1840.
ROS—Continued.			**SHELBY—Continued.**		
DEERFIELD.			GREEN.		
Peter Jackson - - -	84		Samuel Woodward - -	81	Samuel Woodward.
HARRISON.			ORANGE.		
Benjamin Cave - - -	81		Peter L. Hall - - -	77	Peter L. Hall.
			Edward Severns - - -	84	John Barnett.
SANDUSKY COUNTY.					
TOWNSEND.			**STARK COUNTY.**		
Phineas Stevens - - -	87	Zelotus Parkhurst.	TUSCARAWAS.		
Alpheus McIntyre - - -	51	Alpheus McIntyre.	Jonathan Woods - - -	82	Alvah Woods.
			Michael Hahn - - -	95	Michael Hahn.
BALLSVILLE.					
William Seberel - - -	54	William Seberel.	LAKE.		
			John Henry - - -	82	John Henry.
GREEN CREEK.					
Job Wright - - -	80	Job Wright.	SUGAR CREEK.		
Daniel Bates - - -	77	Daniel Bates.	Joseph Kroninger - -	91	Joseph Kroninger.
Allen Waters - - -	81	William Waters.			
William Bundey - - -	66	William Bundey.	BETHLEHEM.		
			Adam Cook - - -	88	Adam Cook.
YORK.					
David Dalrymple - - -	75	Daniel Pierce.	LEXINGTON.		
George Armstrong - - -	83	J. S. Chapman.	William Kingsbury - -	66	John Kingsbury.
			John Shreve - - -	79	Jos. Shreve.
SANDUSKY.					
John Waggner - - -	77	John Waggner.	PLAIN.		
Samuel Thompson - -	45	Samuel Thompson.	Moses Nelson - - -	80	Charles Hortz.
SCIOTO COUNTY.			CANTON.		
BRUSH CREEK.			Jacob Nagle - - -	79	John Black.
Jesse Edwards - - -	85	Jesse Edwards.			
			SUMMET COUNTY.		
CLAY.			NORTON.		
Uriah Barber - - -	78	Uriah Barber.	Henesdale Bates - - -	84	
NILE.			COVENTRY.		
James Dawson - - -	77	Otho Dawson.	Lambert Clement - -	83	
George Hutton - - -	86	John Patton.	John Herrington - -	77	John Herrington.
WAYNE.			HUDSON.		
Robert McClurg - -	86	Samuel J. McClurg.	Jonathan Draper - -	89	A. Draper.
			John Walker - - -	77	John Walker, jr.
JEFFERSON.			John Ellsworth - - -	78	John Ellsworth.
Jacob Hill - - -	83	Jacob Hill.			
			BOSTON.		
PORTER.			Simeon Tappan - -	74	Simeon Tappan.
Benjamin Burt - -	79	Benjamin Burt.			
James Salter - - -	84	Robert Kenady.	TALLMADGE.		
			Reuben Beach - - -	82	Reuben B. Beach.
MADISON.			Isaac Dudley - - -	79	Isaac Dudley.
John Canter - - -	94	John Canter.	Thomas Granger - -	76	L. Granger.
			William Neal - - -	78	William Neal.
SENECA COUNTY.					
ADAMS.			STOW.		
Jere. Williams - - -	81	Jere. Williams.	Charles Wooden - -	85	
			Isaac Steel - - -	76	Isaac Steel.
CLINTON.					
Francis Ditto - - -	90	Francis Ditto.	NORTH AKRON.		
			Elijah Bryan - - -	84	C. Bryan.
HOPEWELL.					
Frederick Shawhen - -	79	Lorenzo Shawhen.	**TUSCARAWAS COUNTY.**		
			BUCKS.		
REED.			Asher Walker - - -	80	
Aaron Deen - - -	73	Aaron Deen.			
			PERRY.		
SENECA.			George Biner - - -	80	George Biner.
Eli Wright - - -	76	Eli Wright.			
			TRUMBULL COUNTY.		
SCIPIO.			BROOKFIELD.		
Peterson Watson - -	75	James S. Sparks.	Ethan Newcomb - -	78	Daniel Newcomb.
Daniel Groscost - -	78	Daniel Groscost.	Henry Taylor - - -	81	Henry Taylor.
SHELBY COUNTY.			COITSVILLE.		
CYNTHIANA.			Amos Loveland - -	78	Daniel Loveland.
Benjamin Morris - -	76	Benjamin Morris.			
			BOURDMAN.		
DINSMORE.			Edward Evans - - -	73	Edward Evans.
Lawrence Curts - -	81	Jacob Click.			
			CANFIELD.		
JACKSON.			Charles Wood - - -	90	Charles Wood.
Timothy Wale - - -	78	Timothy Wale.	Eleazer Gibson - - -	80	Ansel Beaman.

OHIO—Continued.

Names of pensioners for revolutionary or military services.	Ages.	Names of heads of families with whom pensioners resided June 1, 1840.	Names of pensioners for revolutionary or military services.	Ages.	Names of heads of families with whom pensioners resided June 1, 1840.
TRUMBULL—Continued.			**WARREN COUNTY.**		
HARTFORD.			UNION.		
William C. Jones - - -	80	William C. Jones.	Robert Hamilton - - -	80	Robert Hamilton.
YOUNGSTOWN.			Burgan Covert - - -	80	Burgan Covert.
Jonathan Smith - -	86	Jonathan Smith.	TURTLE CREEK.		
VERNON.			Richard Davis - - -	93	Richard Davis, jr.
Joseph De Wolf - -	73	Joseph De Wolf.	Daniel Staggs - - -	68	
Martin Smith - -	78	Martin Smith.	Elijah Pelham - - -	82	
Mary Beach - -	80	Mercy Beach.	Ezekiel Irvin - - -	80	Ezekiel Irvin.
Isaac Rice - - -	78	Phebe Rice.	Leonard Peckinpaugh - -	82	Leonard Peckinpaugh.
GUSTAVUS.			Abraham Storm - - -	85	Abraham Storm.
Wanton Berlingane - -	76	Wanton Berlingane.	WAYNE.		
Stephen Lindsley - -	79	Stephen Lindsley.	George Baine - - -	87	
Elijah Whipple - -	89		CLEAR CREEK.		
Luther Frisby - -	80		Anthony Bradenburg - -	77	
JOHN'S TOWN.			Richard Davis, sen. - -	83	
Sarah Webb - -	80	Nathan Webb.	Thomas Arnett - - -	82	Thomas Arnett.
Josiah Finney - -	84	Joseph Finney.	Peter Kesling - - -	90	Peter Kesling.
VIENNA.			Moses Cropley - - -	83	
Amasa Schoville - -	80	Amasa Schoville.	Daniel Gray - - -	91	
FOWLER.			Stephen Kinney - - -	78	John E. Kinney.
Peter De Wolf - -	82	Betsey Card	HAMILTON.		
Ahira Actley - -	79	Plin Actley	John Scott - - -	80	
Hannah Remmington - -	77	William P. Barnes.	John D. Bowers - - -	80	
Silas Jones - -	78	Silas Jones.	William Marts - - -	76	William Marts.
WARREN TOWNSHIP.			DEERFIELD.		
William Netterfield - -	89	William Netterfield.	John Clark - - -	84	B. Clark.
WARREN VILLAGE.			**WASHINGTON COUNTY.**		
Joseph Reeves - -	85	J. F. Reeves.	BELPRE.		
Oliver Brooks - -	82	Oliver J. Brooks.	Sherebiah Fletcher - -	78	Sherebiah Fletcher.
CHAMPION.			FEARING.		
John Gordon - -	81	Isaac Lane.	Barnabas Otis - - -	83	Barnabas Otis.
BRISTOL.			GRANDVIEW.		
Freeman Gates - -	74	Henry Chaffy.	Henry Franks - - -	91	William Ellis.
FARMINGTON.			LAWRENCE.		
Moses Burrows - -	95	Lorenzo D. Wilber.	Nancy Mitchell - - -	78	Nancy Mitchell.
Peter Bellows - -	83	Eli Young.	MARIETTA.		
SOUTHINGTON.			Christopher Burlingame -	87	John B. Burlingame.
Benjamin Mattsly - -	90	Daniel Mattsly.	NEWPORT.		
LORDSTOWN.			Oliver Woodward - -	91	Eleanor Wright.
Nathaniel Kelley - -	75	Nathaniel Kelley.	ROXBURY.		
JACKSON.			Andrew Dennis - - -	86	William Woodward.
Samuel Calhoon - -	87	Samuel Calhoon.	Ephraim Ellis - - -	76	Ephraim Ellis.
AUSTENTOWN.			SALEM.		
Wendle Grove - -	86	Henry Petre.	Ignatius Waterman - -	82	Ignatius Waterman.
Abraham Searl - -	92	Jesse Bailey.	UNION.		
WEATHERSFIELD.			Nathan Rice - - -	79	Nathan Rice.
John Newell - -	96	John Newell.	WARREN.		
Richard Shaw - -	89	Richard Shaw.	Rufus Inman - - -	77	Aaron Inman.
George Owry - -	87	William Johnston.	WATERFORD.		
MECCA.			John Payne - - -	79	John Payne.
James Cook - -	78	James Cook.	WATERTOWN.		
UNION COUNTY.			Peter Howe - - -	84	Elias H. Wolcott.
MILFORD.			WESLEY.		
James Willard - -	78	James Willard.	William Dunbar - - -	97	Daniel Dunbar.
PARIS.			Thomas Perry - - -	84	Thomas Perry.
Sally Hartwell - -	69	Ambrose Meeker.	Benajah Hays - - -	79	Benajah Hays.
JEROME.			**WOOD COUNTY.**		
Joseph McClung - -	40	Joseph McClung.	HENRY.		
MILL CREEK.			Jos. Badger - - -	83	
William Thompson - -	82	William Thompson.	**WAYNE COUNTY.**		
			PERRY.		
			Barnett Hagerman - -	80	

Names of pensioners for revolutionary or military services.	Ages.	Names of heads of families with whom pensioners resided June 1, 1840.	Names of pensioners for revolutionary or military services.	Ages.	Names of heads of families with whom pensioners resided June 1, 1840.
WAYNE—Continued. PLAIN.			**WAYNE—Continued.** MILTON.		
Augustus Case - - -	87		Benjamin Foster - - -	86	
			Benjamin Cotton - - -	83	William Cotton.
JACKSON.			GREEN.		
Ezra Tryon - - -	80		Conrad Metsker - - -	82	Conrad Metsker.
CANAAN.			EAST UNION.		
Rufus Freeman - - -	78		Jesse Richards - - -	84	James McFadden.
			Simon Goodspead - - -	76	Simpson Goodspead.
WAYNE.			WOOSTER.		
John Davidson - - -	84		Robert Cain - - -	57	
CHIPPEWA.			**WILLIAM COUNTY.**		
Christina Franks - - -	73	Christina Franks.	BRADY.		
Isaac Underwood - - -	74	Isaac Underwood.	James Hagaman - - -	85	John J. Hagaman.

STATE OF INDIANA.

Names of pensioners for revolutionary or military services.	Ages.	Names of heads of families with whom pensioners resided June 1, 1840.	Names of pensioners for revolutionary or military services.	Ages.	Names of heads of families with whom pensioners resided June 1, 1840.
ADAMS COUNTY. WABASH.			**CRAWFORD COUNTY.**		
George Emery - - -	87	William Shepherd.	Alexander Black - - -	80	Alexander Black.
			George Keesucker - - -	90	William Keesucker.
ALLEN COUNTY. WAYNE.			Jesse Toney - - -	78	Jesse Toney.
Michael Crance - - -	97	Michael Crance.	John Ruth - - - -	89	John Ruth.
PERRY.			**CLARK COUNTY.**		
Charles Weeks, sen. - -	79	Charles Weeks, sen.	Jacob Mikesell - - -	83	Jacob Mikesell.
CEDAR.			John Mitchill - - -	79	John Mitchill.
William Berry - - -	76	William Berry.	William Gobin - - -	82	William Gobin.
			John Brenton - - -	79	James McClary.
BARTHOLOMEW COUNTY. WAYNE.			Elias Kelly - - -	78	Jeremiah Perry.
Samuel M. Hall - - -	53	Samuel M. Hall.	Ezekiel Jenkins, sen. -	77	Ezekiel Jenkins, sen.
			Enos Tuttle - - -	78	Solomon Tuttle.
CLIFTY.			John Norris - - -	66	
Jonathan Moore - - -	86	Jonathan Moore.	Elijah Carl - - -	78	
Timothy Brown - - -	78	John Mittan.	Samuel Carr - - -	58	Samuel Carr.
ROCK CREEK.			**CASS COUNTY.**		
John Corney - - -	83	Pleasant Corney.	John W. Sutherland - -	75	Z. Sutherland.
COLUMBUS.			**CLAY COUNTY.** BOWLING GREEN.		
Solomon Tracy - - -	90	James Carter.	John Wheeler - - -	56	John Wheeler.
Stephen Goble - - -	81	Stephen Goble.	WASHINGTON.		
			Benjamin Wheeler - -	92	Benjamin Wheeler.
BLACKFORD COUNTY. LICKING.			JACKSON.		
David Kirkpatrick - -	76		Michael Crooks - - -	80	James Harland.
John Saxson - - -	75	John Saxson.	Lawrence Thompson - -	99	Thomas Wheeler.
			POSEY.		
BOONE COUNTY.			John Yocom - - -	96	Samuel Reffet.
			Richard Cunningham - -	84	Francis Cunningham.
John Kersey - - -	77	John Kersey.	PERRY.		
John McManis - - -	81	John Shelburn.	David Christy, sen. - -	68	David Christy, sen.
Joseph Wheatler - - -	79	Joseph Wheatler.	**DEARBORN COUNTY.**		
John Forgason - - -	86	John Forgason.	Ephraim Robbins - -	79	
Abram Utter - - -	75	Abram Utter.	John Dickson - - -	77	
			Nathan Ricketts - -	81	
BROWN COUNTY. WASHINGTON.			Robert Ricketts - -	75	
Abraham Floyd - - -	85	Abraham Floyd.	Francis McDonough - -	59	
			Timothy Ward, sen. -	89	
JOHNSON.			MANCHESTER.		
David Johnson - - -	85	David Johnson.	John Kiles - - -	84	Thomas Kiles.
William Wilkerson - -	101	William Wilkerson.			

INDIANA—Continued.

Names of pensioners for revolutionary or military services.	Ages.	Names of heads of families with whom pensioners resided June 1, 1840.	Names of pensioners for revolutionary or military services.	Ages.	Names of heads of families with whom pensioners resided June 1, 1840.
DEARBORN—Continued.			**FLOYD—Continued.**		
KELSO.			NEW ALBANY.		
Moses Hendrickson - -	95	Moses Hendrickson.	*Township.*		
James Skates - -	84	William Row.	Richard Jones - - -	73	Richard Jones.
William White, sen. - -	77	William White, sen.	Adam Hart - - -	81	Adam Hart.
MILLER.			William Wells - - -	78	Hiram Miller.
Job Judd - - -	86	Job Judd.	GREENVILLE.		
John C. Gibson - -	74	John C. Gibson.	Reuben Smith, sen. - -	83	Reuben Smith, sen.
Thomas James - -	85	Jehu Goodwin.	Ingram Mitchel - - -	83	Ingram Mitchel.
LAUGHERY.					
Peter Cabah - - -	83	Peter Cabah.	**FAYETTE COUNTY.**		
Samuel Marsh - -	79	Samuel Marsh.	ORANGE.		
John Baker - - -	78	John Baker.	Benjamin Pierce - - -	81	James Stevens.
DAVIESS COUNTY.			POSEY.		
			Nicholas Kemmer - - -	80	Nicholas Kemmer.
William Horrall - - -	86	William Horrall.			
George Lashly - - -	100	George Lashly.	WATERLOO.		
J. Rainey - - - -	83	J. Rainey.	Chris. Cunningham - -	60	Chris. Cunningham.
Charles Kilgore - -	76	Charles Kilgore.	CONNERSVILLE.		
DECATUR COUNTY.			James Justice - - -	90	Rosanna Justice.
Jeremiah J. Dogan - -	77	Jeremiah J. Dogan.	**GREENE COUNTY.**		
Edward Duncan - - -	83	Elijah W. Burris.	Joshua Burnett - - -	87	Joshua Burnett.
Thomas Hooton - - -	88	Hiram Hooton.	James Blevins - - -	79	James Blevins.
John Prichard - - -	78	John Prichard.	Edward Purcell - - -	81	Jesse Purcell.
John Demoss - - -	88	John Demoss.	Daniel Woodsworth - -	88	Daniel Woodsworth.
Elijah Barnes - - -	85	Absalom Barnes.	Joseph Lawrence - - -	86	Joseph Lawrence.
Charles Harry - - -	79	Charles Harry.	Adam Stropes - - -	48	Adam Stropes.
John Gullion - - -	77	Thomas Gullion.	John Buskirk - - -	83	Joseph Buskirk.
Benjamin Gosnell - -	80	Benjamin Gosnell.	John Chaney - - -	82	Henry Burch.
William McCoy - - -	81	William McCoy.	Francis Lang - - -	79	Francis Lang.
Joseph Collins - - -	84	Joseph Collins.	**GIBSON COUNTY.**		
DELAWARE COUNTY.			PATOKA.		
			John Witherspoon, sen. -	83	John Witherspoon, sen.
John Quin - - -	82	John Quin.	Robert Skelton, sen. - -	47	Robert Skelton, sen.
William Williams - -	78	William Williams.	James Wheeler - - -	82	James Wheeler.
William Wicker - -	81	Asa Wicker.	JOHNSON.		
DUBOIS COUNTY.			John Pritchett - - -	84	Elisha Pritchett.
James Harbison, sen. - -	81	James Harbison, sen.	**HARRISON COUNTY.**		
ELKHART COUNTY.			HARRISON.		
			Alexander Gilmore - -	72	Alexander Gilmore.
William Tuffs - - -	92	James Selders.	HEATH.		
John Maxon - - -	49	John Maxon.	Joseph McClelan - - -	75	Joseph McClelan.
William Wilson - -	103	William Wilson.	FRANKLIN.		
FRANKLIN COUNTY.			Patrick Hunter - - -	80	Patrick Hunter.
David Gray, sen. - -	92	David Gray, sen.	WASHINGTON.		
Samuel Meredith - -	85	Samuel Meredith.	Philip Acres - - -	86	Philip Acres.
Hezekiah Stiles - -	79	Freeman Aulger.	POSEY.		
James Ryan - - -	67	James Ryan.	James Johnson - - -	82	James Johnson.
John Mann - - -	90	John Mann.	Hanson Johnson - - -	77	Hanson Johnson.
Joseph Runnels - -	77	Joseph Runnels.	James Case - - -	79	James Case.
William Wiggons - -	97	William Sherwood.	BLUE RIVER.		
Henry Eads - - -	85	John Quick.	Thomas Reneau - - -	80	Thomas Reneau.
John Low - - -	77	John Low.	John Williams - - -	84	John Williams.
William Symes - -	80	Thomas Symes.	**HENDRICKS COUNTY.**		
Zachariah Cookry - -	83	Zachariah Cookry.	Edward Flothers - - -	90	Edward Flothers.
John Colyear - - -	84	John Colyear.	Daniel Higgins - - -	90	Daniel Higgins.
John Portlock - - -	77	John Portlock.	Thomas Hardin - - -	81	Noah Hardin.
Peter Griner - - -	99	Thomas Meredith.	W. Sacree - - -	73	Abram Spicklemore.
FULTON COUNTY.			John Ward - - -	90	John Ward.
James Porter - - -	36	James Porter.	**HENRY COUNTY.**		
FOUNTAIN COUNTY.			PRAIRIE.		
TROY.			Andrew Ice - - -	84	Jesse Ice.
Robert McIntyre - -	75	John Bodly.	FALL CREEK.		
WABASH.			Michael McDormit - -	69	Michael McDormit.
Enos Davis - - -	77	Samuel Campbell.	LIBERTY.		
FLOYD COUNTY.			James Stevenson - - -	86	Robert Boyd.
NEW ALBANY.			Richard Conaway - - -	75	Richard Conaway.
City.					
Epaphras Jones - - -	76	Epaphras Jones.			

INDIANA—Continued.

Names of pensioners for revolutionary or military services.	Ages.	Names of heads of families with whom pensioners resided June 1, 1840.
HENRY—Continued.		
HENRY.		
Aaron Dunn	84	John Dunn.
STONEY CREEK.		
John Pearce	61	John Pearce.
DUDLEY.		
Isaac Cocks	87	William H. Smith.
WAYNE.		
Jacob Morris	78	William Deaver.
HAMILTON COUNTY.		
WHITE RIVER.		
Levi Holloway	107	Ebenezer Holloway.
FALL CREEK.		
John Hare	83	John Hare.
JACKSON.		
Isaac Hamman	79	Isaac Hamman.
ADAMS.		
William Cutts	87	William Cutts.
HANCOCK COUNTY.		
BROWN.		
Mosby Childers	93	Mosby Childers.
JONES.		
Mr. Lawson	57	
CENTRÉ.		
Robert Wilson	95	
JACKSON COUNTY.		
Robert B. Smith	54	Robert B. Smith.
Benjamin Scott	86	John Scott.
Christian Branaman	82	Christian Branaman.
Thomas Prather	78	Basil Prather.
David Benton	76	Walter Benton.
Michael Bierly	82	Michael Bierly.
Daniel Ross	88	Martha Ross.
John Russell	96	John Russell.
Samuel Lee	77	John L. Young.
Philip Langdon	80	Philip Langdon.
JAY COUNTY.		
Peter Mason	76	
James Campbell	77	James Campbell.
JEFFERSON COUNTY.		
LANCASTER.		
David Sutton	64	David Sutton.
SHELBY.		
Samuel Welch	76	Samuel Welch.
Sally Robinson	100	Jos. Tague.
John Conor	88	John Conor.
William Hall, sen.	95	William Hall, sen.
SALUDA.		
Thomas Arbuckel	95	John Arbuckel.
Jos. McCume	87	
JOHNSON COUNTY.		
Matthias Parr	83	James Parr.
Abner Hanks	77	Abner Hanks.
John Parr	81	Abraham Jones.
Joshua Harris	83	Joshua Harris.
John Duke	100	Washington Duke.
James Kerr	84	James Kerr.
JENNINGS COUNTY.		
Samuel Smith	80	James P. Smith.
William Messerve	79	William Messerve.
John Stagg	80	John Stagg.
William Howlett	82	William Howlett.
Amasa Spencer	87	Amasa Spencer.
JENNINGS—Continued.		
Heth Frederick	77	Heth Frederick.
Michael Courtney	83	Woods Courtney.
Charles Haney	81	Charles Haney.
Philo Stodard	75	Philo Stodard.
Frederick Kyser	84	Frederick Kyser.
KNOX COUNTY.		
Moses Knight	87	
Daniel Langton	81	Daniel Langton.
John Parker, sen.	76	John Parker, sen.
William Purcell	79	William Purcell.
Philip Catt	91	Philip Catt.
Michael Thorn	78	Michael Thorn.
William J. Welton	51	William J. Welton.
William McCord	80	
Cornelius Merry	77	Cornelius Merry.
Peter McNelly	85	
George Snapp	89	George Snapp.
LAGRANGE COUNTY.		
VAN BUREN.		
David Cowan	78	David Cowan.
GREENFIELD.		
Morgan Young	85	Morgan Young.
LAPORTE COUNTY.		
Abijah Bigelow	78	Herbert Williams.
Peter Bladley	53	Peter Bladley.
Simeon Wheeler	79	George Bentley.
Frederick Drollinger	87	Gabriel Drollinger.
LAWRENCE COUNTY.		
Zachariah Godfrey	64	Zachariah Godfrey.
John Henderson	79	John Henderson.
David Biles	89	David Biles.
George Sipes	81	George Sipes.
Alexander Reed	85	Alexander Mitchell.
Leonard Houston	48	Leonard Houston.
MONTGOMERY COUNTY.		
BROWN.		
Alexander Foster	83	Alexander Foster.
COLE CREEK.		
Thomas Mason	79	William Mason.
Matthias Hanlon	89	Matthias Hanlon.
MADISON.		
Presley Sims, sen.	90	Presley Sims, sen.
MARION COUNTY.		
FRANKLIN.		
Thomas Wells	74	
James Acheare	71	
James Dobbing	79	
WARREN.		
Joseph Rouse	91	
Thomas Griffin	84	
WAYNE.		
Benjamin Miller	90	James Miller.
Robert Caldwell	85	William McVey.
PERRY.		
Charles Orms	79	Moses Orms.
John M. Johnston	75	John M. Johnston.
Alexander Monroe	85	Jos. Wallace.
John George	84	John Stuck.
Edward Hall	80	Edward S. Hall.
PIKE.		
John Humes	79	Thomas Humes.
WASHINGTON.		
Stephen Pitts	41	Stephen Pitts.

INDIANA—Continued.

Names of pensioners for revolutionary or military services.	Ages.	Names of heads of families with whom pensioners resided June 1, 1840.	Names of pensioners for revolutionary or military services.	Ages.	Names of heads of families with whom pensioners resided June 1, 1840.
MORGAN COUNTY.			**PERRY**—Continued.		
Devoult Keller	86		Thomas Bowlin	77	Thomas Bowlin.
Mordecai Miller	86		Lemuel Mallory	77	Lemuel Mallory.
David Irwin	85		**PARKE COUNTY.**		
Benjamin Utterback	85		David Johnson	79	Isaac Johnson.
George F. Baker	84		Jacobus Hines	78	Jacobus Hines.
Thomas Smith	77		Jesse Duncan	85	William Green.
MARSHALL COUNTY.			Samuel Musgrove	80	Samuel Musgrove.
William Bailey	56	William Bailey.	William Long	80	William W. Clark.
MONROE COUNTY.			Larkin Lane	79	Alexander Lane.
Nicholas Fluner	52		Daniel Stringham	75	R. H. Wedding.
Isaac Buskins	81		Abel Hall	86	Abel D. Hall.
George W. Hardin	46		**PUTNAM COUNTY.**		
John Back	81		CLINTON.		
Andrew Ferguson	82		Thomas Rhoten	85	Thomas Rhoten.
William Wilkison	105		Isaiah Slavens	75	Isaiah Slavens.
MARTIN COUNTY.			FLOYD.		
John Hopper	93		William Shepherd	80	William Shepherd.
Garret Vores	89	Garret Vores.	FRANKLIN.		
ORANGE COUNTY.			Robert Whitehead	79	Robert Whitehead.
PAOLI.			JEFFERSON.		
Zachariah Lindley	64	Zachariah Lindley.	Isaac Armstrong	81	Crawford Tuggle.
Meredith Tongate	51	Meredith Tongate.	GREENCASTLE.		
ORLEANS.			Laban Hall	87	Abel D. Hall.
William Irvin	78	William Irvin.	Peter Stoner, sen.	77	Peter Stoner, sen.
Joshua Nichols	85	Martin Nichols.	Elizabeth Cunningham	69	Benjamin S. Cunningham.
NORTHEAST.			MARION.		
Julius Turner	51	Julius Turner.	Samuel Denny	85	Isaac Storm.
SOUTHEAST.			Benjamin Mehornay	79	Owen Mehornay.
Isam Stroud	49	Isam Stroud.	MADISON.		
OWEN COUNTY.			Nimrod H. Stone	75	Thomas C. Duckworth.
GRAYSON.			John A. Miller	80	John A. Miller.
James Lloyd	50	*James Lloyd.	Andrew McPheters	79	Andrew McPheters.
JEFFERSON.			**POSEY COUNTY.**		
Philip Greenwood	85	Philip Greenwood.	PLYM.		
HARRISON.			John Walker	80	John Walker.
Elijah Lacy	76		George Nelson	80	George Nelson.
WAYNE.			SMITH.		
Bartlet Asher	77		Jos. McReynolds	70	Jos. McReynolds.
Andrew Evans	81		NEW HARMONY.		
MONTGOMERY.			John Six	80	John Six.
John McCully	85		**RIPLEY COUNTY.**		
Samuel Newel	86		JACKSON.		
John Snoddy	82		Edward Pendergast	70	Edward Pendergast.
FRANKLIN.			John Tucker	80	John Tucker.
John Carpenter	85		Jacob Dawers	79	Jacob Dawers.
CLAY.			Conrad Dowers	76	Conrad Dowers.
Obadiah Turpin	81		James Delapp	85	Nathaniel Delapp.
Peter Withirn	77		Henry Myers	93	Lewis Myers.
Hugh Barnes	67		DELAWARE.		
WASHINGTON.			John Burchfield	74	John Burchfield.
James Bryant	91		Robert Burchfield	81	Robert Burchfield.
Thomas Ashbrook	82		Samuel Gookins	78	Asa Gookins.
PORTER COUNTY.			Daniel Welch	77	Esau King.
Henry Battin	91	George W. Turner.	JOHNSON.		
PIKE COUNTY.			Lemuel Chapman	82	
Isaac Fisher	76		Isaac Levi	91	Martin Levi.
PERRY COUNTY.			John Boldry	84	Samuel Boldry.
James Lanman	90	George Lanman.	Samuel Marquest	81	Benjamin Richardson.
Terence Conner	84	Terence Conner.	Ephraim Wilson	84	Henry Wilson.
			RANDOLPH COUNTY.		
			STONEY CREEK.		
			Samuel Ambrom	79	Samuel Ambrom.
			Drummond Smithson (does not draw pension yet)	85	Drummond Smithson.
			NETTLE CREEK.		
			Robert Lumpkin	84	Robert Lumpkin.

INDIANA—Continued.

Names of pensioners for revolutionary or military services.	Ages.	Names of heads of families with whom pensioners resided June 1, 1840.	Names of pensioners for revolutionary or military services.	Ages.	Names of heads of families with whom pensioners resided June 1, 1840.
RANDOLPH—Continued.			**SWITZERLAND—Continued.**		
WASHINGTON.			YORK—Continued.		
William Fitzjerrell -	97	William Fitzjerrell.	Robert Gulion - -	76	Robert Gulion.
GREEN'S FORK.			**SULLIVAN COUNTY.**		
Chris. Borders - -	79	William B. Borders.	Robert Bedwell, sen. -	80	Robert Bedwell, sen.
JACKSON.			Matthew McCammon -	85	Edward Neal.
Jos. Chandler - -	87	Henry Chandler.	James Williams - -	77	Stephen Williams.
Elias Porter - -	84	Elias Porter.	William Dougherty -	78	William Dougherty.
			Jos. Ransford - -	78	William Ransford.
RUSH COUNTY.					
NOBLE.			**ST. JOSEPH COUNTY.**		
Joel Berry - -	86	Holsworth Berry.			
John Carson - -	79	John Carson.	James Wilson - -	59	James Wilson.
Michael Smith - -	77	Hugh Smith.	Isaac Ross - -	80	Isaac Ross.
RICHLAND.			John Mead - -	75	Eli B. Mead.
John Riley - -	89	John Riley.	**SPENCER COUNTY.**		
Henry Smith - -	76	Henry Smith.	Zachariah Bryant -	75	Zachariah Bryant.
ORANGE.			Nicholas Miller -	77	Barney Miller.
John Aldridge - -	79	Nathan Aldridge.	David Chancellor -	84	John Smith.
James Fordice - -	77	Thomas F. Smith.	Lodowick Davis -	76	Lodowick Davis.
RUSHVILLE.			**TIPPECANOE COUNTY.**		
John Robinson -	85	John Robinson, jr.	SHEFFIELD.		
POSEY.			Henry Miller - -	81	Henry Miller.
Mary Collins - -	75	Andrew McRoberts.	John Wright - -	80	John Stean.
JACKSON.			TIPPECANOE.		
James Hunt - -	85	James Hunt.	James Shaw - -	82	James Shaw, sen.
Henry David - -	78	Henry David.	WABASH.		
CENTRE.			Isaac Davidson -	98	William W. Robinson.
George Isham - -	81	Robert Brooks.	**UNION COUNTY.**		
SCOTT COUNTY.			Matthew McClerkin -	85	Matthew McClerkin.
			Rowly McMillan -	96	Rowly McMillan.
William Hopper, sen. -	–	William Hopper, sen.	**VERMILION COUNTY.**		
John McCornent -	55	John McCornent.	HELT.		
John Young - -	–		Francis Malone -	80	Jos. Malone.
Shedrick Pierson, sen. -	86		John Hancrous -	83	Jeremiah Hancrous.
John Clark - -	80		Richard Mack -	74	Richard Mack.
David King - -	51		Abraham White -	78	Abraham White.
Benjamin Spader -	78		**VIGO COUNTY.**		
SHELBY COUNTY.			RILEY.		
ADDISON.			William Ray (since dead) -	90	
John Thomas - -	77	Buckner Candel.	LOST CREEK.		
Joseph Boon - -	72	Joseph Boon.	Walter Dickerson -	78	W. Dickerson.
BLACK HAWK, IN JACKSON.			**VANDERBURG COUNTY.**		
Elisha Collins - -	49	Elisha Collins.	PIGEON.		
LIBERTY.			Charles Harrington -	42	
Isaac Wheeler - -	78	Isaac Wheeler.	**WARREN COUNTY.**		
HANOVER.			John Osborn - -	77	
John Watson - -	81	John Watson.	David Nichols - -	71	
Robert Gordon - -	85	James Vanskoyke.	**WASHINGTON COUNTY.**		
SWITZERLAND COUNTY.			WASHINGTON.		
PLEASANT.			Micajah Callaway -	83	Micajah Callaway.
Stephen Rogers - -	80	Henry Rogers.	FRANKLIN.		
Charles Steward -	82	Charles Steward.	James Gainson -	78	James Gainson.
JEFFERSON.			Thomas Flower -	77	Thomas Flower.
John M. King - -	42	John M. King.	JACKSON.		
POSEY.			Jesse Alvis - -	81	William Johnson.
William Preston -	75	William Preston.	John Galamore -	78	John Galamore.
William Buck - -	77	Morton Buck.	Benjamin Buckman -	81	Benjamin Buckman.
Thomas Mountz -	76	Thomas Mountz.	VERNON.		
COTTON.			William King - -	87	William King.
Andrew Stepleton -	96	Andrew Stepleton.	William Moore -	82	William Moore.
Stephen G. Peabody -	45	Stephen G. Peabody.	MONROE.		
Daniel Heath - -	83	Daniel Heath.	William Bowman -	80	Isabella Stuart.
Thomas Porter -	78	James Porter.	Nathaniel Chambers -	99	Nathaniel Chambers.
YORK.			Buckner Daniels -	79	Buckner Daniels.
Abraham Scudder -	77	William Scudder.			

24

STATE OF INDIANA.

Names of pensioners for revolutionary or military services.	Ages.	Names of heads of families with whom pensioners resided June 1, 1840.	Names of pensioners for revolutionary or military services.	Ages.	Names of heads of families with whom pensioners resided June 1, 1840.
WASHINGTON—Continued.			**WAYNE**—Continued.		
BROWN.			RICHMOND.		
Joel Corkins - - -	81	Joel Corkins.	Francis Jones - - -	75	
Samuel Vest - - -	81	Samuel Vest.	George Holman - - -	77	George Holman.
WAYNE COUNTY.			WAYNE.		
NEW GARDEN.			Richard Rue - - -	81	Henry Ransford.
Benjamin Bishop - -	82		John Dougan - - -	77	John Dougan, jr.
CENTER.			WASHINGTON.		
Abram Hendershot - -	96		Jacob Forry - - -	85	Jacob Forry.
JEFFERSON.			**WARRICK COUNTY.**		
Stephen Fox - - -	81		OHIO.		
GREEN.			John Alexander - -	84	Thomas Alexander.
William Cook - - -	80		HART.		
Nimrod Jester - - -	78		William Williams - -	85	William Williams, jr.

STATE OF ILLINOIS.

Names of pensioners for revolutionary or military services.	Ages.	Names of heads of families with whom pensioners resided June 1, 1840.	Names of pensioners for revolutionary or military services.	Ages.	Names of heads of families with whom pensioners resided June 1, 1840.
ADAMS COUNTY.			**CALHOUN COUNTY.**		
QUINCY CITY.					
Second ward.			Isaac Ruland - - -	54	Isaac Ruland.
Stephen Jones - - -	77	Moses Jones.	**DU PAGE COUNTY.**		
Third ward.					
Israel Walters - - -	55	Israel Walters.	Parker Chase - - -	77	S. Dodge.
Albert Ammerman - -	49	Albert Ammerman.	John Dudley - - -	82	John Dudley.
Richard Rose - - -	81	Richard Rose.	Thomas Mattison - -	86	Stephen Mattison.
Charles Shepherd - -	86	Benjamin Ramsey.	**DEWITT COUNTY.**		
BOND COUNTY.			John Scott - - -	77	John Maxwell.
Joseph McAdams - -	87	James McAdams.	Peter Cartwright - -	81	Samuel Cartwright.
Huldah Briggs - -	73	William H. Draper.	**DEKALB COUNTY.**		
Peter Hubbard - -	84	Peter Hubbard.	None.		
BROWN COUNTY.			**EDGAR COUNTY.**		
Mitchell Kindrick - -	50	Mitchell Kindrick.	James Ewing - - -	35	James Ewing.
BUREAU COUNTY.			Daniel Rowell - - -	80	James Wilson.
			Lucretia Hotchkiss - -	71	Lucretia Hotchkiss.
Aaron Sturgess - -	80	Aaron Sturgess.	William Gannon - -	95	Henry Penington.
CRAWFORD COUNTY.			**EFFINGHAM COUNTY.**		
George Baythe - -	85		Martha J. Brockett - -	85	Thomas J. Brockett.
COLES COUNTY.			**FRANKLIN COUNTY.**		
John Tutwiler - - -	83	A. Wiley.	William McElyea - -	82	William McElyea.
James Ryan - - -	83	James Ryan.	John Scarborough - -	79	John Scarborough.
Joseph Frost - - -	87	Joseph Frost.	Moses Jones - - -	80	Moses Jones.
CLINTON COUNTY.			**FULTON COUNTY.**		
			TOWNSHIP 5.		
Joseph Taylor - - -	55	Joseph Taylor.	Christopher Zoll - -	88	Henry Zoll.
CLAY COUNTY.			James Kitchen - - -	77	William Hall.
Samuel Parks - - -	93		TOWNSHIP 8.		
Moses Johnson - - -	100		Robert Beer - - -	97	Robert Beer.
Nathaniel West - - -	90		Jones Cline - - -	75	Jones Cline.
CLARK COUNTY.			TOWNSHIP 6 N. 5 E.		
			Alexander Wilson - -	47	Alexander Wilson.
Samuel McCure - -	90	Samuel McCure.	Hezekiah Hardesty - -	77	Richison Spencer.
CARROLL COUNTY.			R. C. Rowley - - -	88	R. C. Rowley.
			FAYETTE COUNTY.		
Daniel Christian - - -	85	George W. Christian.	Henry Ginger - - -	94	William Rodger.

ILLINOIS—Continued.

Names of pensioners for revolutionary or military services.	Ages.	Names of heads of families with whom pensioners resided June 1, 1840.	Names of pensioners for revolutionary or military services.	Ages.	Names of heads of families with whom pensioners resided June 1, 1840.
FAYETTE—Continued.			**LA SALLE COUNTY.**		
WESTERN DIVISION.					
James Verdon - - -	88	James Verdon.	Henry Misner, sen. - -	84	Henry Misner, sen.
GREENE.COUNTY.			**MONROE COUNTY.**		
Francis Miller - - -	96	David Miller.	James McRoberts - - -	78	James McRoberts.
John Hewitt - - -	79	John Hewitt.	John Jerrod - - -	48	John Jerrod.
John Clark - - -	75	Absalom Clark.	Peter Rodgers - - -	86	Peter Rodgers.
Allen J. Bridges - - -	80	Allen J. Bridges.	Michael Miller - - -	86	Jesse Wiswell.
James Garrison - - -	99	Edward Flatt.	**MORGAN COUNTY.**		
Jonah Scroggin - - -	77	R. H. Scroggin.	James Wright, sen. - -	84	James Wright, sen.
Adonijah Griswold - - -	88	Adonijah Griswold.	Samuel Jackson - - -	86	Samuel Jackson.
GALLATIN COUNTY.			A. Tanner - - -	86	
Mr. Tong - - -	90	Thomas Tong.	Reuben Ross - - -	78	Reuben Ross.
William Roark - - -	78	Michael Roark.	William Springer - - -	67	
John Barger - - -	46	John Barger.	Samuel Brown - - -	76	
Reuben Bramlett - - -	82	Reuben Bramlett.	**MONTGOMERY COUNTY.**		
Abner Foster - - -	81	Abner Foster.	James Richardson - - -	82	James M. Rutlidge
John Emmet - - -	81	James Barker.	Mason Owen - - -	80	Mason Owen.
Joseph Mings - - -	85	Daniel Miner.	Ezra Bostick - - -	86	Ezra Bostick.
Thomas Hamilton - - -	84	Thomas Hamilton.	**MERCER COUNTY.**		
John Thadowen - - -	85	John Thadowen.	Jane Meadows - - -	71	William Meadows.
William Bolton - - -	40	William Bolton.	**MENARD COUNTY.**		
John Lamb, sen. - - -	84	John Lamb, sen.	Lewis Fergerson, sen. - -	80	Lewis Fergerson, sen.
HAMILTON COUNTY.			Joshua Short - - -	90	James Short.
None.			William Hohimer - - -	42	William Hohimer.
HANCOCK COUNTY.			Benjamin Walker - - -	82	James Walker.
Charles Betteworth - - -	79	D. Betteworth.	**McLEAN COUNTY.**		
Samuel Colwell - - -	77	Samuel Colwell.	Abner Case - - -	64	Abner Case.
JEFFERSON COUNTY.			John C. Karr - - -	81	Tharasco Karr.
George Roper - - -	78	George Roper.	William McGhee - - -	84	William McGhee.
Francis Haney - - -	86	William Hicks.	**McDONOUGH COUNTY.**		
JACKSON COUNTY.			William Willard - - -	89	
Zachariah Linsley - - -	85	Zachariah Linsley.	**MARION COUNTY.**		
Jesse Gordon - - -	85	Jesse Gordon.	Samuel Young - - -	80	Matthew Young.
Robert Fry - - -	85	Robert Fry.	Peter Finn - - -	90	William Layson.
IROQUOIS COUNTY.			Michael Lutrell - - -	89	Elizabeth Sheltor.
Thomas Williamson - - -	79	Thomas Williamson.	**MACOUPIN COUNTY.**		
JO DAVIESS COUNTY.			Uriah Gilmore - - -	99	Seburne Gilmore.
Jeremiah Bettis - - -	49	Jeremiah Bettis.	Robert Busby - - -	84	Lewis Harmon.
JOHNSON COUNTY.			Samuel Brown - - -	76	Alexander Montgomery.
Samuel J. Chapman - - -	46	Samuel J. Chapman.	Joshua Richardson - - -	79	Joshua Richardson.
Hezekiah West - - -	76	Hezekiah West.	**MADISON COUNTY.**		
Daniel Chapman - - -	80	Daniel Chapman.	Michael Deck - - -	89	Michael Deck.
KNOX COUNTY.			William McAdam - - -	83	Aaron Rule.
Samuel Chapin - - -	80	Gustavus Volvridge.	Francis Roach - - -	101	David Roach.
John Strange - - -	94	John Strange.	William Hall, sen. - -	88	William Hall, sen.
KANE COUNTY.			Benjamin Johnson - - -	82	Benjamin Johnson.
Nathan Brown - - -	87	Nathan Brown.	Martin Pruitt - - -	93	Solomon Pruitt.
Daniel Burroughs, sen. - -	85	Daniel Burroughs, sen.	John Cornelison - - -	82	W. C. Johns.
William Bennett - - -	86	William Bennett.	Anthony A. Harrison - -	77	William L. Harrison.
LAWRENCE COUNTY.			Asa Brooks - - -	48	Asa Brooks.
John T. Vandeventer - -	48	J. T. Vandeventer.	William Bates - - -	82	William Bates.
James Thompson - - -	27	James Thompson.	Richard Randle - - -	88	Richard Randle.
William Melton - - -	82	Benjamin Melton.	**OGLE COUNTY.**		
Benjamin Melton - - -	76	Benjamin Melton.	Aaron Payne - - -	50	Aaron Payne.
John Struple - - -	45	A. Andrews.	**POPE COUNTY.**		
James Gibson - - -	49	James Gibson.	Arthur Hagan - - -	41	
Thomas West - - -	52	Thomas West.	Daniel Hancock - - -	78	

ILLINOIS—Continued.

Names of pensioners for revolutionary or military services.	Ages.	Names of heads of families with whom pensioners resided June 1, 1840.	Names of pensioners for revolutionary or military services.	Ages.	Names of heads of families with whom pensioners resided June 1, 1840.
PIKE COUNTY.			**TAZEWELL—Continued.**		
Samuel Reagan	48	Samuel Reagan.	Basil Meeks	79	Basil Meeks.
John Patterson	50	John Patterson.	**UNION COUNTY.**		
Horace S. Holladay	56				
David Kehr	78	Jane Watson.	George Brown, sen.	78	George Brown, sen.
David Callier	48	David Callier.	**VERMILION COUNTY.**		
Elias Scouton	66	Elias Scouton.			
Hugh McNary	79	James McNary.	Martha Hulse	78	John Johnson.
Nathaniel Perrin	78	Nathaniel Perrin.	Huldah Bolton	66	Jonathan Patterson.
			Joseph Coughran	74	William Fields.
PERRY COUNTY.			Jacob Gundy	73	Joseph Gundy.
			Robert Bailey	85	Robert Bailey.
W. C. Murphy	40	William C. Murphy.			
Leonard Lipe	77	Leonard Lipe.	**WILLIAMSON COUNTY.**		
John Banes	80	John Banes.			
			John Painter	84	John Painter.
PEORIA COUNTY.			Benajah Gill	80	Benajah Gill.
			John G. Lumpkins	84	John G. Lumpkins.
William Crow	81	James Crow.			
Winney Rhinearson	51	Winney Rhinearson.	**WILL COUNTY.**		
John Montgomery	75	John Hines.			
Phineas Bronson	76	Phineas Bronson.	Ebenezer Collins	—	John V. Singer.
James Pierce	52				
			WHITESIDE COUNTY.		
RANDOLPH COUNTY.					
			Alexander Thompson	82	Alexander Thompson.
William Sharp	78				
			WHITE COUNTY.		
SANGAMON COUNTY.					
			Nathan Gaggers	81	Anna Driggers.
			Mathias Parr	85	Edmund Thomason.
Philip Crowder	80	Philip Crowder.	Henry Morgan	87	Henry Morgan.
Joel Maxcy	78	Joel Maxcy.	Daniel Powell	48	Daniel Powell.
John Overstrett	80	Dabna Overstrett.	Daniel Chapman	70	Daniel Chapman.
John Lockridge	79	William A. Lockridge.	Joseph Hawthorn	84	William Hawthorn.
Joseph R. Young	32	J. R. Young.			
			WAYNE COUNTY.		
ST. CLAIR COUNTY.					
			John H. Mills	79	John H. Mills.
Moses Land, sen.	76	Moses Land.	Thomas Sloan	79	Thomas Sloan.
Hosea Rigs	80	Hosea Rigs.	James Stuart	78	James Stuart.
			George Clark	84	George Clark.
SHELBY COUNTY.					
			WASHINGTON COUNTY.		
John Jenkins	87	Van. C. Dawson.			
Zebedee Smith	46	Zebedee Smith.	George Brown	88	George Brown.
			M. S. McMillon	33	M. S. McMillon.
SCOTT COUNTY.			Thomas McClerken, sen.	95	Thomas McClerken, sen.
			James Thompson	36	James Thompson.
Margaret Stout	83	Nathaniel Stout.			
John Clarke	69	Jacob Bryan.	**WARREN COUNTY.**		
Louisa McEvers	78	Seneca McEvers.			
			Benjamin Blankenship	80	Benjamin Blankenship.
SCHUYLER COUNTY.			William Willard	89	John Willard.
			David Lynn	76	Samuel Lynn.
Anna Hinman	68	W. Hinman.			
Moses Justice	85	Moses Justice.	**WABASH COUNTY.**		
			Jonathan Goss	80	Jonathan Goss.
TAZEWELL COUNTY.			Nathaniel Hendryx	85	Nathaniel Hendryx.
			Andrew Tuttle	81	Andrew Tuttle.
Norman Newell	79	Thomas Brooks.	Alexander Stewart	90	Alexander Stewart.
Eliot Gray	85	Eri Gray.	Allen Ramsey	76	Allen Ramsey.

STATE OF MISSOURI.

Names of pensioners for revolutionary or military services.	Ages.	Names of heads of families with whom pensioners resided June 1, 1840.	Names of pensioners for revolutionary or military services.	Ages.	Names of heads of families with whom pensioners resided June 1, 1840.
BUCHANAN COUNTY.			**CHARITON COUNTY.**		
MARION.					
Page Stanley - - -	40	Page Stanley.	Charles Finnell - - -	77	
BOONE COUNTY.			**CLAY COUNTY.**		
PERSIA.					
Elizabeth Burks - -	78	George Sexton.	James Wells - - -	78	David Wells.
			James Sewell - - -	80	James Sewell.
MISSOURI.			James Crowley - - -	75	James Crowley.
Robert Lemon - -	85	Robert Lemon.	John Evans - - -	64	John Evans.
Reuben Hatton - -	78	Reuben Hatton.	Richard Simms - -	86	Richard Simms.
William Pennington -	55	William Pennington.	John Majors - - -	81	Elisha Majors.
Samuel Elgin - -	82	Samuel Elgin.	**CARROLL COUNTY.**		
CEDAR.			WACONDA CREEK TOWNSHIP.		
Abrm. Grindstaff -	45	Abrm. Grindstaff.	William Goodson - - -	80	William Goodson.
Gershom Fleeke -	43	Gershom Fleeke.	**COLE COUNTY.**		
COLUMBIA.			JEFFERSON TOWNSHIP.		
Ann Gentry - -	49	Ann Gentry.	William L. Cearnel - -	38	Archibald Cearnel.
William Armstrong -	82	John Reed.	Jos. Kingry - - -	73	Greenbury Kingry.
ROCKY FORK.			Christopher Casey - -	88	Hardin Casey.
Radford McCargo -	78	Radford McCargo.	JEFFERSON CITY.		
John Deavenport -	48	John Deavenport.	Robert Raphael - - -	21	Philip Megerle.
John Connelly -	78	Sanford Connelly.	WALKER.		
John Reams -	58	John Reams.	Enoch Tobe - - -	80	Enoch Tobe.
BARRY COUNTY.			**COOPER COUNTY.**		
SMITH.			CLARK'S FORK.		
William Lumley - -	82	William Lumley.	Edward Robertson - -	85	Edward Robertson.
Augustin Sims - -	78		**LEBANON.**		
Samuel Nelson - -	88		Robert Kirkpatrick - -	77	John Read.
Charles Dildy - -	77	Charles Dildy.	MANITEAU.		
Thomas Walker - -	90	Thomas Walker.	Hugh Larremore - -	81	R. Larremore.
CALLAWAY COUNTY.			James Kelly - - -	86	James Kelly.
BOURBON.			**DAVIESS COUNTY.**		
Robert S. Russel -	79	Robert S. Russel.	John Hamilton - - -	90	
Abel Dood - -	76	Thomas Miller.	**FRANKLIN COUNTY.**		
CEDAR.			BŒUFF.		
Thomas Boyd - -	79	Thomas Boyd.	Judith Miller - - -	75	Nicholas Shukman.
FULTON.			BOWLES.		
Jesse D. Oldham -	48	Jesse D. Oldham.	John Pritchett - - -	48	John Pritchett.
James Thomas -	77	George Thomas.	CALVARY.		
Samuel Bowles -	90	Thomas Bowles.	George W. Elliott - -	48	George W. Elliott.
George Harding -	84	George Harding.	**GREENE COUNTY.**		
NINE MILE PRAIRIE.			Samuel Steel - - -	77	Caleb Headlee.
Henry Overley - -	76	Pearson W. Overley.	Thomas Thompson - -	79	Malcom McDougal.
CÔTE-SANS-DESSEIN.			**GASCONADE COUNTY.**		
Sylvester Baker - -	83	A. J. Baker.	Jesse Evans - - -	81	
CAPE GIRARDEAU COUNTY.			**HOWARD COUNTY.**		
APPLE CREEK.			RICHMOND.		
Thomas Hill - -	79	Thomas Hill.	James Noble - - -	82	Robert Shaw.
BYRD.			PRAIRIE.		
Ithamer Huble - -	78	Ithamer Huble.	Edward Williams - -	79	Edward Williams.
LORANCE.			William Burton - -	84	James Wallace.
James Hutchison - -	82	James Hutchison.	**JEFFERSON COUNTY.**		
RANDLE.			MERRIMAC.		
David McLane - -	82	David McLane.	William Drinning, sen. -	76	William Drinning, sen.
Robert Brevard - -	76	Robert Brevard.	**JACKSON COUNTY.**		
CRAWFORD COUNTY.					
MERRIMAC.			Jacob Stuart - - -	57	Jacob Stuart.
Levi Arthur -	–	Levi Arthur.	**JOHNSON COUNTY.**		
Thomas Snelson - -	84	Mary Snelson.	JACKSON.		
LIBERTY.			Moses Ferguson, sen. -	78	Moses Ferguson, sen.
William Mitchell - -	76	William Mitchell.			
CORTOIS.					
Jarret Bricky - -	83	Jarret Bricky.			
WATKINS.					
John Welch - -	86	John Welch.			

MISSOURI—Continued.

Names of pensioners for revolutionary or military services.	Ages.	Names of heads of families with whom pensioners resided June 1, 1840.	Names of pensioners for revolutionary or military services.	Ages.	Names of heads of families with whom pensioners resided June 1, 1840.
LINCOLN COUNTY.			**POLK COUNTY.**		
HURRICANE.			BENTON.		
James Cannon - - -	82	James Cannon.	Bracket Davison - - -	46	B. Davison.
William Butler - -	84	William Butler.	VAN BUREN.		
			John Burnes - - -	48	John Burnes.
WOODSON.					
Thomas Hampton - -	81	John S. Besser.	**PLATTE COUNTY.**		
Joseph Brown - - -	86	Shadrach Woodson.	Frederic McLinn - - -	46	Frederic McLinn.
CLARK.			Sabert Sellers - - -	84	Mahala Sollers.
John Chambers - - -	110	James Chambers.	James Potter - - -	81	Bently Potter.
Michael Glass - - -	78	Charles Helfly.			
Hezekiah Murphy - -	74	Hezekiah Murphy.	**RAY COUNTY.**		
			RICHMOND.		
MACON COUNTY.			John Sconce - - -	49	John Sconce.
CHARITON.					
Nicholas Tuttle - - -	82	Pleasant Tuttle.	FISHING RIVER TOWNSHIP.		
			Abram Hill - - -	81	William Hill.
LIBERTY.					
Bennet Tilley - - -	89	Bennet Tilley.	**RANDOLPH COUNTY.**		
Henry Linch - - -	80		Daniel Rardin - - -	61	Daniel Rardin.
GOSHEN.					
James Fletcher - - -	83	Elias Fletcher._	**RALLS COUNTY.**		
			SPENCER.		
MADISON COUNTY.			Robert Jamerson - - -	84	Willis M. Jamerson.
LIBERTY.			CLAY.		
Robert Sinclaire - - -	83	Charles Sinclaire.	Rodam Sims - - -	86	Lewis Garnet.
TWELVE-MILE TOWNSHIP.			SALT RIVER.		
Samuel Burks - - -	77	William Burks.	Ignatius Granville - - -	90	William Little.
William Boren - - -	74	Sarah Ann Duncan.	Samuel Turner - - -	87	Samuel Turner.
MARION COUNTY.			**RIVES COUNTY.**		
ROUND GROVE.			LEABO.		
William Jeffries - - -	83	James W. Jeffries.	William Baylis - - -	81	William Baylis.
Anderson Long - - -	80	Anderson Long.			
			ST. LOUIS COUNTY.		
LIBERTY.			CITY OF ST. LOUIS.		
William Pollard - - -	79	William Pollard.	Alphonso Wetmore - - -	–	Alphonso Wetmore.
MILLER COUNTY.			BONHOMME.		
HENRY.			D. Martin - - - -	44	Mrs. Molly Martin.
Andrew Salisbury - -	96	William J. McKay.			
			ST. FERDINAND.		
MONTGOMERY COUNTY.			J. D. Putnam - - -	48	John Putnam.
DANVILLE.					
William Hall - - -	79	William Hall.	**ST. CHARLES COUNTY.**		
			PORTAGE.		
LOWER LOUTRE.			Reuben Bernus - - -	30	James A. Eads.
Peter Rock - - -	92	Andrew Hunter.			
			CUIVRE.		
MONROE COUNTY.			Mary Zumwalt - - -	74	Solomon Zumwalt.
JACKSON.					
John Kippers - - -	79	Samuel Kippers.	ST. CHARLES.		
			William Turney - - -	67	William Turney.
SOUTH FORK.					
Nealey Bybee - - -	77	Nealey Bybee.	**ST. GENEVIEVE COUNTY.**		
			BOVEY.		
MORGAN COUNTY.			William R. Brown - - -	84	John S. Brown.
RICHLAND.			**ST. FRANCOIS COUNTY.**		
John Chitcoat - - -	80	John Chitcoat.	ST. FRANCOIS.		
			James Cunningham - -	84	James Cunningham.
PIKE COUNTY.					
SPENCER.			**SHELBY COUNTY.**		
Zachariah Birch - - -	83	Zachariah Birch.	Jesse Brown - - -	45	Jesse Brown.
CALUMET.					
John Mulherrin - - -	85	William Mulherrin.	**STODDARD COUNTY.**		
William Sherwood - -	80	John Calvin.	Benjamin Taylor - - -	79	Benjamin Taylor.
CUIVRE.					
Cornelius Beazly - - -	82	Jacob Rhoades.	**SALINE COUNTY.**		
			MARION.		
PETTIS COUNTY.			Benjamin Chambers - -	76	Benjamin Chambers.
BOWLING GREEN.			Joshua Roberts - - -	75	Joshua Roberts.
Jonathan James - - -	46	Jonathan James.			
			SCOTT COUNTY.		
FLAT CREEK.			MORELAND.		
George Cathey - - -	85	James McCormick.	Uriah Brock - - -	79	Hartwell Brock.

MISSOURI—Continued.

Names of pensioners for revolutionary or military services.	Ages.	Names of heads of families with whom pensioners resided June 1, 1840.	Names of pensioners for revolutionary or military services.	Ages.	Names of heads of families with whom pensioners resided June 1, 1840.
VAN BUREN COUNTY. OSAGE.			**WASHINGTON COUNTY.** UNION.		
James McHenry - - -	78	John McHenry.	John Bailey - - -	85	John Bailey.
			John Hawkins - - -	80	John Hawkins.
WARREN COUNTY. CHARETTE.			John Paul - - - -	80	John Paul.
Benjamin Sharp - - -	78	Benjamin Sharp.	BELVIEW.		
John Wyatt, sen. - - -	81	John Wyatt, sen.	Edward Thomas - -	85	Reuben Thomas.
			HARMONY.		
			Thomas Sherley - -	85	Jordan Sherley.

STATE OF ARKANSAS.

Names of pensioners for revolutionary or military services.	Ages.	Names of heads of families with whom pensioners resided June 1, 1840.	Names of pensioners for revolutionary or military services.	Ages.	Names of heads of families with whom pensioners resided June 1, 1840.
WASHINGTON COUNTY.			**JACKSON COUNTY.**		
Warren Philipott - - -	84	Warren Phillpott.	Joel Hill - - - -	78	Joel Hill.
Henry Scott - - -	28	Cyrus Galbraith.			
Aaron Smith - - -	75	George Taylor.	**INDEPENDENCE COUNTY.**		
Martin Randleman - - -	79	Jonathan Holden.			
Samuel Gregg - - -	83	Henry Gregg.	Benjamin Harden - -	77	E. L. Harden.
James Leeper - - -	79	James Leeper.			
John Liggett - - -	77	William Mayfield.	**HEMPSTEAD COUNTY.**		
Redding Putman - - -	48	Redding Putman.			
			James Williams - -	78	J. W. Williams.
SCOTT COUNTY.			Eli Collins - - -	83	William R. Collins.
			William Black - -	85	William Black.
Peter Richie - - -	98	James Richie.			
			CRAWFORD COUNTY.		
PIKE COUNTY.					
			William Orrick - -	85	Samuel Orrick.
Wilson Jenkins - - -	80	Jesse Jenkins.			
			BENTON COUNTY.		
MARION COUNTY.					
			John Robinson - -	81	J. H. Morrison.
Obadiah Wood - - -	95	William Wood.			
			RANDOLPH COUNTY.		
MADISON COUNTY.					
			Edward Hutson - -	84	Edward Hutson.
James Gage - - -	86	Jacob Gage.			
James Stewart - - -	87	Pleasant Stewart.	**POPE COUNTY.**		
Daniel Sutherland - -	85	John Holmon.			
			Daniel Cownover - -	77	Daniel Cownover.
LAWRENCE COUNTY.					
			SALINE COUNTY.		
William McKnight, sen. -	80	William McKnight, sen.			
			Asher Bagley - -	89	Asher Bagley.
JOHNSON COUNTY.			Benjamin Bryant - -	80	Benjamin Bryant.
Philip Jones - - -	78	Philip Jones.			

STATE OF MICHIGAN.

Names of pensioners for revolutionary or military services.	Ages.	Names of heads of families with whom pensioners resided June 1, 1840.	Names of pensioners for revolutionary or military services.	Ages.	Names of heads of families with whom pensioners resided June 1, 1840.
ALLEGAN COUNTY.			**LENAWEE COUNTY.**		
MARTIN.			Thomas Gratton - - -	83	
Jeremiah Selerieg - -	-	James Selerieg.	WOODSTOCK.		
BERRIEN COUNTY.			Abram Osborn - - -	85	Samuel Osborn.
BERTRAND.			Thomas Swartwout - -	83	Andrew Swartwout.
John Silsby - - -	56	John Silsby.	RAISIN.		
CASS COUNTY.			Lophario Donaldson - -	75	Lophario Donaldson.
HOWARD.			BLISSFIELD.		
Jonathan Wells - - -	50	Jonathan Wells.	Samuel Black - - -	77	Luther Smith.
SILVER CREEK.			**MONROE COUNTY.**		
James Selleck - - -	78	James Selleck.	RAISINVILLE.		
MASON.			Asher Seaton - - -	78	Salmon Owen.
Jotham Curtiss - - -	84	Jonathan Curtiss.	LONDON.		
CHIPPEWA COUNTY.			William Perryburn - -	84	John G. Thayer.
Abel Bingham - - -	54	A. Bingham.	DUNDEE.		
CALHOUN COUNTY.			Samuel Stone - - -	76	Samuel Stone.
SHERIDAN.			Martin Smith - - -	57	Martin Smith.
Wealthy Chamberlain -	70	Julius Chamberlain.	MONROE CITY.		
MARSHALL.			1st ward.		
Jonathan Babcock - -	76	A. C. Babcock.	George Alfred - - -	76	George Alfred.
ALBION.			4th ward.		
Polly Finch - - -	71	Abel Finch.	Stephen Downing - -	78	Stephen Downing.
BURLINGTON.			**MICHILIMACINAC COUNTY.**		
Charles Meseroll - -	98	John L. Meseroll.	Jonas Stone - - -	60	Jonas Stone.
GENESEE COUNTY.			Nathan Puffer - - -	70	Isaac Blanchard.
Reuben Robinson - -	82	J. N. Robinson.	**MACOMB COUNTY.**		
Samuel Roam - - -	52	Samuel Roam.	CLINTON.		
HILLSDALE COUNTY.			William Olds - - -	69	T. Turner.
CAMDEN.			MACOMB.		
L. Laraby - - -	73	T. Laraby.	B. Howard - - -	70	B. Howard.
READING.			**OAKLAND COUNTY.**		
George Fitzsimmons -	48	George Fitzsimmons.	ADDISON.		
SCIPIO.			Derrick Hulick - - -	81	Dennis Snyder.
Daniel Couch - - -	76	Uriah B. Couch.	ROYAL OAK.		
ADAMS.			Ezra Parker - - -	95	W. M. Parker.
S. Sharp - - -	47	S. Sharp.	TROY.		
SOMERSET.			Zadoc Wellman - -	79	Joel Wellman.
Edmund Pratt - -	87	Heman Pratt.	Esbon Gregory - -	80	Jesse Gregory.
Peter Havens - ⸱ -	78	Peter Havens, jr.	AVON.		
INGHAM COUNTY.			Nathaniel Baldwin - -	79	Freeman Burch.
LE ROY.			HOLLY.		
Mary Brink - - -	74	Lewis S. Rouse.	Elias Cady - - -	80	Elias Cady.
JACKSON COUNTY.			Altamont Donaldson -	77	Altamont Donaldson.
SANDSTONE.			NOVI.		
Catharine Lightall -	108	Benjamin Huntley.	Hooper Bishop - -	85	
EAST PORTAGE.			WHITE LAKE.		
Rhodes Hall - -	82	William Hall.	John Blanchard - -	77	
JACKSON.			Jos. Brace - - -	74	
Abiathar Lincoln - -	82	Jotham Wood.	Benjamin Brace - -	79	
Jos. C. Darling - -	76	Chris. C. Darling.	**SHIAWASSEE COUNTY.**		
John N Van Austin -	65	David Adams.	VERNON.		
John Gibson - - -	88	T. Ruggles.	Ebenezer Brown - -	50	Ebenezer Brown.
William J. Moody - -	44	William J. Moody.	**ST. JOSEPH COUNTY.**		
COLUMBIA.			SHERMAN.		
David Haynes - -	78	P. E. Haynes.	Ahira Brooks - - -	81	Ahira Brooks.
GRASS LAKE.			MOTTVILLE.		
Adam Overocker - -	79	Adam Overocker.	Thaddeus Gilbert - -	88	George Gilbert.
LAPEER COUNTY.			LEONIDAS.		
METAMORA.			Esther Watkins - -	73	Levi Watkins.
James Banker - - ⸱	89	James Banker.	Esther Madden ⸱ - -	75	William Orcutt.

MICHIGAN—Continued.

Names of pensioners for revolutionary or military services.	Ages.	Names of heads of families with whom pensioners resided June 1, 1840.	Names of pensioners for revolutionary or military services.	Ages.	Names of heads of families with whom pensioners resided June 1, 1840.
ST. CLAIR COUNTY.			**WASHTENAW—Continued.**		
CLYDE.			SALINE.		
Richard Bean - - -	49	R. Bean, jr.	Archibald Armstrong - -	81	Archibald Armstrong.
COTTRELLVILLE COUNTY.					
			WAYNE COUNTY.		
Edward Locke - - -	50	Edward Locke.	Jonathan Kearsley - -	54	Jonathan Kearsley.
Thomas Fargo - - -	82	Samuel Ward.	Henry Myers - - -	45	Henry Myers.
VAN BUREN COUNTY.			John Winchell - - -	43	
LAWRENCE.			Elizabeth Trowbridge - -	79	
James Stevens - - -	83	Allen Briggs.	Edward Vickney - - -	–	
DECATUR.			Abram Cook - - -	65	Abram Cook.
William Dyckman - -	77	E. B. Dyckman.	**VAN BUREN.**		
HARTFORD.			Abner Rawson - - -	76	
Ira Allen - - - -	54	Ira Allen.	**DEARBORN.**		
WASHTENAW COUNTY.			Edward Howard - - -	84	Joshua Howard.
			James Randall - - -	45	John McVey.
Martin Dubois - - -	77	J. D. Dubois.	**REDFORD.**		
John Thompson - - -	79		David Smead - - -	74	
Elijah Drake - - -	80	Flemon Drake.	John Woodward - - -	77	
YPSILANTI.			David Warren - - -	60	
Ebenezer Hawkins - -	75	E. Hawkins.	Bennet Joy - - -	45	
SALEM.			**CANTON.**		
Vespasian Hoisington - -	78	Vespasian Hoisington.	Jacob Rutenaw - - -	81	George Rutenaw.
John L. Shear - - -	56	John Shear.	**BROWNSTOWN.**		
YORK.			Michael Vrelandt - - -	80	Curren Vrelandt.
John Stoddard - - -	43	John Stoddard.	**NANKIN.**		
Daniel French - - -	55	Daniel French.	Hubbel Stevens - - -	80	A. L. Stevens.

TERRITORY OF FLORIDA—WESTERN DISTRICT.

Names of pensioners for revolutionary or military services.	Ages.	Names of heads of families with whom pensioners resided June 1, 1840.	Names of pensioners for revolutionary or military services.	Ages.	Names of heads of families with whom pensioners resided June 1, 1840.
WALTON COUNTY.			**ESCAMBIA COUNTY.**		
Joab Horn - - -	86	Joab Horn.	Amanda M. Dade - - -	24	
Aaron Snowden - - -	73	Aaron Snowden.	Mary S. Wilkinson - -	20	

EASTERN DISTRICT.

Names of pensioners for revolutionary or military services.	Ages.	Names of heads of families with whom pensioners resided June 1, 1840.	Names of pensioners for revolutionary or military services.	Ages.	Names of heads of families with whom pensioners resided June 1, 1840.
CITY OF ST. AUGUSTINE.			**NASSAU COUNTY.**		
			Amos Latham - - -	85	Amos Latham.
Ambrose Cooper - - -	35	Ambrose Cooper.	John D. Vaughan - - -	73	John D. Vaughan.
Crecencio Pacetty - - -	29	Crecencio Pacetty.	**DUVAL COUNTY.**		
William Coates - - -	22	Francis Newcomer.			
Martin Stephens - - -	26	Martin Stephens.	John S. Pickitt - - -	26	John S. Pickitt.

CENSUS OF PENSIONERS.

FLORIDA—MIDDLE DISTRICT.

Names of pensioners for revolutionary or military services.	Ages	Names of heads of families with whom pensioners resided June 1, 1840.	Names of pensioners for revolutionary or military services.	Ages.	Names of heads of families with whom pensioners resided June 1, 1840.
LEON COUNTY.			GADSDEN—Continued.		
Rhesa Oliver - - -	84	Rhesa Oliver	John Fletcher - - -	76	Zaberd Fletcher.
HAMILTON COUNTY.			William Rawls - - -	79	Nealle Anderson.
Henry Pennington - - -	38	Henry Pennington.	MADISON COUNTY		
GADSDEN COUNTY.			Charlotte Davis - - -	35	Charlotte Davis.
			Elizabeth Triplet - - -	25	Elizabeth Triplet.
Bozeman Ralph - - -	78	Bozeman Ralph.	Sarah Flinn - - -	35	Sarah Flinn.
			Martha Langford - - -	35	Martha Langford.

APPALACHICOLA DISTRICT.

WASHINGTON COUNTY.			JACKSON COUNTY.		
Josiah Jones - - -	85	Josiah Jones.	Richard Levens - - -	100	
Evans Andrews - - -	74	Evans Andrews.			

TERRITORY OF WISCONSIN.

Names of pensioners for revolutionary or military services.	Ages.	Names of heads of families with whom pensioners resided June 1, 1840.	Names of pensioners for revolutionary or military services.	Ages.	Names of heads of families with whom pensioners resided June 1, 1840.
BROWN COUNTY.			IOWA COUNTY.		
James Singleton - - -	35	James Singleton.	John McNear - - -	45	John McNear.
GRANT COUNTY.			RACINE COUNTY.		
			Helmont Kellogg - - -	77	Seth H. Kellogg.
David Marshall - - -	51	Lemuel Gillham.	JEFFERSON COUNTY.		
Joseph H. Dickson - - -	35	Joseph Dickson.	Eliada Brown - - -	76	Enoch G. Darling.
GREENE COUNTY.			WALWORTH COUNTY.		
George McFadden - - -	35		William F. Lyon - - -	74	William F. Lyon.
Robert Baley - - -	75				

TERRITORY OF IOWA.

Names of pensioners for revolutionary or military services.	Ages.	Names of heads of families with whom pensioners resided June 1, 1840.	Names of pensioners for revolutionary or military services.	Ages.	Names of heads of families with whom pensioners resided June 1, 1840.
LEE COUNTY.			DES MOINES COUNTY		
George Perkins - - -	89	George Perkins.	Daniel Baine - - -	71	Daniel Baine.
CLINTON COUNTY.			John McDonald - - -	86	Hugh McDonald.
John Lepper - - -	79	George Parker.	DUBUQUE COUNTY.		
HENRY COUNTY.			Sarah Hensling -	82	John Dawson.
Charles Shepherd - - -	82	Charles Shepherd.			

CENSUS OF PENSIONERS.

DISTRICT OF COLUMBIA.

Names of pensioners for revolutionary or military services.	Ages.	Names of heads of families with whom pensioners resided June 1, 1840.	Names of pensioners for revolutionary or military services.	Ages.	Names of heads of families with whom pensioners resided June 1, 1840.
WASHINGTON CITY.			**WASHINGTON—Continued.**		
Richard Suter - - -	55	Richard Suter.	Cornelia Lansdale - - -	75	John F. Cox.
Mrs. Eator - - -	26		**ALEXANDRIA CITY.**		
Jacob Gideon, sen., (since dead) -	86	Jacob Gideon, jun.			
			Morriss Pearce - - -	51	Thomas Wiley.
WASHINGTON COUNTY.			John Pipsecow - - -	88	
			Dorcas Henderson - - -	82	John Simms.
Joseph Nourse - - -	87	Joseph Nourse.	Lawrence Hurdle - - -	81	Lawrence Hurdle.

[The return for Carter county, Kentucky, is inserted below, not having been received in time to appear in its proper place.]

STATE OF KENTUCKY—CARTER COUNTY.

Names of pensioners for revolutionary or military services.	Ages.	Names of heads of families with whom pensioners resided June 1, 1840.	Names of pensioners for revolutionary or military services.	Ages.	Names of heads of families with whom pensioners resided June 1, 1840.
Elzaphan Rucker - - -	57	Elzaphan Rucker.	William Bates - - -	77	Rial M. Jones.

A General Index

to

A CENSUS OF PENSIONERS FOR REVOLUTIONARY OR MILITARY SERVICE 1840

Prepared by

THE GENEALOGICAL SOCIETY

of the

Church of Jesus Christ of Latter-Day Saints

Salt Lake City, Utah

Originally Published
Baltimore, 1965

Reprinted
Genealogical Publishing Co., Inc.
Baltimore, 1974, 1989, 1996

Publisher's Notice

This is an index to the pensioners on the rolls in 1840 (as obtained from the population census schedules) who were listed in 1841 in the Department of State's unindexed publication *A Census of Pensioners for Revolutionary or Military Services; with Their Names, Ages, and Places of Residence . . . Under the Act for Taking the Sixth Census.* This *Index* eliminates the tedious requirement of searching out individual names, for it contains all the names in the *Census,* including the heads of families with whom the pensioners resided. The arrangement is alphabetical, with Christian names grouped under the generic family name, followed by the number of the page or pages where the name is found in the *Census.* An asterisk placed after a name indicates that such a person was the head of the famliy with whom the pensioner resided.

The *Index* has been reproduced from a typescript prepared by the Genealogical Society of the Church of Jesus Christ of Latterday Saints in Salt Lake City and kindly lent to us for publication as the companion volume to our former reprint of the unindexed *Census* named above.

Library of Congress Catalogue Card Number 65-25482
International Standard Book Number 0-8063-0346-8

Copyright © 1965
Genealogical Publishing Co., Inc.
Baltimore, Maryland
All rights reserved

Made in the United States of America

A

CENSUS OF PENSIONERS

For

REVOLUTIONARY OR MILITARY SERVICES;

INDEX

Achmet,
    Hamet 59*

Ackart,
    David 51
    Solomon 51

Ackeley,
    Isaac C. 60*

Acker,
    Benjamin 104
    Christian 114

Ackerman,
    Christopher 124
    Cornelius 107*
    John 174*

Ackerson,
    Cornelius 75
    William 75

Ackler,
    Adam 83
    *Amos 126
    Katharial 83
    *Josiahs 83
Ackley,
    Francis 71*
    Marian 49

Acock,
    Robert 167*

Acre,
    Simeon 145

Acree,
    James 154*

Acres,
    Philip 182*

Actley,
    Ahira 180
    Plin 180

Actman,
    John 114

Acton,
    Smallwood 161*

Acuff,
    Mary 157

Adair,
    John 167*

Adam,
    Samuel C. 56*

Adams,
    Aaron 85*, 162*
    Abigail 65*
    Abrazus 15
    Adam 127
    Alanson 61*
    Amos 13
    Ansel 26*
    Benjamin 40, 61*, 64, 164
    Daniel 23, 41
    David 21, 143, 150*, 192
    Dolly 41
    Ebenezer 105*
    Edmond 83
    Elias 38*
    Elijah 174
    Elisha 174
    Elizabeth 45, 171
    Enoch 19, 37
    Esther 19
    Francis 146*
    George W. 164
    Hannah 57
    Hannah P. 8
    Heman 169
    Horace 88
    Horatio 86
    J. 122
    James 124*
    Jedediah 119
    Jemima 8
    Joan 40
    John 15*, 16, 19, 33*, 64, 91*,
      122
    Jonas 21, 71*
    Jonathan 31, 37*
    Joseph 15, 57, 69
    Levi 76*
    Margaret 16
    Martha 18*
    Melas 85
    Micajah 154*
    Miriam 36*
    Molly 21
    Moses 10, 177*

Adams, (cont.)
    Nehemiah 41
    Patty 64
    Peter 24, 28*, 167
    Peter B. F. 167
    Philip 67*
    Rebecca 8
    Reuben 37, 157
    Rhoda 88
    Roswell 54, 69
    Ruth 85
    Samuel 8, 64, 171*
    Silas 171
    Stephen 64
    Sumner 84
    Susan 11
    Susanna 57
    Susannah 10
    Thomas 16, 85*, 172*
    Timothy 37, 71*
    William 31, 40*, 53, 54,
       75*, 120, 163*

Addis,
    Richard 143

Addison,
    Jacob 176*
    John 5
    William 164*

Addoms,
    John T. 78

Adkins,
    David 59
    Edward 165
    Isaiah 125*
    John 134*
    Nathan 137
    Thomas 165, 167*
    William 137

Adley,
    Peter 14*

Adlington,
    John 28*

Adock,
    Joshua (sr.) 137*

Adye,
    Caleb 74

Agard,
    John 177*
    Noah 76

Aggings,
    Hugh 108*

Agly,
    Jacob 122

Aiken,
    Asa 71
    Israel 71
    Martha 16*
    Susanna 71
    Thomas 56

Aikens,
    John 17*, 97
    Mary 97

Aikin,
    James 103*

Ailstock,
    Absalom 136*

Ailsworth,
    George 158*

Ainstead,
    Elizabeth 84

Ainsworth,
    Walcome 64*

Akart,
    Peter 94*

Akeley,
    R. 67
    Thomas 67

Akens,
    James 145*

Akeright,
    Isaac 122*

Akin,
    James 154*

Akins,
    James 144*
    Lyman P. 98
    Miriam 41
    Sarah 98

Akley,
    Samuel 7*

Albaugh,
    Zachariah 175*

Albe,
    Reuben 33*

Albee,
    Ichabod 21*
    John 36

Alber,
    Caleb 39*

Albert,
    William 47*

Albright,
    John 78

Albro,
    Andrew 95*
    Stephen 90

Albu,
    Asa 34
    Asa H. 34

Alcox,
    Lydia 53*

Alden,
    Adam 67
    Eliab 102*
    Elijah 30, 36
    Humphrey 30
    Isaiah 29*
    Judah 29*
    Nathan 29*
    Polly 67
    Simeon 31*

Aldhoff,
    Joseph 116

Aldrich,
    Arnold 39
    Caleb 17*
    Huldah 46*
    Jared C. 88
    Joel 46*
    John 48
    Joshua 77*
    Luke 48
    Mary 5
    Milton 24
    Noah 69*
    Olive 46
    Welcome 46

Aldridge,
    John 185
    Nathan 185

Aldritch,
    G. B. 76
    Nathan 39

Alen,
    Selathial 80

Aleshire,
    Conrad 136
    Henry 136
    John C. 135

Alexander,
    (Mr.) 149*
    Abner 155
    Abram 63*
    Amos 22*
    Bathsheba 92
    Benjamin 90
    Consider 69
    Dorcas 160
    Elijah 156*
    Eliphaz 75*
    Elisha 34
    George 150*
  * H. S. 69
    Jacob 173
    James 137*
    Jeremiah 150
    Jerusha 160
    John 186
    John G. 160
    John T. 160
    Josiah 34
    Mary 69
    Matthew 142, 159*
    McIntosh 90
    Peter 167
    Quartus 69
    Robert 117*, 173*
    Samuel 34, 137*
    Simeon 34
    Sylvester 95
    Thomas 139*, 186
    Thompson 117
    William 24*
    * Jabez 23*
Alfin,
    William 138*

Alford,
    Aber 51*
    Asahel 83
    Cyrus 83
    Elizabeth 62

Alfred,
    George 192*

Alger,
    James 30*
    Rebecca 47

Algiar,
    Sebastian 112

Alky,
    Harry 51

All,
    James 112

Allan,
    Nathan 128*

Allard,
    Samuel H. 18

Allbee,
    Jonathan 14

Allen,
    Abel 80*
    Abigail 43, 52, 104
    Abner 24
    Abraham 81*
    Adam 171
    Ambrose 43*
    Amos 82, 100*
    Ann 128
    Anna 31
    Arnold 50*
    Asaph 64*
    Barsham 3*
    Benjamin 10, 93
    Catharine 44, 129*
    Charles 31, 131, 142*, 158*
    Cynthia 10
    Cyrus 63*
    Daniel 8, 11*, 52, 66
    David 6, 32*
    Diarca 24
    Ebenezer 12, 65
    Electa 59
    Elijah 97
    Elizabeth 31, 47, 160*
    Emery 5
    Esther 66
    Ezra 93
    George 135
    Gideon 74
    Hannah 45, 65*
    Hezekiah 79

Allen,
    Horace 79
    Ira 193*
    Isaac 5*, 43*, 93
    Isaac F. 25
    Jabez 45
    Jacob 3*, 6*, 77*, 100*, 176
    James 131, 145*, 154*
    Jeremiah 88*
    Job 6*
    Joel 80*
    John 10*, 112, 118*, 120
    Joseph 5
    Joshua 111
    Josiah 111
    Luther 43
    Lydia 66, 79*
    Mabel 52*
    Margaret 98
    Mary 21*, 49*, 128
    Moses 158*
    Nathan 30
    Nathaniel 43
    Nehemiah 6
    Nelson 12
    Obed 65
    Oliver 104
    Parthena 24
    Penuel 23
    Peter L. 62*
    Phebe 50
    Philander 24
    Philip 85*
    Phineas 75
    Reuben 6
    Roger 59
    Rufus 8
    Russell 59
    Sally 66
    Samuel 45, 98, 135, 139*
    Samuel G. 71*
    Seth 82*
    Stephen 55*, 73, 98
    Stephen H. 73
    Sumner 75
    Susan 27
    Susannah 8, 176
    Thomas 27*
    William 6, 55*, 87*, 120, 138,
        146*
    William C. 101*
    Zimri 74

Allerson,
    William T. 153

Allerton,
    John 170*

Alley,
　　Ephraim 8
　　Isaiah 155
　　John 8
　　Otis 7
　　Thomas 155

Allgodd,
　　John 153*
　　William 141*

Alling,
　　Timothy 51

Allis,
　　Moses 175
　　Stephen 34*
　　William 175
Allison,
　　Birch 137*
Allmar,
　　Winny 139*

Allread,
　　Elias 146*

Allton,
　　Daniel 57
　　Sarah 57

Almond,
　　John 132*

Almoney,
　　John 154*

Almy,
　　John 47*
　　Peleg 47*
　　Sanford 47*

Alshouse,
　　David 114

Alsobrook,
　　Jesse 149*

Alsworth,
　　Andrew 123
　　James 121

Alvard,
　　Dorothy 36

Alven,
　　Silas 15

Alverson,
　　Elijah 158*
　　John 46*
　　John S. 164*

Alvin,
　　Eliphalet 6

Alvis,
　　Elizabeth 130*
　　Jesse 185

Alvord,
　　Jacob B. 78
　　John 55
　　Nancy 78
　　Nehemiah B. 55

Ambler,
　　Abigail 69*
　　Hannah 55
　　Thomas 55

Ambrom,
　　Samuel 184*

Ament,
　　Anthony 163*

Ames,
　　Abi 66
　　Amos 29
　　Baker 7
　　Daniel 54*
　　David 95
　　Deborah 12
　　Dorcas 41
　　Elijah 97*
　　Elisha 125*
　　Erasmus 54
　　Hannah 54
　　Jacob 13
　　Nathaniel 89*
　　Rufus 58
　　Samuel 7, 59*, 78
　　Simeon 41

Amidon,
　　Titus 44*

Amlaw,
　　Agat 78
　　Mary 78*

Ammerman,
　　Albert 186*

Ammerman, (cont.)
  Powell P. 74
  Richard 74

Amos,
  Henry 169
  Mordecai 169, 173*

Amsdem,
  Elihu 82
  Isaac 82

Amsden,
  Isaac 91
  Noah 85*
  William 91

Amsdill,
  Abner 80

Andas,
  Philip 122

Anders,
  David 145
  Owen 145

Anderson,
  Abigail 49
  Abraham 120
  Addy 120
  Alexander 29, 156, 157
  Allen 16
  Andrew 133*
  Armisted 167
  Armisted D. 167
  Asa 69
  Barton 9
  Charles 102*, 132*
  Daniel 135*
  David 34
  Ellis 61
  Francis 47
  Henry W. 78
  Hiram 97
  Jacob 132*, 136*
  James 34, 145*, 153*, 173*
  John 110*, 118*
  Jordan 129*
  Lemuel 93*
  Michael 44
  Nealle 194
  Norman 50
  Robert 6, 9, 166*
  Sally 163
  Samuel 80

Anderson, (cont.)
  Samuel P. 6
  Sarah 135
  Thomas 16*, 61
  Timothy 50
  William 80, 145*, 178*

Andress,
  Henry 30*
  Samuel 9*

Andrew,
  Ephraim 14

Andrews,
  A. 187
  Asa 6
  Asa W. 78
  Benjamin 16, 58, 94
  Benjamin H. 58

  Betsey 67
  Betty 78
  Carmi 27
  Ebenezer 69
  Eli 89
  Elkaneh 128*
  Ethan 71*
  Evans 194*
  George 48*
  Hugh 139*
  Isaac 20*
  Isham 129*
  Joanna 41*
  John 18*, 116, 117*, 159*
  Jurial 69
  Lemuel 35
  Lois 72
  Mark 82*
  Mary 32
  Moses 34*
  N. 170
  Nathan 27
  Nathan A. 27
  Nathaniel 170
  Olive 27
  Phineas 124*
  Reuben 94
  Rhoda 50
  Richard 76*
  Robert 5*
  Samuel 61, 91*, 138
  Sarah 47*
  Selah 50
  Silas 51
  Solomon 67
  Stephen 35
  Thomas 128*

Andrews, (cont.)
  Timothy 78*
  Varney 132*
  William 42*, 79*
  William F. 42*

Andros,
  Jonathan 49*
  Thomas 27*

Andrus,
  Abigail 51
  Catharine 51
  Henry 51
  Samuel 79
  Sophia 51

Angel,
  John 141*
  Lucy 68*
  Stukely 70

Angell,
  Fenna 45*
  Joshua 46
  Stephen 35

Anger,
  Jesse 63*

Angevine,
  Stephen 91*

Angier,
  Elizabeth 38

Angle,
  Augustus 101*
  Daniel 102
  Jacob 102

Anglin,
  Henry 146*

Angurs,
  Justus 66

Annabel,
  John 42

Annies,
  Jacob 75*

Annin,
  Daniel 105
  Joseph 111*
  Samuel 105

Annis,
  Martha 82
  Sally 44
  William 44

Ansen,
  Phebe 104

Anthony,
  Burrington 45
  Christopher 96
  George 111*
  Gideon 86*
  John 96, 144
  Margaret 48*
  Richard 94*
  Susanna 45

Antle,
  Dorcus 163

Apgar,
  Adam J. 109

Aplin,
  Job 28
  William 45

Apperson,
  Elizabeth (Mrs.) 141
  Thomas 141

Apple,
  Henry 97
  Thiciam 97

Applebee,
  Benjamin 3
  James 17
  Simeon 3
  Thomas 17
  William 17*

Applegate,
  Bartholomew 110*
  Daniel 110
  John R. 109
  Matthias 110
  William 110*
  Zebulon 170

Arant,
  Peter 144*

Arbuckel,
  John 183
  Thomas 183

8

Arbuckle,
    James 160*

Arbuthnot,
    Samuel 117*

Archer,
    E. 165
    Edmund 165
    John W. 100
    Obediah 100
    Stephen 104

Archey,
    Jeremiah 119*

Arey,
    Abraham 140*

Argrove,
    Leven 142*

Arkley,
    Ithamar 80*

Arlin,
    Daniel 18*

Armistead,
    William 149*

Armsbry,
    John 94*

Armsby,
    Brownell 27
    Joseph 97*
    Lemuel M. 27

Armstrong,
    Adam 83
    Archibald 133, 193*
    Bela 82
    Cheney 54
    Ebenezer 176*
    Elijah 95*
    George 179
    Henry 160
    Horatio G. 127
    Isaac 184
    J. M. 98
    James 39, 123*
    Jeremiah 69*
    Jesse 46
    Job 46
    John 79, 127, 130, 156
    Joseph 130
    Launcelot 149

Armstrong, (cont.)
    Matthew .150*
    Meriam 59*
    Nabby 54
    Solomon 73
    Thomas 156
    Timothy 34*
    William 133, 143, 189

Arnett,
    John 147
    Thomas 180*

Arnnusmun,
    Margaret 105

Arnold,
    Alexander 98*
    Caleb 48
    Edward 29, 83*
    Elisha 46*, 131*
    Elizabeth 48
    Francis R. 45
    Galen 29
    Hannah 48
    Henry 120
    Isaac 60*
    Israel 46*
    John 46*, 47, 73, 161*
    Joseph 48, 120
    Nathaniel 46
    Oliver 47*
    Remington 48
    Richard 48*
    Ruth 44*
    Seth 66
    Seth S. 66
    Talcott A. 50
    Thomas 168
    William 168
    Zebra 165

Arnott,
    Henry 135*

Arons,
    William 145

Arrowhood,
    Thomas 178
Arrowood,
    John 137*
Arrowsmith,
    Elizabeth 130

Artherton,
    Matthew 70*

Arthur,
    James 170*
    John 128*
    Joseph 157
    Levi 189*
    William 129*

Artis,
    John 118*

Artist,
    Isaac 119

Ash,
    John 74
    William 19*

Ashbrook,
    Thomas 184

Ashby,
    Nathan 136

Ashcraft,
    William 53

Asher,
    Bartlet 184
    William 161*

Ashley,
    Daniel 57*
    Joseph 57*, 103
    Susan 44

Ashlock,
    Jesse 157*

Ashmore,
    Jabez 109*
    Joseph 109

Ashmun,
    Samuel 78*

Ashport,
    Lydia 30*

Ashton,
    T. C. 82

Ashworch,
    Elizabeth 129*

Ashworth,
    Joel 134*

Askew,
    William 141*

Aspenwall,
    Nancy 12
    Samuel 65*

Aspinwall,
    Elijah 145

Atchley,
    Isaac 96
    Lydia 154
    Noah 154

Atherton,
    Caleb 28
    Freeman 125
    Joel 6*

Atkins,
    Chauncy 91
    David 81*
    Luther 43*
    Oliver 59

Atkinson,
    Daniel 129*
    John 35
    Nathaniel 19*
    Reuben 128, 130
    Robert 130
    Theodore 18
    William 9*

Attwood,
    Lydia 49

Atus,
    Lunun 14*

Atwater,
    Ichabod 59*
    Phineas 97
    Russel 97

Atwell,
    Charles B. 131
    Oliver 36
    Paul 73*
    Samuel 54*

Atwood,
    Ebenezer 97
    Elisha 61
    Isaac 71*

Atwood, (cont.)
    Jonathan 60*
    Moses 23
    Nathan 13
    Philip 22*, 34*
    Roby 46
    Thomas 62*
    Zabeth 13

Aubry,
    Craven 163
    Samuel 163

Augar,
    Archibald 109*

Augler,
    Freeman 182

Aumock,
    John 110*

Austin,
    Abiathar 72
    Ama 99
    Asa 43, 66
    Benjamin 137*
    Eleazer 81
    Ezekiel 48*
    Eli 65
    Frye 41
    George 66*
    Hannah 32
    Isaac 41
    John 62*, 165*
    John A. 111*
    Jedediah 54*
    Lewis 168
    Mary 66
    Moses 16*
    Nathaniel 168
    Phebe 58
    Richard 129
    Samuel 120*, 177
    Saunders 159
    Stephen 159
    Thaddeus 51

Averell,
    Jonathan B. 40

Averile,
    John (Mrs.) 20

Averill,
    Daniel 21*
    Ezekiel 9*

Averill, (cont.)
    Jesse 100

Averrill,
    Moses 15*

Avery,
    Abel 59*
    Abram 86*
    Benjamin 100
    Christopher 126
    Constant 87
    Cyrus 100
    D. 87
    Daniel 61*
    David 54
    Dennison 90*
    E. 74
    Ebenezer 54*
    Elihu 34
    Ezekiel 119*
    George 126, 158*
    George W. 65
    J. B. 85
    John 34*
    John H. 77*
    Jonathan 34
    Joshua 27*
    Mansford 36
    Marietta 74
    Mary 17, 53*, 144
    Nathan 65
    Oliver 54
    Roger 88
    Rufus 53*
    Theodore 32
    Williams 102*

Avis,
    John 134

Axley,
    Benjamin 95*

Axton,
    Bayliss 165

Ayatt,
    Esther 56

Ayer,
    Benjamin 10

Ayers,
    Elihu 132*
    William 156

Aylesworth,
    Polly 77*

Ayres,
    John S. 63
    Robert 109*
    Thomas 102

Babb,
    Jemima 99

Babbett,
    Harry 82
    Joy 85*
    Mary 82

Babbit,
    Adoniram 27
    Edward 33, 57*
    Hiram J. 84
    Isaac 27
    Seth 57
    Snellern 33

Babbitt,
    Edward B. 39
    Mary 39
    Uri 63*

Babcock,
    A. C. 192
    Amy 119
    Benjamin 8, 94
    Caleb 93
    Elisha 34, 77*
    Elsey 48*
    George 100*
    Harvey 77
    Jason 94
    Jonas 92*
    Jonathan 75, 77, 192
    Paul 48*
    Reuben 38, 94*
    Robert 83
    Simon 60*
    Thomas 90
    William 60*

Baccus,
    Andrew 70
    Lucy 83

Baccus,
    Stephen 70
    William 83

Bachelder,
    Jethro 63
    John   16, 20*, 63
    Jonathan 23
    Simon 15
    Stephen 11*

Bacheller,
    Rupee 71

Bachellor,
    Joseph 86*

Back,
    Elisha 85
    Henry 85
    John 184
    Lyman 70*

Backsdale,
    Samuel 128*

Backus,
    Abner 60*
    Elizabeth 54
    Samuel 178
    Timothy 57

Bacon,
    Alvin 51
    Benjamin 100
    Ebenezer 41
    Elijah 98
    Ellen 38
    Francis 51
    Jabez 26*
    Jacob 31
    Jonathan 81*
    Joseph 33*
    Josiah 58
    Lemuel 75
    Moses 92
    Naomi 22
    Rebecca 22*
    Timothy 5*
    William 59, 75, 83*
    William H. 58

Badcock,
    Ichabod 53*

Badger,
    Edmund 33*
    Joseph 180
    Nathaniel 5
    Samuel 63*
    Stephen 19*

Badget,
    Thomas 131*

Bagget,
    Josiah 145

Bagley,
    Asher 191*
    Ephraim 65
    Peter 65*
    Philip 42
    Winthrop 25*

Bagnele,
    Bethiah 28
    Samuel W. 28

Bagwell,
    Frederick 148*
    Jesse 143
    John 143*
    William 143

Bailey,
    Abigail 31*
    Albridge D. 19
    Anselm 132*
    Armstead 129
    Bethia 107
    Callam 160
    Daniel 21*, 107
    Dudley 19
    Ebenezer 80*
    Elisha 160*
    Elkins 138
    Enoch 90*
    George 116
    Henry 116, 133*
    Hezekiah 55*
    Israel 32
    James 41, 71, 144
    Jesse 180
    John 191*
    Jonas 38
    Jonathan 40
    Joseph 49*
    Joshua 64*, 72
    Lucy 5, 41

Bailey, (cont.)
    Michael 59
    Nancy 129
    Philo 59
    Rebecca 6
    Richard 160*
    Robert 188*
    Stephen 138
    Silas 38*
    Thaddeus 12*
    William 143*, 184*
    William T. 160

Bailis,
    Henry 134

Bailow,
    Samuel 98

Baily,
    Amaziah 94
    Bertheany 104
    Evan 116
    James 94
    John 104
    John S. 94

Bain,
    John 113, 175*

Bainbridge,
    Susan 115*

Baine,
    Daniel 194*
    George 180

Bainny,
    Mary 114*

Baird,
    Abijah 79
    David 79
    John 176*
    Jonathan 38*

Baisley,
    Thomas 106, 131*, 144

Baker,
    A. J. 189
    Abel 82
    Abigail 29, 38
    Abner 173
    Allen 80

Baker, (cont.)
    Amos 40
    Annos 48
    Anson 90
    Asa G. 8*
    Beal 146*
    Betsey 48
    Charles 144*
    Daniel 17, 169, 170*
    David 169
    Dempsey 146*
    Dwelly 29
    Enoch 54*
    Ezekiel 90*
    Freeman 94
    George 27*, 122
    George F. 184
    J. 73
    James 40
    James P. 14
    John 79, 100*, 164*, 182*
    Jonathan 90*
    Joshua 73, 102*
    Joshua C. 48
    Judah 99*
    Lois 46, 90
    Mary 4, 6
    Oliver 80*
    Ralph 9
    Richard 115
    Robert 85*
    Samuel 6, 9, 26*, 156
    Samuel W. 24
    Sarah 46*
    Seth 75*
    Silas 14
    Sylvester 189
    Thomas 17, 22*
    Timothy 85*, 173
    Waterman 99*
    William 90

Balch,
    Dorcas 22
    Hart 71
    John 90*
    Joseph 81*

Balcom,
    Joseph 41
    Micah 41

Balcome,
    Ebenezer 46*

Baldwin,
    Aaron 93*
    Abel 51
    Abigail 51*
    Andrew 162
    Anson 52
    Archibald 55
    Asa 54*
    Barret 163
    Cornelius 103
    Desire 52*
    Ebenezer 76
    Edward 163
    Elijah 66
    Erastus 58*
    Esther 40
    Ezekiel 103
    Ezra 66
    Henry 59
    J. 74
    Jacob 22
    James 32*, 58*
    Jane 59
    John 137*
    Jonathan 178*
    Joseph 54*
    Josiah 74
    Kesiah 52
    Levi 127
    Nahum 13*
    Nathaniel 192
    Obadiah 80
    Philemon 54*
    Samuel 127
    Sarah 44
    Sidney 99
    Thomas 57
    Thomas T. 52
    U. 108
    William 22, 40
    William W. 108

Bales,
    John 121
    Sarah 48*

Baley,
    Alfred 50
    Noah 140
    Robert 194
    William H. 103

Ball,
    Aaron 108*

Ball, (cont.)
    Abner 108*
    Anna 51
    Daniel 137*
    Huldah 44*
    John 72
    S. D. 174*
    William 72, 110*

Ballard,
    B. W. 166*
    Betty 14
    Frederick 7
    Jonathan A. 14
    Joseph 41
    Joshua W. 7
    Uriah 7
    William 171*

Ballew,
    Stephen 137*

Ballou,
    Russell 22*
    Sanford 65
    William 65

Ballow,
    Noah 46*

Baloo,
    Richard 164*

Balsley,
    Andrew 91
    James 91

Baltrip,
    Augustin 141*

Baman,
    John 154*

Bamper,
    Ann 107
    Garret A. 107

Bancker,
    Catharine 104

Bancroft,
    Benjamin 36
    Jonathan 40*
    Timothy 22*

Bane,
    John 163*
    Richard 164*

Banes,
    John 188*

Banfill,
    Anna 65

Bangs,
    Allen 6
    Desire 44
    Electa 34*

Banister,
    Jason 70

Banker,
    Frederick 105
    James 192*
    Thomas 105
    Abraham 55
    Charity 77
    Daniel 102*
    Esther 56
    H. L. 142
    Hyat 55*
    John 130, 145
    Mabel 55
    N. 130
    Nathan 55*
    Ruth 55
    Sarah 4*
    Silvanus 11
    William 77

Bannerman,
    George 139

Bannister,
    Jason 70

Bannon,
    Agnes 121

Banta,
    Angelica 81

Barack,
    Nicholas 115*

Barbank,
    Jonathan 24

Barber,
    Abi 51
    Alson 51
    Daniel 48*
    David 101
    Elizabeth 51
    Giles A. 67
    Hiram 101
    Jethro 19*
    Job 62*, 90
    John 25, 144
    Margaret 48
    Moses 48
    Robert 144
    Samuel 109*
    Sarah 24, 79*
    Uriah 179*

Barbes,
    Robert 122*

Barbour,
    Mary 109

Barcalew,
    Runyon 109*

Barce,
    Josiah 86

Barclay,
    James 98
    John 157*
    Robert 148*

Barcus,
    James 173*

Barden,
    Jesse 31

Bardin,
    Sarah 21

Bardine,
    Aaron 46
    Horace 46

Bardwell,
    Ezra 34
    Obadiah 33*
    Reuben 34
    Samuel 34

Barefield,
    James 159*

Barga,
    Peter 92

Barger,
    John 187*

Barham,
    James 167*

Barhour,
    Simeon 58*

Barhydt,
    Jerome 96*

Barhyte,
    James 95*

Barker,
    Abijah 20*
    Barnabas 63*
    Benjamin 6
    Daniel 82
    Edward 136*
    Elizabeth 86*
    George 157
    Hannah 41
    Huldah 51*
    J. Bowen 30*
    James 7*, 47*, 52, 187
    Jesse 6*
    Lewis 141
    Mary 20*, 52
    Moody 20
    Nathan 63*
    S. D. 37
    Sarah 20, 76*
    Stephen 162*
    Theodore 65*
    William 7

Barkhardt,
    John 60

Barkly,
    R. J. D. 146
    William 146

Barley,
    James 136
    Samuel 136

Barlow,
    Abner 91
    Catharine 160
    Joseph 160

Barmer,
    John 139*

Barmore,
    Mashal 100

Barnard,
    Carter 154*
    Edmund 21*
    Elisha 34*
    Enoch 168
    Luther 68
    Moses 93
    Richard 33*
    Rufus 72*
    Sarah 8*
    Stephen 63*
    William 93
    William L. 165*

Barnes,
    (Mrs.) 58
    Abel 51
    Absalom 182
    Amos 18
    Barson 58
    Bathsheba 28*
    Caleb 51
    David 33, 52*
    Elijah 51*, 182
    Hugh 184
    James 151, 155*
    Jesse 116*
    John 177
    Jonathan 89
    Joshua 62
    Lucy 78
    Lyman 29, 51
    Merit 51
    Nathan 53
    Nicodemus 161
    Oliver 51
    Rebecca 6
    Reuben 100*
    Rufus 36
    Sarah 97
    Sibenu 51
    William P. 180

Barnet,
    Michael 153
    Robert 124
    Thomas 139*

Barnett,
    Andrew 163*

Barnett, (cont.)
    James M. 153
    James P. 165
    John 179
    Lewis 161
    Mary 164
    Nathaniel 94*
    Sarah 165
    Sion 146*
    William 153

Barney,
    Asa 100
    John 23*, 84
    Luther 75*
    Mary 84
    Throop 100

Barnham,
    Daniel 76*
    Tamma 57*

Barnhart,
    David 94*
    John 114
    Philip 123*
    Sophia 114

Barnhill,
    Henry 140*
    Samuel 166

Barnhour,
    Philip D. 175

Barns,
    Amos 18
    Baker 114
    Calvin 76*
    Daniel 76*
    Dennis 76
    Israel 58*
    James 137*
    John 103
    Josiah 36
    Lard 154
    Moses 36
    Nathan 58*
    Reuben 21*, 76
    Silas 32
    William 159*

Barnsheeser,
    John 113

Barnum,
>Enoch 168
>Samuel 95
>Stephen 32

Barnwell,
>David 148
>John 144*

Barny,
>Martin 25

Barr,
>John 166*
>William 117*

Barrack,
>Bryant 163*

Barret,
>Elizabeth 84
>Jacob 75*
>James 123
>Lemuel 25*

Barrett,
>Abraham 105*
>Amos 168
>Annah 100
>B. 74
>Benjamin 36, 74, 168
>David 98*
>Elizabeth 170*
>Ezra 25
>H. P. 36
>Joel 70*
>Jonathan 38
>Joseph 105
>Lemuel 25
>Nathaniel 13*
>Oliver 97
>Salsbury 97
>Samuel 105
>Thomas 42*
>Wakeman 56*

Barrister,
>Andrew 36
>Linus 36

Barrit,
>William 104*

Barron,
>Abigail 25
>Benjamin M. 25

Barron, (cont.)
>Fletcher 25
>J. 74
>J. V. 16*
>Joseph 74
>Moses 25
>William 21*

Barrott,
>Solomon 127*

Barrows,
>Eleazer 71
>Jacob 26*
>Joseph 147
>Lemuel 90
>Lucius 71
>Peter 12*
>Philbrook 69*
>Samuel 97
>Samuel S. 24
>Thomas 24, 30

Barrus,
>Alvin 22
>Jeremiah 22

Barry,
>Robert 39

Barsden,
>Edward 135
>John S. 135

Barsha,
>Peter 62*

Barstow,
>Samuel 60*

Bartee,
>David 129

Barter,
>John A. 42
>Joseph 9*
>Mark 9*

Bartholomew,
>Charles 88*
>Charles D. 98
>Daniel 98*
>Isaac 98
>James 50
>James C. 50
>John 138*

Bartholomew, (cont.)
    Joseph 176*
    L. 100
    Ruth 51

Barthwick,
    Stephen 82*

Bartine,
    David 109

Bartlee,
    Thomas 165*

Bartlet,
    E. 175
    Samuel 82

Bartlett,
    Abraham 87
    Adin 64*
    Alfred 63
    Ama 22*
    Ann 105
    Benjamin 75
    Beri 25
    C. M. 85
    Christopher 64*
    Curatia T. 7
    Daniel 35
    David 75*
    Eli 37
    Elijah 34
    Elisha 62
    Hannah 66
    Henry 105
    Isaac 168
    Isaac W. 168
    Joanna 82
    Joel 66
    John 8
    Josiah 17*
    Levi 79
    Mary 37*
    Nathaniel 24
    Orson 62
    Rachel 36
    Rebecca 63
    Thaddeus 7
    William 5

Barton,
    Elisha 130*
    H. H. 67
    Job 125*

Barton, (cont.)
    Josiah 25*
    Lucretia 36*
    Perley 101
    Prudence 94*
    Rhoda 45*
    Robert 93
    Timothy S. 101
    Waldo 67

Bartram,
    Isaac H. 56*

Barwes,
    Olive 58

Basford,
    James 77*

Bashaw,
    Peter 155*

Basket,
    Francis 166
    Jesse 166

Bass,
    Bathsheba 65
    Dutoy 132
    James 156*
    John 38, 129*

Bassett,
    Abel 84*
    Anselm 28
    Caleb 30*
    Cornelius 32*
    Edward 52*
    Isaac 37
    J. P. 37
    Jabez 10
    James 52
    Josiah 52
    Lydia 28, 79*
    Martha 22
    Mary 53
    Nathan 22, 85
    Nathaniel 32*
    Philo 52
    Samuel 10, 12
    Samuel P. 43

Bastian,
    Andrew 139

Bastin,
    Daniel C. 97
    Dorcas 64
    Isaac 64

Batchelder,
    Amos 20*
    Enoch 39
    John H. 11
    Kinsley H. 25
    Levi 39
    Mark 19*
    Phineas 11
    William 10*

Bateman,
    Daniel 108*
    Moses 108*
    Thomas 151
    Zadiack 75*

Baterson,
    Stephen 56*

Bates,
    Aaron 36
    Asa 57*
    Barnabas 93
    Benjamin 30, 108
    Benoni 108
    Cornelius 29*
    Cyrus 10
    Daniel 179*
    Dewitt 93
    Elias 102*
    Elizabeth 32
    Ezra L. 38
    Henesdale 179
    Humphrey 166*
    Jabez R. 10
    Jacob 5*
    John 101
    Lemuel 36
    Mary 10, 30
    Phineas 123*
    Phineas P. 91
    Priscilla 32
    Samuel 56
    Sebeus 33
    Silvia 29*
    Susannah 13*
    Thaddeus 32
    Thomas 11* ,
    William 10, 101*, 187*, 195
    William H. 33

Batholomew,
    Jonathan 52*

Bathurst,
    Henry A. 123
    Lawrence 123

Baton,
    Mary 115

Batterson,
    Mary 59*

Battey,
    Patience T. 45
    Sheldon 45
    William 46*

Battin,
    Henry 184

Battis,
    Sampson 19*

Battle,
    Justice 175
    S. T. 175

Battles,
    Caroline 65
    James 88
    Mary 65
    Naham 30
    Noel 148
    William 148

Batts,
    Rebecca 43

Bauge,
    Lucy B. 69

Baughm,
    Joseph 163

Baulch,
    Marvin 78

Baum,
    Frederick 81
    Jacob F. 81

Baxter,
    Daniel 10
    Eli 69

Baxter, (cont.)
 John 73, 84
 Morris 105*
 Nathan 88*
 Reliance 10
 Rhoda 26
 William 133*

Bay,
 Robert 172

Bayles,
 Elijah 157*
 Jonathan 104

Bayless,
 Elias 73
 John 73

Bayley,
 Benjamin 65
 George 23*
 Joshua 65
 Samuel 65

Baylies,
 Hodizah 28*

Baylis,
 William 190*

Baythe,
 George 186

Bazzell,
 Daniel 20
 William 20

Beach,
 Adnah 102*
 Amos 81
 Asa 95*
 Francis 59*
 John 52, 90
 Julius 59*
 Mary 180
 Mercy 180
 Nathan 125*
 Oble 177*
 Phebe 52
 Reuben 179
 Reuben B. 179
 Rhoda 62
 Rosell 169*
 Thaddeus L. 62

Beadshaw,
 John 130*

Beagle,
 Borick 112

Beakley,
 Charles 102
 Christian 102

Beal,
 Elizabeth T. 5
 George 123*
 Henry 106
 Jarvis 5*
 John 101*
 Joseph 32
 Rebecca 171

Beale,
 Robert 133*

Bealer,
 Jacob 154*

Beals,
 Azariah 32
 Celia 32
 Cyrus 10
 Levi 62
 Lydia 10, 44*

Beam,
 Anthony 111
 Josiah 111
 Michael 174*

Beaman,
 Ansel 179
 Josiah 34

Beams,
 Coonrod 164*

Bean,
 Benjamin 17*
 Daniel 19*
 Ebenezer 18*
 James 163
 James C. 7
 James R. 4*
 Jeremiah 7, 19*
 Leonard 165*
 Lydia 16*
 Margaret 7

Bean, (cont.)
    Oliver 10*
    R. 193
    Richard 193
    Susan 65

Bear,
    Jacob 124

Bearce,
    Benjamin 30

Beard,
    Aaron 55
    Addison 52
    David 90*
    Francis A. 156
    George W. 67
    Joseph 52, 178
    Mary 129
    Susan 52
    William 156, 157, 178

Bearder,
    Andrew 109

Beardslee,
    James 55
    John W. 55
    Josiah 93
    Margaret 55
    Sally 55

Beardsley,
    (N.X.N.) 58
    Agur 59
    Amos 94
    Aram 82
    Benjamin 103
    Dolly 62
    Elijah 103
    Levi 76
    Lewis 62
    Nathan 58
    Thomas 58

Bearse,
    Gideon 7
    Moses H. 26
    Rebecca 26

Bearsly,
    William 95*

Beashamp,
    John W. 158*

Beasley,
    Benjamin 132
    Isom 157*
    Leonard 142*
    Robert 83

Beatty,
    James 169

Beaty,
    David 138*
    James 97
    Joseph 106
    Maria 106
    Mary 153
    Peter 112*
    Robert 112
    Samuel 153
    William 166

Beaumont,
    Daniel 78*

Beavers,
    Samuel 176*

Beazly,
    Cornelius 190
    William 142

Bechtel,
    Philip 115

Beck,
    David 138
    George 161
    Jesse 128*
    Mary 42
    Thomas 161
    William 140*

Becker,
    Jacob 96
    Martin 87*
    Peter 96
    Phillip 96*

Becket,
    Sarah 132

Beckett,
    James C. 169
    John 169

Beckley,
    George 169

Beckley, (cont.)
    Richard 59*
    Zebedee 64*

Beckman,
    John R. 15

Becknell,
    Thomas 164*

Beckwith,
    Benjamin 53
    Byron 23
    Israel 54
    Jemima 23
    Jesse 54
    Job 99*
    Lemuel 99*
    Nehemiah 128*
    Ralzamon 85
    Richard 82
    Samuel 123
    Thomas 82

Beckworth,
    Rice 170

Becraft,
    Francis 96
    Jacob 96

Bedding,
    Henry 122
    Joseph 122

Beddo,
    Thomas 171*

Bedell,
    Isaac 110*

Beden,
    Thomas T. 90

Bedient,
    Isaac 93
    Mordecai 93*

Bedinger,
    Henry 134*

Bedlock,
    Benjamin 125*

Bedlow,
    Hannah 57*

Bedortha,
    Justus 44

Bedwell,
    Robert 185*

Beebe,
    Alexander 92
    Asa 92, 94*
    David 175
    William C. 54*

Beebee,
    Anna 103

Beebel,
    Ezekiel 96

Beech,
    Gabriel 103
    Jedediah 94*

Beecher,
    John P. 84
    Lucy 64
    Marcus 64

Beedle,
    Henry 3*
    John 4

Beels,
    Bashabe 117
    Ezra 117

Beeman,
    Daniel 59*
    Isaac 103
    Moses 178*
    Samuel 100*
    Tracy 59*

Been,
    George 39

Beer,
    James 170
    Robert 186*

Beers,
    Cyrus 56
    Ezra D. 57
    Fanton 56*
    John 52*
    Nathan 51*
    Samuel 56
    Zachariah 175

Beesley,
    William 161*

Beggs,
    William 117*

Belcher,
    Bartlett 153*
    Cyrus 143
    Hannah 41*
    Jacob 41*
    Nathan 54*
    Robert 143
    William 119

Belden,
    Charles 61
    Christina 59*
    Jonathan 68
    Mary 49*, 50
    Norman 81
    Richard 49*

Belding,
    Jonathan 90*

Belknap,
    Ebenezer 101*
    Josiah 71*
    Polly 64

Bell,
    (Mrs.) 144
    Andrew 80
    Archibald 160
    Benjamin 139*
    Daniel 165
    Edward 120
    George 144
    James 159*, 161
    Jane 118*
    John 121*, 165
    Jonathan 20*, 56*
    Joshua 54
    Nelson 144
    Pamela 160
    Phineas 88*
    Richard 140*
    Thadeus 56*
    Thomas 163*
    Walter 33
    William 33, 94*, 157*, 160,
        165
    William W. 160

Bellis,
    Adam 111

Belloat,
    C. S. 158
    James 158

Bellows,
    Almira 54
    Isaac 78
    Lydia 36
    Miles 167
    Peter 180
    Sarah 35
    Stephen 36
    Zebulon 78

Belnap,
    Jesse 122

Belonga,
    Margaret 78

Belsor,
    Anthony 127

Belton,
    Thomas 108*

Beman,
    Aaron 81
    Nathan 81

Bement,
    Benjamin 53*
    Consider 80*

Bemes,
    Susannah 25

Bemis,
    Amasa 38*
    Elijah 38
    Jacob 6*
    Jonas 38*
    Reuben 38
    Thaddeus 7

Bemiss,
    Joseph 95

Bemont,
    Ambrose 50

Bemus,
    Daniel 64*

Bender,
    George 45
    John E. 108
    Lewis 108

Benedict,
    Aaron 53*
    Abraham 82
    Amos 88
    Darius 56
    Elisha 101
    Ira 88
    Isaac 56
    James 81*
    John T. 82
    Joseph 97, 104
    N. G. 101
    Obadiah M. 88
    Samuel 75
    Thomas 99*

Beneham,
    John 53

Benett,
    John 116

Benham,
    Bridget 79
    Ebenezer 51*
    Elizabeth 52*
    Isaac 62*
    Lois 51*
    Matthew 79
    Samuel 85
    Thomas 168*

Benjamin,
    Darius 78
    Dorothy 55*
    Ebenezer 88*
    Elias 78*
    Ira 70
    Jesse 85*
    Jonathan 174
    L. 70
    Mary 70
    Samuel 50*, 107*
    Sarah 116
    Selah B. 98

Benn,
    George 73

Benner,
    Christopher 14

Bennet,
    A. F. 76
    Abram 173*
    Benjamin 17, 76
    Daniel 90*
    David 110*
    Ebenezer 79*
    Elisha 53
    Elizabeth 17, 105
    H. 73
    Henry 73
    Isaac 177
    John 5*, 134*
    Jorial 147
    Mary 49*
    Miles 90*
    Miller 105
    Stephen 57*
    William 136*

Bennett,
    Abigail 81
    Aham 99
    Allen 32
    Arnold 83*
    Asher 47
    Benjamin 55, 99
    Caleb 32*
    Catharine 77
    D. 67
    Daniel 92
    David 20*, 67
    Ebenezer 15
    Eleazer 17
    Elias 56*
    Elisha 81
    Elizabeth 55
    Esther 60
    Ezekiel 93*
    H. 94
    James 39*, 62*, 160
    Jeremiah 19*
    Jesse 94
    John 17, 50, 71, 75*, 105
    John H. 19
    Joseph 157
    Josiah 55*
    Katharine 171*
    Levi 92
    Louis 81
    Martha 105
    Marvin O. 55
    Mary 47*, 48

25

Bennett, (cont.)
    Nathan 77*, 105*
    Polly 93
    Reuben 3, 144*
    Rufus 125*
    Samuel 66*, 70, 110*
    Sarah 71
    Stephen 30*
    Susanna 67
    Temperance 60*
    Thomas 56, 157
    William 187*
    Zebina W. 67

Bensinger,
    Frederick 115

Bensley,
    David 83*

Benson,
    Abel 41*
    Daniel 68*
    Dinah 101*
    Enoch 145*
    Isaac 30*
    Jeptha 13*
    John 153
    Jonah 30*
    Joseph 59
    Matthew 106
    Peter 115
    Sarah 58
    Spencer 153
    Susannah 20*

Bentley,
    Caleb 94*
    E. 98
    George 183
    George W. 54
    J. 156
    Jeremiah 156

Bently,
    Anna 54
    Asahel 78
    Elisha 94
    James 82
    Thomas 140*

Benton,
    Avery 79*
    David 183
    Elijah 25*
    Felix 71*

Benton, (cont.)
    Henry 43
    Howard 24
    Jacob 61*
    Jonathan 103
    Loring 33
    Noah 52*
    Susan 91
    Walter 183
    Zebulon 33

Berdan,
    Henry 107*

Berdens,
    Timothy 3

Bergen,
    Christopher 85
    Jacob 85
    Peter 92*

Berk,
    Elihu 155
    Waster 101

Berker,
    George 119

Berlin,
    Jacob 134
    Philip 134

Berlingane,
    Wanton 180*

Bernard,
    Walter 130*

Bernis,
    Jemima 67
    Joseph 67

Berniss,
    Aaron 95*
    Joseph 95

Bernus,
    Reuben 190

Berrian,
    Jane 102

Berry,
    Abigail 4*
    Andrew 139*

Berry, (cont.)
    Barnabas 81
    Betsey 27*
    Caroline N. 15
    Ebenezer 65*
    Eleanor 19
    Enoch 155*
    Hannah 41*
    Holsworth 185
    James 130
    Joel 185
    John 134*, 137
    Joseph 4, 8
    Josiah 4
    Kellogg 55*
    Lucy (Mrs.) 130
    Nathaniel 10
    Nicholas 105*
    Obadiah 7
    Peter 7
    Philemon 81
    Polly 43
    Robert 130
    Sarah 103, 169
    Seth 74*
    Timothy 4*
    Thomas 7, 176
    Walter 19
    William 181*
    Zebulon 6*

Bertholf,
    John 107
    John S. 107

Bertram,
    William 158*

Besse,
    Alden 7
    Jabez 10*
    Joseph 7

Besser,
    John S. 190

Bessey,
    Constant 29
    Silas 29

Besson,
    John 109

Best,
    Henry 104
    Levi H. 147
    Peter 94*

Bethel,
    John 152*

Betterley,
    William 125*

Betterton,
    Joshua 143

Bettes,
    Leonard 32*

Betteworth,
    Charles 187
    D. 187

Bettis,
    Jeremiah 187*

Betts,
    Daniel 56
    Isaiah 56, 81*
    James 90*
    Warren 77
    William R. S. 110
    Zophar 77

Bevan,
    Philip 116

Bevert,
    John 155*

Bevier,
    Daniel 74

Bevill,
    Edward 148*

Bibb,
    Henry 131*
    James 163
    Robert 163

Bibber,
    James 6*

Bible,
    Adam 169
    Christian 136
    Magdaline 136

Bice,
    Jacob 103*

Bickel,
    Jacob 122
    John 114*

Bickford,
    Abigail 20
    Eli 63*
    John 15
    Paul 65
    Samuel B. 20
    William 8, 9

Bickley,
    William 165*

Bicknal,
    Amy 49*

Bicknell,
    Abner 12
    Nathaniel 7
    Olive 7

Bidlack,
    Philemon 171*

Bidwell,
    Anna 23*
    Eleazer 58
    Elizabeth 50*
    Miles H. 58
    Patience 72*
    Phineas 58

Bierly,
    Michael 183*

Biffle,
    Jacob 157*

Bigbie,
    William 129*

Bigelow,
    Abijah 183
    Alpheus 40*
    Humphrey 36
    John 37
    Jonas 37*
    Lucy 65
    Noah 85*
    Samuel 98
    Timothy 108*
    W. L. 65

Bigford,
    Samuel 81*
    Thomas 67

Biggs,
    Mary 94*

Bigler,
    John 108*

Bigony,
    Ann 116

Biles,
    David 183*

Bill,
    Benajah 53
    Eleazer 54
    Gurdon 53
    James R. 122*
    Joseph 75
    Jonathan 75
    Joshua 53
    Lodowick 53

Billingham,
    Elizabeth 115

Billings,
    Benjamin 28*
    Fletcher 86
    Gilbert 57
    Jesse 33*
    John S. 57
    Lucretia 54
    Nathaniel 44
    Patuma 70
    Sarah 32
    Willard 70

Billingsley,
    C. 149
    Clement 149
    John 167*

Billington,
    Ezekiel 156*
    Thomas 48

Bills,
    Abial 119
    Ann 60
    Benjamin 174

Bills, (cont.)
    Daniel 51*
    Elisha 92*
    Hannah 20*
    Peleg 119
    Sylvanus 51*

Bilow,
    Amable 78
    Joseph K. 78

Biner,
    George 179*

Bingaman,
    John 169

Bingham,
    A. 192
    Abel 192
    Jeremiah 71*
    Mercy 57
    Ozias 126
    Samuel 88
    William 156*

Birch,
    Eddy 175
    Isaiah 94
    James 162
    Oliver 175
    Phebe 94
    Zachariah 190*

Birchard,
    Daniel 56

Bird,
    Edmund 92
    Eve 92
    Frederick A. 72
    John 143
    Joseph 72
    Nathaniel 76*
    William 98

Birdsey,
    Ellen 55

Birdsong,
    John 158*

Birdwell,
    Benjamin 154*

Birge,
    Hosea 103*
    James 58*

Birks,
    John 162*

Birrell,
    Rhoda 58

Birtch,
    Jane 54

Bisbee,
    Benjamin 31*
    Isaac 70*
    John 29*

Bisby,
    Samuel 32

Biscow,
    James 162*

Bishop,
    Abraham 82*
    Alonzo 58
    Anna 51*, 54
    Benjamin 186
    Calvin 90
    Catharine 95
    Daniel 71
    Elisha 163*
    Elizabeth 60
    Ezekiel 46*
    Hooper 192
    Ira 90
    Isaac 82*
    Jacob 56
    James 130*
    John 24, 64*, 79, 104, 144*
    Joseph 10, 90
    Lambert 99
    Lawrence 161*
    Levi 90
    Lewis 90, 92
    Margaret 118
    Mary 99, 118
    Moses 94*
    Newman 43*
    Nicholas 143*
    Robert 54, 71
    Sarah 79, 161
    Seth 58

Bishop, (cont.)
 Solomon 90
 Squire 10
 Sylvanus 92
 Thomas F. 51*
 Zadok 10

Bissel,
 David 48*

Bissell,
 D. H. 85
 Jonathan M. 66*
 Theoda 85
 Thomas 50*

Bitely,
 J. L. 95
 John 95

Bivin,
 Benjamin 96
 Elizabeth 96

Bixby,
 Aaron 58*, 66*
 Daniel 78
 Halsey 58
 Molly 58
 Nathaniel 67*
 Olivia 42
 Sampson 98
 Samuel 24, 36*, 98
 William 24

Black,
 Alexander 181*
 David 148*
 George 134
 Jacob 144*
 John 146*, 179
 John J. 113
 Joseph 142*
 Josiah 4
 Jotham 118*
 Mary Jane 91
 Samuel 145, 192
 William 22*, 145, 191*

Blackbourn,
 Clement 148

Blackburn,
 Eli 164
 Harrison 161
 Samuel 162*
 William 161

Blackford,
 Jacob 119*
 M. 92
 William 41

Blackman,
 David 55
 Elisha 125
 Enoch 78*
 Gain R. 74
 Ira 171
 Jeffrey A. 91
 Samuel 77
 Zachariah 74

Blackmar,
 Jabez 76
 Jacob 58*

Blackmore,
 Isaac 115*
 Timothy 175*

Blackstone,
 Rebecca 9

Blackweel,
 Ann 130
 James 130

Blackwell,
 David 154*

Bladley,
 Peter 183*

Blain,
 Alexander 153
 Elam 171*
 Thomas 96

Blair,
 Abraham 174*
 Benjamin 36
 Daniel P. 106
 Elizabeth 20
 James 91
 John 33, 168
 Mercy 36
 Nancy 128
 Reuben 36
 Robert 106*
 Robert W. 106
 Seth 86*
 Susan 36
 William 91

Blaisdell,
　　Dolly　16
　　Hannah　62
　　Philip　15
　　Samuel　21

Blake,
　　Caleb　28
　　Charles　11, 34
　　Deborah　5
　　Ebenezer　78*
　　Eleazer　22*
　　Eliphalet　23
　　George　44*
　　Isaac　25*
　　J. L.　14
　　Jason　27
　　John　10*, 11, 61
　　Jonathan　44, 61
　　Josiah　14
　　Marcy　28
　　Moses　12
　　Robert　10*
　　Thomas　139
　　W. W.　174
　　William　108
　　Willing　8*

Blakely,
　　Rhodah　86
　　William　142*

Blakeman,
　　Beard　55
　　Gould　55
　　Joemna　55
　　Sarah　55

Blakemore,
　　John　163
　　Lewis　163

Blakeslee,
　　Cooper　171

Blakesly,
　　Samuel　58*

Blakey,
　　George　164*

Blakney,
　　John　144*

Blalock,
　　Charles　158*
　　David　158

Blanch,
　　Harriet　106

Blanchard,
　　A.　78
　　Amos　43*
　　Benjamin　87
　　Betty　48
　　Charles　8
　　David　23
　　Hastings　63
　　Isaac　192
　　Jeremiah　42
　　John　68*, 77*, 192
　　Joseph　23
　　Leonard　10
　　Louis　86
　　Martha　78
　　Mary　32
　　Reuben　75
　　Sarah　9
　　Seth　6*
　　Solomon　8
　　Thomas S.　43
　　Walter　86
　　William　75

Blancitt,
　　William　132

Blanden,
　　Jonathan　25*
　　Samuel　93
　　Zeno　93

Blanding,
　　Martha　28*

Blane,
　　John　109*
　　Thomas　110*

Blank,
　　Peter　118*

Blankenbaker,
　　Luke　166
　　Nicholas　166

Blankenship,
　　Abram　129*
　　Benjamin　188*
　　Reuben　149*

Blanton,
　　Thomas　157*

Blanvette,
    John J. 106*

Blasdell,
    John 119*
    Richard 85

Blauton,
    James 138*

Blauvelt,
    Abraham J. 107
    Clarissa 106
    Cornelius T. 106
    Daniel G. 106
    John A. 107
    John G. 106
    John R. 107
    Sarah 107

Blauvett,
    James J. 107*

Blaylocker,
    John 141*

Blazer,
    Moses 117

Bledsoe,
    Benjamin 144*
    Elijah 161*
    Fanny 138
    Jacob 155*
    Miller 147

Bleeker,
    Leonard 106*

Bleekman,
    Mary 81
    Thomas 81

Blesdill,
    Mary 39

Blevins,
    Henry 153*
    James 182*

Blick,
    Dennis 161
    John 161

Bliss,
    Asa 28*
    Elizabeth 54
    Ezra 50*
    Francis 44*
    Gaius 44*
    Isaac 49*
    John 124*
    John M. 33
    Luther B. 44
    Moses 50
    Nathan 38*
    Susan 33
    William 27*

Bliven,
    Coddington 48
    Mary 72

Blivin,
    Nathan 48*

Blockman,
    Ruth 32

Blodget,
    Abdil 65
    Abijah 61
    Admatha 99*
    Henry 65*
    Jonathan 6*
    Margaret 66
    Nathan 78
    Randolph 66
    Solomon 23

Blodgett,
    Abigail 61
    Amos 17
    Benjamin 65, 91
    James 65
    Joseph 91
    Ludam 91
    Nathan 22
    Solomon 91*
    William 40*

Blood,
    Abel 19
    Asa 78*
    David 24, 67*, 81*
    Ebenezer 40
    Elijah 65
    Elizabeth 83
    Ephraim 68*

32

Blood, (cont.)
Isaac 98
Israel M. 91
John 71*
Jonas 21
Lucy 65
Nathaniel 91

Bloodgood,
John 94*

Bloom,
Peter C. 106*

Bloomer,
Gilbert 164

Bloomfield,
Betsey 88
John W. 88
Thomas 109*

Blose,
Isaac 134
Valentine 134

Bloss,
C. W. 121
Samuel 89*

Blossom,
E. D. 29
Peter 69
Seth 69

Blouk,
Jacob 139*

Blount,
Isaac 146*
Walter 74

Blowees,
Samuel 81
Silas 77
Ephraim 68

Blue,
Hannah 10
Jenett 15
Nathaniel 10

Blunt,
Asher 97
Palmer 97

Blur,
Nicholas 74

Bly,
John 63
Moses 16*

Blyche,
Jacob 156

Boardman,
Amos 65*
Benjamin 24*
Benjamin L. 39
Eleazer J. 70
Elias 39
Elizabeth 70
John H. 42
Mary 18

Boatman,
Bernard 170*
Mitchell 173
William 173

Boaz,
James 132*

Bobo,
Tilmon 143*

Bock,
Isaac 38

Bocker,
Aaron 4

Bodley,
William 178*

Bodly,
John 182
Thomas 112

Bodwell,
Ebenezer 6*

Bogardus,
Henry 91, 102
Henry P. 91
John N. 102
Mary 105*

Bogart,
John G. 106

Boggs,
    Mary 144
    Thomas 144
    William 173
*
Bohon,
    Sarah 165*

Bohonon,
    Ananiah 65*
    Stephen 23*

Boies,
    Betsey 25

Boit,
    Jacob B. 137*

Bolcom,
    David 39*

Bold,
    John R. 177*

Bolden,
    Jeremiah 59
    Joshua 59

Boldman,
    John 98*

Boldry,
    John 184
    Samuel 184

Bolen,
    Charles 171*
    William 154*

Boles,
    Benjamin 139*

Bolich,
    Andrew 115

Boling,
    Jesse 160*

Bollen,
    John 120*

Bolling,
    Jarrett 136*

Bolls,
    Samuel 25

*Bogue,
    John 54

Bolster,
    Berreck 67*
    Joel 67*

Bolt,
    Frederick 135*

Bolton,
    Huldah 188
    James 11
    Nathaniel 93
    Solomon 11
    William 187*

Boman,
    Sherwood 137*

Bomar,
    John 163*

Bond,
    Adonijah 87*
    Arthur 153
    Baly 44
    Bethuel 76*
    John 166*
    Jonas 14
    Joseph 39*
    Lewis 84
    Silas 23
    William 23, 158*
    Wright 153

Bonds,
    Joseph 145*

Bone,
    George 144*
    John 165*

Boner,
    William 134*

Bonfoy,
    Concurrance 60*

Bonner,
    James 149
    John 158*

Bonney,
    Ezekiel 30*, 168
    Isaac 8*

Bonsell,
    Benjamin 115

34

Bonton,
    Azor 100
    Sarah 56
    Seth 56

Bontwell,
    Joseph 39*

Booher,
    Philip 134*

Booker,
    Anna 9
    Samuel 167*

Bookhunt,
    James 90*

Boomer,
    C. 84
    Ephraim 27*

Boon,
    Joseph 185*
    Ralph 171
    Susanna 157*

Boone,
    Anna 167
    H. G. 167
    Samuel 166

Booraem,
    John 109*

Boot,
    Josiah 50

Booth,
    David 55, 73
    Erastus 73
    George C. 157*
    Isaac 91*
    Isaac B. 61

Boothby,
    Elizabeth 4*

Boothe,
    Judson 87
    Simeon 65

Bootle,
    Martha 94

Boovie,
    Jacob 94*

Borders,
    Chdristopher 185
    William B. 185

Bordwell,
    John 82

Boren,
    William 190

Borham,
    Hartwell 141*

Boroughs,
    Zebulon 63*

Borring,
    John 121

Borror,
    Charles 135*

Borst,
    Benjamin 96
    Martinus 96

Boss,
    Augustus 138
    Benjamin 46*
    *James 130
    Sarah 47
    *Jane 130
Boster,
    Jonathan 4

Bostian,
    Jacob 139*

Bostick,
    Elisha 140
    Ezra 187*

Boston,
    Christopher 125*, 153*
    Joel 160
    Reuben 160
    Thomas 4

Bostwick,
    (Dr.) 178*
    Anna 55

Bostwick, (cont.)
    Arthur 62
    Edmund 178
    Eliza 178
    Hiram 74
    J. 73
    John 73
    Reuben 61*

Bosworth,
    Benjamin 70*, 125
    Daniel 14*
    Jacob 57
    Nathaniel 64*
    Tabitha 49

Bothell,
    David 84
    James 84

Bothwick,
    Solomon 36

Botsford,
    Jabez B. 55
    Mary 55
    Samuel 53*

Bottom,
    Bethiah 30

Botts,
    Benjamin 160
    Moses 160

Boughton,
    Asahel 91
    Eleazer 91
    Moses 104
    William 94

Bouldin,
    Joanna 129*

Boultie,
    Samuel F. 6

Bourd,
    Philip 165*

Bourn,
    Huldah 61
    James 165*
    John 29*, 61
    Rachel 49

Bourne,
    Nathaniel 27*
    William 30
    Zuriel 27*

Bourrows,
    Ashley 65
    Lydia 65

Boutell,
    John 74*

Bouton,
    Edwin 104

Bovee,
    Nicholas M. 76
    Philip 168*

Bover,
    Abigail 94

Bowden,
    Elias 159*
    John 140*
    Samuel 43*
    Theodore 13*

Bowe,
    Edward 92*
    Mabel 43

Bowen,
    Barzillar 12
    David 161*
    Eleazer 57
    Elizabeth 62, 128
    Emery 86
    Ephraim 45*
    James 46*
    Jeremiah 25, 65*
    Joel 28*
    John A. 25
    Lyman 47
    M. 128
    Priscilla 28*
    Rose 47*
    Sabia 69
    Samuel 12, 146*
    Sarah 12, 22*
    Simeon 47
    William 24, 128
    William A. 130

Bower,
    Frederick 112
    Joseph 32

Bowers,
    Abiah 40
    Alpheus 58
    Balaam 130*
    Catherine 50
    Cyrus 50
    George 122*
    Harley 59
    James 156*
    Jerahmeel 23
    Joab 103*
    John 140*
    John D. 180
    Leonard 152*
    Mary 28
    Milton 28
    Molly 28
    Peter 40
    Rebecca 60*, 114*
    Reuben 161*
    William W. 167
    Zepheniah 103*

Bowing,
    Jabes 13*

Bowker,
    Amy 75
    Edmond 39*
    John 41, 97*
    Levi 14*, 64
    Paul 5

Bowles,
    Epaphras 79
    Samuel 189
    Thomas 140*, 189

Bowley,
    John 24

Bowlin,
    Thomas 184*

Bowman,
    Daniel 157*
    David 27
    George H. 162
    Godfrey 124*
    John 37*
    Jashua 170

Bowman, (cont.)
    Philip 170
    Sarah 162
    Thaddeus 80
    Thankful 23
    Thornton A. 136
    William 185

Bowne,
    James 110*

Bowsman,
    John 151*

Box,
    Edward 159*
    Samuel 153

Boyce,
    Dwight 26
    William 148

Boyd,
    Alvin 75
    G. W. 167
    George 93*
    James 135*, 151*, 170*
    John 132*
    John M. 167
    Joseph 75
    Mehitable 107
    Robert 121, 176*, 182
    Thomas 189*
    William 128*, 154*, 160*

Boyden,
    (N.X.N.) 101
    John 34*
    Josiah 34*

Boydstun,
    Samuel 151*

Boyed,
    Daniel 139*

Boyer,
    Christian 114*
    Christopher 115
    Evan 116
    Henry 116, 160
    James 55
    James E. 126
    Lewis 177*

Boyington,
    Peltiah 13
    Waterman 13

Boyinton,
    J. 71
    Jewitt 71

Boykin,
    John 141*

Boyles,
    George 15*
    John 141

Boylon,
    Cornelius 96

Boynton,
    Bela 60*
    Berthier 21
    David 21
    Elias 21*
    Moses 12

Boytt,
    William 132*

Brabrook,
    Eunice 99
    William 99

Brace,
    Benjamin 192
    Daniel 61*
    Joseph 192

Brack,
    Janus 59
    Thaddeus 59

Brackets,
    Hezekiah 77*

Brackett,
    Herd 6*
    Isaac 40
    James 14*
    John 5
    Joshua 4*
    Martin 34
    Nathan 9*
    Rebecca 40
    Susanna 34
    Walker 5

Bracy,
    C. 68
    Cornelius 68

Bradberry,
    J. 155
    John 155

Bradbury,
    Daniel 41*
    James 42

Braden,
    John 152*

Bradenburg,
    Anthony 180

Bradesh,
    Edmund 4*

Bradford,
    Archibald 57
    Elisha 78
    Husey 49
    James 45, 137*
    Lewis 5
    Lucy 78, 71
    Mary 44
    Noah 28
    Peabody 5
    Philena 57
    Richard 71
    Susanna 45*

Bradish,
    Daniel 97*

Bradley,
    Abigail 62
    Anne 59*
    Benjamin 19*
    David 97*
    Ebenezer 62
    Eli 33
    Elihu 92*
    Elijah 52*
    Elisha 87
    Gilead 52*
    James 93*, 129*
    John 66, 148*, 149*
    Lent 76*
    Lydia 51
    Samuel 14*
    Thaddeus 172*

Bradley, (cont.)
 Timothy 52
 Timothy M. 62
 William 55

Bradly,
 David 32
 E. S. 32
 John 157*

Bradshaw,
 Benjamin 153*
 Claiborne 165*

Brady,
 Hepzee 82
 John 122*, 160
 William 160

Brag,
 Edward 5

Bragden,
 Enoch 4
 John 4
 Samuel 90
 Thomas 90

Bragdon,
 Aaron 11*
 Amos 17*
 John 6
 Jotham 7*
 Martha 42
 Nathaniel 6

Bragg,
 Lydia 10*, 42
 Moses 70*
 William 71, 152*

Brainard,
 Enoch 24

Brainerd,
 Lydia 60*

Brakenridge,
 James 173

Brakett,
 William 7*

Braman,
 Cyrus 105
 George W. 48

Braman, (cont.)
 James 64*
 Joseph 48
 Sylvanus 27
 Sylvanus B. 27

Bramble,
 Erastus 53
 Robert 53*

Bramblett,
 James 161*
 Reuben 145*, 187

Branaman,
 Christian 183*

Branch,
 Olive 129*
 Samuel 75*
 William 174*

Brandon,
 Benjamin 163
 Josiah 156*

Branham,
 William B. 160*

Brank,
 B. G. 162
 Robert 162

Brann,
 William 133*

Brannon,
 Sarah 117

Branscomb,
 Charles 13
 Rebecca 13

Brant,
 Joseph 80

Brasee,
 Peter 104
 Winneson 104*

Brasel,
 Bird 146*

Brass,
 Lucy 171

Brawner,
    Eli 124*

Bray,
    Enoch 41
    John 109*
    Joseph 13
    Nicholas 5

Brayton,
    Borden 47*
    Francis 47*
    John 47
    Mary 46*
    Patience 47

Brecher,
    James 26

Breck,
    Cyrus 24
    Patience 9
    Samuel 9

Breed,
    Allen 90
    John 92
    Joseph 77*, 92
    Rufus 90

Breedon,
    Enoch 155*

Breese,
    Garret 109*

Breette,
    John 78

Bregins,
    John 159*

Brenton,
    John 181

Bressier,
    Nicholas 123*

Brest,
    John 160*

Breth,
    Amzi 7
    Martin 7

Brett,
    Daniel 27*
    Edmond 106*

Brevard,
    Robert 189*

Brewer,
    Aaron 110
    Barret 149
    Benjamin 152
    David 43
    Elisha 78*
    Henry 173*
    Isaac 32*
    John 77*, 110
    Susan 127*

Brewno,
    Jacob 160
    Moses 160

Brewster,
    Charles 54
    Daniel 126*
    Darius 9*
    Eleanor 20
    Frederick 54*
    Hugh 144
    Isaac 20
    Joseph 95*
    Joshua 29*
    Lucy 12
    Nathan 168*
    Samuel 95*
    William 12, 144

Brey,
    Christopher 114*

Brian,
    James 144*

Briant,
    Betheal 66
    Jacob 111
    Reuben 57*

Briby,
    John 173

Brice,
    Samuel 143

Brick,
    Daniel 69*

Bricker,
    Benjamin 120
    Peter 120

Brickett,
    Barnard 63
    James 16*

Bricky,
    Jarret 189*

Bridge,
    Benjamin 172

Bridges,
    Allen J. 187*
    Daniel 4
    Edmund 13*
    Hannah 43

Bridgham,
    Garnish 5
    John 5
    Lucy 5

Bridgis,
    James 160
    Jane 160

Bridgman,
    Gideon 24
    Sybel 36
    Thomas 24

Briggs,
    Aaron 91*
    Abigail 48
    Abizer 28*
    Allen 80, 193
    Asa 97
    Benjamin 33*
    Deborah 30*, 32
    Elisha 29*, 72
    Elizabeth 28*
    Ephraim 80
    Huldah 186
    James 28*
    Jesse 29*
    Job 47, 48
    Joseph 49*, 66*, 81
    Leonard 30
    Lucy 28
    Naomi 7*

Briggs, (cont.)
    Nathaniel 24*
    Owen 72
    Patience 93*
    Phineas 83
    Samuel 29*
    Sarah 28*, 47
    Solomon 67
    Sweet 48
    Thankful 47
    Thomas 47*, 72

Brigham,
    Alice 38*
    Amariah 36
    Anna 37*
    Betty 41*
    D. C. 61
    Dow C. 61
    Elizabeth 40
    Emma 65
    Eunice 39
    John 23
    Jonathan 76*
    Lydia 172
    Mary 61
    Samuel 65
    Stephen 90*

Brightman,
    Daniel 27
    Mary 53
    Peleg 27*
    Thomas 48*
    William P. 53

Brightwell,
    Charles 132*

Brigs,
    Austin 92
    Joshua 92

Briles,
    Reuben 158

Brimage,
    John 162
    Thomas 162

Brimfield,
    Humphrey 174*

Brimhall,
    Sarah 17

Briney,
  Kellian 121

Briniyion,
  Thomas 8*

Brink,
  Adam 103
  Benjamin 126
  George 76*
  Henry 97
  Jacob 103
  James 103
  John 126
  Margaret 103
  Mary 192
  Moses 99
  William J. 103
  Wilman R. 99

Brinkerhoff,
  Jacob J. 107
  James 107
  Seba 102*

Brinton,
  Asa 22

Bristee,
  Candes Lilly 57
  Theodore 57

Bristol,
  David 52*, 89
  Eli 88*
  Henry 58
  Nathaniel 74
  Reuben 177*

Briton,
  James 64*

Brittian,
  Joseph 96

Brittain,
  William 137*

Britton,
  Abijah 86
  Asa 22
  Jesse 139*
  John C. 90
  Joseph 153*
  Michael 138

Broadway,
  George 142
  John 158*

Brock,
  Bezzent 138*
  Hannah 68
  Hartwell 190
  Headon 143
  Paul 17
  Reuben 143
  Uriah 190

Brockett,
  Giles 52*
  Joel 51*
  Leman 52
  Martha J. 186
  Thomas J. 186

Brockway,
  John 53*
  Martin 97*

Broderic,
  Paul 178

Brodhead,
  Samuel 102

Broga,
  Andrew 32*

Broiles,
  Cornelius 154
  Daniel 154

Brokaw,
  George 169*
  Isaac 111*
  Richard 111*

Bromley,
  Alas 54*
  William 68*

Brondage,
  David 176*

Bronner,
  Felix 83

Bronson,
  Asahel 53*
  Fidelia 50

Bronson, (cont.)
    Hannah 53*
    Isaac 53*, 126*
    Marilla 60
    Phineas 188*
    Selah 52*
    Theodore 50

Brooker,
    Samuel 33*

Brookfield,
    Brown 110*
    William 107

Brooks,
    Abel 148
    Ahira 192*
    Alpheus 71*
    Asa 187*
    Asahael 8
    Bathsheba 132*
    Charles 117*, 176
    E. 37
    Ebenezer 38
    Eleazer 62*
    Eliza 48
    Garry 86
    George 145
    Hanneniah 168
    James 129*
    John 3, 20*, 30, 55*, 92,
      93, 160*, 172
    Jonas 25*
    Littleton 153*
    Nathan 35
    Oliver 180
    Oliver J. 180
    Reuben 33*, 70*
    Robert 185
    Samuel 8, 37
    Samuel L. 86
    Sarah J. 175
    Silas 79*
    Smith 142*
    Thomas 153*, 188
    William 20*, 136*, 140*

Brooksher,
    John 143*

Broom,
    Daniel 78

Brothers,
    Thomas 161*

Brotherton,
    Thomas 139
    William B. 139

Brothwell,
    Benjamin 55*

Brothwill,
    Thomas 55*

Brougham,
    John J. 96
    Margaret 96

Brower,
    Abram 106
    John C. 105
    John H. 106
    Mary 111*
    Rebecca 106

Browin,
    Edward 164

Brown,
    A. G. 168
    Abigail 57*
    Adam 87
    Alexander 156
    Ambrose 57*, 145*
    Amos 93, 138*
    Andrew 10*, 37
    Arabia 162*
    Archibald 164
    Artem 31
    Arthur 158*
    Asa 91, 92
    Asahel 67
    Asenath 12
    Asher 66
    Benjamin 38, 100, 133, 145*, 153*
    Caleb 19*
    Catharine 156
    Charles 18*, 165
    Christopher 48*, 53*
    Cyril 12
    Cyrus 93
    Daniel 86, 87, 101*
    David 28*, 77, 86
    Deborah 50
    E. D. 176
    Ebenezer 40*, 53, 99*, 192*
    Ebenezer J. 80
    Edward 43
    Eleazer 94
    Eli 83*

Brown, (cont.)
    Eliada 194
    Elias 51*
    Elijah 46, 67*, 97, 140
    Elisha 175
    Elizabeth 136
    Elkanah 82
   *Enoch 14
    Esek 46*
    Esther 92
    Ezekiel 171
    Ezra 176
    Fanny 77
    Fracil W. 49
    Francis 162
    George F. 43
    Gersham 35
    Giles R. 83
    Hambleton 149*
    Harvey 60
    Henry 115*, 129*, 145*
    Humphrey 47
    Ira 97
    Isaac 12, 41, 71*, 119
    Isaiah 34*
    Issachar 131*
    Jacob 33*, 113, 118, 154*
    James 3, 19*, 42*, 78, 112,
      117, 125*, 143*
    James P. 12
    Jane 168
    Jeptha 54*
    Jeremiah 11, 15*, 128*, 156*
    Jerusha 52*
    Jesse 49, 133, 138*, 190*
    John 18, 19, 28, 47*, 62*,
      82, 86, 91, 99, 120*, 124*,
      132*, 133*, 144, 147, 150*,
      157*, 177*
    John F. 103
    John R. 99
    John S. 190
    Jonathan 8*, 100*, 103*
    Joseph 32, 81*, 106, 136,
      153*, 190
    Joshua 16*, 48*
    Joshua A. 156
    Josiah 176
    Laban 65
    Lebius 55
    Levi 80*, 85
    Levi K. 112
    Low 136*
    Lydia 24
    Lysander 82
    Mariam 15
  Ephraim 40, 59

Brown, (cont.)
    Martha 129*
    Mary 10, 36, 42*, 43*, 49, 58,
      116, 129
    Mary (Mrs.) 142*
    Mason G. 27
    Matilda 77
    Mehitable 105
    Melville 176
    Moody 4*
    Moses 16, 67
    Nathan 36*, 83*, 187*
    Nathaniel 60*, 82
    Nehemiah 101*
    Oliver 22, 38, 168, 174*
    Oliver (Capt.) 133
    Orthanial 61*
    P. 142
    Park 51
    Peleg 48
    Peter 84, 117, 136
    Pollard 142
    Rachel 104
    Robert 35, 158*
    Rosamond 45
    Samuel 7*, 14, 40*, 107, 168,
      187*
    Sarah 41, 48*, 59, 107
    Solomon 69*
    Stephen 42*, 92*
    Sylvester 91
    Sylvia 52*
    Tarlton 142*
    Thaddeus 6*
    Thomas 15, 20*, 91, 152*, 158*,
      165*
    Thomas C. 162*
    Thomas S. 12
    Timothy 181
    Tristram 24
    Uriah 22
    Waite 46
    Warren 59
    William 8*, 24*, 59, 67, 71, 82,
      94*, 111*, 123, 133*, 134*, 14●
      149*, 156
    William B. 39*
    William G. 10, 123
    William R. 190

Browne,
    James 141*
    William 59

Brownell,
    Abner 47
    Alfred 47
    Deborah 47
    James 47
    Phebe 47*
    Ruth 47
    Stephen 47*

Browning,
    Francis 136*
    Mary 163
    Samuel 48
    Susanna 48

Brownson,
    Edward 68
    Eunice 119

Bruce,
    David 66
    Dexter 36
    George 157
    Hannah 43*
    John 99*, 157*
    Joseph 66
    Silas 34
    William 157*

Brumback,
    Peter 160*

Brumbley,
    Perry 48*

Brumfield,
    John 151
    Fleming 151

Brumley,
    John 118*

Brummett,
    Thomas 152*

Brundage,
    Mary 106

Bruner,
    Ide 152
    Jacob 152
    Peter 113*

Brunson,
    Huldah 82

Brush,
    Ebenezer 97
    Ruth 97

Bruster,
    James 142

Bruton,
    James 139

Bryan,
    C. 179
    Daniel 163
    Elijah 179
    Elisha 136
    Ezekiel 147*
    George 160
    Jacob 188
    John 52, 141*
    Mary 52
    Thomas 163
    William 136
    William S. 160

Bryant,
    Abijah 7*
    Alexander 93*
    Austin 152
    Benjamin 191*
    Betsey 37
    David 37*
    Elizabeth 148
    Ezekiel 28
    H. M. 148
    James 184
    Jesse 141
    John 18, 140, 148*
    Joseph 5*, 174
    Mary 39*
    Paschal G. 164
    Patrick 35
    Reuben 141*
    Robert 152
    Sarah 162*
    Thomas 152*
    William 37
    William O. 137*
    Zachariah 185*

Bryson,
    Daniel 139*

Bubibeer,
    Hannah 39
    John 39

Buccannon,
    James 120

Buchanan,
    George 146*
    James 141
    William 106*

Buchanon,
    David 120*

Bucholter,
    Peter 147

Buck,
    (Mrs.) 41
    Aaron 57*, 83
    Abel 68*
    Asaph 93*
    Betsey 50
    Daniel 89
    Elizabeth 116*
    Ephraim 152*
    George 87
    Ichabod 119*
    Isaac 98, 137*
    J. 175
    John 85
    Jonathan 7, 89, 175
    Morton 185
    Nathan 32
    Samuel 85
    Thomas 98, 136*
    William 185

Bucke,
    Anelm 10

Buckhart,
    George 163
    John 120*

Buckingham,
    G. 94

Buckland,
    George 50*
    Jonathan 61*

Bucklew,
    Peter 121*

Buckley,
    Amelia 55
    Charlotte 55
    D. 50

Buckley, (cont.)
    Eleazer 55*
    Jonathan 125*
    Joseph 55
    Timothy 55

Buckly,
    Daniel 88

Buckman,
    Benjamin 185*
    Elias 24*
    Reuben 32
    William 70*

Buckminster,
    Benjamin M. 20

Budd,
    John 125*

Budlong,
    Anna 48
    Mary A. 48
    Stephen 48

Buel,
    Arphaxed 119
    Charles 58
    David 58*
    Ebenezer 62
    Lucy 33
    Marlin 52*
    Nathan 119
    Sophia 62

Buell,
    Isaac 89*
    John 83
    Timothy 91*
    Ward 65

Buffam,
    Samuel 47

Buffington,
    Luther 45
    Preserved 126*

Buford,
    John 129*, 162*

Bugbee,
    Alanson 61
    George 80*
    Hannah 61

Bugbee, (cont.)
    Hezekiah 58
    Martha 57*
    Mehitable 69
    Sarah 57

Bugber,
    William 100

Bukely,
    Charles 53*

Bucker,
    Israel 169*
    Windsor 50

Bukwith,
    Lydia 53

Buley,
    Benjamin 103

Bull,
    Jesse B. 49
    Joel 80
    John 58
    Martha 58
    Peter 103

Bullard,
    Asa 36
    Elijah 119*
    John 30
    Nathan 19
    Ruth 34

Bullinger,
    Adam 134*

Bullock,
    Charles 138
    Chloe 66
    Comfort 104
    Ebenezer 82*
    John 117
    Major 104
    Peter 24
    Susan 46

Bullough,
    Elias 147
    J. K. 147

Bump,
    Moses 87*
    Reuben 126

Bumphrey,
    Stephen 43*

Bumps,
    Benjamin 12
    Shubal 12

Bumpus,
    Axy 29*
    Daniel 28
    Edward 28
    Edward 28
    Edmund P. 28
    Hannah 7
    Huldah 7
    Mesey 29*
    Nathaniel 7

Bundey,
    William 179*

Bundy,
    Elijah 95
    Elijah H. 59*
    Elizabeth 95
    Phillip E. 24

Bunker,
    Lewis 30
    Rufus K. 7

Bunn,
    Lydia 49

Bunnel,
    (N.X.N.) 50
    Dennis 85
    Elizabeth 115*
    John 50
    Luther 52
    Pehial 85
    Pure 52

Bunnell,
    Abel 58
    John 116
    Samuel 53

Bunster,
    James 145
    William 145

Bunting,
    Mary 116

Bunton,
    William 159*

Burbage,
    Thomas 142*

Burbank,
    Abel 71
    Elizabeth 36
    John 3, 36
    John S. 100
    Judith 100
    Mehitable 41
    Sulivan 39*
    William 18*

Burbeck,
    Henry 53*
    Thomas 39

Burbridge,
    Lincefield 161
    Thomas 161

Burbuk,
    Thomas 40

Burch,
    *Daniel 99
    Henry 182
    Joseph 166*
    *Freeman 192
Burchard,
    Nathaniel 97

Burchart,
    Jacob 123*

Burchfield,
    John 184*
    Robert 184*
    Thomas 121

Burd,
    Andrew 115

Burden,
    Aaron 39
    Bilota 39
    John 136*
    Nathaniel 36*

Burdich,
    Augustus 58
    Isaiah 48
    Joshua 82

Burdick,
    Abner 119
    Robert 74*
    Varnum M. 78

Burdock,
    Adam 63*

Burdwin,
    J. R. 87
    Lois 87

Buren,
    Jeremiah 137

Burge,
    David 161*
    Lot 82*

Burges,
    Jane 43*

Burgese,
    Keziah 10

Burgess,
    James 78, 133*
    John 28*
    Jonathan 10*
    Lucy 28
    Sarah 29*

Burget,
    Lambert 98*

Burgett,
    John 166

Burgh,
    David 96
    Eleanor 96

Burhigh,
    Peter 17
    Sarah 17

Burk,
    Elizabeth 110, 154
    Joseph 68
    Mary 107
    Robert 166*
    Sampson 68

Burkart,
    Frederick 115*

Burke,
    J. 151
    Joseph 152*
    Samuel 166*
    Silas 91*
    Susan 130*
    Wiley B. 151

Burket,
    Christopher 123*

Burkhardt,
    Jacob 117

Burkholder,
    John 136
    William 136

Burkley,
    Rhoda 25

Burks,
    Elizabeth 189
    Samuel 190
    William 190

Burlew,
    John 109
    Ruth 109*

Burley,
    Abigail 16*
    Benjamin 24
    Elizabeth 24

Burlingame,
    Amey 46
    Benjamin 33*
    Christopher 180
    David 46*
    John B. 180
    Nathan 73*
    Pardon 46*

Burlison,
    Edward 88*

Burnam,
    Isaac 170*

Burnap,
    Polly 37*

Burnell,
    Jonathan 5
    Joseph 35

Burnell, (cont.)
    Sophia 69

Burner,
    (N.X.N.) 136
    John R. 136

Burnes,
    John 190*
    William 161

Burnet,
    Robert 106*

Burnett,
    Andrew 45*
    John J. H. 72*
    Joshua 182*
    Richard 164
    William 157*

Burney,
    Samuel 148*
    Sarah 51

Burnham,
    Abner 86*
    Andrew 41
    Asa 75
    Benjamin 42*
    George 16, 47, 106*, 188*
    James 16*
    Jemima 45
    John 16, 42*
    Mehitable 53
    Nathan 60*
    Oliver 59*
    Pike G. 26*
    Roger 50*
    Ruhama 20*
    Ruth 41
    Sarah 42*
    Walcott 72*

Burnheimer,
    Jacob 8
    Joseph 8

Burns,
    James 87
    John 26*, 143*
    Joshua 142
    Lard 154
    Philip 167*

Burnside,
    Andrew 142*
    Robert 164*

Burr,
    Catherine M. 55
    Charles 49
    Elizabeth 27
    Joel 95*
    Mary 32
    Melinda 86
    Rebecca 59
    Sarah A. 55*
    Seth 29
    W. 86
    William 53*
    Zabina 50*

Burrell,
    Benjamin 45*
    Nathan 168

Burret,
    Moses 84

Burrett,
    Nathan 55*
    Sally 55

Burrill,
    John 14*

Burris,
    Elijah W. 182

Burrite,
    Hannah 89

Burroughs,
    Charles 109
    Daniel 187*
    John 109
    Solomon 139*
    Westly 109

Burrows,
    Amos 95
    Caleb 95
    Cathine 53
    Joseph 86
    Moses 180
    Nathaniel 112
    William 97*

Burpee,
    Isaac 21
    Nathaniel 42

Burpey,
    Jonathan 19
    Joseph 19
    Nathaniel 19

Burt,
    Aaron 175*
    Benjamin 179*
    David 44
    Edward 74*
    James 107*
    Joel 36
    John 73
    Reuben 44*
    Richard 111
    Ruth 66
    Warner 66

Burter,
    Jemima 16

Burtis,
    Solomon 124

Burton,
    Asa 33
    Benjamin 63*
    Charles 37
    Elijah 68
    Elizabeth 37
    Henry 70*
    J. E. 86
    Lewis 55
    Naomi 59
    Richard 142*
    Robert 140*
    Samuel 128
    Selah 84
    Simon 76*
    Susannah 21
    Thomas 128
    William 8*, 102*, 141*, 189

Busbee,
    John 62

Busby,
    Needham 142*
    Robert 187

Bush,
    Abijah 94*
    Conrad 90*
    Drury 160*
    Enoch 135*
    Frederick 102
    George 60*

Bush, (cont.)
James 161*
John 87*
John T. 104
Joseph 104, 124
Prescott 147*
Robert 161
Sarah 105
Stephen 76*
Ziba 33*

Bushee,
Austus 27

Bushnel,
Doud 64*

Bushnell,
Jason 88*

Bushong,
George 154*

Buskins,
Isaac 184

Buskirk,
John 182
Joseph 182

Buss,
Ephraim 88*
Lydia 22

Bussel,
Isaac 14
Robert 14

Bussell,
Matilda 63
William 153*

Bussett,
Isaac 51*

Bussey,
James 57
John 31*

Bussle,
Matthew 152*

Buster,
Claudis 133*

Buswell,
Anna 24
Elias 17
Hammond, 24
James 19*
John 16

Butler,
Abigail 42*
Allen 98*
Ann 115
Ann D. 130
Augustus 89
Azariah 44
Catharine 86
David 100*
George 9
J. O. 132
James 149*
Jethro 151*
John 131*, 132
Jonathan 20*
Joseph 22, 132*
Lucinda 46
Lydia 104*
Patty 79
Phineas 9
Reuben 97*
Samuel 59, 115
Sarah 131
Stephen 62*
William 59, 190*
Zachariah 157*

Butman,
Nancy 43
Rebecca 42*

Butrick,
Oliver 82

Butter,
William 58

Butterfield,
Elijah 100*
Jesse 14
Olive 84
Oliver 20
Philip 44
Phineas 20
Rachel 79
Robert 20
Samuel 79

Butterfoss,
    Andrew 109*
    E. 109

Butterworth,
    Noah 46

Buttler,
    Israel 91*

Buttles,
    L. 44
    Olive 44
    R. 44

Button,
    Benjamin 87
    Elijah 44
    Joseph 119
    William 57

Butts,
    Isaac 54
    Lockwood 91
    Pardon 91
    Thomas 27*
    William 91

Buzan,
    John 161*

Buzell,
    Moses 18

Buzzel,
    Joshua 77*

Buzzell,
    Henry 17*
    Jacob P. 17
    Jonathan 17
    Jotham 13*
    Martha 17
    Mary 17

Bybee,
    Nealey 190*

Byer,
    John 112

Byerly,
    Jacob 124*

Byers,
    Frederick 113

Byington,
    Lucy 98

Bynum,
    John 155*

Byrd,
    William 132

Byres,
    John 112

Byvis,
    George 167

Cab,
    Ann 102

Cabah,
    Peter 162*

Cabbage,
    Adam 152*
    John 152

Cable,
    John M. 105

Cabos,
    John 147*

Cadenhead,
    James 149*

Cadle,
    Richard 127

Cadwell,
    E. S. 87
    Phineas 87
    Reuben 78*

Cady,
    Absalom 61
    Chloe 83
    David 86
    Elias 192*
    Elisha 57
    Elizabeth 71
    George 86
    Heny 88
    Isaac 72*

Cady, (cont.)
    Jonathan 36*, 80*
    Lyman 71
    Molly 61
    Richard 57*
    Ruth 88
    Squire 57
    Zadock 75*

Choon,
    Zuba 26*

Cain,
    Jemima 28
    John 161*
    Robert 181
    Samuel 28

Calaham,
    Joel 143*

Calaway,
    Dudley 128

Calb,
    Michael 92

Calder,
    James 45
    John 45, 146*

Claderwood,
    James 12
    John 12

Caldwell,
    Asa 39
    Charles 148
    David 148
    Ezekiel 135
    James 143*
    John 34, 135
    Joseph 143*
    Philip 86*
    Robert 183
    Rufus 34
    William 153*, 168*

Calehoofer,
    Frederick 118*

Calep,
    James 16

Calhoon,
    Samuel 180*

Calhoun,
    Alonzo 62
    James 100*
    Samuel 62

Calkin,
    Eli 69*

Calkins,
    Annis 65
    Esther 44
    John 68
    Mary 44
    Matthew 77*
    Nathaniel 95

Callaway,
    Micajah 185*

Calleham,
    David 129*

Callen,
    Hugh 120*

Callier,
    David 188*

Callis,
    George 132*

Calloway,
    Chesley 165

Calton,
    Elizabeth 148

Calvin,
    Caleb 46
    John 190
    Jotham 9*
    Mary 46
    Sarah 129

Calwell,
    David 46
    John 112
    Willard 46
    William 155*

Cam,
    John 175

Cameron,
    Andrew W. 134
    Rachel 134

Camp,
Andrew 112
Asa 99*
Benjamin 92*
Elah 60
John 58*
Lemuel 60
Manoah 60*
Nicholas 92*
Rejoice 60
Reuben 57*

Campbell,
Alexander 121
Archibald 78*, 86*
Archibald 59*
Archy 142*
Catharine 108
Charles 120, 151
Daniel R. 79*
David 125*, 149*
George 146*
Hugh 151
Isaac 86*
Jacob 93
James 10*, 66, 109, 144*,
152, 153*, 174, 183*
Jeremiah 37*, 123, 152*
John 75*, 130*, 165, 166*,
174, 176*, 177
Joseph 153*
Joshumy 175
Lawrence 163
Mary 121
R. A. 175
Rachel 123
Rice 109
Richard 156*
Robert 120*, 153*, 164*
Samuel 182
Squire 93
Susan 132*
Thomas 117, 148
William 3, 5*, 20, 165*
William C. 68

Camper,
John 133*

Campfield,
John 110*

Candee,
Job 52
Samuel 52*

Candel,
Buckner 185

Candill,
James 166
William 166

Candle,
Absalom 137
Berry 137

Canfield,
Aman 105*
Andrew 119*
Charles 178
Daniel 33*
Dennis 80*
Elijah 178
Henry 60
Israel 110*
L. B. 78
Oliver 125*
Timothy 93*

Cannady,
John 129*

Cannon,
James 190*
John 33
Martha 109
Olive 33
Pugh 159

Canon,
Henry 143*

Canter,
John 179*

Capen,
Samuel 31*

Capevill,
James 48*

Capin,
Ebenezer 67

Caples,
Jesse 59*

Capron,
Elisha 46
Elisha 85

Capron, (cont.)
    Greene 49*, 60
    Joseph 46*
    Sylvester 85

Caps,
    Greenbury 143*
    Hilary 156

Capson,
    Horace 45

Cara,
    Alpha 101
    Isaac 101

Carathers,
    James 152*

Card,
    Betsey 180
    Hugh 148*
    Peleg 48*
    Thomas 93
    Thurston 9*
    William 47*

Carder,
    Robert 135
    Sally 86
    Virginia Page 135

Cardozo,
    S. 142*

Cardwell,
    Perrin 153*

Carey,
    Francis 133
    Henry 68
    Hezekiah 68
    Jabez 88*
    John 125*
    Jonathan 30*
    Joseph 77*, 100*
    Richard 80*
    Samuel 125*

Cargill,
    Thomas 148*

Carhart,
    John 110

Carl,
    Elijah 181
    John 96*
    Samuel 181*

Carle,
    William 14*

Carleton,
    Isaac 42
    Jonathan 10*
    Samuel 42*
    Sarah 42

Carley,
    Jonathan 66
    Joseph 66, 96

Carlisle,
    Deborah 65
    James 142*
    Lydia 21*
    Michael 65
    William 156

Carll,
    Ebenezer 4
    Mary 174
    Robert 4

Carlton,
    Benjamin 41
    Daniel 16
    Ezra 14*
    Jephtha 178
    John 12, 139
    Rebecca 21*, 26
    Ruth 16
    Sarah 41
    Thomas 16*
    Woodman 26

Carmack,
    Cornelius 157
    John 157
    William 135*

Carman,
    Thomas 111*

Carmer,
    Abraham 79*
    Isaac 99*

Carmichael,
    John 177*

Carnagey,
    William 170*

Carnall,
    Patrick 129*

Carner,
    Jacob 96
    Philip 96

Carnes,
    Edward 44
    Godfrey 124
    John 124, 169

Carney,
    John 157*
    Weden 135

Carnine,
    Peter 166*

Carns,
    Ephraim 110*

Carpenter,
    Abel 63
    Benjamin 89, 98, 107
    Bernard 89
    Colonel A. 49
    Daniel 74*, 83
    David 22*
    Elias 65*
    Elijah 87
    Eliphal 57
    Ezra 31
    George 65
    Guy 97*
    Isaiah 90
    Jesse 87
    John 49, 67, 184
    Joseph 46*
    Lemuel 152
    Lewis 67, 85*
    Lucius 57
    Margaret 107
    Mary 113
    Olive 65
    Peggy M. 66
    Richard 57
    Samuel 97, 135*
    Sbubael 172
    Thomas 3*
    Timothy 61*

Carpenter, (cont.)
    Uriah B. 57
    William 97

Carper,
    John 136*

Carr,
    Amos 33*
    Christopher 114
    Daniel 9
    David 18
    Ebenezer 92
    Eli 12
    Gideon 155
    Jesse 19*
    John 47*, 77
    John B. 155
    Jonathan 84
    Joseph 94*, 95
    Levi 90*
    Mary 42
    Mary J. 45
    Moses 138*
    Moses J. 126
    Nathan 23*, 77
    Samuel 113
    William 12, 95, 126, 138*

Carragan,
    Gilbert 104*

Carregan,
    William 137*

Carrell,
    William 175*

Carrington,
    Clement 129*
    George 140*

Carrol,
    Jesse 46*
    John 53*

Carroll,
    Daniel 155
    Dempsey 149*
    Dennis 122
    James 145
    John 163*
    William 172

Carryl,
    Parmelia 23
    Sally 23

Carson,
    Andrew 139*
    James 161*
    John 185*
    Mary 106
    Robert 109, 158
    Seth 14
    Washington 109
    William 144, 160*

Carswell,
    David 171

Carte,
    Alexander 84

Carter,
    Abijah 6*
    Amos 154
    Barnabas 165
    Benjamin C. 101
    Braxton 137*
    Charles 147*, 153*
    Daniel 25
    David 145*
    Elihu 50
    Elizabeth 142*, 152
    Elthir 50
    Ezekiel 152
    George W. 141
    Henry 15, 141, 166*
    Isaac 33*
    Jabez 101
    Jacob 15
    James 40, 84, 132, 137,
      140*, 170*, 181
    Joel 49*
    John 18*, 84, 95*, 129,
      152
    Joseph 124*
    Joshua 36*
    Julia 40
    Lois 50
    Matilda 112
    Michael 20*
    Nathan 19*
    Philip 160*
    Rachel 59*
    Robert 147
    Rufus 90*
    Samuel 154
    Thomas 12*, 123*, 140*
    William 58, 84, 132*,
      165*

Cartmile,
    Henry 133*

Cartwright,
    Peter 186
    Samuel 186

Carvan,
    John 166

Carver,
    Austin 87
    Clifford 27
    John 27
    Mary 30
    Tabitha 60*

Carvill,
    Benjamin 9
    Mercy 8

Cary,
    David 93
    Ebenezer 165*
    Harry 66
    Levi 92
    Luther 8*
    Oliver 73*
    Zenas 92

Case,
    Abel 51*
    Abner 187*
    Augustus 181
    Charles 51
    Clark 54
    Dorcas 90
    Ebenezer 26*
    Ichabod 79*
    Isaac 10*
    James 182*
    John 90
    John M. 51
    Nathan 71*
    Tunis 109*

Casey,
    Charles S. 155
    Christopher 189
    Hardin 189
    John 155
    Joseph 164*
    M. B. 149
    Wanton 49*
    William 149

Cash,
    Ann 145
    Howard 145
    Mary 43

Cash, (cont.)
    Peter 138
    Samuel 26*
    Thomas 161*
    W. P. 163
    Warren 163

Cashman,
    Andrew 10
    Isaac 10

Cashwell,
    William 128*

Casler,
    Adam 87
    Daniel 84
    Delilah 88
    John 88
    Nicholas 87*
    Peter A. 87
    Richard 83*
    Richard J. 83

Cason,
    John 137
    William 133*, 147*

Cass,
    Abel 18
    Joseph J. 59
    Moses 13*
    Nebediah 176*
    Theophilus 24

Cassadey,
    George 124*

Cassady,
    Margaret 91

Cassel,
    William 132

Cassell,
    Abraham 164
    Thomas J. 164

Casselman,
    Barbara 83
    John 83

Cassway,
    John 88

Casterline,
    Daniel 110
    Eunice 110

Castle,
    Isaac B. 53
    Samuel 141

Castleberry,
    Paul 143*

Caswell,
    Barnabas 70
    David 54
    Deliverance 57
    Hannah 43, 54
    Jane 43
    Jedediah 30*
    Joseph 17*
    Phillip 5
    Richard 43, 44
    Samuel 163*
    Simeon 5
    William 15

Cate,
    Elisha 63*
    Samuel 20
    William T. 17

Catham,
    William 43*

Cathcart,
    Enos 82
    Thomas 82

Catherine,
    Meriman 52

Cathey,
    George 190

Catlin,
    Lery 58
    Octural 52
    Sarah 89
    Timothy 34*

Catlins,
    Putnam 119*

Caton,
    Abram 96*
    Leonard 90
    Richard 90

Cator,
    Abm. J. 79
    Cornelius 79
    John C. 79*

Catt,
    Philip 183*

Cattell,
    Jonas 108*

Catun,
    Peter 167*

Caulk,
    Jacob 148

Caulkins,
    Eunice 171

Cauly,
    Francis 157*

Cauney,
    Charity 18

Caurod,
    Benjamin 163

Causland,
    Robert M. 13*

Cave,
    Benjamin 179

Cavenan,
    John 58*

Cavenaugh,
    Edward 116*

Cawthorn,
    Richard 130*

Cayson,
    Edm. 156*
    James 156

Cearnel,
    Archibald 189
    William L. 189

Cease,
    John 79

Cell,
    Philip 139*

Center,
    Emery 8
    Hannah 16

Cetchell,
    Stephen 80

Chase,
    Ezekiel 27*
    Horace 51
    Rebecca 51
    Simeon 27*
    Stephen 46*

Chacy,
    John 110*

Chadbourn,
    Levi 3*
    Seammon 3*
    Simeon 3*

Chadsey,
    Benjamin 95*

Chadwell,
    George 155

Chadwick,
    Abigail 19*
    James 162
    John 49, 162
    Joseph 85
    Joshua 22*
    Levi 174*
    Nathan 92*
    William 85

Chaffee,
    Abiel 58*
    Chester 58*
    Daniel 44
    Ephraim 44
    Joel 59*
    John 62
    Lucy 62
    Mary 50
    Olive 44
    Samuel 50

Chaffin,
    Rodney 7

Chaffy,
Henry 180

Chalker,
Jabez 60*
Moses 60*
Oliver 60*

Challis,
Benjamin 23
Christopher 16
Nathaniel 23

Chamberlain,
Benjamin 67
Chalin 115
Ebenezer 62, 67
Elisha 22*
John 4
Judith 17
Julius 192
Mary 66*
Patience 29
Phineas 75
S. 67
Samuel 109
Thomas 164*
W. 67
Wealthy 192

Chamberlin,
Aaron 110*
Asa 70
C. 70, 93
Calvin 29*
D. 73
Daniel 73, 119
Jiriah 72*
John 85, 110*
Joseph 112
Judah 175*
Molly 29
Moses 66
Nathaniel 33*, 66
O. P. 85
Patience 29
Rufus 59
William 70

Chambers,
Ann 95
Benjamin 190*
Benjamin 74*
David 109
E. O. 159
Ephraim 98*

Chambers, (cont.)
James 110*, 117, 190
John 81*, 120*, 158, 190
Lydia 95
Nathaniel 185*
Sarah 145
Wilson 158

Chambertin,
Mary 3

Chamblee,
Willie 141

Champe,
Phoebe 171*
William 171

Champion,
Daniel 71*
Phebe 53*
Reuben 53*

Champlin,
Adam B. 48*
Elias 103
Elizabeth 74
George 77
Hazard 49
John E. H. 47
Jonathan 77
Joseph 48
Michael 77
Nicholas P. 79
Samuel 74
Silas 53*
Stephen 54, 79*
Susanna 74*
William 69*

Chancellor,
David 185

Chandler,
Abial 25
Abigail 25
Charles C. 97
Dimond 44
Ebenezer 63
Ezra B. 66
Freelove 44
Hannah 11*
Henry 72, 185
Howard 29*
Joan 40
Joel 146

Chandler, (cont.)
John 6*, 9*, 97, 148*,
161
Joseph 185
Joshua 30*
Josiah 117
Lucy 97
Lury 86
Matthew 86
Meshack 143*
Mordecai 143*
Nathaniel 5
Noah 10
Samuel 20*, 29, 142*
Shelldeake 146
Simeon 66
Stephen 97
Theophilus 63
Thomas 29, 134*
Thomas M. 142*
Walter 84
William 40
Zebedee 29*

Chandoin,
S. 130*

Chaney,
Henry 127
John 182

Chapel,
Anna 54
Betsey 54
Guy 54
Jonathan 53
Lucy 54

Chapin,
Benoni 62*
Calvin 50*
David 89*
Esther 62*
Huldah 71
Ichabod 62
Lucy 34
Lydia 71
Mary 67*
Oliver 61*
Paul 44
Samuel 187
Sylvanus 71*
Timothy 98*
Wolcot 71

Chaplain,
Ebenezer 50*

Chaples,
James 8

Chaplin,
John 63*
John S. 6
Lydia 6

Chapman,
Ashbel 61
Benjamin 9, 154*
Dan. 83*
Daniel 97*, 168, 187*, 188*
Ebenezer 100*
Elisha 17*
Esther 57
Frederick 51
George 135
Horace 23
J. S. 179
James 53*, 89
Jason 53
Jedediah 60*
Joel 90
Lemuel 184
Lois 48*
Lucy 155*
Lydia 61
Richard 23
Robert 156
Rufus 89
Salathel 51*
Samuel J. 187*
Sarah 15, 24*
Thomas 75
Valentine 17*

Chappel,
Edward 57
John 143
Noah 117*

Chappell,
Amos 86
Frederick 48
Hiram 87
Lydia 174
Scranton 48
Thomas 48
William 133*

Charles,
    Thomas 44*

Charlesworth,
    Margaret 87

Charlton,
    David 138*
    John 172
    Francis 135*

Charnock,
    John 128*

Chase,
    A. T. 67
    Amariah 176
    Barton 28
    Daniel 56, 101
    Dean 95*
    Ebenezer 8*
    Edmund 3
    Elizabeth 66
    Ezekiel 14*
    George 25
    Gideon 56
    Grindal 38, 49*
    Hezekiah 12
    Isaac 6*, 8, 106
    James 8, 67
    Jared 27*
    Jeremiah 78*
    John 28, 71*
    Joseph 91
    Leonard 26*
    Lydia 41, 42
    Mary 23, 71
    Maxson 48
    Moses 15, 25
    Nathaniel 7
    Oliver 57*
    Parker 186
    Reuben 27*
    Rhoda 58
    Richard 33*
    Robert 8*
    Samuel 25, 26*
    Sarah 21
    Solomon 176
    Thomas 7*, 25
    William 76*

Chatfield,
    Daniel 55
    Lewis 55

Chatman,
    Constant 177
    Henry C. 177
    Nathaniel 50*

Chaudoin,
    Andrew 163*

Cheadle,
    Elijah 81*

Cheatham,
    Benjamin 155*

Check,
    James 136*

Cheek,
    Richard 153*
    William 146*

Cheeney,
    Moses 41

Cheeny,
    Ebenezer 22*

Cheeseman,
    Benjamin 122

Cheever,
    (Mrs.) 43*
    Abijah 42*
    Jacob 39
    Sarah 39

Cheeves,
    William R. 130*

Cheives,
    Joel 133*

Chelfench,
    Hiram 147

Chellis,
    Elizabeth 16

Chemiller,
    David 176

Cheney,
    Benjamin 69
    David 65
    Enoch 65

Cheney, (cont.)
    Hannah 16
    Nathaniel 66*
    Priscilla 71
    Samuel 19
    William 16

Chenoweth,
    Jehu 136
    Mary 136

Cheny,
    Molly 37*

Cherry,
    J. W. 149
    Joshua 149

Chesbrough,
    Perez 54*

Cheshire,
    Richard 137*

Chesley,
    John 15
    Philip 92*
    Samuel 7
    Simon 126*
Chesney,
    Benjamin 135

Chester,
    John 154*, 159*
    Mary 53

Chichester,
    Henry 56

Chick,
    Adrial 4
    Isaac 4

Chickering,
    Esther 30

Chidsey,
    Hannah 52*

Child,
    Abigail 58
    Lyman 65
    Rufus 58
    Salmon 91
    Susanna 36

Child, (cont.)
    Willard 58*
    William 91

Childers,
    Goolsbury 162
    Milliner 146
    Mosby 183*
    Wiley 146

Childress,
    David 154
    John 153*
    Mitchell 153*

Childs,
    Amasa 93
    Amos 10*
    Amy (Mrs.) 103
    Curtis 82
    Ebenezer 14
    Penuel 69*
    Reuben 34*
    Richard D. 103
    Sarah 93
    Solomon S. 73
    Zilpha 33

Chiles,
    James 132*-

Chilton,
    George 155*
    Stephen 167*

China,
    John 142

Chinn,
    Perry 141*

Chipman,
    Elon S. 81
    Jesse 81
    Nathaniel 69*
    William 7*

Chisam,
    Benjamin 166
    Mary 166

Chitcoat,
    John 190*

Chitenden,
    Reuben 93*

Chittenden,
    Abraham 52
    Asel H. 97
    Cornelius 60*
    H. W. 52
    John 60
    Solomon 97
    Nathan 52

Choat,
    Humphrey 16
    James 16

Choate,
    David 24*, 42
    Ebenezer 5*
    Miriam 42

Chopell,
    Samuel 138

Chrishfield,
    Joshua 171

Chrisman,
    Henry 83
    Nicholas 83

Christ,
    Laurence 118

Christian,
    Charles P. 110*
    Daniel 186
    George W. 186
    Henry 104
    Valentine 118*

Christie,
    Daniel 103*

Christmas,
    Richard 146*

Christy,
    David 181*
    Sarah 166*

Chriswell,
    Samuel 98

Chubb,
    Molly 71*

Chubbuck,
    Ebenezer 126

Chunn,
    Sylvester 156*

Church,
    Amos 9*
    Anthony 32
    Arson 82
    Caleb 77
    Charles 14*
    Cyrus 32
    Daniel 82
    Earl 30
    Eba 34
    Eli 77
    Ezra 62
    Gideon 47
    James C. 77, 106
    Jesse 124
    John 18
    Jonathan 30
    Joseph 54*
    Joseph M. 30
    Joshua 38, 70*, 124
    Lemuel 65
    Lydia 47
    Mary 54
    Nathaniel 77*
    Oliver 85
    Rachel 38
    Samuel 89*
    Sarah 30
    Silas 38
    Simeon 72
    Simeon C. 72
    Susannah 13
    Thomas 49*
    Varnum 77
    Willard 100*
    William J. 34

Churchell,
    Jabez 7

Churcher,
    Amos 141*

Churchill,
    Elijah 43
    Francis 66
    Isaac 83*
    Jabez 7
    Joab 7
    John E. 66

Churchill, (cont.)
    Jonas 83*
    Lillis 32
    Lydia 82
    Nathaniel 82
    Samuel 30*
    Seymour 32
    Simeon 29
    Stephen 103*
    William 7*

Cilley,
    Hannah 21
    Joseph 15
    Samuel 19*
    Thomas 21*

Claflin,
    Albert 94
    William 94

Claggett,
    Amie 130
    Asa 127
    Ferdinand 130
    Syntha 16

Clancy,
    Charles 175
    John 175

Clane,
    Reuben 88

Clanning,
    Dorcas 48

Clap,
    David 31
    Theophilus C. 31

Clapp,
    Anna 48
    Benjamin 70*
    Benjamin J. 80
    Betsey 49
    Elizabeth 33
    Isaac 68
    Martha 29
    Oliver 49
    Otis 62
    Rachel 29
    Roswell 23
    Ruth 47
    Simeon 34
    Thomas 29
    Timothy 36

Clapper,
    John 104*

Clapsadale,
    Michael 112

Clapsaddle,
    Dennis 83

Clark,
    A. S. 175
    Abigail 42
    Absalom 187*
    Adna S. 175
    Alexander 81
    Amasa 57*
    Amos 52, 57*, 60*
    Amy 43
    Anna 81
    Anthony 19*
    Arthur 170
    Asa 41
    B. 180
    Benjamin 75*, 80, 154*, 155
    Bethiah 31
    Betsey 86
    Braxton 161
    Burgess 158*
    Cary 60
    Cary C. 60
    Cephas 78
    Champion 59
    Charles 9
    Charles G. 4*
    Daniel 53*, 59*, 71
    David 37, 58
    Edwin 59
    Eliakim 86
    Elias 76
    Elijah S. 63
    Elisha 52, 54
    Elizabeth 42*, 130
    Elizabeth (Mrs.) 130
    Ellen 42
    Ephraim 4
    Esther 35
    Eunice 54
    Ezra 28*, 88
    Flavel 83*
    Francis 81
    G. B. 97
    George 54, 59*, 60*, 100*, 155, 188*
    Hannah 25, 31*, 74, 129
    Henry 110*
    Ichabod 108*
    Ichabod G. 69

Clark, (cont.)
    Isaac 52*
    Jabez 67*
    Jacob 54
    James 10, 11*, 34, 80,
      150
    James H. 30, 107
    James R. 74
    Jemima 60
    Jeremiah 108
    Jerome 93*
    Jerusha 42
    Job 119
    Joel 86*
    John 58, 60*, 63, 90,
      105*, 122*, 139*,
      157*, 161, 178*, 180,
      185, 187
    John S. 84
    Jonas 159*
    Jonathan 4, 23*, 24*, 61*,
      161*
    Joseph 9*, 30*, 60*, 177*
    Joseph C. 52*
    Joshua 43, 82
    Josiah 15, 24*
    Judah 35
    Judith 44*
    Judy 68
    Julia 34
    Justus 34
    Lemuel 36*
    Lewis 148*
    Louis 99
    Lucius W. 42
    Lucy 90
    Lydia 52
    Lyman 58*
    Martha 84
    Mary 54*, 58
    Matthew
    Mehitable 30
    Moses 25, 48*, 106, 162*
    Mumford 86
    Nancy 166
    Nathan 105*
    Nathan W. 62
    Nathaniel 16*
    Nathaniel S. 64*
    Norman 25
    Owen 84
    Parker 107
    Patience 4
    Paul 62
    Peter 43

Clark, (cont.)
    Phebe 89
    Reuben 107*
    Richard 28, 142
    Robert 68
    Roswell 68
    Rufus 60*
    S. S. Field 131
    Sally 17
    Samuel 23, 62
    Samuel H. 70
    Sarah 16*, 77, 80
    Seth 63*
    Shadrach 131
    Stephen 60*
    Submit 36
    Susanna 35
    Sylvanus 34*
    Thaddeus 58
    Theodore E. 90
    Thomas 32*, 117, 162*
    Turner 130
    Wells 86*
    William 3*, 22*, 30, 35, 41, 57,
      77*, 106, 108*, 118*, 144*, 146*
    William W. 184
    Willys 53
    Wilson 151
    Winslow 88*
    Wright 62

Clarke,
    Abijah 31
    George 90
    Hannah 47
    Jacob 61
    John 131*, 188
    Matthew 117
    Mehitable 79
    Pardon 45
    Russell J. 47
    Sally 47
    Samuel 135*
    Sarah 47, 48*
    Thankful 45
    Thomas 145*
    William C. 48*

Clarkson,
    Isaac S. 166
    Phebe 166

Clary,
    David 34*

Clason,
    Smith 104

Clay,
    William 19, 152*

Clayton,
    Elisha 135*
    John 110*

Clearwater,
    Hiram 103
    Sarah 103

Cleary,
    Ed. 128

Cleasby,
    Joseph 19*

Cleaveland,
    Chester 86*
    Cyrus 33
    Henry 33
    Lewis W. 90
    Mason 57
    Nehemiah 90
    Silas 57

Cleaves,
    Abraham 11*
    William 5*

Cleavland,
    Fassett 84
    Gardner 75*
    James 126
    Lydia 65
    Solomon 84

Cleburne,
    George 157
    John 157

Cleland,
    Nathan 76
    Thankful 76

Clement,
    Amos C. 16
    Edward 143
    Hannah 16
    Isaac 64*
    John 25*, 42
    Joseph 91
    Lambert 179

Clements,
    Charles 130*
    Hannah 65
    Roswell 44

Clemmons,
    Clement 142*
    Cornelius 140*
    Jonathan 101*

Clency,
    George 176*

Clenny,
    Jonathan 157

Cleveland,
    Bradford 70
    Charles E. 70
    Elijah 99
    Hannah 70
    Harry 89
    Joseph 91*
    Josiah 99
    Permilla 70
    Roswell 90*
    Stephen 89
    W. 166
    William 166

Click,
    Henry 152*
    Jacob 179

Clifford,
    Isaac 19
    John 108*
    Jonathan 63
    Joseph E. 19
    Nathan 26*

Clift,
    Thankful 53

Clinard,
    Daniel 138

Cline,
    Henry 73
    Jacob 32*
    Jones 186*

Clink,
    (Mrs.) 117
    Jacob 117

Clinkinbeard,
    Isaac 160*

Clinton,
    Allen 56
    James 109*, 164
    Peter 164
    Thomas 127*
    William 144*

Clontz,
    Jeremiah 139
    John A. 139

Clopton,
    Thomas 131

Close,
    Gilbert 56

Clothier,
    A. R. 76
    Jesse 76

Cloud,
    Ezekiel 146*
    William 134*

Clough,
    Aaron 67
    Abner 19*
    Asa 10
    Benjamin 10
    Daniel 41*
    David 70*
    Elizabeth 16
    Gilman 64*
    John 14, 18, 106*
    Joseph 19*
    Josiah 16
    Oliver 18
    Sarah 19
    William 40*

Cloutman,
    Samuel 43

Cloveland,
    Sherman 58

Clowers,
    Daniel 145
    Daniel P. 145

Clows,
    (Miss) 117
    William 117

Cluky,
    Charles 95*

Clunet,
    Anna Maria 116*

Clute,
    Bartholomew 96*
    Geradus 78
    Helen 90*
    Jacob D. 96*
    James 78
    John D. 168

Coakley,
    John 88

Coalman,
    George 121
    John 121*

Coan,
    John 52*

Coaps,
    Lewis 117*

Coates,
    John 43
    William 129*, 193

Coats,
    Beverly E. 155
    John 131*
    William 155

Cobb,
    Abel 99*
    Benjamin 60*
    Daniel 6*, 65
    Deliverance 30
    E. B. 74*
    Elkanah 62
    Isaiah 30*
    Jacob 65*
    Jesse 153
    John 143*
    Justus 71*
    Nathan 28, 65
    Nathaniel 7, 71*
    Nehemiah 28
    Pharaoh 153
    Rowland 6
    Simeon 62
    William 7

Cobbern,
      Betsey 38

Cobbs,
      John 129*
      Joseph 160

Cobleigh,
      Reuben 80*

Cobley,
      Eleazer 67*

Cobson,
      William 86

Coburn,
      Asa 65*
      Hiram 7
      Jephthah 14
      Manly 14
      Mary 40
      Morrell 23
      Moses 6
      N. 121
      Nathaniel 121
      Nathaniel B. 40
      Rachel 40

Cochram,
      Daniel 141*
      David 141*
      Samuel 157*

Cochran,
      Elizabeth 87
      M. 146
      Matthew 146
      Robert 117*
      Samuel 136
      Simon 168*
      Temperance 136
      Thomas 160*
      William 158

Cochrane,
      Aliner 170
      David 127*
      Elizabeth 170
      James 127*

Cock,
      Joel 104

Cocks,
      Isaac 183

Coddington,
      John 111*

Cody,
      Rodolphus 90
      Samuel 90

Coe,
      Abner 63
      Jedediah 63
      John 76*
      Oliver 63
      Richard 106, 127*
      Sarah 106
      Sylvester 58
      Timothy 51*

Coffey,
      Reuben 167*

Coffin,
      Catharine 42
      George 21*
      Huldah 26
      Isaac 3*
      Peter 26*
      Violet 26*

Coffinger,
      David 95

Coffman,
      Chloe 161
      Jacob 161

Cofran,
      Joseph 19

Cofren,
      Robert 10*

Cogar,
      Peter 135

Coger,
      Avis (Mrs.) 103
      Charles P. 103

Coggin,
      Robert 138*

Coghill,
      James 161*

Cognell,
      Thomas 130*

Cogswell,
      Aaron 42
      Joseph B. 16
      Judith 16

Cohoon,
    Luman 79

Coil,
    Mark 127*

Coit,
    Anna 54
    Benjamin 54*
    Erastus 54
    Isaac 35

Colbath,
    George 15*
    Leighton 11*

Colbey,
    Benjamin 13*

Colborn,
    Thomas 15

Colbreath,
    Dependence 88*

Colburn,
    Abigail 21
    Benjamin 24
    Charles 19*
    David 69*
    Edward 11
    Henry 12
    John 21
    John H. 21
    Joseph 40
    Leonard 22*
    Lewis 31
    Mary 21
    Meriam 24
    Nathan 21
    Peter U. 21
    Samuel 61
    Sarah 55
    William 11, 40

Colby,
    Benjamin 19, 21
    Chilis F. 19
    Christopher 117*
    Ebenezer 3*, 17*
    Ichabod 18
    James 8, 9
    John T. G. 18
    Page 63
    Samuel 6*, 9*
    Sarah 24
    Thomas 63
    William 92*

Coldwell,
    William 161

Cole,
    Adonijah 90
    Amos 77*
    Andrew 30*, 49
    Anna 49*
    Benjamin 70
    Charles 29
    Daniel 23, 119
    Dexter 33
    Dorothy 47*
    Edward 12
    Elizabeth 49*, 165*
    Hannah 4
    Henry 68
    Huldah 33
    Ichabod 49
    Jabez 90
    Jacob R. 4
    James 8
    Jeremiah 9
    Job T. 41
    John 68, 84, 90*, 101, 160*
    Joseph 30*
    L. B. 124
    Leroy 94
    Levi 80*
    Lydia 46*
    Major 143
    Mary 56
    Mary C. 8
    Oliver D. 72
    Otis 33
    Royal 125
    Samuel 9, 42*, 125*, 126*
    Seth 49
    Simeon 42*
    Sisson 94
    Sterling 90
    Thomas 24, 84*
    William 135

Colegate,
    Asaph M. 135*

Colegrove,
    C. 94
    Christopher 94
    Stephen 93*

Coleler,
    John 176

Coleman,
    (N.X.N.) 101
    Charles P. 151*

Coleman,
Elethe 34
Hamilton 94
Hannah 107
Hawes 132
Hawes N. 132
Joel 107*
John 60*
Thomas 148
Wesley 132
William 120*, 132

Coles,
Asa 32
Benjamin 32
Thomas 45*

Coley,
William 77*

Colgrove,
Jeremiah 33
Lydia 33
Reuben 67

Colkins,
Nathan S. 35

Collahan,
Josias 147*

Collamer,
Daniel A. 95*
Dolly H. 97
Elizabeth 61
Ira A. 61
Tryphena 97

Collar,
Norris 93*

Collett,
Elizabeth 166
John 166

Colley,
Daniel 24
Elizabeth 43
Joseph 5
Lydia 24
Richard 5
Thomas 19*
Thomas J. 24
William 5

Collier,
Coleman A. 165*
James 178
Jason 36*

Collings,
Abbent 99
Daniel 14
Lemuel 14
Samuel 99

Collingsworth,
William 112

Collins,
Anna 66
Anthony 109*
Benjamin 13*
David 18, 81
Ebenezer 188
Eli 191
Elisha 81*, 185*
Jamaico J. 106
James 106, 135*, 147
Jeffrey 136*
John 67*, 143*, 144*
Jonathan 85
Jonathan C. 85
Joseph 10*, 81, 182*
Josiah 160
Lewis 152*
Mary 185
Mason 131*
Moses 42*
Robert 66
Roby 46
Samuel 168
Sarah 45, 93
Solomon 12
Stephen 164*
W. W. 168
Welcome 45
William 78*, 84
William R. 191

Collister,
Sarah 86

Colly,
Austin 158*
William 158*

Colman,
John 124*
Nancy 31

Colmery,
John 120

Colony,
Isaac 95*

Colt,
    John 64
    Sarah 111*
    Trueman 52

Colter,
    John 174*
    Matthew 165*

Colton,
    Abigail 43
    Charles 66*
    Ebenezer P. 66
    Hannah 66
    Louis 51
    Samuel 51

Colver,
    David 177*

Colvin,
    Elizabeth 46
    Joab 125
    Marcy 125
    Mason 133*
    Moses 46

Colwell,
    Arthur 95*
    John 144*
    Martha 46
    Samuel 187*
    Stephen 133
    Uriah 46

Colyear,
    John 182*

Coman,
    Stephen 87

Combs,
    Amos 30
    George 141*
    Graham 119
    John 36, 119, 147*, 167
    Joshua 101*
    Leslie 164*
    Levi 36
    Robert 130

Comee,
    Oliver 31

Comfort,
    Edward 77*

Comingore,
    John 165*

Compton,
    Cyrus 154
    Jeremiah 154
    Job 110*
    Joseph 169*

Comstock,
    A. 85
    Ann 56
    Anson 85, 101
    Daniel 101
    David 88*
    James 54*
    Martin L. 75*
    Medad 89*
    Samuel 21*
    Sanford 99
    Sarah 54
    Simeon 53
    Thomas 53

Con,
    John 144*

Conable,
    Samuel 83*

Conant,
    Abel 63
    Amos 79
    Artemas 41
    Betsey 67*
    Caleb 24
    Daniel 44
    Elizabeth 41
    Harvey 36
    Israel 91
    James 38*
    John F. 44
    Joseph 63
    Silvanus 8
    Susanna 38
    Sylvanus 60*
    Sylvia 8

Conaway,
    Charles 173*
    Richard 182*

Concklin,
    John D. 85

Condit,
    Japhia 108*
    John 13*

Condra,
    Ephraim M. 15
    Philip 156

Cone,
    Asa 32
    Daniel 33*
    Daniel H. 58
    Elizabeth 85
    Jared 25*
    Joshua 60*
    Noadiah 60*
    Oliver 53, 92
    Samuel 11*
    Timothy 94*
    Waitstill 53

Conets,
    John 90

Congdon,
    George 48*
    Henry 119
    Joseph 86

Conger,
    Benjamin 145*
    Zenas 99*

Conghuet,
    Peter 81

Conhover,
    Isaac 88*

Conk,
    John 110
    William 110

Conkey,
    Alexander 35
    Joshua 97*
    Richard 79*

Conklin,
    Isaac 104*, 105
    James 73
    John 73
    Jonathan 90*
    Mary 106
    Matthew 106

Conley,
    Michael 169*

Conly,
    John 56

Conn,
    Daniel 121
    Elizabeth 121
    Samuel 164

Connant,
    Samuel 40

Connell,
    Christopher 124
    Isaac 124
    Richard 74

Connelly,
    John 189
    Sanford 189

Conner,
    Isaac 166*
    John L. 129
    Joseph 80
    Mary 117
    Nathan 16
    P. 144
    Philemon 144
    Terence 184*
    Thomas 158*
    William 165

Connor,
    Hannah 19

Conor,
    John 183*

Conover,
    Abigail 115
    Ann 110*
    Lewis 110*

Conrad,
    Jacob 112

Conrey,
    Stephen 21*

Conse,
    Henry J. 105
    Jacob 105

Cooledge,
　　John　38

Cooley,
　　Abner　44
　　Charles　44
　　Isaac　126
　　Justin　88*
　　Mary　77
　　Peneller　44
　　Roger　43*
　　Thomas　85*

Coolidge,
　　Daniel　41
　　Joel　41*
　　Joseph　7*

Cooly,
　　James　164
　　William　164

Coombs,
　　John　5
　　Joseph　5
　　Lydia　22
　　Rachel　8
　　Samuel　8
　　William　5

Coomer,
　　John　28

Coon,
　　Abram　96
　　Dennis　119*
　　John　62, 96
　　John C.　157
　　Jonathan　86
　　Peter　103*

Conney,
　　William　104

Coons,
　　Benjamin　165*

Coop,
　　Horatio　155
　　James　155
　　Lydia　92

Cooper,
　　Aaron　76
　　Alexander　158*
　　Ambrose　193*

Cooper, (cont.)
　　Caleb　167*
　　Chauncey　90
　　Dabney　157*
　　E.　153
　　Ebenezer　153
　　Elizabeth　102
　　Frederick　167*
　　Gilbert　102*
　　Henry　93*, 110
　　Isles　130*
　　Jacob　50, 164
　　James B.　108*
　　John　76, 111*, 114, 136, 140
　　Joseph　80*
　　Judah　50
　　Laton　166
　　Levin　164*
　　Samuel　61
　　Sherman　23
　　Smith D.　159
　　Starling　140
　　Sylvanus　96

Coosard,
　　Valentine　178*

Copeland,
　　Amasa　57*
　　Benjamin　156*
　　Charles　8
　　James　8
　　Joseph　45
　　Rebecca　45
　　Richard　158*
　　Ripley　142*
　　Sarah　131*
　　William　145*
　　Zaccheus　153*

Copes,
　　George　116
　　Peter P.　128*

Copland,
　　Asa　31*

Copley,
　　Benjamin　43*
　　Daniel　58*

Copp,
　　Jonathan　18

Coppedge,
　　Thomas　128

Coppernoll,
    Elizabeth 81
    George E. 81

Cor,
    Robert 138

Corathers,
    John 120
    Thomas 120

Corbel,
    Othniel 95

Corbet,
    Edmond 150
    Edward 150
    Jacob 164
    James 164

Corbett,
    John 155

Corbin,
    Carlton 36
    Clement 23
    David 79
    Experience 35
    Ezborn 23
    Joshua 36
    Nathaniel 64
    Stephen 98

Corbit,
    Johnson 133
    Samuel 133

Cord,
    Zaccheus 162*

Corder,
    B. D. 163
    Benjamin D. 163
    John 133*

Cordy,
    James 166
    W. 166

Corey,
    Amasa 77
    Anna 77
    Benjamin 21
    Ebenezer 125
    Elijah 133
    James 113
    Joanna 125

Corey, (cont.)
    Joseph 48*
    Samuel 21, 133
    William 48

Corkins,
    Joel 186*

Corkle,
    Daniel 133

Corley,
    Abner 142
    Alpheus 65
    William 65
    Zaccheus 149*

Corlis,
    Christopher 58

Corliss,
    Eliju 24*
    Emerson 65*

Corn,
    John Peter 138*
    Timothy 165*

Cornelison,
    John 187

Cornelius,
    Charles 150*
    H. W. 125
    Henry W. 125
    William 128

Cornell,
    Martha 47

Corney,
    John 181
    Pleasant 181

Corning,
    Jedediah 54
    Uriah 54

Cornish,
    Gabriel 81*
    George 51*
    John 5*
    Samuel P. 89
    Stephen 89

Cornue,
    Wessel 100*

Cornwall,
    Anna 51
    George 50

Cornwell,
    John 59*
    Samuel 102*
    Seth 59
    William 118*

Corsen,
    David 17
    David M. 17

Corthell,
    Elizabeth 29*

Cortleyou,
    Hendrick 109
    Henry 109

Cortright,
    Moses 91

Cortrite,
    G. 99

Cortwite,
    Charles 77*

Cortwright,
    Lawrence 107*

Corvet,
    Jeremiah 32*

Corwill,
    Zachariah 142*

Corwin,
    Edward 123*
    Samuel 96

Cory,
    Ann 27*
    Jonathan 108
    Oliver 93*
    Samuel 47*

Cosoy,
    John 160*

Cose,
    Abial 58

Cosey,
    David 22

Costen,
    Stephen 140*

Coston,
    Bishop 74
    James 74

Cotherell,
    John 29
    Lydia 29

Cottle,
    Robert 27*

Cotton,
    B. L. 70*
    Benjamin 181
    Elias 45*
    Enoch 65
    James White 164*
    Rowland 82
    Solomon 65
    William 181

Cottorn,
    William 119

Couch,
    Aaron F. 32
    Abraham 56*
    Chester 32*
    Daniel 192
    George 152
    John 10*
    Joshua 55*
    Uriah B. 192
    William 76*

Coughran,
    Joseph 188

Coulter,
    James 117

Coulton,
    Elkanah 139
    Martin 139

Courier,
    Ammi 97*
    Joseph 84*

Courrier,
    Edward 19*

Courter,
    William 107

Courtney,
    James 151*
    Michael 183
    Woods 183

Coux,
    Hontice H. 79

Covel,
    Ebenezer 28*
    Joseph B. 80*
    Thomas 91*
    William 28

Covenhoven,
    Robert 123*

Covert,
    Burgan 180*
    Luke 98*
    Peter 97
    T. 96
    Thomas 96

Covey,
    James 98*

Covill,
    Ebenezer 57*
    Ephraim 90
    Judah 13
    Lorenzo R. 90
    Richard 82*

Covington,
    J. R. 39
    Robert 164*

Cow,
    Phebe 60

Cowan,
    David 183*
    Elizabeth 10
    Isaac 10
    Jane 10*
    W. R. 149*
    William 155

Cowden,
    James 37*
    Robert 150*

Cowdrey,
    Asa 51
    James 51

Cowdry,
    Nathaniel 39*
    Orpha 65
    Submit 65

Cowell,
    Abigail 43*
    Isaac 118*

Cowen,
    John 74*
    William 170*

Cowgill,
    Daniel 162
    George 162
    Nehemiah 108

Cowherd,
    Coleby 163
    James 163*
    Jonathan 163
    Lucy 132*

Cowing,
    Calvin 9*

Cowl,
    Benjamin 104*

Cowles,
    Jabez 50*

Cowley,
    Robert 144*

Cownover,
    Daniel 191*

Cox,
    Andrew 172
    Bartlett 130*, 132*
    Benjamin 176
    Card 153*
    Charles 137*
    Earl 70
    Edward 154
    Elizabeth 54
    George 70*
    John 107, 154*, 167*
    John F. 195
    Jovan 159*
    Mary 107, 121
    Michael 175

Cox, (cont.)
    Moses 147*
    Richard 145*
    Samuel 154
    Thomas 154
    William 91*, 119*, 121, 176

Coxe,
    William 144*

Coy,
    Elisha 73*
    Vine 90
    Willis 35

Coykendall,
    Katharine 171*

Coyle,
    Patrick 167*

Coyt,
    William 96*

Cozart,
    Susanna 91

Crabb,
    Jarrett 141*

Crabbe,
    Abijah 85*

Crabs,
    Philip 174*

Crabtree,
    Isaac 157*
    Jacob 135*
    Richard 152*

Craft,
    Ezekiel 148*

Crafts,
    Elias 39
    Graves 34*
    Mary 30*
    Samuel 7

Crag,
    Thomas 130*

Crage,
    John 95*

Craig,
    A. 36
    Alexander 159*
    David 133*
    Elizabeth 25, 110*
    James 159
    John 143*, 148*, 169
    John H. 160*
    Samuel 160
    Susan 36
    Tappan W. 25
    Thomas 71*
    W. 36
    William 169

Craige,
    Moses 31
    Nathan 38*

Craim,
    Sibbel 79

Crain,
    Amos 70*
    Chester 91
    Elisha 91
    Tryphenia 84*

Cram,
    Betsey 18
    Daniel 5
    Samuel 11

Crammer,
    John 8*

Crampton,
    Thomas 127

Crance,
    Michael 181*

Crandal,
    James 48*
    Jeremiah 90
    Sylvester 62

Crandall,
    Abner 94*
    Benjamin 96*
    Carey 73*
    Catharine 53
    Ethan 48*
    Gideon 70
    Isaiah 73
    Jonathan 68*

Crandall, (cont.)
    Joseph 94*
    Levi 44*
    Richmond 66*
    Tracy 70

Crane,
    Abiatha 27
    Benjamin 108*
    Elihu 122
    Elizabeth 32, 76
    James 71*
    Joanna 27
    Josiah 88
    Mayfield 150
    Moses 8
    Roger 174
    Rufus 8
    Stephen B. 97
    Tower W. 174
    William 143*
    Zebulon 69

Cranson,
    Asa 87*

Cranston,
    Elizabeth 86
    James M. 27
    John 48*
    Mary 45
    Phineas 86
    Samuel 79*
    William 76
    William B. 45
    Zilpha 76

Crapo,
    Jonathan 175*

Crapser,
    Schuyler 105

Crary,
    Amos 72
    Archibald C. 88
    Joseph 12*
    Nathan 97*

Craw,
    Abraham 87
    Catharine 87
    David 86
    Justus 86

Crawford,
    Eleazer 175*

Crawford, (cont.)
    Hannah 55
    John 15, 103*, 173*
    Peter 140*
    Samuel S. 106
    Thomas 171
    William 10*, 110*

Crawl,
    Samuel 117

Crawley,
    G. W. 144
    Thomas 158*

Creary,
    Archibald 130

Creel,
    John 129*

Creesey,
    Benjamin 5*

Crego,
    Abram 77
    Daniel S. 77

Cremer,
    S. (Mrs.) 103
    Sarah 103

Crews,
    James 153*
    Joseph 129

Crider,
    Obadiah 121

Crigger,
    Jacob 176*

Crim,
    Henry 83
    John H. 83

Crinshaw,
    John 154*

Crips,
    Michael 8*

Crisp,
    John 159
    William 159

Criss,
    Nicholas 169*

Crisse,
    Barnet 74*

Crissey,
    John 168

Crist,
    Philip 134*

Criswell,
    David 163*
    Henry 158*
    John 158
    Robert 158

Critchfield,
    Benjamin 174*
    John 173
    William 123*, 169*

Crittenden,
    Ebenezer 91
    Jerusha 55
    Levi 32
    Orrin 91
    William 33
    William S. 33

Crittendon,
    Jerusha 108
    Sophia 108
    William 132*

Croberga,
    Leonard 113

Crocker,
    Anthony 143*
    David 178*
    Dyer 119
    George 27
    Haman 28
    Hannah 91
    J. 170
    James 38*, 42
    Jedediah 170
    Lydia 28
    Noah 70*
    Peter 69
    Polly 42
    Sarah 61
    Solomon 143*
    Theophilus 82*

Crocket,
    Asher 134*
    Samuel 5

Crockett,
    Samuel 5

Crofoot,
    Ephraim 59
    Louis 59
    Archilous 166*

Croft,
    John 75*

Crofts,
    Joseph 92*

Crofut,
    Mos. 55
    Sarah 55

Croker,
    Jesse 133*

Crom,
    Adam 134*

Cromwell,
    Stephen 8

Cronk,
    John 91*

Crook,
    Andrew 25
    John 25, 164
    Kiah 164

Crooker,
    Ruth 5
    William 5

Crooks,
    Charles 74*
    Michael 181

Croom,
    F. J. 139

Cropley,
    Moses 180

Crosby,
    Enoch 91*
    John 40*
    Joseph 20*
    Timothy 78*

Crosman,
    Peggy 26
    Thomas 103*

Cross,
    Abijah 41*
    Abraham 154*
    Augustus L. 72
    Benjamin 92
    David L. 154
    Elijah 154
    John 63
    Joseph 62, 137*
    Moses 19*
    Samuel 10
    Solomon 97*
    William 25*, 152*

Crossing,
    James 175

Crossman,
    Alpheus 46
    Celia 61
    Josiah 86
    Josiah A. 86
    Noah 46

Croswell,
    Andrew 13

Crouch,
    Elijah 38
    John 154

Crouk,
    Dennis 104*
    Garld 124

Crout,
    Andrew 87

Crouter,
    Ruth 103

Crow,
    Elizabeth 135
    Huldah 58
    James 188
    Robert 162
    William 188

Crowder,
    James 166
    Philip 188*

Crowel,
    Aaron 26

Crowell,
    David 16
    Henry 59
    Manoah 10*
    Michael 9*
    Peter 16
    Rachel 59
    Samuel 8
    Washington 26

Crowley,
    Elizabeth 94
    James 189*
    Royal 69*

Crowningshield,
    Mary 39

Croxton,
    Carter 130*

Crozer,
    John 170

Crozier,
    Benjamin 108*

Cruckshank,
    Samuel 88

Cruff,
    Thomas 49*

Crum,
    Henry 105*

Crumb,
    Arnold 48
    Catharine 95
    Elias 81*
    Peter 156*

Crumley,
    Jacob 154

Crumlow,
    Caleb 118*

Crumnet,
    Hannah 17

Crump,
    Joseph 163
    Joshua 163

Crunk,
    John 158*

Crutcher,
    John 162
    N. (Mrs.) 162

Crutchfield,
    John 162
    Mordecai 162

Crutchlow,
    Mary 120*

Crute,
    John 132*

Cry,
    Sarah 152*

Cubbuck,
    Simeon 87*

Cudworth,
    William 27

Cuff,
    Cato 54*
    Will 130*

Culbert,
    James 116
    Jane 116

Culbertson,
    Andrew 143

Culp,
    John 144*

Culva,
    Lucy 51
    Nathan 51

Culver,
    Ansel 75
    Christopher 53
    Corydon 176
    David 101*
    Eliakim 72*
    Elisha 70
    John 24*, 53
    Joseph 75
    Joshua 104

Cumings,
    Alexander 119*
    Clatira 99
    Thomas 123*

Cummings,
    Charles 22
    Elijah 42*
    Hosea 88
    Isaac 38
    Jacob 79, 123
    Jonas 64
    Joseph 30, 158*
    Molly 22
    Noble 28*
    Richard 12*
    Sarah 108*
    Simeon R. 79
    Thomas 88

Cummins,
    Harmon 143*
    John 135*
    William 160*

Cump,
    Nicholas 143*

Cundiff,
    Isaac 128*

Cunill,
    Elizabeth 44

Cuningham,
    Ansell 146*

Cunningham,
    Benjamin S. 184
    Christopher 182*
    Elizabeth 184
    Francis 181
    J. B. 153
    James 153, 190*
    John 132*, 158
    Murril 163
    Phebe 135
    Richard 181
    Samuel 61
    Sarah 101
    Thomas J. 163
    William 136*, 148
    William N. 148

Cupples,
  James 118

Curbo,
  Joseph 145*

Curl,
  Leonard 118*
  Matthew 145*

Curlee,
  Cullin 159

Curler,
  Hiram 71

Currie,
  Duncan 140
  John 88, 140
  Samuel 45*

Currier,
  Abraham 4
  Amos 19
  Asa 17*
  David 23
  Ebenezer 19*, 70
  Elizabeth 24
  Mary 24, 78
  Michael 78
  Moses 16*
  Nancy 19*
  Nathaniel 4
  Samuel 122
  Theophilus 24

Curry,
  John 72
  Robert 99
  William 99

Curtice,
  Jacob 20
  Jeremiah 76
  Thomas 76

Curtis,
  Benjamin 12*, 32
  Caleb 9*
  Charles 36
  Daniel 8
  Dilly 59
  Elisha 103
  Gideon 62*
  Isaac Palmer 24
  James 163*

Curtis, (cont.)
  Job 29
  John 21*, 135
  John G. 87
  Jonathan 63
  Lebus 97
  Lydia 29
  Lysander 59
  Mary 58
  Nancy 29*
  Peter 102
  Philbrick 24
  Philip 30
  Sally 55*
  Silas 105*
  Thomas 31*
  William 25*, 31
  Zarah 175*

Curtiss,
  Asahel 89*
  Elijah 95
  Elijah W. 95
  Everard 55
  Giles 50*
  Isaac 100*, 173*
  Joel 73*
  Jonathan 192
  Jotham 192
  Mary 43*
  Vinson 35

Curts,
  Lawrence 179

Cushing,
  Abel 35
  Alice 29
  Benjamin 46
  Charles 28
  Daniel 16*
  H. 87
  Henry 45
  Jonathan 29*, 44
  Nathaniel 29
  Pyam 29

Cushman,
  Alden 32
  Almon 93
  Bartholomew 28
  Bartlett H. 7
  Benjamin 29
  Daniel 80
  Elizabeth 93
  Frederick 62
  Isiah 8*

Cushman, (cont.)
    Jacob 29*
    James G. 30
    Jonah 32
    Joseph 7, 28, 70*
    Levi 66
    Lucy 69
    Margaret 7
    Mary 35
    Ralph 34
    Roswell 62
    Saba 28
    Sarah 7
    William 7*

Cushmon,
    Gideon 7

Cussell,
    Edmund D. 44
    James 44

Custard,
    Isaac 126*

Custerd,
    Thomas 112*

Custis,
    William 41

Cutler,
    Christopher 40

Cutler,
    Ebenezer 64*
    Gardner 23
    Nathaniel 67
    Oliver 30
    Samuel 59
    Sarah 40
    William H. 37

Cutlip,
    William 134

Cutright,
    Christopher 135
    John 135

Cutter,
    Benjamin 100*
    Betsey 21*
    Haden 23
    Joseph 22*
    Mehitable 42

Cutter, (cont.)
    Rachel 22
    Rebecca 39*
    Seth 21*
    William 39

Cutting,
    E. 77
    Earl 38*
    Eliphalet 77
    Josiah 38

Cutts,
    William 183*

Cutzer,
    Leonard 134*

Cuykendal,
    Martin 74*

Cypert,
    Robert 158

Cyrus,
    Bartholomew 132*

Daball,
    Benjamin 53*

Dabney,
    Lutilda 153

Daboll,
    Anstis 79
    Elias 79

Dacy,
    Mehitable 6

Dade,
    Amanda M. 193
    Fanny 41
    William 41

Dagget,
    Darius 21

Daggett,
    Aaron 10
    Caleb C. 21
    Darius 21

Daggett, (cont.)
    Henry 51*
    Joseph 69
    Mary 45*
    Mayhew 95*
    Sarah 47
    Seril M. 47
    William 28

Daggtt,
    Trustum 14

Dague,
    Mathias 171

Dailey,
    Elijah 127
    Jane 97
    Jesse 131*

Daily,
    Owen 149*
    Silas 98*

Daimwood,
    Richard 74*

Daines,
    Castle 101*

Dains,
    Asa 175
    Jeptha 175
    Leonard 175

Dake,
    Bartlett 98
    Emanuel 97
    John M. 98

Dakin,
    E. 73
    Elisha 73
    Jonathan 129*

Dalby,
    Nathaniel 132

Dale,
    Richard 130*

Dalino,
    Ruth 13

Dalliba,
    John 90
    Sanford 90

Dalloff,
    Thomas 18

Dalloway,
    Elizabeth 103
    Jacob 103

Dalrymple,
    David 179
    Edwin 109
    Elizabeth 109
    James 41*

Dalton,
    Michael 15*
    Thomas 157
    William 140*

Dame,
    Asa 17
    Edward 23
    Joseph 17*
    Martha 24

Damon,
    Abel 172*
    Benjamin 20*
    Daniel 39*
    Isacc 35
    Joseph 39*
    Luther 29*
    Mercy 35

Dan,
    James 105*
    Samuel 105*, 131

Dana,
    Asa 87
    John 103

Dancomb,
    Eleazer 55

Danforth,
    Abner 10
    Cooe 33
    J. 62
    John 40
    Jonathan 62
    Joseph 18
    Lydia 42*
    Peter 72
    Samuel 10
    Sarah 95
    Thomas 27*

Daniel,
    Benjamin 157*
    Beverly 165*
    Christopher 140*
    Elizabeth 132
    Ezekiel 143
    James 155*
    John 145*
    Mecklenburg 132
    Richard 129*

Danielly,
    John 140

Daniels,
    Amariah 178*
    Anna 23
    Benjamin 177*
    Buckner 185*
    Charles S. 83
    Eleazer 83*
    Hiram 23
    Hulda 51
    Job 53*
    John 33*, 97, 106*
    Leonard 77
    Mary 31
    Nathan 31, 77
    Nehemiah 93*
    Samuel 98*
    Sarah 108*
    Sterling G. 51
    Susanna 64

Danielson,
    Luther 176*

Danow,
    Arthur 62*

Darby,
    Dorothy 125
    Richard 147*
    Tabitha 43
    Tiffany 125

Dare,
    Mary 107
    Philip 107

Darkam,
    Abigail 56

Darling,
    Acenath 70*
    Benjamin 90*

Darling, (cont.)
    Christopher C. 192
    Daniel G. 34
    David 63
    Enoch G. 194
    Hiram 62
    J. M. 64
    James 135
    Jerusha 46*
    John 34
    Jonathan 25
    Joseph C. 192
    Judith 63
    Levi 62
    Mary 38
    Priscilla 44
    Samuel 31*
    Zelek 39*

Darnes,
    Elizabeth 157*

Darrah,
    John 137*

Darrow,
    Benjamin 155*
    Ebenezer 53*
    Grace 55*
    James 104*
    John 119*
    Zaccheus 82*

Dart,
    Agnes 123
    David 54*
    Hannah 123
    Julius 44
    Levi 44*
    Lucretia 54

Dasenbury,
    Gabriel 98
    Seth 98

Dates,
    Abraham 75

Daugherty,
    Andrew 121*
    James 10, 123
    John 123

Davenport,
    A. 167*
    Adson 86

Davenport, (cont.)
    Calvin 33
    Elizabeth 86
    Ezekiel 106
    Henry 106
    James 103*
    Joel 136*
    Joseph 128
    Moses 42
    Noah 79
    Phebe 52*
    Squire 172*
    William 129

Davey,
    Edmund H. 108

David,
    Henry 185*
    John 16

Davids,
    Peter 104
    William 104

Davidson,
    Giles 128*
    H. B. 167
    Hannah 52*
    Isaac 185
    James 32*, 127*
    John 32*, 146*, 155*, 181
    Joseph 57*, 113, 132*
    Joshua 169
    Matthew 81
    Peter 82

Davis,
    (Mrs.) 64
    Aaron 8*, 22
    Abel 38, 40*
    Abigail 55
    Abiger 33
    Abner 15
    Amos 67
    Anderson 159
    Andrew 103*, 152*
    Augustus 34
    Azariah 119*
    Benjamin 107*
    Betsey 41
    Bryant 166
    Burrell 141
    Calvin 70
    Catharine 119
    Channey 89
    Charlotte 194*

Davis, (cont.)
    Cyrus 138
    Daniel 21*, 95, 120*, 172
    David 23, 106*
    Deborah 53
    Ebenezer 74
    Edmund 28
    Edward 119, 141
    Elijah 89
    Elisha 89*
    Enos 182
    Ezra D. 48
    Felard 3
    Francis 64, 137*
    Gabriel 163
    Gashum 7*
    George 121
    Hannah 42
    Harriet 40
    Harvey 79
    Henry 67*, 116, 120*
    Hugh 133*
    Ichabod 53
    Isaac 5*, 82, 164
    J. S. 69
    Jackson 168
    Jacob 18, 20, 81*, 121
    James 52*, 91*, 119, 153*, 160*
        161
    James B. 64
    James S. 167*
    Jesse 162
    Joel 71, 153*
    John 57*, 69, 117, 120*, 121,
        130*, 135, 138*, 145*, 152*,
        155, 161, 166*, 170, 176*
    John B. 137*
    John J. 103
    John S. 50
    Jonathan 15, 19*, 143*
    Joseph 38, 67, 74, 163
    Joshua 7*
    Josiah 3, 19*, 119*
    L. B. 154
    Leonard 136
    Levi 169*
    Lewis 19, 130
    Lodowick 185*
    Lucy 41, 54, 86
    Margaret 35
    Marmaduke S. 169*
    Martha 138
    Martha (Mrs.) 138
    Mary 60, 84, 109, 132*
    Michael 153
    Moses 18, 41
    Nancy 166

Davis, (cont.)
    Nathan 106*
    Perry 28
    Philip 10
    Porter 89
    Priscilla 46
    Prisly 166
    Rebecca 57
    Richard 106, 180*
    Robert 141*
    Ruth 33
    Samuel 6*, 17*, 18, 24,
       40*, 64*, 67, 108, 148*,
       171
    Sarah 124*
    Silas 67
    Simeon 62*
    Squire 38
    Stephen R. 46
    Susan 41, 129*
    Susanna 22
    Temperance 106
    Thomas 37, 57, 69, 123, 131*,
       144*, 147*, 156*, 174*, 177*
    Thomas P. 154
    Timothy 41, 71
    Tolover 146*
    Tryphena 70
    Wells 19
    Weltham 82
    William 11*, 12, 118*, 130*,
       134, 135*, 151, 162, 168,
       176*
    Winthrop 17*

Davison,
    B. 190
    Bracket 190
    Daniel 63*
    John 72

Davoe,
    Anthony 94*

Dawers,
    Jacob 184*

Dawes,
    Jacob 33
    John 33

Dawley,
    Elizabeth 45
    Perry 31
    Welthon 45

Daws,
    Amos 87
    Nicholas 87
    Reuben 29

Dawson,
    James 173, 179
    John 170*, 194
    Otho 179
    Titus 99
    Van C. 188
    William 169*

Day,
    Aaron 78*
    Abraham 9
    Annis 57*
    Anthony 74*
    Asa 97*
    Benjamin 120*
    David 62
    Eliza 100
    George 57
    Horatio 62
    Jesse 165
    John 21*, 38, 59
    Joseph 38
    Levi 24
    Lewis 85*, 178
  * Mehitable 4
    Nathaniel 7*
    Noah 100*
    Rebecca 165
    Reuben 143
    Solomon 100, 178
    Susanna 57
    William 143
  * Mildred 130
Daylay,
    John 111
    Philip 111

Dayley,
    Dennis 167*

Dayton,
    Denra 55
    Ephraim 53
    Jerusha 55
    Mary 47*
    Nathan 72*

Dea,
    Charles 177*

Deab,
    George 8

Deake,
    William G. 73*

Dean,
    A. 68
    Adena 31
    Alanson 99
    Apollos 27
    Archelaus 68
    David 57*, 69, 108*
    David B. 44
    Ebenezer 13, 56*
    Edmund 7*
    Enos 28*
    Ethel 59
    George 5
    Gideon 14*
    Jeremiah 70*
    John 12*
    Leander B. 28
    Lemuel 28*
    Martha 59
    Mary 28*, 104
    Richard 148*
    Samuel 56*
    Seth 27*
    Silas 61*
    Susanna 134*
    Temperance 28
    William 75, 124*

Deane,
    Josiah R. 38

Dear,
    Charles H. 59

Dearborn,
    Anna 65
    Asa 99
    Edmund 19
    Hannah 17
    Joseph 15*
    Nathaniel 99
    Simon 10
    Wilder 65

Dearman,
    Thomas M. 149*

Deatly,
    James 133*

Deatz,
    Henry 172

Deavenport,
    John 189*

Deaver,
    William 183

Debow,
    Harvey 91
    John 91

Debruler,
    John 160

DeCamp,
    John 102*
    Rachel 108*

Decamp,
    Samuel 133

DeCato,
    Francis 65

Decer,
    John 162*

Deck,
    Joseph 116
    Michael 187*

Decker,
    Ephraim 79
    George 166*
    Jacob 76*, 114*
    James B. 76, 126
    Levi 126
    Martin 79
    Pamelia 76
    Thomas 8*

DeComcy,
    William 161*

Deeds,
    George 172*

Deeker,
    (Mrs.) 114
    Jacob 114

Deemer,
    P. 115
    Philip 115

Deen,
    Aaron 179*
    John 161*

Defer,
    William 165

DeForest,
    Abel 73*
    Gideon 93*
    Mary 95
    Mills 65
    William C. 95

Deforest,
    Abraham 125
    Isaac 125

Defriese,
    Ann 153

Degges,
    Dudley 131
    Seneca T. P. 131
    William 132*

DeGolier,
    Anthony 95

Degolyea,
    James 81
    Joseph 81

Degraff,
    Haronymus 87
    John 87

Degraw,
    Luke 111*

Degroot,
    Jacob 111*

DeHaven,
    Edward 162
    John 162

Deily,
    George 114

Deitz,
    Jacob 72
    Johan Jost 72

Delamater,
    Abram J. 79

Delamater, (cont.)
    Elizabeth 79
    Lafayette 102

Deland,
    Jacob 97

Delano,
    Jabez 7*
    Jeptha 29*
    Jesse 29
    Margaret 29
    Nathan 98*
    Oliver 29*
    Peggy 8
    Susanna 29*

Delapier,
    Bartholomew 101*

Delapp,
    James 184
    Nathaniel 184

Delaway,
    John 62

Delbridge,
    Thomas 129*

Deldine,
    J. 154
    Jonathan 154

Deloach,
    Simon 155*

Delong,
    Daniel 82*
    Francis 78*

Demarest,
    Peter 110
    Peter D. 107*
    Philip 101*
    Sarah 107
    Sarah P. 107

Demary,
    Rebecca 24

Demask,
    Ebenezer 101*

Demey,
    David C. 154*

Deming,
    Benjamin 63*
    Daniel 76*
    Gideon 72

Demming,
    David 89*
    Edmina 59
    Edmund 59*
    M. 97
    Mary 95*

Demoranville,
    Simeon 27*

Demoriest,
    Peter 99

Demoss,
    John 182*
    Peter 166*

Deneen,
    Alexander 169
    James 169

Denham,
    Harden 165*
    Washington 153*

Denike,
    Samuel 107*

Dening,
    Anna 77

Denio,
    Aaron 68*

Denison,
    Charles 75
    Foreman 79
    James 53*
    James P. 77
    John 84
    Nathaniel 77
    Prudence 54*
    Stanton 83

Denman,
    Matthias 108*

Dennett,
    Orin 4

Denning,
    Carrol 176
    Solomon 176

Dennis,
    Adonijah 37*
    Andrew 180
    Hannah 105
    John 146*, 170*
    Moses 20*
    William 132

Dennison,
    Andrew 112*
    David 5
    Hiram 99
    Isaac 41*
    John 107
    Lucy 57
    Margaret 107
    Mary 72
    Nathan 69

Denniston,
    Joseph 120*

Denny,
    Absalom 90
    Elijah 166*
    Samuel 184
    William 157*

Denslow,
    Benjamin 93*
    Elihu 49
    Elijah 51*

Denson,
    Thomas 142*

Dent,
    George 127
    James 138
    John 135*
    William 127

Denton,
    John 153

Deny,
    Richard 131

Depew,
    Cornelius 106*
    Peter 96*

Depoister,
    John 163

Depoy,
    Christopher 178

Depuy,
 Aaron 114
 John 103

Deram,
 Thomas 113

Derby,
 Asa 80
 Sarah 80

Derham,
 John 177*

Derning,
 Abigail 50
 Lucy 50

Derr,
 Elizabeth 114*
 John 122

Derrah,
 Robert 135*

Derrell,
 Benjamin 101

Deshazer,
 Henry 165*

Deshlu,
 Charles 114*

Deshon,
 Moses 3*

Desmarkes,
 E. 150

Deum,
 Christopher 116

Deuse,
 (Mrs.) 84*

Deusenbury,
 William 75*

Devars,
 James 135*

Devauss,
 John 177*

Dever,
 Reuben 137
 William 137

Deveraux,
 Alanson 62
 John 62

Devereux,
 Elizabeth 43
 Erastus 89

Devericks,
 John (sr.) 135*

Devin,
 William 165*

Devinell,
 Sarah 22*

Deviney,
 James 121*

Devore,
 J. W. 142

Devose,
 Enos 176*

Devou,
 Helen 78*

Dewees,
 Samuel 127

Dewett,
 Martin 143*

Dewey,
 Abijah 102
 Abram 85
 Asahel 65
 Darius 70
 Ebenezer 70*
 Elijah 99
 Jemima 60
 Lydia 60, 85
 Mary 24
 Peleg 100
 Silas 50*
 Timothy 65
 Trueman 71
 William 71

Dewing,
 Elijah 31*

Dewitt,
 Abraham 98*
 Cornelius 75*
 Egbert 75*

DeWitt,
 Garritt, 51*

Dewolf,
 Benjamin 174*
 Edward 73*

DeWolf,
 Jabez 89
 Joseph 180*
 Peter 180
 Susan 89

Dexter,
 Daniel 45
 David 66*
 John S. 46*
 Nathan 36
 Stephen 63

Dey,
 Daniel 87
 James 87

Deyo,
 Benjamin A. 102
 Bridget 102*

Diamond,
 Abigail 16
 John 20
 Obadiah 16
 Rebecca 20

Dibble,
 John 56

Dick,
 Henry 104*
 William 113

Dicken,
 John 163*

Dickens,
 Joseph 161
 Levi 161
 Thomas 137*

Dickenson,
 Griffeth 132*
 Lucy 50
 Thomas 72

Dickerman,
 John 77
 William 77

Dickerson,
 Asa 60
 Benjamin 176
 David 103*
 George 173
 Hamsah 101
 Ichabod 54*
 Isaac 111
 John 126
 Moses 108*
 Samuel C. 101
 Solomon 165*
 Vachel 174
 W. 185
 Walter 185
 Walter S. 110
 William 119

Dickey,
 Adam 65*
 Eleazer B. 12*
 Elias 20
 James 36*, 126*
 Jennett 20
 William 20*

Dickinson,
 Abel 22
 Charles 94
 Ebenezer 35
 Edward 115
 Erastus 22
 Eunice 22
 Jefferson 66
 John 35
 Levi 35
 Lucy 50, 88*
 Mary 49, 52
 Samuel 38
 Samuel W. 52
 Simeon 35
 Solomon 66
 Willard 38

Dickson,
 Francis 93*
 James 122
 John 101*, 139*, 181
 Joseph 194
 Joseph H. 194
 Miniran 115
 Rachel 39*
 William 132*, 156*

Diefendorf,
 Jacob A. 87*

Diffenderfer,
    David 113
    Jacob 113

Dike,
    Joanna 37*

Dikeman,
    Daniel 55
    Frederick 68*
    Rebecca 56

Dilano,
    Amasa 5*

Dilday,
    Joseph 138
    Seth 138

Dildy,
    Charles 189*

Diley,
    Philip 115*

Dill,
    George 123
    John 90, 137*
    Mary 29
    Milcah 29*
    Runnels 143*
    Samuel 90

Dillard,
    John 147*

Dilley,
    Martin 135

Dillingham,
    Elisha 45*
    John 5*
    Paul 64*

Dillon,
    Henry 157

Dilly,
    Ephraim 172*

Dilts,
    John 109
    William 109*

Diman,
    William 49

Dimmick,
    Benjamin 95
    Giles 95
    John 61

Dimmock,
    Braddock 27*

Dimock,
    Daniel 172
    Priscilla 172

Dimond,
    Elizabeth 49

Dine,
    John 113

Dingee,
    Elijah 56

Dingley,
    Levi 5*

Dingman,
    Adolphus 96
    Harmonious 89
    Jerradus 89
    Killian 96

Dinsmoor,
    Elijah 18
    Fox 18
    Phebe 70

Dinsmore,
    John 19
    Mary 20
    Samuel 19*, 20
    William W. 13

Dinturff,
    Philip 101*

Dirnick,
    Joseph 97*

Disbro,
    Samuel 55

Disbrow,
    Philena 82*

Dismoor,
    J. R. 70

Ditto,
	Francis 179*

Ditty,
	John 158*

Divelly,
	Elizabeth 47*

Divine,
	Matthew 165

Dix,
	Abigail 11
	Amy 66
	Elijah 11
	Jonathan 66

Dixan,
	John B. 149
	Thomas 90*

Dixley,
	Edward 43

Dixon,
	Amos 105*
	John 86
	John B. 86
	Lydia 84
	Robert 89*
	Thomas 162*

Doane,
	Amos 11
	Edward 11
	Mary 26
	Oliver 11

Dobbin,
	Hugh W. 91*
	James 5*

Dobbing,
	James 183

Dobbins,
	David 157
	James 140*

Dobs,
	Nathan 145*

Dobson,
	O. L. 142

Docken,
	Hannah 18

Dockstader,
	Frederick 83
	John 83

Dodd,
	Isaac 108*
	Susanna 49*
	William 143*, 152

Dodds,
	Z. 73
	Zachariah 73

Dodge,
	Abraham 42
	Betsey 12
	Clark 22, 84
	Eunice 22
	Francis 87*
	Isaac 86
	Joel 84
	Lucretia 54
	Lyman 96
	Nathan P. 12
	S. 186
	Shadrach 168
	Simeon 66
	Thomas 42
	William 101*

Dodson,
	George 155*

Doe,
	Henry 9
	Olive 12
	Raymond S. 12
	Simon 13*

Dogan,
	Jeremiah J. 182*

Doggett,
	William 140

Dolbear,
	Joel 38
	Mary 38

Dolbeer,
	Mary 108*

Dolbie,
    Pardon 98*

Dole,
    Matilda 11
    Molly 41
    Moses 34
    Rebecca 40
    William H. 11

Dollar,
    James 137*
    William 140*

Dollestun,
    Esther 97

Dollinger,
    John 115

Dolliver,
    William 41*

Dolloff,
    John 7
    Miles 18*
    Richard 7

Dollsberry,
    Lyles 136*

Dolly,
    John 140*

Dolton,
    Thomas 140*

Dom,
    Daniel O. 142*

Donald,
    James 124
    William 124, 158

Donaldson,
    Alexander 155
    Altamont 192*
    Calvin 93
    Eli 93
    Lophario 192*
    Timothy 93

Donehugh,
    John 100

Donley,
    Samuel 120

Donnell,
    Abigail 4
    Deborah 4
    Lester F. 116

Donnow,
    James 51*

Donoho,
    Keziah 137*

Dony,
    John 99
    William 99

Dood,
    Abel 189

Doolittle,
    David 125*
    Obed 59*
    Uriah 89

Dooly,
    Jacob 164*
    James 166

Doran,
    Alexander 134
    Joseph 134
    Leonard 98

Dorathy,
    Mary 34

Dorchester,
    Alfred 84
    Anna 84
    Eliakim 90
    Reuben 90

Dorcy,
    John G. 128

Dore,
    Bennaiah 17*
    Jonathan 17*

Doremus,
    James 110

Dorland,
    Margaret 110*

Dorr,
    Edward 42*
    John 9
    William 9

Dorrance,
    William R. 57

Dorse,
    William 155*

Dorsett,
    Oliver 58

Doss,
    J. C. 86
    John 129
    William 167*

Dosset,
    Mary 53

Doten,
    Samuel 6*

Dotey,
    Daniel 25*

Dotson,
    James 136
    Richard 136

Doty,
    Abigail 103
    Asa 168
    Azariah 152
    Danforth 84*
    Ebenezer P. 103
    Ephraim 152, 174
    Ezra 88
    Isaac 100
    J. 69
    Jacob 99
    James 108*
    Jerchamell 69
    Jeremiah 99
    John 74
    Levi 100
    Palmer 74
    Peter 174
    Samuel 63*
    Samuel S. 111
    Susanna 30
    Thomas T. 148*
    Z. S. 88
    Zebulon 122

Doud,
    Benjamin 85
    Eli 85
    John 147*

Dougan,
    John 186*

Dougherty,
    Patrick 115
    William 185*

Doughty,
    Christopher 117
    David 5
    Ichabod 5*
    James 5

Douglass,
    David 90*
    Elisha 12*
    James 103*
    John 7*, 116*, 154*
    John R. 172
    Thomas 155*

Doup,
    Dilman 114*

Douthard,
    Silas 162*

Dove,
    George 132
    Thomas 153*
    William 132*

Dow,
    Benjamin 63*
    David 64
    Elenor 10
    Eunice 21*
    James B. 63
    Jesse 24
    John 16*
    Joseph 20*
    Moses 62*
    Nathaniel 20, 63
    Ruth 16
    Samuel 45
    Zebulon 15

Dowd,
    Samuel 174*
    Solomon 54*

Dowell,
    Hannah 42

Dowers,
    Conrad 184*

Downe,
    Mary H. 11*

Downer,
    James 24
    Jason 24*
    Zachariah 93*

Downes,
    John 39
    Naomi 39

Downey,
    Samuel 163*

Downing,
    Daniel 54*
    Henrietta 166
    John 5*, 16, 88, 166
    Jonathan 19
    Lewis 18
    Samuel 6*, 95*
    Stephen 192*

Downs,
    Aaron 4*
    Daniel 91
    Edward 107*
    Jabez 23
    Joseph 55*
    Noah 86
    Sally 142

Dows,
    Joseph 39*

Dowton,
    John 141*

Doxcy,
    Jeremiah 159
    Stephen H. 159

Doxtater,
    Peter 84*

Doy,
    Ebenezer 122

Drace,
    Catharine 114

Drake,
    Adam 27
    Benjamin 31
    Chloe 31

Drake, (cont.)
    Cynthia K. 27
    Elijah 193
    Eliphalet 17
    Flemon 193
    Hannah 20
    Hiram 126
    Jacob 111*
    James 20, 126
    John 17*
    Joshua 155
    Josiah 84*
    Lot 35
    Noah 58*
    Ruth 28*
    William 30*

Drakely,
    Abiram 175

Drane,
    Joel 60*

Draper,
    A. 179
    Anna 23
    Elisha 128*
    James 147*
    Jonathan 179
    Joshua 156
    Simeon 36*
    William H. 186

Dremren,
    James A. 112

Drennan,
    Hugh 162*

Drennen,
    Thomas 117
    William M. 117

Drenning,
    William 118*

Dresser,
    Aaron 5
    Benjamin 42
    Elijah 8
    Job A. 7
    Levi 7
    Paul 4
    Richard 4
    Susanna 42
    Trius 8

Drew,
Andrew 17*
Jerusha 7
Levi 145
Mercy 7
Oliver 105*
Thankful D. 28
Thomas C. 22*
Wealthy 29*
Wilson 145

Drewin,
Samuel 131*

Drewry,
Eleazer 37*

Driggers,
Anna 188

Dring,
Susanna 47
Thomas 47

Drinkard,
Archibald 129

Drinning,
William 189*

Driscoll,
Asa 53

Driskill,
David 161
Green 161

Drollinger,
Frederick 183
Gabriel 183

Drown,
Betsey 47*
Jonathan J. 49*
Sarah 28*

Drumheller,
L. 128*

Drummond,
Mary 133*

Drury,
Ephraim 37
J. (Major) 129
Lucien B. 41

Drury, (cont.)
Luther 78*
William 37*

Dryden,
Artemas 37*

Dubledee,
Asahel 70

Dubois,
Conrad 103
Garret 103
J. D. 193
John 105
Martin 193

Dubose,
Peter 142*

Ducker,
John 164*
John B. 151

Duckworth,
John 137*
Thomas C. 184

Duclous,
Francis 262
Philip W. 62

Dudley,
Abel 17
Anna 17
Benjamin 67*
Eber 56
Harmon 60*
Isaac 179*
Jared 52*
Joel 80
John 67*, 186*
Nathan 141
Polly 17
Roswell 77*
Samuel 17, 135*
Thomas 80

Duff,
John 160*

Duggan,
William 153*

Dugless,
Robert 113

Duher,
    Godfried 115

Duke,
    Doctor M. 141
    Harden 131*
    Henry 164*
    James 139*
    John 183
    Washington 183
    William 141

Dukes,
    David 161*

Dumas,
    Lewis 64

Dumm,
    Catharine 178

Dumph,
    Frederick 72

Dun,
    Joshua 6*

Dunbar,
    Amos 120*
    Daniel 180
    David 13*
    Elijah 9
    George 94
    Jacob 14
    John 93*
    Jonathan 45
    Josiah 35
    Nabby 29
    Philippi 29
    Thomas 164*
    William 180

Duncan,
    Charles 96
    Edward 182
    Elijah 155*
    Gabriel 164*
    George 140*
    James 124
    Jesse 184
    John 124, 148
    Robert 143*, 148
    Samuel 164*
    Sarah Ann 190
    Thomas 153*

Dunckle,
    George 87
    George G. 87
    Nicholas 87*

Dungin,
    John 17*
    Willoughby 17

Dunham,
    Ammi 8
    Calvin 89
    Daniel 92
    David 92
    Ebenezer 84*
    Eber 68
    Edward 86
    Enoch 109*
    Experience 28*
    Ezekiel 89
    Gideon 82*
    Henry 126
    James 61*
    John 108*
    Louis 68
    Lydia 91
    Martha 126
    Mercy 97
    Moses 7
    Reuben 97
    Richardson 73*
    S. C. 70
    Salathiel 99*
    Samuel 60*
    Seneca 86
    Solomon 23
    Stephen 61*

Dunkle,
    Ruth 66

Dunlap,
    Dorcas 9*
    James 10*, 165*
    Jonathan 147*
    Joseph 152
    William 165

Dunn,
    (Widow) 38
    Aaron 183
    Isaac 118*
    James 128*
    James T. 109*
    Jane 131
    John 38, 102*, 183
    John P. 161

Dunn, (cont.)
    Joseph 161
    Rachel 40
    Thomas 147*
    Timothy 77*
    William 152

Dunning,
    Abel 81*
    John 95, 100
    Josiah 100

Dunscomb,
    Mary 101*

Dunsett,
    Azabia 33

Dunstead,
    Jason 80

Dunster,
    Martin 38

Dunton,
    Abner 12
    James 38
    Mary 68
    Silas 36*
    William B. 68

Dunworth,
    George 57

Dupee,
    Aaron 102

Dupey,
    Mary 132*

Duplex,
    George 99
    Lament 99

Durand,
    Alyron 80
    Fisk 76*
    Joseph 80
    Samuel 52*
    Susanna 52*
    William 51*

Durant,
    Isaac 40
    Sally 15
    Susan 15

Durdan,
    Jacob 145*

Durfee,
    Ebenezer 80*
    H. 74
    John 74
    Joseph 27*
    Mary 47*
    Richard 47*
    Walter 78*

Durgin,
    Hannah 17
    Richard 18

Durham,
    James 141*
    John 160*
    Mastin 167*
    Simeon 93
    Stephen 84*

Durkee,
    A. 65
    Asa 68*
    Asahel 65
    Daniel 78
    Ebbe 178
    Joel 178
    John 24*
    Nathan 82*
    Nathaniel 78
    William 57*
    Zelia 24

Durnbauch,
    Anna Mary 118*

Dusenberry,
    William 177*

Dusler,
    Isaac 81
    Marcus 81

Dustin,
    Moses 76*
    Sarah 20

Dutcher,
    Simeon 83*

Dutrich,
    Legal 113

Dutton,
    Amasa 54*
    Daniel 176
    Ephraim 71
    Ira 80
    Richard 77
    Ruth 79
    Street 79
    Zelotus 71

Duty,
    Jonah 158

Duval,
    William 129*

Dwelley,
    Allen 12*

Dwelly,
    John 12

Dwight,
    Mary A. 51
    Timothy 51

Dwinnell,
    Hannah 36
    Henry 64*
    Solomon 36

Dyal,
    John 164*

Dyckman,
    E. B. 193
    William 193

Dye,
    M. K. 163
    William H. 109

Dyer,
    Catherine 5
    Elisha 145
    Esek 46*
    Hannah 5
    Henry 14
    Isaac 4
    James 14
    John 145, 154
    Jonathan 70, 76
    Joseph 50*
    Leonard 5
    Mary 5
    Ruth 29*

Dyer, (cont.)
    Sarah 45*
    Stephen 71*

Dygart,
    Sylvanus 98*

Dygert,
    Anne 83
    John B. 83

Dyke,
    Calvin 175*
    Samuel 71*

Dysart,
    John 156*

Dyson,
    John 129*

Eads,
    Henry 182
    James A. 190

Eager,
    Jason 80*
    Nahum 38
    Seraphina 38
    William 38

Eagle,
    William 135*

Ealter,
    John 157*

Eames,
    James 6*, 89*
    Jonathan 22*, 39*

Earl,
    David 70
    Harrison 88
    Joseph 87*
    Roswell 70

Earle,
    Cornelius 103*
    Moses 102*

Earnest,
    Elisha 146
    George 146

Earskins,
    John 92*

Easland,
    John 32*

Easpe,
    Abednego 141*

Eastas,
    Abraham 164*

Easterbrooks,
    Aaron 49*

Easterly,
    James 75

Easters,
    Jesse 5

Eastes,
    Mary 161

Eastman,
    Asahel 94
    Charles 173*
    Daniel 4*
    Deliverance 176
    Dorothy 65
    Henry 23
    Isaiah F. 94
    J. M. 176
    Jacob 3*
    James 25
    Joseph 89
    Joseph S. 89
    Moses 25
    Olive 16
    Samuel 19*
    Samuel F. 65
    Susanna 26
    William 26
    Zechariah 6*

Eastmony,
    Sarah 7

Easton,
    Anna 85
    Giles 127
    Henry 85
    Lewis 127
    Obadiah 47*
    Richard 117*

Eastward,
    Abram 74

Eastwood,
    Israel 144

Eaton,
    (Mrs.) 195
    Abner 89
    Abram 69
    Benjamin 98
    Benjamin H. 106
    Cyrel 91*
    Daniel 66*
    David 16, 76*
    Ebenezer 41*
    Eliab 14
    Eunice 51
    Jacob 70
    Jere. 66
    John 19*, 23, 83
    Jonathan 98
    Joseph 20
    Joseph T. 64*
    Joshua T. 14
    Josiah 44*, 57*, 66*
    Luther 41*
    Mary 76
    Maverick 66
    Nathan 68
    Peter 98*
    Sally 71
    Samuel 20*
    Sarah 15
    Solomon 61*
    Sylvanus 16
    True 64
    William 3*, 18, 141*

Ebbs,
    Emanuel 121*

Eberhad,
    David 114

Eberhart,
    Jacob 147*

Ebills,
    John 134*

Ebley,
    Douglass 136

Eccleston,
    Daniel 77

Ecclestone,
    Caleb 54
    Elizabeth 54
    Gershom 54*

Echard,
    Charles 32

Eckard,
    Andrew 135*

Ecker,
    George 88*

Eckerson,
    Abram 106
    Mary 106

Eckert,
    John 115*

Eckleburger,
    David 159

Eddee,
    Conrad 83*

Eddey,
    Willard 94
    William 94

Eddleman,
    Aaron 163
    Leonard 163

Eddy,
    Adolphus 86
    Asa 91*
    Barnard 45*
    Benjamin 45*
    Bryant 84
    Celia 11
    Elisha 28
    Gilbert 94*
    James 69*
    Jarvis 46
    Joel 67
    John 27
    Mary 46, 57
    Noah 92
    Reuben 98
    Rhoda 86

Eddy, (cont.)
    Samuel 33*
    Thomas 78*
    William 92
    William R. 174*

Edenfield,
    David 145*

Edes,
    Emery 6
    Thomas 6

Edgar,
    Richard 41

Edgarton,
    Roger 77

Edgecomb,
    G. 79
    Gilbert 79
    Jabez 53*
    Samuel 53*

Edgell,
    Moses 24

Edgerly,
    Richard 4

Edgerting,
    Jedediah 69*

Edgerton,
    James 53*

Edgington,
    Averriler 162
    B. P. 162

Edick,
    George 90*
    Jacob C. 83

Edman,
    Samuel 174*

Edmonds,
    Asa E. 36
    Daniel 136
    Eliphalet 86*
    James 88*
    John 36, 39*, 42*
    William 138*

Eldred,
 Judah 83
 Robert 48*
 Rebecca 46*
 Zenas 83

Eldredge,
 Ebenezer 26
 Jacob 26
 James 119

Eldreg,
 Francis 3

Eldrege,
 Elisha 99
 Hulah 99

Eldridge,
 Abba 28*
 John 110*
 Jonathan 71
 Joseph 71
 Melinda 26
 Rhoda 50
 Rolfe 129
 Simeon 153*

Eldrige,
 Cynthia 22*

Eley,
 Gabriel 125
 Horatio G. 125

Elgin,
 Samuel 189*

Elindorf,
 John 104

Eliot,
 Jacob 16*

Elkins,
 Joshua 165*
 Josiah 10
 Martha 162
 Shadrach 159

Ellege,
 Abraham 148*

Eller,
 John 103*
 John Melchor 140*

Ellery,
 Sally 41
 William 41

Ellet,
 Jarvis 148

Ellethorp,
 Amy 61

Ellington,
 David 165*

Elliot,
 Gideon 87*
 Jacob 5
 John 6, 18*, 27
 Lewis 172
 Percy 87*
 Rebecca 172
 Richard 43*
 Samuel 64*
 Stephen 8

Elliott,
 Alexander 160*
 Andrew 24
 Benjamin 99
 Eleanor 75
 Elizabeth 135
 George W. 189*
 Ira 57
 Jacob 5
 Jedediah 6
 John 116*
 Joseph 126*
 Samuel 126
 Thomas 57
 William 24, 75, 116, 126
 Zachariah 147*

Ellis,
 Asa 89
 Carey 10
 Charles 97
 Clarke 39
 Daniel 89
 Desiah 49*
 Duncan 166
 Eben 30*
 Ebenezer 30
 Elijah 145
 Ephraim 180*
 Ezekiel 101*
 Gamaliel 66
 Hannah 30

Ellis, (cont.)
 Jacob 90*
 Jane 167
 Jesse 168*
 Joel 28*
 John 70*, 75*, 124*, 147
 Joseph 66, 152*
 Lyman 84*
 Mary 145
 Nancy 166
 R. 34*
 Robert 10
 Samuel 160*
 Shadrach 147
 Stephen 119*
 Willard 29
 William 180

Ellison,
 Charles 157*
 Francis H. 106*
 John 116

Ellisson,
 John 158*

Ellsbury,
 Lindsey 144

Ellsworth,
 John 95*, 179*
 John C. 63
 Oliver 25

Elmendorf,
 John. 103*

Elmer,
 Ebenezer 107*
 Joel 73*
 Nathan 108*
 Nelson L. 58
 Oliver S. 49
 Ruth 49
 Stephen 50*

Elmondorf,
 Hulbert 103

Elseroad,
 Samuel 118*

Elsey,
 Patrick 178
 Thomas 178

Elsworth,
 John 77*
 William 170*

Elton,
 Grace 50
 James 50

Eltz,
 Samuel F. 116

Elwell,
 Elizabeth 41
 Jeremiah 6*
 John 99
 L. 68
 Thankful 68

Elwood,
 Abigail 79
 Hezekiah 79

Ely,
 Andrew 102*
 Ashley 178
 Darius 178
 Enoch 44*
 Ephraim 61
 Gurdon 60*
 Horace 83
 Jabez 82*
 Joseph 44*
 Jube 44*
 Simeon 83
 Wells 105
 William 124, 135*
 William S. 53

Emerick,
 Wilhelmus 103
 William H. 103

Emerson,
 Charles L. 93
 Elizabeth 16
 Hannah 17
 Harry 139
 Henry 139, 143*
 James 21
 Joseph 47, 174*
 Joshua F. 17
 Mark 20
 Mary 66
 Peter 21
 Phebe 37

Emerson, (cont.)
    Polly 93
    Samuel 4*, 42
    Stephen 99*
    William 39*

Emert,
    Elizabeth 152
    George 152

Emery,
    Alexander 12
    Benjamin 13
    Caleb 13
    Daniel 19
    George 181
    John 13, 22*, 25
    Joseph 12

Emes,
    Olive 35

Emmes,
    Joshua 174*
    Nathaniel 44*

Emmet,
    John 187
    Martha 110

Emmons,
    Chester 58
    Daniel S. 60*
    Harry 70
    John 97, 135*
    Joseph 85
    Prudence 70
    Samuel 60

Emory,
    Stephen 38

Enderly,
    Michael 103

Enders,
    James 108

English,
    Catharine 95
    John 123

Engly,
    Joseph 39
    Lovina 39

Eno,
    Chester 51
    Loisa 51

Enoe,
    Martin 61*

Enos,
    Alva 83
    David 69*
    Sarah 83

Ensign,
    Daniel 91*
    Otis 76*
    Rhoda 90

Ensworth,
    Jedediah 61
    Mary 61

Ent,
    Daniel 109*

Entreken,
    William 143*

Eoff,
    Isaac 155*
    William 155

Epes,
    Peter 130*

Eply,
    John 159*

Epner,
    Rachel 96

Epperson,
    Chesley 162
    Francis 162

Erb,
    Jacob 114*

Ernest,
    George 116

Errickson,
    Thomas 110*

Errington,
    Martha 122

Ervin,
    James 102, 164*
    John B. 102

Erwin,
    George 155
    James 169*
    John 97*, 155*
    Richard 155*
    William 138*

Erwine,
    Henry 118*

Escridge,
    George 134

Esh,
    John 114

Eshleman,
    Abraham 113*
    Jacob 113

Eskridge,
    Elizabeth 133

Esletyne,
    Jacob 104*

Espy,
    John 144

Esseck,
    Joseph 138

Essick,
    Jacob 115

Estabrook,
    Nathan 97

Esteen,
    John 47*

Esterbrooks,
    Benjamin 96*

Esters,
    Abram 161*
    Joseph 75

Estes,
    John 131*

Estler,
    John 110

Etchison,
    Edmond 138*

Ethel,
    Anthony 130*

Etherage,
    Jane 18

Etherton,
    (Mrs.) 162

Ethforth,
    Samuel 45*

Ethridge,
    Joel 144

Etres,
    Samuel 146

Evaets,
    Mary 59*

Evans,
    Allen 59
    Andrew 184
    Asa 103
    Benjamin 46*
    Daniel 34
    Ebenezer 39
    Edward 179*
    Elisha 137*
    Evan 112*, 173
    Hannah 76
    Huldah 18*
    James 127, 128
    James P. 10*
    Jane 155
    Jesse 189
    John 156*, 189*
    Joseph 19
    Milla 103
    Moses 50*
    Nathaniel 21*
    Noah 90
    Perry 143*
    Philip 143*
    Sampson 129*
    Samuel 83, 154
    Silas S. 83
    Thomas 155
    William 90, 147*

Eveans,
    William 7

Eveleth,
    J. 43
    Joseph 43

Evellon,
    Daniel 118*

Evens,
    Alva 117

Everest,
    Benjamin 71*
    Zadoc 71

Everet,
    Joseph 120*

Everett,
    Abner 59*
    Daniel 98*
    Josiah 14*
    Levi 19*
    William 154*

Everhart,
    John 112
    Laurence 127*

Everingham,
    William 107*

Everly,
    George 155
    John 155

Everritt,
    John 134*

Everton,
    Quinda 31
    Thomas 176

Everts,
    George 71
    Lorain 71

Every,
    George 23
    Stephen 83*
    Peter 53*

Eves,
    Abraham 126

Evings,
    Mary 69*

Ewen,
    Rufus 68

Ewens,
    Alexander 156*

Ewing,
    Alexander 122
    George 152
    James 112, 122*, 186
    John 122
    Robert 124

Ezell,
    Balaam 167*

Fackenthall,
    Michael 112*

Fagg,
    Joel 157*

Failing,
    Jacob 81
    John J. 81*
    Nicholas 81
    Phebe 81

Fain,
    Ebenezer 145*
    John 153*

Fair,
    Samuel 176

Fairbank,
    Prudence 67

Fairbanks,
    Abel 62
    Benjamin 62
    Cyrus 37
    George W. 10
    Jacob 37
    John 41
    Levi 38*
    Lydia 10
    Pearly 66*
    William 31, 151*

Fairchild,
    Abraham 110*
    Joseph 77*
    Nathan 55
    Sherman 171

Fairfield,
    Samuel E. 61

Fairman,
    Roswell 75*

Fairwether,
    Samuel 56*

Faison,
    William 146*

Falconer,
    Francis 162
    Joseph 162

Falcounbury,
    Levi 100
    Levi W. 100

Fales,
    Jonathan 49*
    Keziah 38
    Martha 45

Falkner,
    David 153*

Fall,
    Aaron 168*
    Henry H. 84*
    Judith 18

Fallett,
    Samuel 35

Falum,
    Jonas P. 115

Fanbush,
    John 164*

Fancher,
    James 149

Fanin,
    John 8*

Fanner,
    David 161

Fanning,
    Jonathan 85
    Susan 54
    William 127*

Fannington,
    John 11*

Fanrington,
    Aaron 31*

Fanschelt,
    William 116*

Fanton,
    Hannah 56

Farchild,
    Abijah 93

Fardin,
    Dudley 162*

Farebank,
    Beulah 31
    Leonard 31

Fareclauth,
    Benjamin 145*

Fargo,
    Polly 94
    Samuel 33, 60*
    Thomas 193

Faris,
    Martin 130*

Farley,
    James 14
    Susan S. 42*

Farman,
    Daniel 57*

Farmer,
    Benjamin 63
    David 19
    Ezekiel 171
    Gilbert 40
    Jesse 141
    Naomi 18
    Uriah 63

Farnam,
    Aaron 62
    Lydia 62

Farnham,
    Chloe 57
    Daniel 87
    Dorcas 8
    Elijah 87
    John 8, 66*
    Joseph 94*
    Nathaniel 13*
    Ralph 4*
    Urania 82

Farnsworth,
    Abigail 8
    Amos 40*
    Ebenezer 70*
    Edmund 74*, 80
    Isaac 24
    Thomas 80

Farnum,
    Israel 21
    Royal 45
    Rufus 30*
    Simeon 11

Farr,
    Alvin 85
    E. F. (Mrs.) 143*
    Nathaniel 71*
    Sarah 85

Farrar,
    Francis 144
    Isaac 20*
    John 74*
    Judson 63*
    Thomas 143*

Farrell,
    Ithamar 98

Farren,
    J. 170
    Jared 170

Farrer,
    Abel 132*
    Joseph 92*

Farrington,
    Abner 8
    Abraham 70
    Ebenezer 20*, 70
    Ithamas 7*
    March 79

Farris,
    Elijah 167*
    Moses 166
    Robert 66*
    William 9*

Farrow,
    John 142*

Farwell,
    Eleazer 40*
    Samuel 40

Fast,
    Christian 178*

Faudre,
    Vachael 161*

Faulkenburg,
    David 155

Faulkner,
    Ammi 36
    Cyrus 36
    Eunice 22*

Faunce,
    Hope 30

Fauver,
    Frederick 107*

Favor,
    Emerson 20

Fawn,
    Elizabeth 138*

Faxan,
    E. 62
    Francis 62

Faxon,
    James 23*
    Priscilla 46
    Rachel 31
    Sarah 30
    William 30

Fay,
    Anna 38
    Apollos 37
    Chloe 24
    Joseph 24

Fay, (cont.)
     Martha 38*
     Moses 74*
     Patty 38
     Sarah 22*

Feagles,
     Charles 123

Fearing,
     S. L. 29

Fears,
     Patience 41*

Feaster,
     Henry 108*

Featherly,
     John 100*

Featherston,
     Charles H. 128

Fecter,
     William 83*

Fee,
     John 122*
     Michael 120*

Feighly,
     Peter 127*

Felch,
     Edward 65*
     James B. 57*
     Nicholas 15

Felker,
     Joseph 13*

Fell,
     David 97

Felley,
     Eleanor 50
     Horace 50

Fellows,
     Augustus 92
     David D. 90
     Ezekiel 24
     Isaac 92
     Jari 97

Fellows, (cont.)
     John 17
     Jonathan 97
     Joseph 24
     Josiah 23
     Molly 88*
     Moses 19*

Felt,
     Jehial 85*
     Joseph 22*
     Naomi 22*

Felter,
     Tunis 111*

Felton,
     Ebenezer 34
     John 43
     Mathias 22*
     Stephen 34

Fenn,
     Benjamin 53*

Fenne,
     Aaron 80

Fenner,
     Ann 159*
     Cornelius G. 45
     John 114
     Lydia 45
     Richard 46
     Welcome 46

Fennin,
     Richard 10

Fenton,
     Adonijah 76
     Nathaniel 75*
     Samuel 100*
     Solomon 61*

Fentress,
     James 156*

Fenwick,
     James W. 166

Fer,
     Mary 50

Ferdand,
    Joseph F. 44

Fergerson,
    Lewis 187*

Fergeson,
    Mary G. 109*

Ferguson,
    Abraham 162*
    Andrew 184
    Daniel 20
    Elizabeth 113
    Gilbert 83*
    H. 73
    Hans 120
    Isaac 158*
    James 116*
    John 20, 122
    Moses 189*
    Thomas 75

Fergusson,
    Moses 129*

Ferhune,
    Daniel 162*

Feriole,
    Alexander 78*

Ferl,
    John C. 114*-

Fernald,
    Elizabeth 4
    Hiram 4
    Mark 4

Fero,
    Abraham 98
    Peter 98

Ferrel,
    David 135*
    Gabriel 139*
    William 156*

Ferrell,
    James 108*, 175
    James S. 136*
    John 175

Ferril,
    Smith 157*

Ferrin,
    Hannah 25
    Jonathan 25
    Moses 18

Ferris,
    Harry 75
    John A. 77*
    John T. 74
    L. 96
    Richard 99*
    Samuel 96

Ferro,
    Peter 80*

Ferry,
    Thaddeus 44

Ferubee,
    Samuel 138*

Fessenden,
    Peter 37*

Fetterly,
    Thomas 84*

Fickett,
    John 5
    Lucy 5
    Zebulon 14*

Fiddler,
    John 91

Fidler,
    John 109*

Field,
    Benjamin 109, 161*
    Dennis 109*
    Edward 52*
    Galen 7
    George 99
    Hendrick 111*
    Isaac 45
    John 52*
    Joseph 28
    Lucy 45*
    Mary 52
    Medad 34
    Michael 109
    Rachel 7
    Ruby 7
    Seth 36*
    Zipporah 45*

Fielding,
    Daniel 177*

Fields,
    Bartholomew 149*
    John 21
    Thomas 14*
    William 136*, 188

Fifield,
    Abraham 19
    Daniel 19
    John 7

Figgins,
    James 170

Filer,
    Julia 58
    Oris 124
    Polly 58

Files,
    A. J. 149
    Adam J. 149
    Esther 5*
    J. 148
    Jeremiah 148

Fillebrown,
    Cato 28
    John 44
    Thomas 11*

Filley,
    Jemima 49

Filmore,
    Sarah 38

Filyou,
    James 152

Finch,
    Abel 192
    Amos 102*
    Elnathan 95*
    Ira 171
    Isaac 80*
    John 105*
    Polly 192
    Reuben 96
    Ruth 53
    William 147*, 172

Finck,
    Christian 75
    Phebe 75

Findley,
    David 176*

Fink,
    John L. 107*

Finley,
    Paul 142*
    Robert 134*

Finn,
    Peter 187

Finnell,
    Charles 189

Finney,
    Jonathan 79*
    Joseph 180
    Josiah 180
    Moses 80*

Finton,
    Asahel L. 68
    Isaac 68
    John 151*
    Joseph 101*

Fires,
    John 164
    William 164

Fish,
    Aaron 92
    Allen 27
    Caleb 95
    Eleazer 21
    Job 30
    John 62, 67
    John K. 101
    Jonathan 84*, 101
    Joseph 103*
    Nathan 35
    Pardon 119
    Rebecca 28*
    Sally 78
    Simeon 9*
    Sylvanus 27*
    Thomas 27*
    Ursula 30
    William 26

Fishburn,
    Ludwig 113
    Philip 113

Fisher,
    Aaron 34
    Asa 31
    Cyrus 31
    Elias 165*
    Elijah 7*
    Frederick 156*
    George 114, 171
    Isaac 184
    Israel 34
    J. 34
    Jacob 4*, 134, 171
    Jane 28
    Jesse 104
    John 57, 173*, 177
    John B. 165*
    Jeremiah 62*
    Josiah 80*
    Laben 57
    Lemuel 27
    Leonard 31
    Mehitable 20
    Oliver 30
    Richard 20
    Susan 31
    Thomas 20
    Timothy 31*, 66
    William 109, 132*, 137

Fishley,
    George 15*

Fisk,
    Abner 80, 89
    Amey 46*
    Artemas 65
    Betsey 41
    David 20*
    Ebenezer 63*
    Ephraim 18*
    Eunice 57*
    Jacob 33*
    John 82*
    Moses 38
    Ruth 65
    Seberry 36
    Stephen 70*
    Susan 44
    William 26
    Zedekiah 34*

Fiske,
    James 62*
    Job W. 46

Fitch,
    Abigail 54, 60
    Asa 89, 100*
    Daniel 108*
    Elijah 60
    Erastus S. 86
    Esther 56
    Giles 95*
    Jabez 54
    John 51, 62*, 88*
    R. W. 76
    Roswell W. 76
    Walter 93*
    William 103*

Fite,
    Henry 155
    John 155
    Leonard 155*

Fitherman,
    John 120

Fitts,
    Abigail 10
    Dolly 16
    John 42
    Nathaniel 16

Fitz,
    Robert W. 132
    Tandy W. 132

Fitzgerald,
    Benjamin 132*
    James 95
    Sarah 95

Fitzhue,
    Elizabeth 101*

Fitzjerrell,
    William 185*

Fitzpatrick,
    James 165*
    Michael 106*

Fitzsimmons,
    George 192*
    William 123

Fitz Simmons,
    John 77*

Fitz Strasburg,
Michael 113

Flack,
James 167*

Flagg,
Abijah 49*
Elijah 97*
John 9
Jonathan 37*
Nathaniel 97
Patty 36
Peter 83*
Samuel A. 9

Flaharty,
Amasa 178
Nicholas 178

Flanagan,
Andrew 119
Timothy O. 72
William 146*

Flanders,
Abner 19
Augustus 81*
Daniel 41
David 19
Henry 88
J. C. 35
John 88
Mary 24
Moses 24
Philip 12

Flanigan,
Daniel 147

Flatt,
Andrew 122*
Edward 187

Fleeke,
Gershom 189*

Fleming,
Isaac N. 146
John 120*
Robert 119*
Samuel 149*
William 146

Flemming,
Robert 145*
Stephen 122*

Flerrin,
Samuel 18

Fletcher,
Ann 115
Benjamin 84
Catharine 70*
Cyrus 8
Daniel 70*
Elias 190
Elizabeth 8
James 190
Joel 23
John 77*, 194
Joseph 66, 67
Joshua 37*
Josiah 40*
Luke 97*
Oliver 91*
Peter 20*
Roland 71
Samuel 18
Sherebiah 180*
Simeon 20*
Thomas A. 153
William 40
Zaberd 194
Zebina 44

Fling,
Abel 71*

Flinn,
Sarah 194*

Flint,
Aaron 57*
Augustus 65
Austin 37*
Charles 40
Daniel 65
Davis 64
Elizabeth 40
Jabez 105*
Jerusha 32*
John 49
Jonah 65
Joshua C. 60
Levi 9
Mary 39*
Nathaniel 65
Rebecca 37*
Sarah 60
Tilly 37*
William 43*

Flitcher,
    John 99
    Joseph 99

Flood,
    John G. 42
    Richard 60*
    Rufus 64
    Samuel 42

Florance,
    J. T. 158

Flory,
    David 114

Flothers,
    Edward 182*

Flournoy,
    Jacob 129*

Flower,
    Thomas 185*
    Zephon 126*

Flowers,
    Absalom 133*
    Anna 155

Floyd,
    Abraham 181*
    Davis 162
    John 162
    Samuel 116

Fluner,
    Nicholas 184

Fobes,
    John 97*

Fog,
    William 24

Fogg,
    Benjamin 111
    Charles 20
    Charles M. 31
    E. T. 29
    George 10*
    Hannah 5*
    Jeremiah 20
    Lydia 16
    Michal 8
    Samuel 13*
    Sarah 15

Fogg, (cont.)
    Stephen 18
    Susanna 31
    William 4

Folandt,
    Philip 103

Folck,
    Daniel 134*

Follansbee,
    Eleanor 20
    Enoch 41
    John 20
    Nathan 24*
    Nehemiah 41*
    Sarah 41*

Follett,
    Andrew 94
    Benjamin 66*
    Lewis 46
    William 46*

Folliard,
    John 94*

Follinsbee,
    John 16

Follis,
    Isaac 165*

Folsom,
    Asa 15
    Mary 16*
    Olive 42

Fonda,
    Eldert 81

Fontaine,
    Ann 131
    Edmund 131

Foot,
    Albert 100
    Allen 71
    Beeri 100
    Daniel 71*
    Darius 58*
    Ebenezer 90
    Edwin 52
    Elihu 52
    Elizabeth 32
    Freeman 71

Foot, (cont.)
    Joseph 103*
    Miles 51
    Noel 88
    Salmon 32
    Samuel S. 88
    Simeon 125*
    Thankful 88

Foote,
    Erastus 77
    Jehiel 90*
    Jesse 81*

Forbes,
    Abiah 30*
    Alexander 156*
    Catharine 85
    Eli 52*
    Eunice 34
    Ezra 30
    Mary 30
    William 11*, 34

Forbs,
    Samuel 81*

Forbus,
    Hugh 139*

Force,
    Ameriah 31*
    J. P. 163
    Peter 163

Ford,
    Amos 57*
    Ann 157*
    Anna 92
    Asher 100*
    Billy 30*
    Charles 8*
    Dabney 136
    Elisha 28, 132*
    Eunice 51
    Frederick K. 136
    Gilbert 32
    Isaac 126*
    John 152*
    Joseph 166
    Joshua 157
    Loyd 154*
    Mary 174
    Micah 65
    Nathaniel 89*
    Polly 166

Ford, (cont.)
    Sanborn 95*
    Sarah 166
    Stephen B. 51
    Thomas 90
    William 92, 161*

Fordice,
    James 185

Foreman,
    (Dr.) 150
    Peter 113*

Forest,
    Mary 89

Forestall,
    Joseph 23*

Forgason,
    John 181*

Forman,
    Thomas M. 127*

Forney,
    Abraham 139*

Forrester,
    Robert 152*
    William 152

Forry,
    Jacob 186*

Forseth,
    Jonathan 54

Forsyth,
    Joseph 117*
    William 53*

Forsythe,
    Thomas 113

Fort,
    Sherwood 137*

Forte,
    Albert 143*

Fortner,
    Ezekiel 159*

Fox, (cont.)
    Simon 122*
    Stephen 186
    Thomas 51*
    Vaniah 76*
    William 13, 174

Foy,
    John L. 10

Foye,
    Moses 4*

Fradenburgh,
    Jacob 101
    James 101

Frailey,
    John 116*

Frame,
    John 131*

France,
    Adam 103*
    Jacob 96*
    John 133*
    Wilhelmus 102*

Frances,
    Samuel C. 83

Francis,
    Aaron 82*
    Elijah 50*
    Job 87*
    Robert 33*
    Stephen 50

Francisco,
    Anne 83
    J. F. 151
    Levi 86*
    Mary G. 108

Frank,
    (Mrs.) 88
    Catharine 88, 99
    John 99
    Peter 176

Franklin,
    Jonathan 24*
    Lewis 131*
    Moses 94*
    Nathan 92*

Franklin, (cont.)
    Reuben 161
    Thomas 129*
    Thomas P. 129*

Franklyn,
    Ezra 57*

Franks,
    Abraham 119
    Christina 181*
    Henry 180

Frary,
    Seth 36

Frasey,
    William 118*

Frashier,
    James 142*

Frasier,
    Alexander 156
    C. P. 142

Frayer,
    Charles 102
    David 102

Frazier,
    Henrietta 128
    Henry 153*
    James 127
    Levin 128*
    Solomon 127
    Thomas 159*

Frazure,
    John 162*

Freas,
    Marlain 114

Fredenburgh,
    A. 74
    Aaron 74

Frederick,
    Cabler 155
    Heth 183*

Fredrigal,
    Thomas 118

Freed,
    Jacob 178
    Jonas 114

Freeland,
    Solomon 125*

Freeman,
    Aaron 53
    Alden 65
    Alexander 88
    Almond B. 66
    Andrew 30*
    Bradford 65
    Charles 28
    Deborah 26
    Elisha 30
    Elizabeth 103
    Enoch 24*
    Hardy F. 161
    Hersey 5
    Job 172
    John 10*, 30, 129*, 142,
        169*
    Judith 161
    Michael 161*
    Nathan 178
    Nathaniel 33
    Richard 142*
    Rufus 181
    S. M. 36
    Salsbury 46*
    Sampson 10*
    Samuel 172
    Solomon 174
    Stephen R. 178
    Stiles 90*
    Thomas 24, 70*
    William 174
    William A. 28
    Wyott 141
    Zadoc 154*

Freeney,
    Jane W. 149

Freer,
    Solomon 161*

French,
    Asa 18*, 35
    C. 32
    Charles 8, 70*
    Christopher 32
    Daniel 193*
    Ebenezer 91

French, (cont.)
    Edward 30
    George 24
    Gideon F. 32
    J. 73
    Jacob 70
    Jeremiah 99*
    Jonas 40*
    Jonathan 24*, 86, 103
    Joseph 10, 70, 83*
    Lucy 27
    Mary 15, 174
    Molly 29
    Nancy 15
    Nathan 174*
    Nathaniel 29, 32
    Noah 84*
    Polly 27*
    Rachel 21
    Reuben 25*
    Roger 70*
    Samuel 37, 87
    Sarah 8
    Susanna 65
    Sylvanus 31
    Thomas 157*
    Warren 174
    William 7*, 40*, 44, 87, 166*

Fretwell,
    Richard 147*

Frey,
    Ad. 115
    J. 115
    Jacob 115

Friday,
    Coonrad 87*

Fridley,
    Ludwig 117*

Friend,
    Nathaniel 42*

Frieze,
    Peter 139

Frigate,
    John H. 166*

Frink,
    Amos 92
    Harvey 76
    Nathan 89*

Frink, (cont.)
    Samuel 37*
    Thomas 76

Frisbee,
    Asahel 103*
    Gideon 79
    Levi 80*
    Lewis 103
    Sarah 103
    Thomas 72*

Frisbie,
    Abraham 116

Frisburn,
    Michael 112

Frisby,
    Ichabod C. 50*
    Luther 180

Frist,
    Adam 114

Fritter,
    Travers 133*

Fritts,
    George 138*

Fritz,
    Nicholas 113

Frizzell,
    Nathan 161
    William 161

Frizzle,
    Eliakim 65
    Martha 65

Frolick,
    C. 87

Frost,
    Charles A. 40
    Charles J. 75
    Eli C. 76
    Elliot 4*
    George P. 103*
    Hiram 126
    John 80
    Joseph 76, 186*
    Joshua 4

Frost, (cont.)
    Mary 134
    Micajah 164*
    Obadiah E. 9
    Phinehas 7*
    Richard 43*
    Sarah 4
    Simon 134
    Thomas 75

Frothingham,
    Elizabeth 94*
    Samuel 59*

Froxil,
    J. 148
    Jacob 148

Frun,
    Thomas 59*

Fruse,
    Gordon 15

Fry,
    Andrew 49*
    Catharine 113
    Christopher 105
    Conrad 112
    John 33, 173
    Nicholas 137
    Peter 112
    Robert 187*
    William 105

Frye,
    Lucy 41

Fryer,
    John 134*

Fudge,
    Jacob 144*

Fuinster,
    William 139*

Fulham,
    Elisha 86

Fulherson,
    Joseph 177*

Fulk,
    Simon 113

Fulkerson,
   John 121
   Richard 121

Fuller,
   Aaron 6*
   Abigail 88
   Amasa 69*
   Amos 29
   Azariah 37
   Benjamin 42
   Betsey 74
   Catharine 125
   Charles C. 39
   Chase 74
   Chester 61
   Cyrus 59
   Daniel 20*, 62*
   David 57, 81*, 85*, 148
   Ebenezer 54*
   Eleanor 39
   Elijah 71
   Elkney 82*
   Enoch 11
   Eunice 61
   George 154*
   H. 70
   Hannah 8
   Henry 51
   J. 68
   James 42*, 153*
   John 59, 61*, 68, 82*
   Jonathan 36, 74*
   Joseph 23, 27*, 174*
   Joshua 75
   Josiah 60*
   Lemuel 23*
   Lot 88*
   Mary 7
   Nathan 57*, 82
   Nathaniel 42*
   Noah 23*, 68*
   Orrin 88
   Rufus 19
   Ruth 119
   Samuel 73*
   Silas 49*
   Stephen 145*
   Wealthy 54*
   William 10*, 82

Fullerton,
   John 59

Fullington,
   Jane 67
   John 67

Fullinsbury,
   Olive 116

Fullum,
   Elizabeth 37*

Fulton,
   A. 144*
   J. B. 144
   Joseph 118*
   Robert 19
   Thomas 148*

Fults,
   Conrad 88
   George 88

Furber,
   Betsey 15
   Elizabeth 16
   Hannah 18
   Joshua 16

Furbush,
   Rachel 41*

Furgison,
   James 154
   Samuel 154

Furguson,
   Betty 18
   John 174*

Furnald,
   Samuel 7

Furnish,
   James 162*

Furniss,
   Sarah 43

Furr,
   Enoch 131*
   Henry 137*

Fye,
   John 123

Gabbard,
   George 165*

Caganus,
Reuben 140

Gage,
Aaron D. 156
Abel 21*
Amos 6, 91
Daniel 7*
David 19, 85
Elizabeth 21
Jacob 191
James 191
John 41*
Jonathan 42
Louis 6
Moses 85
Nathan 21
Nathaniel 91
Reuben 172
Thaddeus 19, 85*
Zenas 26*

Gaggers,
Nathan 188

Gaild,
Hannah 9

Gaines,
Edward L. 166
James 139*

Gains,
Thomas 163*
William 145*

Gainsey,
David 96

Gainson,
James 185*

Gainy,
William 141*

Galamore,
John 185*

Galaspy,
James 149
John O. 149

Galbraith,
Cyrus 191

Gale,
Anthony 164

Gale, (cont.)
Hiram 64
James H. (Major) 127*
Jane B. 94
Robert 166
Robert F. 166
W. A. 164

Galespie,
Daniel 149

Gall,
George 173*
Polly 171

Gallatin,
Samuel 72

Gallenton,
Abraham 119

Gallespie,
Jacob 153*

Gallop,
Rufus 94*

Galloway,
Charles 161*
James 165*

Gallup,
Amos 54*
Andrew 53*
Nehemiah 53*
Robert 77
William 89

Galpin,
Abel 99
Amos 58*
Daniel 50*
Simeon 99

Galusha,
John 100
Thomas 100

Galutia,
Abiram 101
Reuben 101

Galway,
Richard 111*

Gambel,
John 70*

Gamble,
    Archibald 21
    James 178
    Samuel 21

Gamblin,
    James 157*
    Joshua 162*

Gammon,
    Harris 153
    Jesse 153*
    Joshua 5
    Lewis 153

Gammond,
    Joseph 7
    Seba 7

Gamsey,
    Joel 73*

Gandy,
    David 107
    Ephraim 143*

Ganett,
    Frances 74

Gangewer,
    George 114*

Gangwer,
    Andrew 114*

Gann,
    William 144

Gannon,
    William 186

Ganoe,
    Daniel 166*

Gant,
    Erasmus 134*

Gantley,
    Secon 104

Garberich,
    John 114*

Gardener,
    James M. 61

Gardiner,
    John 126
    Moses 14

Gardner,
    Abigail 48*
    Andrew 34, 120
    Benjamin 49
    Betsey 80
    Carswell 112
    Charles 54
    Christopher 23
    Cranston 48
    Daniel 34, 126*
    David 29
    Deborah 35
    Francis P. 53
    George 132*
    James A. 48
    John 7*, 27, 123, 139*
    Josiah 82*
    Mary 47*, 108
    Perez 29*
    Richard C. 80
    Samuel 29*
    Samuel J. 108
    Sarah 7, 34
    Sarah Ann 48
    Sidney 54
    Silas 48
    Varnum 48
    Waity 48

Garfield,
    Elisha 23
    Samuel 21, 23

Garick,
    Adam 142*

Garison,
    Silas 150
    Stephen 150

Garland,
    Ham 17
    Hannah 17
    James 17
    John 161*
    Richard 26*

Garlen,
    Nathaniel 135*

Garlinghouse,
    Benjamin 91*

Garman,
    William 137*

Garner,
    John 149
    John W. 133
    Joseph 148*
    Sturdy 148*
    Willie 137

Garnet,
    Lewis 190

Garnett,
    Ruth 30*

Garnsey,
    Abner 25
    Chauncey 59*
    David 25

Garretson,
    John 123*

Garrett,
    John 97, 103
    Robert 165*
    William 139*

Garrigus,
    John 110*

Garrison,
    Aaron 107
    Abraham H. 107*
    Benjamin 163
    Elizabeth 106
    Harry 104
    James 187
    John 97, 158*
    Peter A. 107

Garriz,
    Sihez 165*

Garter,
    Barnabas 165

Gartington,
    Christopher 151

Garvin,
    James 134
    John 16

Garvy,
    Francis 72
    Isaac J. 72

Garwood,
    Samuel 120

Gary,
    Enos 73
    Jonas 22
    Peter 123*

Gaskins,
    Jeremiah 179

Gass,
    John 152*
    Patrick 133*

Gassett,
    David 71
    Nahum 40*
    Vashti 71

Gaston,
    David 144
    James A. H. 144
    Jane 144

Gatchell,
    William 5*

Gates,
    Asa 47*
    Daniel F. 67
    Elias 103
    Ezra 25, 103
    Fanny 44
    Freeman, 180
    George 20
    Henry 44
    Jonah 65*
    Lyman 21
    Maria 87
    Micah 21
    Oldren 96*
    Samuel 64*
    Simon 37*
    William 26*, 41*, 89

Gatewood,
    Edmund 129*
    Fletcher 160
    John 166*
    Nancy 160
    William 129*, 131*

Gatlin,
Stephen 145*

Gattes,
Alexander 140*

Gatting,
Edward 140
Elizabeth 140

Gaudy,
Rachel 116

Gauff,
Samuel 138*

Gault,
Daniel 20
James 84
John 20

Gauss,
Benjamin 91*

Gavon,
Michael G. 177

Gawen,
Mary 3

Gay,
Abiel 12
Allen 145*
Asel 54*
Edward 79
James 85
Thomas 31
Willard 33
William 79

Gayle,
Bartlett 132
Joice 132
Mathias 132*

Gayler,
William 102

Gaylor,
Harvey 103*

Gaylord,
Ambrose 125*
Asaph 90
Chancy 90
Deodate 56
E. 74
Elijah 74

Gaylord, (cont.)
Harvey R. 168
Jedediah 79*
John 177*
Levi 168
Patience 43*

Gearon,
Thomas 110*

Gearran,
Solomon 154*

Geary,
Martha 36
William 109

Geasling,
Charles 149*

Gee,
A. 78
John 78
Moses 172*

Geeman,
James 99*

Geer,
Allen 94
Charles 96*
Eleanor 50
Elias 94
John 33*

Geidner,
Timothy 114

Geissenger,
John 122*

Gelats,
George 119*

Gellengwaters,
James 134
John 134

Gelston,
William 60*

Gemshorn,
Catharine 113

Gent,
Charles 157
James W. 157

Gentner,
    Andrew 8*

Gentry,
    Ann 189*
    David 157*
    George 128
    James 128*
    John 153
    Richard 164*

Genung,
    Isaac 110*

George,
    Britton 159*
    Francis 10*
    Hannah 31
    Jesse 175*
    John 183
    Jordan 166*
    Leonard 25
    Margaret 9
    Moses S. 85*
    Nathaniel 16
    Petteford 138
    Samuel 16, 23
    William 156*

German,
    Lewis 59
    William 130

Gerould,
    Zubah 21

Gerry,
    Seth 91*

Geryl,
    Jemima 67

Gest,
    Jane 170

Getchel,
    Joshua 53

Getchell,
    Sarah 14
    Seth 11

Geter,
    Lyttleton 162

Getman,
    Elizabeth 81
    Mary 83*
    Peter 81*
    Peter C. 81

Gibbons,
    Lucius 44
    Mary 136
    Samuel 136
    Timothy 44

Gibbs,
    Abigail 39
    Catharine 45
    Churchill 131*
    Ebenezer F. 155
    Elijah 67*
    Frederick 88, 89
    Gershom 58
    Isaac 34
    Jesse 70
    John 155
    Joseph 29*, 126*
    Josiah 70
    Lemuel 70
    Luman 135*
    Patience 58
    Pelatiah 7
    Philo 85*
    Solomon 58*
    William 58*, 143*
    Willis 58

Gibson,
    David 21
    Eleazer 179
    Elisha 166
    Erasmus 142*
    George 45, 167*
    Gideon 120*
    Henry 106*
    Hugh 139
    James 187*
    Jesse 161
    John 37, 156*, 161, 192
    John C. 182*
    Joseph 139
    Peter 69
    Thomas 37
    William 156, 159*

Giddings,
    Achsah 51*
    Affiah 51
    Hiram 71

Giddings, (cont.)
 Isaac 41*
 Mary 54
 Nabby 71
 Niles 83*

Gideon,
 Jacob 195*

Gifford,
 Elihu 47*
 Jeremiah 89*
 John 81*, 85*
 Lewis 27*
 Stephen 75
 William 122

Giffords,
 Absalom 83
 William 83

Gilbert,
 Allen 92
 Benjamin 59*
 Catharine 162
 Charles 162
 E. B. 81
 Elim 62
 Esther 36
 Franklin 58
 George 192
 Hannah 43, 82
 Hooker 50*
 Jabez H. 92
 James 146*
 John 24*
 Jonathan 82, 83*
 Joseph 73, 95*, 131*
 Josiah 34*
 Margaret 80
 Margaretta 178
 Mary 58, 93*
 P. R. 60
 Reuben 85*
 Ruth 36
 Samuel 7*, 135*
 Sarah 69
 Sewell 174*
 Thaddeus 192
 Thomas 55
 Truman 176

Gilbreth,
 Benjamin 9*

Gildersleeve,
 Polly 91

Gileot,
 Athnel 58*

Giles,
 John 165*
 Samuel 81
 Thomas 86*

Gilford,
 John 4*

Gilkey,
 William 71*

Gill,
 Benajah 188*
 Daniel 168
 Dixon L. 37
 George (Colonel) 144*
 John 84, 133*
 Jones 128*
 Joseph 168
 Sarah S. 164

Gillaspie,
 William 178*

Gilleland,
 Susan 145

Gillert,
 Stephen 104*

Gillespie,
 Sarah 107*
 William 150

Gillet,
 Anna 93
 B. F. 53
 Benjamin 51*
 Chester 81
 Hannah 103
 Israel 80*
 John D. 82
 Joseph 53, 98*
 Rufus 104*
 Samuel 98*
 Stephen 81

Gillett,
 Benoni 50*, 51*
 Ephraim 51
 James 51
 Jennett 50
 Jonathan 59*
 Joseph 66

Gillett, (cont.)
    Nehemiah 55
    Simon 66

Gillham,
    Lemuel 194

Gilliam,
    Jacob 157*

Gillmore,
    Daniel 31
    James 22
    John 97
    Reuben 171

Gillott,
    Alpheus 126*

Gillpatrick,
    Joseph 4*

Gills,
    John 129

Gillum,
    John P. 164*

Gilman,
    Abigail 23, 80
    Charles 102*
    David 11
    Edmund 131*
    Eliphalet F. 16
    James 21*
    Jeremiah 23
    John 131*
    Jonathan 18
    Joshua 65
    Moses 17*
    Nathaniel 11
    Polly 18
    Sally 18
    Samuel 17, 70
    Sarah 11
    Tabatha 18

Gilmer,
    James 146*

Gilmor,
    Alexander 134*
    Samuel 134

Gilmore,
    Alexander 182*

Gilmore, (cont.)
    Charles 102*
    Daniel 144*
    John 27*, 149
    Samuel 11*
    Seburne 187
    Uriah 187

Gilpatrick,
    Joshua 3

Gilreath,
    Alexander 141*

Gilson,
    Eleazer 21
    John 21*
    Nathaniel 21
    Solomon 67*

Ginger,
    Henry 186

Ginings,
    Eliphalet 14

Gist,
    Joseph 165*

Gitchel,
    Nathaniel 12*

Given,
    John 158

Givens,
    James 159*
    Samuel 139*

Givins,
    David G. 135
    Robert 164
    Robert H. 164
    William 163*

Gladden,
    Elizabeth 51*
    Solomon 119*, 178

Gladding,
    John 45
    Phebe 45

Glandens,
    Major 138

Glascow,
    Lemuel 140
    Miles 140

Glasgow,
    James 118
    John 159
    Richard 159
    William 145*

Glason,
    Patrick 159

Glass,
    Consider 14*
    Frederick 112
    John 125
    Lucy 29
    Michael 190
    Nancy 29

Glaze,
    Thomas 148*

Glazier,
    Asa 93*
    Oliver 37*

Glean,
    Anthony 95*

Gleason,
    Anson 54
    Eli R. 57
    Fisher 79
    Levi 64
    Lovina 79
    Phineas 22*
    Wilson 22

Gleeson,
    Eleanor 19
    Jeremiah 19

Glenis,
    Eli 18
    Thomas 18

Glenn,
    A. 165
    Andrew 165
    Joseph B. 157
    Thomas 147*

Glenney,
    Mary 51
    William 51

Glidden,
    Arnold, 11
    Joseph W. 97

Glines,
    William 19

Glinn,
    John 166

Glontz,
    John 123*

Glover,
    Joseph 162*
    Nancy 31*
    Warde 142

Gloyd,
    J. 84
    Joseph 35
    Rachel 35

Glynn,
    F. T. 67
    Sarah 25*

Goad,
    William 154*

Goar,
    Isaac 162

Goattey,
    John 161*

Gobin,
    William 181*

Goble,
    Stephen 181*

Godard,
    Arsepheus 50
    Ebenezer 50
    Grove 51
    John 51

Goddard,
    Edward 78*
    Joseph 162*

Goddard, (cont.)
    Samuel 41

Goddarel,
    Nancy 38

Godding,
    Samuel 6

Godfrey,
    Benjamin 54
    George G. 28
    Jerusha 28*
    Jonathan 56
    Mary 15
    Reuben 54
    Sarah 142
    Sewel 65
    Wiltha 28
    Zachariah 183*

Godsey,
    Ankey 154
    J. 140
    William 140

Goff,
    Benjamin 78
    Daniel 160
    Gideon 50*
    Hezekiah 62*
    Israel 28*
    James 5, 172*
    Job 134*
    John 83
    Orange 83
    Raymond P. 48
    Richard 77
    Samuel 78
    Simeon 33*
    William 5

Goforth,
    Benjamin 164
    Humphrey 158
    Zachariah 158

Going,
    William 141*

Goins,
    Charles 162*

Golden,
    Deborah 109

Goldin,
    Amos 95*

Goldsmith,
    Jonathan 174
    Nehemiah 43

Goldthwait,
    Timothy 9*

Golpin,
    Samuel 59*

Gonech,
    Catharine 113
    Peter 113

Gonter,
    John 113*

Gontz,
    John 113

Gooch,
    John 65

Good,
    Joseph 167
    Thomas 134*
    Thomas (Colonel) 159*

Goodale,
    Ephraim C. 71
    Hiram 60
    James 43
    John S. 50
    Josiah 64

Goodall,
    Richard 130*

Goode,
    Lemuel 163
    Rebecca 163
    William 129*

Goodell,
    Amos 57
    David 41
    Peninah 44
    Sarah 44
    Susanna 57
    William 41, 79

Goodenough,
 Adino 90
 John B. 90
 Sally 95

Goodhue,
 Thomas 24

Goodin,
 John 7
 Robinson 139

Goodman,
 Jacob 165*
 Littleberry 160
 Thomas 160

Goodmon,
 John 7

Goodnight,
 Christopher 134*
 David 155
 Henry 155

Goodno,
 Asa 71
 Calvin 71

Goodnough,
 Abigail 77
 David 77
 Henry 67
 Mima 67

Goodnow,
 Abner 33*
 Eber. 97*
 Harriet 13
 John 40*
 Phebe 41

Goodrich,
 Abijah 37
 Alfred 34
 Allen 68*
 Azim M. 72
 Betsey 21
 Chauncey 51
 Deborah 49
 Draco 21
 Edward P. 33
 Eleazer 68
 Elijah 90
 George 34
 Hezekiah 24, 70

Goodrich, (cont.)
 Icabod 50
 Jacob 90, 95
 James 52
 Jasper 50
 Joseph 52
 Joshua 37
 Josiah 80
 Mabel 70
 Michael 32
 Roswell 80
 Simeon 68
 Walter 32
 Zenas 103*

Goodrum,
 John 130*

Goodsel,
 Abigail 52

Goodsell,
 Samuel P. 89*
 Thomas 88*

Goodson,
 Benjamin 151*
 William 189*

Goodspeed or Goodspead
 Gardner 78*
 Simon 181
 Simpson 181

Goodwin,
 A. D. 14
 Abel 175
 Abigail 88
 Amaziah 3
 Benjamin 3, 177
 Caleb 140
 Caroline 68
 David 176
 Eunice 3
 George 14
 Israel T. 88
 James 3, 19
 Jehu 182
 John 140
 L. 144
 Lewis 144
 Martin S. 58
 Mary 4*, 23
 Matthew 68
 Reuben 3, 4*
 Ruth 4*

Goodwin, (cont.)
    Samuel 19
    Seth 176
    Thaddeus 20*
    Theophilus 134
    Wells 63*
    Wentworth 4

Goodyear,
    Stephen 51*

Googins,
    Alexander 3
    Stephen 3

Gookins,
    Asa 184
    Samuel 184

Goold,
    Alexander 4*
    Hiram 4
    John 4

Gordon,
    Abner 153*
    Altha 85
    David 110*
    Eliphalet 86
    G. W. 167
    J. V. 85
    James 74*
    Jesse 187*
    John 180
    Joseph 12, 78*
    Josiah 157
    Mary 118
    Nathaniel B. 122
    Richard 156*
    Robert 185
    Samuel 167
    William 157

Gorden,
    Abigail 18
    Hannah 18
    John 133

Gordin,
    Josiah 14

Gore,
    Sarah 126*

Gorham,
    G. G. 166

Gorham, (cont.)
    George 43
    John 37*
    John A. 166
    Josiah 8*
    Julia 51
    Phineas 58*
    Russel 43

Gorrell,
    Andrew 127

Gorton,
    Mary 48*
    Phebe 48

Gose,
    George 136

Gosnell,
    Benjamin 182*

Goss,
    Conrad 72*
    Cyrus 19
    Dorcas 100
    Ephraim 20*
    Jonathan 188*
    Joshua 43
    Oliver 64*
    Ruth 19

Gossett,
    William 143*

Gott,
    Joshua 43*
    Sarah 103*
    Story 103*

Gould,
    Aaron 56
    Aaron P. 25
    Amos 25
    Amos G. 70
    Asa 80*
    Benjamin 42
    Daniel 7*, 120*
    Denizen 20
    Eli 33*
    Elijah 80*
    George 20
    Jacob C. 45
    John 67*, 70
    Jonathan 36*
    Josiah 108*

Gould, (cont.)
    Levi 11
    Lucy 13
    Mary 20, 91
    Millie 35
    Perham 15
    Peter 68*
    Robert 111*
    Sarah 56
    Seth 66*
    Silas 15
    Timothy 108*
    William 73*, 74*, 108*,
      168

Gove,
    Ebenezer 25
    Elijah 24
    Lois 4
    Martha 14*
    William 25

Govit,
    Benajah 48
    Desire 48

Gowdy,
    E. 73
    Henry 50
    John 73
    Roxannah 50

Gowell,
    Susan 4

Gowers,
    Abel 145*

Gowing,
    Eliab 74
    Jonathan 74

Goyer,
    John 113

Grace,
    Elizabeth 94*
    Huldah 8
    John 3
    Manuel 79
    Moses 3
    Nimrod B. 123*

Gracy,
    James B. 139
    Robert 139

Graff,
    Deborah 81
    Robert D. 95
    Samuel 124*

Graffam,
    Joseph 5
    Sarah 5

Gragg,
    Henry 149*

Graham,
    Aaron 7
    Addison 171
    Amos 167*
    Charles 158
    David 173
    Isaac 158
    Jemima 51
    Jesse 60*
    John 117, 138*
    Thomas 165*
    William 75, 171

Grandy,
    Asa 80*
    Jesse 71

Granger,
    Daniel 14*
    John 100*
    L. 179
    Thomas 179
    Zaccheus 130
    Zebe 93*

Grannis,
    Frederick 52
    Jared 52
    Joseph 52

Grant,
    Abigail 4
    Bridgeman 67
    Deborah 121
    Dorothy 20
    Elihu 67
    Elizabeth 46
    Elnathan 61*
    Gustavus 50
    H. 32
    Hannah 54
    Harvey 50
    Hezekiel 32
    John 15*, 20, 139*, 160*, 165*

Grant, (cont.)
    Joseph 146
    Joshua 4
    Lydia 43
    Lucius 50
    Lucy 50
    Peter 3
    Silas 3
    Simon 73
    William 143*

Grantham,
    Richard 152*

Grants,
    Marks 83*

Granville,
    Ignatius 190

Grate,
    Nicholas 112

Gratton,
    Crary 82*
    David M. 82
    Thomas 82, 192

Grave,
    Timothy 52*

Graves,
    Asa 88
    Benjamin 78*
    Chauncey 62*
    Ebenezer 86
    Elizabeth 84
    Erastus 80
    Henry 44
    Henry C. 55
    Hobert 89*
    Jacob 18
    James 164*
    Job 33*
    John 46, 162*
    Oliver 34*, 80
    Reuben 34*, 156*
    Rhoda 35
    Roxana 88
    Simeon 81*
    Thaddeus 62*
    Thomas 166*
    Thomas H. 166*
    Timothy 94*
    William 23*, 80

Gravis,
    Ambrose 21

Gray,
    Abraham 169
    Alexander M. 136*
    Amos 66*
    Christopher 94
    Daniel 136, 180
    David 182*
    Eliot 188
    Eri 188
    Frazier 176*
    Gabriel 129*
    George 140
    Isaac 167*
    Jacob 109*
    James 130*, 141*
    James B. 21
    Job 47
    John 17*, 100, 103, 118, 169
    Joseph 21, 55*, 80*, 109*
    Josiah 108*
    Margaret 100*
    Mary 121
    Nathan 176
    Phebe 118
    Robert 34
    Samuel 75*
    Sarah 44, 63
    Tabitha 41
    William 100, 103, 161*, 165*,
      177*

Greeley,
    Matthew 24*
    Reuben 19
    Rhoda 42*

Greely,
    John 80*

Green,
    Abigail 86
    Asahel 50
    Ann 113
    Anne 89
    Asa 71*
    Benjamin 71
    Betsey 21
    Bradbury 24
    Chaffe 92*
    Charles 133*
    Daniel 73, 87, 88*, 93
    Deborah 40
    David 139*

Green, (cont.)
Ebenezer 82*
Eleazer 89
Elias 67
Elijah 160
Elizabeth 22*, 109
Ezra 16*
Francis 22
George 40, 89, 130, 138*
George J. 130
Grace 50
Hall 89
Harry 22
Henry 33*, 91*
Horace 93
Isaac R. 101
Jabez 83*
James 76*, 89, 101
James B. 109
Jehiel 176*
Jesse 107, 174
John 81, 86, 90*, 136, 141*
John T. 81
Jonathan 27*
Joseph 15, 71, 84, 108*, 174
Lawrence 136
Lodowick 89
Lydia 85
Marsha 154*
Mary 15, 24, 107
Nathan 159*
Northrup 91
Samuel 34*, 43*, 141
Susanna 45*
Stephen 105
Thaddeus K. 105
Thomas 160*
Timothy 81*
Wardwell 94*
Willard 85
William 40*, 53, 128, 184
Zachariah 106*

Greene,
Benjamin 48*, 49
Charles K. 48
Christopher C. 48
Ebenezer 58
Elisha B. 174*
Esther 48
James 48
Oliver 48
Samuel 58
Sarah 46

Greene, (cont.)
Stephen 48*
William 48

Greenfield,
James 53*

Greening,
Nehemiah 130*

Greenlaw,
John 7*

Greenleaf,
Benjamin 9*
Daniel 13
Israel 123*
John 13*
Mary 19*

Greenman,
Asa 80
Gideon 48*

Greenwell,
John 163

Greenwood,
Abel 41
Abigail 41
Benjamin 127
Philip 184*
Sally 41
William 22

Greer,
George 117
James 12*
James C. 155
Thomas 117

Gregg,
Henry 191
Samuel 191

Gregory,
Abram 140*
Alexander 122
Asahel 119
Berry 157*
Christian 133
Elias 56
Elizabeth 46
Elnathan 33
Esbon 192
George 153*

139

Gregory, (cont.)
    Isaac 143*
    Jesse 126, 192
    John 55*, 122, 167*
    Josiah 55*, 64
    Luther 12*
    Matthew 72*
    Nathan 53*
    Samuel 119
    Sarah 56
    Stephen 93, 94*, 126
    Thomas 129*, 138*, 141*
    Uriah 95*
    William 157*

Grewer,
    John 148*

Grey,
    Joseph 154*

Gribbins,
    John 169
    William D. 169

Grider,
    Martin 161*

Gridley,
    Adney 99
    Anna 96
    Chloe 90
    Elijah 90*
    John 96
    Leander 90
    Ruel 51
    Thomas 99

Grier,
    John 154

Griffeth,
    Cheseham, 130*

Griffin,
    Anna 18
    Benjamin 16*
    Daniel 20
    David 60*
    Gordon 160*
    H. 60
    Hannah 20
    James 21, 140
    Jesse 142
    John 140, 149*
    Joseph 142
    Nathan 97

Griffin, (cont.)
    Nica 168
    Richard 139*
    Sherrod 163*
    Thomas 86*, 183
    William 133*
    Zachariah 129*

Griffing,
    Nathaniel 101
    Stephen 101

Griffis,
    Abner 93

Griffith,
    A. 75
    Elisha 134
    Ellis 67
    Eunice 168
    Evan 128
    Jeremiah 75
    Nathan 169*
    Otis 87
    Paul 87

Griffiths,
    Charles 48

Grigg,
    Josiah 130
    Theoderick H. 130

Griggs,
    Benjamin 109*
    Daniel 61
    Hannah 24
    Jedida 57
    Joseph 44
    Orlando 44
    Reuben 109

Grigsby,
    Aaron 155
    Amos 155
    Benjamin 165
    James 165

Grilley,
    David S. 89

Grim,
    Henry 112

Grimes,
    James 169*

Grimett,
    Josiah 156*

Grimm,
    Daniel 117

Grimmer,
    Jacob 158*

Grimsley,
    Abraham 157

Grinder,
    Martin 124

Grindstaff,
    Abraham 189*
    Jacob 164

Grinean,
    Louis 80

Griner,
    Peter 182

Grinnell,
    John 47
    William 27

Grinstead,
    William 130

Grisel,
    Samuel 101

Grisham,
    David 147*
    Kindness 166

Grisnold,
    Jarvis 58

Grissel,
    Thomas 101

Griswold,
    Abel 43*
    Adonijah 187*
    Amy 32
    Anna 54
    David 69*, 77*
    Edward 99
    Elijah 51*
    Joel 71
    John 88*, 116

Griswold, (cont.)
    Joseph A. 54
    M. 68
    Mehitaole 44*
    Samuel 68
    Simeon 94*

Groat,
    Beruch C. 96
    Dinah C. 96
    Nicholas 79*
    Rebecca 96

Groff,
    J. P. 84

Groom,
    Major 161*

Groomer,
    Moses 165

Grooms,
    Jonathan 128

Gron,
    Ambrose 90

Groscost,
    Daniel 179*

Gross,
    Benjamin 13*
    Deborah 29
    Hannah 46
    Isaac 128*
    Lewis 29
    Peter 114*
    Stephen 46

Grostcost,
    Jacob 121*

Grote,
    Isaac 72

Grout,
    Abel 66*
    Aseneth 35
    Hilkiah 69*
    Susanna 40
    William C. 40

Grove,
    Amaziah 65

Grove, (cont.)
George 117*
Philip 123*
Wendle 180

Grover,
B. 68
Benjamin 68, 79
Daniel 144
David 28
Ebenezer 61*
Edsel 14
Elizabeth 14
George W. 7
Peter 144
Robert B. 28
Simeon 28

Groves,
Elizabeth 109
Jacob 81*
John 109
William 127*

Grovier,
Nehemiah 101*

Grow,
David 65*
Luther 4

Grub,
E. 117

Grubb,
Peter 120

Grubbs,
Hensley 131
Nathan 132*

Gruber,
Margaret B. 142*

Grubs,
(Miss) 117
Andrew 117

Grumbine,
Peter 116

Grumblin,
Benjamin 149

Grummond,
Joanna 87

Grummond, (cont.)
Rachel 104

Guess,
Benjamin 148

Guest,
William 143*

Guffey,
Alexander 164*

Guild,
Amos 31*
Anthony 23
Jesse 66*
John 66*
Joseph 36
Samuel 31, 89*

Guile,
Alford 54
Eunice 54
Hawley 89*

Guilford,
Simeon 33

Guill,
John 166*
William 131*

Guillo,
Francis 27*

Guin,
Johnson 80
Obed 80

Guinn,
John 173

Gulick,
John 109*

Gulion,
Robert 185*

Gullion,
John 182
Thomas 182

Gully,
Richard 145

Gum,
    Isaac J. 51
    Roger 134
    Sterling 137*

Gump,
    Frederick 170*

Gumph,
    C. 113
    Christopher 113
    Michael 113*

Gundy,
    Jacob 188
    Joseph 188

Gunn,
    Abel 105*
    Betsey 55*
    Henry A. 34
    John 158*
    Moses 34*
    Salmon 34
    Uriel 55

Gunnell,
    Jonathan 124
    William R. 144*

Gunney,
    Levi 30*
    Samuel 30
    Thankful 30

Gunnison,
    Samuel 41*

Gunter,
    Charles 146*
    George 113

Gurley,
    Jer. 148
    John 148

Gurn,
    Samuel 51

Gurnee,
    Samuel 75*

Gurner,
    Frances 81*

Gurney,
    Asa 29*
    Daniel 30
    Jacob 7
    Jane 30
    Joseph 34
    Joseph P. 29*
    Josiah 34
    Samuel 5*
    Zachariah 30*

Gutherage,
    Nathan 164
    Nathaniel 164

Guthin,
    Chauncey 126

Guthrie,
    Abel 89*
    Joseph 77*

Gutridge,
    William 170*

Gutterson,
    Mary 16
    Rhoda 16

Guyse,
    John 146*

Guyton,
    Aaron 143*

Gwartney,
    Michael 133
    Zachariah 133

Gwin,
    Elizabeth 172

Gwinnup,
    George 172

Hackendorn,
    David 121*

Hacket,
    Daniel 77

Hacket, (cont.)
    John 133
    Josiah 77

Hackett,
    Allen 168
    Daniel 65
    Ephraim 65
    George 30*
    James M. 168
    Joseph 25*
    Zebedee 70

Hackly,
    John 160

Hackney,
    Adam 87
    D. W. 156
    John 136*
    Samuel 165*
    Thomas 156
    William 87

Hackwith,
    R. 162
    Thomas 162

Haden,
    Bartholomew 167*
    Edward 50
    George 152*
    Zerviah 50

Hadley,
    John 63*
    Phebe 20
    Thomas 20
    William 24

Hadlock,
    Thomas 77*

Hagadom,
    William 83*

Hagaman,
    Henry 111
    James 181
    John J. 181

Hagan,
    Arthur 187
    Gardener 92

Hagar,
    John 38
    Washington 38

Hager,
    Aaron 38
    Abraham 37
    Henry 96*
    Jesse 38
    Simon 139*

Hagerdy,
    George 120

Hagerman,
    Barnett 180

Hagg,
    Nathaniel 40

Haggard,
    Henry 149
    William 162*

Hagget,
    Abner 20

Hagner,
    Aaron 38

Hags,
    Edmond 140*

Hahn,
    Michael 179*
    Valentine 100*

Haifley,
    Elizabeth 161
    Jacob 161

Haight,
    David D. 104
    Hannah 104
    James 83
    James F. 83
    Jane 101

Hail,
    John 152*

Haile,
    Bernard 49

Hailey,
 Ambrose 129*

Hailing,
 Philip 98*

Haily,
 Pleasant 165*

Haines,
 Christopher 160*
 Hannah 64*
 Peter 134
 Samuel 19
 Thomas 18*

Hains,
 John 112

Hair,
 Daniel 133
 James 120
 John (Dr.) 120, 170

Haislip,
 John S. 130*

Hakes,
 John D. 75

Haladay,
 C. 67
 Roger 100*

Halbert,
 Horace 62

Halbrook,
 David 12*

Hale,
 Aaron 24
 Amon 154*
 Benjamin 6*
 Calvin 38
 Daniel 19*
 Enoch 3
 Isaac 156*
 Israel 6*
 John 24
 Nicholas 155*
 Oliver 6*
 Simeon 50
 Sylvester 72
 Theda 50
 William 21
 William P. 21

Haley,
 George 110*
 James 155*
 Randall 162
 Randolph 162

Haliday,
 Revell 133*

Halister,
 Hartley 69
 Jennett 69

Hall,
 (Mrs.) 162
 Abel 184
 Abel D. 184*
 Abigail 27
 Alanson 58
 Alpheus 61*
 Andrews 52*
 Anson 94*
 Anthony 162*
 Asa 69, 135*
 Betsey H. 53
 Charles 5, 94*
 Daniel 77
 David 27, 79*, 109*
 Ebenezer 59
 Edward 183
 Edward S. 183
 Eleanor 26*, 42
 Elias 68*
 Elisha 83*
 Elizabeth 5*, 23, 107
 Enoch 89*
 Ephraim 66, 90*
 Erastus 83
 Gad 101*
 Hannah 9
 Henry 26, 71
 Hiram 26, 82
 Isaac 8, 12*, 48*
 Isham 129*
 Jabez 33
 Jacob 69*, 109
 James 9, 132*
 Jesse 44*, 135
 John 58*, 107*, 111, 129*, 131*,
  158*, 177
 John B. 89
 John L. 135
 Jonathan 24, 71*, 86
 Joseph 17, 164*
 Joshua 76
 Josiah 31
 Jotham 86

Hall, (cont.)
    Laban 184
    Levi 9, 62
    Lucy 95
    Lydia 26*
    Lyman 33
    Mary 32, 66*
    Mercy 82
    Moses 85*
    Nathaniel 24, 48*, 62
    Oso 99
    Peter L. 179*
    Rhoda 12
    Rhodes 192
    Richard 127
    Robert 49
    Russell 46*
    Ruth 52*, 95
    S. 142
    Samuel 42, 72*
    Samuel M. 181*
    Sarah 76
    Silas 24, 76
    Simeon 97
    Solomon 142
    Stephen 64*
    Susanna 142*
    Sylvester 76
    Thomas 132*
    Timothy 19*, 50*
    Wildman 56*
    William 40, 75*, 121, 163,
        183*, 186, 187*, 190*,
        192
    Zachariah 45
    Zebulon 75

Hallet,
    Elisha 11
    Jonathan 11
    Solomon 11*, 77*

Hallett,
    Benjamin 26*

Halley,
    John 129

Hallock,
    Daniel 105
    Micah W. 105
    Thomas 102
    Ruth 52

Hallowell,
    John 11

Hallowell, (cont.)
    Mary 11
    Miles 167*
    Richard 116

Halsapple,
    John 104
    Nicholas 104*
    William 104

Halsey,
    Hamutual 105
    Henry 51, 137*
    Hugh 105
    John 72*
    Mathew 98
    Philip 51
    Sylvanus 105*

Halsted,
    John 172
    Joseph 89*

Haly,
    Anthony 175*

Ham,
    Benjamin 17*
    John 10, 164
    Joseph 164
    Nathaniel 5

Haman,
    Alexander 146*

Hamblet,
    F. M. 44

Hambleton,
    David 159*
    Reuben 144
    Thomas 139*

Hamblett,
    Benjamin 22
    Phineas 22

Hamblin,
    Abner J. 86
    Benjamin 58*
    Hannah 86

Hamby,
    William 152

Hames,
       John 146*

Hamestreet,
       Benjamin 87
       Philip 87

Hamet,
       Caleb 80

Hamilton,
       Alexander 133
       B. 165
       David 165
       Eliakim 99*
       George 124*, 127
       Hemdon 159*
       James 137*, 152*, 167*
       John 3*, 106*, 160*, 189
       Jonathan 3
       Joshua 154*
       M. 93
       Robert 180*
       Thomas 149*, 154*, 187*
       William 6*, 122
       William R. 149

Hamingway,
       Mary 22

Hamlen,
       John 35

Hamler,
       Henry 165*

Hamlett,
       William P. 129*

Hamlin,
       Hannah 88
       Russell 55*

Hamman,
       Isaac 183*

Hammer,
       Henry 136*

Hammerty,
       James 166*

Hammock,
       John 152*

Hammon,
       Gideon 30*

Hammon, (cont.)
       Josiah 11

Hammond,
       David 19*
       Esther 19
       Esther D. 19
       Hinsdell 98
       John 48
       John 48
       John D. 43
       Lewis 93
       Mary 104
       Robert 80*
       Samuel 149*
       Samuel (Colonel) 142*
       Simeon 98
       Stephen 83*
       Thomas 69

Hammonds,
       Peter 164*

Hamond,
       John 172

Hamonds,
       Absalom 136
       Sarah 136

Hampton,
       Thomas 190

Hamson,
       Hannah 43

Hanbeck,
       Samuel 74*

Hanchell,
       Ezra 50*

Hanchett,
       J. 175
       Jonah 175

Hancock,
       Ann 45, 129
       Austin 131*
       Daniel 187
       Henry K. 45
       Jane 129
       Joel 76*
       Samuel 129
       Thomas 31*
       Wealthy 44*

Hancox,
    Charles 77
    Phebe 77

Hancrous,
    John 185
    Jeremiah 185

Hand,
    Aaron 108
    Abram 173*
    Elizabeth 93
    Isaac M. 108
    James 158
    James S. 166
    Jane 166
    Jonathan 108*, 111
    Samuel 158

Handerson,
    Abigail 23

Handford,
    Betsey 55

Handley,
    John 155
    Samuel 155

Handy,
    Charles 33
    John 98
    Levi 30
    Lois 30
    Lucy 14
    Mary 33
    Nancy 128*
    Thomas 28

Haneson,
    B. 131
    J. 131
    John 131

Haney,
    Charles 183*
    Daniel 7
    Francis 187
    Susannah 128

Hanford,
    Levi 79
    William B. 79

Haniford,
    Nancy 19

Haniman,
    James 25

Hankins,
    Abraham 153*

Hanks,
    Abner 183*
    Jotham 79*
    Mary 174
    Richard 139*

Hanlon,
    Matthias 183*

Hanmer,
    Peter 98

Hanna,
    John 173
    Robert 100

Hannah,
    Andrew 154*
    John 99
    Robert 144
    William 99

Hannahs,
    Daniel 94

Hanning,
    John 119*

Hannis,
    Margaret 96

Hannon,.
    Eusom 136*

Hannum,
    Anna 36

Hansbrough,
    John 134*

Hanscom,
    George 6
    Nathan 14
    Robert 4
    Sally 4

Hanscomb,
    Uriah 3

Hansford,
    Charles 161
    William 161

Hanson,
    Aurt 95*
    Edmund 5
    Gersham 18
    Isaac 17*
    Jabez 99*
    John 17
    Nathaniel E. 17
    Sarah 16, 42
    Silvester 102

Hanting,
    Moses 38

Hapgood,
    Hannah 38

Haptonstall,
    Abraham 172

Haradon,
    Joseph 20

Harber,
    Jeremiah 163*

Harbison,
    James 182*
    John 124

Harbour,
    Hartwell 131
    Noah 131

Harde,
    John P. 103

Harden,
    Benjamin 191
    Cato 119
    E. L. 191
    Henry 147*
    John 119*
    Phebe 12
    William 119

Hardenbergh,
    Jacobus 103
    James 103

Hardenbrook,
    Edgar 109

Hardesty,
    Elijah 136
    Hezekiah 186
    Richard 169*

Hardey,
    William 119

Hardie,
    Abrom T. 104
    John 104

Hardin,
    (Mrs.) 164
    George W. 184
    Noah 182
    Seth 12
    Susan 163
    Thomas 167*, 170, 182

Harding,
    Abby 53
    Abial 92*
    Abijah 33*
    Chloe 98*
    George 189*
    Henry 27
    Isaac 116
    Jemima 58
    Lydia 125
    Mary 27*
    Nathan 27*
    Stephen 125
    William 45*
    William B. 45

Hardison,
    James 157*

Hardman,
    Benjamin 135

Hardwick,
    George 164

Hardwood,
    Nancy 42*

Hardy,
    Asa 63
    Benjamin 63
    Elias 22
    Jesse 25*
    Lucy 22, 28
    P. B. 151*
    Sarah 20, 80
    Thomas 152*

Hare,
> John 183*
> Michael 122
> Richard 132*

Harford,
> Clotilda 80

Hargan,
> Joseph 163
> Michael 163

Hargee,
> William 52

Haring,
> Garret F. 107*
> John 114

Heris,
> Benjamin 144

Harkness,
> Elizabeth 12
> John 126*
> Mercy 33
> Robert 12

Harland,
> James 181

Harley,
> Ambrose 131
> Lewis 131

Harloe,
> George 166*

Harlow,
> James 28*, 79
> Nathaniel 130*
> Sylvanus 11
> William 70

Harman,
> Adam 154*
> Alvah 78
> John 139*
> Titus 101*

Harmon,
> Charles 156*
> Edward 5
> Elizabeth 121
> Gideon 150*

Harmon, (cont.)
> Jehiel 50*
> John 103
> Lewis 187
> Moses 18*
> Oliver 174*
> Pelatiah 18*
> Rawson 32
> William 6*

Harmony,
> George 113

Harnes,
> Robert 48

Harper,
> John W. 173
> Joseph 127*
> Richard 152*
> Squire J. 152
> William 147*

Harple,
> (Mrs.) 114
> Lewis 112*
> Mary 114

Harrar,
> Daniel 114

Harrell,
> George 176*
> Kadar 138*

Harring,
> John A. 102*

Harrington,
> Aaron 70
> Amasa 33
> Charles 185
> Eleanor 37*
> Elizabeth 64
> Freelove 47*
> Halloway 36
> Job 49*
> John 77*
> Jonas 67*
> Jonathan 36*
> Joseph D. 64
> Josiah 47*
> L. 70
> Levi 39*
> Martha 89

Harrington, (cont.)
    Micah 37*
    Noah 37
    Peleg 47
    Pernilepa 47
    Relief 36
    Reuben 67
    S. 77
    Samuel 69*
    William 163

Harris,
    Abijah 105*
    Abraham 111
    Absalom 25
    Aby 25
    Alfred 67
    Andrew 143
    Ann 42
    Benjamin 147*
    Daniel 66*, 75
    David 135*
    Elisha 66
    Eunice 18
    Ithran 36*
    J. 68
    James 32*, 129, 132, 141
    John 8*, 66*, 129, 143,
      153
    John C. 129
    John R. 160
    Joseph 75
    Joshua 100*, 183*
    Leah 71
    Liddy 160
    Luke 71
    Mary 87
    Matthew 145*
    Moses 142*
    Nathaniel 136*
    Oliver 46*
    Patey 162
    Philip 89
    Relief 31*
    Richard 148, 164*
    Robert 144*
    Robin 141*
    Russell 46
    Salathiel 67
    Samuel 111, 162
    Stephen 46, 65, 145*
    Thomas 67, 161*
    Walter 19*
    William 48, 86, 128*, 141,
      151*, 162*, 174*
    Winans 107*

Harrison,
    Abijah 108*
    Anthony A. 187
    Henry 108
    James 135
    John S. 147
    Moses 18, 108*
    Richard 128*
    Robert 98*
    Thomas 89*, 108
    William 129
    William L. 187

Harriss,
    Hannah 43
    Hugh 154*
    Martha 16
    Mary 108
    Mary C. 43
    Nathaniel 160
    Samuel D. 108

Harrow,
    Jacob 134*

Harry,
    Charles 182*

Hart,
    Adam 182*
    Asa 91
    Benjamin 50
    Charles 165*
    Christopher 118*
    Dean 109
    George 95
    Gilbert 90
    Hannah 27
    Henry 94, 149*
    Hezekiah 50
    Horace 50
    Jacob 162
    Jane 109
    Job 91
    John 14*, 161*
    John R. 109
    Joseph 48
    Martin 32*
    Mary 52, 146
    Nancy Ann 136*
    Philo D. 69
    Ruth 50, 59
    Seth 70*
    Sarah 50
    Titus 58*
    Zachariah 62*

Harter,
    Richard 68*

Hartford,
    Lucy 50

Hartgrove,
    Howel 140*

Hartley,
    Daniel 144*
    John 81
    Leban 158

Hartman,
    Adam 113
    John 118*, 136*
    Michael 83, 121*
    Philip 136

Hartshorn,
    Betsey 31
    David 31
    Hannah 86
    Jeremiah 31
    Jesse 31
    Samuel 23

Hartwell,
    Abiel 30
    Benjamin 40*
    Daniel 29*
    Edward 13
    George 40
    Mary 40
    Oliver 11
    Sally 180
    Samuel 13, 93

Harvey,
    Anna 44
    Benjamin 83*, 134
    Benjamin W. 67
    George 54*, 129
    James 11*, 99*
    John 148*
    Jonathan 89*
    Libby 4*
    Moses 100*
    Nancy 136
    Paul 80*
    William 120

Harvin,
    Edward 131*

Harward,
    James 141

Harwick,
    Hannah 84
    Jacob B. 84

Harwood,
    Ebenezer 66
    Jacob 34*
    Joel 66

Hasford,
    Franklin 73
    Joseph 73

Hasgatt,
    Davis 13*

Haskell,
    Admiral 173
    Benjamin 27
    Charles 41
    Charlotte 142
    Ednah 42
    James 33
    Josiah 9*, 38*
    Prince 173
    Roger 33*
    William 41

Hasket,
    John 153*

Haskew,
    John 144*

Haskill,
    James 33
    John 71
    John C. 71
    Lepha 46*
    Mary 12
    Nathaniel 12
    Samuel 46

Haskins,
    Aaron 80*
    Apollos 30
    Edward 28
    Elijah 28
    Ezra 69
    Henry 28
    Hopestill 79
    Ira 30

Haskins, (cont.)
    J. G. 91
    James F. 98
    John 32*
    Joshua 30
    Preserved 28
    Preserved 28
    Richard 69
    Samuel 28, 98

Hass,
    Christian 134
    Eleanor 77
    Peter 134

Hasting,
    Francis M. 99

Hastings,
    A. 68
    Benjamin 21*
    Charles 37
    Ephraim 68
    Jonas 36*
    Joseph P. 37
    Libbeus 25
    Lucretia 36
    Moses 68
    Sarah 16*
    Theophilus 37*
    Timothy 98*

Hasty,
    James 140*
    John 16

Hatch,
    Abigail 58
    Alexander 140*
    Ann 7
    Anthony 29*
    Asa 65*
    Benjamin 87*
    D. C. 67
    Daniel 59
    David 3*
    Deborah 35
    Ede 99*
    Edmund 76
    Heman 73
    Jeremiah 72*
    John 59
    Joseph 27
    Leonard 64
    Lewis 100*
    Luther 29*
    Mary M. 142

Hatch, (cont.)
    Mary R. 142
    Micah 64
    Molly 71
    Nathan 76, 100*
    Nathaniel 71
    Philip 8*
    Samuel 5
    Sarah 70*
    Seenee 70
    Thomas 25*
    Timothy 64*, 77*
    Walter 12
    Washington 58
    William 89*

Hatchel,
    Elijah 96

Hatcher,
    Seth 132*

Hatchet,
    Archer 155

Hatchkiss,
    Eben 53*
    Elijah 51*

Hatfield,
    Daniel 108*

Hathaway,
    Ebenezer 75*
    Erastus 62
    Harry 62
    Jabez 27*
    John 27*
    Levi 37*
    Robert 36*
    Stephen 43
    Timothy 37*
    Tryphena 62
    Zenas 81

Hatter,
    Michael 160*

Hatton,
    Basil 127*
    Reuben 189*

Hauffman,
    Jonas 121

Haugh,
    Lorenzo 96

Hawley, (cont.)
Elijah 33
Isaac 78
Joseph C. 92
Lucy 55*
Nathan 62
Thomas 56*

Hawly,
Lavina 58

Haws,
Ezekiel 151*
Joseph 6

Hawthorn,
Joseph 188
William 188

Hay,
Alexander 81*
Betsey 39*
Jane 91
John 172
Joseph 6
Philip C. 91

Haycraft,
Margaret 163

Hayden,
Ann 35
David 13
Elizabeth 45
Jacob 86*
Joel 32
John 26*
Jonathan 13
Lewis 38*
Nathaniel 45*

Haydon,
Benjamin 163*
Jeremiah 162*

Hayes,
Aaron 33*

Hayes, (cont.)
Amos M. 6*
Benjamin 90*
David 65, 137*
Dudley 51*
Enoch 58*
Isaac 68
Israel 68
Jesse 58*
Joanna 19
Joseph 55*
Robert 65
Samuel 135*

Hayford,
Nathaniel 18
Warren 18
William 7*

Hayhew,
Holmes 34

Hayley,
Martha 15

Hayman,
Anthony W. 112*

Haymore,
Dinah 43

Haynes,
Abigail 67
Benjamin 157
David 192
Edmund 129
James 159*
John 129
Joseph 156
P. E. 192
Reuben 38*
Simeon 12*
Thomas 157

Hays,
Benajah 180*
Charles 110

Hays, (cont.)
    Elizabeth 110
    James 175
    John 142*
    John W. 175
    Plinn 125*
    Robert 117
    Thomas 143*, 160
    William 141*

Hayse,
    Robin 157*
    William 167*

Hayship,
    G. H. 147

Haythorn,
    John 125

Hayward,
    Ambrose 10
    Edmund 10
    Ephraim 81*
    Orson 103
    Susanna 10

Haywood,
    John A. 127
    Josiah 73
    Sarah H. 45*
    Thomas 127

Hazelton,
    Mary 24

Hazen,
    Hannah 10*
    Jacob 5
    Solomon 69*

Heacock,
    Esther 126
    Reuben 126

Head,
    Britton 99*
    Charlotte 142

Head, (cont.)
    Drusilla 18
    Henry 95
    Henry G. 95
    James W. 8*
    John 108
    Leavit 72
    Moses 69
    Ralph 89

Headlee,
    Caleb 189

Headley,
    Joseph 174
    Stephen 108*

Heady,
    John 59
    Mary 59

Heal,
    James 9

Heald,
    John W. D. 83
    Thomas 40

Healey,
    Comfort 63*
    Jabez 97
    John 63*

Heall,
    Levi 9

Healy,
    Dolly 36
    Mary 48

Heape,
    Archibald 127

Heaps,
    John 127

Heard,
    Elizabeth 18
    Richard 40*

Hearl,
   John 3*

Hearn,
   Drewry 142*

Heath,
   Abial 41
   Anne 49*
   Augustine 133*
   Benjamin 75*
   Charles 14
   Cyrus 63
   Daniel 65*, 185*
   Elizabeth 25
   Eunice 23
   Hugh 108
   Isaac 9
   J. 73
   John 16*, 73
   Mary 53*
   Patience 73
   Rebecca 47*
   Richard 16*, 109*
   Samuel C. 25
   William 12, 13, 33*

Heaton,
   Oliver 22

Heavner,
   Charles 8*

Hebard,
   Dyer 65

Hebb,
   S. B. 172

Heckman,
   (N.X.N.) 115
   Charles 115

Hecox,
   Ebenezer 178
   Joshua 178

Hector,
   George T. 160*

Hedden,
   G. 95
   Job 95

Hedge,
   Thankful 26*

Hedgepeth,
   Abram 139*

Hedges,
   Hannah 105
   Robert 105, 162*

Heesick,
   Benjamin 96

Hefflebower,
   Jacob 112

Hefner,
   Valentine 122*

Heft,
   Henry 112*

Hegdon,
   Charles 133*

Heidler,
   Joshua 112

Heiffner,
   Jacob 178*

Heilman,
   George 114*

Heim,
   Jacob 114*

Heiner,
   William 92*

Helery,
   Osburn 120*

Helfly,
   Charles 190

Heliker,
   John 98*

Hellems,
   Hyram 115
   Samuel 115

Helm,
   George 155*

Helmeck,
   Nicholas 172*

Helsey,
    Heth 77

Helton,
    Edward 157

Hemenway,
    Elihu 34
    P. 34

Hemminger,
    John J. 124

Hemmingway,
    Jesse 21

Hemrod,
    Andrew 171

Hemted,
    David D. 104

Henareck,
    James 132

Hendershot,
    Abram 186

Henderson,
    Abraham 3
    Benjamin 9
    David 156*
    Dorcas 195
    Ezekiel 143*
    George 157*
    James 138
    James M. 158
    Jesse 138
    John 183*
    Margaret 75
    Pleasant 158
    Richard 149*
    Samuel 139
    Thomas 143*
    Wiley 146

Hendley,
    Charles 40*
    E. K. 164*
    Lucy 40

Hendrick,
    Daniel 129*
    Elizabeth 106
    Francis 110
    Moses 94*
    Obadiah 132*
    William 164

Hendricks,
    Albert 157*
    Hilary 150*
    Moses 164*

Hendrickson,
    James 110*
    Moses 182*
    P. 87
    Peter 87
    William 173

Hendrix,
    Solomon 152*

Hendrixon,
    Peter 110*

Hendry,
    Selina 168

Hendryx,
    Esther 94
    I. J. 94
    Nathaniel 188*

Henebarger,
    John 113

Henfield,
    John 43

Henick,
    Sarah 6

Hening,
    Henry 117*

Henley,
    John 156*

Henlick,
    John 170

Henman,
    John 99
    Sarah 53*

Henniss,
    Benjamin 160

Henny,
    Moses 164

Henrel,
    Rebecca 162

Henry,
    Allen 3
    David 157*
    Fanny 52*
    Francis 22*
    James T. 139*
    John 153*, 168, 179*
    Joseph 138*
    Lucinda 176
    Moses 136*
    Nicholas 135
    Peter 123*, 135
    William 91, 136*

Henrys,
    Samuel 46*

Henseley,
    Samuel 136*

Henshaw,
    Josiah 36
    Sarah 36

Hensley,
    Robert 153

Hensling,
    Sarah 194

Henson,
    Elijah 138
    Nicholas 161*
    William 102*

Henzell,
    William 113

Heoner,
    Nicholas 139*

Heran,
    Samuel 177*

Herbert,
    James 25
    Samuel 25, 110*
    William H. 110

Herd,
    Nathaniel 42

Hereford,
    John 135*

Herendeen,
    Silas 72

Heriman,
    David 177

Herlinger,
    Martin 112

Herman,
    Frederick 63
    Frederick W. 63

Herndon,
    Edward 129*
    George 164

Herns,
    Jonathan 119
    William 119

Heron,
    William 134*

Herrendeen,
    Hezekiah 58*

Herrick,
    Daniel 79
    David 98
    Ebenezer 22*
    Elijah 87*
    Ephraim 76*
    Hezekiah 79
    Jonathan 95
    Josiah 20*
    L. D. 65
    Lucy 95
    Mary 21
    Miles 95
    Oliver 8, 9
    Stephen 65
    Timothy 57

Herriman,
    Joseph 65

Herring,
    Anna Maria 123
    James 128*, 162
    Robert 14

Herringdon,
    Joseph 145*

Herrington,
 Comfort 76
 Elisha 77
 Henry B. 90
 James 90
 John 179*
 Jonathan 124*
 Parley 94
 S. P. 94
 Susanna 93*

Herringway,
 Enos 52*

Herron,
 John 163*
 Oswell 166

Hersey,
 Ezekiel 29*
 Zadok 14*

Hersom,
 Nathaniel 4
 Samuel 4

Hervey,
 Daniel 24
 Samuel 24

Heselton,
 Elizabeth 11
 Joseph 11

Hess,
 David 174*
 George 114*
 Joseph 83

Hesser,
 Frederick 115

Hessey,
 W. A. 29

Hester,
 Robert R. 164

Heth,
 Aaron 32
 Alvah 32
 Thomas 59*

Hetrich,
 John 114*

Hevener,
 Peter 87

Heverland,
 Nathaniel 104

Hewell,
 Jesse W. 147
 Wyatt 147

Hewes,
 Benjamin 61
 William 61

Hewet,
 Patrick 157

Hewett,
 Ebenezer 137

Hewing,
 Joseph 32*

Hewit,
 Barney 101*
 Jeptha 78*

Hewitt,
 Andrew 69*
 Charles E. 54
 Elisha 75*
 Henry 75*
 James 84
 John 134*, 187*
 Orin 69
 Randall 96
 Richard 99*
 Sally 119
 Simeon 54
 Stanton 54
 Sterry 94*
 Thomas 28*

Hewlet,
 Nehemiah 100*

Hewlett,
 Cynthia 68

Hews,
 Betsey 70

Heyer,
 Cornelius 8*

Heywood,
    Ella 21
    John 21
    Samuel 37*

Hibbard,
    Burnham 88
    David 64
    Ebenezer 58
    Elisha 25
    Hezekiah 85
    Rufus 85
    Ruth 88
    Vine T. 82*

Hice,
    Leonard 138

Hickey,
    James 115

Hickman,
    Adam 136*
    Edwin 140*
    Jacob 138
    James 166*
    Thomas 155*

Hickock,
    Nathaniel 172

Hickok,
    Ebenezer 128*
    Joel 78

Hicks,
    Barney 84
    Benjamin 26*
    Daniel 79, 132*
    Durfee 100
    Gardner 100
    John 77*, 79, 153*
    Jesse 142*
    Mary 164
    Miles 138*
    Nathan 28*
    Polly 94*
    Samuel 51
    Simeon 68*
    Stephen 84
    William 187

Hicky,
    (Mrs.) 117
    James 117

Hidecker,
    John A. 149

Higbey,
    Seba 101*

Higby,
    Brewster 176
    Curtis 85
    Cyrus 176
    Samuel 51*

Higdon,
    Margaret 160*

Higginbottom,
    William 159*

Higgins,
    Daniel 182*
    David 105
    Ebir 82
    Edmund 6*
    Elisha 66
    Elizabeth 105
    Ichabod 66
    James 155*, 173
    Nancy 142
    Rebecca 43*
    Thomas 77*
    Uriah 62
    Walter 4
    William 173

High,
    Nathan 176
    Rachel 137*

Highfill,
    Leonard 166*

Highland,
    Amasa 22
    Ira 22

Hight,
    James 122
    John 98, 122, 170*

Higley,
    Joel 97
    Obed 51*

Hilborn,
    Ira 5
    Lucy 5

Hildreth,
    Reuben 83
    Simeon 23
    Thaddeus 83

Hiles,
    John 166*

Hill,
    Abraham 52*
    Abram 139*, 190
    Alice 87
    Amasa 174*
    Ann 160
    Anna 29*
    Benijah 100*
    Caleb 174
    Cyrus 63
    Daniel 21*, 159*
    David 22, 45, 68
    Ebenezer 17*, 87
    Ellen 33*
    Hannah 46
    Henry 74*
    Herman 166*
    Humphrey 129*
    Ira 68*
    Jacob 179*
    James 46
    James A. 46
    Joel 66*, 191*
    John 16, 17, 146*
    John N. 137
    Jonas 155*
    Lewis 45*
    Lucy 17
    Nicholas 87
    Noah 4*, 39*
    Orison 36
    Rebecca 4, 41
    Reuben 146
    Rosilla 22
    Ruth 67
    Samuel 63
    Sarah 38*
    Solomon 34*, 82
    Stephen 76
    Stukely 48*
    Thomas 39, 46, 67, 85, 91*,
        158, 189*
    Uriah 103
    William 48, 120*, 129*,
        132*, 190
    Winkfield 158

Hilland,
    David G. 136
    James 136

Hillard,
    David 95

Hillecoss,
    George 88

Hiller,
    Timothy 30*

Hilles,
    John 156
    Samuel 156

Hillhouse,
    William 149*

Hilliard,
    Hannah 55
    Henry 98
    John 65
    Jonathan 16
    Jonathan B. 16
    Peter 142*
    Thomas 141*

Hillier,
    Joseph W. 41

Hillman,
    John 117*

Hills,
    Carine 85
    Daniel 90*
    Heman 76
    Jacob 44*
    Josiah 88
    Mary 72
    Mille 171
    Nathaniel 66
    Samuel 81
    Sarah 42
    Sylvester 81
    William 24, 66
    Zimri 76

Hillyer,
    Mary 109
    Seth 168*

162

Hilsabeek,
    Jacob 140
    Joseph 140

Hilsinger,
    Michael 93

Hilt,
    Daniel 12

Hilton,
    Abram 155*
    Hale 42*
    Joseph 3*
    Otis 54
    Richard 72
    William 13
    William H. 13

Hilyard,
    Joshua 78*
    Miner 69*
    Rebecca 78*

Hinchman,
    Lewis 44

Hinckley,
    Benjamin 26
    Chloe 26*
    Edith 13
    John 91*
    Prince 26*
    Robert W. 13
    Samuel 35, 37*
    Sylvanus 26

Hincley,
    George 112

Hindman,
    James 117*

Hinds,
    Eli 67*
    Jesse 73*
    Joshua 168
    Samel 9
    Samuel 9

Hines,
    Jacobus 184*
    James 152*
    John 188

Hingon,
    F. 139

Hinkley,
    Asa 25*
    Joseph 73
    Josiah 73

Hinkson,
    Jonn 42, 160*

Hinman,
    Anna 188
    Isaac 63*
    Maria 90
    Mercy 56
    Rebecca 86
    Timothy 63*
    W. 188

Hinsey,
    George 117

Hinson,
    Charles 137*
    John 144*

Hipple,
    Frederick 120
    John 120

Hiscock,
    Jesse 15
    Luther 90
    Richard 90

Hiscox,
    Clarke 48*

Hisle,
    Samuel 163*

Histed,
    Thaddeus 122

Histle,
    Younger 161

Hitchcock,
    Aaron A. 52
    Abraham 104
    Gaas 64
    Harvey 89
    Henry 70
    Isaac 99

Hitchcock, (cont.)
    Jonathan 76*
    Levi 89*
    Nathan 70
    Samuel 50*

Hitchcok,
    Abijah 75*

Hite,
    Julius 131*

Hitt,
    Abigail 79
    Isaac 79

Hix,
    John 30

Hizer,
    George 113

Hoadley,
    Culpepper 53*
    Ebenezer 51*

Hoadly,
    Samuel 175*

Hoag,
    Maria A. 102

Hoaglan,
    Aaron 178*

Hoagland,
    Abraham 87
    Jacob 87

Hoar,
    Edmund 82*
    Leonard 40*
    Mary 30
    William 49

Hoard,
    Isaac 101*
    Jonathan 72*

Hobart,
    Edmund 29*
    John 24
    Jonathan 65
    Joseph 65
    Mason 52*
    N. 43

Hobart, (cont.)
    Nathaniel 30*
    Noah 43

Hobbs,
    Abigail 3
    James 3
    Josiah 5*

Hobert,
    Solomon 62*

Hobson,
    Lawson 156*
    Sarah 42

Hodgden,
    John 26
    Phineas 26

Hodgdon,
    Ann 16
    Caleb 9
    Hanson 16
    Stephen 6*
    Thomas 9

Hodge,
    Bednego 130
    George 137*
    Joseph 6
    Philo 58*
    Robert 44

Hodges,
    B. 74
    Benjamin 45
    Eliphalet 82*
    Ephraim 74
    Jacob 87
    Job 56
    Leonard 27, 62*
    Miles 101
    Nathaniel 29
    Philemon 146
    Prudence 84
    Rufus 27
    Samuel K. 146
    William 31, 144*
    Willis 157*

Hodgkins,
    Abigail 8
    Eunice 41*
    John 15*
    Phineas 80
    William 63*

Hodgman,
    Abel 21*
    Joseph 71
    W. L. 71

Hodgson,
    Alexander 115
    Mary 115

Hodsdon,
    Andrew 5
    Benjamin 5

Hodskins,
    John 23
    Frederick S. 23

Hoffman,
    Henry 115
    Joseph H. 116

Hoffner,
    Martin 140*

Hoffses,
    James 8
    Margaret 8

Hogan,
    Anna 91*

Hogeboom,
    Bartholomew 176
    John 176

Hogert,
    Ephraim 84

Hogg,
    Abner 20*
    Thomas 130*
    William 16, 21

Hoggard,
    John 137*

Hoghstrasser,
    Jacob 72

Hogins,
    Abraham 155
    Archibald D. 155

Hogland,
    Catharine 109
    James 131
    John 131

Hogstrasser,
    Paul J. 72

Hohimer,
    William 187*

Hoid,
    Amos 19

Hoisington,
    Vespasian 193*

Hoit,
    Elisha 21
    Hannah 21
    Jonathan H. 18
    Levi 67
    Nathaniel 11*
    Samuel 97

Hoke,
    Jacob 94
    Merrit 94

Hokum,
    Joel 174*

Holanes,
    Sally 163

Holben,
    Lorenz 114
    Solomon 114

Holbert,
    Dolpheas D. 135
    Robert 130*

Holbrook,
    Abel 52
    Amos 32
    Calvin 58*
    Ebenezer 36
    James 31
    Jesse 145*
    Lucy 32
    Martha 15
    Meriam 66*
    Molly 31
    Moses 31
    Nathaniel 31*
    Olive 36
    Sally 41
    Sarah 20
    Thomas C. 52
    Thomas G. 20

Holcomb,
Abraham 59
Ahinoam 50
Chloe 50
Ebenezer S. 50
Elam 124
Elihu E. 50
John 144*
Jordan 143
Joseph 35
Levi 98*
Mary 50*
S. 95
Timothy 134
W. K. 95
William 143

Holden,
Aaron 80
Aaron G. 23
Abigail 34
Abijah 64
Abraham 80
Abram 85
Amos 32
Asa 23, 102*
Daniel 8
Ebenezer M. 93*
Eli 64
Elijah 64
Henry 6
J. B. 34
Jemima 70
Jonathan 191
Joseph S. 70
Levi 38
Luther 8, 69
Nathaniel 64
Octavius A. 126
Sarah 69
Sartile 126
Stephen 92

Holder,
Daniel 143*

Holdgate,
William 114

Holdredge,
Hannah 53

Holdrege,
Hannah 53

Holdridge,
Ephraim 71*
Jehiel 62*
Robert 60*

Holdron,
Henry 111

Holems,
George 21

Holenbeck,
John 81

Holiday,
Amos 98*

Holister,
David 75

Holladay,
Horace S. 188

Holland,
Charles 150*
James 22*, 138*
Joseph 10*
Michael 5
Park 11*
Thomas 141, 148*, 165

Hollester,
Nathan 177*

Holley,
Benjamin F. 46
Mary 26
Paul P. 72
William 20*

Holliday,
James 135*
John 159*
William 160
Zachariah 160

Hollingshead,
James 118*

Hollingsworth,
Elizabeth 141
H. 141
Henry 141

Hollis,
    James   143
    Thomas   143

Hollista,
    Horace   59
    Joseph   59

Hollister,
    Lucy   68
    Smith   93*

Holloway,
    Ebenezer   183
    Levi   183
    Rachel   154
    Rebecca   154

Holly,
    John D.   72*
    Paul P.   72

Hollydeoke,
    Ann   127*

Holman,
    George   186*
    John   101*
    Samuel   92*
    Susanna   36
    Thomas   168*

Holme,
    William   143

Holmes,
    Abijah   105*
    Anthony   110*
    Catel   105
    Cornelius   30*
    David   28, 105*
    Eliza   16
    Ezekiel   11
    Ezra   86*
    George W.   36
    Gersham   5
    Gershom D.   5
    Jabez   96
    James   99*, 130*
    John   105
    Lazarus   26*
    Lydia   30
    Marcus   85
    Mary Ann   143*
    Mercy   7*
    Moses   82

Holmes, (cont.)
    Nathaniel   30
    Noah   17
    Oliver   30
    Robert   28*
    Samuel N.   28*
    Seth   90*
    Silence   31*
    Thomas   50*
    Uriah   27
    William   82
    Zack   139*

Holmon,
    John   191

Holms,
    Elisha   54

Holsclau,
    James   139*

Holsey,
    Sandford   35

Holt,
    Abby   54
    Anna   57
    Asa   37
    Asahel   70*
    C.   148
    Charles   148
    Claburn   143*
    Darius   7
    Edith   47
    Elijah   177
    Elizabeth   71*
    Ephraim   38
    Eunice   37
    Hiriam   7
    James   139*
    John   174*
    Leona   67
    Lydia   7
    Miriam   18
    Nathaniel   47
    Oliver   74, 83
    Pleamon   7
    Thomas   118

Holton,
    Arad   67
    W.   67

Homan,
    (Mrs.)   43

Homan, (cont.)
    John 43, 45
    Sarah 25, 43*

Homans,
    Sarah 45

Homes,
    Ebenezer 27

Homsher,
    Adam 114

Honey,
    John 153*
    Tobias 148

Hood,
    David 93
    Jacob 153
    Jared 95
    John 93, 98, 154*, 167*
    Norton 95

Hook,
    Josiah 168
    Leavitt 20*

Hooker,
    Charles 71
    Daniel 51*
    Gilbert 100
    Hannah 36, 43*, 50*
    Israel 90*
    James 69*
    Jerusha 140
    Mary 71
    Nathaniel 49*
    Seth 50
    Simeon 62
    Zibeon 40
    Zina 100

Hooper,
    Absalom 138
    Asa 43
    Rachael 5

Hoose,
    Nicholas 102*

Hooton,
    Elijah 155
    Hiram 182
    Thomas 182

Hoover,
    Andrew 114*
    Henry 157*
    Jacob 133*
    Michael 135*

Hope,
    John 131
    William 159*

Hopkins,
    Abraham 171
    Benjamin 47
    Ezekiel 47*
    George 88*
    Isaac J. 48
    James 132*
    Jesse 158*
    John 26*, 99
    M. L. 79
    Martha 12
    Mary 165
    Moses 116
    Peleg 47*
    Peter 47*
    Phebe 171
    Reliance 26*
    Reuben 34
    Robert S. W. 46
    Roderick 89*
    Richard 12
    Seth 34
    Solomon 4
    William 20*, 144*, 165*
    William G. 143*

Hopkinson,
    Caleb 4
    Uriah 41
    William 10

Hopper,
    Harmon 152
    John 152, 184
    John A. 107*
    William 185*

Hoppin,
    Mary 45

Hoppis,
    Adam 137*

Horfland,
    John 139*

Horn,
Daniel 4
Ebenezer 18*
Elisha 136
Frederick 4
Hannah 18
Ichabod 17*
Joab 193*
Jonathan 3
Joseph 173
Susan 161

Hornbeck,
Abraham 103*
Peter 103*

Horne,
George 174
Jesse 174

Horr,
Hannah 84
Zebina 28

Horrall,
William 182*

Horris,
Jesse 141*

Horsaw,
Jonathan 4*

Horsham,
John 117

Horter,
Z. 141*

Horton,
Abel 69
Benjamin 106
David 110*
Hopkins 69
Isaac 145*, 158*
Jeremiah 106
John 94*
John B. 164
Lemuel 42
Polly 32
Samuel 85*
Thomas 98*
William 88, 164

Hortz,
Charles 179

Hoskins,
Ambrose 51*
David 58
Eli 25*
James 165*
Lyman 58
Samuel 38*
Thenas 163

Hosley,
Sampson 95*

Hosmer,
David 36*
Prosper 104
Samuel 40*

Hossum,
Ebenezer 41*

Hotchkiss,
Asahel 59*
Harvis 123*
Lucretia 186*
Lyman 52
Roswell 70*
Samuel 51*, 98*
Simeon 100
Temperance 52

Houchins,
Edward 165*

Houck,
George M. 133

Hough,
Clark 24
John 137*
Lydia 24
Martha 57, 171
Owen 171
Samuel L. 57
Susan 93

Houghton,
A. L. 66
Anna 176
Elijah 67*
Jonas 38*
Joseph S. 13
Oliver 176
Peter 71
Samuel 36
Sarah 66
Shevah 100
Sibel 71

Houk,
    Peter 114*

Houke,
    Nicholas 166

Houland,
    Joseph 79

House,
    Benjamin 61*
    Chris. John 83
    Esther 50
    George 152
    Giles 50
    John 106*
    Louis 50
    Mary 88
    Nancy 94
    Sarah 71
    Thomas 5
    Washington 152
    William 106*

Houser,
    Andrew 142*

Houston,
    Charles 24
    James 152
    Leonard 183*
    Ruth 24
    William 152*
    Margaret 78*

Houx,
    Lawrence 164

Hovey,
    Dudley 57*
    Z. 68
    Zacheus 68

How,
    David 20*, 41*
    Isaac 41
    Israel 61*
    John 73
    Micah 19*
    Polly 19

Howard,
    Adam 178
    Allen 67
    Andrew 35
    B. 192*
    Benjamin 22*

Howard, (cont.)
    Bethiah 67
    Claborn 139
    Daniel 30
    Darius 14, 101*
    Dorothy 47*
    Edward 31*, 193
    Elijah 25
    Enos 95*
    George 170
    George F. 147
    Hannah 34
    Hepsibah 31
    Hope 77
    Ichabod 46
    J. 43
    James 18*, 47*, 129*, 143*
  * Jesse 148
    John 43, 154*, 175*
    John M. 165*
    Jonas 30
    Jonathan 34*
    Joseph 7
    Joshua 193
    Levi 20
    Lydia 25
    Lyman 100
    Martha 32
    Mary 20, 46
    Mary H. 170
    Oliver 30, 61*
    Peter 175*
    Phebe 76
    Robert 150
    Samuel 21, 124*
    Sarah 21
    Simeon 97, 100
    Solomon 70*
    Stephen 78*
    Thomas 31
    Uriah 14
    Willard 30
    Ziba 80*
  * Job 38*

Howe,
    Amasa 172*
    Asa 125*

Howe,
    Azor 30*
    Benjamin 21
    Cady 83
    Daniel 117
    David 95*
    Ebenezer 6, 20
    Ezekiel 41*
    Farnham 41

Howe, (cont.)
    Gardner 66*
    George 54
    Joel 38*
    John 37*, 82, 109
    Jonathan 24*, 41
    Jotham 37
    Lucy 24
    Mary 14, 59*
    Molly 37
    Nancy 88
    Peter 180
    Phebe 78
    Robert P. 105
    Samuel 64
    Solomon 71*
    William 56

Howel,
    Charles 129
    Gideon 129
    Mills 146*

Howell,
    Elizabeth 112*
    James 134
    Jeremiah 110*
    John 141*
    Jonathan 178
    Martha 130*, 142
    William 85*, 175

Howes,
    Bethiah 34
    David 34
    Elijah 65
    Elizabeth 76
    O. 87

Howland,
    Elizabeth 37*
    John 45*
    Joseph 33*
    Thomas A. 49

Howle,
    William 142*

Howlett,
    William 183*

Hows,
    Benjamin 38
    Sylvenus 10*

Hoxie,
    John 35

Hoxsie,
    Lodowick 48

Hoxworth,
    Edward 114

Hoyt,
    Abner H. 63
    Betty 42
    Daniel 56
    Daniel S. 84
    Ebenezer 56*
    Enoch 102*
    Job 105
    John 65
    Joseph B. 19*
    Moses 16*
    Nathan 24
    Nathaniel 105*
    Robert 37
    Samuel 63
    Sarah 17*
    Thomas 63
    Warren 56
    William 42, 82*

Hoytt,
    Enoch 65*

Hubbard,
    Abel 69
    Bildad 178
    Caleb 34*, 60
    Ephraim 173
    George 44*
    Hannah 92
    Israel 178
    John 82*, 93
    Jonathan 4
    Joseph 34, 37*, 132*
    Joseph A. 75
    Martha 88
    Mary 7*, 66, 69
    Mehitable 11
    Nathaniel 21
    Orange 66
    Peter 186*
    Samuel 84
    Thomas 148*
    Titus 44*
    William 34, 131*, 143

Hubbed,
    Josiah 55

Hubbel,
    Abijah 92*

Hubbel, (cont.)
Silliman 58
Sillimon 58

Hubbell,
Aaron 55*, 68*
Abijah 176*
Chester 59
Elizabeth 59
G. L. 160
Isaac 56
Lemuel 93*
Mary 55*
Richard 160
Thaddeus 55*

Hubbert,
Caspar 113*

Hubbs,
Jacob 161*
Samuel 87*

Hubburt,
John 19

Huber,
Christian 112*

Huble,
Ithamer 189*

Huckins,
John 17
Ruth 17

Huddleston,
Robert 139*

Huderal,
Thomas 168*

Hudgens,
Ambrose 142
John 142

Hudgins,
Hugh 132*

Hudnall,
John 128*

Hudson,
Charles 131, 132*
David 13
Hilary 131

Hudson, (cont.)
James 106
John 106, 131*, 154, 172
Joshua 170*
Peter 131*
Richard 87
Samuel 25*
Sarah 37
Thomas 136*, 156

Hudspeth,
Airs 150*

Huey,
George 119*
Lewis 163*

Huff,
Daniel 4*, 8*
Joel 51
Moses 8*
N. 96
Nicholas 96
P. J. 96
Peter 165*
Richard 96
Stephen 143

Huffman,
Ambrose 160
Ann 131
Henry 160
Jacob 174
James 176
Joseph 174
William 75

Hufnoglo,
Christian 87

Huges,
John 16
Mehitable 16

Hugeley,
Charles 163*

Huggins,
Anna 23
Nathaniel 82
Samuel 142*

Hugh,
John 64*

Hughes,
    Absalom 160*
    Andrew 143
    David 154*
    Elias 175
    James 141*, 143*
    Jonathan 134, 175
    Samuel 86
    Welthan 46*
    William 143

Hughs,
    Francis 152
    Margaret 152
    Martin 167
    Parley 125*

Hulbert,
    Augustus 97
    Polly 97

Hulet,
    Asa 176
    Fletcher 176
    John 176
    Joseph 71

Hulett,
    Lemuel 163*

Hulfish,
    John 109*

Hulgan,
    H. 140

Hulick,
    Derrick 192

Huling,
    Andrew 136

Hull,
    Abner 68*
    Agrippa 32*
    Asel 102
    Benjamin 59
    Chester 102
    David 92*
    Elizabeth 45
    Hazzard 61
    Isaac P. 102
    Jeremiah 52*
    John 68
    Joseph 23, 61

Hull, (cont.)
    Libeus 99
    Mabel 51
    Nathaniel 102
    Peleg 45*
    Sally 80
    Samuel 99
    Turner 108
    William H. H. 80

Hulse,
    Margaret 109*
    Martha 188

Hulsey,
    Jesse 146*

Hulshart,
    Matthew M. 110*

Hults,
    Isaac 104
    Stephen 104

Hume,
    Richard 33
    Stephen 33

Humes,
    John 183
    Thomas 183

Hummel,
    Frederick 121
    George 121

Hummell,
    Elijah 109*

Humphrey,
    Abraham 87
    Daniel 32
    David 173
    Deborah 32
    Elizabeth 49*
    George C. 106
    Hugh 32
    John 45, 161*, 173
    Levi 51*
    Lydia 47*
    Mercy 91
    Merrett 165*
    Oliver 91*
    Robert 106
    Sally 82

Humphrey,
 Samuel 90*
 William 62*
 Willis 87

Humphreys,
 Aley 162
 Henry 38
 James 31*
 Royal 38

Humphries,
 John 127

Hundley,
 Elizabeth 154
 Joseph 132

Hungerford,
 Green 82
 Hanley 56
 Hannah 56
 John P. 59
 Olive 60*
 Uriel 56

Hunn,
 Samuel 50*

Hunnewell,
 Abigail 6

Hunsden,
 Elizabeth 72
 Robert 72

Hunt,
 Abijah 75*
 Abner 35
 Abram 167*
 Alva 94
 Anna 16
 Anthony 35
 Benjamin 72
 Betsey 47*
 Calvin 34
 David 80
 Ephraim 32
 Esther 59
 Hannah 79
 Hiram 79
 Humphrey 115
 Israel 21*, 109*
 Jacob 16, 135
 James 185*
 John 59, 135

Hunt, (cont.)
 John D. 68
 Jonathan 44*, 160*
 Julius 129*
 Littleton 145
 Moses 63*
 Nathan 22*
 Noah 40*
 Oliver 109
 Pardon 47
 Roswell 64*
 William 94, 99*
 Winifred 29*
 Zaccheus 80

Hunter,
 Andrew 190
 Ann 163
 Calvin 44
 Daniel 117
 Francis 133*
 J. M. 106
 Jacob 166*
 James 144
 John 164*
 Mary 71, 109
 Mary S. 109
 Nathaniel 59*
 Patrick 182*
 R. James 144
 S. R. 79
 Thomas 10*, 152*
 William 9

Hunting,
 S. F. 86

Huntington,
 Andrew 86*
 Erastus 100
 Gilbert 54
 John S. 99*
 Joseph 94*
 Rebecca 61*
 Roger 69*
 Samuel 82
 Thomas 100
 William 16

Huntley,
 Benjamin 192
 Hoell 53
 Howell 53
 Naomi 53*
 Solomon 90*

Huntly,
Dennis 63
Ezra 77
Moses 63
Reuben 77

Huntoon,
Aaron 15
George 26*
Judith 25
Moses 26
Reuben 78*
Susanna 23

Huntress,
Ann 15
Mary 15*

Huntt,
William 8

Hupres,
Harrison 162

Hurd,
(N.X.N.) 68*
Adam 68
Benjamin 60*
Crippen 60*
Elnathan 60*
Esther 171
Isaac 40*, 84
Jacob 60*
Lewis 68
Merrit 103
Richard 80
Robert L. 73*
Wilson 52*

Hurdle,
Lawrence 195*

Hurlbert,
J. 73
Josiah 84*
Sarah 73

Hurlburt,
Amasa 24
Amy 24
Benjamin F. 88
Clemence 88

Hurlbut,
Abiram 98*
Christopher 98

Hurlbut, (cont.)
Elizabeth 98
James 49
Mahetible 49
Roswall 49
Seymour 60*

Hurley,
Joshua 139*
Margaret 158

Hurn,
Henry 124
John 124

Hursey,
James 8*

Hurt,
John 161*
Washington 136
William 160*
Zachariah 136

Hurton,
John 3*

Husstullar,
G. 148
George 148

Huston,
James 122
William 86

Hutchason,
Robert 11

Hutchens,
Abigail 3*

Hutcherson,
Elizabeth 64
John 128*
Cornelius 122*

Hutchings,
Margaret 108
Pearl K. 24
William 13*

Hutchins,
Alpheas 26*
Levi 18*
Samuel 18
Shubal 57*

175

Hutchins, (cont.)
    Solomon 17*
    Thomas 140*

Hutchinson,
    Abijah 85
    Asa 10*
    Francis 127
    Hannah 21
    Isaac 135
    James 16, 85
    Jerome 70*
    John 70, 135
    Jonathan 43*
    Lucy 54
    Mehitable 16
    Mary 10, 20
    Samuel 71*
    Solomon 11
    Titus 25

Hutchison,
    James 189*

Hutson,
    Edward 191*
    John 64*
    Samuel 128

Hutt,
    Gerald 133*

Huttinack,
    S. Francis 78
    Stephen F. 78

Hutton,
    Christopher 104
    Elizabeth 96
    George 96, 179
    Isaac 104
    James 112
    John 106*

Hutts,
    Leonard 130*

Huyck,
    William 126*

Huzzy,
    Susanna 67*

Hyatt,
    Charles 93
    Judy 93
    Stephen 56

Hyde,
    Abigail 55
    Catharine 40*
    Ebenezer 53
    Jarid 64
    Joel 54*
    Joseph 64
    Laurens 53
    Olive 57
    Samuel 40
    Zenas 67*

Hyden,
    William 154*

Hyder,
    John 140*

Hyland,
    William 29

Hyler,
    John 123*

Hyse,
    Jacob 135*

Hysmith,
    Moses 140*

Ice,
    Andrew 182
    Jesse 182

Ide,
    Anna 33*
    James 95*
    Jesse 62*
    Nathan 28*

Imax,
    Isaac 96*

Ingalls,
    Caleb 80*
    Edward 67
    Edmond 67
    Henry 84
    Hermance 13
    Jacob 73*
    Luther 24
    Moses 26*
    Nathaniel 21*

Ingalls, (cont.)
    Phebe 13
    Phineas 5*
    Solomon 84
    Sylvester 24

Ingell,
    Jonathan 28*

Ingersol,
    Margaret 69

Ingersoll,
    James 98

Ingham,
    Isaac 76
    Lucy 76
    Mary 71
    S. 73
    Samuel 73

Ingle,
    Adam 154*

Inglee,
    Ebenezer 14*

Inglis,
    Robert 79
    William 79

Ingraham,
    Daniel 172
    Hezekiah 54*
    Jonathan 33*
    Levi 81
    Simeon 45*

Ingram,
    Abraham 165
    Edwin 140
    Harriet 163
    Jeremiah 163
    Meredith 118

Inman,
    Aaron 180
    Rufus 180

Inmon,
    Joanna 47

Inmorn,
    Jefferson 45

Inskeep,
    Sarah 115*

Ipock,
    Samuel 137*

Irelan,
    Dayton 108*

Ireland,
    Joel 7*

Ires,
    Ichabod 52*

Ireson,
    Samuel J. 43
    Sarah 43

Iris,
    Thomas 7

Irisbie,
    Josiah 52*

Irish,
    Andrew 76
    Cornelius 8

Irvin,
    Ezekiel 189*
    James 160
    John 102*, 160
    William 184*

Irvine,
    Thomas 137*

Irvins,
    William 173

Irwin,
    David 184
    James 113, 169*

Isaacs,
    Samuel 156*

Isaman,
    Christian 124

Isbell,
    Benjamin 130
    H. 130
    Henry 130
    Z. 130

Iseley,
      Philip 145*

Isham,
      Asahel 62
      Daniel 62*
      George 185
      Jehiel 61*
      William 62

Ives,
      Amos 84
      Chauncey 94
      Isaac 96
      John 69
      Levi 96
      Martha 52
      Mary 69
      Phineas T. 52
      Stephen 52
      Thomas 154*

Ivey,
      David 158*

Ivins,
      Daniel 107

Jack,
      James 178*

Jacklin,
      Hannah 50

Jackman,
      Perkinson 155*
      Richard 10*
      Royal 25*
      Samuel 18*

Jacks,
      Ann 142

Jackson,
      Alfred 154
      Asa 81
      Benjamin 174*
      Caleb 42*
      Chesley 151
      Daniel 55
      Dorothy 17
      Edward 145*

Jackson, (cont.)
      Eliphalet 81
      Elizabeth 37, 154
      Ephraim 17, 69
      Hannah 30, 69
      Isaac 138*
      James 163*
      John 93*, 140, 147
      Joseph 157*, 160*
      Joshua 119*
      Lewis 147
      Martha 18
      Peter 179
      Robert 86*
      Samuel 59*, 187*
      Sarah 23
      Thomas 151
      Timothy 89
      Vincent 153
      Whitney 55
      William 19, 155*

Jackways,
      William 100*

Jacobs,
      Asa 58*
      Elizabeth 115, 125
      George 115
      Hepribeth 3
      John 10*, 40*, 125, 166*
      Jonathan 116*
      Lemuel 29*
      Molly 17
      Nathaniel 64*, 92*
      Sarah 88*
      Theodore 3
      Thomas 140*

Jacoby,
      Jacob 160

Jacocks,
      Peter 50

Jamerson,
      Robert 190
      Willis M. 190

James,
      Abner 140*
      Amos 94*
      Charles 98
      Edwin 72
      Isaac 134*
      Jabez 16*

James, (cont.)
    John 106*, 142*
    John D. 112
    Jonathan 190*
    Lovisa 59*
    Martha 154
    Mary 43
    Nathan 112
    Paul 78
    Phebe 49*
    Sheffield 78
    Thomas 182
    William 112, 130*, 155*,
      160

Jameson,
    Benoni 163*
    Joseph 144*

Jamieson,
    John 122

Jane,
    Ebenezer 166*

Janes,
    David 93*
    Josiah 60
    Phebe 51*
    Ruth 60

Janson,
    Blandinah 103

Janvier,
    Isaac 126*

Jaqrua,
    Daniel 59
    Olive 59

Jaques,
    Daniel 40
    Eunice 17*
    Hannah 40
    Parker 41
    Richard 13*

Jaquins,
    Candy 104
    John 104
    William 32*

Jared,
    Joseph 156*

Javens,
    John 121
    Thomas 121

Jay,
    Ivory 3
    Jedediah 29
    Jesse 76
    Lydia 3

Jefferd,
    Samuel 3
    Samuel M. 3

Jeffers,
    Jacob 128

Jefferson,
    Alva 82

Jeffords,
    Elizabeth 142

Jeffries,
    Alexander 130
    George 130
    James W. 190
    William 163*, 190

Jeffrys,
    John 107
    Nicholas 107

Jefts,
    Joseph F. 21

Jelliff,
    James 56

Jellyers,
    Henry 83

Jameson,
    William 44*

Jencks,
    Abigail 46*
    Jedediah 46
    L. 85
    Mary 46
    Susanna 85

Jenison,
    Elias 66
    Hannah 66

Jenkins,
    Abiathar 125*
    Alvan 26*
    Calvin 29*
    Charles S. 91
    David 21*, 76*
    Elisha 163
    Elizabeth 104
    Enoch 82*
    Ezekiel 181*
    Isaac 104
    Jesse 191
    John 71, 147*, 188
    Jonathan 136
    Kesiah 163
    Lemuel 9*, 62*
    Lewis 146*
    Nathaniel 79*
    Solomon 79*
    William 14, 77, 141, 147
    Wilson 191

Jenks,
    Andrew N. 66
    Boomer 66
    Jacob 168
    John S. 125*

Jennerson,
    Joseph 67
    Judith 67

Jenness,
    John 63*

Jennings,
    Benjamin 123*
    Burret 59
    Elisha 61
    Isbuel 176*
    J. W. 144
    John 59, 136
    Justus 95*
    Nathan 61
    Nathan B. 116*
    Noah 96
    Peter 55*, 157*
    Seth 103*
    William 55*

Jennison,
    Levi 23*
    Moses 40*

Jepherson,
    Jedediah 39*

Jepherson, (cont.)
    John 39*

Jepson,
    Bradbury T. 8, 9

Jernegan,
    Stephen 137

Jerolomon,
    Margaret 96

Jerome,
    Anthony 53*

Jerrod,
    John 187*

Jervis,
    Sands 72

Jesse,
    William 132*

Jessup,
    Ebenezer 56*

Jester,
    Nimrod 186
    Thomas 137*

Jeter,
    Fielding 164*

Jethro,
    Martin 51*

Jett,
    William 129*
    William S. 133
    William Starke 133

Jevidend,
    Mary 163*

Jewel,
    Elisha 77
    Gilbert 77

Jewell,
    Edwin 22
    Ephraim 172*
    John 44
    Joseph 161
    William 153*

Jewet,
    David   33
    Oliver   33

Jewett,
    Benjamin 16*
    Enoch   21
    Joseph   37*
    Joseph M. 168*
    Mary   13
    Samuel S. 13
    Sarah   24

Jewit,
    Nathan H. 53

Jewitt,
    Alpheus   59*
    John   99*

Jinker,
    Benjamin 53*

Jinkins,
    Jesse   156
    Samuel B. 165

Jillson,
    David   66*
    George   43

Jinney,
    James H. 72

Jinnings,
    Abner   124*

Jipson,
    D.   68
    David   68

Joel,
    Betsey   30*

Johns,
    Jacob   118*
    W. C.   187
    W. E.   164

Johnson,
    A.   68
    Abigail   20
    Abner   157*
    Abraham W. 52
    Adrian   109*
    Alexander 137*
    Amos   92

Johnson, (cont.)
    Archibald 163
    Benjamin   12, 187*
    Benoni   58
    Betsey   80
    Bulkley   101
    Caleb   151*
    Calvin   70*
    Catharine 45*
    Cave   160*
    Comfort   97
    Daniel   12, 77, 147
    David   75*, 181*, 184
    Ebenezer   102*
    Edward   85*
    Eleanor   41, 102
    Eleazer   44
    Elisha   66*
    Elizabeth 130*, 137
    Ezekiel   48*
    Francis   137*
    George   100
    Gideon   155
    Hannah   24
    Hanson   182*
    Henry   25, 110
    Hezekiah   85
    Howell   143*
    Hugh   63
    Huldah   52*
    Ira   61
    Isaac   184
    Isaac S.   80
    Isaiah   83*
    Jacob   118
    James   6, 96, 129, 131*, 138*,
                 163*, 167, 182*
    James A.   128
    James B.   45
    Jeremiah   105
    Job J.   78
    John   15, 41, 60*, 62, 105*,
                 176, 188
    Joseph   6, 24*, 147
    Joshua   41*, 63*
    Justus   90*
    Lambert   110
    Laurence   99*
    Lawton   49
    Lewis   71, 109*
    Lucenia   75*
    Lydia   37*
    Maria   96
    Mary   39*, 45, 149
    Michael   25*
    Moses   186
    Nathaniel 40, 52*, 62

Johnson, (cont.)
    Obadiah 132*
    Ozias 68*
    P. 163
    Peter 107*, 134*, 152*
    Peter M. 110*
    Philip 81*
    Phineas 17*, 52
    Rachel 106*
    Rebecca 60*
    Richard 148*, 149*, 157
    Robert 153*
    Roland 146
    Rowland 143*
    S. 151
    Samuel 25, 61, 63, 65, 99*,
      110*, 136*
    Samuel N. 92
    Sarah 6
    Seth 77
    Silas 35
    Sylvester 48*
    Timothy 52*
    Usual 53*
    William 39*, 69*, 79, 87,
      90*, 137*, 150*, 161*,
      185
    Windsor 71

Johnston,
    Ellis 143
    George B. 19
    Jacob 108
    Jacob S. 108
    James 77, 121*, 131*
    John 14, 124
    John M. 183*
    Thomas 133*
    Tobias 119
    William 77, 112, 122*, 180

Johnstone,
    Benjamin 11
    Hepzebah 63
    Ruth 11

Johonnet,
    Oliver 44*

Johonnett,
    Oliver 49

Jolly,
    Henry 174
    Saving 140

Jones,
    Abraham 108, 183
    Abram 129*
    Absalom 121
    Alathea 60
    Alexander 132
    Amos 12*, 86*
    Anna 105*
    Asa 22*, 54
    Azuba 40
    Benjamin 73*, 117, 141, 157,
      164
    Benson 67
    Berryman 134*
    Betsey 86
    Britton 140*
    Charles 86, 98
    Charles B. 44
    Clements 109
    Cornelius 8*
    Daniel 110*, 153*
    Darling 154*
    David 93, 157*
    Dennis 100
    Dudley W. 16
    E. 78
    E. B. 155
    Eleanor 61
    Elias 85*
    Elisha 132
    Eliza 128
    Elizabeth 6*, 141
    Elkanah 174
    Enoch 93
    Epaphras 182*
    Ethal 116
    Ezekiel 39*, 90*
    Fanny M. 49
    Francis 186
    George 20, 58*, 177
    Gray 129*
    Hannah 100
    Harrison 150
    Hizar 155
    Income 67
    Isaac 44, 117*, 147*
    Israel 62*, 66*
    J. C. 164
    Jacob 143
    James 133*, 135*, 157*, 161*,
      166*, 167*
    Jesse 139*
    Joel 124*
    Johanna 171*
    John 22*, 60*, 99*, 104, 113,
      128*, 152*, 155, 165, 170*

Jones, (cont.)
Joseph 99*, 146, 155*,
178*
Joshua 134*, 162*
Josiah 109, 194*
Levi 134
Lydia 44, 59
Martha 165
Marybee 95
Mehitable 10
Morris 52*
Morton 155*
Moses 104, 186*
Musgroves 137*
Nathaniel 143*
Noah 72*
Peregrine 125*
Philip 191*
Phineas 38*
Pliny 44
Prescott 21
Reuben 76
Rial M. 195
Richard 155*, 182*
Robert 79, 165*
Samuel 15, 38, 44, 75,
90*, 103*, 143*
Sarah 20
Silas 180*
Simeon 157
Stephen 34*, 186
Stephen L. 163
Sylvester 10*
Tavner 131*
Thomas 14*, 140*, 154*
Thomas C. 148*
Thomas R. 133*
Timothy 44
Weldon 150
Westword A. 159
William 44, 72*, 77*, 112*,
138*, 146*, 159
William (Mrs.) 20
William C. 180*
Zelotus 171
Zemis 77

Jordan,
Amos 175*
Charles B. 145
Edmund 33
Elijah 117
Edmund 33
Elizabeth 145
Fountain 147*
George 160*
Hugh 125

Jordan, (cont.)
James 5, 120*
Jesse 143*
Joanna 5*
John 107
John P. 7
Joshua 70*
Solomon 117
Thomas 177*
Timothy 7
William 47, 128*

Jorden,
Benjamin 25*

Jordon,
David 6*
Henry 125*
William 132*

Joscelyn,
David 103*

Jose,
Jamima 58

Joslin,
David 22
Josiah 70
Luke 21
Nathaniel 21*
Rebecca 21
Sarah 22

Joslyn,
Eleazer 93
Sarah 21*

Josselyn,
John 43
Mary 30*

Jourdan,
Hannah 12
John 111*

Jourdon,
Ammon 64
Susanna 165*

Jowner,
John 52

Joy,
Abraham 84
Bennet 193
David 64

Joyall,
    John B. 62*

Joyner,
    Joshua 133*

Judd,
    (N.X.N) 59
    Anthony 79
    Daniel 71
    Demas 96*
    Esther 50
    Henry 50
    Jesse 79
    Job 182*
    Lydia 71
    Oliver 32*
    Sarah 52*
    Solomon 61*
    Thomas 52*, 59

Judkins,
    Leonard 13
    Philip 13
    Richard 10
    Samuel 65*

Judson,
    Albert 56
    Naomi 55*
    Nehemiah 58*

Juiss,
    Benjamin 52
    Joseph 52

Jump,
    John 162*

Jumper,
    Daniel 5*

June,
    Benjamin 90*
    Sarah 97

Justice,
    Amy 162*
    Elizabeth 121
    George 121
    James 182
    Joseph 78
    Moses 186*
    Rosanna 182
    Simon 166*
    Walcott 78

Justin,
    Gershom 72
    Lucy 85

Kaler,
    Nathaniel 87*

Kane,
    Angelica 96
    James 122

Kanna,
    Lucy 98

Karr,
    John C. 187
    Tharasco 187
    Walter 110*

Kay,
    John 101*

Kea,
    Henry 138*

Keaner,
    Jacob 114*

Kearns,
    Thomas 102
    William 160*

Kearsley,
    Jonathan 193*

Keblinger,
    Adam 128*

Kee,
    Andrew 116

Keech,
    Rachel 46
    Stephen 46

Keefer,
    Ann Maria 113
    Frederick 113

Keel,
    Richard 155*

Keeler,
    Hezekiah 62
    Jeremiah 104*
    John 118*
    Lewis 62, 107
    Philip B. 86

Keen,
    Benjamin 27*
    Isaac 9
    John 8*, 164*
    Josiah 9
    Lydia 30*
    Meshack 8
    Tulob 8

Keener,
    Adam 116*
    George 117*

Keeney,
    Richard 50*

Keep,
    Stephen 44*

Keer,
    David 166

Keesucker,
    George 181
    William 181

Keeth,
    John 147*

Keeton,
    David 172

Kehl,
    George 113

Kehm,
    Michael 114*

Kehr,
    David 188

Keith,
    Asa 36*
    Caleb 24*

Keldar,
    Henry 103
    Penelope 103

Keler,
    Henry 13*

Kelicott,
    Thomas 92

Kell,
    Alexander 145
    James 145
    Robert 146
    William 146

Kellar,
    Henry 96*

Keller,
    (Mrs.) 113
    Alexander 9
    David 9
    Devoult 184
    Frederick 121*
    George 135
    Jacob 113
    John 117, 135

Kelley,
    Allen 153*
    Betsey 49
    David 47
    Edmund 79
    Giles 146*
    Jeremiah M. 59
    John 176*
    Jonathan 18
    Martin 79
    Micajah 16
    Nancy 166*
    Nathaniel 180*
    Richard 152*
    Samuel G. 16
    Sarah 10
    Timothy 23*
    William 145*

Kellog,
    Nathaniel 98*

Kellogg,
    Alpheus 66
    Ebenezer 83
    Elijah 6
    Eliphalet 116*
    Enoch 80
    Helmont 194
    James 80

Kellogg, (cont.)
    Jerusha 66
    Joseph 6
    Levi 88
    Loomis 88*
    Luvitia 69
    Medad 61*
    Nathaniel 98
    Seth H. 194
    Spencer 88
    Thomas 83

Kellum,
    Luther 119*

Kelly,
    Abel 69
    Abraham 118
    Edmund 142
    Elias 181
    Elizabeth 88
    Griffin 160
    James 72, 118, 121, 159*,
      189*
    John 88
    Mary 43
    Nathaniel 63
    Richard 127
    Robert 121, 142
    Samuel 167*
    Stephen 78*
    Thomas D. 141
    William 165*

Kelsey,
    Aaron 67
    Joel 23
    John 97
    Lucy 67
    Roswell 68

Kelso,
    Elizabeth 106
    James 106

Kelton,
    Amos 28*

Kelty,
    Catharine 128

Kemball,
    Samuel 46

Kemerer,
    Frederick 114

Kemmer,
    Nicholas 182*

Kemp,
    Benjamin 21
    David 21
    Dudley B. 40*
    Eliakim 21
    Tryphena 21

Kemper,
    Daniel 109*

Kempor,
    John 104*

Kempton,
    Peter 108

Kemuston,
    Nancy 17

Kenady,
    Robert 179

Kendall,
    Abigail 13
    Asa 39*
    Balah 66
    John 175*
    Joshua 77*
    Josiah 20
    Lemuel 24
    Mary 4
    Nathan 20*, 41*
    Noah 38*
    Peter 82*
    Samuel 65
    Timothy 65

Kendell,
    George 22
    Mary 22

Kenderhine,
    Eli 116

Kenderick,
    Nathaniel 24

Kendred,
    Palmore 156

Kendrick,
    Daniel 24

Keneday,
    Sherwood 138*

Kenistan,
    David 18

Keniston,
    David 8
    Ebenezer 15
    William 8*

Kennada,
    Agnes 57
    Charles 57

Kennaday,
    Thomas 138*

Kennair,
    John 139

Kennaird,
    David 133*

Kennan,
    Joseph 111
    Mary 111
    William 158

Kennear,
    William 119*

Kenneda,
    Lucy 57

Kennedy,
    David 162*
    Deborah 81*
    J. 148
    Joseph 156, 164*
    Samuel 81*
    William 148, 158*

Kenner,
    Rodham 164*

Kenney,
    Daniel 97*
    Isaac 52
    Samuel 66
    William 52

Kennon,
    David 78
    Isaac 78

Kenny,
    Edward D. 166*
    Mehitable 30

Kent,
    Abigail 29*
    Alexander 131
    Arad 65
    Charles 101*
    Ezekiel 78
    Hannah 45
    Jacob 108
    Jerome 78
    John 33*, 176*
    John K. 50*
    Lucretia 126
    Peter 152*
    Sarah 109
    Simon 108
    Thomas 170*

Kenter,
    Richard 63*

Kentfield,
    Erastus 35

Kenyon,
    Martha 48*
    William 48*

Kephart,
    Henry 163
    Jacob 163

Kepner,
    Barnard 115

Kerby,
    Jesse 167*

Kerkendall,
    Henry 103
    Wilhelmus 103

Kerner,
    Philip 178

Kerr,
    Andrew 144*
    Elizabeth 139
    James 120, 183*
    Robert 139*

Kerring,
    Sarah 30

Kersey,
    John   29, 135*, 181*
    Peter   29*
    S. S.   29

Kersy,
    John   158

Kesler,
    Peter   176*

Kesling,
    Peter   180*

Kesterson,
    John   152*
    John S.   133

Ketcham,
    Samuel   107*
    Solomon   105

Ketchum,
    Ezra   95
    Jonathan   93
    Samuel   93

Keth,
    Simeon   70

Kettell,
    Jonathan   42

Ketterman,
    Daniel   134*

Key,
    Sarah   160

Keyes,
    Aaron   70
    Elias   170*
    Ezekiel   25*
    Ezra   68*
    Israel   38
    James   136
    Jemima   15
    Lorenzo   15
    Nathaniel   69*
    Robert   136
    Thomas   62*

Keys,
    Ariel   57
    Jeremiah   154*

Keyser,
    George   134
    Pamela   134

Kibbe,
    Mary   91

Kibbee,
    Ruth   65*

Kibber,
    Frederick   61*

Kibbey,
    P. W.   23

Kibby,
    Thomas   34*

Kibling,
    John   70

Kidd,
    James R.   106
    Keziah Ann   106
    William   147*

Kidder,
    Aaron B.   22
    Hannah   39
    Phineas   20*

Kider,
    John   67*

Kidney,
    Jonathan   72*

Kidwell,
    M.   165
    Matthew   165

Kieth,
    Anna   31
    Peter   77*
    Sally   67
    Scot   67

Kifer,
    Henry   122*

Kiker,
    George   139*

Kilbee,
    Hannah   69

Kilbern,
    Calvin 38

Kilborn,
    Elizabeth 49
    Evelin 58
    John 5*
    Samuel 86

Kilbourn,
    Eliphaz 72*

Kolburn,
    Eliphalet 19*
    James 65
    John 38*

Kilburne,
    William 61*

Kilby,
    John 49

Kiles,
    John 181
    Thomas 181

Kilgore,
    Charles 182*
    James 7*
    John 6*

Killgoar,
    John 144

Killin,
    John 168*

Killogg,
    Calvin 103

Killom,
    Daniel 20*
    Thomas 20*

Killpatrick,
    Robert 142
    Thomas 142

Kilmer,
    Mary 104

Kilton,
    Edward 11*
    John 45
    Margaret 45

Kimbal,
    Nathaniel 11*

Kimball,
    Abel 174*
    Abigail 25
    Benjamin 41*
    Daniel 20*, 24
    David 22*
    Elisha 24
    Jabez 24
    John 24, 81
    Joseph 5*
    Samuel 25
    Sargent 18
    Thomas 42*
    Tristram 16
    Willis 24

Kimber,
    Elizabeth 107, 163

Kimdle,
    E. 92
    Ephraim 92

Kinard,
    Barnett 148
    John 148

Kinby,
    James 137*

Kincaid,
    John 9*

Kindred,
    Thomas 154*
    William 164*

Kindrick,
    Mitchell 186*

King,
    Ada 110*
    Anna H. 95
    Apollos 91*
    Aury 108*
    Austin 50
    Benjamin 75
    Benjamin H. 154
    David 141*, 185
    Drury 141
    E. A. 74
    Ebenezer 75
    Elihu 35

King, (cont.)
    Elizabeth 116
    Esau 72, 184
    Foster 34
    George 120, 127*, 161*
    George H. 77*
    Hannah 35
    Hugh 155*
    Isaac 67
    Isabell 144
    Jackson 72
    Jacob 77
    James 25*, 142
    Jane 60
    Jason 10
    Jeremiah 163*
    Jesse 133*
    John 39*, 77*, 100*, 134*,
      136*, 143*, 146*, 160*
    John M. 185*
    Joseph 34
    Josiah 27*
    Martin 144
    Mary 5, 108*
    Moses R. 108
    Ormel 95
    Peter 35
    Philip 74, 160*
    R. L. 37
    Reuben 67, 73
    Richard 147*
    Robert 123*
    Simeon 126
    Stephen 72*
    Thomas 154*
    William 66*, 77, 154, 160*,
      185*

Kingman,
    Alexander 171*
    Ann 142*
    Relief 31*

Kingry,
    Greenbury 189
    Joseph 189

Kingsberry,
    Jabez 61*

Kingsbury,
    Austin 175
    John 179
    Joseph 175
    Lemuel 173*
    Mary 49*

Kingsbury, (cont.)
    Nathaniel 30
    Thomas 78
    William 179

Kingsley,
    Alpheus 54*
    Anne 48
    Austin 5
    Azael 5
    Daniel 5*
    Elias 97*
    George 81
    Hezekiah 57*
    Jaben 57*
    Martin 124*
    Rufus 119*
    Timothy 35
    Uriah 81
    Walter 57
    William 95*

Kingsly,
    Jonathan 100*

Kinion,
    Anthony 137*

Kinkead,
    Thomas 135*

Kinman,
    Lucy 83

Kinnard,
    John 149*

Kinnecutt,
    Lydia 49

Kinnehorn,
    William 128*

Kinneson,
    Joseph 65*

Kinney,
    Abijah 8*
    Anna 79
    Avery 57
    Daniel 97
    Elisha 54
    Freelove 57
    Hannah 70
    Jesse 92*
    John E. 180

Kinney, (cont.)
    Jonathan 70
    Joseph 29, 126*
    L. S. 70
    M. (Major) 114
    Peabody 97
    Stephen 180

Kinsley,
    Abiel 81*
    Francis 78

Kinsman,
    William 42*

Kinyon,
    Alexander 78*
    Griffin 99
    John 92*

Kippers,
    John 190
    Samuel 190

Kirby,
    Andrew J. 148
    F. F. 128
    Leonard 167*
    Martin 135
    William 135

Kirk,
    Benjamin 165
    John 134*
    Prudence 71
    William 71

Kirkendoll,
    Matthew 161*

Kirker,
    John 124*

Kirkland,
    Edwin S. 100
    Henry F. A. 88*
    John 100

Kirkpatrick,
    David 181
    Robert 189

Kirtland,
    Nathan 60*

Kise,
    Peter 110*

Kitchen,
    James 186
    John 117, 150

Kittle,
    Abraham 111
    Jacob 136*, 143*

Kittredge,
    Jeremiah 63
    Solomon 21*
    Zephaniah 21*

Kline,
    Adam 115

Kling,
    John 96*

Klingaman,
    Peter 122*

Klingeman,
    John P. 118

Knap,
    Benjamin 101*
    John C. 36
    Margaret 31

Knapp,
    Benjamin 85
    Charles 77
    Codema 175
    Cyrus 68
    Edward N. 28
    Ephraim 97
    H. G. 70
    Hannah 68
    Hezekiah 56*
    Isual 106*
    Jared 83*
    John 56
    Justus 119
    Moses 90*, 97
    Nathan 56
    Nathaniel W. 56
    Philip 27*
    Samuel 99*
    Sarah 43
    Susanna 28
    William 56*, 99*

Kneeland,
    John 126

Knerr,
    Andrew 114*

Knight,
    Abiah 25
    Abraham 6*
    Ann 56
    Betsey 163
    Comfort 46
    Daniel 7*
    David 48
    Elbridge 71
    Elijah 22*, 78
    Elizabeth 4*, 42*, 49
    Esther 71
    Grant 163
    Israel 46*
    J. 78
    Jacob 5*
    Joel 67*
    John 6*, 142
    Jonathan 3, 19*, 46
    Moses 25, 183
    Nathan 48
    Peter 134*
    Prince 37
    Sally 94*
    Sarah 25
    Sheldon 46
    Silas 37
    Simeon C. 3
    Thomas 107*
    William 133*, 140

Knights,
    Caleb S. 47
    James 95*

Knittle,
    Abraham 115

Knower,
    Ann 37
    Thomas 37

Knowles,
    Caleb C. 10
    Dorothy 16
    Eleazer 16
    Ezekiel 15
    Heppy 49
    Hepsebah 49
    John 18
    Joseph 18
    Lydia 10
    Mary 133
    Rhoda 168

Knowlton,
    Andrew 9
    Dorcas 4*
    Frederick 57*
    Harry 93
    Joseph 12
    Joseph F. 12
    Nathan 36, 41*
    Stephen 38*
    Thomas 61*

Knox,
    Benjamin 140
    Henry 97
    James 139*
    John 97
    Molly 20*
    Robert 140
    Robert S. 169
    Samuel 155
    Thomas 118
    William 169

Koch,
    John 116*

Kolb,
    John 143*

Kollock,
    Cornelius 31
    Susan 115

Koon,
    Lawrence 121*

Koonce,
    Philip 156*

Koontz,
    John 138*
    Philip 136*

Kopenhaver,
    Thomas 114
    William 114

Krebs,
    George 116*

Kreeger,
    George 140*

Kress,
    Conrad 123*

Kretcher,
    Elizabeth 81
    Henry 81

Krewson,
    Simon 116

Krick,
    Francis 127*

Kroninger,
    Joseph 179*

Krouse,
    John 113

Krun,
    Benjamin A. 103
    Cornelius 103
    James C. 103

Kudisilly,
    Henry 175

Kulby,
    John 165

Kumble,
    Rachel 81

Kump,
    George 121
    Henry 134*

Kunck,
    Hendrick 87*

Kuran,
    Michael G. 102
    Peter 102

Kurtus,
    John 153*

Kuter,
    Valentine 115

Kuton,
    Isaac 165*

Kyle,
    Thomas 165*

Kyser,
    Frederick 183*
    John H. 96

Labar,
    Daniel 114

Lacey,
    Betsey 56
    Jesse 56

Lackey,
    Elizabeth 140
    George 139*
    Isaac 67
    Robert 115*
    Thomas 139*
    William 140, 148*

Lacky,
    Elizabeth 154

Lacy,
    Eleanor 112
    Elijah 184

Ladd,
    Samuel 18
    Sarah 65*

Lafar,
    Catharine 142*

Lafferly,
    John 118

Lafferty,
    John 74

Laffoon,
    Anderson 162
    James 162

Lagran,
    John N. 145*

Lain,
    Charles 152*
    John 118*
    Joseph 152*

Lake,
    Burden 66
    Christopher 47

Lake, (cont.)
    Crapo 105
    Daniel 102*
    David **47***
    Elnathan 28
    Enos 22
    Gideon 33*
    Giles 47
    Hannah 75
    Henry 87*
    Hepsabeth 22
    John C. 105
    John E. 22*
    Peter 105
    Samuel 47
    Samuel C. 105
    William 101*

Lakeman,
    Rachel 42*

Lakin,
    David 40*
    Winslow 20*

Laman,
    John 82*

Lamatus,
    John 167

Lamb,
    Calvin 36
    David 36
    Ira 10
    Israel 100*
    James 9*, 10
    Johiel 73*
    John 187*
    Joseph 62
    Nahum 36
    Nathan 62
    Nathaniel 23*
    Silas 53*
    Susan 38

Lambert,
    Christopher 128
    Elijah 44
    James 108*
    John 167*
    Lois 59*
    Lucy 44
    Peter 87*
    Samuel 111*
    Sarah 42

Lambkin,
    Mary 129*

Lamberson,
    David 109*
    Thomas 109*

Lambertson,
    Simon 102*

Lament,
    Cornelius 78
    Hiram 78

Lamon,
    Noah 84

Lamont,
    John 168
    William 76*

Lamphear,
    David 69
    Elizabeth 69*
    Reuben 69

Lampher,
    Ezra 92*

Lamphere,
    Elizabeth 57
    Solomon 57

Lamphier,
    Benjamin 123
    G. 79
    William 123

Lamprey,
    Daniel 15*

Lamson,
    Betsey 21
    Jonathan 21
    Joseph 20*

Lanabee,
    Daniel 21

Lancaster,
    John 9*
    Joseph 5*
    Levi 11
    Nathaniel 24
    Samuel 42*

Lancey,
    Elizabeth 13

Land,
    John 164*
    Joseph 150
    Lewis 143*
    Moses 188*

Landerkin,
    Daniel 8*

Landers,
    Ebenezer 77
    John 148*
    Mehitable 95
    Moses 95
    Solomon 77

Landis,
    Peter 113
    David 113

Landon,
    Ebenezer 171*
    Henry 59
    Rufus 59

Landpher,
    Oliver 54

Landrim,
    Thomas 154*

Landrum,
    Whitfield 147

Lane,
    Alexander 125*, 184
    Anson G. 53
    Asa 33
    Asaph 22*
    Benjamin 97
    Caleb 29, 41*
    David 39*
    Edward 141
    Elisha 22
    Gisbin 155
    Henry 108*
    Ira 93
    Isaac 93*, 153*, 180
    Isham 164*
    J. 178
    Jane 178
    John 141
    Jonathan 53

Lane, (cont.)
    Larkin 184
    Leavitt 30
    Matthias 74*
    Meny 16
    Nathaniel 53
    Samuel 22, 121*, 174*
    Sylvester R. 58
    Tide 153*
    Turner 157*

Lanfair,
    Robert 33
    Roswell 33

Lang,
    Francis 182*

Langden,
    F. 175
    Joseph 92
    Submit 175

Langdon,
    John 106*
    John W. 172
    Mary 83
    Philip 183*

Langford,
    Jonathan 53*
    Martha 194*

Langley,
    Betsey 15
    James 17, 149*
    Peter 45

Langmade,
    William 74

Langton,
    Daniel 183*

Laning,
    Mary 109
    Ralph 109*

Lanman,
    George 184
    James 184

Lanneau,
    Basil 142

Lanphire,
    Wheeler 91*

Lansdale,
    Cornelia 195
    Isaac 148*

Lanson,
    Martha 12
    William 12

Lapham,
    Asa 29*
    Lemuel 30*
    Rachel 105

Laplace,
    J. J. 151
    John J. 151

Larabee,
    Bethshebee 30
    John 175*
    Samuel 67*

Laraby,
    David 89
    Elias 99*
    L. 192
    Ruth 89
    T. 192

Larance,
    Margaret 117

Laraway,
    Isaac 96*
    Jacob 72*

Larbree,
    Daniel 10
    Mary 10

Larcham,
    Sarah 152

Lard,
    John 3
    Samuel 108*

Lare,
    Joseph 116

Larel,
    Daniel 31
    Lavina 31

Large,
    Joseph 153*

Laria,
    Isiah 8
    James 8

Larkcom,
    Arvillas C. 178
    Paul 178

Larkin,
    Elam 78
    Ephraim 27
    James 135
    John 38*, 96*
    Lorin 78

Larkins,
    Evan 139

Larnard,
    Jonas 36
    Sylvanus 63*

Larned,
    John 36*
    Moses 66
    Nathan 66
    Sarah 45*
    Thomas 36*

Larns,
    Eleanor 139

Larose,
    Jacob 176*

Larrabe,
    Jacob 5*

Larrabee,
    Adam 53
    Anna 42
    Charles 51
    Sarah 42

Larremore,
    Hugh 189
    R. 189

Larreson,
    James 109

Larribee,
    Adam 53

Law, (cont.)
    Mason 100*
    Reuben 21
    Richard 53*
    Sarah 22

Lawless,
    John 162

Lawrance,
    Anna 39*

Lawrence,
    Amon 97*
    Amos 8, 69
    Ebenezer 39*
    Elizabeth 97
    Hiram 97
    Isaac 11*
    Jacob 119*, 156
    John 145*, 156
    Jonathan 81
    Joseph 182*
    Joshua 8
    Josiah 33
    Luther 22
    M. A. 115
    Marvil 57*
    Melatiah 27
    Neely 166
    Nicholas 71*
    Oliver 20, 124*
    Sidney 81
    Silas 27*
    Stephen 107
    Submit 22
    Susan 40
    Thomas 33, 51
    William 116, 135*, 166

Laws,
    David 141*

Lawson,
    (Mr.) 183
    Chesley 167
    David 154
    Ebenezer 61
    Elizabeth 140
    Jacob 102*
    James 162*
    John 165*
    Momon 153
    Nathan 167
    Peter 153
    Sarah 57

Lawson, (cont.)
    Thomas 139*
    William 136*

Lawton,
    Caleb 48
    Israel 66*
    Job 54
    William 47*

Lawyer,
    Luke 13*

Lay,
    Edward 103*
    John 53*
    Thomas 152*

Layman,
    Jacob 154*
    William 127

Layne,
    A. 130*

Layport,
    Jacob 95*

Layson,
    William 187

Layton,
    William H. 163, 165

Lazarus,
    Marks (Mrs.) 142
    Rachel (Mrs.) 142

Lazell,
    Joseph 75
    Luther 29*
    Sarah 75

Lazendry,
    Elisha 92
    Samuel 92

Lea,
    Jacob 167*

Leach,
    Comfort 15
    Elizabeth 19
    George 5*
    Harvey 57
    John 14

Leach, (cont.)
    Jeremiah 14
    Joshua 169*
    Josiah 22
    Nancy 166
    Phebe 57
    S. 73
    Samuel 19, 73
    Sibal 69*
    Thomas 136
    William 19*

Leadbetter,
    Ezra 10
    Increase 10

Leader,
    George 114*

Leadford,
    Peter 138*

League,
    James 128

Leak,
    John M. 157*
    Walter 140*

Lear,
    Hannah 130
    James 130
    Samuel 17*, 20
    Samuel L. 20

Learnard,
    John 69

Learned,
    Abijah 124
    Silvanus 124

Leasure,
    Abraham 120*
    John 122

Leathers,
    Enoch 14
    Paul 166

Leathhead,
    Robert 13

Leavett,
    Barron T. 18
    Polly 18

Leavitt,
    Amos 18
    Andrew 21
    Betsey 3
    Jonathan 18*
    Mary 4*, 20*
    Simon 15
    Thomas C. 15
    William 21

Leayre,
    Harriet 108*

Leckey,
    Andrew 161*

Leckie,
    W. 157
    William 157

Ledbetter,
    Johnson 146
    Richard 140, 146

Ledbitter,
    Mary 143

Ledmon,
    William 154*

Lee,
    Adam 109
    Daniel 58
    David 58, 169*
    Eber 60
    Elisha 88
    Ellen 62*
    Enoch 88
    Francis B. 54
    G. W. 67
    Henry 138*
    Isaac 43*
    Israel 76
    James 139*
    Jeptha 99*
    John 77*, 138
    John S. 76
    Jonathan 52*
    Joshua 163
    Levi 46*
    Matthew 162
    Nathan 18*
    Richard 173
    Samuel 183
    Thomas 50, 109
    William 97*
    Zebulon 173

Leech,
     Elijah 160

Leeds,
     Joseph H. 56
     Thomas 31*

Leeman,
     Henry 10

Leeper,
     James 191*

Lefferts,
     Esther 95*

Lefler,
     John 123
     Mary 123

Leftwich,
     (General) Joel 129
     Rug 129

Legg,
     Daniel 39
     David 39
     Joel 92

Legget,
     Abraham 102

Legrange,
     John 106*

Lehman,
     John 113

Lehnhart,
     Philip 112

Lehr,
     Philip 114*

Leighton,
     Ephraim 9*
     Hannah 40
     Jacob 17*
     Mary 17
     Thomas 5

Leister,
     John P. 110*

Leland,
     John 39*

Leland, (cont.)
     John V. 36
     Lydia 70
     Phineas 70
     Thomas 176*
     Timothy 41

Lemangon,
     Philip 91

Lemaster,
     George 135*

Lemen,
     William S. 98*

Lement,
     Thomas 8*

Lemmex,
     William 69

Lemmon,
     Jacob 133*
     John 121*

Lemon,
     James 97
     Margaret A. 166
     Robert 189*
     Warner C. 44

Lemons,
     Robert 140*

Lemuir,
     Mary 44

Lenard,
     Abna 121
     Esther 121

Lendall,
     Anna 43

Leney,
     John 33

Lenhart,
     Jacob 122
     Peter 122

Lenox,
     James 120

Lent,
    Isaac 95
    Jacob 105, 106*
    Moses 101*

Lentz,
    Elizabeth 114
    Jacob 114*

Lenusford,
    Eaton 159

Leob,
    Henry 114
    Margaretta 114

Leonard,
    Amasa 59
    Asenath 27
    Caleb 11
    Dwight 43
    Elizabeth 38
    F. B. 94
    Frederick 136
    George 113*
    Henry 136
    Hiram 90
    Isaac 121*
    Jacob 30*
    John 110, 153*
    Martin 30
    Mary 68, 94
    Nathan B. 45
    Nehemiah 30
    Noah 89*
    Olive 99
    Paul 34
    Phineas 43
    Robert 102*
    Samuel 30*, 171
    Silas 59
    Solomon 100*
    William 138*
    Ziba 34

Lepkichler,
    Michael 115

Leport,
    Jacob 96*

Lepper,
    Jacob F. 87
    John 194
    Mary 87

Leray,
    Bridget 54*

Lercy,
    Peter 103

Leroy,
    Simeon 78

Lerry,
    David 13
    Edward L. 13

Lesley,
    John 134

Leslie,
    Peter 155*
    Thomas 117
    William 117

Lester,
    Guy 103*
    Martha 67
    Nathan 103

Lettis,
    Jacob 87
    James 87

Letts,
    Chester 89
    Daniel 89
    Francis 109
    John 92*

Letz,
    Abigail 106

Levally,
    Phebe 48

Levay,
    George 146*

Levens,
    Richard 194

Levering,
    Ann 42
    Mary 116
    Nathaniel 11*

Levi,
    Bessie 52
    Isaac 184
    Martin 184

Levick,
    Robert 108*

Levings,
    Noah 88

Levingston,
    David 123*
    Jacob 99*

Levingstone,
    John 113

Lewin,
    Thomas 27*

Lewis,
    Aaron 149*
    Abel 50*
    Abiah 55
    Abner 66*
    Albert 32
    Alva 111
    Andrew 135*
    Anna 109
    Augustus 94*
    Augustus J. 48
    Axiom 149
    Bayles W. 144
    Channey 50*
    Charity 55*
    Christopher 88
    Clark 54
    Darius 32
    Eli 72*
    Elizabeth 53
    Enoch 48*
    Esther 32
    Ezekiel 91, 120*
    George 26
    Hannah 31*
    Hurbart 137
    Isaac 44*
    Jacob 136*
    James 139*, 163
    Jesse 128*
    John 23, 134*, 144, 172*
    John T. 116*
    Jonathan 32, 63*
    Joseph H. 48
    Justice 93*
    Lemuel 81
    Martha 22*
    Martin 80*
    Mary 109
    Merrick 40

Lewis, (cont.)
    Morgan 105*
    Nathan 55
    Oliver 88
    Patience 55*
    Peleg 57
    Phebe 25
    Polly 127
    Reuben 103*
    Richard 26*
    Ruel 129*
    Sally 54
    Sarah 60*
    Solomon 152
    Thomas 165*
    Wait 82
    William 23, 69*, 81, 129*, 140*

Lewter,
    Hardy 137*

Lezotte,
    Joseph 78
    Mary 78

Libbey,
    Enoch 17
    George 15, 24
    James 23

Libby,
    Abigail 6*
    Daniel 6
    Dorothy 6
    Edward 5*
    Ephraim 14
    Hiram 6
    Joseph 14
    Mark 6*
    Nathaniel 4*
    Robert 5
    Samuel 19*
    Sherley 6
    Theophilus 5*

Liddell,
    John 150

Liggett,
    James 121
    John 191
    Thomas 121

Light,
    John 153*

Lightall,
    Catharine 192

Lightfoot,
    Tapley M. 158*

Lighthall,
    George 83

Ligon,
    Joseph 156*
    William 166

Lile,
    Ephraim 147*

Liles,
    Robert 154
    Robert D. 154

Lilley,
    Elisha 65*

Lillibridge,
    Daniel 61
    Ellis 61
    Gideon 48*

Lillie,
    Mary 65

Lilly,
    Caleb 68
    Elijah 69
    Hannah 44
    Hiram 69
    Jerusha 68
    John 44, 122
    Mary 90

Limon,
    Moses 84

Linam,
    Andrew 160*

Linch,
    Henry 190

Lincolm,
    (N.X.N.) 57

Lincoln,
    Abiather 192
    Amasa 66

Lincoln, (cont.)
    Anna 27
    Elizabeth 32, 66
    Isaac 36
    Jacob 38
    John 120
    Loved 9*
    Nathaniel 28
    Patterson 120
    Rachel 29*
    Ruama 69
    Ruth 28
    Sally 28
    Samuel 65*
    Sherman 9*
    Susanna 29

Lindal,
    Mary 27

Lindley,
    Zachariah 184*

Lindsay,
    James 10*
    John 113

Lindsey,
    Benjamin 142*
    Catharine 49*
    Deborah 43*
    Mary 134
    Palmela 49*
    Stephen 84

Lindsley,
    John 52
    Sarah 52
    Stephen 180*

Lindsly,
    David 110*

Line,
    Jacob 113
    John 169*
    Joseph S. 121*

Lines,
    Benjamin 51*
    Rufus 93
    Sarah 53

Lingle,
    John 113

Lingo,
      William 159*

Link,
      Simon 112

Linn,
      John 122*, 162*
      Joseph 11*

Linnen,
      Thomas 8*

Linsley,
      Zachariah 187*

Lint,
      Isaac 140

Linton,
      Hugh 149
      John 149
      Joseph 26

Lints,
      Jacob 83
      Phillips 83

Linvill,
      William 146*

Lipe,
      Leonard 188*

Lipes,
      Sarah 109

Lipford,
      Anthony P. 132*
      Henry 132

Lipp,
      John 116

Lippencot,
      Samuel 170*

Lippenwill,
      Reuben 66*

Lippet,
      Moses 57
      Nathaniel 57

Lippincott,
      Amelia 110*

Lippitt,
      Charles 45*

Lipscomb,
      Norvell 155

Liscum,
      Samuel 106*

Lisle,
      Jackson 155*

List,
      Jacob 163*

Lister,
      William 144*

Liston,
      Hugh 158
      John K. 101

Liswell,
      Jeremiah 43
      Thomas 43

Litchfield,
      Alfred 29
      Caleb 71*
      Francis 29
      Hannah 29
      Paul 29

Litchford,
      Arthur 129*

Litteral,
      Richard 133*

Little,
      Christy 109*
      Daniel 16
      David 68
      Ebenezer 110*
      George 134*
      James 68
      John 8*, 56*
      John L. 165
      Joseph 19*
      Luther 29*
      Robert 111*
      Tristram 16
      William 190

Littlefield,
    Aaron 31*
    Daniel L. 3
    Dorothy 4
    Elijah 4
    Isaac 19*
    Jesse 84
    Joanna 4*
    Joseph 3
    Miriam 3
    Moses 11
    Rebecca 31*
    Simeon 68*
    Susannah 4
    Timothy 10*

Littlehale,
    Lydia 23

Littleton,
    Charles 148 *

Livermore,
    Braddyll 37*
    David 20*
    Elisha 36
    M. 74
    Solomon 84

Living,
    Stephen 149*

Lloyd,
    George E. 174
    James 59, 184*
    Joseph 161*

Loas,
    John 121*

Lobbdell,
    Simeon 73

Lobdell,
    Joseph 83

Lock,
    James 138
    John 138
    Mary 16

Lockard,
    William 128*

Locke,
    Abigail 39

Locke, (cont.)
    Edward 193*
    Elisha 86*
    John 110*
    Levi 20
    Richard 143*
    Simeon P. 20

Lockett,
    Royall 132*

Lockhart,
    James 142*

Lockheart,
    John 158
Lockhust
    Philip 129

Lockinghour,
    Jacob 138

Lockridge,
    James 157 *
    John 188
    William A. 188

Lockwood,
    Abm. 79
    Abraham 121*
    Alfred 103
    Darius 73
    David 58*, 169*
    Gilbert 75
    Jemima 103
    Job 99
    John 98
    Messenger 56*
    Nathan 102*
    Noah 56*

Loder,
    Henry 81
    John 81

Logan,
    Alexander 128*
    James 163
    James R. 163
    John 167
    Joseph 167
    Timothy 162*

Logee,
    Rachel 47

Loghery,
    William A. 98

Logue,
    William 120

Lohr,
    Peter 133*

Lombard,
    Jedediah 6*
    John 5*, 6

Lommis,
    Oliver 102
    Willis 102

Lomoreaux,
    Joseph 126

London,
    Archibald 112
    George 52

Lone,
    Pheniz 87

Long,
    A. G. 121
    Alexander 121
    Anderson 190*
    Benjamin 118
    David 82*, 157*
    George 117*
    Hannah 118
    Henry 127
    Jacob 113*, 131*
    James 26
    Jonathan 153*
    Joseph 22
    Moses 19*
    Nancy 34, 127
    Nicholas 121*, 161
    Phebe 22
    Reuben S. 24
    Richard 156*
    Robert 142*
    Stephen 34
    William 184

Longfellow,
    Mary 12*
    Sarah 24

Longley,
    Asa 13*
    Edmund 34
    Nathaniel 38*
    Thomas 34
    William 154*

Longnecker,
    John 113
    Molly 113

Longstaff,
    Henry 109
    James 109

Longstreth,
    Salome 118
    Thomas 118

Look,
    Alden 30
    Elijah 76*
    James 88
    Jane 30

Looker,
    Othniel 172

Loomies,
    Isaiah 54
    John 54
    Simon 54

Loomis,
    Alva 78
    Anson 89
    Daniel 61*
    Elijah 90*
    Elsea 44*
    Epaphious 92
    Ezra 78
    Ira 58
    Jacob 43*
    Joseph 25*
    Oliver 168
    Orville P. 89
    Samuel 89
    Simon 99*
    Thomas 77

Looveland,
    Abner 175
    S. H. 175

Lorance,
    William 166
    William H. 166

Loraway,
    Philip 100
    Phipps 100

Lord,
    Abigail 7
    Anna 55
    Caroline 39
    Daminicus 4*
    Daniel 19
    Elizabeth 3*
    Frederick 49*
    Hannah 4*
    Ichabod 178*
    Jesse 82
    John 4
    Polly 15
    Samuel 4*, 60*, 124*
    Thomas 18*
    Wentworth 3*
    William 92*

Loree,
    Job 110*

Lorentz,
    Ann E. 128
    Ann Elizabeth 128

Loring,
    Lydia 30
    Solomon 54*
    Thomas 44

Lorring,
    Theophilus 16

Losee,
    Abraham 36

Losell,
    John 57
    Lydia 57

Losey,
    Abraham 76*
    William 174*

Lothrop,
    Solomon 27*

Lott,
    John 87, 109*

Loud,
    Anna 32
    David 31*
    Sylvanus 32
    William 32

Loudon,
    John 93*

Loudy,
    Theophilus 142

Lougee,
    John 16*
    Jonathan 66*
    Mary 17

Louk,
    Margaret 94*

Loundsberry,
    James 87
    Nathan M. 69
    William 87

Lounsbury,
    Ebenezer 103*
    Prudence 52

Lourey,
    Thomas 161*

Loury,
    Jacob 123

Louther,
    Joel 168

Louthworth,
    Massa 55

Love,
    Charles 177*
    Henry 172
    James 157*
    John 141*
    Levi 76
    Lovey 147
    Robert 76, 135*, 138*
    Thomas 147
    Thomas C. 80*

Lovejoy,
    Abner 74
    Almond 74
    Andrew 103
    Daniel 70*
    Lydia 21
    Samuel 21
    Stephen 21
    William 21

Lovelace,
    Nancy B. 164

Lovelady,
    Thomas 136

Loveland,
    Amos 179
    Daniel 179
    Fredrick 172*
    George 67
    R. 67

Lovelass,
    David 125*

Loveless,
    Gershom 109*

Lovell,
    Jacob 29
    Mary 36, 45
    Olive 29
    Ruth 29
    Silvanus 30

Lovering,
    Ebenezer 15*

Lovin,
    Edmund 153
    James 153

Loving,
    Simeon 29*

Lovis,
    John 19

Low,
    A. 96
    Aaron 42
    Abraham 74, 96
    Alvin C. 97

Low, (cont.)
    Betty 43
    E. 43
    Hannah 103*
    Henry 136*
    Jacob G. 91*
    John 182*
    Lydia 97
    Mary 8, 45*
    Robert 7
    Simon 20*
    Thomas 66*
    Warren 42
    William 113

Lowcy,
    Jesse 123*

Lowden,
    Daniel 68*

Lowe,
    Abraham 72
    Barton 170*
    Basil 142*
    Charlotte 37
    Dennis 142
    James L. 72
    John 41*

Lowell,
    Benjamin B. 10
    Ezra 24
    John 10
    Olive 23*
    Thomas 11*

Lowery,
    Levi 146*

Lowry,
    Thornton 130*
    Jacob 123
Loyd,
    Alexander 93
    John 64
    Martin 44
    Thompson C. 160*
    William 59

Lucado,
    Isaac 130
    Littlebury 130

Lucas,
Basil 134*
Betsey 28, 29
Charles 29
David 125
George 125
George W. 26*
Jerima 28
John 17
Mary 135, 149
Reubah 28
Sally 17
Wilson 135

Luce,
Anna 26
Ivory 82*
Joshua 61
Leverett 61
Mehitable 26*
Nathaniel 57*
Shubael 26
Thomas 26*
Uriah 93

Luck,
John 139*

Luckey,
Hugh 158*

Lucus,
Isaac 120
John 120

Ludden,
Samuel 31*

Luddington,
Jesse 52

Luddon,
Enos 74*

Ludington,
Jason 44
Naomi 44

Ludlow,
John 108
Margaret 108

Ludwick,
Elizabeth 116*

Ludwig,
Samuel 113

Luffman,
John 104
Thomas 104

Lufkin,
Benjamin 7
Moses 41*

Luke,
Cheney 83
Daniel 71
Jonathan 71
Samuel 83

Lull,
Mary 21
Moses 21

Lum,
Jesse 121*

Lumbard,
Emery 8
Hannah 8

Lumberton,
James 35

Lumbnot,
Mary 30

Lumley,
William 189*

Lumpkin,
Joseph 138
Moore 132*
Robert 184*
Wilson 131

Lumpkins,
John G. 188*

Lumsden,
John 138*

Lund,
Hosea 24
Stephen 24

Lunduz,
Asahel 33*

Lunn,
Thomas 174

Lunshum,
John 116

Lunt,
A. F. 28
Daniel 5*
Hannah 42
John 6*
Moses 65
William 48*

Luscombe,
Samuel 82

Luther,
Aaron 27
Allen 49
Benjamin 49
Elisha 93
Elizabeth 140*
Frederick 49
Josias L. 45
Martin 49*
Mary 64
Moses 64
Philip 99
Samuel 49
Stephen 27*
Sylvester 49
Thomas 45
Waity 46
Zadoc 46

Lutrell,
Michael 187

Luty,
Catharine 113

Lutz,
Peter 84

Lyans,
Mercy 99

Lydston,
John 4

Lye,
Ann 43*

Lyford,
C. L. 7
Fifield 63*

Lyle,
John 149
William W. 112

Lyles,
David 156

Lyman,
Eleazer 100
Elisha 53
Ezekiel 84
Giles 35, 85*
Johanna 59
Martin 60
Mary 60
Mehitable 64
Philomela 65
Richard 64
Thomas 35

Lynch,
William 127*

Lynds,
Aaron P. 71
Hannah 71

Lynes,
David 96
Samuel 96

Lynn,
David 188
Dewalt 121*
James 148*
John 90*
Samuel 188

Lyon,
Aaron 75
Chloe 87
Daniel 119
Elan 9
Eliphaz 87
Isaac 30
Jacob 58, 141*
James 172
Johanna 108*
John 110
Joseph 108*
Joshua 56*
Lydia 30
Moses 79
Naomi 110
Nehemiah 56
Nehemiah W. 56
R. 77
Richard 79
Stephen 108*
Thomas 31*, 104
William F. 194*

Lyons,
Isaac 103
Mary 103
Samuel 170*
William 164

McAdam,
    William 187

McAdams,
    James 186
    John 157*
    Joseph 186

McAdew,
    Andrew 127*

McAffee,
    Benjamin 126*

McAlexander,
    Alexander 132

McAlister,
    Reuben 71*
    Richard 12*

McAllister,
    William 152*

McAlvin,
    William 20*

McArthur,
    Peter 81*

McBee,
    Israel 152*

McBride,
    John 138*

McCain,
    Harrison 144

McCaine,
    James 120*

McCalister,
    Daniel 166*

Macalister,
    John 140*

McCall,
    Charles S. 158
    Lycurgus 158
    Samuel 120*

McCalla,
    Joseph 163

McCalla, (cont.)
    Thomas 163

McCammon,
    Matthew 185

McCan,
    James 136

McCann,
    James 166
    Patrick 162*

McCargo,
    Radford 189*

McCarter,
    James 149*
    Robert 100

McCarton,
    James 132

McCarty,
    Daniel 105, 165*
    Michael 149*
    Stephen 105

McCaskill,
    Kenneth 151*

McCaslin,
    Alexander 13*
    John 155
    William 98

McCather,
    Duncan 126

McCauly,
    Isabel 19
    James 19
    John 136*

McCausland,
    Mary 10*
    Thomas 10

McChesany,
    Abigail 92
    J. A. 92

McClain,
    Abijah 119*
    William 177*

McClain, (cont.)
    William H. 115

McClanan,
    Samuel 45*

McClanen,
    Thomas 117*

McClary,
    Benjamin 100*
    James 181
    Sarah 20

McClehany,
    James 160*

McClelan,
    Joseph 182*

McClelland,
    Anna M. 125
    Carey 174
    James 170*
    Peter 125

McClenden,
    Jesse 151
    Shadrach 151

McClerken,
    Thomas 188*

McClerkin,
    Matthew 185*

McCleskey,
    James 145*

McClintock,
    Eleanor 44
    Hugh 165*
    Tryphena 44

McCloud,
    Anguish 26
    John 67*
    Samuel 176*

McClung,
    John 157*
    Joseph 180*

McClure,
    Alexander 135

McClure, (cont.)
    Andrew 118*
    John 143*
    Manly 20
    Martha 20, 23
    Mehitable 16
    Samuel 23
    Thomas 137

McClurg,
    Robert 179
    Samuel J. 179

McCohan,
    Thomas B. 177

McCollans,
    Daniel 146

McColler,
    Alexander 159
    Alexander N. 159

McColley,
    Samuel 152

McCollough,
    James 117

McConell,
    Joseph 161*

McConnel,
    Ware 25*

McConnell,
    Edward 160*
    Emanuel 156*
    James 148*
    William 133

McCorcle,
    Archibald 159*

McCord,
    William 183

McCormack,
    Joseph R. 148*
    Rebecca 166
    Robert 152
    Thomas 147*

McCormahay,
    John 128*

McCormick,
    Dennis 81
    James 190
    Sarah 77

McCornent,
    John 185*

McCosklin,
    Andrew 149*

McCown,
    Susan 165*

McCoy,
    Daniel 157
    E. 98
    John 98, 106*, 153
    Jonathan 19
    Rachel 118
    Redden 142*
    Robert 118, 152*
    Samuel 145*
    Sarah 171
    Stephen 19
    William 75*, 85, 153, 182*

McCrackin,
    John 118

McCravy,
    John 148

McCraw,
    Sarah 134

McCrory,
    James 149
    Robert 149

McCroskey,
    John 154*

McCubbin,
    N. 140
    Nicholas 140

McCuffe,
    Pompey 57*

McCuller,
    Chloe 174

McCullock,
    Alexander 158

McCullock, (cont.)
    Andrew 121
    James 33*
    Robert 90*

McCullough,
    Ann G. 101
    James 135
    John 120*
    Joseph 135

McCully,
    John 184

McCumber,
    Joseph 178*

McCume,
    Joseph 183

McCune,
    James 173
    Thomas 173

McCurdy,
    Archibald 137*

McCure,
    Samuel 186*

McCutcheon,
    Frederick 24
    George 99*

McCutchin,
    James 133

McCutchin,
    John 133, 155*

McDadde,
    John 145

McDaffee,
    John 17

McDaniel,
    Edward 169*
    James 153*
    Susannah 4

McDarmit,
    Daniel 117
    Joseph 117

McDerment,
    Joseph 148

McDill,
    James 144
    John 144

McDonald,
    Campbell 176*
    Charles 104*
    Hugh 194
    Jacob 117
    James 152*
    James A. 95*
    John 5, 105, 142*, 149, 162*, 194
    Joseph 120*
    Peltiah 6*

McDonell,
    James 148*

McDonough,
    Andrew 152
    Ann 152
    Francis 181

McDormat,
    William 110

McDormit,
    Michael 182*

McDougal,
    Malcom 189

McDougle,
    Alexander 178
    John A. 178

McDowel,
    Daniel 75*

McDowell,
    James 162
    John 115*
    John L. 162
    R. 144
    Robert 144

McDuffin,
    David 11*

McDugle,
    Alexander 119*, 163

McEithan,
    John 137

McElhany,
    Felix 171*

McElhenny,
    Samuel 144
    Stephen 144*

McElroy,
    John 173*

McElwel,
    John 144*

McElyea,
    Patrick 155
    William 186*

McEntire,
    Charles 134

McEvers,
    Louisa 188
    Seneca 188

McEwen,
    John 55

McFadden,
    George 194
    James 181

McFallen,
    James 102

McFalls,
    David D. 157

McFarland,
    Sarah 41

McFarlen,
    James 45*

McFarlin,
    James 65

McFerren,
    Samuel 159

McFerrin,
    William 159

McFladden,
    Manassa 120*

McGaughy,
    Samuel 148*

McGavock,
    Hugh 136*

McGaw,
    William 124*

McGee,
    Henry 117
    Margaret (Mrs.) 117
    Mary 109
    Samuel 102*
    Thomas 136
    William 109

McGhee,
    William 187*

McGill,
    Harvey 153
    Hugh 97, 124*
    James 153
    Martha 5*

McGlassen,
    Nancy 164*

McGlaughlin,
    James 119

McGlotholin,
    John 136*

McGown,
    Stephen 93*

McGowns,
    Edward 27

McGrann,
    Elizabeth 113

McGregor,
    Alexander 85
    James L. 169
    Joel 23

McGriger,
    James 118

McGuigan,
    Nancy 75

McGuin,
    Samuel 19

McGuire,
    Allegany 159
    Barney 85*
    Halladay 159
    Hugh 79
    John 169

McHatton,
    James 166*

McHenry,
    James 191
    John 191
    William 122*

McIlroy,
    James 160
    William B. 160

McInally,
    Jonah 148*

McIntire,
    Jacob 20*
    Jesse 43
    John 26*, 65
    Mary 46
    Reuben 65
    Thomas 110
    William 110

McIntosh,
    Jeremiah 31*
    Thomas 167
    Timothy 100*
    William 83*, 142*, 150

McInturff,
    John 152

McIntyre,
    Alpheus 179*
    Heman 32
    Robert 182

McJemkin,
    Major Joseph 143*

McKay,
    Thomas 144*
    William J. 190

McKeddy,
        Thomas 154
        William 154

McKee,
        Elizabeth 50*
        James 158*
        John 117, 162*
        Samuel 165*
        Thomas 117

McKeen,
        Hugh 73
        John 23*
        S. 73
        Samuel 23, 94*

McKeeven,
        Catharine 134
        Elizabeth 134

McKenney,
        Edmund 141*
        Jonathan 6
        Rufus 3
        Sarah 3
        Solomon 10

McKenny,
        Isaac 13
        Jonathan 6
        Joseph 10

McKensey,
        James 152
        William 152

McKenzie,
        George 99*
        James 178*
        John 158*
        Mary 72
        William 72

McKillip,
        A. 93
        Archibald 93

McKinlay,
        Alexander 81
        Sarah 81

McKinney,
        John S. 8

McKinney, (cont.)
        Margaret 8
        Peter 120*

McKinny,
        Edmund 141*
        James 106

McKinstry,
        Amos 67
        George 67
        Paul 82
        Porter 82

McKnight,
        Adam 171*
        Benjamin 136
        Emos 157
        Robert 85*
        William 191*

McKown,
        John 135*
        William 93

McKoy,
        James 133
        James C. 133

McLain,
        John 147*

McLane,
        Arthur 127
        David 189*
        John 71*
        Thomas 147*

McLaughlin,
        David 94
        Hannah 6*
        James 134
        John 140
        Lydia 23
        Robert 140

McLaughlon,
        Stephen 153*

McLayne,
        Henry 132*

McLean,
        James 50

McLean, (cont.)
　　John 127*
　　Ogden 50

McLeary,
　　Michael 139*

McLellan,
　　John 6*
　　William 5*

McLellen,
　　John 11

McLemore,
　　John 153
　　William 153

McLeod,
　　Abner 152*
　　Malcom 137
　　William 139*

McLewin,
　　John 101
　　W. F. 101

McLinn,
　　Frederic 190*

McMahan,
　　Archibald 143*
　　Peter 143*

McMahon,
　　Peter 127*

McManis,
　　John 181

McManners,
　　John 168*

McMannus,
　　Daniel 5*
　　John 5

McManus,
　　Christopher 76*

McMikle,
　　John 106*

McMillan,
　　James 91

McMillan, (cont.)
　　Rowly 185*

McMillen,
　　John 171*

McMillion,
　　Elizabeth 44

McMillon,
　　M. S. 188*

McMurphy,
　　Alexander 23
　　Daniel 23

McMurry,
　　John 144*

McMurtry,
　　John 157*

McNabb,
　　Elizabeth 153
　　William 153

McNair,
　　A. 124
　　Archibald 124
　　Robert 101

McNally,
　　Arthur 9
　　Michael 9

McNamara,
　　James 124*

McNary,
　　Hugh 188
　　James 188

McNatt,
　　James 140*

McNatt,
　　John 154*

McNeal,
　　Abigail 17
　　Jacob 130*
　　Neal 83

McNear,
　　John 194*

McNeely,
    John 140*

McNeil,
    Lucy 20
    Solomon 20

McNelly,
    Mary 73*
    Peter 183

McNey,
    John 118*

McNichols,
    Ann 116

McNiel,
    Henry 88*

McNish,
    Sarah 100
    William 100

McNitt,
    John 77*

McNorton,
    Patrick 151*

McNott,
    Charles 156
    John 156

McNutt,
    Alexander 172

McPeeters,
    Charles 141
    Jonathan 141

McPeters,
    Joseph 154*

McPherrin,
    Clark 120*

McPherson,
    James 138
    Mark 164*
    Mary E. 131
    Matthew 138

McPheters,
    Andrew 184*

McPike,
    John 168*

McQuiddy,
    John 167*

McQuigg,
    Daniel 99

McReynolds,
    John 148
    Joseph 184*

McRight,
    William 145*

McRoberts,
    Andrew 185
    James 187*

McSpadden,
    Samuel 153
    Thomas 153

McVaugh,
    John 116*

McVey,
    John 193
    William 183

McWherter,
    James 143*

McWhorter,
    Benjamin 144
    George 139*
    Henry 134

McWilliams,
    George 124
    John 124, 133
    Samuel 123*

Maberry,
    George 149*

Mabgly,
    Robert 150
    Varder 150

Mabie,
    Cornelius 106

Mabon,
    Jeanette 167

Mabry,
    John 167*

Mace,
    Andrew 10*
    Moulton 21
    Samuel 71

Mack,
    Abraham 100
    Archibald 67*
    John 100
    Mary 60
    Nicholas 116
    Richard 185*

Mackey,
    Benjamin 119*

Macomber,
    Elijah 27*
    John 62*
    Josiah 27
    Sylvester 87
    Venus 27

Macomeson,
    John 145*

Macvin,
    Hannah 56

Madcaff,
    David 6

Madden,
    David 76
    Elizabeth 162
    Esther 192
    Jeremiah 162

Maddin,
    John 12

Madding,
    Daniel 159
    Francis 159

Maddocks,
    Samuel 13*

Maddox,
    Delilah 166
    Jacob 153*
    John 130*, 165*

Madill,
    David 177

Madison,
    Jesse J. 98
    William 129*, 131*

Madlock,
    Jacob 116

Maffett,
    Elizabeth 130
    John A. 130

Magars,
    George 62*

Magdalena,
    Mary 131

Magee,
    John 93*
    Ralph 164*

Maggot,
    Henry 154*

Magoon,
    Edward 63
    Edward M. 63
    John 68*
    Josiah 18

Magoun,
    Joshua 30*

Mahappy,
    Andrew 173
    John 173

Mahew,
　　Peter V.　65

Mahony,
　　Huldat　45

Maiden,
　　Lawrence　139

Mailick,
　　John　134*

Main,
　　David　54*
　　Perris　171*
　　Sandford　54

Maine,
　　Ezekiel　119*
　　William　9

Mains,
　　David　154

Mairs,
　　Lewis　111

Maize,
　　Samuel　110

Major,
　　Samuel　130*

Majors,
　　Elisha　189
　　John　189
　　Robert　155*

Makepiece,
　　William　31

Malarkey,
　　Daniel　120*

Male,
　　Wilmore　134*

Malett,
　　Isaac　159

Mallard,
　　John　71

Mallby,
　　Degrasse　52

Mallery,
　　David　59*

Mallet,
　　Miles　52*
　　Thomas　8

Mallett,
　　Ann　55*
　　Isaac　9
　　William　9

Mallison,
　　Roswell　79*

Mallory,
　　Edward E　52
　　Gill　90
　　Henry H.　148
　　James　74
　　Joel　90
　　John　130*, 148
　　Lemuel　184*
　　M.　74
　　Nathaniel　122

Malone,
　　Cornelius　148*
　　Francis　185
　　Joseph　185
　　William　148*

Malory,
　　Benajah　88*

Malpas,
　　James　139

Mamsel,
　　John　70

Man,
　　David　61
　　Grace　45*

Manby,
　　Roswell　178

Manchester,
　　Abraham　47*
　　Barzilla　27
　　Elias　75*
　　Ephraim　47
　　Esther　47
　　Giles　47*

Manchester, (cont.)
    Margaret 47
    Nabby 46
    Nathaniel 89
    Nehemiah 46
    Phebe 47
    Stephen 89*

Mandell,
    Abigail 37
    Martin 37

Mandigo,
    Archibald 102
    Jeremiah 102

Mane,
    William 75*

Mangam,
    John 150*

Manis,
    Seth 153*

Mankins,
    William 170

Manley,
    Addison 83

Manly,
    Elizabeth 68
    William 68

Mann,
    Andrew 60, 88
    Anna 46
    Billie 66
    Ebenezer 37*
    Harriet N. 101
    John 115*, 182*
    Jonas 90
    Joseph 60*
    Martha 20*
    Mary 30*
    Mehitable 38
    Nathan 82, 140*
    Patience 30
    Phebe 46
    Robert 11*
    Sarah 46
    William 38

Manning,
    Abigail 35
    Andrew 61
    Gamaliel 57
    Isaac 108*
    Joel 68
    John 33*
    Joseph 69
    Lathrop 61
    Mansur 57
    Mary 57
    Sarah 21, 57
    Seabry 57
    Thomas 170*
    William 40*, 68

Manow,
    David 150

Manross,
    Elisha 51
    Martha 51

Mansell,
    Joseph 11*

Mansfield,
    Amos 62*
    George 133*
    Martha 66
    Mary 43*

Mansir,
    Nathaniel R. 39

Manteath,
    Samuel 139*

Manton,
    Catharine 46*
    Jeremiah 46*

Manuel,
    Christopher 141*

Mapes,
    Elijah 76
    John 108*
    Joseph 171*
    William 76

Maple,
    Stephen 118*
    William 119*

Maples,
    Charles G. 75
    Jonah 75
    Marmaduke 139*

Maps,
    Zebel 110

Marble,
    Henry 38*
    Jabez 37
    Joel 37
    Lydia 34
    P. C. 95
    Sally 21
    Samuel 13

Marcellus,
    Garrett 85*

March,
    Matthias 5*
    Newhall P. 11
    William 11

Marcum,
    Josiah 164

Marcy,
    Elizabeth 70*
    Paul 34
    Stephen 91*

Marden,
    Ann 16*
    David 17
    James 17

Marical,
    Christian 118*

Marion,
    Samuel 135*

Mariquot,
    Jacob 103*

Mark,
    Susanna 79*

Markham,
    Asa 81*
    Elizabeth 32
    John 60*

Markham, (cont.)
    L. 148
    Lewis 148
    Samuel 44

Markhams,
    Isaac 99*

Markle,
    Jacob P. 103*

Marks,
    Abigail 103*
    Hezekiah 103

Marler,
    John 141*

Marlow,
    George 131

Marquest,
    Samuel 184

Marr,
    Lydia 3

Mars,
    Mary 93

Marsa,
    Thomas 164

Marsden,
    John 123*

Marsh,
    Betsey 21
    Daniel 22*
    Deliverence 36
    Enos 34
    Henry 70, 158*
    Hiram 21
    Jacob 21
    Jasper 76*
    John 93*
    Joseph C. 78*
    Lois 45
    Lot 29*
    Lucius 34
    Lucretia 84
    Mabel 50
    Marcus 50
    Michael 43

Martin, (cont.)
    Stephen 132
    Thomas 105*, 167
    Ward 99
    William 25*, 65, 134*, 156*
    William L. 118

Martindale,
    Ebenezer 82*
    James 172*
    Stephen 68*
    Theodore 33
    Uriah 33

Martine,
    Daniel 106

Martling,
    Abraham 104*
    Abraham B. 101*

Marton,
    Andrew 168

Marts,
    William 180*

Martyn,
    Richard 65

Marven,
    Patrick 163*

Marvin,
    Benjamin 95
    Clarissa 78
    Hiram 78
    James 58
    Ozias 88*
    Stephen 62
    Timothy 95

Mash,
    Edmund 25
    John 58*
    Newton 25

Mason,
    A. 87
    Aaron 7
    Abigail 18
    Alexander 28*
    Ashbel 87
    Benjamin M. 18

Mason,
    Caleb 155
    Calvin 168
    Deborah 24
    E. 92
    Ebenezer 10*, 100
    Elijah 58
    Elisha 58*, 176
    Eunice 7
    John 149*
    Joseph 58
    L. 73
    Luther 73
    Lydia 22
    Mary 92
    Michael 100
    Nathan 168
    Noah 106*
    Pardon 45*
    Patrick 131*
    Peter 183
    Philip 121, 140
    Rufus 80*
    Samuel B. 18
    Simeon 36
    Simon 20
    Thomas 164*, 183
    Tilley 13
    William 17, 139*, 183

Massey,
    Edmund 164

Massman,
    Aaron 9
    Memik 9*

Masten,
    Abraham 103

Masters,
    Enoch 137*
    James 124
    William 118

Mastin,
    Ezekiel 103
    Jacob 103*

Maston,
    Exekiel 103

Matfield,
    Chester 52

Matha,
Samuel 56*

Matheny,
Peter 158
William 158

Mather,
Caroline 93*
Huldah 66
John 76
Joseph 76
Nathaniel 75*
Reuben 83
Rufus 66

Mathers,
Sally 15

Mathews,
Desire 10
Hardy 137*
Isaac 146
James 10
Loisa Ann 85
Marty G. 142
Milton 146
Nancy 129*
Samuel 129*
William 146*

Mathewson,
Abigail 46
E. 126
Elizabeth 126
John 47
Lydia 47
Mathias 142
Otis 46

Matkins,
James 137
John 137

Matlock,
George 153
Henry 153*
Richard 153

Matteson,
Ashahel 48
Benjamin A. 48
Cory 48
D. J. 76

Matteson, (cont.)
Dorcas 48
Henry A. 48
Jesse 77
Jonathan 84
Lucy 48
Phebe 48
Rhoda 48
Richard 46
Rufus 48
Samuel 84
Sarah 76
Stephen 48*
Susanna 48
Thankful 77

Matthew,
Isaac 136*

Matthews,
Amos 161
Amos V. 161
Asahel 37
Benjamin 76, 148*
Caleb 76
John 110*
Joseph 57
Nathan 57
Philip 144*
Sarah 20
Thomas 20, 76

Matthewson,
Betty 46
Charles 23
Horace 23

Matthias,
Elizabeth 116

Mattice,
Adam 96

Mattis,
Christian 114*

Mattison,
Andrew 41*
Dyer 87*
Samuel 82*
Stephen 186
Thomas 186

Mattocks,
Peter 124*

Matton,
    William 127

Mattoon,
    Ebenezer 35

Mattox,
    Ebenezer 175*

Mattsly,
    Benjamin 180
    Daniel 180

Mauck,
    Henry 135

Maul,
    Jacob 104*
    Jacob J. 104
    John 104

Maupin,
    William 128*

Maurer,
    Peter 113

Mauton,
    Joseph P. 10

Mauzy,
    Peter 162*

Mavier,
    Silas 178

Mawin,
    David 56

Maxam,
    Adonijah 59
    Clark 59

Maxcy,
    Joel 188*

Maxen,
    Leah 110
    William 110

Maxfield,
    Alexander 44
    Daniel 11*
    Daniel P. 20

Maxfield, (cont.)
    Reuben 6
    Rhoda 20
    Richard 20*
    Robert 6

Maxham,
    Esther 78

Maxon,
    John 182*
    Phinehas 97
    Torrey 23*

Maxson,
    John 78
    Stephen 86*
    Zacheus 73

Maxwell,
    James 119
    John 159*, 186
    Priscilla 24
    Robert 5*
    William 5*

May,
    Calvin 21
    Deborah 38
    Eleazer 37*
    Elisha 66
    Eunice 23, 87
    Hepzibah 6
    John 23, 140*
    Luke 86
    Major 157
    Rebecca 50
    Sally 86
    Samuel 36
    Stephen 66
    Sylvester 50
    Thomas 159*
    William 154*, 157

Mayberry,
    William 6*

Maybin,
    Matthew 138*

Maybourn,
    John 155

Mayers,
    Samuel 157*

Mayfield,
    Elijah 156*
    Sutherland 166*
    William 191

Mayhew,
    Ann 115
    Enoch 115
    Hannah 34
    J. B. 29
    James 11*

Maynadier,
    Henry 127*

Maynard,
    A. F. 53
    Ebenezer 53
    Joseph 13*
    Lebues 53
    Lemuel 74*
    Needham 96
    Samuel 20

Maynerd,
    Jabez 60*

Mayo,
    Axom 146
    Eunice 26
    John 146
    Stephen 130*

Mays,
    Elizabeth 47*

Meach,
    Jacob 54*

Meacham,
    Chloe 93*
    Elijah 135*

Mead,
    Amos 99*
    Benjamin 37
    Betsey 22
    Bradley 22
    David 73, 105
    Eli 85
    Eli B. 185
    Eliza 22*
    Ezra 56*
    James 75*

Mead, (cont.)
    Jeremiah 56
    John 185
    Jonathan 101
    Jotham 85*
    Lewis 111*
    Marthall S. 34
    Samuel 135*
    Sarah 23, 73
    Seeley 56
    Seth 56
    Smith 56
    Stephen 174*
    Thaddeus 56
    Thomas 56*
    Tilby 37*
    Uriah 56*, 97
    William 37

Meade,
    William 134

Meador,
    Jason 144*

Meadowes,
    Barbara 161*

Meadows,
    Green 135
    James 136*
    Jane 187
    John 147
    Joseph 147
    Josiah 135
    William 187

Meanon,
    David 121

Means,
    James 12*

Meares,
    (Mrs.) 163

Mears,
    Russell 40

Medbury,
    Martha 47

Medlin,
    Bradley 159

Meeder,
    Edward S. 66*

Meek,
    Alexander 150*

Meeker,
    Ambrose 180
    Comfort 77
    Cory 120*
    Elijah 77
    Ichabod 77
    Joseph 55
    Michael 108*
    Sarah 108
    Silas 55
    Zadock 108

Meeks,
    Basil 188*
    John 131*

Meers,
    Moses 163

Mefford,
    Jacob 161*

Megee,
    John 164*
    Sylvester 127

Megerle,
    Philip 189

Meggs,
    Mary 143*

Mehaffy,
    Samuel 124

Mehornay,
    Benjamin 184
    Owen 184

Meigs,
    Daniel B. 62*
    Isaac 52
    Mabel 52

Meily,
    Martin 114*

Melendy,
    John 63*

Melendy, (cont.)
    Luther 20
    Thomas 20

Mellen,
    Thomas 65*

Melott,
    Prater 169
    Theodore 169

Melton,
    Benjamin 187*
    Robert 147
    William 147, 187

Melvin,
    Jonathan 91*

Menard,
    Daniel 70

Mendenhall,
    Joseph 119*

Mendum,
    Anna 4
    William 4

Mengle,
    Adam 115

Menkler,
    Herman 102

Menow,
    Margaret 6

Mentzer,
    Japhet 175

Merack,
    Moses 137
    Tabitha 137

Meraman,
    Marcus 51*

Merb,
    Josiah 8*

Mercellis,
    Catharine 96*

Merchant,
    Joel 56*

Merchant, (cont.)
>Joseph 88*
>Samuel 59
>Tabitha 59

Merchants,
>Joseph 34*

Meredith,
>Henry 142*
>John W. 177*
>Samuel 182*
>Thomas 120, 182

Meriam,
>David 69
>John 37*, 100
>Joseph 37*

Merick,
>John 128
>William 128

Meriman,
>Mary 50

Merit,
>Ensign 8
>Mary 8
>William 14*

Merrell,
>Elijah F. 52
>Sarah 52

Merriam,
>Amasa 52*
>John 84
>S. S. 69
>Samuel S. 69

Merrick,
>Constant 22*
>John 149*

Merril,
>Roger 10*

Merrill,
>Abner 14*
>Anna 23*
>Annis 25*
>Asa 90*
>Daniel 140*

Merrill, (cont.)
>David 23
>Ebenezer 65
>Enoch 11
>Enos 87
>Eunice 18
>Ezekiel 103
>Hugh 116
>Ira 86
>Jacob 4*
>James 95*
>Jared 53*
>John 5, 9, 81
>Martha 40
>Mead 79
>Nathan L. 9
>Sally 81
>Simeon 100*
>True 24

Merrills,
>Hosea 33*
>Nathaniel 59*

Merriman,
>Anne 59
>George 78
>George F. 59
>Israel 86
>Lois 51*

Merrit,
>George 113
>John 53
>Polly 113
>William 140*

Merritt,
>Amos 36*
>Ann 110
>Daniel 141*
>Ezekiel 87*
>Hannah 55
>Molly 88
>Noah 68*
>Stephen 160*

Merry,
>Cornelius 183*
>Rose 130

Merserell,
>Abraham 109

Miles, (cont.)
James 98
Joel 22
John 135*
Levi 79*
Lucinda 52
Mercy 53
Noah 22
Patterson 157
Samuel 59
Thomas 128*
William 122

Milford,
Thomas 142*

Miliken,
John 12

Milikin,
Samuel 92

Millard,
Joseph 51*
Leavitt 60*
M. 32
Samuel 86*
Stephen 101*

Miller,
Abijah 90
Abner 105*
Abraham 77, 168
Ada 85*
Adam 154*
Alexander 99
Alva 89
Andrew 116*
Ann 132
Barney 185
Benjamin 119*, 150, 183
Bethiah 27*
Christian 112, 127*
Clark 108*
David 187
Dennis 69
Ebenezer 58*
Edward 166
Eliakim 89
Elizabeth 105
Elsa 119
Enoch 108*
Ephraim 95
Eunice 49
Eve 106

Miller, (cont.)
Francis 187
Frank 8
Frederick 114, 158*
George 8, 63, 122*
Giles 81
Harry 62
Henry 185*
Hiram 182
Isaac 22, 44
J. B. 157
Jacob 95, 154, 163*, 178
James 8, 49*, 164, 183
James B. 164
Jason 86
Jefferson 158
Jemima 104
Jeremiah 102
Jesse 44
John 50, 86, 105, 112, 114*
115, 152*, 161*
John A. 184*
John B. 157
John H. 157*
Joseph 110*, 133, 135
Joseph B. 75*
Joseph P. 119
Joshua 5
Judith 189
Leisure 102
Lemuel 4*
Leonard 150
Levi 93
Luke 110*
M. 115
Mark 158
Michael 187
Mordecai 184
Moses 65
Nathan 48
Nathaniel 80*
Nicholas 185
Noah 12*
Peter 81
Phebe 65
Philip 136*
Robert 166
Rosanna 50
Roswell 51*
Samuel 104*, 133, 135
Samuel J. 132
Solomon S. 62
Stephen 154
Thomas 173, 189
Valentine 118*

Millet,
    James 41*
    John 4*

Millikan,
    William 33*

Milliken,
    John 12
    Lydia 6
    Margaret 6
    Sewall 6

Millikin,
    Adams 23
    James 166

Milliner,
    A. 79
    Alexander 79

Mills,
    Andrew 7
    Banajah 87
    Catherine 55
    Cephas 44*
    Ebenezer A. 168
    Francis 135*
    James R. 18*
    Jane 39
    John H. 188*
    Jonathan 105
    Karen Hapuck 145
    Morgan 149*
    Nabby 33
    Peter 73*
    Samuel 61*
    Samuel D. 106*
    Samuel J. 84*
    Sarah 18
    Soloman 56*
    Stephen 99*, 104
    William 45*
    William S. 39

Millun,
    William 143*

Milner,
    Beverly 173*

Milton,
    Alexander 150
    Nathaniel 154*

Milum,
    Jerdon 156*

Miner,
    Daniel 187
    James 63*, 102
    Jeremiah 166*
    John 170*
    Joseph 53*
    Rachel 23*
    Rhoda 53
    Samuel 59
    Seth 53*
    Thomas 102

Mings,
    Joseph 187

Mink,
    John C. 8*

Minor,
    David 98
    Isaac 26*
    Jedediah 98
    Sylvanus 80
    T. 129*

Minter,
    Mary 132*

Minthorn,
    Walter S. 126*

Minyard,
    John 163
    Richard 163

Mires,
    Francis 109
    John 109

Misner,
    Henry 187*·

Mitchel,
    Abigail 17
    Amos 172
    Day 41*
    Eli 55
    Ingram 182*
    Nazra 140*
    Samuel 17
    Thomas 80*
    William 157*

Mitchell,
A. 148
Alexander 183
Alice 19
Ammi 7*
Benjamin 8
Charles 166
Edward 109
Elijah 177
Elizabeth 47
Eve 169
Frederick A. 20
George K. 163*
Gideon 166
Hepsebah 97
Horatio 97
Isaac 97*
Jacob 109
James 120, 157*
James M. 8
Jesse 148*
John 76*, 167*
John B. 62*, 142
Joseph 19, 47
Nancy 180*
Pammey 8*
Robert 131*
Sarah 49
William 74, 145*, 148, 189*

Mitchill,
John 181*

Mittan,
John 181

Mix,
Amny 49*
Amos 126, 176*
Hiram 126
Jeremiah 138
Jesse 64*
Josiah 178
Ransom 52*
Samuel R. 178

Mixer,
Grant 84
Samuel 84

Mixter,
Daniel 44

Moffit,
Judah 69*

Moffitt,
Eli 98*

Mohler,
Casper 175*

Mohorn,
John 131*

Moke,
John 127

Molsbey,
William 153*

Molton,
Prudence 69
William 23

Moncam,
John 64*

Money,
Jacob 120
John 137

Monk,
Anna 91
Christopher 91
Elias 7
James 139*
John 84*

Monn,
Timothy 31

Monro,
John 52

Monroe,
Abraham 89*
Alexander 183
George 153
Isaac 40
John L. 27*
Joseph 104*
Joshua 99*
Sereny 140
Susanna 56*
William 136*

Monson,
A. E. 51
Eneas 51

Moore, (cont.)
    Zephaniah S. 66

Moores,
    David 10*

Moorhead,
    Joseph 122

Mooring,
    John 137*

Moors,
    Abraham 20
    Hubbard 22
    Isaac A. 20
    Jonathan 6
    Joseph 22, 83*
    Michael 160
    Relief 6
    Savil 89*
    Silas 160
    Timothy 20*

Moran,
    Alexander 101

Moray,
    Charles 95

Morcon,
    Sybel 38

More,
    Andrew W. 98
    Asa 76
    Eli 144
    Henry 79
    John 162, 171*
    Joseph 173
    Joseph R. 76
    Sally 162

Morehead,
    John 165
    Rebecca 165
    Walter 143
    William 143

Morehouse,
    Abraham 55*
    Ann 55*

Moreland,
    Charles 152

Moreland, (cont.)
    Moses 118*
    Wright 152

Mores,
    Hannah 84
    Levi 84

Morey,
    Daniel 28
    Israel 24*
    Joseph 114
    Katharine 171
    Sarah 28
    Thomas 65
    William 13

Morford,
    Noah 107*

Morgan,
    Abigail 61
    Andrew 38*
    Asa 19*
    Benjamin 155*
    Charles 54, 61
    Cooning 89
    Daniel 60*, 172
    Desire 54
    E. H. 175
    Elias 80
    Erastus 44*
    Evan 135*
    Ezra 20
    George 169*
    Gideon 153*
    Griswold A. 54
    Henry 188*
    Isaac 162
    James 150*, 154*
    John 150*, 166
    Jesse 116, 175
    Jonathan 54, 110*
    Lucy 94*
    Nancy 132*
    Nathan 140*
    Nicholas 53*
    Oliver 53
    Pelatiah 171
    Peter 118*
    Reuben 18
    Russel 55
    Samuel 158
    Skiff 61*
    Thomas 152*, 167

Morse, (cont.)
Horace 77
Isaac 91
Jacob 10
Joel 119
Joseph 26*, 66
Josiah 16
Leonard 25
Levi 8*, 30
Mark 20, 42*
Mary 46
Michael 82
Moses 51
Nancy 18
Nathan 91
Obadiah 25*
Orlando 91
Philip 10*
Samuel 19*, 25, 38, 39*
Sarah 50
Seth 7, 175
Simeon 39*
Stephen 25*
William 50, 156
William H. 66

Morsell,
Lydia 65*

Mortimore,
Joseph 118

Morton,
Benjamin 6*
Bryant 11
David 143*
Edward 135*
Ezra D. 28*
James 130
Joel 78
Oliver 146*
Richard 137*
Ruth 50*
Thomas 5*, 159*
Timothy 59
William S. 130

Mosby,
Edward C. 132
Hezekiah 79*
Joseph 162*
Susanna 132*
William 160*

Moseley,
Ann 129
Catharine 83

Mosely,
Enoch 78
Mary 129

Moser,
John 120*

Moses,
Abraham 67*
Esther 58
John 62
Jonathan 62
Martin 58*
Seba 103*
Thomas 135

Mosher,
David 73
Helen 105
Jabez 73

Moshier,
Tunis 91

Mosier,
Josiah 89
S. Emerson 89

Mosley,
Joseph 99
Joseph J. 99

Mosman,
Ezra 41*
Jesse 66

Moss,
Daniel 172
E. 148*
Gilly 144
Isaac 175
James 132*
Levi 170
Martha 58
Nathan 119
Samuel 132*, 144
Simeon 100*
Stephen 58
Thomas 167

Mott,
    Mary 103, 105*
    Thomas 103

Motte,
    Isaac (Mrs) 142*

Mottsinger,
    Felix 138

Moulton,
    Anna 15*, 25
    David 25
    Ebenezer 6
    Jonathan 25*
    Joseph 6*
    Josiah 18
    Nathan 3
    Noah 25
    Rebecca 43
    Rinaldo 25
    Salmon 88*
    Stephen 88*
    William 15

Moultrup,
    Moses 90*

Mount,
    Catharine 110
    Ezekiel 110
    Jesse 110
    John 83*, 87*
    John H. 110
    Mathias 99*

Mountfort,
    Elizabeth 6*

Mountz,
    Thomas 185*

Mourey,
    Nathaniel 33*

Moury,
    Jeremiah 47
    Silas 47

Mowdy,
    John 178*

Mower,
    Alfred 36

Mower, (cont.)
    Calvin 10
    J. 37
    John 10
    Jonathan 37
    Samuel 10*

Mowers,
    Conrad 77
    Henry 77
    Peter 89*

Mowry,
    Abel 46*
    Henry 39*
    Jeremiah 46*
    Jonathan 46
    Olney 46
    Susanna 46*

Moyer,
    (Mrs.) 113
    Andrew C. 96
    Christopher 96
    Lodowick 83*

Mozingo,
    George 133*

Mud,
    Joseph 79

Mugford,
    John 6*
    W. 43
    William 43

Mugs,
    Elizabeth 50

Muir,
    John 110

Mulford,
    Charles L. 72
    Mathew 72

Mulherrin,
    John 190
    William 190

Mulholon,
    Daniel 98*

Mulikin,
    Edward 10

Mulkins,
    Mary 54

Mullen,
    Henry B. 43
    James 43

Mullet,
    Elizabeth 20*

Mulligan,
    Patrick 14*

Mullin,
    Philip 103*
    Thomas 150

Mullins,
    Flower 153*
    Gabriel 166
    James 129
    Joshua 164*
    Malone 146*
    Patrick 166

Mulloy,
    Hugh 170*

Mun,
    Joseph 5

Munday,
    Benjamin H. 130*
    Gabriel 109

Mundy,
    Isaac M. 110
    J. Martin 110

Munger,
    Abner 84
    Lorrin 23
    Louisa 84
    Nancy 44

Munn,
    Amos 11*
    Calvin 44, 67*
    Elisha 34*
    Lois 83
    Sarah 44

Munnerling,
    L. R. 143
    Thomas M. 143

Munro,
    Bosworth 49
    Joseph 49*

Munroe,
    Catharine 103
    John 103
    Josiah 69*

Munsell,
    Eunice 51
    Hezekiah 50*
    Rodney 51

Munson,
    Ceba 52
    Chauncy 52
    Hiram 100
    John 102
    Jonathan 52
    Josiah 100
    Mabel 53*
    Medad 58*
    Orange 102
    Samuel 76*

Murdock,
    Elisha 39
    James 5*
    John 103
    Lucretia 103
    Matthew 120
    Thomas 106
    Thomas H. 145
    William 145

Murphey,
    Bartholomew 159*
    Joseph 3
    Samuel 121*
    Thomas 3

Murphy,
    Aaron 75*
    Catharine 156
    Daniel 159
    Daniel H. 159
    David 21
    Hezekiah 190*
    Hiram 8

Murphy, (cont.)
    John 115*, 164*
    Mary 86
    Sarah 21
    Smith 48*
    Stephen 85
    W. C. 188
    William 153
    William C. 188

Murray,
    Alexander 85*
    Andrew 79
    Barnabas 166*
    Benjamin B. 89
    Catharine 95
    Cotton 5*
    David 90*
    George 90
    Hannah 56
    James 155*
    Lucretia 89
    Martha 95
    Samuel 92
    Sarah 42, 108
    Stephen 68*

Murrell,
    George 138*

Murtins,
    John 53*

Musgrove,
    Samuel 184*
    William 169*

Music,
    Jonathan 149

Muson,
    John G. 53*

Musselwhite,
    Nathan 140

Musser,
    Adam 117
    Christian 169*
    John 136*
    Paul 115

Muzzy,
    Benoni 41

Muzzy, (cont.)
    Joseph 67*
    Nathan 178*

Myatt,
    Reddick 155

Myers,
    Andrew 175
    Christopher 174
    Ephraim 103
    Frederick 102*
    Henry 184, 193*
    Henry S. 95
    John 96, 97, 138*
    John S. 103
    Lewis 184
    Lydia 89
    Peter L. 96
    Stephen 96
    William E. 89

Mygatte,
    Henry 51

Myres,
    Abraham 104
    Andrew 118*
    Samuel 104

Myrick,
    Brazilla 80*
    Matthew 159*

Nabers,
    Sarah 149

Nadeau,
    Bozziel 78
    Francis 78

Nagle,
    Elizabeth 115*
    Jacob 179
    John P. 112

Nalls,
    Richard 156*

Nance,
    Sherwood 143*
    William M. 132*

Napp,
    Rosina 75

Narramore,
    Asa 61
    John 152*
    Samuel L. 61

Narsh,
    John 5

Nasan,
    Betsey 3*

Nash,
    Anna 42*, 55
    Betsey 30
    Daniel 93*
    Isaac 95
    Jacob 35
    Job 32
    Jonathan 5, 28*, 95
    Keeler 55
    Michael 137*
    Samuel 37*
    Silas 76*
    Timothy 32
    Zebulon 30

Nason,
    Edward 4
    George E. 47
    James 4
    Stephen 18

Nay,
    John 134
    Oliver 134

Nayson,
    John 12

Neace,
    Martin 159*

Neagles,
    Sarah 45

Neal,
    Benjamin 165*
    Edward 185
    Isaac 12*
    John 17, 132*
    Joseph 32
    Joshua 17
    Sarah 24
    William 179*

Nealey,
    Benjamin 3*

Nealley,
    Andrew 18

Nealy,
    Andrew 18

Nearing,
    Henry 58*
    Joseph 93*

Neavel,
    Henry 114

Nee,
    John 133*

Needham,
    Daniel 42*
    Francis 101*
    Jefferson 7
    Mary 7

Neel,
    John M. 134
    William 134

Neely,
    Hannah 75

Newbury,
    Stedman 53*

Newby,
    Levi 129*
    Thomas 129*

Newcom,
    John 166

Newcomb,
    Bryant 31*
    Daniel 179
    Ethan 179
    James 27, 163
    Jeremiah 27*
    Justice 66
    Rhoda 45*

Newcomer,
    Francis 193

Newel,
    Franklin 12
    Samuel 184

Newell,
    Benjamin 171
    Ezekiel 61
    John 44, 180*
    Moses 36
    Norman 188
    Rebecca 24
    Ruth 37
    Stephen 36, 44
    Welcome 37

Newhall,
    Daniel 34*
    James 43*
    Sarah 43*
    William 43

Newkirk,
    Catharine 88
    Caty 88
    John 106*

Newland,
    (N.X.N.) 120
    David 89
    Jabez 67*
    Joseph 75
    Josiah 89
    Lemuel A. 75

Newlin,
    John 171
    Nicholas 171

Newman,
    Abner 129*
    Abram 84*
    Anna 119
    Daniel 147*
    Ed. (Col.) 163
    Edmund 153*, 163
    Isaac 81
    Jacob 156
    John 104, 157*
    Joseph 157
    Reuben 143*
    Richard 102
    Walter 171

News,
    William 139*

Newton,
    Abigail 79
    Alice 172
    Anson 86
    C. L. 37
    Ebenezer 38
    Eleanor 23
    Elizabeth 38*
    George 81
    Gideon 70*
    Henry 93
    Hezekiah 37
    J. S. 92
    James 92
    Jason 69*
    Jeremiah 33*
    John 35
    Judith 131
    Minott 31
    Versalla 86
    William 21, 131

Nichels,
    John 8*

Nichelson,
    Thomas 43

Nichol,
    William 134

Nicholas,
    Laura 128*

Nicholas, (cont.)
    Nicholas 102

Nicholls,
    William 125

Nichols,
    Aaron 80
    Abigail 32
    Asa 34*
    Bathsheba 71
    Charles 39
    Clark 80
    David 44*, 80, 185
    Dorcas 65
    Enos 55*
    Ephraim 55*
    Estor 8
    Ezra 40
    Isaac 65
    John 74
    Joshua 184
    Jonathan 39
    Lydia 32
    Martha 16
    Martin 184
    Mary 48*
    Moses 28*
    Rebecca 37*, 38
    Reuben 80
    Samuel 74, 77*, 87*
    Sarah 80
    Stephen 44
    Stiles 55*
    Susan 16
    Sylvamus 59*
    Thaddeus 59*
    Thankful 36*
    William 71*
    William B. 24

Nicholson,
    John 146*
    Sarah 121*

Nickens,
    James 133*

Nickerson,
    (N.X.N.) 12
    E. 79
    Edward 79
    Moses 10*
    Patience 28*

Nickerson, (cont.)
    Salathel 26*
    Stephen 26*

Nickols,
    Betsey 64
    Enoch 24
    Fortunatus 38*
    Jonas 64
    Peter 64
    William 64*

Nicks,
    John 164*

Nicolson,
    James 51*

Niffin,
    Amos 104
    Charles 104

Niles,
    Elisha 60*, 89
    Elizabeth 116
    Enoch 98
    Ephraim 63
    Jehial 74*
    John 31
    Oliver 63
    Peter 23
    Stephen 66
    William 72*

Nimley,
    Robert 166*

Nimon,
    Jacob 112
    Philip 112

Nims,
    Daniel 101*
    Edmund 21

Nisbeth,
    Teunis 95

Nitzer,
    Jacob 109*

Nix,
    George 141*
    John 146

Nixon,
     George 170
     Richard 102*
     Thomas 41*

Noble,
     Hannah 43
     Jabez B. 83
     James 14, 68*, 189
     John 14, 59
     Lyman 83
     Roswell 51
     Roswell F. 51

Nobles,
     William 142*
     Zilpha 142

Noel,
     John 117

Noland,
     Barbara 162
     Silas 162

Nolen,
     James 145
     Shadrach 159*

Nolton,
     Robert 83*

Norman,
     Hannah 109
     William 153*

Norris,
     Andrew 172
     Bethnal 172
     Greenlief K. 10
     James F. 10*
     John 181
     Jonathan 70*
     Lucy 26
     Ruth 10
     William 146*
     Ziba 111*

Norriss,
     John 101*

North,
     Abijah 162*
     Caleb (Col.) 112*

North, (cont.)
     Levi 50*
     Ruth 72*

Northamer,
     Adam 113

Northern,
     Joseph 138
     Reuben 161*

Northrop,
     Abigail 90
     Anna 51
     Clarina 55*
     David 117
     Gideon 117
     Isaac 52
     Jacob 90
     Joseph 63
     Lemmel 63

Northrup,
     George A. 79
     Joel 83
     Joseph 93*, 174
     Stephen 87*

Northup,
     Sylvester 48*
     Zebulon 48

Northway,
     Zenas 91*

Norton,
     Anna 50
     Asher 170
     Azuba (Mrs.) 170
     Christopher 83
     Darius 8
     David 12
     Electar 43
     Elihu 14
     Elon 89*
     H. 92
     Henry 50
     James 162*
     Jared 126*
     Leverett 178
     Love 26
     Martin 68*
     Mary 8
     Nathaniel 9*

Nye, (cont.)
    Nathan 65
    Solomon 64*

Oakes,
    John 11*

Oakley,
    Bennett 176
    Miles 176
    Susan 158*

Oakly,
    Catharine 94

Oakman,
    Constant 29
    Hatel 29

Oaks,
    Ebenezer 14
    Ephraim 105
    Isaac 149
    Jesse 105
    Joshua 14

Oatley,
    Mary 48

Obanks,
    Ezekiel 56*

O'Blennis,
    Mary 106*

Oblinger,
    Amos 177
    John 177

O'Brian,
    Tillotson 140*

O'Brien,
    John 51

O'Brien,
    Joseph C. 100
    Mary 100

O'Brion,
    John 4
    William L. 4

O'Bryon,
    William 125*

Ockington,
    Mary 22

Odall,
    John 21*

Odam,
    Levi 143*

Odell,
    Aaron 104
    Amos 104
    Arthur 98
    Griswold 55
    Nathan 56
    Richard 74*

Odem,
    Lewis 162
    Willis 162

Odenheimer,
    William H. 116

Odle,
    John 170

Odom,
    James 139

O'Donnel,
    Isaac 113

O'Donnell,
    James 116

Ogden,
    David 79*
    Jonathan 86*
    Joseph 98*
    Sally 55*
    Samuel 133*
    Stephen 173

Ogilvie,
    Kimbrough 161*

Ogle,
    William 92

Oglesby,
    Jesse 164*

O'Harra,
    Susan 127
    William 127

Ohl,
    John 115*

Ohlin,
    Palmer 87

Okes,
    Samuel 80

Olcott,
    Asa 101
    Jared 84*
    Jonathan 49*

Olden,
    Thomas 120

Oldham,
    Jesse D. 189*

Olds,
    George 62
    Philo 32
    Reuben 36*
    William 192

Oliver,
    Alva 131
    Catharine 103
    Douglas 152*
    Isaac 164
    James C. 128
    Joel 161
    John 40*, 144*
    Keziah 107
    Mary 8
    Rhesa 194*
    Richard 161, 164
    Stephen 122
    William 128

Olmstead,
    Henry 25
    James 76
    Philo 100
    Roger 100
    Susan 25
    Timothy 51

Olmsted,
    Archibald 104
    Ashbel 74
    Jeremiah 56
    Joseph 95*
    Matthew 56
    Nehemiah 85*
    Oliver 89
    Rosanna 89

Olney,
    Esick 77*
    James 46*
    Sarah 45

Olny,
    Richard 46

Olympia,
    Mary 128

Omans,
    Thomas 87*

Ommuck,
    William 110*

O'Neal,
    Darius 152*

O'Neill,
    Sarah 115

Oney,
    Isaac 136
    Joseph 136

Onison,
    John 131

Oosterhoudt,
    Henry T. 103*

Oram,
    Darby 109*

Orcott,
    Perley 65

Orcutt,
    Michael 44
    Ruth 32
    Sally 71
    Samuel 34*
    Stephen 61*
    William 57, 161*, 192

Ordway,
    Edward 19

Orear,
    Daniel 144*

Ores,
    Jacob H. 84*

Organ,
    Eliza 43

Orgin,
    Catharine 117

Orms,
    Charles 183
    Moses 183

Ormsby,
    Alanson 92
    Almon 92
    Experience 92
    Philander 92

Orr,
    James 139
    James J. 139
    John 162

Orrick,
    Samuel 191
    William 191

Orris,
    David 58
    Samuel 98*

Orsborne,
    Eliada 58*

Orsbourn,
    Nathaniel 154

Orton,
    Darius 122
    Sibel 171

Osborn,
    Abner 101
    Abram 192
    Eli 99*
    Elizabeth 59
    Ephraim 37*
    Ezra 175
    Hugh 175
    Isaac 75*
    Ithamar 101
    J. B. 108*
    J. H. 108*
    Jeremiah 55*
    Jeriah 176
    John 55*, 142*, 185
    Joseph 82*
    Nathan 79
    Nehemiah 110*
    Samuel 192
    Susanna 59
    White 86
    William 99
    William F. 59

Osborne,
    Abraham 50*
    Abram 76
    Daniel 76*
    Isaac 51*
    John 35

Osbourn,
    Willis 149

Osburn,
    John 30
    John U. 30
    Stephen 138

Osgood,
    Jeremiah 116
    Josiah 62
    Levi 123
    Nathan 69
    Oliver 71*
    Thomas 63*

O'Shields,
    Geoffrey 143*
    John 143*

Ostean,
    David 155*

Ostrander,
    Catharine 102*
    John 94
    Sarah 94

Oswell,
    Ruth 45

Otey,
    Samuel 135

Otis,
    Barnabas 180*
    Jacob 107*
    John 62
    John T. 54*
    Joseph 62

Otiss,
    Paul 16

Ott,
    Andrew 112
    Beulah 9, 12

Otterson,
    James 19*

Ours,
    Cichman 134*

Ousley,
    John 152*

Ousterhoudt,
    Stephen 103

Outerkirk,
    Frederick 94*

Ovelman,
    George 127*

Overley,
    Henry 189
    Pearson W. 189

Overocker,
    Adam 192*

Overstreet,
    Henry 163

Overstrett,
    Dabna 188
    John 188

Overton,
    Jonathan 137
    Justus 106*
    Samuel 137

Oviatt,
    Nathan 51*
    Samuel 58*

Owen,
    Avarilla 131
    Bailey 155*
    Benjamin C. 100*
    Calvin W. 86
    Catharine 116
    Eleazer 35
    Elisha 61*
    Frederick 143*
    Hugh 10
    James D. 131
    Joseph 72*
    Lucy 86
    Lydia 90
    Mason 187*
    Philip 5
    Salmon 192
    Shedrick 143*

Owens,
    Albert 165
    David 109*
    John 76, 148
    Jonathan 102
    Reuben 76
    Ruth 102
    William 165

Owney,
    William 133

Owry,
    George 180

Ozies,
    Christopher 116*

Pace,
George W. 132
Robert 130*
William 155

Pacetty,
Crecencio 193*

Pachen,
Jacob 56*

Packard,
Asahel 93
Benjamin 27
Caleb 34, 38
Freelove 27
Isaac 92*
James 12
Jesse 30
Job 7*
Louis 15
Lucy 38
Luke 35
Mercy 77
Nehemiah 5*
O. H. 77
Parley 38
Philip 35
Rebecca 98
Relief 30
Thankful 27
Willard 34

Packer,
Hannah 53*
John 53*, 107*
Nancy 77
Sabina 53*

Packes,
Ebenezer 57*
Moses 57

Paddleford,
Abigail 28
James 28

Padrick,
Isaac 81

Page,
Amos 67
Benjamin 19*, 71
Daniel 25*

Page, (cont.)
David 52, 97*, 101
Dorcas 165
Elizabeth 45
Ephraim 61*
Isaac 101
John 162*
Lucy 62
Parker 67
Reuben 65*
Timothy 87*
Woodward 52

Pages,
John 139*

Paige,
Benonah 79*
Osgood 21

Pailer,
John W. 138
William 138

Paine,
Amos 68
Betsey 45
Edward 174
Jabez 66*
Jesse 65*
Margaret 47
Mary 49
Nathaniel B. 47
Rhoda 28
Richard 7, 64*
Sally M. 174
Simon 46
Susan 26
Susanna 26
Thomas 6*, 124*, 137*
William 13*

Painter,
Deliverance S. 58
Henry 58
John 165, 166, 188*
Thomas 52

Paitsell,
Jacob 130*

Pakham,
Marcy 46

Palhaines,
    Abraham 123
    Sarah 123*

Pallman,
    Peleg 8*

Pally,
    David 166
    Edmund 166

Palmer,
    Abram 103
    Andrew 91
    Benjamin 8, 57*
    Christopher 93
    D. W. 63
    Daniel 42, 101*, 143*
    Dorothy 72
    Edward 75
    Elijah W. 82
    Elisha 54*
    Emblem 47
    Ephraim 176*
    George 62
    Hannah 50, 93
    Hiram 67
    Humphrey 93*
    Ichabod 24
    Iriphena 52
    Isaac 67, 161*
    Israel 47
    James 85*, 136
    Job 142
    John 63, 94*, 173
    John L. 159
    Jonathan D. 47
    Joshua 21*
    Margaret 67
    Moses 96
    R. W. 67
    Reuben 59*
    Robert 62
    Robert M. 54
    Royatt 82
    Samuel 96, 104
    Sarah 8, 75
    Simon 11*
    Simeon 72
    Susanna 159
    Sybil 23
    Thomas 97*, 153*
    William 140*

Palmiter,
    Asenath 91
    William 91

Palms,
    Samuel 60*

Pamplin,
    Henry 156
    William 156

Pangburn,
    Samuel 80

Pangman,
    Adonijah 59
    Gideon P. 59

Pannel,
    Benjamin 167*
    John 153*

Parcher,
    Ivory 3

Pardee,
    Abigail 91
    Henry 91
    Rosanna 52

Parder,
    Samuel 86

Pardu,
    Daniel 50*

Pardy,
    Peter 117
    Thomas 117

Parent,
    William 110*

Parham,
    Daniel 141
    David H. 84
    Lewis 156*

Parish,
    Cypnam 174
    Jeremiah 74*
    John 100*
    Levi H. 85*
    Lewis 174

Park,
Abigail 126
Daniel 108
John 36
Mathias 99
Thomas 126
William 40

Parke,
Zebulon 124

Parker,
Aaron 6, 39*
Abel 62*
Abraham 157*
Alva 89
Amos 89*
Asa 61*, 63*
Asel 98
Bailey 19
Benjamin 6, 75
Catharine 108*
Daniel 24*
David 10, 39, 69*
Ebenezer 97
Edward 86
Elisha 43*
Ephraim 69*
Eunice 66
Ezra 192
Free G. 13
George 111*, 194
Hannah 36
Humphrey 139*
Ira 44
Isaac 27*
Isaiah 131
Jabez 131
James 89
Joanna 19
John 64, 68, 132, 143, 173, 183*
Joseph 69, 109*
Joseph T. 110
Joshua 40*
Josiah 13*
Lucia 77
Lucretia 67
Luther 98
Mary 44, 79
Nathan 122
Nehemiah 38
Obadiah 71
Peter 93*
Phineas 98

Parker, (cont.)
Rebecca 64
Richard 33
Robert 143
Samuel 25, 43, 66, 69, 82*
Sarah 77
Silas 71
Solomon 25
Stephen 37*, 52
Stiles 171*
Susanna 45*
Theodore 4
Thomas 159*
Timothy 157*
W. M. 192
William 20*, 22*, 39*, 85*, 154
William F. 71

Parkers,
Richard 154*

Parkerson,
J. 147
Jacob 147

Parkham,
Drury 143*

Parkhurst,
Benjamin 70, 174
Daniel 88
David 86*
Gilbert 92*
Isaac 70
Joseph 40
Samuel 40*
Simon 70
Zelotus 179

Parkinson,
James 128
Joseph 131*
Sylvanus 74

Parkman,
Hannah 104
William E. 104

Parks,
Aaron 81
Anna 103*
David 87*
Ebenezer 75*

Parks, (cont.)
    Eunice 40
    George W. 175*
    Harry C. 81
    Jacob 105
    Jonas 40
    Jonathan 37*
    Jonathan A. 111
    Josiah 40*
    Michael 173*
    Nathan 172*
    Peter 43, 165*
    Rufus 94*
    Samuel 186

Parlin,
    Elezer 14

Parmalee,
    Constant 60*
    James 60*

Parmele,
    Giles 97

Parmely,
    James 91*

Parmenter,
    Alvin 126
    Caleb 28
    Draper 28
    Ebenezer 40*
    John 75
    Nathaniel 20*
    Oliver 80
    Phineas 75

Parmer,
    Jared 93*
    Lydia 58

Parmeter,
    Luther 38
    M. 37
    Nathan 97*
    Nathaniel 97*

Parmetor,
    Abraham 172

Parmley,
    John 167*

Parr,
    Benjamin 144
    James 183
    Jesse 111
    John 183
    Matthias 183, 188

Parris,
    Josiah 7
    Sarah 115*

Parrish,
    B. 76
    Ebenezer 125*
    James 169
    Thomas 157*

Parrons,
    Arel 100
    Sarah 100

Parrot,
    A. 78
    Adoniran 78
    Catharine 110*
    Samuel 177*

Parrott,
    William 130*

Parshal,
    Reuben S. 100

Parsley,
    Ira 17
    Samuel 17
    Thomas 166*

Parsons,
    Abraham 16*
    Amos 66*
    Andrew 58
    Bartholomew 32*
    Ebenezer 42*
    Eleazer 7*
    Ephraim 60
    George 154*, 170
    John 83, 170
    L. 115
    Leonora 115
    Mary 35
    Mercy 68
    Molly 41*

Patteson, (cont.)
    William B. 73

Pattie,
    William 130*

Pattison,
    Nelly 79

Patton,
    David 144*
    Jacob 153*
    James 162
    John 162, 179
    Joseph 154*
    Mary 33
    Samuel 137*
    William 121*

Pau,
    Nusom 131*

Paul,
    David 9*
    John 191*
    Kiles 70*
    Trueman 33
    Zeniah 33

Paulding,
    John 104
    Joseph 98*
    Peter 104

Paulk,
    Ammi 61

Paull,
    Hannah 27*

Paviton,
    William 110*

Paxton,
    Martin R. 145

Payne,
    Aaron 187*
    Ann 134
    John 166*, 180*
    Mathey 150*
    Richard 129*
    Solomon 178*

Payns,
    William 32

Paysons,
    Samuel 8*

Peabody,
    Benjamin 42
    Charles 11*
    Francis 43
    J. 43
    Jane 43
    Joel R. 42
    John 37*
    Lydia 42
    Rachel 44*
    Sarah 42
    Stephen G. 185*

Peacock,
    Uriah 147*

Peak,
    Abel 154*

Peale,
    Jeremiah 132*

Pear,
    Isaac 108*

Pearce,
    Ann 28
    Anna 28
    George 122, 166
    George W. 166
    Ichabod 47*
    Isaac 28
    Job 122
    John 183*
    Martha 48
    Michael 101*
    Morriss 195
    Obed 128
    Thomas 28, 119*

Pearl,
    Austin 61
    Frederick 61*
    John 8*
    Lois 61
    Philip 57

Pearsal,
    Sampson 121

Pearson,
Abel 158
Charles 155
Ellis 155
Joseph 38
Mesheck 166*
Sarah 42
Silas 41
Sterling 155
William 155

Pease,
Abigail 50
Anna 61
Chauncey 91
David H. 101
Ebenezer 126*
Edward 65*
Heber 50
James 74*
Jerusha 101
Joel 168*
John 50*
Oliver 61
Patty 44
Sarah 61*
Simeon 50*

Peatfield,
James 42

Peavey,
John 17*

Peavy,
Enoch 17
John S. 11*
Mary 17

Peck,
Abijah 53*, 95*
Benjamin 28, 45*, 56*
Charles 81
Daniel 90*
Eliphalet 82*
Elizabeth 103
Ellen 55
Hannah 24*
Henry H. 96*
Ichabod 81*
Jeremiah 28*
Job 55
John 164*
Jonathan 46*

Peck, (cont.)
Joseph 44, 96
Levi 55
Lewis D. 96
Lois 51*
Lucy 49*
Mary 28, 55
Olive 48*
Peleg 82*
Peter 152*
Phebe 53
Reuben 71*, 75
Samuel 52*
Sarah 53*
Solomon L. 44
Tabithia 93
Thomas 105*
Ward 53*

Peckham,
Daniel 47*
Josiah 62*
Mary 48
Pardon 80*
Timothy 48*

Peckinpaugh,
Leonard 180*

Pect,
Elijah 55*

Peddy,
Andrew 137*

Peden,
Alexander 143
Robert 143

Pedrick,
Joseph 19*

Peirce,
Eliab 83*
Hannah 3*
Nathaniel 11*
Peace 3
Phebe 30
Samuel 3

Pelham,
Elijah 180
Isabella 165
John 165

Pell,
    Josiah 125*

Pelton,
    David M. 24
    Hannah 176
    Joel 14*
    Joseph 89*
    Samuel 175*
    Stephen 94

Pemar,
    B. 139*

Pember,
    Eli 175*
    Elisha 60

Pemberton,
    John 158

Pendegrass,
    Spencer 148*

Pendergast,
    Edward 184*

Pendergrass,
    Candace 137
    Mary 137

Pendexter,
    Thomas 3*

Pendleton,
    Gurdon 54
    Micass 132*
    P. 133
    Phil. 133
    Stephen 78

Penfield,
    James 55*
    Samuel 76*
    Simeon 60*

Penington,
    Henry 186

Penly,
    Joseph 5*

Pennefill,
    Heister 127

Pennell,
    Robert 80*

Pennett,
    William 86

Penney,
    Arba 11
    Henry 171*
    Pelatiah 17
    Salathiel 11

Pennfield,
    William O. 89

Penniman,
    Gardner 31
    Huldah 29

Pennington,
    Henry 194*
    John 111*
    Kenchen 139*
    William 189*

Penny,
    Benjamin 3*
    Edmund 5

Penock,
    Human 25
    Jefferson 25

Pentacost,
    Thomas 158

Peoples,
    Isham 144*

Peory,
    John 33*

Pepper,
    (Mrs.) 56
    Stephen 35

Perady,
    Love 94

Perey,
    Lucy 20*

Perham,
    David 11

Perham, (cont.)
Joel F. 67*
Oliver 20*
Peter 11

Perigo,
Eunice 97
Joseph H. 92
Robert 92

Perine,
William 85*

Perkegs,
Robert 45

Perkenson,
Ezekiel 129*

Perkins,
Aaron 125*
Abigail 42
Abraham 42*
Benjamin 18
Caleb 87
Daniel 67
David 42
Ebenezer 7
Edmund 20
Edwin 44
Eli 134*
Eliab 103
Elizabeth 16*
Ezekiel 74*
Francis 69*
George 194*
Hannah 21, 69
Harlow 82
Hezekiah B. 42
Hiram 21, 91
Isham 145
John 159
Judith 44
Leonard 82
Luther 7
Mark D. 21
Mary 28, 30, 174
Mehitable 7
Moses 145
Nathaniel 63*
Oliver 4*
Pelatiah 4*
Reuben 87
Rufus 79*

Perkins, (cont.)
Sarah 7
Simeon 7, 30
Wesley 174
William 80

Perley,
James 64*
Solomon 42

Perot,
Lewis 116

Perren,
Henry S. 24

Perrien,
James D. 111

Perrigo,
Frederick 78
James D. 78
Mary 54

Perrin,
John 45*
Nathaniel 188*

Perrine,
Peter 120*

Perry,
A. P. 66
Abel 41
Alice 44
Anna 66
Arthur 32
Betsy 129*
Calvin P. 66*
Chandler 6
Charity 107
David 9
David B. 55
Elizabeth 30*
Elizabeth C. 47*
Elizabeth M. 47
Elnathan 86*
Freeman 80
Hamilton 154
Henry 81
Jeremiah 86*, 181
Jesse 153
Job 9
John 27*, 44, 81

Perry, (cont.)
    Joseph 9*
    Lewis 153
    Lydia 28*
    Mary 40, 55*, 96
    Nathaniel 55*
    Roxanna 78
    Samuel 55, 84
    Seth 30*
    Silas 22*
    Stephen 80
    Thomas 134*, 180*

Perryburn,
    William 192

Perryman,
    William 166*

Persinger,
    Jacob 133*

Persons,
    Benjamin P. 156*
    Chesterfield 84
    Jeremiah 64
    Lois H. 39
    Stephen 64
    William E. 82*

Peter,
    Hannah 60
    William 5

Peterman,
    (Mrs.) 113
    Joseph 113

Peters,
    Amos 109
    Cornelius 75
    Harman 75
    J. P. 76
    John 109, 134*
    Joseph P. 76
    Mary 55
    Will 153

Peterson,
    Amos 97
    Betsey 28
    John 104*
    Jonathan 33
    Joseph 7*

Peterson,
    Philip 87*
    Priscilla 29
    Rebecca 29
    Reuben 111
    Ruth 29
    Sylvanus 33

Pethey,
    Samuel 82

Petigrew,
    James 149*

Petingal,
    Benjamin 92*

Petit,
    Samuel 81*

Petre,
    Henry 180

Petree,
    Peter 167*

Pette,
    Andrew 93

Pettee,
    Abigail 13
    Barry 13

Pettengill,
    Obadiah 10*
    William 10*

Pettes,
    Joseph 54

Pettey,
    Daniel 45

Pettibone,
    Amos 33*
    Daniel 90*
    Eli 68*
    Jacob 83*

Pettingell,
    John 84*

Pettingill,
    Hugh 40

Pettingill, (cont.)
    Samuel 93
    William 21*, 93

Pettis,
    Benjamin 60*
    Ebenezer 98*

Pettit,
    Lucy 129
    Thomas 163*

Petton,
    Thomas 44

Petty,
    Daniel 109
    Francis 165
    Francis R. 75
    John 153
    Joshua 27
    Moses 27
    Pickney 165
    Roadham 160*
    Samuel B. 160
    Theophilus 149*
    Thomas 158*

Petway,
    Micajah 138*

Pew,
    Reuben C. 166*
    Richard 130*

Peyton,
    Yelverton 164*

Phares,
    Robert 109

Phariss,
    Robert 154

Phelps,
    Abijah 172
    Ada 79
    Alexander 74
    Amos 60*
    Anson 75
    Augustus 126
    Bissel 64
    Calvin C. 92
    Cornelius 76*

Phelps, (cont.)
    Daniel 60*
    David 64
    Edward 21*
    Elijah 33
    Elisha 94
    Elizabeth 34, 50*
    Elnathan 98*
    Francis 66*
    Horace 79
    Ira 172
    Israel 95*
    John 58*, 73
    Jonathan 76*
    Lavina 171*
    Mary 87
    Oliver 62*, 123*
    R. L. 60
    Ralph R. 74
    Richard 172
    Richard T. 161
    Roger 60
    Rowena 126
    Silas 92
    Theodoma 35
    Zarnah 59*

Philbric,
    Nathaniel 7*

Philbrick,
    Ephraim 15
    Ruth 20*
    William 12*

Philbrook,
    Simon 18

Philburk,
    Thomas 45

Philhower,
    Christopher 109

Philips,
    Abraham 81
    Deborah 28*
    Elkanah 81
    Evan 72*
    John 66*
    Lucinda 81
    Mary 61
    Samuel 81
    Sarah 116
    Squire 117*

Philler,
    Andrew 116
    Mary T. 116

Phillips,
    A. A. 87
    Abiezar 84
    Abigail 8
    Adam 87
    Anna 25
    Bradford 54
    Daniel 74
    David 156*
    Deborah 8
    Ebenezer 84*
    Eharer 46
    Elihu 92
    Elizabeth 66, 128
    George 4, 66, 87
    Gideon 22
    Henry C. 25
    Henry W. 104
    Hugh 142*
    John 22*, 125*, 131*, 138
    Jarius 8
    Levi 143*
    M. 84
    Martha S. 54
    Mary 4
    Naomi 26*
    Nehemiah 63*
    Olive 22, 47
    Pain 66
    Phebe 48
    Richard 22
    Russell 16
    Samuel 168*
    Sarah T. 108*
    Silence 8
    Stephen 127*
    Susanna 27*
    Thomas 76*
    Timothy 41*
    William 104, 157*
    William A. B. 11*

Phillpott,
    Warren 191*

Phillsbury,
    Merrill 63*

Philo,
    Nathan 125

Philops,
    Jedediah 31*

Philpot,
    Eliza 16
    John 16
    Joseph 161

Phinney,
    John 5*
    Zenas 37*

Phipps,
    Hannah 41
    Richard 145
    Samuel 74*

Phips,
    Samuel 178

Pickarel,
    Jonas 91

Pickens,
    Andrew 158
    J. S. 158

Pickerill,
    Samuel 169*

Pickering,
    Artemas C. 36
    Benjamin 39*
    David 39*
    Lovey 15

Pickert,
    Emelias 83

Picket,
    Phineas 51*
    Adolphus 84*

Pickett,
    Henry 163
    John 168
    Judith 42*
    Samuel 33
    William 6*

Pickinson,
    Oliver 58*

Pickitt,
    John S. 193*

Pineo,
  Joseph 24
  Oramel 24

Pingrey,
  Hoyet 7
  John 40
  Stephen 40

Pingue,
  Hezekiah 6

Pinkey,
  Peter 113

Pinn,
  David 153

Pinney,
  Isaac 70*
  Lemuel 61

Pinson,
  Calvin 97

Pipen,
  Richard 141

Piper,
  Andrew 83*
  David 18*
  John 13

Pipes,
  Joseph 120*
  Mary 165*

Pippin,
  Robert 136*

Pipsecow,
  John 195

Pitcher,
  John 30

Pitchford,
  Daniel 160*

Pitkin,
  Emily 50
  Russell 80*

Pitman,
  Ambrose 164*

Pits,
  Mexico 162*

Pitsch,
  Anthony 127*

Pitt,
  Henry 157*

Pittman,
  William 121*

Pitts,
  Henry 142*
  James 146*
  James C. 9
  John 3
  Sarah 53*
  Seth 9*
  Shubael 9
  Stephen 183*

Pittsley,
  Mercy 27

Pitzer,
  Anthony 175*

Pixley,
  Alexander 24*
  Joseph 90
  Olive 80

Placard,
  Christian 170

Place,
  Ann 168
  Azariah 97
  Calvin 57
  Griffin 97
  Jeremiah 49*
  John 48*
  Reuben 47*
  Simon 57

Plaisted,
  Lydia 6
  Samuel 4

Plant,
  Anna 55
  David 55
  John 156*

Plasted,
 Roger 4*

Platt,
 Ely 88
 Gillen 55*
 James 103*
 Joseph 55*
 Joseph S. 105
 Lydia 105
 Richard 75
 William 89

Platz,
 George 123*

Plemmons,
 Jacob 139
 Thomas 139

Plidden,
 David 100*

Pliley,
 Casper 178
 William 178

Plimpton,
 Anna 36*
 Lydia 36*
 Mary 36*

Pliney,
 Barnabas 29
 Deborah 29

Plinley,
 Henry 102*

Plott,
 John 125
 Joseph 125

Plough,
 Henry 96

Plum,
 Ann 108*
 George 60*
 John 126*

Plumb,
 Elisha 74*
 Joseph 53
 William 59*

Plumby,
 Allen J. 75
 Ebenezer 75

Plumer,
 Isaac 14*
 William 117

Plumley,
 Samuel 67*
 William 67

Plummer,
 Daniel 12
 Edward 9*
 John 12

Poe,
 D. W. 176
 Elizabeth 176
 John 178
 Virgil 162

Pofford,
 William 141*

Poindexter,
 Chapman 152*
 Thomas 131*

Poland,
 Anna 41
 Asa 67*
 Peter 171
 Sarah 24

Pollard,
 Chatten D. 152*
 Edward 25*
 Hepsebeth 68
 James 162
 Kesiah 86
 Leanna 162
 Olive 21
 Robert 131*
 Samuel 13
 Walter 70*
 William 190*

Polley,
 Ebenezer 97*
 Foster 97
 John 97*

Pollock,
    David 122

Pollord,
    Hepsebeth 68

Polly,
    David 77
    John 166*
    Joseph 55*

Polmentier,
    Isaac 98*

Pomeroy,
    Ebenezer 35
    Elisha 80*
    I. 74
    Ichabod 172
    Ira 74
    Jacob 36
    Luther 35
    Noah 172
    Simeon 71
    Simson 44*
    Thomas M. 71

Pomroy,
    Joel 90
    Joseph 11*
    Medad 122

Pond,
    Barnabas 88*
    Bartholomew 89
    Benjamin 41
    Elaher 31
    Ezekiel 62
    Ezra 78
    Jabez 31
    James 157
    Merritt 89
    Moses 53
    Zebulon 69

Pool,
    Abigail 52
    Colwell 139
    Henry 125
    Job 5*
    John 156
    Joshua 7
    Lucinda 156
    Matthew 149
    Samuel 149

Poole,
    Abigail 53

Poor,
    Abigail 42
    Charles 19
    Daniel 19
    Mary 20*
    Ruth 70
    Samuel 19*
    Thomas W. 70

Poore,
    Jane 162
    Robert C. 162

Poorman,
    Christian 121

Pope,
    Elnathan 27*
    Harwood 138*
    Henry 142
    Mary 111*
    Philip 157*
    Richard 137*
    Simeon 63*
    Thomas 30
    William 29

Popham,
    William 102
    William S. 102

Popinoe,
    Daniel 107*

Poplin,
    George 139*
    Lucy 139

Popple,
    Gideon 57*

Porch,
    Henry 167*

Porgan,
    Andrew 131

Porter,
    Aaron 43*
    Abel 89
    Abijah 50*
    Asa 22

Porter, (cont.)
Asahel 23
Benjamin 82, 92
Benjamin J. 12*
David 102*
Ebenezer 85
Elias 185*
Elizabeth 133
George 66*
Hancock 143*
Harvey 43
James 20, 149*, 182*, 185
John 24, 34, 58, 100, 162*, 170
John N. 100
Joseph 170
Mary 42*, 43, 50*
Martin 88*
Nathaniel 26*
Nehemiah 6
Penelope 154
Philo 82*
Rachel 58
Rhodolphus 31
Rufus 6
Samuel 43
Sarah 72
Silas 36
Stephen 97*
Thomas 185
Tyler 5*
William 24*, 30*

Porterfield,
Catharine 6
John 139*
Richard 153*
Robert 133*

Portler,
Oliver 64
William 64

Portlock,
John 182*

Portwood,
John 163
Page 152*

Posey,
Hezekiah 148*
Samuel 142

Post,
David 178

Post, (cont.)
Esther 59*
Ezra 91
Jacob 71*
Jimmy 60*
John 178
John C. 107
John H. 111*
John J. 107*
John P. 107
Simeon 69
William 91

Pott,
Thomas 105*

Potter,
Abel 84*
Abijiah 26
Almon 89
Balden 82
Bently 190
Borden 73
Caleb 90*
Cyrus 83
David 55*
Ebenezer 22*
Edward 50
Ezra 60
George W. 24
Gideon 81
Henry 94
Hugh 10*
Income 57*
Jacob 108*
James 8, 33, 37*, 190
Jesse 8
John 52, 93*, 165*
Joseph 28, 82, 125*
Loury C. 49
Lovey 37
Martha 48
Mary 48, 89
Mary G. 46
Matthew 81
Medad 52
Nancy 24
Nicholas 75*
Noel 62, 88*
Reuben 48
Rhoda 37
Robert 83
Russell 52
Samuel R. 47*
Sarah 49, 94

Potter, (cont.)
    Stephen 94*
    Thaddeus 63*
    Thankful 58
    Thomas 18
    Varnum 81
    William 80
    Zebedee 90*
    Zebina 82

Potterson,
    John 163*

Pottle,
    Betsey 91

Potts,
    James 158*

Powel,
    Abner 140*
    Asel 87*
    Mary 139*
    William 159*

Powell,
    Ambrose 162*
    Benjamin 24
    Charles 138*
    Daniel 188*
    Egbert 67
    Felix 84
    George 138*
    Jeremiah 89
    John 163
    Lewis 137*
    Liberty 89
    Peyton 148*
    Sarah 163
    Thomas 87*
    Trueman 67
    William 81*

Powelson,
    Henry 134*

Power,
    Robert 166

Powers,
    Asahel 71*
    Charles 17
    Chester 93
    Corbin W. 80

Powers, (cont.)
    David 89*
    Eshi 117
    Hartwell 71
    John 37*
    John D. 70
    Jonathan 63*
    Joseph 93
    Leonard 93
    Peter 69
    Rachel 23
    Rebecca 71
    Sarah 92
    Stephen 35
    Walter 23
    William 135*

Prather,
    Basil 183
    Thomas 183

Pratt,
    Aaron 32
    Abel 97*
    Abigail 59*
    Abijah 99
    Asa 71*
    Augustus 102*
    Betty 32
    Caleb 45*
    Charles 88
    Dan 8*
    David 9, 24*, 34
    Dexter 29
    Dier 28*
    Ebenezer 20*
    Edmund 192
    Elizabeth 41, 65*
    Elnathan 168
    Ephraim 80*, 168
    Ervin 69
    George 13, 14*
    Hannah 32
    Heman 192
    Hiram 70
    Isaac 32, 40
    James 13, 69
    Jesse 34*
    Joel 38
    John 86, 177*
    John D. 37
    Jonathan 132*
    Joseph 13
    Levi 21

Pratt, (cont.)
    Luther 168
    Lydia 13
    Martha 72
    Mary 45*, 99
    Nathan 36*, 70
    Noah 86
    Patience 32, 44*
    Ranseller S. 168
    Rebecca 37
    Remember 73
    Ruth 31*
    S. H. 73
    Simeon 30*
    Solomon C. 40
    Stephen 76*, 90, 167*
    Thaddeus 7
    Thomas 13
    Thomas J. 42
    William 27, 29, 50, 71
    William H. 50

Pray,
    Abraham 10*
    John 32
    Sarah 13
    Thomas 13

Preble,
    Edward D. 6
    John 129*
    Mary 6

Predgin,
    Francis 139*

Preewitt,
    John 165*

Pren,
    Ryal 154*

Prentice,
    Daniel 40*
    Elisha 54*
    Elizabeth 98
    Joseph 98

Prentiss,
    Daniel 59
    Thomas 71*

Presbrey,
    John 28*

Prescot,
    E. 94
    Mary 16
    Phebe 94

Prescott,
    Abel 40*
    Phebe 20
    Richard 142
    Samuel 10*
    William 40

Presey,
    John 24

Presler,
    Jonathan 91

Presley,
    Andrew 152

Presnell,
    John 148*

Pressey,
    John 42*
    Moses 90
    Phebe 90

Preston,
    Amasiah 28
    Amos 62*
    Benjamin 24*
    Calvin 88
    Daniel 94
    Ebenezer 126
    Elizabeth 162
    Ezra 73
    James P. 135*
    Jeffrey 162
    Joan 94
    John 31, 73
    Levi 126
    Othniel 86*
    Philip 88
    Shubal 90*
    Stillman 92
    William 25*, 185*

Prewet,
    Solomon 161*

Prewett,
    Joshua 167*

Pribble,
    James 166*

Pribou,
    Amasa 5*

Price,
    Aaron L. 78
    Daniel 136*
    David 75*
    E. 145*
    Ebenezer 103*
    Hannah 78
    Isaac 92
    Jacob 119*
    John 116, 131*
    Matthew 48
    Ruth 92
    Sampson 178*
    Thomas 153*
    William 139, 177*

Prichard,
    John 182*
    Jonas 21

Prichards,
    Stephen 134

Priddy,
    John 171

Pride,
    Absalom 54*

Priest,
    Aaron 22
    Asa 89*
    Daniel 20
    Joel 64*
    John 66*
    John (Mrs.) 20
    Joseph 63*
    Mary 20

Prigen,
    William 137

Prikhe,
    William 114

Prillainan,
    Jacob 177

Primes,
    Henry 119*

Prince,
    Benjamin 5*
    Dinah 4
    Joseph 89, 133*
    Philip 54

Prindle,
    Mary Ann 100
    Samuel 69*, 90*

Prior,
    Alva 67
    Ebenezer 50*
    Elizabeth 67

Pritchard,
    Nathaniel 174*
    Phoebe 160*

Pritchett,
    Elisha 182
    John 182, 189*

Pritt,
    Thomas 135

Procter,
    John 21
    Josiah 6*

Proctor,
    Abel 40
    Joseph 162*
    Levi 40*
    Polly 43
    Sally 71
    Samuel 71*
    Sarah 16
    Silas 69*
    Stilman 71
    William 162*

Pronty,
    John 96

Prossy,
    W. 43

Prout,
    Chloe 59*

Prouty,
 Amos 66
 Burpy 69*
 Eli 38
 Fosdick 66
 Harris G. 29
 Johnson 23
 Prudence 37*
 Rebecca 38

Provost,
 David 110*
 Samuel 56*

Pruett,
 Joshua 143
 Reuben 157*
 William 143

Pruit,
 Zachariah 132*

Pruitt,
 Martin 187
 Solomon 187

Pryor,
 Samuel 139*
 Simon 162*

Pucket,
 John 155*
 Josiah 156*
 William 142

Puckett,
 Nathaniel 129*

Puff,
 John 99
 Peter 99

Puffer,
 Ebenezer 85
 Esther 66
 Nathan 192
 Sally 66
 Sarah 85

Pugh,
 Ann 132
 John 132*
 John M. 132
 Josiah 132*
 William 119

Pugsley,
 John 5

Pukham,
 Peleg 48*

Pulcifer,
 Joseph 8*

Pulleam,
 R. M. 131

Pullen,
 Oliver 12

Pullin,
 Elisha 160
 George 160
 Loftus 164*
 Robert 145
 Robert R. 145
 Thomas 128*
 William 149

Pulver,
 Catharine 104

Pumpilly,
 Allen 8
 Elizabeth 8

Purbeck,
 A. 43
 Aaron 43

Purce,
 Francis 161*

Purcell,
 Edward 182
 George 130
 Jesse 182
 William 183*

Purdy,
 Isaac 86
 Jeremiah 77*
 Josiah 86
 Martha 68
 Samuel 104*

Purkins,
 Anthony 164*

Purnell,
    Dryden 128
    John 128

Purple,
    John 20

Purrington,
    Joshua 8
    Sylvanus 72

Purse,
    William 142*

Purviance,
    Joseph 159*

Pushee,
    David 24
    Harvey 24

Putman,
    Nelly 81
    Olive 17
    Peter 81
    Redding 191*

Putnam,
    Benjamin 11
    Catharine 49
    Daniel 70
    Ezra 70
    Francis 39
    Hannah 66
    Hezekiel 44
    Hiram S. 67
    Israel 65*
    J. D. 190
    John 22*, 64*, 125, 190
    Luman 125
    P. B. 66
    Silas 39
    Stephen 66*
    Tamar 11
    William B. 17

Putney,
    Esther 18*
    James 24
    John 23*
    Jonas K. 40
    Joseph 19*, 101
    Samuel 81*

Pyncheon,
    George 32

Pyncheon, (cont.)
    Mary 32

Pyott,
    Lloyd 169*

Pyrow,
    William 139*

Quackenbuss,
    Caty 88
    Isaac 88
    John 88
    Magdalem 88

Qualls,
    Elizabeth 167

Queen,
    John 134
    Stephen 134
    Thomas 148*

Quick,
    Christopher 97
    Cornelius 103*
    Elizabeth 131*
    John 182
    Margaret 111
    Peter J. 111*
    Philip 103

Quigley,
    Cary 117
    William 170*

Quill,
    David 43*

Quillin,
    John 141*

Quimby,
    Charles S. 125
    John 82
    Moses 64

Quimby, (cont.)
    Samuel 125

Quin,
    John 182*

Quinn,
    Daniel 144

Quint,
    John 3*

Quintard,
    Hannah 56

Raburn,
    Henry 135

Race,
    Philip 104

Radford,
    Miles 142

Radforth,
    Sarah 95

Radloff,
    James 28
    Sarah 28

Raduback,
    Katharine 176
    Thomas 176

Ragan,
    Larkin 155*

Rager,
    Conrad 119
    Jacob 119

Ragsdale,
    Benjamin 158
    James 158

Rahn,
    Jonathan 145

Raignsbearger,
    John 169*

Rainer,
    John 165
    Thomas 39

Rainey,
    J. 182*

Rains,
    Cullen 143
    James 165*
    John 135, 153*
    Letitia 154
    Robert 148*, 154

Raley,
    Lewis C. 164

Ralf,
    Jeremiah 14*

Ralph,
    Bozeman 194*
    Sarah 46*

Ralston,
    David 136*
    John 124*
    William 85

Ramage,
    John 117*

Ramond,
    Lucretia 54

Rampson,
    Ann 106

Ramsay,
    David 25
    John 72*
    Thomas 123

Ramsdall,
    Ebenezer 14*

Ramsdell,
    Catharine 51
    George 43

Ramsdell, (cont.)
Lydia 29*
Mary L. 51

Ramsden,
Reuben 44
Sarah 44

Ramsey,
Allen 188*
Andrew 139*
Benjamin 186
Daniel 156*
Frances Ann 164
Francis 166*
James 144*, 164, 165
Joel 136*
John 163*
Joseph 136*
Mary 46
Robert 14*, 159*
Thomas 162*
William 169*

Rand,
Ephraim 78
Israel 78
Mary 39

Randal,
Alfred 142
Caleb 10
Jacob 101
Moses 101
Phebe 142
Samuel 63*

Randall,
Alexander 127
Allen 84
Barton 47
Benjamin 84
Benjamin F. 94
Charles 58*
Deborah 127
Elisha 74*
Gersham 35
Jack 59*
Jacob 134*
James 193
Jedediah 77*
John Y. 15*
Mary 46
Oliver 11, 46

Randall, (cont.)
Rachel 16
Reuben 178*
Rodley 83
Sarah 15*, 46*
Shubal 79
Simeon 71
Stephen 46*
Timothy 58*
William 11

Randle,
Richard 187*

Randleman,
Martin 191

Randolph,
Henry 158
Hosey 84
Hugh 148
James 124*
Thomas F. 108

Raney,
John 153*
Solomon 79

Ranger,
William 90

Ranken,
William 139*

Rankhorn,
Joseph 155*

Rankin,
Catharine 83*
James 84
Joseph 169
Robert 159*
Thomas 112*

Rankins,
Abigail 12*

Rann,
Jeremiah 16, 69

Ransford,
Henry 186
Joseph 185
William 185

Ransin,
George 90*

Ransom,
Amos 49*
George P. 125*
James 54*
L. 70
Nathaniel P. 94

Ranson,
Silas 82*

Rape,
Gustavus 155*

Rapellee,
John 98*

Raphael,
Robert 189

Rapp,
Christian 87*

Rappole,
George 84
Henry 84

Rardin,
Daniel 190*

Rasson,
Jane 162*

Rathban,
Edmund 170*

Rathbone,
John 54
Ruth 54

Rathbun,
Jonathan 53*

Rathburn,
Benjamin 101
Joseph 168*
Nathaniel 73

Ratnom,
George 87*

Rauson,
Elizabeth 45

Rauson, (cont.)
Joseph 45

Rawles,
William 130*, 194

Rawson,
Abner 193
Bailey 66*
Caleb 36
Esther 91
John 140*
Joseph 91
William 36

Rawzon,
Anna 80
Josiah H. 80

Ray,
Archibald 158
Benjamin 136
Caleb 50
Ebenezer 42*
Eunice 6
Francis 137
Gershom 57*
Gideon 48, 54
Gilbert 97
Hannah 93
Reuben 70*
Roswell 95*
Samuel 5
Sarah 48
Timothy 91*
William 89*, 185
Zachariah 95*

Rayban,
Joshua 10

Rayburn,
Eleanor 121
James 121

Raymond,
Almeda 27
David 56
Deborah 28*
Dorothy 65
Edward 57
Elisha 68
Elizabeth 70
Gould 56
James 105*

Raymond,
    Lemuel 102*
    Loisa 57
    Nap 142
    Nathan 3, 10
    Nathaniel 56
    Newcomb 77*
    Sands 103*
    Simon 65
    William 10
    Zacheus 117*
    Zadok 56

Rayner,
    Amos 138*

Raynolds,
    Margaret 57
    Matilda 57

Raynor,
    David 83

Razey,
    Pelatiah 89*

Rea,
    Joshua 120
    Mary 39

Read,
    Caroline M. 28
    Daniel 66*
    George 9*
    James 121
    John 110*, 189
    John P. 9*
    Thomas 67*
    Zalmon 56*

Reader,
    Benjamin 157

Reading,
    Polly (Mrs.) 162

Reagen,
    Samuel 188*
    William 136*

Ream,
    Andrew 113
    Harry 113

Reams,
    John 189*

Rease,
    Mary 154*

Reason,
    James 166
    M. 166

Reaves,
    John 141*
    William A. 137

Recaud,
    L. M. 127

Reckard,
    Abner 74

Record,
    Abigail 7
    Jane 7
    Jonathan 7
    Lewis 7
    Simon 7

Recruitz,
    Dragoon 116

Recter,
    James 137

Rector,
    John 152
    Maximilian 153*

Red,
    William S. 106

Redd,
    John 131*

Reddick,
    John 176*

Redding,
    William H. 156*

Redell,
    Margaret 105

Redick,
    Joseph 123

Redington,
    Asa 11*

Redman,
    Richard 134
    Robert 13

Reed,
    Albert 29
    Alexander 183
    Amelia 107
    Amos 92*
    Asa 38
    Benjamin 173
    Bethia 86
    David 8, 67
    Ebenezer 74*
    Effa 107
    Elihu 40
    Elijah 27, 94*
    Elnathan 71*
    Ezekiel 85
    Garrett 77*
    George 28*
    Hinds 64
    Huldah 67
    Isaac 34, 39*, 69, 135*, 145
    J. W. 41
    Jacob 8
    James 111*
    Jesse 29
    John 27*, 93*, 171*, 189
    Joseph 101*, 109, 145
    Joshua 39*, 67*
    Josiah 40*, 93, 159*
    Justice 58*
    Keziah 23*
    Kitchel 86
    Lemuel 27*
    Martha 120
    Matthew 121
    Moses 34
    Polly 77
    Robert 148
    Samuel 34*, 43, 49, 61*, 86*
    Samuel F. 43
    Sarah 29
    Solomon T. 69
    Stephen 71*
    Supply 23
    Thomas 31, 33*, 95*
    Trueman L. 69
    William 124*
    William F. 91

Reed, (cont.)
    William W. 11*
    Zachariah 83
    Zanthy 77

Reede,
    Thomas 141*

Reeder,
    Charles 109
    Sarah 109
    William F. 76

Reefer,
    Henry 120*

Reeger,
    Nathan 135
    Philip 135

Reehordron,
    Abner 101*

Reeks,
    Sarah 149

Reel,
    David 117

Reeler,
    Asa 55
    David 55*
    Huldah 56

Reep,
    Michael 139*

Rees,
    William 163

Reese,
    L. 149
    Littleton 149

Reeve,
    Irad 105
    William 145*

Reeves,
    J. F. 180
    John 155
    Joseph 166, 180
    Luther 168*
    Manassah 75

Reeves,
    Nathaniel 170*
    Puryer 75
    William 169*
    Willis 166

Reffet,
    Samuel 181

Refinburgh,
    D. 93

Regg,
    Benjamin 177*

Regna,
    Abraham 104*

Reid,
    Josiah 5
    William 153

Reiley,
    F. 168
    J. 168
    James 168

Reily,
    John 169*

Reinert,
    Jacob 115

Reins,
    John 134*

Rekord,
    Elijah 23

Reley,
    John 136

Remer,
    George 105

Remick,
    Phebe 13
    Seth D. 13

Remicks,
    Sarah 16*

Remington,
    Benedict 49*

Remington, (cont.)
    Chauncey 175
    Hannah 180
    John 39*, 47
    Joseph M. 171
    Thomas 47*

Rencill,
    Elizabeth 120*

Reneau,
    Thomas 182*

Benedict,
    Rumas 56

Reneval,
    William 104

Renfrew,
    John 113

Renfro,
    John 160
    Joseph 160

Rennison,
    William 169

Renolds,
    James 17*
    Miles 17*

Renson,
    Abigail 11

Rentzall,
    George 128

Rermick,
    Mary 17

Ressinger,
    Michael 122

Revel,
    John 116*

Revenburg,
    Peter 96

Rexford,
    Amos 93*

Rexroad,
    Solomon 135
    Zachariah 135

Reynold,
    Elizabeth 48

Reynolds,
    Benedict 120*
    Benjamin 14, 102*, 126*
    Benoni 90*
    Charity 168*
    Charles 10
    David 10, 48*
    Deborah 104
    Eliphalet 14
    Elisha 63*
    Elizabeth 48
    Emily 48
    Ezekiel 155
    George 125
    Hannah 50*
    Hardy 117
    Jacob 155*
    James 48*
    Jeremiah 105*
    Job 95
    Joel J. 75*
    John 27, 65*, 119*
    Jonathan 49*, 100
    Mary 85
    Michael 155
    Nathaniel 104*, 168
    Nicholas 100
    Peter 68
    Samuel 155*
    Simeon 119*
    Thomas 78*
    William 48*, 128
    Zachariah 100

Rhay,
    Henry 144*

Rhea,
    Robert 152*

Rhett,
    James 142

Rhiam,
    George 121

Rhinearson,
    Winney 188*

Rhoades,
    Elisha 80
    Jacob 190
    Samuel P. 90

Rhodes,
    Anthony 83
    Catharine 48
    Ezekiel 77*
    Isaac 95
    Jacob 4*
    James 48
    John 95
    Joseph 84*, 102*
    Mary 48
    Moses 3*
    Stephen F. 95
    Zachariah 45*

Rhodus,
    Rhosmantu 51

Rhoten,
    Thomas 184*

Rhyne,
    Manuel 139

Riant,
    Thomas 14

Ribbet,
    William 110*

Riblet,
    Christian 178*

Rice,
    Abiah 71*
    Alpheus 44
    Amos 36*, 72
    B. P. 37
    Bailey 136*
    Christian 123*
    Edmund 40*
    Ephraim 66*
    Ezra 36
    Francis 86
    Hannah 22
    Henry B. 142*
    Holman 160*
    Isaac 180
    Israel 86
    Jacob 74
    Jason 70*, 168

Richie,
    James 191
    Peter 191

Richmond,
    Amaziah 66*
    Asa 28
    Ezra 36*
    Eunice 28
    Isaac 89
    James 27*
    Lydia 27
    Mary 47
    Nancy 77
    Nathaniel 70*
    Phebe 27
    Priscilla 27
    Rachel 57
    Seth 77
    Susanna 44
    Thomas 36*
    Vial 52*
    William 134
    Zimri 44

Rickard,
    John 138*

Ricker,
    George W. 3
    Noah 3*
    Rebecca 3
    Reuben 16*
    Tobias 7

Rickerd,
    John 113*

Rickerson,
    Benjamin 147*

Ricketts,
    Nathan 181
    Robert 181
    William 137*

Rickey,
    Submit 79
    Thomas 79

Ricknell,
    Mary 32

Rid,
    John 139*

Riddle,
    James 92
    John 140
    Joseph 129
    Ran. 140
    Robert 120*

Ridean,
    John 118

Rideout,
    Stephen 8*

Rider,
    Benjamin 103
    Daniel 87*
    Elizabeth 25
    Esther 62*
    Putnam 92
    Stephen 9, 30
    Timothy 92

Ridgway,
    James 44

Ridington,
    Jacob 98
    Nathaniel A. 98

Ridley,
    John 168*
    Samuel 64*

Ridlow,
    Mary 11

Ridner,
    Joseph 148
    Samuel 148

Riely,
    John 166*

Rierson,
    Stephen 140*

Riffel,
    Melchor 116*

Rigbee,
    James 141*

Rigby,
    John 138*

Riggan,
    Frances 141*

Riggans,
    Jacob 138
    Joel 138

Riggins,
    James 153*

Riggs,
    Samuel 153*

Right,
    Abigail 15

Righter,
    John C. 116
    Phebe 116*

Rightmyer,
    George D. 83
    H. 87
    Henry 87

Righton,
    Joseph 142*
    N. 93
    Nicholas 93

Rigs,
    Hosea 188*

Rigsbee,
    Frederick 141*

Riker,
    John 98
    Tunis 99*

Riley,
    James 145*
    John 185*
    Sarah 50
    William 142

Rillough,
    Samuel 157*

Rimhart,
    Mathias 72

Rimiston,
    David 84

Rinchold,
    Henry 113

Rinehart,
    George 169
    George S. 113
    Martin 169

Riney,
    John 174*

Ring,
    Abijah 15
    Thomas 140*

Ringe,
    Richard 64

Ringo,
    Burtis 162*

Ringoe,
    John 166*

Rinker,
    Catharine 116*

Ripley,
    Asa 88*
    Calvin 45
    Charles 45, 84*
    Eliphalet 57*
    Hezekiah 28*
    Jerusha 29
    Lucy 12
    Mary 28
    Nahum 12
    Nehemiah 57*
    Pelham W. 91*
    Pyram 74
    Rebecca 32
    Susan 33
    William 28

Rising,
    Benjamin 175
    Oliver 175

Risley,
    Asa 24*
    Cynthia 88*
    Eli 89*
    George 61*
    Richard 92

Risner,
    William 85*

Rist,
    Rebecca 66
    Samuel 66

Ritch,
    Lott 141*

Ritchey,
    Esau 165*
    James 119*

Ritchie,
    George W. 171

Rittenhouse,
    Jacob 125*

Ritter,
    Ezra 71*
    Hannah 87
    Henry 83
    John K. 87
    Joseph 83
    William 153

Rix,
    Nathan 83*
    Nathaniel 25*
    Peter 43*

Rixford,
    Elizabeth 84
    Henry 36
    William 22*

Roach,
    Abigail 15
    David 187
    Francis 187
    James 132*
    James M. 130
    Jeremiah 174
    Martha 130
    Thomas 53*
    William 174

Roads,
    Jane 136
    John H. 136

Roam,
    Samuel 192*

Roark,
    Michael 187
    William 187

Robarge,
    Peter 78*

Robb,
    James 120

Robbards,
    Jesse 162*

Robbe,
    Henry 86
    Mary 86

Robberts,
    Love 4*

Robbin,
    Joseph 22*

Robbins,
    Abigail 20
    Abner 26
    Amos 57
    Asa 11
    Charles D. 20
    Clark 89
    Consider 28
    Daniel 62*
    Ebenezer 57*
    Edmund 28
    Ephraim 181
    George 85
    Huldah 40
    J. L. 78
    Jedediah 40
    John 173*
    Lorin 89
    M. 78
    Oliver 89
    Peter 98
    Samuel 30*
    Stephen 57
    William 28

Robenson,
    Benjamin 165

Roberds,
    Cornelius 91*

Roberson,
    (Mrs.) 113

Roberson, (cont.)
John 113

Roberts,
Aaron 141
Abigail 50
Alford J. 12
Annath 82
Chester 51
Daniel 50*
Ebenezer 59, 92*
Ed. 153
Edmond 153
Elijah 59*
Eliza 78
Elizabeth 17*
Horace 50
Horatio 34
Isaac 50
Jackson 165
James C. 17
Jeremiah 3*
Joel 63*
John 16, 17, 78*, 87*, 95,
    133*, 151
John T. 40
Jonathan 14
Joseph 12, 17*
Joshua 139*, 190*
Levi M. 77*
Lucretia 50*
Martha 16
Naman 162
Nathaniel 3
P. 142
Paul 3
Peter 142
Philip 163*
Rebecca 49
Reuben 146*, 158*
Richardson 166
Samuel 78, 143*
Sayres 108*
Tabitha 36
Thomas 134*, 145
William 13, 137*

Robertson,
Alanson 56
Allen 144
Daniel 23
David 61
Edward 189*
Hannah 56

Robertson, (cont.)
Isaac 129*
James 160*
John 132*
Matthew 166*
Peter 81, 104*
Richard 130*
Robert 146*
Sarah 55*
Thomas 163*
William 67*, 145

Robeson,
Andrew 114
Joshua 114

Robins,
Allen 49
John 76
Peter 98
Thomas 38, 57*
Zeruviah 57*

Robinson,
(N. X. N.) 71
Abigail 27*
Alpheus 89
Amasa 57*
Andrew 57*
Andrew L. 12
Ann 28
Anna 28
Benjamin 40, 129
Caleb 89
Chandler 125*
Chloe D. 36
Daniel 5
Daniel T. 13
Deborah 4
Dennis 75
Ebenezer 28*, 71*
Eli P. 102*
Eliakim 4
Elizabeth 78, 135
Ephraim 69*
Esther 68
Evan 8
Ezra 71
Hannah 45
Henry 96, 97
Isaac 97*
Issachar 79
J. N. 192
James 15*

Robinson, (cont.)
    Jedediah 10
    Jeriah 145
    John 52*, 99*, 126*, 144*,
        150, 185*, 191
    John L. 12
    John R. 67
    Jonathan 41*, 57*, 64*
    Joseph 15
    Keen 74
    L. 78
    Levi 18, 32*
    Lewis 173
    Luke 39, 145
    Mary 70, 89, 112
    Naomi 44*
    Nathaniel 69*, 70, 94*
    Noah 67
    Obed 28*
    Peter 178
    Phebe 5*
    Randal 91
    Reuben 57*, 192
    Richard 156
    Robert 91
    Sally 183
    Stafford 68
    Susanna 38*
    William 54*, 109*, 150
    William W. 185
    Zaccheus 41*

Robison,
    James 121*
    Michael 115
    William 115

Roby,
    Henry 70*

Rochester,
    Ann 143*

Rock,
    Peter 190

Rockwell,
    Clapp 56
    George R. 33
    Joseph 59*
    Samuel 89*

Rockwood,
    Anna 31

Rockwood, (cont.)
    Frost 37*
    Samuel 68*

Rodenboh,
    Jacob 114

Rodger,
    William 186

Rodgers,
    Benjamin 115
    Daniel 142*
    E. H. 144
    Isaac 27*
    J. 37
    James 110*, 119*, 149*
    Jonathan 37
    Joseph 168*
    Penley 99*
    Peter 187*

Roe,
    Hannah 136
    James 134
    Jesse 171
    Matthew 138*
    Susanna 134
    William 86

Roebuck,
    George 143

Roen,
    John 140*

Roff,
    Christopher 79*

Rogan,
    Barnet 116

Roger,
    David 113
    James 113

Rogers,
    Aaron 41
    Abigail 61
    Ahaz 144*
    Alvah 26
    Asa 26
    Bethial 29*
    Bias 137*
    Bolen 135*

Rogers, (cont.)
    Daniel 26, 105, 159*
    David 70, 152
    Dorothy 162
    Ebenezer 52, 54*
    Eli 109
    Eliphalet 69*
    Elizabeth 45
    Erastus 174
    Ethan 102*
    Eunice 24
    Francis 78*
    George 167*
    Gideon 53*
    Hannah 26*
    Heman 52*
    Henry 185
    Hezekiah 26
    Hooma 58
    J. 73
    James 100*, 167*
    John 19, 72, 73, 143*
    Josiah 125*, 171*
    Leonard 60*
    Louisa 43
    Martha 52, 152
    Nathaniel 74, 84*
    Patty 41
    Rachel 29
    Rebecca 42
    Rhodam 134
    Richard 26
    Ruth 52
    Samuel 41, 58, 95*, 174*
    Simeon 89*
    Stephen 185
    Sylvanus 28
    Thomas 29, 54*, 69*
    Timothy 105
    William 84*, 170*
    Wilson 156
    Yates 26

Roherts,
    Gideon 122

Rohr,
    George W. 163

Rohrer,
    Martin 176*

Roise,
    Silas 64*

Roiser,
    John 67

Roiser, (cont.)
    Robert 147*

Roland,
    Fendal 157
    James 159*

Roles,
    James 85*

Rollen,
    Abel 141*

Rollins,
    Aaron 79
    Anthony 11
    Benjamin 63
    Bern 79
    David 10*
    Eliphalet 19*
    Francis 15
    Henry 136
    Jabez 10*
    John 9*, 17*
    Joseph 10
    Josiah 9
    Moses 136
    Nicholas 15
    Robert 25
    Samuel 17
    Sarah 15, 63
    Susannah 11
    T. J. 143

Rollings,
    Charles 140*

Rolly,
    Eli S. 96*

Rolo,
    Daniel 93*

Romaine,
    Albert 107
    Samuel 107

Roman,
    Alexander 88

Romine,
    Benjamin 110

Ronald,
    William S. 135

Rood,
    Eli 104*

Roof,
    John 87*

Rooke,
    Amos 105*

Roome,
    Henry 107*

Roosa,
    Christian 102
    Jacob J. 103*
    John E. 103

Root,
    Amos 91
    Azariah 171*
    Billa 73*
    Dinah 88*
    Elias 35
    Erastus 88*
    Garry 175
    Israel 91
    Joel 32*
    John 104*
    Joseph 92*
    L. 122
    Lemuel 122
    Lucy 34, 100
    Nathaniel 61*, 90*
    Polly 70
    Rufus 71*
    Sally 100
    Salmon 85*
    Sarah 85
    Stephen E. 70
    Thomas 82
    William 77
    Zenas 33*

Roots,
    Hiram H. 59
    Lucy 59

Rootz,
    Michael 136

Roper,
    Elizabeth 38
    George 187*
    John 148

Roper, (cont.)
    Mary 166*
    Stephen 148
    Sylvester 38

Rorack,
    Letitia 153*

Rorick,
    Caspar 111*

Rosa,
    Abram 78
    Rufus 78

Rosacrontz,
    Jacob 107
    Jane 107

Rosakrans,
    James 102*

Rose,
    Abraham 20*
    Achsa 174
    Ambrose P. 4
    Amy 106
    C. C. 174
    Chauncey 80
    Elanson 73
    Eunice 67
    George 67
    Hannah 52*
    Hiram 103
    James 136
    John 141*
    Joseph 4, 80
    Maria 124
    Mary 53*
    Peter 86*
    Phineas 106
    Richard 186*
    Sterling 141*
    Thomas 28*
    William 73

Roseboon,
    Hendrick 178

Rosebraugh,
    John 134*

Rosefelt,
    Henry 96

Rosenbery,
    Michael 177

Rosengrant,
    Mary 76

Rosensteel,
    Jacob 117*

Rositer,
    Noah 32

Ross,
    A. 160*
    Amos 169
    Arthur 47
    Benjamin 97
    Daniel 42*, 183
    David 137
    David P. 164
    Elizabeth 43
    Ezekiel 169
    George 159*
    George B. 155
    Gideon 3
    Henry 106*
    Isaac 6*, 185*
    James 112, 137
    Jeremiah 42
    John 23, 110*, 155, 157*, 164
    Jonathan 3
    Martha 183
    Reuben 187*
    Robinson 158*
    Samuel 101*
    Sarah 5
    Simon 3
    Thankful 36
    Thomas 24, 42*
    Timothy 42
    Walter 149*
    Williamson 139*

Rossiter,
    Noah 32
    Timothy 146*

Rosson,
    Reuben 129*

Roth,
    Susan 113

Rothbone,
    Solomon 76*

Rothwell,
    Fountain 162

Round,
    Nathaniel 57*

Roundey,
    Benjamin 9*
    Jane 43*
    Sarah 43*

Rounds,
    Amos 28*
    Charles 175
    David 68
    James 169*
    Nathaniel 175

Roundtree,
    William 131*

Rouse,
    Joseph 183
    Lewis S. 192
    Nicholas 98*

Roush,
    George 176*
    Jonas 176

Routon,
    James 129

Row,
    John 162*
    William 182

Rowdon,
    William 102*

Rowe,
    Benjamin 156*
    Betsey 43
    Charles 140*
    Daniel 149
    Enoch 15*
    Isaac 43
    John 7, 52*
    Joseph 16
    Joshua 149
    Martin 146
    Solomon 41
    Thaddeus 82
    Webber 5*
    Zebulon 6*

Rowell,
    Daniel 26, 186
    Jesse 144*
    William 16

Rowen,
    Jacob 25
    John 68
    Sarah 25

Rowland,
    John 83
    Samuel 83

Rowley,
    Joseph R. 174
    R. C. 186*
    Seth 93
    Silas 51*
    Thomas 36, 174
    William 98

Roy,
    James 153

Royalty,
    John 161*

Royce,
    Chauncey 51
    Chester 70
    Elijah 70
    John 51
    Samuel 88*
    Solomon 160*

Royel,
    Lemuel 23*

Rucker,
    Elzaphan 195*
    Lemuel 177*

Ruckman,
    John 120*

Rudd,
    Bezaleel 105*
    Enos 68
    Eunice 57
    John W. 32
    Nathaniel 32
    Sarah 68

Rudder,
    James 129

Ruddle,
    Robinson 167

Rude,
    Phebe 54
    Rix 54
    William 46*

Rudolph,
    George 112

Rudy,
    Jacob 116*

Rue,
    John 109
    Joseph J. 109
    Richard 186

Ruffeam,
    Simeon 119

Rugar,
    John 77

Ruger,
    John 102*

Rugg,
    Isaac 74*
    Joshua 72
    Mary 89

Ruggles,
    Gardner 37
    James 63
    John 9
    Lucy 37, 55*
    Martin 37
    Olive 37
    S. O. 29
    Seth 69*
    T. 192

Ruland,
    Isaac 186*

Rule,
    Aaron 187

Rulin,
    Benjamin 96

Rulin, (cont.)
    Rueben 96

Rulshart,
    John 110*

Rumels,
    Samuel 17

Rumery,
    Jonathan 88*

Rumfeldt,
    Elizabeth 114
    George 114

Rummell,
    John 84

Rumney,
    Stephen 64*

Rumrill,
    Joseph 39*

Rumsey,
    David 76*
    Jeremiah 123*
    John 68*

Rundal,
    David 105*

Rundell,
    Reuben 102*

Rundle,
    Phineas 56

Rundlet,
    Lydia 20
    Thomas 20

Rundlets,
    Nathaniel 15

Rundlett,
    Reuben 24*

Runkle,
    Edwin 116

Runnell,
    Thomas 31

Runnells,
    Thomas 6*

Runnels,
    Ebenezer 62
    Enos 42*
    John 171
    Joseph 18*, 182*
    Sarah 62
    Thomas 143

Runnion,
    Elijah 135*

Runnolds,
    Luke 54
    Sally 54

Runyan,
    Hugh 110*
    Richard 110*

Rupert,
    George 171

Rupp,
    Andrew 114

Ruse,
    Aaron 170*

Rush,
    Jacob 123*
    Michael 118
    William 118

Rushing,
    Berrill 159
    Philip 159
    Richard 159*

Rushon,
    Catharine 114

Russel,
    Andrew 13
    Asa 33
    Burnham 20
    Robert S. 189*
    Solomon 13
    William 93

Russell,
    Abigail 100

Russell,
Amos 40
Benjamin 6*
Bill 39*
Calvin 13*
Chandler 31
Daniel 20
David 61*
David A. 52
Ebenezer 20
Eleazer 88
Enoch 173
Esther 176
Eunice 52
Hannah 8, 105
Harvey 44
Henry 42*
James 105
James G. 145*
Jedediah 20
John 59*, 84*, 131*, 153*, 183*
Jonathan 11, 18
Lorica 61*
Luther 14
Moor 25*
Moses 176
Paul 116*
Peabody 42
Rebecca 42
Robert 136*
Samuel 63*
Sarah 43
Simeon 84*
Stephen 61*
Thomas 8, 148*
Whiting 99
William 11, 93*

Rust,
Abel 83
Elizabeth 43
Hiram 83
Huldah 74
Jerusha 41*
John 165
Justin 74
Lucy 71
Martin 58
Mason 165
Oliver 71
S. 73
Stephen 73
William 22

Rutan,
Abraham 111*

Rutenaw,
George 193
Jacob 193

Ruth,
John 181*

Rutherford,
Absalom 153*
John 42, 92*
Robert 134
Thomas 134

Rutland,
Abednego 158
Joseph 158

Rutledge,
Joseph 145

Rutlidge,
James M. 187

Ryall,
Peter 84*

Ryan,
Elizabeth 78
Harris 154*
James 182*, 186*
Jonathan 78
Peter O. 141*
Samuel 40
William 138*

Ryckman,
Albert 72
Wilhelmus 72

Ryder,
Mary 91

Rymer,
George 135*

Rynearson,
Cornelius 119
Isaac 119

Ryon,
Charles 97

Ryphenburgh,
    Adam 105
    Jeremiah 105

Sabin,
    Eldad 80
    Erastus W. 80
    Jonathan 60*
    Lewis 12

Sabins,
    Samuel 27

Sackett,
    Benjamin 59*
    Martha 51*
    Skene D. 168
    William 96
    Zavan 124*

Sacks,
    Jacob 69*

Sacree,
    W. 182

Saddler,
    David 143*
    John 8*

Safford,
    Abigail 82*
    Hiram 78

Sage,
    Daniel 77
    Elias 84*
    Elizabeth W. 59*
    Rodney 32
    Silas 32
    Simeon 59*
    Stephen 32
    Thaizer 96*

Sager,
    Ganet J. 72
    G. J. 72

Sailor,
    Peter 114*

St. John,
    Agnes 129
    David 56
    Enoch 56
    J. 74
    Jacob A. 129
    Jesse 56

Salada,
    John 114*

Sales,
    Samuel 31

Salesbury,
    Amey 46

Salisberry,
    William 126

Salisbury,
    Andrew 190
    Benjamin F. 91

Sallvy,
    Daniel 31

Salmon,
    Gershom 91
    John 130*
    Stephen 91
    Stephen D. 44

Salpaugh,
    Catharine 104
    Philip 104
Salsburg,
    Harmon 72
    John 72

Salsbury,
    Abel 46
    Lucas 87*

Salter,
    James 179
    John 60*
    Michael 162*

Salts,
    Benjamin 97*

Salyers,
    Dunn 164*

Sammis,
    Lester 33

Sammons,
    Benjamin 81
    Jacob 81
    Joseph 129*

Samons,
    Margaret 107*

Sampels,
    Jesse 148*

Sample,
    John 85*, 121
    William 121

Sampson,
    Abner 29*
    Andrew 29*
    Benjamin 64*
    Bristol B. 119*
    George 70*
    Howland 29*
    Isaiah 30
    Isiah 30
    James 6
    Jonathan 37*
    Luther 10*
    Philemon 70*
    Reuben 6
    Samuel 30*

Samson,
    Amos 39*

Sanbern,
    Elizabeth 63

Sansberry,
    John 136*

Sanbone,
    Benjamin 23*

Sanborn,
    Anna 20*

Sanborn, (cont.)
    Benjamin 14
    Dolly 17*
    Hannah 5
    Josiah 17
    Lucy 25
    Lydia 25
    Mary 16
    Matthew P. 13
    Nathaniel 14
    Noah J. 18
    Simon M. 16

Sanburn,
    John 12*
    Paul 85*

Sandefer,
    Martha 165

Sanders,
    Avery 78*
    Elizabeth 97
    Henry 32
    Isaac D. 160*
    J. 74
    John 17*, 130, 166*
    Joseph 74
    Joshua 77
    Lydia 23
    Peter 57*
    Philemon 160*
    Samuel H. 130*
    W. A. 157
    William 170
    Zachariah 167*

Sanderson,
    Artimas 70
    Asa 34*
    Isaac 34*, 69
    Jonathan 38
    Lyman 100
    Phineas 70
    Rachel 34
    Rufus 13*
    Sarah 100
    Sophia 38
    William M. 88*

Sandford,
    Archibald 53*
    David 32
    Elisha 52*

Sandford, (cont.)
George 51
J. 74
Jarius 51*
Joseph 74
Stephen 32

Sandon,
Horace 82

Sands,
Andrew 122*
Dinah 16*
Rebecca 50*

Sandusky,
John 156

Sanford,
Abiah 56
Ebenezer 56*
Eunice 58
James 56*
John 8*, 110*
Sela 89*
Strong 58*
Zalmon 56

Sanger,
Daniel 33*

Sanmon,
Peter 54

Santell,
Asa 12
John 12

Sardam,
Sylvia 59

Sardom,
Solomon 59

Sargeant,
Sarah 17

Sargeants,
Jacob 80*

Sargent,
Caleb 19
Charity 4
Charles 3*

Sargent, (cont.)
Chase 4
Elijah 172
Eunice 20
George W. 23
Henry 4
Jacob 49*
James 175*
Joseph 19
Joshua 20*
Phineas 23
William 4, 19*, 160*

Sarles,
Richard 99*
Sutton 105

Sartin,
Ely 153*

Sartwell,
M. 67
Sylvanus 67

Sarzedas,
David 142

Sasser,
Benjamin 137

Sassor,
William 151

Satterlee,
Cynthia 126
J. F. 126
James 126*

Satterwhite,
Robert 129*

Saully,
Eunice 55

Saunders,
Christopher 99
Cornelius 157*
Daniel 130*
David 129*
Eliza 157
George 129*
James 155, 157
Jesse 130*
Joseph 155

Saunders, (cont.)
Luke 99
M. 43
Noah 61*
Thomas 55*
William 113, 138*

Savage,
Amasa 50
Elijah D. 9
Hiel 95
John 13
Margaret 43*
Robin 143*
Sarah 13
Selah 50*
Seth 50

Savel,
Mary 115*

Savery,
Thomas 72
William 72

Sawin,
Abigail 41
Abner 37*
Levi 30

Sawins,
Jerome 71*

Sawtelle,
Eunice 11

Sawtle,
Benjamin 170
Sybil 170

Sawyer,
Abel 24
Benjamin 22*, 38*, 97
Ebenezer 4*, 63, 84*
Edmund 19
Edward 19
George 13*, 75
Israel 16
Jabez 4*
Jacob 11
James B. 10
Jemima 97
John 6*
John E. 10

Sawyer, (cont.)
Jonathan P. 24
Joseph 22
Joshua 38
Jude 38*
Lydia 61*
Manasseh 98
Martha 16
Mary 21, 46*
Moses H. 64
Nabby 64
Polly 36
William 10, 63

Sawyers,
Joseph 140

Sawyner,
Ebenezer 4

Saxon,
Solomon 146*

Saxson,
James 159
John 181*

Saxton,
Lucinda 145

Sayers,
Robert 166*

Saylers,
Michael 156
Thomas 156

Sayles,
Abigail 46
Angell 47
Artemas 88
Daniel 31
Elisha 47
Rose 46*
Smith 46*
Stukely 88

Saylor,
Philip 175*

Sayre,
Isaac 109*
James 105*
Job 106*

Scofield, (cont.)
    Josiah W. 56
    Mary 105
    N. 95
    Nathaniel 74
    Selah 75

Sconce,
    John 190*

Scoonover,
    James 177*

Scott,
    Abraham 118*
    Amey 46*
    Benjamin 100, 183
    Charles T. 24
    Daniel 95*
    Deborah 31
    Elizabeth 120*
    Ethiel 62*
    Eunice 34
    Ezekiel 100*
    Henrietta 47
    Henry 191
    James 97, 85*, 134, 135*
    James T. 42
    John 112, 125, 126, 138, 152
        163, 180, 183, 186
    Joseph 61, 63*, 130*
    Mary 22, 24, 126
    Mehitable 42
    Oliver 172*
    Olney 46
    Phineas 34*
    Richard 66
    Robert 117*, 161*
    Ruth 61
    Sarah 121
    Thomas 97
    Uri 52*
    William 160*, 163
    William F. 132*
    Zerah 119*

Scouten,
    Jacob 125

Scouton,
    Elias 188*

Scovell,
    David 174
    Rachel 174

Scovil,
    Henry 86
    Lydia 86

Scovill,
    Chester 53
    Matthew 89
    Westol 119

Scoville,
    Jacob 59*
    S. M. 73
    Samuel 73

Scowfield,
    Jesse 161*

Scranton,
    Jerry 52*
    Timothy 52*

Scribner,
    Aaron 174
    Esther 78
    Jeremiah 78
    Jonathan 65, 78*
    Samuel 19
    Thaddeus 95*

Scriggins,
    Thomas 4

Scripture,
    Samuel 22*

Scriver,
    William 94*

Scrivner,
    Caleb W. 94
    James 94

Scroder,
    John 106

Scroggin,
    Jonah 187
    R. H. 187

Scroggins,
    W. 142
    Willis 142

Scroggs,
    John 139

Scruggs,
    Elizabeth 162
    Thomas M. 162
    Timothy 129*

Scudder,
    Abraham 185
    William 185

Scutt,
    William 104*

Seabott,
    Henry 86

Seabrook,
    Stephen 110

Seager,
    Darius 91*
    Harlow B. 168

Seaght,
    Henry 109

Seagraves,
    Edward F. 39

Seales,
    Samnet 5

Seaman,
    Andrew 96*

Seamans,
    Isaac 99*
    Jemima 84*

Seamore,
    Thomas 158
    William 158

Searcy,
    John 166

Seares,
    Barnabas 35
    David 57*

Searey,
    James 160

Seargeant,
    Mary 66

Searl,
    Abraham 180
    Brentnal 12

Searle,
    Benjamin B. 62*

Searles,
    Curtis 41
    Hannah 40
    Samuel 40

Sears,
    Abigail 34
    Allen 73
    Asarelah 34
    David 60*
    Earl 30*
    Ebenezer 66*
    Hannah 37*
    Jacob 106
    John 106
    Mercy 30
    Roland 35
    Samuel 106*
    William 30

Seat,
    James 139*

Seaton,
    Asher 192
    George 160
    William K. 160

Seaver,
    Anna 76
    Calvin 70
    Ichabod 119*
    Josiah W. 3
    Obed 46
    Otis 70
    R. W. 76

Seavey,
    Daniel 19*
    Jonathan 15*

Seavy,
    Ebenezer 7*

Seay,
    James 131*, 143*
    Matthew 131*

Seberel,
    William 179*

Sechler,
    Michael 123*

Secor,
    Andrew 72*
    John 77*

Secrest,
    John 158*

Sedgewick,
    Lucy 49
    Martha 49
    William 49

Sedgley,
    John 8

Seeber,
    Andolph 87
    Henry 83
    Sylvanus 83

Seekell,
    William 28

Seeley,
    Benjamin 83*
    Ebenezer 56*
    Isaac 89
    Joseph 56*
    Lucinda 89
    Samuel 126
    Zadock 105*

Seely,
    Abigail 116
    Abram 32
    T. 92

Segar,
    Caleb 36
    Elijah 69*
    Joseph 59*

Seger,
    Edward 93
    Ezekiel 93
    Mehitable 40
    Nathaniel 7

Seifert,
    William 115

Seigler,
    George 142*

Seip,
    Frederick 113

Selden,
    Asa 34
    Jesse 34

Selders,
    James 182

Selerieg,
    James 192
    Jeremiah 192

Self,
    Guy 161
    John 161

Selfridge,
    John 100

Selingham,
    Jacob 25*

Sellech,
    Stephen 82*

Selleck,
    James 192*
    Joseph 56*
    Peter 89*

Sellers,
    James 152*

Selman,
    Abigail 44

Semel,
    Elias 114

Semmon,
    Conrad 133
    George 133

Semmons,
    Alexander 140*

Sent,
  Jacob 82*

Sentar,
  Tandy 154*

Senter,
  Isaac 6
  Sally 6

Seppius,
  Abraham 96

Septer,
  Frederick 124

Seratt,
  Allen 152*

Sergeant,
  George 126
  John 68*

Sergent,
  Eunice 24

Servace,
  William G. 170*

Servall,
  Henry 9*

Serviss,
  John 87
  Samuel 87

Sessions,
  Hannah 61
  Joanna D. 61

Settlemyre,
  Godfrey 125*

Sevanson,
  Levi 165*

Sever,
  Henry 72
  James 28
  Peter 72

Severance,
  Abel 19
  Benjamin 17, 175*
  Elizabeth 11

Severance, (cont.)
  John 19
  Joseph S. 11
  Mehitable 17

Severence,
  Asa 80
  Azuba 126
  Samuel 126

Severns,
  Edward 179

Severson,
  Nicholas 78
  Richard 78

Sevey,
  Eliakim 4
  John 4

Sevier,
  Abraham 157
  Abraham R. 157*
  James 154*
  Nasma 152

Sewall,
  Stephen 6

Sewank,
  Jacob 118*

Seward,
  Daniel 162
  Jedediah 73*
  John 178*
  Leverett 82*
  Lucinda 162
  Olive 22
  S. 73
  Silas 73
  Swain 92*
  Timothy 52*

Sewel,
  James 161*, 189*

Sewell,
  Rebecca 127*

Sexton,
  Charles 74, 171
  David 144
  Esther 154

Sexton, (cont.)
Ezra 168
George 189
John 152*
Lois 74
Mary 116
Oliver 70
Silas W. 116
Timothy 154
William C. 168

Seymond,
Rebecca 56
Seth 56

Seymour,
Eliza 90
Elizabeth 49*
John 76
Nathan 61
Nathaniel 95
Rebecca 58*
Susan 58
Thomas 95
William 51, 61, 72*, 76
Zadock 90

Shackelford,
John P. 131
Richard 131

Shackford,
Christopher 3
Samuel 3

Shackleford,
Leonard 131*
William 131*

Shade,
Jacob 134*

Shafer,
Adam 125*
Angelica 96
Christian H. 96
Frederick 178
Henry 96*
Philip 178*

Shaffer,
Frederick 152*
John 136
Samuel 136

Shaffer, (cont.)
Thomas 120
Thomas S. 120

Shaid,
John 114

Shall,
Anna Eve 83
David J. 83
John 83*
Michael 121*

Shalley,
John 114*

Shalluck,
Mary 67

Shammon,
Benjamin 135

Shands,
William 133*

Shank,
J. D. 174

Shankland,
William 86*

Shannon,
A. B. 159*
Elizabeth 117
John 16
Lydia 16
Thomas 16*

Shaper,
Andrew 173*

Sharon,
John 84
Samuel 166*

Sharp,
Adam 140*
Andrew 123*
Benjamin 191*
Daniel 70*
Garret 90
Isham 166*
Isom 160
Reuben 57*

Sharp,
S. 192*
Susanna 160
William 152*, 188

Sharpe,
Joseph 139*

Sharpnack,
Peter 119

Sharpton,
Margaret 142

Shattuck,
Abraham 23*
David 54
Giles 54
James 9
James M. 64
Joseph 41*
Mary 68
Oliver 44
Phebe 64

Shaver,
Henry 83*
Jacob 90*
John 79*, 81*

Shaw,
Abiather 22*
Abraham 4*
Amos 103
Andrew 11
Asa 35
Basil 146
Benjamin 158
Crispas 68*
Daniel 97*
Darling 94*
David 124
Ede 103
Elisha 62*
George 9, 11, 30, 33*
George M. 48
Hannah 70
Ichabod 125
Jacob 91
James 72, 156*, 185*
John 9, 20*, 44, 94
Jorius 7*
Joseph 5, 15, 27*, 97, 141
Josiah 35, 79*

Shaw, (cont.)
Lydia 27*
Margaret E. 116
Nathaniel 8*, 28
Noah 47*
Polly 6*
Richard 180*
Robert 189
Samuel 3, 34
Samuel M. 3
Sarah 32
Shipman 34
Sylvanus 70*
William 5, 77, 144*, 156*

Shawhen,
Frederick 179
Lorenzo 179

Shay,
Sears 125*
Thomas 113*

Shea,
Stephen 127

Sheaffer,
Peter 113

Shear,
John 193
John L. 193

Shearer,
David 119
Jeremiah 117*
Samuel 119
Thomas 80
William 80

Shearin,
Frederick 141*

Shed,
Daniel 11*
Joel 40*

Shedd,
David 80*

Sheffer,
Adam 123

Sheffield,
    Joseph 77*
    Nathan 75*

Sheftall,
    Sheftall 147*

Shehane,
    Edward 42

Shelburn,
    John 181

Shelden,
    Eli 42
    Elisha 91*
    Nathaniel 98

Sheldin,
    Roger 48*

Sheldon,
    Aaron 68*
    Caleb 62*
    Cephas 64*
    Ephraim 12*
    Ezekiel 94
    Isaac 77
    John 33
    Josiah 62*
    Moses 68
    Nathaniel 46*

Sheles,
    Joseph 88

Shellan,
    Samuel 92

Shelldin,
    Asa 47*

Shelly,
    Rebecca 95

Shelor,
    Daniel 134
    George 134

Shelters,
    Philip 62*

Shelton,
    Jane 165*
    Joseph 130*

Sheltor,
    Elizabeth 187

Shelts,
    Christopher 98*

Shenefelt,
    Anna 175
    John 175

Shennick,
    Jacob 127

Shepard,
    Amos 34
    Charles 20
    David 60*
    Elijah 89
    Eunice 20
    Horace 87
    John 91*, 109
    Joseph 34
    Lucinda 87
    Phineas 170*
    Riley 89
    Samuel 57*, 66*, 158*
    Schuyler 28
    Valentine 139*

Shepardson,
    Thaddeus 13

Shepherd,
    Albert 104
    Charles 186, 194*
    Enos 34
    James 8, 104
    Joel 34
    John 38
    Levi 10*
    Mary 8
    Mary Ann 165*
    Morrill 19*
    Prudence 38
    R. S. 149
    Thomas 75*
    William 181, 184*

Shepperd,
    Jacob 129*

Shepperson,
    David 136*

Shipman,
James 137*
William 119

Shipper,
Solomon 47*

Shippey,
Daniel 87*

Shippy,
James 110
William 110

Shirley,
Harry 22
Job 75
John 22

Shirman,
Enoch 68

Shirtleff,
Noah 178
Selah 178

Shirts,
Matthias 170*
Peter 109*

Shive,
Lewis 116*

Shively,
Catharine 114

Shoals,
Abel 54*

Shober,
Susan 134*

Shockley,
Joseph 30
Thomas 158
William 158*

Shoecraft,
Elizabeth 86

Shoemaker,
Abraham 118*
Elizabeth 83
Henry 96
J. M. 76
Randle 139*
Samuel 76

Shoff,
Frederick 115
Frederick R. 115

Sholes,
John 44
Sarah 89*

Sholl,
Joseph 83

Shook,
Andrew 138
Jacob 121

Shores,
Thomas 130*, 134

Shorey,
Samuel 10*

Short,
Anna 49
Archibald 132
James 49, 187
John 69, 161
Joshua 187
Moses 41

Short, (cont.)
    Philip 49
    Samuel 93*
    Seth 57

Shortridge,
    Andrew 155*

Shory,
    John 18
    Lyford 18

Shotwell,
    Elijah 108*

Shoufler,
    Valentine 114*

Shoultes,
    Jacob 72*

Shoup,
    Ludwick 115*

Showell,
    Judith 16

Shreve,
    John 179
    Joseph 179

Shrieve,
    Benjamin 163

Shroat,
    Michael 164

Shropshire,
    Abner 160*

Shrum,
    Margaret 117*

Shuck,
    Matthias 163*

Shufelt,
    William 119*

Shuffield,
    William 146*

Shukman,
    Nicholas 189

Shults,
    C. J. 85
    Jacob 85

Shumway,
    Benjamin 33
    L. 36
    Lucy 36
    Samuel 36*

Shurmon,
    Philip 152*

Shurnway,
    Harmon 57

Shurr,
    John 145*

Shurtleff,
    Benoni 71*

Shurtliff,
    Gideon 28
    Sarah 29
    Timothy 63

Shute,
    Benjamin 16*

Shutts,
    Diadama 165
    Henry 176
    Joseph 165

Sibley,
    Arculaus 57*
    Chauncey 86
    Daniel 39*
    Ezra 86
    John 151*

Siesco,
    Abraham 87*

Sifard,
    Andrew 177*

Sigmon,
    George 166*

Sikes,
    Gideon 50*
    Josiah 139

Silaman,
    Thomas 115*

Silick,
    Elizabeth 104
    Nathaniel 104

Sill,
    Elisha N. 51*

Sillaman,
    Benjamin 51

Silley,
    Benjamin 12*

Silloway,
    Patience 42

Silsbe,
    David 98*

Silsbee,
    David 111*

Silsbury,
    Jonathan 87*

Silsby,
    John 192*
    Lassell 23

Silver,
    Daniel 41*

Silvernail,
    John 104

Silverthorn,
    Charles 116

Silvestre,
    Etienne 151*

Simkins,
    Charles 135*

Simmon,
    George 97

Simmons,
    Abner 47*
    Benjamin 86*
    Caleb 89
    Calvin 49
    George 130*
    Gideon 87
    Horace 174*
    Ichabod 47
    Isaac 47, 89
    James 57*, 153*, 154*
    James P. 159
    Jehu 132*
    Jeremiah 141*
    John 100*, 105
    Peleg 29
    Perry 47
    Polly 159
    Samuel 24
    Thomas 169*
    William 47, 163*, 165

Simms,
    Jer. 177*
    John 153, 195
    Richard 189*

Simonds,
    Bridget 24
    Eliza 43*
    Hiram A. 24
    James 25*
    Joseph 77*
    Lucy 38

Simons,
    (N. X. N.) 58
    Allen E. 106
    Asa 134*
    Frederick 118*
    John 87, 106
    Joseph 68
    L. A. 65
    Lucy 57, 61
    Mehitable 58

Simonson,
    Christopher 126

Simonson, (cont.)
    Garret 126
    Hannah 107
    Simon 107

Simpson,
    Anderson 100
    Andrew 98*
    David 11
    James 41*, 103*, 133, 148
    John 103*, 164*, 171
    Lucy 4*
    Maria 95
    Mary 133
    Peter 102*
    Stephen 118*
    Thomas 66*
    William 148

Sims,
    Augustin 189
    John 160*
    Presley 183*
    Rebecca 48
    Rodam 190
    William 48, 150

Simson,
    Simeon 11

Sinclair,
    Joshua 11*

Sinclaire,
    Charles 190
    Robert 190

Sinclare,
    Noah 26*

Sincler,
    Rachel 18

Singer,
    John V. 188

Singleton,
    Edmond 146
    James 194*
    Overstreet 146

Singletory,
    Josiah 137*

Sink,
    Abraham 130
    John 130

Sipe,
    John 121*

Sipes,
    George 183*

Sippell,
    Peter 89*

Sischo,
    Samuel 23*

Sisco,
    Giles 110*
    Nathaniel 110*
    Peter J. 110*

Sisk,
    Bartlett 152
    Lawson 152

Sisson,
    Elizabeth 53
    George 47*
    Lebeas 48
    Seabury 49
    Sophia 47*
    Susanna 47
    Thomas 48

Sitts,
    Henry 94
    Peter 87*

Siveat,
    Terrill 159

Siver,
    John 83, 162

Sivzer,
    Sevia 44*

Six,
    John 184*

Sixbury,
    Benjamin 87

Sizer,
    Anthony 43*

Skaats,
    James 172

Skaggs,
    Henry 162
    James 162

Skanes,
    Adam 149*

Skates,
    James 182

Skeel,
    Amos 78*

Skeele,
    Amos 44*

Skeen,
    Jonathan 136

Skelp,
    House 106*

Skelton,
    Robert 182*
    William 129*, 153*

Skiff,
    Lucy 35

Skimmel,
    Richard 83*

Skinner,
    Andrew 9
    Ashbel 97
    Barton 22
    Chester 72
    Cleopatra 51*
    Daniel 103*
    David 60*
    Eli 97
    Elizabeth 50*, 72
    Hannah 168
    Henry 132
    Isaac 70*, 161*
    James 127*
    John 8, 39
    Jonathan 80
    Joseph 37
    O. S. 97
    Rhoda 97

Skinner, (cont.)
    Sarah 37
    Temperance 70
    Timothy 22
    Ursula 50

Skinners,
    Hiram 79

Skully,
    Jacob 113

Slack,
    Charles 140
    Margaret 140

Slade,
    Abner 58*
    Allen 21
    John 65*
    Samuel 21*
    William 21

Slason,
    Jonathan 68*

Slater,
    Andrew 96*
    Esther 51
    Jacob 102
    Nicholas 77

Slaughter,
    Ephraim 43
    Jacob 154*
    John 85
    Lucy 133
    Mary 162
    Philip 129
    Philip C. 129
    Robert 133
    Sylvanus 43
    William 154

Slavens,
    Isaiah 184*

Slavin,
    John 162*

Slawson,
    Eleazar 105
    John 90*
    Nathan 105*

Sledd,
    John 132*
    William 141*

Sleeper,
    Betsey 23
    Colby 23
    Elizabeth 23

Sleght,
    Andrew 91

Sleight,
    Abraham 105*

Slick,
    William 118*

Slingerland,
    Peter 93

Sliter,
    William 94*

Sloan,
    Asahel 24
    Ezekiel 84*
    J. 142
    Joan 142
    John 157*
    Lyman G. 87
    Sarah 87
    Temperance 24
    Thomas 188*

Sloane,
    William 136*

Slocum,
    Elizabeth 45, 49

Slocumb,
    Ezekiel 141*
    John 146
    John C. 146
    Lucy 61

Slone,
    William 127

Sloper,
    Henry 24

Slorum,
    Bethiel 31

Sloughter,
    George 145*

Sloughton,
    Eleanor 50
    Flora 50
    Horace 50
    Mehitable 50*
    William 50

Slover,
    John 109

Sluper,
    Benjamin 17
    Joseph 17

Sly,
    Samuel 106*

Smaledge,
    Elizabeth 44

Small,
    Amos 8
    Daniel 4*, 6*
    Elisha 14
    Elizabeth 4*
    Ephraim 8
    James 6*, 172*
    Luther 12
    Samuel 9
    William 14

Smalley,
    Reuben 100*

Smart,
    Dudley 20*
    Elijah 25
    Jonathan 17
    Moses 25*
    Richard S. 20
    Ruth 25
    Samuel 23, 24*

Smawley,
    Josiah 104*

Smead,
    David 193
    Oliver 174
    Samuel 174

Snow, (cont.)
    Jeremiah 72*
    John 22*
    Jonathan 5
    Joseph 22, 91
    Levi 32
    Lucy 57
    Marcy 27*
    Mary 65
    Richard 128*
    Sherman 91
    Shubal 32*
    Simpkins 75
    Solomon 35
    Stephen 32
    Z. 64

Snowden,
    Aaron 193*
    David 162

Snowdeul,
    Edward 9
    Elizabeth

Snyder,
    Adam 115
    Christian 127
    Christopher 103*
    Daniel 83
    Dennis 192
    Jacob 116
    Jeremiah 114
    Margaret 83
    Martin 103
    Peter 103
    William 104*, 170*

Sodown,
    Jacob 146
    Jacob W. 146

Solace,
    Joseph 60

Soliday,
    Mary 120

Sollers,
    Mahala 190
    Sabert 190

Solomon,
    John 165

Solomons,
    Asell 56*

Somerby,
    Moses 42

Somes,
    Lucy 41

Sones,
    Peter 123*

Sonner,
    Anthony 173*

Soper,
    David 85
    Jesse 69*
    Timothy 84

Sorel,
    John 161*

Sorrill,
    John 133

Soul,
    Alethea 29

Soule,
    Ivory 22*
    James 5
    Jonathan 5
    Lathrop L. 7
    Polly 7

Southall,
    Henry 141*

Southard,
    Henry 98, 111

Southell,
    Asahel 119
    Hannah 119

Souther,
    Laban 29*

Southerland,
    Silas 104

Southwick,
    David 78*
    Isaac 36

Southworth,
    Asa 84
    Erastus 75
    Isaac 69*
    Lucy 129*
    Samuel 65
    William 122

Soverence,
    Eanice 69

Sowel,
    John 153

Sowle,
    Job 27*

Sowtell,
    Joseph 40*
    Nathaniel 40*

Spader,
    Benjamin 185

Spafford,
    Jacob 82*

Spain,
    Peter D. 163*
    William 140*

Spalding,
    Aaron 33
    Bela 70
    Carlton 63
    Daniel 73
    Ezra 70
    George 165*
    Philip 23
    Reuben 70*
    Samuel 63
    Wealthy Ann 126
    Zebulon R. 126

Spann,
    Charles 142*

Sparger,
    John W. 173*

Sparks,
    Ebenezer 66
    Eleanor 61
    Elijah 50

Sparks, (cont.)
    Isaac 158
    James S. 179
    John 141
    Lavina 124
    Matthew 158
    Reuben 141
    Roxana 61
    William 124

Sparlin,
    Anson 85

Sparling,
    George 174*

Sparrow,
    Henry 165*
    J. 74

Sparrows,
    Jabez 26*

Spats,
    Michael 112

Spaulden,
    Phineas 99

Spaulding,
    Abel 171
    Benjamin 32*
    Emma 23
    Gardner 23
    John 71*, 171
    Joseph 11*
    Josiah 13*
    Samuel 12, 67*
    Stephen 80*
    William 13*

Spaunberg,
    George 73
    Jacob 73

Spear,
    Elizabeth 31, 45*
    Hiram 80
    Jonathan 70*
    Luther 34, 38
    Rhoda 80
    Stephen 64*

Spears,
    James 124

Spears,
John 124, 129*, 146*
Joseph 156*
Luther 34
Obadiah 142*
Thomas 64*
William 145*

Speckard,
George 173*

Speed,
Henry 104*
Martha 15*

Speer,
Mary 108

Speller,
John 100

Spelman,
Mary 45
Stephen 44

Spencer,
Amasa 183*
Ansel 53*
Anthony 49
Benjamin 137*
Daniel 87*, 125
David 57*
Ebenezer 63*
Elam 125
Eleanor 5
Elihu 53*
Elijah 95*
Ezra 49
F. 142
Gardiner 60*
Hannah 53
Henry 53
Isaac 49*
James 61*
Joel 60*
John 49, 76, 132*
Joshua 4, 71
Lucy 129
Mary 49, 93, 134*
Matthias D. 105
Mehitable 76
Mitchel 58*
Moses 131
Noah 97*

Spencer,
Oliver 53
Orange 122
Orrin 49
Peleg 103*
Richard 49
Richison 186
Sarah 49
Seth 24*
Simeon 125
Theodore 49*
Thomas 81
William W. 129

Sperry,
Abigail 23
Chauncey 78
Ebenezer 23
Enoch 32*
Jonathan 99
Rexford 99

Spicely,
James 130*

Spicer,
Joseph 131*
Michael 80*
Patrick 156
William 141*

Spicklemore,
Abram 182

Spights,
Levi 146

Spike,
Daniel 98*

Spiller,
Annes 42*
Thomas 42*

Spindle,
Emanuel 26

Spink,
Nicholas 83
Oliver 48*
Ruth 45

Spinney,
Hannah 4
Jeremiah 8*

Spohn,
    Melchoir 115*

Spontnable,
    Elizabeth 81
    J. I. 81

Spooner,
    Benjamin 71*
    Charles 70*

Spore,
    John 98*

Sprague,
    Andrew 95
    Daniel P. 46
    Delia 46
    Elkanah 95
    Hosea 63*
    James 38, 176*
    Jonathan 63*
    Paschal 39
    Philip 69*
    Seth 29*
    Uriah 29*
    William 9, 74*, 85*

Spring,
    Alpheus 7
    Marshal 7
    Thomas 7

Springer,
    John 47
    Knight 47*
    Martin 94
    William 187

Springs,
    Micajah 141*

Springsteen,
    John 110

Sprinkle,
    Thomas 140

Sproul,
    Jean 8

Sprout,
    Nathan 35

Sprowls,
    William 120

Spurr,
    Enoch 6*

Squairs,
    Thomas 56*

Squares,
    Anson 84

Squire,
    Daniel 50
    David 50
    Ephraim 57*
    Frederick 97*
    Joel 94*
    Philip 57*

Squires,
    Abner 49*
    Ambrose 74*
    Betsey 175
    Calvin 50
    Charles 126
    Ebenezer 69
    Isaac 56
    Joanna 56
    Mary 126
    Thomas 35
    William 119

Staat,
    Binear 111

Stacey,
    Caleb 44*
    Eunice 4
    Nancy 43
    Rebecca 21
    William 21

Stackhouse,
    Amos 168

Stacpole,
    Absalom 3*

Stackpole,
    Susan 11

Stacy,
    Eunice 4

Stacy, (cont.)
    John 38, 61*
    Malin 64*
    Nathaniel 38
    Sarah 35
    William 97

Stafford,
    Aaron 89*
    Andrew 77*
    David 69
    James 48
    Jared 48
    Job 81*
    John 162*
    Joseph 81*
    Orpah 48
    Samuel 66*

Stagg,
    John 183*

Staggers,
    Abraham 118

Staggs,
    Daniel 180

Stahler,
    Eve Mary 118

Stallard,
    Randolph 129*

Stam,
    Henry 87

Stambaugh,
    Peter 113

Stanard,
    Elizabeth 51
    Ezra 73

Stanbro,
    J. 78
    John 78

Stanbry,
    James 48*

Stanbury,
    Samuel 111

Stancliff,
    Comfort 122
    Samuel 122

Stanclift,
    John 80*

Standish,
    Amos 76
    J. 74
    Samuel 100*

Standley,
    David S. 46

Stanert,
    Sarah 115

Stanford,
    Ebenezer 33
    Jemima 33
    John 5*
    Thomas 148

Staniford,
    Mary 42*

Stanley,
    Adin 11*
    Freeman 33
    George 32
    Jacob 75
    Jonathan L. 11
    Page 189*
    Rial 11
    Sally 26*

Stanly,
    Moses 129*
    V. C. 168
    William 168

Stannard,
    Alvan 87
    Elijah 60*
    Job 60*
    John 32*, 60*
    Pliny 72
    Siblius 87

Stansberry,
    Solomon 164*

Stansbury,
    Gitty 105

Stansbury, (cont.)
  Luke 153*

Stanton,
  Charles P. 54
  Elijah 83
  Gilbert 47
  Hannah 54
  Jason 116
  Moses 104
  Paul 6
  Robert 124*
  Sarah 48
  Thomas 87
  William 6, 104

Staples,
  B. 154
  Betsey 154
  Gideon 14
  Isaac 90*
  John 4, 114
  Louisa 4*
  Lydia 39, 119
  Roswell 69
  Ruth 46
  Simon 46

Stapp,
  Achilles 166*

Star,
  Thaddeus 55*

Starbird,
  John 17*

Starcher,
  Adam 135

Stark,
  John 21
  Joseph 81
  Nathan 24
  William 132*

Starkey,
  Waitstill 22

Starks,
  Eunice 62
  Pardon 169*
  Samuel 92*
  Tryphina 33

Starks, (cont.)
  Willard 33
  William 129

Starkweather,
  A. S. 43
  B. 73
  Billing 73
  Elijah 75

Starling,
  Seth 70*

Starr,
  Henry 107
  John 144
  Samuel M. 172*
  William 174*

Starret,
  Benjamin 158*

Starrett,
  Jacob 112

Starring,
  John H. 83

Statham,
  Nathaniel 147*

Stauffer,
  Henry 116

Staver,
  Susanna 173

Steadman,
  Hannah 47
  Luther 84

Stean,
  John 185

Stearnes,
  Sarah 67

Stearns,
  Abigail 21
  Alice 35
  Asa 78
  Daniel 176
  Elias 25*
  Ephraim 22

Stearns, (cont.)
George 40
Isaac 40
Israel 87*
John 15, 67, 176
Jonathan 67*
Mary 37
Nathaniel 30
P. 37
Reuben 67*
Stephen 22
William 67*
William B. 67

Stears,
Jenny 133
Richard 133

Stebbens,
Lavis 56

Stebbins,
David 44*
James 44
John 89*
Jotham 66*
Louisa 32
Timothy 43*

Stedham,
James H. 144
Zachariah 144

Stedman,
B. L. 85
Selah 85
William 66

Steel,
Andrew 141
Ann 116
Francis 141
George C. 108
Isaac 120*, 179*
Phebe 108
Samuel 153*, 189
William 141

Steele,
Bradford 52*
David 133
Eldad 175*
Jemima 61
John 111*, 133

Steele,
Jonathan 20
Oliver W. 61

Steen,
Edward 165

Steere,
Mary 47*
Samuel 47

Steers,
Hugh 160*

Stegall,
William 130

Steighwalt,
Peter 115

Steiner,
John 116

Steinmetz,
P. 115

Stelle,
Samuel 109

Stellwagon,
Elizabeth 119*

Stent,
Othiel 52*

Stephens,
David 107*
Elias 4
Elnathan 80
Enos 80
Henry 153
Jacob 166*
Jared 50
John 4, 165*
Jowel 4
Laurence 134*
Luther 4
Martin 193*
Mary 43
Michel 167*
Moses 93, 99*
Reuben 149*
Sophia 120

Stevenson, (cont.)
    James 164*, 182
    John 44*

Stever,
    Henry 93

Steves,
    Jeremiah 88
    Joshua S. 88

Steward,
    Amasa 13*
    Charles 185*
    Eli 161
    George 89
    Henry 99*
    James 90*, 114
    John 143*, 177*
    Sally 11
    William 171

Stewart,
    Alexander 188*
    Alfred 170*
    Archibald 120
    Charles 73, 178*
    D. 168
    Daniel 168
    Edward 134*, 138*
    Henry 147*
    James 145, 191
    James A. 81
    Jesse 79
    John 94*, 133*, 141*, 145
     151, 159
    Nathan 87*
    Oliver 87*, 104*
    Pleasant 191
    Robert 100*
    Samuel 56
    Thomas 129
    William 57*, 136, 146*

Stickles,
    Nicholas 104
    Peter 104, 112

Stickney,
    Abigail 41
    Abijah 84
    Benjamin 10*
    Charles 24*
    Daniel 24

Stickney, (cont.)
    Elizabeth 18
    Hiram 24
    Mary 15
    Polly 14
    William 41

Stiger,
    Peter 112

Stiles,
    Aaron 79
    Hezekiah 182
    Job 126*
    Lincoln 71*
    Philo 84
    Reuben 78*
    Samuel 67, 79

Stillman,
    George W. 93
    Getchell 14
    Harriet 49
    Joseph 49

Stills,
    John 33*

Stillson,
    Sarah 17
    William 17

Stillwell,
    John 119
    Joseph 119
    Margaret 87

Stilwell,
    Jarret 101*

Stimpson,
    Andrew 21*
    Lemuel 37
    Leonard 37

Stimson,
    David 71*

Stinard,
    Ogis B. 107

Stinchcomb,
    Sarah 127

Stincuphor,
    Joseph 154*

Stine,
    Henry 112

Stinson,
    Abiah 10
    David 144*
    Janette 19
    John 19
    Samuel 13*
    William 115

Stitt,
    Samuel H. 165*

Stivers,
    Daniel 175
    John 168
    Robert 168

Stockbridge,
    Horatio 46
    Lebbeus 30
    Sarah 8*

Stockdale,
    William 117*

Stocking,
    Luther 50
    Samuel 53

Stockman,
    Jonathan 42*
    Moses 108
    Nancy 108

Stockton,
    Mary H. 109

Stockwell,
    A. 67
    Calvin 36
    Eli 39*
    Elijah 21
    Elizabeth 44
    Jesse 174
    Levi 78*

Stodard,
    Philo 183*

Stoddard,
    Asa 25
    Brownell 47
    Daniel 53*
    Frederick 54*
    Hiram E. 49
    John 193*
    Joseph 91*
    Lemuel 25
    Lucy 29
    Lydia 29
    Mary 29
    Noah 27*
    Philo 69*
    Robert 53
    Stephen 53
    Susan 29*

Stodder,
    Lucy 44

Stokeham,
    Reuben 95*

Stoker,
    Edward 165*
    William 158

Stokes,
    John 144
    Richard 60*, 137*
    Samuel 136*
    William 131*

Ston,
    Jedediah 52*
    Molly 51

Stone,
    Albey 57*
    Ambrose 35
    Amos 98*
    B. 166
    Baltus 116
    Benjamin 66*, 135*
    Brant 166
    Cudbeth 162*
    Daniel 59*
    David 8, 22
    Elizabeth 131
    Esther 45
    Ethan 45
    Ezekiel 154

Stow,
Alvin 25
Ithamar 36
Joshua 59*
Ruth 41*

Stowe,
Anne 10
Ithamar F. 10

Stowell,
Asa 80*
David 80*
Isaac 62
Israel 29*
Permela 23
Samuel 92*

Stowers,
Lewis 145*
Samuel 1

Strader,
John 140*

Stragler,
Moses 171

Straight,
Henry 168*
Nathan 49*
William 93*

Straighter,
John 172*

Strain,
Alexander 123

Straley,
Andrew 134
James 134

Strame,
Richard 159*

Strane,
Andrew 139*

Strange,
David 128*
John 166*, 173*, 187*

Strattan,
Seth 166*

Stratten,
Hussy 103

Stratton,
Benjamin 131
Harvey 34
James 74, 131
Martha 37
Milton 134
Nehemiah 9*
Polly 22
Samuel 37, 55, 121
Stephen 103
Thomas 55, 121
Warren 34
William 140*
Zebulon 74

Straw,
Mary 23
Moses 23
Richard 19*

Street,
David 131*
Isaac 155*
Waldegrave C. 146

Streeter,
Aldrich 36
Alvin 36
Nathan 36
Rhoda 39
Samuel 35

Streeton,
Nancy 168

Stremback,
Jacob 115*

Strickland,
John 136
Joseph 136
Naomi 44
Simeon 85*
Stacy 145

Strickler,
David J. 136
Sarah 136

Stricklin,
Lot 140
Calvin 140

Striker,
    Dennis 102*
    Phillip 110
    Sarah 110

Stringer,
    John 161*

Stringham,
    Daniel 184

Stritzel,
    Margaret 116*

Strobeck,
    John A. 96
    Paul 96

Stroble,
    David 142
    Elizabeth 142

Strobridge,
    William 62*

Stroman,
    John 116*

Strong,
    Charles 147*
    Christopher 155*
    David 60*
    Elizabeth 50
    Ephraim 51
    Hiram 50
    Joel 99*
    John 58*, 59*, 109
    Johnson 148*
    Levi 35
    Lydia 125
    Mendwell 70
    Nathan 98
    Nathan S. 98
    Rachel 60*
    Stephen 18*
    Trueman 103
    William 51

Stronnan,
    Barbary 119

Stropes,
    Adam 182*

Strother,
    George 131*
    James 131

Stroud,
    Hampton 151
    Isam 184
    John 119
    William 151

Stroup,
    Daniel 123
    Eve 123

Struple,
    John 187

Strutton,
    Frances 133

Stuard,
    William 130*

Stuart,
    Allen 63
    Daniel 3
    Hannah 11
    Henry 12
    Isabella 185
    Jacob 189*
    James 134, 188*
    John 134*
    Joseph 3
    Margaret 166
    St. Clair 134

Stubbs,
    Joseph 12
    Lewis 144*

Stuck,
    John 183

Stucky,
    Frederick 113

Studder,
    Abel 107

Studevent,
    Charles 147*

Studley,
    Alvin 29
    John 29*

Studwell,
    Henry 75

Stuffleban,
    John 162

Stufflebun,
    Ann M. 104

Stull,
    Andrew 112*

Sturcher,
    William R. 135

Sturdavant,
    Hosea 18

Sturdevant,
    Andrew 10*
    James 98*
    Jonathan 76*

Sturdifant,
    Abigail 30

Sturdivant,
    Joel 130*

Sturges,
    Benjamin 110*

Sturgess,
    Aaron 186*

Sturman,
    William 163*

Sturtavant,
    Seth 8*

Sturtevant,
    Abigail 30
    Barseliel 39*
    Isaac 63
    John 30
    Leonard 7
    Lot 11
    Mary 7
    Reward 11
    Sarah 7
    W. B. 79
    Zenas 30*

Stutler,
    Robert 134

Styles,
    Henry 112
    William 41

Sublett,
    Abraham 164*
    John S. 163*

Suddeth,
    James N. 145
    Jared 145

Suddith,
    Isaac 173

Sufferance,
    Ruth 12

Sugg,
    William 160

Suits,
    Catharine 89*

Sullard,
    Benjamin 109*

Sullenger,
    James 161*

Sullivan,
    Aaron 134
    Benjamin 18*
    Cornelius 162
    Daniel 137
    David 73*
    E. D. 137
    John 133*
    Peter 134
    Samuel 74*

Sumers,
    John 144

Sumett,
    George 136
    Patrick 136

Summers,
    Daniel 55
    Enoch 52

Swartwood,
    Barnadus 115
    James 76
    Moses 114

Swartwout,
    Andrew 192
    Daniel 89
    James 99
    Moses 89
    Thomas 192
    William 99

Swartz,
    Philip 115

Swartzlander,
    Conrad 122
    George 122

Sweat,
    Abraham P. 19*
    Allen 159*
    Jonathan 168*

Sweatland,
    James 12
    Rebecca 10
    Stephen 12

Sweatt,
    Aden 24
    Stockman 24

Sweeney,
    Joseph 167*

Sweet,
    Benjamin 27
    Elizabeth 48*
    Freeborn 94*
    James 49*, 68*
    Jeremy 46*
    Jonathan 98
    Mary 45*
    Sarah 83
    Thomas 79
    Valentine 79
    Vaughn 83
    Waity 49

Sweeter,
    Benjamin 85

Sweeting,
    Lewis 90*
    Nathaniel 89
    Philip B. 89

Sweetland,
    E. L. 60
    Ebenezer L. 60

Sweetser,
    Cornelius 39
    John 39*
    Richard 10
    Stephen 39

Sweigan,
    Barbara 113

Sweney,
    James 178*
    John 88*
    William 166*

Swetland,
    Huldah 45*

Swett,
    David W. 7
    Eben 9
    John 6*
    Joshua 5*
    Samuel 5*
    Thomas R. 20*
    William 7*

Swezey,
    Daniel 110*

Swift,
    Henry 91
    Joseph 7*
    Lot 91
    Lyman 76
    Orpha 36
    Rebecca 27
    Rowland 86
    Susanna 76

Swingle,
    George 162
    John 162

Swinington,
    Adin A. 71
    Joseph 71

Swink,
    John 137*

Switzer,
    George 116

Sword,
    Michael 136*

Swords,
    James 147*

Sycks,
    Henry 118*

Sydevant,
    Gary 139

Sykes,
    Ashbel 68
    Harry 68*
    James 136
    John 136

Sylvester,
    Caleb 40*
    Joseph 30*
    Levi 76*
    N. B. 29

Symes,
    Thomas 182
    William 182

Symmes,
    Edward 39
    Elizabeth 39

Symms,
    James 152
    John 152

Symonds,
    Ashna 50*

Sypert,
    W. L. 158
    William L. 158

Taber,
    Martha 47
    Mary 86
    Nancy 47
    Thomas 27

Tabor,
    John 10
    Philip 23
    Ruth 19*
    William 150*

Tacke,
    John 155*

Tackles,
    Alexander 82

Taff,
    John P. 147

Taft,
    Artemus 69
    Enos 39*
    George 39
    Israel 36*
    Josiah 38*
    Martha 36
    Moses 39
    Newell 39
    Relief 15
    Stephen 92

Taggart,
    Elizabeth 47*
    Lydia 70*

Tague,
    Joseph 183

Tailor,
    Editha 84
    Mary 127

Talbee,
    Stephen 49*

Talbot,
    Benjamin 145*
    Joseph 5
    Josiah 30

Talbott,
    Martha 166

Talcott,
    Chester 61
    Justus 60*
    Rebecca 61

Tallmadge,
    Rhoba 99

Tallman,
    Rachel 106
    Tunis 106

Talmadge,
    J. 73
    Seymour 73

Talmage,
    Samuel 52*
    Sarah 52*
    Stephen 105*

Talman,
    Daniel 106
    James 27
    Rachel 106

Talton,
    William 139*

Tandy,
    R. M. 161

Tanner,
    A. 187
    Abram 131*
    Betsey 49
    Ebenezer 59
    Henry 37
    John 152*
    Lydia 59
    Quain 94*
    William 37

Tanney,
    Michael 147*

Tanno,
    Michael 112

Tansler,
    Andrew 136
    Henry 136

Taple,
    John Nickolas 79*

Tapley,
    Rachel 43

Tapp,
    Vincent 133*

Tappan,
    James 103
    John 103
    Peter 102*
    Simeon 179*
    William 42

Tarbox,
    Abigail 43
    Carll 4
    Gilbert 4
    Samuel 5*

Tarebant,
    Juletta 31

Tarket,
    Francis 103
    Mary 103

Tarlton,
    Eleanor 166

Tarpinning,
    Lawrence 119*

Taber,
    David 86

Tarr,
    Abram 9
    Annis 43*
    Jabez 43*
    Joseph 8*

Tarrant,
    James 149*

Tarrey,
    Susanna 29

Tart,
    Thomas 141*

Tarver,
    Samuel 153*

Task,
    Henry 91

Tays,
 Samuel 157*

Teach,
 Elizabeth 119

Teag,
 William 158

Teal,
 Ezekiel 116
 Ezekiel H. 116
 Joseph 105
 Oliver 86*

Tebbets,
 Ephraim 4
 James 4
 William 82

Tebbetts,
 Ephraim 17
 Robert 17*

Tedford,
 Robert 152*
 Robert A. 152

Teeks,
 Joseph 104

Teem,
 Adam 143*

Teerpening,
 William 102*

Teetu,
 Conrad 99*

Telford,
 Alexander 177
 James 177

Teller,
 Ahasuerus 89*

Tellinghart,
 Catharine 91

Telt,
 Joseph 43

Temple,
 Chancy L. 65*

Temple, (cont.)
 E. 68
 Ebenezer 68
 Ephraim 38
 Jabez 67
 Joel 37
 John 8*, 32
 Mary 33
 Samuel 133*
 Stephen 33*

Templeman,
 Samuel 133*

Ten Broeck,
 Leonard W. 104
 Maria 104
 Samuel 104

Teneick,
 Sarah 79

Ten Eyck,
 Conrad 82

Tennal,
 George 164*

Tennant,
 Russell 88

Tenney,
 David 24*
 Edmund 21
 Gideon 34*
 Molly 23
 Rufus 40

Tenny,
 Edmund 21
 James 135*

Terfastz,
 John 121

Termilgar,
 Samuel 79

Terrel,
 Elihu 175
 Eunice 175
 Wyllis 175

Terrell,
 Horace 53

Theobald,
  James 162*

Thing,
  Abner 3

Thissell,
  Thomas 21*

Thomas,
  Aaron 139*
  Abraham 145
  Abram 177*
  Alexander 12, 138*
  Arispa 30
  Averick 30
  Benjamin 63
  Caleb 168
  Catlett 129*
  Cephas 11
  Charles 5, 161*
  Ebenezer S. 30
  Edward 30, 191
  Eleazer 30
  Elijah 33*, 79*
  Gardner 27*
  George 9, 36, 112, 189
  Giles 135
  Henry 75*
  Henry L. 29
  Ichabod 14
  Isabella 28*
  Jacob 86
  James 60*, 112*, 129*, 132*
    134, 189
  Jason 92*
  Jesse 63, 140
  John 58, 129, 149, 185
  John A. 52*
  John C. 129
  John J. 160
  Josiah 176
  Leman 59
  Lodowick 82*
  Mary 9
  Nathan 51
  Nicholas 46
  Noah 29
  Notley 153*
  Reuben 191
  Richard 160*
  Richard R. 46
  Sarah 42
  Seneca 30

Thomas, (cont.)
  Seth 30
  Soloman 35
  Spencer 4*, 7*
  William 135, 160, 176

Thomason,
  Edmund 188
  George 138*
  John C. 147
  William 147

Thomaston,
  George 137

Thompson,
  Aaron 108*
  Alexander 188*
  Alice 55*
  Allen 84
  Barnabas 70
  Benjamin 4, 19*, 30*, 112
  Betsey 50*
  Charles M. 59
  Charles W. 57
  Daniel 60
  David 16*
  Deborah 30
  Dexter C. 30
  Dorcas 18
  E. 148*
  Ebenezer 30, 58
  Ethan 88
  Festus L. 48
  George 91
  H. 157
  Hannah 91, 109*
  Hudson 157
  Isaac 105
  Isaac C. 9
  J. 43, 75
  Jabez 30
  Jacob 134*
  James 4*, 46, 54*, 75*, 105
    106*, 146*, 178, 187*, 188*
  Jennings 132*
  Job 178
  Joel 9, 105
  John 7*, 18*, 20, 93*, 131*
    171, 193
  John C. 18
  Joseph 43, 50, 65, 166*, 169
  Joseph M. 4
  Lawrence 181

Thwing,
Nicholas 40

Tibbets,
Benjamin 12
Edmund 17*
Ichabod 12
James 18
Margaret 16
Nathaniel 16
Silvester 3
Simeon 3
Stephen 8*

Tibbetts,
John 14
Nathaniel 14

Tibbits,
Daniel 91*

Tice,
Peter 98*
Richard 106*
William 65

Tichenor,
David 108*
Isaac T. 108
James 110
Joseph D. 110

Tidd,
Jonathan 39
William 39

Tidmore,
John 149*

Tiffany,
Asa 160
Daniel 48
Joel 85
Noah 99
Philemon 99
Thomas 119
Timothy 51*
Trueman 85

Tiffney,
Amasa 94*

Tifft,
Amasa S. 91*

Tifft, (cont.)
Augustus 47
Green 94
Rufus 94
Sally 47

Tift,
Caleb 84*
Soloman 53

Tilbals,
Elin 59
Orrin 59

Tilcomb,
Sarah 17

Tilden,
David R. 64
Josiah 69*
Lydia 30*
Wales 29*

Tileston,
Cornelius 35

Tilghman,
Anna Marie 128
Tench 128

Tilley,
Bennet 190*
James 39

Tillotson,
Abigail 86
Ephraim 86
Jacob 77

Tillson,
William 9
William F. 9

Tilly,
Hannah 75*

Tilotson,
Daniel 51
Edward 51

Tilton,
Daniel 18
James 107
John 15, 107, 178*

Tilton, (cont.)
    Judith 18
    Timothy 15

Tilue,
    John 108*

Timberlake,
    Joseph 163

Timmanson,
    Henry 142
    William T. 142

Timmonds,
    George 163*

Tinch,
    William 132*

Tindley,
    Thomas 43*

Tiney,
    Richard 175*

Tingley,
    Lemuel 111*
    Mason 119
    Samuel 28*

Tinker,
    John 78
    Mary 54, 58
    William 53*

Tinkham,
    Elizabeth 30
    Hezekiah 64*
    Seth 70*

Tinner,
    James 155*

Tinney,
    Festus 82
    Temperance 82

Tinsley,
    John 131*

Tippy,
    Uriah 168*

Tipton,
    James 158
    Jonathan 158
    Luke 169
    Thomas 170
    William 152*

Tirrell,
    Benjamin 32

Tisdale,
    Barney 24*

Titlow,
    John 114*
    Philip 153*

Titman,
    Philip 139

Titus,
    Abel 69*
    Benjamin 118*
    John 80*
    Joseph 28, 57, 59,* 111
    Samuel 86
    Simon 57

Tivis,
    R. 117
    Rossin 117

Tobe,
    Enoch 189*

Tobey,
    George 8
    Mary 8

Toby,
    Elnathan 74
    Isaac 34
    John 34

Todd,
    Alexander 173
    Asa 35
    Benjamin 157*
    Darling 79
    Jehiel 93
    John 20*
    Joseph 164*
    Lewis 138*

Todd, (cont.)
    Samuel 79, 161*
    Samuel B. 163*
    Thomas 100*
    William 111*, 173

Toland,
    John 168*

Tolbert,
    Samuel 148*

Tolbot,
    Abram 9*

Toler,
    Richard 130*

Tolles,
    Horace 59

Tollifero,
    John A. 149
    Mildra 149

Tolly,
    John 159*

Tolman,
    Benjamin 23*
    Thomas 63

Tolty,
    Daniel 130*

Tomblin,
    John W. 84
    Timothy 84

Tombs,
    Charles 129
    Clifton 132*
    Elizabeth 129

Tomlinson,
    Agur 55
    Jabez H. 55*
    John 160*
    Joseph 177*
    Lucy 52
    Phebe 55
    Richard 137*
    Samuel 107
    William H. 53

Tompkins,
    Abraham 73
    Benjamin 47
    Evi S. 111
    Ichabod 111
    James 102
    Jonathan 102
    Mary 47*, 86
    Philip 86
    Stephen M. 83
    Stephen V. 73
    Thomas G. 47

Tompson,
    Ellis 46

Toney,
    Jesse 181*

Tong,
    (Mr.) 187
    Thomas 187

Tongate,
    Meredith 184*
    Uriel 162

Tooker,
    Joseph 106*

Toothaker,
    Seth 5*

Topliff,
    James 70

Topping,
    William 85

Torney,
    Bilb 99*

Torrance,
    Richard 85
    Thomas 85

Torrey,
    Abigail 86
    Philip 29*

Torry,
    Joseph 35
    Oliver 57*
    Timothy 82*

Toser,
    Elias 22
    Mary 22

Tothingham,
    Deborah 66

Totman,
    George 78
    Lorenzo 78
    Stoddard 33

Toulin,
    John 111

Tourgie,
    Desire 95

Tourjee,
    William 48*

Tourtelott,
    Joseph 58*

Tourtlotle,
    Leah 11

Tower,
    Amos 69
    Bethsheba 29
    Calvin 45*
    Charles 41
    Hannah 46
    Isaac 36*
    Isaiah 95*
    James 107
    Jerusha 29
    Lear 35
    Lucy 119
    Mary 41
    Moses 29
    Reuben (Mrs.) 89
    Rial 119
    Savia 69

Town,
    Ebenezer 42
    Edmund 62
    Elisha 68
    Ira 62
    John 22
    Joshua 42
    Lucy 67
    Nehemiah 67

Town, (cont.)
    Spencer 65
    William 57, 100

Towne,
    Elisha 21
    J. 43
    Joseph 4
    Matthew W. 21

Towner,
    Elijah 102*, 126
    Joseph 126

Townley,
    Catharine 99
    Charlotte 108
    Henry 99

Townly,
    Charlotte 108

Towns,
    John 154
    Moses 20*
    Noah 10*
    Thomas 154

Townsel,
    Joshua 148*

Townsend,
    Abraham 64
    David 22*, 24
    Ebner 103
    Hannah 103, 104
    James 109
    Jeremiah 93
    Joshua 103
    M. 43
    Margaret 37
    Molly 64
    Moses 43
    Reuben 37
    Robert 5, 176
    William 104
    William A. 88

Townsley,
    Dan. 34
    Daniel 34

Towle,
    Ira 65

Towle, (cont.)
    Jonathan 18*
    Nella 65
    Thomas 3*

Towles,
    Elizabeth 133
    Henry 160*

Towls,
    Betsey 96

Towser,
    Jeremiah 108

Tozer,
    Julius 126*

Trabal,
    Daniel 163

Tracey,
    Solomon 84*

Tracy,
    Ahira 62
    Cyrus 65
    Eleazer 54
    Elias 75*
    Gamaliel 54
    Gilbert 75*
    Hannah 54
    James R. 54
    Jarrett 127*
    Lemuel 72*
    Levi 73
    Phebe 69
    Sidney 92
    Solomon 181

Traffarn,
    Cromwell 89*

Trafton,
    Elias D. 45*

Train,
    Isaac 98

Trainor,
    James R. 133

Trammel,
    David 152

Trammel, (cont.)
    Dennis 152
    William 145*

Trant,
    Christian 166*

Trash,
    Samuel 31

Trask,
    Asa 10
    Ebenezer 10
    Jesse 34
    John 46*
    Retire 171
    William 36

Trausu,
    Philip 114

Traux,
    Hester 118

Traver,
    Adam 103

Travers,
    Sylvanus 97

Traverse,
    Lydia 40

Travis,
    Arthur 164*
    Nathaniel 103
    Philip B. 79*
    Robert 102
    Uriah 102

Treace,
    Michael 153*

Treadway,
    David 94
    Elijah 54*
    Jonathan 80
    Thomas J. 80

Treadwell,
    Benjamin 56*
    Cato 56
    Joshua E. 4
    Susan 4
    Susanna 42*

Trowell,
    James 152*

Truair,
    John 90
    Manuel 90

Truax,
    David 177
    Sarah 118

Truby,
    Michael 121*

True,
    Benjamin 16
    Jabez 19*
    John 10, 20*
    Jonathan 14
    Martin 157*
    Obadiah 7
    Osgood 16
    Polly 14
    Robert 7
    Samuel 11
    William 8, 9

Truesdell,
    Phebe 87

Truesden,
    Hiel 84

Truman,
    Shem 85

Trumbell,
    John 51

Trumbull,
    B. W. 104
    Robert 63*
    Sarah 54

Trussell,
    Moses 19*

Tryon,
    Clarissa 51
    Ezra 181
    Joseph 50*
    Thomas 90*

Tschoop,
    John 121

Tubbs,
    Benjamin 123
    Lemuel 62
    Samuel 91*, 123

Tubs,
    John 53*
    Samuel 108*
    Sylvester 51

Tuck,
    Edward 131
    John 23
    Mary 23
    Thomas 131

Tuckee,
    Daniel 52

Tucker,
    Aaron 14*, 57
    Anna 8*
    Benjamin 39*, 65*
    Daniel 30
    David 157
    Drusilla 47*
    Eunice 68
    Experience 41
    Ezra 24, 44
    Henry 172
    Ira 92
    Jemima 46
    Joel 44
    John 11, 92, 156*, 184*
    Joseph 70
    Morriss 94*
    Nancy 46
    Nathaniel 41*
    Robert 57*
    Sarah 42
    Silas 57
    Sylvia 157
    Thomas 132*
    William 129*
    Woodward 30
    Zaith 101*

Tuesdell,
    Bethiah 99
    Jonathan 99

Tuffs,
    William 182

Tuttle, (cont.)
    Edmund 55
    Elizabeth 51, 87
    Enos 181
    Isaac 51
    Jesse 73*
    John 140*
    Joseph 17
    Lucius 53
    Lucy 97
    Mary 110*
    Nicholas 190
    Olive 97
    P. 87
    Pleasant 190
    Roxana 91
    Solomon 181
    Sylvester 67

Tutwiler,
    John 186

Tuyman,
    William 131*

Twambly,
    Ebenezer 26*

Twig,
    Daniel 167*

Twilager,
    Josiah 77
    Rachael 77

Twining,
    Nathan 21*

Twiss,
    Peter 20

Twist,
    Stephen 43*

Twitchell,
    Eli 7*
    Peter 7

Twombly,
    John 17
    Lydia 16

Tyle,
    Hannah 104

Tyler,
    Abraham 3*
    Alfred 162
    Andrew 12
    Anna 52
    Benjamin F. 12
    Bishop 54*
    Charles 162
    Cyral 52
    Daniel 173*
    David M. 175
    Jacob 174
    James 66*
    James W. 150
    Jeremiah 66
    John 51*
    Julia 50*
    Mabel 52
    Moses 38*, 119*
    Nehemiah 60*
    Peter 98
    Silas 116
    Simeon 12, 104
    William 52, 86*, 104
    William M. 66
    Zelotes 46

Tylor,
    Jonathan 25

Tyner,
    Nicholas 139*

Tyrell,
    Jacob 34*

Tyrrell,
    Eunice 100*

Ufford,
    Samuel 55
    Samuel H. 55

Ullery,
    George 119*

Ulmer,
    George 12

Ulrich,
    Samuel 122

Umphrey,
    John S. 151
    John Spencer 151

Unash,
    Gideon 54*

Uncas,
    John 54

Underhill,
    Augustus 100

Underwood,
    Howell 155
    Isaac 181*
    J. 73
    James 109
    Jonas 73
    Lucy 58
    Nathan 26*
    Russel 66
    Russell 25
    Samuel R. 79
    Silas 79
    William 138

Union,
    John 43
    Peter 43

Upchurch,
    Charles 146*

Updike,
    Daniel 49*
    James 48*
    Levi 109
    William 109

Upham,
    Asa 94
    George 126

Upton,
    George 148*
    Jerusha 39
    Nathaniel 39
    Paul 39
    Samuel 34

Uran,
    Jonathan 18*

Urgeburger,
    J. 86

Usher,
    Anna 60
    Sophron 60

Utley,
    Abigail 57
    James 57
    Sally 35

Utman,
    Frederick 96*

Utter,
    Abram 181*
    Jesse 79
    Stephen 79

Utterback,
    Benjamin 184

Uxford,
    Gibson W. 50
    John 50

Vail,
 Christopher 54*
 Peter 105*

Valendenham,
 W. 144
 William 144

Valentine,
 Elijah F. 39

Vales,
 Sames 159
 Samuel 159

Vallandingham,
 Lewis 166*

Vallet,
 John 48*

Van,
 Jacob 101

Van Aken,
 Peter 102

Vanalstine,
 Cornelius 91

Van Alstine,
 Jacob 87*

Vananaken,
 Margaret 114

Vananken,
 Elias 98

Van Antwerp,
 John L. 94
 P. Y. 94
 Rachael 81

Vanarsdale,
 Cornelius O. 165*

Vanarsdall,
 Cornelius 174
 Minedred W. 174

Van Atten,
 James 81*

Van Austin,
 John N. 192

Van Benthuysen,
 William 94*

Van Brockle,
 Jacob 110

Van Buren,
 Abraham 94*
 John 88
 Martin 88

Van Camp,
 Isaac 76
 Joseph 76

Van Campen,
 Daniel 76*
 Moses 85*

Vance,
 James 166
 Peyton A. 150
 William 10*, 150

Van Cleaf,
 Dinah 111
 Jacob S. 111
 Joseph 110
 William J. 110

Vancliver,
 Matthew 139*

Vandal,
 Abraham 134
 E. D. 134

Vandegriff,
 Garrett 146*

Vandenburg,
 Minardt P. 72

Van Densen,
 Henry 59

Vanderbick,
 Rynear 107

Vanderburgh,
 Clarion F. 79

Van Horne,
    Philip 94
    Thomas 94

Van Hosen,
    Rachel 72

Vanhouten,
    Abram 106
    Abram J. 106
    Jane 106
    John 106*
    John T. 106

Van Houten,
    John A. 107*

Van Ingen,
    Joseph 84*

Vaninwagen,
    Gradis 99

Vankirk,
    John 120

Van Meter,
    Rebecca 163
    Sarah 90

Vanmetre,
    Isaac 162*

Vanner,
    Andrew 8
    Catherine 8

Vannest,
    Jeronimus 86

Van Netter,
    Margaret 87

Vanorden,
    Hannah 106
    Peter S. 106*

Van Ormum,
    R. 97
    Richard 97

Van Orsdoll,
    Jane 106*

Van Osdol,
    Oakey 170*

Van Ostead,
    William 81*

Van Patten,
    Frederick 96

Vanpelt,
    Agnes 136
    Jacob 136

Van Pelt,
    Rulif 111*

Van Rensselaer,
    Nicholas 94*

Van Sanford,
    A. 72
    Anthony 72

Vansant,
    Felix 141*

Van Santford,
    C. L. 96*

Van Sciven,
    Benjamin 107
    Daniel 107

Van Scoy,
    Abel 105*
    Abraham 105*
    Daniel 125
    Samuel 125
    Timothy 105*

Van Sice,
    John Cornelius 103

Van Sickel,
    Hannah 111*

Vansickle,
    Peter 171

Van Sickler,
    Mary 81*

Vanskoyke,
    James 185

Vanskyhock,
    Timothy 122*

Vanslyke,
    Abigail 87
    William 73*

Vansyche,
    Cornelius 110*

Van Tassel,
    Elizabeth 104
    Jacob 101*
    John 104
    Stephen 104

Vantine,
    Abraham 109

Van Tyne,
    Ellen 111*

Van Valin,
    Oliver 102

Van Valkenburgh,
    Barrust 104
    James 104
    William 104*

Van Vechten,
    Derrick 87

Van Veghten,
    Heman 91

Van Voast,
    Catharine 81
    John 81, 96

Van Volkenburgh,
    Eli 72

Van Voorhis,
    William 107

Van Vorst,
    James 96*

Van Vranken,
    Evert E. 95*
    Richard 81*

Van Wagenen,
    Conrad 96

Van Wagenen, (cont.)
    R. 96

Van Wager,
    Gershom 79

Van Wart,
    A. 94
    Isaac 94

Van Winkle,
    Elias 119*

Vanwinkle,
    William 173*

Van Worken,
    Martin 122

Van Wort,
    Jacob 93

Van Wyck,
    Edward 101

Van Zandt,
    Peter 97

Varbenscoter,
    C. 102
    Elias 102

Varick,
    Marie 101*

Varner,
    John 125*
    Joseph 132*

Varnum,
    Joel 14*

Vars,
    Augustus 93
    Joseph 93
    William 47

Vasney,
    Eli 72

Vass,
    Philip 133*
    Vincent 159

Vas Sise,
    Abraham   101

Vathier,
    Charles   172*

Vattier,
    C.   151

Vaughan,
    Ably   45
    Almond   129*
    J.   34
    Jesse   129
    Joel   151
    John   46, 82
    John D.   193*
    John M.   129
    John W.   82
    Mary   45
    William   137*, 142*

Vaughen,
    Joseph   17

Vaughn,
    Frederick   76
    Isaac   28
    William   134*

Veach,
    Elijah   165

Veasey,
    Joshua   15

Veazey,
    Lydia   17*

Vedder,
    Albert   87*
    H.   94
    Richard   94
    Sarah   96*

Veeder,
    Nicholas G.   96
    William   96

Verbryck,
    Ralph   106
    Rebecca   165*
    Samuel G.   106*

Verdon,
    James   187*

Vergason,
    Molly   54

Vergison,
    Daniel   123*

Vermillion,
    Jesse   136*

Vermilye,
    John   75*

Vermilyea,
    William   91*

Verner,
    David   143
    John   143*

Vernon,
    Leonard   158
    Richard   158
    Thomas   153*

Vermum,
    Enoch   120*

Versill,
    Samuel   5

Vest,
    George   160*
    Samuel   186*

Viah,
    Gideon   172
    Samuel   172

Vial,
    Nathaniel   28*, 68
    Samuel   68

Vicar,
    Jane   104

Vick,
    John   156*
    Joseph   155*

Vickers,
    John R.   156*

Vickery,
    Polly 77

Vickney,
    Edward 193

Viles,
    Wentworth 13

Ville,
    Maria 104

Vincamp,
    Delilah 165

Vinceint,
    Thomas 163

Vincent,
    David 34*
    George 163
    Joshua 34
    Orain 34
    Stephen 25
    Thomas 25

Viner,
    Isaac 33
    Sarah 33

Vinson,
    Aaron 128*
    Nathan 147*
    Rebecca 32
    Thomas 32

Vinton,
    Abiathar 74*
    Seth 61*

Violet,
    John 177*

Virgil,
    Ziporah 99

Virgin,
    John 18

Virgina,
    Jeremiah 62*

Vise,
    Sarah 165

Vittum,
    Jonathan 18

Vliet,
    David 109*

Volentine,
    Stephen 74*

Volvridge,
    Gustavus 187

Vookers,
    Abraham 82*

Voorhees,
    A. D. 98
    Aaron 110*
    David 109*
    James 91*
    Paul 111
    Peter 111
    Tunis 76

Vores,
    Garret 184*

Vosburgh,
    Abraham 72*, 87
    Elizabeth 104
    John 87
    John P. 104

Vose,
    Gilman 65
    Jane 46
    Jeremiah 46*
    William 22*

Vosseller,
    Lucius 111*

Voudy,
    William 4

Vought,
    Godfrey 126*
    Henry C. 104

Vowles,
    Ann 130
    Newton 130

Vreedenburg,
    A. 72
    Abraham 72

Vreeland,
    Abraham 111*
    Garret G. 111*
    Ichabod 107*
    John 73

Vrelandt,
    Curren 193
    Michael 193

Vroom,
    Henry 111*

Vrooman,
    Simon J. 92*

Waaliver,
    R. 84

Waddill,
    James 159

Waddle,
    Martin 152*

Wade,
    Asa 168
    Charles 46
    Claiborn 128*
    Edward 92*
    John 12*
    Joshua 62*
    Molly 46
    Oliver 46
    Richard 161*
    Willard 46*

Wadeworth,
    Ruth 31

Wadkins,
    Samuel 158*

Wadleigh,
    John 18*

Wadsworth,
    Benjamin 36, 59
    Drusbury 29*
    Epaphras 125*
    Hezekiah 73
    Israel 71
    Joseph 29, 36
    Joseph F. 29
    Nela 59
    Trueman C. 73
    William 140*

Wadworth,
    Thomas 88*

Waffle,
    John H. 87

Wager,
    Hannah 110*

Wages,
    Benjamin 165
    John 165

Wagg,
    James 5
    John 137*

Waggner,
    John 179*

Waggoner,
    Abraham S. 83
    John 135
    Samuel 135
    Solomon 83

Waiger,
    George T. 95
    J. S. 95

Waiscott,
    John 46

Wait,
    Gardner 63*

Wait, (cont.)
 Judith 35
 Pain 86
 Samson 64
 William H. 149

Waite,
 Edmund 43
 Nathaniel 64
 Rebecca 37
 Sally N. 6
 Sarah 37*
 William 64

Waits,
 James 169*

Waitt,
 Elizabeth 43
 Samuel 43

Wakefield,
 Abigail 68
 Hannah 4
 Henry 157*
 Joshua 4
 Peter 174*
 Thomas 155*
 Timothy 39*

Wakelee,
 Arad 119
 Charles H. 51
 Mary 51, 119

Wakeley,
 Aelel 102
 Russel 102

Wakely,
 Deborah 68*

Wakeman,
 George 55
 Gershon 55
 Jabez 79, 103
 Mary 56
 Stephen 88*

Waklee,
 John 123
 Mary 123

Walborn,
 Catharine 114

Walborn, (cont.)
 John 114

Walch,
 James 9*

Walcomb,
 John 142

Walcot,
 Benjamin 44

Walcott,
 Sabia 45
 Thomas 39

Walden,
 James 47*
 John 162*
 N. 86
 Nathan 86

Waldo,
 David 75*
 John 134*
 Nathan 82*
 Sarah 70
 Warren 70

Waldon,
 John 125

Waldron,
 Ann 26
 Elizabeth 70
 Gilford 28
 Nathaniel 83
 Warren 26

Waldroup,
 David 145
 James 145

Waldson,
 Solomon 17

Wale,
 Timothy 179*

Walen,
 Richard 99

Wales,
 Amos A. 31
 Anson 65

Wales, (cont.)
Eleazer 91
John 31
Lydia 65
Mary 31, 70*
Nathaniel 31
Samuel 31*
Solomon 91
Thomas 30

Walford,
John 101

Walizer,
John 121
Michael 121

Walker,
(Mrs.) 61
Aaron F. 110
Abel 63
Alexander 117
Alvin 89
Andrew 139*
Asher 179
Assenath 36
Benjamin 19, 187
Betsey 34
Bliss 66
Bruce 24
Calvin 34
Charles 5*
Daniel 47
Edward 66, 77*
Eliakim 19
Elisha 130*
Frances 130
G. 148
George 28*, 38, 143*
Green 138
Hannah 17, 88
Henry 138
Hiram 68
Isaac 155*
James 28*, 35, 41*, 44*, 69
78*, 121*, 155, 164*, 187
Jason 36*
John 4, 17, 141*, 150, 157
169*, 179*, 184*
Joseph 41, 122
Josiah 6*
Lewis 28
Lois 36, 41
Maria 68

Walker, (cont.)
Micajah 146
Moses 28*
Nathaniel 24, 122
Rane 129
Richard 27, 28
Robert 156*, 159
S. 37
Sally 25, 29
Samuel 8, 68, 132*, 154
Samuel C. 13
Sarah 21*, 46
Silas 37, 86
Simeon 63
Solomon 130*
Temperance 15*
Thankful 71*
Thomas 135*, 150, 189*
Timothy 12
William 13, 57, 112*, 129*
130*, 148
William J. 128*
William S. 137*
William W. 157*
Zenith 37

Walkup,
George 33*
Samuel 164*

Wall,
Jacob 141
Joseph 141
Martha 127*
Mary 110
Peter 132*
Richard 142*

Wallace,
Charles 84, 112
Ebenezer 84
George 117
Jacob 96
James 117*, 189
John 25*, 139*, 149*, 163
Joseph 183
Joshua 163
Samuel 97*
Waymouth 18
William 172*

Wallbridge,
Joshua 44*

Wallen,
    Daniel 110*

Waller,
    Ashabel 169*
    Nathaniel 138*

Wallice,
    Frederick 64
    Thankful 64

Walling,
    David 150*
    John 107*

Wallis,
    Sarah 61
    William 136

Wallradt,
    Henry 83

Walls,
    George 133
    Reuben 165*

Walrop,
    Asey 140

Walson,
    Mary 82

Walsworth,
    Elijah 84*

Walter,
    C. 94
    Christer 94
    George 81*
    Isaac 90
    Jacob 112
    John 91, 117*
    Luman 91
    Marlin 90

Walters,
    Frederick 173*
    Israel 186*
    John 177*

Walthal,
    Harry 129*

Walton,
    Abram 125

Walton, (cont.)
    Benjamin 11*
    Martin 157*
    Oliver 39*
    William 125

Walworth,
    Elijah 95*

Wambaugh,
    Philip 117

Wandle,
    Sarah 95*

Waoner,
    John 58*

Ward,
    Abigail 83
    Abner 19*
    Alven 101
    Andrew 163*
    Barnard 62*
    Benjamin 27, 37, 168*
    C. 44
    Caleb 24, 34
    Christopher 44
    Daniel A. 75
    Edward 177*
    Elijah 168
    Elizabeth 162
    Ephraim 38
    Federal 55
    H. 162
    Henry 96, 106
    Hopper 130
    Ichabod 54*
    Israel 83, 172
    J. 175
    Jacob 101
    James 164
    James L. 108
    Jedediah 71
    John 12, 101*, 165, 182*
    Josiah 88, 175
    Leonard S. 134
    Luther 34, 66
    Mary 88
    Nathan 83
    Nehemiah 11*, 170*
    Nicholson 47*
    Obadiah 168
    Sally 108
    Samuel 147*, 193

Ward, (cont.)
Sarah 27
Simon 25*
Thomas 118*
Timothy 181
William 37, 145

Wardaline,
Mary 102

Warden,
John 107*
Samuel 148
Thomas 80*
W. B. 163*

Wardrop,
Edward 141
Solomon 141

Wardwell,
A. 95
Ahasuerus 95
Joseph 7

Ware,
David 21
Elias 31
Jerson 8
Thomas 111, 132*
Vinal 8
William 38

Warfield,
Elizabeth 127
Ephraim 50
Job 33
N. D. 127
Prudence 33
Samuel 39*

Warford,
Benjamin 160

Warick,
Charles 119*

Waring,
Joseph 104

Warker,
Anna 23

Warna,
Rhoda 51

Warnack,
William 160*

Warne,
Abraham 111
Elijah 111*

Warner,
Alanson 81
Benjamin 16*, 80
Daniel 38*, 68
Deborah 63
Eleazer 88*
Elias 38*
Elihu 57*
Elisha 67
Elizabeth 32
Esther 60*
Gad 32
Hessibah 59
Huldah 86
Israel 100*
J. I. 62*
Jemima 47*
John 50, 120*
Jonathan 67
L. A. 66
Lewis 130
Loomis 51
M. 86
Michael 116
Moses 122, 170*
Nathaniel 41, 76*
Oliver A. 63
Omer 80*
Phineas 37*
Richard 50*
Samuel 50*, 51, 80
Seth 102*
Stephen 44, 51
Stephen W. 44
Thomas 51
Thomas A. 86
William 59

Warnock,
John 143*

Warren,
Aaron 3, 92*
Abijah 8*
Ashbel 50*
Caleb 100*
Charles 10, 33
Daniel 4*, 89*

Warren, (cont.)
David 193
Elijah 37, 39, 159
Experience 92
George W. 12*
Henry E. 37
Jared 10
Jeduthan 37*
John 20, 89
Joseph 83*
Joshua 4*
Josiah 20
Jotham 67
Keziah 3
Nathan 5
Pelatiah 10
Phebe 28*
Phineas 12, 33
Richard 10
Samuel 92, 143*
Silas 39
Stephen 34*
Thomas 5
Timothy 34
Uriah 93*
Walter 3
William 159

Warrener,
Lucy 82*

Warriner,
Gad 43*

Warrington,
William 171*

Warson,
John 13*

Warters,
Moses 140

Warthin,
Greene H. 147

Wartrons,
John B. 54*

Washam,
Charles 167*
John 150*

Washburn,
Abiel 30

Washburn, (cont.)
Abner 65
Abraham 33*
Barzaliel 27*
Benjamin 166*
Ebenezer 7*
Eli 24
Eliel 67
Elizabeth 37
Ephraim 13, 28
Francis 28
Freeman 89
Hannah 37
Israel 27*
Jennet 7
Lettice 27*
Lucy 28
Luther 89
Patience 35
Sarah 18*
Thomas 29*
William 76*
Zenus 29

Washington,
John 119*

Wason,
John 16*

Wasson,
James 75*

Water,
William 179

Waterbury,
Enos 56*
Frederic 56
Mary 56
William 56*

Waterfield,
Orville E. 161
Peter 161

Waterhouse,
Ambrose 60*

Waterman,
Abraham 70*
Anstress 46
Calvin 90*
Charlotte 83
Darius 79

Waterman, (cont.)
    David 88*
    Edward 46*
    Esther 46*
    Henry 46, 83
    Ignatius 180*
    Jerusha 29*
    Phebe 168
    Resolved 46
    Ruth 70
    Sarah 70
    William 48, 70*

Waters,
    Allen 179
    Amos 93
    Asa 31*, 36
    Benjamin 168*
    Benjamin C. 155*
    Champlen 152
    David 146
    Deborah 16
    James 156*
    John 162*
    Mindwell 33*
    Olive 93

Watford,
    Barnabas 149
    Joseph 149
    William 137*

Watkins,
    Abial 41
    Benedict 162*
    Elanson 90
    Esther 192
    Gideon 51
    James 148*
    James B. 27
    John 141, 155*
    Joseph D. 130*
    Levi 192
    Mary 127
    Spencer 153*
    Stephen 63*
    Susanna 131
    Thomas 127
    Thomas G. 141
    Willard 57
    William 155
    William E. 155

Watley,
    William 39

Watmough,
    John G. 115*

Watrous,
    Benjamin 98
    John 98

Watson,
    Abiah 49*
    Alice 17*
    Allen T. 130
    David 15, 119
    Ebenezer 63*
    Eunice 8
    George 58
    Hannah 86
    James 117
    Jane 188
    Johanna 132
    John 18, 60*, 160, 185*
    John M. 160
    Joseph 164
    Judith 57
    Levi 58*
    Lucy 38
    Major 91
    Mary 16, 17
    Nathan 17
    Nathaniel 153*
    Patience 17
    Peterson 179
    Robert 172
    Samuel 16, 156
    Simeon 150*
    Thomas 13, 23, 58
    Walter 128
    William 38, 164, 169

Watt,
    James 123

Watten,
    Chandler 58

Watter,
    David 80
    Harry 80

Watterhouse,
    Hannah 4
    Joseph 4

Wattles,
    William 75*

Watts,
    Ann 133
    Daniel 43*
    Eleanor 23
    John 21*
    Martha 105
    Peter D. 122
    Samuel 14*

Waugh,
    Bethsheba 13
    John 13
    Joseph 21, 178
    Lemmon 178
    Michael 124
    Ruth 58*

Way,
    Abner 52*
    Asa 75*
    Elisha 53*
    Lucy 53

Wayland,
    Joseph 164

Weare,
    Jeremiah 4*

Weatherbee,
    Isaac 95
    John 95

Weatherby,
    Amos 70
    Daniel 71*
    Newel 70
    Thomas 71*

Weatherhead,
    Amaziah 46
    Daniel 46
    Leah 46
    Whipple 46

Weatherington,
    Joseph 159*

Weathers,
    Elisha 139*
    Valentine 147*

Weatherstone,
    David 83
    Margaret 83

Weaver,
    Abigail 47*
    Adam 124*
    Amasa 88
    Benjamin 131
    Caleb 71
    Denison 99
    Dute 49
    Gate Root 88
    Jacob 84, 114
    John 158*
    Joseph 27*
    Lodowick 99
    Mary 114
    Olive 49
    Samuel 158
    Shadrach 156*
    Thomas 89

Webb,
    Abigail 105
    Anna 29
    Azariah 64
    Benjamin 90
    Daniel 32*
    E. H. 64
    Ebenezer 81
    Edward 5
    Elizabeth 85*
    Grace 137*
    Hannah 79
    Isaac 78
    J. R. 64
    Jesse 153*
    John 32, 82*, 105, 135, 138*
        146
    John T. 146
    Joseph 79*
    Lewis 165*
    Moses 56
    Nathan 180
    Paul 29
    Samuel 81
    Sarah 180

Webber,
    Abigail 9
    Benjamin 41*
    Ezekiel 8*
    John 39*
    Rinaldo 86*
    William 90*

Weber,
    Nancy 8

Weber, (cont.)
    Noah 8

Weble,
    Abner 57*

Webster,
    Aaron 86
    Allen 78
    Alpha 63
    Anna 18
    Atkinson 18
    Benjamin 73
    Chauncey 76
    David 62
    George 5
    Hannah 17*
    Hiram 78
    John 69
    John H. 148
    John S. 62
    Keziah 104*
    Lydia 16
    Mehitable 63
    Milton 61
    Moses 69
    Samuel 86
    Simeon 61
    Stephen 18
    Thomas 16
    William 15

Wedding,
    R. H. 184

Weden,
    Peleg 49*

Wedgwood,
    Lot 3
    Noah 3

Weed,
    Abraham 95*
    Abram 59
    Anna 55*
    Benjamin 56*
    Daniel 56, 79
    David 55*
    Dorothy 65
    Elnathan 105*
    Gilbert 85*
    Henry 56*
    Isaac 65

Weed, (cont.)
    John 56
    Jonathan 56*
    Mary 56
    Reuben 74*
    Sally 92
    Susanna 79

Weeden,
    Enos H. 45
    George 47
    Jonathan 95

Weekley,
    Thomas 136*

Weeks,
    Bethiah 10
    Charles 181*
    Harry 100
    James 9*
    John 18
    Lydia 15
    Samuel 100
    Sarah 75*
    William 19*

Weels,
    Sailor 82*

Weest,
    Christian 113

Weir,
    John 118*

Weiser,
    Justina 113

Weitzel,
    Elizabeth 121

Welch,
    Abel 5
    Andrew 134*
    Anna 15
    Benjamin 77
    Daniel 184
    David 163*, 174
    Edward 63*
    James 5
    John 3, 58*, 59*, 94*, 130
        189*
    Jonas 38*, 44

Welch, (cont.)
Nicholas 86*
Peter 174
Prudence 57
Roswell 87
Samuel 183*
Thomas 77, 158*
William 9

Weld,
Susanna 45*

Welford,
Lewis 144*

Wellcome,
Stephen 10

Weller,
Frederick 87*
Lucinda 100*
Phillip 111*

Wellington,
Benjamin F. 74
Ebenezer 22
William 22

Wellis,
J. Hubbard 50

Wellman,
Abraham 175*
Benoni 93
Deluis 66
Fanny 8
Joel 192
Jonathan 60
Mary 8
Rebecca 175
Timothy 66
Zadoc 192

Wells,
Abraham 97
Anne 82
Asa 77
Benjamin 169*
Bolling 130*
Charles D. 173*
David 189
Eleazer M. P. 45
Eli 136
Elias 64, 86

Wells, (cont.)
Elisha 89
Elisha R. 49
Ira 89
Jacob 139
James 160*, 189
Jesse 153
John 10, 92*
Jonathan 192*
Josiah 71
Leonard 145*
Little Berry 163*
Lucy 45
Mary 10, 43*
Matthew 86
Nicholas C. 70
Noah 81
Rebecca 62*
Redman 145*
Richard 128
Samuel 55*
Sarah 18, 91, 136
Silas 88
Simon 49*
Thomas 53*, 139, 183
William 164*, 182

Welman,
William 93

Welsh,
Isaiah 129*
John 120*
Robert 172
Stillman 49

Welton,
Sarah 53
William J. 183*

Weltshire,
Joseph 136

Wemple,
John 87

Wendell,
Hannah 83
Jacob 83

Wentworth,
Benning 178*
Bulah 64
Foster 8, 9

Wentworth, (cont.)
    Ichabod 3*
    James 163
    Joseph 26
    Josiah W. 102
    Lemuel 12
    Nathaniel 32
    Paul 12
    Paul (Mrs.) 12
    Rachel 32
    Samuel 4
    Samuel S. 26
    Stephen 12
    Timothy 4*

Wesby,
    John 131*

Wescott,
    Abigail 15
    Daniel 56

Wesley,
    Margaret 29

Weslick,
    Josiah 124*

Wesner,
    Samuel 74*

West,
    Anson 80
    Benjamin 146*, 173
    Bransford 132*
    Butcher 148
    Caleb 80*
    Charles 36*
    Clement 178*
    Daniel 66
    Edward 64*
    Elias 110
    Hannah 131
    Hezekiah 187*
    Ichabod 32*
    James 169
    John 43, 173
    Joseph 127*, 142*, 173
    Martha 80
    Nathaniel 186
    Robert 169
    Samuel 148
    Thomas 187*
    William 143*, 166
    Willoughby 138*

Westbrook,
    Abraham 123*

Westcott,
    James 93
    Joseph 78*
    Josiah 46
    Lydia 46
    Mary 46
    Niles 46
    Sarah 45*
    Stephen 46
    Thomas R. 46

Westerman,
    Easter 156

Westervelt,
    Benjamin P. 107*

Westfall,
    Diana 169
    Simeon 169

Westgate,
    Joseph E. 67
    Thomas 27*
    William 67

Westmoreland,
    T. A. 156

Weston,
    Abigail 29*
    Charles 40
    Edman 65
    Eliphus 30
    Huldah 65
    James 29*, 138*
    Levi 29*
    Mary 93
    Rachel 116
    William 73*

Wetherbee,
    Daniel 37*
    Jacob 22*

Wetherby,
    Ebenezer 25
    Sally 35

Wetherel,
    Obadiah 9

Wethwell,
    Joseph D. 80

Wetmore,
    Alphonzo 190*
    Elisha 79

Weycoff,
    Alice 104

Weygint,
    Tobias 90*

Weyman,
    John 127*

Weymouth,
    James 12*

Whaley,
    Alanson 82
    Hannah 56
    James 119*
    Jerusha 48
    Jonathan 48*
    Reynolds 82
    T. 92*

Whalon,
    Joseph 27*

Whaly,
    James 176*

Wharton,
    Samuel 130, 131*

Whatley,
    Daniel 146*

Wheat,
    Bridgett 24
    Joseph 24, 38*

Wheatler,
    Joseph 181*

Wheatley,
    Reuben 63
    Ward 63

Wheaton,
    Benjamin 79
    Jeremiah 57

Wheaton, (cont.)
    Jeremiah S. 57
    Jesse 31
    Joseph 28*, 57
    Rachel 37
    Reuben 96
    Roswell 58*
    William 73, 96

Wheedon,
    Rufus 69

Wheeler,
    Aaron 92*, 96
    Ann 31
    Anna 57
    B. 68
    Benjamin 96, 181*
    Betsey 77
    Bronson 53
    Caroline M. 55
    Celia 91
    Comfort 64*
    Isaac 185*
    James 56*, 92, 146*, 182*
    Jarvis 28
    Jeremiah 67*
    Jesse 77
    John 21, 35, 86, 170, 181*
    John W. 33
    Jonathan 54*
    L. A. 92
    Lavinia 24
    Martha 83
    Meribath 33
    Merritt 77
    Micass 132*
    Nichols C. 55
    Peter 40*
    Prosper 68
    Roby 28
    Salisbury 23
    Samuel 34*, 76*, 77, 104*
        136*
    Simeon 183
    Thomas 181
    Valentine 75*
    William 19*, 28, 170
    Zenas 32*

Wheelock,
    Asa 66*
    Davis 36
    Dennison 36

Wheelock, (cont.)
    Eleazer 69
    Ephraim 38
    Gershom B. 90
    Ithamar 22
    Jonathan 18
    Joseph 39
    Lyman 27*
    Obadiah 88*
    Paul 38
    Ralph 90

Wheelwright,
    Abraham 42
    Joseph 3*

Wheldon,
    Abram 52*
    J. 72
    Joshua 72

Wheler,
    John 15

Whelpley,
    Ebenezer 105*

Wherren,
    Peggy 4

Whetmore,
    John 85*
    Polly 106*

Whetson,
    John 123

Whimley,
    John 82

Whipple,
    Benjamin 19
    Caleb C. 92*
    David 35
    Eliab 46
    Elijah 180
    George 47*
    Isaac 54
    Joseph 46
    Lavina 46
    Nathan 46
    Oliver 22
    Rufus 22
    Ruth 48

Whipple, (cont.)
    Sarah 19
    Solomon 35
    Stephen 23
    Sylvia 46*
    Welcome 46
    Zebulon 178*

Whiston,
    Elizabeth 97

Whitaker,
    Abel 28*, 47
    Abraham 102, 126
    Henry 126
    James 129*, 165
    James S. 102
    Joel 28
    Mark 161*
    Nathaniel 111*
    Peter 28, 172
    Robert L. 138*
    Stephen 61*

Whitbeck,
    Jacob 104

Whitcher,
    Anna 16
    Joseph 65
    Timothy 16

Whitcomb,
    Abijah 22
    Abraham 41*
    Asa 70
    David 21
    Enoch 21
    Francis 66
    Hiram 71
    Jonathan 71
    Oliver 19
    Rachel 31*
    Rosewell 22
    Samuel 74*
    Sarah 41
    Simeon 68, 73*
    Susan 31

White,
    Abigail 31
    Abijah 87*
    Abraham 185*
    Adam 103

White, (cont.)
Alexander 86
Andrew 148*
Ann 157*
Asa 29*, 58
Azor 125
Bela 27
Benjamin 137*
Bethiah 30*
Caleb 126, 165
Charles 12, 22, 127
Chary 22
Christopher 150
Cynthia 84
Daniel 25, 40, 59, 79*, 154
David 39*, 40, 119*, 126
Delano 58
Dorothy 132*
Ebenezer 19
Elijah 72, 148
Elizabeth 132*
Ephraim 58
Esther 59, 75
Fortune C. 89*
George 121*, 146
Giles 102
Hannah 60*
Henry 105*
J. R. 79
James 33*, 76*, 150, 171
Jane 22
Jedediah 32
Jenkins 100
Jeremiah 77
Jesse 146*
John 22, 28*, 69, 75*, 93*, 100
137*, 138*, 157*, 165, 176
Jonathan 167*
Joseph 18*, 28, 37, 128*
Juliana 78
Laurence 78*
Lewis 44
Lucinda 57*
Lyman P. 72
Martha 79
Martin 58
Mary 53*, 83
Matilda 28*
Micah 31*
Milton 83
Nancy 58
Nathaniel 84
Patience 31
Paul 72

White, (cont.)
Philip 60*
Potter 124*
Rebecca 26
Reuben 33*, 102
Rhoda 123
Richard 131*
Robert B. 96*
Samuel 23, 26, 57*, 86*, 166*
Samuel B. 148
Sherwood 150
Silas 18*, 22
Solomon 70*
Stephen 22, 157*
Thaddeus 65*
Theophilus 77
Thomas 33, 37, 47*, 58*, 127
160*
Timothy 28*
Trueman 79*
Uriah 79
William 12, 65*, 78*, 122*
131*, 182*
William D. 132*

Whiteaker,
Ann 163
James 163
Josiah 163

Whitecar,
Josiah 175

White Cotton,
James 164*

Whitehead,
Burwell 141
David 59*
James 151*
Lazarus 141
Robert 184*

Whitehorne,
Ruth 48

Whitehouse,
James 17
Nathaniel 17
Susannah 13*

Whiteman,
George 171*

Whiten,
    Samuel 15
    Thomas B. 15

Whitesides,
    John 158
    William 158

Whitford,
    Constant 80*
    Job 49*
    Stephen 86

Whitid,
    John 95*

Whiting,
    Deborah 35
    Elkanah 31
    Erastus 90
    Jared 30
    John 13
    Joshua 31
    Leonard 13
    Nathan 67
    Sampson 7*
    Samuel 39*
    William 83*

Whitington,
    Grief 151*

Whitley,
    Dorcas 44*
    Joseph 101*

Whitlock,
    Charles 131
    James 131*
    John 131
    Phebe 56
    Thomas 129*

Whitlook,
    Justus 56*

Whitman,
    Abial 67*
    Abigail 49*
    Benjamin 71*
    Benjamin R. 45
    Caleb 48*
    David 24*
    Deborah 48*

Whitman, (cont.)
    Henry 45
    Jacob 7
    Lucretia 46
    Peleg 49*
    Randall 86

Whitmarsh,
    Samuel 32
    Susanna 29*

Whitmash,
    Anna 49

Whitmore,
    Benjamin 70
    Daniel 12
    Edward 62*
    Enoch 37, 38*
    Gideon 95
    Hezekiah 50*
    Isaac 37
    James 77*
    Jesse 12
    Joseph 13*

Whitney,
    Abijah 40
    Benjamin 70, 80
    Betty 24
    David 22, 71*, 102
    Ebenezer 9*, 34*
    Eleanor 9
    Eleazer 66
    Elijah 65*
    Elisha 59
    Enos 119*
    Ezekiel 102
    Hannah 32
    Hackaliah 39*
    Henry 76
    Isaac 8, 9, 24, 101
    Jacob 14*, 101
    Joel 22
    Jonathan 66
    Joshua 73*
    Lydia 24
    Martha 37*
    Olive 59
    Reuben 38
    Richard 76*
    Samuel 57
    Sarah 22
    Seth 79*

Whitney, (cont.)
  Seth 79*
  Silas 24, 25*
  Walter 72*
  Warren 57

Whiton,
  Horace 57
  Israel 29
  Otis 57

Whitring,
  Elijah 100*

Whittaker,
  Ephraim 94*

Whitteker,
  Ebenezer 25
  Peter 25

Whittemore,
  Prentiss 21
  Prudence 21

Whitten,
  Jane 9
  Joseph 8
  Philip 145
  Richard 12*
  Solomon 13

Whittier,
  Thomas 24

Whittington,
  Faddy 147*

Whittle,
  John 21
  Rachel 21

Whorry,
  Daniel 84*

Wiard,
  Darius 76*

Wibber,
  Amy 40

Wicker,
  Asa 182
  William 182

Wickes,
  Abel 48*
  Oliver 49*

Wickham,
  Daniel 73
  James S. 49
  Margaret 85
  Sarah 49

Wickhams,
  Isaac 27*

Wicknire,
  Grant 58*

Wickoff,
  Garret 110*
  Garret W. 110
Wicks,
  Alexander 106*
  Samuel 35
  Zophar 79*

Wickum,
  Benjamin 159

Wickwire,
  Alvan 59
  Sarah 59

Wickwise,
  Willard 54

Wicoff,
  Joachim 133

Widener,
  Michael 136*

Widick,
  L. 92

Widington,
  Benjamin 131*

Widrig,
  Jacob 83*

Wier,
  John 22

Wier,
  Rebecca 22

Wiggin,
    Benjamin 17*
    Daniel 172*
    James 17*
    Nathan 3*
    Winthrop 16

Wiggington,
    Henry 160

Wiggins,
    Catharine 107
    Eldridge 10
    Sarah 19
    William 43*

Wigginton,
    John 129*

Wiggons,
    William 182

Wiggs,
    John 141*

Wight,
    Abigail 40
    Caleb 40
    Eliab 31*
    Joseph 6*
    Luther 168

Wigington,
    George 150*

Wilbar,
    Isaac 30
    Joanna 30
    Joseph 28

Wilber,
    Benjamin 87
    Elizabeth 89*, 93*
    John 26*, 45*, 126*
    Joseph 32*, 54
    Lorenzo D. 180
    Thomas 13*

Wilbor,
    Francis 47
    Samuel 47*

Wilbour,
    Daniel 46*

Wilbour, (cont.)
    Hannah 45*
    Thankful 47*

Wilbur,
    Asa 9
    Benjamin 31
    Curtis 94
    David 9
    Joseph 103
    Sarah 94
    Thomas 27*

Wilcott,
    Zebulon 35

Wilcox,
    Alvan 51
    Asa 21
    Benjamin 90
    Borden 82*
    Daniel 110*
    Edward 86
    Elisha 65*
    Ephraim 75
    Hollis 21
    Jacob 51
    James 108*
    Jehiel 171*
    Johiah 51
    John 10, 49, 62
    John M. 64
    Joseph 90, 170
    Josiah A. 51
    Lucy 50*
    Mary 47
    Nanny 62
    Nathan 64
    Norris 51
    Pardon 47*
    Peleg 47
    Rebecca 49
    Reuben 89*
    Rosanna 51
    Sandford 86
    Stephen 75
    Thomas 47*
    Washington 10

Wilcutt,
    Catharine 35
    Susanna 32

Wild,
    Eunice 67

Willsey,
    Isaac 96*

Willson,
    Abigail 37*
    George 91*
    Henry 160
    Hughey 97*
    James 160
    John 100*, 143*
    N. W. 100
    Robert 16, 17
    Sarah 100
    T. 74
    Thomas 74
    William 47*

Wilmarth,
    Joseph 24

Wilmer,
    Henry 116

Wilmouth,
    Huldah 62

Wilsey,
    Catharine 59
    Margaret 73

Wilson,
    Abraham 133*
    Alexander 103, 122, 186*
    Almira 90
    Andrew 106*
    Ann 155
    Ann (Mrs.) 155
    Artemas 22
    Asa 136*
    Augustin 143*
    Benjamin 22, 55
    Betsey 4*
    Chester 78
    David (Capt.) 112*
    Delia 51
    Eleanor 56
    Eli 51
    Eli B. 135*
    Elias 147
    Elizabeth 87
    Enoch 31
    Ephraim 184
    George 70, 144
    Henry 184

Wilson, (cont.)
    Isaac 170*
    Isham 143
    Israel 172
    James 81, 156*, 185*, 186
    Jane 164*, 176
    Jared 31
    Jesse 93
    Joab 51
    John 13*, 55*, 59*, 73*, 78*
      87, 111*, 112, 120*, 143*
      147, 166*
    John G. 81
    John J. 81
    John L. 66
    Jonathan 148
    Joseph 37, 90, 120*, 135
    Joshua 149*
    Maria 103
    Mary 77, 165*
    Matthew 175*
    Mercy 58
    Moor 98*
    Nathaniel 58*
    Newman 143
    Noah 125*
    Paul 95*
    Richard J. 89*
    Robert 144*, 183
    Robert M. 116
    Samuel 21, 55*, 119*, 139*
    Solomon 70
    Submit 51
    Wallace 131
    Walter 56*, 84
    Warren 24*
    William 21, 70, 117*, 135*
      153*, 182*

Wilt,
    Andrew 114
    Jacob 114, 118
    Thomas 118

Winans,
    Benjamin 177
    John 96, 177

Winch,
    Abijah 80
    Anna 14

Winchel,
    John 58*

Winchell,
    Jacob 91
    Jedediah 91
    John 193

Winchester,
    Anne 105
    David 105
    Franklin 66
    Richard 163*
    Sarah 66
    William 34

Windham,
    Eleanor 127
    Sarah 127, 169*

Wines,
    Stephen 109

Winfield,
    Abraham 103*
    Emanuel 100
    William 107*

Winfree,
    Philip 160
    Reuben 160

Wing,
    Abner 71
    Israel 43
    Thruston 105

Wingate,
    Jeremiah 17
    Jonathan 3
    Mary 17

Wingo,
    John 143
    William 143

Wink,
    Jacob 112

Winkler,
    Susan 161
    William 161

Winn,
    Ashley 154
    John 37*

Winne,
    Christopher 72
    Cornelius 102*

Winney,
    Henry 81

Winship,
    Abel 22
    John 6*

Winslow,
    Amos 7
    Elizabeth 5
    Jonathan 36
    Samuel 63

Winsor,
    Hannah 46
    Samuel 46

Winstead,
    Francis 153
    Manley 163*
    Margaret 153

Winston,
    Nathaniel 157*

Winter,
    Jacob 80*
    John 114

Winters,
    Jacob 74*
    Juvenile 76*
    N. 92
    Nicholas 92

Winthworth,
    Paul 7

Winton,
    Bradley 124
    Nathan 124
    Zar 55

Wintworth,
    John 124*

Wintzell,
    Charles 111*

Winy,
    James 33*

Wires,
    Miriam 35

Wiscarver,
George 118

Wise,
Bartlett 23
Daniel 4*, 22
Eunice 51*
George 128
Jacob 121*, 142*
John 147
Joseph 152
Leonard 22
Mary 24
Peter 152
William 51

Wiser,
Michael 130*

Wisinger,
George 125
Ludwick 125

Wisner,
David 88*
Jacob 112*

Wiswell,
Jesse 187
John 22
Joseph 25

Wit,
Bergiss 153*

Wite,
Jesse 130*
John P. 130

Wited,
John 164*

Witham,
Elizabeth 4
Jedediah 4
Sally 15

Withee,
Uzizeel 13
Zoe 14

Witherell,
John 10
Rufus 10

Witherington,
Solomon 137*
William 137*

Withers,
Spencer 133*

Witherspoon,
John 182*

Withington,
Daniel 138*
John 19
Lemuel 31
Thomas 30, 31

Withirn,
Peter 184

Witing,
John 109
Nathaniel 109

Witmoyer,
F. 114
Peter 114
Philip 114*

Witt,
Anes 167
Eunice 22*
Phoebe 161
Samuel 167
Silas 161

Witten,
James S. 136
Thomas 136

Witter,
Jonah 54*

Witters,
Conrad 176*

Witty,
James 170*

Wolcott,
Benjamin 126
Chester 50
David 178*
Elias H. 180
Margaret 126

Workman,
    Hugh 120*

World,
    Nicholas 110*

Wormoth,
    Thaddeus 162*

Wormwood,
    James 4*

Wormworth,
    Mary 83
    William 83

Wornack,
    Abner 161*

Worrell,
    Sally 138

Worsham,
    Charles 161

Worsley,
    Abigail 22

Worster,
    Samuel 3
    William 3

Wort,
    Israel B. 171
    John 171

Worth,
    Susan 26

Worthen,
    Michael 16*

Worthing,
    Isaac 12
    Nathan 12

Worthington,
    Thomas 127
    William 164*, 172

Worthley,
    Samuel 21

Wotring,
    Peter 171

Wray,
    Benjamin 130*

Wrenn,
    John 133*

Wrid,
    Elizabeth 56

Wright,
    Aaron 112
    Abigail 49*
    Abijah 91*
    Abraham 99
    Asa 82*
    Asher 61*
    Azel 68*
    Betsey 88
    Beverly B. 160
    Chloe 35
    D. 132*
    David 24, 150
    Dennis 92
    Ebenezer 29*
    Edward 139*
    Eldad 34
    Eleanor 180
    Eleazer 79*
    Eli 179*
    Elisha 91*
    Elizabeth 40, 160*
    Ephraim 84*
    Francis 21
    George 118, 167*
    George E. 29
    Henry J. 51
    Isaac 99*
    J. N. 123
    Jacob 23*, 94
    James 187*
    James H. 144
    Jane 103*
    Job 179*
    John 9*, 60*, 102, 120, 130*
        135, 141*, 148*, 167, 185
    Joseph 9*, 28, 29, 49, 166
    Levi 29*
    Lewis 118*
    Mabel 50*
    Margaret 51
    Mary 68, 163
    Mercy 123
    Moses 23*
    N. 92
    Nancy 64

Wright, (cont.)
    Nathan 40, 86
    Nehemiah 22*
    Noah 40*
    Oliver 22, 69*
    Patience 29
    Peter 21, 40*
    Philemon 22*
    Reuben 9, 45*, 76*
    Russel 136
    Samuel 58
    Samuel D. 123
    Solomon C. 88
    Stephen 35
    Susan 28
    Thaddeus 88
    Thomas 138*, 141*
    Tilman 64
    William 169*
    William A. 152

Wrin,
    James 68*

Wutting,
    Thomas 14, 15

Wyatt,
    Edward 154
    Elizabeth 166*
    John 191*

Wyckoff,
    Jacob 109
    John C. 111*
    Peter 109

Wyckum,
    John 80*

Wycoff,
    Samuel 173

Wygant,
    James 124*

Wykle,
    William 152

Wyley,
    Joseph 170

Wylie,
    Francis 144*

Wylie, (cont.)
    Peter 67*

Wyman,
    Almira 40
    Aphia 21
    Asa 67
    Asa M. 67
    John 13, 67, 68*
    Lydia 18, 67
    Reuben 13*
    Samuel 89
    William 13

Wysor,
    Henry 136*

Yadon,
    Joseph 152*

Yager,
    Solomon 158*

Yainter,
    Huldah 37*

Yale,
    James 102*
    Moses 89
    Sarah 89

Yancy,
    Francis 136*
    Lewis D. 146*

Yansen,
    Daniel 115*

Yanson,
    Henry 96
    John 96
    Margaret 96

Yarbell,
    Thomas 40

Yarbell, (cont.)
    William 40*

Yarborough,
    Agnes 129*
    Jephtha 139*

Yarbrough,
    Henry 159*
    Joseph 137*

Yarrow,
    John 9
    Worster 9

Yates,
    David 141
    Jemima 141
    John 131*
    Uriah 100
    William 168*

Yeager,
    George 113
    John 112

Yeagley,
    Anna Barbara 114*

Yearger,
    Israel 122

Yearly,
    Alexander 128

Yeates,
    Samuel 152*

Yeaton,
    George 18
    Leavitt 16
    Moses 16

Yelles,
    Henry 114

Yelton,
    James 166*

Yeomans,
    Martha 47*

Yeomany,
    David 54
    Elizabeth 54

Yeoumans,
    Nathaniel 106*

Yerks,
    John 104*
    Letty 104

Yetman,
    James 110

Yocom,
    John 181

Yoho,
    Henry 135*

Yonker,
    Hannah 81*
    Jacob 81*

York,
    Benjamin 25*
    Benjamin R. 7*
    Gashum 65
    Isaac 6*
    Isaac Ilsley 26*
    Jeremiah 54*
    John 102*
    Sarah 75
    W. 65
    William 23, 48
    William R. 5*

Young,
    Alpheus 47
    Amos 7
    Andrew 167*, 171
    Barker C. 29
    Bela 25*
    Benjamin 13*
    Caleb 25
    Charles 134*, 178
    Christopher 178
    Clark 70*
    Daniel 132*
    David 38
    Eleazer 16*
    Eli 94*, 180
    Elias 49
    Gideon 29, 87*
    H. H. 174*
    Hannah 4*
    Henry 116, 151
    Henry P. 30
    J. R. 188

Young, (cont.)
    Jacob W. 157*
    James 10*, 89, 93*, 124*, 143
    John 25, 46, 124, 135*, 143
     149, 185
    John C. 87
    John L. 183
    Joseph 25*, 26*
    Joseph R. 188
    Mary 78
    Matthew 187
    Matthias 178
    Michael 178
    Morgan 171, 183*
    Nancy 94
    Nathan 103*
    Othenial 47
    Patty 4*
    Peter 87*
    Philip 121
    Ralph 167*
    Robert 135
    Salathiel 94
    Samuel 47*, 149, 187
    Stephen 27*, 46*
    Thomas 143*
    William 13*, 140*
    Yanacca 25

Younger,
    Kennard 167*

Younglove,
    Daniel 86
    John 86

Younglowe,
    Polly 104

Youngman,
    Abigail 21
    Thomas 68

Youngs,
    Barnabas 83*
    Christopher 106
    Jesse 99*
    John 174
    Neuter 106

Yourn,
    Frank 157

Yournans,
    Abijah 98

Yournans, (cont.)
    Jonas 98

You,
    Sarah 67

Yungst,
    Peter 120*

Zeah,
    David 96*

Zeck,
    John 157*

Zeglar,
    Leonard 140*

Zegman,
    George 115

Zepporah,
    Marsh 35

Zimerman,
    Abraham 115

Zoll,
    Christopher 186
    Henry 186

Zollinger,
    Peter 127*

Zombro,
    Jacob 112

Zophar,
    Brack 59

Zouldthwait,
    Elizabeth 4

Zumwalt,
    Mary 190
    Solomon 190

No Surname
    Abigail 54
    Amos 53
    David 58*, 59
    Jonathan 58*
    Levy 58*